Frommer's
France 2002

P9-AEU-154

The Dordogne is the site of some of Europe's oldest settlements. In this southeastern region of France, you can see cave paintings as well as the natural beauty that surrounds the medieval towns and beautiful châteaux. See chapter 20. © Tom Kirkman Photography.

The views of Paris are spectacular from La Tour Eiffel, which stretches 1,056 feet into the air. See chapter 5. © Bob Krist Photography.

Visitors take a break to decide what masterpiece they'll see next at the Louvre in Paris, one of the world's great museums. See chapter 5. © Dave Bartruff Photography.

To enter the Louvre, you must pass through this 71-foot glass pyramid, designed by I.M. Pei. See chapter 5. © Kevin Galvin Photography.

The facade of the Cathédrale Notre-Dame is one of the most beautiful sights in Paris. See chapter 5. © Kevin Galvin Photography.

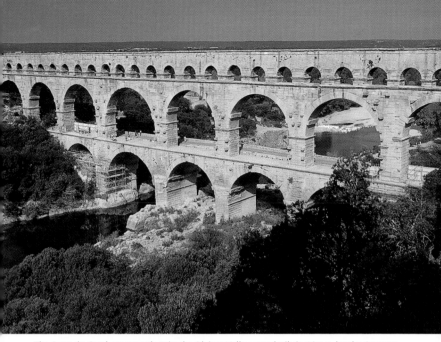

The Pont du Gard, an aqueduct in the Rhône Valley, was built in 19 B.C. by the Romans. See chapter 13. © Tom Kirkman Photography.

A typical street in Alsace, the "least French of French provinces." See chapter 11.
© Markham Johnson/Robert Holmes Photography.

In Giverny, you can stroll through Monet's gardens and see the waterlilies that inspired this great painter. See chapter 6. © Dave G. Houser/Houserstock, Inc.

The Château de Chambord, built during the height of the French Renaissance, is the largest château in the Loire Valley. See chapter 7. © Kevin Galvin Photography.

The Provence countryside takes on a purplish hue just before the midsummer harvest. Lavender fields blossom straight out to the horizon. See chapter 15. © Uwe Schmid/The Stock Market.

Vineyards unfold as you drive through the winding landscape of the Rhône Valley. See chapter 13. © Brigitte Merle/Tony Stone Images.

Half-timbered houses from the 17th century line the streets of Rouen. See chapter 8.
© Dave G. Houser/Houserstock, Inc.

A Renaissance masterpiece, the Château de Chenonceau spans the river Cher in the Loire Valley. The castle was a gift from Henri II to his mistress, Diane de Poitiers. See chapter 7.
© Kindra Clineff Photography.

The abbey of Mont-St-Michel is one of Europe's most important Gothic monuments. See chapter 8. © *Kindra Clineff Photography.*

The remains of 9,386 American soldiers are buried here at the Normandy American Cemetery at Omaha Beach. The markers commemorate those who died here during the D-day invasion. See chapter 8. © *Yannick Le Gal/The Image Bank.*

In Rocamadour in the Dordogne Valley, towers, old buildings, and oratories rise in stages up the side of a cliff. See chapter 20. © Markham Johnson/Robert Holmes Photography.

The landscape in Burgundy seems almost surreal. See chapter 12 for a full itinerary on how to explore this area by car. © *Kindra Clineff Photography.*

The produce is fresh on market day in Dijon. See chapter 12. © Len Kaufman Photography.

During the Great Schism from 1378 to 1417, a succession of popes ruled here at the Palais des Papes in Avignon, while others simultaneously held on to power in Rome. See chapter 15. © Nik Wheeler Photography.

Visitors are welcome at wineries throughout La Route du Vin in Alsace-Lorraine (chapter 11), Burgundy (chapter 12), and the Beaujolais country (chapter 13). © Tom Kirkman Photography.

Residents of St-Paul-de-Vence on the Cote d'Azur enjoy a game of pétanque. See chapter 16. © Nik Wheeler Photography.

Nice is the capital of the Riviera, attracting artists and writers with its brilliant sunshine and relaxed living. See chapter 16. © Richard Passmore/Tony Stone Images.

Sunflower fields like this one in Burgundy inspired van Gogh and countless other artists. See chapter 12. © Bob Krist Photography.

A New Star-Rating System & Other Exciting News from Frommer's!

In our continuing effort to publish the savviest, most up-to-date, and most appealing travel guides available, we've added some great new features.

Frommer's guides now include a new **star-rating system.** Every hotel, restaurant, and attraction is rated from 0 to 3 stars to help you set priorities and organize your time.

We've also added **seven brand-new features** that point you to the great deals, in-the-know advice, and unique experiences that separate travelers from tourists. Throughout the guide look for:

Finds	Special finds—those places only insiders know about
Fun Fact	Fun facts—details that make travelers more informed and their trips more fun
Kids	Best bets for kids—advice for the whole family
Moments	Special moments—those experiences that memories are made of
Overrated	Places or experiences not worth your time or money
Tips	Insider tips—some great ways to save time and money
Value	Great values—where to get the best deals

We've also added a **"What's New"** section in every guide—a timely crash course in what's hot and what's not in every destination we cover.

Other Great Guides for Your Trip:

Frommer's Paris

Frommer's Paris from $80 a Day

Frommer's Memorable Walks in Paris

Frommer's Irreverent Guide to Paris

Frommer's Portable Paris

Frommer's Provence & the Riviera

Frommer's Europe

Frommer's Europe from $70 a Day

Frommer's Gay & Lesbian Europe

France
2002

by Darwin Porter & Danforth Prince

Here's what the critics say about Frommer's:

"Amazingly easy to use. Very portable, very complete."

—Booklist

"The only mainstream guide to list specific prices. The Walter Cronkite of guidebooks—with all that implies."

—Travel & Leisure

"Complete, concise, and filled with useful information."

—New York Daily News

"Hotel information is close to encyclopedic."

—Des Moines Sunday Register

Hungry Minds™

Best-Selling Books • Digital Downloads • e-Books • Answer Networks •
e-Newsletters • Branded Web Sites • e-Learning
New York, NY • Cleveland, OH • Indianapolis, IN

About the Authors

France is a second home to **Darwin Porter,** a native of North Carolina, and **Danforth Prince,** who lived in France for many years. Darwin, who worked in television advertising and as a bureau chief for the *Miami Herald,* wrote the original edition of this guide back in 1971. Danforth, who began his association with Darwin in 1982, worked for the Paris bureau of the *New York Times* between renovations of a 14th-century château in the Loire Valley. Both these writers know their destination well, for they have made countless annual trips through the countryside and have lived and worked from Brittany to Provence.

Published by:

Hungry Minds, Inc.

909 Third Avenue
New York, NY 10022

ISBN 0-7645-6478-1
ISSN 0899-3351

Editors: Ron Boudreau, Vanessa Rosen, Leslie Shen, and Kathleen Warnock
Special thanks to Matthew Kiernan and Alice Fellows
Production Editor: Tammy Ahrens
Cartographer: Roberta Stockwell
Photo Editor: Richard Fox
Production by Hungry Minds Indianapolis Production Services
Chapter 2 illustrations by Rashell Smith and Karl Brandt

Special Sales

For general information on Hungry Minds' products and services, please contact our Customer Care department; within the U.S. at 800-762-2974, outside the U.S. at 317-572-3993 or fax 317-572-4002. For sales inquiries and reseller information, including discounts, bulk sales, customized editions, and premium sales, please contact our Customer Care department at 800-434-3422.

Manufactured in the United States of America

5   4   3   2   1

Contents

5 Exploring Paris   131

6 Side Trips from Paris: Versailles, Chartres & the Best of the Île de France   185

17 Languedoc-Roussillon   600

18 The Basque Country   642

19 Bordeaux & the Atlantic Coast   664

20 The Dordogne & Périgord: Land of Prehistoric Caves, Truffles & Fine Wine   692

21 The Massif Central   709

List of Maps

An Invitation to the Reader

In researching this book, we discovered many wonderful places—hotels, restaurants, shops, and more. We're sure you'll find others. Please tell us about them, so we can share the information with your fellow travelers in upcoming editions. If you were disappointed with a recommendation, we'd love to know that, too. Please write to:

Frommer's France 2002
Hungry Minds, Inc. • 909 Third Avenue • New York, NY 10022

An Additional Note

Please be advised that travel information is subject to change at any time—and this is especially true of prices. We therefore suggest that you write or call ahead for confirmation when making your travel plans. The authors, editors, and publisher cannot be held responsible for the experiences of readers while traveling. Your safety is important to us, however, so we encourage you to stay alert and be aware of your surroundings. Keep a close eye on cameras, purses, and wallets, all favorite targets of thieves and pickpockets.

New! Frommer's Star Ratings & Icons

Every hotel, restaurant, and attraction listing in this guide has been ranked for quality, value, service, amenities, and special features by using a star-rating scale. In country, state, and regional guides, we also rate towns and regions to help you narrow down your choices and budget your time accordingly. Hotels and restaurants in the Very Expensive and Expensive categories are rated on a scale of one (highly recommended) to three stars (exceptional). Those in the Moderate and Inexpensive categories rate from zero (recommended) to two stars (very highly recommended). Attractions, towns, and regions are rated according to the following scale: zero stars (recommended), one star (highly recommended), two stars (very highly recommended), and three stars (must-see).

In addition to the rating system, we also use seven icons to highlight insider information, useful tips, special bargains, hidden gems, memorable experiences, kid-friendly venues, places to avoid, and other useful information:

| Finds | Fun Fact | Kids | Moments | Overrated | Tips | Value |

The following abbreviations are used for credit cards:

AE	American Express	DISC Discover	V Visa
DC	Diners Club	MC MasterCard	

FROMMERS.COM

Now that you have the guidebook to a great trip, visit our website at **www.frommers.com** for travel information on nearly 2,000 destinations. With features updated regularly, we give you instant access to the most current trip-planning information available. At Frommers.com, you'll also find the best prices on airfares, accommodations, and car rentals—and you can even book travel online through our travel booking partners. At Frommers.com you'll also find the following:

- Daily Newsletter highlighting the best travel deals
- Hot Spot of the Month/Vacation Sweepstakes & Travel Photo Contest
- More than 200 Travel Message Boards
- Outspoken Newsletters and Feature Articles on travel bargains, vacation ideas, tips & resources, and more!

What's New in France

As France moves deeper into the millennium, a new currency, the euro, isn't the only new development. Change, usually for the better, is in the air from Paris to the French Riviera.

SETTLING INTO PARIS

ACCOMMODATIONS There was a time when a man would slip into the **Hôtel Saint Merry,** 78 rue de la Verrerie, 4e (✆ **01-42-78-14-15**), with a gleam in his eye. According to management, "All known sexual passions could be satisfied." Today, that decadence is history. The newly restored hotel is one of the most charming of the small hotels near the Beaubourg. It has only a dozen rooms, so reservations are imperative.

Well-heeled lovers of French *luxe* are again booking into the **George V,** 31 av. George V, 8e (✆ **800/332-3442**), after 2 years of renovation. Now a Four Seasons hotel, the George V has reduced the number of rooms from 300 to 245, but all are large and comfortable (no more maid's rooms).

Just when Parisians thought that no one could come up with another town-house hotel to rival existing competition, along comes the **Hôtel Sofitel Trocadéro Dokhan's,** 117 rue de la Lauriston, 16e (✆ **01-53-65-66-99**). There's no place in Paris that feels more like a family pied-à-terre. On the ground floor, you'll find the only champagne bar in the city.

If you want a snug nest, the 26-room **Hôtel Verneuil,** 8 rue de Verneuil, 7e (✆ **01-42-60-82-14**), comes to the rescue. For those who think size doesn't matter, this restored

17th-century charmer is a gem. At your doorstep await the pleasures of Paris, including the Musée d'Orsay and the Seine, just 2 blocks away.

See chapter 4 for details.

DINING Parisians are flocking to **Georges** (✆ **01-44-78-47-99**), the fashionable new restaurant atop the Centre Pompidou, place Georges-Pompidou, 4e. This chic rendezvous commands miles of space, including a trio of gigantic aluminum "pods" shielding the kitchen. At sandblasted-glass tables, diners feed on an elegantly refined cuisine that mixes the French and Italian kitchens and also turns to Asia for inspiration.

The great five-star Michelin chef, Alain Ducasse, has moved into the Hôtel Plaza Athénée, where he operates **Restaurant Plaza Athénée,** 25 av. Montaigne, 8e (✆ **01-53-67-66-65**). The gourmets of Europe and America are following him to his swank new quarters. From the lightest of dishes to those made with lard, Ducasse is still the king of Paris chefs.

See chapter 4 for details.

EXPLORING PARIS

SHOPPING In the summer of 2000, the Paris Art Market, at the foot of the Montparnasse Tower, emerged as "the place to go" on Sundays. It attracts everyone from painters and sculptors to jewelers and hat makers. See chapter 5 for details.

PARIS AFTER DARK The creators of Buddha Bar, the hottest table reservation in Paris, now have a place to invite you after dinner. It's the **Barrio**

Latino, 46 rue du Faubourg St-Antoine, 12e (✆ **01-55-78-84-75**). The club is spread over four levels of a gutted Eiffel building near place de la Bastille. See chapter 5 for details.

SIDE TRIPS FROM PARIS

The gardeners of **Versailles** claim that it's an ill wind that doesn't blow some good. Before a crippling storm on Christmas 1999, many of their trees had become too tall, weak, aged, or diseased. The storms took care of that, uprooting such classics as Marie Antoinette's Virginia tulip tree, planted in 1783. With a $40 million renovation, the park is being restored to the way it was in the day of the Sun King, Louis XIV. When the work is completed, the grounds of Versailles will look more spectacular than ever. See chapter 6 for details.

THE LOIRE VALLEY

Long known as a pricey part of France, **Tours** is the major center for visiting France's châteaux district. A bistro has opened to help diners keep costs trimmed: **La Souris Gourmande,** 100 rue Colbert (✆ **02-47-47-04-80**), offering half a dozen fondues, each made with cheese from a different region of France. See chapter 7 for details.

BRITTANY

Art lovers and seekers of tranquility are showing up at the tiny Breton village of **Pont-Aven,** where Gauguin, after struggling in Paris, retreated before he sailed to Tahiti. The French artist found inspiration here, as did the post-Impressionists who came to the village, forever changing it. Today the scenery that inspired Gauguin awaits you, along with good inns, galleries, and the **Musée Municipal de Pont-Aven,** place de l'Hôtel-de-Ville (✆ **02-98-06-14-43**), the venue

for changing exhibits related to the Pont-Aven school. See chapter 9 for details.

PROVENCE

A genuinely charming restaurant has opened in the historic Provençal city of Arles—**L'Olivier,** 1 bis rue Réattu (✆ **04-90-49-64-88**), built on foundations from the 12th century. Menu items change with the season but always include what's freshest at the market. For details, see chapter 15.

THE FRENCH RIVIERA

Foreign visitors to **St-Tropez** are flocking to the hot new hangout, **Kelly's Irish Pub,** sur le Port (✆ **04-94-54-89-1**). Homesick Parisians, on the other hand, show up at the restored **Café des Arts,** place des Lices (✆ **04-94-97-02-25**), since it reminds them of the city they left behind.

In **Cannes,** a sophisticated crowd visits **Le Whatnut's,** 7 rue Marceau (✆ **04-93-68-60-58**), for traditional French food, including some of the resort's best grilled fish. This place is on the see-and-be-seen circuit.

Over in **Monaco,** when Alain Ducasse lost a Michelin star in 2001 at his **Louis XV** restaurant in the Hôtel de Paris, place du Casino (✆ **92-16-30-01**), it made headlines throughout France. The good news is that the restaurant is just as fine as always, and there's no discernible difference in the cuisine in spite of the loss of that star.

See chapter 16 for details.

THE BASQUE COUNTRY

In Pau, in the western Pyrénées, visitors are flocking to the **Musée de la Confiture,** 48 rue du Maréchal-Joffre (✆ **05-59-27-69-51**), where M. Miot, France's recognized "best jam maker and best candy maker," sells all sorts of goodies. For details, see chapter 18.

The Best of France

France presents visitors with an embarrassment of riches—you may find yourself bewildered at all the choices you'll have. We've tried to make the task easier by compiling a list of our favorite experiences and discoveries. In the following pages, you'll find the kind of candid advice we'd give our closest friends.

1 The Best Travel Experiences

- **Hunting for Antiques:** The 18th-and 19th-century French aesthetic was gloriously different from that of England and North America, and many objects bear designs with mythological references to the French experience. It's estimated there are more than 13,000 antiques shops throughout the country. Stop wherever the sign ANTIQUAIRE or BROCANTE is displayed.

- **Dining Out:** The art of dining is still serious business in France. Even casual bistros with affordable menus are likely to offer fresh (seasonal) ingredients in time-tested recipes that may add up to a memorable meal. Food here is as cerebral as it is sensual. For our favorite restaurants in all of France, see "The Best Upscale Restaurants" and "The Best Affordable Restaurants," later in this chapter.

- **Biking in the Countryside:** The country that invented La Tour de France offers thousands of options for leisurely bike trips. For a modest charge, trains in France will carry your bicycle to any point you specify. Some of the best excursions are offered by **Euro-Bike Tours,** in DeKalb, Illinois (© **800/321-6060**). They feature tours of some of the most desirable regions, including Provence, Burgundy, and the Loire Valley. See also "Special-Interest Vacations," in chapter 3.

- **Cruising on a Luxury Barge:** Take a cruise on the canals and waterways of Burgundy, Brittany, Alsace, Languedoc, the Dordogne, or Provence. Many barges have been upgraded into luxury craft with superb dining facilities and comfortable accommodations. Sit back and enjoy the scenery, perhaps stopping here and there to sightsee or to visit local wineries. Contact **Première Selections,** a division of the Kemwel Company (© **800/234-4000**). Inclusive fares begin at $1,650 for 3 nights and $2,812 for 6 nights. See also "Special-Interest Vacations," in chapter 3.

- **Shopping in Parisian Boutiques:** The French guard their image as Europe's most stylish people. The citadels of Right Bank chic are along rue du Faubourg St-Honoré and its extension, rue St-Honoré. The most glamorous shops sprawl along these streets, stretching between the Palais Royal (to the east) and Palais de l'Elysée (to the west). Follow in the footsteps of Coco Chanel, Yves Saint Laurent, and Karl Lagerfeld for a shopper's tour of a lifetime. See chapter 5.

- **Strolling Along the Seine in Paris:** Lovers still walk hand in hand along the river, while on its banks the *bouquinistes* peddle their postcards, or some 100-year-old pornography or a tattered history of Indochina. Some visitors walk the full 7-mile stretch of the river through the city, but you can confine your stroll to central Paris, passing the Tuileries, the Louvre, and Notre-Dame and crossing the historic bridges, like pont Neuf, over the Seine and onto Île de la Cité or Île St-Louis. See chapter 5.

- **Exploring the Loire Valley:** Exploring the châteaux among the valley's rich fields and forests will familiarize you with the French Renaissance's architectural aesthetics and with the intrigues of the French kings and their courts. Nothing conjures up the aristocratic *ancien régime* better than a tour of these legendary châteaux. See chapter 7.

- **Climbing to the Heights of Mont-St-Michel:** Straddling the tidal flats between Normandy and Brittany, this is the most spectacular fortress in northern Europe. Believed to be protected by the archangel Michael, most of this Gothic marvel stands as it did during the 1200s. See chapter 8.

- **Paying Tribute to Fallen Heroes on Normandy's D-day Beaches:** On June 6, 1944, the largest armada ever assembled departed on rough seas and in dense fog from England. For about a week the future of the civilized world hung in a bloody and brutal balance between the Nazi and Allied armies. Today you'll see only the sticky sands and wind-torn, gray-green seas of a rather chilly beach. But even if you haven't seen *Saving Private Ryan* or *The Longest Day,*

you can picture the struggles of the determined soldiers who paid a terrible price to establish a beach-head on the Nazi-occupied continent of Europe. See chapter 8.

- **Touring Burgundy During the Grape Gathering:** Medieval lore and legend permeate the harvests in Burgundy, when thousands of workers (armed with vintner's shears and baskets) head over the rolling hills to gather the grapes that have made the wines of Burgundy so famous. You can sample the local wines in any of the area restaurants, which always stock impressive collections. See chapter 12.

- **Schussing Down the Alps:** France offers world-class skiing and luxurious resorts. Our favorites are Chamonix, Courchevel, and Megève. Here you'll find cliffs only experts should brave, as well as challenging runs for intermediates and beginners. The aprés-ski scene roars into the wee hours. See chapter 14.

- **Marveling at the Riviera's Modern-Art Museums:** Since the 1890s, when Signac, Bonnard, and Matisse discovered St-Tropez, artists and their patrons have been drawn to the French Riviera. Experience an unforgettable drive across southern Provence, interspersing museum visits with wonderful meals, people-watching, lounging on the beach, and stops at the area's architectural and artistic marvels. Highlights are Aix-en-Provence (Cézanne's studio and the Vasarély Museum), Biot (the Léger Museum), Cagnes-sur-Mer (the Museum of Modern Mediterranean Art), Cap d'Antibes (the Grimaldi Château's Picasso collection), La Napoule (the Henry Clews Museum), and Menton (the Cocteau Museum). Nice, St-Paul-de-Vence, and St-Tropez all have impressive modern-art collections. See chapters 15 and 16.

- **Partying on the Côte d'Azur:** Until Edwardian escapists "discovered" it about a century ago, the coastline of Provence was dotted with sleepy fishing villages; today it's famous for its glamour and hedonism, despite its overcrowding (and impossible traffic jams). Our vote for best beach goes to the Plage de Tahiti, just outside St-Tropez, where there's lots of topless (and bottomless) action. If you bother to wear a bikini, it should be only the most daring. See chapter 16.

2 The Best Romantic Escapes

- **Deauville** (Normandy): Using the resort of Deauville to propel herself to stardom, Coco Chanel added greatly to its sense of glamour and romance. Try your hand at the casinos, ride horses, stroll along the discreetly elegant boardwalk, or simply revel in the resort's wonderful sense of style and nostalgia. See chapter 8.
- **La Baule** (Brittany): Consider an escape with your significant other to La Baule, a coastal resort in southern Brittany. The salt air; the moody, windswept Atlantic; and the Belle Époque architecture help justify the name of its 5-mile beach, La Côte d'Amour. See chapter 9.
- **Talloires** (The French Alps): The bracing climate, the history that goes back to the early Middle Ages, and the Gallic flair of the innkeepers make for a memorable stay in Talloires. Accommodations range from a converted medieval monastery to an intimate B&B.

The cuisine is world-class, as is the opportunity for quiet, relaxed romance. See chapter 14.

- **Les Baux** (Provence): During the Middle Ages, troubadours in southern Europe presented their love ballads to audiences at the craggy fortress of Les Baux. The romantic tradition continues today, with escapists from all over congregating in the weirdly eroded, rocky, arid Les Baux landscapes. The town has an abundance of hideaways where you can concentrate on romance. See chapter 15.
- **St-Tropez** (Côte d'Azur): Any blonde manages to feel like Brigitte Bardot in sunny St-Tropez, and the number of scantily clad satyrs and nymphs who slink through town in summer could perk up the most sluggish libido. The real miracle here is that the charm of the place manages to survive its own hype and the hordes of visitors. See chapter 16.

3 The Best Driving Tours

- **La Route des Crêtes** (Alsace-Lorraine): The Vosges are one of the oldest mountain ranges in France, and once formed one of the country's boundaries with Germany. Richly forested with tall hardwood trees and firs, they skirt the western edge of the Rhine and resemble Germany's Black Forest. La Route des Crêtes, originally chiseled out of the mountains as a supply line, begins west of Colmar, at the Col du Bonhomme. High points are Münster (home of the cheese), Col de la Schlucht (a resort with panoramas as far as the Jura and the Black Forest), and Markstein. At any point along the way, you can stop and strike out on some of the well-marked hiking trails. See chapter 11.

- **La Côte d'Or** (Burgundy): Stretching only 37 miles from Santenay to Dijon, this route is for wine lovers. Rows of terraced vines rise in tiers above the D122/N74/D1138 highways (La Route des Grands Crus), passing through the towns of Puligny-Montrachet, Volnay, Beaune, Nuits-St-Georges, Vosne-Romanée, Gevrey-Chambertin, and Marsannay–la-Côte. Travel at your leisure, stopping to sample and purchase the noble vintages whose growers are identified by signs sprouting from the sides of the highway. See chapter 12.

- **The Gorges of the Ardèche** (The Rhône Valley): The river that carved these canyons (the Ardèche, a tributary of the Rhône) is the most temperamental of any French waterway: Its ebbs and flows have created the Grand Canyon of France. Riddled with alluvial deposits, grottoes, caves, and canyons more than 950 feet deep, the valley is one of the country's most unusual geological spectacles. A panoramic road (D290) runs along one rim of these canyons, providing views over a striking, arid landscape. Plan to park and walk for a few minutes on some of the well-marked paths. The drive, which you can do in a day even if you make frequent stops, stretches in a southeast-to-northwest trajectory between the towns of Vallon–Pont-d'Arc and Pont St-Esprit. See chapter 13.

- **La Route des Grandes Alpes** (The French Alps): One of the most panoramic drives in western Europe stretches southward from the lakefront town of Evian to coastal Nice. You'll see Alpine uplands, larch forests, glaciers, and the foothills of Mont Blanc. Plan on spending anywhere from 2 to 6 days for the drive, stopping in such towns as Morzine, Avoriaz, Chamonix, and Megève. The route covers some 460 miles and crosses about 20 of France's dramatic mountain passes. Some sections are passable only in midsummer. See chapter 14.

4 The Best Châteaux & Palaces

- **Château de Chantilly** (Île de France): Anne de Montmorency, a constable of France, who advised six monarchs, began this palace in 1528. To save costs, she ordered that her new building be placed atop the foundations of a derelict castle. Her descendants enlarged and embellished the premises, added the massive stables, and hired Le Nôtre to design gardens that later inspired Louis XVI to create similar (though larger) ones at Versailles. See chapter 6.

- **Château de Vaux-le-Vicomte** (Île de France): Vaux-le-Vicomte symbolizes the dangers of conspicuous consumption. Built in 1661 for Nicolas Fouquet, Louis XIV's finance minister, its lavishness made many wonder if some of the money for it had been pilfered from the treasury—it had. This did not amuse the Sun King, who had Fouquet jailed and his château confiscated. Then Louis hired the complex's designers to design his own palace and gardens at Versailles. See chapter 6.

- **Château de Versailles** (Île de France): This is the most spectacular palace in the world. Its construction was riddled with ironies and tragedies, and its costs can be partly blamed for the bloodbath of the French Revolution. Ringed with world-class gardens and a network of canals whose excavation required an army of laborers, the site also contains the Grand and Petit Trianons as well as miles of ornate corridors lined with the spoils of a vanished era. See chapter 6.

- **Palais de Fontainebleau** (Île de France): Since the earliest Frankish kings, the forest has served as a royal hunting ground. Various dwellings had been erected for medieval kings, but in 1528, François I commissioned the core of the building that would be enlarged and embellished by subsequent monarchs, including Henri II, Henri III, Catherine de Médici, Charles IX, and Louis XIII. Napoléon declared it his favorite château, delivering an emotional farewell to his troops from its staircase after his 1814 abdication. See chapter 6.

- **Château d'Azay-le-Rideau** (The Loire Valley): Many visitors thrill to this château's fairy-tale beauty. Poised above the waters of the Indre, it boasts decorative remnants of medieval fortifications and an allure that prefigured the Renaissance embellishments of later Loire Valley châteaux. See chapter 7.

- **Château de Chambord** (The Loire Valley): Despite the incorporation (probably by Michelangelo) of feudal trappings in its layout, this château was built for pleasure—a manifestation of the successes of the 21-year-old François I. Begun in 1519 as the Loire Valley's most opulent status symbol, Chambord heralded the end of the feudal age and the debut of the Renaissance. After military defeats in Italy, a chastened François rarely visited, opting to live in châteaux closer to Paris. See chapter 7.

- **Château de Chenonceau** (The Loire Valley): Its builders daringly placed this palace on arched stone vaults above the rushing river Cher. Built between 1513 and 1521, Chenonceau was fought over by two of France's most influential women, each of whom imposed her will on Renaissance politics and the château's design. Henri II gave the palace to his mistress, Diane de Poitiers. After the king's death, his widow, Catherine de Médici, forced Diane to a less prestigious château nearby (Chaumont), humiliating her in the process. See chapter 7.

- **Château de Villandry** (The Loire Valley): Built in 1538, Villandry is a truly dignified palace, but the real attraction is its 17 acres of formal gardens. Brought to their full magnificence after 1906 by the noted French scholar Dr. Carvallo, they're a mandatory stop for anyone who wants to tour the great gardens of Europe. See chapter 7.

5 The Best Museums

- **Centre Pompidou** (Paris): Back in business after a long restoration, "the most avant-garde building in the world" is a citadel of 20th-century art, with a rotating exhibition drawn from more than 40,000 works. Everything is here, from Calder's 1928 *Josephine Baker* (one of his earliest versions of the mobile) to the re-created Jazz Age studio of Brancusi. See chapter 5.

- **Musée d'Orsay** (Paris): The spidery glass-and-iron canopies of an abandoned railway station were adapted into one of Europe's most thrilling museums. Devoted to 19th-century art, it contains paintings by most of the French Impressionists, and thousands of sculptures and decorative objects whose design changed forever the way Europe interpreted line, movement, and color. See chapter 5.

- **Musée du Louvre** (Paris): The Louvre's exterior is a triumph of grand French architecture, while its interior contains an embarrassment of artistic riches, with more paintings (around 300,000) than can be displayed at any one time. The collection manages to retain its dignity despite the thousands of visitors who traipse through the corridors every day, looking in particular for the *Mona Lisa* and the *Venus de Milo*. In the 1980s, the grandeur of its Cour Carrée was neatly offset by I. M. Pei's controversial Great Pyramid. See chapter 5.

- **Musée de la Tapisserie de Bayeux** (Bayeux, Normandy): This museum's star is a 900-year-old tapestry named in honor of medieval Queen Mathilda. Housed in a glass case, the Bayeaux tapestry is a long band of linen embroidered with depictions of the war machine that sailed from Normandy to conquer England in 1066. See chapter 8.

- **Musée Historique Lorrain** (Nancy, Alsace-Lorraine): Few other French museums reflect a specific province as well as this one. Its collections include 16th-century engravings, 17th-century masterpieces by local painters, exhibits devoted to Jewish history in eastern France, antique furniture, wrought iron, and domestic accessories. See chapter 11.

- **Fondation Maeght** (St-Paul-de-Vence, Côte d'Azur): Established as a showcase for modern art by collectors Aimé and Marguerite Maeght, this museum is an avant-garde compendium of works by Giacometti, Chagall, Braque, Miró, Matisse, and Barbara Hepworth. Built on many levels in a design by the architect José Luís Sert, it boasts glass walls with views of the surrounding Provence landscapes. See chapter 16.

- **Musée Île-de-France** (St-Jean-Cap-Ferrat, Côte d'Azur): This breathtaking villa is loaded with paintings and furniture that have remained in their original positions since the donor's death in 1934. The source of the museum's collection was the baronne Ephrussi, who scoured Europe for treasures. See chapter 16.

- **Musée Fabre** (Montpellier, Languedoc): This museum occupies a villa where Molière once presented some of his plays. Today it boasts one of the worthiest collections of French, Italian, and Spanish paintings in the south of France. See chapter 17.

- **Musée Toulouse-Lautrec** (Albi, Languedoc): The artist Toulouse-Lautrec was born in Albi in 1864. Much to his family's horror, he opted to move to a scandalous neighborhood in Paris, where his depictions of the Belle Époque scene are treasures today. Also on view here are works by Degas, Bonnard, and Matisse. See chapter 17.

- **Musée Ingres** (Montauban, the Dordogne): This museum, housed in a 17th-century archbishop's palace, was created in 1867 when Jean-Auguste-Dominique Ingres (one of the most admired classicists since the Revolution) bequeathed the city more than 4,000 drawings and paintings. See chapter 20.

6 The Best Cathedrals

- **Notre-Dame de Paris** (Paris): A triumph of medieval French architecture, this structure's stone walls symbolize the power of Paris in the Middle Ages. Begun in 1163, Notre-Dame is the cathedral of the nation. It's dazzling in the early morning and at sunset, when its image is reflected in the Seine. See chapter 5.

- **Notre-Dame de Chartres** (Chartres, Île de France): No less a talent than Rodin declared this cathedral a French acropolis. Its site was holy for both the prehistoric Druids and the ancient Romans. One of the first High Gothic cathedrals, the first to use flying buttresses, Chartres is one of the largest cathedrals in the world. It also contains what might be the finest stained-glass windows in history, more than 3,000 square yards of glass whose vivid hues and patterns of light are truly mystical. See chapter 6.

- **Notre-Dame de Rouen** (Rouen, Normandy): Consecrated in 1063 and rebuilt after a fire in 1200, this cathedral was immortalized in the late 19th century, when Monet spent hours painting a series of impressions of the facade at various times of day. Some sections are masterpieces of the Flamboyant Gothic style; others are plainer, though as dignified. See chapter 8.

- **Notre-Dame d'Amiens** (Amiens, the Ardennes): A lavishly decorated example of High Gothic architecture, this cathedral boasts a soaring nave whose roof is supported by 126 breathtakingly slender pillars. It was begun in 1220 to house the head of St. John the Baptist, brought back from the Crusades; at 469 feet long, it is the largest church in France. It escaped destruction during the bombings of the world wars, despite the fierce fighting nearby. See chapter 10.

- **Notre-Dame de Reims** (Reims, Champagne): One of France's first Christian bishops, St. Rémi, baptized Clovis, king of the Franks, on this site in 496. The church memorializing the event was conceived as a religious sanctuary where the French kings would be anointed; it was large, spectacular, and (in our eyes) rather cold. The coronation of every king between 1137 and 1825 was celebrated here. Damaged by World War I bombings, the cathedral was restored by American donations during the 1920s and 1930s. See chapter 10.

- **Notre-Dame de Strasbourg** (Strasbourg, Alsace-Lorraine): One of the the most architecturally harmonious Gothic cathedrals of the Middle Ages was built of russet-colored stone between 1176 and 1439, and is a symbol of Alsatian pride and one of our favorite cathedrals. Its 16th-century astrological clock is a showstopper, gathering crowds daily for its 12:30pm exhibition of figures from myth and fable. See chapter 11.

7 The Best Vineyards & Wineries

A terrific source of information on French wines is the **Centre d'Information, de Documentation, et de Dégustation sur le Vin (CIDD),** 30 rue de la Sablière, 75014 Paris (© **01-45-45-44-20;** fax 01-45-42-78-20). This self-funded school presents about a dozen courses addressing all aspects of wine tasting, producing, buying, and merchandising. Conducted in French, Japanese, and English, there are classes for both amateurs and professionals. You can sign up for as few as four courses, each lasting 3 hours, for 1,500F (228, $217.50), or take a 300-hour curriculum whose diploma is recognized throughout the industry.

If your primary interest lies with the wines of Bordeaux, contact the **Maison du Vin de Bordeaux,** 1 cours de 30 Juillet, 33075 Bordeaux (© **05-56-00-22-88;** www.vins-bordeaux.fr), which offers appealing 2-day courses that cost 2,070F (314.65, $300.15) per person, double occupancy (including room and board).

- **Couly-Dutheil** (Chinon; © 02-47-97-20-20): The cellars here are medieval, many carved into the rock undulating through the area's forests. Most of this company's production involves Chinon wines (mostly reds), though two they're justifiably proud of are Borgeuil and St-Nicolas de Borgeuil, whose popularity in North America has grown in recent years. See chapter 7.
- **Champagne Taittinger** (Reims; © **03-26-85-45-35**): Taittinger is a grand *marque* of French champagne, one of the few whose ownership is still controlled by members of the family who founded it in 1930. It's one of the most visitor-friendly of the champagne houses. See chapter 10.
- **Domaines Schlumberger** (Guebwiller, near Colmar; © 03-89-74-27-00): Established by Schlumberger in 1810, these cellars are an unusual combination of early-19th-century brickwork and modern stainless steel; a visit will enhance your understanding of the subtle differences among wines produced by the seven varieties of grape cultivated in Alsace. See chapter 11.
- **Domaine Protheau** (Château d'Etroyes, Mercurey; © **03-89-74-85-75**): The 150 acres of grapevines straddle at least two appellations contrôlées, so you'll have a chance to immerse yourself in the subtle differences among reds (both pinot noirs and burgundies), whites, and rosés produced under the auspices of both Rully and Mercurey. The headquarters of the organization is a château built in the late 1700s and early 1800s. See chapter 12.

Two miles away, you can visit the **Château de Rully,** site of the **Domaine de la Bressande** (© **03-85-87-20-89**), a well-respected producer of white and, to a lesser extent, red burgundies. Originally built in the 12th century as a stronghold of the comtes de Ternay, it offers tours of its cellars, winemaking facilities, and vineyards. See chapter 12.

- **The Wine-Growing Region Around Bordeaux:** This region is among the most glamorous in France, with a strong English influence, thanks to centuries of wine buying by London- and Bristol-based dealers. One of the area's prestigious growers is the **Société Duboscq,** Château Haut-Marbuzet, 33180 St-Estephe (© **05-56-59-30-54**), which welcomes visitors daily. Free visits to the cellars are followed by a complimentary *dégustation des vins* of whichever of the company's products a visitor requests. See chapter 19.

8 The Best Luxury Hotels

- **Le Ritz** (Paris; ✆ **800/223-6800** in the U.S. and Canada, or 01-43-16-30-30): This hotel occupies a palace overlooking the octagonal borders of one of the most perfect plazas in France: place Vendôme. The decor is pure opulence. Marcel Proust wrote parts of *Remembrance of Things Past* here, and Georges-Auguste Escoffier perfected many of his legendary recipes in its kitchens. See chapter 4.

- **Hôtel de Crillon** (Paris; ✆ **800/223-6800** in the U.S. and Canada, or 01-44-71-15-00): This hotel's majestic exterior was designed by the 18th-century architect Jacques-Ange Gabriel and forms part of the backdrop for place de la Concorde. The decor covers the reigns of Cardinal Richelieu and Marie Antoinette, and a battalion of well-trained attendants polishes nearly every surface weekly. See chapter 4.

- **Château d'Artigny** (Montbazon, Loire Valley; ✆ **02-47-34-30-30**): The perfume king François Coty once lived and entertained lavishly at this mansion outside Tours—and you can do the same today in one of the poshest hotels in the Loire Valley. Live in the grandeur once enjoyed by Elizabeth Taylor and other celebs, taking in the popular weekend soirées and musical evenings. See chapter 7.

- **L'Oustau de Beaumanière** (Les Baux, outside Marseille, Provence; ✆ **04-90-54-33-07**): This Relais & Châteaux stands in the valley at the foot of Les Baux de Provence. The cuisine is superb, as are the accommodations, some of which are in buildings dating from the 16th and 17th centuries. See chapter 15.

- **Grand Hôtel du Cap-Ferrat** (St-Jean-Cap-Ferrat, Côte d'Azur; ✆ **800/225-4255** in the U.S., or 04-93-76-50-50): The Grand Hôtel occupies 14 prime acres on one of the world's most exclusive peninsulas. It's housed in a Belle Époque palace and, since the turn of the 20th century, has been the temporary home for royals, aristocrats, and wealthy wannabes. See chapter 16.

- **Hôtel du Cap–Eden Roc** (Cap d'Antibes, Côte d'Azur; ✆ **04-93-61-39-01**): Built during the grand Second Empire and set on 22 acres of splendidly landscaped gardens, this hotel is legendary, evoking shades of the F. Scott Fitzgerald classic *Tender Is the Night.* Swimmers will revel in a pool blasted from the dark rock of the glamorous coastline of Cap d'Antibes. See chapter 16.

- **Hôtel Négresco** (Nice, Côte d'Azur; ✆ **04-93-16-64-00**): Built in 1913 as a layered wedding cake in the château style, the Négresco was a lavish escape for the Edwardian era's most respected and most notorious figures, including Lillie Langtry, the long-term mistress of Britain's Edward VII. After her fall from grace, she sat in the Négresco's lobby, swathed in veils, refusing to utter a word. Following renovations, the hotel is better now than it was during its Jazz Age heyday. See chapter 16.

- **Hôtel du Palais** (Biarritz, Basque Country; ✆ **800/223-6800** in the U.S. and Canada, or 05-59-41-64-00): Delectably beautiful, this place was built in 1845 as a pink-walled summer palace for Napoléon III and his empress, Eugénie. Adept at housing such guests as Edward VII of England, Alfonso XIII of Spain, and the duke of Windsor, it's a Belle Époque fantasy. See chapter 18.

9 The Best Affordable Hotels

- **Hôtel de Lutèce** (Paris; ✆ 01-43-26-23-52): It slumbers on Paris's "other island," the Île St-Louis, which usually avoids the crush of visitors on the more popular Île de la Cité, just across the bridge. You'll still be right in the city, but can imagine yourself in a country inn at this tasteful retreat on the Seine. See chapter 4.

- **Hostellerie Lechat** (Honfleur, Normandy; ✆ 02-31-14-49-49): It overlooks a Norman 18th-century port favored by the French novelist Flaubert. The amenities here aren't grand, but you'll get the feeling that Madame Bovary herself may be about to roll into view in her notorious carriage. The setting, which includes a rustically appealing restaurant, is charming and—even more surprising—the price tag is reasonable. See chapter 8.

- **Hôtel d'Avaugour** (Dinan, Brittany; ✆ 02-96-39-07-49): Its exterior looks as antique as the fortifications ringing the medieval harbor, but a radical restoration transformed the interior into a cozy getaway on the Norman coast. Add its aesthetic appeal and the old-time flavor of Dinan's winding alleys and views of the Channel, and you've got the ingredients for an affordable escape. See chapter 9.

- **Ostellerie du Vieux-Pérouges** (Pérouges, Rhône Valley; ✆ 04-74-61-00-88): This hotel, described as a museum of the 13th century, is one of the most significant in central France. Composed of a group of much-restored 13th-century buildings with low ceilings and thick walls, it evokes the France of another day and doesn't overcharge. See chapter 13.

- **Hôtel Clair Logis** (St-Jean-Cap-Ferrat, Côte d'Azur; ✆ 04-93-76-04-57): The real estate that surrounds this converted 19th-century villa is among the most expensive in Europe, but this hotel manages to keep its prices beneath levels that really hurt. When you check into your room (named after a flower in the 2-acre garden surrounding the place), you'll be in good company: Even General de Gaulle, who knew the value of a centime, stayed here. See chapter 16.

- **Hôtel du Donjon** (Carcassonne, Languedoc; ✆ 800/528-1234 in the U.S. and Canada, or 04-68-11-23-00): Built into the bulwarks of Carcassonne, one of France's most perfectly preserved medieval fortresses, is this small-scale hotel whose furnishings provide a vivid contrast to the crude stone shell that contains them. A stay here allows you personal contact with a site that provoked battles between medieval armies. See chapter 17.

- **La Réserve** (Albi, Languedoc; ✆ 05-63-60-80-80): This dignified farmhouse is surrounded by scrublands, vineyards, groves of olives, and cypresses. It's less expensive than many of the ultra-luxurious hideaways along the nearby Côte d'Azur and has the benefit of a location just outside the center of one of our favorite fortified sites in Europe, the town of Albi. See chapter 17.

- **Tulip Inn Le Bayonne Etche-Ona** (Bordeaux, Atlantic Coast; ✆ 05-56-48-00-88): Like much of the rest of the neighborhood, this hotel was conceived during the 18th century as a showcase for French neo-classicism. Today, after a recent renovation, it offers modern comforts in an antique setting—and it's a great value. See chapter 19.

10 The Best Historic Places to Stay

- **Hôtel Trianon Palace** (Versailles, Île de France; ☏ **01-30-84-50-00**): Louis XIV nearly bankrupted France during the construction of his nearby palace, but this hotel overlooking its gardens might have been even more influential. In 1919, the Versailles Peace Treaty was ratified by delegates who stayed in the same rooms that today house guests. You'll be pampered at this plush, elegant hotel, which boasts its own spa. See chapter 6.

- **Château de Locguénolé** (Hennebont, Brittany; ☏ **02-97-76-76-76**): No professional decorator could ever have accumulated the array of furnishings and artifacts that 500 years' occupancy by generations of the same family have managed to cram into this Breton manor house. Some visitors think it's the most charming hotel in southern Brittany, a fact that's easy to believe once you experience its style and charm. See chapter 9.

- **Manoir du Stang** (La Forêt-Fouesnant, Brittany; ☏ **02-98-56-97-37**): Even the ivy that twines across the facade of this 16th-century Breton manor house looks as though it had been planted by someone very important, very long ago. Formal gardens segue into forested parkland; modern amenities are juxtaposed with enviable antiques—the place is a gem that happens to be a glamorous hotel. Some of the staff wear traditional Breton costumes. See chapter 9.

- **Château de Rochegude** (Rochegude, Provence; ☏ **04-75-97-21-10**): During the thousand years of this château's existence, its owners have included popes, dauphins, and less prominent aristocrats who showered it with taste and money. Today each room is outfitted in a style inspired by a specific emperor or king. The setting is 20 acres of parkland adjacent to the Rhône, outside Orange. See chapter 15.

- **Château de Roussan** (St-Rémy-de-Provence, Provence; ☏ **04-90-92-11-63**): One of this château's outbuildings was the home of the psychic Nostradamus, and its main building, sheltered by a stone neoclassical facade erected in 1701, is among the most beautiful in Provence. The château evokes another time and place, with none of the artificiality of the nearby Côte d'Azur. See chapter 15.

- **Château de Brindos** (Anglet, Basque Country; ☏ **05-59-23-17-68**): Built between 1923 and 1926 by the heiress to an American railway fortune (Virginia Gould) with her English husband (Reginald Wright), this château has an Art Deco facade, 14th-century Gothic ruins in its garden, and fireplaces and ceilings imported from other Renaissance palaces. Today, it offers an alluring combination of the Gilded Age as interpreted by the Jazz Age, plus superb food and spectacular architectural adornments. See chapter 18.

- **Château de la Vallée Bleue** (La Châtre, Massif Central; ☏ **02-54-31-01-91**): If you happen to stay in a room here named for Liszt, Chopin, Flaubert, or Delacroix, it's probably because they slept in the same spot. The château was built by a doctor committed to the well-being of his nearby patient, George Sand, author and feminist trendsetter whose masquerades as a man still provoke curiosity in this part of France. See chapter 21.

11 The Best Upscale Restaurants

- **Restaurant Plaza Athénée (Alain Ducasse)** (Paris; ☎ 01-53-67-66-65): Achieving a coveted three-star rating from Michelin seemed hardly to challenge this brash chef. Ducasse is the world's first five-star chef (three for Paris and two for his Louis XV in Monte Carlo). He's the darling of foodies and the spiritual heir of the legendary Escoffier. Who can outdo his pasta bathed in cream, sweetbreads, truffles, and (get this) the combs and kidneys of a proud, strutting cock? See chapter 4.
- **Le Grand Véfour** (Paris; ☎ 01-42-96-56-27): Amid the arcades of the Palais Royal, this has been a dining spot since the reign of Louis XV, attracting such notables as Colette, Victor Hugo, and the forever-loyal Jean Cocteau. Jean Taittinger, of the champagne family, runs it today, and his kitchen brings originality to French classics—everything from pigeon in the style of Rainier of Monaco to French-roasted sole and sea scallops in a velvety pumpkin sauce. See chapter 4.
- **Taillevent** (Paris; ☎ 01-44-95-15-01): Dining here is still the social and gastronomic high point of a Paris visit. Its premises (an antique house near the Arc de Triomphe) are suitably grand, and its cuisine appropriately stylish to the Jackie Onassis look-alikes who dine here. See chapter 4.
- **Boyer-les-Crayères** (Reims, Champagne; ☎ 03-26-82-80-80): This restaurant's setting is a lavish but dignified château with soaring ceilings and a French Empire decor. Built in 1904 as the home of the Pommery family (of champagne fortune) and surrounded by a 14-acre park, it's maintained by an impeccable staff that appreciates the nuances of service rituals. You can retire directly to your room after consuming a bottle or two of the region's famous bubbly. See chapter 10.
- **Auberge de l'Ill** (near Colmar, Alsace-Lorraine; ☎ 03-89-71-87-87): After a meal here, you'll understand why France and Germany fought for control of Alsace. Set amid farmland on the edge of the river Ill, this half-timbered manor house presents an idyllic setting. The food and wine served are rich, lush, and rooted in the vineyards surrounding the place. See chapter 11.
- **À la Côte St-Jacques** (Joigny, Burgundy; ☎ 03-86-62-09-70): Set on the edge of Burgundy, beside the river Yonne, this is the quintessential *restaurant avec chambres*. Indulge your taste for well-prepared food and wine; then totter off to one of about a dozen carefully furnished guest rooms among several buildings in this historic compound. One of our favorite dishes is cassolette of morels and frogs' legs, sublime when accompanied by a half bottle of red burgundy. See chapter 12.
- **L'Espérance** (Vézelay, Burgundy; ☎ 03-86-33-39-10): Housed in a farmhouse at the base of a hill (La Colline de Vézelay) that has been a holy site for thousands of years, L'Espérance is run by one of Europe's most famous chefs, Marc Meneau, and his wife, Françoise. The place combines country comforts with world-class sophistication. See chapter 12.
- **Paul Bocuse** (Collonges-au-Mont-d'Or, near Lyon, Rhône Valley; ☎ 04-72-42-90-90): Bocuse was the *enfant terrible* of French gastronomy through most of his youth. Today he's the

Impressions

Who can help loving the land that has taught us six hundred and eighty-five ways to dress eggs?

—Thomas Moore, *The Fudge Family in Paris* (1818)

world's most famous chef, catering to Europe's hardest-to-please customers. The cuisine is ostensibly Lyonnais, but Bocuse has never been limited by provincialism, and his mind wanders the world for inspiration. He creates signature dishes for his international fans—ranging from pigeon in puff pastry with foie gras to his celebrated black truffle soup. See chapter 13.

- **Hôtel-Restaurant Troisgros** (Roanne, Rhône Valley; © 04-77-71-66-97): The setting is the dining room of a once-nondescript hotel near a train station. The cuisine is a joyfully lush celebration of the agrarian bounty of France. Mingling specialties from all the regions, it attracts diners from as far away as Paris and Brussels. Years after they dine here, many

still speak reverently of their meal. See chapter 13.

- **Auberge du Père-Bise** (Talloires, French Alps; © 04-50-60-72-01): A mysterious alchemy transformed what was a simple lakeside chalet into an illustrious restaurant. Set beside Lac d'Annecy in eastern France, it's outfitted as the provincial home of local gentry, yet it serves elegant food favored by generations of people, including the Rothschilds. See chapter 14.
- **Le Moulin de Mougins** (Mougins, Côte d'Azur; © 04-93-75-78-24): Occupying a 16th-century olive mill in a Provence forest, this restaurant is the creation of chef Roger Vergé, the most sophisticated media genius in the French culinary world. See chapter 16.

12 The Best Affordable Restaurants

- **Crémerie-Restaurant Polidor** (Paris; © 01-43-26-95-34): For many Parisians, the cuisine here evokes memories of dinners their grandmothers might have concocted in the days after World War II. The unpretentious setting, where lace curtains filter the sunlight, drew even such iconoclasts as André Gide. See chapter 4.
- **Les Vapeurs** (Trouville, Normandy; © 02-31-88-15-24): An anomaly among the Norman coast's high-priced brasseries, this restaurant overlooking the port is no-frills, from its Art Deco decor to its fresh, well-priced seafood. Patrons enjoy the festive ambience. See chapter 8.

- **Chez La Mère Pourcel** (Dinan, Brittany; © 02-96-39-03-80): The references this place makes to someone's grandmother (Mère Pourcel) are justified, since the cuisine hasn't changed much in decades. That's just fine with its guests, many of whom drive from Paris for a day in the countryside and a well-priced dinner. See chapter 9.
- **Brasserie de l'Ancienne Douane** (Strasbourg, Alsace-Lorraine; © 03-88-15-78-78): In a city known for its Alsatian cuisine, this colorful restaurant is a frontrunner in the moderate category. In a medieval building, you can feast on the famous sauerkraut

and foie gras of the region, as well as on a particularly succulent specialty, chicken in Riesling wine. See chapter 11.

- **Au Chalet de Brou** (Bourg-en-Bresse, Rhône Valley; ℂ 04-74-22-26-28): Located in a town famous for its poultry, this restaurant sits across from the village church. It offers amazingly low prices on the local birds, and many food critics travel here from all over France for the hearty roast chicken. See chapter 13.
- **Le Bistro Latin** (Aix-en-Provence, Provence; ℂ 04-42-38-22-88): The deal here lies in the fixed-price menus, as carefully composed as a symphony. Prices are low, flavors are sensational, and hints of Italian zest pop up in dishes like risotto with scampi. See chapter 15.
- **Le Safari** (Nice, Côte d'Azur; ℂ 04-93-80-18-44): This ever-popular brasserie overlooking the cours Saleya market soaks up the Riviera sun. Dressed in jeans, waiters hurry back and forth, serving regulars and the visitors alike on the sprawling terrace. This place makes one of the best salade Niçoise in town, as well as a drop-dead delicious spring lamb roasted in a wood-fired oven. See chapter 16.

A Traveler's Guide to France's Art & Architecture

by Reid Bramblett

France's art treasures range from medieval stained glass and Ingres portraits to Monet's Impressionist waterlilies; its architecture encompasses Roman ruins and Gothic cathedrals as well as Renaissance châteaux and postmodern buildings like the Centre Pompidou. This brief overview will help you make sense of it all.

1 Art 101

PREHISTORIC, CELTIC & CLASSICAL (25,000 B.C.–A.D. 500)

After England's Stonehenge, Europe's most famous prehistoric remains are France's **Paleolithic cave paintings.** Created 15,000 to 20,000 years ago, they depict mostly hunting scenes and abstract shapes. Whether these paintings served in religious rites, or were simply decorative is anybody's guess.

Important examples of ancient art include:

- **Cave art.** The **caves at Lascaux,** the Sistine Chapel of prehistoric art, have been closed since 1963, but experts have created a replica, Lascaux II. To see the real stuff, visit **Les Eyzies-de-Tayac,** which boasts four caves (Font de Gaume is the best). In neighboring Lot Valley, outside Cahors, is the **Grotte du Pech-Merle,** with France's oldest cave art (about 20,000 years old).
- **Celtic & classical art.** Little remains of the art of **Celtic** (ca. 1,000 B.C.–A.D. 125) and **Roman** (A.D. 125–500) Gaul. What has survived—small votive bronzes, statues, jewelry, and engraved weapons and tools—is spread across France's **archaeology museums.** Burgundy preserves the most of Celtic Gaul, including sites at **Dijon, Châtillon-sur-Seine, Alise-Ste-Reine,** and **Auxerre.** For Roman Gaul, visit the southern towns of **Nîmes, Arles, Orange, St-Rémy-de-Provence,** and **Vienne.** You'll also find some sculptures in Paris's **Musée de Cluny.**

ROMANESQUE (900–1100)

Artistic expression in early medieval France was largely church-related. Because mass was recited in Latin, images were used to communicate the Bible's lessons to the illiterate masses. **Bas-reliefs** (sculptures that project slightly from a flat surface) were used to illustrate key tales that inspired faith in God and fear of sin (*Last Judgments* were favorites). These reliefs were wrapped around column capitals and fitted into the **tympanums** (the arched spaces above doorways; the complete door, tympanum, arch, and supporting pillars assemblage is the **portal**).

Worshipers were also interested in the bevy of specialized saints associated with everyday matters, such as crops, marriage, animals, and health. Chapels were built to house silver and gold **reliquaries** displaying bits of saints to which worshipers could pray. Saintly **statues** also began appearing on facades, though this became more of a Gothic convention.

The best examples of Romanesque art include:

- **Sculptures & statues.** The best surviving examples are a *Last Judgment* tympanum by Gislebertus at **St-Lazare** in Autun; 76 Romanesque cloister capitals and one of France's best-carved 11th-century portals at **St-Pierre Abbey** in Moissac near Montauban; the tympanum over the inner main portal of huge **Ste-Madeleine** in Vézelay; reliefs of *Christ and the Evangelists* by Bernard Guildin in the crypt of **St-Semin** in Toulouse; and the wonderfully detailed facade frieze and statues of **St-Pierre** in Angoulême.
- **Wall paintings & frescoes.** You'll find rare examples at **Nôtre-Dame** in Le Puy (ca. 1000), **St-Savin** near Poitiers (1100), and **Berzé-la-Ville** (1100) near Cluny.
- **Bayeaux Tapestry (1066–1077).** The one notable example of Romanesque artistry is the Bayeaux Tapestry, 230 feet of embroidered linen telling the story of William the Conqueror's famous defeat of the English.

GOTHIC (1100–1400)

Late-medieval French art remained largely ecclesiastical. Church facades and choir screens were festooned with **statues and carvings,** and the French became masters of **stained glass.** Many painterly conventions began on windowpanes or as elaborate designs in **illuminated manuscript** margins, which developed into altarpieces of the colorful, expressive **International Gothic** style of posed scenes and stylized figures.

In Gothic painting and sculpture, figures tended to be more natural than in the Romanesque, but were also highly stylized, flowing, and rhythmic. The features and gestures were usually exaggerated for symbolic or emotional emphasis.

The best examples of Gothic art include:

- **Sculpture & statues.** The best-preserved examples are at the cathedrals of **Chartres, Amiens,** and **Reims** (also see "Architecture 101," below), and at **Strasbourg,** which boasts one of the most elaborate Gothic portals and rose windows in France.
- **Stained glass.** All of the above churches (especially **Chartres**) contain some of the most stunning stained glass in Europe—though first prize goes to Paris's **Sainte-Chapelle.**
- **Painting.** Burgundy was the first French area to embrace the High Gothic painting style of its Flemish neighbors. The great **van der Weyden** left works in **Dijon** and **Beaune** as well as at the **Louvre.** The Dutch **Limbourg Brothers'** *Les Très Riches Heures* (1413–16, finished after their deaths), now in **Château de Chantilly,** is considered a touchstone of the International Gothic style. **Enguerrand Quarton** was the most important French painter of the period. His only documented paintings are *Virgin of Mercy* (1452) at **Chantilly** and a work at the **Musée de l'Hospice** in Villeneuve-lez-Avignon, but most scholars also attribute to him the **Louvre's** *Villeneuve Pietà* (1460).
- **Unicorn Tapestries (1499–1514).** Now in Paris's **Musée de Cluny,** these tapestries shine brightly as a statement of medieval sensibilities while borrowing some burgeoning Renaissance conventions.

THE RENAISSANCE & BAROQUE (1450–1800)

Renaissance means "rebirth," in this case of classical ideals. Humanist thinkers rediscovered the wisdom of ancient Greece and Rome, while artists strove for naturalism, using newly developed techniques like linear perspective. The French had little to do with this movement, which started in Italy and was picked up only in Germany and the Low Countries. However, many Renaissance treasures are in French museums, thanks to collectors such as **François I**.

Not until the 17th-century **baroque** did a few native French masters emerge. This period is hard to pin down. In some ways a result of the Catholic Counter-Reformation, it reaffirmed spirituality in a simplified, monumental, and religious version of Renaissance ideals. In other ways, it delved even deeper into classical modes and a kind of superrealism based on using peasants as models and the *chiaroscuro* (contrast of light and dark) of Italian painter Caravaggio.

Some view those two baroque movements as extensions of Renaissance experiments and find the true baroque in later, complex compositions—all explosions of dynamic fury, movement, color, and figures—that are still well balanced but in such cluttered abundance as to appear untamed. **Rococo** is this later baroque art gone awry: frothy and chaotic.

Paris's **Louvre** is filled with Renaissance works by Italian, Flemish, and German masters, including **Michelangelo** (1475–1564) and **Leonardo da Vinci** (1452–1519), whose *Mona Lisa* (1503–1505), perhaps the world's most famous painting, hangs there. Great baroque and rococo artists include

- **Nicolas Poussin (1594–1665).** While his mythological scenes presaged the Romantic Movement, on a deeper level his balance and predilection to paint from nature had closer connection to (and greater influence on) Impressionists like Cézanne. Find his works in the **Louvre** and in **Nancy.**
- **Antoine Watteau (1684–1721).** A rococo painter of colorful, theatrical works now in the **Louvre,** Watteau began the short-lived *fête galante* style of china-doll figures against stylized landscapes of woodlands or ballrooms.
- **François Boucher (1703–70).** Louis XV's rococo court painter, Boucher studied Watteau and produced decorative landscapes and genre works, now at the **Louvre.**
- **Jean-Honoré Fragonard (1732–1806).** Boucher's student and master of rococo pastel scenes, Fragonard painted an overindulgence of pink-cheeked, wispy, genteel lovers frolicking against billowing trees. His famous *The Bathers* hangs in the **Louvre.** More work is in Amiens's **Musée de Picardie.**

NEOCLASSICAL & ROMANTIC (1770–1890)

As the baroque got excessive and the rococo got cute, and as the somber Counter-Reformation got serious about imposing limits on religious art, several artists, like Jacques-Louis David, looked to the ancients. Viewing new excavations of Greek and Roman sites (Pompeii, Paestum) and statuary became integral parts of the Grand Tour through Italy, while the Enlightenment (and growing revolutionary) interest in Greek democracy beat an intellectual path to the distant past. This gave rise to a **neoclassical** style that emphasized symmetry, austerity, clean lines, and classical themes, such as depictions of historical or mythological scenes.

The **Romantics,** on the other hand, felt that both the ancients and the Renaissance had gotten it wrong and that the Middle Ages were the place to be. They idealized tales of chivalry and held a deep respect for nature, human rights, and the nobility of peasantry, as well as a suspicion of progress. Their paintings were heroic, historic, and (melo)dramatic.

The greatest artists and movements of the era include:

- **Jacques-Louis David (1744–1825).** David dropped the baroque after a year of study in Rome exposed him to neoclassicism, which he brought back to Paris and displayed in such paintings as *The Oath of the Horatii* (1784) and *Coronation of Napoléon and Joséphine* (1805–08), both in the **Louvre.**
- **Jean-Auguste-Dominique Ingres (1780–1867).** Ingres, who trained with David, from whom he broke to adapt a more Greek style, became a defender of the neoclassicists and the Royal French Academy, and opposed the Romantics. His *Grand Odalisque* (1814) hangs in the **Louvre.**
- **Théodore Géricault (1791–1824).** One of the early Romantics, Géricault painted the dramatic *The Raft of the Medusa* (1819), which served as a model for the movement. This large history painting hangs in the **Louvre.**
- **Eugène Delacroix (1798–1863).** Painted in the Romantic style, his *Liberty Leading the People* (1830), in the **Louvre,** reveals experimentation in color and brushstroke.
- **The Barbizon School.** This group of landscape painters, founded in the 1830s by **Théodore Rousseau** (1812–67), painted from nature at Barbizon, where the **Musée Ganne** is devoted to Rousseau's works. The paintings of **Jean-François Millet** (1814–75), who depicted classical scenes and peasants, still hang in his studio nearby and in Paris's **Musée d'Orsay.** You'll find works by **Jean-Baptiste-Camille Corot** (1796–1875), a sort of idealistic proto-Impressionist, in the **Louvre.**

IMPRESSIONISM (1870–1920)

Formal, rigid neoclassicism and idealized romanticism rankled some late-19th-century artists interested in painting directly from nature. Seeking to capture the fleeting *impression* of light reflecting off objects, they adopted a free, open style, characterized by deceptively loose compositions; swift, visible brushwork; and often light colors. For subjects, they turned away from the historical depictions of previous styles to landscapes and scenes of daily life. Unless otherwise specified below, you'll find some of their best works in the **Musée d'Orsay.**

Impressionist greats include:

- **Edouard Manet (1832–83).** His groundbreaking *Picnic on the Grass* (1863) and *Olympia* (1863) weren't Impressionism proper, but helped inspire the movement with their realism, visible brushstrokes, and thick outlines.
- **Claude Monet (1840–1926).** The Impressionist movement began with an 1874 exhibition in which Monet exhibited his loose, Turner-inspired *Impression, Sunrise* (1874), now in the **Musée Marmottan,** which one critic picked to lambaste the whole exhibition, deriding it all as "Impressionist." Far from being insulted, the show's artists adopted the word for their movement. Monet's *Water Lilies* hangs in the basement of Paris's **Musée de l'Orangerie.** You can visit his studio and gardens at **Giverny,** north of Paris.
- **Pierre-Auguste Renoir (1841–1919).** Originally Renoir was a porcelain painter, which helps explain his figures' ivory skin and chubby pink cheeks.
- **Edgar Degas (1834–1917).** Degas was an accomplished painter, sculptor, and draftsman—his pastels of dancers and bathers are memorable.
- **Auguste Rodin (1840–1917).** The greatest sculptor of the Impressionist era, Rodin crafted remarkably expressive bronzes, refusing to idealize the human figure as had his neoclassical predecessors. The **Musée Rodin,** his

former Paris studio, contains among other works, his *Burghers of Calais* (1886), *The Kiss* (1886–98), and *The Thinker* (1880).

POST-IMPRESSIONISM (1880–1930)

Few experimental French artists of the late 19th century were considered Impressionists, though many were friends with those in the movement. The smaller movements or styles are usually lumped together as "post-Impressionist."

Again, you'll find the best examples of their works at Paris's **Musée d'Orsay,** although the pieces mentioned below by Matisse, Chagall, and the Cubists are found in the **Centre Pompidou** instead.

Important post-Impressionists include:

- **Paul Cézanne (1839–1906).** Cézanne adopted the short brushstrokes, landscapes, and light color palette of his Impressionist friends, but his style was more formal and deliberate. He sought to give his art monumentality and permanence, even if the subjects were still lifes (*Nature Morte: Pommes et Oranges,* 1895–1900), portraits (*La Femme a la Cafetière,* 1890–95), and landscapes (*La Maison du Pendu Auvers-sur-Oise,* 1873).

- **Paul Gauguin (1848–1903).** Gauguin could never settle himself or his work, trying Brittany, where he developed **synthetism** (black outlines around solid colors), and hopping around the South Pacific, where he was inspired by local styles and colors, as in *Femmes de Tahiti sur la Plage* (1891).

- **Georges Seurat (1859–91), Paul Signac (1863–1935), and Camille Pissaro (1830–1903).** These artists developed **divisionism** and its more formal cousin, **pointillism.** Rather than mixing yellow and blue together to make green, they applied tiny dots of yellow and blue right next to one another so that the viewer's *eye* mixed them together to make green. His best work in the Orsay is *Le Cirque* (1891), though the lines are softer and subjects more compelling in the nude studies called *Les Poseuses* (1886–87).

- **Henri de Toulouse-Lautrec (1864–1901).** He's most famous for his work with thinned-down oils to create paintings and posters of wispy, fluid lines anticipating Art Nouveau, often depicting the bohemian life of Paris (dance halls, cafes, and top-hatted patrons at fancy parties), as in the barely sketched out *La Danse Mauresque* (1895); the pastel *Le Lit* (1892) shows his quieter, more intimate side.

- **Vincent van Gogh (1853–90).** Although Dutch by birth, van Gogh spent most of his artistic career in France. He combined divisionism, synthetism, and a touch of Japanese influence and painted with thick, short strokes. Never particularly accepted by any artistic circle, he is the most popular painter in the world today, even though he sold only one painting in his short life. The Orsay contains such famous works as *Le Chambre de Van Gogh à Arles* (1889), a self-portrait (1887), a portrait of his psychiatrist *Docteur Paul Gachet* (1890), and *La Méridienne* (1889–90).

- **Henri Matisse (1869–1954).** Matisse took a hint from synthetism and added wild colors and strong patterns to create **Fauvism** (a critic described those who used the style as *fauves,* meaning "wild beasts"), such as *Interior, Goldfish Bowl* (1914). He continued exploring these themes even when most artists were turning to Cubism. When his health failed, he assembled brightly colored collages of paper cutouts (such as the Pompidou's *Sorrow of the King,* 1952). You'll find several of his works in the **Musée Matisse** in Nice and his masterpiece, the **Chapelle du Rosaire** (1949–51), a chapel designed and decorated by him, near Vence.

- **Georges Braque (1882–1963) and Pablo Picasso (1881–1973).** French-born Braque and Spanish-born Picasso painted objects from all points of view at once, rather than using tricks like perspective to fool viewers into seeing three dimensions (in the Pompidou, Braque's *Man with Guitar,* 1914, and Picasso's 1907 study for *Les Demoiselle d'Avignon*). The result was called **Cubism** and was expanded upon by the likes of **Fernand Léger** (1881–1955; *Wedding* 1911) and the Spaniard **Juan Gris** (1887–1927; *Le Petit Déjeuner*, 1915). Braque developed the style using collage (he added bits of paper and cardboard to his images), while Picasso moved on to other styles. You can see all of Picasso's periods at museums dedicated to him in **Paris, Antibes,** and **Vallauris,** where Picasso revived the ceramics industry.
- **Marc Chagall (1889–1985).** This Hasidic Jewish artist is hard to pin down. He traveled widely in Europe, the United States, Mexico, and Israel; and his painting started from Cubism and picked up inspiration everywhere to fuel a brightly colored, allegorical, often whimsical style. You'll find a museum devoted to him in **Nice,** several of his stained-glass windows in the **Cathédrale Notre-Dame d'Amiens,** his painted ceiling in Paris's **Opéra Garnier,** and *To Russia, the Asses and the Others* (1911) in the Pompidou.

2 Architecture 101

While each architectural era has its own distinctive features, there are some elements, floor plans, and terms common to many of the eras.

From the Romanesque period on, most **churches** consist of either a single wide **aisle** or a wide central **nave** flanked by two narrow aisles. The aisles are separated from the nave by a row of **columns,** or more accurately by square stacks of masonry called **piers,** connected by **arches.** Sometimes—especially in the Romanesque and Gothic eras—there's a second level to the nave, above these arches (and hence above the low roof over the aisles) punctuated by windows called a **clerestory.**

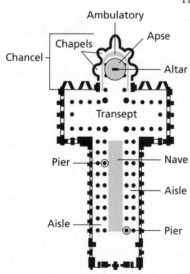

Church Floor Plan

This main nave/aisle assemblage is usually crossed by a perpendicular corridor called a **transept,** placed near the far, east end of the church so that the floor plan looks like a **Latin Cross** (shaped like a crucifix). The shorter, east arm of the nave is called the **chancel;** it often houses the stalls of the **choir** and the **altar.** If the far end of the chancel is rounded off, it is termed an **apse.** An **ambulatory** is a curving corridor outside the altar and the choir area, separating them from the ring of smaller chapels radiating off the chancel and apse.

Some churches, especially those built after the Renaissance, when mathematical proportion became important, have a **Greek Cross** plan, with each axis the same length—like a giant plus sign (+).

Very few buildings (especially churches) were built in one particular style. Massive, expensive structures often took centuries to complete, during which time tastes would change and plans would be altered.

ANCIENT ROMAN (125 B.C.–A.D. 450)

Provence was Rome's first transalpine conquest, and the legions of Julius Caesar quickly subdued the Celtic tribes across France, converting it into Roman Gaul.
Roman architectural innovations include:

- **The load-bearing arch.**
- **The use of concrete, brick, and stone.**

Nîmes preserves from the 1st century B.C. a 20,000-seat **amphitheater,** a **Corinthian temple** called the "Square House," a fine **archaeology museum,** and the astounding **Pont du Gard,** a 158-foot-long, three-story aqueduct made of cut stones fitted together without mortar.

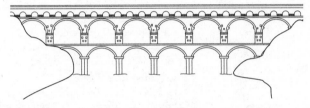

Pont du Gard

From the Augustan era of the 1st century A.D., **Arles** preserves a 25,000-seat **amphitheater,** a rebuilt **theater,** and a decent **museum.** The nearby **Glanum** excavations outside St-Rémy-de-Provence (which houses its **archaeology museum**) offer a complete, albeit highly ruined, glimpse of an entire Roman provincial town: from a few pre-Roman Gallic remnants and a 20 B.C. arch to the last structures sacked by invading Goths in A.D. 480.

ROMANESQUE (800–1100)

Romanesque churches were large, with a wide nave and aisles to accommodate the faithful who came to hear mass and worship at the altars of various saints. But to support the weight of all that masonry, the walls had to be thick and solid (meaning they could be pierced by only a few small windows) and had to rest on huge piers, giving Norman churches a dark, somber, and often oppressive feeling.
Some of the features of this style include:

- **Rounded arches.** These load-bearing architectural devices allowed the architects to open up wide naves and spaces, channeling all the weight of the stone walls and ceiling across the curve of the arch and down into the ground via the columns or pilasters.
- **Thick walls.**
- **Infrequent and small windows.**
- **Huge piers.**

The **Cathédrale St-Bénigne** in Dijon was the first French Romanesque church, but of that era only the crypt remains. The **Cathédrale St-Pierre** in

Angoulême has a single large nave, a rounded apse with small radiating chapels, and a pair of transept mini-apses.

GOTHIC (1100–1500)

By the 12th century, engineering developments freed architecture from the heavy, thick walls of the Romanesque and allowed ceilings to soar, walls to thin, and windows to proliferate. The Gothic was France's greatest homegrown architectural style, copied throughout Europe.

Instead of dark, relatively unadorned Romanesque interiors that forced the eyes of the faithful toward the altar, the Gothic interior enticed the churchgoers' gaze upward to high ceilings filled with light. The priests still conducted mass in Latin, but now peasants could "read" the stories told in stained-glass windows.

The squat, brooding exteriors of the Romanesque fortresses of God were replaced by graceful buttresses and soaring spires, which rose from town centers like beacons of religion.

Some identifiable Gothic features include:

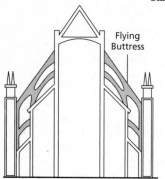

Cross Vault

- **Pointed arches.** The most significant development of the Gothic era was the discovery that pointed arches could carry far more weight than rounded ones.

- **Cross vaults.** Instead of being flat, the square patch of ceiling between four columns arches up to a point in the center, creating four sail shapes, sort of like the underside of a pyramid. The X separating these four sails is often reinforced with ridges called **ribbing**.

- **Flying buttresses.** These free-standing exterior pillars connected by graceful, thin arms of stone help channel the weight of the building and its roof out and down into the ground. Not every Gothic church has evident buttresses.

Flying
Buttress

- **Stained glass.** The multitude and size of Gothic windows allowed them to be filled with Bible stories and symbolism told in the colorful patterns of stained glass. The use of stained glass was more common in the later Gothic periods.
  - **Rose windows.** These huge circular windows, often the centerpieces of facades, are filled with elegant tracery and "petals" of stained glass.
  - **Tracery.** Lacy spider webs of carved stone curlicues grace the pointy end of windows and sometimes the spans of ceiling vaults.

Cross Section of Gothic Church

  - **Spires.** These pinnacles of masonry seem to defy gravity and reach toward Heaven itself.
- **Gargoyles.** These are drain spouts disguised as wide-mouthed creatures or human heads.
- **Choir screen.** Serving as the inner wall of the ambulatory and the outer wall of the choir section, the choir screen is often decorated with carvings.

The **Basilique St-Denis** (1140–1144), today in a Paris suburb, was the world's first Gothic cathedral. The statuary, spire, and some 150 glorious stained-glass windows of the **Cathédrale de Chartres** (1194–1220) make it a must-see, while the **Cathédrale Notre-Dame de Reims** (1225–90) sports over 2,300 exterior statues and stained glass from 13th-century rose window originals to 20th-century windows by Marc Chagall. The **Cathédrale Notre-Dame d'Amiens** (1220–36) is pure Gothic, its festival of statues and reliefs built with remarkable speed.

Paris's **Cathédrale de Nôtre-Dame** (1163–1250) has good buttresses, along with a trio of France's best rose windows, portal carvings, a choir screen of carved reliefs, and spiffy gargoyles (though many are actually 19th-century neo-Gothic). The *sine qua non* of stained glass is Paris's **Sainte-Chapelle** (1240–50).

Cathédrale de Chartres

RENAISSANCE (1500–1630)

In architecture as in painting, the Renaissance came from Italy and was only slowly Frenchified. And as in painting, its rules stressed proportion, order, classical inspiration, and precision to create unified, balanced structures.

Some identifiable Renaissance features include:

- **A sense of proportion.**
- **A reliance on symmetry.**
- **The use of classical orders.** This specifies three types of column capitals: Doric, Ionic, and Corinthian.

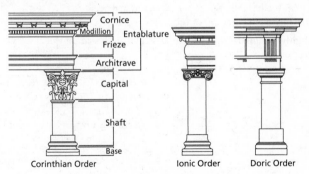

Classical Orders

- **Steeply pitched roofs.** They often feature **dormer windows** (upright windows projecting from a sloping roof).

The Loire Valley and Burgundy are well supplied with Renaissance **châteaux**. Foremost is the Loire's **Château de Chambord** started in 1519, probably according to plans by Leonardo da Vinci (who may have designed its double helix staircase). In contrast, the **Château de Chenonceau** (home to many a French king's wife or mistress) is a fanciful fairy tale built in the middle of a river. The best example in Burgundy is the **Château de Tanlay,** east of Chablis.

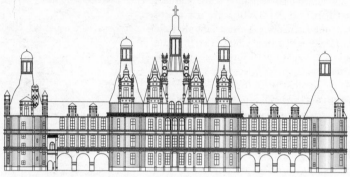

Château de Chambord

CLASSICISM & ROCOCO (1630–1800)

While Italy and Germany embraced the opulent baroque, France took the fundamentals of Renaissance **classicism** even further, becoming more imitative of ancient models—this represents a change from the Renaissance preference of finding inspiration in the classic era.

During the reign of Louis XIV, art and architecture were subservient to political ends. Buildings were grandiose and severely ordered on the Versailles model. Opulence was saved for the interior decoration, which increasingly (especially from 1715 to 1750, after the death of Louis XIV) became a detailed and self-indulgent **rococo** (*rocaille* in French). Externally, rococo is noticeable only by a greater elegance and delicacy.

Rococo tastes didn't last long, and soon a **neoclassical** movement was raising structures, such as Paris's **Pantheon** (1758), that were even more strictly based on ancient models than the earlier classicism had been.

Some identifiable features of classicism include:

- **Highly symmetrical, rectangular structures based on the classical orders.**
- **Projecting central sections topped by triangular pediments.**

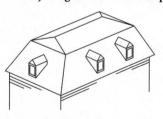

Mansard Roof

- **Mansard roofs.** A defining feature and true French trademark developed by **François Mansart** (1598–1666) in the early 15th century, a mansard roof has a double slope, the lower being longer and steeper than the upper.
- **Dormer windows.**
- *Oeil-de-bouef* ("ox-eyes"). These small, round windows poke out of the roof's slope.

The early-15th-century Parisian architect **François Mansart** built town houses, châteaux, and churches (**Val-de-Grâce** in Paris; the **Palais du Tau** in Reims) and laid out Dijon's **place de la Libération.** But he's chiefly remembered for his steeply sloping namesake, **"mansard" roofs.**

Louis Le Vau (1612–70) was the chief architect of the Louvre from 1650–1670 and also of the **Château de Vaux-le-Vicomte** (1656–61) outside Paris, a gig that put him and his collaborators—including Mansart, interior decorator **Charles Le Brun** (1619–90), and unparalleled landscape gardener **André Le Nôtre** (1613–1700)—on Louis XIV's radar and landed them the commission to rebuild **Versailles** (1669–85). Versailles is France's—indeed, Europe's—grandest palace.

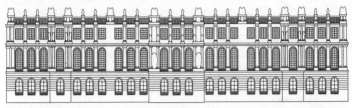

Versailles

Rococo is tough to find in architecture. In Paris, seek out Delamair's Marais town house, the **Hôtel de Soubise** (1706–12), and the prime minister's residence, the **Hôtel Matignon** (1721) by Courtonne. For rococo decor, check out the **Clock Room** in Versailles.

THE 19TH CENTURY

Architectural styles in 19th-century France began in a severe classical mode. Then they dabbled with medieval revival, delved into modern urban restructuring, and ended with an identity crisis torn between industrial-age advancements and Art Nouveau organic.

The 19th century saw several distinct styles, including:

- **First Empire.** Elegant neoclassical furnishings—distinguished by strong lines often accented with a simple curve—during Napoléon's reign.
- **Second Empire.** Napoléon III's reign saw the eclectic Second Empire reinterpret classicism in a dramatic mode. Paris was restructured by **Baron Haussmann** (1809–91), who cut broad boulevards through the city's medieval neighborhoods.
- **Third Republic/early industrial.** Expositions in Paris in 1878, 1889, and 1900 were the catalysts for constructing huge glass-and-steel structures that showed off modern techniques and the engineering prowess of the Industrial Revolution. This produced such Parisian monuments as the **Tour Eiffel** and **Sacré-Coeur.**
- **Art Nouveau.** Architects and decorators rebelled against the Third-Republic era of mass production by stressing the uniqueness of craft. They created asymmetrical, curvaceous designs based on organic inspiration (plants and flowers) in such mediums as wrought iron, stained glass, tile, and wallpaper.

Napoléon spent his imperial decade (1804–14) refurbishing the **Palais de Fontainebleau** in First Empire style. The ultimate paean to the classical was the **Arc de Triomphe** (1836), Napoléon's imitation of a Roman triumphal arch.

In the Second Empire, Napoléon III commissioned **Baron Haussmann** in 1852 to re-map Paris according to modern urban-planning theories—clearing out the tangles of medieval streets to lay out **wide boulevards** radiating off **grand squares** (the **Étoile** anchored by the Arc de Triomphe is his classic).

In 1889, the French wanted to show how far they had come since the Revolution. They hired **Gustave Eiffel** (1832–1923) to build the world's tallest structure, a temporary 1,051-foot-high tower made of riveted steel girders. Everyone agreed it was tall; most thought it was ugly and lacking in aesthetics. Its usefulness as a radio transmitter saved Eiffel's tower from being torn down.

Art Nouveau was less an architectural mode than a decorative movement, though you can still find some of the original Art Nouveau Métro entrances designed by **Hector Guimard** (1867–1942) in Paris. (A recently renovated entrance is at the Porte Dauphine station on the no. 2 line.)

THE 20TH CENTURY

France commissioned some ambitious architectural projects in the last century, most of them the *grand projets* of the late François Mitterrand. Most were considered controversial, outrageous, or even offensive. Other than a concerted effort to break convention and look stunningly modern, nothing unifies the look of this architecture—except that much of it was designed by foreigners.

Tour Eiffel

Britain's **Richard Rogers** (b. 1933) and Italy's **Renzo Piano** (b. 1937) turned architecture inside-out—literally—to craft the eye-popping **Centre Pompidou** (1977), Paris's modern art museum. Exposed pipes, steel supports, and plastic-tube escalators wrap around the exterior.

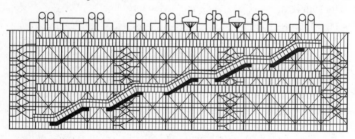

Centre Pompidou

Chinese-American maestro **I. M. Pei** (b. 1917) was called in to cap the Louvre's new underground Métro entrance with **glass pyramids** (1989), placed smack in the center of the Palais du Louvre's 17th-century courtyard.

In 1989, Paris's opera company moved into the curvaceous, dark glass mound of space of the **Opéra Bastille** (1989), designed by Canadian **Carlos Ott.** (Unfortunately, the acoustics have been lambasted.)

3

Planning Your Trip to France

In the pages that follow, we've compiled everything you need to know to handle the practical details of planning your trip: what documents you'll need, how to use French currency, how to find the best airfare, when to go, and more.

1 The Regions in Brief

Though France covers only 212,741 square miles (making it slightly smaller than Texas), no other country has such a fabulous diversity of sights and scenery into such a compact area. It offers examples of all the characteristics of Europe: the north's flat, fertile lands; the Loire Valley's rolling green hills; the east's alpine ranges; the towering Pyrénées; the Massif Central's plateaus and rock outcroppings; and the southeast's semitropical Mediterranean coast. Even more noteworthy are the cultural and historic differences that define each region.

And all these contrasts beckon within easy traveling range of Paris (located in the center of the country) and one another. The train trip from the capital is just 4 hours to Alsace, 5 to the Alps, 7 to the Pyrénées, and 8 to the Côte d'Azur. **French National Railroads (SNCF)** operates one of the finest lines in the world, with fast service to and from Paris (though trains tend to crawl on routes unconnected with the capital).

You'll find some 44,000 miles of roadway, most in good condition for fast long-distance driving. (But try not to go by the Route Nationale network all the time. Nearly all of France's scenic splendors lie along secondary roads, and what you lose in mileage you'll make up for in enjoyment.)

A "grand tour" of France is nearly impossible for the visitor who doesn't have a lifetime to explore the country. If you want to get to know a province in depth, it's good to devote a week to a specific region if you can; you may have a more rewarding trip if you concentrate on getting to know two or three areas at a leisurely pace rather than racing around, trying to cram in too much. You're going to be faced with hard choices about where to go in your limited time, so to help you decide, we've summarized the highlights of each region for you.

ÎLE DE FRANCE (INCLUDING PARIS) The Île de France is an island only in the sense that its boundaries (about a 50-mile radius from the center of Paris) are delineated by rivers with odd-sounding names like Essonne, Epte, Aisne, Eure, and Ourcq, plus a handful of canals. It was in this temperate basin that France was born. This region's attractions include **Paris, Versailles, Fontainebleau, Notre-Dame de Chartres,** and **Giverny,** it also incorporates dreary suburbs and even Disneyland Paris. Despite creeping industrialization, pockets of verdant charm remain, including the forests of Rambouillet and Fontainebleau and the artists' hamlet of Barbizon. For more information, see chapters 4, 5, and 6.

THE LOIRE VALLEY This area includes two ancient provinces, Touraine (centered on Tours) and Anjou (centered on Angers). It was beloved by royalty and nobility until Henry IV moved his court to Paris. Head here to see the most magnificent castles in France. Irrigated by the Loire River and its many tributaries, this valley produces many superb and reasonably priced wines. For more information, see chapter 7.

NORMANDY This region will forever be linked to the 1944 D-day invasion. Some readers consider a visit to the D-day beaches the most emotionally worthwhile part of their trip. Normandy boasts 372 miles of coastline and a maritime tradition. It's a popular weekend getaway from Paris, and many hotels and restaurants thrive here, especially around the casino town of **Deauville.** This area has hundreds of half-timbered houses reminiscent of medieval England, charming seaports like **Trouville,** and mighty ports like **Le Havre,** where the Seine flows into the English Channel. Normandy's great attractions include **Rouen** cathedral, the abbey of **Jumièges,** and medieval **Bayeux.** For more information, see chapter 8.

BRITTANY Jutting out into the Atlantic, the westernmost (and one of the poorest) regions of France is known for its rocky coastlines, Celtic roots, frequent rains, and ancient dialect, akin to the Gaelic tongues of Wales and Ireland. Many French vacationers love the seacoast (rivaled only by the Côte d'Azur) for its sandy beaches, cliffs, and relatively modest prices (by French standards). Highlights of the region are **Carnac** (home to ancient Celtic dolmens and burial mounds) and fishing ports like Quimper, Quiberon, Quimperlé, and Concarneau. The region's most sophisticated resort, **La Baule,** is near some of Brittany's best beaches. For more information, see chapter 9.

CHAMPAGNE Every French monarch since A.D. 496 was crowned at **Reims,** and much of French history revolved around this holy site and the fertile hills ringing it. Joan of Arc was burned at the stake due partly to her efforts to lead her dauphin through enemy lines to Reims. In the path of any invader wishing to occupy Paris, both Reims and the fertile Champagne district have seen much bloodshed through the centuries, including the World War I battles of Somme and Marne. There are industrial sites among patches of verdant forest, and the steep sides of valleys are sheathed in vineyards. The 78-mile road from Reims to Vertus, one of the three **Routes du Champagne,** takes in a trio of wine-growing regions that produce 80% of the world's bubbly. For more information, see chapter 10.

THE ARDENNES & NORTHERN BEACHES This northern region is often ignored by North Americans (which is why we feature it as a side trip from Reims in Champagne). In summer, French families arrive by the thousands to visit Channel beach resorts like **Le Touquet-Paris-Plage.** This district is quite industrialized and (like Champagne) has always been suffered in wars. The region's best-known port, **Calais,** was a bitterly contested English stronghold on the French mainland for centuries. Ironically, Calais is the port of disembarkation for the ferries, hydrofoils, and Channel Tunnel arrivals from Britain. **Notre-Dame Cathedral** in **Amiens,** the medieval capital of Picardy, is a treasure, with a 140-foot-high nave—the highest in France. Other than Amiens, the town holding the most interest is **Laon,** 74 miles southeast; it's still surrounded by medieval ramparts, which are the northeast's most rewarding attraction. For more information, see chapter 10.

ALSACE-LORRAINE Between Germany and the forests of the Vosges

The Regions of France

ENGLAND

English Channel

Strait of Dover

BELGIUM

Calais
Boulogne Lille
Cherbourg
THE
ARDENNES Arras
Amiens
GERMANY
LUXEMBOURG
Le Havre Rouen Oise
Caen ÎLE DE FRANCE
Golfe de
St-Malo NORMANDY Reims Metz ALSACE-
LORRAINE
Brest
Versailles ★ PARIS Marne Nancy
Quimper BRITTANY Rennes Chartres CHAMPAGNE Strasbourg
Le Mans Orléans Troyes Colmar
Belle-Ile Angers LOIRE VALLEY Yonne Mulhouse
St-Nazaire Nantes Loire Dijon Besançon
Indre Bourges
ATLANTIC Saône
OCEAN BURGUNDY
La Rochelle SWITZERLAND
Ile d'Oléron Lake
Geneva
Limoges Vichy Annecy
Bay Clermont- Lyon Mont
of Angoulême Ferrand Blanc
Biscay Périgueux MASSIF St-Etienne RHÔNE
Bordeaux CENTRAL VALLEY
Dordogne Grenoble
THE DORDOGNE FRENCH ITALY
& PÉRIGORD Valence ALPS
BORDEAUX Cahors
& THE Agen
ATLANTIC Montauban Nîmes Avignon
COAST Albi Montpellier PROVENCE Nice
Biarritz Toulouse FRENCH MONACO
Pau BASQUE LANGUEDOC- RIVIERA Cannes
Lourdes Carcassonne ROUSSILLON Marseille
COUNTRY Golfe du Toulon
Lion
ANDORRA MEDITERRANEAN SEA

SPAIN

0   100 mi
0   100 km

is the most Teutonic of France's provinces: Alsace, with cosmopolitan **Strasbourg** as its capital. Celebrated for its cuisine, particularly its foie gras and *choucroute* (sauerkraut), this area is home to villages whose half-timbered designs will make you think of the Black Forest. If you travel the *Route de Vin* (**Wine Road**), you can visit historic towns like Colmar, Riquewihr, and Illhaeusern, all famous to those who love great food and wine. **Lorraine,** birthplace of Joan of Arc,

witnessed countless bloody battles during the world wars. Its capital, **Nancy,** is the proud guardian of a grand 18th-century plaza: place Stanislas. The much-eroded peaks of the Vosges forest, the closest thing to a wilderness left in France, offer rewarding hiking. For more information, see chapter 11.

BURGUNDY Few trips will prove as rewarding as several leisurely days spent exploring Burgundy, with its splendid old cities like **Dijon.** Besides its famous cuisine (*boeuf* and *escargots à la bourguignonne*), the district contains, along its Côte d'Or, hamlets whose names (Mercurey, Beaune, Puligny-Montrachet, Vougeot, and Nuits-St-Georges) are synonymous with great wines. For more information, see chapter 12.

THE RHÔNE VALLEY   A fertile area of alpine foothills and sloping valleys in eastern and southeastern France, the upper Rhône Valley ranges from the cosmopolitan French suburbs of the Swiss city of Geneva to the northern borders of Provence. The district is thoroughly French, unflinchingly bourgeois, and dedicated to preserving the gastronomic and cultural traditions that have produced some of the most celebrated chefs in French history.

Only 2 hours by train from Paris, the region's cultural centerpiece, **Lyon**, is France's "second city." North of here, you can travel the Beaujolais trail or head for Bresse's ancient capital, **Bourg-en-Bresse,** which produces the world's finest poultry. You can explore the Rhône Valley en route from northern climes to Provence and the south. Try to visit the medieval villages of **Pérouges** and **Vienne,** 17 miles south of Lyon; the latter is known for its Roman ruins. For more information, see chapter 13.

THE FRENCH ALPS   This area's resorts rival those of neighboring Switzerland and contain incredible scenery: snowcapped peaks, glaciers, and alpine lakes. **Chamonix** is a famous ski resort facing **Mont Blanc,** Western Europe's highest mountain. However, **Courchevel** and **Megève** are more chic. During the summer, you can enjoy such spa resorts as **Evian** and the calm, restful 19th-century resorts ringing **Lake Geneva.** For more information, see chapter 14.

PROVENCE   One of France's most fabled regions flanks the Alps and the Italian border along its eastern end, and incorporates a host of sites the rich and famous have long frequented. Premier destinations are **Aix-en-Provence,** associated with Cézanne; **Arles,** "the soul of Provence," captured brilliantly by van Gogh; **Avignon,** the 14th-century capital of Christendom during the papal schism; and **Marseille,** a port city established by the Phoenicians (in some ways more North African than French). Provence gems are the small villages, like **Les Baux, Gordes,** and **St-Rémy-de-Provence,** birthplace of Nostradamus. The strip of glittering coastal towns along Provence's southern edge is known as the **Côte d'Azur** (the French Riviera; see the following section). For more information, see chapter 15.

THE FRENCH RIVIERA (CÔTE D'AZUR)   The fabled gold-plated *Côte d'Azur* (Blue Coast) has become quite overbuilt and spoiled by tourism. Even so, the names of its resorts still evoke glamour: **Cannes, St-Tropez, Cap d'Antibes, and St-Jean-Cap-Ferrat.** July and August are the most crowded, but spring and fall can be a delight. **Nice** (pronounced "niece") is the biggest city, and the most convenient for exploring the area. The independent principality of **Monaco,** the most fabled piece of real estate along the Côte d'Azur, occupies less than a square mile. Along the coast are some sandy beaches, but many are rocky or pebbly. Topless bathing is common, especially in St-Tropez, and some of the restaurants here are fabled citadels of conspicuous consumption. This is not just a place for sun and fun. Dozens of artists and their patrons have littered the landscape with world-class galleries and art museums. For more information, see chapter 16.

LANGUEDOC-ROUSSILLON
Languedoc may not be as chic as

Provence, but it's less frenetic and more affordable. **Roussillon** is the rock-strewn arid French answer to ancient Catalonia, just across the Spanish border. The **Camargue** is the name given to the steaming marshy delta formed by two arms of the Rhône River. Rich in bird life, it's famous for its flats of tough grasses and for fortified medieval sites as **Aigues-Mortes.** Also appealing are **Auch,** the capital of Gascony; **Toulouse,** the bustling pink capital of Languedoc; and the "red city" of **Albi,** birthplace of Toulouse-Lautrec. **Carcassonne,** a marvelously preserved walled city with fortifications begun around A.D. 500, is the region's highlight. For more information, see chapter 17.

THE BASQUE COUNTRY   Since prehistoric times, the rugged Pyrénées have formed a natural boundary between France and Spain. Sheltered within the valleys flourished one of Europe's most unusual cultures: the Basques. In the 19th century, resorts like **Biarritz** and **St-Jean-de-Luz** attracted the French aristocracy—the empress Eugénie's palace at Biarritz is now a hotel. The **Parc National des Pyrénées** is crisscrossed with hiking trails, and four million Catholics annually make pilgrimages to the city of Lourdes. In the villages and towns of the Pyrénées, the old folkloric traditions, strongly permeated with Spanish influences, continue to thrive. For more information, see chapter 18.

THE ATLANTIC COAST   Flat, fertile, and frequently ignored by North Americans, this region includes towns pivotal in French history (**Saintes, Poitiers, Angoulême,** and **La Rochelle**) as well as wine- and liquor-producing villages (**Cognac, Margaux, St-Emilion,** and **Sauternes**) whose names are celebrated around the world. **Bordeaux,** the district's largest city, has an economy based on wine merchandising and boasts grand 18th-century architecture. For more information, see chapter 19.

THE DORDOGNE & PÉRIGORD
The land of *foie gras* and truffles is the site of some of Europe's oldest prehistoric settlements. For biking or just indulging in gourmet meals, the region is among the top vacation spots in France. In the Périgord, traces of Cro-Magnon settlements are evidenced by the cave paintings at **Les Eyzies.** The Dordogne is the second-largest *département* (French equivalent of an American state). Some of France's most unusual châteaux were built in the valley during the early Middle Ages, and many towns that grew here are spectacularly beautiful. The region is no longer undiscovered, as retirees from abroad have moved into the elegant stone houses dotting the banks of the many rivers. Highlights are the ancient towns of **Périgueux, Les Eyzies-de-Tayac, Sarlat-le-Canéda, Beynac-et-Cazenac,** and **Souillac.** For more information, see chapter 20.

THE MASSIF CENTRAL   The rugged heartland of south-central France, this underpopulated district contains ancient cities, unspoiled scenery, and an abundance of black lava, from which many area buildings were created. According to Parisians, the Massif Central is provincial—and the locals work hard to keep it that way. The largest cities are historic **Clermont-Ferrand** and **Limoges**—the medieval capitals of the provinces of the Auvergne and the Limousin. **Bourges,** a gateway to the region and once capital of Aquitaine, has a beautiful Gothic cathedral. For more information, see chapter 21.

2 Visitor Information

Your best source of information before you go is the **French Government Tourist Office** (**www.fgtousa.org**), which can be reached at the following addresses:

- **In the United States,** contact 444 Madison Ave., 16th floor, New York, NY 10022 (© **212/838-7800**); 676 N. Michigan Ave., Suite 3360, Chicago, IL 60611-2819 (© **312/751-7800**); or 9454 Wilshire Blvd., Suite 715, Beverly Hills, CA 90212-2967 (© **310/271-6665**). To request information, you can try **France on Call** (© **410/286-8310**).
- **In Canada,** contact the Maison de la France/French Government Tourist Office, 1981 av. McGill College, Suite 490, Montréal H3A 2W9 (© **514/288-4264**; fax 514/845-4868).
- **In the United Kingdom,** contact the Maison de la France/French Government Tourist Office, 178 Piccadilly, London W1V 0AL (© **020/7399-3500**; fax 020/9221-8682).
- **In Ireland,** call the Maison de la France/French Government Tourist Office, 10 Suffolk St., Dublin 2 (© **01/679-0813**).
- **In Australia,** contact the French Tourist Bureau, 6 Perth Ave., Xarralumia, NSW 2000 (© **02/6216-0100**; fax 02/9221-8682).
- **In New Zealand,** there's no representative, so call the Australia phone or fax number above.

3 Entry Requirements & Customs Regulations

DOCUMENTS

All foreign (non-French) nationals need a valid passport to enter France.

The French government no longer requires visas for **U.S. citizens,** providing they're staying in France for less than 90 days. For longer stays, U.S. visitors must apply for a long-term visa, residence card, or temporary-stay visa. Each requires proof of income or a viable means of support in France and a legitimate purpose for remaining in the country. Applications are available from the **Consulate Section of the French Embassy,** 4101 Reservoir Rd. NW, Washington, DC 20007 (© **202/944-6000**), or from the visa section of the French Consulate at 10 E. 74th St., New York, NY 10021 (© **212/606-3689**). Visas are required for students planning to study in France even if the stay is for less than 90 days.

Border Crossings to Monaco

Tiny Monaco (1.21 square miles in all) is an independent nation, but you'd hardly know it. Document requirements for travel to Monaco are the same as those for France, and there are virtually no border patrols or passport formalities at the Monégasque frontier. (You will, however, need a coat and tie if you wish to wager at the upscale casinos in Monte Carlo.)

If you'd like information specifically about the principality of Monaco, contact the **Monaco Government Tourist and Convention Bureau,** 565 Fifth Ave., 23rd floor, New York, NY 10017 (© **212/286-3330**; fax 212/286-9890). In the United Kingdom, contact the office at 3/18 Chelsea Garden Market, The Chambers, Chelsea Harbour, London SW10 OXF (© **020/7352-9962**; fax 020/7352-2103).

At the moment, citizens of **Britain, Canada, New Zealand, Switzerland, Japan,** and **European Union** countries do not need visas.

Australians need visas to enter France. They're available from the French Consulate, Consulate General, 31 Market St., 26th floor, Sydney, NSW 2000 (✆ **02/9261-5779**).

South Africans also need visas to enter France. They're available from the French Consulate, 40 Queen Victoria St., Cape Town 8001 (✆ **021/423-82-84;** fax 021/423-09-35).

Residents of all other countries can check with the nearest French government tourist office. See "Visitor Information," above.

CUSTOMS

WHAT YOU CAN BRING INTO FRANCE Customs restrictions for visitors entering France differ for citizens of the European Union (EU) and non-EU countries. Non-EU nationals can bring in duty-free 200 cigarettes, 100 cigarillos, 50 cigars, or 250 grams (87.50 oz.) of smoking tobacco. This amount is doubled if you live outside Europe. You can also bring in 2 liters of wine and 1 liter of alcohol over 22 proof, and 2 liters of wine 22 proof or under. In addition, you can bring in 50 grams (17.5 oz.) of perfume, a quarter liter of eau de toilette, 500 grams (175 oz.) of coffee, and 200 grams (70 oz.) of tea. Visitors ages 15 and over can bring in other goods totaling 300F (45.60, $43.50); for those 14 and under, the limit is 600F (91.20, $87). (Customs officials tend to be lenient about general merchandise, realizing that the limits are unrealistically low.)

Citizens of EU countries can bring in any amount of goods as long as these goods are intended for their personal use and not for resale.

WHAT YOU CAN BRING HOME Returning **U.S. citizens** who have been away for 48 hours or more are allowed to bring back, once every 30 days, $400 worth of merchandise duty-free. You'll be charged a flat rate of 10% duty on the next $1,000 worth of purchases. Have your receipts handy. On gifts, the duty-free limit is $100. You cannot bring fresh foodstuffs into the United States; canned foods, however, are allowed. For more information, contact the **U.S. Customs Service,** 1301 Constitution Ave. (P.O. Box 7407), Washington, DC 20044 (✆ **202/927-6724;** www.customs.ustreas.gov), offers a free pamphlet, *Know Before You Go.*

Citizens of the United Kingdom who are returning from a European Community (EU) country will go through a separate Customs Exit (called the "Blue Exit") especially for EU travelers. In essence, there is no limit on what you can bring back from an EU country, as long as the items are for personal use (this includes gifts) and you have already paid the necessary duty and tax. However, customs law sets out guidance levels. If you bring in more than these levels, you may be asked to prove that the goods are for your own use. Guidance levels on goods bought in the EU for your own use are 800 cigarettes, 200 cigars, 1kg smoking tobacco, 10 liters of spirits, 90 liters of wine (of this not more than 60 liters can be sparkling wine), and 110 liters of beer. For more information, contact **HM Customs & Excise,** Passenger Enquiry Point, 2nd floor Wayfarer House, Great South West Road, Feltham, Middlesex, TW14 8NP (✆ **020/8910-3744** or 44/20-8910-3744 from outside the U.K.; www.hmce.gov.uk).

Citizens of Canada can find a summary of the rules at the comprehensive website of the Canada Customs and Revenue Agency (www.ccra-adrc.gc.ca). You can also write for the booklet *I Declare,* issued by **Revenue Canada,** 2265 St. Laurent Blvd., Ottawa K1G 4KE (✆ **506/636-5064**).

Canada allows its citizens a $750 exemption, and you're allowed to bring back duty-free 200 cigarettes, 50 cigars, 2.2 pounds of tobacco, and 1.5 liters of liquor. In addition, you're allowed to mail gifts to Canada from abroad at the rate of Can$60 a day, provided they're unsolicited and don't contain alcohol or tobacco (write on the package "Unsolicited gift, under $60 value").

Citizens of Australia should request the helpful Australian Customs brochure *Know Before You Go,* available by calling ℂ **02/921-32-000** from within Australia, or 612/ 6275-6666 from abroad. For more information, point your browser to www.customs.gov.au and click on "Hints for Australian Travelers." The duty-free allowance is A$400; for those under 18, A$200. In addition, Australian citizens can bring back 250 cigarettes or 250 grams of loose tobacco, and 1.125 liters of alcohol.

Citizens of New Zealand can obtain customs information from the **New Zealand Customs Service,** 50 Anzac Ave., P.O. Box 29, Auckland (ℂ **09/359-6655;** www.customs.govt. nz). The duty-free allowance is NZ$700. Citizens over 17 can bring in 200 cigarettes or 50 cigars or 250 grams of tobacco (or a mixture of all three if the combined weight is less than 250g); plus 4.5 liters of wine and beer, or 1.125 liters of liquor.

4 Money

France is one of the world's most expensive destinations. To compensate, it often offers top-value food and lodging. Part of the cost is the value-added tax (VAT in English, or TVA in French), which adds between 6% and 33% to everything.

It's expensive to rent and drive a car (gasoline is costly, too), and flying within France costs more than flying within the United States. Train travel is relatively inexpensive, however, especially if you purchase a railpass.

Remember prices in Paris and on the Riviera will be higher than in the provinces. Three of the most touristed areas—Brittany, Normandy, and the Loire Valley—have reasonably priced hotels and many restaurants offering superb food at moderate prices.

If you need a check in French francs before your trip (for example, for a hotel room deposit), contact **Ruesch International** (ℂ **800/424-2923;** www.ruesch.com). Ruesch offers a variety of conversion-related services, usually for $5 to $15 per transaction. You can also inquire at a local bank.

CURRENCY

During part of the life of this edition, France will have two currencies—the old French franc and the new euro adopted by 11 nations of the European Union. French currency is based on the **franc (F),** which consists of 100 **centimes (c).** Coins come in units of 5c, 10c, 20c, and 50c (usually referred to as a half-franc coin) and 1F, 2F, 5F, and 10F. Notes come in denominations of 20F, 50F, 100F, 200F, 500F, and 1,000F.

The franc will remain France's currency until early 2002. Then the **euro,** which became the official single currency of France and 11 other countries in 1999, will take over. (See "The World's Greatest Financial Merger: The Euro," below.)

All banks are equipped for foreign exchange, and you'll find exchange offices at the airports. Banks are open Monday through Friday from 9am to noon and 2 to 4pm. Major banks also open their exchange departments on Saturday from 9am to noon.

When converting your home currency into French francs or euros, be

The World's Greatest Financial Merger: The Euro

The adoption of a single European currency called the **euro ( )** is a contentious move within Europe. Though most of Western Europe has been interconnected as an economic and trade unit for years, the official merger of its national currencies is another matter. Up until the last minute, all the countries involved jockeyed for the best deal for their nation before the final papers were signed, and even now the euro is an official currency, they're still fighting over the details of how it will be phased in.

In 1999, the countries that adopted the euro—Austria, Belgium, Finland, France, Germany, Ireland, Italy, Luxembourg, the Netherlands, Portugal, and Spain—locked their exchange rates together and switched most business transactions and computer and credit-card banking to the new currency, which, after some ups and significant downs, seems leveled out just below parity with the dollar ($1 = 1.07). Greece joined the group in 2001. Several countries, including Britain, Denmark, and Sweden, have opted out of switching for the time being (though Denmark and Sweden seem to be moving closer to voting it in). Switzerland is not part of the EU.

The euro as physical banknotes and coins will be issued on December 15, 2001 (but not officially to be used until January 1, 2002), and the various national currencies won't be fully withdrawn until February 28—down from the 6 months previously announced. Exceptions: France and Ireland plan to phase out francs and pounds by mid-February, and Germany is cutting things close by doing away with deutsche marks on New Year's Eve 2001.

Because you'll still be juggling francs alongside euros until then, the prices in this book are quoted in the old national currencies, the new euros, and dollars: for example, 330F (50, $47). Note that most Europeans will still think in local currencies and settle their prices in round numbers of francs, then merely convert that to the euro amount. Expect when the euro actually exists that the euro price will be the one rounded off. Therefore (just this once!) the rates quoted in this edition may be a little off.

aware that rates vary. Your hotel will probably offer the worst exchange rate. In general, banks offer the best rate, but even they charge a $2 to $5 commission, depending on the transaction. Whenever you can, stick to the big Paris banks, like Crédit Lyonnais, which usually offer the best rates and charge the least commission.

ATMs

ATMs are linked to a national network that most likely includes your bank at home. **Cirrus/MasterCard** (✆ **800/424-7787;** www.mastercard. com) and **PLUS/Visa** (✆ **800/843-7587;** www.visa.com) are the two most popular networks; check the back of your ATM card to see which network your bank belongs to. Use the 800 numbers to locate ATMs in your destination. Cirrus is linked to **Credit Lyonnais, Banque Nationale de Paris, Ceile de France,** and **Société Generale.** PLUS is linked to **Société**

The French Franc, the U.S. Dollar, the British Pound & the Euro

Because exchange rates fluctuate, this table should be used as a general guide.

At press time, $1 U.S. = approximately 6.89F (or 1F = 14.5¢). This was the rate of exchange used to calculate the dollar values given in this book. At this writing, £1 = approximately 10.34F (or 1F = 9.7 pence). As a rough guideline, subject to multiple revisions as Europe's newest currency increases in usage, 1 = about 6.57F, 91¢, or 63 U.K. pence.

FF	US$	UK	Euro	FF	US$	UK	Euro
1	0.15	0.10	0.15	75.00	10.88	7.28	11.4
2	0.29	0.19	0.30	100.00	14.50	9.70	15.20
3	0.44	0.29	0.46	125.00	18.13	12.13	19.00
4	0.58	0.39	0.61	150.00	21.75	14.55	22.80
5	0.73	0.49	0.76	175.00	25.38	16.98	26.60
6	0.87	0.58	0.91	200.00	29.00	19.40	30.40
7	1.02	0.68	1.06	225.00	32.63	21.83	34.20
8	1.16	0.78	1.22	250.00	36.25	24.25	38.00
9	1.31	0.87	1.37	275.00	39.88	26.68	41.80
10	1.45	0.97	1.52	300.00	43.50	29.10	45.60
15	2.18	1.46	2.28	350.00	50.75	33.95	53.20
20	2.90	1.94	3.04	400.00	58.00	38.80	60.80
25	3.63	2.42	3.80	500.00	72.50	48.50	76.00
50	7.25	4.85	7.60	1000.00	145.00	97.00	152.00

Generale, Banque National de Paris, Carte Bleue Group, and Credit Lyonnais. You can also ask your bank for a list of overseas ATMs. Be sure to check the daily withdrawal limit. Also, make sure you have a PIN you can use in Europe. Depending on the number of digits in your PIN, you may not be able to use your ATM abroad; to get cash at ATMs in France, your PIN must be 4 digits long.

TRAVELER'S CHECKS

Traveler's checks are something of an anachronism from the days before the ATM made cash accessible at any time. These days, traveler's checks seem less necessary because most cities have 24-hour ATMs that allow you to withdraw cash as needed right from your own bank account, although you might be subject to a small fee for doing so. But some travelers still prefer the security offered by traveler's checks, because you can get a refund if they're lost or stolen, if you've kept a record of their serial numbers.

You can get traveler's checks at almost any bank. American Express offers checks in denominations of $10, $20, $50, $100, $500, and $1,000. You'll pay a service charge ranging from 1% to 4%. You can also get American Express traveler's checks by calling © 800/221-7282 or 800/721-9768, or going online to www.americanexpress.com. Gold or platinum cardholders can avoid paying the fee by ordering over the phone; platinum cardholders can also purchase checks fee-free at AmEx Travel Service locations (check the website for the office nearest you). American Automobile Association (AAA) members can obtain checks fee-free at most AAA offices.

Visa offers traveler's checks at **Citibank** branches and other financial institutions; call ✆ **800/227-6811** for a location near you. **MasterCard** also offers traveler's checks through **Thomas Cook Currency Services;** call ✆ **800/223-7373** for a location near you.

If you carry traveler's checks, keep a record of the serial numbers separately from the checks, so you're ensured a refund in case they're lost or stolen.

CREDIT CARDS

Credit cards are invaluable when traveling. They're a safe way to carry money and provide a record of all your expenses. You can also withdraw cash advances from your credit cards at any bank (though you'll start paying interest on the advance the moment you receive the cash, and you won't receive frequent-flyer miles on an airline credit card). At most banks, you don't even need to go to a teller; you can get a cash advance at the ATM if you know your PIN. (If you've forgotten your PIN or didn't know you had one, call the credit card company and ask them to send it to you.

Almost every credit-card company has an emergency toll-free number you can call if your card is stolen. The company may be able to wire you a cash advance off your credit card immediately, and in many places, can deliver an emergency credit card in a day or two. Citicorp Visa's U.S. emergency number is ✆ **800/336-8472.** American Express cardholders and traveler's check holders should call ✆ **800/233-5439.** MasterCard holders should call ✆ **800/307-7309.**

5 When to Go

July and August are the worst months. Parisians desert their city, leaving it to the crowds of tourists and the businesses that cater to them.

The best time to visit Paris is off-season, in the long spring (April through June) or the equally extensive fall (September through November), when the tourist trade is a manageable flow and everything is easier to come by—from Métro seats to good-tempered waiters. The weather is temperate throughout the year.

Hotels used to charge off-season rates during the cold, rainy period from November through February, when tourism slowed; now, they're often packed with business clients, trade fairs, and winter tour groups and there's less incentive for hoteliers to offer reductions. Airfares, however, are still cheaper in these months, and more promotions are available. They rise in the spring and fall, peaking in the heavily trafficked summer months when tickets cost the most.

Don't come to Paris in the first 2 weeks of October without a confirmed hotel reservation. The weather's fine, but the city is jammed for the auto show, when the French indulge their passion for cars.

WEATHER

France's weather varies considerably from region to region and sometimes from town to town as few as 12 miles apart. Despite its northern latitude, Paris never gets very cold—snow is a rarity. The hands-down winner for wetness is Brittany, where Brest (known for the mold that adds flavor to its bleu cheeses—probably caused by the constant rainfall) receives a staggering amount of rain between October and December. The rain usually falls in a kind of steady, foggy drizzle and rarely lasts more than a day. May is the driest month.

The Mediterranean coast in the south has the driest climate. When it does rain, it's heaviest in spring and autumn. (Cannes sometimes receives more rainfall than Paris.) Summers are comfortably dry—beneficial to humans but deadly to vegetation, which (unless it's irrigated) often dries and burns up in the parched months.

Provence dreads *le mistral* (an unrelenting, hot, dusty wind), which most often blows in winter for a few days but can last for up to 2 weeks.

HOLIDAYS

In France, holidays are *jours fériés*. Shops and many businesses (banks and some museums and restaurants) close on holidays, but hotels and emergency services remain open.

The main holidays—a mix of both secular and religious—include New Year's Day (January 1), Easter Sunday and Monday, Labor Day (May 1), V-E Day in Europe (May 8), Whit Monday (May 19), Ascension Thursday (40 days after Easter), Bastille Day (July 14), Assumption of the Blessed Virgin (August 15), All Saints' Day (November 1), Armistice Day (November 11), and Christmas (December 25).

FRANCE CALENDAR OF EVENTS

January

Monte Carlo Motor Rally. The world's most venerable car race. For information, call ⓒ **92-16-61-66.** Usually mid-January.

International Ready-to-Wear Fashion Shows (Le Salon International de Prêt-à-porter), Parc des Expositions, Porte de Versailles, Paris 15e (ⓒ **01-44-94-70-00**). Here you'll see what the public will be wearing in 6 months. Mid-January to mid-February.

February

Carnival of Nice. Parades, boat races, street music, balls, and fireworks are all part of this ancient celebration. The climax is the 113-year-old tradition of burning King Carnival in effigy, an event preceded by *Les Batailles des Fleurs* (Battles of the Flowers), during which opposing teams pelt one another with flowers. Make your hotel reservations well in advance. For information, contact the Nice Convention and Visitors Bureau (ⓒ **04-92-14-48-00;** fax 04-92-14-48-03). Mid-February to early March.

March

Foire du Trône, on the Neuilly Lawn of the Bois de Vincennes, Paris. This mammoth amusement park operates daily from 2pm to midnight. Call ⓒ **01-46-27-52-29.** End of March to late May.

April

The 24-hour Le Mans Motorcycle Race. For information, call Automobile Club de l'ouest (ⓒ **02-43-40-24-24**). June 17 and 18.

International Marathon of Paris. Runners from around the world compete. Call ⓒ **01-41-33-15-68.** First weekend in April.

Son-et-Lumière (Sound-and-Light) Shows, Loire Valley. April to September.

May

Anniversary of the End of World War II, Paris and Reims. Though the Nazis' surrender was signed on May 7, 1945, the celebration lasts several days in Paris, with more festivity in Reims. ⓒ **08-36-48-31-12** in Paris. May 5 to 8.

Cannes Film Festival. Movie madness transforms this city into a media circus, with daily melodramas acted out in cafes, on sidewalks, and in hotel lobbies. Reserve early and make a deposit. Admission to the prestigious films is by invitation only. There are box-office tickets for the other films, which play 24 hours. Contact the Festival International du Film (FIF), 99 bd. Des Malesherbes, 75008 Paris (*①* 01-45-61-66-00; fax 01-45-61-87-60). Two weeks before the festival, the event's administration moves to the Palais des Festivals, esplanade Georges-Pompidou, 06400 Cannes (*①* 04-93-39-01-01). May 9 to 20.

French Open Tennis Championship, Stade Roland-Garros, 16e (Métro: Porte d'Auteuil). The Open features 10 days of Grand Slam men's, women's, and doubles tennis on the hot, red, slow, dusty courts. For tickets, call *①* 01-97-43-48-00. Late May to mid June.

June

Monaco Grand Prix. Hundreds of cars race through the narrow streets and winding roads in a surreal blend of high-tech machinery and medieval architecture. Call *①* 01-42-96-12-23. Early June.

Le Prix du Jockey Club (June 1 at 2pm) and the **Prix Diane-Hermès** (June 8 at 2pm), Hippodrome de Chantilly. Thoroughbreds from as far away as Kentucky and Brunei compete in a genteel race that's talked about in horsey circles around the world. On race days, as many as 30 trains depart from Paris's Gare du Nord for Chantilly, where they're met by free shuttle buses to the track. Alternatively, buses depart on race days from Place de la République and Porte de St-Cloud. Call *①* 01-49-10-20-30 for information on this and on all other equine events in this calendar.

Cinéscénie de Puy du Fou, son-et-lumière at the Château du Puy du Fou, Les Epesses (Poitou-Charentes). The achievements of the Middle Ages are celebrated by a cast of 650 actors, dozens of horses,

and laser shows. Call *①* 02-51-64-11-11. Early June to early September.

Les Nocturnes du Mont-St-Michel. This is a sound-and-light tour through the stairways and corridors of one of Europe's most impressive medieval monuments. Call *①* 02-33-89-80-00 for more information. Performances are Monday through Saturday evenings from June to mid-September. In the off-season, performances are on Saturday and Sunday only.

Festival de St-Denis. This series presents 4 days of music in the burial place of the French kings, a grim early Gothic monument in Paris's industrialized northern suburb of St-Denis. Call *①* 01-48-13-06-07; Métro: St-Denis-Basilique. June 6 to July 5.

Paris Air Show. This is where the military-industrial complex of France shows off enough high-tech hardware to make anyone think twice about invading La Patrie. Fans, competitors, and industrial spies mob the halls of Le Bourget Airport. Call *①* 01-53-23-33-33. Mid-June in alternate years. The 2002 dates are June 15 to June 19.

The 24-Hour Le Mans Car Race. For information, contact Automobile Club de l'ouest (*①* 02-43-40-24-24). June 17 to 18.

Festival Chopin, Paris. Everything you've ever wanted to hear by the Polish exile, who lived most of his life in Paris. Piano recitals are held in the Orangerie du Parc de Bagatelle. Call *①* 01-45-00-22-19. June 17 to July 14.

Gay Pride Parade, place de l'Odéon to place de la Bastille, Paris. A week of expositions and parties climaxes in a parade patterned after those in New York and San Francisco. It's followed by a dance at the Palais de Bercy. For details, contact Christian Spadone or Rene Lalement at ✆ **06-14-17-21-28** or www.france.qrd.org/assocs/lgp-idf.

La Villette Jazz Festival. Some 50 concerts are held in churches, auditoriums, and concert halls in the Paris suburb of La Villette. Past festivals have included Herbie Hancock, Shirley Horn, and other artists from around Europe and the world. Call ✆ **08-03-30-63-06.** Late June to early July.

Les Chorégies d'Orange, Orange. One of southern France's most important lyric festivals presents oratorios, operas, and choral works by master performers whose voices are amplified by the ancient acoustics of France's best-preserved Roman amphitheater. Call ✆ **04-90-34-24-24.** June 21 to August 14.

July

Colmar International Music Festival, Colmar. Classical concerts are held in public buildings of one of the most folkloric towns in Alsace. Call ✆ **03-89-20-68-92.** July 4 to July 15.

Le Grand Tour de France. Europe's most prominent, highly contested, and televised bicycle race pits crews of wind-tunnel-tested athletes along an itinerary that detours deep into the Massif Central and ranges across the Alps. The race is decided at a finish line drawn across the Champs-Elysées. Call ✆ **01-41-33-15-00.** July 7 to 29.

Festival d'Avignon. One of France's most prestigious theater events, this world-class festival has a reputation for exposing new talent to critical acclaim. The focus is usually on avant-garde works in theater, dance, and music by groups from around the world. Make hotel reservations early. For information,

call ✆ **04-90-27-66-50** or fax 04-90-82-95-03. July 5 to July 30.

Festival d'Aix-en-Provence. A musical event par excellence, featuring everything from Gregorian chant to melodies composed on synthesizers. For operas and concerti, the audience sits on the lawns of the 14th-century papal palace. Recitals are performed in the medieval cloister of the Cathédrale St-Sauveur. Make advance hotel reservations. Expect heat, crowds, and traffic. Contact the Festival International d'Art Lyrique et Academie Europeénne de Musique (✆ **04-42-17-34-34;** fax 04-42-66-13-74). July 3 to 29.

Bastille Day. Celebrating the birth of modern-day France, the nation's festivities reach their peak in Paris with street fairs, pageants, fireworks, and feasts. In Paris, the day begins with a parade down the Champs-Elysées and ends with fireworks at Montmartre. No matter where you are, by the end of the day you'll hear Edith Piaf warbling *"La Foule"* (The Crowd), the song that celebrated her passion for the stranger she met and later lost in a crowd on Bastille Day. July 14.

Paris Quartier d'Eté. These 4 weeks of music evoke the style of the pop orchestral music of an English village green. The setting is either the Arènes de Lutèce or the Cour d'Honneur at the Sorbonne, both in the Quartier Latin. The dozen or so concerts are usually grander than the outdoorsy setting would imply, and include performances by the Orchestre de Paris, the Orchestre National de France, and the Baroque Orchestra of the European Union. Spin-offs of this include plays and jazz concerts. Call ✆ **01-44-94-98-00** or fax 01-44-94-98-01. July 15 to August 15.

Nice Jazz Festival. This is the biggest and most prestigious jazz festival in Europe. Concerts begin in early afternoon and go on until late at night (sometimes all night in the clubs) on the Arènes de Cimiez, a hill above the city. Reserve hotel rooms way in advance. Contact the Grand Parade du Jazz, Cultural Affairs Department of the city of Nice (✆ **04-93-92-82-82**; fax 04-93-92-82-85). July 22 to 29.

St-Guilhem Music Season, St-Guilhem le Désert (Languedoc). This festival of baroque organ and choral music is held in a medieval monastery. Call ✆ **04-67-63-14-99.** July 24 to August 25.

August

Festival Interceltique de Lorient, Brittany. Traditional Celtic verse and lore are celebrated in the Celtic heart of France. The 150 concerts include classical and folkloric musicians, dancers, singers, and painters. Traditional Breton *pardons* (religious processions) take place in this once-independent maritime duchy. Call ✆ **02-97-21-24-29.** August 3 to 12.

Festival International de Folklore et Fête de la Vigne (Les Folkloriades), Dijon, Beaune, and about 20 villages of the Côte d'Or. At the International Festival of Folklore and Wine in Dijon, dance troupes from around the world perform, parade, and participate in folkloric events in celebration of the famous wines of Burgundy. Contact the

Festival de Musique et Danse Populaires (✆ **03-80-30-37-95;** fax 03-80-30-23-44; www.folkloriades.org). Late August and early September.

September

Festival Musique en l'Île. A series of concerts, mostly dignified masses composed between the 17th and late 19th centuries, are given within medieval churches in the 4th, 5th, and 6th arrondissements. Sites include St-Louis-en-l'Île, St-Severin, and St-Germain-des-Prés. Call ✆ **01-43-55-47-09.** September 5 to October 17.

Festival d'Automne, Paris. One of France's most famous festivals is one of its most eclectic, focusing mainly on modern music, ballet, theater, and modern art. Contact the Festival d'Automne (✆ **01-53-45-17-00;** fax 01-53-45-17-01). During the festival itself, call ✆ **01-53-45-17-00** to reserve tickets. Mid-September to mid-December.

International Ready-to-Wear Fashion Shows, (Le Salon International de Prêt-à-porter), Parc des Expositions, Porte de Versailles, Paris. Call ✆ **08-36-68-31-12** in Paris. Late September.

Paris Auto Show, Parc des Expositions, near the Porte de Versailles in western Paris. This is the showcase for European car design, complete with glistening metal, glitzy attendees, lots of hype, and the latest models from world automakers. Check *Pariscope* for details, contact the French Government Tourist Office (see "Visitor Information," earlier in this chapter), or call (✆ **01-56-88-22-40.** September 28 to October 13.

October

Perpignan Jazz Festival. Musicians from everywhere jam in what many consider Languedoc's most appealing season. Call (✆ **04-68-35-37-46.** Throughout October and November.

Festival d'Automne, Paris. See description under "September," above. Throughout October.

Prix de l'Arc de Triomphe, Hippodrome de Longchamp, Paris 16e ((✆ **01-49-10-20-30**). France's answer to England's Ascot is the country's most prestigious horse race, culminating the equine season in Europe. Early October.

November

Festival d'Automne, Paris. See description under "September," above. Throughout November.

Armistice Day, nationwide. In Paris, the signing of the controversial document that ended World War I is celebrated with a military parade from the Arc de Triomphe to the Hôtel des Invalides. Call (✆ **8-36-68-31-12** in Paris. November 11.

Les Trois Glorieuses, Clos-de-Vougeot, Beaune, and Meursault. The country's most important wine festival is celebrated in three Burgundian towns. Though you may not gain access to many of the gatherings, there are enough tastings and other amusements to keep you occupied. Reserve early or visit as day trips from any of several nearby villages. Contact the Office de Tourisme de Beaune ((✆ **03-80-26-21-30**). Third week in November.

City of Paris's Festival of Sacred Art. This dignified series of concerts is held in five of the oldest and most recognizable Paris churches. Call (✆ **01-44-70-64-10.** Mid-November to mid-December.

December

Festival d'Automne, Paris. See description under "September," above. Through late December.

The Boat Fair (Le Salon International de la Navigation de Plaisance). Europe's most visible exposition of what's afloat occurs at the Parc des Expositions, Porte de Versailles, Paris 15e ((✆ **01-41-90-47-10;** fax 01-41-90-47-19; Métro: Porte de Versailles). 8 days in early December.

Christmas Fairs, Alsace (especially Strasbourg). More than 60 Alsatian villages celebrate a traditional Christmas. The events in Strasbourg have continued for some 430 years. Other towns with celebrations are Munster, Selestat, Riquewihr, Kaysersberg, Saverne, Wissembourg, and Than. Call (✆ **03-88-52-28-28.** Late November to December 24.

Fête des Lumières, Lyon. In honor of the Virgin Mary, lights are placed in thousands of windows throughout the city. Call (✆ **04-72-77-69-69.** December 8 until sometime after Christmas.

Foire de Noël, Mougins. Hundreds of merchants, selling all kinds of Christmas ornaments and gifts, descend on Mougins, a small village in Provence. Call (✆ **04-93-75-87-67.** December 11 and 12.

Fête de St-Sylvestre (New Year's Eve), nationwide. In Paris, it's most boisterously celebrated in the Quartier Latin around the Sorbonne. At midnight, the city explodes. Strangers kiss and boulevard St-Michel and the Champs-Elysées become virtual pedestrian malls. Call (✆ **08-36-68-31-12.** December 31.

6 Special-Interest Vacations

BALLOONING   The world's largest hot-air-balloon operator is **Bombard Society,** 333 Pershing Way, West Palm Beach, FL 33401 (© **800/862-8537** or 561/837-6610; fax 561/837-6623). It maintains about 3 dozen hot-air balloons, some stationed in the Loire Valley and Burgundy. The 5-day tours, costing $5,988 per person (double occupancy), incorporate food and wine tasting and include all meals, lodging in Relais & Châteaux hotels, sightseeing, rail transfers to and from Paris, and a daily balloon ride over vineyards and fields.

Bonaventura Balloon Co., 133 Wall Rd., Napa, CA 94558 (© **800/ 359-6272**), meets you in Paris and takes you via high-speed train to Burgundy, where your balloon tour begins, carrying you over the scenic parts of the region. Guests stay in a 14th-century mill, now an inn owned by a three-star chef. A 9-day trip is $2,595 per person, including sightseeing in Paris, two balloon trips, lodging, cooking classes, wine tasting, and at least one meal per day.

BARGE   CRUISES   Before the advent of the railways, many of the crops, building supplies, raw materials, and finished products of France were barged through a series of rivers, canals, and estuaries. Many of these waterways are still graced with their old-fashioned locks and pumps, allowing shallow-draft barges easy access through the idyllic countryside.

French Country Waterways, P.O. Box 2195, Duxbury, MA 02331 (© **800/222-1236** or 781/934-2454; www.fcwl.com), leads 1-week tours through Burgundy and Champagne. For double occupancy, the price ranges from $2,995 to $4,795.

Le Boat, 45 Whitney Rd., Suite C-5, Mahwah, NJ 07430 (© **800/ 992-0291** or 201/560-1941; fax 201/ 560-1945; www.leboat.com), focuses

on regions of France not covered by many other barge operators. The company's luxury crafts are of a size and shape that fit through the narrow canals and locks of Camarque, Languedoc, and Provence. Each 6-night tour has 10 passengers in five cabins outfitted with mahogany and brass, plus meals prepared by a Cordon Bleu chef. Prices are highly variable; 6 nights in the Upper Loire begin at $1,690 per person, rising to $4,000 in summer.

European Waterways, 140 E. 56th St., Suite 4C, New York, NY 10022 (© **800/546-4777** or 212/688-9489; fax 212/688-3778), operates Great Island Voyages, featuring river cruise ships that ply Europe's historic rivers. The *Lafayette, Litote,* and *Escargot* traverse France's Burgundy region. Fares range from $1,990 to $3,500 per person (double occupancy) for a 1-week cruise, including room, breakfast, and dinner. Bicycles are carried on board for sightseeing trips. This company also offers cruises in the Loire Valley and the south of France.

Premier Selections, 106 Calvert St., Harrison, NY 10528 (© **800/ 234-4000** or 914/835-5555; fax 914/ 835-8756), lets you travel the waterways of France aboard a hotel barge. Enjoy fine wines and cuisine, bicycling, and walking. Visit châteaux, old towns, and timeless villages. The fleet can accommodate individuals as well as groups and offers an array of cruising areas, including Burgundy, Champagne, the Upper Loire, Alsace-Lorraine, and the south of France. Inclusive fares per person for 3 nights (double occupancy) begin at $1,650, with 6 nights beginning at $2,825, for room, breakfast, and dinner.

BICYCLING   TOURS   Holland **Bicycling Tours,** P.O. Box 6086, Huntington   Beach,   CA   92615 (© **800/852-3258;** fax 714/593-1710;

www.hollandbicyclingtours.com), leads 10-day tours through Brittany and Normandy, with visits to medieval monasteries, Romanesque and early Gothic cathedrals, past jagged granite coastlines. The price of the land portion (without airfare) is $1,850 per person. A 10-day tour through Provence, with views of van Gogh's sunflowers, Roman ruins, and fields of lavender, thyme, and basil is $1,950 per person. Both include double-occupancy hotel accommodations, breakfasts and dinners, bike rentals, the services of a tour leader, and van rides when necessary.

Classic Adventures, P.O. Box 143, Hamlin, NY 14464 (© **800/777-8090;** www.classicadventures.com), sponsors 7- to 11-day spring and fall tours of the Loire Valley, Burgundy, and the Dordogne. Accommodations are upscale, and all tours are van-supported and escorted. The 7-day tours, including room, breakfast, and dinner, are $1,889 per person for the Loire Valley and $1,889 per person for Burgundy; an 11-day tour of the Dordogne costs $2,489.

Euro-Bike & Walking Tours, P.O. Box 990, DeKalb, IL 60115 (© **800/321-6060;** www.eurobike.com), offers 10-day tours in the Dordogne ($2,495 per person), 11-day tours in Provence ($3,195 per person), 6-day tours of Burgundy ($1,895 per person), and 8-day tours of the Loire Valley ($2,485 per person). All are escorted, and include room, breakfast, and dinner.

Uniquely Europe (a division of Europe Express), 1805 N. Creek Parkway, Suite 100, Bothell, WA 98011 (© **800/426-3615**), has biking and walking tours of Alsace, Burgundy, the Dordogne, the Loire Valley, and Provence. A 7-day guided bike tour is $2,350 to $2,600 per person, double occupancy; a 7- or 8-day self-guided bike tour is $1,190 to $2,150. All tours include overnight accommodations and most meals. Guided tours

include van support and a guide; on non-guided tours, you'll always have the name of an English-speaking local contact.

COOKING SCHOOLS If you've always wanted to learn to cook *à la française,* you can take those all-important lessons from Maxime and Eliane Rochereau at their hotel/restaurant, **Le Castel de Bray-et-Monts,** Brehemont, 37130 Langeais (© **02-47-96-70-47;** fax 02-47-96-57-36; www.cooking-class-infrance.com). Before settling on the banks of the Loire, in the heart of château country, the Rochereaus spent 15 years living and working in the United States—Maxime as chef de cuisine at Chicago's Ritz-Carlton and Palm Beach's Breakers, and Eliane as a caterer for the Palm Beach jet set. Maxime now offers classes in classic French cooking at an 18th-century manor surrounded by a garden in the charming village of Brehemont. Classes are in English; the price, including a week's accommodation and full board, is 11,000F (1,672, $1,595) per person, double occupancy. No classes are conducted during December and January.

The famous/infamous Georges-Auguste Escoffier (1846 to 1935) taught the Edwardians how to eat. Today Le Ritz, the site of many of Escoffier's meals, maintains the **Ritz-Escoffier École de Gastronomie Française,** 38 rue Cambon, 75001 Paris (© **01-43-16-30-50;** www.ritz paris.com), offering demonstration classes of the master's techniques Monday, Tuesday, and Thursday afternoons. These cost 290F (44.10, $42.05) each. Courses, taught in French and English, start at 6,000F (912, $870) for 1 week, up to 34,400F (5,228.80, $4,988) for 6 weeks.

Le Cordon Bleu, 8 rue Léon-Delhomme, 75015 Paris (© **800/457-CHEF** in the U.S., or 01-53-68-22-50;

www.cordonbleu.net). Established in 1895, it is the most famous French cooking school—this is where Julia Child learned to perfect her *paté brisée* and *mousse au chocolat.* Bon appétit! Its best-known courses last 10 weeks, at the end of which certificates are issued. Many gourmet enthusiasts prefer a less intense immersion and opt for either a 4-day workshop or a 3-hour demonstration class. Enrollment in either of these first-come, first-served; costs are 240F (36.50, $34.80) for a demonstration and around 5,200F (790.40, $754) for the 4-day workshop. Classes are in English.

LANGUAGE   SCHOOLS The **Alliance Française,** 101 bd. Raspail, 75270 Paris, CEDEX 06 (© **01-42-84-90-00;** fax 01-42-84-91-00), is a state-approved nonprofit organization with a network of 1,100 establishments in 138 countries, offering French-language courses to some 350,000 students. The school in Paris is open all year; month-long courses range from $1,630 to $3,260, depending on the number of hours per day. Request information and application forms at least 1 month before your departure. In North America, the largest branch is the **Alliance Française,** 2819 Ordway St. NW, Washington, DC 20008 (© **800/6-FRANCE;** fax 202/362-1587).

A clearinghouse for information on French-language schools is **Lingua Service Worldwide,** 75 Prospect St., Suite 4, Huntington, NY 11743 (© **800/394-LEARN** or 631/424- 0777; www. linguaserviceworldwide.com). Its programs are available not only Paris but also Aix-en-Provence, Antibes, Avignon, Bordeaux, Cannes, Nice, St. Malo, Tours, as well as other cities. They range from $425 to $993 for 2 weeks, depending on the city, the school, and the accommodations.

7 Health & Insurance

STAYING HEALTHY

If you suffer from a chronic illness, consult your doctor before your departure. For conditions like epilepsy, diabetes, or heart problems, wear a **Medic Alert Identification Tag** (© **800/825-3785;** www.medicalert. org), which will alert doctors to your condition and give them access to your records through Medic Alert's 24-hour hot line. Membership is $35, plus a $15 annual fee.

Pack prescription medications in carry-on luggage. Bring along copies of your prescriptions in case you lose your pills or run out. Bring written prescriptions in generic, not brand-name, form, and keep all medications in their original vials.

Contact the **International Association for Medical Assistance to Travelers,** or **IAMAT** (© **716/754-4883** or 416/652-0137; www.sentex.net/ -iamat). They offer tips on travel and health concerns in countries you'll be visiting, and list many local English-speaking doctors.

TRAVEL INSURANCE

There are three kinds of travel insurance: trip-cancellation, medical, and lost-luggage coverage. **Trip-cancellation insurance** is a good idea if you have paid a large portion of your vacation expenses up front (say, by purchasing a package deal). However, if you're buying a package vacation, don't buy your trip-cancellation insurance from your tour operator. Buy it from an outside vendor instead.

The other types of insurance don't make sense for most travelers. Check your existing policies before you buy any additional coverage. Your existing health insurance should cover you if you get sick while on vacation—though if you belong to an HMO, check to see whether you are fully covered when away from home. For independent travel health-insurance providers, see below.

Your homeowner's or renter's insurance should cover stolen luggage. The airlines are responsible for losses of up to $2,500 on domestic flights if they lose your luggage; if you plan to carry anything more valuable than that, keep it in your carry-on bag.

The differences between **travel assistance** and insurance are often blurred, but in general, the former offers on-the-spot assistance and 24-hour hot lines (mostly oriented toward medical problems), while the latter reimburses you for travel problems (medical, travel, or otherwise) after you have filed the paperwork. The coverage you should consider will depend on how much protection is already in your existing health insurance or other policies. Some credit and charge card companies may insure you against travel accidents if you buy plane, train, or bus tickets with their cards. Before purchasing additional insurance, read your policies and agreements carefully. Call your insurers or credit card companies if you have any questions.

Some credit cards (American Express and certain gold and platinum Visa and MasterCards) offer automatic **flight insurance** for death or dismemberment in case of an airplane crash, and allow you to purchase additional coverage through them.

If you require additional insurance, try one of the companies listed below—but don't pay for more than you need. If you need only trip-cancellation insurance, don't purchase coverage for lost or stolen property. Trip-cancellation insurance costs approximately 6% to 8% of the total value of your vacation.

Reputable issuers of travel insurance include **Access America** (© 800/284-8300; www.accessamerica.com); **Travel Guard International** (© 800/826-1300; www.noelgroup.com); and **Travelex Insurance Services** (© 800/228-9792; www.travelex-insurance.com).

8 Tips for Travelers with Special Needs

FOR TRAVELERS WITH DISABILITIES   Facilities for travelers with disabilities are certainly above average in Europe, and nearly all modern hotels in France now provide accessible rooms. However, older hotels (unless they've been renovated) may not provide such features as elevators, special toilet facilities, or ramps for wheelchairs.

The new high-speed TGV trains are wheelchair accessible; older trains have compartments for wheelchair boarding. On the Paris Métro, those with disabilities are able to sit in wider seats provided for their comfort. Guide dogs ride free. However, some stations don't have escalators or elevators, so these present problems.

Knowing which hotels, restaurants, and attractions are accessible can save you a lot of frustration—firsthand reports from other travelers with disabilities are the best.

The **Association des Paralysés de France,** 17 bd. Auguste-Blanqui, 75013 Paris (© 01-40-78-69-00), is a privately funded organization that provides documentation, moral support, and travel ideas for individuals who use wheelchairs. In addition to the Paris office, it maintains an office in each of the 90 *départements* (small "mini-states" into which France is divided) of France and can help find accessible hotels, transportation, sightseeing, house rentals, and (in some cases) companionship for paralyzed or partially paralyzed travelers. It's not, however, a travel agency.

Travelers with disabilities may want to consider joining a tour that caters specifically to them. One of the best operators is **Flying Wheels Travel,** 143 West Bridge (P.O. Box 382), Owatonna, MN 55060 (*©* **800/535-6790;** www.flyingwheelstravel.com). It offers escorted tours and cruises, with an emphasis on sports, as well as private tours in minivans with lifts.

Other helpful organizations are the **American Foundation for the Blind,** 11 Penn Plaza, Suite 300, New York, NY 10001 (*©* **800/232-5463** or 212/502-7600; www.afb.org); **The Lighthouse, Inc.,** 111 E. 59th St., New York, NY 10022 (*©* **800/829-0500** or 212/821-9200; www.lighthouse.org); and the **New York Society for the Deaf,** 817 Broadway, 7th floor, New York, NY 10003 (*©* **212/777-3900** TTY/voice; www.nysd.org).

In the United Kingdom, **RADAR** (Royal Association for Disability and Rehabilitation), Unit 12, City Forum, 250 City Rd., London ECIV 8AF (*©* **020/7250-3222;** www.radar.org.uk), publishes holiday "fact packs" (three in all), which sell for £2 each or a set of all three for £5. The first provides general information on planning and booking a holiday, insurance, finances, and useful organization and holiday providers. The second outlines transport and equipment, transportation available when going abroad, and equipment for rent. The third deals with specialized accommodations.

Another resource is **Holiday Care,** 2nd floor, Imperial Buildings, Victoria Road, Horley, Surrey RH6 7PZ, UK (*©* **01293/774-535;** fax 01293/784-647; www.holidaycare.org.uk), a national group that advises on accommodations for the elderly and persons with disabilities. Members receive a newsletter and access to a free reservations network for hotels in Britain and, to a lesser degree, Europe and the rest of the world.

FOR GAY & LESBIAN TRAVELERS Paris vies with London and Amsterdam as Europe's gay and

lesbian capital. France is one of the world's most tolerant countries, and Paris is the center of French gay life, though gay and lesbian establishments exist throughout the country as well, especially on the Riviera. Before your trip, you might want to pick up a copy of *Frommer's Gay & Lesbian Europe.*

SOS Écoute Gay (*©* **01-44-93-01-02**) is a gay hot line, theoretically designed as a way to counsel persons with gay-related problems—the phone is answered by volunteers, some of whom are not as helpful as others. A counselor responds to calls Monday and Wednesday from 8am to 10pm; Tuesday, Thursday, and Friday from 6 to 8pm.

Another helpful source is **La Maison des Femmes,** 163 rue de Charenton, Paris 12e (*©* **01-43-43-41-13;** Métro: Reuilly-Diderot). This organization offers information about Paris for lesbians and bisexual women, and sometimes sponsors informal dinners and get-togethers. Call for a recorded announcement that gives the hours when someone will be available that particular week.

Gai Pied's publication *Guide Gai* (revised annually) is the best source of information on gay and lesbian clubs, hotels, organizations, and services—even restaurants. Lesbian or bisexual women might also pick up a copy of *Lesbia,* if only to check out the ads. These publications and others are available at Paris's largest and best-stocked gay bookstore, **Les Mots à la Bouche,** 6 rue Ste-Croix-de-la-Bretonnerie, Paris 4e (*©* **01-42-78-88-30**). Hours are Monday through Saturday from 11am to 11pm, Sunday from 2 to 8pm. Both French- and English-language publications are available.

If you want help planning your trip, the **International Gay & Lesbian Travel Association,** or IGLTA (*©* **800/448-8550** or 954/776-2626; www.iglta.org), can link you up with the appropriate gay-friendly service organization or tour specialist. With around 1,200 members, it offers quarterly newsletters, marketing mailings, and a membership directory that's updated quarterly. Members are kept informed of gay and gay-friendly hoteliers, tour operators, and airline and cruise-line representatives.

Out and About (© 800/929-2268 or 415/229-1793; www.outandabout. com) has been hailed for its reporting on gay travel. It offers a monthly newsletter packed with information on the global gay and lesbian scene. There are also two good biannual English-language gay guidebooks, both focused on gay men but which include information for lesbians as well. You can get the *Spartacus International Gay Guide* or *Odysseus* from most gay and lesbian bookstores, or order from Giovanni's Room (© 215/923-2960; www.giovannis-room.com) or A Different Light Bookstore (© 800/343-4002 or 212/ 989-4850; www.adlbooks.com). Lesbians and gays might want to pick up *Gay Travel A to Z* ($16). The *Ferrari Guides* (www.ferrariguides.com) is another good series of gay and lesbian guidebooks.

General gay and lesbian travel agencies include **Above and Beyond Tours** (© 800/397-2681) and **Kennedy Travel** (© 800/988-1181 or 516/ 352-4888.

FOR SENIORS Many discounts are available for seniors—men and women of the "third age," as the French say. For more information, contact the French Government Tourist Office (see "Visitor Information," earlier in this chapter).

At any rail station in the country, seniors (60 and over, with proof of age) can obtain **A La Carte Senior.** The pass costs 285F (43.30, $41.35) and is good for a 50% discount on unlimited rail travel throughout the year. The carte also offers reduced prices on

some regional bus lines and half-price admission at state-owned museums. There are some restrictions—for example, you can't use it between 3pm Sunday and noon Monday and from noon Friday to noon Saturday. There's no discount on the Paris network of commuter trains.

The domestic airline **Air France** offers seniors a 10% reduction on its regular nonexcursion tariffs. Some restrictions apply. Discounts of around 10% are offered to passengers ages 62 and over on selected Air France international flights. Be sure to ask for the discount when booking.

Members of the **American Association of Retired Persons (AARP),** 601 E St. NW, Washington, DC 20049 (© 800/424-3410 or 202/ 434-AARP; www.aarp.org), get discounts on hotels, airfares, and car rentals. The AARP offers members a wide range of benefits, including *Modern Maturity* magazine and a monthly newsletter, at $10 for 1 year, $27 for 3 years.

Grand Circle Travel (© 800/ 221-2610 or 617/350-7500; www. gct.com) is one of the hundreds of agencies specializing in vacations for seniors. Many of these packages, are of the tour-bus variety, with free trips thrown in for those who organize groups of 10 or more. Seniors seeking more independent travel should probably consult a regular travel agent.

SAGA International Holidays, 222 Berkeley St., Boston, MA 02116 (© 800/343-0273; www.sagaholi-days.com), offers inclusive tours for those 50 and older. SAGA also sponsors the more substantial "Road Scholar Tours" (© 800/621-2151), which are fun-loving tours with an educational bent.

If you want something more than the average vacation or guided tour, try **Elderhostel** (© 877/426-8056 or 617/426-7788; www.elderhostel.org) or the University of New Hampshire's

Interhostel (© **800/733-9753** or 603/862-1147; www.learn.unh.edu), both variations on the same theme: educational travel for senior citizens. On these escorted tours, the days are packed with seminars, lectures, and field trips, and academic experts lead all sightseeing. The courses in these programs are ungraded, involve no homework, and often focus on the liberal arts. They're not luxury vacations, but are fun and fulfilling.

FOR STUDENTS The best resource is the **Council on International Educational Exchange,** or CIEE (© **212/822-2700;** www.ciee.org), 6 Hamilton Place, Boston, MA 02108. It can set you up with an ID card (see below), and its travel branch, **Council Travel Service** (© **888/COUNCIL;** www.counciltravel.com), is the biggest student-travel operation in the world. It can get you discounts on plane tickets, railpasses, and the like. Ask for a list of CTS offices in major cities to keep the discounts

flowing (and aid lines open) as you travel.

From CIEE, you can obtain the student traveler's best friend, the $20 **International Student Identity Card** (ISIC). It's the only officially acceptable form of student ID, good for cut rates on railpasses, plane tickets, and more. It also provides basic health and life insurance, and a 24-hour help line. If you're no longer a student but still under 26, you can get a GO 25 card, which will get you the insurance and some of the discounts (but not student prices at museums).

In Canada, **Travel CUTS,** 200 Ronson St., Suite 320, Toronto, ONT M9W 5Z9 (© **800/667-2887** or 416/614-2887; 020/7528-6113 in London; www.travelcuts.com), offers similar services. **Usit Campus,** 52 Grosvenor Gardens, London SW1W 0AG (© **0870/240-1010;** www.usitcampus.co.uk), opposite Victoria Station, is Britain's leading specialist in student and youth travel.

9 Flying to France from North America

Flying time to Paris is about 7 hours from New York or Washington, D.C., 8 hours from Atlanta or Miami, 9 hours from Chicago, and 11 hours from Los Angeles.

The two Paris airports—Orly and Charles de Gaulle—are about even in terms of convenience to the city's center, though taxi rides from Orly might take a bit less time than those from de Gaulle. Orly, the older of the two, is 8 miles south of the center, whereas Charles de Gaulle is 14 miles northeast. In April 1996, the last of Air France's flights to Orly from North America was rerouted to Charles de Gaulle (Terminal 2C). U.S. carriers land at both airports in equal measure.

Most airlines divide their year into roughly seasonal slots, with the lowest fares between November 1 and March 13. Shoulder season (October and

mid-March to mid-June) is only slightly more expensive. We think it's the ideal time to visit France.

THE MAJOR AIRLINES

American Airlines (© **800/433-7300;** www.aa.com) offers daily flights to Paris from Dallas/Fort Worth, Chicago, Miami, Boston, and New York.

British Airways (© **800/AIRWAYS;** www.britishairways.com) offers flights from 18 U.S. cities to Heathrow and Gatwick airports in England. From there, you can book any number of British Airways flights to Paris.

Continental Airlines (© **800/231-0856;** www.continental.com) provides nonstop flights to Paris from Newark and Houston. Flights from Newark depart daily; flights from Houston depart four to seven times a week, depending on the season.

Delta Air Lines (© 800/241-4141; www.delta.com) is one of the best choices for those flying from the southeastern United States or the Midwest. There's a nonstop from Atlanta to Paris every evening. Delta also operates daily nonstop flights from Cincinnati and New York. Delta is the only airline offering nonstop service from New York to Nice.

US Airways (© 800/428-4322; www.usairways.com) offers daily non-stop service from Philadelphia to Paris.

The French national carrier, **Air France** (© 800/237-2747; www.air france.com), offers daily or several-times-a-week flights between Paris and such North American cities as Atlanta, Boston, Chicago, Cincinnati, Houston, Los Angeles, Mexico City, Miami, Montréal, New York, Newark, San Francisco, Toronto, and Washington, D.C.

Canadians usually choose **Air Canada** (© 888/247-2262 in North America; www.aircanada.ca), offering daily nonstop flights to Paris from Toronto and Montréal. Two of Air Canada's flights from Toronto are shared with Air France and use Air France aircraft.

FINDING THE BEST AIRFARES

- Watch for **sales.** You'll almost never see them during the peak months of July and August, or during the Thanksgiving or Christmas seasons; at other times, however, you can get great deals. In the last couple of years, there have been amazing sales on winter flights to Paris. If you already hold a ticket when a sale breaks, it may even pay to exchange your ticket, which usually incurs a charge of between $50 and $150, depending on the airline and the ticket.

- If your schedule is flexible, ask if you can secure a cheaper fare by **staying an extra day** or by **flying midweek.** (Many airlines won't volunteer this information.)

- **Consolidators,** also known as bucket shops, buy seats in bulk from the airlines and then sell them back to the public at prices below even the airlines' discounted rates. Their ads usually run in the Sunday travel section of your newspaper. **Council Travel** (© 888/COUNCIL; www.council travel.com) and **STA Travel** (© 800/781-4040; www.statravel. com) cater especially to young travelers, but their bargain prices are available to people of all ages. **1-800-AIR-FARE** (© 800/AIR-FARE; www.1800airfare.com) was formerly owned by TWA but now offers the deepest discounts on many other airlines. Other reliable consolidators include **1-800-FLY-CHEAP** (www.1800flycheap. com); **TFI Tours International** (© 800/745-8000 or 212/736-1140; www.tmn.com), which serves as a clearinghouse for unused seats; or "rebators" such as **Travel Avenue** (© 800/333-3335 or 312/876-1116; www.travelavenue. com).

- Book a seat on a **charter flight.** Most charter operators advertise and sell their seats through travel agents, making these local professionals your best source of information for flights. Before deciding to take a charter, however, check the restrictions: You may be asked to purchase a tour package, pay in advance, be subject to a change in the day of departure, pay a service fee, and pay harsh penalties if you cancel—but are stuck if the charter doesn't fill and is canceled up to 10 days before departure. Summer charters fill more quickly than others and are almost sure to fly, but if you book a charter flight, seriously consider cancellation and baggage insurance.

- **Search for deals online.** It's possible to get great deals on airfare, hotels, and car rentals via the Internet. See "Planning Your Trip Online" below for more information.

10 Packages & Escorted Tours

Package tours are not necessarily the same thing as escorted tours. They are simply a way of buying your airfare and accommodations at the same time—and can save you lots of money. In many cases, a package that includes airfare, hotel, and rental car can cost less than the hotel alone if you'd booked it yourself, because packages are sold in bulk to tour operators, who resell them to the public.

It pays to comparison shop, though. Some packages offer better hotels than others; some provide the same hotels for lower prices. Some feature flights on scheduled airlines, while others book charters. In some packages, your choice of accommodations and travel days may be limited. Some let you choose between escorted vacations and independent vacations; others allow you to add on just a few excursions or escorted day trips without booking an entirely escorted tour.

For more vacation ideas, see "Special-Interest Vacations," earlier in this chapter.

Delta Air Lines, for example, through its tour division, Delta Dream Vacations (© **800/872-7786;** www.delta.com), offers a full 10-night package called "Jolie France," costing from $1,925 to $2,140 per person (double occupancy), depending on the season. It takes in not only Paris, but also some of the regional highlights of France, including Tours, Bordeaux, Carcassonne, Nice, Nîmes, and Dijon. All hotels, airfare from the U.S. East Coast, tours, and breakfasts are included, plus four dinners.

The French Experience, 370 Lexington Ave., Room 812, New York, NY 10017 (© **212/986-1115;** fax 212/986-3808; www.frenchexperience. com), offers inexpensive airfares to Paris on most scheduled airlines. Several tours use varied types and categories of country inns, hotels, private châteaux, and bed-and-breakfasts. They take reservations for about 30 small hotels in Paris and arranges short-term apartment rentals in the city or farmhouse rentals in the countryside. It also offers all-inclusive packages to Paris as well as prearranged package tours of various regions of France. Tours can be adapted to suit individual needs.

American Express Vacations (© **800/241-1700;** www.american express.com) is another option. Check out the **Last Minute Travel Bargains** site, offered in conjunction with **Continental Airlines** (www.american express.com/travel/lastminutetravel/default.asp), with deeply discounted vacation packages and reduced airline fares that differ from the E-savers bargains that Continental e-mails weekly to subscribers.

Among the airline packages, yet another option includes **American Airlines FlyAway Vacations** (© **800/321-2121;** www.aavacations.com).

Escorted tours are a different animal. Some people love having all the details taken care of for them; others hate the structure and loss of spontaneity. Before you book, ask hard questions about the cancellation policy, the size of the group, how action-packed the itinerary is, and exactly what's included.

Globus/Cosmos Tours, 5301 S. Federal Circle, Littleton, CO

80123-2980 (© **800/338-7092;** www.globusandcosmos.com), offers escorted coach tours of various regions of France lasting from 8 to 16 days. You must book tours through a travel agent, but you can call the above number for brochures.

Tauck Tours, 276 Post Rd. W., Westport, CT 06880 (© **800/468-2825;** www.tauck.com), provides first-class, fully escorted coach grand tours of France as well as 1-week general tours of specific regions within France. Its 14-day tour of France covering the Normandy landing beaches, the Bayeux Tapestry, and Mont-St-Michel costs $3,750 per person, double occupancy (land only), while an 8-day trip beginning in Nice and ending in Paris costs $2,400 per person.

11 Getting There from Elsewhere in Europe

BY PLANE

From London, **Air France** (© **0845/084-5111**) and **British Airways** (© **0345/222111** in the U.K. only) fly frequently to Paris with a trip time of only 1 hour. These airlines alone operate up to 17 flights daily from Heathrow, one of the busiest air routes in Europe. Many commercial travelers also use regular flights originating from the London City Airport in the Docklands. A ballpark for rates is London to Paris $36 one way.

Direct flights to Paris also exist from other cities in the United Kingdom, such as Manchester, Edinburgh, and Southampton. Contact Air France, British Airways, or **British Midland** (© **0870/607-0555;** www.flybmi.com) for details. Daily papers often carry advertisements for cheap flights. The highly recommended **Trailfinders** (© **020/7937-5400;** www.trailfinder.com) sells discounted fares.

You can reach Paris from any major European capital. Your best bet is to fly on the national carrier, Air France, with more connections into Paris from European capitals than any other airline. From Dublin, try **Aer Lingus** (© **800/223-6537;** www.aerlingus.com), with the most flights into Paris from Ireland. From Amsterdam, the convenient choice is **KLM** (© **800/374-7747;** www.klm.nl).

BY TRAIN

Paris is one of Europe's busiest rail junctions, with trains arriving at and departing from its many stations every few minutes. If you're in Europe, you may want to go to Paris by train. The cost is relatively low—especially in comparison to renting a car.

Railpasses as well as individual rail tickets within Europe are available at most travel agencies or at any office of **Rail Europe** (© **800/4-EURAIL** in the U.S.; www.raileurope.com) or **Eurostar** (© **800/EUROSTAR** in the U.S.; www.eurostar.com).

BY BUS

Bus travel to Paris is available from London as well as many other cities on the Continent. In the early 1990s, the French government established incentives for long-haul buses not to drive into the center of Paris. The arrival and departure point for Europe's largest operator, **Eurolines France,** is a 35-minute Métro ride from central Paris, at the terminus of Métro line 3 (Métro: Gallieni), in the eastern suburb of Bagnolet. Despite this inconvenience, many people prefer bus travel. Eurolines France is located at 28 av. du Général-de-Gaulle, 93541 Bagnolet (© **08-36-69-52-52;** www.eurolines.fr).

Long-haul buses are equipped with toilets, but they also stop at mealtimes for rest and refreshment. The price of a round-trip ticket between Paris and London (a 7-hour trip) is 470F (71.45, $68.15) for passengers 26 and over, and 420F (63.85, $60.90) for passengers under 26.

Because Eurolines does not have a U.S. sales agent, most people buy their ticket in Europe. Any European travel agent can arrange these purchases. If you're traveling to Paris from London, you can contact **Eurolines (U.K.) Ltd.,** 52 Grosvenor Gardens, Victoria, London SW1; or call ☎ **0990/ 143219** for information or for credit-card sales.

BY CAR

The major highways into Paris are the A1 from the north (Great Britain and Benelux); the A13 from Rouen, Normandy, and northwest France; the A10 from Bordeaux, the Pyrénées, France's southwest, and Spain; the A6 from Lyon, the French Alps, the Riviera, and Italy; and the A4 from Metz, Nancy, and Strasbourg in eastern France.

BY FERRY FROM ENGLAND

Ferries and hydrofoils operate day and night, in all seasons, with the exception of last-minute cancellations during particularly fierce storms. Many Channel crossings are carefully timed to coincide with the arrival and departure of major trains (especially those between London and Paris). Trains let you off a short walk from the piers. Most ferries carry cars, trucks, and freight, but some hydrofoils take passengers only. The major routes include at least 12 trips a day between Dover or Folkestone and Calais or Boulogne. Hovercraft and hydrofoils make the trip from Dover to Calais, the shortest distance across the Channel, in just 40 minutes during good weather, while the ferries might take several hours, depending on the weather and tides. If you're bringing a car, it's important to make reservations, as space below decks is usually crowded. Timetables can vary depending on weather conditions and many other factors.

The leading operator of ferries across the channel is **P&O Stena Lines** (BritRail ☎ **800/677-8585** in North America, or 0870/600-0600 in the U.K.). It operates car and passenger ferries between Portsmouth, England and Cherbourg, France (three departures a day; 4¼ hours each way during daylight hours, 7 hours each way at night); between Portsmouth and Le Havre, France (three a day; 5½ hours each way). Most popular is the route between Dover, England and Calais, France (25 sailings a day; 75 minutes each way), costing $41 U.S. one-way.

The shortest and most popular route across the Channel is between Calais and Dover. **Hoverspeed** runs at least 12 hovercraft crossings daily; the trip takes 35 minutes. It also runs a SeaCat (a catamaran propelled by jet engines) that takes longer to make the crossing between Boulogne and Folkestone; the SeaCats depart about four times a day on the 55-minute voyage. For reservations and information, call Hoverspeed (☎ **800/677-8585** in North America, or 08705/240-241 in the U.K.; www.hoverspeed.com). Typical one-way fares are 250F (37.50, $36.25) per person.

If you plan to transport a rental car between England and France, check with the rental company about license and insurance requirements and drop-off charges. Many companies, for insurance reasons, forbid transport of their vehicles over the water between England and France. Transport of a car begins at 678F (102, $98) each way. A better idea is to ask about a car exchange program (Hertz's is called "Le Swap"), in which you drop off a right-hand drive car and pick up a left-hand drive vehicle at Calais.

Under the Channel

Queen Elizabeth and the late French president François Mitterrand opened the Channel Tunnel in 1994, and the *Eurostar Express* has daily passenger service from London to Paris and Brussels. The $15-billion tunnel, one of the great engineering feats of our time, is the first link between Britain and the Continent since the Ice Age. The 31-mile journey takes 35 minutes, with the actual time spent in the Chunnel 19 minutes.

Eurostar tickets are available through **Rail Europe** (✆ 800/4-EURAIL). A round-trip nonrefundable ticket costs between $180 and $330 (£120 and £220) in first class, and between $105 and $165 (£70 and £110) in second class, depending on when you travel and how far in advance you pay for your ticket.

In London, make reservations for Eurostar (or any other train in Europe) at ✆ 0990/848-848. In Paris, call ✆ 08-36-35-35-39, and in the United States, call ✆ 800/EUROSTAR. Chunnel train traffic is competitive with air travel, if you calculate door-to-door travel time. Trains leave from London's Waterloo Station and arrive in Paris at Gare du Nord. London/Paris one-way passenger fare is $139 second class, $279 first class.

The Chunnel accommodates not only trains, but also passenger cars, charter buses, taxis, and motorcycles from $149 each way for a small car. **Le Shuttle,** a half-mile-long train carrying motor vehicles under the English Channel (✆ 0990/353535 in the U.K.; www.eurodrive.co.uk), connects Calais, France, with Folkestone, England. It operates 24 hours a day, 365 days a year, running every 15 minutes during peak travel times and at least once an hour at night.

Before boarding Le Shuttle, you stop at a toll booth to pay, and then pass through Immigration for both countries at one time. During the ride, you travel in air-conditioned carriages, remaining in your car or stepping outside to stretch your legs. An hour later, in France, you simply drive off.

12 Getting Around France

BY TRAIN

With some 50 cities linked by the world's fastest trains, you can get from Paris to just about anywhere else in the country in hours. With 24,000 miles of track and about 3,000 stations, SNCF (French National Railroads) is fabled throughout the world for its on-time performance. You can travel in first or second class by day and in *couchette* or sleeper by night. Many trains carry dining facilities.

INFORMATION   If you plan much travel on European railroads, get the latest copy of the *Thomas Cook European Timetable of Railroads.* This comprehensive 500-plus-page book documents all of Europe's mainline passenger rail services with detail and accuracy. It's available in North America from the **Forsyth Travel Library,** 226 Westchester Ave., White Plains, NY 10604 (✆ 800/367-7984; www.forsyth.com), at a cost of $27.95, plus $4.95 postage ($6.95 U.S. for shipments to Canada).

In the United States: For more information and to purchase railpasses before you leave, contact **Rail Europe,** 500 Mamaroneck Ave., Suite 314, Harrison, NY 10528 (℡ **800-4-EURAIL;** fax 914/682-3712).

In Canada: Rail Europe offices are at 2087 Dundas St. E., Suite 105, Mississauga, ON L4X 1M2 (℡ **800/361-7245** or 905/602-4195; fax 905/602-4198).

In London: SNCF has offices at **Rail Europe,** 179 Piccadilly, London W1V 0BA (℡ **0990/848-848**).

In Paris: For information or reservations, call **SNCF** at ℡ **08-36-35-35-39.** You can also go to any local travel agency. A simpler way to buy tickets is to use the *Billetterie* (ticket machines) in every train station. If you know your PIN, you can use a credit card to buy your ticket.

FRANCE RAILPASSES Working cooperatively with SNCF, Air Inter Europe, and Avis, Rail Europe offers three flexible railpasses that can reduce travel costs considerably.

The **France Railpass** provides unlimited rail transport in France for any 3 days within 1 month, at $210 in first class and $180 in second. You can purchase up to 6 more days for an extra $30 per person per day. Costs are even more reasonable for two adults traveling together: $342 for first class and $292 for second. Children 4 to 11 travel for half price.

The **France Rail 'n' Drive Pass,** available only in North America, combines good value on both rail travel and Avis car rentals, and is best used by arriving at a major rail depot, then striking out to explore the countryside by car. It includes the France Railpass (see above), and use of a rental car. A 3-day rail pass (first class) and 2 days' use of the cheapest rental car (with unlimited mileage) is $199 per person (assuming two people traveling together). It's $169 per person for the second-class rail pass and the same car; you can upgrade to a larger car for a supplemental fee. Solo travelers pay from $269 for first class and $239 for second.

EURAILPASSES In-the-know travelers take advantage of one of Europe's greatest travel bargains: the **Eurailpass,** which permits unlimited first-class rail travel in any country in Western Europe except the British Isles (good in Ireland). Passes are sold only in North America and are non-transferable. A Eurailpass costs $554 for 15 days, $718 for 21 days, $890 for 1 month, $1,260 for 2 months, and $1,558 for 3 months. Children 3 and under travel free providing they don't occupy a seat (otherwise they're charged half fare); children 4 to 11 are charged half fare.

If you're under 26, you can purchase a **Eurail Youthpass,** entitling you to unlimited second-class travel for $388 for 15 days, $499 for 21 days, $623 for 1 month, $882 for 2 months, and $1,089 for 3 months. Regardless of the pass, you'll have to pay an extra supplement for the high-speed TGV train anywhere in France.

Reservations are required on some trains (and cost an additional $8 per person). Many trains have *couchettes* (sleeping cars), which also cost extra. Obviously, the 2- or 3-month traveler gets the greatest economic advantages; the Eurailpass is ideal for extensive trips. You can visit all of France's major sights, from Normandy to the Alps, then end your vacation in

Norway, for example. Eurailpass holders are entitled to reductions on certain buses and ferries as well.

Travel agents everywhere, and railway agents in such major cities as New York, Montréal, and Los Angeles, sell Eurailpasses. You can purchase them at the North American offices of CIT Travel Service, the French National Railroads, the German Federal Railroads, and the Swiss Federal Railways.

The **Eurail Flexipass** allows you to visit Europe with more flexibility. It's valid in first class and offers the same privileges as the Eurailpass. However, it provides a number of individual travel days you can use over a longer period of consecutive days. That makes it possible to stay in one city for a while without losing days of rail travel. There are two passes: 10 days of travel in 2 months for $654, and 15 days of travel in 2 months for $862.

With many of the same qualifications and restrictions as the Flexipass is a **Eurail Youth Flexipass.** Sold only to travelers under 26, it allows 10 days of travel within 2 months for $458, and 15 days of travel within 2 months for $599.

BY CAR

The most charming châteaux and best country hotels always seem to lie away from the main cities and train stations. You'll find that renting a car is often the best way to travel around France, especially if you plan to explore in depth and not stick to the standard Paris-Nice route.

But Europe's rail networks are so well developed and inexpensive, we recommend you rent a car only for exploring areas little serviced by rail, such as Brittany, rural Burgundy, and the Dordogne. Or take trains between cities and rent a car on the days when you want to explore independently.

Driving time in Europe is largely a matter of conjecture, urgency, and how much sightseeing you do along the way. Driving time from Paris to Geneva is 5½ hours minimum. It's 2½ hours from Paris to Rouen, 3½ hours to Nantes, and 4 hours to Lyon. The driving time from Marseille to Paris is a matter of national pride, and tall tales abound about how rapidly the French can do it. Flooring it, you might conceivably make it in 7 hours, but we always make a 2-day journey of it.

RENTALS   Renting a car in France is easy. You'll need to present a passport, a driver's license, and a credit card. You'll also have to meet the minimum age requirement of the company. (For their least expensive cars, this is 21 at Hertz, 23 at Avis, and 25 at Budget. More expensive cars at any of the above-mentioned might require that you be at least 25.) It usually isn't obligatory, at least within France, but certain companies, especially the smaller ones, have at times asked for the presentation of an International Driver's License, even though this is becoming increasingly superfluous in Western Europe.

Note: The best deal is usually a weekly rental with unlimited mileage. All car-rental bills in France are subject to a 19.6% government tax, among the highest in Europe. And

---

Tips Have a Seat

Remember that a train ticket itself does not guarantee you a seat; it merely gets you transportation from one place to another. On crowded trains and during busy times, you'll have to make a **seat reservation** (and pay for the privilege) if you want to be sure of sitting somewhere other than on top of your luggage. Seat reservations cost $8 per person.

though the rental company won't usually mind if you drive your car across the French border—into, say, Germany, Switzerland, Italy, or Spain—it's often forbidden to transport your car by ferry, including across the Channel to England.

Unless it's already factored into the rental agreement, an optional **collision-damage waiver (CDW)** carries an extra charge of 110F to 125F (16.70 to 19, $15.95 to $18.15) per day for the least expensive car. Buying this will usually eliminate all but $250 of your responsibility in the event of accidental damage to the car. Because most newcomers aren't familiar with local driving customs and conditions, we recommend that you buy the CDW, though you should check with your credit-card company first to see if it will cover this automatically when you rent with its card. (It may cover damage, but not liability, so make sure you understand this clearly.) At some companies, the CDW won't protect you against theft, so if this is the case, ask about buying extra theft protection. This cost is 55F (8.35, $8) extra per day.

Automatic transmission is considered a luxury in Europe, so if you want it you'll have to pay dearly.

Budget (© **800/472-3325** in the U.S. and Canada; www.budgetrent-acar.com) has about 30 locations in Paris, with its largest branch at 81 av. Kléber, 16e (© **01-47-55-61-00;** Métro: Trocadéro). For rentals of more than 7 days, you can pick up a car (in most cases) in one French city and drop it off in another, but there are extra charges. Drop-offs in cities within an easy drive of the French border (including Geneva and Frankfurt) incur no extra charge; however, you can arrange drop-offs in other non-French cities for a reasonable surcharge.

Hertz (© **800/654-3001** in the U.S. and Canada; www.hertz.com)

maintains about 15 locations in Paris, including offices at the city's airports. The main office is at 27 rue St-Ferdinand, 17e (© **01-45-74-97-39;** Métro: Argentine). Be sure to ask about any promotional discounts.

Avis (© **800/331-2112** in the U.S. and Canada; www.avis.com) has offices at both Paris airports and an inner-city headquarters at 5 rue Bixio, 7e (© **01-44-18-10-50;** Métro: école-Militaire) near the Eiffel Tower.

National (© **800/227-3876** in the U.S. and Canada; www.nationalcar.com) is represented in Paris by Europcar, whose largest office is at 165 bis rue de Vaugirard (© **01-44-38-61-61;** Métro: St-Sulpre). It has offices at both Paris airports and at about a dozen other locations. For the lowest rates, reserve in advance from North America.

Two U.S.-based agencies that don't have Paris offices but act as booking agents for Paris-based agencies are **Kemwel Holiday Auto** (© **800/678-0678;** www.kemwel.com) and **Auto Europe** (© **800/223-5555;** www.autoeurope.com). These can make bookings in the United States only, so call before your trip.

GASOLINE Known in France as *essence,* gas is quite expensive for those accustomed to North American prices. All but the least expensive cars usually require an octane rating that the French classify as *essence super,* the most expensive variety. Depending on your car, you'll need either leaded (*avec plomb*) or unleaded (*sans plomb*). Filling a medium-size car will cost between $55 and $75.

Beware the mixture of gasoline and oil called *mélange* or *gasoil* sold in some rural communities; this mixture is for very old two-cycle engines.

Note: Sometimes you can drive for miles in rural France without encountering a gas station, so don't let your tank get dangerously low.

DRIVING RULES   Everyone in the car, in both the front and the back seats, must wear seat belts. Children under 12 must ride in the back seat. Drivers are supposed to yield to the car on their right, except where signs indicate otherwise, as at traffic circles.

If you violate the speed limit, expect a big fine. Those limits are about 80 mph (130kmph) on expressways, about 60 mph (100kmph) on major national highways, and 56 mph (90 kmph) on country roads. In towns, don't exceed 37 mph (60 kmph).

MAPS   For France as a whole, most motorists opt for Michelin map 989. For regions, Michelin publishes a series of yellow maps that are quite good. Big travel-book stores in North America carry these maps, and they're commonly available in France (at lower prices). In this age of congested traffic, one useful feature of the Michelin map is its designations of alternative *routes de dégagement,* which let you skirt big cities and avoid traffic-clogged highways.

Another recommended option is *Frommer's Road Atlas Europe.*

BREAKDOWNS/ASSISTANCE   A breakdown is called *une panne* in France. Call the police at © 17 anywhere in France to be put in touch with the nearest garage. Most local garages offer towing. If the breakdown occurs on an expressway, find the nearest roadside emergency phone box, pick up the phone, and put a call through. You'll be connected to the nearest breakdown service facility.

BY PLANE

Regrettably, there are few competitors in the world of domestic air travel within France. **Air France,** which recently acquired Air Inter Europe, is the 800-pound gorilla, serving about eight cities in France and eight others in Europe. Airfares tend to be much higher than for comparable distances in the U.S., and discounts are few. Sample round-trip fares from Paris are 2,300F (349.60, $333.50) to Nice, 2,240F (340.50, $324.80) to Bordeaux, and 2,260F (343.50, $327.70) to Toulouse. Travel time from Paris to most anywhere in France is about an hour.

13 Planning Your Trip Online

With a mouse, a modem, and a certain do-it-yourself determination, Internet users can tap into the travel-planning databases that were once accessible only to travel agents. Sites such as **Travelocity, Expedia,** and **Orbitz** allow you to comparison shop for airfares, book flights, learn of last-minute bargains, and reserve hotel rooms and rental cars.

But don't fire your travel agent just yet. Although online booking sites offer tips and data, they can't endow you with the experience that makes a seasoned travel agent an invaluable resource, even in the Internet age. And for consumers with a complex itinerary, a trusty travel agent is still the best

way to arrange the most direct flights to and from the best airports.

Still, there's no denying the Internet's emergence as a powerful tool in researching and plotting travel time. The benefits of researching your trip online can be well worth the effort:

- **Last-minute specials** (E-savers), such as weekend deals or Internet-only fares, are offered by airlines to fill empty seats. Most of these are announced on Tuesday or Wednesday and must be purchased online. They're valid only for travel that weekend, but some can be booked weeks or months in advance. Sign up for weekly e-mail alerts at airline websites (see p. 51) or check mega-sites that compile comprehensive lists of E-savers, such as **Smarter Living** (smarterliving.com) and **Web-Flyer** (www.webflyer.com).

- Some sites will send you **e-mail notification** when a cheap fare to your destination becomes available. Some will also tell you when fares to a place are lowest.
- The best of the travel-planning sites are now **highly personalized;** they track your frequent-flier miles and store your seating and meal preferences, tentative itineraries, and credit-card information, letting you plan trips or check agendas quickly.
- All major airlines offer **incentives**—bonus frequent-flier miles, Internet-only discounts, sometimes even free cell phone rentals—when you purchase online or buy an e-ticket. You might also check to see if you can purchase frequent-flier miles from an airline if you are close to the number needed for award travel.
- Advances in mobile technology provide business travelers and other frequent travelers with the **ability to check flight status, change plans, or get specific**

directions from handheld computing devices, mobile phones, and pagers. Some sites will e-mail or page a passenger if a flight is delayed.

TRAVEL PLANNING & BOOKING SITES

The best travel-planning and booking sites cast a wide net, offering domestic and international flights, hotel and rental-car bookings, news, destination information, and deals on cruises and packages. Keep in mind that free (one-time) registration is often required. Because several airlines are no longer willing to pay commissions on tickets sold by online travel agencies, be aware that these online agencies will either charge a $10 surcharge if you book a ticket on that carrier or will not carry those airlines' offerings.

This section isn't intended to be a comprehensive list, but rather a discriminating selection of sites to get you started. Recognition is given to sites based on their content value and ease of use and isn't paid for—unlike some rankings, which are based on payment. Remember: This is a press-time snapshot of leading websites—some undoubtedly will have evolved or moved by the time you read this.

 Frommers.com: The Complete Travel Resource

For an excellent travel planning resource, we highly recommend **Arthur Frommer's Budget Travel Online** (www.frommers.com). We're a little biased, but we guarantee you'll find the travel tips, reviews, monthly vacation giveaways, and online-booking capabilities thoroughly indispensable. Among the features are **Ask the Expert** bulletin boards, where Frommer's authors answer your questions via online postings; **Arthur Frommer's Daily Newsletter,** for the latest travel bargains and inside travel secrets; and Frommer's **Destinations archive,** where you'll get travel tips, hotel and dining recommendations, and advice on the sights for more than 200 destinations around the globe Once your research is done, the **Online Reservation System** (www.frommers.com/booktravelnow) takes you to Frommer's favorite sites for booking your vacation at affordable prices.

- **Travelocity** (www.travelocity.com or www.frommers.travelocity.com) and **Expedia** (www.expedia.com) are the most longstanding and reputable sites, each offering excellent selections and searches for complete vacation packages. Travelers search by destination and dates coupled with how much they're willing to spend.
- The latest buzz in the online travel world is about **Orbitz** (www.orbitz.com), launched by United, Delta, Northwest, American, and Continental airlines. It shows all possible fares for your trip, with fares lower than those available through travel agents. (At press time, travel-agency associations were waging an antitrust battle against this site.)
- **Qixo** (www.qixo.com) is another powerful search engine that allows you to search for flights and hotel rooms on 20 other travel-planning sites (such as Travelocity) at once. Qixo sorts results by price, after which you can book your travel directly through the site.

SMART E-SHOPPING

The savvy traveler is one armed with good information. Here are a few tips to help you navigate the Internet successfully and safely:

- **Know when sales start.** Last-minute deals may vanish in minutes. If you have a favorite booking site or airline, find out when last-minute deals are released to the public. (For example, Southwest's specials are posted every Tuesday at 12:01am central standard time.)
- **Shop around.** Compare results from different sites and airlines—and against a travel agent's best fare. If possible, try a range of times and alternate airports before you make a purchase.

- **Follow the rules of the trade.** Book in advance and choose an off-peak time and date if possible. Some sites will tell you when fares to a destination are cheapest.
- **Stay secure.** Book only through secure sites (some airline sites aren't secure). Look for a key icon (Netscape) or a padlock (Internet Explorer) at the bottom of your web browser before you enter credit card information or other personal data.
- **Avoid online auctions.** Sites that auction airline tickets and frequent-flier miles are the number-one perpetrators of Internet fraud, according to the National Consumers League.
- **Maintain a paper trail.** If you book an e-ticket, print out a confirmation or write down your confirmation number and keep it safe and accessible—or your trip could be a virtual one!

ONLINE TRAVELER'S TOOLBOX

Veteran travelers usually carry some essential items to make their trips easier. Following is a selection of online tools to bookmark and use:

- **Visa ATM Locator** (www.visa.com/pd/atm) or **MasterCard ATM Locator** (www.mastercard.com/atm). Find ATMs in hundreds of cities in the U.S. and around the world.
- **Foreign Languages for Travelers** (www.travlang.com). Learn basic terms in more than 70 languages and click on any underlined phrase to hear what it sounds like. *Note:* Speakers and free audio software are required.
- **Intellicast** (www.intellicast.com). Weather forecasts for all 50 states and cities around the world. *Note:* Temperatures are in Celsius for many international destinations.

- **Mapquest** (www.mapquest.com). The best of the mapping sites lets you choose a specific address or destination and will quickly return a map and detailed directions.
- **Cybercafes.com** (www.cybercafes. com) or **Net Café Guide** (www. netcafeguide.com/mapindex.htm). Locate Internet cafes at hundreds of places around the globe. Answer your e-mail and log onto the Web for a few dollars per hour.

- **Universal Currency Converter** (www.xe.net/currency). See what your dollar or pound is worth in more than 100 other countries.
- **U.S. State Department Travel Warnings** (www.travel.state.gov/ travel_warnings.html). Reports on places where health concerns or unrest might threaten U.S. travelers. It also lists the locations of U.S. embassies around the world.

14 Tips on Accommodations

The French government rates hotels on a one- to four-star system. One-star hotels are budget accommodations; two-star lodgings are quality tourist hotels; three stars go to first-class hotels; and four stars are reserved for deluxe accommodations. In some of the lower categories, the rooms may not have private bathrooms; instead, many have what the French call a *cabinet de toilette* (hot and cold running water and maybe a bidet). In such hotels, bathrooms are down the hall. Nearly all hotels in France have central heating, but, in some cases, you might wish the owners would turn it up a little on a cold night.

RELAIS & CHÂTEAUX Now known worldwide, this organization of deluxe and first-class hostelries began in France for visitors seeking the ultimate in hotel living and dining in a traditional atmosphere. Relais & Châteaux establishments (there are about 150 in France) are former castles, abbeys, manor houses, and town houses converted into hostelries or inns and elegant hotels. All have a limited number of rooms, so reservations are imperative. Sometimes these owner-run establishments have pools and tennis courts. The Relais part of the organization refers to inns called *relais,* meaning "post house." These tend to be less luxurious than the

châteaux, but are often charming. Top-quality restaurants are *relais gourmands.* Throughout this guide, we've listed our favorite Relais & Châteaux, but there are many more.

For an illustrated catalog of these establishments, send $8 to **Relais & Châteaux,** 11 E. 44th St., Suite 704, New York, NY 10017. For information on and reservations for individual properties, call © **800/735-2478** or 212/856-0115. Check out the website at www.integra.fr/relaischateaux.com.

BED & BREAKFASTS Called *gîtes—chambres d'hôte* in France, these may be one or several bedrooms on a farm or in a village home. Many offer one main meal of the day as well (lunch or dinner).

There are at least 6,000 of these accommodations listed with **La Maison des Gîtes de France et du Tourisme Vert,** 59 rue St-Lazare, 75009 Paris (© **01-49-70-75-75**). Sometimes these B&Bs aren't as simple as you might think: Instead of a bare-bones farm room, you might be in a mansion in the French countryside.

In the United States, a good source for this type of accommodation is **The French Experience,** 370 Lexington Ave., Room 812, New York, NY 10017 (© **212/986-1115;** fax 212/ 986-3808; www.frenchexperience. com), which also rents furnished houses for as short a period as 1 week.

CONDOS, VILLAS, HOUSES & APARTMENTS   If you can stay for at least a week and don't mind doing your own cooking and cleaning, you might want to rent a long-term accommodation. The local French Tourist Board might help you obtain a list of agencies that offer this type of rental (which is popular at ski resorts). In France, one of the best groups of estate agents is the **Fédération Nationale des Agents Immobiliers,** 129 rue du Faubourg St-Honoré, 75008 Paris (✆ **01-44-20-77-00**).

In the United States, **At Home Abroad, Inc.,** 405 E. 56th St., Apt. 6H, New York, NY 10022-2466 (✆ **212/421-9165;** fax 212/752-1591; www.athomeabroadinc.com), specializes in villas on the French Riviera and in the Dordogne as well as places in the Provençal hill towns. Rentals are usually for 2 weeks. For a $25 registration fee (applicable to any rental), you'll receive photographs of the properties and a newsletter.

A worthwhile competitor is **Vacances en Campagne,** British Travel International, P.O. Box 299, Elkton, VA (✆ **800/327-6097;** fax 540/298-2347; www.britishtravel.com). Its $4 directory contains information on more than 700 potential rentals across Europe, including France.

If you want to rent an apartment in Paris, the **Barclay International Group,** 150 E. 52nd St., New York, NY 10022 (✆ **800/845-6636;** www.barclayweb.com), can give you access to about 3,000 apartments and villas throughout Paris (plus 39 other cities in France), ranging from modest modern units to the most stylish. Units rent from 1 night to up to 6 months; all have TVs and kitchenettes, and many have concierge staffs and lobby-level security. The least expensive units cost around $90 per night, double occupancy. Incremental discounts are granted for a stay of 1 week or 3 weeks. Rentals must be prepaid in U.S. dollars or with a major U.S. credit or charge card.

Hometours International, Inc., P.O. Box 11503, Knoxville, TN 37939 (✆ **800/367-4668** or 865/690-8484), offers more than 400 moderately priced apartments, apartment hotels, and B&Bs in Paris. On the Riviera, you can rent villas, all with pools, at reasonable rates. For budget travelers, they offer a prepaid voucher program for the Campanile hotels, a chain of about 350 two-star family-run hotels throughout France. Rates begin as low as $90 double. This is an excellent alternative to B&B hotels because some chain members provide a buffet breakfast for only 35F (5.30, $5.10) per person. B&B catalogs ($9) and free apartment brochures are available from the address above.

HOTEL CHAINS   One good moderately priced choice is the **Mercure** chain, an organization of simple but clean and modern hotels offering values throughout France. Even at the peak of the tourist season, a room at a Mercure in Paris rents for as little as $95 per night (admittedly, a rarity). For more information on Mercure hotels and a its 100-page directory, call **Accor** (✆ **800/221-4542** in the U.S.; www.mercure.com).

Formule 1 hotels are bare-bones and basic but clean and safe, offering rooms for up to three people, for around $30 per night. Built from prefabricated units, these air-conditioned, soundproofed hotels are shipped to a site and reassembled, often on the outskirts of cities like Paris (27 in the suburbs alone). There are 150 of these low-budget hotels throughout the rest of France.

Mercure and Formule 1 are both owned by the French hotel giant Accor, corporate parent of Motel 6, to which Formule 1 bears a resemblance. The chain finds that the low cost of Formule 1 makes it unprofitable and impractical to allow customers to pre-reserve these rooms from the United States—so you'll have to reserve upon arrival in France. For a directory, write to Formule 1/ETAP Hotels, 6–8 rue du Bois-Briard, 91021 Evry CEDEX (℡ **01-69-36-75-00**).

Other worthwhile economy bets, sometimes with a bit more charm, are the hotels and restaurants of the **Fédération Nationale des Logis de France,** 83 av. d'Italie, 75013 Paris (℡ **01-45-84-70-00**). This is an association of 4,000 hotels, usually country inns convenient for motorists, most rated one or two stars. They publish an annual directory.

15 Tips on Shopping

France is the market of continental Europe—a jumble of products, colors, crafts, and cutting-edge style. Though its retail reputation has grown through fashion and style, the truth is that this is a country where shopping at the local produce market is a quasi-religious experience, where the dime stores are as much fun as (if not more than) the department stores, and where many of the best things in life can be found in a *parapharmacie*—a newfangled concept that marries tons of drugstore, health-care, and beauty products with a discount system.

Factory outlets are opening up *droit* and *gauche.* The old factories continue to sell wares straight from their home-towns (like Limoges), and the new factories have opened boutiquelike shops to hawk overruns.

Add to all this a tradition of the finest antiques in the world (plus heaps of fun junk and what locals call *brocante*), and you have the makings of a spree even a nonshopper will love.

THE BEST BUYS IN FRANCE

BEAUTY PRODUCTS Designer makeup at retail may be the same price in France as in the U.S.—or possibly more expensive. But at a "duty-free" (nonairport variety) store or a discounter where you can qualify for *détaxe* (see "How to Get Your VAT Refund," below), you'll see anywhere from 20% to 45% melt off your bill. Paris offers the most duty-free stores and bigger discounts on name-brand goods, but any city with a tourist business, such as Nice, Cannes, Monaco, or Biarritz, will have at least one discounter. If you know you'll be qualifying for détaxe by spending 1,200F (182.40, $174) or more, ask at each parfumerie you visit until you find one that has the selection you need and the new détaxe program.

CRAFTS The main **faïence** (earthenware) cities are in the north, stretching from Rouen in the northeast to Quimper on the Atlantic coast. (For specific shops in Quimper, see chapter 9.) You'll find **tiles** in the south; check out Salernes, and Moustier Ste-Marie in Provence is known for a specific type of faïence with animals. **Soap making** is an art in the south of France, with soap makers dotting Marseille and Provence. L'Occitane, a Provençal brand, is now sold in its own boutiques in assorted Provence towns and in Paris.

You'll find **copper cooking pots** in northern France, especially in a Normandy village called Villedieu-les-Poêles, 22 miles south of St-Lô, not far from Mont-St-Michel. Copper-lined cookware has been manufactured here since the 1700s, and dozens of stores along the main street sell huge amounts of the stuff. To watch the artisans at work, stop by **Les Ateliers du Cuivre et de l'Argent,** 54 rue du Général-Huard, outside of Villedieu-les-Poêles, beside the main road to Mauviel (℡ **02-33-51-31-85**). A factory store sells at prices much lower than the retail stores in Paris.

Hours are Monday through Saturday from 9am to noon and 1:30 to 5:30pm.

Northeastern France, near Strasbourg, is the home of **Baccarat crystal,** whereas Burgundy is known for its large hand-carved (and very heavy) pieces of **furniture.**

FASHION You can find knockoffs of the latest trends all over, at more than affordable prices, in the two major dime-store chains. Every major city has a **Monoprix** (owned by Galeries Lafayette) or **Prisunic** (owned by Au Printemps); or both.

If you can't leave France without buying something from that icon Hermès, the sorry news is that you may find better deals outside France; London currently has a better price structure (depending on the rate of exchange for your dollar). You'll qualify for a détaxe refund if you buy a scarf at Hermès, but you'll have to buy three ties or two ties and a pocket square to get a tax break.

SIZE CONVERSION CHART

WOMEN'S CLOTHING

American	6	8	10	12	14	16
Continental	36	38	40	42	44	46
British	8	10	12	14	16	18

WOMEN'S SHOES

American	5	6	7	8	9	10
Continental	36	37	38	39	40	41
British	4	5	6	7	8	9

CHILDREN'S CLOTHING

American	3	4	5	6	6X
Continental	98	104	110	116	122
British	18	20	22	24	26

CHILDREN'S SHOES

American	8	9	10	11	12	13	1	2	3
Continental	24	25	27	28	29	30	32	33	34
British	7	8	9	10	11	12	13	1	2

MEN'S SUITS

American	34	36	38	40	42	44	46	48
Continental	44	46	48	50	52	54	56	58
British	34	36	38	40	42	44	46	48

MEN'S SHIRTS

American	14½	15	15½	16	16½	17	17½	18
Continental	37	38	39	41	42	43	44	45
British	14½	15	15½	16	16½	17	17½	18

MEN'S SHOES

American	7	8	9	10	11	12	13
Continental	39½	41	42	43	44½	46	47
British	6	7	8	9	10	11	12

FOOD You can bring **cheeses** into the United States that have aged more than 90 days—this basically means hard and moldy cheeses, not soft, runny ones. No fresh fruit or vegetables are allowed. You'll be safer with

Tips How to Get Your VAT Refund

French sales tax, or VAT (value-added tax), is a hefty 19.6%, but you can get most of that back if you spend 1,200F (182.40, $174) or more at any participating retailer. Most stores participate, though discount perfume shops usually peg the minimum at 1,200F net, which works out to an equivalent pretax amount of 1,600F to 1,700F (243.20 to 258.40, $232 to $246.50). They then deduct the 20% discount so you're back where you started, at 1,200F. This sounds more complicated than it is, so ask!

The name of the refund is *détaxe*, meaning exactly what it says. You never really get the full 19.6% back, but you can come close.

After you spend the required minimum amount, ask for your détaxe papers; fill out the forms before you arrive at the airport and allow at least half an hour for standing in line. All refunds are processed at the final point of departure from the EU, so if you're going to another EU country, you don't apply for the refund in France.

Mark the paperwork to request that your refund be applied to your credit card so you aren't stuck with a check in francs. Even if you made the purchase in cash, you can still get the refund on a credit card. This ensures the best rate of exchange. While you can get cash in some airports, if you don't take the cash in French francs you'll lose money on the transaction.

If you're considering a major purchase, especially one that falls between 1,200F to 2,000F (182.40 to 304, $174 to $290), ask the store policy before you get too involved—or be willing to waive your right to the refund.

mustards; Dijon is brimming with choices, but any French grocery store will have a large selection of choices of the Maille brand.

You can buy **chocolates** in grocery stores, but these are commercial chocolates. If you want to know what everyone's raving about, save up a few francs and head to the chocolatiers in Lyon or Paris, preferably in the cooler months, and begin your own taste test. You should consume handmade fresh chocolate within 3 days. In Paris, the big outlets are **La Maison du Chocolat** and **Christian Constant.** For more information, see chapter 5.)

KITCHENWARE Innovative kitchen appliances are promoted all over France, but their electricity requirements aren't compatible with North America's. However, the ubiquitous copper-lined casseroles and thick-walled roasters might last a lifetime once you recover from the shock of their prices. If you happen to be touring Normandy and want to pick up the best copper-lined saucepans available, head for the hamlet of Villedieu-les-Poêles (see "Crafts," above). You can buy used copperware at almost any flea market and then clean it up yourself. Copper polish is sold at markets as well. In Paris, hit rue Montmartre in the 2nd arrondissement (not in Montmartre) for a choice of kitchen and restaurant suppliers that sell to the public.

PERFUME Note that French perfume lasts longer than the U.S. counterpart of the same scent (it's made with potato alcohol, not grain alcohol), and most new scents are launched in France before they come to the States. French perfume makers, especially the top-of-the-line designer names such as Chanel and Dior, are cracking down on the recent move toward discounting. Some stores will discount other brands and not these premium ones; some outlets will give a smaller discount on the big names.

If you don't qualify for détaxe (see "How to Get Your VAT Refund," above), you should be able to get a flat 20% discount in duty-free stores in Paris and in major cities in the provinces. The airport offers a 13% discount. Don't buy American brands of fragrance in Europe, even at a duty-free shop—they're more expensive than at home. If a store offers a 10% discount, ask what else you get for free—there could be free samples and maybe a tote bag or promotional kit thrown in that the airport can't match.

PORCELAIN   For delicate porcelains, head for Limoges (in the Limousin), where factory shops sell local wares and a few seconds. Note that factory shops are closed from noon to 2pm. In Limoges, look for Bernardaud and Raynaud; in nearby Aixe-sur-Vienne, there's the Ancienne Manufacture Royale de Limoges. (For more information, see chapter 21.)

For earthenware, or faïence, see "Crafts," above. If driving to the French provinces doesn't suit your itinerary, head for rue de Paradis in Paris, where you'll find suppliers with massive displays from all the big French factories. You'll eliminate any savings if you have to ship back to the U.S., but if you can carry a piece with you, you may save 20% to 25%.

WINE & CHAMPAGNE   Searching out unusual vintages from small vintners is great fun. Any wine outlet inventories an overwhelming selection from Bordeaux, Burgundy, Alsace, the Rhône Valley, and Champagne. You'll find lots of sales outlets for exotic burgundies in and around Beaune, Brouilland, Montbard, and Gevrey-Chambertin, and any wine store in Dijon will be amply stocked. If bubbly is your thing, head for Epernay and Reims, where all sorts of champagnes are sold at decent prices—though they may be no cheaper than those in Paris or in the States, depending on promotions and the time of year. (For more information, see chapter 10.)

While all the big *maisons* (stores) sell to visitors, they discount only a smidgen, and only for three or six bottles and no more. Prices in the local hypermarché or at any branch of the French wine-shop chain Nicolas may rival prices offered by the maisons.

Alsace, Provence, and the Bordeaux region retain thousands of cases of their local vintages for sale (at favorable prices). Bottles of unusual cognacs, often with labels scrawled in the shaky script of an old vintner, are for sale in out-of-the-way corners around southwestern France and in centre-ville Cognac.

If after-dinner liqueurs are your thing, in Normandy you'll find bottles of Calvados (the famous apple-based liqueur) everywhere in the region.

For information on Customs and how much alcohol you can bring home, see "Entry Requirements & Customs Regulations," in this chapter.

SHIPPING IT HOME

Shipping costs will possibly double your cost on goods; you'll also pay U.S. duties on the items if they're valued at more than $50. The good news is that détaxe is automatically applied to any item shipped to an American destination—no need to worry about the 1,200F minimum. However, some stores have a $100 minimum for shipping. You can also walk into any PT&T (post office) and mail home a packet or small box of goodies. French do-it-yourself boxes can't be reopened once closed.

FAST FACTS: *France*

For Paris-specific information, see "Fast Facts: Paris," in chapter 4.

Auto Clubs The Association Française des Auto Clubs, 14 av. de la Grand-Armée, 17e (© **01-40-55-43-00;** Métro: Porte-Maillot), provides limited information to members of U.S. auto clubs like AAA.

Business Hours Business hours are erratic, as befits a nation of individualists. Most banks are open Monday through Friday from 9:30am to 4:30pm. Many, particularly in small towns or villages, take a lunch break at varying times. Hours are usually posted on the door. Most museums close 1 day a week (often Tuesday), and they're generally closed on national holidays. Usual hours are 9:30am to 5pm. Some museums, particularly the smaller ones, close for lunch from noon to 2pm. Refer to the individual listings. See "When to Go" in this chapter for a list of recognized holidays

Generally, offices are open Monday through Friday from 9am to 5pm, but always call first. In Paris or other big French cities, stores are open from 9 or 9:30am (but often 10am) to 6 or 7pm without a break for lunch. Some shops, particularly those operated by foreigners, open at 8am and close at 8 or 9pm. In some small stores, the lunch break can last 3 hours, beginning at 1pm. This is more common in the south than in the north.

Drugstores If you need one during off-hours, have your concierge get in touch with the nearest Commissariat de Police. An agent there will have the address of a nearby pharmacy open 24 hours a day. French law requires that the pharmacies in any given neighborhood display the name and location of the one that remains open all night.

Electricity In general, expect 200 volts or 50 cycles, though you'll encounter 110 and 115 volts in some older establishments. Adapters are needed to fit sockets. Many hotels have two-pin (in some cases, three-pin) sockets for electric razors. It's best to ask your hotel concierge before plugging in any appliance.

Embassies/Consulates If you have a passport, immigration, legal, or other problem, contact your consulate. Call before you go, as they often keep odd hours and observe both French and home-country holidays. The Embassy of the **United States**, at 2 av. Gabriel, 8e (© **01-43-12-22-22;** Métro: Concorde), is open Monday through Friday from 9am to 6pm. Passports are issued at its consulate at 2 rue St-Florentin (© **01-43-12-22-22;** Métro: Concorde). The Embassy of **Canada** is at 35 av. Montaigne, 8e (© **01-44-43-29-00;** Métro: F.-D.-Roosevelt or Alma-Marceau), open Monday through Friday from 9am to noon and 2 to 5pm. The Embassy of the **United Kingdom** is at 35 rue Faubourg St-Honore, 8e (© **01-44-51-31-00;** Métro: Concorde or Madeleine), open Monday through Friday from 9:30am to 1pm and 2:30 to 5pm. The consulate is at 18 bis rue d'Anjou, 8e (© **01-44-66-29-79;** Métro: Concorde or Madeleine), open Monday through Friday from 9am to noon and 2 to 5pm. The Embassy of **Ireland** is at 4 rue Rude, 16e, 75116 Paris (© **01-44-17-67-00;** Métro: Etoile), open Monday through Friday from 9:30am to noon and 2:30 to 5:30pm. The Embassy of **Australia** is at 4 rue Jean-Rey, 15e (© **01-40-59-33-00;** Métro: Bir-Hakeim), open Monday through Friday from 9:15am to noon and 2:30 to 4:30pm. The embassy of **New Zealand** is at 7 ter rue Léonard-de-Vinci, 75116 Paris (℃ **01-45-00-24-11;** Métro: Victor Hugo), open Monday through Friday from 9am to 1pm and 2:30 to 6pm. The Embassy of **South Africa** is at 59 quai d'Orsay (℃ **01-53-59-23-23;** Métro: Invalides), open Monday through Friday from 8:45 to 11am.

Emergencies In an emergency while at a hotel, contact the front desk. Most staffs are trained in dealing with a crisis and will call the police, summon an ambulance, or do whatever is necessary. If the emergency involves something like a stolen wallet, go to the police station in person. Otherwise, you can get help anywhere in France by calling ℃ **17** for the police or ℃ **18** for the fire department (*pompiers*). For roadside emergencies, see "Getting Around France," earlier in this chapter.

Mail Most post offices in Paris are open Monday through Friday from 8am to 7pm and Saturday from 8am to noon. Allow 5 to 8 days to send or receive mail from your home. Airmail letters within Europe cost 3F (.45, 45¢); to the United States and Canada, 4.40F (.65, 65¢). Airmail letters to Australia and New Zealand cost 5.20F (.80, 75¢).

You can exchange money at post offices. Many hotels sell stamps, as do local post offices and cafes displaying a red TABAC sign outside.

Police Call ℃ **17** anywhere in France.

Restrooms If you're in dire need, duck into a cafe or brasserie to use the lavatory. It's customary to make some small purchase if you do so. Paris Métro stations and underground garages usually contain public restrooms, but the degree of cleanliness varies. France still has some "hole-in-the-ground" toilets, so be warned.

Safety Much of the country, particularly central France, the northeast, Normandy, and Brittany, remains relatively safe, though no place in the world is crime-free. Those intending to visit the south of France, especially the Riviera, should exercise caution—robberies and muggings here are commonplace. It's best to check your baggage into a hotel and then go sightseeing instead of leaving it unguarded in the trunk of a car, which can easily be broken into. Marseille is among the most dangerous French cities.

Taxes Watch it: You could get burned. As a member of the European Union, France routinely imposes a value-added tax (VAT in English; TVA in French) on many goods and services. The standard VAT is 19.6% on merchandise, including clothing, appliances, liquor, leather goods, shoes, furs, jewelry, perfumes, cameras, and even caviar. Refunds are made for the tax on certain goods and merchandise, but not on services. The minimum purchase is 1,200F (182.40, $174) in the same store for nationals or residents of countries outside the EU. See "How to Get Your VAT Refund," earlier in this chapter, for details.

Telephone You'll find public phones in cafes, restaurants, Métro stations, post offices, airports, train stations, and occasionally on the street. Pay phones accept coins of ½F, 1F, 2F, and 5F; the minimum charge is 2F (.30, 30¢). Pick up the receiver, insert the coin(s), and dial when you hear the tone, pushing the button when there's an answer.

The French also use a *télécarte*, a phone debit card, which you can purchase at rail stations, post offices, and other places. Sold in two versions, it allows you to use either 50 or 120 charge units (depending on the card) by inserting the card into the slot of most public phones. Depending on the type of card you buy, the cost is 41F to 98F (6.25 to 14.90, $5.95 to $14.20).

If possible, avoid making calls from your hotel, as some French establishments will double or triple the charges.

To call France from North America, dial **011,** then **33** (the country code for France), the area code, and the eight-digit number. Although French area codes are two digits (the first digit is always a 0), you do not dial the zero when calling from abroad. For example, the Hôtel Négresco (℃ **04-93-16-64-00**) contains the area code for southeastern France (04). **To call long-distance within France,** you simply dial this 10-digit number. But if you call from North America, you would dial ℃ **011-33-4-93-16-64-00.**

To call North America from France, an easy and relatively inexpensive way is to use USA Direct/AT&T WorldConnect. From within France, dial any of the following numbers: ℃ **0800/99-0011, -1011, -1111,** or **-1211.** Follow the prompt, which will ask you to punch in the number of your AT&T credit card or a MasterCard or Visa. The countries that participate in the system—referred to as WorldConnect—include the United States, Canada, the United Kingdom, Ireland, Australia, New Zealand, and South Africa. By dialing the number you want in any of these countries, you'll avoid the surcharges imposed by the hotel operator. At any time, an AT&T operator will be available to help you. The country code for the U.S. and Canada is **1.** Great Britain is **44,** Ireland is **353,** Australia is **61,** New Zealand is **64,** and South Africa is **27.**

For information, dial ℃ **12.**

Time The French equivalent of daylight saving time lasts from April to September, which puts it 1 hour ahead of French winter time. France is usually 6 hours ahead of U.S. eastern time, except in October, when U.S. clocks are still on daylight time; then France is only 5 hours ahead. The rest of the year, when it's 9am in New York, it's 3pm in France.

Tipping All bills, as required by law, are supposed to say *service compris,* which means that the tip has been included. But French diners often leave some small change as an additional tip, especially if service has been exceptional.

Here are some general guidelines: for hotel staff, tip 6F to 10F (.90 to 1.50, 85¢ to $1.45) for every item of baggage the porter carries on arrival and departure, and 10F (1.50, $1.45) per day for the chambermaid. In cafes, service is usually included. Tip taxi drivers 10% to 15% of the amount on the meter. In theaters and restaurants, give cloakroom attendants at least 5F (.75, 75¢) per item. Give restroom attendants about 2F (.30, 30¢) in nightclubs and such places. Give cinema and theater ushers about 2F (.30, 30¢). For guides for group visits to museums and monuments, 5F to 10F (.75 to 1.50, 75¢ to $1.45) is a reasonable tip.

Water Drinking water is generally safe, though it's occasionally been known to cause diarrhea. If you ask for water in a restaurant, it'll be served bottled (for which you'll pay) unless you specifically request tap water (*l'eau du robinet*). Your waiter may ask if you'd like your water *avec gas* (carbonated) or *sans gas* (without bubbles).

4

Settling into Paris

Stroll along the Seine and the broad tree-lined boulevards, browse the chic shops and relax over coffee or wine at the sidewalk cafes; visit the museums, monuments, and cathedrals; sample the legendary cuisine; attend an opera or a concert; and enjoy the nightlife. Despite the turmoil behind the scenes, Paris is still the City of Light—and it always manages to live up to its reputation as one of the world's most romantic cities.

Ernest Hemingway referred to the many splendors of Paris as a "moveable feast" and wrote, "There is never any ending to Paris, and the memory of each person who has lived in it differs from that of any other."

1 Orientation

ARRIVING

BY PLANE Paris has two major international airports: Aéroport d'Orly, 8½ miles south of the city, and Aéroport Roissy–Charles de Gaulle, 14¼ miles northeast. A shuttle, which is 80 F (12.15, $11.60), makes the 50- to 75-minute journey between the two airports about every 30 minutes.

Charles de Gaulle Airport (Roissy) At Charles de Gaulle (© 01-48-62-22-80), foreign carriers use Aérogare 1, while Air France wings into Aérogare 2. From Aérogare 1, you take a moving walkway to the passport checkpoint and the Customs area. The two terminals are linked by a *navette* (shuttle bus).

The shuttle also transports you to the **Roissy rail station,** from which fast RER (Réseau Express Régional) trains leave every 15 minutes heading to such Métro stations as Gare du Nord, Châtelet, Luxembourg, Port-Royal, and Denfert-Rochereau. A typical fare from Roissy to any point in central Paris is 69F (10.50, $10) in first class, 49F (7.45, $7.10) in second class.

You can also take an **Air France shuttle bus** to central Paris for 75F (11.40, $10.93). It stops at the Palais des Congrès (Port Maillot), then continues on to place Charles-de-Gaulle-étoile, where subway lines can carry you to any point in Paris. That ride, depending on traffic, takes between 45 and 55 minutes. The shuttle departs about every 12 minutes between 5:40am and 11pm.

Another option is the **Roissybus** (© 01-48-04-18-24), departing from the airport daily from 5:45am to 11pm and costing 48F (7.30, $6.95) for the 45- to 50-minute ride. Departures are about every 15 minutes, and the bus will take you near the corner of rue Scribe and place de l'Opéra in the heart of Paris.

A **taxi** from Roissy into the city will cost about 250F (38, $36.25), but from 8pm to 7am the fares are 40% higher. Long lines for taxis form outside each of the airport's terminals and are surprisingly orderly.

Orly Airport Orly (© 01-49-75-15-15) has two terminals—Orly *Sud* (south) for international flights and Orly *Ouest* (west) for domestic flights. They're linked by a free shuttle bus (trip time: 15 min.).

Air France buses leave from Exit E of Orly Sud and from Exit F of Orly Ouest every 12 minutes between 5:45am and 11pm for Gare des Invalides; the fare is 45F (6.85, $6.55). Returning to the airport, buses leave the Invalides terminal for Orly Sud or Orly Ouest every 15 minutes, taking about 30 minutes.

Another way to get to central Paris is via the free **shuttle bus** that leaves both of Orly's terminals about every 15 minutes for the nearby Métro and RER train station (Pont-de-Rungis/Aéroport-d'Orly). RER trains take 35 minutes for rides into the city center. A trip to Les Invalides, for example, is 47F (7.15, $6.80).

A **taxi** from Orly to central Paris costs about 200F (30.40, $29), more at night. Don't take a meterless taxi from Orly—it's much safer (and usually cheaper) to hire a metered cab, which are under the scrutiny of a police officer.

BY TRAIN   Paris has six major train stations: **Gare d'Austerlitz,** 55 quai d'Austerlitz, 13e (servicing the southwest with trains to and from the Loire Valley, Bordeaux, the Pyrénées, and Spain); **Gare de l'Est,** place du 11-Novembre-1918, 10e (servicing the east with trains to and from Strasbourg, Nancy, Reims, and beyond to Zurich, Basel, Luxembourg, and Austria); **Gare de Lyon,** 20 bd. Diderot, 12e (servicing the southeast with trains to and from the Côte d'Azur [Nice, Cannes, St-Tropez], Provence, and beyond to Geneva, Lausanne, and Italy); **Gare Montparnasse,** 17 bd. Vaugirard, 15e (servicing the west with trains to and from Brittany); **Gare du Nord,** 18 rue de Dunkerque, 15e (servicing the north with trains to and from London, Holland, Denmark, Belgium, and northern Germany); and **Gare St-Lazare,** 13 rue d'Amsterdam, 8e (servicing the northwest with trains to and from Normandy). Buses operate between the stations. Each has a Métro stop, making the whole city accessible. Taxis are also available at designated stands—look for the signs that say TÊTE DE STATION. For train information and to make reservations, call ✆ **08-36-35-35-35** between 7am and 8pm daily. One-way to Tours 160–200F (24.30– 30.40, $23.20–$29); one way to Strasbourg 220F (33.45, $31.90) .

Warning: The stations and surrounding areas are usually seedy and frequented by pickpockets, hustlers, hookers, and addicts. Be alert, especially at night.

BY BUS   Most buses arrive at the **Gare Routière Internationale du Paris-Gallieni,** 28 av. du Général-de-Gaulle, in the suburb of Bagnolet (✆ **01-49-72-51-51;** Métro: Gallieni).

⎛Tips   The New Airport Shuttle

Cheaper than a taxi for one or two people but more expensive than airport buses and trains, the **Airport Shuttle** (✆ **01-43-21-06-78;** fax 01-43-21-35-67; www.paris-anglo.com/clients/ashuttle.html) will pick you up in a minivan at Charles de Gaulle or Orly and take you to your hotel for 120F (18.25E, $17.40) for one person or 89F (13.55, $12.90) per person for parties of two or more. It'll take you to the airports from your hotel for the same price. The **Paris Airport Service** (✆ **01-49-62-78-78;** fax 01-49-62-78-79) offers a similar service. It charges 145F (22.05, $21.05) for one person or 180F (27.35, $26.10) for two or more going to Charles de Gaulle, and 115F (17.50, $16.70) for one person or 135F (20.50, $19.60) for two or more to Orly. Both companies accept Visa and MasterCard, with 1-day advance reservations required.

Paris by Arrondissement

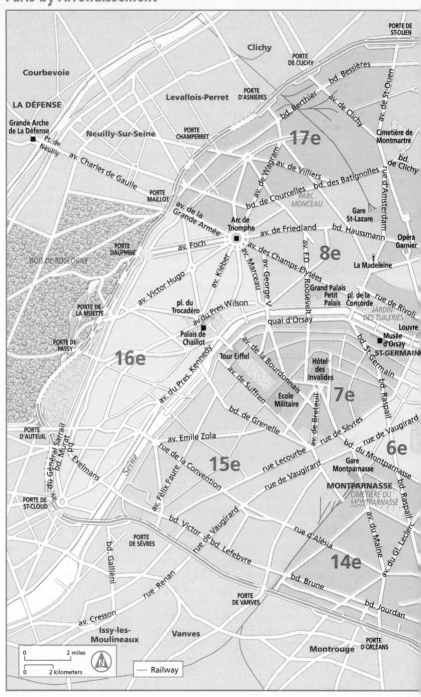

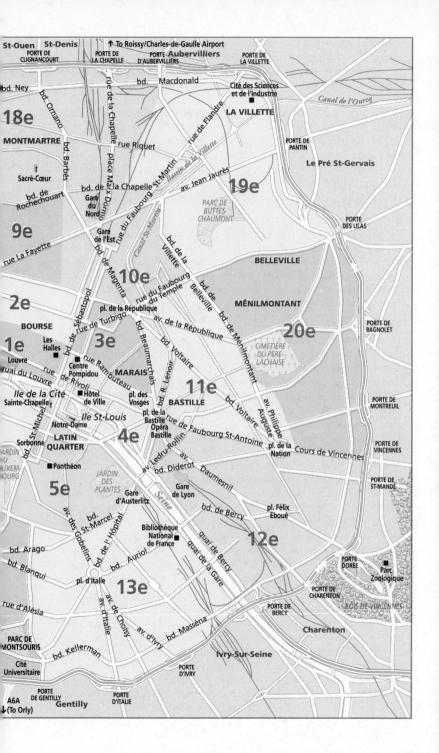

BY CAR Driving in Paris is *not* recommended. Parking is difficult and traffic dense. If you drive, remember that Paris is encircled by a ring road, the *périphérique.* Always obtain detailed directions to your destination, including the name of the exit on the périphérique (exits aren't numbered). Avoid rush hours.

Few hotels, except the luxury ones, have garages, but the staff will usually be able to direct you to one nearby.

The major highways into Paris are A1 from the north (Great Britain and Benelux); A13 from Rouen, Normandy, and other points of northwest France; A10 from Spain, the Pyrénées, and the southwest; A6 and A7 from the French Alps, the Riviera, and Italy; and A4 from eastern France.

VISITOR INFORMATION

The **main tourist information office** is at 127 av. des Champs-Elysées, 8e (© **08-36-68-31-12;** Métro: George V), where you can get details about Paris and the provinces. It's open April to October, daily from 9am to 8pm (closed May 1), and November to March, daily from 11am to 6pm (closed December 25).

Welcome Offices in the city's rail stations (except Gare St-Lazare) and at the Eiffel Tower can give you free maps, brochures, and *Paris Selection,* a French-language monthly listing current events and performances.

CITY LAYOUT

Paris is surprisingly compact. Occupying 432 square miles, it's home to more than 10 million people. The river Seine divides Paris into the ***Rive Droite*** **(Right Bank)** to the north and the ***Rive Gauche*** **(Left Bank)** to the south. These designations make sense when you stand on a bridge and face downstream (west), watching the waters flow out toward the sea—to your right is the north bank, to your left the south. A total of 32 bridges link the Right Bank and the Left Bank, some providing access to the two small islands at the heart of the city—**Île de la Cité,** the city's birthplace and site of Notre-Dame, and **Île St-Louis,** a moat-guarded oasis of 17th-century mansions. These islands can cause confusion to walkers who think they've just crossed from one bank to the other, only to find themselves in an almost-medieval maze of narrow streets and old buildings.

The "main street" on the Right Bank is, of course, **avenue des Champs-Elysées,** beginning at the Arc de Triomphe and running to place de la Concorde. Avenue des Champs-Elysées and 11 other avenues radiate like the arms of an asterisk from the Arc de Triomphe, giving it its original name, place de l'étoile (*étoile* means "star"). It was renamed place Charles-de-Gaulle following the general's death; today, it's often referred to as place Charles-de-Gaulle-étoile.

FINDING AN ADDRESS Paris is divided into 20 municipal wards called *arrondissements,* each with its own city hall, police station, and post office; some have remnants of market squares. Arrondissements spiral out clockwise from the 1st, in the geographical center of the city. The 2nd through the 8th form a ring around the 1st, while the 9th through the 17th form an outer ring around the inner ring. The 18th, 19th, and 20th are at the far northern and eastern reaches of the Right Bank. Arrondissements 5, 6, 7, 13, 14, and 15 are on the Left Bank.

Most city maps are divided by arrondissement, and addresses include the arrondissement number (in Roman or Arabic numerals and followed by "e" or "er"). Paris also has its own version of a zip code. The proper mailing address for a hotel is written as, for example, "75014 Paris." The last two digits, 14, indicate that the address is in the 14th arrondissement—in this case, Montparnasse.

Numbers on buildings running parallel to the Seine usually follow the course of the river—east to west. On perpendicular streets, numbers on buildings begin low closer to the river.

MAPS   If you're staying more than 2 or 3 days, purchase an inexpensive pocket-size book called *Paris par arrondissement,* available at all major newsstands and bookshops; prices start at 40F (6.10, $5.80). These guides provide you with a Métro map, a foldout map of the city, and maps of each arrondissement, with all streets listed and keyed.

THE ARRONDISSEMENTS IN BRIEF

Each of Paris's 20 arrondissements possesses a unique style and flavor. Do note, however, that in this guide, we cover only those hotels in central Paris; for a wider selection of accommodations in the outer arrondissements, see *Frommer's Paris 2002.*

1er (Musée du Louvre/Les Halles) One of the world's great museums, the **Louvre** lures hordes to the 1st arrondissement on the Right Bank. This area is home to rue de Rivoli and the **Jeu de Paume** and **Orangerie** museums. Walk through the **Jardin des Tuileries,** laid out by Louis XIV's gardener. Pause to take in the beauty of **place Vendôme.** Jewelers and art dealers are plentiful, and memories of Chopin are evoked at no. 12 on the square where he died. Zola's "belly of Paris" (Les Halles) is no longer the food-and-meat market; it has become the **Forum des Halles,** a center of shopping, entertainment, and culture.

2e (La Bourse) Home to the **Bourse (stock exchange),** this Right Bank district lies between the Grands Boulevards and rue Etienne-Marcel. On weekdays, the shouts of brokers echo across place de la Bourse until lunchtime, when they continue their hysteria in the district's restaurants. Much of the east end of the 2nd is devoted to the **garment district (Le Sentier),** where items are sold to buyers from stores all over Europe. You'll find gems amid the commercialism—none finer than the **Musée Cognacq-Jay,** 25 bd. des Capucines, featuring work by every artist from Watteau to Fragonard.

3e (Le Marais) This district embraces much of **Le Marais (the Swamp),** one of the best loved of the old Right Bank neighborhoods. Over the centuries, kings have called Le Marais home, and its salons have echoed with the witty, devastating remarks of Racine, Voltaire, Molière, and Mme de Sévigné. Allowed to fall into decay for decades, it came back in the 1990s, with galleries and trendy boutiques. One of its chief draws is the **Musée Picasso,** a great repository of 20th-century art. Le Marais is also the center of Paris's gay and lesbian scene. Rue des Rosiers, with its Jewish restaurants, remains as a memory of the hundreds of Jewish residents who used to reside in Le Marais.

4e (Île de la Cité/ Île St-Louis & Beaubourg) The 4th has it all: not only the Île de la Cité, with **Notre-Dame,** the **Sainte-Chapelle,** and the **Conciergerie,** but the Île St-Louis, with aristocratic town houses, courtyards, and antiques shops. Île St-Louis, a former cow pasture and dueling ground, is home to 6,000 lucky Louisiens, its permanent residents. Of course, the whole area is touristy and overrun. As the heart of medieval Paris, the 4th evokes memories of Danton and Robespierre, even of Charlotte Corday stabbing Marat in his bath.

You get France's finest **bird and flower markets,** plus the **Centre Georges-Pompidou.** After all this, you can retreat to **place des Vosges,** a square of perfect harmony where Victor Hugo penned many masterpieces from 1832 to 1848.

5e (Latin Quarter) The Quartier Latin on the Left Bank is Paris's intellectual soul. Bookstores, schools, churches, jazz clubs, student dives, Roman ruins, publishing houses, and boutiques characterize the district. The quarter got its name because the students and professors at the **Sorbonne** (founded in 1253) spoke Latin. As the center of "bohemian Paris," it was the setting for Henry Murger's novel *La Vie Bohème* (later the Puccini opera *La Bohème.*

For sure, the old Latin Quarter is gone. Changing times have brought Greek, Moroccan, and Vietnamese immigrants, among others, hustling everything from couscous to fiery-hot spring rolls and souvlaki. The 5th borders the Seine, so you'll want to stroll along **quai de Montebello,** where vendors sell everything from antique Daumier prints to yellowing copies of Balzac's *Père Goriot.* The 5th also stretches to the **Panthéon,** the resting place of Rousseau, Zola, Hugo, Braille, Voltaire, and Jean Moulin, the Resistance leader tortured to death by the Gestapo. Marie Curie is buried here as well.

6e (St-Germain/ Luxembourg) This heartland of Paris publishing is, for some, the most colorful Left Bank quarter. You can see earnest young artists emerging from the **École des Beaux-Arts.** Strolling the boulevards of the 6th, including **St-Germain,** has its own rewards, but the secret of the district lies in its narrow streets and hidden squares as well as the **Jardin du Luxembourg,** a classic garden overlooked

by Marie de Médici's **Palais du Luxembourg.** To be really authentic, stroll these streets with an unwrapped loaf of sourdough bread from the wood-fired ovens of **Poilâne,** 8 rue du Cherche-Midi. Everywhere you'll encounter historic and literary associations, as on **rue Jacob,** where Racine, Wagner, Ingres, and Hemingway all once lived. Today's big name could be filmmaker Spike Lee checking into his favorite, La Villa Hôtel, at 29 rue Jacob.

7e (Eiffel Tower/Musée d'Orsay) The **Eiffel Tower** dominates the 7th on the Left Bank. The tower is one of the most recognizable landmarks in the world, but many Parisians hated it when it was unveiled in 1889. The 7th is home to other imposing monuments, including the **Hôtel des Invalides,** which contains Napoléon's Tomb and the Musée de l'Armée (the world's greatest army museum). But there's much hidden charm as well. Even visitors with no time to explore the 7th at least rush to the **Musée d'Orsay,** the world's premier showcase of 19th-century French art and culture.

8e (Champs-Elysées/ Madeleine) The 8th is the heart of the Right Bank and its prime showcase is **avenue des Champs-Elysées,** linking the **Arc de Triomphe** with the Egyptian obelisk on **place de la Concorde.** Here you'll find the top fashion houses, elegant hotels, expensive restaurants and shops, and fashionably attired Parisians. By the 1980s, it had become a garish strip, with too much traffic and too many fast-food joints. But in the 1990s, the mayor of Paris (now president of France), Jacques Chirac, launched a cleanup. The major change has been broadened sidewalks, with new rows of trees.

The area is known for having France's (perhaps the world's) best, grandest, and most impressive: the best restaurant (**Taillevent**), the sexiest strip joint (**Crazy Horse Saloon**), the most splendid square (**place de la Concorde**), the best rooftop cafe (at **La Samaritaine**), the grandest hotel (**Crillon**), the most impressive triumphal arch (**Arc de Triomphe**), the most expensive residential street (**avenue Matignon**), the oldest Métro station (**Franklin-D.-Roosevelt**), and the most ancient monument (**Obelisk of Luxor,** 3,300 years old). Also here is **La Madeleine** church, looking like a Greek temple.

9e (Opéra Garnier/Pigalle) Everything from the Quartier de l'Opéra to the strip joints of Pigalle (the infamous "Pig Alley" for the G.I.s of World War II) is within the 9th on the Right Bank. It was radically altered by Baron Haussmann's 19th-century redevelopment, and the *grands boulevards* are among the most obvious of his works. Boulevard des Italiens is home to **Café de la Paix,** opened in 1856, once the meeting place of Romantic poets like Théophile Gautier and Alfred de Musset. Later, de Gaulle, Dietrich, and 2 million Americans started showing up.

Another major attraction is the **Folies-Bergère,** where can-can dancers have been kicking since 1868 and such entertainers as Mistinguett, Piaf, and Chevalier have appeared, along with the Josephine Baker. But more than anything, it was the **Opéra** (now the Opéra Garnier or Palais Garnier), once the haunt of the Phantom, that made the 9th the last hurrah of Second Empire opulence.

10e (Gare du Nord/Gare de l'Est) Gare du Nord and Gare de l'Est, along with cinemas, porno houses, and dreary commercial zones, make the 10th on the Right Bank one of the least desirable arrondissements for tourists. We try to avoid the 10th, except for two longtime favorite restaurants: **Brasserie Flo,** 7 cour des Petites-Ecuries (go for *la formidable choucroute*—a heap of sauerkraut with everything); and **Julien,** 16 rue du Faubourg St-Denis (called the poor man's Maxim's because of its belle-époque interior and moderate prices).

11e (Opéra Bastille) For many years, this Right-Bank quarter seemed to sink lower and lower. However, the 1989 opening of the **Opéra Bastille** gave it a new lease on life. The "people's opera house" stands on the landmark **place de la Bastille,** where on July 14, 1789, Parisians stormed the fortress, seized the ammunition depot, and released the prisoners.

The area sandwiched between the Marais, Ménilmontant, and République is now being called "blue-collar chic," as the *artistes* of Paris have been driven from the costlier sections and can be found walking the sidewalks of rue Oberkampf. Hip Parisians in search of a more cutting-edge experience are living and working among the decaying 19th-century apartments and the 1960s public housing with graffiti-spattered walls.

12e (Bois de Vincennes/Gare de Lyon) Few out-of-towners came here on the Right Bank until a French chef opened **Au Trou Gascon.** Then the world started showing up. The major attraction is the **Bois de Vincennes,** a sprawling park on the eastern periphery of Paris. It has been a longtime favorite of families who enjoy its zoos and museums, its château and lakes, and the Parc Floral de Paris, whose springtime rhododendrons and autumn dahlias are among the city's major lures. The dreary **Gare de Lyon** lies in the 12th, but going here is worthwhile even if you don't have to take a train. **Le Train Bleue** is the station's restaurant, whose ceiling frescoes and Art Nouveau decor are national artistic treasures—and the food's good, too. The 12th, once a depressing neighborhood, is moving toward a resuscitation, with new housing, shops, gardens, and restaurants.

13e (Gare d'Austerlitz) Centering around the grimy Gare d'Austerlitz, the 13th on the Left Bank may have its fans, though we've yet to meet one. British snobs who flitted in and out of the station were among the first foreign visitors, and they wrote the 13th off as a dreary working-class district. But there's at least one reason to come: the **Manufacture des Gobelins,** 42 av. des Gobelins—this is the tapestry factory that made the word *Gobelins* world famous.

14e (Montparnasse) The northern end of this district on the Left Bank is **Montparnasse,** home of the Lost Generation. One of its major monuments is the Rodin statue of Balzac at the junction of boulevard Montparnasse and boulevard Raspail. At this corner are famous **literary cafes** like La Rotonde, Le Sélect, La Dôme, and La Coupole. Perhaps Gertrude Stein didn't come here (she loathed cafes), but all the other American expats, including Hemingway and Fitzgerald, arrived for a drink or four. At 27 rue de Fleurus, Stein, and Toklas collected their paintings and entertained T. S. Eliot and Matisse. At its southern end, the 14th contains neighborhoods filled with well-designed apartment buildings, many constructed between 1910 and 1940.

15e (Gare Montparnasse/Institut Pasteur) A mostly residential district beginning at Gare Montparnasse, the 15th on the Left Bank stretches west to the Seine. It's the largest arrondissement, but attracts few visitors and has few attractions, except for the **Parc des Expositions** and the **Institut Pasteur.** Institut Pasteur at 25 rue du Dr. Roux (*℡* **01-45-68-82-82;** Metro: Pasteur), founded by Louis Pasteur in 1887, is a biochemical research center. Parc des Expositions is a fairgrounds where special exhibitions are staged.

16e (Trocadéro/Bois de Boulogne) Highlights of the 16th on the Right Bank are the **Bois de Boulogne, Jardins du Trocadéro, Musée de Balzac, Musée Guimet** (famous for its Asian collections), and the **Cimetière de Passy,** resting place of Manet, Talleyrand, Giraudoux, and Debussy. One of the largest arrondissements, it's known for its well-heeled bourgeoisie, upscale rents, and posh residential boulevards. Prosperous and conservative addresses include **avenue d'Iéna** and **avenue Victor-Hugo;** also prestigious is **avenue Foch,** the widest boulevard, with homes that at various periods were maintained by Aristotle Onassis, the shah of Iran, Debussy, and Prince Rainier of Monaco. The 16th also includes the best place in Paris to view the Eiffel Tower from afar: **place du Trocadéro.**

17e (Parc Monceau/Place Clichy) Flanking the northern periphery of Paris, the 17th on the Right Bank is one of the most spread-out arrondissements, incorporating the northern edge of glamorous place de Charles-de-Gaulle-étoile in the west, the bourgeois place Wagram at its center, and the tawdry place Clichy in the east. Highlights are **Parc Monceau,** the **Palais des Congrès** (of interest only if you're attending a convention or special exhibit), and the **Porte Maillot Air Terminal**. More exciting than any of those are two great restaurants: **Guy Savoy** and **Michel Rostang** (see "Dining," later in this chapter).

18e (Montmartre)   The 18th at the far end of the Right Bank is the most famous outer arrondissement, embracing **Montmartre** and associated with such names as the **Moulin Rouge, Sacré-Coeur,** and **place du Tertre** (a tourist trap if there ever was one). Utrillo was its native son, Renoir lived here, and Toulouse-Lautrec adopted the area as his own. Today, place Blanche is known for its prostitutes, and Montmartre is filled with honky-tonks, souvenir shops, and bad restaurants. Go for the attractions and *mémoires*. The **Marché aux Puces de Clignancourt** flea market is another landmark.

19e (La Villette)   Visitors come to what was once the village of La Villette to see the **Cité des Sciences et de l'Industrie,** a spectacular science museum and park built on a site that once was devoted to slaughterhouses. Mostly residential, this district at the far end of the Right Bank is one of the most ethnic in Paris, home to workers from all parts of the former Empire. A highlight is **Les Buttes Chaumont,** a park where kids can enjoy puppet shows and donkey rides.

20e (Père-Lachaise Cemetery)   Also at the far end of the Right Bank, this district's greatest landmark is the **Père-Lachaise Cemetery,** resting place of Piaf, Proust, Wilde, Duncan, Stein and Toklas, Bernhardt, Colette, Jim Morrison, and many others. Nostalgia buffs sometimes visit Piaf's former neighborhood, Ménilmontant-Belleville, but it has been almost totally rebuilt. The district is home to many Muslims and hundreds of members of Paris's Sephardic Jewish community, many of whom fled from Algeria or Tunisia. With turbaned men selling dates and grains on the street, this arrondissement seems more North African than French.

2 Getting Around

Paris is a city for strollers, whose greatest joy is rambling through unexpected alleys and squares. If you have a choice, try to hoof it on your own two feet. How else can you rub elbows (literally) with Parisians and experience the real Paris?

BY MÉTRO (SUBWAY)   The Métro (© 08-36-68-77-14) is the most efficient and fastest means of transportation in Paris. All lines are numbered, and the final destination of each line is clearly marked on subway maps, in the underground passageways, and on the train cars.

The Métro runs daily from 5:30am to around 1:15am. It's reasonably safe at any hour, but beware of pickpockets.

To familiarize yourself with Paris's Métro system before you leave, check out the map on the inside back cover of this book. Most stations display a map of the Métro at the entrance. To make sure you catch the correct train, find your destination, then follow the rail line it's on to the end of the route and note the name of the final destination—this final stop is the direction. To find your train in the station, follow the signs labeled with your direction in the passageways until you see it labeled on a train.

Transfer stations are known as *correspondances*—some require long walks; Châtelet is the most difficult—but most trips will require only one transfer. When transferring, follow the bright-orange CORRESPONDANCE signs until you

---

Tips **Discount Passes**

The **Paris-Visite** (© **01-44-68-20-20**) is a pass valid for 1, 2, 3, or 5 days on the public transport system, including the Métro, buses, and RER trains. The funicular ride to the top of Montmartre is also included. Its cost ranges from 60F (9.10, $8.70) for 1 day to 185F (28.10, $26.85) for 5 days. Get it at RATP (Régie Autonome des Transports Parisiens) offices, the tourist office, and the main Métro stations.

Another discount pass is **Carte Mobilis,** which allows unlimited travel on all bus, subway, and RER lines during a 1-day period for 32F to 74F (4.85 to   11.25, $4.65 to $10.75), depending on the zone. Ask for it at any Métro station.

Most economical of all, for anyone who happens to arrive in Paris early in the week, is a **Carte Orange.** Sold at large Métro stations, it allows 1 week of unlimited Métro or bus transit within central Paris for 85F (12.90, $12.35). They're valid from any Monday to the following Sunday, and are sold only on Mondays Tuesdays, and Wednesdays. You'll have to submit a passport-sized photo.

---

reach the proper platform. Don't follow a SORTIE (Exit) sign or you'll have to pay another fare to resume your journey.

Many of the larger stations have easy-to-use maps with push-button indicators that light up your route when you press the button for your destination.

On the urban lines, it costs the same to travel to any point: 8F (1.20, $1.15). On the Sceaux, Boissy-St-Léger, and St-Germain-en-Laye lines serving the suburbs, fares are based on distance. A *carnet* (book of coupons) is the best buy—10 tickets for 58F (8.80, $8.40).

At the turnstile entrances to the station, insert your ticket and pass through. At some exits, tickets are also checked, so hold on to yours. There are occasional ticket checks on trains and platforms and in passageways, too.

BY BUS Buses are much slower than the Métro, and the majority run only from 7am to 8:30pm (a few operate until 12:30am, and 10 operate during early-morning hours). Service is limited on Sundays and holidays. Bus and Métro fares are the same, and you can use the same carnet tickets on both. Most bus rides require one ticket, but there are some destinations requiring two (never more than two within the city limits).

At certain bus stops, signs list the destinations and numbers of the buses serving that point. Destinations are usually listed north to south and east to west. Most stops along the way are also posted on the sides of the buses. During rush hours, you may have to take a ticket from a dispensing machine, indicating your position in the line at the bus stop.

If you intend to use the buses a lot, pick up an RATP bus map at the office on place de la Madeleine, 8e, or at the tourist offices at RATP headquarters, 53 bis quai des Grands-Augustins, 6e. For detailed recorded information (in English) on bus and Métro routes, call © **08-36-68-41-14.**

The same organization that runs the Métro and the buses, the **RATP** (© **08-36-68-77-14**), also offers the **Balabus,** big-windowed orange-and-white motor coaches that, unfortunately, run only during limited hours: Sundays and national holidays from noon to 9pm, from April 15 to the end of September only. Itineraries run in both directions between Gare de Lyon and the Grande Arche de La Défense, encompassing some of the city's most beautiful vistas. It's a great deal—two Métro tickets for 16F (2.45, $2.30) will carry you the entire route. You'll recognize the bus and the route it follows by the *Bb* symbol emblazoned on each bus's side and on signs posted beside the route it follows.

BY TAXI   It's impossible to get one at rush hour, so don't even try. Taxi drivers are organized into a lobby that keeps their number limited to 15,000.

Watch out for the common rip-offs. Always check the meter to make sure you're not paying the previous passenger's fare. Beware of cabs without meters, which often wait outside nightclubs for tipsy patrons, or settle the tab in advance. You can hail regular cabs on the street when their signs read LIBRE. Taxis are easier to find at the many stands near Métro stations.

The flag drops at 14F (2.15, $2.05), and from 7am to 7pm you pay 3.87F (.60, 55¢) per kilometer. From 7pm to 7am, expect to pay 6.32F (.95, 90¢) per kilometer. On airport trips, you're not required to pay for the driver's empty return ride.

You're allowed several small pieces of luggage free if they're transported inside and don't weigh more than 5 kilograms (11 lb.). Heavier suitcases carried in the trunk cost 6F to 10F (.90 to 1.50, 85¢ to $1.45) apiece. Tip 12% to 15%—the latter usually elicits a *merci.* For radio cabs, call ✆ **01-44-52-23-86** or 01-44-52-23-58—note that you'll be charged from the point where the taxi begins the drive to pick you up.

BY BOAT   The **Batobus** (✆ **01-44-11-33-44**) is a 150-passenger ferry with big windows. Every day between May and September, the boats operate along the Seine, stopping at points of interest: from west to east, the **Eiffel Tower, Musée d'Orsay,** the **Louvre, Notre-Dame,** and the **Hôtel de Ville** (from east to west, the order is reversed). Transit from one stop to another is 20F (3.05, $2.90), and departures are about every 30 minutes from 10am to 7pm. Unlike on the Bâteaux-Mouche (see chapter 5), there's no recorded commentary. The Batobus isn't really a sightseeing tour (though the views are panoramic); instead, it simply offers a way to move from one attraction to another.

 FAST FACTS: Paris

For additional practical information, see "Fast Facts: France," in chapter 3.

American Express With a grand Paris office at 11 rue Scribe, 9e (✆ **01-47-77-77-07**; Métro: Opéra, Chaussée-d'Antin, or Havre-Caumartin; RER: Auber), AmEx is quite busy with customers buying and cashing traveler's checks (at not the best rates), picking up mail, and solving travel problems. It's open Monday through Friday from 9am to 6pm; the bank is also open Saturday from 9am to 5:30pm, but the mail-pickup window is closed. A less-busy office is at 38 av. de Wagram, 8e (✆ **01-42-27-58-80**; Métro: Ternes), open Monday through Friday from 10am to 5pm.

Area Code There isn't one as North Americans think of it. All French telephone numbers now consist of 10 digits, the first two of which are sort of like an area code. If you're calling anywhere in France from within France, just dial all 10 digits—no additional codes are needed. If you're calling from the United States, drop the initial 0 (zero).

Currency Exchange American Express can fill most banking needs. Most banks in Paris are open Monday through Friday from 9am to 4:30pm, but only a few are open Saturday; ask at your hotel for the location of the one nearest you. For the best exchange rate, cash your traveler's checks at banks or foreign-exchange offices, not at shops and hotels. Most post offices will change traveler's checks or convert currency. Currency exchanges are also found at Paris airports and train stations and along most of the major boulevards. A small commission is charged.

Some exchange places charge favorable rates to lure you into their stores. For example, **Paris Vision,** 214 rue de Rivoli, 1er (✆ **01-42-86-09-33;** Métro: Tuileries), maintains a minibank in the back of a travel agency, open daily from 9am to 2:30pm and 3:30 to 6pm (closes at 4:30pm on Sunday). Its rates are only a fraction less favorable than those offered for very large blocks of money as listed by the Paris stock exchange.

Dentists For emergency dental service, call **S.O.S. Dentaire,** 87 bd. du Port-Royal, 13e at (✆ **01-43-37-51-00;** Métro: Port-Royal), Monday through Friday from 8pm to midnight and Saturday and Sunday from 9:30am to midnight. You can also call or visit the **American Hospital,** 63 bd. Victor-Hugo, in suburb of Neuilly-sur-Seine outside Paris (✆ **01-46-41-25-25;** Métro: Pont-de-Levallois or Pont-de-Neuilly; Bus: 82).

Doctors Some large hotels have a doctor on staff. If yours doesn't, try the **American Hospital,** 63 bd. Victor-Hugo, Neuilly (✆ **01-46-41-25-25;** Métro: Pont-de-Levallois or Pont-de-Neuilly; Bus: 82), which operates a 24-hour emergency service. Blue Cross and other American insurance plans are accepted by the bilingual staff.

Drugstores After regular hours, have your concierge contact the Commissariat de Police for the nearest 24-hour pharmacy. French law requires one pharmacy in any given neighborhood to stay open 24 hours. You'll find the address posted on the doors or windows of all other drugstores. One of the most central all-nighters is **Pharmacy "Derhy,"** 84 av. des Champs-Elysées, 8e (✆ **01-45-62-02-41;** Métro: George-V).

Embassies/Consulates See "Fast Facts: France," in chapter 3.

Emergencies For the police, call (✆ **17;** to report a fire, call (✆ **18.** For an ambulance, call the fire department at (✆ **01-45-78-74-52;** a fire vehicle rushes cases to the nearest emergency room. **S.A.M.U.** is an independently operated, privately owned ambulance company; call (✆ **15.**

Hospitals See "Doctors," above.

Police In an emergency, call (✆ **17.** For nonemergency situations, the principal Préfecture is at 9 bd. du Palais, 4e (✆ **01-53-73-53-71** or 01-53-73-53-73; Métro: Cité).

Safety Beware of child pickpockets, who prey on visitors around sites such as the Louvre, the Eiffel Tower, Notre-Dame, and Montmartre, and who especially like to pick pockets in the Métro, often blocking the entrance and exit to the escalator. A band of these young thieves can clean out your pockets even while you try to fend them off. They'll get very close, sometimes ask for a handout, and deftly help themselves to your money, passport, or whatever. Women should hang on to their purses.

3 Accommodations

Although Paris hotels are shockingly expensive, there is some good news. Scores of lackluster, cheap Paris lodgings, where the wallpaper dated from the Napoleonic era, have been renovated and offer much better value in the moderate-to-inexpensive price range. The most outstanding example of this is in the **7th arrondissement,** a normally pricey district of Paris where several good-value hotels have blossomed from dives that couldn't be recommended until now.

By now, the Paris "season" has almost ceased to exist. Most visitors, at least those from North America, come in July and August. Since many French are on vacation then, and trade fairs and conventions come to a halt, there are usually plenty of rooms, even though these months have traditionally been the peak season for European travel. In most hotels, February is just as busy as April or September because of the volume of business travelers and the increasing number of tourists who've learned to take advantage of the off-season discount airfares.

Hot weather doesn't last long in Paris, so most hotels, except the deluxe ones, don't provide air-conditioning. If you're trapped in a Paris garret on a hot summer night, you may have to sweat it out. To avoid the noise problem when you have to open windows, request a room in the back when making a reservation.

Most hotels offer a continental breakfast of coffee, tea, or hot chocolate; a freshly baked croissant and roll; and limited quantities of butter and jam or jelly. Though nowhere near as filling as a traditional English or American breakfast, it does have the advantage of being quick to prepare—it'll be at your door a few moments after you call down for it and can be served at almost any hour. The word "breakfast" in the following entries refers to this continental version.

Service and value-added tax are included in rates quoted, unless otherwise specified. Unless otherwise specified, all hotel rooms have a private bathroom.

RIGHT BANK: 1ST ARRONDISSEMENT (MUSÉE du LOUVRE/LES HALLES)
VERY EXPENSIVE

Hôtel Costes ✦✦✦ Fashion types gravitate toward this hotel for its grand style and location close to the headquarters of some of Paris's most upscale shops and the offices of *Harper's Bazaar*. This may not be the Ritz, but is one of the shining stars of Paris. The town house–style premises was a *maison bourgeoise* (upper middle-class home) for generations. In 1996, it was adorned with jewel-toned colors, heavy swagged curtains, and lavish Napoléon III accessories. Everything about it evokes the rich days of the Gilded Age, especially the guest rooms. Some are small, but cozy and ornate, with one or two large beds, CD players, and fax machines. Beds are large with custom-made French mattresses, and suites are spacious with large sitting areas and often theme designs such as "Moroccan nights." For ultimate luxury, ask for one of the duplex units with split-level layouts.

239 rue St-Honoré, 75001 Paris. ✆ **01-42-44-50-50.** Fax 01-42-44-50-01. 83 units. 3,000F–3,500F (456– 532, $435–$507.50) double; from 7,500F (1,140, $1,087.50) suite. AE, DC, MC, V. Métro: Tuileries or Concorde. **Amenities:** Restaurant; bar; pool; gym; car rental; 24-hr. room service; baby-sitting; laundry/dry cleaning; in-room massage. *In room:* A/C, TV, fax, minibar, hair dryer, CD player.

Hôtel de Vendôme ✦✦ This jewel box was the former Embassy of Texas when that state was a nation. The hotel opened in 1998 and stands at one of the world's most prestigious addresses. It is comparable and almost as good as Costes. Though the guest rooms are moderate in size, they're opulent and

Heart of the Right Bank Hotels

Au Palais de Chaillot Hôtel **4**
Four Seasons Hôtel George V **4**
Galileo Hôtel **4**
Hôtel Britannique **13**
Hôtel Burgundy **3**
Hôtel Costes **6**

Hôtel de Crillon **5**
Hôtel de Lutèce **19**
Hôtel des Chevaliers **15**
Hôtel des Deux-Iles **17**
Hôtel de Vendôme **7**
Hôtel du Jeu de Paume **18**

Hôtel du Louvre **11**
Hôtel du Ministère **1**
Hôtel du 7e Art **16**
Hôtel Mansart **9**
Hôtel Queen Mary **2**
Hôtel Ritz **8**

Hôtel Saint Merry **14**
Hôtel St-Louis **20**
Hôtel Sofitel Trocadero Dokhan's **4**
Résidence Lord Byron **4**
Timhôtel Louvre **12**
Timhôtel Palais Royal **10**

designed in classic–Second Empire style with luxurious beds, and well-upholstered, hand-carved furnishings. Suites have not only generous space but also such extras as blackout draperies and quadruple glazing as well as custom-made plump mattresses. The security is fantastic, with TV intercoms. This new version of the hotel replaces a lackluster one that stood here for a century, and its facade and roof are classified as historic monuments by the French government.

1 place Vendôme, 75001 Paris. **©** **01-42-60-32-84.** Fax 01-49-27-97-89. reservations@hoteldevendome. com. 29 units. 2,800F–3,200F (425.60– 486.40, $406–$464) double; 4,500F–5,500F (684– 836, $652.50–$797.50) suite. AE, DC, MC, V. Métro: Concorde or Opéra. **Amenities:** Restaurant, bar; 24-hr. room service; laundry. In room: A/C, TV, minibar, hair dryer.

Hôtel du Louvre ✯ *Kids*

When Napoléon III inaugurated the hotel in 1855, journalists described it as "a palace of the people, rising adjacent to the palace of kings." In 1897, Camille Pissarro moved into a room with a view that inspired many of his landscapes. The hotel is located between the Louvre and the Palais Royal. Its decor features marble, bronze, and gilt. The guest rooms are quintessentially Parisian, filled with souvenirs of the belle époque along with elegant fabrics, excellent carpeting, double-glazed windows, comfortable beds, and traditional wood furniture. Suites provide greater dimensions and better exposures, as well as such upgrades as antiques, trouser presses, and robes.

Place André-Malraux, 75001 Paris. **©** **800/888-4747** in the U.S. and Canada, or 01-44-58-38-38. Fax 01-44-58-38-01. www.hoteldulouvre.com. 195 units. 2,350F–5,280F (357.20– 802.55, $340.75–$765.60) double; from 6,000F (912, $870) suite. Ask about midwinter discounts. AE, DC, MC, V. Parking 120F (18.25, $17.40). Métro: Palais Royal or Louvre-Rivoli. **Amenities:** 2 restaurants, 2 bars; pool; health club; boutiques; room service; in-room massage; laundry/dry cleaning. In room: A/C, TV, minibar, hair dryer, safe.

Hôtel Meurice ✯✯✯

After a 2-year renovation, the landmark Meurice, which reopened in mid-2000, is better than ever. The hotel is now more media hip, style conscious, and better located than the George V, its closest rival. Since the early 1800s, it has welcomed the royal and the rich and even the radical: the deposed king of Spain, Alfonso XIII, once occupied suite 108; the mad genius Salvador Dalí made the Meurice his headquarters, as did General von Cholritz, the Nazi who ruled Paris during the occupation. The mosaic floors, plaster ceilings, hand-carved moldings, and Art Nouveau glass roof atop the Winter Garden look like new. Each room is individually decorated with period pieces, fine carpets, Italian and French fabrics, marbles, and modern features like fax and Internet access. Louis XVI and Empire styles predominate. Our favorites and the least expensive are the sixth-floor dormer rooms. Some have painted ceilings of puffy clouds and blue skies along with canopied beds. Suites are among the most lavish in France—"fit for a king" as the expression goes, and indeed kings have occupied them. Royalty, among others, still do. Beds are sumptuous, furnished in luxurious fabrics with deluxe custom-made French mattresses.

228 rue de Rivoli, Paris 75001. **©** **01-44-58-10-10.** Fax 01-44-58-10-15. www.meuricehotel.com. 160 units. 4,300F–4,600F (653.60– 699.20, $623.50–$667) double; from 5,900F (896.80, $855.50) suite. AE, DC, MC, V. Parking 120F (18.25, $17.40). Métro: Tuileries or Concorde. **Amenities:** Two restaurants, bar; gym; full-service spa; 24-hr. room service; baby-sitting; laundry/dry cleaning. In room: A/C, TV, fax, dataport, mini-bar, hair dryer, safe.

Hôtel Ritz ✯✯✯

The Ritz is Europe's greatest hotel, an enduring symbol of elegance on one of Paris's most beautiful and historic squares. César Ritz, the "little shepherd boy from Niederwald," converted the Hôtel de Lazun into a luxury hotel in 1898. With the help of the culinary master Escoffier, he made the Ritz a miracle of luxury. In 1979, the Ritz family sold the hotel to Mohammed al Fayed, who refurbished it and added a cooking school. (You may remember that his son, Dodi, and Princess Diana dined here before they set out on their fateful drive.) Two town houses were annexed, joined by a long arcade lined with miniature display cases representing 125 of Paris's leading boutiques. The public salons are furnished with museum-caliber antiques. Each guest room is uniquely decorated, most with Louis XIV or XV reproductions; all have fine rugs, marble fireplaces, tapestries, brass beds, and more. The spacious marble bathrooms are the city's most luxurious, with deluxe toiletries, scales, private phones, cords to summon maids and valets, robes, full-length and makeup mirrors, and dual basins. Ever since Edward VII got stuck in a too-narrow bathtub with his lover of the evening, the tubs at the Ritz have been deep and big.

15 place Vendôme, 75001 Paris. © **800/223-6800** in the U.S. and Canada, or 01-43-16-30-30. Fax 01-43-16-31-78. www.ritzparis.com. 175 units. 4,000F–4,560F (608– 693.10, $580–$661.20) double; from 5,415F (823.13, $785.23) suite. AE, DC, MC, V. Parking 230F (34.95, $33.35). Métro: Opéra, Concorde, or Madeleine. **Amenities:** Two restaurants, two bars; pool; health club; boutiques; 24-hr. room service, in-room massage, laundry/dry cleaning. *In room:* A/C, TV, minibar, hair dryer, safe.

MODERATE

Hôtel Britannique *Value* Conservatively modern and plush, this is a much-renovated 19th-century hotel near Les Halles, the Pompidou, and Notre-Dame. The place not only is British in name but also seems to have cultivated an English graciousness. The guest rooms are small, but immaculate and soundproof, with comfortable beds. A satellite receiver gets U.S. and U.K. television shows. The reading room is a cozy retreat.

20 av. Victoria, 75001 Paris. © **01-42-33-74-59.** Fax 01-42-33-82-65. www.hotel-britannic.com. 40 units. 820F–1,130F (124.65– 171.75, $118.90–$163.85) double. AE, DC, MC, V. Parking 100F (15.20, $14.50). Métro: Châtelet. **Amenities:** Room service. *In room:* TV, minibar, hair dryer, safe.

Hôtel Burgundy ★ *Value* The Burgundy is one of the best values in this expensive area. The frequently renovated building began as two adjacent town houses in the 1830s, one a pension where Baudelaire wrote poetry in the 1860s, the other a bordello. They were linked by British-born managers who insisted on using the English name. Renovated in 1992, with improvements in 2001, the hotel hosts many North and South Americans and features conservatively decorated rooms, each with a bathroom with full tub and shower. The Charles Baudelaire restaurant is open for lunch and dinner Monday through Friday.

8 rue Duphot, 75001 Paris. © **01-42-60-34-12.** Fax 01-47-03-95-20. www.perso.wanadoo.fr/hotel.burgundy. 89 units. 1,000F–1,150F (152– 174.80, $145–$166.75) double; 1,600F–1,900F (243.20– 288.80, $232–$275.50) suite. AE, DC, MC, V. Métro: Madeleine or Concorde. **Amenities:** Restaurant, bar; baby-sitting, room service. *In room:* A/C, TV, minibar, hair dryer.

Hôtel Mansart *Value* After operating as a glorious wreck for decades, this hotel—designed by its namesake—was renovated in the 1990s and offers some of the lowest rates in a pricey area. The public rooms contain Louis reproductions and floor-to-ceiling geometric designs inspired by the inlaid marble floors (or formal gardens) of the French Renaissance. The small- to medium-size guest rooms are subtly formal and comfortable, though only six of the suites and most expensive rooms overlook the famous square. Twenty rooms are air-conditioned, and all come with tub/shower bathrooms. Breakfast is the only meal served.

5 rue des Capucines, 75001 Paris. © **01-42-61-50-28.** Fax 01-49-27-97-44. www.123france.com. 57 units. 980F–1,800F (148.95– 273.60, $142.10–$261) double; 1,500F–1,800F (228– 273.60, $217.50–$261) suite. AE, DC, MC, V. Métro: Opéra or Madeleine. **Amenities:** Bar; baby-sitting; laundry/dry cleaning. *In room:* TV, minibar, safe.

Kids Family-Friendly Hotels

Hôtel de Fleurie (*see p. 98*) In the heart of St-Germain-des-Prés, this has long been a family favorite. You can rent its *chambres familiales*—two connecting rooms with two large beds. Children 12 and under stay free in their parents' room.

Hôtel du Louvre (*see p. 88*) This hotel has welcomed families to Paris since 1855—well, rich families anyway. It's well situated near the Louvre and the Palais Royal and offers generally spacious rooms, many large enough to accommodate families. Baby-sitting can be arranged.

Lord Byron (*see p. 94*) Families who want a moderate place to stay off the Champs-Elysées often book into this residence. It's old fashioned but affordable, and the welcome to families is genuine.

Timhôtel Louvre (*see p. 90*) This hotel is especially great for families, since it offers some rooms with four beds; children under 12 are welcome to stay in their parents' room for free.

Timhôtel Palais-Royal (*see p. 90*) operates in the same kid-friendly style.

INEXPENSIVE

Timhôtel Louvre *Kids* This hotel and its sibling, the Timhôtel Palais-Royal, are mirror images, at least inside; they're part of a new breed of two-star family-friendly hotels cropping up in France. These Timhôtels share the same manager and temperament. Though the rooms at the Palais-Royal branch are a bit larger than the ones here, this branch is so close to the Louvre it's almost irresistible. The ambience is modern, with monochromatic rooms and wall-to-wall carpeting upgraded in 1998. Each unit's bathroom comes with a tub and shower.

The **Timhôtel Palais-Royal** is at 3 rue de la Banque, 75002 Paris (✆ **01-42-61-53-90;** fax 01-42-60-05-39; Métro: Bourse).

4 rue Croix des Petits-Champs, 75001 Paris. ✆ **01-42-60-34-86.** Fax 01-42-60-10-39. www.paris-france-hotel.net. 56 units. 700F–800F (106.40– 121.60, $101.50–$116) double. Children under 12 stay free in parents' room. AE, DC, MC, V. Métro: Palais Royal. **Amenities:** Baby-sitting; laundry/dry cleaning. *In room:* A/C, TV.

RIGHT BANK: 3RD ARRONDISSEMENT (LE MARAIS)
MODERATE

Hôtel des Chevaliers Half a block from the edge of place des Vosges, this hotel occupies a dramatic corner building whose 17th-century vestiges have been elevated into high art. These include the remnants of a stone-sided well in the cellar, a stone barrel vault covering the breakfast area, and Louis XIII accessories that'll remind you of the hotel's origins. Each guest room is comfortable and well maintained, and all bathrooms come with both tub and shower. Units on the top floor have exposed ceiling beams. Some rooms are larger than others, with an extra bed making them suitable for parents traveling with a child or three companions on the road together.

30 rue de Turenne, 75003 Paris. ✆ **01-42-72-73-47.** Fax 01-42-72-54-10. www.myhotel.inparis.com. 24 units. 680F–820F (103.35– 124.65, $98.60–$118.90) double; 895F–995F (136.05– 151.25, $129.80–$144.30) triple. Parking 60F (9.10, $8.70). Métro: Chemin Vert or St-Paul. *In room:* TV, minibar, hair dryer, safe.

RIGHT BANK: 4TH ARRONDISSEMENT
(ÎLE DE LA CITE/ÎLE ST-LOUIS & BEAUBOURG)
EXPENSIVE

Hôtel du Jeu de Paume ✻   This hotel is small-scale and charming, with a layout that includes an interconnected pair of 17th-century town houses accessible via a timbered passageway from the street outside. The rooms are a bit larger than those within some of the nearby competitors. Originally, the hotel was a "clubhouse" used by members of the court of Louis XIII, who amused themselves with *Les jeux de paume* (an early form of tennis) on a lot nearby. Bedrooms are outfitted in a simple version of Art Deco. The first-class mattresses have recently been renewed, and the suites, though not the most spacious, are elegantly furnished and beautifully maintained, enough to justify their higher price range. The aesthetics here will remind you more of the Marais than of the Quartier Latin to the south. There's an elevator on the premises.

54 rue St-Louis en l'Isle, 75004 Paris. ✆ **01-43-26-14-18.** Fax 01-40-46-02-76. www.travel-in-paris.com. 30 units. 1,365F–1,650F (207.50– 250.80, $197.95–$239.25) double; 2,500F–2,750F (380– 418, $362.50–$398.75) suite. Parking 120F (18.25, $17.40). AE, DC, MC, V. Metro: Pont-Marie. **Amenities:** Fitness center; sauna; baby-sitting; laundry/dry cleaning. *In room:* TV, minibar, hair dryer, safe.

Hôtel de Lutèce ✻   This hotel feels like a country house in Brittany. The lounge, with its old fireplace, is furnished with antiques and contemporary paintings. Each of the guest rooms boasts antiques, adding to a refined atmosphere that attracts celebrities like the duke and duchess of Bedford. Many units were renovated in 1998, and each comes with either tub or shower. The beds contain first-class mattresses. The suites, larger than the doubles, of course, are often like doubles with extended sitting areas. Each is tastefully furnished, with an antique or two. The hotel is comparable in style and amenities to the Deux-Iles (see below), under the same ownership.

65 rue St-Louis-en-l'Ile, 75004 Paris. ✆ **01-43-26-23-52.** Fax 01-43-29-60-25. www.france-hotel-guide.com/h75004lutece.htm. 23 units. 890F (135.30, $129.05) double; 1,100F (167.20, $159.50) triple. AE, MC, V. Métro: Pont Marie or Cité. **Amenities:** Laundry/dry cleaning. *In room:* A/C, TV, hair dryer.

Hôtel des Deux-Iles ✻   This hotel is housed in a restored 18th-century town house. The decor is elaborate, with bamboo and reed furniture and French provincial touches. Overall, this is an unpretentious but charming choice with a great location. The guest rooms are on the small side, however. Beds contain quality French mattresses renewed as frequently as needed. A garden of plants and flowers off the lobby leads to a basement breakfast room with a fireplace.

59 rue St-Louis-en-l'Ile, 75004 Paris. ✆ **01-43-26-13-35.** Fax 01-43-29-60-25. www.myhotel.inparis.com. 17 units. 910F (138.30, $131.95) double. AE, MC, V. Métro: Pont Marie. **Amenities:** Laundry/dry cleaning. *In room:* A/C, TV, hair dryer.

Hôtel St-Louis ✻ *Value*   Proprietors Guy and Andrée Record maintain a charming family atmosphere at this antique-filled hotel in a 17th-century town house. Despite a renovation completed in 1998, it represents an incredible value considering its prime location on Ile St-Louis. Expect cozy, slightly cramped rooms. Beds have fine mattresses of medium thickness. With mansard roofs and old-fashioned moldings, the top-floor units sport tiny balconies with sweeping views. The breakfast room is in the cellar, with 17th-century stone vaulting.

75 rue St-Louis-en-l'Ile, 75004 Paris. ✆ **01-46-34-04-80.** Fax 01-46-34-02-13. www.hotelsaintlouis.com. 21 units. 815F–1,300F (123.90– 197.60, $118.20–$188.50) double. MC, V. Métro: Pont Marie. **Amenities:** Baby-sitting; laundry. *In room:* TV, hair dryer, safe.

MODERATE

Hôtel Saint-Merry ★ *Finds* The rebirth of this once-notorious brothel as a charming, upscale hotel is another example of how the 8e has been gentrified. It contains only a dozen rooms, each relatively small, but charmingly accented with exposed stone, 18th-century ceiling beams, and lots of quirky architectural details. (Each was preserved by a team of architects and decorators.) Suites, much larger than doubles, have upgraded furnishings and more comfort. According to the staff, the clientele here is estimated to be about 50% gay males; the other half straight and involved in the arts scene that flourishes in the surrounding neighborhood. Before it became a bordello, incidentally, this place was conceived as the presbytery of the nearby Church of Saint-Merry.

78 rue de la Verrerie. 75004 Paris. © **01-42-78-14-15.** Fax 01-40-29-06-82. www.myhotel.inparis.com. 12 units. 900F–1,300F (136.80– 197.60, $130.50–$188.50) double; 1,900F (288.80, $275.50) suite. Metro: Hôtel de Ville or Châtelet. *In room:* TV.

INEXPENSIVE

Hôtel de la Place des Vosges ★ *Value* Built about 350 years ago, during the same era as the construction of the majestic square it's named for (a 2-minute walk away), this is a well-managed, small-scale property with reasonable prices and lots of charm. Many of the small guest rooms have beamed ceilings, tiled bathrooms (with tub or shower), small TVs hanging from the ceiling, and a sense of cozy, well-ordered efficiency. Beds contain first-class quality mattresses which are renewed every year or so. There are patches of chiseled stone at various parts of the hotel, a decorative touch that helps evoke the era of Louis XIII.

12 rue de Birague, 75004 Paris. © **01-42-72-60-46.** Fax 01-42-72-02-64. www.bparis.com. 16 units. 660F–690F (100.30– 104.90, $95.70–$100.05) double. MC, V. Métro: Bastille. *In room:* TV, hair dryer.

Hôtel du 7e Art The structure that contains this place is one of many 17th-century buildings in this neighborhood that are classified as historic monuments. Don't expect grand luxury: bedrooms are cramped but clean, and outfitted with the simplest of furniture, relieved by 1950s-era posters promoting the glories of old Hollywood. Each has white walls, and some—including those under the sloping mansard-style roof—have exposed ceiling beams. All have small, shower-only bathrooms. There's a lobby bar and a breakfast room, but be warned in advance that there's no elevator for access to any of this place's five stories. The hotel is named after the 7th Art, a French reference to filmmaking.

20 rue St-Paul. 75004 Paris. © **01-44-54-85-00.** Fax 01-42-77-69-10. www.chez.com/hotel7art. 23 units. 460F–592F (69.90– 90.030, $66.70–$85.85) double; 789F (119.95, $114.40) suite. AE, DC, MC, V. Parking 100F (15.20, $14.50). Métro: St-Paul. *In room:* TV.

RIGHT BANK: 8TH ARRONDISSEMENT (CHAMPS-ELYSÉES/MADELEINE)
VERY EXPENSIVE

Four Seasons Hotel George V ★★★ Even in its latest reincarnation, with all its glitz and glamour, this hotel is for the merely rich. Both the Bristol and Plaza Athénée accurately claim they have more class. Its history is as gilt-edged as they come: opened in 1928 in honor of the George V of England, and noted for grandeur that managed to survive the Depression and two world wars, it was designated as an official branch of the now-defunct League of Nations. During the liberation of Paris, it housed Dwight D. Eisenhower. After its acquisition by Saudi Prince Al Waleed, and a 2-year renovation, it was reopened late in 1999 under the banner of Toronto-based Four Seasons. The guest rooms are about as close as you'll come to residency within a well-upholstered private home where teams of decorators lavished vast amounts of attention and money. The beds rival those at the Ritz and Meurice in comfort. It's deluxe all the way. The renovation reduced the number of units from 300 to 245, which now come in three sizes. The largest are magnificent; the smallest are, in the words of a spokesperson, *"très agreeable."* Security is tight—a fact appreciated by sometimes notorious guests.

31 ave George V, 75008 Paris. © **800/332-3442** in the U.S. or Canada, or 01-53-53-28-00. Fax 01-49-52-70-20. www.fourseasons.com. 245 units. 4,264F–5,706F (648.15– 867.30, $618.30–$827.35) double; from 8,200F (1,246.40, $1,189) suite. Parking 263F (40.00, $38.15). AE, DC, MC, V. Metro: George V. **Amenities:** Two restaurants, bar; pool; fitness center; 24-hr. room service. *In room:* A/C, TV, minibar, hair dryer, safe.

Hôtel de Crillon ⭐⭐⭐ The Crillon, one of Europe's grand hotels, sits across from the U.S. Embassy. Although some international CEOs and diplomats treat it as a shrine, those seeking less pomposity might prefer the Plaza Athenée or the Ritz. The 200-plus-year-old building, once the palace of the duc de Crillon, has been a hotel since the early 1900s and is now owned by Jean Taittinger, of the champagne family. The salons boast 17th- and 18th-century tapestries, gilt-and-brocade furniture, chandeliers, fine sculpture, and Louis XVI chests and chairs. The guest rooms are large and luxurious. Some are spectacular, like the Leonard Bernstein Suite, which has one of the maestro's pianos and one of the grandest views of any hotel room in Paris. The marble bathrooms are sumptuous, with deluxe toiletries, dual sinks, robes, and (in some) thermal taps. The furniture, including the beds, offers grand comfort . The boudoir luxury was overseen by Sonia Rykiel doing her take on Louis XV and Madame Pompadour.

10 place de la Concorde, 75008 Paris. © **800/223-6800** in the U.S. and Canada, or 01-44-71-15-00. Fax 01-44-71-15-02. www.crillon.com. 160 units. 3,950F–4,650F (600.40– 706.80, $572.75–$674.25) double; from 6,800F (1,033.60, $986) suite. AE, DC, MC, V. Free parking. Métro: Concorde. **Amenities:** Two restaurants, bar, tearoom; gym; 24-hr. room service; laundry/dry cleaning. *In room:* A/C, TV, minibar, hair dryer, safe.

MODERATE

Galileo Hotel ⭐ *Finds* This is one of the 8th's most charming hotels, run by Roland and Elisabeth Buffat, who have won friends from all over with their Hôtel des Deux-Iles and Hôtel de Lutèce on St-Louis-en-l'Ile (see above). A short walk from the Champ-Elysées, the town-house is the epitome of French elegance and charm. The rooms are medium and a study in understated taste, decorated in cocoa and beige. Beds are queen size or twin with plush mattresses. The most spacious are rooms 501 and 502, with a glass-covered veranda you can use even in winter. For this neighborhood, the prices are moderate.

54 rue Galilée, 75008 Paris. © **01-47-20-66-06**. Fax 01-47-20-67-17. 27 units. 950F (144.40, $137.75) double. AE, DC, MC, V. Parking 150F (22.80, $21.75). Métro: Charles de Gaulle–Etoile or George V. **Amenities:** Limited room service (drinks and snacks); baby-sitting; laundry/dry cleaning. *In room:* A/C, TV, minibar, hair dryer, safe.

Hôtel Queen Mary ⭐ Meticulously renovated inside and out, this early-1900s hotel is graced with an iron-and-glass canopy, ornate wrought iron, and the kind of detailing normally reserved for more expensive hotels. The public rooms have touches of greenery and reproductions of mid-19th-century antiques; guest rooms contain upholstered headboards, comfortable beds, and mahogany furnishings, plus a carafe of sherry. All units were fully renovated in 1998, and most come with a tub/shower combination (five units have shower-only bathrooms). Suites are only slightly more spacious than the regular doubles but are meticulously maintained and beautifully furnished in a classic motif.

9 rue Greffulhe, 75008 Paris. ☏ **01-42-66-40-50.** Fax 01-42-66-94-92. www.hotelqueenmary.com. 36 units. 780F–995F (118.55– 151.25, $113.10–$144.330) double; 1,400F (212.80, $203) suite. AE, DC, MC, V. Parking 100F (15.20, $14.50). Métro: Madeleine or Havre-Caumartin. **Amenities:** Bar; business center; room service; baby-sitting. *In room:* A/C, TV, minibar, hair dryer, safe.

INEXPENSIVE

Hôtel du Ministère *(★)*   The Ministère is a winning choice near the Champs-Elysées, though it's far from Paris's cheapest budget hotel. It used to be a family hotel, but in 1999, the new owners began refurbishing the place, making it better than ever. The guest rooms are on the small side, but each is comfortably appointed and well maintained; many have oak beams and furnishings that, though worn, are still serviceable. Try to avoid a room on the top floor, as you'll be too cramped. Each unit's bathroom is equipped with a tub-shower combo. Junior suites are only slightly larger than the regular doubles. But since the doubles are a bit small, you may want to pay extra for this added living space.

31 rue de Surène, 75008 Paris. ☏ **01-42-66-21-43.** Fax 01-42-66-96-04. www.argia.fr/hotel-ministere. 28 units. 890F–990F (135.30– 150.50, $129.05–$143.55) double; from 1,090F (165.70, $158.05) junior suite. AE, MC, V. Parking 11F (16.70, $15.95). Métro: Madeleine or Miromesnil. **Amenities:** Bar; laundry/dry cleaning. *In room:* A/C, TV, minibar, hair dryer, safe.

Résidence Lord Byron *(Kids)*   Off the Champs-Elysées on a curving street of handsome buildings, the Lord Byron may not be as grand as other hotels in the neighborhood, but it's more affordable. Unassuming and a bit staid, it's exactly what repeat guests want: a sense of luxury, solitude, and understatement, a fine choice for families. Beds are old-fashioned with well-worn but still-comfortable mattresses. Families often book the suites because of the larger living space. You can eat breakfast in the dining room or in the shaded inner garden.

5 rue de Chateaubriand, 75008 Paris. ☏ **01-43-59-89-98.** Fax 01-42-89-46-04. www.escapade-paris. com. 31 units. 910F–1,015F (138.30– 154.30, $131.95–$147.20) double; 1,430F–1,730F (217.35– 262.95, $207.35–$250.85) suite. AE, DC, MC, V. Parking 75F (11.40, $10.90). Métro: George V. RER: Etoile. **Amenities:** Room service; baby-sitting; dry cleaning. *In room:* A/C, TV, minibar, hair dryer, safe.

RIGHT BANK: 16TH ARRONDISSEMENT (TROCADÉRO/BOIS DE BOULOGNE)
EXPENSIVE

Hôtel Sofitel Trocadero Dokhan's *(★★)*   Except for the fact that porters tend to walk through its public areas carrying luggage, you might suspect that this well-accessorized hotel was a private home. It's housed within a stately looking 19th-century building vaguely inspired by Palladio, and it contains the kind of accessories that would look appropriate on the set of a Viennese operetta. This includes antique paneling, Regency-era armchairs, gilded chandeliers, and a pervasive sense of good, upper-bourgeois taste. Each bedroom benefits from a different decorative style, and each has antiques or good reproductions, ornamental swags and curtains above the headboards, lots of personalized touches, and triple-glazed windows. Beds are often antique reproductions with state-of-the-art custom-built mattresses. Suites have not only larger living space but spacious bathrooms with such extras as makeup mirrors and *luxe* toiletries.

117 rue Lauriston, 75116 Paris. ☏ **01-53-65-66-99.** Fax 01-53-65-66-88. hotel.trocadero.dokhans@ wanadoo.fr. 45 units. 2,300F–2,700F (349.60– 410.40, $333.50–$391.50) double; 5,000F (760, $725) suite. Parking 90F (13.70, $13.05). Metro: Trocadero. AE, DC, MC, V. **Amenities:** Restaurant (lunch only), champagne bar. *In room:* A/C, TV, fax, minibar, hair dryer, CD player.

INEXPENSIVE

Au Palais de Chaillot Hôtel   When Thierry and Cyrille Pien, brothers trained in the States, opened this hotel, budget travelers came running. Located between the Champ-Elysées and Trocadéro, the town house was restored from top to bottom and the result is a contemporary yet informal variation on Parisian chic. The guest rooms come in various shapes and sizes and are furnished with a light touch, with bright colors and wicker. Rooms 61, 62, and 63 afford partial views of the Eiffel Tower. Each comes with a neatly tiled, shower-only bathroom.

35 av. Raymond-Poincaré, 75016 Paris. ℂ **01-53-70-09-09.** Fax 01-53-70-09-08. www.chaillotel.com. 28 units. 625F (95, $90.65) double; 755F (114.75, 109.530) triple. AE, DC, MC, V. Parking 90F (13.70, $13.05). Métro: Victor Hugo or Trocadéro. **Amenities:** Laundry/dry cleaning. *In room:* TV, hair dryer.

LEFT BANK: 5TH ARRONDISSEMENT (LATIN QUARTER)
MODERATE

Grand Hôtel St-Michel   Built in the 19th century, this hotel is larger and more businesslike than many town house–style inns nearby. It basks in the reflected glow of Brazilian dissident Georges Amado, whose memoirs recorded his 2-year literary sojourn in one of the rooms. In 1997, the hotel completed a renovation and moved from two- to three-star status. The public areas are tasteful, with portraits and rich upholsteries. All but four of the rooms have tub-shower combinations. The improvements enlarged some rooms, lowering their ceilings and adding amenities, but retained old-fashioned touches like wrought-iron balconies (on the fifth floor). Beds have been renewed with medium-thick mattresses offering much comfort. Triple rooms have an extra bed and are suitable for families or people traveling together. Others have only shower, toilet, and sink. Sixth-floor rooms offer interesting views over the rooftops.

19 rue Cujas, 75005 Paris. ℂ **01-46-33-33-02.** Fax 01-40-46-96-33. www.parisserve.com. 46 units. 890F (135.30, $129.05) double; 1,290F (196.10, $187.05) triple. AE, DC, MC, V. Métro: Cluny–La Sorbonne. RER: Luxembourg or St-Michel. **Amenities:** Bar; baby-sitting; laundry/dry cleaning. *In room:* TV, minibar, hair dryer, safe.

Hôtel Abbatial St-Germain   The origins of this hotel run deep: interior renovations have revealed such 17th-century touches as dovecotes and massive oak beams. In the early 1990s, a restoration made the public areas appealing and brought the small bedrooms, furnished in faux Louis XVI, up to modern standards. All the beds are fitted with quality French mattresses and immaculate linens. All windows are double-glazed, and the fifth- and sixth-floor units enjoy views over Notre-Dame. The neatly kept bathrooms are equipped with showers.

46 bd. St-Germain, 75005 Paris. ℂ **01-46-34-02-12.** Fax 01-43-25-47-73. www.abbatial.com. 43 units. 760F–880F (115.50E– 133.75, $110.20–$127.60) double. AE, MC, V. Parking 110F (16.70, $15.95). Métro: Maubert-Mutualité. **Amenities:** Baby-sitting; laundry/dry cleaning. *In room:* A/C, TV, minibar, hair dryer, safe.

Hôtel-Résidence St-Christophe   This hotel, in one of the Latin Quarter's undiscovered but charming areas, offers a gracious English-speaking staff. It was created in 1987 when a derelict hotel was connected to a butcher shop. All the small- to medium-size rooms were successfully renovated in 1998, with Louis XV–style furniture, wall-to-wall carpeting, and firm mattresses. Half of the bathrooms have tubs in addition to showers.

17 rue Lacépède, 75005 Paris. ℂ **01-43-31-81-54.** Fax 01-43-31-12-54. hotelstchristophe@compuserve. com. 31 units. 700F (106.40, $101.50) double. AE, DC, MC, V. Parking 100F (15.20, $14.50). Métro: Place Monge. **Amenities:** Laundry/dry cleaning. *In room:* TV, minibar, hair dryer.

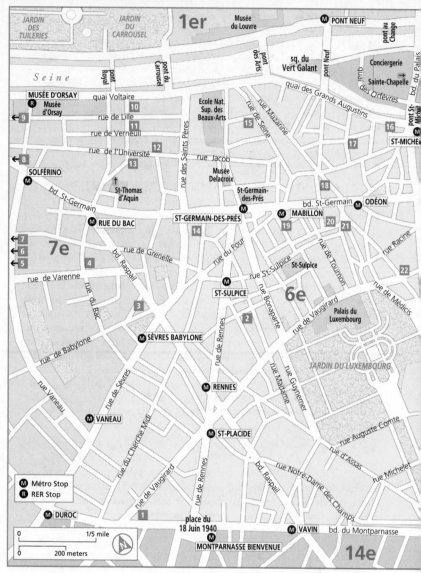

INEXPENSIVE

Familia-Hôtel   As the name implies, this is a hotel that has been family-run for decades. Many personal touches make the place unique, and it was lavishly renovated in 1998. The walls of 14 rooms are graced with finely executed sepia-colored frescoes of Parisian scenes. Eight units have restored stone walls, and seven boast balconies with delightful views over the Latin Quarter. Half of the bathrooms come with tubs as well as showers. Mattresses are more comfortable than in many hotels nearby thanks to a dynamic family-ownership that likes to keep this place up and running, renovating bedrooms are often as needed.

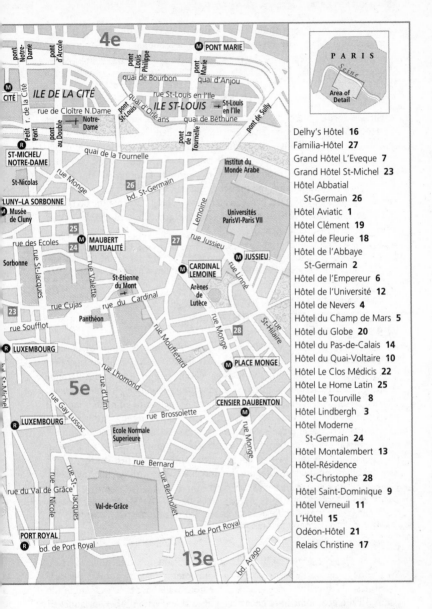

11 rue des Ecoles, 75005 Paris. ℂ **01-43-54-55-27.** Fax 01-43-29-61-77. www.myhotel.inparis.com. 30 units. 550F–665F (83.60– 101.10, $79.75–$96.45) double. Rates include breakfast. AE, DC, MC, V. Métro: Jussieu or Maubert-Mutualité. *In room:* TV, minibar, hair dryer.

Hôtel Le Home Latin *Value* This is one of Paris's most famous budget hotels, known since the 1970s for its simple lodgings. The blandly functional rooms were renovated in 1999; some have small balconies overlooking the street. Those facing the courtyard are quieter than those fronting the street. The elevator only goes to the fifth floor, but to make up for the stair climb, the sixth floor's *chambres mansardées* offer a romantic location under the eaves and panoramic rooftop views. Forty-seven units come with a shower only; the rest have a tub-shower combo. Mattresses are of medium thickness but are frequently renewed.

15–17 rue du Sommerard, 75005 Paris. ✆ **01-43-26-25-21.** Fax 01-43-29-87-04. www.homelatinhotel.com. 54 units. 595F–650F (90.45– 98.80, $86.30–$94.25) double; 750F (114, $108.75) triple; 860F (130.70, $124.70) quad. AE, DC, MC, V. Parking 85F (12.90, $12.35). Métro: St-Michel or Maubert-Mutualité. *In room:* Hair dryer, no phone.

Hôtel Moderne St-Germain ✶   Situated in the heart of the Latin Quarter, the Hôtel Moderne is better than ever since it ended the 20th century with a complete overhaul. Though the rooms are small, this is still one of the neighborhood's better three-star hotels. Its charming owner, Mme Gibon, welcomes guests to her spotless accommodations. In the units fronting rue des Ecoles, double-glazed windows hush the traffic. About half of the bathrooms have a tub as well as a shower. The hotel has a greater comfort level now that the bed linens and mattresses have all been renewed. Guests enjoy access to the sauna and Jacuzzi at the Hôtel Sully next door.

33 rue des Ecoles, 75005 Paris. ✆ **01-43-54-37-78.** Fax 01-43-29-91-31. www.abpromhotels.com. 45 units. 650F–950F (98.80– 144.40, $94.25–$137.75) double; 1,200F (182.40, $174) triple. AE, DC, MC, V. Parking 150F (22.80, $21.75). Métro: Maubert-Mutualité. **Amenities:** Use of sauna and Jacuzzi next door; laundry/dry cleaning. *In room:* A/C, TV, minibar, hair dryer.

LEFT BANK: 6TH ARRONDISSEMENT (ST-GERMAIN/LUXEMBOURG)
VERY EXPENSIVE

Relais Christine ✶✶   The Relais Christine welcomes you into what was a 16th-century Augustinian cloister. You enter from a narrow cobblestone street into a symmetrical courtyard and then an elegant reception area with baroque sculpture and Renaissance antiques. Each room is uniquely decorated with wooden beams and Louis XIII–style furnishings; the rooms come in a range of styles and shapes, and some are among the Left Bank's largest, with extras like mirrored closets, plush carpets, thermostats, and even some balconies facing the outer courtyard. The least attractive, smallest, and dimmest rooms are those in the interior. Each comes with a complete tub and shower. Bed configurations vary but all are on the soft side, offering much comfort with quality linens.

3 rue Christine, 75006 Paris. ✆ **01-40-51-60-80.** Fax 01-40-51-60-81. www.relais-christine.com. 51 units. 2,000F–2,600F (304– 395.20, $290–$377) double; 3,000F–4,500F (456– 684, $435–$652.50) duplex or suite. AE, DC, MC, V. Free parking. Métro: Odéon. **Amenities:** Honor bar in lobby; baby-sitting; laundry/dry cleaning. *In room:* A/C, TV, minibar, hair dryer, safe.

EXPENSIVE

Hôtel de Fleurie ✶ *Kids*   Off boulevard St-Germain on a colorful little street, the Fleurie is one of the best of the "new" old hotels; its statuary-studded facade recaptures a 17th-century elegance, and the stone walls have been exposed in the salon. All the bedrooms have been renewed in a renovation program launched back in 1999. Many have elaborate draperies and antique reproductions, and all of them come with comfortable French mattresses. Some of the rooms have tub and shower combinations, others a full bath except for a tub (shower stalls instead). Because some of the rooms are larger than others and contain an extra bed for one or two children, the hotel has long been a family favorite.

32–34 rue Grégoire-de-Tours, 75006 Paris. ✆ **01-53-73-70-00.** Fax 01-53-73-70-20. www.hotel-de-fleurie. tm.fr. 29 units. 1,700F–1,800F (258.40– 273.60, $246.50–$261) double; 1,700F–1,800F (258.40– 273.60, $246.50–$261) family room. Children 12 and under stay free in parents' room. AE, DC, MC, V. Métro: Odéon or St-Germain-des-Prés. **Amenities:** Bar; car rental; room service; laundry/dry cleaning. *In room:* A/C, TV, minibar, hair dryer.

Hôtel de l'Abbaye St-Germain ⭐ This is one of the district's most charming boutique hotels, a convent in the early 18th century. Its brightly colored rooms have traditional furniture like you'd find in a private club, plus touches of sophisticated flair. In front is a small garden and in back a verdant courtyard with a fountain, raised flowerbeds, and masses of ivy and climbing vines. If you don't mind the expense, one of the most charming rooms has a terrace overlooking the upper floors of neighboring buildings. Bedrooms come with tiled, full bathrooms. Mattresses are on the same comfort level of a top hotel, and suites are generous in size and full of Left Bank charm, often with antique reproductions.

10 rue Cassette, 75006 Paris. ⓒ **01-45-44-38-11.** Fax 01-45-48-07-86. www.hotel-abbaye.com. 46 units. 1,260F–1,860F (191.50– 282.70, $182.70–$269.70) double; 2,440F–2,540F (370.90– 386.10, $353.80–$368.30) suite. Rates include breakfast. AE, MC, V. Métro: St-Sulpice. **Amenities:** Room service; baby-sitting; laundry/dry cleaning. *In room:* A/C, TV, hair dryer, safe.

L'Hôtel ⭐ Ranking just a notch below the Relais Christine, this is one of the Left Bank's most charming boutique hotels. It was once a 19th-century fleabag called the Alsace, whose major distinction was that Oscar Wilde died here, broke and in despair. But today's guests aren't anywhere near poverty row: This was the sophisticated creation of late French actor Guy-Louis Duboucheron, and show business and fashion celebrities love it. The guest rooms vary in size, style, and price, from quite small to deluxe, but all have nonworking fireplaces and fabric-covered walls. An eclectic collection of antiques pops up here and there: One spacious room contains the original furnishings and memorabilia of stage star Mistinguette, a frequent performer with Maurice Chevalier and his on-again–off-again lover. Her pedestal bed is set in the middle of the room, surrounded by mirrors, as she liked to see how she looked at all times. About half the bathrooms are small, tubless nooks. All the sumptuous beds with their tasteful fabrics, crisp linens, and custom-made mattresses have recently been renewed.

13 rue des Beaux-Arts, 75006 Paris. ⓒ **01-44-41-99-00.** Fax 01-43-25-64-81. www.l-hotel.com. 27 units. 2,500F–4,800F (380– 729.60, $362.50–$696) double; from 5,000F (760, $725) suite. AE, DC, MC, V. Métro: St-Germain-des-Prés or Mabillon. **Amenities:** 24-hr. room service; baby-sitting; laundry/dry cleaning. *In room:* A/C, TV, minibar, hair dryer.

Odéon-Hôtel ⭐ Reminiscent of a modernized Norman country inn, the Odéon offers rustic touches like exposed beams, stone walls, high crooked ceilings, and tapestries mixed with contemporary fabrics, mirrored ceilings, and black leather furnishings. Located near both the Théâtre de l'Odéon and boulevard St-Germain, the Odéon stands on the first street in Paris to have pavements (1779) and gutters. By the 20th century, this area, which had drawn the original Shakespeare & Co. bookshop to no. 12 rue de l'Odéon, began attracting such writers as Gertrude Stein and her coterie. The guest rooms are small to medium but charming, and each comes with a combo tub and shower. The beds are excellent with reading lamps, firm mattresses, and bedside controls.

3 rue de l'Odéon, 75006 Paris. ⓒ **01-43-25-90-67.** Fax 01-43-25-55-98. www.odeonhotel.fr. 33 units. 950F–1,400F (144.40– 212.80, $137.75–$203) double; 1,500F (228, $217.50) suite. AE, DC, MC, V. Parking 100F (15.20, $14.50). Métro: Odéon. **Amenities:** Baby-sitting. *In room:* A/C, TV, hair dryer, safe.

MODERATE

Hôtel Aviatic Completely remodeled, this is a bit of old Paris in an interesting section of Montparnasse, with an inner courtyard and a vine-covered wall lattice, surrounded by cafes popular with artists, writers, and musicians. It has been a family-run hotel for a century and has an English-speaking staff. The reception lounge boasts marble columns, brass chandeliers, antiques, and a petite salon. The guest rooms were renovated throughout the 1990s, and each comes with a shower or tub/shower combo. The old mattresses were tossed out and new ones installed, giving you more comfort than this place has had in a decade.

105 rue de Vaugirard, 75006 Paris. ℂ **01-53-63-25-50.** Fax 01-53-63-25-55. www.aviatic.fr. 43 units. 950F (144.40, $137.75) double. AE, DC, MC, V. Parking 120F (18.25, $17.40). Métro: Montparnasse-Bienvenue or St-Placide. **Amenities:** Room service; baby-sitting; laundry/dry cleaning. *In room:* A/C, TV, minibar, hair dryer.

Hôtel du Pas-de-Calais

The Pas-de-Calais goes back to the 17th century. Its elegant facade, with wooden doors, has been retained. Novelist Chateaubriand lived here from 1811 to 1814, but its most famous guest was Jean-Paul Sartre, who struggled with the play *Les Mains Sales* (Dirty Hands) in room 41. The hotel is a bit weak on style, but as one longtime guest confided, despite the updates, "We still stay here for the memories." The guest rooms were renovated in 2000; inner rooms surround a courtyard with two garden tables and several trellises. Each bathroom comes with a tub and shower. As in the case of the hotel above, all the mattresses have been replaced, giving a great deal of comfort.

59 rue des Sts-Pères, 75006 Paris. ℂ **01-45-48-78-74.** Fax 01-45-44-94-57. 40 units. 850F–920F (129.20–139.85, $123.25–$133.40) double. AE, DC, MC, V. Parking 110F (16.70, $15.95). Métro: St-Germain-des-Prés or Sèvres-Babylone. **Amenities:** Room service (drinks and snacks); baby-sitting; laundry/dry cleaning. *In room:* A/C, TV, hair dryer, safe.

Hôtel Le Clos Médicis

The location of this hotel across from the Jardin du Luxembourg is a major advantage. You'll find a verdant garden with lattices and exposed stonewalls, a lobby with modern spotlights and simple furniture, and a multilingual staff. The warmly colored guest rooms, small to medium in size, are comfortable, and each comes with a neatly tiled bathroom with combination tub and shower. Mattresses are infrequently renewed, but there is nonetheless a good comfort level here. The best way to live here is to book one of the multi-level suites with spacious living areas and tasteful furnishings.

56 rue Monsieur-le-Prince, 75006 Paris. ℂ **01-43-29-10-80.** Fax 01-43-54-26-90. www.select-paris.com/hotels. 38 units. 790F–1,200F (120.10– 182.40, $114.55–$174) double; 1,400F (212.80, $203) duplex suite. AE, DC, MC, V. Parking 150F (22.80, $21.75). Métro: Odéon. RER: Luxembourg. **Amenities:** Laundry. *In room:* A/C, TV, minibar, hair dryer.

INEXPENSIVE

Delhy's Hôtel

It's an oldie but goodie. On a narrow crooked alley in the Latin Quarter's densest part, this building was built around 1400, and acquired by François I as a home for one of his mistresses. Don't expect luxury, but look for charming touches that help compensate for the lack of an elevator. The staircase is listed as a national relic, and most of the compact guest rooms still have the original, almost fossilized, timbers and beams. The rooms were for the most part renovated in the late 1990s. If you get one without a bathroom, you'll have to go down to the ground floor for access to the public facilities.

22 rue de l'Hirondelle, 75006 Paris. ℂ **01-43-26-58-25.** Fax 01-43-26-51-06. www.travelocity.com/paris. 21 units, 7 with private bathroom. 376F (57.15, $54.50) double without bathroom; 466F (70.85, $67.55) double with bathroom; 636F (96.65, $92.20) triple with bathroom. Rates include breakfast. AE, DC, MC, V. Métro: St-Michel. *In room:* TV.

Hôtel Clément

This hotel sits on a quiet narrow street, within sight of the twin towers of St-Sulpice church. The building dates back to the 1700s, but it was renovated several years ago. The guest rooms are simple and small, in some cases not much bigger than the beds they contain. Mattresses are a bit thin but beds are neatly maintained with crisp linen. Since many of the regular doubles are small you may want to ask for a suite with better furnishings and more space. Most of the bathrooms contain tubs; only two units have shower-only bathrooms.

6 rue Clément, 75006 Paris. ℂ **01-43-26-53-60.** Fax 01-44-07-06-83. www.123france.com. 31 units. 590F–710F (89.70– 107.90, $85.55–$102.95) double; 810F (123.10, $117.45) suite. AE, DC, V. Métro: Mabillon. *In room:* A/C, TV, hair dryer, safe.

Hôtel du Globe This 17th-century building is located on an evocative street, and inside you'll find most of the original stonework and dozens of original timbers and beams. There's no elevator (you'll have to lug your suitcases up a very narrow antique staircase) and no breakfast area (trays are brought to your room). Each guest room is decorated with individual old-fashioned flair. The rooms with tubs are almost twice as large as those with shower stalls. The largest and most desirable are rooms 1, 12 (with a baldaquin-style bed), 14, 15, and 16. The room without a bathroom is a single that goes for 330F (50.15, $47.85).

15 rue des Quatre-Vents, 75006 Paris. ℂ **01-46-33-62-69.** Fax 01-46-33-62-69. 15 units, 5 with bathroom. 430F–655F (65.35– 99.55, $62.35–$95) double. MC, V. Closed 3 weeks in Aug. Métro: Mabillon, Odéon, or St-Sulpice. **Amenities:** Laundry/dry cleaning. *In room:* TV.

LEFT BANK: 7TH ARRONDISSEMENT (EIFFEL TOWER/MUSÉE D'ORSAY)
VERY EXPENSIVE
Hôtel Montalembert ✿✿ Unusually elegant for the Left Bank, the Montalembert dates from 1926 when it was built in the beaux-arts style. It was restored most recently in 2001, borrowing sophisticated elements of Bauhaus and postmodern design in beiges, creams, and golds. The guest rooms are spacious, except for some standard doubles, which are small unless you're a very thin model. Frette linens decorate roomy beds topped with cabana stripe duvets crowning deluxe French mattresses. The bathrooms are luxurious with deep tubs, chrome fixtures, Cascais marble, and tall pivoting mirrors.

3 rue de Montalembert, 75007 Paris. ℂ **800/786-6397** in the U.S. and Canada, or 01-45-49-68-68. Fax 01-45-49-69-49. www.montalembert.com. 56 units. 2,200F–2,700F (334.40– 410.40, $319–$391.50) double; 3,500F (532, $507.50) junior suite; 4,400F (668.80, $638) suite. AE, DC, MC, V. Parking 120F (18.25, $17.40). Métro: Rue du Bac. **Amenities:** Restaurant, bar; privileges at nearby health club; 24-hr. room service; baby-sitting; laundry/dry cleaning. *In room:* A/C, TV, minibar, hair dryer, safe.

MODERATE
Hôtel de l'Université ✿ Long favored by well-heeled parents of North American students studying in Paris, this 300-year-old, antiques-filled town house enjoys a location in a discreetly upscale neighborhood. Room 54 is a favorite, containing a rattan bed and period pieces. Another charmer is room 35, which has a fireplace and opens onto a courtyard with a fountain. The most expensive unit has a small terrace overlooking the surrounding rooftops. Beds have plush comfort and discreet French styling. You'll sleep well here.

22 rue de l'Université, 75007 Paris. ℂ **01-42-61-09-39.** Fax 01-42-60-40-84. www.hoteluniversite.com. 28 units. 850F–1,300F (129.20– 197.60, $123.25–$188.50) double. AE, MC, V. Métro: St-Germain-des-Prés. **Amenities:** Baby-sitting; laundry/dry cleaning. *In room:* A/C, TV, hair dryer, safe.

Hotel Le Tourville ✿ This is a well-managed, personalized "hotel de charme" in a desirable town house between the Eiffel Tower and Les Invalides.

It originated in the 1930s as a hotel, and was revitalized and reconfigured during the 1990s into the stylish charmer you see today. Bedrooms contain original artworks, antique furnishings or reproductions, and traditional wooden furniture covered in modern, sometimes bold, upholsteries. Four of the rooms, including the suite, have private terraces for soaking up the Parisian sunshine. Rooms 16 and 18 are the most desirable. Beds are queens or twins, each with a recently renewed, medium-size French mattress. The staff is well trained, with the kind of personalities that make you want to linger at the reception desk. Breakfast is the only meal served, but you can get a drink in the lobby if you'd like.

16 av. de Tourville, 75007 Paris. ℂ **01-47-05-43-90.** Fax 01-47-05-43-90. www.hoteltourville.com. 30 units. 890F–1,390F (135.30– 211.30, $129.05–$201.55) double; 1,990F (302.50, $288.55) suite. AE, DC, MC, V. Metro: École Militaire. **Amenities:** Bar. *In room:* A/C, TV, hair dryer.

Hôtel Verneuil ⭐ *(Finds*   Small-scale and personal, this hotel, in the words of a recent critic, "combines modernist sympathies with nostalgia for *la vieille France.*" Within what was built in the 1600s as a town house, it offers a creative and intimate jumble of charm and coziness. Expect a mixture of antique and contemporary furniture, lots of books, and, in the bedrooms, trompe l'oeil ceilings, antique beams, quilts, and walls covered in fabric that comes in a rainbow of colors. The medium-size mattresses offer acceptable comfort, nothing special. Some bathrooms have showers only.

8 rue de Verneuil, 75007 Paris. ℂ **01-42-60-82-14.** Fax 01-42-61-40-38. www.france-hotel.com. 26 units. 850F–1,100F (129.20– 167.20, $123.25–$159.50) doubles and suites. Parking 120F (18.25, $17.40). AE, DC, MC, V. Metro: St-Germain-des-Prés. **Amenities:** Bar; baby-sitting; laundry/dry cleaning. *In room:* TV, minibar, hair dryer.

INEXPENSIVE

Grand Hôtel L'Eveque   Built in the 1930s, this hotel draws lots of English-speaking guests, many of whom appreciate its proximity to the Eiffel Tower. In 2000, the interior was renovated and repainted, with all the carpets changed. The pastel-colored guest rooms retain an Art Deco inspiration, just enough space to be comfortable, with double-insulated windows overlooking a courtyard in back or the street in front. Suites are only slightly larger double rooms, and mattresses are no better than a standard roadside motel. The small bathrooms contain showers.

29 rue Cler, 75007 Paris. ℂ **01-47-05-49-15.** Fax 01-45-50-49-36. www.hotel-leveque.com. 50 units. 400F–500F (60.80– 76E, $58–$72.50) double; 600F (91.20, $87) suite. AE, MC, V. Métro: Ecole Militaire. *In room:* TV, hair dryer, safe.

Hôtel de l'Empereur   This hotel was built in the early 1700s and enjoys a loyal group of repeat visitors. There's an elevator to haul you to one of the smallish but attractive guest rooms, most with shower-only bathrooms. You get a good bed for the night, not any grand comfort. Some of the rooms are large enough to hold more guests, but other than offering more space, they are the same as the doubles. In 1998, the two top floors were renovated. There's no restaurant or bar, but a nearby restaurant will send up platters of food on request.

2 rue Chevert, 75007 Paris. ℂ **01-45-55-88-02.** Fax 01-45-51-88-54. www.hotelempereur.com. 38 units. 475F–505F (72.20– 76.75, $68.90–$73.25) double; 660F (100.30, $95.70) triple; 760F (115.50, $110.20) quad. AE, DC, MC, V. Parking 150F (22.80, $21.75) across the street. Métro: Latour-Maubourg. **Amenities:** Laundry/dry cleaning. *In room:* TV, fridge, hair dryer.

Hôtel de Nevers   This is one of the neighborhood's most historic choices—it was a convent from 1627 to 1790, when it was disbanded by the Revolution.

In 2000, many aspects of this place were upgraded and renovated. The building is *classé*, meaning any restoration must respect the original architecture. That precludes an elevator, so you'll have to use the beautiful white staircase. The cozy, pleasant guest rooms contain a mix of antique and reproduction furniture. In recent renovations, all the mattresses were renewed. Rooms 10 and 11 are especially sought after for their terraces overlooking a corner of rue du Bac or a rear courtyard. About half of the units have full bathrooms.

83 rue du Bac, 75007 Paris. © **01-45-44-61-30**. Fax 01-42-22-29-47. www.imageol.com/paris. 11 units. 500F–560F (76– 85.10, $72.50–$81.20) double. No credit cards. Métro: Rue du Bac. *In room:* TV, minibar, hair dryer.

Hôtel du Champ de Mars
Favored by families, this hotel sits close to the park flanking the base of the Eiffel Tower. It offers clean, simple guest rooms frilly and pretty enough to be referred to as "coquettish" by the manager. In 1998, most rooms were redecorated, retaining their charm and cramped dimensions. Mattresses are often old-fashioned, but with some life left in them; others have been recently renewed. The suites are roomy and old-fashioned, but with some of the grandest views of the Seine in all of Paris. The most memorable of the public areas is a stone-sided breakfast room, which serves the hotel's only meal.

7 rue du Champ de Mars, 75007 Paris. © **01-45-51-52-30**. Fax 01-45-51-64-36. www.hotel-du-champ-de-mars.com. 25 units. 440F–470F (66.90– 71.45, $63.80–$68.15) double. MC, V. Parking 100F–150F (15.20– 22.80, $14.50–$21.75) in nearby public parking lot. Métro: Ecole Militaire. *In room:* TV.

Hôtel du Quai-Voltaire
Built in the 1600s as an abbey, then transformed into a hotel in 1856, the Quai-Voltaire is best known for its illustrious guests, like Wilde, Wagner, and Baudelaire, who occupied rooms 47, 55, and 56, respectively. Camille Pissarro painted Le Pont Royal from the window of his fourth-floor room. Many guest rooms in this modest inn have been renovated; most overlook the bookstalls and boats of the Seine. Each unit comes with a small, shower-only bathroom.

19 quai Voltaire, 75007 Paris. © **01-42-61-50-91**. Fax 01-42-61-62-26. info@hotelduquaivoltaire.com. 33 units. 750F–800F (114– 121.60, $108.75–$116) double; 870F (132.25, $126.15) triple. AE, DC, MC, V. Parking 110F (16.70, $15.95) nearby. Métro: Musée d'Orsay or Rue du Bac. **Amenities:** Bar; room service; laundry. *In room:* TV, hair dryer.

Hôtel Lindbergh
About a 3-minute walk from St-Germain-des-Prés, this hotel offers streamlined and simple guest rooms. About two thirds of the bathrooms contain tubs as well as showers. Breakfast is the only meal served, but the staff will point out worthy restaurants nearby—an inexpensive bistro, Le Cigale, is a few buildings away.

5 rue Chomel, 75007 Paris. © **01-45-48-35-53**. Fax 01-45-49-31-48. linhotel@club-internet.fr. 26 units. 580F–660F (88.15– 100.30, $84.10–$95.70) double; 790F–880F (120.10– 133.75, $114.55–$127.60) triple; 840F–930F (127.70– 141.35, $121.80–$134.85) quad. AE, DC, MC, V. Parking 110F (16.70, $15.95). Métro: Sèvres-Babylone or St-Sulpice. **Amenities:** Laundry/dry cleaning. *In room:* TV, hair dryer.

Hôtel Saint-Dominique
Part of this place's charm derives from its division into three buildings connected through an open-air courtyard. The most visible of these was an 18th-century convent—you can still see its battered ceiling beams and structural timbers in the reception area. The guest rooms aren't large, but each is warm and simply decorated; many have wallpaper in nostalgic patterns. About a third of the bathrooms have full shower-tub combinations.

62 rue St-Dominique, 75007 Paris. © **01-47-05-51-44**. Fax 01-47-05-81-28. www.all-hotels-in-paris.com. 34 units. 700F–850F (106.40– 129.20, $101.50–$123.25) double. AE, DC, MC, V. Métro: Latour-Maubourg or Invalides. *In room:* TV, minibar, safe.

NEAR THE AIRPORTS
ORLY

Climat de France Boxy and contemporary-looking, and interconnected with Orly by frequent free, 10-minute shuttle-bus rides, this 1990s hotel offers standardized, not particularly imaginative guest rooms. Each is comfortable, insulated against noises from the airport, and a bit larger than you might expect. All units have shower-only bathrooms.

58 voie Nouvelle, near the Parc Georges Mélliès. 94544 Orly. © 01-41-80-75-75. Fax 01-41-80-12-12. airplus@club-internet.fr. 72 units. 390F–425F (59.30– 64.60, $56.55–$61.65) double. Free parking. AE, DC, MC, V. Transit to and from airport by complimentary shuttle-bus. **Amenities:** Restaurant. *In room:* TV.

Hilton Paris Orly Airport ☆ Boxy and bland, the Hilton at Orly is a well-maintained business hotel that's especially convenient. Incoming planes can't penetrate the guest rooms' sound barriers, giving you a decent shot at a night's sleep. (Unlike the 24-hour Charles de Gaulle Airport, Orly is closed to arriving flights from midnight to 6am.) The rooms are standard for a chain hotel; each was renovated in the late 1990s. Mattresses provide the standard Hilton comfort.

Aéroport Orly, 267 Orly Sud, 94544 Orly Aerogare Cedex. © 800/445-8667 in the U.S. and Canada, or 01-45-12-45-12. Fax 01-45-12-45-00. www.hilton.com. 353 units. 720F–920F (109.45– 139.85, $104.40–$133.40) double; 1,200F (182.40, $174) suite. AE, DC, MC, V. Parking 90F (13.70, $13.05). Free shuttle bus between hotel and both Orly terminals. **Amenities:** Restaurant, bar; fitness center; nearby tennis court; sauna; room service; laundry/dry cleaning. *In room:* A/C, TV, minibar, hair dryer.

ROISSY/CHARLES DE GAULLE

Hôtel Campanile de Roissy This hotel is less expensive than most other lodgings near the airport. Its cement-and-glass design is barely masked by a thin overlay of cheerful-looking and rustic artifacts, but generally, this is an efficiently decorated and not particularly stylish place to stay, with a well-meaning but overworked staff. Each unit comes with a small, shower-only bathroom. Mattresses are a bit thin but provide reasonable comfort for the night.

Parc de Roissy, 95700 Val-d'Oise. © 01-34-29-80-40. Fax 01-34-29-80-39. 224 units. 425F–525F (64.60– 79.80, $61.65–$76.15) double. Rates include breakfast. AE, DC, MC, V. Free parking. Free shuttle van to and from Roissy. **Amenities:** Restaurant; room service. *In room:* TV.

Hôtel Sofitel Paris Aéroport CDG ☆ Many travelers shuttle happily through this bustling, somewhat anonymous member of the nationwide French chain. It employs a multilingual staff accustomed to accommodating constantly arriving and departing international business travelers. Renovated in 1998, the conservative guest rooms are soundproof havens against the all-night roar of jets. Suites are larger and have more comfort, although they are not especially elegant, more chain formatted. Mattresses, however, in all rooms are first class.

Aéroport Charles de Gaulle, Zone Central, B.P. 20248, 95713 Roissy. © 800/221-4542 in the U.S. and Canada, or 01-49-19-29-29. Fax 01-49-19-29-00. www.accor.com. 352 units. 980F–1,500F (148.95– 228, $142.10–$217.50) double; from 2,250F (342, $326.25) suite. AE, DC, MC, V. Parking 164F (24.95, $23.80). Free shuttles to and from airport. **Amenities:** Restaurant, bar; pool; sauna; business center; 24-hr. room service. *In room:* A/C, TV, minibar, hair dryer.

4 Dining

Our best piece of advice—even if your budget is lean—is to splurge on one grand classic French meal. (You'll need to make reservations weeks or even months in advance.) A meal at a place such as **La Tour d'Argent** ✰✰✰, **Taillevent** ✰✰✰, **Alain Ducasse** ✰✰✰, or **Violon d'Ingres** ✰✰✰ will be a memory you'll always carry.

Three-star dining remains quite expensive in Paris. The $100 main course (*entree* means appetizer in French so don't get them confused) is no longer a novelty, and first courses can top $50; in the top Michelin-starred dining rooms, the total bill easily tops $175 per person. But you can get around that high price tag in many places by ordering a fixed-price menu, perhaps for a mere $90, or heading for one of the not-so-celebrated but equally stellar dining rooms—**Pierre Gagnaire** ★★★, for example, instead of the legendary Alain Ducasse.

One question we're often asked is if you can dine badly in Paris. The answer is an emphatic yes! We get complaints from readers who cite haughty service and mediocre food at outrageous prices. Often, complaints are about places catering mostly to tourists. We'll help you avoid them by sharing our favorite discoveries. While others are fighting it out for a table at one of the less-than-wonderful places along the Champs-Elysées, you can enjoy finer fare off the beaten track.

Changes are in the Paris air. In the past, suits and ties were a given, and women always wore smart dresses or suits. Well, you can kiss your suits *au revoir*—these days. Except in first-class and deluxe places, attire has become more relaxed. Relaxed doesn't mean sloppy jeans and workout clothes, however. Parisians still value style, even when dressing informally.

Restaurants are still required by law to post their menus outside, so peruse them carefully. The prix-fixe menu remains a solid choice if you want to have some idea of what your bill will be when it's presented by the waiter (whom, by the way, you should call *monsieur*, not *garçon*).

Part of the fun of a trip to Paris is enjoying the experience of an old-fashioned, family-run bistro. And just when you thought bistros were dying off, new-wave chefs are moving in, hoping to revive them with excellent food at affordable prices. A trend that developed in the early 1990s—that of the "baby bistro"—continues into the 21st century. These babies are reasonably priced spin-offs of some of Paris's ultra-deluxe restaurants. We've recommended some of the best of them, including Jacques Cagna's **Rôtisserie d'en Face** ★.

RIGHT BANK: 1ST ARRONDISSEMENT (MUSÉE DU LOUVRE/LES HALLES)
VERY EXPENSIVE

Carré des Feuillants ★★★ MODERN FRENCH   This is a bastion of perfection, an enclave of haute gastronomy between the Place Vendôme and the Tuileries. When chef Alain Dutournier turned this 17th-century convent into a restaurant, it was an overnight success. The interior is like an early-1900s bourgeois house with several small salons opening onto a sky-lit courtyard, across from a glass-enclosed kitchen. You'll find a sophisticated reinterpretation of cuisine from France's southwest, using seasonally fresh ingredients and lots of know-how. Examples are roasted veal kidneys cooked in their own fat; grilled wood pigeon with chutney and polenta; and roasted leg of suckling lamb from the Pyrénées with autumn vegetables. Lighter dishes are scallops wrapped in parsley-infused puff pastry served with cabbage and truffles, and mullet-studded risotto with lettuce. For dessert, try the pistachio cream cake with candied tangerines.

> **Tips   Check, Please**
>
> It's considered somewhat provincial these days to request *l'addition* (the bill). Chic Parisians ask for *la note*.

Heart of the Right Bank Restaurants

Angélina **2**	Aux Lyonnais **15**	Chez Janou **31**
Aquarius **35**	Benoit **25**	Chez Jean **11**
À Sousceyrac **27**	Blue Elephant **26**	Chez Jo Goldenberg **33**
Au Bascou **24**	Bofinger **30**	Chez Pauline **16**
Au Clair de Lune **20**	Brasserie Flo **14**	Chez Vong **23**
Au Gourmet de l'Ile **36**	Buddha Bar **5**	China Club **28**
Au Petit Riche **13**	Carré des Feuillants **3**	Georges **34**
Au Trou Gascon **29**	Chez Georges **19**	Goumard **6**

14 rue de Castiglione (near place Vendôme and the Tuileries), 1er. ✆ **01-42-86-82-82.** Fax 01-42-86-07-71. Reservations required far in advance. Main courses 260F–340F (39.50– 51.70, $37.70–$49.30); fixed-price lunch 360F (54.70, $52.20). AE, DC, MC, V. Mon–Fri noon–2:30pm; Mon–Sat 7:30–10pm. Closed first 3 weeks in Aug. Métro: Tuileries, Concorde, Opéra, or Madeleine.

Goumard ✰✰✰ SEAFOOD   Opened in 1872, this landmark is one of Paris's leading seafood restaurants. It's so devoted to the fine art of preparing fish that other food is banned from the menu (if you happen to dislike fish, the staff will verbally present a limited roster of meat dishes). The decor consists of an unusual collection of Lalique crystal fish displayed in artificial aquariums. Even more unusual are the men's and women's restrooms, now classified as historic monuments; the commodes were designed by the Art Nouveau master cabinet-maker Majorelle in the early 1900s. Much of the seafood is flown in from Brittany daily. Examples are a *craquant* (crispy) of crayfish in its own herb salad, lobster soup with coconut, a grilled turbot salad on a bed of artichokes with tarragon, and poached turbot with hollandaise sauce, with leeks in vinaigrette. In all these dishes, nothing (no excess butter, spices, or salt) is allowed to interfere with the natural flavor of the sea. Be prepared for some unusual food—the staff will help translate the menu items for you.

9 rue Duphot, 1er. ✆ **01-42-60-36-07.** Fax 01-42-60-04-54. Reservations required far in advance. Main courses 190F–390F (28.90– 59.33, $27.55–$56.55); fixed-price lunch 250F (38, $36.25). AE, DC, MC, V. Mon–Sat 12:30–2:30pm and 7:30–10:30pm. Closed 3 weeks in Aug. Métro: Madeleine or Concorde.

Le Grand Véfour ✰✰✰ TRADITIONAL FRENCH   This is the all-time winner: a great chef; the most beautiful restaurant decor in Paris; and a history-infused citadel of classic French cuisine. This restaurant has been around since the reign of Louis XV, though not under the same name. Napoléon, Danton, Hugo, Colette, and Cocteau have dined here—as the brass plaques on the tables testify—and it's still a gastronomic experience. Guy Martin, chef for the past decade, bases many dishes on recipes from the French Alps. His best preparation is roast lamb in a juice of herbs. Other specialties are noisettes of lamb with star anise, Breton lobster, and the unusual cabbage sorbet in dark-chocolate sauce. The desserts are often grand, like the *gourmandises au chocolat* (medley of chocolate), served with chocolate sorbet.

17 rue de Beaujolais, 1er. ✆ **01-42-96-56-27.** Fax 01-42-86-80-71. Reservations required far in advance. Main courses 310F–390F (47.10– 59.30, $44.95–$56.55); fixed-price menu 430F (65.35, $62.35) lunch, 1,050F (159.60, $152.25) dinner. AE, DC, MC, V. Mon–Fri 12:30–2pm; Mon–Thurs 8–10pm. Métro: Louvre-Palais Royal.

EXPENSIVE

Chez Pauline ✰ *Finds* BURGUNDIAN/FRENCH   Fans say this *bistrot de luxe* is a less expensive, less majestic version of Le Grand Véfour. The early-1900s setting is grand enough to impress a business client and lighthearted enough to attract a roster of VIPs. You'll be ushered to a table on one of two levels, amid polished mirrors, red leather banquettes, and memorabilia of long-ago Paris. The emphasis is on the cuisine of central France, especially Burgundy, shown by the liberal use of wines in favorites like cassoulet of Burgundian snails with bacon and tomatoes, *boeuf bourguignonne* (braised beef in red-wine sauce) with tagliatelle, terrine of parslied ham, and salmon steak with green peppercorns. Also wonderful is the roasted Bresse chicken with dauphinois potatoes. Dessert may include a *clafoutis* (pastry) of apricots and raspberries sautéed in sugar as well as caramelized rice pudding. Owner/chef André Genin is an author of children's books, some on the value and techniques of French cuisine.

5 rue Villedo, 1er. ℂ **01-42-96-20-70**. Reservations recommended. Main courses 190 F–400 F (28.90E–60.80E, $27.55–$58); fixed-price menu 220 F (33.45E, $31.90). AE, CB, DC, V. Mon–Fri 12:15–2:30pm and 7:30–10:30pm, Sat 7:30–10:30pm. Closed Sat–Sun May to early Sept. Métro: Palais Royal.

MODERATE

Chez Vong ⋆ CANTONESE   This is the kind of Les Halles restaurant you head for when you've had your fill of grand French cuisine and grander culinary pretensions. The decor is a soothing mix of greens and browns, steeped in a Chinese-colonial ambience that evokes early-1900s Shanghai. Menu items feature shrimp and scallops served as spicy as you like, including a super-hot version with garlic and red peppers; "joyous beef" with pepper sauce; chicken in puff pastry with ginger; and a tempting array of fresh fish dishes. The whims of fashion have decreed this one of the restaurants of the moment, so it's full of folks from the worlds of entertainment and the arts.

10 rue de la Grande-Truanderie, 1er. ℂ **01-40-26-09-36**. Reservations recommended. Main courses 88F–200F (13.40– 30.40, $12.75–$29); fixed-price lunch Mon–Fri 150F (22.80, $21.75). AE, DC, MC, V. Mon–Sat noon–2:30pm and 7pm–midnight. Métro: Etienne-Marcel or Les Halles.

Il Cortile ⋆⋆ ITALIAN/MEDITERRANEAN   Flanking the verdant courtyard of a small hotel, this much-talked-about restaurant serves the best Italian food in Paris. In warm weather, tables are set up in an enclosed patio—a luxury in this congested neighborhood. The cuisine is fresh, inventive, and seasonal. Dishes are from throughout Italy, with emphasis on the north, as shown by a special promotion of wines of Tuscany and the Piedmont. Look for items like farfalle pasta with squid ink and fresh shellfish, fettuccine with *pistou* (pasta in a soup made from vegetables), and an award-winning version of guinea fowl (spit-roasted and served with artfully shaped slices of the bird's gizzard, heart, and liver, it comes with polenta). The service is flawless: the Italian-speaking staff is diplomatic and good-humored. If you want to see what's cooking, ask for a seat with a view of the rotisserie, where hens and guinea fowl slowly spin.

In the Hôtel Castille, 37 rue Cambon, 1er. ℂ **01-44-58-45-67**. Reservations recommended. Main courses 100F–150F (15.20– 22.80, $14.50–$21.75); fixed-price menu 270F (41.05, $39.15). AE, DC, DISC, MC, V. Mon–Fri noon–2:30pm and 7:30–10:30pm. Métro: Concorde or Madeleine.

Joe Allen ⋆ *Kids* AMERICAN   The first American restaurant in Les Halles is aging well. Joe Allen long ago invaded the place with his hamburger. Though the New York restaurateur admits "it's a silly idea," it works, and it's Paris's best burger. While listening to the jukebox, you can order savory black-bean soup, spicy chili, sirloin steak, barbecued ribs, or apple pie. Joe Allen is getting more sophisticated, catering to modern tastes with dishes like grilled salmon with coconut rice and sun-dried tomatoes. His saloon is the only place in Paris serving New York cheesecake and real pecan pie, and thanks to French chocolate, he feels his brownies are better than in the States. Giving them tough competition are the California chocolate-mousse pie and strawberries Romanoff. If you haven't made a reservation for dinner, expect a wait of at least 30 minutes at the New York Bar.

30 rue Pierre-Lescot, 1er. ℂ **01-42-36-70-13**. Reservations recommended for dinner. Main courses 75F–140F (11.40– 21.30, $10.90–$20.30); fixed-price menu 140F (21.30, $20.30). AE, MC, V. Daily noon–12:30am. Métro: Etienne-Marcel.

Le Fumoir ⋆ INTERNATIONAL   Stylish and breezy, this upscale brasserie is set in an antique building a few steps from the Louvre. Currently, it's one of the most fashionable places in Paris to be seen eating or drinking. You can order salads, pastries, and drinks at off-hours, and platters of more substantial food at conventional mealtimes. Examples are codfish with onions and herbs, sliced rack of veal simmered in its own juices with tarragon, calf's liver with onions, and herring in mustard-flavored cream sauce.

6 rue de l'Amiral-Coligny, 1er. ℂ **01-42-92-00-24**. Reservations recommended. Main courses 90F–120F (13.70– 18.25, $13.05–$17.40). Salads, pastries, and snacks daily 11am–2pm; full menu daily noon–3pm and 7–11:30pm. AE,and V. Métro: Louvre-Rivoli.

INEXPENSIVE

Angélina TEA/TRADITIONAL FRENCH   In the high-rent area near the Inter-Continental (on a section of rue de Rivoli that's getting scuzzy), this *salon de thé* (tea salon) combines fashion-industry glitter and bourgeois respectability. The carpets are plush, the ceilings high, and the gilded accessories have the right amount of patina. This place has no equal when it comes to viewing the lionesses of haute couture over tea and sandwiches. The overwrought and slightly snooty waitresses bear silver trays with pastries, drinks, and tea or coffee to marble-topped tables. Lunch usually offers a salad and a *plat du jour* like chicken salad, steak tartare, sole meunière, or poached salmon. The specialty, designed to go well with tea, is the Mont Blanc, a combination of chestnut cream and meringue.

226 rue de Rivoli, 1er. ℂ **01-42-60-82-00**. Reservations accepted for lunch, not for teatime. Pot of tea for one 35F–36F (5.30– 5.45, $5.10–$5.20); sandwiches and salads 58F–98F (8.80– 14.90, $8.40–$14.20); main courses 68F–150F (10.35– 22.80, $9.85–$21.75). AE, V. Mon–Fri 9am–7pm; Sat–Sun 9am–7:30pm (lunch 11:45am–3pm). Métro: Tuileries or Concorde.

La Fermette du Sud-Ouest ✯ SOUTHWESTERN FRENCH   This restaurant, which occupies the site of a 1500s convent, is in the heart of one of Paris's most ancient neighborhoods. After the Revolution, the convent was converted into a coaching inn, preserving the original stonework and massive beams. La Fermette prepares rich, savory stews and confits celebrating agrarian France, serving them on the ground floor and on a mezzanine resembling a choir loft. Menu items include an age-old but ever-popular magret of duckling with flap mushrooms, *andouillette* (chitterling sausages), and a sometimes startling array of *cochonailles* (pork products and byproducts) you probably need to be French to appreciate. Cassoulet and pot-au-feu are enduring specialties.

31 rue Coquillière, 1er. ℂ **01-42-36-73-55**. Reservations recommended. Main courses 85F–130F (12.90– 19.75, $12.35–$18.85); fixed-price menu (at lunch and at dinner before 9pm) 120F–145F (18.25– 22.05, $17.40–$21.05). MC, V. Mon–Sat noon–2pm and 7:30–10pm. Métro: Les Halles.

RIGHT BANK: 2ND ARRONDISSEMENT (LA BOURSE)
MODERATE

Chez Georges TRADITIONAL FRENCH   This bistro is something of a local landmark. It was opened in 1964 near La Bourse (stock exchange), and is run by three generations of the same family. Naturally, at lunch it's packed with stock exchange members. The owners serve what they call *la cuisine bourgeoise* (comfort food). Waiters bring around bowls of appetizers, like celery rémoulade, to get you started. You can follow with sweetbreads with morels, duck breast with cèpe mushrooms, classic cassoulet, or *pot-au-feu* (beef simmered with vegetables). A delight is sole filet with a sauce made from Pouilly wine and crème fraîche. Beaujolais goes great with this hearty food.

1 rue du Mail, 2e. ℂ **01-42-60-07-11**. Reservations required. Main courses 130F–160F (19.75– 24.30, $18.85–$23.20). AE, MC, V. Mon–Sat noon–2:15pm and 7–9:45pm. Closed 3 weeks in Aug. Métro: Bourse.

INEXPENSIVE
Au Clair de Lune ALGERIAN/FRENCH   This neighborhood staple has flourished in the heart of Paris's garment district since the 1930s, when Algeria was a distinct part of the French-speaking world. It represents a pocket of a long-gone, French-colonial ambition. You'll dine in a long, narrow room whose walls are hung with Berber carpets, and whose patrons are likely to include shop workers from the nearby wholesale clothiers. On the menu is always the Algerian staple of couscous, as well as an array of oft-changing daily specials such as veal stew, shoulder or rack of lamb, grilled fish, and roast chicken. The portions are large, so come hungry. The wines are from throughout France and North Africa.

13 rue Française, 2e. ℂ **01-42-33-59-10.** Main courses 58F–80F (8.80– 12.15, $8.40–$11.60); fixed-price menu 70F (10.65, $10.15). MC, V. Daily noon–2:30pm and 7:30–11pm. Métro: Etienne-Marcel or Les Halles.

Aux Lyonnais ✿ LYONNAIS/FRENCH   A LYON LE COCHON EST ROI! proclaims the sign. Pig may be king at this fin-de-siècle bistro (with walls molded with roses and garlands, brass globe lamps, potted palms, and etched glass), behind La Bourse, but the kitchen staff does everything well. After a meal here, you'll know why Lyon is called the gastronomic capital of France. Launch your repast with some Lyonnais sausages, or one of our favorites—a chicory salad with bacon and slices of hot sausages. Poached eggs in red-wine sauce and grilled pig's feet still appear on the menu. Pike dumplings are always prepared to perfection and served in white-butter sauce. Wash it down with Beaujolais. The upside-down apple pie with crème fraîche is the dessert of choice.

32 rue St-Marc, 2e. ℂ **01-42-96-65-04.** Reservations required. Main courses 90F–200F (13.70– 30.40, $13.05–$29). AE, DC, MC, V. Mon–Sat 11:30am–3pm and 6:30–11:30pm. Métro: Bourse or Richelieu-Drouot.

RIGHT BANK: 3RD ARRONDISSEMENT (LE MARAIS)
INEXPENSIVE
Au Bascou ✿ *Finds* BASQUE   The succulent cuisine of France's "deep southwest" is the specialty in this restaurant, where art objects and oil paintings celebrate the beauty of the region, and hanging clusters of pimentos add spice to the air. The Basque food here is as good as it gets. For a ray of sunshine in your life, try the *piperade basquaise*, a spicy omelet loaded with peppers and onions; pimentos stuffed with a purée of codfish; and an axoa of veal (shoulder of calf served with a pimento-and-pepper-based green sauce.) Because all starters are priced at 55F (8.35, $8.03), and all desserts at 40F (6.10, $5.80), a three-course meal at this place, without wine, adds up to 180F (27.35, $26.10).

38 rue Réaumur, 3e. ℂ **01-42-72-69-25.** Reservations recommended. All main courses 85F (12.90, $12.35). AE, DC, MC, V. Tues–Fri noon–3pm; Mon–Sat 8–11pm. Closed 1 week in Aug. Métro: Arts-et-Métiers.

Chez Janou PROVENÇAL   On one of the narrow 17th-century streets behind place des Vosges, this unpretentious bistro operates from a pair of cramped but cozy dining rooms filled with memorabilia from Provence. The service is brusque and sometimes hectic. But the food here is like a visit to your favorite French grandmother's kitchen, where she'll regale you with time-tested dishes like large shrimp with pastis sauce, *brouillade des pleurotes* (baked eggs with oyster mushrooms), velouté of frogs' legs, fondue of ratatouille, gratin of mussels, and a simple but savory *daube provençale*, sometimes compared to pot roast. You can enjoy all these specialties on a covered terrace.

2 rue Roger-Verlomme, 3e. ℂ **01-42-72-28-41.** Reservations recommended. Main courses 68F–92F (10.35– 14, $9.85–$13.35). No credit cards. Daily noon–3pm and 7:30pm–midnight. Métro: Chemin-Vert.

L'Ambassade d'Auvergne ✿ AUVERGNAT/FRENCH   You enter this rustic tavern through a busy bar with heavy oak beams, hanging hams, and ceramic plates. This favorite showcases the culinary generosity of France's most isolated region, the Auvergne, whose pork products are widely celebrated. The best examples are a chicory salad with apples and pieces of country ham; pork braised with cabbage, turnips, and white beans; grilled tripe sausages with mashed potatoes and cantal cheese with garlic; and pork jowls with green lentils. The cholesterol is intense, but devotees love this type of food. Nonpork specialties are pan-fried duck liver with gingerbread, perch steamed in verbena tea, and roasted rack of lamb with wild mushrooms. Dessert might be a poached pear with crispy almonds and caramel sauce or a wine-flavored sorbet.

22 rue de Grenier St-Lazare, 3e. ✆ 01-42-782-31-22. Reservations recommended. Main courses 86F–120F (13.05– 18.25, $12.45–$17.40); fixed-price menu 170F (25.85, $24.65). AE, MC, V. Daily noon–2pm and 7:30–11pm. Closed 2 weeks in Aug. Métro: Rambuteau.

RIGHT BANK: 4TH ARRONDISSEMENT (ÎLE DE LA CITÉ/ÎLE ST-LOUIS& BEAUBOURG)
VERY EXPENSIVE

L'Ambroisie ✿✿✿ TRADITIONAL & MODERN FRENCH   One of Paris's most talented chefs, Bernard Pacaud draws world attention with his vivid flavors and expert culinary skill. Expect perfection at this 17th-century town house in Le Marais, with two high-ceilinged salons whose decor resembles an Italian palazzo. In summer, there's outdoor seating. Pacaud's tables are nearly always filled with diners who come back again and again to see where his imagination will take him next. The dishes change seasonally and may include fricassee of Breton lobster with a civet and red-wine sauce, served with a purée of peas; turbot braised with celery, served with a julienne of black truffles; or one of our favorite dishes in all Paris, *poulard de Bresse demi-deuil homage à la Mè Brazier* (chicken roasted with black truffles and truffled vegetables in a style invented by a Lyonnais matron after World War II). An award-winning dessert is the *tarte fine sablée* (a delicate small biscuit) served with bitter chocolate and vanilla-flavored ice cream.

9 place des Vosges, 4e. ✆ 01-42-78-51-45. Reservations required far in advance. Main courses 370F–610F (56.25– 92.70, $53.65–$88.45). AE, MC, V. Tues–Sat noon–1:30pm and 8–9:30pm. Métro: St-Paul or Chèmin Vert.

EXPENSIVE

Benoit ✿ TRADITIONAL FRENCH   There's something traditional and weighty about this old-fashioned historical monument; every mayor in Paris has dined here since the restaurant was founded in 1912 by the grandfather of the present owner. He's one of the last *bistrotiers* who purchases Beaujolais in casks and bottles it in his own cellars. The setting is theatrical, and the service can be intensely attentive or arrogant, depending on a delicate chemistry that only long-time fans of this place understand. Prices are higher, a lot higher, than you'd expect for bistro fare, but all seems part of the self-satisfied norm here, and clients keep coming back for more. Cuisine is rich, full of flavor, and satisfying, based on time-tested classics that rarely get modernized. Traditional crowd-pleasers include salmon that's both marinated and smoked; snails served in their shell with garlic butter; and cassoulet, a white bean and pork dish from France's southwest that's absolutely fabulous on a cold day. A dessert that earns raves is the *Sainte-Eve*, pears layered with macaroon-flavored cream enclosed in puff pastry.

20 rue St-Martin, 4e. © **01-42-72-25-76**. Reservations required. Main courses 180F–250F (27.35– 38, $26.10–$36.25); fixed-price lunch 200F (30.40, $29). AE. Daily noon–2pm and 8–10pm. Metro: Châtelet or Hôtel-de-Ville.

MODERATE

Bofinger ☆ ALSATIAN/FRENCH Opened in the 1860s, Bofinger is the oldest Alsatian brasserie in town and certainly one of the best. It's a belle-époque dining palace, resplendent with shiny brass and stained glass. Weather permitting, you can dine on an outdoor terrace. Affiliated today with La Coupole, Julien, and Brasserie Flo, the restaurant has updated its menu, retaining only the most popular of its traditional dishes, like sauerkraut and a well-prepared sole meunière. Recent additions have included roasted leg of lamb with a fondant of artichoke hearts and a purée of parsley, grilled turbot with a *brandade* of fennel, and stingray with chives and burnt-butter sauce. Shellfish, including an abundance of fresh oysters and lobster, is almost always available in season.

5–7 rue de la Bastille, 4e. © **01-42-72-87-82**. Reservations recommended. Main courses 90F–160F (13.70– 24.30, $13.05–$23.20). AE, DC, MC, V. Mon–Fri noon–3pm and 6:30pm–1am; Sat–Sun noon–1am. Métro: Bastille.

Georges ☆ INTERNATIONAL Thanks in part to this restaurant, the Centre Pompidou is again in the spotlight; all of artsy Paris is talking about this place. It's a very large space on the top floor of Paris's most comprehensive arts complex, with views through bay windows over most of the city. The decor is minimalist and postmodern, with lots of brushed aluminum and stainless steel. Tables are made from sandblasted glass, lit from below, and accessorized with hypermodern cutlery. Menu items are mostly continental, with hints of Asia. Some combinations come as a surprise—macaroni with lobster, for example. Others seem exotic, including roasted ostrich steak. Aside from these dishes, some of the best items on the menu are the roasted scallops with lemon butter and a tuna steak spiced up with coriander. There's also a luscious version of sole meunière. (May that dish never go out of style!) To get here, head for the exterior elevator to the left of the Pompidou's main entrance, and know that unless you identify your reservation to the guard, you might not be permitted to go up.

On the uppermost (6th) floor of the Centre Georges Pompidou, 19 rue Beaubourg, 4e. © **01-44-78-47-99**. Reservations imperative for dinner, strongly recommended for lunch. Main courses 45F–180F (6.85– 27.35, $6.55–$26.10). AE, DC, MC, V. Wed–Mon noon–6pm and 7pm–2am. Metro: Les Halles.

INEXPENSIVE

Aquarius VEGETARIAN Housed in a 17th-century building whose stonework forms part of the earthy decor, this is one of the best-known vegetarian restaurants in Le Marais. The owners serve a limited array of (strictly organic) wine, and smoking is forbidden. Flavorful meals are healthfully prepared and come in generous portions. Choose from a variety of soups and salads; a galette of wheat served with crudités and mushroom tarts; or a country plate composed of fried mushrooms and potatoes, garlic, and goat cheese, served with a salad.

54 rue Ste-Croix-de-la-Bretonnerie, 4e. © **01-48-87-48-71**. Main courses 45F–64F (6.85– 9.75, $6.55–$9.30); fixed-price menu 95F (14.45, $13.83). MC, V. Mon–Sat noon–10:15pm. Métro: Hôtel de Ville. RER: Châtelet–Les Halles.

Au Gourmet de l'Ile ☆ *Value* TRADITIONAL FRENCH Locals swear by the cuisine at Au Gourmet de l'Ile, whose fixed-price meals are among Paris's best bargains. The setting is beautiful, with a beamed ceiling, walls from the

1400s and candlelit tables. In the window is a sign emblazoned with AAAAA, which, roughly translated, stands for the Amiable Association of Amateurs of the Authentic Andouillette. Their chitterling sausages are soul food to the French. Popular and tasty too are *la charbonnée de l'Ile*, a savory pork with onions, and stuffed mussels in shallot butter. The fixed-price menu includes a choice of 15 appetizers, 15 main courses, salad or cheese, and 15 desserts.

42 rue St-Louis-en-l'Ile, 4e. ℂ **01-43-26-79-27.** Reservations required. Main courses 75F–120F (11.40– 18.25, $10.90–$17.40); fixed-price menu 155F–195F (23.55– 29.65, $22.50–$28.30). AE, MC, V. Wed–Sun noon–2pm; daily 7–10:30pm. Métro: Pont Marie.

Chez Jo Goldenberg ⭐ *Finds* JEWISH/CENTRAL EUROPEAN   This is the best-known restaurant on the "Street of the Rose Bushes." Albert Goldenberg, the doyen of Jewish restaurateurs in Paris, long ago moved to choicer surroundings (69 av. de Wagram, 17e), but his brother, Joseph, has remained here. Dining is on two levels, one for nonsmokers. Look for the collection of samovars, the white fantail pigeon in a wicker cage, and the interesting paintings. The *carpe farcie* (stuffed carp) is a preferred selection, but the beef goulash is also good. We like the eggplant moussaka and the pastrami. The menu offers Israeli wines, but M. Goldenberg admits they're not as good as French wines. Live Yiddish music is presented every night beginning at 9pm, and special menus are offered during Jewish holidays—reservations are a must.

7 rue des Rosiers, 4e. ℂ **01-48-87-20-16.** Reservations required. Main courses 75F–110F (11.40– 16.70, $10.90–$15.95). AE, DC, MC, V. Daily noon–1am. Métro: St-Paul.

RIGHT BANK: 8TH ARRONDISSEMENT (CHAMPS-ELYSÉES/MADELEINE)
VERY EXPENSIVE

Les Elysées du Vernet ⭐⭐⭐ PROVENÇAL   This restaurant is fast becoming a gastronomic wonder of Paris. It's the darling of the media and of *tout Paris*. It has one of the neighborhood's most panoramic glass ceilings, a gray and green translucent dome designed by the architect (Gustav Eiffel) who conceived Paris's famous tower. That, plus the fact that the Montpellier-born chef, Alain Solivérès, was recently awarded two Michelin stars, keeps the crowds lined up. Menu items are focused on Provençal models and change every 2 months, based on whatever is fresh. During our midwinter visit, award-winning examples included scallops with truffles, tournedos Rossini (a slab of beef layered with foie gras), and a *cocotte* (small stew-pot) of lobster. There's also a melt-in-your-mouth version of apple charlotte, and even a newfangled black-truffle ice cream, a dish that traditionalists consider far-fetched. Candles illuminate the place at night, and during the dinner hour, there's a harpist or a pianist, whose music reverberates pleasantly off the glass dome.

In the Hôtel Vernet, 25 rue Vernet, 8e. ℂ **01-44-31-98-98.** Reservations required. Main courses 280F–670F (42.55– 101.85, $40.60–$97.15). AE, DC, MC, V. Mon–Sat 12:30–2pm and 7:30–9pm. Metro: George V.

Lucas-Carton (Alain Senderens) ⭐⭐⭐ MODERN FRENCH   This is one of the city's temples of French gastronomy, right up there with Taillevent. When Alain Senderens took over this landmark belle-époque restaurant, he added some welcome modern touches and a brilliant culinary repertoire. The dining rooms boast mirrors, bouquets of flowers, and wood paneling that has been polished every week since its installation in 1900. All dishes are influenced by Senderens's creative flair. Menu items, which change seasonally, include polenta with black truffles, duckling Apicius (roasted with honey and spices), and pastillade of rabbit. Senderens is constantly experimenting—his latest sensations are lobster roasted with vanilla and *poularde demi-deuil,* a Bresse hen whose flesh has been scored with black truffles (the resulting black-and-white flesh is supposed to be "in partial mourning"); it's accompanied by saffron-flavored rice. The chestnuts purée is the perfect way to end a meal.

9 place de la Madeleine, 8e. ℂ **01-42-65-22-90.** Fax 01-42-65-06-23. Reservations required several days ahead for lunch and several weeks ahead for dinner. Main courses 240F–700F (36.50– 106.40, $34.80–$101.50); fixed-price lunch 395F (60.05, $57.30); fixed-price dinner 1,200F (182.40, $174). AE, DC, MC, V. Tues–Fri noon–2:30pm; Mon–Sat 8–10:15pm. Closed 3 weeks in Aug. Métro: Madeleine.

Pierre Gagnaire ✫✫✫ MODERN FRENCH   If you're able to get a reservation here, it's worth the effort. The menus are seasonally adjusted to take advantage of France's rich bounty; Pierre Gagnaire, the owner, demands perfection, and the chef has a dazzling way of blending flavors and textures. Stellar examples are freshwater crayfish cooked tempura style with thin-sliced flash-seared vegetables and sweet-and-sour sauce, as well as turbot cooked in a bag and served with fennel and Provençal lemons. Chicken with truffles is part of a two-tiered service—first the breast in a wine-based aspic, second the thighs chopped into roughly textured pieces. For dessert, try the chocolate soufflé served with a frozen parfait and Sicilian pistachios.

6 rue Balzac, 8e. ℂ **01-44-35-18-25.** Fax 01-44-35-18-37. Reservations are imperative and difficult to make. Main courses 310F–460F (47.10– 69.90, $44.95–$66.70); fixed-price menu 520F–650F (79.05– 98.80, $75.40–$94.25) lunch, 1,250F (190, $181.25) dinner. AE, DC, MC, V. Mon–Fri 12:30–2:15pm and 7–10pm. Métro: George V.

Restaurant Plaza Athénée (Alain Ducasse) ✫✫✫ MODERN & TRADITIONAL FRENCH   Few other chefs in the history of French cuisine have been catapulted to international fame as quickly as Alain Ducasse. The most recent setting for his cuisine is in a world-renowned hotel, the Plaza Athénée. There's a lot of marketing and glitter associated with this *marriage de convenience,* but what you'll find is a lobby-level hideaway that top-notch decorator Patrick Jouin transformed with layers of pearl-gray paint and yards of translucent organdy. The five-star Michelin chef divides his time between Paris and Monaco, though he insists he doesn't repeat himself in either of his famous eateries. He seeds his dishes with produce from every corner of France—rare local vegetables, fish from the coasts, and dishes incorporating cardoons, turnips, celery, turbot, cuttlefish, and Bresse fowl. His French cuisine is contemporary and Mediterranean, yet not new. Though many dishes are light, Ducasse isn't afraid of lard, as he proves by his thick, oozing slabs of pork grilled to a crisp. The wine list is superb, with some selections deriving from the best vintages of France, Germany, Switzerland, Spain, California, and Italy.

In the Hotel Plaza Athénée, 25 Ave. Montaigne, 8e. ℂ **01-53-67-66-65.** Fax 01-53-67-65-12. Reservations required 2 months in advance. Main courses 360F–558F (54.70– 84.80, $52.20–$80.90); fixed-price menus 985F–1,490F (149.70– 226.50, $142.85–$216.05). AE, DC, MC, V. Thurs–Fri noon–2pm; Mon–Fri 8–10:30pm. Closed mid-July to mid-Aug and Dec 22–30. Métro: FDR or Alma-Marceau.

Taillevent ✫✫✫ MODERN & TRADITIONAL FRENCH   This is the Parisian *ne plus ultra* of gastronomy. Taillevent opened in 1946 and has climbed steadily in excellence; today it ranks as Paris's outstanding all-around restaurant, challenged only by Lucas-Carton and Pierre Gagnaire in this highly competitive area. It's set in a grand 19th-century town house off the Champs-Elysées, with paneled rooms and crystal chandeliers. The place is small, as the owner wishes, since it permits him to give personal attention to every facet of the operation and maintain a discreet atmosphere. You might begin with a *boudin* (sausage) of

Breton lobster à la Nage, cream of watercress soup with Sevruga caviar, or duck liver with spice bread and ginger. Main courses include red snapper with black olives, Scottish salmon cooked in sea salt with a sauce of olive oil and lemons, and cassolette of crayfish from Brittany. Dessert might be a *nougatine glacé* with pears. The wine list is among the best in Paris.

15 rue Lamennais, 8e. © **01-44-95-15-01.** Fax 01-42-25-95-18. Reservations required weeks, even months, in advance for lunch and dinner. Main courses 290F–330F (44.10– 50.15, $42.05–$47.85). AE, DC, MC, V. Mon–Fri noon–2:30pm and 7–10pm. Closed Aug. Métro: George V.

EXPENSIVE

Buddha Bar ✦ FRENCH/PACIFIC RIM   This place is hot, hot, hot—and still remains Paris's restaurant of the moment, even though it's been around for a while. A location on a chic street near the Champs-Elysées and place de la Concorde, and an allegiance to a fusion of French, Asian, and Californian cuisines attract trendy diners devoted to the whims of fashion. The vast dining room is presided over by a giant Buddha, and the culinary theme combines Japanese sashimi, Vietnamese spring rolls, lacquered duck, sautéed shrimp with black bean sauce, grilled chicken skewers with orange sauce, sweet-and-sour spareribs, and crackling squab à l'orange. There are two sittings for dinner: 7 to 9pm and 10:30pm to 12:30am. Many come here just for a drink in the carefully lacquered bar, upstairs from the street-level dining room.

8 rue Boissy d'Anglas, 8e. © **01-53-05-90-00.** Reservations required far in advance. Main courses 115F–260F (17.50– 39.50, $16.70–$37.70). AE, MC, V. Mon–Fri noon–3pm; daily 7pm–12:30am. Métro: Concorde.

Ladurée ✦ TRADITIONAL FRENCH   Ladurée, acclaimed since 1862 as one of Paris's grand cafes (located near La Madeleine), is now installed on the Champs-Elysées, adding a touch of class to the neighborhood. This offshoot caters to an international set wearing everything from Givenchy to Gap. The belle-époque setting is ideal for sampling Ladurée's macaroons—not the coconut version familiar to Americans but two almond meringue cookies, flavored with vanilla, coffee, strawberry, pistachio, or another flavor, held together with butter cream. The menu of talented chef Philippe Dandrieux is adjusted to take advantage of the freshest daily ingredients. It may include a crisp and tender pork filet with potato-and-parsley purée and marinated red mullet on a salad of cold ratatouille. If you're looking for a pick-me-up to accompany your tea and macaroons, consider a *plaisir sucre,* a chocolate confection decorated with spun sugar. The only downside: service isn't always efficient.

75 av. des Champs-Elysées, 8e. © **01-40-75-08-75.** Reservations required for restaurant, not for cafe. Main courses 150F–250F (22.80– 38, $21.75–$36.25); pastries from 28F (4.25, $4.05). AE, DC, MC, V. Daily 7:30am–1am.

Shozan ✦ FRENCH/JAPANESE   East and West form a perfect synthesis in this Franco-Japanese alliance. It's not for the traditionalist, but trendy young Parisians enjoy the new flavors. For example, the classic foie gras appears as foie-gras sushi with sansho pepper, and the roast lamb comes with a green-tea crust. The roast tuna with buckwheat seed and the scampi concoction are delectable. A chef's specialty is lobster with white-sesame sauce spiked with sweet sake. Famous interior designer Christian Liaigre created the stunning setting, dominated by wood and leather.

11 rue de la Trémoille, 8e. © **01-47-23-37-32.** Reservations recommended far in advance. Main courses 165F–220F (25.10– 33.45, $23.95–$31.90); fixed-price menu 195F (29.65, $28.30) lunch, 395F (60.05, $57.30) dinner. AE, DC, MC, V. Mon–Fri noon–2:30pm; Mon–Sat 7–10:30pm. Closed 15 days in Aug. Métro: Alma-Marceau.

ugglers, dancers and an assortment of acrobats fill the street.

he shoots you a wide-eyed look as a seven-foot cartoon character approaches.

Vhat brought you here was wanting the kids

o see something magical while they still believed in magic.

With 700 airlines, 50,000 hotels and over 5,000 cruise and vaca-

tion getaways, you can now go places you've always dreamed of.

Travelocity.com
A Sabre Company
Go Virtually Anywhere.

"WORLD'S LEADING TRAVEL WEB SITE, 5 YEARS IN A ROW" WORLD TRAVEL AWARDS

I HAVE TO CALL THE TRAVEL AGENCY AGAIN. DARN, OUT TO LUNCH. NOW HAVE TO CALL THE AIRLINE. I HATE CALLING THE AIRLINES. I GOT PUT ON HOLD AGAIN. "INSTRUMENTAL TOP 40" ... LOVELY. I HATE GETTING PUT ON HOLD. TICKET PRICES ARE ALL OVER THE MAP. HOW DO I DIAL INTERNATIONALLY? OH SHOOT, FORGOT THE RENTAL CAR. I'M STILL ON HOLD. THIS MUSIC IS GIVING ME A HEADACHE. I WONDER IF SOMEONE ELSE HAS CHEAPER FLIGHTS. FORGET IT, CAN'T TAKE IT ANYMORE ... I'M HANGING UP

YAHOO! TRAVEL
100% MUZAK-FREE

Booking your trip online at Yahoo! Travel is simple. You compare the best prices. You click. You go have fun. Tickets, hotels, rental cars, cruises & more. Sorry, no muzak.

YAHOO!
Travel
travel.yahoo.com

Spoon, Food & Wine INTERNATIONAL   This hypermodern venture of superstar chef Alain Ducasse is hailed as a "restaurant for the millennium" and condemned by some Parisian food critics as surreal and a bit absurd. The claustrophobic dining room evokes stylish Paris and California, and the cuisine roams the world for inspiration, with such middlebrow offerings as American macaroni-and-cheese, a BLT, barbecued ribs, chicken wings, and pastrami. Other dishes evoke Italy, Latin America, Asia, and India. The steamed lobster with mango chutney is a winner. Pasta comes with a selection of five sauces.

In the Hôtel Marignan-Elysée, 14 rue Marignan, 8e. © **01-40-76-34-44.** Reservations recommended far in advance. Main courses and vegetable side dishes each 135F–185F (20.50– 28.10, $19.60–$26.85). Mon–Fri noon–2pm and 7–11pm. AE, DC, V. Métro: Franklin-D.-Roosevelt.

RIGHT BANK: 9TH ARRONDISSEMENT (OPÉRA GARNIER/PIGALLE)
EXPENSIVE

Au Petit Riche ★ LOIRE VALLEY (ANJOU)   No, that's not Flaubert or Balzac walking through the door. But should they miraculously come back, the decor of old Paris with the original gas lamps and time-mellowed paneling would make them feel at home. When it opened in 1865, this bistro was the food outlet for the Café Riche next door; today, it offers yesterday's grandeur and simple, well-prepared food. You'll be ushered to one of five areas crafted for maximum intimacy, with red banquettes, ceilings painted with allegorical themes, and accents of brass and frosted glass. The wine list favors Loire Valley vintages that go well with such dishes as *rillettes* and *rillons* (potted fish or meat, especially pork) in Vouvray wine aspic, poached fish with buttery white-wine sauce, old-fashioned blanquette of chicken, and seasonal game dishes like civet of rabbit.

25 rue Le Peletier, 9e. © **01-47-70-68-68.** Reservations recommended. Main courses 88F–160F (13.40– 24.30, $12.75–$23.20); fixed-price menu 165F (25.10, $23.95) lunch, 140F–180F (21.30– 27.35, $20.30–$26.10) dinner. AE, DC, MC, V. Mon–Sat noon–2:15pm and 7pm–midnight. Métro: Le Peletier or Richelieu-Drouot.

Chez Jean FRENCH   The crowd is young, the food is good, and the vintage brassiere aura of the 1950s makes you think that the Parisian expat novelist James Baldwin will arrive for his table any minute. There's been a brasserie on this site since around 1900. Amid well-oiled, pine-wood panels and carefully polished copper, you can choose from some of grandmother's favorites as well as more modern dishes like risotto with lobster and squid ink, scallops with endive fricassée, lamb roasted with basil, "nougat" of oxtails with balsamic vinaigrette, and pavé of duckling with honey sauce and exotic mushroom fricassée. The changing menu attracts fans that consider the food a lot more sophisticated than that served at other brasseries. (The chefs gained their experience in upscale restaurants.)

8 rue St-Lazare, 9e. © **01-48-78-62-73.** Reservations recommended far in advance. Main courses 130F–245F (19.75– 37.25, $18.85–$35.55); fixed-price menu 195F (29.65, $28.30). MC, V. Mon–Fri noon–2:30pm and 7–11pm; Sat–Sun 7–11pm. Métro: Notre-Dame de Lorette, Opéra, or Cadet.

Wally Le Saharien ALGERIAN   Head to this dining room—lined with desert photos and tribal artifacts crafted from ceramics, wood, and weavings— for an insight into the spicy, slow-cooked cuisine that fueled the colonial expansion of France into North Africa. The fixed-price dinner menu begins with a trio of starters: a spicy soup, stuffed and grilled sardines, and a savory *pastilla* of pigeon in puff pastry. This can be followed by any of several kinds of couscous or a *méchouia* (slow-cooked tart) of lamb dusted with an optional coating of sugar, according to your taste. *Merguez,* the cumin-laden spicy sausage of the North African world, factors importantly into any meal, as does home-made (usually honey-infused) pastries. End your meal with traditional mint-flavored tea.

36 rue Rodier, 9e. ☎ **01-42-85-51-90.** Reservations recommended. A la carte main courses (available only at lunch) 85F–138F (12.90– 21, $12.35–$20); fixed-price dinner 250F (38, $36.25). MC, V. Tues–Sat noon–2pm; Mon–Sat 7–10pm. Métro: Anvers.

RIGHT BANK: 10TH ARRONDISSEMENT (GARE DU NORD/GARE DE L'EST)
MODERATE

Brasserie Flo ⭐ ALSATIAN   This remote restaurant is a bit hard to find, but once you arrive (after walking through passageway after passageway), you'll see that *fin-de-siècle* Paris lives on. The restaurant opened in 1860 and has changed its decor very little since. The house specialty is *la formidable choucroute* (a mound of sauerkraut with boiled ham, bacon, and sausage) for two. The onion soup and sole meunière are always good, as are the warm foie gras and guinea hen with lentils. Look for the *plats du jour,* ranging from roast pigeon to veal fricassée with sorrel.

7 cour des Petites-Ecuries, 10e. ☎ **01-47-70-13-59.** Reservations recommended. Main courses 90F–168F (13.70– 25.55, $13.05–$24.35); fixed-price menu 138F–179F (21– 27.20, $20–$25.95) lunch, 189F (28.75, $27.40) dinner; fixed-price late-night supper (after 10pm) 142F (21.60, $20.64). AE, DC, MC, V. Daily noon–3pm and 7pm–1:30am. Métro: Château d'Eau or Strasbourg–St-Denis.

RIGHT BANK: 11TH ARRONDISSEMENT (OPÉRA BASTILLE)
EXPENSIVE

Blue Elephant ⭐ ASIAN   At this Paris branch of a chain of stylish Thai restaurants, the decor evokes the jungles of Southeast Asia, interspersed with Thai sculptures and paintings. The menu items are succulent, infused with lemon grass, curries, and the aromas that make Thai cuisine distinctive. Examples are a salad made with *pomelo,* a Thai fruit that's larger and tarter than a grapefruit, studded with shrimp and herbs; salmon soufflé served in banana leaves; chicken in green-curry sauce; and grilled fish with passion fruit. Although most of the cuisine is Thai, there's a scattering of Szechuan and Indonesian dishes as well.

43 rue de la Roquette, 11e. ☎ **01-47-00-42-00.** Reservations recommended far in advance. Main courses 85F–160F (12.90– 24.30, $12.35–$23.20); fixed-price dinner 285F (43.30, $41.35). AE, DC, MC, V. Mon–Fri noon–2:30pm and 7pm–midnight; Sun noon–2:30pm and 7–11pm. Métro: Bastille.

À Sousceyrac TRADITONAL FRENCH   Its name is derived from a village (in the Lotte region of southwestern France) that has always been associated with rich cuisine, traditional values, and literature. (*Le Déjeuner de Sousceyrac,* by Père Benoît, was a best-selling ode to French nostalgia in the 1970s.) You can capture some of that feeling at this charmer, whose decor and menu have changed very little since 1925. Even the nicotine stains in the old-fashioned paneling might have been made by previous clients such as former French president Mitterand and the current holder of the office, Jacques Chirac. Classic menu examples include slices of velvety foie gras; mousse of grouse; and roasted rabbit *à la royale,* cooked in a blend of red wine, a puréed medley of its innards, and its own blood. Dishes like this demand accompaniment by a strong red wine, of which the restaurant lists many.

26 rue Faidherbe, 11e. ☎01-43-71-65-30. Reservations recommended. Main courses 120F–165F
(18.25– 25.10, $17.40–$23.95). DC, MC, V. Mon–Fri noon–2pm; Mon–Sat 7:30–9:45pm. Closed Aug and
1 week in April. Métro: Charonnes or Faidherbe.

RIGHT BANK: 12TH ARRONDISSEMENT
(BOIS DE VINCENNES/GARE DE LYON)
EXPENSIVE

Au Trou Gascon ★★★ GASCONY   One of Paris's most acclaimed chefs,
Alain Dutournier lures fashionable palates to an unchic area. He launched his
career in southwest France's Gascony region. His parents mortgaged their inn to
allow Dutournier to open an early-1900s bistro in an unfashionable part of the
12th arrondissement. At first he got little business, but word eventually spread
of a savant in the kitchen who practiced authentic *cuisine moderne.* His wife,
Nicole, is the welcoming hostess, and the wine steward has distinguished himself for his exciting cave containing several little-known wines along with a fabulous collection of Armagnacs. Start with fresh duck foie gras cooked in a terrine
or Gascony-cured ham cut from the bone. The best main courses include fresh
tuna with braised cabbage, the best cassoulet in town, and chicken from the
Chalosse region of Landes, which Dutournier roasts and serves in its own
drippings.

40 rue Taine, 12e. ☎ 01-43-44-34-26. Reservations required far in advance. Main courses 145F–165F
(22.05– 25.10, $21.05–$23.95); fixed-price menu 200F (30.40, $29) lunch, 320F (48.65, $46.40)
dinner. AE, DC, MC, V. Mon–Fri noon–2pm; Mon–Sat 7:30–10pm. Closed Aug. Métro: Daumesnil.

MODERATE

China Club ★ CHINESE/CANTONESE   Evoking 1930s Hong Kong, this
favorite is still going strong, still laughing at upstart new Asian restaurants, and
serving some of the best Asian cuisine in Paris. It's our favorite—we always
imagine we're James Bond when we dine here. The food is mainly Cantonese,
prepared with flair. The menu is vast, with plenty of choices. Nearly everything
is good, especially the sautéed shrimp and calamari, Shanghai chicken, and red
rice sautéed with vegetables. Before dinner, you might want to enjoy a drink in
the upstairs smoking lounge. Downstairs, the Sing Song club has live music,
including something called Sino-French jazz on Fridays and Saturdays.

50 rue de Charenton, 12e. ☎ 01-43-43-82-02. Main courses 70F–190F (10.65– 28.90, $10.15–$27.55);
fixed-price dinner 160F (24.30, $23.20); fixed-price Sun dinner 115F (17.50, $16.70). AE, MC, V. Sun–Thurs
7pm–2am; Fri–Sat 7pm–3am. Closed Aug. Métro: Bastille or Ledru-Rollin.

RIGHT BANK: 16TH ARRONDISSEMENT
(TROCADÉRO/BOIS DE BOULOGNE)
VERY EXPENSIVE

Jamin ★★★ TRADITIONAL FRENCH   This is where Paris's great chef of
the 1980s, Joël Robuchon, made his mark. Now in charge is Robuchon's long-
time second in command, Benoit Guichard, who is inspired by his master but
an imaginative chef in his own right. Guichard has chosen pale-green panels and
pink banquettes as a soothing backdrop to his brief but well-chosen menu.
Lunches can be relatively simple, though each dish, like a beautifully seasoned
salmon tartare, is done to perfection. Classic technique and an homage to tradition characterize the cuisine, with offerings like John Dory with celery and
fresh ginger; pigeon sausage with foie gras, pistachios, and mâche lettuce; and
beef shoulder so tender it has obviously been braising for hours. A particularly
earthy dish celebrates various parts of the sow that are usually rejected, blending

the tail and cheeks on a platter with walnuts and fresh herbs. Finish with a *tarte tatin.*

32 rue de Longchamp, 16e. ℂ **01-45-53-00-07.** Fax 01-45-53-00-15. Reservations required far in advance. Main courses 210F–430F (31.90– 65.35, $30.45–$62.35); fixed-price menu 280F–410F (42.55– 62.30, $40.60–$59.45) lunch, 410F (62.30, $59.45) dinner. AE, DC, MC, V. Mon–Fri 12:30–2pm and 7:45–10pm. Métro: Trocadéro.

MODERATE

La Butte Chaillot ⟨★⟩ ⟨Value⟩ TRADITIONAL FRENCH   This baby bistro showcases culinary high priest Guy Savoy and draws a busy crowd from the affluent neighborhood's many corporate headquarters. Diners congregate in posh but congested areas tinted in salmon and dark yellow. Menu items change weekly (sometimes daily) and betray a strange sense of mass production not unlike that found in a luxury cruise liner's dining room. Examples are a sophisticated medley of terrines; a "low-fat" version of chunky mushroom soup; a salad of snails and herbed potatoes; succulent rack of lamb; and roasted rabbit with sage and a compote of onions, bacon, and mushrooms. A starkly contemporary stainless-steel staircase leads to extra seating in the cellar.

110 bis av. Kléber, 16e. ℂ **01-47-27-88-88.** Reservations recommended. Main courses 98F–118F (14.90– 17.95, $14.20–$17.10); fixed-price menu 150F–195F (22.80– 29.65, $21.75–$28.30). AE, DC, MC, V. Daily noon–2:30pm and 7pm–midnight. Métro: Trocadéro.

RIGHT BANK: 17TH ARRONDISSEMENT (PARC MONCEAU/PLACE CLICHY)
VERY EXPENSIVE

Guy Savoy ⟨★★★⟩ TRADITONAL FRENCH   Consistently named one of the hottest chefs in Europe, Guy Savoy serves the kind of food he likes to eat, prepared with consummate skill. We think he has a slight edge over his rival, Michel Rostang (see below), though Ducasse surpasses them both. Although the food is superb and meals comprise as many as nine courses, the portions are small; you won't necessarily be satiated at the end. The menu changes with the seasons, but may include a light cream soup of lentils and crayfish, duckling foie gras with aspic and gray salt, and red snapper with a liver-and-spinach sauce served with crusty potatoes. If you come in the right season, you may have a chance to order masterfully prepared game like mallard and venison. Savoy is fascinated with mushrooms and has been known to serve a dozen types, especially in autumn. An example includes a delectable pan-fried combination of mussels and wild mushrooms.

18 rue Troyon, 17e. ℂ **01-43-80-40-61.** Fax 01-43-80-36-22. Reservations required 1 week in advance. Main courses 335F–580F (50.90– 88.15, $48.60–$84.10); *menu dégustation* (tasting menu) 1,050F (159.60, $152.25). AE, DC, MC, V. Mon–Fri noon–2pm; Mon–Sat 7:30–10:30pm. Métro: Charles de Gaulle–Etoile or Ternes.

Michel Rostang ⟨★★★⟩ TRADITIONAL & MODERN FRENCH   Michel Rostang is one of Paris's most creative chefs, the fifth generation of a distinguished French "cooking family." His restaurant contains four dining rooms paneled in mahogany, cherry, or pearwood; some have frosted Lalique crystal panels. Changing every 2 months, the menu offers modern improvements on *cuisine bourgeoise.* Truffles are the dish of choice in midwinter, and you'll find racks of suckling lamb from the salt marshes of France's western seacoasts in spring; in game season, look for sophisticated preparations of pheasant and venison. Three year-round staples are quail eggs with a coque of sea urchins,

Kids Family-Friendly Restaurants

Crémerie-Restaurant Polidor *(see p. 127)*   This is one of the most popular restaurants on the Left Bank. It is so family-friendly, it even calls its food *cuisine familiale*. This might be the best place to introduce your child to French cuisine.

Joe Allen *(see p. 109)*   Joe Allen delivers everything from chili to chocolate-mousse pie. This place in Les Halles serves real American cuisine, including the best hamburgers in Paris.

fricassée of sole, and young Bresse chicken with crusty mushroom purée and a salad composed of the chicken's thighs.

20 rue Rennequin, 17e. ✆ **01-47-63-40-77**. Fax 01-47-63-82-75. Reservations required far in advance. Main courses 198F–385F (30.10– 58.50, $28.70–$55.85); fixed-price menu 385F–750F (58.50– 114, $55.85–$108.75) lunch, 750F–880F (114– 133.75, $108.75–$127.60) dinner. AE, DC, MC, V. Tues–Fri 12:30–2:30pm; Mon–Sat 8–10:30pm. Closed 3 weeks in Aug. Métro: Ternes.

MODERATE

La Rôtisserie d'Armaillé ★ *Value* TRADITIONAL FRENCH   The impresario behind this attractive baby bistro is Jacques Cagna, who established his role as a gastronomic star long ago from his headquarters in the Latin Quarter (see below). The chic place is popular for business lunches and dinners, also drawing residents and shoppers from the grand neighborhood. It's ringed with light wood paneling and banquettes with patterns of pink and green. At lunch, the menu includes a main course and a starter or dessert; the pricier dinners include a starter, main course, and dessert. Either way, you'll have many choices. Examples are wild-mushroom flan with red-wine sauce, a salad of sweetbreads and crayfish, and rack of lamb with parsley and sage, with apple beignets and champagne-drenched pineapple-and-mango soup for dessert. The artwork features cows, pigs, and lambs that are likely to figure among the grilled steaks and chops featured on the menu.

6 rue d'Armaillé, 17e. ✆ **01-42-27-19-20**. Reservations recommended. Fixed-price menu 75F (11.40, $10.90) lunch, 240F (36.50, $34.80) dinner. AE, DC, MC, V. Mon–Fri noon–2:30pm; Mon–Sat 7:30–11pm. Métro: Charles de Gaulle–Etoile.

RIGHT BANK: 18TH ARRONDISSEMENT (MONTMARTRE)
INEXPENSIVE

Marie-Louise TRADITIONAL FRENCH   Opened in an unfashionable neighborhood in 1957 and named after the matriarch who first owned it, this bistro offers Paris views rarely seen by visitors who gravitate toward the Seine. The decor evokes old-time France with allusions to the establishment's birth in the age of Sputnik. Opt for a table on the busy main floor or on the quieter floor above. Again and again, longtime fans order *boeuf à la ficelle* (poached beef filet tied with string and served in its natural juices). Also popular are the sautéed monkfish with pasta, *coq au vin*, chicken Marie-Louise (with rice and paprika cream sauce), and grilled sirloin steak with pepper or béarnaise sauce.

52 rue Championnet, 18e. ✆ **01-46-06-86-55**. Reservations required. Main courses 75F–110F (11.40– 16.70, $10.90–$15.95); fixed-price menu 105F–155F (15.95– 23.55, $15.25–$22.50). V. Tues–Sat noon–2pm and 7:30–10pm. Closed Aug. Métro: Simplon or Porte de Clignancourt.

LEFT BANK: 5TH ARRONDISSEMENT (LATIN QUARTER)
VERY EXPENSIVE

La Tour d'Argent ★★★ TRADITIONAL FRENCH   This penthouse restaurant, a national institution, serves up an amazing view over the Seine and the apse of Notre-Dame. Although La Tour d'Argent's reputation as the best in Paris has been eclipsed, dining here remains an unsurpassed event. A restaurant of some sort has stood on this site since at least 1582: Mme de Sévigné refers to a cafe here in her celebrated letters, and Dumas used it as a setting for one of his novels. The fame of La Tour d'Argent spread during its ownership by Frédéric Delair, who started the practice of issuing certificates to diners who ordered the house specialty—*caneton* (pressed duckling). The birds are numbered: the first was served to Edward VII in 1890, and now they're up over 1 million! Under the sharp eye of current owner Claude Terrail, the cooking is superb and the service impeccable. A good part of the menu is devoted to duck, but the kitchen does know how to prepare other dishes. We especially recommend starting with the pheasant consommé or the pike-perch quenelles André Terrail; follow with the ravioli with foie gras or the salmon and turbot *à la Sully*.

15–17 quai de la Tournelle, 5e. ✆ **01-43-54-23-31.** Fax 01-44-07-12-04. Reservations required far in advance. Main courses 270F–515F (41.05– 78.30, $39.15–$74.70); fixed-price lunch 350F (53.20, $50.75). AE, DC, MC, V. Tues–Sun noon–2:30pm and 7:30–10:30pm. Métro: St-Michel or Pont Marie.

MODERATE

Brasserie Balzar ★ TRADITIONAL FRENCH   Opened in 1898, Brasserie Balzar is battered but cheerful, with some of Paris's friendliest waiters. The menu makes almost no concessions to nouvelle cuisine; it includes pepper steak, sole meunière, sauerkraut with ham and sausage, pig's feet, and fried calf's liver served without garnish. Be warned that if you want just coffee or a drink, you probably won't get a table at meal hours. But the staff will be happy to serve you if you want to have a full dinner in the midafternoon, accustomed as they are to the odd hours of their many patrons. Former guests have included both Sartre and Camus (who often got in arguments), James Thurber, countless professors from the nearby Sorbonne, and numerous English and American journalists.

49 rue des Ecoles, 5e. ✆ **01-43-54-13-67.** Reservations strongly recommended. Main courses 75F–125F (11.40– 19, $10.90–$18.15). AE, MC, V. Daily noon–midnight. Métro: Odéon or Cluny–La Sorbonne.

Campagne et Provence PROVENÇAL   This restaurant is across from Île de la Cité. Bouquets of dried flowers garnish the pale blue walls, and the upholstery hints of Provence's blue sky. The waiters are likely to speak with the accents of southern France. The savory food includes a salad of wild Provençal mesclun garnished with Parmesan, *compôté d'oignons* (Provençal tart) flavored with onions or a combination of sardines and red mullet, and grilled fish with risotto. A tasty dessert is the anise-flavored crème brûlée.

25 quai de la Tournelle, 5e. ✆ **01-43-54-05-17.** Reservations recommended. Fixed-price menu 120F (18.25, $17.40) lunch, 195F (29.65, $28.30) 2-course dinner, 230F (34.95, $33.35) 3-course dinner. V. Tues–Fri noon–2pm; Mon–Sat 7:30–11pm. Métro: Maubert-Mutualité.

INEXPENSIVE

Coco de Mer ★ *Finds* SEYCHELLE ISLANDS   The theme of this restaurant tugs at the emotions of the thousands of Parisians who have spent their holidays on the legendary beaches of the Seychelle Islands in the Indian Ocean. It contains several dining rooms, one of which is outfitted like a beach, with a sand-covered floor, replicas of palm trees, and a scattering of conch shells. Menu items feature such exotic dishes as tartare of tuna flavored with ginger, olive oil, salt, and pepper; and smoked swordfish, served either as a carpaccio or in thin slices with mango mousse and a spicy sauce. Main courses focus on fish, including a species of delectable red snapper (*boirzoes*) that is imported from the Seychelles. Dessert might consist of a *crème de banana gratinée.*

354 bd St-Marcel, 5e. ℭ **01-47-07-06-64.** Reservations recommended. Main courses 90F–110F (13.70– 16.70, $13.05–$15.95). AE, DC, MC, V. Tues–Sat noon–3pm; Mon–Sat 7:30pm–midnight. Metro: Les Gobelins or St-Marcel.

La Petite Hostellerie ⭐ *Value* TRADITIONAL FRENCH This 1902 restaurant offers a ground-floor dining room that's usually crowded and a larger upstairs one with attractive 18th-century woodwork. People come for the cozy ambience and decor, decent French country cooking, polite service, and excellent prices. The fixed-price dinner might feature favorites like *coq au vin*, duckling *à l'orange*, and steak with mustard sauce. Start with onion soup or stuffed mussels and finish with cheese, peach Melba, or an apple tart.

35 rue de la Harpe (a side street north of bd. St-Germain, just east of bd. St-Michel), 5e. ℭ **01-43-54-47-12.** Fixed-price menu 65F–89F (9.90– 13.55, $9.45–$12.90). Tues–Sat noon–2pm; Mon–Sat 6:30–11pm. Closed 2 weeks in Feb and 3 weeks in Aug. AE, DC, MC, V. Métro: St-Michel or Cluny–La Sorbonne.

Perraudin TRADITIONAL FRENCH Everything about this place—decor, cuisine, price, and service—attempts to duplicate an early-1900s bistro. This one was built in 1870 as an outlet for coal and wine. Eventually, it evolved into the wood-paneled bistro you see today, where little has changed since Zola was buried in the Panthéon nearby. The walls look like they've been marinated in tea; the marble-topped tables, old mirrors, and Parisian vaudeville posters have been here forever. Reservations aren't made in advance: Instead, diners usually drink a glass of kir at the zinc-topped bar as they wait. (Tables turn over quickly.) The menu includes roast leg of lamb with dauphinois potatoes, *boeuf bourguignonne*, and grilled salmon with sage sauce. The onion tart, pumpkin soup, or terrine are all good appetizers.

157 rue St-Jacques, 5e. ℭ **01-46-33-15-75.** Main courses 59F (8.95, $8.55); fixed-price menu 65F (9.90, $9.45) lunch, 150F (22.80, $21.75) dinner. No credit cards. Tues–Fri noon–2:15pm; Mon–Sat 7:30–10:15pm. Closed 2 weeks in Aug. Métro: Cluny–La Sorbonne. RER: Luxembourg.

LEFT BANK: 6TH ARRONDISSEMENT (ST-GERMAIN/LUXEMBOURG)
VERY EXPENSIVE

Jacques Cagna ⭐⭐⭐ TRADITIONAL & MODERN FRENCH St-Germain knows no finer dining than at Jacques Cagna, a sophisticated restaurant in a 17th-century town house with massive timbers, burnished paneling, and 17th-century Dutch paintings. Cagna is one of the best classically trained chefs in Paris, though he's become a half-apostle to *cuisine moderne*. This is evident in his delectable carpaccio of pearly sea bream with caviar-lavished *céleric rémoulade* (celery root in mayonnaise with capers, parsley, gherkins, spring onions, chervil, chopped tarragon, and anchovy essence). Also sublime are the rack of suckling veal with ginger-and-lime sauce, Challons duckling in burgundy sauce, and fried scallops with celery and potatoes in truffle sauce. The menu is forever changing, according to the season and Cagna's inspirations, but if you're lucky it will include his line-caught sea bass served with caviar in a potato shell.

14 rue des Grands-Augustins, 6e. ℭ **01-43-26-49-39.** Fax 01-43-54-54-48. Reservations required far in advance. Main courses 180F–350F (27.35– 53.20, $26.10–$50.75); fixed-price menu 260F–490F (39.50– 74.50, $37.70–$71.05) lunch, 490F (74.50, $71.05) dinner. AE, DC, MC, V. Tues–Fri noon–2pm; Mon–Sat 7:30–10:30pm. Closed 3 weeks in Aug. Métro: St-Michel or Odéon.

Heart of the Left Bank Restaurants

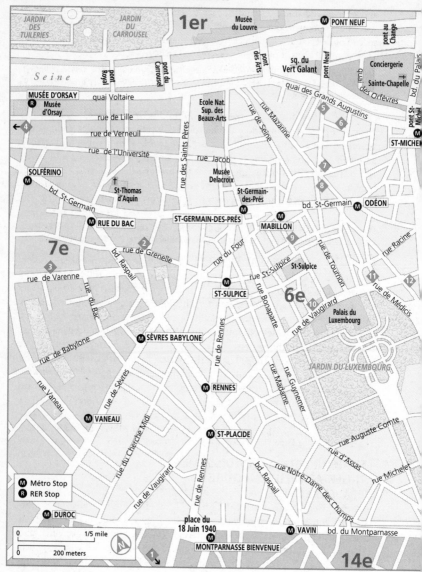

EXPENSIVE

Closerie des Lilas ⭐ TRADITIONAL FRENCH   Opened in 1847, the Closerie was a social and culinary magnet for the avant-garde. The famous people who have sat in the "Pleasure Garden of the Lilacs" are countless: Gertrude Stein and Alice B. Toklas, Ingres, Henry James, Chateaubriand, Picasso, Hemingway, Apollinaire, Lenin and Trotsky (at the chess board), Whistler, and others. Today, the crowd is likely to include a sprinkling of stars and the starstruck. The place resounds with the sometimes rather loud sounds of a jazz pianist, making the interior seem more claustrophobic than it already is. It can be tough

Alcazar Bar & Restaurant **8**
Allard **7**
Aux Charpentiers **9**
Brasserie Balzar **14**
Campagne et Provence **16**
Chez Diane **10**
Closerie des Lilas **19**
Coco de Mer **18**
Crémerie-Restaurant
    Polidor **12**
Jacques Cagna **6**
L'Arpége **3**
La Bastide Odéon **11**
La Cagouille **1**
La Petite Chaise **2**
La Petite Hostellerie **15**
La Rôtisserie d'en Face **5**
La Tour d'Argent **17**
Le Violon d'Ingres **4**
Perraudin **13**

to get a seat in what's called the *bateau* (boat) section, but you can make the wait more enjoyable by ordering the world's best champagne julep at the bar. It's also possible to have just coffee or a drink at the bar, though the food is better than ever. Try the veal kidneys with mustard, veal ribs in cider sauce, steak tartare, or pike-perch quenelles.

171 bd. du Montparnasse, 6e. © 01-40-51-34-50. Reservations recommended far in advance (for restaurant only). Restaurant main courses 120F–220F (18.25– 33.45, $17.40–$31.90); brasserie main courses 90F–180F (13.70– 27.35, $13.05–$26.10). AE, DC, V. Restaurant daily noon–3pm and 7:30–11pm. Brasserie daily 11:30am–1am. Métro: Port Royal or Vavin.

MODERATE

Alcazar Bar & Restaurant ✩ MODERN FRENCH Paris's most high-profile *brasserie de luxe* is this artfully high-tech place funded by British restaurateur Sir Terence Conran. (His chain of restaurants in London has captivated a tough audience of jaded European foodies.) It features an all-white futuristic decor in a large street-level dining room and a busy upstairs bar. The menu includes grilled entrecôte with béarnaise sauce and fried potatoes; Charolais duckling with honey and spices; sashimi and sushi with lime; monkfish with saffron in puff pastry; and a collection of shellfish and oysters from the waters of Brittany. The wines are as stylish and diverse as you'd expect, and the trendy crowd tends to wear a lot of black.

62 rue Mazarine, 6e. ℂ **01-53-10-19-99.** Reservations recommended. Main courses 90F–170F (13.70– 25.85, $13.05–$24.65); fixed-price lunch 140F–160F (21.30– 24.30, $20.30–$23.20). AE, DC, MC, V. Daily noon–3pm and 7pm–2am. Métro: Odéon.

Allard ✩ TRADITIONAL FRENCH Long missing from this guide, this old-time bistro, opened in 1931, is back and as good as ever following a long decline. It was once the leading bistro, although today the competition is too great to reclaim that reputation. The front room's zinc bar has been a haven preferred by many celebrities over the years, including Mme Pompidou and actor Alain Delon. All the old Allard specialties are still offered, with quality ingredients deftly handled by the kitchen. Try the snails, foie gras, veal stew, or frogs' legs. We head here on Mondays for the *boeuf à la mode* (beef braised in red wine with carrots) and on Wednesdays for the *coq au vin*. The *cassoulet Toulousain* (casserole of white beans and goose and other meats) remains one of the Left Bank's best. For dessert, we vote for the *tarte tatin*.

41 rue St-André-des-Arts, 6e. ℂ **01-43-26-48-23.** Reservations required. Main courses 120F–200F (18.25– 30.40, $17.40–$29); fixed-price menu 150F (22.80, $21.75) lunch, 150F–200F (22.80– 30.40, $21.75–$29) dinner. AE, DC, MC, V. Mon–Sat 12:30–2:30pm and 7:30–11:30pm. Métro: St-Michel or Odéon.

La Rôtisserie d'en Face ✩ *Value* TRADITIONAL FRENCH This is Paris's most frequented baby bistro, operated by Jacques Cagna, whose vastly expensive restaurant (see above) is across the street. The informal place features a postmodern decor with high-tech lighting and black lacquered chairs. The simply prepared food is very good and employs high-quality ingredients. It includes several types of ravioli, paté of duckling *en croûte* with foie gras, *friture d'éperlans* (tiny fried freshwater fish), and smoked Scottish salmon with spinach. Cagna's Barbary duckling in red-wine sauce is incomparable.

2 rue Christine, 6e. ℂ **01-43-26-40-98.** Reservations recommended. Fixed-price menu 145F–165F (22.05– 25.10, $21.05–$23.95) lunch, 245F (37.25, $35.55) dinner. AE, MC, V. Mon–Fri noon–2:30pm, Mon–Sat 7–11:30pm. Métro: Odéon.

INEXPENSIVE

Aux Charpentiers TRADITIONAL FRENCH This old veteran bistro, which opened more than 130 years ago, attracts those seeking the Left Bank Paris of yesteryear. It was once the rendezvous spot of the master carpenters, whose guild was next door. Nowadays, it's where young men take their dates. Though the food isn't imaginative, it's well prepared in the best tradition of *cuisine bourgeoise*—hearty but not refined. Appetizers include paté of duck and rabbit terrine. Recommended as a main course is the roast duck with olives. The *plats du jour* recall French home cooking: salt pork with lentils, *pot-au-feu*, and stuffed cabbage. The wine list has a selection of Bordeaux, including Château Gaussens.

10 rue Mabillon, 6e. ☏ **01-43-26-30-05.** Reservations required. Main courses 90F–130F (13.70– 19.75, $13.05–$18.85); fixed-price menu 120F (18.25, $17.40) lunch, 158F (24, $22.90) dinner. AE, DC, MC, V. Daily noon–3pm and 7–11:30pm. Métro: St-Germain-des-Prés.

Chez Diane TRADITIONAL & MODERN FRENCH   Come here for restaurant food at simple bistro prices. Designed to accommodate only 40 diners, this place is illuminated by Venetian glass chandeliers and paved with old-fashioned floor tiles. The deep ochres and terra cottas are redolent of Provence's landscapes and villas. Chez Diane's offerings change with the seasons and the owners' inspirations. Recently, we enjoyed sweetbreads in flap mushroom sauce, nuggets of wild boar in honey sauce, minced salmon terrine with green peppercorns, and a light-textured modern adaptation of *hachis Parmentier*, a meat loaf lightened with parsley, chopped onions, and herbs. To finish, we recommend the *charlotte au fromage blanc*, a cheesecake with blueberry sauce.

25 rue Servandoni, 6e. ☏ **01-46-33-12-06.** Reservations recommended for groups of four or more. Main courses 100F–140F (15.20– 21.30, $14.50–$20.30); fixed-price menu 160F (24.30, $23.20). V. Mon–Fri noon–2pm; Mon–Sat 8–11:30pm. Métro: St-Sulpice.

Crémerie-Restaurant Polidor ★ (Kids) TRADITIONAL FRENCH   Crémerie Polidor is the most traditional bistro in the Odéon area, serving *cuisine familiale.* Its name dates from the early 1900s, when it specialized in frosted cream desserts, but the restaurant itself can trace its history back to 1845. The Crémerie was André Gide's favorite, and Joyce, Hemingway, Valéry, Artaud, and Kerouac also dined here. The place is still frequented by students and artists, who head for the rear. Peer beyond the lace curtains and brass hat racks to see drawers where repeat customers lock up their cloth napkins. Overworked but smiling waitresses serve the 19th-century cuisine. Try the pumpkin soup followed by *boeuf bourguignonne,* Basque-style chicken, or *blanquette de veau.* For dessert, get a chocolate, raspberry, or lemon tart—the best in all Paris.

41 rue Monsieur-le-Prince, 6e. ☏ **01-43-26-95-34.** Main courses 40F–78F (6.10– 11.85, $5.80–$11.30); fixed-price menu (Mon–Fri) 55F (8.35, $8) lunch, 110F (16.70, $15.95) dinner. No credit cards. Daily noon–2:30pm; Mon–Sat 7pm–12:30am; Sun 7–11pm. Métro: Odéon.

La Bastide Odéon ★ (Finds) PROVENÇAL   The sunny climes of Provence come through in the pale yellow walls, heavy oaken tables, and artful bouquets of wheat and dried roses. Chef Gilles Ajuelos prepares a market-based cuisine. His simplest first courses are the most satisfying, like sardines and seared sweet peppers with olive oil and pine nuts, grilled eggplant with herbs and oil, and eggplant-stuffed roasted rabbit with olive toast and balsamic vinegar. Main courses include wild duckling with pepper sauce and exotica like lamb's feet and giblets. A winning dessert is the almond pie with prune and Armagnac ice cream.

7 rue Corneille, 6e. ☏ **01-43-26-03-65.** Reservations recommended. Fixed-price menu 154F–194F (23.40– 29.54, $22.35–$28.15). MC, V. Tues–Sat 12:30–2pm and 7:30–11pm. Métro: Odéon. RER: Luxembourg.

LEFT BANK: 7TH ARRONDISSEMENT (EIFFEL TOWER/MUSÉE D'ORSAY)
VERY EXPENSIVE

L'Arpège ★★★ MODERN FRENCH   L'Arpège is best known for Alain Passard's adventurous specialties—no restaurant in the 7th serves better food.

Across from the Musée Rodin in a residential neighborhood, L'Arpège has claimed the site of what for years was the world-famous L'Archestrate, where Passard worked in the kitchens. Amid a modern decor of etched glass, burnished steel, monochromatic oil paintings, and pearwood paneling, you can enjoy innovative specialties like Breton lobster in sweet-and-sour rosemary sauce, scallops with cauliflower and lime-flavored grape sauce, and pan-fried duck with juniper and lime sauce. The signature dessert is a candied tomato stuffed with 12 kinds of dried and fresh fruit, served with anise-flavored ice cream.

84 rue de Varenne, 7e. ℂ **01-47-05-09-06.** Fax. 01-44-18-98-39. Reservations required far in advance. Main courses 350F–820F (53.20– 124.65, $50.75–$118.90); fixed-price menu 590F (89.70, $85.55) lunch, 1,400F (212.80, $203) *menu dégustation* (tasting menu). AE, DC, MC, V. Mon–Fri 12:30–2pm and 8–10pm. Métro: Varenne.

EXPENSIVE

Le Violon d'Ingres ★★★ TRADITIONAL & MODERN FRENCH   This restaurant is Paris's pièce de résistance. Chef/owner Christian Constant is "the new Robuchon." Those fortunate enough to dine in Violon's atmosphere of rose-colored wood, soft cream walls, and elegant chintz fabrics rave about the cleverly artistic dishes. They range from a starter of pan-fried foie gras with gingerbread and spinach salad to more elegant main courses like lobster ravioli with crushed vine-ripened tomatoes; roasted veal in a light and creamy milk sauce served with tender spring vegetables; and even a selection from the rotisserie, like spit-roasted leg of lamb rubbed with fresh garlic and thyme. A well-chosen selection of wine is offered. The service is charming and discreet.

135 rue St-Dominique, 7e. ℂ **01-45-55-15-05.** Fax 01-45-55-48-42. Reservations required at least 3–4 days in advance. Main courses 190F–230F (28.90– 34.95, $27.55–$33.35); *menu dégustation* (tasting menu) 590F (89.70, $85.55). AE, MC, V. Mon–Sat 7–11pm. Métro: Ecole Militaire.

MODERATE

La Petite Chaise TRADITIONAL FRENCH   This is Paris's oldest restaurant, opened as an inn in 1680 by the baron de la Chaise at the edge of what was a hunting preserve. (According to lore, the baron used the upstairs bedrooms for afternoon dalliances, between fox and pheasant hunts.) Very Parisian, the "Little Chair" invites you into a world of cramped but attractive tables, old wood paneling, and ornate wall sconces. A vigorous chef has brought renewed taste and flavor to this longtime favorite, and the four-course set menu offers a large choice of dishes in each category. Examples are a salad with duck breast strips on a bed of fresh lettuce, seafood-and-scallop ragout with saffron, and poached fish with steamed vegetables served in a sauce of fish and vegetable stock and cream.

36–38 rue de Grenelle, 7e. ℂ **01-42-22-13-35.** Reservations recommended. Fixed-price menu 160F–195F (24.30– 29.65, $23.20–$28.30). AE, V. Daily noon–2pm and 7–11pm. Métro: Sèvres-Babylone or Rue du Bac.

LEFT BANK: 14TH ARRONDISSMENT (GARE MONTPARNASSE)
MODERATE

La Cagouille ★ *Finds* FRENCH/SEAFOOD   Don't expect to find meat at this temple of seafood—owner Gérard Allamandou refuses to feature it on his menu. Everything about La Cagouille is a testimonial to a modern version of the culinary arts of La Charente, the flat sandy district hugging the Atlantic south of Bordeaux. In a trio of simple oak-sheathed dining rooms with marble-topped tables, you'll sample seafood prepared as naturally as possible, with no fancy sauces or elaborate cooking techniques. Allamandou's preferred fish is red mullet, which might appear sautéed in a bland oil or baked in rock salt. The name of the place derives from the regional symbol of La Charente: the sea snail, whose preparation here is elevated to a fine culinary art. Look for a vast assemblage of all-French, mostly white wines and at least 150 cognacs. In the summer, there's a partially concealed terrace for outside dining.

10–12 place Constantine-Brancusi, 14e. ⓒ 01-43-22-09-01. Reservations recommended. Main courses 120F–180F (18.25– 27.35, $17.40–$26.10); fixed-price menu 150F–250F (22.80– 38, $21.75–$36.25). AE, V. Daily noon–2pm and 5:30–10:30pm. Métro: Gaité.

L'Assiette SOUTHWESTERN FRENCH   Everything about this place appeals to a nostalgic crowd seeking down-to-earth prices and flavorful food. You'll recognize it by the bordeaux-colored facade and plants in the windows. The place was a *charcuterie* (pork butcher's shop) in the 1930s, and maintains some of its old accessories. Mitterrand used to drop in with his cronies for oysters, crayfish, sea urchins, and clams. The food is inspired by Paris's long tradition of bistro cuisine, with a few twists. Examples are chanterelle mushroom salad; *rillettes* (a roughly textured paté) of mackerel; roasted guinea fowl; and homemade desserts, including a crumbly version of apple cake with fresh North African figs. Particularly delicious is a *petit salé* (stew with vegetables) of duckling with wine from the Poitou region of west-central France.

181 rue du Château, 14e. ⓒ 01-43-22-64-86. Reservations recommended. Main courses 150F–200F (22.80– 30.40, $21.75–$29); fixed-price menu 200F (30.40, $29). AE, MC, V. Wed–Sun noon–2:30pm and 8–10:30pm. Closed Aug. Métro: Gaité.

5 The Top Cafes

To a Parisian, a cafe is a club, tavern, and snack bar. Whatever your pleasure—reading a newspaper, meeting a lover or a friend, doing your homework, writing your memoirs, nibbling at a hard-boiled egg, or drinking yourself into oblivion—you can do it all at a French cafe. (For the top wine bars in Paris, see "Paris After Dark," in chapter 5.)

Brasserie Lipp, 151 bd. St-Germain, 6e (ⓒ **01-45-48-53-91;** Métro: St-Germain-des-Prés), has an upstairs dining room, but it's more fashionable to sit in the back room. For breakfast, order the traditional black coffee and croissants. At lunch or dinner, the house specialty is pork and *choucroute* (sauerkraut)—the best in Paris. Open daily from 9am to 2am, although restaurant service is available only from 11am to 1am—it's fashionable to arrive late.

Across from the Centre Pompidou, the avant-garde **Café Beaubourg,** 100 rue St-Martin, 4e (ⓒ **01-48-87-63-96;** Métro: Rambuteau or Hôtel-de-Ville), boasts soaring concrete columns and a minimalist decor by the architect Christian de Portzamparc. In summer, tables are set on the sprawling terrace, providing a panoramic view of the neighborhood's goings-on. Open Sunday through Thursday from 8am to 1am and Friday and Saturday from 8am to 2am.

Jean-Paul Sartre came to **Café de Flore,** 172 bd. St-Germain, 6e (ⓒ **01-45-48-55-26;** Métro: St-Germain-des-Prés), during the war. It's said he wrote his trilogy, *Les Chemins de la Liberté* (The Roads to Freedom) here. The cafe is still going strong, though the celebrities have moved on. Open daily from 7am to 2am.

Café de la Paix, place de l'Opéra, 9e (ⓒ 01-40-07-30-20; Métro: Opéra), has been a popular American enclave since U.S. troops marched through Paris in their victory parade after World War II. No one can remember de Gaulle dining here, but a messenger arrived and ordered a "tinned" ham for the general's first supper when he returned after the Liberation. Open daily from noon to midnight.

Café Marly, 93 rue de Rivoli, 1er (② **01-49-26-06-60;** Métro: Palais-Royal-Musée-du-Louvre), occupies the Louvre's historic cour Napoléon. It's accessible only from a point close to the pyramid and has become a favorite refuge for Parisians escaping the roar of traffic. Anyone is welcome to sit for just a *café au lait* whenever meals aren't being served (from 11am to 1am). Menu items, served in three Louis-Philippe–style rooms, include club sandwiches, oysters and shellfish, steak *au poivre* (pepper steak), and upscale bistro food. In summer, outdoor tables overlook the majestic courtyard. Open daily from 8am to 2am.

At **La Coupole,** 102 bd. Montparnasse, 14e (② **01-43-20-14-20;** Métro: Vavin), the crowd ranges from artists' models to young men dressed like Rasputin. Perhaps order a coffee or cognac VSOP at one of the sidewalk tables. The dining room looks like a railway station and serves food that is sometimes good, sometimes indifferent. But people don't really come here for the cuisine; it's more on the see-and-be-seen circuit. Try the sole meunière, *carré d'agneau* (lamb), or cassoulet. A buffet breakfast is served Monday through Friday from 7:30 to 10:30am. Open daily from 7:30am to 2am.

The legendary **Deux Magots,** 6 place St-Germain-des-Prés, 6e (② **01-45-48-55-25;** Métro: St-Germain-des-Prés), is still the hangout for sophisticated neighborhood residents and a favorite for visitors in summer. Inside are two large Asian statues that give the cafe its name. Open daily from 7:30am to 1:30am.

Fouquet's, 99 av. des Champs-Elysées, 8e (② **01-47-23-50-00;** Métro: George-V), is the premier cafe on the Champs-Elysées. The outside tables are separated from the sidewalk by a barricade of potted flowers. Inside is an elegant grill room with leather banquettes and rattan furniture, private rooms, and a restaurant. The cafe and grill room are open daily from 9am to 2am; the restaurant is open daily from noon to 3pm and 7pm to 1am.

5

Exploring Paris

Paris is one of those cities where the street life—shopping, strolling, and hanging out—should claim as much time as sightseeing in churches and museums. A gourmet picnic in the Bois de Boulogne, a sunrise pilgrimage to the Seine, an afternoon at the flea market—Paris bewitches you with these experiences. For all the Louvre's beauty, you'll probably remember the Latin Quarter's crooked alleyways better than the 370th oil painting of your visit.

The best way to discover Paris is on foot—it won't cost you a franc to explore the streets of the City of Light. Walk along the avenue des Champs-Elysées, tour the quays of the Seine, wander the Île de la Cité and Île St-Louis, browse the countless shops and stalls, stroll through the squares and parks. If you're an early riser, a stroll at dawn can be enthralling as you see the city come to life: shop fronts are washed clean, cafes begin serving hot coffee and croissants, and vegetable and fruit vendors start setting up their stalls and arranging their produce.

Paris is also a shopper's city—with everything from tony boutiques to colorful street markets. We've covered the best of the best in this chapter.

For sheer variety, there's nothing like its nightlife. Nowhere else will you find such nightclubs, bars, dance clubs, cabarets, jazz dives, music halls, and honky-tonks. (For Paris's cafe scene, see chapter 4.)

ORGANIZED TOURS

Before plunging into sightseeing on your own, you might like to take the most popular get-acquainted tour in Paris: **Cityrama,** 147–149 rue St-Honoré, 1er (② **01-44-55-61-00;** Métro: Palais-Royal-Musée-du-Louvre). On a double-decker bus with enough windows for Versailles, you're taken on a 2-hour ride through the city. Because you don't go inside any attractions, you must settle for a look at the outside of such places as Notre-Dame and the Eiffel Tower, but it'll help you get a feel for the city if this is your first visit. Individual earphones are distributed with commentary in 10 languages. Tours depart daily at 9:30am, 10:30am, 1:30pm, and 2:30pm. There are additional tours every Saturday and Sunday at 11:30am, and between March and October, there are two tours every day at 3:30 and 4:30pm. A 2-hour orientation tour is 150F (22.80, $21.75).

A morning tour with interior visits to Notre-Dame and the Louvre costs 295F (44.85, $42.78). Half-day tours to Versailles at 330F (50.15, $47.85) and Chartres at 275F (41.80, $39.90) represent good value and remove some of the hassle associated with visiting those monuments. A joint ticket that includes both Versailles and Chartres costs 500F (76, $72.50). Another offering, a tour of the nighttime illuminations, leaves daily at 10pm in summer or at 7pm in winter and costs 150F (22.80, $21.75); it tends to be tame and touristy.

The same entity that maintains Paris's network of Métros and buses, **RATP** (② **08-36-68-41-14**), operates the **Balabus,** a fleet of orange-and-white big-windowed motorcoaches. The only drawback is their limited operating hours:

Paris Attractions

Opéra Bastille **32**
Opéra Garnier **24**
Palais de l'Elysée **14**
Palais du Luxembourg **54**
Palais Royal **21**
Panthéon **51**
Parc Monceau **12**
Place de la Bastille **31**

Place de la Concorde **15**
Place de l'Alma **8**
Place des Vosges **34**
Place Vendôme **23**
Sainte-Chapelle **44**
Sewers of Paris (entrance) **8**
Tour Montparnasse **2**
University of Paris (Sorbonne) **50**

Information (i)

PARIS

Seine

Area of Detail

Sundays only, from noon to 9pm (and the afternoons of some national holidays). Itineraries run in both directions between Gare de Lyon and the Grand Arche de La Défense. Three Métro tickets will carry you along the entire route. You'll recognize the bus, and the route it follows, by the *Bb* symbol emblazoned across its side and on signs posted beside the route it follows.

A boat tour on the Seine provides sweeping vistas of the riverbanks and some of the best views of Notre-Dame. Many of the boats have open sun decks, bars, and restaurants. **Bateaux-Mouche** (© **01-42-25-96-10** for reservations, or 01-40-76-99-99 for schedules; Métro: Alma-Marceau) cruises depart from the Right Bank of the Seine, adjacent to pont de l'Alma, and last about 75 minutes. Tours leave daily at 20- to 30-minute intervals from 10am to 11:30pm between May and October. Between November and April, there are at least nine departures every day between 11am and 9pm, with a schedule that changes frequently according to demand and the weather. Fares are 45F (6.85, $6.55) for adults and 20F (3.04, $2.90) for children 5 to 15. Dinner cruises depart daily at 8:30pm, last 3 hours, and cost between 500F to 700F (76 to 106.40, $72.50 to $101.50), depending on which of the fixed-price menus you order. Aboard dinner cruises, jackets and ties are required for men.

Batobus (© **01-44-11-33-44**) are 150-passenger ferries with big windows. Daily between April and September, they operate east-west along the Seine, stopping at six points en route. Departures occur at 25-minute intervals between 10am and 7pm. (The boats don't run between October and March.) Stops include the Eiffel Tower, Musée d'Orsay, points on both the Left Bank and the Right Bank opposite the Louvre, Notre-Dame, and the Hôtel de Ville. These ferries weren't conceived as sightseeing vehicles, and unlike on the *bateaux-mouches,* there's no recorded commentary. Fares between any two stops are 20F (3.04, $2.90) for the first segment, and 10F (1.52, $1.45) for each segment after that, though frankly we consider the Batobus an expensive way to cross a river that's already crisscrossed with a network of bridges. More appealing is to pay 65F (9.90, $9.45) per adult or 35F (5.30, $5.10) per child 11 and under (children under 3 ride free) for a day ticket that allows you to enter and exit from the boats as many times as you like (and ride as long as you like) during any single day. The views are panoramic, and the boat allows you to move from one history-rich neighborhood to another bypassing the Métro and street traffic.

SUGGESTED ITINERARIES

These itineraries are obviously intended for the first-time visitor, but even those making their 30th trip to Paris will want to revisit attractions like the Louvre, where you could spend every day of your life and always see something new. Use these tips as a guide, not a bible. Paris rewards travelers with guts and independence of mind, those who will pull open the doors to a chapel or an antiquarian's shop not because they're listed on a souvenir map but because they look intrinsically interesting. In Paris, they usually are.

If You Have 1 Day

Get up early and begin walking the streets in the neighborhood of your hotel. Find a little cafe, where you can enjoy a Parisian breakfast of coffee and croissants. If you're a museum and monument junkie, the two most popular museums are the **Musée du Louvre** and the **Musée d'Orsay.** The three most enduring monuments are the Eiffel Tower, the Arc de Triomphe, and Notre-Dame (which you can see later in the day, since it's not imperative that you go inside). If it's a toss-up between the Louvre and the d'Orsay, we'd make it the Louvre because it holds a greater variety of works. If you feel the need to choose between monuments, we'd opt for the **Eiffel Tower** for the city view. If you feel your day is too short to visit museums or wait in lines for the tower, we suggest you spend your time strolling the streets. The most impressive neighborhood is **Île St-Louis.** After exploring this island and its mansions, wander through such Left Bank districts as **St-Germain-des-Prés** or around **place St-Michel,** the heart of the student quarter. As the sun sets, head for **Notre-Dame,** a good place to watch shadows fall over Paris as the lights come on. Afterward, walk the banks of the **Seine,** where vendors sell books and souvenir prints. Promise yourself a return visit and have dinner in a Left Bank bistro.

If You Have 2 Days

Take in the glories of the Right Bank. Begin at the **Arc de Triomphe** and stroll down the **Champs-Elysées,** the main boulevard of Paris, until you reach the Egyptian obelisk at **place de la Concorde.** This is one of the most famous walks in the world. Place de la Concorde affords terrific views of the Madeleine, the Palais-Bourbon, the Arc de Triomphe, and the Louvre. Take a break in the **Jardin des Tuileries,** directly west and adjacent to the Louvre. Give your feet a rest at lunch in a Right Bank bistro. Then for a total contrast, go for a walk in the Marais. Our favorite stroll is along the rue des Rosiers, a street

that's the heart of the **Jewish community.** And don't miss **place des Vosges.** After a rest, select one of the restaurants in **Montparnasse,** following in Hemingway's footsteps. This area is livelier at night.

If You Have 3 Days

Many visitors will target the restored **Centre Pompidou** as one of their major sightseeing goals. Others wander the sculpture garden of the **Musée National Auguste-Rodin.** Or if you prefer the **Musée Picasso,** you can use part of the morning to explore a few art galleries of the Marais. Following in the trail of Descartes and Mme de Sévigné, select a cafe here for lunch. Reserve the afternoon for **Île de la Cité,** where you'll get to see not only Notre-Dame again but also the **Conciergerie,** where Marie Antoinette and others were held before they were beheaded. See the stunning stained glass of **Ste-Chapelle** in the Palais de Justice. Even if you've been saving money up until now, our final suggestion is that you go all out for one grand French meal at a fabulous restaurant. It's a memory you'll treasure long after you've recovered from paying the tab. After dinner, sample Paris's nightlife—the dancers at the **Lido** or the campy **Folies-Bergère** or a Left Bank jazz club. If you'd like to sit and have a drink, Paris has some of the most elegant hotel bars in the world at such places as the **Crillon** and **Plaza Athenée.**

1 The Top Attractions

Eiffel Tower ✹✹✹   This may be the single most recognizable structure in the world—it's the symbol of Paris. Weighing 7,000 tons but exerting about the same pressure on the ground as an average-size person sitting in a chair, the tower was not meant to be permanent. It was built for the Universal Exhibition of 1889 by Gustave-Alexandre Eiffel, the engineer whose fame rested mainly on his iron bridges. (He also designed the framework for the Statue of Liberty.)

The tower, including its 55-foot TV antenna, is 1,056 feet tall. On a clear day you can see it from 40 miles away. Its open-framework construction ushered in

---

Tips **A Timesaving Tip**

Museums require that you check shopping bags and book bags, and some-times these lines can be longer than the ticket lines. If you value your time, leave these bags behind or do your shopping afterward. Ask if a museum has more than one coat line; if so, avoid the main one and go to the less crowded ones.

---

the almost-unlimited possibilities of steel construction, paving the way for the 20th century's skyscrapers. Skeptics said it couldn't be built, and Eiffel actually wanted to make it soar higher. For years it remained the tallest man-made struc-ture on earth, until such skyscrapers as the Empire State Building came along. The advent of wireless communication in the early 1890s preserved the tower from destruction.

You can visit the tower in three stages: Taking the elevator to the first land-ing, you'll have a view over the rooftops of Paris. Here you'll find a cinema museum, restaurants, and a bar open year-round. The second landing provides a panoramic look at the city (on this level is Le Jules Verne restaurant, a great place for lunch or dinner). The third landing offers the best view, allowing you to identify monuments and buildings. On the ground level, in the eastern and western pillars, you can visit the 1899 elevator machinery when the tower is open.

To get to **Le Jules Verne** (© 01-45-55-61-44), you take a private south foun-dation elevator. You can enjoy an aperitif in the piano bar, then take a seat at one of the dining room's tables, all of which provide an inspiring view. The menu changes seasonally, offering fish and meat dishes that range from filet of turbot with seaweed and buttered sea urchins to veal chops with truffled vegetables. Reservations are recommended.

Insider tip: The least expensive way to see the tower is to walk up the first two floors at a cost of 18F (2.75, $2.60). That way, you also avoid the long lines waiting for the elevator.

Champ de Mars, 7e. © 01-44-11-23-23. www.tour-eiffel.fr. Admission to first landing 24F (3.65, $3.48), second landing 45F (6.85, $6.53), third landing 62F (9.40, $9). Stairs to second floor 18F (2.75, $2.61). Sept–May daily 9:30am–11pm; June–Aug daily 9am–midnight. Fall and winter, stairs open only to 6:30pm. Métro: Trocadéro, Ecole Militaire, or Bir-Hakeim. RER: Champ de Mars–Tour Eiffel.

Musée du Louvre ★★★   The Louvre is the world's largest palace and one of the world's largest and greatest museums. It's more beautiful than ever since the facade has been thoroughly cleaned. The $1.2-billion Grand Louvre Project, a 15-year-long project, is officially complete, but refurbishment of individual gal-leries and paintings continues. For up-to-the-minute data on what is open or about to open, you can check out the Louvre's website at **www.louvre.fr**.

The Louvre's collection is staggering. You'll have to resign yourself to missing certain masterpieces because you simply can't see everything. People on one of those "Paris-in-a-day" tours try to break track records to glimpse the two famous ladies: the *Mona Lisa* and the *Venus de Milo.* Those with an extra 5 minutes go in pursuit of *Winged Victory,* that headless statue discovered at Samothrace and dating from about 200 B.C.

To enter the Louvre, you pass through the 71-foot **I. M. Pei glass pyra-mid** in the courtyard. Commissioned by Mitterrand and completed in 1989, it received mixed reviews. The pyramid allows sunlight to shine on an

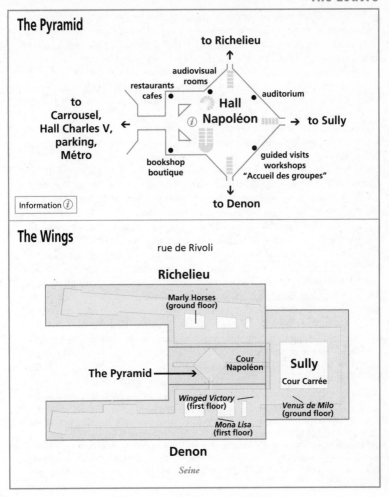

The Pyramid

to Richelieu

audiovisual rooms

restaurants cafes

to Carrousel, Hall Charles V, parking, Métro

auditorium

Hall Napoléon

to Sully

bookshop boutique

guided visits workshops "Accueil des groupes"

to Denon

Information ⓘ

The Wings

rue de Rivoli

Richelieu

Marly Horses (ground floor)

The Pyramid →

Cour Napoléon

Sully

Cour Carrée

Winged Victory (first floor)

Venus de Milo (ground floor)

Mona Lisa (first floor)

Denon

Seine

underground reception area and shelters shops and restaurants beneath the Jardin du Carrousel. The renovation also increases the Louvre's gallery space by 80% and provides underground garages for the tour buses that used to jam rue de Rivoli.

Tips on tickets: If you don't want to wait in line for tickets at the entrance of the pyramid or use the new automatic ticket machines, you can order tickets over the phone (see below) with a credit card. You can also order advance tickets (and take a virtual tour of the museum from your desk) at the website. Tickets can be mailed to you in the U.S., or you can pick them up at any FNAC location in Paris.

Those with little time should go on a **guided tour** (in English), which lasts about 1½ hours. These start under the pyramid at the station marked ACCEIL DES GROUPES.

The collections are divided into seven departments: Asian antiquities; Egyptian antiquities; Greek, Etruscan, and Roman antiquities; sculpture; paintings; prints and drawings; and objets d'art. In 1997, President Jacques Chirac inaugurated 107,000 square feet of gallery space, most of it in the eastern Sully wing, including a new presentation of the Louvre's collection of Egyptian antiquities. This innovation means 60% more space for the world of the pharaohs, a culture that has fascinated the French since Napoléon's occupation of Egypt in 1798.

Other new areas include freshly restored and newly occupied rooms of Greek, Etruscan, and Roman antiquities. The Grand Galerie, a 600-foot hall opening onto the Seine, is dedicated to mostly Italian paintings from the 1400s to the 1700s, including works by Raphael and Leonardo da Vinci.

The **Richelieu Wing** houses the museum's collection of northern European and French paintings, decorative arts, French sculpture, Oriental antiquities (a rich collection of Islamic art), and the grand salons of Napoléon III. Originally constructed from 1852 to 1857, this wing has been virtually rebuilt. In its 165 rooms, plus three covered courtyards, some 12,000 works of art are displayed. Of the Greek and Roman antiquities, the most notable (aside from *Venus* and *Winged Victory*) are fragments of the Parthenon's frieze.

Of course we love Mona and Venus, but our eternal passion burns for Jacques-Louis David's *Portrait of Madame Récamier,* depicting Napoléon's opponent at age 23; on her comfortable sofa, she reclines in the style of classical antiquity. Other favorites of ours are *Ship of Fools,* by Hieronymous Bosch, tucked in the Flemish galleries; *Four Seasons,* by Nicolas Poussin, the canonical work of French classicism; Eugène Delacroix's *Liberty Leading the People,* perhaps the ultimate endorsement of revolution (Louis-Philippe purchased the painting and hid it during his reign); and Paolo Veronese's gigantic *Wedding Feast at Cana,* showing (if nothing else) how stunning colors can be when applied by a master.

When you tire of strolling the galleries, you might like a pick-me-up at the Richelieu Wing's **Café Richelieu** or **Café Marly,** 93 rue de Rivoli, 1er (⟨ℂ⟩ **01-49-26-06-60**). Boasting Napoléon III opulence, the Marly offers a perfect oasis. Try a cafe crème, a club sandwich, a pastry, or something from the bistro menu.

34–36 quai du Louvre, 1er. Main entrance in the glass pyramid, Cour Napoléon. ⟨ℂ⟩ **01-40-20-53-17,** or 01-40-20-51-51 for recorded message, or 08-03-80-88-03 for advance credit card sales. www.louvre.fr. Admission 46F (7.04, $6.67) before 3pm, 30F (4.55, $4.35) after 3pm and on Sun, free for children 17 and under, free first Sun of every month. Mon and Wed 9am–9:45pm (Mon short tour only); Thurs–Sun 9am–6pm. (Parts of the museum begin to close at 5:30pm.) 1½-hour English-language tours leave Mon and Wed–Sat at various times for 17F (2.63, $2.47); children 12 and under free with museum ticket. Métro: Palais Royal–Musée du Louvre.

Musée d'Orsay ⟨★★★⟩ The neoclassical Gare d'Orsay train station has been transformed into one of the world's great museums. It contains an important collection devoted to the pivotal years from 1848 to 1914. Across the Seine from the Louvre and the Tuileries, it is a repository of works by the Impressionists as well as the Symbolists, Pointillists, Realists, and late Romantics. Artists represented include van Gogh, Manet, Monet, Degas, and Renoir. It houses thousands of sculptures and paintings across 80 galleries, plus Belle-Époque furniture, photographs, objets d'art, architectural models, and a cinema.

One of Renoir's most joyous paintings is here: *Moulin de la Galette* (1876). Another celebrated work is by the American James McNeill Whistler—*Arrangement in Gray and Black: Portrait of the Painter's Mother.* The most famous piece in the museum is Manet's 1863 *Déjeuner sur l'herbe* (*Picnic on the Grass*), which created a scandal when it was first exhibited; it depicts a nude woman nonchalantly picnicking with two fully clothed men in a forest. Two years later, his *Olympia,* lounging on her bed wearing nothing but a flower in her hair and high-heeled shoes, met the same response.

1 rue de Bellechasse or 62 rue de Lille, 7e. ℂ **01-40-49-48-14.** www.musee-orsay.fr. Admission 40F (6.13, $5.80) adults, 30F (4.55, $4.35) ages 18–24 and seniors, free for children 17 and under. Tues–Wed and Fri–Sat 10am–6pm; Thurs 10am–9:45pm (June 20–Sept 20 from 9am). Sun 9am–6pm. Métro: Solférino. RER: Musée d'Orsay.

Musée National Auguste Rodin ★★   This beautiful house and its gardens are a repository of the work of Auguste Rodin (1840 to 1917), the undisputed master of French 19th-century sculpture (though his works were first thought obscene). After his death, the government purchased Rodin's gray-stone 18th-century mansion, where he had his studio from 1910 until 1917. The rose gardens were restored to their original splendor, making a perfect setting for Rodin's most memorable works.

In the courtyard are three world-famous creations: *The Gates of Hell, The Thinker,* and *The Burghers of Calais.* Rodin's first major public commission, *The Burghers* commemorated the heroism of six burghers who in 1347 offered themselves as hostages to Edward III in return for his ending the siege of their port. *The Thinker,* in Rodin's own words, "thinks with every muscle of his arms, back, and legs, with his clenched fist and gripping toes." Inside the mansion, the sculptures, plaster casts, reproductions, originals, and sketches reveal the freshness and vitality of this remarkable man. Many works appear to be emerging from marble into life. Everybody is drawn to *The Kiss.* Upstairs are two versions of the celebrated and condemned nude of Balzac, his bulky torso rising from a tree trunk. Included are many versions of his *Monument to Balzac* (a large one stands in the garden), Rodin's last major work. Generally overlooked is a room devoted to Camille Claudel, Rodin's mistress and a towering artist in her own right. His pupil, model, and lover, she created such works as *Maturity, Clotho,* and (donated in 1995) the *Waltz* and the *Gossips.*

In the Hôtel Biron, 77 rue de Varenne, 7e. ℂ **01-44-18-61-10.** www.musee-rodin.fr. Admission 28F (4.25, $4.05) adults, 18F (2.75, $2.60) ages 18–25, free for children 17 and under. Apr–Sept Tues–Sun 9:30am–5:45pm; Oct–Mar Tues–Sun 9:30am–4:45pm. Métro: Varenne.

Musée Picasso ★★★   When it opened in the beautifully restored Hôtel Salé in the Marais, the press hailed it as a "museum for Picasso's Picassos," meaning those he chose not to sell. Superior to a similar museum in Barcelona, it offers an unparalleled view of the artist's long and varied career and different periods, including his fabled gaunt blue figures and harlequins. This museum remains one of Paris's most popular attractions. The world's greatest Picasso collection, acquired by the state in lieu of $50 million in inheritance taxes, consists of 203 paintings, 158 sculptures, 16 collages, 19 bas-reliefs, 88 ceramics, and more than 1,500 sketches and 1,600 engravings, plus 30 notebooks. These works span some 75 years of Picasso's life and changing styles.

The range of paintings includes a remarkable 1901 self-portrait and embraces such masterpieces as *Le Baiser* (*The Kiss*). Another masterpiece is *Reclining Nude and the Man with a Guitar.* It's easy to stroll through seeking your favorite work—ours is the delightfully wicked *Jeune garçon à la langouste* (*Young Man*

Finds **Looking for a Quick Escape?**

The little alley behind the Musée Rodin winds its way down to a pond with fountains and flower beds and even sandpits for children. It's one of the most idyllic hidden spots in Paris.

with a Lobster). The museum also owns several studies for *Les Demoiselles d'Avignon,* the painting that launched Cubism in 1907.

In the Hôtel Salé, 5 rue de Thorigny, 3e. ✆ **01-42-71-25-21.** www.paris.org/Musees/Picasso. Admission 30F (4.55, $4.35) adults, 20F (3.04, $2.90) ages 18–25 and seniors, free for children 18 and under. Apr–Sept Wed–Mon 9:30am–6pm; Oct–Mar Wed–Mon 9:30am–5:30pm. Métro: St-Paul, Filles du Calvaire, or Chemin Vert.

Notre-Dame ★★★   This cathedral is one of the world's most famous houses of worship. For 6 centuries, it has stood as a fabled Gothic masterpiece of the Middle Ages. Although many disagree, we feel that Notre-Dame is more interesting outside than in. You'll have to walk around the entire structure to appreciate this "vast symphony of stone" with its classic flying buttresses. Better yet, cross the bridge to the Left Bank and view it from the quay.

From square parvis (the courtyard in front of the church), you can view the trio of 13th-century sculpted portals. On the left, the Portal of the Virgin depicts the signs of the zodiac and the Virgin's coronation. The central Portal of the Last Judgment is divided into three levels: the first shows Vices and Virtues; the second, Christ and his Apostles; and the third, Christ in triumph after the Resurrection. On the right is the Portal of Ste- Anne, depicting such scenes as the Virgin enthroned with Child. It's Notre-Dame's most perfect piece of sculpture. Over the central portal is a remarkable rose window, 31 feet in diameter, forming a showcase for a statue of the Virgin and Child. Equally interesting is the Cloister Portal (around on the left), with its dour-faced 13th-century Virgin, a unique survivor of the many that originally adorned the facade. (Unfortunately, the Child she's holding is decapitated.)

If possible, view the interior at sunset. Of the three giant medallions that warm the austere cathedral, the north rose window in the transept, from the mid-13th century, is best. The interior is typical Gothic, with slender, graceful columns. The carved-stone choir screen from the early 14th century depicts biblical scenes. Near the altar stands the 14th-century Virgin and Child. Behind glass in the treasury is a display of vestments and gold objects, including crowns. Notre-Dame is especially proud of its relic of the True Cross and the Crown of Thorns.

To visit those grimy gargoyles immortalized by Victor Hugo (where Quasimodo lurked), you have to scale steps leading to the twin square towers, rising to a height of 225 feet. Once here, you can closely inspect those devils (some sticking out their tongues), hobgoblins, and birds of prey.

Approached through a garden behind Notre-Dame is the **Memorial des Martyrs Français de la Déportation,** jutting out on the tip of the Île de la Cité. This memorial honors the French martyrs of World War II, who were deported to camps like Auschwitz and Buchenwald. In blood red are the words (in French):

⌒ *Moments*   **A Nighttime Walk & an "Abomination"**

When Viollet-le-Duc designed the flying buttresses of the cathedral of Notre-Dame, they were denounced as "horrendous," "a blight of Paris," and an "abomination." Now they're a reason to go walking at night after a meal in a bistro. On the Île de la Cité, wander through the garden in the rear of the cathedral. Near the square Jean XXIII, cross the pont de l'Archevêche and walk along quai de Montebello along the Left Bank of the Seine for a wonderful perspective, especially when the *bateaux-mouches* light up the buttresses as they pass along. You'll end up at the place St-Michel, where one of the cafes awaits you for your nightcap.

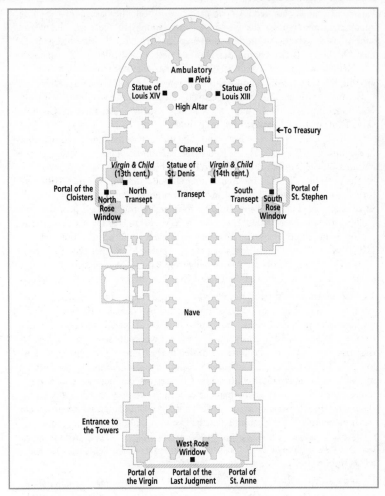

Ambulatory
Pietà
Statue of
Louis XIV
Statue of
Louis XIII
High Altar
←To Treasury
Chancel
Virgin & Child
(13th cent.)
Statue of
St. Denis
Virgin & Child
(14th cent.)
Portal of the
Cloisters
North
Transept
Transept
South
Transept
Portal of
St. Stephen
North
Rose
Window
South
Rose
Window
Nave
Entrance to
the Towers
West Rose
Window
Portal of
the Virgin
Portal of the
Last Judgment
Portal of
St. Anne

"Forgive, but don't forget." It's open Monday through Friday from 8:30am to 9:45pm, Saturday and Sunday from 9am to 9:45pm. Admission is free.

6 place du parvis Notre-Dame, 4e. © **01-42-34-56-10**. www.paris.org/Monuments/NDame. Admission free to cathedral; towers 35F (5.30, $5.10) adults, 23F (3.50, $3.35) ages 12–25 and seniors, free for children under 12; treasury 15F (2.28, $2.18) adults, 10F (1.50, $1.45) ages 12–25 and seniors, free for children under 12. Cathedral open year-round daily 8am–6:45pm. Towers and crypt Apr–Sept daily 9:30am–6pm; Oct–Mar daily 10am–5:15pm. Museum Wed and Sat–Sun 2:30–5pm. Treasury Mon–Sat 9:30–11:30am and 1–5:45pm. Métro: Cité or St-Michel. RER: St-Michel.

2 Musée de Louvre/Les Halles: The First Arrondissement (Right Bank)

The first arrondissement is first for a reason: it's where most visitors make a bee-line upon arrival in Paris. Several of the city's top attractions are here, including the **Louvre** (see "The Top Attractions," above) and the Tuileries. It's also home to **Les Halles,** for 8 centuries the major fruit, meat, and vegetable market of

Paris. The smock-clad vendors, the carcasses of beef, the baskets of the most appetizing vegetables in the world—all that belongs to the past. Today, the action has moved to the modern steel-and-glass structure at Rungis, a suburb near Orly. Here is **Les Forum des Halles** (Métro: Les Halles; RER: Châtelet-Les Halles), which opened in 1979. This large complex, much of it underground, houses dozens of shops, plus several restaurants and movie theaters.

For many visitors, a night on the town still ends in the wee hours with the traditional bowl of onion soup at Les Halles, usually at **Au Pied de Cochon** (Pig's Foot) or **Au Chien Qui Fume** (Smoking Dog).

There's still much to see in Les Halles, beginning with the **Église St-Eustache,** 2 rue du Jour, 1er (☎ **01-42-36-31-05;** Métro: Les Halles), with another entrance on rue Rambuteau. In the old days, cabbage vendors came here to pray for their produce. The Gothic-Renaissance church dates from the mid-16th century yet wasn't completed until 1637. It has been known for its organ recitals since Liszt played here in 1866. Inside is the black marble tomb of Jean-Baptiste Colbert, the minister of state under Louis XIV. A statue of the statesman rests on top of his tomb, flanked by Coysevox's *Abundance* (a horn of flowers) and J. B. Tuby's *Fidelity.* The church is open from April to September daily from 8am to 8pm, and from October to March daily from 9am to 7pm; mass is at 9:30am, 11am, and 6pm Sunday, and there's also an organ concert Sunday at 5:30pm.

Galerie Nationale du Jeu de Paume Jeu de Paume, in the northeast corner of the Tuileries (see below), was constructed by Napoléon III as a court on which to play *jeu de paume,* a precursor to tennis. For years it was one of Paris's treasured addresses, displaying some of the finest works of the Impressionists. To the regret of many, the collection was moved to the Musée d'Orsay in 1986. Following a $12.6-million face-lift, the Second Empire building has been transformed into a new gallery with state-of-the-art display facilities and a video screening room. There's no permanent collection; every 2 or 3 months a new show is mounted. Sometimes the works of little-known contemporary artists are on display; other times established artists like Jean Dubuffet are featured.

In the northeast corner of the Jardin des Tuileries/1 place de la Concorde, 1er. ☎ **01-47-03-12-50.** Admission 45F (6.85, $6.55) adults, 35F (5.30, $5.08) students, free for children 13 and under. Tues noon–9:30pm; Wed–Fri noon–7pm; Sat–Sun 10am–7pm. Métro: Concorde.

Jardin des Tuileries ★★ These spectacular, statue-studded gardens are as much a part of Paris as the Seine. They were designed by Le Nôtre, Louis XIV's gardener and planner of the Versailles grounds. About 100 years before that, Catherine de Médici ordered a palace built here, connected to the Louvre; other occupants have included Louis XVI and Napoléon. Twice attacked by Parisians, it was burned to the ground in 1871 and never rebuilt. The gardens, however, remain. In orderly French manner, the trees are arranged according to designs, and the paths are arrow-straight. Breaking the sense of order and formality are bubbling fountains.

Seemingly half of Paris can be found in the Tuileries on a warm spring day, listening to the birds and admiring the daffodils and tulips. As you walk toward the Louvre, you'll enter the **Jardin du Carrousel,** dominated by the **Arc de Triomphe du Carrousel,** at the Cour du Carrousel. Pierced with three walkways and supported by marble columns, the monument honors Napoléon's Grande Armée, celebrating its victory at Austerlitz on December 5, 1805. The arch is surmounted by statuary, a chariot, and four bronze horses.

Bordering place de la Concorde, 1er. ☎ **01-44-50-75-01.** Métro: Tuileries.

Musée des Arts Décoratifs   In the northwest wing of the Louvre's Pavillon de Marsan, this museum holds a treasury of furnishings, fabrics, wallpaper, objets d'art, and other items displaying living styles from the Middle Ages to the present. Notable on the first floor are the 1920s Art Deco boudoir, bath, and bedroom done for couturière Jeanne Lanvin by the designer Rateau, plus a prestigious collection of the works donated by Jean Dubuffet. Decorative art from the Middle Ages to the Renaissance is on the second floor; rich collections from the 17th, 18th, and 19th centuries occupy the third and fourth floors. The fifth floor has specialized centers, such as wallpaper and drawings, and documentary centers detailing fashion, textiles, toys, crafts, and glass trends.

Palais du Louvre, 107, rue de Rivoli, , 1er. ☎ 01-44-55-57-50. Admission 35F (5.25, $5.08) adults, 25F (3.75, $3.63) ages 18–25, free for children 18 and under. Tues and Thurs–Fri 11am–6pm; Wed 11am–9pm; Sat–Sun 10am–6pm. Métro: Palais Royal or Tuileries.

Palais Royal   At the demolished Café Foy in the Palais Royal, the outraged Camille Desmoulins once jumped on a table and shouted for the mob "to fight to the death." The date was July 13, 1789. The renown of the Palais Royal goes back even farther. The gardens were planted in 1634 for Cardinal Richelieu, who presented them to Louis XIII. The property later became the residence of the ducs d'Orléans. Philippe-Egalité, a cousin of Louis XVI, built his apartments on the grounds and subsequently rented them to prostitutes. By the 20th century, those apartments were rented by such artists as Cocteau and Colette. (A plaque at 9 rue Beaujolais marks the entrance to Colette's apartment, which she inhabited until her death in 1954.) Today, the Palais Royal contains apartments, some discreet shops, and a few great restaurants such as **Le Grand Véfour;** for more information, see chapter 4. Note sculptor Daniel Buren's prison-striped columns, added in 1986, and Pol Bury's steel-ball sculptures decorating the fountains.

Rue St-Honoré, on place du Palais-Royal, 1er. Métro: Palais-Royal/Musée du Louvre.

3 Le Marais: The 3rd Arrondissement (Right Bank)

When Paris began to overflow the confines of the Île de la Cité in the 13th century, the citizenry settled in the Marais, the marsh that used to be flooded regularly by the high-rising Seine. By the 17th century, the Marais had reached the pinnacle of fashion, becoming the center of aristocratic Paris. At that time, most of its great *hôtels particuliers* (mansions)—many now restored or being spruced up today—were built by the finest craftspeople in France.

In the 18th and 19th centuries, the fashionable deserted the Marais in favor of the expanding Faubourg St-Germain and Faubourg St-Honoré. Industry eventually took over the quarter, and the once-elegant hôtels were turned into tenements. There was talk of demolishing this blighted sector, but in 1962, the alarmed Comité de Sauvegarde du Marais saved the district. The regeneration of the neighborhood was sparked by the Pompidou Center.

No longer "the Swamp" (its English name), the Marais in the 3rd arrondissement (and part of the 4th) is trendy once again, filled with tiny twisting streets, bars for both gays and straights, and cutting-edge designer shops.

In **place de la Bastille** on July 14, 1789, a mob of Parisians attacked the Bastille and sparked the French Revolution. Nothing remains of the historic Bastille, built in 1369, for it was torn down. Many prisoners—some sentenced by Louis XIV for "witchcraft"—were kept within it, the best known being the "Man in the Iron Mask." When the fortress was stormed, only seven prisoners were discovered (the marquis de Sade had been transferred to the asylum 10 days

earlier). Authorities had discussed razing it anyway, so the attack was more symbolic than anything else. What it signified, however, and what it started will
never be forgotten. Bastille Day is celebrated every July 14. In the center of the
square is the **Colonne de Juillet** (July Column), which doesn't commemorate
the Revolution; rather, it honors the victims of the 1830 July Revolution, which
put Louis-Philippe on the throne. The tower is crowned by the God of Liberty,
a winged nude with a star emerging from his head.

Not far away, **place des Vosges** ★★★, 4e (Métro: St-Paul or Chemin-Vert),
is Paris's oldest square and once its most fashionable. It was called the Palais
Royal in the days of Henri IV, who planned to live here—but his assassin,
Ravaillac, had other intentions. Henri II was killed while jousting on the square
in 1559, in the shadow of the Hôtel des Tournelles. His widow, Catherine de
Médici, had the place torn down. Place des Vosges, once a dueling ground, was
one of Europe's first planned squares. Its grand siècle red-brick houses are ornamented with white stone, and its covered arcades allowed people to shop at all
times, even in the rain—an innovation at the time. In the 18th century, chestnut trees were added, sparking a controversy that continues to this day: critics
say that the addition spoils the perspective.

As you stroll the Marais, you might want to seek out the following hôtels. The
Hôtel de Rohan, 87 rue Vieille-du-Temple (✆ 01-40-27-60-09), was once
occupied by the fourth Cardinal Rohan, who was involved in the scandal that
framed Marie Antoinette for buying a priceless diamond necklace. The first
Cardinal Rohan, was reputed to be the son of Louis XIV. The main attraction is
the 18th-century Salon des Singes (Monkey Room). In the courtyard is a stunning bas-relief of a nude Apollo and four horses against exploding sunbursts.
The hotel can be visited only during special exhibitions announced in Paris
newspapers.

At 47 rue Vieille-du-Temple is the **Hôtel des Ambassadeurs de Hollande,**
where Beaumarchais wrote *The Marriage of Figaro*. It's one of the most splendid
mansions in the area—and was never occupied by the Dutch embassy. It's not
open to the public.

Although the facade of the 17th-century **Hôtel de Beauvais,** 68 rue François-
Miron, was damaged during the Revolution, it remains one of the most charming in Paris. A plaque commemorates the fact that Mozart inhabited the
mansion in 1763. To visit inside, speak to the Association du Paris Historique,
on the ground floor of the building, any afternoon.

Hôtel de Sens, a landmark at 1 rue de Figuier (✆ 01-42-78-14-60), was built
from the 1470s to 1519 for the archbishops of Sens. Along with the Hôtel de
Cluny, it's the only domestic architecture remaining from the 15th century. Long
after the archbishops had departed in 1605, it was occupied by the scandalous
Queen Margot, wife of Henri IV. Her "younger and more virile" new lover slew
the discarded one as she looked on. Today, the mansion houses the Bibliothèque
Forney. The gate is open Tuesday through Saturday from 1:30 to 8pm.

Work began on the **Hôtel de Bethune-Sully,** 62 rue St-Antoine (✆ 01-
44-61-20-00), in 1625. In 1634, it was acquired by the duc de Sully, who had
been Henri IV's minister of finance. After a straitlaced early life, Sully broke
loose, adorning himself with diamonds and garish rings—and a young bride who
had a preference for younger men. The hôtel was acquired by the government
after World War II and hosts the National Office of Historical Monuments and
Sites. Recently restored, the relief-studded facade is appealing. There's daily
admittance to the courtyard and the garden that opens onto place des Vosges.

The **rue des Rosiers (Street of the Rosebushes),** is one of the most colorful of the streets remaining from the old Jewish quarter. The Star of David shines here, Hebrew letters flash (in neon), couscous is sold from the shops run by Moroccan or Algerian Jews, bearded men sit in doorways, restaurants serve kosher meals, and signs appeal for Jewish liberation.

Shoppers will delight in such places as **Passage de Retz,** 9 rue Charlot (*C* **01-048-04-37-99**), established in 1994, an avant-garde gallery with the most amusing exhibitions in the Marais. At **Hier, Aujourd'hui, and Demain,** 14 rue de Bretagne (*C* **01-42-77-69-02**), you'll fall in love with 1930s Art Deco.

The 3rd arrondissement is also home to the **Picasso Museum** (see "The Top Attractions," earlier in this chapter).

Musée Carnavalet ✦   The history of Paris comes alive here in intimately personal terms—down to the chessmen Louis XVI used to distract himself in the days before he went to the guillotine. A renowned Renaissance palace, the hôtel was built in 1544 by Pierre Lescot and Jean Goujon and acquired by Mme de Carnavalet. The great François Mansart transformed it between 1655 and 1661. It's best known because one of history's most famous letter writers, Mme de Sévigné, moved here in 1677. Fanatically devoted to her daughter (until she had to live with her), she poured out nearly every detail of her life in letters, virtually ignoring her son. A native of the Marais, she died at her daughter's château in 1696. It wasn't until 1866 that the city turned it into a museum.

23 rue de Sévigné, 3e. *C* **01-44-59-58-58**. Admission 35F (5.30, $5.08) adults, 18F (2.75, $2.61) ages 7–26, free for children under 7. Tues–Sun 10am–5:40pm. Métro: St-Paul or Chemin-Vert.

4 Where Paris Was Born: Île de la Cité & the 4th Arrondissement

Medieval Paris, that architectural blending of grotesquerie and Gothic beauty, began on this island in the Seine. Explore as much of it as you can, but if you're in a hurry, try to visit at least **Notre-Dame** (see "The Top Attractions," earlier in this chapter), the Ste-Chapelle, and the Conciergerie. The 4th arrondissement is on the right bank, opposite the island.

Centre Pompidou ✦✦✦   Relaunched in January 2000, in what was called in the 1970s "the most avant-garde building in the world," the newly restored Pompidou Centre is packing in the art-loving crowds again.

The dream of former president Georges Pompidou, this center for 20th-century art, designed by Richard Rogers and Renzo Piano, opened in 1977 and became the focus of loud controversy. Its bold exoskeletal architecture and the brightly painted pipes and ducts crisscrossing its transparent facade (green for water, red for heat, blue for air, and yellow for electricity) were jarring in the old Beaubourg neighborhood. Perhaps the detractors were right all along—within 20 years, the building began to deteriorate so badly that a major restoration was called for.

The Centre Pompidou encompasses four separate attractions. The **Musée National d'Art Moderne** (National Museum of Modern Art) offers a large collection of 20th-century art. With some 40,000 works, this is the big draw, although only some 850 works can be displayed at one time. If you want to view some real charmers, see Alexander Calder's 1926 *Josephine Baker,* one of his earlier versions of the mobile, an art form he invented. Marcel Duchamp's *Valise* is a collection of miniature reproductions of his fabled Dada sculptures and drawings; they're displayed in a carrying case. And every time we visit Paris we have to see Salvador Dali's *Portrait of Lenin Dancing on Piano Keys.*

In the **Public Information Library,** the public has free access to a million French and foreign books, periodicals, films, records, slides, and microfilms in nearly every area of knowledge. The **Center for Industrial Design** emphasizes the contributions made in the fields of architecture, visual communications, publishing, and community planning; and the **Institute for Research and Coordination of Acoustics/Music** brings together musicians and composers interested in furthering the cause of music, both contemporary and traditional.

Finally, you can also visit a re-creation of the jazz-age studio of Romanian sculptor Brancusi (**l'Atelier Brancusi**), which is configured as a mini-museum that's slightly separate from the rest of the action.

Place Georges-Pompidou, 4e. © 01-44-78-12-33. www.centrepompidou.fr. Admission 30F (4.55, $4.35) adults, 20F (3.04, $2.90) students, under age 18 free. Special exhibits 50F (7.60, $7.25) adults, 30F (4.55, $4.35) students, under age 13 free. Wed–Mon 11am–9pm. Métro: Rambuteau, Hôtel de Ville, or Châtelet–Les Halles.

Conciergerie ★★ The Conciergerie is the most sinister building in France. Though it had a long, regal history before the Revolution, it's visited today chiefly by those wishing to bask in the Reign of Terror's horrors. The Conciergerie conjures images of the days when tumbrils pulled up daily to haul off the fresh supply of victims to the guillotine.

You approach the Conciergerie through its landmark twin towers, the Tour d'Argent and Tour de César, though the 14th-century vaulted Guard Room is the actual entrance. Also from the 14th century is the vast, dark, foreboding Salle des Gens d'Armes (People at Arms), chillingly transformed from the days when the king used it as a banqueting hall.

Few of the prisoners in the Conciergerie's history endured the tortures of Ravaillac, who assassinated Henri IV in 1610. He got the full treatment— pincers in the flesh, hot lead and boiling oil poured on him. This was also where Marie Antoinette was brought to await her trial and eventual beheading.

1 quai de l'Horloge, 1er. © 01-53-73-78-50. www.monum.fr. Admission 36F (5.45, $5.20) adults, 23F (3.50, $3.34) ages 18–25 and seniors, free for children under 12. Apr–Sept daily 9:30am–6:30pm; Oct–Mar daily 10am–5pm. Métro: Cité, Châtelet, or St-Michel. RER: St-Michel.

Ste-Chapelle ★★★ Go here if for no other reason than to see one of the world's greatest examples of Flamboyant Gothic architecture—"the pearl among them all," as Proust called it—and brilliant stained-glass windows with a lacelike delicacy. The reds are so red that Parisians have been known to use the phrase "wine the color of Ste-Chapelle's windows." Ste-Chapelle is Paris's second most important monument of the Middle Ages (after Notre-Dame); it was erected to enshrine relics from the First Crusade, including what were believed to have been the Crown of Thorns, two pieces from the True Cross, and the Roman lance that pierced the side of Christ. St. Louis (Louis IX) acquired the relics from the emperor of Constantinople and is said to have paid heavily for them, raising money through unscrupulous means.

Viewed on a bright day, the 15 stained-glass windows depicting Bible scenes seem to glow ruby red and Chartres blue. The walls consist almost entirely of the glass. Built in only 5 years, beginning in 1246, the chapel has two levels. You enter through the lower chapel, supported by flying buttresses and ornamented with fleurs-de-lis. The lower chapel was used by the servants of the palace, the upper chamber by the king and his courtiers; the latter is reached by ascending a narrow spiral staircase. At the top, you're sure to ooh and aah at the sight.

Ste-Chapelle stages **concerts** most nights in summer, with tickets at 120F to 150F (18.25 to 22.80, $17.40 to $21.75). Call ℂ **01-42-77-65-65** between 11am and 6pm daily for details.

Palais de Justice, 4 bd. du Palais, 1er. ℂ **01-53-73-78-50**. www.monum.fr. Admission 35F (5.30, $5.08) adults, 23F (3.50, $3.35) ages 18–25, free for children 17 and under. Apr–Sept daily 9:30am–6:30pm; Oct–Mar daily 10am–5pm. Métro: Cité, St-Michel, or Châtelet–Les Halles. RER: St-Michel.

ANOTHER ISLAND IN THE STREAM: ÎLE ST-LOUIS

As you walk across the iron footbridge from the rear of Notre-Dame, you descend into a world of tree-shaded quays, aristocratic town houses and court-yards, restaurants, and antiques shops.

The Île St-Louis (Métro: Sully-Morland or Pont-Marie), the sibling island of the Île de la Cité, is primarily residential; those who live here guard their her-itage, privileges, and special position. It was originally two "islets," one named Island of the Heifers, until the two were ordered joined by Louis XIII. The num-ber of famous people who have occupied these patrician mansions is legend. Plaques on the facades make it easier to identify them: Madame Curie, for exam-ple, lived at 36 quai de Bethune, near pont de la Tournelle, from 1912 until her death in 1934.

The most exciting mansion is the **Hôtel de Lauzun,** built in 1657, at 17 quai d'Anjou; named after a 17th-century rogue, the duc de Lauzun, lover and on-again/off-again favorite of Louis XIV. The poet Charles Baudelaire lived here in the 19th century with his "Black Venus," Jeanne Duval. Baudelaire brought such artists as Delacroix and Courbet to his apartment, which was often filled with the aroma of hashish. Occupying another apartment was Théophile Gau-tier ("art for art's sake"), who's remembered today for his *Mademoiselle de Maupin.*

Voltaire lived in the **Hôtel Lambert,** 2 quai d'Anjou, with his mistress, Emi-lie de Breteuil, the marquise du Châteley, who had an "understanding" husband. Louis Le Vau built the mansion in 1645 for Nicolas Lambert de Thorigny, the president of the Chambre des Comptes. For a century, it was the home of the royal family of Poland, the Czartoryskis, who entertained Chopin, among others.

At 9 quai d'Anjou, is the house where **Honoré Daumier** (the painter, sculp-tor, and lithographer) lived from 1846 to 1863. From here he satirized the petite bourgeoisie. His caricature of Louis-Philippe netted him a 6-month jail sentence.

5 The Champs-Elysées, Paris's Grand Promenade: The 8th Arrondissement (Right Bank)

In late 1995, after two hard, dusty, and hyperexpensive years of construction, several important improvements in Paris's most prominent triumphal prome-nade were unveiled. The *contre-allées* (side lanes that had always been clogged with parked cars) were removed (new underground garages alleviate the horren-dous parking problem), new lighting was added, the pedestrian sidewalks were widened, and new trees were planted. Now the Grand Promenade truly is grand again . . . except for all those fast-food joints.

Arc de Triomphe ✦✦✦   At the western end of the Champs-Elysées, the Arc de Triomphe is the largest triumphal arch in the world, about 163 feet high and 147 feet wide. To reach it, don't try crossing the square, the busiest traffic hub in Paris. (Death is certain!) Instead, take the underground passage. With a dozen streets radiating from the "Star," the traffic circle is vehicular roulette.

The arch has witnessed some of France's proudest moments—and some of its more humiliating defeats, notably those of 1871 (when Paris capitulated in the Franco-Prussian War) and 1940. The memory of German troops marching under the arch—who can forget the 1940 newsreel footage of the Frenchman openly weeping as the Nazi stormtroopers goose-stepped down the Champs?—is still painful to the French so many years later.

Commissioned by Napoléon in 1806 to commemorate his Grande Armée's victories, the arch wasn't completed until 1836, under Louis-Philippe. Four years later, Napoléon's remains—brought from his grave on St. Helena—passed under the arch on their journey to his tomb at the Hôtel des Invalides. Since then it has become the focal point for state funerals. It's also the site of the tomb of the unknown soldier, where an eternal flame is kept burning.

Of the sculptures decorating the monument, the best known is Rude's *Marseillaise,* also called *The Departure of the Volunteers.* J. P. Cortot's *Triumph of Napoléon in 1810,* along with the *Resistance of 1814* and *Peace of 1815,* both by Etex, also adorn the facade. The arch is engraved with the names of hundreds of generals who commanded troops in Napoléonic victories.

You can take an elevator or climb the stairway to the top, where there's an exhibition hall with lithographs and photos depicting the arch throughout its history. From the observation deck, you have a panoramic view of the Champs-Elysées as well as such landmarks as the Louvre, Eiffel Tower, and Sacré-Coeur.

Place Charles de Gaulle–Etoile, 16e. (℄) **01-55-37-73-77.** www.monuments.fr. Admission 42F (6.430, $6.09) adults, 26F (3.95, $3.77) ages 18–25, free for children 11 and under. Apr–Sept daily 9:30am–11pm; Oct–Mar daily 10am–10:30pm. Métro: Charles de Gaulle–Etoile.

Musée Jacquemart-André ★★ (Finds) This is the best decorative-arts museum in Paris, though it's no place to take the kids (unless they're aspiring decorators). Give it at least 2 hours. The museum derives from the André family, prominent Protestants in the 19th century. The family's last scion, Edouard André, spent most of his life as an officer in the French army stationed abroad, returning to marry Nélie Jacquemart, a well-known portraitist. Together they compiled a collection of rare French 18th-century decorative art and European paintings in an 1850s town house, which they continually upgraded and redecorated according to the fashions of their time.

In 1912, Mme André willed the house and its collections to the Institut de France, which paid for extensive renovations and enlargements completed in 1996. The collection's pride are works by Bellini, Carpaccio, and Uccelo, Houdon busts, Gobelin tapestries, Savonnerie carpets, della Robbia terra cottas, awesome antiques, and works by Rembrandt (*The Pilgrim of Emmaus*), van Dyck, Rubens, Watteau, Fragonard, and Boucher. After a major restoration, one of the most outstanding exhibits is a group of three mid-18th-century frescoes by Giambattista Tiepolo; this is the only museum in France with frescoes by the Venetian master. The works depict spectators on balconies viewing Henri III's arrival in Venice in 1574. Take a break from the gilded-age opulence with a cup of tea, or a tart in Mme André's dining room, with 18th-century tapestries.

158 bd. Haussmann, 8e. (℄) **01-45-62-11-59.** Admission 50F (7.60, $7.25) adults, 38F (5.83, $5.51) children 7–17, children under 7 free. Daily 10am–6pm. Métro: Miromesnil or St-Philippe-du-Roule.

Palais de l'Elysée The "French White House" occupies a block along fashionable Faubourg St-Honoré and since 1873 has been occupied (officially, if not physically) by the president of France. You can admire the palace from the outside (about a block away), but can't enter without an official invitation. Built in

ALPS   ASPEN

AT&T Direct® Service

The easy way to call home from anywhere.

Global
connection
with the AT&T
Network

AT&T
direct
service

For the easy way to call home, take the attached wallet guide.

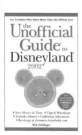
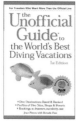
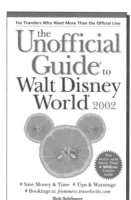

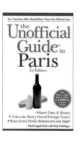
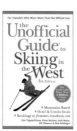
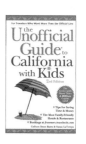
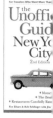

Where the Royal Heads Rolled

The eastern end of the Champs-Elysées is **place de la Concorde,** an octagonal traffic hub built in 1757 to honor Louis XV. It's one of the world's grand squares. The statue of the king was torn down in 1792 and the name changed to place de la Révolution. Floodlit at night, it's dominated by an **Egyptian obelisk** from Luxor, the oldest man-made object in Paris; it was carved circa 1200 B.C. and given to France in 1829 by the viceroy of Egypt.

During the Reign of Terror, Dr. Guillotin's little invention was erected on this spot, where it claimed thousands of lives—from Louis XVI, who died bravely, to Mme du Barry, who went kicking and screaming. Before the leering crowds, Marie Antoinette, Robespierre, Danton, Mlle Roland, and Charlotte Corday lost their heads here. (You can still lose your life on place de la Concorde—if you try to chance the frantic traffic and cross over.)

For a spectacular sight, look down the Champs-Elysées—the view is framed by Coustou's Marly horses, which once graced the gardens at Louis XIV's Château de Marly. (These are copies; the originals are in the Louvre.) On the opposite side, the gateway to the Tuileries is flanked by Coysevox's winged horses. On each side of the obelisk are two fountains with bronze-tailed mermaids and bare-breasted sea nymphs. Gray-beige statues ring the square, honoring the cities of France. To symbolize that city's fall to Germany in 1871, the statue of Strasbourg was covered with a black drape that wasn't lifted until the end of World War I. Two of the palaces on place de la Concorde are today the Ministry of the Marine and the deluxe Hôtel de Crillon. They were designed in the 1760s by Jacques-Ange Gabriel.

1718 for the comte d'Evreux, it had many owners before the Republic purchased it. Mme de Pompadour once owned it. When she "had the supreme delicacy to die discreetly at the age of 43," she bequeathed it to the king. After her divorce from Napoléon, Joséphine lived here. A grand dining hall was built for Napoléon III, and an orangerie (now a winter garden) was constructed for the duchesse du Berry.

Rue du Faubourg St-Honoré, 8e. Métro: Miromesnil.

Place Vendôme ★★   Always aristocratic and often royal, place Vendôme enjoyed its golden age during the Second Empire. Fashion designers such as Worth introduced the crinoline here. Louis Napoléon lived here, wooing his empress, Eugénie de Montijo, at the Hôtel du Rhin. In its halcyon days, Strauss waltzes echoed across the plaza. In time they were replaced by cannon fire. The square is dominated by a column crowned by Napoléon. There was a statue of the Sun King here until the Revolution, when it was replaced briefly by *Liberty.*

Then came Napoléon, who ordered that a sort of Trajan's Column be erected in honor of his victory at Austerlitz. It was made of bronze from captured Russian and Austrian cannons. After Napoléon's downfall, the statue was replaced by one of Henri IV, everybody's favorite king and every woman's favorite man. Later Napoléon mounted it again, in uniform and without the pose of a Caesar.

The Communards of 1871, who detested royalty and the false promises of emperors, pulled down the statue. Courbet is said to have led the raid. For his part in the drama, he was jailed and fined the cost of restoring the statue. He couldn't pay it, of course, and was forced into exile in Switzerland. Eventually, the statue of Napoléon, wrapped in a Roman toga, finally won out.

Place Vendôme, 8e. Métro: Opéra.

6 Montmartre: The 18th Arrondissement (Right Bank)

From the 1880s to just before World War I, Montmartre enjoyed its golden age as the world's best-known art colony, where *la vie de bohème* (bohemian life) reigned supreme. Following World War I, the pseudoartists flocked here in droves, with camera-snapping tourists hot on their heels. The real artists had long gone to such places as Montparnasse.

Before its discovery, Montmartre was a sleepy farming community, with windmills dotting the landscape. Those who find the trek up to Paris's highest elevations too much of a climb may prefer to ride **Le Petit Train de Montmartre,** that passes all the major landmarks; it seats 55 passengers and offers English commentary. Board at place du Tertre (at the Église St-Pierre) or place Blanche (near the Moulin Rouge). From June to September, trains run daily from 10am to 10pm; off-season, daily from 10am to 6pm. For information, contact **Promotrain,** 131 rue de Clignancourt, 18e (© **01-42-62-24-00**).

The simplest way to reach Montmartre is to take the Métro to Anvers, then walk up rue du Steinkerque to the funicular, which runs to the precincts of Sacré-Coeur every day from 5:30am to 12:30am. Except for Sacré-Coeur (see below), Montmartre has only minor attractions; it's the historic architecture and the atmosphere that are compelling.

Specific attractions to look for include the **Bateau-Lavoir (Boat Warehouse),** place Emile-Goudeau. Although gutted by fire in 1970, it has been reconstructed. Picasso once lived here and, in the winter of 1905 to 1906, painted one of the world's most famous portraits, *The Third Rose* (Gertrude Stein).

Espace Montmartre Salvadore-Dalí, 11 rue Poulbot, 18e (© **01-42-64-40-10**), presents Dalí's phantasmagorical world with 330 original works, including his 1956 *Don Quixote* lithograph. It's open daily from 10am to 6pm, charging 40F (6.10, $5.80) for adults.

One of the most famous churches here is the **Église St-Pierre,** rue du Mont-Cenis, originally a Benedictine abbey. The church was consecrated in 1147; two of the columns in the choir stall are the remains of a Roman temple. Among the sculptured works, note the nun with the head of a pig, a symbol of sensual vice. At the entrance are three bronze doors sculpted by Gismondi in 1980: the middle door depicts the life of St. Peter; the left is dedicated to St. Denis, first bishop of Paris; and the right is dedicated to the Holy Virgin.

Musée de Vieux Montmartre, 12 rue Cortot, 18e (© **01-46-06-61-11**), exhibits a wide collection of mementos. This 17th-century house was once occupied by Dufy, van Gogh, Renoir, and Suzanne Valadon and her son, Utrillo. It's open Tuesday through Sunday from 11am to 6pm. Admission is 25F (3.80, $3.63) for adults and 20F (3.04, $2.90) for students.

Basilique du Sacré-Coeur ★★★   Montmartre's crowning achievement is Sacré-Coeur, though its view of Paris takes precedence over the basilica itself. Like other Parisian landmarks, it has been the subject of much controversy. One Parisian called it "a lunatic's confectionery dream." Zola declared it "the basilica

Fun Fact   **La Grande Arche de La Défense**

Designed as the architectural centerpiece of the sprawling futuristic suburb of La Défense, this massive steel-and-masonry arch rises 35 stories. It was built with the blessing of the late François Mitterrand and ringed with office buildings and a circular avenue (*périphérique*), patterned after the one surrounding the Arc de Triomphe. This deliberately overscaled archway is one of the latest major landmarks to dot the Paris skyline, along with the Cité de la Musique in the city's northwestern section. High enough to shelter Notre-Dame below its canopy, the monument was designed as an extension of the panorama that connects the Louvre, Arc de Triomphe du Carrousel, Champs-Elysées, Arc de Triomphe, avenue de la Grande-Armée, and place du Porte-Maillot into a magnificent straight line. An elevator carries you to an observation platform, from which you can see the carefully conceived geometry of the street plan. Note that the netting you'll see has been placed there to catch any falling fragments of the arch. Watch your head.

The arch is located at 1 place du parvis de La Défense, outside the city limits, beyond the 17th arrondissement. To get here, take the RER to La Défense. Call (C) **01-49-07-27-57** for information. Admission is 46F (7.00, $6.67) for adults. It's open daily from 10am to 6pm.

of the ridiculous." Sacré-Coeur's supporters included the Jewish poet Max Jacob and the artist Maurice Utrillo, who never tired of drawing and painting it. The two of them came here regularly to pray.

Its gleaming white domes and *campanile* (bell tower) tower over Paris like a Byzantine church of the 12th century. But it's not that old: after France's defeat by the Prussians in 1870, the basilica was planned as an offering to cure the country's misfortunes; rich and poor alike contributed to build it. Construction began in 1873, but the church wasn't consecrated until 1919. The interior of the basilica is decorated with mosaics, the most striking of which are the ceiling depiction of Christ and the mural of the Passion at the back of the altar. The crypt contains a relic of what some believe is a piece of the sacred heart of Christ—hence the church's name.

On a clear day, the vista from the dome can extend for 35 miles. You can also walk around the inner dome of the church, peering down like a pigeon (a few will likely be there to keep you company).

Place St-Pierre, 18e. (C) **01-53-41-89-00.** www.paris.org/Monuments/Sacre.Coeur/. Admission free to basilica; joint ticket to dome and crypt 30F (4.55, $4.35) adults, 16F (2.45, $2.32) students and children. Daily 9am–7.45pm. Métro: Abbesses; take the elevator to the surface and follow the signs to the *funiculaire*, which goes up to the church for the price of a Métro ticket.

Cimetière de Montmarte ⊛ Novelist Alexandre Dumas and Russian dancer Vaslav Nijinsky are just a few of the famous composers, writers, and artists interred here. The remains of the great Stendhal are here, Hector Berlioz, Heinrich Heine, Edgar Degas, Jacques Offenbach, and even François Truffaut. We like to pay our respects at the tomb of Alphonsine Plessis, the courtesan on whom Dumas based his Marguerite Gautier in *La Dame aux Camélias*. Émile

Zola was interred here, but his corpse was taken to the Panthéon in 1908. In 1871, the cemetery became the site of the mass burials of victims of the Siege and the Commune.

20 av. Rachel (west of the Butte Montmartre and north of bd. de Clichy), 18e. ☎ **01-43-87-64-24**. Sun–Fri 8am–6pm; Sat 8:30am–6pm (closes at 5:30pm in winter). Métro: La Fourche.

7 La Villette: The 19th Arrondissement (Right Bank)

Cité des Sciences et de l'Industrie ★★ *Kids*   In 1986, this opened as the world's most expensive ($642 million) science complex, designed to "modernize mentalities" as part of the process of modernizing society. The place is so vast, with so many options, that a single visit will give you only an idea of its scope. Some exhibits are couched in an overlay of Gallic humor, including seismographic activity as presented in the comic-strip adventures of a jungle explorer. The silver-skinned Géode (a geodesic dome) shows the closest thing to a 3-D cinema in Europe on the inner surfaces of its curved walls. It's a 112-foot sphere with a 370-seat theater. Explora, a permanent exhibit, is spread over the three upper levels; its displays revolve around four themes: the universe, life, matter, and communication. The Cité also has a multimedia library and a planetarium. An "inventorium" is for children.

At Cinaxe, sophisticated stereo systems and larger-than-normal screens combine to enhance the sensations of the scenes being presented in the film. The experience includes episodes representing what you'd see, for example, in an airplane flying over mountains or if you were on the nose cone of a rocket.

The *Argonaut* is a submarine originally built in 1905 as part of a scientific experiment and a forerunner of the giant nuclear subs whose construction was partially based on ideas developed here. It was disarmed in 1982 and would have been demolished but for its purchase by the Musée de la Villette. Today, it's a nationalistic source of pride, although it's firmly mounted on concrete and is never submerged.

La Cité des Enfants is divided into two sections: one for ages 3 to 5, the other for ages 6 to 12. This is an adventure playground, with water sports, a butterfly greenhouse, robots, an ant farm, interactive TVs, and even a Techno Cité where kids are given an explanation of the workings of computers and other machines. There are also visual exhibits on such subjects as electricity.

The Cité is in **La Villette** park, Paris's largest park, with 136 acres of greenery. You'll find a belvedere, a video workshop for children, and information about exhibitions, along with a cafe and restaurant.

In the Parc de La Villette, 30 av. Corentine-Cariou, La Villette, 19e. ☎ **01-40-05-80-00**. Cité Pass (entrance to all exhibits) 50F (7.60, $7.25) adults, free for children 7 and under; Géode 57F (8.65, $8.27). Tues–Sat 10am–6pm; Sun 10am–7pm. Métro: Porte de La Villette.

Musée de la Musique   Contained in the stone-and-glass Cité de la Musique, this museum serves as a tribute to the rich musical traditions of many ages and cultures. You can view 4,500 instruments, from the 17th century to the present, as well as paintings, engravings, and sculptures that relate to musical history. One appealing section of mandolins, lutes, and zithers evokes music from 400 years ago. It's all here: cornets disguised as snakes, antique music boxes, and even an electric guitar. As part of the permanent collection, models of the world's great concert halls and interactive display areas give you a chance to hear and better understand the art and technology of musical heritage.

In the Cité de la Musique, 221 av. Jean-Jaurès, 19e. ✆ **01-44-84-44-84**. www.cite-musique.fr. Admission 40F (6.130, $5.80) adults, 30F (4.55, $4.35) students and seniors, 15F (2.330, $2.20) children 17 and under; visits with commentary, 60F (9.10, $8.70) adults, 45F (6.85, $6.53) students and seniors, 20F (3.05, $2.90) children 17 and under. Tues–Thurs noon–6pm; Fri–Sat noon–7:30pm; Sun 10am–6pm. Métro: Porte de Pantin.

8 The Latin Quarter: The 5th Arrondissement (Left Bank)

This is the Left Bank precinct of the **University of Paris** (a.k.a. the **Sorbonne**), where students meet and fall in love over coffee and croissants. Rabelais called it the *Quartier Latin* because the students and professors spoke Latin in the classrooms and on the streets. The sector teems with belly dancers, exotic restaurants (from Vietnamese to Balkan), sidewalk cafes, bookstalls, and *caveaux* (basement nightclubs).

A good starting point is **place St-Michel** (Métro: Pont-St-Michel), where Balzac used to get water from the fountain when he was a youth. This center was the scene of much Resistance fighting in the summer of 1944. The quarter centers on **boulevard St-Michel** ("Boul Mich"), to the south.

La Sorbonne   The University of Paris—everybody calls it the Sorbonne—is one of the most famous institutions in the world. Founded in the 13th century, it had become the most prestigious university in the West by the 14th century, drawing such professors as Thomas Aquinas. Reorganized by Napoléon in 1806, the Sorbonne is today the premier university of France. At first glance it may seem architecturally undistinguished; it was rather indiscriminately reconstructed at the turn of the century. Not so the **Église de la Sorbonne,** built in 1635 by Le Mercier at the center of the Sorbonne. It contains the marble tomb of Cardinal Richelieu, a work by Girardon based on a Le Brun design. At his feet is the remarkable statue *Science in Tears*.

Bd. St-Michel. Métro: St-Michel.

Musée National du Moyen Age (Musée de Cluny) ✦✦   There are two reasons to come here: the world's finest collection of art from the Middle Ages, including jewelry and tapestries; and it's all displayed in a well-preserved manor house built atop Roman baths. In the cobblestone Cour d'Honneur, you can admire the flamboyant Gothic building with its clinging vines, turreted walls, gargoyles, and dormers with seashell motifs. Along with the Hôtel de Sens in the Marais, this is all that remains in Paris of domestic medieval architecture.

The Cluny was the mansion of a 15th-century abbot. By 1515, it was the home of Mary Tudor, the widow of Louis XII and daughter of Henry VII of England and Elizabeth of York. Seized during the Revolution, it was rented in 1833 to Alexandre du Sommerard, who adorned it with medieval works of art. On his death in 1842, the building and the collection were bought by the government.

Most people come primarily to see the **Unicorn Tapestries** ✦✦✦, the world's most outstanding tapestries. They were discovered a century ago in the Château de Boussac in the Auvergne. Five seem to deal with the senses (one depicts a unicorn looking into a mirror held by a maiden). The sixth shows a woman under an elaborate tent, her pet dog resting on an embroidered cushion beside her. The lovable unicorn and its friendly companion, a lion, hold back the flaps. The red and green background forms a rich carpet of spring flowers, fruit-laden trees, birds, rabbits, donkeys, dogs, goats, lambs, and monkeys.

Downstairs are the ruins of the Roman baths, dating from around A.D. 200. You can wander through a display of Gallic and Roman sculptures and an interesting marble bathtub engraved with lions.

Insider tip: Just inaugurated is a new garden that's a return to the Middle Ages. It was inspired by the luxuriant detail of the museum's most fabled treasure, the 15th-century tapestry of *The Lady of the Unicorn.* It's small, but richly planted.

In the Hôtel de Cluny, 6 place Paul-Painlevé, 5e. © **01-53-73-78-00.** Admission 30F (4.55, \$4.35) adults, 20F (3.04, \$2.90) ages 18–25, free for children 17 and under. Wed–Mon 9:15am–5:45pm. Métro: Cluny–La Sorbonne.

Panthéon ★★ Some of the most famous men in the history of France (Victor Hugo, for one) are buried in austere grandeur, on the crest of the mount of Ste-Geneviève. In 1744, Louis XV made a vow that if he recovered from a mysterious illness, he would build a church to replace the decayed Abbaye de Ste-Geneviève. He recovered—and Mme de Pompadour's brother hired Soufflot for the job. He designed the church in the form of a Greek cross, with a dome reminiscent of St. Paul's in London. When Soufflot died, his pupil Rondelet carried out the work, completing the structure 9 years after his master's death.

Following the Revolution, the church was converted into a "Temple of Fame:" ultimately a panthéon for the great men of France. Mirabeau was buried here, though his remains were later removed. Likewise, Marat was a temporary tenant. Voltaire's body was exhumed and placed here—and allowed to remain. In the 19th century, the building changed roles so many times—first a church, then a panthéon, again a church—it was hard to keep its function straight. After Victor Hugo was buried here, it became a panthéon once more. Other men entombed within include Jean-Jacques Rousseau, Soufflot, Émile Zola, and Louis Braille.

In spring 1995, the ashes of scientist Marie Curie were entombed, "the first lady so honored in our history for her own merits," in the words of François Mitterrand. Madame Curie had been denied membership in the all-male Academy of Sciences. Another woman, Sophie Bertholet, was buried here first, alongside her chemist husband, Marcellin, and not as a personal honor to her.

The finest frescoes, the Puvis de Chavannes, are at the end of the left wall before you enter the crypt. One illustrates Ste-Geneviève bringing supplies to relieve the victims of the famine. The best depicts her white-draped head looking out over moonlit medieval Paris, the city whose patroness she became.

Place du Panthéon, 5e. © **01-44-32-18-00.** Admission 42F (6.430, \$6.09) adults, 23F (3.50, \$3.34) ages 18–25, free for children 17 and under. Apr–Sept daily 9:30am–6:30pm; Oct–Mar daily 10am–6:15pm (last entrance 45 min. before closing). Métro: Cardinal Lemoine or Maubert-Mutualité.

9 St-Germain-des-Prés: The 6th Arrondissement (Left Bank)

This was the postwar home of existentialism, associated with Jean-Paul Sartre, Simone de Beauvoir, Albert Camus, and the intellectual, bohemian crowd that gathered at the Café de Flore, the Brasserie Lipp, and Les Deux-Magots. The black-clad poet Juliette Greco was known as *la muse de St-Germain-des-Prés,* and to Sartre she was the woman with "millions of poems in her throat." Her long hair and uniform of black slacks, black turtleneck sweater, and sandals launched a fashion trend adopted by young women from Paris to California.

In the 1950s, new names appeared—Françoise Sagan, Gore Vidal, and James Baldwin—but by the 1960s, the tourists had become firmly entrenched at the cafes. Today, St-Germain-des-Prés retains a bohemian street life, full of bookshops, art galleries, *caveaux* (basement) nightclubs, bistros, and coffeehouses.

Église St-Germain-des-Prés ★★ Outside it's a handsome early-17th-century town house; inside it's one of Paris's oldest churches, dating from the 6th century when a Benedictine abbey was founded on the site. The marble columns

---

Moments **Gregorians Unplugged**

Église St-Germain-des-Prés stages wonderful concerts on the Left Bank; it boasts fantastic acoustics and a marvelous medieval atmosphere. The church was built to accommodate an age without microphones, and the sound effects will thrill you. For more information, call ℭ **01-43-25-41-71.** Arrive about 45 minutes before the performance if you'd like a front-row seat. Ticket are 120F to 250F (18.25 to 38, $17.40 to $36.25).

---

in the triforium are all that remain from that period. Restoration of the Chapelle St-Symphorien—the site of a panthéon for Merovingian kings, at the entrance of the church—began in 1981. During that work, unknown Romanesque paintings were discovered on the chapel's triumphal arch. The Romanesque tower, topped by a 19th-century spire, is the most enduring landmark in the village of St-Germain-des-Prés. Its church bells, however, are hardly noticed by the patrons of Deux-Magots across the way.

The Normans nearly destroyed the abbey at least four times. The present building has a Romanesque nave and a Gothic choir with fine capitals. Among the people interred at the church are Descartes (well, his heart at least) and Jean-Casimir, the king of Poland who abdicated his throne.

When you leave the church, turn right onto rue de l'Abbaye and have a look at the 17th-century (and very pink) Palais Abbatial.

3 place St-Germain-des-Prés, 6e. ℭ 01-43-25-41-71. Free admission. Daily 8am–8pm. Métro: St-Germain-des-Prés.

Église St-Sulpice ✲✲   Pause first on the rue St-Sulpice. The 1844 fountain by Visconti displays the sculpted likenesses of four bishops of the Louis XIV era: Fenelon, Massillon, Bossuet, and Flechier. Work on the church itself, once Paris's largest, began in 1646 as part of the Catholic revival in France. Although the body of the church was completed in 1745, work on the bell towers continued until 1780, when one was finished, the other left incomplete. One of the most notable treasures inside is Servandoni's rococo Chapelle de la Vierge (Chapel of the Madonna), which contains a Pigalle statue of the Virgin. The church houses one of the world's largest organs; it has 6,700 pipes and has been played by such musicians as Charles-Marie Widor and Marcel Dupré.

The main draw at St-Sulpice is the Delacroix frescoes in the Chapel of the Angels (on your right as you enter). Seek out his Jacob wrestling (or is he dancing?) with an angel. On the ceiling, St. Michael has his own troubles with the devil, and another mural depicts Heliodorus being driven from the temple. Painted in the final years of his life, the frescoes were a high point in the baffling career of Delacroix.

Rue St-Sulpice, 6e. ℭ 01-46-33-21-78. Free admission. Daily 7:30am–7:30pm. Métro: St-Sulpice.

10 The Eiffel Tower/Musée d'Orsay: The 7th Arrondissement (Left Bank)

From place du Trocadéro, you can step between the two curved wings of the Palais de Chaillot and gaze out on a panoramic view. At your feet lie the Jardins du Trocadéro, centered by fountains. Directly in front, pont d'Iéna spans the Seine, leading to the **Eiffel Tower** (see "The Top Attractions," earlier in this chapter). Beyond, stretching as far as your eye can see, is the **Champ-de-Mars,**

Frommer's Favorite Paris Experiences

Strolling Along the Seine. Lovers still walk hand in hand alongside it, and vendors on its banks still peddle everything from postcards to 100-year-old pornography. Some energetic types walk the full 7-mile stretch of the river, but you may want to confine your stroll to central Paris, passing the Louvre, Notre-Dame, and pont Neuf.

Window Shopping Along the Faubourg St-Honoré. In the 1700s, this was home to the wealthiest of Parisians; today, it's home to the stores that cater to them. Even if you don't buy anything, you'll enjoy some great window shopping with all the big names, like Hermès, Larouche, Lacroix, Lanvin, Courrèges, Cardin, St-Laurent, and Lagerfeld.

Enjoying an Afternoon of Cafe-Sitting. The Parisian cafe is an integral part of the city's life. Even if it means skipping a museum, spend some time at a cafe. Whether you have one small coffee or the most expensive cognac in the house, nobody will hurry you, and you can see how the French really live. See our recommendations in chapter 4.

Taking Afternoon Tea à la Française. Skip London's cucumber-and-watercress sandwiches and get down to the business of rich, luscious desserts like Mont Blanc, that creamy purée of sweetened chestnuts. Try the grandest Parisian tea salon of them all: **Angelina,** 226 rue de Rivoli, 1er (see chapter 3). A close rival is the **Salon de Thé Bernardaud,** 11 rue Royale, 8e (© **01-42-66-22-55;** Métro: Concorde), run by the Limoges-based manufacturer of fine porcelain. Teatime here is unique: A staff member presents you with five porcelain patterns and you choose the one in which you'd like your tea served.

Attending an Opera or a Ballet. In 1989, the acoustically perfect Opéra Bastille was inaugurated to compete with the grande dame of Paris's musical scene, the Opéra Garnier, which then was reserved for dance

once a military parade ground, now a garden with arches, grottoes, lakes, and cascades. Also combined with these sights are the **Musée d'Orsay** and the **Musée Rodin** (see "The Top Attractions," earlier in this chapter).

Hôtel des Invalides (Napoléon's Tomb) ✸✸✸   The glory of the French military lives on in the Musée de l'Armée, the world's greatest army museum. It was the Sun King who decided to build the "hotel" to house soldiers who had been disabled by war. It wasn't entirely a benevolent gesture, because these veterans had been injured, crippled, or blinded while fighting Louis's battles. This massive building program was launched in 1670. Eventually the structure was crowned by a Jules Hardouin-Mansart gilded dome.

The best way to approach the Invalides is from the Right Bank across the pont Alexandre-III. Among the collections (begun in 1794) are Viking swords, Burgundian basinets, 14th-century blunderbusses, Balkan khandjars, American Browning machine guns, war pitchforks, salamander-engraved Renaissance serpentines, musketoons, and grenadiers. As a sardonic touch, there's even General Daumesnil's wooden leg. Outstanding are the suits of armor worn by kings and only and eventually closed for renovations. Now the Garnier has reopened, and opera has returned to its rococo splendor. A night here will take you back to the Second Empire, beneath a ceiling by Chagall. Whether for a performance of Bizet or Tharp, check out these two major Paris landmarks. Dress with pomp and circumstance.

Discovering Hidden Montmartre. This is the most touristy part of Paris. But far removed from the area's top draw, Sacré-Coeur, another neighborhood unfolds—that of the true Montmartrois. Wander on any of the backstreets away from the souvenir shops. Arm yourself with a good map and seek out such streets as rue Lepic (refresh yourself at the Lux Bar at no. 12), rue Constance, rue Tholozé (with its view over the rooftops of Paris), lively rue des Abbesses, and rue Germain-Pilon. None of these is famous, none is crowded with hordes of visitors, but each is flanked with buildings whose detailing shows the pride and care that permeates Paris's architecture. You'll discover dozens of other streets on your own.

Checking Out the Marchés. A daily Parisian ritual is ambling through one of the open-air markets to purchase fresh food to be consumed that day—some ripe and creamy Camembert or a pumpkin-gold cantaloupe is at its peak. You can partake of this tradition and gather supplies for a picnic in one of the city's parks. The vendors arrange their wares into a mosaic of vibrant colors. Sanguine, an Italian citrus whose juice is the color of an orange sunset; ruby-red peppers; and golden yellow bananas from Martinique—all dazzle the eye. Our favorite market is on rue Montorgeuil, beginning at rue Rambuteau, 1er (Métro: Les-Halles). See "Shopping," later in this chapter, for other markets to check out.

dignitaries. The famous "armor suit of the lion" was made for François I. The displays of swords are among the world's finest.

Crossing the Cour d'Honneur (Court of Honor), you'll come to Église du Dôme, designed by Hardouin-Mansart for Louis XIV. He began work on the church in 1677, though he died before its completion. The dome is Paris's second-tallest monument. In the Napoléon Chapel is the hearse used at the emperor's funeral on May 9, 1821.

To accommodate the Tomb of Napoléon—made of red porphyry, with a green granite base—the architect Visconti had to redesign the high altar. First buried at St. Helena, Napoléon's remains were returned to Paris in 1840 then locked inside six coffins. Surrounding the tomb are a dozen Amazonlike figures representing his victories. Almost lampooning the smallness of the man, everything is made awesome: You'd think a real giant was buried here, not a symbolic one. The statue of Napoléon in his coronation robes stands 8½ feet tall.

Place des Invalides, 7e. ℂ 01-44-42-37-72. Admission to Musée de l'Armée, Napoléon's Tomb, and Musée des Plans-Reliefs 40F (6.130, $5.80) adults, 30F (4.55, $4.35) children 12–18, free for children 11 and under. Oct–Mar daily 10am–5pm; Apr–May and Sept daily 10am–6pm; June–Aug daily 10am–7pm. Closed Jan 1, May 1, Nov 1, and Dec 25. Métro: Latour-Maubourg, Varenne, or Invalides.

Fun Fact **The Little Corporal's Little Corporal**

Legends abound that some of Napoléon's body parts went missing when he was reburied at the Invalides, notably his penis and heart. According to scholars, the two doctors who dissected the emperor placed all his body parts in an urn positioned between his legs. However, one wealthy gentleman in Connecticut frequently exhibits a penis preserved in alcohol, claiming it was once attached to the emperor.

11 Montparnasse: The 14th Arrondissement (Left Bank)

For the Lost Generation, life centered on the cafes here. Hangouts like the Dôme, Coupole, Rotonde, and Sélect became legendary. Artists, especially American expatriates, turned their backs on touristy Montmartre. Picasso, Modigliani, and Man Ray came this way, and Hemingway. Fitzgerald was here when he was poor (when he was in the chips, he hung out at Le Ritz). Faulkner, Isadora Duncan, Miró, Joyce, Ford Madox Ford, and even Trotsky came here.

The life of Montparnasse still centers around its cafes and nightclubs, many only a shadow of what they used to be. Its heart is at the crossroads of boulevards Raspail and du Montparnasse, one of the settings of Hemingway's *The Sun Also Rises*. Rodin's controversial statue of Balzac swathed in a large cape stands guard over the prostitutes who cluster around the pedestal. Balzac seems to be the only one in Montparnasse who doesn't feel the impact of time and change.

Tour Montparnasse ★★ Towering over the entire arrondissement is the Tour Montparnasse, rising 688 feet—like the Eiffel Tower, a landmark on the Paris skyline. Completed in 1973, it was denounced by some critics as "bringing Manhattan to Paris." The city passed an ordinance outlawing any further structures of this size in the heart of Paris. Today, the tower houses a mammoth underground shopping mall and even a train station. You can ride an elevator to the 56th floor, then climb three flights to the rooftop terrace. At viewing tables at the top, you can pick out all the landmarks, from Sacré-Coeur and Notre-Dame to the new Défense area in the distance. A bar and restaurant are on the 56th floor.

33 avenue du Main, 15e. ✆ **01-45-38-52-56.** Admission 46F (7, $6.65) adults, 38F (5.80, $5.51) seniors, 35F (5.30, $5.08) students, 30F (4.55, $4.35) children 5–14, children under 5 free. Apr–Sept daily 9:30am–11:30pm; Oct–Mar Mon–Fri 9:30am–10:30pm. Métro: Montparnasse-Bienvenue.

Cimetière du Montparnasse ★ In the shadow of the Tour Montparnasse lies this burial ground of yesterday's celebrities, debris-littered and badly maintained. A map (the left of the main gateway) directs you to the most famous occupants: the shared grave site of Simone de Beauvoir and Jean-Paul Sartre. Others buried here include Samuel Beckett, Guy de Maupassant, Alfred Dreyfus, auto tycoon André Citroën, Camille Saint-Saëns, and Man Ray.

3 bd. Edgar-Quinet, 14e. ✆ **01-44-10-86-50.** Mon–Fri 8am–6pm; Sun 9am–6pm. Closes at 5:15pm Nov–Mar. Métro: Edgar-Quinet.

12 Gare Montparnasse/Institut Pasteur: The 15th Arrondissement (Left Bank)

Musée Bourdelle ★ Here you can see works by the prime student of Rodin, Antoine Bourdelle (1861 to 1929). The museum displays the artist's drawings, paintings, and sculptures, and lets you wander through his studio, garden, and house. The most notable exhibits are the 21 studies he did of Beethoven. The original plaster casts of some of his greatest works are also on display. Though some of the exhibits are badly captioned, you'll still feel the impact of Bourdelle's genius.

18 rue Antoine-Bourdelle, 15e. ℭ 01-49-54-73-73. Admission 25F (3.80, $3.65) adults, 22F (3.35, 3.19) students, 15F (2.30, 2.30) children. Tues–Sun 10am–5:40pm. Métro: Falguière.

13 Parks, Gardens & Cemeteries

See section 2, "Musée de Louvre/Les Halles," for details on the **Tuileries.** **Cimetière du Montmartre** can be found in section 6, "Montmartre"; the **Cimetière de Montparnasse** is covered in section 11, "Montparnasse."

Jardin du Luxembourg ★★ *Kids* Hemingway told a friend that the Jardin du Luxembourg "kept us from starvation." He told how in his poverty-stricken days in Paris, he wheeled a baby carriage through the gardens because it was known "for the classiness of its pigeons." When the gendarme left to get a glass of wine, the writer would eye his victim, lure it with corn and snatch it. "We got a little tired of pigeon that year," he confessed, "but they filled many a void."

Before it became a feeding ground for struggling artists in the 1920s, the Luxembourg Gardens knew greater days. They are the finest formal gardens on the Left Bank (some say in all of Paris). Marie de Médici, the much-neglected wife and later widow of the roving Henri IV, ordered the **Palais du Luxembourg** built on this site in 1612. She planned to live here with her "witch" friend, Leonora Galigäi. A Florentine by birth, the regent wanted to create another Pitti Palace, she told the architect, Salomon de Brosse. She wasn't entirely successful, though the overall effect is most often described as Italianate.

The queen didn't get to enjoy the Luxembourg Palace for very long. She was forced into exile by her son, Louis XIII, after he discovered that she was plotting to overthrow him. She died in Cologne in poverty, quite a comedown from the luxury she'd known in the Luxembourg. (Incidentally, the 21 paintings she commissioned from Rubens were intended for her palace but are now in the Louvre.) For 50F (7.60, $7.25), you can visit the palace the first Sunday of each month at 10:30am, but you must call ℭ **01-44-61-21-66** to make a reservation. There is no information number for the park itself.

The main draw here is not the palace but the gardens. They're mostly in the classic French style: well groomed and laid out, the trees planted in designs. The large central water basin is encircled by urns and statuary—one statue honors Ste-Geneviève, the patroness of Paris, depicted with pigtails reaching to her thighs. Come here to soak in the atmosphere, and bring the kids if you have any. You can sail a toy boat, ride a pony, or attend a Grand Guignol puppet show. Best of all, play boules with a group of elderly men who aren't afraid of looking like a cliché from 1928, complete with black berets and Gauloises.

6e. Métro: Odéon. RER: Luxembourg.

Bois de Boulogne ★★ *Kids* This is one of the most spectacular parks in Europe. Horse-drawn carriages traverse it, or you can stroll its many hidden pathways. If you had a week to spare, you could spend it all in the Bois de Boulogne and still not see everything.

Porte-Dauphine is the main entrance, but you can take the Métro to Porte-Maillot as well. West of Paris, the park was once a forest for royal hunts. In the late 19th century, it was very much in vogue: carriages bearing elegant Parisian damsels with their foppish escorts rumbled along avenue Foch. Nowadays, it's more likely to attract middle-class picnickers.

When Napoléon III gave the grounds to the city in 1852, they were developed by Baron Haussmann. Separating Lac Inférieur from Lac Supérieur is the Carrefour des Cascades (you can stroll under its waterfall). The Lower Lake contains two islands connected by a footbridge. From the east bank, you can take a boat to these grounds, perhaps stopping at the cafe-restaurant on one of them. Restaurants in the Bois are numerous, elegant, and expensive. The Pré-Catelan contains a deluxe restaurant of the same name and a Shakespearean theater in a garden said to have been planted with trees mentioned in the bard's plays.

The **Jardin d'Acclimation,** at the northern edge of the park, is for children, with a small zoo, amusement park, and a narrow-gauge railway. Two racetracks, **Longchamp** and **Auteuil,** are in the park. The annual Grand Prix is run in June at Longchamp (site of a medieval abbey). Fashionable Parisians turn out, the women attired in their finest haute couture and hats. To the north of Longchamp is the Grand Cascade, the artificial waterfall of the Bois de Boulogne.

In the 60-acre **Bagatelle Park,** the comte d'Artois (later Charles X), brother-in-law of Marie Antoinette, made a wager with her that he could erect a small palace in less than 3 months. He hired nearly 1,000 craftsmen and irritated the local populace by requisitioning all shipments of stone and plaster arriving through the west gates of Paris. He hired ébenistes, painters, and the Scottish landscape architect Thomas Blaikie—and won his bet. If you're in Paris in late April, go to the Bagatelle to look at the tulips. In late May, one of the finest and best-known rose collections in all of Europe is in full bloom. If you can, visit in September, when the light is less harsh than in summer, or even in February, when, stripped of much of its greenery, the park's true shape can be seen. *Note:* Beware of muggers and knife-carrying prostitutes at night.

Porte-Dauphine, 16e. ☏ **01-40-67-90-82.** Métro: Les-Sablons, Porte-Maillot, or Porte-Dauphine.

Parc Monceau An American expatriate once said that all babies in Parc Monceau were respectable. Whether or not babies like the park, their mothers and nurses seem fond of wheeling their carriages through it. Much of the park is ringed with 18th- and 19th-century mansions, some evoking Proust's *Remembrance of Things Past.* The park was opened to the public during Napoléon III's Second Empire. It was built in 1778 by the duc d'Orléans, or Philippe-Egalité, as he became known.

Parc Monceau was laid out with an Egyptian-style obelisk, a medieval dungeon, a thatched alpine farmhouse, a Chinese pagoda, a Roman temple, an enchanted grotto, various chinoiseries, and a waterfall. These fairy-tale touches have largely disappeared except for a pyramid and an oval *naumachie* fringed by a colonnade. Many of the fantasies have been replaced by solid statuary and monuments, one honoring Chopin. In spring, the red tulips and magnolias alone are worth the airfare to Paris.

8e. ☏ **01-42-27-39-56.** Métro: Monceau or Villiers.

Cimetière du Père-Lachaise ★★ When it comes to name-dropping, this cemetery has been called the "grandest address in Paris." Everybody from Sarah Bernhardt to Oscar Wilde (his tomb by Epstein) was buried here. So were Balzac, Delacroix, and Bizet. Colette was taken here in 1954 (legend has it that cats replenish the red roses found on her black granite slab). In time, the "little sparrow," Edith Piaf, followed. The lover of George Sand, poet Alfred de

Royal Remains at St-Denis

In the 12th century, Abbot Suger placed an inscription on the bronze doors of St-Denis: "Marvel not at the gold and expense, but at the craftsmanship of the work." The first Gothic building in France that can be dated precisely, St-Denis was the "spiritual defender of the State" during the reign of Louis VI ("The Fat"). The facade, with its crenelated parapet on the top similar to the fortifications of a castle, has a rose window. The windows, in stunning colors—mauve, purple, blue, and rose—were restored in the 19th century.

St-Denis, the first bishop of Paris, was patron saint of the French monarchy. Royal burials began here in the 6th century and continued until the Revolution. The sculptures around the four tombs—some two stories high—span the country's artistic development from the Middle Ages to the Renaissance. The guided tour (in French only) takes you through the crypt. François I was entombed at St-Denis. His funeral statue is nude, although he demurely covers himself with his hand. Other kings and queens here include Louis XII and Anne of Brittany, as well as Henri II and Catherine de Médici. Revolutionaries stormed through, smashing many marble faces and dumping royal remains in a lime-filled ditch in the garden. They were reburied under the main altar during the 19th century. The basilica stands today in a northern suburb of Paris, but it's easily reached by the Métro. Free organ concerts are presented on Sundays at 11:15am.

The Basilique St-Denis is located at Place de l'Hôtel-de-Ville, 2 rue de Strasbourg (*C* **01-48-09-83-54**). Admission is 32F (4.80, $4.65) for adults and 21F (3.15, $3.05) for seniors and students, children 11 and under are admitted free. It's open Monday through Saturday from 10am-7pm and on Sundays from 12-7pm April through September. October to March, it's open 10am-5pm Monday through Saturday, and 12-5pm Sundays, closed January 1, November 1 and 11, and December 25. The closest Métro is St-Denis Basilique.

Musset, was buried under a weeping willow. Napoléon's marshals Ney and Masséna were entombed here, and Chopin and Molière. Marcel Proust's black tombstone rarely lacks a bunch of violets; Proust wished to be buried with his friend and lover, composer Maurice Ravel, but their families wouldn't allow it.

Some tombs are sentimental favorites: that of rock star Jim Morrison reportedly draws the most visitors—and causes the most disruption. The dancer Isadora Duncan rests in a "pigeonhole" in the Columbarium, where bodies have been cremated and then "filed." If you search hard enough, you can find the tombs of Abélard and Héloïse, the ill-fated lovers of the 12th century. At Père-Lachaise, they've found peace at last. Other famous lovers rest here: one stone is marked Gertrude Stein on one side, Alice B. Toklas on the other.

Spreading over more than 110 acres, Père-Lachaise was acquired by the city in 1804. Nineteenth-century French sculpture abounds, each family trying to outdo the others in ornamentation and cherubic ostentation. Some French socialists still pay tribute at the Mur des Fédérés, the anonymous gravesite of the

Communards who were executed on May 28, 1871. The French who died in the Resistance or in Nazi concentration camps are also honored by several monuments.

Note: A free map is available at the newsstand across from the main entrance; it will help you find the well-known grave sites.

16 rue de Repos, 20e. ⓒ **01-55-25-82-10.** Mon–Fri 8am–6pm; Sat 8:30am–6pm; Sun 9am–6pm. Nov to early Mar closes at 5:30pm. Métro: Père-Lachaise.

14 Paris Underground

Les Catacombs ⓐ★ Every year an estimated 50,000 tourists explore some 1,000 yards of underground tunnel to look at six million ghoulishly arranged skeletons. First opened to the public in 1810, this "empire of the dead" is now illuminated by overhead electric lights throughout its entire length.

In the Middle Ages, the Catacombs were originally quarries, but in 1785, city officials decided to use them as a burial ground. The bones of several million persons were moved here from their previous resting places, since the overcrowded cemeteries were considered health menaces. In 1830, the prefect of Paris closed the Catacombs to the viewing public, considering them obscene and indecent. He maintained that he could not understand the morbid curiosity of civilized people who wanted to gaze upon the bones of the dead. Later, in World War II, the Catacombs were the headquarters of the French Resistance.

1 place Denfert-Rochereau, 14e. ⓒ **01-43-22-47-63.** www.multimania.com/houze. Admission 33F (5, $4.80) adults, 23F (3.50, $3.34) seniors, 17F (2.63, $2.47) ages 7–25, children under 7 free. Tues–Fri 2–4pm; Sat–Sun 9–11am and 2–4pm. Métro: Denfert-Rochereau.

The Sewers of Paris (Les Égouts) ⓐ★ Some sociologists assert that the sophistication of a society can be judged by the way it disposes of waste. If that's true, Paris receives good marks for its network of sewers. Victor Hugo is credited with making these sewers famous in *Les Misérables.* "All dripping with slime, his soul filled with a strange light," Jean Valjean makes his flight through the sewers of Paris. Hugo also wrote, "Paris has beneath it another Paris, a Paris of sewers, which has its own streets, squares, lanes, arteries, and circulation."

In the early Middle Ages, drinking water was taken directly from the Seine, while wastewater was poured onto fields or thrown onto the then-unpaved streets, transforming the urban landscape into a sea of rather smelly mud.

ⓒ*Moments* **Memorial to a Princess**

Place de l'Alma (Métro: Alma-Marceau) has been turned into a tribute to the late Diana, princess of Wales, killed in an auto accident August 31, 1997, in the nearby underpass. The bronze flame in the center is a replication of the flame in the Statue of Liberty and was a 1987 gift from the *International Herald Tribune* to honor Franco-American friendship. Many bouquets and messages (and even graffiti) are still placed around the flame, which seems to have come to represent the princess.

Paris has also opened the **Center for Nature Discovery, Garden in Memory of Diana, Princess of Wales,** at 21 rue des Blancs-Manteaux in the Marais. The small park, which you can visit daily during daylight hours, is devoted to teaching children about nature and gardening, and contains flowers, vegetables, and decorative plants.

Around 1200, the streets of Paris were paved with cobblestones, with open sewers down the center. These helped spread the Black Death, which devastated the city. In 1370, a vaulted sewer was built in the rue Montmartre, draining effluents into a tributary of the Seine. During the reign of Louis XIV, improvements were made, but waste disposal in Paris remained deplorable.

During the early 1800s, under the reign of Napoléon, 18½ miles of sewer were added beneath the Parisian landscape. By 1850, as the Industrial Revolution made the manufacture of iron pipe and steam-digging equipment more practical, Baron Haussmann developed a system that used separate underground channels for both drinking water and sewage. By 1878, it was 360 miles long. Beginning in 1894, under the guidance of Belgrand, the network was enlarged, and new laws required that discharge of all waste and storm water runoff be funneled into the sewers. Between 1914 and 1977, an additional 600 miles of sewers were added beneath the pavements of a burgeoning Paris.

Today, the city boasts some memorable statistics regarding its waste disposal. The network of sewers, one of the world's best, is 1,300 miles long. Within its cavities, it contains freshwater mains, compressed-air pipes, telephone cables, and pneumatic tubes. Every day, 1.3 million cubic yards of wastewater are processed by a plant in the suburb of Achères. One of the largest in Europe, it's capable of treating more than 2.18 million cubic yards of sewage per day.

The *égouts* (sewers) of the city, as well as telephone and telegraph pneumatic tubes, are constructed around four principal tunnels, one 18 feet wide and 15 feet high. It's like an underground city, with the street names clearly labeled. Further, each branch pipe bears the number of the building to which it is connected.

Tours of the sewers begin at Pont de l'Alma on the Left Bank, where a stairway leads into the bowels of the city. However, you often have to wait in line as much as half an hour. Visiting times may change in bad weather, as a storm can make the sewers dangerous. The tour consists of a movie on sewer history, a visit to a small museum, and a short trip through the maze.

Pont de l'Alma, 7e. *€* **01-53-68-27-81**. Admission 25F (3.80, $3.63) adults, 20F (3.04, $2.90) students, seniors, and children 5–12, children under 5 free. May–Oct Sat–Wed 11am–5pm; Nov–Apr Sat–Wed 11am–4pm. Closed 3 weeks in Jan. Métro: Alma-Marceau. RER: Pont de l'Alma.

15 Shopping

Shopping is the local pastime of Parisians; some would even say it reflects the city's very soul. The City of Light is one of the rare places in the world where you don't go anywhere in particular to shop—shopping surrounds you on almost every street. The windows, stores, and people (and yes, even their dogs) brim with energy, creativity, and a sense of visual expression. You don't have to buy anything to appreciate shopping in Paris—just soak up the art form the French have made of consumerism. Peer in the *vitrines* (display windows), absorb cutting-edge ideas, witness new trends—and take home an education in style.

BUSINESS HOURS

Shops are usually open Monday through Saturday from 10am to 7pm, but the hours vary, and Paris doesn't run at full throttle on Monday mornings. Small shops sometimes take a 2-hour lunch break and may not open until after lunch on Mondays. While most stores open at 10am, some open at 9:30am or even

11am. Thursday is the best day for late-night shopping, with stores open until 9 or 10pm.

Sunday shopping is currently limited to tourist areas and flea markets, though there's growing demand for full-scale Sunday hours, à la the United States and the United Kingdom. The big department stores are now open for the five Sundays before Christmas; otherwise, they're dead on *dimanche*.

The Carrousel du Louvre, an underground mall adjacent to the Louvre, is open and hopping on Sundays but closed on Mondays. The tourist shops that line rue de Rivoli across from the Louvre are open on Sundays, as are the antiques villages, flea markets, and several good food markets in the streets. The Virgin Megastore on the Champs-Elysées pays a fine in order to stay open on Sunday. It's *the* teen hangout.

GREAT SHOPPING AREAS

1er & 8e These two *quartiers* adjoin each other and form the heart of Paris's best Right Bank shopping neighborhood. This area includes the famed **rue du Faubourg St-Honoré,** with the big designer houses, and **avenue des Champs-Elysées,** where the mass-market and teen scenes are hot. At one end of the 1er is the **Palais Royal**—one of the city's best shopping secrets, where an arcade of boutiques flanks the garden of the former palace.

At the other side of town, at the end of the 8e, is **avenue Montaigne,** 2 blocks of the fanciest shops in the world, where you float from one big name to another.

2e Right behind the Palais Royal lies the **Garment District** (Sentier), as well as a few upscale shopping secrets like **place des Victoires.** This area also hosts a few old-fashioned *passages,* alleys filled with tiny stores such as **Galerie Vivienne** on rue Vivienne.

3e & 4e The difference between these two arrondissements gets fuzzy, especially around **place des Vosges,** center stage of the Marais. Even so, they offer several dramatically different shopping experiences.

On the surface, the shopping includes the real-people stretch of **rue de Rivoli** (which becomes **rue St-Antoine**). Two department stores are in this area: **La Samaritaine,** 19 rue de la Monnaie (© **01-40-41-20-20**), occupies four noteworthy buildings erected between 1870 and 1927. **BHV** (Bazar de l'Hôtel de Ville), which opened in 1856, has seven floors loaded with merchandise; it lies adjacent to Paris's City Hall at 52–64 rue de Rivoli (© **01-42-74-90-00**).

Hidden in the Marais is a medieval warren of tiny, twisting streets chockablock with cutting-edge designers and up-to-the-minute fashions and trends. Start by walking around place des Vosges for galleries, designer shops, and fabulous finds, then dive in and get lost in the area leading to the Musée Picasso.

Finally, the 4e is also home of **place de la Bastille,** an up-and-coming area for artists and galleries where the newest entry on the retail scene, the **Viaduc des Arts** (which actually stretches into the 12e), is situated.

6e & 7e Whereas the 6e is one of the most famous shopping districts in Paris—it's the soul of the Left Bank—much of the good stuff is hidden in the zone that becomes the wealthy residential 7e. **Rue du Bac,** stretching from the 6e to the 7e in a few blocks, stands for all that wealth and glamour can buy. The street is jammed with art galleries, home-decor stores, and gourmet-food shops.

9e To add to the fun of shopping the Right Bank, 9e sneaks in behind 1er, so if you choose not to walk toward the Champs-Elysées and the 8e, you can head to the city's big department stores, built in a row along **boulevard Haussmann** in the 9e. Here you'll find not only the two big French icons, **Au Printemps** and **Galeries Lafayette,** but also a large branch of Britain's **Marks & Spencer.**

SHOPPING A TO Z

ANTIQUES   Directly across from the Louvre, **Le Louvre des Antiquaires,** 2 place du Palais-Royal, 1er (✆ **01-42-97-00-14;** Métro: Palais-Royal), is the largest repository of antiques in central Paris. More than 250 dealers display their wares on three floors, specializing in objets d'art and small-scale furniture of the type that might have been favored by Mme de Pompadour. You may find 30 matching Baccarat crystal champagne flutes from the 1930s, a Sèvres tea service dated 1773, or a small Jean Fouquet pin of gold and diamonds. Too stuffy? No problem. There's always the 1940 Rolex with the aubergine crocodile strap.

Village St-Paul, 23–27 rue St-Paul, 4e (no phone; Métro: St-Paul), isn't an antiques center but a cluster of individual dealers in their own hole-in-the-wall hideout; the rest of the street, stretching from the river to the Marais, is lined with dealers, most of which are closed on Sundays. The Village St-Paul, however, *is* open on Sunday, and hopping. Inside the courtyards and alleys are every dreamer's visions of hidden Paris: many dealers selling furniture and other decorative items in French provincial and, to a much lesser extent, formal styles.

ART   **Galerie Adrien Maeght,** 42 rue du Bac, 7e (✆ **01-45-48-45-15;** Métro: Rue-du-Bac), is among the most famous names, selling contemporary art on a very fancy Left Bank street. In addition to major works of art, it sells posters beginning at 30F (4.55, $4.35), signed and numbered lithographs from 500F (76, $72.50), and books on art and artists.

The **Viaduc des Arts,** 9–147 av. Daumesnil (between rue de Lyon and av. Diderot), 12e (✆ **01-44-75-80-66;** Métro: Bastille, Ledru-Rollin, Reuilly-Diderot, or Gare-de-Lyon), occupies a long 2-block stretch from the Opéra Bastille to the Gare de Lyon, and features art galleries and artisans in individual boutiques within the arches of an old train viaduct. As you can tell from the number of Métro stops that serve the address, you can start at one end and work your way to the other, or even start in the middle.

BOOKS   The most famous bookstore on the Left Bank was **Shakespeare and Company,** on rue de l'Odéon, home to the legendary Sylvia Beach, "mother confessor to the Lost Generation." Hemingway, Fitzgerald, and Gertrude Stein were all patrons. Anaïs Nin often stopped in. At one point she helped Henry Miller publish *Tropic of Cancer,* a book so notorious in its day that returning Americans trying to slip a copy through Customs often had it confiscated as

---

Finds **An Open-Air Canvas Gallery**

The **Paris Art Market** is "the place to go" on Sunday. The Art Market at the foot of Montparnasse Tower is like an open-air gallery and has done much to restore the reputation of Montparnasse (14e) as a *quartier* for artists. Some 100 artists participate, including painters, sculptors, and photographers, even jewelers and hat makers. Head for the mall along the boulevard Edgar Quinet for the best of work. Go any time on Sunday between 10am and 7:30pm. Métro: Montparnasse.

---

pornography. Long ago, the shop moved to 37 rue de la Bûcherie, 5e (no phone; Métro: St-Michel), where expatriates swap books and literary gossip.

Tea and Tattered Pages, 24 rue Mayet, 6e (✆ **01-40-65-94-35**; Métro: Duroc), is one of the largest stores in Paris specializing in used English-language books.

Scattered over two floors of tightly packed inventory, **The Village Voice Bookshop,** 6 rue Princesse, 6e (✆ **01-46-33-36-47**; Métro: Mabillon), specializes in new English-language books, so it's a favorite among expat Yankees and Brits. It's near some of the Left Bank gathering places described in Gertrude Stein's *The Autobiography of Alice B. Toklas.*

W. H. Smith France, 248 rue de Rivoli, 1er (✆ **01-44-77-88-99**; Métro: Concorde), is France's largest store devoted to English and American books, magazines, and periodicals. You can get the *Times* of London and the Sunday *New York Times,* available every Monday afternoon. There's a fine selection of maps and travel guides.

CHILDREN'S CLOTHES, SHOES & TOYS

Au Nain Bleu, 406 rue St-Honoré, 8e (✆ **01-42-60-39-01**; Métro: Concorde), is the world's fanciest toy store. But don't panic; in addition to the expensive stuff, there are rows of penny candy–style cheaper toys in jars.

Bonpoint, 15 rue Royale, 8e (✆ **01-47-42-52-63**; Métro: Concorde), is part of a well-known chain that helps parents transform their darlings into models of well-tailored conspicuous consumption. Though you'll find some garments for real life, the primary allure of the place lies in its tailored, traditional—and very expensive—garments designed by the "Coco Chanel of the children's garment industry," Marie-France Cohen. The shop sells clothes for boys and girls from newborns to 16-year-olds.

The prices are a whole lot lower at **Dipaki,** 18 rue Vignon, 9e (✆ **01-42-66-24-74**; Métro: Madeleine), which carries selections for toddlers to 12-year-olds. Kids will love the fashions, which are wearable, washable, and affordable. It's only a short walk from place de la Madeleine.

Natalys, 92 av. des Champs-Elysées (midway between Planet Hollywood and the Lido), 8e (✆ **01-43-59-17-65**; Métro: Franklin-D.-Roosevelt), is part of a French chain with about 15 stores in Paris. It's an upscale mass-marketer of maternity clothes and garments for kids up to 6 years old. The styles have just enough French panache without going over the top in design or price. There's also a wide inventory of strollers, cribs, bassinets, and car seats.

CHINA & CRYSTAL

Purveyor to kings and presidents of France since 1764, **Baccarat,** 30 bis rue de Paradis, 10e (✆ **01-47-70-64-30**; Métro: Gare-de-l'Est), and 11 place de la Madeleine, 8e (✆ **01-42-65-36-26**; Métro: Madeleine), produces world-renowned full-lead crystal in dinnerware, jewelry, chandeliers, and statuary. The rue Paradis address is the more historic, while the Madeleine branch is more glamorous but less well stocked. The Madeleine showroom stocks porcelain and crystal from other manufacturers like Christofle.

Lalique, 11 rue Royale, 8e (✆ **01-53-05-12-12**; Métro: Concorde), famous for its clear- and frosted-glass sculpture, Art Deco crystal, and perfume bottles, has recently branched out into sales of other types of merchandise—like silk scarves meant to compete with Hermès and leather belts with Lalique buckles.

And then there's **Limoges-Unic & Madronet,** at 34 and 58 rue de Paradis, 10e (✆ **01-47-70-54-49** or 01-47-70-61-49; Métro: Gare-de-l'Est). In two shops a 3-minute walk from each other on the same street, you'll find Limoges china and anything else you might need for the table—glass, crystal, and silver. It pays to drop into both stores before making a purchase, as their inventories vary slightly according to the season and the whims of the buyers.

CHOCOLATE   Some of Paris's most delicious chocolates can be found at **Christian Constant,** 37 rue d'Assas, 6e (✆ **01-53-63-15-15;** Métro: St-Placide). Particularly appealing are combinations of chocolate meringue, chocolate mousse, and the bitter chocolate *feuilles d'automne* (autumn leaves).

Racks and racks of chocolates are priced individually or by the kilo (2.2 lbs) at **La Maison du Chocolat,** 225 rue du Faubourg St-Honoré, 8e (✆ **01-42-27-39-44;** Métro: Ternes), though it'll cost you nearly or over 500F (76, $72.50) for a kilo. Note the similarity to Hermès when it comes to the wrapping and ribbon (and prices). The chocolate pastries are affordable; the store even has its own chocolate milk! There are five other branches around Paris.

CRAFTS   One of the few regional handcrafts stores in Paris worth going out of your way to find, **La Tuile à Loup,** 35 rue Daubenton, 5e (✆ **01-47-07-28-90;** Métro: Censier-Daubenton), carries beautiful pottery and fäience from many regions of France. Look for figures of Breton folk on the fäience of Quimper as well as garlands of fruits, leaves, and flowers from the *terre vernissée* (varnished earth, a charming way to define stoneware) from Normandy, Savoy, Alsace, and Provence. Prices begin at 10F (1.52, $1.45) for a sachet of Provençal lavender and climb as high as 4,000F (608, $580) for a bulky but undeniably beautiful wall plaque.

DEPARTMENT & DIME STORES   After you've admired the architecture of one of Europe's most famous department stores, step inside **Au Printemps,** 64 bd. Haussmann, 9e (✆ **01-42-82-50-00;** Métro: Havre-Caumartin; RER: Auber), for a view of all it offers. Inside the main building is Printemps de la Mode, which occupies the bulk of the structure, and an affiliated housewares shop, Printemps de la Maison. Upstairs are floors of wares of every sort, especially clothing. An affiliated store, under the same management but across the street, is **Brummel,** the menswear division. Directly behind the main store is a branch of **Prisunic,** Printemps's workaday but serviceable dime store, which contains a grocery. Be sure to check out the magnificent stained-glass dome, built in 1923, through which kaleidoscopic light cascades into the sixth-floor cafe. English-speaking interpreters are stationed throughout the store and at the Welcome Desk in the basement of the main building. *Note:* Foreign visitors who show their passport will receive a flat 10% discount.

A two-part department store, **Au Bon Marché,** 22 and 28 rue de Sèvres, 7e (✆ **01-44-39-80-00;** Métro: Sèvres-Babylone), is on the Left Bank in the midst of all the chic boutiques. Number 28 houses a gourmet grocery store; no. 22 is a source for all your general shopping needs.

Colette, 213 rue St-Honoré, 1er (✆ **01-55-35-33-90;** Métro: Palais-Royal), is Paris's new store of the moment, a swank citadel for à la mode fashion that has made the elegant but staid rue St-Honoré less stuffy. For cutting-edge design, this is the place to go; you'll see fashions by young talents like Marni and Lucien Pellat-Fimet, furnishings by such designers as Tom Dixon, and even zany Japanese accessories. Here's a tip: Even if you don't buy any of the merchandise, head for the tea salon downstairs for fresh quiches, salads, and cakes.

At **Galeries Lafayette,** 40 bd. Haussmann, 9e (✆ **01-42-82-34-56;** Métro: Chaussée-d'Antin; RER: Auber), take a minute to stand under "the Dome"—a stained-glass cupola that towers above the arcaded store. Built in 1912, Galeries

Lafayette is now divided into several stores: **Galfa** men's store, **Lafayette Sports,** and two other general-merchandise stores, both known simply as **"GL."** Next door is a branch of the dime store **Prisunic,** which the chain also owns. Above Prisunic is one of the fanciest grocery stores in town, **Gourmet Lafayette,** with prices half those at Fauchon.

FASHION: CUTTING-EDGE CHIC   Azzadine Alaïa, 7 rue de Moussy, 4e (© **01-42-72-19-19;** Métro: Hôtel-de-Ville), showcases the collection of the darling of French fashion in the 1970s. Alaïa revived body consciousness and put the ooh-la-la in Paris chic; he specializes in evening dresses. If you can't afford the current collection, try the stock shop around the corner at 18 rue de Verrerie (© **01-40-27-85-58;** Métro: Hôtel-de-Vil), where last year's leftovers are sold at serious discounts.

   Jean-Charles de Castelbajac, 26 rue Madame, 6e (© **01-45-48-40-55;** Métro: St-Sulpice), is the bad boy of French fashion, known for flamboyant yet amusing gear in primary colors, often with big bold sayings scribbled across the clothes. His store is in a cluster of designer shops that's great for gawking.

   Jean-Paul Gaultier, 6 rue Vivienne, 2e (© **01-42-86-05-50**; Métro: Bourse), tucked in one of Paris's most famous passageways, this boutique features the typical fare of this master punk turned tailor: street fashion made high fashion. A newer branch of the store, featuring exactly the same inventory, is at 30 rue du Faubourg St-Antoine, 12e (© **01-44-68-84-84**; Métro: Bastille).

FASHION: VINTAGE COUTURE   At Didier Ludot, 24 Galerie de Montpensier, in the arcades surrounding the courtyard of the Palais-Royal, 1er (© **01-42-96-06-56;** Métro: Palais-Royal), fashion historians salivate when they're confronted with an inventory of the *haute couture* of yesteryear. In this frenetically stylish shop, at prices that rival what you'd expect to pay for a serious antique, you'll find a selection of gowns and dresses created between 1900 and 1980 for designing women who looked *faaabulous* at Maxim's, at chic cocktail parties on the Avenue Foch, in Deauville, or wherever.

FASHION: DISCOUNT & RESALE   Anna Lowe, 104 rue du Faubourg St-Honoré, 8e (© **01-42-66-11-32;** Métro: Miromesnil), is one of the premier boutiques for the discriminating woman who wishes to purchase a little Chanel or perhaps a Versace…at a discount, *bien sur.* Many clothes are runway samples; some have been gently worn.

   The inventory at **Réciproque,** 88–123 rue de la Pompe (between av. Victor-Hugo and av. Georges-Mandel), 16e (© **01-47-04-30-28;** Métro: Pompe), is scattered over five buildings in a residential neighborhood. Everything it carries is secondhand, clustered into sections devoted to Chanel, Versace, Lacroix, Hermès, and Mugler. Women will find gowns, suits, sportswear, and shoes. Men should go to no. 101. Although everything here has already been worn, in some cases that means only on runways or during photo shoots.

   French film stars often shop at **Défilé des Marques**, 171 rue de Grenelles, 7e (© **01-45-55-63-47**; Métro: Latour-Maubourg), but anyone can pick up discounted Laurent, Dior, Lacroix, Prada, Hermès, and others at a fraction of the price. Yes, discounted Hermès scarves are sold here as well.

   L'Annex des Createurs, 19 rue Godot de Mauroy, 9e (© **01-42-65-43-40;** Métro: Madeleine or Aubert), is the place to go to stock up on last year's luxurious brands from the collection of Versace, Dolce & Gabbana, Sophie Sitbon, and the like. All merchandise is discounted from 40% to 70%.

Hidden away in a second-floor apartment, **L'Une et L'Autre,** 24 rue Feydeau, 2e (✆ **01-44-76-03-03;** Métro: St-Paul), offers very luxurious clothing at amazing discounts. For example, an item that might sell for 3,500F (532, $507.50) in a boutique is sold here for 1,500F (228, $217.50).

FASHION FLAGSHIPS   If you can't have the sun, the moon, and the stars, at least buy something with Coco Chanel's initials on it—either classic Chanel, or something with Karl Lagerfeld's rather interesting twist. The **Chanel** boutique is at 31 rue Cambon, 1er (✆ **01-42-86-28-00;** Métro: Concorde or Tuileries).

During the decade (1947 to 57) that he directed his empire, **Christian Dior,** 30–32 av. Montaigne, 8e (✆ **01-40-73-54-44;** Métro: Franklin-D.-Roosevelt), was the only couturier whose name was known throughout the Western Hemisphere. The house continues to thrive since its reorganization into a small-scale version of a department store, with sections devoted to men's, women's, and children's clothing; gift items; makeup and perfume; and so on. Unlike some of the other big-name fashion houses, Dior is very approachable.

One of the most recognizable accessories in France is a lavishly opulent silk scarf or tie from **Hermès,** 24 rue du Faubourg St-Honoré, 8e (✆ **01-40-17-47-17;** Métro: Concorde). You'll find them in abundance, along with everything else (bags, purses, and suitcases) endorsed by the legendary saddlemaker, at the flagship branch, which occupies the most prestigious shopping street in France.

Louis Vuitton, 6 place St-Germain-des-Prés, 6e (✆ **01-45-49-62-32;** Métro: St-Germain-des-Prés), is the most interestingly decorated branch of Vuitton in Paris. Antiques and fine hardwoods evoke the grand age of travel, when steamships and railway cars hauled the affluent to exotic places. It stocks a wide inventory of purses, suitcases, and trunks with the traditional monogram, plus new lines of Vuitton leather goods crafted from beige cowhide. The store also sells writing instruments as well as a Carnet du Voyage, a do-it-yourself scrapbook with watercolors and space in which to jot down your own memories.

FOOD   At the place de la Madeleine stands one of the most popular sights in the city—not La Madeleine church but **Fauchon,** 26 place de la Madeleine, 8e (✆ **01-47-42-60-11;** Métro: Madeleine), which offers a wider choice of upscale gourmet products than anyplace else in the world. Distinct areas are devoted to candy, pastries, and bread; fresh fruits and veggies; dry and canned goods; fresh fish and meats; awe-inspiring take-away food; and wine.

Fauchon's main competitor, **Hédiard,** 21 place de la Madeleine, 8e (✆ **01-43-12-88-77;** Métro: Madeleine), opened in 1854. It was recently renovated and transformed into a series of salons filled with almost Disneyesque displays meant to give the store the look of a turn-of-the-20th-century spice emporium. Upstairs is the solidly reliable **Restaurant de l'Epicerie.**

More intimate than its larger competitors, **Albert Ménès,** 41 bd. Malesherbes, 8e (✆ **01-42-66-95-63;** Métro: St-Augustin or Madeleine), serves the Parisian upper crust with jams, confiture, sugared almonds, teas, and assorted gourmet foodstuffs, many from small-scale producers from the provinces. Virtually everything can be shipped or packed for easy transport. A specialty food basket for the holidays is a status treat and can be made in virtually any price range.

Le Maison du Miel, the House of Honey, at 24 rue Vignon, 9e (✆ **01-47-42-26-70;** Métro: Madeleine, Havre-Caumartin, or Opéra), has been a family tradition since before World War I. The entire store is devoted to products made from honey: honey oil, honey soap, regional varieties of nougat, and various honeys to eat. It's around the corner from Fauchon and worth the walk.

JEWELRY Well-dressed women around the world wear fabulous gemstones from **Van Cleef & Arpels,** 22 place Vendôme, 1er (✆ **01-53-45-45-45;** Métro: Opéra or Tuileries). One of the firm's specialties is yellow diamonds whose color resembles amber but whose fire is unmistakably brilliant. Floral motifs, set into platinum or gold with vibrant hues, are also a trademark.

LEATHER A cult hero in France yet virtually unknown elsewhere, **Didier Lamarthe,** 219 rue St-Honoré, 1er (✆ **01-42-96-09-90;** Métro: Tuileries), is famous for his handbags and small leather goods in funky fashion shades like melon or mint. Sure, he does more conservative colors like navy and black, but if you want the world to know you've been to Paris and that you're totally *branché* (plugged in), spring for one of the more risqué shades.

Longchamp, 404 rue St-Honoré, 1er (✆ **01-43-16-00-12;** Métro: Concorde), is known for high-quality leather and strong everyday durables that come in basic as well as fashion shades. Except for a handful of men's accessories (briefcases, belts, and ties), most of the inventory is designed for women.

LINGERIE The undergarments sold and manufactured by **Cadolle,** 14 rue Cambon, 1er (✆ **01-42-60-38-37;** Métro: Concorde), are among the world's most comfortable and opulent. Herminie Cadolle invented the brassiere nearby in 1889, and in 1911, she moved to this location near the former headquarters of Coco Chanel, whose "emaciated" styles she disliked. Today, the store is managed by her great-granddaughters. What's new here? The magic word is corsets, preferably in black, worn with long skirts or slacks. Fashioned from everything from velvet to satins, they're almost guaranteed to turn heads day or night.

MALLS At **Carrousel du Louvre,** 99 rue de Rivoli, 1er (no phone; Métro: Palais-Royal-Musée-du-Louvre), you can combine a convenient location, a food court, handy boutiques, and plenty of museum gift shops with a touch of culture. Always mobbed, this is one of the few venues allowed to stay open on Sundays. The easiest way to get here is to enter from rue de Rivoli. There's a Virgin Megastore, the Body Shop, and several big-name boutiques, like Courrèges and Lalique. Check out Diane Claire for the fanciest souvenirs you've ever seen. A branch of the French Government Tourist Office is next door to Virgin.

Forget about the street address of **Forum des Halles,** 1–7 rue Pierre-Lescot, 1er (no phone; Métro: Etienne-Marcel or Châtelet-Les-Halles). This mall fills an entire block where the great old produce market, Les Halles, once stood. Now it's a crater of modern metal with layers of boutiques around a courtyard. There's one of everything here—but the feel is sterile, without a hint of *joie de vivre.* It's near the Centre Pompidou if you need access to a lot of stores in a hurry.

MARKETS Artists love to paint the **Marché aux Fleurs,** place Louis-Lépine, on Île de la Cité, 4e (Métro: Cité); photographers love to click away. The stalls are ablaze with color, each a showcase of flowers (most of which escaped the fate of being hauled to the perfume factories of Grasse in the French Riviera). The Flower Market is along the Seine, behind the Tribunal de Commerce. On Sundays, this is a bird market.

Paris's most famous flea market is a grouping of more than a dozen flea markets. **Marché aux Puces de Clignancourt,** av. de la Porte de Clignancourt (no phone; Métro: Porte-de-Clignancourt; then turn left, cross bd. Ney, and walk north on av. de la Porte de Clignancourt), is a complex of 2,500 to 3,000 open stalls and shops in St-Ouen, a suburb just north of the 18th arrondissement. It sells everything from antiques to junk, from new to vintage clothing.

The first clues that you're here are the stalls of cheap clothing along avenue de la Porte de Clignancourt. As you proceed, various streets will tempt you. Hold off until you get to rue des Rosiers, then turn left. Vendors start bringing out their offerings around 9am and take them in around 6pm. Hours are a tad flexible, depending on weather and crowds. Monday is traditionally the best day for bargain seekers, as there is smaller attendance and a greater desire on the part of the merchants to sell.

First-timers at the flea market always ask two things: "Will I get any real bargains here?" and "Will I get fleeced?" It's all relative. Obviously, the best buys have been skimmed by dealers (who often have a prearrangement to have items held for them). And it's true that the same merchandise displayed here will sell for less out in the provinces. But for the visitor who has only a few days to spend in Paris—and only half a day for shopping—the flea market is worth the experience. Vintage French postcards, old buttons, and bistroware are quite affordable; each market has its own personality and an aura of Parisian glamour that can't be found elsewhere. Most of the markets have toilets; some have a central office to arrange shipping. Cafes, pizza joints, and even a few real restaurants are scattered throughout. Beware of pickpockets and troublemakers.

Then there's the **Marché aux Puces de la Porte de Vanves,** av. Georges-Lafenestre, 14e (Métro: Porte-de-Vanves). Like a giant yard sale, this weekend event sprawls along two streets and is Paris's best flea market—dealers swear by it. There's little in terms of formal antiques and few large pieces of furniture. You'll do better if you collect old linens, secondhand Hermès scarves, toys, costume jewelry, or perfume bottles. Asking prices tend to be high, as dealers prefer to sell to nontourists. On Sundays, there's a food market one street over.

Marché Buci, rue de Buci, 6e (Métro: St-Germain-des-Prés), is a traditional French food market held at the intersection of two streets. It's only 1 block long, but what a block! Seasonal fruits and vegetables dance across tabletops while chickens spin on the rotisserie. One stall is devoted to big bunches of fresh flowers. Avoid Monday mornings, since very little is open then.

MUSIC The chain called **FNAC,** with a branch at 136 rue de Rennes, 6e (✆ **01-49-54-30-00;** Métro: St-Placide), is for anyone looking for CDs, records and tapes, computers, photography equipment, TVs, and stereos. It's known for its wide selection and competitive prices. The ticket service sells tickets for most of the venues and concerts in the city. There are eight other locations in Paris.

The showcase **Virgin Megastore,** 52–60 av. des Champs-Elysées, 8e (✆ **01-49-53-50-00;** Métro: Franklin-D.-Roosevelt), is one of the anchors that helped rejuvenate the Champs-Elysées. The landmark building on Paris's famed strip houses the city's largest music store as well as a bookstore and cafe. The ticket service can make reservations for plays, concerts, and sporting events. Other Virgin branches are in the Carrousel du Louvre (see "Malls," above), at both airports, and in Gare Montparnasse.

PERFUME, COSMETICS & TOILETRIES Just about every working woman around place de la Madeleine shops at **Catherine,** 7 rue Castiglione, 1er (✆ **01-42-61-02-89;** Métro: Concorde). They appreciate its discounts and lack of pretension. It resembles a high-volume pharmacy more than a chichi boutique; *flacons* of perfume move in and out of the premises very fast. You get a 30% discount on most brands of makeup and perfume and a 20% discount on brands like Chanel and Dior.

You'll find some of the best deals in cosmetics at **maki,** 9 rue Mansart, 9e (© **01-42-81-33-76**; Métro: Blanche). Located in the middle of a theater area, it's the place where French actors and models come for quality products at discounted prices. The staff will often give advice on makeup.

Though you can buy its scents in any discount parfumerie, we recommend visiting the source of some of the world's most famous perfumes: **Caron,** 34 av. Montaigne, 8e (© **01-47-23-40-82**; Métro: Franklin-D.-Roosevelt). Established in 1904, it gained a reputation as the choice of temptresses; the *Scent of a Woman* that Al Pacino fell in love with was Caron's Fleurs de Rocaille.

A specialist in products for skin and hair, **Annick Goutal,** 14 rue de Castiglione, 1er (© **01-42-60-52-82**; Métro: Tuileries), or 12 place St-Sulpice, 6e (same phone; Métro: St-Sulpice), sells everything a person would need to stay young-looking (or at least try): herbal shampoos, liquid soaps, bubble bath, oils, and creams.

At the rear of a courtyard, halfway between place de la Madeleine and the Champs-Elysées, is **Makeup Forever,** 5 rue de la Boetie, 8e (© **01-42-66-01-60;** Métro: St-Augustin). Established in the 1980s, its products were quickly endorsed by professional stylists. Its purse-sized makeup case, at about 100F (15.20, $14.50), has become a mini status symbol for French yuppies and fashionable types.

At **Octée,** 12 rue des Quatre-Vents, 6e (© **01-46-33-18-77;** Métro: Odéon), the collection of fragrances is color-coded to your personality, skin type, and mood. Prices are reasonable, with any scent costing 185F (28, $26.83) for a purse-sized vial. Though most of the scents were conceived for women, a limited number are meant for men, the most popular of which is Black Cedar.

TABLEWARE & MORE   Much about the **Conran Shop,** 117 rue du Bac, 7e (© **01-42-84-10-01;** Métro: Sèvres-Babylone), may remind you of an outpost of the British Empire, valiantly imposing British aesthetics and standards on the French-speaking world. Inside, you'll find articles for the home, kitchen- and tableware, vases, stationery, postcards, and even a selection of chocolates, teas, and coffees. It's adjacent to the sprawling department-store racks of Bon Marché (at the top of a street), known for its charming shops.

Looking for the perfect tableware to make your dinner party unique? **Geneviève Lethu,** 95 rue de Rennes, 6e (© **01-45-44-40-35;** Métro: St-Sulpice), a Provençal designer, has shops all over France. Her clever and colorful designs seem to reflect what happens when Pottery Barn style goes French Mediterranean. Her moderately priced goods are also sold in major department stores.

WINES   Les Caves Taillevent, 199 rue du Faubourg St-Honoré, 8e (© **01-45-61-14-09;** Métro: Charles-de-Gaulle-Étoile), is a temple to the art of making fine French wine. Associated with one of Paris's grandest restaurants, Taillevent, it occupies the street level and cellar of an antique building in a neighborhood awash with memories of the French empire. Stored here are more than half a million bottles of wine—some at around 26 F(3.95, $3.77); others, rare vintages at 20,000F (3,044, $2,900).

16 Paris After Dark

THE PERFORMING ARTS

Announcements of shows, concerts, and operas are on kiosks all over town. You can find listings of what's playing in *Pariscope,* a weekly entertainment guide, or the English-language *Boulevard,* a bimonthly magazine. Performances start later in Paris than in London or New York—anywhere from 8 to 9pm—and Parisians tend to dine after the theater. (But you may not want to follow suit, since many of the less expensive restaurants close as early as 9pm.)

There are many ticket agencies in Paris, but most are found near the Right Bank hotels. *Avoid them if possible.* You can buy the cheapest tickets at the theater box office. Remember to tip the usher who shows you to your seat in a theater or movie house 3F (.46, 44¢).

For information on and tickets to just about any show in Paris (also Dijon, Lyon, and Nice), **Global Tickets** has a New York office if you'd like to make arrangements before you go. It's at 234 W. 44th St., Suite 1000, New York, New York 10036 (℃ **800/223-6108** or 914/328-2150). It also has an office in Paris at 19 rue des Mathurins, 9e (℃ **01-42-65-39-21;** Métro: Havre-Caumartin). A personal visit isn't necessary; Global will mail tickets to your home, fax confirmation, or leave tickets at the box office in Paris. There's a markup of 20% (excluding opera and ballet) over box-office price, plus a U.S. handling charge of $8. Hotel and theater packages are also available.

Several agencies sell tickets for cultural events and plays at discounts of up to 50%. One is the **Kiosque Théâtre,** 15 place de la Madeleine, 8e (no phone; Métro: Madeleine), offering leftover tickets for about half price on the day of performance. Tickets for evening performances are sold Tuesday through Friday from 12:30 to 8pm and Saturday from 2 to 8pm. For matinees, tickets are sold Saturday from 12:30 to 2pm or Sunday from 12:30 to 4pm.

For easy access to tickets for festivals, concerts, and the theater, try one of two locations of the **FNAC** department-store chain: 136 rue de Rennes, 6e (℃ **01-49-54-30-00;** Métro: Montparnasse-Bienvenue), or in the Forum des Halles, 1–7 rue Pierre-Lescot, 1er (℃ **01-40-41-40-00;** Métro: Châtelet-Les-Halles).

The Top Venues

The **Opéra Garnier,** place de l'Opéra, 9e (℃ **01-40-01-17-89;** Métro: Opéra), is the premier stage for dance and opera. Because of the competition from the Opéra Bastille, the original opera has made great efforts to present more up-to-date works, including choreography by Jerome Robbins, Twyla Tharp, and George Balanchine. This rococo wonder was designed by the young architect Charles Garnier in the heyday of the empire. The facade is adorned with marble and sculpture, including *The Dance,* by Carpeaux. Painstaking restorations have returned the Garnier to its former glory: its boxes and walls are again lined with flowing red and blue damask, the gilt gleams, the ceiling (painted by Marc Chagall) has been cleaned, and air-conditioning has been added. The box office is open Monday through Saturday from 11am to 6:30pm.

The controversial building known as the **Opéra Bastille,** place de la Bastille, 120 rue de Lyon (℃ **01-43-43-96-96;** Métro: Bastille), was designed by the Canadian architect Carlos Ott, with curtains created by fashion designer Issey Miyake. The showplace was inaugurated in July 1989 (for the Revolution's bicentennial), and on March 17, 1990, the curtain rose on Hector Berlioz's *Les Troyens.* Since its much-publicized opening, the opera house has presented masterworks like Mozart's *Marriage of Figaro* and Tchaikovsky's *Queen of Spades.* The main hall is the largest of any French opera house, with 2,700 seats, but music critics have lambasted the acoustics. The building contains two additional concert halls, including an intimate room with only 250 seats, usually used for chamber music. Both traditional opera performances and symphony concerts are presented here. There are sometimes free concerts on French holidays; call before your visit.

For the best orchestra performances in France, try **Maison de Radio France,** 116 av. du Président-Kennedy, 16e (✆ **01-56-49-21-80;** Métro: Passy-Ranelagh), which offers top-notch concerts with guest conductors. It's the home of the Orchestre Philharmonique de Radio France and the Orchestre National de France. The box office is open Monday through Saturday from 11am to 6pm.

The Art Deco **Théâtre des Champs-Elysées,** 15 av. Montaigne, 8e (✆ **01-49-52-50-50;** Métro: Alma-Marceau), which attracts the haute-couture crowd, hosts both national and international orchestras as well as operas and ballets. Events are held year-round, except in August. The box office is open Monday through Saturday from 11am to 7pm.

Conceived by the Mitterrand administration, **Cité de la Musique,** 221 av. Jean-Jaurès, 19e (✆ **01-44-84-45-00,** or 01-44-84-44-84 for tickets and information; Métro: Porte-de-Pantin), has been widely applauded. At the city's northeastern edge in what used to be a run-down neighborhood, the $120-million stone-and-glass structure, designed by architect Christian de Portzamparc, incorporates a network of concert halls, a library and research center for the study of music from around the world, and a museum. The complex hosts a rich variety of concerts, ranging from Renaissance to 20th-century programs.

Even those with only a modest understanding of French can still delight in a sparkling production of Molière at the **Comédie-Française,** 2 rue de Richelieu, 1er (✆ **01-44-58-15-15;** Métro: Palais-Royal-Musée-du-Louvre), established to keep the classics alive and to promote important contemporary authors. The box office is open daily from 11am to 6pm, but the hall is dark from July 21 to September 5. In 1993, a Left Bank annex was launched, the **Comédie-Française-Théâtre du Vieux-Colombier,** 21 rue du Vieux-Colombier, 4e (✆ **01-44-39-87-00;** Métro: Sèvres-Babylone, Saint-Sulpice). Although its repertoire can vary, it's known for presenting some of the most serious French dramas in town.

International stars appear in the cavernous **Olympia,** 28 bd. des Capucines, 9e (✆ **01-47-42-25-49;** Métro: Opéra or Madeleine). Yves Montand appeared once—the performance was sold out 4 months in advance. Today you're more likely to catch Gloria Estefan. A typical lineup might include an English rock group, Italian acrobats, a well-known French singer, a dance troupe, an American juggler or comedy team (doing much of their work in English), plus the featured star. A witty emcee and an onstage band provide smooth transitions between acts.

CHANSONNIERS

The *chansonniers* (literally songwriters) provide a bombastic musical satire of the day's events. This combination of parody and burlesque is a time-honored Gallic amusement and a Parisian institution. Songs are often created on the spot, inspired by the "disaster of the day." You'll need to understand French to get most of the humor.

Au Caveau de la Bolée   To enter this bawdy boîte, you descend into the catacombs of the early-14th-century Abbey of St-André, once a famous literary cafe that attracted Verlaine and Oscar Wilde, who downed (or drowned in) glass after glass of absinthe here. The singing is loud and bawdy, just the way the young student regulars like it. Occasionally the audience sings along. You'll enjoy this place a lot more if your French is pretty good, but even if it's not, there are enough visuals (magic acts and performances by singers) to amuse. A fixed-price dinner, served Monday through Saturday at 8:30pm, is followed by at least four entertainers, usually comedians. The cabaret starts at 10:30pm, and in lieu of paying admission, you can order dinner. If you've already eaten, you can just order a drink. 25 rue de l'Hirondelle, 6e. ✆ **01-43-54-62-20.** Fixed-price dinner 300F (45.60, $43.50) Mon–Fri; 350F (53.20, $50.75) Sat. Cover 150F (22.80, $21.75) Mon–Sat if you don't order dinner. Métro: St-Michel.

Au Lapin Agile   Picasso and Utrillo once patronized this little cottage near the top of Montmartre, formerly known as the Café des Assassins. It has been painted by numerous artists, including Utrillo, and was used as a setting for a Steve Martin play. For decades, it has been the heart of French folk music. You'll sit at wooden tables in a dimly lit room with walls covered by bohemian mem-orabilia, listening to French folk tunes, love ballads, army songs, sea chanteys, and music-hall ditties. You're encouraged to sing along, even if it's only the "oui, oui, oui—non, non, non" refrain of "Les Chevaliers de la Table Ronde." The best singalongs are on weeknights after tourist season ends. The place is open Tuesday through Sunday nights from 9:15pm to 2am. 22 rue des Saules, 18e. ✆ **01-46-06-85-87.** Cover (including the first drink) 130F (19.75, $18.85). Métro: Lamarck.

NIGHTCLUBS & CABARETS

These places are all outrageously expensive, but they provide some of the most lavish, spectacular floor shows anywhere.

Chez Michou   The setting is blue, the emcee wears blue, and the spotlights shining on the stage bathe the cross-dressing performers in a celestial blue light. The creative force behind all this is Michou, veteran impresario whose 20-odd belles bear names like Hortensia and DuDuche, and lip-synch their way through songs by Whitney Houston, Diana Ross, and Tina Turner and such French luminaries as Mireille Mathieu, Sylvie Vartan, "Dorothée," and the immortal Brigitte Bardot. 80 rue des Martyrs, 18e. ✆ **01-46-06-16-04.** Reservations required for din-ner. Dinner and show (including aperitif, wine, and coffee) 600F(91, $87); show only (at bar) 220F (33.45, $31.90). Métro: Pigalle.

Crazy Horse Saloon   This sophisticated strip joint has thrived for decades thanks to good choreography and a sly, flirty theme that celebrates and exalts the female form. Each number features gorgeous girls, girls, girls, outfitted in out-rageous costumes. If you opt for dinner, it will be a tasteful, well-prepared event served with flair at Chez Francis, a restaurant under separate management a few steps from the cabaret itself. Shows, which last 1¾ hours, are attended by men-folk and, to a lesser extent, women, from around Europe and the world. 12 av. George-V, 8e. ✆ **01-47-23-32-32.** Cover (including two drinks) 450F–560F (68.40– 85.10, $65.25–$81.20); dinner spectacle 660F (100.30, $95.70). Métro: George-V or Alma-Marceau.

Folies-Bergère   Folies-Bergère is a Paris institution; foreigners have been flocking here since 1886. Josephine Baker, the legendary African-American singer who used to throw bananas into the audience, became "the toast of Paris" here. According to legend, the first G.I. to reach Paris at the 1944 Liberation asked for directions to the club.

Don't expect the naughty and slyly permissive skin-and-glitter revue that used to be the trademark of this place. In 1993, that all ended with a radical restora-tion of the theater and a reopening under new management. The site functions as a conventional 1,600-seat theater, presenting musical revues filled with a sense of nostalgia for old Paris. You're likely to witness an intriguing, often charming, but not particularly erotic repertoire of songs, mostly in French but sometimes in English, interspersed with the banter of an emcee. A restaurant serves bland fixed-price dinners in an anteroom to the theater. The experience probably isn't worth the staggering cost, but for many a first-timer, a visit to Paris without going to the Folies-Bergère would be no visit at all. 32 rue Richer, 9e. (C) **01-44-79-98-98.** Cover 160F–350F (24.30– 53.20, \$23.20–\$50.75); dinner and show 370F–550F (56.25– 83.60, \$53.65–\$79.75). Métro: Rue-Montmartre or Cadet.

Lido de Paris As it moves deeper into the millennium, the Lido has changed its feathers and modernized its shows; it competes with the best Las Vegas has to offer. Its \$15 million production, *C'est Magique,* reflects a dramatic reworking of the classic Parisian cabaret show, with eye-popping special effects, water technology using more than 60,000 gallons per minute, and bold new themes, even aerial and aquatic ballet. The show, the most expensive ever produced in Europe, uses 70 performers, \$4 million in costumes, and a \$2 million lighting design with lasers. There's even an ice rink and swimming pool that appear and disappear. The 45 Bluebell Girls, those legendary showgirls, are still here. Now that chef Paul Bocuse is the consultant for the culinary offerings, the cuisine is better than ever. 116 bis av. des Champs-Elysées, 8e. (C) **800/227-4884** in the U.S., or 01-40-76-56-10. Dinner dance (8pm) and show (10pm) 815F–1,015F (123.90– 154.30, \$118.20–\$147.20); Show only (10pm and midnight) 460F–560F (69.90– 85.10, \$66.70–\$81.20). Prices include a half bottle of champagne per person. Métro: George-V.

Moulin Rouge This is a camp classic. The establishment that Toulouse-Lautrec immortalized is still here, but the artist would probably have a hard time recognizing it today. Colette created a scandal here by offering an on-stage kiss to Mme de Morny, but shows today have a hard time shocking audiences. Try to get a table, as the view is much better on the main floor than from the bar. What's the theme—the strip routines and saucy sexiness of *la belle époque,* and of permissive, promiscuous Paris between the world wars. Handsome men and girls, girls, girls, virtually all topless, keep the place going. Dance finales usually include two dozen of the belles ripping loose with a topless can-can. place Blanche, 18e. (C) **01-53-09-82-82.** Cover including champagne 520F–580F (79.05– 88.15, \$75.40–\$84.10); 7pm dinner and show 790F (120.10, \$114.55); for seats at the bar, cover (including two drinks) 370F (56.25, \$53.65). Revues nightly at 9 and 11pm. Métro: Blanche.

Villa d'Este In the past, this club booked Amalia Rodrigues, Portugal's leading fadista, and the French chanteuse Juliette Greco. Today, you're more likely to hear the French singer François de Guelte or other top talent from Europe and America. Villa d'Este has been around for a long time, and the quality of its offerings remains high. You'll probably hear some of the greatest hits of such beloved French performers as Piaf, Aznavour, Brassens, and Brel. 4 rue Arsène-Houssaye, 8e. (C) **01-42-56-14-65.** Cover (including first drink) 190F (28.90, \$27.55); dinner (including wine) and show 340F–750F (51.70– 114, \$49.30–\$108.75). Métro: Charles-de-Gaulle-Étoile.

LE COOL JAZZ

The great jazz revival that long ago swept America is still going strong here, with Dixieland or Chicago rhythms being pounded out in dozens of jazz cellars, mostly called *caveaux.* Most clubs are crowded on the Left Bank near the Seine, between rue Bonaparte and rue St-Jacques.

For the latest details, see *Jazz Hot, Jazz Magazine,* or *Pariscope.*

Au Duc des Lombards Comfortable and appealing, this jazz club replaced an earlier club 9 years ago and has thrived in a low-key way ever since.

Performers begin playing nightly at 9pm and continue (with breaks) for 5 hours, touching on everything from free jazz to more traditional forms like hard bop. Unlike at many of its competitors, tables can be reserved here and will usually be held until 10:30pm. 42 rue des Lombards, 1er. ℂ **01-42-33-22-88.** Cover 100F–120F (15.20– 18.25, $14.50–$17.40). Métro: Châtelet.

Baiser Salé   Set within a cellar lined with jazz-related paintings, a large central bar and an ongoing roster of videos that show great jazz moments (Charlie Parker, Miles Davis) of the past, this is an appealing and musically varied club. Everything is very mellow and laid-back, with an emphasis on the music. Genres include Afro-Caribbean, Afro-Latino, salsa, merengue, rhythm and blues, and, less frequently, fusion. 58 rue des Lombards, 1er. ℂ **01-42-33-37-71.** Cover 50F–150F (7.60– 22.80, $7.25–$21.75) Wed–Sun; free Mon–Tues. Métro: Châtelet.

Le Bilboquet/Club St-Germain   This restaurant/jazz club/piano bar, where the film *Paris Blues* was shot, offers some of the best music in the city. Jazz is featured on the upper level in the restaurant, Le Bilboquet, a wood-paneled room with a copper ceiling, brass-trimmed bar, and Victorian candelabra. The menu is limited but classic French, and a dinner will run you 180F to 300F (27.35 to 45.60, $26.10 to $43.50). Under separate management is the downstairs disco, Club St-Germain, which charges no cover—but drinks cost a staggering 100F (15.20, $14.50). You can walk from one club to the other, but have to buy a new drink each time you change venues. 13 rue St-Benoît, 6e. ℂ **01-45-48-81-84.** No cover. Métro: St-Germain-des-Prés.

New Morning   Jazz maniacs come to drink, talk, and dance at this enduring club. It's sometimes a scene, attracting such guests as Spike Lee and Prince. The place is especially popular with jazz groups from Central and South Africa. 7–9 rue des Petites-Ecuries, 10e. ℂ **01-45-23-51-41.** Cover 100F–180F (15.20– 27.40, $14.50–$26.10). Métro: Château-d'Eau.

Slow Club   One of the most famous jazz cellars in Europe, capped with medieval ceiling vaults that make the music reverberate in an evocative way, this venue hosts a revolving set of artists who tend to focus on New Orleans–style jazz. The hip folks who flock here tend to be in their 30s and early 40s. 130 rue de Rivoli, 1er. ℂ **01-42-33-84-30.** Cover 80F–100F (12.15– 15.20, $11.60–$14.50). Métro: Châtelet.

DANCE CLUBS

The area around the Église St-Germain-des-Prés is full of dance clubs. They come and go so quickly that last year's Disco Inferno could be a hardware store by now—but new ones will spring up to take the place of the old. For the most up-to-date information, see *Time Out, Pariscope,* or *L'Officiel des Spectacles.*

Batofar   The hippest after-dark dive in town is actually on a barge in the Seine. This boat was once a lighthouse, and from its innards a cavernous nightclub has been carved, including a dance floor packed with a gyrating crowd mostly in their 20s. House, garage, techno, and live jazz round out the bill. This music is spun by the city's best DJs. The club is open in summer only, Tuesday through Sunday from 6pm on. Facing 11 Quai François Mauriuac, 13e. ℂ **01-56-29-10-33.** Cover 100F (15.20, $14.50). Métro: Quai de la Gare.

La Balajo   Established in 1936, this dance club is remembered as the place where Edith Piaf won the hearts of thousands of Parisian music lovers. Today, Le Balajo is hardly as fashionable, though it continues its big-band traditions on

Sunday afternoons, when a crowd mostly 45 and over dances to an eclectic mix of World War II–era swing and bebop. Thursday to Saturday nights, the focus is on disco and, to a lesser degree, reggae, salsa, rock, and rap. 9 rue de Lappe, 11e. ℂ **01-47-00-07-87.** Cover (including first drink) 100F (15.20, $14.50) Thurs-Sat nights; 50F (7.60, $7.25) Sun afternoon. Métro: Bastille.

La Java   Once this bal-musette dance hall was one of the most frequented in Paris; Piaf and Maurice Chevalier made their names here. Today, you can still dance the waltz on what one critic called "retro fetish night," or perhaps even tango on a Sunday afternoon. Brazilian and Latin themes predominate on some nights. Overall, it's one of the best places in Paris for the old-fashioned pleasures of couples arm-in-arm on a dance floor. 105 rue du Faubourg du Temple, 11e. ℂ **01-42-02-20-52.** Cover 80F (12.15, $11.60) Thurs; 100F (15.20, $14.50) Fri–Sat; 40F (6.13, $5.80) Sun. Métro: Belleville.

Le New Riverside   This Left Bank cellar attracts droves of jaded veteran club-goers, who appreciate the indestructible premises and classic rock from the '70s. Expect a crowd ages 25 to 40; women, especially when unaccompanied, are almost always admitted free. 7 rue Grégoire-de-Tours, 6e. ℂ **01-43-54-46-33.** Cover (including first drink) 90F (13.730, $13.05) for men at all times, and for women only after midnight Fri–Sat. Métro: St-Michel or Odéon.

Le Saint   Occupying three medieval cellars deep in the university area, this place attracts a crowd in their 20s and 30s who dance (to music from both the U.S. and Europe), drink, and generally soak up the Left Bank student-dive scene. Vacationers will enjoy this fun spot, and its "Young-Love-Beside-the-Seine" vibe can be a hoot. 7 rue St-Severin, 5e. ℂ **01-43-25-50-04.** Cover (including first drink) 60F–90F (9.10– 13.730, $8.70–$13.05). Métro: St-Michel.

Les Bains   This chic spot has been pronounced "in" and "out" many times, but lately it's very in, attracting a good-looking, local crowd and growing a bit more gay. 7 rue du Bourg-l'Abbé, 3e. ℂ **01-48-87-01-80.** Cover (including first drink) 120F (18.25, $17.40). Métro: Réaumur.

Les Coulisses   There are more tourist traps in Montmartre than anywhere else in Paris, but this fairly new club has some legitimacy, providing a good spot for drinking and dancing in the heart of the district. It's comprised of a basement-level dance club, a first-floor bar, and a restaurant on the second floor. The decor changes all the time, but management usually sticks to baroque and medieval themes. The club stays open until dawn. 5 rue du Mont-Cenis (place du Tertre), 18e. ℂ **01-42-62-89-99.** Cover 160F (24.30, $23.20) Fri–Sat; no cover for those who eat in the restaurant. Métro: Abbesses.

ROCK

Bus Palladium   Set in a single room with a very long bar, this rock-and-roll temple has varnished hardwoods and fabric-covered walls that barely absorb the reverberations of nonstop recorded music. You won't find techno, punk, jazz, blues, or soul here. It's rock-and-roll for hard-core, mostly heterosexual, rock wannabes ages 25 to 35. Alcoholic drinks of any kind cost 80F (12.15, $11.60), except for women on Tuesday, when they can drink for free. 6 rue Fontaine, 9e. ℂ **01-53-21-07-33.** Cover 100F (15.20, $14.50) all the time for men, and Fri–Sat only for women. Métro: Blanche or Pigalle.

SALSA

Les Étoiles   Since 1856, this red-swabbed old-fashioned music hall has shaken with the sound of performers at work and patrons at play. Its newest incarnation is as a restaurant discothèque where the music is exclusively salsa and the food Cubano. Expect simple but hearty portions of fried fish, shredded pork or beef, rice, beans, and flan, as bands from Venezuela play to a crowd that already knows or quickly learns how to dance to South American rhythms. 61 rue du Château d'Eau, 10e. ✆ 01-47-70-60-56. Cover (including first drink) 120F (18.25, $17.40). Métro: Château d'Eau.

WINE BARS

Many Parisians now prefer the wine bar to the traditional cafe or bistro—the food is often better and the ambience more inviting.

Au Sauvignon   This tiny spot has tables overflowing onto a covered terrace and a decor featuring old ceramic tiles and frescoes done by Left Bank artists. Wines range from the cheapest beaujolais to the most expensive Puligny-Montrachet. A glass of wine costs 22F to 32F (3.35 to 4.85, $3.20 to $4.65), with an additional charge of 2F (.30, 30¢) to consume it at a table. To go with your wine, choose an Auvergne specialty, like goat cheese or a terrine. The fresh Poîlane bread is ideal with the ham, pâté, or goat cheese. 80 rue des Sts-Pères, 7e. ✆ 01-45-48-49-02. Closed Aug. Métro: Sèvres-Babylone.

Juveniles   This is a spin-off of one of Paris's most successful wine bars, Willi's (see below), which is nearby. Louder, less formal, more animated, and (to wine lovers) more provocative than its sibling, it prides itself on experimenting with wines. There's no stuffiness at this British-owned spot, where high-quality but less well-known wines from Spain, France, California, and Australia go for between 19F and 49F (2.90 and 7.45, $2.75 and $7.10) a glass. Anything you like, including bottles of the "wine of the week," can be hauled away uncorked from a wine boutique on the premises. And if you get hungry, savory tapas-style platters are available for 35F to 65F (5.30 to 9.90, $5.10 to $9.45). de Richelieu, 1er. ✆ 01-42-97-46-49. Métro: Palais-Royal.

Les Bacchantes   This place prides itself on offering more wines by the glass—at least 50—than any other wine bar in Paris; prices range from 14F to 30F (2.15 to 4.55, $2.05 to $4.35). It also does a hefty restaurant trade in well-prepared *cuisine bourgeoise.* Its cozy, rustic setting—with massive exposed beams, old-fashioned paneling, and chalkboards announcing both the vintages and the platters—attracts dozens of theatergoers before and after performances at the nearby Théâtre Olympia, as well as anyone interested in carefully chosen vintages from esoteric or small-scale winemakers. Wines derive mainly from France, but you'll also find examples from neighboring countries of Europe. 21 rue Caumartin, 9e. ✆ 01-42-65-25-35. Métro: Havre-Caumartin.

Willi's Wine Bar   Journalists and stockbrokers head for this increasingly popular wine bar in the center of the financial district. About 250 kinds of wine are offered, including a dozen "wine specials" you can taste by the glass for 22F to 82F (3.35 to 12.45, $3.20 to $11.90). Lunch is the busiest time; on quiet evenings, you can better enjoy the warm ambience. Daily specials are likely to include lamb brochette with cumin or Lyonnais sausage in truffled vinaigrette, plus a spectacular dessert like chocolate terrine. 13 rue des Petits-Champs, 1er. ✆ 01-42-61-05-09. Métro: Bourse, Louvre, or Palais-Royal.

BARS & PUBS

Bar du Crillon   Though some visitors consider the Bar du Crillon too stuffy and self-consciously elegant, the social and literary history of this bar is remarkable. Hemingway set a climactic scene of *The Sun Also Rises* here, and over the

After-Dark Diversions: Dives, Drag & More

On a Paris night, the cheapest entertainment, especially if you're young, is "the show" staged at the southeasterly tip of Île de la Cité, behind Notre-Dame. A sort of Gallic version of the Sundowner Festival in Key West, Florida, it attracts just about everyone who ever wanted to try their hand at performance art. The entertainment is strictly sponta-neous and usually includes magicians, fire eaters, jugglers, mimes, and music makers from all over, performing against the backdrop of the illu-minated cathedral. This is one of the greatest places in Paris to meet other young people in a sometimes moderately euphoric setting.

Also popular is a stroll along the Seine after 10pm. Take a graveled pathway down to the river from the Left Bank side of pont de Sully, close to the Institut du Monde Arabe, and walk to the right, away from Notre-Dame. This walk, which comes to an end near place Valhubert, is the best place to see spontaneous Paris in action at night. Joggers and saxophone players come here, and many Parisians arrive for impromptu dance parties.

To quench your thirst, wander onto Île St-Louis and head for the **Café-Brasserie St-Regis,** 6 rue Jean-du-Bellay, 4e, across from pont St-Louis (℃ **01-43-54-59-41;** Métro: Musée du Louvre). If you want to linger inside, you can order a *plat du jour* or a coffee at the bar. But try doing as the Parisians do: get a 13F (1.95, $1.90) beer to go (*une bière à emporter*) in a plastic cup and take it with you on a stroll around the island. The little cafe is open daily until 2am.

If you're caught waiting for the Métro to start running again at 5am, try the **Sous-Bock Tavern,** 49 rue St-Honoré, 1er (℃ **01-40-26-46-61;** Métro: Pont Neuf), open daily from11am to 5am. Young drinkers gather here to sample 400 varieties of beer. If you want a shot of whiskey, there's a choice of 150 varieties. The dish to order is a platter of mussels—curried, with white wine, or with cream sauce; they go well with the brasserie-style fries.

If you're looking for the most flamboyant drag in Paris, head to **Madame Arthur,** 75 bis rue des Martyrs, 18e (℃ **01-42-54-40-21;** Métro: Abbesses or Pigalle). It's the longest-running transvestite show in town,

years it has attracted a crowd of diplomats from the U.S. Embassy as well as vis-iting heiresses, stars, starlets, and wannabes. Under its new owner, the Concorde Group, the bar has been redecorated by Sonia Rykiel. Another option down the hall is the Edwardian-style **Jardin d'Hiver,** where, amid potted palms and upscale accessories, you can order tea, cocktails, or coffee. In the Hôtel de Crillon, 10 place de la Concorde, 8e. ℃ **01-44-71-15-00.** Métro: Concorde.

Bar Hemingway/Bar Vendôme In 1944, during the Liberation of Paris, Ernest Hemingway made history by ordering a drink at the Ritz Bar while gun-fire from retreating Nazi soldiers was still audible in the streets. Today, basking in the literary glow, the Ritz commemorates this event with bookish memora-bilia, rows of newspapers, and stiff drinks. Look for the bar's entrance, and homages to other writers such as Proust, near the hotel's rue Cambon entrance.

attracting both straights and gays. The creative force behind the affair is Mme Arthur, who's no lady and whose stage name during her shticks as emcee is Chantaline. The performances include 9 to 11 artists with names like Vungala, Lady Lune, and Miss Badabou. You can visit just to drink or dine from a fixed-price menu (reservations required). The club is open daily from 9 to 10:30pm for dinner, with the show beginning at 10:30pm. Additional shows, according to demand, are held Friday and Saturday at 7pm, with dinner beginning at 6pm. After the last show, around 12:30am, the place becomes a disco. Cover (including the first drink) is 165F (25.10, $23.95); dinner and the show is 295F (44.85, $42.83) Sunday through Thursday; and 395F (60.05, $57.33) Friday and Saturday.

If drag shows aren't your cup of tea, how about *Last Tango in Paris*? At **Le Tango,** 13 rue au Maire, 3e (© **01-42-72-17-78**; Métro: Arts et Métiers), memories of Evita and Argentina live on. This dive with a bordello decor features zouk music from the French Caribbean and Africa, as well as house, garage, and virtually every form of high-energy dance music known in New York and Los Angeles. Most patrons are gay and lesbian and in their 20s and 30s. The cover is 40F (6.13, $5.80). It's open Friday and Saturday from midnight to 5am. Another fun and trendy dance spot is **La Guinguette Pirate,** Quai de la Gare, 13e (© **01-44-24-89-89**; Métro: Quai de la Gare), a Chinese junk moored off the banks of the Seine. This is the latest version of the fabled *guinguette* (river cafe), offering great jazz, zouk, and salsa. Cover is 50F (7.60, $7.25).

If you're looking for a sophisticated, laid-back venue without the high-energy exhibitionism of nightclubs, consider the **Sanz-Sans,** 49 rue du faubourg St-Antoine, 4e (© **01-44-75-78-78**; Métro: Bastille). It's a multiethnic playground where the children of prominent Parisians mingle, testifying to the unifying power of jazz. In this red-velvet duplex, the most important conversations seem to occur over margaritas on the stairway or the back-room couches. The later it gets, the sexier the scene becomes. There's no cover.

If you develop a thirst in the daytime, when the Bar Hemingway isn't open, head for the Bar Vendôme, near the hotel's main (place Vendôme) entrance. The setting is just as cozy and woodsy, albeit a bit more grand. In Le Ritz, 15 place Vendôme, 1er. © **01-43-16-30-30**. Métro: Opéra.

Barrio Latino   It would be easy to spend an entire evening at this multi-storied emporium of good times, Gallic flair, and Latino charm. It occupies a space designed by Gustav Eiffel in the late 19th century, and which operated until very recently as a furniture store. Tapas bars and dance floors are located on the street level (*rez-de-chausée*) and third floor (*2eme étage*); a Latino restaurant is on the second floor (*1er étage*). Staff members roll carts loaded with tapas around the floors, selling them like hot dogs at an American baseball game. The restaurant specializes in food that jaded French palates sometimes find refreshing:

Argentinian steaks, Brazilian *fejoiada*, and Mexican chili con carne, all of which taste wonderful with beer, caipirinhas, Cuba Libres, or rum punches. Clientele is very mixed, mostly straight, partly gay, and 100% blasé about matters such as an individual's sexuality. 46 rue du Faubourg St-Antoine, 4e. ℭ **01-55-78-84-75.** Cover 50F (7.60, $7.25) for non-diners Fri–Sat after 9pm. Métro: Bastille.

China Club   Designed to recall France's 19th-century colonies in Asia or a bordello in 1930s Shanghai (on the ground floor) and England's empire-building zeal in India (upstairs), the China Club will allow you to chitchat or flirt with the singles who crowd into the street-level bar, then escape to calmer, more contemplative climes upstairs. You'll see regulars from the worlds of fashion and the arts, along with a pack of postshow celebrants from the nearby Opéra Bastille. A street-level Chinese restaurant serves dinner daily from 7pm to 12:30am; in the more animated (and occasionally raucous) cellar bar, live music is presented every Friday and Saturday from 10pm to 3am. 50 rue de Charenton, 12e. (ℭ **01-43-43-82-02).** Métro: Bastille or Ledru Rollin.

Harry's New York Bar   *Sank roo doe noo,* as the ads tell you to instruct your cabdriver, is the most famous bar in Europe—quite possibly in the world. Opened on Thanksgiving Day 1911 by an expat named MacElhone, it's the spot where members of the World War I ambulance corps drank themselves silly. In addition to being Hemingway's favorite, Harry's is legendary for other reasons: the white lady and sidecar cocktails were invented here, and it's also the alleged birthplace of the Bloody Mary and the headquarters of a loosely organized fraternity of drinkers known as the International Bar Flies (IBF).

The place's historic core is the street-level bar, where CEOs and office workers loosen their ties on more or less equal footing. Daytime crowds are from the neighborhood's insurance, banking, and travel industries; evening crowds include pre- and post-theater groupies and night owls who aren't bothered by the gritty setting and unflattering lighting. A softer, somewhat less macho ambience reigns in the cellar, where a pianist provides music every night from 10pm to 2am. 5 rue Daunou, 2e. ℭ **01-42-61-71-14.** Métro: Opéra or Pyramides.

Le Bar de l'Hôtel   This is the city's most romantic bar, located in a hotel on the Left Bank. Oscar Wilde checked out long ago, but the odd celebrity still shows up: We were once 15 minutes into a conversation before realizing we were speaking to French actress Jeanne Moreau. Drinks are expertly mixed, the place is sleek and chic, and conversations are held at a discreet murmur. There's no better place for a romantic rendezvous. In L'Hôtel, 13 rue des Beaux-Arts, 6e. ℭ **01-44-41-99-00.** Métro: St-Germain-des-Prés.

Le Fumoir   At Le Fumoir, the well-traveled crowd that lives or works in the district provides a kind of classy raucousness. The decor is a lot like that of an English library, with about 6,000 books providing an aesthetic backdrop to the schmoozing. A Danish chef prepares an international menu featuring meal-size salads (the one with scallops and lobster is great), roasted codfish with zucchini, and roasted beef in red-wine sauce. More popular are the stiff mixed drinks, the wines and beers, and the dozen or so types of cigars for sale. 6 rue de l'Amiral-de-Coligny, 1er. ℭ **01-42-92-00-24.** Métro: Louvre-Rivoli.

Maito Habana   The macho brown-and-green decor evokes a private men's club. You can drink Cuba libres, cognac, or coffee; eat platters of food; or puff away at any of the cigars stocked for the pleasure of the patrons. 19 rue de Presbourg, 16e. (ℭ **01-45-00-60-63).** Métro: Etoile.

Man Ray   This chic rendezvous off the Champs-Elysées is dedicated to Man Ray, the photographer and American Dadaist, who usually felt more comfortable roaming Montparnasse than the 8th. Many of Man Ray's photos decorate the club. The discreet entry is through large wrought-iron doors with virtually no sign. In the basement is a bustling brasserie presided over by two winged Asian goddesses. The bar upstairs is big and bustling, and jazz is often presented here. 34 rue Marbeuf, 8e. ℂ 01-56-88-36-36. Métro: Franklin-D.-Roosevelt.

Pub St-Germain-des-Prés   With nine rooms and 650 seats, this is the largest pub in France, offering 450 brands of beer—don't ask your server to name them—and 26 on draft. The deliberately tacky decor, which has seen a lot of beer swilled and spilled since its installation, consists of leather booths, gilt-framed mirrors, hanging lamps, and a stuffed parrot in a gilded cage. It gets *really* fun between 10:30pm and 4am, when live rock turns everything louder, sudsier, and rowdier. 17 rue de l'Ancienne-Comédie, 6e. ℂ 01-43-29-38-70. Métro: Odéon.

Rosebud   The popularity of this place known for a bemused and indulgent attitude toward anyone looking for a drink and some talk hasn't diminished since the 1950s. The name refers to the beloved sled of Orson Welles's *Citizen Kane*. Around the corner from Montparnasse's famous cafes and thick in associations with Sartre and de Beauvoir, Ionesco, and Duras, Rosebud draws a crowd ages 35 to 65, though the staff has recently remarked on the appearance of students. Drop in at night for a glass of wine, a shot of whiskey, or a hamburger or chili con carne. 11 bis rue Delambre, 14e. ℂ 01-43-35-38-54. Métro: Vavin.

GAY & LESBIAN CLUBS

Gay life is centered around Les Halles and Le Marais, with the greatest concentration of gay and lesbian clubs, restaurants, bars, and shops between the Hôtel-de-Ville and Rambuteau Métro stops. Gay dance clubs come and go so fast that even the magazines devoted somewhat to their pursuit—*3 Keller* and *Exit*, both distributed free in the gay bars and bookstores—have a hard time keeping up. *Lesbia*, a monthly national lesbian magazine, focuses on women's issues.

Banana Café   This is the most popular gay bar in the Marais, a required stop for gay Europeans (mostly male) visiting or doing business in Paris. Occupying two floors of a 19th-century building, it has walls the color of an overripe banana, dim lighting, and a well-publicized policy of raising drink prices after 10pm, when the joint becomes really interesting. On theme nights such as Valentine's Day, expect the entire premises to be plastered with pink crêpe paper. There's a street-level bar and a dance floor in the cellar that features a live pianist and recorded music. On many nights, go-go dancers perform. 13 rue de la Ferronnerie, 1er. ℂ 01-42-33-35-31. Métro: Châtelet-Les-Halles.

Bar Hotel Central   Bar Hotel Central is one of the leading bars for men in the Hôtel-de-Ville area. The club has opened a small hotel upstairs. Both the bar and its hotel are in a 300-year-old building in the heart of the Marais. The establishment caters mostly to gay men, less frequently to lesbians. 33 rue Vieille-du-Temple, 4e. ℂ 01-48-87-99-33. Métro: Hôtel-de-Ville.

La Champmeslé   With dim lighting, background music, and comfortable banquettes, La Champmeslé offers a cozy meeting place for women and to a much lesser extent (about 5%), "well-behaved" men. Paris's leading women's bar is in a 300-year-old building with exposed stone, ceiling beams, and 1950s-style furnishings. Every Thursday night, one of the premier lesbian events in Paris, a cabaret, begins at 10pm (with the same cover and drink prices as on any other day). 4 rue Chabanais, 2e. ⓒ **01-42-96-85-20.** Métro: Pyramides or Bourse.

Le Bar   Covering the street level and cellar of a sprawling building in a neighborhood known for its serious pickup scene, this is the largest gay bar in Paris. You'll find three bars on the premises, and an ambience that's more sexually charged and explicit in the cellar than on the street level. The average age of most patrons is around 32, and the majority are gay and male. 5 rue de la Ferronerie, 1er. ⓒ **01-40-41-00-10.** Métro: Châtelet.

Le Pulp   This is one of the most popular (and fun) lesbian discos in Paris, welcoming women of all ages. After a change in management, the club's seedy past is now a memory; today, this replica of a late-19th-century French music hall is chic, with all types of cutting-edge music. It's best to show up before midnight. What if you're a gay male who wants to hang with the girls? Head for the side entrance, where a "separate but equal facility" called Le Scorp welcomes gay guys into a roughly equivalent place that never manages to be as much fun as Le Queen. 25 bd. Poissonnière, 2e. ⓒ **01-40-26-01-93.** Métro: Rue-Montmartre.

Le Queen   Should you miss gay life à la New York, follow the flashing purple sign near the corner of avenue George-V. This place is often mobbed, primarily by gay men and, to a lesser degree, chic women who work in fashion and film. Look for drag shows, muscle shows, striptease from danseurs who gyrate atop the bars, and everything from Monday '70s-style disco nights to Tuesday-night foam parties (only in summer), when cascades of mousse descend onto the dance floor. Go very, very late: The place stays open until 6 or 7am, but doesn't even open until midnight. 102 av. des Champs-Elysées, 8e. ⓒ **01-53-89-08-90.** No cover Tues–Thurs and Sun; 50F (7.60, $7.25) Mon; 100F (15.20, $14.50) Fri–Sat. Métro: Franklin-D.-Roosevelt.

6

Side Trips from Paris: Versailles, Chartres & the Best of the Île de France

Château de Versailles, the Cathédrale Notre-Dame de Chartres, and the Palais de Fontainebleau draw countless tour buses to this region. They're the stars of the Île de France and need no selling from us. However, some lesser-known but equally stunning spots await you in this greenbelt around Paris. You can find everything from Romanesque ruins, Gothic cathedrals, and feudal castles to 18th-century châteaux, forests like Fontainebleau and Chantilly, sleepy villages, and an African game reserve. To top it off, there's Disneyland Paris if your kids must see Mickey and Minnie with a Gallic twist. Plus, because this region is also a haven for artists, you can visit the painted worlds of Corot, Renoir, Degas, Monet, and Cézanne.

Everything described can be seen on a day trip from Paris or an overnight excursion.

1 Versailles ✦

13 miles SW of Paris, 44 miles NE of Chartres

Back in the grand siècle, all you needed was a sword, a hat, and a bribe for the guard at the gate. Providing you didn't look as if you had smallpox, you'd be admitted to the Château de Versailles, where you could stroll through salon after glittering salon and watch the Sun King, gossiping, dancing, plotting, and flirting. Louis XIV was accorded about as much privacy as an institution.

Today, Versailles needs the return of Louis XIV and his fat treasury. You wouldn't believe it to look at the glittering Hall of Mirrors, but Versailles is down-at-the-heels. It suffers from a lack of funds, which translates into a shortage of security. You get to see only half its treasures; the rest are closed to the public, including the Musée de France, with its 6,000 paintings and 2,000 statues. Some 3.2 million visitors arrive annually, and on average they spend 2 hours here.

ESSENTIALS

GETTING THERE　To get to Versailles by **train** from Paris, catch the RER line C at the Gare d'Austerlitz, St-Michel, Musée d'Orsay, Invalides, Pont-de-l'Alma, Champ-de-Mars, or Javel station and take it to the Versailles Rive Gauche station, from which you can walk or take a shuttle bus to the château. The 35F (5.30, $5.08) round-trip takes about 35 to 40 minutes; Eurailpass holders travel free on the train, but pay 20F (3.04, $2.90) for a ride on the shuttle. Regular SNCF trains also make the run from Paris to Versailles: One set of trains departs from the Gare St-Lazare for the Versailles Rive Droite RER station; another departs from the Gare Montparnasse for Versailles Chantiers station, a 15-minute walk from the château. You can take bus B from Versailles Chantiers to the château for 8F (1.22, $1.16) each way if you don't want to walk.

If you're **driving,** exit the périphérique on N10 (or avenue du Général-Leclerc), which will take you straight to Versailles; park on place d'Armes in front of the château.

VISITOR INFORMATION   The **Office de Tourisme** is at 7 rue des Réservoirs (℃ **01-39-24-88-88;** fax 01-39-24-88-89).

EVENING SPECTACLES   The French government offers a program of fireworks and illuminated fountains, "Les Fêtes de Nuit de Versailles" (Rêve de Roi), on 7 to 10 dates throughout the summer. Two hundred actors in period costume portray Louis XVI and his *ancien régime* court. In July, the 90-minute shows begin at 10:30pm; in August and September, they start at 9:30pm. Spectators sit on bleachers at the palace's boulevard de la Reine entrance, adjacent to the Fountain (Bassin) of Neptune. The most desirable seats cost 250F (38, $36.25); standing room is 70F (10.65, $10.15). Gates to the bleachers open 90 minutes before showtime. For information, call ℃ **01-30-83-78-88.**

Tickets can be purchased in advance at the tourist office in Versailles—inquire by phone, fax, or mail, or in central Paris at any branch of the FNAC department stores. (FNAC's central phone number is ℃ **01-55-21-57-93.**) You can also take your chances and buy tickets an hour prior to the event itself from a kiosk adjacent to the boulevard de la Reine entrance to the bleachers.

SUNDAY-AFTERNOON PROMENADES IN THE PARK   Every Sunday between early April and mid-October, and every Saturday between early July and late August, from 11am to noon and again from 3:30 to 5:30pm, the government broadcasts classical music throughout the park and opens all the valves of every fountain at Versailles. The effect during these Grandes Eaux Musicales duplicates the landscaping vision of the 18th-century architects who designed Versailles. You won't be confined to a seat but are encouraged to walk around the park, enjoying the juxtapositions of grand architecture with lavish waterworks and music by Mozart, Haydn, and such French-born composers as Couperin, Charpentier, and Delalande. Admission to the park during these events is 25F (3.80, $3.65) per person. Call ℃ **01-30-83-78-88** for information.

EXPLORING THE CHÂTEAU & GARDENS

Château de Versailles   Within 50 years, the Château de Versailles was transformed from Louis XIII's hunting lodge into an extravagant palace. Begun in 1661, its construction involved 32,000 to 45,000 workmen, some of whom had to drain marshes and move forests. Louis XIV set out to build a palace that would be the envy of Europe, and he created a symbol of pomp and opulence

---

Tips **By the Clock**

It takes an hour to go through the Grands Appartements and a minimum of 3 hours (or more if you have the time) to tour the château. You can easily spend another 3 hours touring the Trianons and strolling through the gardens. Our recommendation? Make Versailles a daylong event.

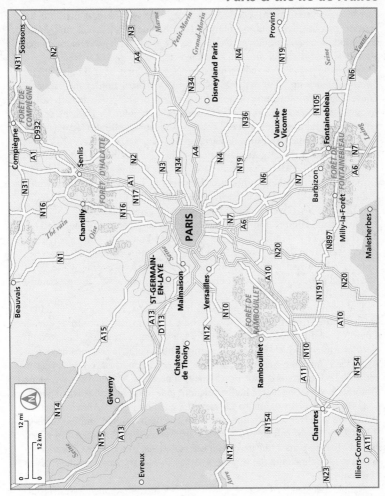

that was to be copied, yet never quite duplicated, all over Europe and even in America.

So he could keep an eye on the nobles of France (and with good reason), Louis XIV summoned them to live at his court. Here he amused them with constant entertainment and lavish banquets. To some he awarded such tasks as holding the hem of his robe. While the aristocrats frivolously played, often in silly intrigues and games, the peasants on the estates sowed the seeds of the Revolution.

When Louis XIV died in 1715, he was succeeded by his great-grandson, Louis XV, who continued the outrageous pomp, though he is said to have predicted the outcome: "Après moi le déluge" (After me, the deluge). His wife, Marie Leczinska, was shocked by the blatant immorality at Versailles.

Louis XVI found his grandfather's behavior scandalous—in fact, on gaining the throne he ordered that the "stairway of indiscretion" (secret stairs leading up to the king's bedchamber) be removed. This dull, weak king (who did have good intentions) and his queen, Marie Antoinette, were well liked at first, but the queen's frivolity and wild spending led to her downfall. Louis and Marie Antoinette were at Versailles on October 6, 1789, when they were notified that mobs were marching on the palace. As predicted, *le déluge* had arrived.

Napoléon stayed at Versailles but never seemed fond of it. Louis-Philippe (who reigned from 1830 to 1848) prevented the destruction of the palace by converting it into a museum dedicated to the glory of France. To do that, he had to surrender some of his own riches. Decades later, John D. Rockefeller contributed toward the restoration of Versailles, and work continues today.

The six magnificent **Grands Appartements** ✦✦✦ are in the Louis XIV style, each named after the allegorical painting on the room's ceiling. The best known and largest is the **Hercules Salon** ✦✦, with a ceiling painted by François Lemoine, depicting the Apotheosis of Hercules. In the **Mercury Salon** (with a ceiling by Jean-Baptiste Champaigne), the body of Louis XIV was put on display in 1715; his 72-year reign was one of the longest in history.

The most famous room at Versailles is the 236-foot-long **Hall of Mirrors** ✦✦✦. Begun by Mansart in 1678 in the Louis XIV style, it was decorated by Le Brun with 17 arched windows matched by corresponding beveled mirrors in simulated arcades. On June 28, 1919, the treaty ending World War I was signed in this corridor. Ironically, the German Empire was also proclaimed here in 1871.

The royal apartments were for show, but Louis XV and Louis XVI retired to the **Petits Appartements** ✦✦ to escape the demands of court etiquette. Louis XV died in his bedchamber in 1774, a victim of smallpox. In a second-floor apartment, which you can visit only with a guide, he stashed away first Mme de Pompadour and then Mme du Barry. Attempts have been made to return the Queen's Apartments to their appearance in the days of Marie Antoinette, when she played her harpsichord in front of specially invited guests.

Louis XVI had a sumptuous **Library**, designed by Jacques-Ange Gabriel. Its panels are delicately carved, and the room has been restored and refurnished. The **Clock Room** contains Passement's astronomical clock, encased in gilded bronze. Twenty years in the making, it was completed in 1753. The clock is supposed to keep time until the year 9999. At age 7, Mozart played for the court in this room.

Gabriel designed the **Opéra** ✦✦ for Louis XV in 1748, though it wasn't completed until 1770. In its heyday, it took 3,000 candles to light the place. With gold-and-white harmony, Hardouin-Mansart built the **Royal Chapel** in 1699, dying before its completion. Louis XVI, when still the dauphin (crown prince), married Marie Antoinette here in 1770. Spread across 250 acres, the **Gardens of Versailles** ✦✦✦ were laid out by the landscape artist André Le Nôtre. At the peak of their glory, 1,400 fountains spewed forth. *The Buffet* is an exceptional one, designed by Mansart. One fountain depicts Apollo in his chariot pulled by four horses, surrounded by tritons rising from the water to light the world. Le Nôtre created a Garden of Eden using ornamental lakes and canals, geometrically designed flowerbeds, and avenues bordered with statuary. On the mile-long Grand Canal, Louis XV—imagining he was in Venice—used to take gondola rides with his favorite of the moment.

A walk across the park will take you to the **Grand Trianon** ✦✦, in pink-and-white marble, designed by Hardouin-Mansart for Louis XIV in 1687. Traditionally it has been a lodging for important guests, though de Gaulle wanted to turn it into a weekend retreat. Nixon once slept here in the room where Mme

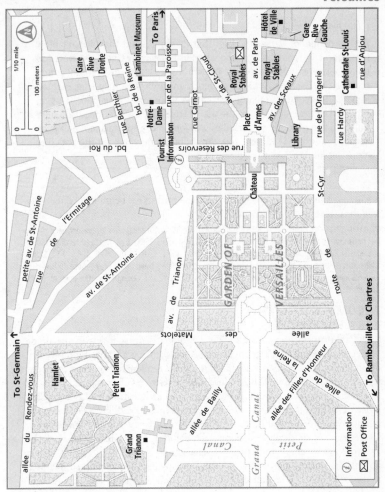

de Pompadour died. Mme de Maintenon also slept here, as did Napoléon. The original furnishings are gone, with mostly Empire pieces here today.

Gabriel, the designer of place de la Concorde in Paris, built the **Petit Trianon** ✹✹ in 1768 for Louis XV. Louis used it for his trysts with Mme du Barry. In time, Marie Antoinette adopted it as her favorite residence, a place to escape the rigid life at the main palace. Many of the current furnishings, including a few in her rather modest bedchamber, belonged to the ill-fated queen.

On Christmas night of 1999, one of the worst storms in France's history destroyed some 10,000 historic trees on the grounds of the Château de Versailles. Blowing at 100 miles per hour, gusts uprooted 80% of the trees planted during the 18th and 19th centuries. These included pines from Corsica planted during the reign of Napoléon, tulip trees from Virginia, and a pair of junipers planted in honor of Marie Antoinette. Versailles had never undergone such a natural catastrophe, and it will take years to rebuild the park. Nonetheless, there

> **Fun Fact** Your Own Tree at Versailles
>
> The gardeners of Versailles claim that it's an ill wind that doesn't blow some good. Before that crippling storm in 1999, many trees here were too tall, weak, aged, and diseased. The storms took care of that, uprooting such classics as Marie Antoinette's much-loved Virginia tulip tree, planted in 1783. With a $40 million restoration in progress, the park is being returned to the way it was in the day of Louis XIV, the Sun King. When it's finished, the grounds of Versailles will look more spectacular than ever. For a donation of $155, you, too, can sponsor a new tree for the park. For more details, check out www.chateauversailles.fr.

is still much that remains to enchant, and the gardens get better and better every month.

© **01-30-83-78-00.** Palace 46F (7, $6.65) adults, 35F (5.30, $5.10) adults after 3:30pm and ages 18–25, free for seniors 60 and over; Grand Trianon 25F (3.80, $3.63) adults, 15F (2.28, $2.18) adults after 3:30pm and ages 18–25, free for seniors 60 and over; Petit Trianon 15F (2.28, $2.18) adults, 10F (1.52, $1.45) adults after 3:30pm and ages 18–25. Everything free for children 17 and under. May 2–Sept 30 Tues–Sun 9am–6:30pm (until 5:30pm rest of the year). Trianons maintain same closing hours, but open at 10am. Grounds daily dawn–dusk.

ACCOMMODATIONS
VERY EXPENSIVE

Hôtel Trianon Palace ★★★ This *luxe* hotel is the grandest in the Île de France. It was built in 1910 on land that had sheltered a Capucine monastery during the the *ancien régime*. In 1919, it was the headquarters of the peace conference where Woodrow Wilson, Lloyd George, Georges Clemenceau, and other world leaders gathered. Since then, guests have included John D. Rockefeller, Queen Elizabeth II, and Marlene Dietrich, who made headlines by entering the dining room wearing pants. Today, the hotel dwarfs the competition in town. It's housed in a classically designed palace, connected to a circa-1990 annex (Le Pavillon) via an underground tunnel. The setting is lovely—the 5-acre garden borders the gardens of Trianons at Versailles. Japanese owners restored the place in the early 1990s to the tune of $60 million. Public rooms are splendid. Accommodations in both buildings are decorated in traditional styles with reference to château living, using rich fabrics and a mixture of antiques and fine reproductions. Mattresses, amenities, and electronic accessories are top-of-the-line, without equal in Versailles. The hotel has joined the Phytomer, one of the top names in French beauty care, to create an outstanding spa.

1 bd. de la Reine, 78000 Versailles. *©* **800/228-3000** in the U.S. and Canada, or 01-30-84-50-00. Fax 01-39-49-00-77. www.westin.com. 200 units. 2,600F–3,500F (395.20– 532, $377–$507.50) double; 3,500F–6,500F (532– 998, $507.50–$942.50) suite. AE, DC, DISC, MC, V. Free parking. **Amenities:** 3 restaurants; indoor pool; tennis courts; health club; spa; 24-hour room service; baby-sitting; laundry/dry cleaning. *In room:* A/C, TV, minibar, hair dryer, safe.

MODERATE

Novotel Versailles Le Chesnay A 15-minute walk north from one of the side wings of the château, this hotel, built in 1988 as part of a nationwide chain, has a modern facade with columns and large windows. It's not too expensive and makes a convenient choice for visitors to Versailles. The guest rooms are practical and were recently renovated in 1998.

4 bd. St-Antoine, 78150 Le Chesnay. (℡ **01-39-54-96-96.** Fax 01-39-54-94-40. h1022@accor-hotels.com. 105 units. 650F–750F (98.80– 114, $94.25–$108.75) double. Children 16 and under stay free in parents' room. AE, DC, MC, V. Parking 50F (7.60, $7.25). **Amenities:** Restaurant, bar. *In room:* TV, minibar.

INEXPENSIVE

Hôtel Paris *Value* This is the best deal in town. The nondescript wood-and-stucco hotel was built late in the 19th century and has been modernized into a clean, well-maintained, if not exciting design. The price is hard to beat, especially considering the great location, a 10-minute walk due east of the château

---

Finds **Peaches & Peas Fit for a King**

Between 1682 and 1789 (except for 8 years during the time of Louis XV), Versailles housed a royal entourage of 3,000 people. To feed them, the kitchens employed a permanent staff of 2,000. Without benefit of running water or electricity, they labored over the banquets that became day-to-day rituals at the most glorious court since the collapse of ancient Rome.

The fruits and vegetables that adorned the royal tables were produced on site, in *Les Potagers du Roi* (the King's Kitchen Gardens). The gardens have survived and can be found a 10-minute walk south of the château's main entrance, at 10 rue du Maréchal-Joffre, across from the Cathédral Saint-Louis. Here, 23 acres are arranged into parterres and terraces as formal as the Gardens of Versailles with flowers, fountains, and statuary.

Meals at Versailles were quite a ritual. The king almost always dined in state, alone, at a table visible to hundreds of observers and, in some cases, other diners, who sat in order of rank. Fortunately for gastronomic historians, there are many detailed accounts of what Louis XIV ingested and how much he consumed: addicted to salads, he ate prodigious amounts of basil, purslane, mint, and wood sorrel. He loved melons, figs, and pears. He found peaches so desirable that he rarely waited to cut and peel them, preferring to let the juices flow liberally down his royal chin. The culinary rage, however, was peas—imported from Genoa for the first time in 1660. According to Mme de Maintenon, Louis XIV's second wife, the entire court was obsessed with "impatience to eat them."

Today, about half a dozen gardeners under the direction of the École Nationale du Paysage maintain Les Potagers du Roi. It manages to intersperse the fruits and vegetables once favored by the monarchs with experimental breeds and hundreds of splendidly espaliered fruit trees.

The kitchen gardens can be visited between April and October, daily from 10am to 6pm. Adults pay an admission of 40F (6.10, $5.80); children under 18 pay 20F (3.04, $2.90). Look for the entrance at 10 rue Maréchal-Joffre (℡ **01-39-24-62-00**), about a quarter-mile south of the palace. Free 1-hour guided tours of the garden, in French, depart once an hour beginning at 10:30am. On the premises is a kiosk where the fruits and vegetables grown here are for sale, as they would be at a farmers' market.

at the corner of rue des États-Généraux. Even the least expensive bedrooms have showers and sinks (although no toilets). The cheapest of the rooms with private bathrooms are the best value; if you upgrade to the 400F (60.80, $58) rate, all you'll get is a bathtub instead of a stall shower. The staff is helpful.

14 av. de Paris, 78000 Versailles. ℭ **01-39-50-56-00.** Fax 01-39-50-21-83. 38 units, 35 with private bathroom. 220F (33.45, $31.90) double without bathroom; 360F–400F (54.70– 60.80, $52.20–$58) double with bathroom. AE, DC, MC, V. *In room:* TV.

Relais Mercure Versailles Château   The interior of this 18th-century building (a 10-minute walk from the château) was gutted in 1994, leaving only the awesomely thick walls. The chain hotel that now stands here provides all the modern comforts, but few frills. Each unit has a well-maintained bathroom with tub and shower combo. The service is brisk and efficient, very much what you'd expect. Breakfast is the only meal served.

19 rue Philippe-de-Dangeau, 78000 Versailles. ℭ **800/221-4542** in the U.S. and Canada, or 01-39-50-44-10. Fax 01-39-50-65-11. www.mercure-versailles.com. 60 units. 540F (82.10, $78.30) double. AE, DC, MC, V. Parking 50F (7.60, $7.25). *In room:* TV.

DINING
VERY EXPENSIVE

Les Trois Marchés 𝕉𝕉𝕉 MODERN FRENCH   The food here is of the highest order—and so are the prices. Chef Gérard Vié, known for the inventiveness of his *cuisine bourgeois,* serves the finest food in Versailles. His soaring greenhouse-inspired dining room is remarkable for its expanses of glass and its intimate size (only 55 seats). In summer, you can dine under the canopy on the front terrace. Begin with the lobster salad flavored with fresh herbs and served with an onion soufflé; the foie gras of duckling; a galette of potatoes with bacon, chardonnay, and sevruga caviar; or the citrus-flavored scallop bisque. The chef is a great innovator, especially when it comes to main courses: pigeon roasted and flavored with rosé and accompanied with celeriac and truffles, or filet of sea bass with a "cake" of eggplant. If you can't choose a single dessert, opt for the assortment. Note that some have found the staff a bit too stiff and patronizing.

In the Hôtel Trianon Palace, 1 bd. de la Reine. ℭ **01-39-50-13-21.** Reservations required. Fixed-price menus 350F–850F (53.20– 129.20, $50.75–$123.25) lunch, 650F–850F (98.80– 129.20, $94.25–$123.25) dinner. AE, DC, MC, V. Tues–Sat noon–2pm and 7:30–10pm. Closed Aug.

MODERATE

La Flottille TRADITIONAL FRENCH   This is the only restaurant inside the park, occupying an enviable position at the head of the Grand Canal with a sweeping view over some of Europe's most famous landscaping. It was built in 1896 as a bar for laborers who maintained the gardens. Today, tables for lunch are placed outside in warm weather, and there's a pavilion-inspired dining room. A brasserie or snack bar serves sandwiches, omelets, crêpes, salads, and ice cream. Specialties include snail-stuffed ravioli with chablis sauce, sweetbreads braised in port, and a ballotine of chicken "in the old-fashioned style."

In the Parc du Château. ℭ **01-39-51-41-58.** Reservations recommended. Restaurant, main courses 98F– 125F (14.90– 19, $14.20–$18.15); fixed-price menu 135F–148F (20.50– 22.50, $19.60–$21.45). Brasserie, snacks 60F–90F (9.10– 13.70, $8.70–$13.05). AE, MC, V. Restaurant open daily noon–3:30pm; brasserie open daily 8:30am–sundown for coffee, ice cream, and snacks.

Le Potager du Roy 𝕉 MODERN FRENCH   Philippe Letourneur has emerged as a formidably talented chef after spending years perfecting a distinctive cuisine and now adding novelty to the dining scene in Versailles. Letourneur rotates his skillfully prepared menu with the seasons. Examples are foie gras with a vegetable-flavored vinaigrette, roasted duck with a navarin of vegetables, and roasted codfish with roasted peppers in the style of Provence. Looking for something unusual and more earthy? Try the fondant of pork jowls with a confit of fresh vegetables.

1 rue du Maréchal-Joffre. ℭ **01-39-50-35-34.** Reservations required. Fixed-price menu 145F (22.05, $21.05) lunch, 189F–285F (28.75– 43.30, $27.40–$41.35) dinner. AE, MC, V. Tues–Fri noon–2:30pm; Tues–Sat 7–10:30pm.

INEXPENSIVE

Le Quai No. 1 ✦ *Value* SEAFOOD/FRENCH This is the informal seafood bistro associated with the much grander, more expensive Les Trois Marchés (see above). Mega-chef Gérard Vié is the creative force here, lending his credentials and glamour to the 18th-century building overlooking the western facade of France's most famous château. The dining room is decorated with lithographs and wood paneling; there's also a summer terrace. Though the cuisine isn't opulent, it is charming, very French, and reasonable in price. The fixed-price menus make Le Quai a bargain in Versailles. Specialties are seafood sauerkraut, seafood paella, bouillabaisse, and home-smoked salmon. The chef recommends the *plateau de fruits de mer.* Carnivores appreciate the three meat-based main courses, the best of which is magrêt of duckling dressed with aged vinegar. An enduringly popular platter is an upscale version of surf-and-turf: grilled Breton lobster and a sizzling sirloin, just like you'd expect in North America. Care and imagination go into the cuisine, and the service is professional and polite.

1 av. de St-Cloud. ℭ **01-39-50-42-26.** Reservations required. Main courses 90F (13.70, $13.05); fixed-price menus 120F (18.25, $17.40) lunch, 150F–220F (33– 45, $21.75–$31.90) dinner. MC, V. Tues–Sun noon–2:30pm; Tues–Sat 7:30–11pm.

VERSAILLES AFTER DARK

O'Paris Pub, 15 rue Colbert, off place d'Armes (tel. **01-39-50-36-12**), is a British pub where music plays in the background; here you can order the best brews in town. A bit more upmarket, **Bar à Vins-Restaurant Le Ducis,** 13 rue Ducis (ℭ **01-39-49-96-51**), offers a mellow atmosphere on a summer evening, with tables spilling out onto a side street. A bottle of wine and a good companion should get you through an evening, enhanced perhaps by a plate of food selected from the chalkboard menu.

2 The Forest of Rambouillet ✦

34 miles SW of Paris, 26 miles NE of Chartres

Georges Pompidou used to visit the château here, as did Louis XVI and Charles de Gaulle. Dating from 1375, it's surrounded by a park in one of the most famous forests in France, with over 47,000 acres of greenery stretching from the valley of the Eure to the valley of Chevreuse, the latter rich in medieval and royal abbeys. The lakes, deer, and wild boar are some of the attractions of this beautiful area.

Allow 2 hours to see the forest.

ESSENTIALS

GETTING THERE   Trains depart from Paris's Gare Montparnasse every 20 minutes throughout the day. One-way passage costs 42F (6.40, $6.10) for the ride of about 35 minutes. For train information and schedules, contact La Gare de Rambouillet, place Prud'homme (ℭ **01-53-90-20-20**).

VISITOR INFORMATION   The **Office de Tourisme** is at the Hôtel de Ville, place de la Libération (📞 **01-34-83-21-21**).

SEEING THE CHATEAU

Château de Rambouillet 🌲   This is one of the royal châteaux of France, though it offers no serious competition to Fontainebleau or Versailles. François I, the Chevalier King, died of a fever at Rambouillet in 1547 at the age of 52. When the château was later occupied by the comte de Toulouse, Rambouillet was often visited by Louis XV, who was amused (in more ways than one) by the comte's witty and high-spirited wife. Louis XVI acquired the château, but his wife, Marie Antoinette, was bored with the place and called it "the toad."

Napoléon's second wife, Marie-Louise, came here in 1814, after leaving him. She was on her way to Vienna with the exiled king of Rome, her son, Napoléon II. Napoléon slept here before leaving on the long voyage into exile at St. Helena.

In 1830, Charles X, Louis XVI's brother, abdicated after the July Revolution. Following that, Rambouillet became privately owned. At one time it was a fashionable restaurant that attracted Parisians, who could also go for rides in gondolas. Napoléon III, however, returned it to the Crown. In 1897, it was designated as a residence for the presidents of the Republic.

Today, it's used as a vacation retreat by the president. When he is not in residence, the rooms can be visited on a self-guided tour. Superb woodwork is used throughout, and the walls are adorned with tapestries, many dating from the era of Louis XV. Although there are no guided tours of the Rambouillet forest, you can get a map at the tourist office and go hiking, biking, or driving through it.

Parc du Château. 📞 **01-34-94-28-00**. Admission 36F (5.45, $5.20) adults, 23F (3.50, $3.35) ages 12–25, free for children 11 and under. April–Sept Wed–Mon 10–11:30am and 2–4:30pm; Oct–March Wed–Mon 10am–11:30am and 2–3:30pm.

Finds   **Through an Enchanted Forest**

If you've exhausted the idea of a ramble through the gardens that surround the château of Rambouillet (or if they're closed because of a visit by the president), consider a visit to the **Rochers d'Angennes,** rocky hillocks that left over from the Ice Age. Park your car where you see the sign pointing to the **Rochers et Étang d'Angennes** on the D107, about 3 miles north of the hamlet of Épernon. From here, walk along the marked trail, through a pine forest, to reach a rocky plateau overlooking the hills and a pond nestled into the surrounding countryside. Round-trip, from your car to the plateau and back, this takes 30 to 45 minutes.

An alternative escape involves parking your car in St-Hubert, beside the N191 about 5 miles southwest of the village of Montfort-l'Amaury. A 10-minute walk south of St-Hubert, along paths pointing to l'**Étang de St-Hubert,** takes you to serpentine-shaped ponds dug out and dammed on orders of Louis XIV in the 18th century, as part of a series of irrigation and flood-control measures. There was an elaborate hunting lodge built by Louis XV, which was destroyed during the Revolution. The promenade, about 15 minutes from your car to the lake and back, encompasses views of massive colonies of waterlilies, part of the legacy of gardeners who tried to beautify the lake for the French kings.

ACCOMMODATIONS

Hotel Amarys Built in 1988, this stone-fronted hotel sits in the forest about half a mile north of the town center. Although the hotel is affordable, it caters mainly to business travelers. The rooms are comfortable, the bathrooms boxy and motel-standard, each with a shower. About half of the bathrooms also have tubs.

Lieu-Dit la Louvière, rue de la Louvière, 78120 Rambouillet. ℰ **01-34-85-62-62.** Fax 01-30-59-23-57. www.hotel-amarys-rbt.com. 66 units. 285F–310F (43.30– 47.10, $41.35–$44.95) double. AE, DC, MC, V. Get off N10 at the Dampierre Chevreuse exit. **Amenities:** Restaurant, bar; outdoor heated pool; tennis court; fitness center; baby-sitting. *In room:* TV, iron, coffeemaker.

DINING

La Poste TRADITIONAL FRENCH If you can't get an invitation to dine with the president at the château, this is the next best option. Located on a street corner in the town's historic center, across from the Sous-Préfecture de Police, this restaurant has been serving food since the mid–19th century, when it was a coaching inn. The dining rooms have rustic beams and old-fashioned accents that complement the flavorful, old-fashioned food, such as homemade terrines of foie gras and freshly made pastries. Main courses range from fricassée of chicken with crayfish to noisettes of lamb with copious amounts of red wine and herbs.

101 av. du Général-de-Gaulle. ℰ **01-34-83-03-01.** Reservations recommended Sat–Sun. Main courses 120F–156F (18.25– 23.70, $17.40–$22.60); fixed-price menu 125F–195F (19– 29.65, $18.15–$28.30). AE, CB, V. Tues–Thurs and Sat noon–2pm; Tues–Sun 7–10pm.

3 The Glorious Cathedral of Chartres ✯✯✯

60 miles SW of Paris, 47 miles NW of Orléans

Many observers feel that medieval architecture reached its pinnacle in the world-renowned cathedral at Chartres. Come to see its architecture, its sculpture, and—most of all—its stained glass, which gave the world a new color, Chartres blue.

The ancient town of Chartres also played a role in World War II. There's a monument to Jean Moulin, the Resistance hero and friend of de Gaulle. Under torture, he refused to sign a document stating that French troops committed atrocities. The Gestapo killed him in 1943 (he's buried in the Panthéon in Paris). From the cathedral, head down rue du Cheval-Blanc until it becomes rue Jean-Moulin (the monument is up ahead on your right). Other street names, including boulevard de le Résistance, also commemorate the World War II Resistance.

Allow 1 hour for the cathedral, 1½ hours for the town.

ESSENTIALS

GETTING THERE From Paris's Gare Montparnasse, **trains** run directly to Chartres, taking less than an hour. Tickets cost 144F (21.90, $20.90) round-trip. Call ℰ **08-36-35-35-35** for information. If you're **driving,** take A10/A11 southwest from the périphérique and follow the signs to Le Mans and Chartres. (The Chartres exit is clearly marked.)

VISITOR INFORMATION The **Office de Tourisme** is on place de la Cathédrale (ℰ **02-37-18-26-26**).

SEEING THE CATHEDRAL

Cathédrale Notre-Dame de Chartres ✯✯✯ Reportedly, Rodin once sat for hours on the edge of the sidewalk, admiring this cathedral's Romanesque sculpture. His opinion: Chartres is the French Acropolis. When it began to rain, a kind soul offered him an umbrella—which he declined, so transfixed was he by the magic of this place.

The cathedral's origins are uncertain; some have suggested that it grew up over an ancient Druid site that later became a Roman temple. It is known that as early as the 4th century, there was a Christian basilica here. A fire in 1194 destroyed most of what had then become a Romanesque cathedral, but it spared the western facade and crypt. The cathedral you see today dates principally from the 13th century, when it was rebuilt with the combined efforts and contributions of kings, princes, churchmen, and pilgrims from all over Europe. One of the world's greatest High Gothic cathedrals, it was the first to use flying buttresses.

French sculpture in the 12th century broke into full bloom when the **Royal Portal** ✫✫✫ was added. It's a landmark in Romanesque art. The sculptured bodies are elongated, often formalized beyond reality, in their long, flowing robes. But the faces are amazingly (for the time) lifelike, occasionally betraying Mona Lisa smiles. In the central tympanum, Christ is shown at the Second Coming, with his descent depicted on the right, his ascent on the left. Before entering, admire the Royal Portal and walk around to both the North Portal and the South Portal, each dating from the 13th century. They depict such scenes as the expulsion of Adam and Eve from the Garden of Eden.

Inside is a celebrated choir screen (parclose screen); work on it began in the 16th century and lasted until 1714. The niches, 40 in all, contain statues illustrating scenes from the life of the Madonna and Christ—everything from the massacre of the innocents to the coronation of the Virgin.

But few rushed visitors ever notice the screen: they're too transfixed by the light from the **stained glass** ✫✫✫. Covering an expanse of more than 3,000 square yards, the glass is without peer and is truly mystical. It was spared in both world wars because of a decision to remove it painstakingly piece by piece. Most of it dates from the 12th and 13th centuries. It's difficult to single out one panel or window of special merit—and depending on the position of the sun, the images all change constantly; however, an exceptional one is the 12th-century *Vierge de la Belle Verrière* (Virgin of the Beautiful Window) on the south side. Of course, there are three fiery rose windows, but you couldn't miss those even if you tried.

The nave—the widest in France—still contains its ancient labyrinth. The wooden *Notre-Dame du Pilier* (Our Lady of the Pillar), to the left of the choir, dates from the 14th century. The crypt was built over 2 centuries, beginning in the 9th. Enshrined within is *Notre-Dame de Sous Terre* (Our Lady of the Crypt), a 1976 Madonna that replaced one destroyed during the Revolution.

Try to get a tour conducted by Malcolm Miller (© **02-37-28-15-58;** fax 02-37-28-33-03), an Englishman who has spent 3 decades studying the cathedral and giving tours in English. His rare blend of scholarship, enthusiasm, and humor will help you understand and appreciate the cathedral. He usually conducts 75-minute tours at noon and 2:45pm Monday through Saturday for a fee of 40F (6.10, \$5.80) per person. Tours are cancelled in the event of pilgrimages, religious celebrations, and large-scale funerals. French-language tours costing 35F (5.30, \$5.10) are conducted at 10:30am and 3pm from Easter to October and at 2:30pm the rest of the year.

If you're fit enough, don't miss the opportunity, especially in summer, to climb to the top of the tower. Open the same hours as the cathedral, except for a lunch closing between noon and 2pm, it costs 25F (3.80, \$3.65) for adults

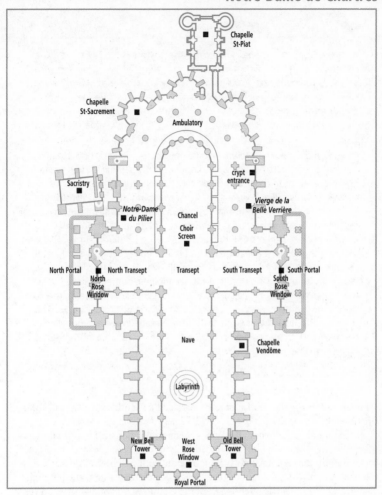

and 15F (2.30, \$2.20) for students. You can visit the crypt, gloomy and somber but rich with medieval history, only as part of a French-language tour conducted whenever there's enough demand. The cost is 11F (1.65, \$1.60) per person.

16 Cloître Notre-Dame. ☎ **02-37-21-56-33**. Free admission to cathedral (see above for tour, crypt, and tower charges). Mon–Sat 7:30am–7pm, Sun 8:30am–7pm.

EXPLORING THE TOWN

Next door to the cathedral is the **Musée des Beaux-Arts de Chartres** ⋆, 29 Cloître Notre-Dame (☎ **02-37-36-41-39**), open October 31 to May 2, Wednesday through Monday from 10am to noon and 2 to 5pm; the rest of the year, until 6pm. Admission is 15F (2.30, \$2.20) for adults and 7.50F (1.15, \$1.10) for children. Installed in a former episcopal palace, the building at times competes with its exhibitions. One part dates from the 15th century and encompasses a courtyard. The permanent collection covers mainly the 16th to the 20th

To Taste a Madeleine

And suddenly the memory returns. The taste was that of the little crumb of madeleine which on Sunday mornings at Combray (because on those mornings I did not go out before church-time), when I went to say good day to her in her bedroom, my aunt Léonie used to give me, dipping it first in her own cup of real or of lime-flower tea.

—Marcel Proust,
Remembrance of Things Past

Illiers-Combray, a small town 54 miles southwest of Paris and 15 miles southwest of Chartres, was once known simply as Illiers. Then Proust groupies started to come and signs were posted: ILLIERS, ILLIERS, LE COMBRAY DE MARCEL PROUST. Illiers was and is a real town, but Marcel Proust in his imagination made it world-famous as Combray in his masterpiece, *À la recherche du temps perdu* (*Remembrance of Things Past*). So today the town is known as Illiers-Combray.

It was the taste of a madeleine that launched Proust on his immortal recollection. To this day, readers from all over the world flock to the pastry shops in Illiers-Combray to eat a madeleine dipped in lime-flower tea. Following the Proustian canon, you can explore the gardens, streets, and houses he wrote about and visited until he was 13. The town is epitomized by its Église St-Jacques, where Proust as a boy placed hawthorn on the altar, and which he later referred to in his novels as l'Église St-Hilaire.

centuries, offering the works of old masters like Zurbarán, Watteau, and Brosamer. Of particular interest is David Ténier's *Le Concert*.

At the foot of the cathedral, the lanes contain gabled houses. Humped bridges span the Eure River. From the Bouju Bridge, you can see the lofty spires in the background. Our favorite stroll is along **rue du Pont-St-Hilaire** ⚐, as it offers the best vista of the old rooftops that lie beneath the towering cathedral itself. The street of St-Hilaire is reached east of the Gothic church of St-Pierre, on rue St-Pierre, a 10-minute stroll south of the cathedral. Two evocative streets of old Chartres, each reached after a 3-minute walk south of the cathedral, are **rue du Cygne** and **rue des Écuyers.** To the east of the cathedral, the most charming old *quartier* is **St. André,** once home to merchants such as cobblers and tanners. Most of the buildings here are now restored but date from the 1700s, and are known for their embossed doorways crowned by bull's-eye glass.

SHOPPING   Your best shopping bet in Chartres is place des Épars. This pedestrian area is home to most of the apparel shops, even some haute-couture boutiques. Along rue Noël-Balay is a small mall with about 15 shops you might find interesting, especially if it's raining. Many of the shops selling regional items are along the narrow streets that fan southeast from the cathedral.

At **Galerie du Vitrail,** 17 Cloître Notre-Dame (✆ 02-37-36-10-03), you'll find a huge selection of stained glass in every size and style. **Lassaussois Antiquités,** 17 rue des Changes (✆ 02-37-21-37-74), specializes in antique objets d'art and contemporary furnishings. If antique lace is your passion, stop by

Some members of Proust's family had lived in Illiers for centuries. His grandfather, François, was born on rue du Cheval-Blanc. At 11 place du Marché, opposite the church, he ran a small candle shop. His daughter, Elisabeth, married Jules Amiot, who ran a shop a few doors away. Down from Paris, young Marcel would visit his aunt at 4 rue du St-Esprit, which has been renamed rue du Docteur-Proust, honoring Marcel's grandfather.

Musée Marcel Proust/Maison de Tante Léonie, 4 rue du Docteur-Proust (℡ **02-37-24-30-97**), contains the world's most concentrated dose of Proust memorabilia and the objects and memories that helped spark his creative vision. In his novels, this was Aunt Léonie's home, filled with antimacassars and antiques, and typical of the solid bourgeois comforts of its day. Upstairs, you can see the bedrooms where the young Marcel and his Aunt Léonie slept. Today, they contain souvenirs of key episodes in his novels. Also important is a re-creation of the Salon Rouge, which Proust maintained in his second-to-last residence, at 102 Bd. Haussmann, Paris, 8e, filled with furniture owned by his parents and grandparents. The museum can be visited only as part of French-language guided tours that are conducted at 2:30 and 4pm, Tuesday through Sunday. Tours are 30F (4.55, $4.35) for adults, 2 F (3.05, $2.90) for students, and free for children under 12. Closed mid-December to mid-January.

In the center of town, a sign will guide you to further Proustian sights, each of which is open 24 hours a day without charge.

Ariane, 39 rue des Changes (℡ **02-37-21-20-68**), which also sells handmade sweaters, elegant linens, costume jewelry, and children's clothing.

ACCOMMODATIONS

Grand Monarque Best Western   The leading hotel of Chartres is housed in a classical building that surrounds a courtyard. Functioning as an inn almost since its original construction, and expanded over the centuries, it still attracts guests who enjoy its old-world charm—such as Art Nouveau stained glass and Louis XV chairs in the dining room. The guest rooms are decorated with reproductions of antiques; most have sitting areas. There is solid and reliable comfort here, but not great style. The hotel also has an old-fashioned, unremarkable restaurant.

22 place des Epars, 28005 Chartres. ℡ **800/528-1234** in the U.S. and Canada, or 02-37-21-00-72. Fax 02-37-36-34-18. www.bw-grand-monarque.com. 54 units. 630F–760F (95.75– 115.50, $91.35–$110.20) double; 1,150–1,1410F (174.80– 214.30, $166.75–$204.45) suite. AE, DC, MC, V. Parking 50F (7.60, $7.25). **Amenities:** Restaurant, bar; room service; laundry/dry cleaning. *In room:* TV, minibar, hair dryer.

Hotel Châtelet   This modern hotel has many traditional touches. The rustic guest rooms are inviting, with reproductions of Louis XV and Louis XVI furniture. The larger, more expensive units face a garden and avoid street noise. But many windows along the front (street) side of the hotel open onto a view of the cathedral. In chilly weather, there's a log-burning fire in one of the salons. Breakfast is the only meal served, but there are numerous restaurants close by.

Moments **A Free Concert**

If you visit Chartres on a Sunday afternoon in July and August, the church features free hour-long organ concerts at 4:45pm, when the filtered light makes the cathedral's western windows come thrillingly alive.

6–8 av. Jehan-de-Beauce, 28000 Chartres. Tel. **02-37-21-78-00**. Fax 02-37-36-23-01. 48 units. 395F–510F (60.05– 77.50, $57.30–$73.95) double. Extra person 60F (9.10, $8.70). AE, DC, MC, V. Free parking. *In room:* TV, minibar, hair dryer.

Hôtel de la Poste *(Value* This modest late-19th-century hotel in the center of town, a member of the Logis de France chain, offers one of the best values in Chartres—even though its starkly renovated rooms are short on charm. Each is soundproofed and comfortably outfitted, with wall-to-wall carpeting. Bathrooms contain cramped shower stalls and rather thin towels (about half the units have tubs as well). The one drawback: group tours often flood the place.

3 rue du Général-Koenig, 28003 Chartres. (**02-37-21-04-27**. Fax 02-37-36-42-17. www.hotelposte-chartres.com. E-mail: hotelposte.chartres@wanadoo.fr. 57 units. 330F–360F (50.15– 54.70, $47.85–$52.20) double. AE, DC, MC, V. Parking 45F (6.85, $6.55). **Amenities:** Restaurant, bar. *In room:* TV.

DINING

Note that the restaurant at the **Hôtel de la Poste** (see above) serves good, reasonably priced food.

La Truie qui File (Choukroune) ★★★ MODERN FRENCH At last Chartres offers a worthy restaurant comparable to some of the more stellar choices in Paris. The blue-and-yellow interior contains modern furniture and art set beneath the ceiling beams of a building erected in the 15th century. That, coupled with the savory cuisine of Gilles and Geneviève Choukroune, create a combination that bustles with good cheer and repeat visitors. The only option for diners is a fixed-price menu with five choices for the starter, main course, and dessert. Items change with the season and the inspiration of the chef, but are likely to include foie gras with spice bread, a combination of crayfish and snails in a blanquette, oxtail stewed in Loire valley wine, and roasted scallops with coriander oil. The signature dessert combines fresh clementines with cumin. There's a certain charm and fragrance to every dish.

Place Poissonnerie. (**02-37-21-53-90**. Reservations recommended. Fixed-price menu 230F (34.95, $33.35). AE, MC, V. Tues–Sun noon–2pm; Tues–Sat 7:30–9:30pm. Closed Aug.

Le Buisson Ardent *(Value* TRADITIONAL FRENCH In a charming 300-year-old house in the most historic section of town, this restaurant is one floor above street level in the shadow of the cathedral. From its location, you might expect it to be a tourist trap—but it isn't, and it refuses to follow many of the fads that sweep through restaurants in nearby Paris. The fixed-price menu changes about once a month and, like the à la carte dishes, is based on strictly fresh meats, produce, and fish. Bestsellers are escalope of warm foie gras with apples and Calvados, and émincée of roasted pigeon with sweetbreads and honey sauce. A dessert specialty is crispy hot pineapples with an orange and passion-fruit salad.

10 rue au Lait. (**02-37-34-04-66**. Reservations recommended. Main courses 90F–142F (13.70– 21.60, $13.05–$20.64); fixed-price menu 145F–250F (22.05– 38, $21.05–$36.25). MC, V. Thurs–Tues noon–2pm and 7:30–9:30pm.

CHARTRES AFTER DARK

For a formal evening of theater or modern dance, try the **Théâtre Municipal,** 1 place de Ravenne (© **02-37-18-27-27**), which offers presentations from September to June. From time to time, you can catch a jazz or rock concert here as well. **Forum de la Madeleine,** 1 Mail Jean-de-Dunois (© **02-37-88-45-00**), presents lighter fare and usually has a busier performance season.

For a relaxing drink, try **La Bodega,** 20 place des Halles (© **02-37-36-05-05**). It has one of the best selections of beer in town, with a Cuban-salsa atmosphere and live entertainment on weekends. The most popular drink? Rum and fresh lime. For dancing the night away, go to **Le Privilège,** 1 place St-Pierre (© **02-37-35-52-02**), where you'll find a wide range of dance music from zouk to funk and even disco.

4 Barbizon: The School of Rousseau ⊛⊛

35 miles SE of Paris, 6 miles NW of Fontainebleau

In the 19th century, the Barbizon school of painting gained world renown. This village on the edge of the Forest of Fontainebleau was a refuge for artists like Rousseau, Millet, and Corot, many of whom couldn't find acceptance in the more conservative Paris salons. In Barbizon, they turned to nature and painted more realistic pastoral scenes, without nude nymphs and dancing fauns. These artists attracted a school of lesser painters, including Daubigny and Diaz. Charles Jacques, Decamps, Paul Huet, Troyon, and others followed. Today, Barbizon attracts fashionable Parisians for *le weekend.* Some complain about its prices, but others just enjoy Barbizon's sunshine and clean air. Even with hordes of galleries and souvenir shops, the town retains much of its traditional atmosphere.

ESSENTIALS

GETTING THERE   Barbizon doesn't have a railway station of its own, so the most direct **train route** involves traveling from Paris to Fontainebleau (see below), and from there, taking one of only two buses a day that double back a few miles to Barbizon. The round-trip fare to Fontainebleau is 94F (14.30, $13.65). Bus fare to Barbizon costs 13F (2, $1.90) each way. For information and schedules, call © **01-64-23-71-11.**

VISITOR INFORMATION   The **Office de Tourisme** is at 55 Grande-Rue (© **01-60-66-41-87**).

MUSEUMS

Maison et Atelier de Jean-François Millet   This museum stands adjacent to the Hostellerie Les Pléiades (see below). Its premises are devoted to the best-known Barbizon painter, who settled here in 1849. Millet painted religious, classical, and especially peasant subjects. See his etching of *The Man with the Hoe,* as well as some of his original furnishings.

29 Grande-Rue. © **01-60-66-21-55.** Free admission. Wed–Sat and Mon 10am–12:30pm and 2–5:30pm.

Musée Ganne   The inn that housed most of the Barbizon artists during their late-19th-century sojourns here was L'Auberge du Père-Gannes. In the mid-1990s, through collaboration with Paris's Musée d'Orsay, it was transformed into the Musée Ganne, a showcase for Rousseau, who began painting landscapes directly from nature (novel at the time) and settled in Barbizon in the 1840s.

92 Grande-Rue. ✆ **01-60-66-22-27.** Admission 25F (3.80, $3.65) adults, 13F (2, $1.90) students, free for children under 12. April–Oct Wed–Mon 10am–12:30pm and 2–6pm; Nov–March Wed–Mon 10am–12:30pm and 2–5pm.

ACCOMMODATIONS

Hostellerie du Bas-Bréau 🐾🐾🐾   Dwarfing the local competition, this member of Relais & Châteaux is one of France's great old inns, set amid shade trees and courtyards. After its inauguration in the 1840s, many artists and writers stayed here, notably Robert Louis Stevenson, who scattered anecdotes of the inn throughout his novels. Napoléon III and his empress, Eugénie, came here for a day in 1868 to purchase some paintings from the Barbizon school. Since then, several enlargements and refurbishments have maintained the hotel's role as a glamorous competitor within the district. It's furnished with provincial antiques and fantastic reproductions. In the colder months, guests gather around the brick fireplace in the living room. The bedrooms contain antiques and comfortable mattresses; units in the rear building open directly onto semi-private terraces. All rooms are equipped with luxurious bathrooms with tub and shower combos.

22 Grande-Rue, 77630 Barbizon. ✆ **01-60-66-40-05.** Fax 01-60-69-22-89. www.basbreau.com. 20 units. 1,500F–2,200F (228– 334.40, $217.50–$319) double; 2,600F–3,200F (395.20– 486.40, $377–$464) suite. AE, MC, V. **Amenities:** Restaurant, bar; limited room service; laundry/dry cleaning. *In room:* A/C, TV, minibar, hair dryer, safe.

Hostellerie La Clé d'Or   Encircled by a stone wall, the grounds of this 100-year-old hotel include a garden and an intimate stone terrace full of plants that flower in a wash of pinks and yellows in spring and summer. The terrace leads to many of the bedrooms, which are modern but quite small, with upholstered chairs and simple tables. Other rooms provide a bit more architectural flair and sport A-frame ceilings with exposed heavy wooden beams. Note that in some units, a curtain of sorts has been used in lieu of a bathroom door. Guest rooms were renovated in 1996, and intermittent repairs have kept everything in good shape since. Bathrooms are small, about half equipped with only a shower.

73 Grande-Rue, 77360 Barbizon. ✆ **01-60-66-40-96.** Fax 01-60-66-42-71. www.chateauhotels.com/lacledor. 17 units. 420F–470F (63.85– 71.45, $60.90–$68.15) double; 750F–870F (114– 132.25, $108.75–$126.15) suite. AE, DC, MC, V. **Amenities:** Restaurant, English-style bar; limited room service; baby-sitting, laundry/dry cleaning. *In room:* TV, minibar.

Hostellerie Les Pléiades 🐾 *Finds*   Les Pléiades combines antique decor with modern comforts in what was originally built in the 1850s as the forest hideaway of the respected 19th-century landscape painter Charles François Daubigny. Today, the three-story villa offers a cozy, conservative, and homey atmosphere. It's also the seat of a series of art, music, and history conferences, which attract important politicians, artists, and writers. Bedrooms come in various shapes and sizes. Most were renovated in 2000 and 2001, and each has a bathroom with a tub and shower combo. The place is run and directed by the daughter, Sophie Vermersch, of its original founder, Roger Karampournis.

21 Grande-Rue, 77630 Barbizon. ✆ **01-60-66-40-25.** Fax 01-60-66-41-68. les.pleiades.barbizon@wanadoo.fr. 23 units. 370F–650F (56.25– 98.80, $53.65–$94.25) double. AE, DC, MC, V. Free parking. **Amenities:** Restaurant, bar; baby-sitting. *In room:* TV, hair dryer.

DINING

We also recommend the restaurants at the **Hostellerie du Bas-Bréau** and **Hostellerie Les Pléiades** (see "Accommodations," above).

Le Relais (*Value*) TRADITIONAL FRENCH   Many prefer dining at this down-to-earth restaurant to meals at the more pricey inns, such as the Bas-Bréau. Offering excellent value, Le Relais is a corner tavern in a building boasting 300-year-old walls, with a provincial dining room centering on a small fireplace. In sunny weather, tables are set in the rear yard, with a trellis, an arbor, and trees. Typical choices are *quenelle* (a kind of dumpling) *de brochet,* roast quail with prunes, *coq au vin,* breast of duckling with cherries or seasonal fruit, grilled beef, and, in autumn, different preparations of venison, rabbit, and pheasant.

2 av. Charles-de-Gaulle. ✆ 01-60-66-40-28. Reservations recommended on weekends. Main courses 90F–120F (13.70– 18.25, $13.05–$17.40); fixed-price menu 160F–215F (24.30– 32.70, $23.20–$31.20). MC, V. Thurs–Tues noon–2:30pm; Thurs–Mon 7–9:30pm. Closed 1 week at Christmas and last week of Aug.

5 Fontainebleau—Refuge of Kings ★★★

37 miles S of Paris, 46 miles NE of Orléans

Napoléon called the Palais de Fontainebleau the house of the centuries. Much of French history has taken place behind its walls, perhaps no moment more memorable than when Napoléon stood on the horseshoe-shaped exterior staircase and bade farewell to his army before his departure to exile on Elba. That scene has been the subject of countless paintings, including Vernet's *Les Adieux.*

After the glories of Versailles, a visit to Fontainebleau can be a bit of a letdown. Fontainebleau, although a grand château, actually looks like a place at which a king could live, whereas Versailles is more of a production. French kings originally came to Fontainebleau because of its proximity to great hunting. It was François I who converted it from a hunting lodge into a palace fit for a king. Versailles, on the other hand, is the creation of the French monarchy at its triumphant pinnacle of splendor, prestige, and power.

Set in 50,000 acres of verdant forest, Fontainebleau remains a country retreat for Parisians, even for those who have seen the château a dozen times. Visitors come to the grounds for horseback riding, picnicking, and hiking. Since it's not as crowded with tourists, it's more peaceful here than in Versailles.

Allow 2½ hours to see everything in Fontainebleau.

ESSENTIALS

GETTING THERE   **Trains** to Fontainebleau depart from the Gare de Lyon in Paris. The trip takes from 45 to 60 minutes each way and costs 94F (14.30, $13.65) round-trip. Fontainebleau's railway station lies 2 miles from the château, within the suburb of Avon. A local bus (it's marked simply "Château") makes the trip to the château at 15-minute intervals Monday through Saturday, and at 30-minute intervals on Sunday, for 10F (1.50, $1.45) each way. If you're **driving,** take A6 south from Paris, exit onto N191, and follow the signs.

VISITOR INFORMATION   The **Office de Tourisme** is at 4 rue Royale in Fontainebleau (✆ 01-60-74-99-99).

SEEING THE CHâTEAU & GARDENS

Musée National du Château de Fontainebleau ★★★   Napoléon joined in the parade of French rulers who used the Palais de Fontainebleau as a resort, hunting in its magnificent forest. Under François I (who reigned from 1515 to 1547), the hunting lodge was enlarged into a royal palace (as at Versailles under

Louis XIV), in the Italian Renaissance style. The style got botched up, but many artists, including Cellini, came from Italy to work for the French monarch.

Under François I's patronage, the School of Fontainebleau (led by the painters Rosso Fiorentino and Primaticcio) increased in prestige. These artists adorned one of the most outstanding rooms at Fontainebleau: the 210-foot-long **Gallery of François I** ★★★. (Restorers under Louis-Philippe didn't completely succeed in ruining it.) Surrounded by pomp, François I walked the length of his gallery while artisans tried to tempt him with their wares; job seekers asked favors; and courtesans attempted to lure him from the duchesse d'Étampes. The stucco-framed panels depict such scenes as Jupiter carrying off Europa, the Nymph of Fontainebleau (with a lecherous dog peering through the reeds), and the king holding a pomegranate, a symbol of unity. However, the frames compete with the pictures. Everywhere is the salamander, symbol of the Chevalier King.

If it's true that François I built Fontainebleau for his mistress; then Henri II, his successor, left a fitting memorial to the woman he loved, Diane de Poitiers. Sometimes called the Gallery of Henri II, the **Ballroom** ★★★ is in the Mannerist style, the second splendid interior of the château. The monograms H & D are interlaced in the decoration. At one end of the room is a monumental fireplace supported by two bronze satyrs, reproduced in 1966 (the originals were melted down in the Revolution). A series of frescoes, painted between 1550 and 1558, depict mythological subjects.

An architectural curiosity is the **Louis XV Staircase** ★★. Originally, the ceiling was decorated by Primaticcio for the bedroom of the duchesse d'Étampes. When an architect added the stairway, he simply ripped out her bedroom floor and used the ceiling to cover the stairway. Of the Italian frescoes that were preserved, one depicts the Queen of the Amazons climbing into Alexander the Great's bed.

Fontainebleau found renewed glory under Napoléon. You can wander much of the palace on your own, visiting sites that evoke his 19th-century heyday. They include the throne room, the room where he abdicated (the abdication document displayed is a copy), his offices, his bedroom (look for his symbol, a bee), and his bathroom. Some of the smaller rooms, especially those containing his personal mementos and artifacts, are accessible by guided tour only. The furnishings in the grand apartments of Napoléon and Joséphine are marvelous.

Musée Chinois (Chinese Museum) holds the Empress Eugénie's collection of stunning Chinese treasures, including Far Eastern porcelain, jade, and crystal.

After your long trek through the palace, visit the **gardens** and, especially, the carp pond; the gardens, however, are only a prelude to the Forest of Fontainebleau and not nearly as spectacular as those surrounding Versailles.

Place du Général de Gaulle. ℂ 01-60-71-50-70. Combination ticket including the private appartements 35F (5.30, $5.10) adults, 23F (3.50, $3.35) students 18–25; ticket to appartements and the Napoléonic rooms 16F (2.45, $2.30) adults, 12F (1.80, $1.75) students 18–25, free for children 17 and under. June–Sept Wed–Mon 9:30am–6pm; Oct–May Wed–Mon 9:30am–5pm.

ACCOMMODATIONS

Grand Hôtel de l'Aigle-Noir (The Black Eagle) ★   This mansion, once the home of Cardinal de Retz, sits opposite the château. The formal courtyard entrance has a high iron grille and pillars crowned by black eagles. It was converted into a hotel in 1720 and has recently been remodeled, making it the finest lodging in Fontainebleau, far superior in amenities and style to the Hôtel Napoléon (see below). The rooms are decorated with Louis XVI, Empire–, or

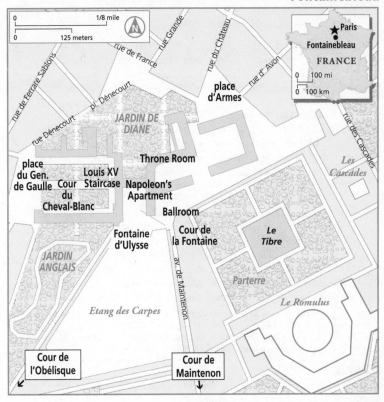

Restoration-era antiques or reproductions with plush mattresses and elegant bathroom amenities. All but four of the units have a complete tub and shower combination. Enjoy a drink in the Napoléon III–style piano bar before dinner.

27 place Napoléon-Bonaparte, 77300 Fontainebleau. ℂ **01-60-74-60-00.** Fax 01-64-23-42-22. www.hotel aiglenoir.fr. 56 units. 1,210F–1,420F (183.90– 215.85, $175.45–$205.90) double; from 2,400F (364.80, $348) suite. AE, DC, MC, V. Parking 55F (8.35, $8). **Amenities:** Restaurant, bar; indoor pool; exercise room; sauna; room service; baby-sitting; laundry/dry cleaning. *In room:* A/C, minibar, coffeemaker, hair dryer.

Hôtel de Londres   Set behind a historic 1830s-era facade, and owned and managed by several generations of the same family since 1932, this hotel enjoys one of the best locations in town for anyone who's fascinated by the architecture of the Chateau of Fontainebleau. It's positioned directly in front of the *Cour des Adieux,* site of Napoléon's farewell to his troops, just before his exile to the Isle of Elba. Only two of the building's three floors are occupied by the hotel, but each of the rooms is tastefully, even cozily outfitted in Louis XVI furniture, with extra-long beds and tiled, shower-only bathrooms. Other than breakfast, no meals are served here, but the Colombier family will direct you to nearby restaurants.

1 place du Général de Gaulle, 77300 Fontainebleau. ℂ **01-64-22-20-21.** Fax 01-60-72-39-16. www. hoteldelondres.com. 12 units. 680F–880F (103.35– 133.75, $98.60–$127.60) double. AE, MC, V. Closed Christmas–Jan 10 and 1 week in Aug. *In room:* TV.

> **Finds In the Footsteps of French Kings**
>
> If you visit the Forest of Fontainebleau, you can hike along the same paths
> that French kings used for hiking expeditions. A guide to these trails
> called *Guide des Sentiers* is offered at the tourist information center (see
> above). You can also find bike paths. Bikes rentals are available at the
> Fontainebleau-Avon rail depot. At the station, go to the kiosk, **MBK**
> (© **01-64-22-36-14**). The cost of a bike is 60F (9.10, $8.70) per half day,
> going up to 120F (18.25, $17.40). Open daily, on weekdays to 6pm and
> weekends to 7pm. The most scenic route is the trail to **Tour Denecourt**,
> 3 miles northeast of the château. Along the way, you can take in views of
> the beeches, birches, and pines—a truly idyllic setting.

Hôtel Napoléon　This classically designed hotel—the number-two choice in
Fontainebleau—is a short walk from the château. The lobby has Oriental rugs,
arched windows overlooking the street, and a garden tearoom. An inviting bar
features an ornate oval ceiling, Louis-Philippe chairs, and a neoclassical fireplace.
The bedrooms are filled with reproductions of antiques and flowered headboards. All are comfortable, but those facing the courtyard are larger and more
tranquil. There are full tub and shower combos in half the bedrooms.

9 rue Grande, 77300 Fontainebleau. © **01-60-39-50-50**. Fax 01-64-22-20-87. www.hotelnapoleon-
fontainebleau.com. 57 units. 770F–890F (117.05– 135.30, $111.65–$129.05) double; 1,200F (182.40,
$174) suite. AE, DC, MC, V. Parking 50F (7.60, $7.25). **Amenities:** Restaurant, bar; limited room service;
baby-sitting; laundry/dry cleaning. *In room:* TV, minibar, hair dryer.

DINING

In addition to the options below, **La Table des Maréchaux,** in the Hôtel
Napoléon (see above), is a superb choice.

Le Caveau des Ducs TRADITIONAL FRENCH　This reasonably priced
restaurant is in a former storage cellar (used by the château). It sits deep underground, beneath a series of 17th-century stone vaults built by the same masons
who laid the cobblestones of rue de Ferrare upstairs. Although the food is simple, the setting—with lots of wood and flickering candles—is dramatic. Menu
items include staples like snails in garlic butter, roast leg of lamb with garlic-and-
rosemary sauce, and virtually everything that can be concocted from the body
of a duck (terrines, magrêt, and confits). The filet of rumpsteak is quite tasty,
especially when served with brie sauce, as are the platters of sole, crayfish tails,
and salmon on a bed of pasta. Especially flavorful are strips of veal in a morel-
studded cream sauce on a bed of fresh pasta. The helpful staff adds a nice touch.

24 rue de Ferrare. © **01-64-22-05-05**. Reservations recommended. Main courses 95F–130F (14.45–
19.75, $13.80–$18.85); fixed-price menu 135F–250F (20.50– 38, $19.60–$36.25). AE, MC, V. Daily
noon–2pm and 7–10pm.

Le François-1er ⋆ TRADITIONAL FRENCH　The premier dining choice
in Fontainebleau has Louis XIII decor, winemaking memorabilia, and walls that
the owners think are about 200 years old. If weather permits, sit on the terrace
overlooking the château and the cour des Adieux. In game season, the menu
includes hare, duck liver, and partridge. Other choices include cold salmon with
cèpes (flap mushrooms), *rognon de veau* (veal kidneys) with mustard sauce, and a
salad of baby scallops with crayfish. The cuisine is meticulous, with an undeniable flair. The *magrêt de canard* (duck) flavored with cassis is delicious.

3 rue Royale. ② **01-64-22-24-68.** Reservations required. Main courses 80F–135F (12.15– 20.50, $11.60–$19.60); fixed-price menu 160F–250F (24.30– 38, $23.20–$36.25). AE, DC, MC, V. Mon–Sat noon–2:30pm and 7:30–10pm; Sun noon–2:30pm.

6 Vaux-le-Vicomte: Life Before Versailles

29 miles SE of Paris, 12 miles NE of Fontainebleau

Though it's so close to Paris, it's tough to reach Vaux-le-Vicomte without a car. Once you get here, allow 2 hours to see the château. By car, take N-6 southeast from Paris to Melun, which is 3¾ miles west of the château. By train, you'll need to take the 45-minute ride from Gare de Lyon to Melun first, and then take one of the taxis lining up at the railway station for the 4-mile ride to Vaux-le-Vicomte (150 F [22.80, $21.75] each way). A rail ticket costs 86F (13.05, $12.45) round-trip. For information, call ② **01-53-90-20-20.**

The office de Tourisme is at 2 av. Gallieni (② **01-64-37-11-31**).

SEEING THE CHâTEAU

Château de Vaux-le-Vicomte ★★★ The château was built in 1656 for Nicolas Fouquet, Louis XIV's ill-fated finance minister. Louis wasn't pleased that Fouquet was able to live so extravagantly here, hosting banquets that rivaled the king's. Then Louis discovered that Fouquet had embezzled funds from the country's treasury. Fouquet was arrested, and Louis then hired the same artists and architects who had built Vaux-le-Vicomte to begin the grand task of creating Versailles. If you visit both, you'll see the striking similarities between the two.

The view of the château from the main gate reveals the splendor of 17th-century France. On the south side, a majestic staircase sweeps toward the gardens, designed by Le Nôtre. The grand canal, flanked by waterfalls, divides the greenery. The château's interior, now a private residence, is furnished with 17th-century pieces. The great entrance hall leads to 12 staterooms, including the oval rotunda. Many rooms are hung with Gobelin tapestries and decorated with painted ceiling and wall panels by Le Brun, with sculpture by Girardon. A self-guided tour of the interior includes Fouquet's personal suite, the huge basement with its wine cellar, the servants' dining room, and the copper-filled kitchen.

Included in the price of admission is entrance to the château's carriage museum (Musée des Équipages), which is housed in the stables. Some 25 perfectly restored 18th- and 19th-century carriages are on display here, each accessorized with mannequin horses and people.

From May to mid-October, candlelight evenings (Des Soirées à Chandelles) are held every Saturday between 8pm and midnight. During those events, all electricity to the château is cut off, and thousands of candles are lit within both the château and its gardens. The effect has been called mystical—a memorable re-creation of the way of life that prevailed during the building's heyday. Cost of admission during the candlelit evenings is 80F (12.15, $11.60) for adults, 70F (10.65, $10.15) for children 6 to 15. children under 6 free.

77950 Maincy. ② **01-64-14-41-90.** www.vaux-le-vicomte.com Admission 65F (9.90, $9.45) adults, 50F (7.60, $7.25) children 6–15, children under 6 free. Mid-March to mid-Nov daily 10am–6pm. Rental of a recorded audio-guide 15F (2.30, $2.20).

DINING

Auberge de Crisenoy MODERN FRENCH You are more likely to find locals from Melun at this auberge than fellow tourists, and that's part of its charm. Behind the solid stone walls of a former private home, the two dining rooms (on separate floors) overlook a garden. The menu items are based on modern interpretations of French classics and change every 3 weeks. Examples include oysters in puff pastry with asparagus coulis; warm foie gras with a purée of figs; and a well-seasoned cassolette of crayfish with spinach and mussels, served in a copper pot placed directly on the table.

Grande Rue, Crisenoy. ℂ **01-64-38-83-06.** Reservations recommended. Main courses 85F–140F (12.90– 21.30, $12.35–$20.30); fixed-price menu 168F–275F (25.55– 41.80, $24.35–$39.90); lunch menus (Mon–Tues and Thurs–Fri only) 120F–275F (18.25– 41.80, $17.40–$39.90). AE. Thurs–Tues noon–3pm and 7:30–9:30pm. Closed 3 weeks in Aug. From Vaux-le-Vicomte, follow N36 toward Meaux for 1½ miles.

Le Table Saint-Just TRADITIONAL FRENCH Dine here, and you're bound to be charmed. Still intact is the original masonry from the 17th-century farmhouse, including artfully crafted structural beams. Menu items change with the seasons, but might include foie gras in puff pastry, served with a confit of celery and acidified apples; lobster with red-wine sauce; and a roasted rack of lamb with a moussaka of fresh vegetables.

Rue de la Libération, in the nearby village of Vaux-le-Pénil. ℂ **01-64-52-09-09.** Reservations recommended. Main courses 95F–150F (14.45– 22.80, $13.80–$21.75); fixed-price menu 150F–320F (22.80– 48.65, $21.75–$46.40). AE, V. Mon–Fri noon–1:30pm; Tues–Sat 7:30–9:30pm. Closed Aug. From the château of Vaux-le-Vicomte, drive 3½ miles west, following the signs to Melun, then to Maincy, then to Vaux-le-Pénil.

7 Disneyland Paris ✶✶✶

20 miles E of Paris

After provoking some of the most enthusiastic and controversial reactions in recent French history, the multimillion-dollar Euro Disney Resort opened in 1992 as one of the world's most lavish theme parks. Conceived on a scale rivaling that of Versailles, the project didn't begin auspiciously: European journalists delighted in belittling it and accused it of everything from cultural imperialism to the death knell of French culture.

But after goodly amounts of public relations and financial juggling, the resort is now on track. Disneyland Paris (the name change was also a boon) has become France's number-one tourist attraction, with 50 million annual visitors. Disney surpasses the Eiffel Tower and the Louvre in the number of visitors and accounts for 4% of the French tourism industry's foreign currency sales. Figures reveal that 40% of the visitors are French, half of them from Paris. Disneyland Paris looks, tastes, and feels like its parents in California and Florida—except for the $10 cheeseburgers *"avec pommes frites."*

Situated on a 5,000-acre site (about one-fifth the size of Paris) in the suburb of Marne-la-Vallée, with a European flair, the park incorporates the most successful elements of its Disney predecessors.

In terms of the other Disney parks, Disneyland Paris definitely lies in the middle, with top honors going to Florida. The California Disneyland emerges as a distant third. The park in Florida is larger than the Paris property, with a greater number of fun options, attractions, and rides. But Disneyland Paris does a decent job of recreating the Magic Kingdom. In 2002, the Paris park will add Walt Disney Studios, which will focus on the role of movies in popular culture.

Take 1 day for the highlights, 2 days for more depth.

ESSENTIALS

GETTING THERE The resort is linked to the RER commuter express **rail network** (Line A), with a stop within walking distance of the park. Board the

RER at such inner-city Paris stops as Charles-de-Gaulle-Étoile, Châtelet-Les Halles, or Nation. Get off at Line A's last stop, Marne-la-Vallée/Chessy, 45 minutes from central Paris. The round-trip fare is 80F (12.15, $11.60). Trains run daily, every 10 to 20 minutes from 5:30am to midnight.

Shuttle buses connect Orly and Charles de Gaulle airports with each hotel in the resort. Buses depart the airports at intervals of 30 to 45 minutes. One-way transport to the park from either airport is 85F (12.90, $12.35) per person.

If you're **driving,** take A4 east from Paris and get off at Exit 14, where it's marked DISNEYLAND PARIS. Parking begins at 40F (6.10, $5.80) per day. A series of moving sidewalks speeds up pedestrian transit from the parking areas to the park entrance. Parking is free for guests of any of the hotels in the resort.

VISITOR INFORMATION   All the hotels we recommend offer general information on the theme park. For details on Disney and for reservations at any of its hotels, contact the **Disneyland Paris Guest Relations Office,** located in City Hall on Main Street, U.S.A. (℡ **01-60-30-60-53** in English, or 01-60-30-60-30 in French; www.disneylandparis.com). For information on Disneyland Paris and specific details on the many other attractions and monuments in the Île de France and the rest of the country, contact the **Maison du Tourism,** Disney Village (B.P. 77705), Marne-la-Vallée CEDEX 4 (℡ **01-60-43-33-33**).

ADMISSION   Admission varies depending on the season. A 1-day ticket costs 170F to 220F (25.85 to   33.45, $24.65 to $31.90) for adults and 140F to 175F (21.30 to   26.60, $20.30 to $25.40) for children 3 to 12; free for children under 3. Peak season is mid-June to mid-September as well as Christmas and Easter weeks. Entrance to Village Disney is free, though there's usually a cover at the dance clubs.

HOURS   In July and August, the park is open daily from 9am to 11pm; September to June, Monday through Friday from 10am to 6pm and Saturday and Sunday from 9am to 8pm. Opening and closing hours vary with the weather and the season. It's usually good to phone the information office (see above).

SEEING DISNEYLAND

Disneyland Paris is a total vacation destination. Clustered into one enormous unit, the Disneyland Park includes five "lands" of entertainment, six massive well-designed hotels, a campground, an entertainment center (Festival Disney), a 27-hole golf course, and dozens of restaurants, shows, and shops.

Visitors from all over Europe stroll amid flowerbeds, trees, reflecting ponds, fountains, and a large artificial lake flanked with hotels. An army of smiling employees and Disney characters—many of whom are multilingual, including Buffalo Bill, Mickey and Minnie Mouse, and, of course, the French-born Caribbean pirate Jean Laffite—are on hand to greet the thousands of *enfants.*

Main Street, U.S.A., is replete with horse-drawn carriages and barbershop quartets. Steam-powered railway cars embark from the Main Street Station for a trip through a Grand Canyon diorama to **Frontierland,** with its paddle-wheel steamers reminiscent of Mark Twain's Mississippi River. Other attractions are a petting zoo, the Critter Corral, at the Cottonwood Creek Ranch and the Lucky Nugget Saloon, inspired by the gold-rush era; ironically, the steps and costumes of the can-can show originated in the cabarets of turn-of-the-20th-century Paris.

The park's steam trains chug past **Adventureland**—with its swashbuckling pirates, Swiss Family Robinson tree house, and reenacted *Arabian Nights* legends—to **Fantasyland.** Here you'll find the **Sleeping Beauty Castle**

(*Le Château de la Belle au Bois Dormant*), whose soaring pinnacles and turrets are an idealized (and spectacular) interpretation of the châteaux of France. In its shadow are Europeanized versions of *Blanche neige et les sept nains* (Snow White and the Seven Dwarfs), Peter Pan, Dumbo, Alice (from Wonderland), the Mad Hatter's Teacups, and Sir Lancelot's Magic Carousel.

Visions of the future are found at **Discoveryland,** whose tributes to invention and imagination are drawn from the works of Leonardo da Vinci, Jules Verne, H. G. Wells, the modern masters of science fiction, and the *Star Wars* series.

As Disney continues to churn out animated blockbusters, look for all their newest stars to appear in the theme park. You'll see characters from *Aladdin, The Lion King, Pocahontas,* and *Toy Story.*

In addition to the theme park, Disney maintains the **Village Disney** entertainment center. Illuminated inside by a spectacular gridwork of lights suspended 60 feet above ground, the complex contains dance clubs, shops, restaurants (one of which offers a dinner spectacle based on the original *Buffalo Bill's Wild West Show*), bars for adults trying to escape their children for a while, a French Government Tourist Office, a post office, and a marina.

ACCOMMODATIONS

The resort contains six hotels, each evoking a different theme but all sharing a reservations service. For more information in North America, call (C) **407/ 934-7639.** For information or reservations in France, contact the Central Reservations Office, Euro Disney S.C.A. (B.P. 105), F-77777 Marne-la-Vallée CEDEX 4 ((C) **01-60-30-60-30**). In correspondence, Euro Disney Resort (not Disneyland Paris) remains the official designation. For travelers with Internet access, all Disneyland Paris hotels can be reached through one website: **www. disneylandparis.com**.

Since the transportation links between Paris and Disneyland Paris are excellent, you don't need to spend the night here. Of course, this all depends on how much Disney you think you need in one trip.

Disneyland Hotel ★★   Mouseketeers who have rich daddies and mommies check in at Disney's poshest resort, which charges Paris Ritz tariffs. The resort's flagship hotel, positioned at the entrance, resembles a massive Victorian resort hotel, with red-tile turrets and jutting balconies. The large, plush guest rooms come complete with cartoons and candy-stripe decor. The luxury bathrooms have marble vanities and twin basins. Units in the rear face Sleeping Beauty's Castle and Big Thunder Mountain; less desirable rooms open onto a parking lot. Guests on the "Castle Club" floor have access to free newspapers, all-day beverages, and a well-equipped private lounge.

Disneyland Paris, B.P. 105, F-77777 Marne-la-Vallée CEDEX 4. (C) **01-60-45-65-00.** Fax 01-60-45-65-33. 496 units. 2,260F–3,320F (343.50– 504.65, $327.70–$481.40) double; from 4,950F (752.40, $717.75) suite. AE, CB, DC, DISC, MC, V. Rates include breakfast. Children stay free in parents' room. **Amenities:** Two restaurants, two bars; indoor and outdoor pool; health club; Jacuzzi; sauna; room service; baby-sitting; laundry/dry cleaning. *In room:* A/C, TV, minibar, hair dryer.

Hotel Cheyenne & Hotel Santa Fe *Kids*   These buildings, near a re-creation of Texas's Rio Grande, look like they were inspired by old Hollywood westerns. If you're a family who attends rodeos together, check in here. The living's rustic, and the prices aren't like the "Goofy" tariffs charged at the other Disney hostelries—these are the least expensive places to stay at the resort (except for the campgrounds). The Cheyenne accommodates visitors in 14 two-story buildings along Desperado Street, whereas the Santa Fe, sporting a desert theme,

---

Tips **Avoiding Those Long Lines**

Disneyland Paris recognizes that long lines tend to frustrate families and cause ill will. Their response, in 2000, involved inaugurating the **Fast Pass** system, where participants go to the various rides and receive a reservation for a 1-hour time block within which they should return. Within that 1-hour time block, waiting times are usually no longer than 8 minutes.

---

encompasses four "nature trails" winding among 42 adobe-style pueblos. Although these are the least elegant of the Disney hotel properties, the comfort level is high. The Cheyenne is a favorite among families, offering a double bed and bunk beds. Children will find an array of activities, including a play area in a log cabin with a lookout tower and a section where you can explore the "ruins" of an ancient Anasazi Village. There's a mariachi atmosphere in the Rio Grande Bar, and country music in the Red Garter Saloon Bar. The only drawback is the lack of a pool. Tex-Mex specialties are offered at La Cantina (Santa Fe), while barbecue specialties predominate at the Chuck Wagon Café (Cheyenne).

Disneyland Paris, B.P. 115, F-77777 Marne-la-Vallée CEDEX 4. © **01-60-45-62-00** for the Cheyenne, or **01-60-45-78-00** for the Santa Fe. Fax 01-60-45-62-33 for the Cheyenne, or 01-60-45-78-33 for the Santa Fe. 2,000 units. 1,100F–1,760F (167.20– 267.50, $159.50–$255.20) double in Hotel Santa Fe; 1,200F–1,850F (182.40– 281.20, $174–$268.25) double in Hotel Cheyenne. AE, DC, DISC, MC, V. Rates include a 2-day pass and breakfast. **Amenities:** Two restaurants, bar; two tennis courts; health club; sauna; solarium; massage; ice-skating rink in winter; room service; baby-sitting; laundry/dry cleaning. *In room:* A/C, TV, minibar, hair dryer, safe.

Hotel New York ⭐⭐ Picture Art Deco New York of the 1930s, and you have the Hotel New York. You can see the influence of the Big Apple in the design of the hotel—the nine-story central "skyscraper" is flanked by the Gramercy Park Wing and the Brownstones Wing. (The exteriors of both wings resemble row houses.) Because the hotel caters to convention groups, it is not as family-friendly as the other Disney properties. The guest rooms are comfortable, with Art Deco accessories, New York–inspired memorabilia, and roomy combination bathrooms with twin basins. The most desirable units are called "Castle Club" and lie on the upper floors. Try for one of the rooms fronting Lake Buena Vista instead of those opening onto the parking lot.

Disneyland Paris, B.P. 100, F-77777 Marne-la-Vallée CEDEX 4. © **01-60-45-73-00.** Fax 01-60-45-73-33. 563 units. 1,650F–2,420F (250.80– 367.85, $239.25–$350.90) double; from 3,350F (509.20, $485.75) suite. Rates include 2-day pass and breakfast. AE, DC, DISC, MC, V. **Amenities:** 2 restaurants; bar; laundry/dry cleaning; room service, baby-sitting, indoor pool, health club, sauna. *In room:* A/C, TV, minibar, hair dryer, safe.

Newport Bay Club ⭐⭐ You might expect to see the reincarnation of old Joe Kennedy walking along the veranda of this hotel, with its slated roofs, awnings, and pergolas. This is the biggest hotel in France, designed with a central cupola, jutting balconies, and a large front porch with comfortable rocking chairs. Ringed by verdant lawns, it's inspired by a turn-of-the-20th-century resort hotel in New England. The corner guest rooms are the largest. Bathrooms are roomy with deluxe toiletries and tub and shower combinations. The upscale Yacht Club and less formal Cape Cod are the dining choices here.

Disneyland Paris, B.P. 105, F-77777 Marne-la-Vallée CEDEX 4. © **01-60-45-55-00.** Fax 01-60-45-55-33. 1,098 units. 1,520F–2,160F (231.05– 328.30, $220.40–$313.20) double; from 2,970F (451.45, $430.65) suite. AE, DC, MC, V. Rates include a 2-day pass and breakfast. **Amenities:** Two restaurants, bar; indoor and outdoor pool; health club; sauna; room service; baby-sitting; laundry/dry cleaning. *In room:* A/C, TV, minibar, hair dryer.

DINING

There are at least 45 restaurants and snack bars in the resort, each trying to please thousands of European and North American palates. Here are three recommendations:

Auberge de Cendrillon TRADITIONAL FRENCH   The most visible and whimsical French restaurant is a fairy-tale version of Cinderella's sumptuous country inn, with a glass couch in the center. A master of ceremonies, in a plumed tricorne hat and an embroidered tunic and lace ruffles, welcomes you. There are corny elements here, but the chefs go out of their way to make a big deal out of French cuisine. For the most part, they succeed. The appetizers set the tone. Our favorites are the warm goat-cheese salad with lardons and the smoked-salmon platter. Either will put you in the mood for some of the classics of the French table, especially loin of lamb roasted under a mustard coating or tender sautéed veal medallions. An aromatic chicken is perfectly roasted in puff pastry. The only drawback is its location in the theme park, limiting its accessibility to its seasonal schedules. Lunches are usually easier to arrange than dinners.

In Fantasyland. ☎ **01-64-74-24-02**. Reservations recommended. Main courses 110F–140F (16.70–21.30, $15.95–$20.30); fixed-price menu 175F (26.60, 25.40). AE, DC, DISC, MC, V. Thurs–Mon 11:30am–90 min before the park closes.

The California Grill ★★ CALIFORNIA/FRENCH   The California Grill is the showcase restaurant of this vast Disney world. Chef Eric Leaty prepares food that's the equivalent of a one-Michelin-star restaurant. Focusing on the lighter specialties for which the Golden State is famous, with many concessions to French palates and tastes, this airy, elegant establishment manages to accommodate both adults and children. Even French critics are impressed by the oysters with leeks and salmon. We also embrace the appetizer of foie gras with roasted red peppers, as well as the roasted pigeon with braised Chinese cabbage and black-rice vinegar. Fresh salmon was another winning selection, roasted over beechwood and served with a sprinkling of walnut oil, sage sauce, asparagus, and a fricassée of forest mushrooms. Children will appreciate "Mickey's Pizzas," spaghetti Bolognese, and grilled ham with fries. *Note:* If you're looking for a quiet, mostly adult venue, go here as late as your hunger pangs will allow.

In the Disneyland Hotel. ☎ **01-60-45-65-00**. Reservations required. Main courses 55F–205F (8.35–31.15, $8–$29.75); children's menu from 85F (12.90, $12.35). AE, DC, DISC, MC, V. Sun–Fri 7–11pm; Sat 6–11pm.

Inventions (Value INTERNATIONAL   This might be the only buffet restaurant in Europe where animated characters from the Disney films go table-hopping, in a way you'd expect from a family-friendly restaurant in Los Angeles. The restaurant contains four enormous buffet tables devoted to starters, shellfish, main courses, and desserts. Selections are wide, portions can be copious, and absolutely no one leaves this place hungry. Don't expect *grande cuisine*—that's the domain of the more upscale (and recommended) California Grill, within the same hotel. What you'll get here is a sense of American bounty and culinary generosity, with ample doses of cartoon fantasy thrown in for seasoning.

In the Disneyland Hotel. ☎ **01-60-45-65-83**. Reservations not necessary. Lunch buffet 180F (27.35, $26.10) adults, 110F (16.70, $15.95) children 7–11, 95F (14.45, $13.80) children 3–6, children under 3 are free; dinner buffet 250F (38, $36.25) adults, 140F (21.30, $20.30) for children 7–11, 95F (14.45, $13.80) children 6 and under. AE, DC, MC, V. Daily noon–3pm and 6–10:30pm.

DISNEYLAND AFTER DARK

The premier theatrical venue of Disneyland Paris is **Le Légende de Buffalo Bill,** in the Disney Village (© **01-60-45-71-00**), a twice-per-night stampede of entertainment that recalls the show that traveled the West with Buffalo Bill and Annie Oakley. You'll dine at tables that ring a riding rink where sharpshooters, stage coaches, and dozens of horses and Indians ride very fast and perform some alarmingly realistic acrobatics. A Texas-style barbecue, served assembly-line-style by waiters in 10-gallon hats, is part of the experience. Despite its cornpone elements, it's not without its charm and an almost mournful nostalgia for a way of life of another continent and another century. Wild Bill himself is dignified, and the Indians suitably brave. Two shows are staged at 6:30 and 9:30pm. The cost (with dinner included) is 325F (49.40, $47.15) for adults and 195F (29.65, $28.30) for children 3 to 11. Children under 3 are free.

8 Provins: City of Roses ★★

50 miles SE of Paris, 30 miles E of Melun

Feudal Provins, the "city of roses," is one of this region's most interesting towns. Historic, romantic, and beautiful, Provins soared to the pinnacle of its power and prosperity in the Middle Ages, then fell to ruin in the Hundred Years' War (1337 to 1453). Given its proximity to Paris, it's surprising that Provins remains so little known by foreigners.

Once one of the largest towns in France, after Paris and Rouen, its Champagne Fair rivaled that of Troyes. But it sits high and dry today with its memories. Provins is also known for its Damask Rose, brought back from the Crusades by Thibault IV. When the duke of Lancaster, through marriage, became the comte de Provins, he included the rose in his coat-of-arms. A century later, the red rose of Lancaster confronted the white rose of York in the War of the Roses.

If you're looking for a particular green tree to sit under, within the medieval core of Provins, head for **Le Jardin Garnier** and its "Allées d'Aligre." A flat, symmetrically laid-out city park bounded by rue des Jacobins, allées d'Aligre, avenue de Verdun, and rue Saint-Thibault, adjacent to the Église Ste-Croix, it offers the kind of verdant space that encourages quiet reflection.

Take 2½ hours to see Provins.

ESSENTIALS

GETTING THERE   **Trains** depart from Paris's Gare de l'Est six times a day. The trip is 80 minutes each way (a bit longer if a transfer is required en route in the town of Longueville). Tickets cost 125 F (19E, $18.15) round-trip. For information and schedule, call © **01-53-90-20-20.**

VISITOR INFORMATION   The **Maison du Visiteur** (tourist office) is on chemin de Villecran (© **01-64-60-26-26;** www.provins.net), adjacent to the entrance to the medieval ramparts.

EXPLORING THE TOWN

With its towers and bastions, Provins was surrounded in the 13th century by ramparts that protected it from the vast plains of Brie. The fortifications are so well preserved that scholars refer to Provins as the "Carcassonne of the North." The best site for viewing the ramparts is the **Porte Jouy,** on the Upper Town's northwestern edge, at the end of rue de Jouy. A staircase rises to the top. Though the ramparts no longer make a circuit of the town, you can still promenade along the top, enjoying the military, secular, and ecclesiastical architecture from the Middle Ages. Entrance is free, and you can climb any time you want.

Ville Haute (Upper Town) is perched on a promontory, and Ville Basse (Lower Town) is crossed by two rivers, the Durteint and the Voulzie, the latter an effluent of the Seine.

Tour César ★★ This tower, dating from the 12th century, is the pride of the town. Today, it is the bell tower of the nearby Église St-Quiriace, which dates from the 13th century. When a fire destroyed that church's bell tower in the 17th century, the church was restored with a vaguely baroque-looking dome and the Tour César then became the bell tower of the rejuvenated church. In 1998, the tower's masonry was restored at great expense as part of a general overhaul of Provin's historic monuments. The church today contains a majestic, primitive Gothic choir and modern dome. Joan of Arc stopped here on her way to Orléans. The church is open day and night, charging no admission.

Rue de la Pie. ✆ **01-64-60-26-26.** Admission 20F (3.05, $2.90) adults, 12F (1.80, $1.75) children 5–12, children under 5 free. Nov 1–Apr 6 daily 2–5pm; Apr 7–Oct 31 daily 10am–6pm.

Grange-aux-Dîmes (Tythe Barn) This historic building was used first as a covered marketplace for the medieval merchants who sold their goods here; then as lodgings for the merchants who traveled from far away. Later it was a warehouse for the tithes the Catholic church extracted from the corps of its faithful. In 1995, a permanent exhibition was added: Provins aux Temps des Foires de Champagne (Provins during the Trade Fairs of Champagne).

Rue St-Jean. ✆ **01-64-60-26-26.** Admission to exhibition 20F (3.05, $2.90) adults, 12F (1.80, $1.75) children. June–Aug Mon–Fri 11am–6pm, Sat–Sun and holidays 10am–6pm; Apr–May and Sept–Oct Mon–Fri 2–6pm, Sat–Sun 11am–6pm; Nov–Mar Sat–Sun and holidays 2–5pm.

Les Souterrains de Provins (The Tunnels of Provins) 𝐹𝑖𝑛𝑑𝑠 The bedrock below the medieval streets of Provins is the site of a network of underground passageways that interconnect more than 150 separate subterranean "rooms." Many of these spaces are listed by the French government as historically important because of their graceful medieval architecture; others are more crude, with vaulting that was chiseled randomly out of the bedrock. Town historians don't completely understand the long-ago function of these tunnels. Possible explanations of why they were dug, between the 12th and the 13th century, include the following: a particular type of mineral was extracted from the porous soil for the treatment of the textiles manufactured during that era; the tunnels were used to escape enemy forces during sieges; they were used to conceal treasures; or they were used as a secret meeting place for Freemasons. A guided tour of the labyrinth begins and ends at the Hôtel-Dieu and lasts 45 minutes.

Tours begin from the Hôtel-Dieu (Town Hall) on rue de Jouy. The tourist office (see above) will provide information. Guided tour 20F (3.05, $2.90) adults, 14F (2.15, $2.05) children. Spring and autumn tours Sat–Sun and holidays 11am–6pm, Mon–Fri 1 tour at 2:30pm; June–Aug Mon–Fri 2–6pm, Sat–Sun 11am–6pm; winter tours Sat–Sun and holidays at 2, 3, and 4pm.

ACCOMMODATIONS & DINING

Aux Vieux Remparts This is the best choice for dining or lodging in Provins, and it also charges reasonable prices. The inn is an oasis of provincial French charm in the center of the old town. The building dates from the 17th century; it was enlarged and improved in 1988. There's a charming garden as well. Each well-furnished bedroom has a faux medieval decor; most are equipped with bathrooms with tub and shower. The best units open onto the

Tour Cesar and the rooftops of old Provins. Even if you're not spending the night, you can enjoy the town's finest cuisine. Stellar dishes include red snapper in puff pastry in a potato galette and served with a charlotte of vegetables and fresh tatatouille.

3 rue Couverte, 77160 Provins. ⓒ 01-64-08-94-00. Fax 01-60-67-77-22. www.auxvieuxremparts.com. Doubles from 395F–750F (60.05– 114, $57.30–$108.75). Restaurant open daily noon–2:30pm and 7:30–9:30pm. Set menus 150F–360F (22.80– 54.70, $21.75–$52.20); main courses 150F–230F (22.80– 34.95, $21.75–$33.35). AE, DC, MC, V. **Amenities:** Restaurant, bar, room service. *In room:* TV.

9 Malmaison: Love Nest of Joséphine

10 miles W of Paris, 3 miles NW of St-Cloud

In the 9th century, the Normans landed in this area and devastated the countryside, hence the name of this Paris suburb, which translates to "bad house." History abounds at the country retreat, the Château de Malmaison.

SEEING THE CHÂTEAU

Musée National du Château de Malmaison ★★   Few sites in France carry as strong a dose of the intimate moments of Napoléon Bonaparte, albeit within a period of his life that wasn't noted for its marital happiness. Construction on the château, used as a country retreat far removed from the Tuileries or Compiègne (other Napoleonic residences), began in 1622. It was purchased in 1799 by Napoléon's wife, Joséphine, who had it restored and fashionably decorated as a love nest. She then enlarged the estate (but not the château).

Today, Malmaison is filled with mementos from Napoléon's early days as a general shortly after the Revolution and during his rise to power as first consul of France. The veranda and council room were inspired by the tent he occupied on his military campaigns and are filled with Empire furnishings. His study and desk are in the library. Marie-Louise, his second wife, took Napoléon's books when she left France; they were later purchased by an English couple that presented them to the museum here. Most of the furnishings are originals; some came from the Tuileries and St-Cloud. Napoléon always attached a sentimental importance to Malmaison, and he spent a week here before his departure for St. Helena.

Many of the portraits and sculptures immortalize a Napoleonic deity—for example, David's equestrian portrait of the emperor and also a flattering portrait of Joséphine by Gérard.

After her divorce in 1809 (she couldn't bear Napoléon an heir), Joséphine retired here and was devoted to her roses until her death in 1814, at the age of 51. Her deathbed is exhibited, as is her toilette kit, including her toothbrush.

Also here is the small Château de Bois-Préau, which was closed for restorations at press time, but which should reopen in late 2001 or 2002. To reach it, follow the signs through the park; it's a 5-minute walk from the main building. Built in 1700 and acquired by Joséphine in 1810, it's smaller, sadder, and less architecturally distinguished than Malmaison. The château (more of a villa since its reconstruction in 1854), is a museum and shrine to the emperor's exile on St. Helena, after his fall from grace. For better coverage of the years between his rise to power (as exhibited at Malmaison) and his disgrace and death on St. Helena, see the Napoleonic museum at the Musée National du Château de Fontainebleau listed under section 5, "Fontainebleau—Refuge of Kings," earlier in this chapter.

Av. du Château. (☎ 01-41-29-05-55. Admission to Malmaison, which includes entrance to Bois Préau (if it's open), adults 30F (4.57, $3.90) Mon–Sat, Sun admission reduced to 20F (3.05, $2.60); students ages 18–25 20F (3.05, $2.60) daily; persons under 18 enter free daily. May–July Wed–Mon 10am–5pm; Apr, Aug, and Sept Mon and Wed–Fri 10am–noon and 1:30–5pm, Sat–Sun 10am–5:30pm; Oct–Mar Mon and Wed–Fri 10am–noon and 1:30–4:30pm, Sat–Sun 10am–5pm. The actual museum closes 45 to 60 min. after the last ticket sale. Free tours Mon and Wed–Fri at 10am, 2pm, and 3:30pm, Sat–Sun every 15 min. (Bois-Préau will reopen after renovations sometime in 2002.) Take the RER A-1 line to La Défense. Transfer to bus 258 for the 6-mile ride to the château.

10 The Remarkable Zoo of Château de Thoiry

25 miles W of Paris

Château et Parc Zoologique de Thoiry ★★ This major attraction drew more visitors in a single year than the Louvre or Versailles. The 16th-century château, owned by the vicomte de La Panouse family (now run by son Paul and his wife, Annabelle), displays two unpublished Chopin waltzes, antique furniture, and more than 343 handwritten letters of French or European kings, as well as the original financial records of France from 1745 to 1750. But these aren't as much a draw as the Parc Zoologique.

The château's grounds have been turned into a game reserve with elephants, giraffes, zebras, monkeys, rhinoceroses, alligators, lions, tigers, kangaroos, bears, and wolves—more than 1,000 animals and birds roam at liberty. The reserve and park cover 300 acres of the 1,200-acre estate.

In the French gardens, you can see llamas, Asian deer and sheep, and many types of birds, including flamingos and cranes. In the tiger park, a promenade has been designed above the tigers. Paul and Annabelle are also restoring the 300 acres of 17th-, 18th-, and 19th-century gardens as well as creating new ones.

To see the animal farm, you can drive your own car, providing it isn't a convertible (an uncovered car may be dangerous). The park is most crowded on weekends, but if you want to avoid the crush, visit early in the morning.

78770 Thoiry-en-Yvelines. (☎ 01-34-87-52-25. www.thoiry.pm.fr. Admission to château, 38F (5.80, $5.50) adults, 30F (4.55, $4.35) children 3–12, children under 3 are free; reserve or gardens, 105F (15.95, $15.25) adults, 80F (12.15, $11.60) children 3–12, children under 3 are free. Château, Feb 3–Nov 11 Mon–Sat 2–6pm, Sun 10am–8pm; closed Nov 12–Feb 2. Park, year-round Apr–Oct daily 10am–6pm; Nov–Mar, daily 10am–5pm. Take the Autoroute de l'Ouest (A13) toward Dreux, exiting at Bois-d'Arcy. Then get on N12, following the signs on D11 to Thoiry.

ACCOMMODATIONS

Auberge de Thoiry This rustic hotel was built more than 200 years ago and retains many of its original wall and ceiling beams, as well as much of its original masonry. Bedrooms were renovated in the late 1990s, just before new owners bought the place and added their own touches. Each unit is well furnished and comfortable, with a tiled, shower-only bathroom. The hotel is less than 500 yards from the entrance to the park, making it a good spot for refreshments.

38 rue de la porte St-Martin, 78770 Thoiry. (☎ 01-34-87-40-21. Fax 01-34-87-49-57. 12 units. 245F–325F (37.25– 49.40, $35.55–$47.15) double. AE, DC, MC, V. Free parking. **Amenities:** Restaurant, bar. *In room:* TV.

11 Giverny: In the Footsteps of Monet

50 miles NW of Paris

On the border between Normandy and the Île de France, the Claude Monet Foundation is where the great painter lived for 43 years. The restored house and its gardens are open to the public.

Budget 2 hours to go to Giverny.

ESSENTIALS

GETTING THERE   If you're going by **train,** take the Paris-Rouen line (Paris-St-Lazare) to the Vernon station. A **taxi** can take you the 3 miles to Giverny. **Bus tours** are operated from Paris by American Express (© **01-42-27-58-80**) and Cityrama (© **01-44-55-61-00**).

If you're **driving,** take the Autoroute de l'Ouest (Port de St-Cloud) toward Rouen. Leave the autoroute at Bonnières, then cross the Seine on the Bonnières Bridge. From here, a direct road with signs will bring you to Giverny. Expect it to take about an hour; try to avoid weekends. Another way is to leave the highway at the Bonnières exit and go toward Vernon. Once here, cross the bridge over the Seine and follow the signs to Giverny or Gasny (Giverny is before Gasny). This is easier than going through Bonnières, where there aren't many signs.

SHOW ME THE MONET

Claude Monet Foundation ★★★   Born in 1840, the French Impressionist was a brilliant innovator, excelling in presenting the effects of light at different times of the day. Some critics claim that he "invented light." His paintings of the Rouen cathedral and of waterlilies, which one critic called "vertical interpretations of horizontal lines," are just a few of his masterpieces.

Monet first came to Giverny in 1883. Many of his friends used to visit him here at Le Pressoir, including Clemenceau, Cézanne, Rodin, Renoir, Degas, and Sisley. When Monet died in 1926, his son, Michel, inherited the house, but left it abandoned until it decayed. The gardens became almost a jungle, inhabited by river rats. In 1966, Michel died and left it to the Académie des Beaux-Arts. It wasn't until 1977 that Gerald van der Kemp, who restored Versailles, decided to work on Giverny. A large part of it was restored with gifts from U.S. benefactors, especially the late Lila Acheson Wallace, former head of *Reader's Digest.*

You can stroll the garden and view the thousands of flowers, including the *nymphéas.* The Japanese bridge, hung with wisteria, leads to a setting of weeping willows and rhododendrons. Monet's studio barge was installed on the pond.

Rue Claude-Monet. © 02-32-51-28-21. Reservations required. Admission 35F (5, $5.10) adults, 20F (3.05, $2.90) children. Gardens only, 25F (3.80, $3.65) adults, 10F (1.50, $1.45) children. Apr–Oct Tues–Sun 10am–6pm; closed Nov–Mar.

DINING

Auberge du Vieux Moulin TRADITIONAL FRENCH   This is a convenient lunch stop near the Monet house. The restaurant is housed in a stone building with a pair of flowering terraces. The Boudeau family maintains a series of dining rooms filled with original Impressionist paintings. Since you can walk here from the museum in about 5 minutes, leave your car in the museum lot. Specialties range from escalope of salmon with sorrel sauce to aiguillettes of duckling with peaches. The kitchen doesn't pretend that the food is anything more than good, country fare with a dash of panache. The charm of the staff helps a lot, too.

21 rue de la Falaise. © 02-32-51-46-15. Main courses 74F–98F (11.25– 14.90, $10.75–$14.20); fixed-price menu 135F–155F (20.50– 23.55, $19.60–$22.50). MC, V. Tues–Sun noon–3pm and 7:30–10pm. Closed Jan.

12 Chantilly—A Day at the Races ✸✸✸

26 miles N of Paris, 31 miles SE of Beauvais

This is a resort town for Parisians who want a quick weekend getaway. Known for its frothy whipped cream and its black lace, it also draws visitors to its race-track and château. The first two Sundays in June are the highlight of the turf season, bringing out an exceedingly fashionable crowd.

Two of the great horse races of France, **Le Prix du Jockey Club** (the first Sunday in June) and the **Prix Diane-Herès** (the second Sunday in June), take place at the Hippodrome de Chantilly. Thoroughbreds from as far away as Kentucky and Brunei, as well as mounts sponsored by the old and new fortunes of Europe, compete in a very civil format that's broadcast throughout France and talked about in horse circles around the world. On race days, as many as 30 trains depart from Paris's Gare du Nord for Chantilly (the ride takes about 30 minutes); from there, free shuttle buses take fans to the track. Or you can take a 45-minute ride on the RER line D from Métro stop Châtelet-Les Halles to Chantilly. Buses also depart on race days from Place de la République and Porte de St-Cloud. Call ✆ **01-49-10-20-30** for information.

ESSENTIALS   Getting There Trains depart frequently for Chantilly from Gare du Nord in Paris; the ride takes about 30 minutes; cost is 84F (12.75, $12.20) round trip. Alternatively, RER line D will get you from metro stop Châtelet-Les Halles to Chantilly in about 45 minutes.

VISITOR INFORMATION The Office Tourisme is at 60 av. du Maréchal-Joffre (✆ **03-44-57-08-58**).

SEEING THE CHÂTEAU & MUSEUMS

Château de Chantilly/Musée Condé ✸✸✸   Once the seat of the grand Condé, a cousin of Louis XIV and head of the Bourbon-Condé dynasty, the Château de Chantilly and the Musée Condé (within the château) are on an arti-ficial carp-stocked lake. You approach via the same forested drive that Louis XIV rode along for a banquet prepared by Vatel, one of the best-known French chefs. (One day when the fish didn't arrive on time, Vatel committed suicide.) The château is French Renaissance, with gables and towers, but part was rebuilt in the 19th century. It's skirted by a forest once filled with stag and boar.

In 1886, the château's owner, the duc d'Aumale, bequeathed the park and palace to the Institut de France, along with his art collection and library. The château houses sumptuous furnishings as well as works by artists like Memling, van Dyck, Botticelli, Poussin, Watteau, Ingres, Delacroix, Corot, Rubens, and Vernet. See especially Raphael's *Madonna of Lorette, Virgin of the House d'Orléans,* and *Three Graces* (sometimes called the *Three Ages of Woman*). The foremost French painter of the 15th century, Jean Fouquet, is represented here by a series of about 40 miniatures. A copy of the rose diamond that received worldwide attention when it was stolen in 1926 is on display in the jewel col-lection. One of the most celebrated Condé library acquisitions is the Limbourg brothers' *Très Riches Heures du Duc de Berry,* a 15th-century illuminated manu-script illustrating the months of the year.

The château was built about 1560 by Jean Bullant for one of the members of the Montmorency family. The stables (see below), a hallmark of French 18th-century architecture, were constructed to house 240 horses, with adjacent kennels for 500 hounds. If you have time, take a walk in the garden laid out by Le Nôtre. A hamlet of rustic cottages and the Maison de Sylvie, a graceful building constructed in 1604 and rebuilt by Maria-Felice Orsini, are in the park. If you don't want to see the château (Musée), you can visit just the garden for 17F (2.60, $2.45) per adult, 10F (1.50, $1.45) per child.

Chantilly. ✆ **03-44-62-62-62.** Admission (including guided tour) 42F (6.40, $6.10) adults, 37F (5.60, $5.35) students 12–18, 15F (2.30, $2.30) children 3–11, children under 3 free. Mar–Oct Wed–Mon 10am–6pm; Nov–Feb Wed–Mon 10:30am–12:45pm and 2–5pm.

Les Grandes Écuries/Musée Vivant du Cheval ★★   This museum occupies the restored *Grandes Écuries,* the stables built between 1719 and 1735 for Louis-Henri, prince de Bourbon and prince de Condé, who occupied the château. Besides being fond of horses, he believed in reincarnation and expected to come back as a horse in his next life; so he built the stables fit for a king.

The stables and an adjoining kennel fell into ruin, but they've been restored as a museum of the living horse, with thoroughbreds housed alongside old breeds of draft horses, Arabs and Hispano-Arabs, and farm horses. Yves Bien-aimé, the riding instructor who established the museum, presents exhibitions tracing the horse's association with humans, as well as a blacksmith shop and displays of saddles, equipment for the care of horses, and horse-race memorabilia.

The three daily equestrian displays (from April to October) last about half an hour and explain how the horse is ridden and trained. A restaurant on the premises, Le Carrousel Gourmand (✆ **03-44-57-19-77;** www.musee-vivant-du-cheval.fr), features the specialties of Picardy, and does so exceedingly well. Reservations are required.

7 rue du Connétable. ✆ **03-44-57-40-40.** Admission 50F (7.60, $7.25) adults, 35F (5.30, $5.10) children 4–12, children under 4 free. Sept–Apr Wed–Mon 10:30am–6:30pm; May–June daily 10:30am–6:30pm; July–Aug Wed–Mon 10:30am–6:30pm, Tues 2–5pm. Equestrian displays Apr–Oct daily 11:30am, 3:30pm, and 5:15pm; Nov–March 3:30pm. Special equestrian exhibitions (cheval, rêve, and poesie) presented first Sun of the month at 3:30pm for 100F (15.20, $14.50) adults, 90F (13.70, $13.05) children 4–12, children under 4 free.

ACCOMMODATIONS

Best Western Hôtel du Parc   This modern hotel is in the center of town, close to a host of restaurants and sights. There are grander châteaux in Chantilly, but if you want a midtown location, this is your finest choice. The contemporary lobby, dominated by mirrors and chrome, gives way to a more inviting English-style bar, with plenty of dark wood and leather. The medium-size guest rooms have built-in furnishings and glass doors that open onto private balconies. Each comes with a small bathroom, about half of which are equipped with both tub and shower. Overall, expect a no-frills experience that's pleasant but nothing special.

36 av. du Maréchal-Joffre, 60500 Chantilly. ✆ **800/528-1234** in the U.S. or Canada, or 03-44-58-20-00. Fax 03-44-57-31-10. www.bestwestern.fr. 57 units. 520F (79.05, $75.40) double; 600F (91.20, $87) suite. AE, DC, MC, V. Parking 50F (7.60, $7.25) per day. *In room:* TV.

Château de Chaumontel ★   Northeast of Luzarches and south of Chantilly is this hotel/restaurant from the late 16th century. Accented with conical towers and slate roofs, it has had many aristocratic owners and was once the hunting lodge of the prince de Condé. In 1956, it was turned into a hotel, with well-furnished accommodations whose decor ranges from rooms with high, sloping ceilings with massive antique beams to elegant replicas of the kind of room you'd find in a privately owned manor house. Most bathrooms have a tub and shower. Surrounded by a moat and a landscape dotted with wildflowers, the château is as evocative a site as any in this region. The rustic dining room serves excellent meals. There's an Indian restaurant on the property as well.

21 rue André-Vassord, 95270 Chaumontel. ℂ **01-34-71-00-30.** Fax 01-34-71-26-97. www.chateau-chaumontel.fr. 20 units. 560F–900F (85.10– 136.80, $81.20-$130.50) double; 1,290F (196.10, $187.05) suite. Rates include breakfast and dinner. AE, MC, V. Take N16 south for 4 miles. **Amenities:** Restaurant, bar, bike rentals, room service. *In room:* TV hair dryer (at reception).

Château de la Tour ⭐⭐   An even finer and more elegant château is this turn-of-the-20th-century hotel with a 12-acre park built as a weekend getaway by a wealthy Parisian banking family. During World War II, it became the home of the German l'État Major, and in 1946, it was transformed into a luxury hotel. The likes of Edith Piaf, Tino Rossi, and Jean Gabin would meet and mingle in the restaurant. Today, many celebrities and sports personalities still frequent the château. In 1990, a new wing was added, giving guests the opportunity to choose rooms with a modern flavor or a more traditional ambience. In either case, all units are large and feature hardwood floors, high ceilings, and first-class furnishings. Most of the well-maintained bathrooms contain a tub and shower combination. Public areas feature two wood-burning fireplaces.

Chemin de la Chaussée, 60270 Chantilly-Gouvieux. ℂ **03-44-62-38-38.** Fax 03-44-57-31-97. www.lechateaudelatour.wanadoo.fr. 41 units. 690F–980F (104.90– 148.95, $100.05-142.10) double. AE, DC, MC, V. Free parking. **Amenities:** Restaurant, bar; outdoor pool; tennis court; laundry service. *In room:* TV, minibar, safe.

DINING

The restaurant at the **Château de la Tour** (see above) is open to the public. You can enjoy an haute French cuisine at both lunch and dinner, with meals ranging in price from 250F–350F (38– 53.20, $36.25–$50.75). Chefs use only market-fresh, quality ingredients, which they feature into a menu that is changed daily and is always based on the best in any season.

La Ferme de Condé TRADITIONAL FRENCH   The most appealing restaurant in Chantilly occupies a 100-year-old stone-sided former Anglican church. It's on the periphery of town, about a mile north of the château. It's the most popular restaurant in town, thanks to excellent food and a rustic, informal decor. Antique farm implements, racks of wine bottles, and barrels give the space a cozy feel. Cuisine is old-fashioned, with variations based on seasonal ingredients and the chef's inspiration. Examples include a terrine *de basse cour,* which combines poultry, rabbit, and duck; and a succulent version of suckling pig roasted on a spit and served with fresh thyme and veal kidneys in a mustard-flavored cream sauce. Also look for a fricassée of scallops with white wine and herbs; and salmon *verdurette,* served with cream sauce and fresh local herbs.

42 av. du Maréchal Joffre. ℂ **03-44-57-32-31.** Reservations recommended. Main courses 70F–125F (10.65– 19, $10.15–$18.15); fixed-price menu 98F–125F (14.90– 19, $14.20–$18.15). DC, MC, V. Daily noon–2:30pm and 7–10:15pm.

13 Senlis ⭐⭐

32 miles S of Paris, 62 miles S of Amiens

Sleepy Senlis, which some Parisians treat as a suburb of Paris, remains a quiet township surrounded by forests. No history has been made here in a long time, but its memories are many and regal. Barbarians no longer threaten its walls as they did in the 3rd century; and gone, too, are those kings of France, from Clovis to Louis XIV, who either passed through or took up temporary residence here. You can tie a visit to this northern French town with a trek to Chantilly (see above). Today, the core of Vieux Senlis is an archaeological bonanza that attracts visitors from all over the world.

Budget 2 hours to see Senlis.

ESSENTIALS

GETTING THERE   Take any of the approximately 20 **trains** that depart every day from Paris's Gare du Nord for Chantilly (see above). In front of the railway station in Chantilly, bus no. 15 (marked "Senlis") maintains departures that are timed to coincide with the arrival of trains from Paris. Round-trip fares from the Gare du Nord to the center of Senlis, combining transit aboard both the bus and the train, cost 98F (14.90, $14.20) per person. Total travel time from downtown Paris to the heart of Senlis takes between 45 and 60 minutes.

VISITOR INFORMATION   The **Office de Tourisme** is on place parvis Notre-Dame (© **03-44-53-06-40;** www.ville-senlis.fr).

SEEING THE SIGHTS

Medieval streets loaded with antique masonry and evocative doorways run throughout the city. One of the most interesting is the **rue du Chat-Harét,** from the center of which there's a view over the ruined château and the Gallo-Roman foundations it sits on. There's also the **rue des Cordelier,** site of a (since demolished) medieval convent. Nos. 14 and 10 along that street are particularly beautiful and old, but neither can be visited.

Cathédrale Notre-Dame de Senlis 🟊🟊   Notre-Dame has a graceful 13th-century spire that towers 256 feet and dominates the countryside. The severe western facade contrasts with the Flamboyant Gothic southern portal. A fire swept the structure in 1504 and much rebuilding followed. A 19th-century overlay was applied to the original structure, which was begun in 1153. Before entering, walk around to the western porch to see the sculptures. Depicted in stone is a calendar of the seasons, along with scenes showing the ascension of the Virgin and the entombment. The builders of the main portal imitated the work at Chartres. In the forecourt are memorials to Joan of Arc and Marshal Foch.

Place Notre-Dame. © **03-44-53-01-59.** Free admission. Daily 8am–7pm.

Château Royal et Parc and Musée de la Vénerie (Hunting Museum) 🟊
A short walk from the Cathédrale, you'll find the Château Royal et Parc. Built on the ruins of a Roman palace, the castle followed the outline of the Gallo-Roman walls, some of the best preserved in France. Once inhabited by such monarchs as Henri II and Catherine de Médici, the château (now in ruins) encloses a complex of buildings. Of the 28 towers built against the Gallo-Roman walls, 16 remain. One ruin houses the King's Chamber, the boudoir of French monarchs since the time of Clovis. In the complex is the Prieuré St-Mauritius, a priory that not only honors a saint but also was founded by one, Louis IX.

The Musée de la Vénerie (Hunting Museum), in the Château Royal, is housed in an 18th-century prior's building in the middle of the garden and displays hunting-related works of art from the 15th century to the present— paintings, drawings, engravings, old hunting suits, arms, horns, and trophies.

Senlis. © **03-44-53-06-40,** ext. 1315. Admission 16F (2.45, $2.30) adults, 8F (1.20, $1.15) students, free for children 16 and under. Wed 2–6pm, Thurs–Mon 10am–noon and 2–5pm. All visits of the Musée de la Vénerie include an obligatory guided tour, in French, that begins every hour on the hour. Closed mid-Dec to Jan.

Musée d'Art de Senlis　No other site in Senlis depicts the ancient Roman occupation of Gaul in such vivid terms. Set within the partially Gothic former home of the local bishop, and inaugurated in 1989, it contains most of the archaeological artifacts of the Gallo-Romans in the region. It also includes rare sculptures and church art from the Middle Ages. One floor above street level, you'll find paintings, some by local artists working in an untrained style that art historians refer to as "naive," executed between the 17th and 20th centuries.

Place Notre-Dame. ✆ **03-44-53-00-80**. Admission 16F (2.45, $2.30) adults, 8F (1.20, $1.15) students under 25, free for local residents and children under 16. Wed 2–6pm, Thurs–Mon 10am–noon and 2–6pm (closes at 5pm Nov–Jan).

ACCOMMODATIONS & DINING
Hostellerie de la Porte Bellon　In a town of lackluster inns, this is a good oasis for the night. The stately-looking but relatively inexpensive hotel was built as a convent 300 years ago, and later functioned as a coaching inn for the lodging of mail carriages. Set a short walk east of Senlis's historic core, it has three floors of big-windowed bedrooms and a facade that's dotted with old-fashioned shutters and window boxes filled with pansies and geraniums. Prefacing the entrance is an unusual 19th-century glass vestibule inspired by an English greenhouse. Bedrooms have comfortable mattresses, but are a bit spartan despite the cheerful wallpaper. Most of them come with a complete tub and shower combination.

51 rue Bellon, 60300 Senlis. ✆ **03-44-53-03-05**. Fax 03-44-53-29-94. 20 units. 400F (60.80, $58) double; 990F (150.50, $143.55) three-bedroom suite. MC, V. Closed Dec 21–Jan 5. **Amenities:** Restaurant, bar; baby-sitting; laundry. In room: TV, minibar.

Vieille Auberge (Value) TRADITIONAL FRENCH　This is the town's best value. Each candlelit dining room, with its stone walls and heavy tables, offers a refined, rustic ambience. During warm months, guests can sit on a small terrace. The staff takes pride in serving classic French dishes, which may include such favorites as monkfish tournedos in a piquant pepper sauce; filet of beef in a country wine sauce accompanied by a vegetable crêpe; and duck filet with foie gras and whole-grain mustard sauce. Though the cuisine isn't worth a special drive from Paris, the restaurant is memorable for its atmosphere and perfectly prepared dishes.

8 rue Long Filet. ✆ **03-44-60-95-50**. Reservations recommended Fri–Sat. Main courses 85F–110F (–12.90–16.70, $12.35–$15.95); fixed-price menu 120F–190F (18.25– 28.90, $17.40–$27.55). AE, DC, MC, V. Daily noon–2pm; Mon–Sat 7–10pm.

14 Compiègne ★★★

50 miles N of Paris, 20 miles NE of Senlis

A visit to this Oise River valley town is usually combined with an excursion to Senlis (see above). The most famous dance step of all time was photographed in a forest about 4 miles from town: Hitler's "jig of joy" on June 22, 1940, which heralded the ultimate humiliation of France and shocked the world.

Like Senlis, this is another town north of Paris that lives for its memories—not all pleasant. Many Parisians come for the 35,000-acre Forest of Compiègne. With its majestic vistas, venerable trees and ponds, it merits exploration.

ESSENTIALS
GETTING THERE　There are frequent **trains** from the Gare du Nord in Paris. The ride takes 50 minutes. The station is across the river from the town

center. A ticket costs 140F (21.30, $20.30) round-trip. If you're **driving,** take the northern Paris-Lille motorway (A1 or the less convenient E15) for 50 miles.

VISITOR INFORMATION   The **Office de Tourisme** is on place Hôtel-de-Ville ((*C* **03-44-40-01-00**).

SEEING THE SIGHTS

An imposing statue of **Joan of Arc,** who was taken prisoner at Compiègne by the Burgundians on May 23, 1430, before she was turned over to the English, stands in the town square.

Musée National du Château de Compiègne ★★★   In the town's heyday,

royalty and two Bonaparte emperors flocked here. But this wasn't always a place of pageantry. Louis XIV once said: "In Versailles, I live in the style befitting a monarch. In Fontainebleau, more like a prince. At Compiègne, like a peasant." But the Sun King returned again and again. His successor, Louis XV, started rebuilding the château, based on plans by Gabriel. The king died before work was completed, but Louis XVI and Marie Antoinette expanded it.

Napoléon's second wife, Marie-Louise, arrived at Compiègne to marry him, and in a dining room, which you can visit only on the guided tour, she had her first meal with the emperor. Accounts maintain that she was paralyzed with fear of this older man (Napoléon was in his 40s, she was 19). After dinner, he seduced her and is said to have only increased her fears.

It wasn't until the Second Empire that Compiègne reached its pinnacle. Under Napoléon III and Eugénie, the autumnal hunting season was the occasion for balls and parties, some lasting 10 days without a break. It was the "golden age": Women in elegant hooped gowns danced with their escorts to Strauss waltzes, Offenbach's operas echoed through the chambers and salons, and Eugénie, who fancied herself an actress, performed in the palace theater for her guests.

On the tour, you'll see the gold-and-scarlet Empire Room, where Napoléon spent many a troubled night, and his library, known for its secret door. In the Queen's Chamber, the "horn of plenty" bed was used by Marie-Louise. The furniture is by Jacob, and the nude on the ceiling by Girodet. Dubois decorated the Salon of Flowers, while the largest room, the Ball Gallery, was adorned by Girodet. In the park, Napoléon ordered the gardeners to create a green bower to remind Marie-Louise of the one at Schönbrunn in Vienna, where she grew up.

Various wings of the château contain a handful of museums, entrance to which is included in the château admission. They include the Musée National de la Voiture (National Automobile Museum), which will be closed for renovations throughout most of 2002; it exhibits about 150 vehicles from Ben-Hur chariots to bicycles to a Citroën "chain-track" vehicle. The château also contains a series of rooms defined as either the Musée de l'Imperatrice Eugénie, the Musée du Second Empire, or the Musée Napoléon III, according to whoever happens to be talking about it. It's devoted to sculpture, paintings (including some by Carpeaux), and furniture, as well as mementos and documents showcasing life, politics, values, and morals of France's Industrial Revolution and its Gilded Age.

Place du Palais. (*C* **03-44-38-47-00.** Admission (including the museums) 35F (5.30, $5.10) adults, 23F (3.50, $3.35) students, free for children under 18. Wed–Mon 10am–5:15pm.

Musée de la Figurine Historique (Museum of Historical Figurines) ★

One of Compiègne's finest monuments is the Flamboyant Gothic Hôtel de

Ville. Built from 1499 to 1503, with a landmark belfry that's visible from far away, it houses a unique museum of great interest to students of the wars that have raged across northern France. The Museum of Historical Figurines offers a unique collection of about 100,000 tin soldiers, from a Louis XIV trumpeter to a soldier from World War II. The Battle of Waterloo, staged in miniature form on a landscape with thousands of figurines, is depicted in all its gore.

Place de l'Hôtel-de-Ville. ☎ **03-44-40-72-55.** Admission 12F (1.80, $1.75) adults, 6F (.90, 85¢) students, seniors, and children. Tues–Sat 9am–noon and 2–6pm; Sun 2–6pm (closes 5pm Nov–Feb).

Château de Pierrefonds ★★   One of the Compiègne forest's most evocative medieval buildings lies 7½ miles north of Compiègne. (To reach it from the town center, follow the signs to Soissons.) Originally built in the 1100s as a château-fortress, it was later bought by Napoléon, who intended to transform it into one of his private homes. Surrounded by a moat, it boasts a feudal look, with rounded towers capped by funnel-shaped pointed roofs. Artifacts from the Middle Ages are displayed within its interior. Save time for a stroll through the tiny village of Pierrefonds at the base of the château. Here, half-timbered houses evoke the life of the château's medieval heyday.

In the Forêt de Compiègne. ☎ **03-44-42-72-72.** Admission 35F (5.30, $5.10) adults, 21F (3.30, $3.05) students 18–26, free for children under 18. May–Aug daily 10am–5:15pm; Sept–Apr daily 10am–12:30pm and 2–5:15pm.

Wagon de l'Armistice (Wagon du Maréchal-Foch) ★★   In 1940, at the peak of his power, in one of the most ironic twists of fate in European history, Hitler forced the vanquished French to capitulate in the same rail coach where German officials signed the Armistice on November 11, 1918. The then-triumphant Nazis transported the coach to Berlin, and then to Ordüff in the Thuringian Forest, where an Allied bomb destroyed it in April 1945. In Compiègne's suburb of Rethondes, 4 miles to the south, you can visit a replica that retells the events of both 1918 and 1940 in graphic detail, assisted by newspapers, photos, maps, and slide shows.

Route de Soissons, in the village of Rethondes. ☎ **03-44-85-14-18.** Admission 18F (2.75, $2.60) adults; 9F (1.35, $1.30) children 7–14, children under 7 free. April–mid Oct Wed–Mon 9am–12:15pm and 2–6:15pm; mid Oct–Mar Wed–Mon 9am–11:45am and 2–5:30pm.

ACCOMMODATIONS

The **Rôtisserie du Chat Qui Tourne** (see "Dining," below) also rents rooms.

Au Relais Napoléon   This modern hotel outside of town is near sports complexes and the border of the forest, surrounded by a sunny terrace, green lawns, and even a small vineyard. The interior is First Empire style, with honeycomb ceilings, tiled floors, and dark woodwork. The medium-size guest rooms offer a relaxing ambience with rich colored walls, reproduction furniture, and firm mattresses, plus tiled bathrooms with tub and shower.

Av. de l'Europe, 60200 Compiègne. ☎ **03-44-20-11-11.** Fax 03-44-20-41-60. contact@relaisnapoleon.com. 47 units. 450F (68.40, $65.25) double. AE, DC, MC, V. Free parking. Head west on av. Berthelot, which becomes av. de l'Europe, a 10-min. trip. **Amenities:** Restaurant, bar; baby-sitting; laundry. *In room:* TV, hair dryer.

Hostellerie du Royal-Lieu ★   If you wish to stay close to the town, this is the best choice for food and lodging. Monsieur and Madame Bonechi have decorated the rooms in this rambling half-timbered inn about 1¼ miles from town. They have names like Madame de Pompadour, Madame Butterfly, and La

Goulue; less fancifully named rooms are done in a scattering of different "Louis" periods or Empire style. Bedrooms are medium in size and sleekly designed. The tiled bathrooms are tidily organized with shower and tub combinations. Both the rooms and the restaurant's terrace look out over a garden. Meals in the elegantly rustic dining room may include four-fish stew with red butter, brochette of quail with black olives and polenta, and filet of beef with morels in cream sauce. They range from 200F–360F (30.40– 54.70, $29–$52.20). Dessert soufflés are available if you order them 30 minutes in advance.

9 rue de Senlis, 60200 Compiègne. (℃ 03-44-20-10-24. Fax 03-44-86-82-27. E-mail: hostellerieduroyallieu@ bigfoot.com. 26 units. 544F (82.70, $78.90) double; 688F (104.60, $99.75) suite. AE, DC, MC, V. Follow the signs southwest toward Senlis until you reach rue de Senlis, a 5-min drive east from the town center. **Amenities:** Restaurant, bar, room service. *In room:* TV, hair dryer.

DINING

Note that the restaurants in both hotels above are open to the public.

Rôtisserie du Chat Qui Tourne TRADITIONAL FRENCH   The name, "Inn of the Cat That Turns the Spit," dates from 1665. The bar and a traditional country inn–style dining room are downstairs. The proprietor believes in judicious cooking and careful seasoning and prices her table d'hôte menus to appeal to a wide range of budgets. The *menu gastronomique* is likely to include *foie gras de canard* (duck), then *cassolette de Roguens* (veal kidneys), followed by either *poulet rôti* (roast chicken) *à la broche* or tournedos of salmon with wild mushrooms, and finally a cheese and a dessert. Mme Robert also rents 22 clean and well-maintained rooms, each with private bathroom, TV, and phone. Doubles cost 170F to 390F (25.85 to 59.30, $24.65 to $56.55).

In the Hôtel de France, 17 rue Eugène-Floquet, 60200 Compiègne. (℃ 03-44-40-02-74. Reservations recommended. Main courses 78F–120F (11.85– 18.25; $11.30–$17.40); fixed-price menus 80F–250F (12.15– 38, $11.60–$36.25), 140F–250F (21.30– 38, $20.30–$36.25) dinner. MC, V. Daily noon–2:15pm and 7:15–9:15pm.

The Loire Valley

Bordered by vineyards, the winding Loire Valley cuts through the land of castles deep in France's heart. Medieval crusaders returning here brought news of the opulence of the East, and soon they began rethinking their surroundings. Later, word came from Italy of a great artistic flowering led by Leonardo da Vinci and Michelangelo. So when royalty and nobility built châteaux throughout this valley during the French Renaissance, sumptuousness was uppermost in their minds. An era of excessive pomp reigned until Henri IV moved his court to Paris, marking the Loire's decline.

The Loire is blessed with attractions—from medieval, Renaissance, and classical châteaux to Romanesque and Gothic churches to treasures like the Apocalypse Tapestries. There's even the castle that inspired *Sleeping Beauty.* Our warnings about driving in Paris don't apply to the Loire Valley. While there's train service to some towns, the best way to see this region is by car.

REGIONAL CUISINE Patricia Wells, author of *The Food Lover's Guide to France,* said that the Loire's cuisine reminds her of "the daffodil days of spring and blue skies of summer." Particularly superb are rose-fleshed salmon from the Loire River, often served with sorrel. The region's rivers are stocked with other fish, including pike, carp, shad, and mullet.

Various types of *rillettes* (potted pork) begin most meals. Gourmets highly prize *pâté d'alouettes* (lark pâté) and *matelote d'anguille* (stewed eel). From the mushroom-rich Sologne emerges wild boar, along with deer, miniature quail, hare, pheasant, and mallard duck. Two popular poultry dishes are chicken casserole in red-wine sauce and spit-roasted capon.

The valley's Atlantic side produces a variety of grapes, used to make wines from dry to lusciously sweet, from still to sparkling and fruity. The best whites are Vouvray (ideal with Loire salmon) and Montlouis. Red Anjou wines, including Rouge de Cabernet and Saumur-Champigny, have a slight raspberry flavor. Dry Sancerre wines, with plenty of backbone, are superb with the Loire's goat cheese and white-water fish.

1 Orléans ✪

74 miles SW of Paris, 45 miles SE of Chartres

After suffering much damage in World War II, many Orléans neighborhoods were rebuilt in dull styles, so visitors who hope to see how it looked when the Maid of Orléans was here are likely to be disappointed. There are still rewarding sights, though, and a jazz festival held the first week of July significantly livens the place up. Today, this city of 200,000 has lost a lot of its former importance to Tours, but signs of urban restoration bring hope for the future.

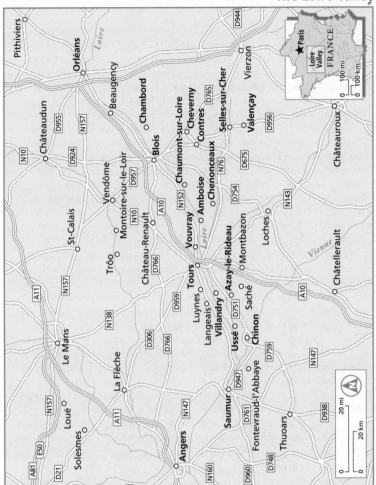

The Loire Valley

ESSENTIALS

GETTING THERE   Ten **trains** per day arrive from Paris's Gare d'Austerlitz (trip time: 1¼ hours); there are also a dozen connections from Tours (trip time: 1½ hours). The one-way fare from Paris is 91F ($14.55, $13.20); from Tours it's also 91F ($14.55, $13.20). Orléans lies on the road between Paris and Tours. If you're **driving** from Paris, take A10 south; from Tours, take A10 north.

VISITOR INFORMATION   The **Office de Tourisme** is on place Albert, 1er (© **02-38-24-05-05;** www.ville-orleans.fr).

EXPLORING THE TOWN

Orléans is the chief town of Loiret, on the Loire, and beneficiary of many associations with the French aristocracy—even giving its name to ducs and duchesses who influenced the course of the nation's history. In 1429, **Joan of Arc** relieved the city from attacks by the Burgundians and the English. That

---

Finds **Biking Your Way Through the Loire**

Once you're in Tours, you can rely on public transport to see much of the Loire; you can also rent a bicycle—the region is relatively flat. Try **Amster 'Cycle,** 5 rue des Remparts, in Tours (© **02-47-61-22-23**), which rents mountain bikes and all-purpose road bikes for 80F (12.15, $11.60) per day. A deposit is required: either a passport, 1,500F (228, $217.50), or a credit card. The shop is only 50 yards from the rail station.

An excellent itinerary for bikers involves heading 10½ miles west of Tours to the Jardins de Villandry. The road will take you along the bank of the Cher River. It's very agreeable, relatively flat, and most scenic. From here, you can continue another 5 miles to the château of Langeais, also a lovely route. If you want to head east from Tours, consider the 15-mile excursion to Amboise. This route is a bit more densely trafficked and not as bucolic. The tourist office will provide bikers with maps.

---

deliverance is celebrated every year on May 8, the anniversary of her victory. An equestrian statue of Jeanne d'Arc stands on place du Martroi, which was created by Foyatier in 1855. From the square, you can drive down rue Royal (rebuilt in 18th-century style) across pont George-V (erected in 1760). From there, you'll have a good view of the town. A simple cross marks the site of the Fort des Tourelles, which Joan of Arc and her men captured.

If you're looking for a unique gift indigenous to the area, go to **La Chocola-terie Royale,** 53 rue Royale (© **02-38-53-93-43**), where you'll find jars of *cotignac,* an apricot-colored jelly made from quince. While in the store, you can also stock up on fine handmade chocolates.

Near rue Royale is place du Châtelet, with its many boutiques, including a Galeries Lafayette. Look for fashionable clothing, jewelry, books, and leather goods. For antiques, walk along rue de Bourgogne, where you'll find a host of dealers offering everything from objets d'art to furniture.

Cathédrale Ste-Croix ✭ Begun in 1287 in the High Gothic period, the cathedral was burned by the Huguenots in 1568. Henri IV laid the first stone on the present building in 1601, and work continued until 1829. The cathedral boasts a 17th-century organ and magnificent woodwork from the early 18th century in its chancel, the masterpiece of Jules Hardouin-Mansart and other artists of Louis XIV. You'll need to take the guided tour to see the chancel, the crypt, and the treasury, with its Byzantine enamels, goldwork from the 15th and 16th centuries, and Limoges enamels.

Place Ste-Croix. © **02-38-77-87-50.** Free admission, but you should tip the guide. Daily 10am–noon and 2–5pm (May–Sept until 6pm). Guided visits, in French only, can be arranged by the tourist office for 25F (3.80, $3.65) per person. Tours given May–Sept at 3, 4, and 5pm.

Hôtel Groslot This Renaissance mansion was begun in 1550 and embel-lished in the 19th century. François II (first husband of Mary, Queen of Scots) lived in it during the fall of 1560 and died on December 5 the same year. Between the Revolution and the mid-1970s, it functioned as the town hall until it was replaced with something less dramatic but more functional. Despite that, marriage ceremonies, performed by the town's magistrates, still occur here. Romance is nothing new to this building: It was here that Charles IX met his lovely Marie Touchet. The statue of Joan of Arc praying (at the foot of the flight

of steps) was the work of Louis Philippe's daughter, Princesse Marie d'Orléans. In the garden you can see the remains of the 15th-century Chapelle St-Jacques.

Place de l'Étape (northwest of the cathedral). ☏ **02-38-79-22-30.** Free admission. July–Sept Sun–Fri 9am–7pm, Sat 5–9pm; Oct–June Mon–Fri 10am–noon and 2–6pm, Sat 4:30–6pm.

Église St-Aignan One of the most frequently altered churches in the Loire Valley, St-Aignan was consecrated in 1509 in the form you see today. It possesses one of France's earliest vaulted hall crypts, complete with polychromed capitals. Scholars of pre-Romanesque art view the place with passionate interest, for its 10th- and 11th-century aesthetics are rare. Above ground, the church's Renaissance-era choir and transept remain, but the Protestants burned the nave during the Wars of Religion. In a gilded wood-carved shrine are the remains of the church's patron saint.

Place St-Aignan. (No phone; ask at tourist office). Free admission. Hours are erratic—usually open only during masses. To visit the crypt, inquire at tourist office (see above).

Musée des Beaux-Arts ✦✦ This is primarily a picture gallery of French and (to a lesser degree) Dutch and Flemish works from the 16th to the late 19th centuries. Some of the works once hung in Cardinal Richelieu's château. The collection includes busts by Pigalle and a fine array of portraits, including one of Mme de Pompadour. Among non-French works, the undisputed star is a lovely Velásquez commemorating the Apostle St. Thomas.

1 rue Fernand-Rabier. 📞 02-38-79-21-55. Admission 20F (3.05, $2.90) adults, 10F (1.50, $1.45) children. Sun and Tues 11am–6pm, Wed 10am–8pm, Thurs–Sat 10am–6pm.

ACCOMMODATIONS

Hôtel d'Arc   This six-story hotel, with its Art Deco facade, sits in the middle of the town center and is close to nearly everything. Built in the 1920s, it's near the railway station and the pedestrian-only shopping streets. The bedrooms feature ceiling moldings and paneling, each in a different decorative theme. Most are of average size; the largest units have numbers that end in 2. Half of the bathrooms come with a tub and shower. Most rooms are peaceful, but avoid those that face rue de la République, as they tend to be noisy. Although the hotel has no restaurant, it serves breakfast in an ornate room with a carved marble fireplace.

37 rue de la République, 45000 Orléans. 📞 **02-38-53-10-94.** Fax 02-38-81-77-47. 35 units. 390F–410F (59.30– 62.30, $56.55–$59.45) double. AE, DC, MC, V. **Amenities:** Laundry/dry cleaning. *In room:* TV, minibar.

Hôtel Mercure Orléans 🍸   If you seek modern comfort, this is the town's finest address. Along the river, adjacent to pont Joffre, this eight-story bandbox structure is within walking distance of place du Martroi and its Joan of Arc statue. Though rather impersonal—it's favored by businesspeople—it offers the best rooms in the city, each recently refurbished. Most units are in chain-hotel style and of medium size. All are equipped with tiled bathrooms with tubs and showers. The restaurant, Le Chaland, serves French and Loire Valley specialties.

44–46 quai Barentin, 45000 Orléans. 📞 **02-38-62-17-39.** Fax 02-38-53-95-34. 108 units. 650F (98.80, $94.25) double. AE, DC, MC, V. **Amenities:** Restaurant (French); bar; heated pool;, room service; baby-sitting. *In room:* A/C, TV, minibar.

Hôtel St-Martin *Value*   If you prefer simplicity to opulence and think of a hotel room only as a place to sleep and shower, then this is the choice for you. The 80-year-old three-story building has spacious rooms, sparsely furnished with firm mattresses and built-in armoires. Only three units have bathrooms with both tub and shower. Half the rooms are blessed with windows that look out onto the garden behind the hotel, where you can sit and enjoy a refreshing nonalcoholic drink. The place is well scrubbed, the rooms old-fashioned with a battered charm.

52 bd. Alexandre-Martin, 45000 Orléans. 📞 **02-38-62-47-47.** Fax 02-38-81-13-28. 22 units, 15 with bathroom. 190F (28.90, $27.55) double without bathroom, 260F–270F (39.50– 41.05, $37.70–$39.15) double with bathroom. AE, DC, V. *In room:* TV.

DINING

La Vieille Auberge TRADITIONAL FRENCH   One of the most dignified-looking restaurants in Orléans occupies an ivy-covered stone house originally built in the 1600s, and which today offers its formal garden as a verdant hideaway for dining. Menu items depend on the season, the ingredients that are available, and the whim of the chef, but expect sophisticated treatments of Loire Valley whitefish, game, and local produce. All of these are accompanied by regional wines that blend flavorfully with the cuisine.

2 rue de Faubourg St-Vincent. 📞 02-38-53-55-84. Reservations recommended. Main courses 90F–140F (13.70– 21.30, $13.05–$20.30); fixed-price menu 130F–320F (19.75– 48.65, $18.85–$46.40). AE, MC, V. Tues–Sun noon–2pm and 7:30–10pm.

Les Antiquaires ★★★ CLASSIC FRENCH This rustically elegant stone-sided 14th-century mansion is on a narrow street near the river. The original ceiling beams highlight the cozy, appealing interior. Owners Philippe and Pascale Bardau, cooking and tending the dining room, create a virtually flawless cuisine based on modern interpretations of traditional French recipes, each of which changes with the seasons. Savor the Loire Valley's abundance of wild game, if you arrive in autumn or winter, in dishes like an estouffade of wild boar with red-wine sauce. In spring, look for dishes such as ravioli of fresh morels with asparagus tips; roasted baby goat served with tagliatelle and sweet garlic sauce; and an orange-and-Grand-Marnier-flavored soufflé served with sorbet in puff pastry. Everything is very creative, and the staff most attentive.

2–4 rue au Lin. ⓒ **02-38-53-52-35.** Reservations required. Main courses 100F–170F (15.20– 25.85, $14.50–$24.65); fixed-price menu 220F–320F (33.45– 48.65, $31.90–$46.40). AE, MC, V. Tues–Sun noon–2:30pm; Tues–Sat 7:30–10pm.

ORLÉANS AFTER DARK

You'll find most of the after-dark action in the bars along rue de Bourgogne and the handful of places that spill over onto rue Bannier. A trendy young crowd dances and drinks the night away at the **Ka Club,** Les Halles Châtelet (ⓒ **02-38-53-08-79**). A few streets over is one of the better jazz clubs, **Paxton's Head,** 264 rue de Bourgogne (ⓒ **02-38-81-23-29**), with a down-home English pub feel. The mid-20s crowd enjoys a live comedian every night at the **Majestic Café,** 2 rue des Trois-Maries (ⓒ **02-38-54-68-68**); housed in a 13th-century building, it looks like a church on the inside with its stone walls and vaulted ceilings. If you want to drink beer and shoot pool, head for **Bar Darlington,** 3 rue du Colombier (ⓒ **02-38-54-67-98**), where there's an easygoing ambience.

2 Châteaudun

64 miles SW of Paris, 27 miles SW of Chartres

Austere and foreboding, **Château de Châteaudun** ★★, place Jean-de-Dunois (ⓒ **02-37-94-02-90**), rises on a stonebound table over a tributary of the Loire. Although begun in the Middle Ages, the château is a mix of medieval and Renaissance architecture, with towering chimneys and dormers. After a fire in the 18th century, Hardouin, Louis XV's architect, directed the town's reconstruction and indiscreetly turned over the castle to the homeless, who stripped it of its finery. In 1935, the government acquired the fortress and launched a major restoration. Even today, it's not richly furnished, but fine tapestries depicting scenes like the worship of the golden calf now cover its walls. The château's most admirable features are two carved staircases. Inside the Ste-Chapelle, dating from the Middle Ages, are more than a dozen 15th-century robed statues.

The château is open daily, April to September from 9:30am to 6pm and October to March from 10am to 12:30pm and 2 to 5pm. Admission is 36F (5.45, $5.20) for adults, 23F (3.50, $3.35) for ages 18 to 25, and free for children 17 and under. Allow 1½ hours to see the château.

ESSENTIALS

GETTING THERE **Buses** run frequently from Chartres, and there are about six **trains** per day, departing from Paris's Gare d'Austerlitz, charging around 100F (15.20, $14.50) each way, and arriving 90 minutes later in Châteaudun. Check with the Office de Tourism for schedules. If you're **driving** from Paris, head southwest along the A10 and exit at Phivars. Then take the N10, following the signs for Châteaudun.

VISITOR INFORMATION   The **Office de Tourism** is at 1 rue de Luynes (*©* **02-37-45-22-46**).

ACCOMMODATIONS

Hôtel de Beauce   This clean, modern hotel is utterly without pretense. Built in the 1950s, it's set in a quiet residential neighborhood about a 2-minute walk from the edge of town. Though it lacks a restaurant, it does have a small cocktail lounge for guests only. The guest rooms are furnished in a simple contemporary style. Most come with a somewhat cramped, shower-only bathroom.

50 rue Jallans, 28200 Châteaudun. *©* **02-37-45-14-75.** Fax 02-37-45-87-53. 24 units, 18 with bathroom. 160F (24.30, $23.20) double without bathroom, 250F (38, $36.25) double with bathroom. MC, V. Closed Sun evening and Dec 20–Jan 10. Parking 26F (3.95, $3.75). **Amenities:** Lounge. *In room:* TV.

Hôtel St-Michel   This hotel's tradition of welcoming guests extends to the early 19th century, when it served as a coaching inn. Today, under the direction of Pierre Le Menestrel, with the help of his hardworking staff and the stellar location on the town's main square, this is Châteaudun's best inn. Bedrooms, which have been undergoing renovations since the early 1990s, are simply furnished and comfortable. Most have a small, shower-only bathroom. Breakfast is served in the lounge, in your room, or in the greenhouse-style winter garden.

28 place du 18-Octobre and 5 rue Péan, 28200 Châteaudun. *©* **02-37-45-15-70.** Fax 02-37-45-83-39. www.groupcitotel.com/hotels/michel.html. 19 units, 15 with bathroom. 210F (31.90, $30.45) double without bathroom, 250F–310F (38– 47.10, $36.25–$44.95) double with bathroom. AE, DC, V. Parking 32F (4.85, $4.65). **Amenities:** Gym; sauna. *In room:* TV.

3 Beaugency *©*

93 miles SW of Paris, 53 miles NE of Tours

Situated on the right bank of the Loire, the town of Beaugency boasts a 14th-century bridge that's unusual because each of its 26 arches is in a different style. The heart of this Loire Valley town is an archaeological garden called the City of the Lords, named after the counts who enjoyed great power in the Middle Ages. A major event in medieval Europe took place here: the 1152 annulment of the marriage between Eleanor of Aquitaine and her cousin, Louis VII. This remarkable woman later became queen consort of Henry II of England, bringing southwestern France as her dowry. She was the mother of Richard the Lion-Hearted. (These events are retold in the film *The Lion in Winter;* Katharine Hepburn as Eleanor won the Academy Award.) Allow 2 hours to see Beaugency.

The 15th-century **Château Dunois,** 2 place Dunois (*©* **02-38-44-55-23**), contains a folklore museum of the Orléans district. The collection includes antique toys, hairpieces, furniture, costumes, paintings, and sculpture found in the district. The museum is open Wednesday through Monday from 10am to noon and 2 to 5pm (to 6:30pm in summer). Admission is 22F (3.35, $3.24) for adults, 10F (1.50, $1.45) for children 6 to 17, and free for children under 5. Included in the cost of admission is a free (mostly French-language) guided tour, offered daily at 10am, 11am, 2pm, 3pm, and 4pm, with an additional tour at 5pm offered between April and September. Near the château is the Voûte St-George (St. George's Vault), a gate of the former castle of the Lords of Beaugency, which opened from the fortress onto the Rû Valley and the lower part of town.

Église Notre-Dame would have been a good example of 12th-century Romanesque architecture if Gothic touches hadn't been added. Originally, it was attached to a Benedictine abbey. Nearby is the Tour St-Firmin, all that remains of a church that stood on place St-Firmin. A trio of bells is sheltered in this tower, whose spire rises 180 feet. From here you'll have a panoramic view of the valley.

In the archaeological garden, the Hôtel-Dieu (hospital) is one of the oldest buildings in Beaugency, dating to the 11th century. The Église St-Etienne, also from the 11th century, is one of the oldest churches of France, and the Tour César is a fine example of the period's military art.

ESSENTIALS

GETTING THERE   If you're **driving** from Blois to Beaugency, take D951 northeast. About 20 **trains** per day run between Beaugency and either Blois or Orléans; each trip takes 20 minutes and costs from 38F (5.80, $5.50) one-way. For railway information, call ℭ **08-36-35-35-35.** From Orléans, there are about eight **buses** a day making the trip to Beaugency.

VISITOR INFORMATION   The **Office de Tourisme** is at 3 place du Dr.-Hyvernaud (ℭ **02-38-44-54-42;** www.ville-beaugency-fr.

ACCOMMODATIONS & DINING

Abbaye de Beaugency ⚑   This three-star hotel offers the finest and most historic accommodations in Beaugency. Built in 1640 as a monastery on the southern fringe of town, it retains the stone window and door frames of its original construction, and an elegant brick facade that might remind you of a château. Functioning as a hotel since 1935, it occupies a small tract of land beside the Loire, within view of the town's oldest bridge. Guest rooms are large and bright, and each bathroom has both tub and shower.

2 quai de l'Abbaye, 45190 Beaugency. ℭ 02-38-44-67-35. Fax 02-38-44-87-92. www.hotelroomsplus.com/france/centre/beaugency/htm. 17 units. 550F–590F (83.60– 89.730, $79.75–$85.55) double. AE, DC, MC, V. **Amenities:** Restaurant, bar. In room: TV.

Tonnellerie ⚑ *Finds*   Set about a mile from the center of Beaugency, this well-managed hotel's owners are proud to present an unpretentious setting that's not (by their own admission) fabulously posh, but intimate and charming. It was originally built as a manor house in the 19th century, and retains its original L-shaped design, walled garden, and sense of the conservative bourgeoisie of the era of Balzac and Flaubert. This favorite offers simply furnished, comfortable, and traditional rooms. Bathrooms are small, most with shower stalls. The Pouey family can arrange visits to the château, golf, hiking, cycling, or a trip to a winery.

12 rue des Eaux-Bleues, Tavers, 45190 Beaugency. ℭ 02-38-44-68-15. Fax 02-38-44-10-01. www.chateaux-france.com/-latonnellerie. 20 units. 490F–1,050F (74.50– 159.60, $71.05–$152.25) double; 1,050F–1,290F (159.60– 196.10, $152.25–$187.05) apt or suite. AE, MC, V. Closed Jan–Feb. Take A10, exit at Beaugency, then take N152 to Beaugency/Tavers. **Amenities:** Restaurant, bar for guests only; pool; room service; baby-sitting. In room: TV, hair dryer.

4 Chambord

118 miles SW of Paris, 11 miles E of Blois

When François I used to say, "Come on up to my place," he meant the **Château de Chambord** ⚑⚑⚑ at 41250 Bracieux (ℭ **02-54-50-40-40**), not Fontainebleau or Blois. Some 2,000 workers began to piece together "the pile" in 1519. What emerged after 20 years was the pinnacle of the French Renaissance, the largest château in the Loire Valley. It was ready for the visit of Charles V of Germany, who was welcomed by nymphets in transparent veils tossing wildflowers in his path. Monarchs like Henri II and Catherine de Médici, Louis XIII, and Henri III came and went from Chambord, but none developed an affection for it to match François I's. The state acquired Chambord in 1932.

The château is set in a park of more than 13,000 acres, enclosed by a wall stretching some 20 miles. Four monumental towers dominate Chambord's facade. The three-story keep has a spectacular terrace from which the ladies of the court used to watch the return of their men from the hunt. The keep also encloses a corkscrew staircase, superimposed so that one person may descend at one end and a second ascend at the other without ever meeting. The apartments of Louis XIV, including his redecorated bedchamber, are also in the keep.

The château is open daily: January to March and October to December from 9am to 5:15pm, April to June from 9am to 6:15pm, and July to August from 9am to 7:15pm. Admission is 40F (6.10, $5.80) for adults, 25F (3.80, $3.65) for ages 12 to 25, and free for children under 11. At the tourist office, you can pick up tickets for the summertime *son-et-lumière* presentation, called *Jours et Siècles* (Days and Centuries). The price is 50F (7.60, $7.25). Allow 1½ hours to go through the château.

ESSENTIALS
GETTING THERE   It's best to **drive** to Chambord. Take the D951 northeast from Blois to Ménars, turning onto the rural road to Chambord. You can also rent a **bicycle** in Blois and ride the 11 miles to Chambord, or take one of the **tours** to Chambord leaving from Blois in summer. From June 15 to September 15, **Point Bus,** 2 place Victor Hugo (© **02-54-78-15-66**), operates bus service to Chambord, leaving Blois at 9:10am and again at 1:20pm with returns at 1 and 6:10pm.

VISITOR INFORMATION   The **Office de Tourisme** is on place St-Michel (© **02-54-20-34-86**).

ACCOMMODATIONS & DINING
Hôtel du Grand-St-Michel   Across from the château, and originally built as a kennel for the hounds of the French kings, this inn is the only one of any substance in town. Try for a front room overlooking the château, which is dramatic when floodlit at night. Accommodations are plain but comfortable, with provincial decor. Most visitors arrive for lunch, which in summer is served on a shaded terrace. The regional dishes are complemented by a marvelous collection of Loire wines so good they almost overshadow the cooking itself. High points from the menu include a stew of wild boar (in late autumn and winter), breast of duckling in a green peppercorn sauce, and several of the local pâtés and terrines, including the coarsely textured and very flavor-filled rillettes of regional pork.

103 place St-Michel, 41250 Chambord, near Bracieux. © **02-54-20-31-31.** Fax 02-54-20-36-40. 39 units. 290F–450F (44.10– 68.40, $42.05–$65.25) double. MC, V. Free parking. Closed Nov 14–Dec 20. **Amenities:** Restaurant, lounges. *In room:* TV.

5 Blois

112 miles SW of Paris, 37 miles NE of Tours

This little town of 55,000 people at the gateway to the Valley of the Loire receives half a million visitors yearly, primarily to visit its notorious château (see

"Exploring the Town & the Château," below). If time remains after a visit to the château, you might want to walk around the town itself. It is a piece of living history, with cobblestone streets and well-restored white houses with slate roofs and red-brick chimneys. Blois (pronounce it "Blwah") enjoys a scenic setting on the right bank of the Loire hugging a hillside overlooking the river. Some of its "streets" are mere alleyways originally laid out in the Middle Ages, or lanes linked by a series of stairs.

Allow 1½ hours to see Blois.

ESSENTIALS

GETTING THERE   The Paris–Austerlitz line via Orléans delivers six **trains** per day from Paris (trip time: 2 hours), costing 190F (28.90, $27.55) one-way; from Tours, five trains arrive per day (trip time: 30 minutes), at a cost of 75F (11.40, $10.90) one-way; and from Amboise, 10 trains arrive per day (trip time: 20 minutes), costing 55F (8.35, $8) one-way. For information and schedules, call ℂ **08-36-35-35-35.** The train station is at place de la Gare. Once here, you can take **buses** operated by **T.L.C.,** route de Vendôme (ℂ **02-54-58-55-44**), to tour various châteaux in the area, including Chambord, Chaumont, Chenonceau, and Amboise. Buses depart from the train station from June to September only. If you're **driving** from Tours, take RN152 east to Blois.

VISITOR INFORMATION   The **Office de Tourisme** is in the Pavillon Anne-de-Bretagne, 3 av. Jean-Laigret (ℂ **02-54-90-41-41**).

EXPLORING THE TOWN & THE CHÂTEAU

If you have time for shopping, head for the area around rue St-Martin and rue du Commerce. Shops here offer high-end items like clothing, perfumes, shoes, and jewelry. For high-quality reproductions of works of contemporary art, visit **Art Cadre,** 18 rue Denis-Papin (ℂ **02-54-74-80-10**). If you're in the market for a one-of-a-kind piece of jewelry or want to have something created to suit your tastes, go to the master jeweler **Philippe Denies,** 3 rue St-Martin (ℂ **02-54-74-78-24**). If you prefer antique jewelry, stop by **Antebellum,** 12 rue St-Lubin (ℂ **02-54-78-38-78**), and browse its selection of precious and semiprecious stone jewelry set in gold and silver. For something a little less serious, stop at **Le Paradis des Enfants,** 2 rue des Trois-Clefs (ℂ **02-54-78-09-68**), where, within a restored 15th-century house, you'll find toys in every shape and size. And if you want to acquire a historically accurate copy of the tapestries you might have admired at nearby châteaux, you'll find a wide range at **Tapisserie Langlois,** Voûte du Château (ℂ **02-54-78-04-43**). Tapestries cost from 1,000F to 15,000F (152 to   2,280, $145 to $2,175), depending on size and intricacy.

Château de Blois ✸✸✸   A wound in battle earned him the name *Balafré* (Scarface), but he was quite a ladies' man. In fact, on the cold, misty morning of December 23, 1588, the duc de Guise had just left a warm bed and the arms of one of Catherine de Médici's ladies-in-waiting. His archrival, King Henri III, had summoned him, but when the duke arrived, Henri was nowhere to be seen; only the king's minions were about. The guards moved toward the duke with daggers. Wounded, the duke made for the door, where more guards awaited him. Staggering, he fell to the floor in a pool of his own blood. Only then did Henri emerge from behind the curtains. "Mon Dieu," he reputedly exclaimed, "he's taller dead than alive!" The body couldn't be shown: The duke was too popular. Quartered, it was burned in a fireplace.

The murder of the duc de Guise is only one of the memories evoked by the Château de Blois, begun in the 13th century by the comtes de Blois. Blois reached the apex of its power and prestige in 1515, when François I moved the royal residence to the chateau. For that reason, Blois is often called the "Versailles of the Renaissance," the second capital of France, and the "city of kings." Blois soon became a palace of exile. Louis XIII banished his interfering mother, Marie de Médici, to the chateau, but she escaped by sliding into the moat down a mound of dirt left by the builders.

If you stand in the courtyard, you'll find the château is like an illustrated storybook of French architecture. The Hall of the Estates-General is a beautiful 13th-century work; the Charles d'Orléans gallery was actually built by Louis XII from 1498 to 1501, as was the Louis XII wing. The Gaston d'Orléans wing was constructed by Mansart between 1635 and 1637. Most remarkable is the François I wing, a French Renaissance masterpiece, containing a spiral staircase with elaborately ornamented balustrades and the king's symbol, the salamander. In the Louis XII wing, seek out paintings by Antoine Caron, Henri III's court painter, depicting Thomas More's persecution.

The château presents a *son-et-lumière* (sound-and-light) show in French from May to September, beginning in most cases at 10:30pm, but in rare instances, including throughout the month of May, at 9:30 or 10:15pm, depending on the school calendar. As a taped lecture is played, and colored lights and dramatic readings evoke the age in which the château was built. The show costs 60F (9.10, $8.70) for adults, 30F (4.55, $4.35) for children 7 to 15.

© 02-54-90-33-33. Admission 35F (5.30, $5.10) adults, 25F (3.80, $3.65) students 6–20, children 6 and under are free. July–Aug daily 9am–8pm; mid-March to June and Sept daily 9am–6:30pm; Oct to mid-March daily 9am–12:30pm and 2–5:30pm.

ACCOMMODATIONS

Note that some of the best rooms in town are at **Le Médicis** (see "Dining," below).

Holiday Inn Garden Court *(Kids)* This leading hotel, built in 1996 in the commercial heart of town, offers all the modern amenities as well as a respect for traditional charm. The rooms are furnished with a contemporary flair and a chain-hotel instinct for standardized comfort, and each unit comes with a well-equipped bathroom with tub and shower. La Vallière is the well-managed on-site restaurant. In summer, guests flock to a terrace overlooking the hotel garden.

26 av. Maunoury, 41000 Blois. © 800/465-4329 in the U.S. or Canada, or 02-54-55-44-88. Fax 02-54-74-57-97. www.holiday-inn.com/blois. 78 units. 470F–540F (71.45– 82.10, $68.15–$78.30) double. Children 12 and under stay free in parents' room. AE, DC, MC, V. Bus: 1. **Amenities:** Restaurant; bar; baby-sitting; laundry/dry cleaning. *In room:* A/C, TV, minibar, hair dryer.

Hôtel le Savoie This modern 1930s-era hotel is both inviting and livable, from its courteous staff to its guest rooms, which are small but nonetheless quiet and cozy. They were last renovated in 1999. In the morning, a breakfast buffet is set up in the bright dining room.

6–8 rue du Docteur-Ducoux, 41000 Blois. © 02-54-74-32-21. Fax 02-54-74-29-58. www.citote.com. 26 units. 250F–300F (38– 45.60, $36.25–$43.50) double. MC, V. *In room:* TV, hair dryer.

Mercure Centre *(★)* This is the newest and best-located hotel in Blois—three stories of reinforced concrete and big windows beside the quays of the Loire, a 5-minute walk from the château. Rooms never rise above the chain-style format and are very roadside motel in look, but they are roomy and soundproofed. Bathrooms come with a combination shower and tub.

28 quai St-Jean, 41000 Blois. © **02-54-56-66-66.** Fax 02-54-56-67-00. www.mercure.blois.fr. 96 units. 600F–625F (91.20– 95, $87–$90.65) double; 660F–695F (100.30– 105.65, $95.70–$100.80) suite. AE, DC, MC, V. Parking 40F ($6, $5.80). Bus: Quayside marked PISCINE. **Amenities:** Restaurant, bar; pool; Jacuzzi; sauna; room service; baby-sitting; laundry/dry cleaning. *In room:* A/C, TV, minibar, hair dryer.

DINING

Le Médicis ☆ TRADITIONAL FRENCH   Christian and Annick Garanger maintain one of the most sophisticated inns in Blois—ideal for a gourmet meal or an overnight stop. Fresh fish is the chef's specialty. Typical main courses are asparagus in mousseline sauce, scampi ravioli with saffron sauce, and supreme of perch with morels. Chocolate in many manifestations is the dessert specialty. In addition, the Garangers rent 12 elegant rooms. The rates are 500F to 700F (76 to 106.40, $72.50 to $101.50) double; there's one suite that goes for 700F (106.40, $101.50).

2 allée François-1er, 41000 Blois. © **02-54-43-94-04.** Fax 02-54-42-04-05. www.le-medicis.com. Reservations required. Main courses 80F–165F (12.15– 25.10, $11.60–$23.95); fixed-price menus 128F (19.45, $18.55), 168F (25.55, $24.35), 285F (43.30, $41.35), and 420F (63.85, $60.90). AE, MC, V. Daily noon–2pm and 7–10pm. Closed Jan. Bus: 2.

Rendezvous des Pecheurs ☆ TRADITIONAL FRENCH   This restaurant occupies a 16th-century house a 5-minute walk from the château. The chefs here, the finest in this part of France, continue to maintain their reputation for quality ingredients, generous portions, and creativity. The chef prepares only two or three meat dishes, including roasted chicken with a medley of potatoes and mushrooms and a confit of garlic. These appear alongside a much longer roster of fish and seafood dishes, such as a poached filet of zander served with fresh oysters, or filet of sea bass served with a champagne sauce on a bed of sea urchins.

27 rue du Foix. © **02-54-74-67-48.** Reservations recommended. Main courses 96F–130F (14.60– 19.75, $13.90–$18.85); fixed-price menu 150F (22.80, $21.75). MC, V. Mon 7:30–10pm; Tues–Sat noon–2pm and 7:30–10pm. Closed 3 weeks in Aug and 1 week in Feb.

BLOIS AFTER DARK

Although Blois doesn't offer the booming nightlife that you can find in France's larger towns, there's still a healthy selection of clubs. If you prefer the bars, saunter on down to the fun and friendly **Pub Mancini,** 1 rue du Puits-Châtel (© **02-54-56-07-84**), with its 100 brands of beer and 40 brands of whiskey; or **Riverside,** 3 rue Henri-Drussy (© **02-54-78-33-79**).

Our particular favorite is **Le Boucchanier,** Promenade du Mail (© **02-54-74-37-23**). Set aboard a coal barge that's moored to the side of the river, it has a nautical decor inspired by the fishing traditions of the Loire Valley, stiff drinks, and an ambience that's better suited than any other in town for making and developing dialogues with strangers. There's no cover. Beers go for 25F (3.80, $3.65).

6 Cheverny

119 miles SW of Paris, 12 miles SE of Blois

The upper crust still heads to the Sologne area for the hunt, just as if the 17th century had never ended. However, 21st-century realities—like formidable taxes—can't be entirely avoided, so the **Château de Cheverny** ☆☆☆ (© **02-54-79-96-29**) must open some of its rooms to visitors. At least that keeps the tax collector at bay and the hounds fed in winter.

Unlike most of the Loire châteaux, Cheverny is occupied by the descendants of the original owner, the vicomte de Sigalas. The family's lineage can be traced back to Henri Hurault, the son of the chancellor of Henri III and Henri IV, who built the first château here in 1634. Upon finding his wife Françoise carrying on with a page, he killed the page and offered his spouse two choices: She could swallow poison or have his sword plunged into her heart. She elected the less bloody method. Perhaps to erase the memory, he had the castle torn down and the present one built for his second wife. Designed in classic Louis XIII style, it boasts square pavilions flanking the central pile.

Inside, you'll be impressed by the antique furnishings, tapestries, and objets d'art. A 17th-century French artist, Jean Mosnier, decorated the fireplace with motifs from the legend of Adonis. The Guards' Room contains a collection of medieval armor; also on display is a Gobelin tapestry depicting the abduction of Helen of Troy. In the king's bedchamber, another Gobelin traces the trials of Ulysses. Most impressive is the stone stairway of carved fruit and flowers.

The château is open daily: November to February from 9:30am to noon and 2:15 to 5pm; in March, the last part of September, and October, it closes at 5:30pm; in April and May, at 6:30pm; and from June to mid-September, at 6:45pm. Admission is 35F (5.30, $5.10) for adults, 17F (2.60, $2.45) for children 7 to 14, and 6 and under are free. Allow 2 hours to see Cheverny.

ESSENTIALS

GETTING THERE   Cheverny is 12 miles south of Blois, along D765. It's best reached by **car** or on an organized **bus tour** from Blois. From the railway station at Blois, there's a bus that departs for Cheverny once a day, at noon, returning to Blois 4 hours later, according to an oft-changing schedule that varies by the season and the day of the week. Frankly, most visitors find it a lot easier to take their own car or a **taxi** from the railway station at Blois.

ACCOMMODATIONS & DINING

Les Trois Marchands TRADITIONAL FRENCH   This much-renovated coaching inn, more comfortable than St-Hubert, has been handed down for many generations. Today, Jean-Jacques Bricault owns the three-story building with awnings, a mansard roof, a glassed-in courtyard, and sidewalk tables with bright umbrellas. In the tavern-style dining room, the menu might include foie gras, lobster salad, frogs' legs, fresh asparagus in mousseline sauce, or fish cooked in a salt crust. The inn rents 37 well-furnished, comfortable rooms, costing 270F to 360F (41.05 to 54.70, $39.15 to $52.20) for a double with bathroom.

Place de l'Eglise, 41700 Cour-Cheverny. © **02-54-79-96-44.** Fax 02-54-79-25-60. Main courses 70F–185F (10.65– 28.10, $10.15–$26.85); fixed-price menu 127F–260F (19.30– 39.50, $18.40–$37.70). AE, DC, MC, V. Tues–Sun noon–2:15pm and 7:30–9:15pm. Closed Feb 1–March 15. **Amenities:** Restaurant; laundry/dry cleaning. *In room:* TV.

St-Hubert TRADITIONAL FRENCH   About 500 yards from the château, this inn was built in the 1950s in the provincial style. The least expensive menu might include terrine of quail, pike-perch with beurre blanc, some cheeses, and a homemade fruit tart. The most expensive menu may offer lobster, an aiguillette of duckling prepared with grapes, salmon braised in local white wine, casserole of seafood with shellfish sauce, and, in season, wild boar in cream sauce. The St-Hubert offers 19 conservatively decorated rooms with bathroom, charging 250F to 330F (38 to 50.15, $36.25 to $47.85) for a double.

Route Nationale. 41700 Cour-Cheverny. © **02-54-79-96-60.** Fax 02-54-79-21-17. Main courses 75F–110F
(11.40– 16.70, $10.90–$15.95); fixed-price menu 80F–220F (12.15– 33.45, $11.60–$31.90).
AE, MC, V. Daily 12:15–2pm and 7:30–9:30pm. Closed Feb and Sun nights in off-season. **Amenities:** Restaurant. *In room:* TV.

7 Valençay

145 miles SW of Paris, 35 miles S of Blois

One of the Loire's most handsome Renaissance châteaux, the **Château de
Valençay** *★★* (© **02-54-00-10-66**) was acquired in 1803 by Talleyrand on the
orders of Napoléon, who wanted his minister of foreign affairs to receive dignitaries in style. In 1838, Talleyrand was buried at Valençay, and the château
passed to his nephew, Louis de Talleyrand-Périgord. The d'Estampes family built
Valençay in 1550. The dungeon and west tower are of this period, as is the main
body of the building, but other wings were added in the 17th and 18th centuries. The effect is grandiose, with domes and turrets.

The private apartments are open to the public; they're sumptuously furnished, mostly in the Empire style but with Louis XV and Louis XVI trappings
as well. A star-footed table in the main drawing room is said to have been the
one on which the Final Agreement of the Congress of Vienna was signed in June
1815 (Talleyrand represented France).

Visits to Valençay are more detailed (and last about 45 minutes longer) than
those to other châteaux in the valley. The Musée de Talleyrand that used to stand
on the premises is now closed, but some of the collection is displayed in the new
rooms of the castle. In the park is a museum of 60 antique cars (ca. 1890–1950).
After your visit to the main buildings, you can walk through the garden and deer
park. On the grounds are many exotic birds, including flamingos.

Admission to the castle, the antique-car museum, and the park is 50F (7.60,
$7.25) for adults, 37F (5.60, $5.35) for seniors, students, and children 17 and
under. The prices goes up to 53F (8.05, $7.70) in July and August. It's open
April through June and September through October, daily from 10am to 6pm;
July and August, daily from 9:30am to 6:30pm; and November through March,
on Saturday, Sunday, and school holidays from 2 to 5pm. Allow 1½ hours to see
the castle.

ESSENTIALS
GETTING THERE   If you're **driving** from Tours, take N76 east, turning
south on D956 to Valençay. From Blois, follow D956 south. There are frequent
SNCF rail connections from Blois. For train information and schedules, call
© **08-36-35-35-35.**

VISITOR INFORMATION   The **Office de Tourisme** is on route de Blois
(© **02-54-00-04-42**).

ACCOMMODATIONS & DINING
Hôtel d'Espagne   This former coaching inn is maintained by the Fourré family, which provides an old-world ambience. The unique rooms are named after
different ancestral manor houses in the region. Bathrooms are exceedingly well
maintained, equipped with combination shower and tubs and hair dryers.
Lunch is served in the dining room or gardens Tuesday through Sunday. The
cuisine is Loire/French, and specialties include noisettes of lamb with tarragon
and sweetbreads with morels. Fixed-price menus range from 180F to 260F
(27.35 to 39.50, $26.10 to $37.70). Reservations are recommended.

9 rue du Château, 36600 Valençay. ℂ **02-54-00-00-02.** Fax 02-54-00-12-63. 16 units. 450F–650F (68.40–98.80, $65.25–$94.25) double; 900F (136.80, $130.50) suite. AE, DC, MC, V. Parking 25F (3.80, $3.65). Closed Feb. **Amenities:** Restaurant. *In room:* TV.

8 Chaumont-sur-Loire

124 miles SW of Paris, 25 miles E of Tours

On the morning when Diane de Poitiers crossed the drawbridge, the **Château de Chaumont** ✹✹ (ℂ 02-54-51-26-26) looked grim, with its battlements and pepper-pot turrets crowning the towers. Henri II, her lover, had recently died. The king had given her Chenonceau, but his angry widow, Catherine de Médici, forced her to trade her favorite château for Chaumont. Inside, portraits reveal that Diane truly deserved her reputation as forever beautiful. Another portrait—of Catherine looking like a devout nun—invites unfavorable comparisons.

Chaumont (Burning Mount), was built by Charles d'Amboise during the reign of Louis XII. Overlooking the Loire, it's approached by a long walk up from the village through a tree-studded park. It was privately owned until the state acquired it in 1938. The castle spans the period between the Middle Ages and the Renaissance, and its prize exhibit is a collection of medallions by the Italian artist Nini. A guest of the château, he made medallion portraits of kings, queens, and nobles—even Benjamin Franklin, who once visited. In the bedroom occupied by Catherine de Médici, you can see a portrait of the Italian-born queen, painted when she was young. The superstitious Catherine always kept her astrologer, Cosimo Ruggieri, at her beck and call, housing him in one of the tower rooms (a portrait of him remains). He reportedly foretold the disasters awaiting her sons, including Henri III. In Ruggieri's room, an unusual tapestry depicts Medusa with a flying horse escaping from her head.

The château is open January to mid-March and October to December, daily from 10am to 4:30pm; mid-March to September, daily from 9:30am to 6pm. Admission is 32F (4.85, $4.65) for adults, 21F (3.20, $3.05) for children 12 to 17, and children 11 and under are free. Allow 2 hours to see Chaumont.

ESSENTIALS

GETTING THERE   Seventeen **trains** per day travel to Chaumont from Blois (trip time: 15 minutes) and Tours (trip time: about 45 minutes). One-way fares are 20F (3.05, $2.90) from Blois or 46F (7.00, $6.65) from Tours. The railway station servicing Chaumont is in Onzain, 1½ miles north of the château, a nice walk. For transportation information, call ℂ **08-36-35-35-35.**

VISITOR INFORMATION   The **Office de Tourisme** is on rue du Maréchal-Leclerc (ℂ 02-54-20-91-73).

ACCOMMODATIONS & DINING

Domaine des Hauts de Loire ✹✹✹   Less than 2 miles from the Château de Chaumont, on the opposite side of the Loire, this Relais & Châteaux property is a manor house built by the owner of a Paris-based newspaper in 1840 and called, rather coyly at the time, a "hunting lodge." It's the most appealing stopover in the neighborhood, with a roster of intensely decorated rooms in Louis Philippe or Empire style. About half the rooms are in the less desirable half-timbered annex that was originally the stables.

The stately dining room is open to nonguests who phone in advance. Its well-prepared food is a local favorite. Menus include a salad of marinated eel with shallot-flavored vinaigrette; oysters on a layered sheet of sardines; roasted filet of Loire Valley whitefish (sandre) served with parsley-flavored cream sauce and cabbage stuffed with a compote of snails; and the ultimate Loire Valley main course, a filet of smoked eel prepared with Vouvray wine.

Route d'Herbault, 41150 Onzain. © **02-54-20-72-57.** Fax 02-54-20-77-32. 35 units. 700F–1,500F (106.40– 228, $101.50–$217.50) double; from 1,850F (281.20, $268.25) suite. AE, DC, MC, V. Closed Dec–Feb. **Amenities:** Restaurant, bar. *In room:* TV, minibar, hair dryer.

9 Amboise

136 miles SW of Paris, 22 miles E of Tours

Amboise is on the banks of the Loire in the center of vineyards known as Touraine-Amboise. Unlike Tours, this is still a real Renaissance town. That's the good news. The bad news: Because it is so beautiful, it's overrun by tour buses, especially in summer. Many townspeople still talk about Mick Jagger's recent purchase of a nearby château. A much earlier resident of Amboise was Leonardo da Vinci, the quintessential Renaissance man, who spent his last years here.

ESSENTIALS

GETTING THERE   Amboise lies on the main Paris-Blois-Tours rail line, with 14 **trains** per day arriving from both Tours and Blois. The trip from Tours takes only 20 minutes and costs 30F (4.55, $4.35) one-way; the trip from Blois also takes 20 minutes and costs 34F (5.15, $4.95). About five conventional trains per day depart from Paris's Gare d'Austerlitz from Paris (trip time: 2½ hours), and several high-speed TGV trains depart from the Gare Montparnasse for the village of St-Pierre-des-Corps, less than a mile from Tours. From St-Pierre-des-Corps, you can transfer onto a conventional train bound for Amboise. Fares from Paris to Amboise, depending on which route and which method you opt for, cost from 142F to 263F (21.60 to 40, $20.64 to $38.15). For information, call © **08-36-35-35-35.**

If you prefer to travel to Amboise by bus, **Autocars de Touraine** (© **02-47-05-30-49**), which operates out of the Gare Routière in Tours, just across from the town's railway station, runs about six **buses** every day between Tours and Amboise. Each takes about 40 minutes and costs 13F (2.00, $1.90) one-way.

If you're **driving** from Tours, take N152 east to D32 and then turn south, following the signs to Amboise.

VISITOR INFORMATION   The **Office de Tourisme** is on quai du Général-de-Gaulle (© **02-47-57-09-28**).

EXPLORING THE TOWN

Château d'Amboise ✦✦   This 15th-century château, which dominates the town, was the first in France to reflect the Italian Renaissance. A combination of both Gothic and Renaissance styles, it is mainly associated with Charles VIII, who built it on a rocky spur separating the valleys of the Loire and the Amasse.

You enter via a ramp that opens onto a panoramic terrace fronting the river. At one time, this terrace was surrounded by buildings; fêtes were staged in the enclosed courtyard. The castle fell into decline during the Revolution, and today only about a quarter remains of this once-sprawling edifice. You first come to the Flamboyant Gothic Chapelle de St-Hubert, distinguished by its lacelike tracery. Today, tapestries cover the walls of the château's grandly furnished rooms. The *Logis du Roi* (king's apartment) escaped destruction and is open to visitors.

It was built against the Tour des Minimes (it's also known as the Tour des Cavaliers), and was noteworthy for its ramp that horsemen could ride up. The other notable tower is the Heurtault, which is broader than the Minimes, with thicker walls.

© 02-47-57-00-98. Admission 41F (6.25, $5.95) adults, 34F (5.15, $4.95) students, 22F (3.35, $3.20) children, free for children 6 and under. July–Aug daily 9am–7:30pm; April–June daily 9am–6:30pm; Sept–Oct daily 9am–6pm; Nov–March daily 9am–noon and 2–5:30pm.

Clos-Lucé ☆ Set within a 2-mile walk from the base of Amboise's château, this brick-and-stone building was constructed in the 1400s, and later served as a retreat for Anne de Bretagne, who, according to legend, spent a lot of her time here praying and meditating. Later François I installed "the great master in all forms of art and science," Leonardo himself. Venerated by the Chevalier King, Leonardo da Vinci lived here for 3 years, until his death in 1519. (Those paintings of Leonardo dying in François's arms are probably symbolic; the king was supposedly out of town at the time.) Today, the site functions as a small museum, offering insights into the life of da Vinci and a sense of the decorative arts of this era.

2 rue de Clos-Lucé. © 02-47-57-62-88. Admission 39F (5.95, $5.65) adults, 32F (4.85, $4.65) students, 20F (3.05, $2.90) children 6–15, free for children 6 and under. Daily 9am–6pm. Closed Dec 25.

ATTRACTIONS ON THE OUTSKIRTS

The region around Amboise has recently been accented with attractions that resemble a mix of Disney's Animal Kingdom and the court of the Renaissance kings. The most frequently visited lies 6 miles west of Amboise, the **Aquarium de Touraine, Parc des Mini-Châteaux** (© **02-47-23-44-44**). Opened in 1994, it contains tanks and aquariums whose water surface covers more than 4,000 square yards. More than 10,000 freshwater and saltwater fish, including about a half-dozen sharks, live within replicas of their natural habitats. Entrance to the aquarium costs 59F (8.95, $8.55) for adults and 39F (5.95, $5.65) for children under 16. At the same address (and same phone) is the Parc des Mini-Châteaux, where small-scale replicas of France's most famous castles have been built at ¹⁄₂₅ the size of the originals. Chambord, for example, is reduced to a maximum height of less than 11 feet. It's all very patriotic—a sort of learning game that teaches French schoolchildren the glories of their native *patrimoine,* and provides architecture enthusiasts with an easy-to-compare digest of some of the most celebrated architecture in Europe. Admission is 65F (9.90, $9.45) for adults and 45F (6.85, $6.55) for children, free for children 5 and under. Hours for both of these sites vary from week to week, according to the season and schedule of special exhibits—do call in advance to reconfirm the hours. To get here from Amboise, follow the signs to Tours and take RD751 along the southern bank of the Loire. The aquarium is half a mile beyond the village of Lussault-sur-Loire (it's clearly marked on the highway). Whereas the aquarium is open year-round, the Parc des Mini-Châteaux is open only from April to mid-November.

ACCOMMODATIONS

Belle-Vue This modest inn lies at the bridge crossing the Loire at the foot of the château. Rooms are furnished in an old-fashioned French style, with low beds and rather thin mattresses. Try to stay in the main building, which has more charm and character than the less convenient annex across the river. Breakfast is the only meal served.

12 quai Charles-Guinot, 37400 Amboise. © 02-47-57-02-26. Fax 02-47-30-51-23. 32 units. 446F (67.80, $64.65) double. Rates include breakfast. MC, V. Closed Nov 15–Mar 15. *In room:* TV.

Hostellerie du Château-de-Pray ★
One mile west of the town center, this château from 1224 resembles a tower-flanked castle on the Rhine. Inside, you'll find antlers, hunting trophies, and a paneled drawing room with a fireplace and a collection of antique oils. Rooms in the main building were renovated in 1998 and are conservative and comfortable. The more spacious chambers are near the ground floor. Small but well-organized bathrooms contain tubs and showers. Try to avoid the four rooms in the 1990s annex; they're rather impersonally furnished and lack character. The restaurant, open to nonguests, offers Loire cuisine and fixed-price menus of excellent quality; reservations are required.

Route de Chargé (D-751), 37400 Amboise. © 02-47-57-23-67. Fax 02-47-57-32-50. www.chateauxethotels.com. 19 units. 590F–1,020F (89.70– 155.05, $94.40–$163.20) double; 990F–1,290F (150.53–196.13., $158.40–$206.40) suite. Breakfast and dinner 500F (76, $72.50) per person extra. AE, DC, MC, V. Closed Jan 2–Feb 10. Free parking. **Amenities:** Restaurant; baby-sitting; laundry/dry cleaning. *In room:* TV, hair dryer.

Le Choiseul ★★★
There's no better address in Amboise and no better place for cuisine than this 18th-century hotel, set in the valley between a hillside and the Loire River. Guest rooms, 16 of which are air-conditioned, are luxurious; though recently modernized, they've retained their old-world charm. The small bathrooms contain combination tub and showers. The formal dining room has a view of the Loire and welcomes nonguests who phone ahead. The food is better than that in Tours or the surrounding area. The formal dining room, the best in town, offers views of the Loire and the garden with flowering terraces; nonguests who phone ahead for a table are welcome. The cuisine is deluxe, international, classic French, and regional, utilizing only the freshest of ingredients and high-quality products. On the grounds is a garden with flowering terraces.

36 quai Charles-Guinot, 37400 Amboise. © 02-47-30-45-45. Fax 02-47-30-46-10. www.choiseul.com. 32 units. 950F–1,450F (144.40– 220.40, $137.75–$210.25) double; 1,550F–1,950F (235.60– 296.40, $224.75–$282.75) suite. AE, DC, MC, V. Closed Dec 16–Feb 3. **Amenities:** Restaurant, bar; pool; tennis court; room service; baby-sitting; laundry/dry cleaning. *In room:* A/C, TV, minibar, hair dryer.

Le Fleuray ★ *Finds*
One of the most appealing hotels in the region is this well-maintained, pink-stucco manor house administered by English expatriates Peter and Hazel Newington. Built in the mid-1800s as the centerpiece for a large farm, it's a marvel of country-living grandeur, partly because of the masses of geraniums, marigolds, and flowering vines that adorn the masonry in warm weather. Mick Jagger has discovered the place; he stays here whenever he feels another nervous breakdown coming on. Bedrooms are cozy and homey, dotted with antique accessories evoking an elegant but not terribly formal country house in England. Although rooms come with phones, don't expect a lot of modern amenities. Bathrooms are compact but well organized, each with a shower.

There's a restaurant on the premises that would be a mistake for you to miss; local residents flock here for the excellent food. Menu items include dates stuffed with warm Roquefort cheese; pork pâté with onions and chutney; and Creole-style chicken in a curry-flavored cream sauce garnished with pineapples.

37530 Cangey. © 02-47-56-09-25. Fax 02-47-56-93-97. www.lefleurayhotel.com. 14 units. 475F–580F (72.20– 88.15, $68.90–$84.10) double. MC, V. Free parking. From Amboise, take the N152 northeast of town, following the signs to Blois. Turn onto the D74, direction Cangey, which you'll reach after a total distance from Amboise of 7½ miles. **Amenities:** Restaurant.

DINING

The finest dining choice is **Le Choiseul.** The restaurant at **Le Fleuray** is also excellent (see "Accommodations," above).

Le Manoir St-Thomas ✦ TRADITIONAL FRENCH   The best food in town outside of Le Choiseul is served at this Renaissance house in the shadow of the château. Set in a pleasant garden, the elegant dining room is richly decorated with a polychrome ceiling and a massive stone fireplace. Owner and chef François Le Coz's specialties include truffles with foie gras, lamb filet with port, and red mullet filet with cream of sweet pepper sauce. The tender saddle of hare is perfectly flavored. Some unique culinary delights are the goose liver pâté wrapped in a combination of truffles and wild black mushrooms, and duck flavored with honey, cinnamon, and ginger.

Place Richelieu. tel] **02-47-57-22-52.** Reservations required. Main courses 130F–150F (19.75– 22.80, $18.85–$21.75); fixed-price menu 179F–305F (27.20– 46.35, $25.95–$44.25). AE, DC, MC, V. Tues 7:15–9:30pm; Wed–Sat 12:15–2:30pm and 7:15–9:30pm; Sun 12:15–2:30pm. Closed Jan 15–March 15.

10 Chenonceaux

139 miles SW of Paris, 16 miles E of Tours

A Renaissance masterpiece, the **Château de Chenonceau** ✦✦✦ (**©** **02-47-23-90-07**) is best known for the *dames de Chenonceau,* who once occupied it. (Note that the village, whose year-round population is less than 300, is spelled with a final "x," but the château isn't.)

In 1547, Henri II gave Chenonceau to his mistress, Diane de Poitiers, 20 years his senior. For a time this remarkable woman was virtually queen of France, infuriating Henri's dour wife, Catherine de Médici. Diane's critics accused her of using magic to preserve her celebrated beauty and to keep Henri's attentions from waning. Apparently Henri's love for Diane continued unabated, although she was in her 60s when he died in a jousting tournament in 1559.

When Henri died, Catherine became regent (her eldest son was still a child) and wasted no time in forcing Diane to return the jewelry Henri had given her and to abandon her beloved home. Catherine added her own touches, building a two-story gallery across the bridge—obviously inspired by her native Florence.

Today, Chenonceau is one of the most remarkable castles in France because it spans an entire river. The way the waters of the Cher river surge and foam beneath its vaulted medieval foundations has been described as mystical by visitors, many of whom consider it their favorite château in all of France.

Many of the château's walls are covered with Gobelin tapestries, including one depicting a woman pouring water over the back of an angry dragon. The chapel contains a marble Virgin and Child by Murillo as well as portraits of Catherine de Médici in her traditional black and white, looking like Whistler's mother. There's even a portrait of the stern Catherine in the former bedroom of her rival, Diane de Poitiers, obviously disapproving of the what took place here between Diane and Henri II. In François I's Renaissance bedchamber, the most interesting portrait is that of Diane as the huntress Diana.

The history of Chenonceau is related in 15 tableaux in the **Musée de Cire** (wax museum), located in a Renaissance-era annex a few steps from the château. Open during the same hours as the château, it charges an admission of 10F (1.50, $1.45) for adults, students, and children. Diane de Poitiers, who, among other activities, introduced the artichoke to France, is depicted in three tableaux. One portrays Catherine de Médici tossing out her husband's mistress.

The château is open daily, mid-March to mid-September from 9am to 7pm; the rest of the year, it closes between 4:30 and 6pm. Admission is 50F (7.60, $7.25) for adults and 35F (5.30, 5.10) for children 7 to 15. A *son-et-lumière* spectacle, *The Era of the Ladies of Chenonceaux,* is staged daily in summer at 10:15pm; admission is 50F (7.60, $7.25) for adults, 35F (5.30, 5.10) for children, and children 6 and under are free. Allow 2 hours to see this château.

ESSENTIALS

GETTING THERE   There are four daily **trains** from Tours to Chenonceaux (trip time: 30 minutes), costing 32F (4.85, $4.65) one-way. The train deposits you at the base of the château; from here, you can either walk or take a taxi.

VISITOR INFORMATION   The **Syndicat d'Initiative** (tourist office) is at 1 rue Bretonneau (© **02-47-23-94-45**), open from Easter to September.

ACCOMMODATIONS

Hôtel du Bon-Laboureur et du Château ★★   This inn is within walking distance of the château and is your best bet for a comfortable night's sleep and some of the best cuisine in the Loire Valley. Founded in 1786, the hotel maintains the flavor of that era, thanks to thick walls, solid masonry, and a scattering of antiques. Most bedrooms are small, especially those on the upper floors. The rear garden has a little guest house and formally planted roses. The place is noted for its restaurant, which receives fewer bus groups than many of its competitors. In fair weather, tables are set up in the courtyard, amid trees and flowering shrubs. Fixed-price menus cost 170F to 370F (25.85 to 56.25, $24.65 to $53.65).

6 rue du Dr. Bretonneau, Chenonceaux, 37150 Bléré. © **02-47-23-90-02**. Fax 02-47-23-82-01. bon-laboureur.fr@lemel.fr. 29 units. 420F–850F (63.85– 129.20, $60.90–$123.25) double; 850F–1,000F (129.20– 152, $123.25–$145) suite. AE, DC, MC, V. **Amenities:** Restaurant, bar; pool; room service; babysitting; laundry/dry cleaning. *In room:* A/C, TV, kitchenette, hair dryer.

La Roseraie ★ *Value*   Thanks to hoteliers Laurent and Sophie Fiorito, who upgraded this hotel in 1993, La Roseraie is the most charming in Chenonceaux, with individually decorated rooms and well-kept gardens. In the 1940s, its guests included Winston Churchill, Eleanor Roosevelt, and Harry Truman. Some of the finest meals in town are served at lunch and dinner in the restaurant, which is open to the public. Our favorites include house-style foie gras; magret of duckling with pears and cherries; and an unusual and delicious invention—*emincée* (a dish made with braised meat) of rump steak with wine-marinated pears.

7 rue du Dr. Bretonneau, Chenonceaux, 37150 Bléré. © **02-47-23-90-09**. Fax 02-47-23-91-59. 17 units. 280F–800F (42.55– 121.60, $40.60–$116) double; 1,100F (167.20, $159.50) suite. AE, DC, MC, V. Closed Dec to mid-Feb. **Amenities:** Restaurant, bar; pool; laundry/dry cleaning. *In room:* TV, hair dryer.

DINING

Note that **La Renaudière,** 24 rue du Dr.-Bretonneau (© **02-47-23-90-04**), and **La Roseraie** (see above) boast very good restaurants.

Au Gateau Breton TRADITIONAL FRENCH   The sun terrace in back of this Breton-type inn, a short walk from the château, is a refreshing place for dinner or tea. Gravel paths run among beds of pink geraniums and lilacs, and the red tables are adorned with bright umbrellas. In cool months, meals are served in the rustic dining rooms. Make a meal of the home cooking and cherry liqueur—a specialty of the region. Specialties include small chitterling sausages of Tours, chicken with Armagnac sauce, and *coq au vin*. The medallions of veal with mushroom-cream sauce are excellent. Tasty pastries are sold in the front room.

16 rue du Dr. Bretonneau. (℃ **02-47-23-90-14.** Fax 02-47-23-92-57. Reservations required July–Aug. Fixed-price menu 68F (10.35, $9.85), 180F (27.35, $26.10). MC, V. May–Sept Tues 7–9:30pm, Wed 11:30am–2pm, Thurs–Mon 11:30am–2pm and 7–9:30pm; Oct–Apr Thurs–Tues 11:30am–2:30pm and 7–9:30pm.

11 Tours (★)

144 miles SW of Paris, 70 miles SW of Orléans

Though it doesn't boast a major château, Tours, at the junction of the Loire and Cher rivers, is the traditional center for exploring the valley. The devout en route to Santiago de Compostela in northwest Spain once stopped off here to pay homage at the tomb of St-Martin, the Apostle of Gaul, who was bishop of Tours in the 4th century. One of the most significant conflicts in world history, the 732 Battle of Tours, checked the Arab advance into Gaul.

With a population of 130,000, Tours is a major city, known for its fine food and wine. Because many of its buildings were bombed in World War II, ugly 20th-century apartment towers have taken the place of stately châteaux. However, since Tours is at the doorstep of some of the most magnificent châteaux in France, it makes a good base from which to explore. Most Loire Valley towns are rather sleepy, but Tours is where the action is centered, as you'll see by its noisy streets and cafes. A quarter of the residents are students, who add a vibrant, active touch to a soulless commercial enclave.

Allow a morning or an afternoon to see Tours.

ESSENTIALS

GETTING THERE   Tours is a 55-minute TGV **train** ride from Paris's Montparnasse. Nearly 10 trains per day make this run, costing 207F to 264F (31.45 to 40.15, $30 to $38.30) one-way. Trains arrive at place du Maréchal-Leclerc, 3 rue Edouard-Vaillant (℃ **08-36-35-35-35** for information and schedules). If you're **driving,** take highway A10 to Tours.

VISITOR INFORMATION   The **Office de Tourisme** is at 78 rue Bernard-Palissy (℃ **02-47-70-37-37**).

EXPLORING THE CITY

The heart of town is place Jean-Jaurès. The principal street is rue Nationale, running north to the Loire River. Head west along rue du Commerce and rue du Grand-Marché to Vieux Tours/Vieille Ville (Old Town).

In the pedestrian area of rue de Bordeaux, starting to the right of the magnificent train station (facing the station) and running to rue Nationale, you'll find dozens of mall-type shops and department stores selling clothes, shoes, jewelry, leather goods, and the like. Up rue Nationale toward the river are more stores, more upscale for clothing, as well as a small, mall with chain boutiques. Rue Nationale continues across the river, but turn left on rue du Commerce toward the old town center. You'll want to explore this district's small streets and courtyards for regional specialties, books, toys, and crafts. A hotbed for antiques is east of rue Nationale (toward the cathedral), along rue de la Scellerie. If you like to search through secondhand items, place de la Victoire is the place to be every Wednesday and Saturday from 7am to 5pm for an open-air flea market.

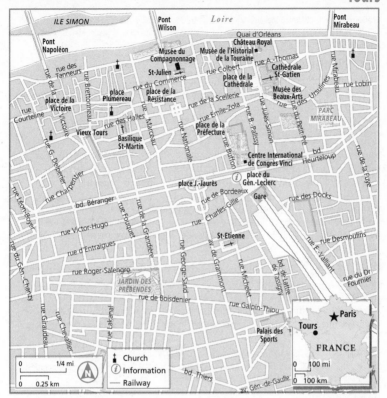

Cathédrale St-Gatien   This cathedral, which honors a 3rd-century evangelist, has a flamboyant Gothic facade flanked by towers with bases from the 12th century, though the lanterns are Renaissance. The choir is from the 13th century, with new additions built each century through the 16th. Sheltered inside is the handsome 16th-century tomb of Charles VIII and Anne de Bretagne's two children. Some of the glorious stained-glass windows are from the 13th century.

5 place de la Cathédrale. ℂ **02-47-71-21-00.** Free admission. Daily 9am–7pm.

Musée des Beaux-Arts   This fine provincial museum is in the Palais des Archevêques, which would be worth a visit to see its lovely rooms and gardens. There are old masters here as well, including works by Degas, Delacroix, Rembrandt, and Boucher. The sculpture collection includes works by Houdon and Bourdelle. You can tour the gardens for free daily from 7am to 8:30pm.

18 place François-Sicard. ℂ **02-47-05-68-73.** Admission 30F (4.55, $4.35) adults, 15F (2.30, $2.20) children under 16. Wed–Mon 9am–12:45pm and 2–6pm.

Musée de l'Historial de la Touraine (Musée Grévin)   This museum traces the tormented tides of change that have swept over the Loire Valley. It depicts the region's history in 31 kitschy but evocative scenes with 165 wax figures. They follow 1,500 years of interaction between locals and such personalities as Charlemagne and his queen, Luitgarde; St-Martin and assorted bishops; Clovis, king of the Visigoths; and Joan of Arc. Other scenes simulate the death of Henry V and the hangings of the Huguenots during the Wars of Religion.

Château Royal, 25 av. André-Malraux. ℂ **02-47-61-02-95**. Admission 35F (5.30, $5.10) adults, 20F (3.05, $2.90) children 7–15, children 6 and under free. July–Aug daily 9am–6:30pm; May 16–June and Sept–Oct daily 9am–noon and 2–6pm; Nov–March 15 daily 2–5:30pm.

ACCOMMODATIONS

The most sumptuous rooms, as well as the finest cuisine, are found at the **Parc de Belmont** (see Château Belmont under "Dining," below).

Best Western Le Central Set off the main boulevard, this old-fashioned hotel is within walking distance of the river and cathedral, surrounded by gardens, lawns, and trees. Built in 1850, it is a more modest but economical choice than others in town. The Tremouilles family offers comfortable rooms at reasonable rates. Accommodations come in a variety of shapes and sizes; a renovation in 1999 improved them and updated the plumbing in the small bathrooms.

21 rue Berthelot, 37000 Tours. ℂ **800/528-1234** in the U.S. or Canada, or 02-47-05-46-44. Fax 02-47-66-10-26. www.tour-online.com/central-hotel. 40 units, 38 with bathroom. 450F–550F (68.40– 83.60, $65.25–$79.75) double without bathroom, 580F–750F (88.15– 114, $84.10–$108.75) double with bathroom. AE, DC, MC, V. Parking 40F (6.10, $5.80). Bus: 1, 4, or 5. **Amenities:** Bar; room service; baby-sitting; laundry/dry cleaning. *In room:* A/C, TV, minibar, hair dryer.

Hôtel de l'Univers This hotel, on the main artery of Tours, was erected in 1853, making it the oldest in town. The guest rooms, decorated partly with modern pieces and partly with Art Deco pieces, are beginning to look a bit worn, although this remains the city's most popular traditional hotel. On weekdays, it's filled with business travelers, while on weekends, it hosts many area brides.

5 bd. Heurteloup, 37000 Tours. ℂ **02-47-05-37-12**. Fax 02-47-61-51-80. www.hotel-univers.loirevalley.com. 85 units. 910F (138.30, $131.95) double. AE, DC, MC, V. Parking 50F (7.60, $8). Bus 1, 4, or 5. **Amenities:** Restaurant, bar; room service; baby-sitting; laundry/dry cleaning. *In room:* A/C, TV, hair dryer.

Hôtel du Manoir On a quiet street near the train station with shops and restaurants, this 19th-century residence provides guests with a comfortable place. The cheerful reception area is an indication of the quality of the rooms. Though small to average, all units have windows that let in lots of light and afford views of the neighborhood or the hotel's courtyard. Most have simple furnishings.

2 rue Traversière, 37000 Tours. ℂ **02-47-05-37-37**. Fax 02-47-05-16-00. 20 units. 270F–290F (41.05– 44.10, $39.15–$42.05) double. DC, MC, V. Parking 15F (2.30, $2.40) per day. Bus: 3, 70. *In room:* A/C, TV.

DINING

Restaurants in Tours can be pricey, but you can keep costs low at **La Souris Gourmande,** 100 rue Colbert (ℂ **02-47-47-04-80**), where the chef is hung up on the diversity of cheese. Try it in half a dozen fondues, each made from a different region of France. You might be asked to join a communal table. Main courses cost from 40F to 82F (6.10 to 12.45, $5.80 to $11.90). The raffish but cheerful bistro **Le Lapin qui,** 90 rue Colbert (ℂ **02-47-66-95-49**), serves cheap eats costing from 76F to 150F (11.55 to 22.80, $11 to $21.75).

VERY EXPENSIVE

Parc de Belmont (Jean Bardet) ✦ MODERN FRENCH Set in three rooms of a 19th-century château, this restaurant is the creation of the Michelin two-star chef Jean Bardet, who considers all meals here to be "an orchestration of wines, alcohol, food, and cigars." That's not to say that you must partake of all four to have one of the best meals in the region. Spectacular specialties include a lobster ragout, sliced sea bass with a confit of tomatoes and artichoke hearts, and scallops with a purée of shallots and truffle cream. The duck giblets and lobster accompanied by a red wine and orange sauce is reason enough to visit.

The rest of the château has been transformed into a luxury hotel and is the domain of chef Bardet's wife, Sophie. The spacious rooms are individually decorated and have high ceilings, cozy fireplaces, and antique furnishings. Some have private balconies that open onto the gardens. A double room ranges from 750F to 1,500 F(114 to 228, $120 to $240), while suites cost from 1,800F to 2,200F (273.60 to 334.40, $288 to $352).

57 rue Groison, 37100 Tours. ✆ **02-47-41-41-11.** Fax 02-47-51-68-72. Reservations recommended. Main courses 210F–380F (31.90– 57.75; $33.60–$60.80); fixed-price menu 250F–750F (38– 114, $40–$120). AE, DC, MC, V. Nov–March Tues–Sat noon–2pm and 7:30–9:30pm, Sun noon–2:30pm; Apr–Oct Tues–Sun noon–1:30pm and daily 7:30–9:30pm. Bus: 9. *In room:* A/C, TV, minibar, hair dryer.

EXPENSIVE

La Roche le Roy ★★ MODERN FRENCH   One of the hottest chefs in town, Alain Couturier, blends new and old techniques at this restaurant in a 15th-century manor south of the town center. Couturier's repertoire includes scalloped foie gras with lentils, cod with saffron cream, and pan-fried scallops with a truffle vinaigrette. His masterpiece is suprême of pigeon with "roughly textured" sauce, and a matelote of eel with chinon wine. For dessert, try his mélange of seasonal fruit with sabayon made from Vouvray Valley wine, or a hot orange soufflé.

55 rte. St-Avertin. ✆ **02-47-27-22-00.** Reservations recommended. Main courses 130F–205F (19.75– 31.15, $18.85–$29.75); fixed-price menu 250F–380F (38– 57.75, $36.25–$55.10). AE, MC, V. Tues–Sat 12:15–1:45pm and 7–10pm. Closed 3 weeks in Aug and 2 weeks in Feb. From the center of town, take av. Grammont south (follow signs to St-Avertin-Vierzon). The road crosses a bridge, but doesn't change names. The restaurant is beside that road, on the southern periphery of Tours.

MODERATE

La Rôtisserie Tourangelle TRADITIONAL FRENCH   This is a local favorite, where you can dine on the terrace in summer (though there's not much to see). It's better to concentrate on the ever-changing menu, which may include homemade foie gras and whitefish caught in the Loire served with *beurre blanc* (white butter sauce). Regional ingredients mix well with the local wines, as exemplified by pike-perch with sabayon and *magret de fillet de canard* (duckling) served with a "jam" of red Chinon wine. In summer, strawberry parfait with raspberry coulis is a perfect end to the meal.

23 rue du Commerce Tours. ✆ **02-47-05-71-21.** Reservations required. Fixed-price menu only; 160F–240F (24.30– 36.53, $25.60–$38.40) and 300F (45.60, $48). Tues–Sun 12:15–1:30pm and 7:15–9:30pm. Bus: 1, 4, or 5.

INEXPENSIVE

Le Relais Buré TRADITIONAL FRENCH   A 5-minute walk east of the center of Tours, this brasserie specializes in shellfish and regional recipes, though it's somewhat unimaginative. It has a busy bar and a front terrace, with tables scattered inside on the street level and mezzanine. Menu items include six well-flavored versions of sauerkraut; a wide choice of grilled meats, including steak au poivre; foie gras and smoked salmon; and a tempting array of desserts.

1 place de la Résistance. ✆ **02-47-05-67-74.** Main courses 68F–115F (10.35– 17.53, $10.93–$18.40), fixed-price menu (Mon–Fri only) 120F (18.25, $19.20). AE, DC, MC, V. Daily noon–2pm and 7pm–midnight. Bus: 1 or 5.

Les Tuffeaux *Value* TRADITIONAL FRENCH   This 18th-century house contains one of the best restaurants in Tours, although the cuisine at La Rôtisserie Tourangelle (see above) has a slight edge. Menu items change about once a month, depending on the inspiration of chef Gildas Marsollier, who prepares a roster of French classics but also experiments with noisettes of roasted rabbit with bacon and almonds, fricassée of chicken livers with raspberry vinegar, and braised turbot with a gratinated *viennoise* of Comté cheese. Roasted filet of pigeon with pink grapefruit is an enduring favorite. The 115F (17.50, $16.70) fixed-price menu is the best bargain in town.

19 rue Lavoisier. (C) **02-47-47-19-89.** Reservations required. Main courses 85F–110F (12.90– 16.70, $12.35–$15.95); fixed-price menu 115F–210F (17.50– 31.90, $16.70–$30.45). AE, MC, V. Tues–Sat noon–1:45pm; Mon–Sat 7–9:30pm. Bus: 1, 4, or 5.

NEARBY ACCOMMODATIONS & DINING

Château d'Artigny ★★★   This is the grandest address in the Loire Valley. About a mile west of the hamlet of Montbazon, this château was built between 1912 and 1920 for perfume and cosmetic king François Coty, who lived and entertained lavishly. The 18th-century Italianate design was inspired by an obscure villa, the Château de Champlatreux, near Paris. Set in a forest, overlooking formal gardens, this château is a combination of Jazz Age ostentation and the 18th-century French aesthetic. The drawing room and corridors are furnished with fine antiques, Louis XV–style chairs, and bronze statuary. The grounds contain acres of park and a large garden with reflecting pool.

Guest rooms are outfitted in period styles, sometimes with marble wall sheathings, many antiques, comfortable mattresses, and all the perks of upscale country living. Only 33 units are in the main building; 23 others are within three annexes that were originally built as a chapel, a gatehouse, and a mill.

Rte. d'Azay-le-Rideau (the D-17), 37250 Montbazon. (C) **02-47-34-30-30.** Fax 02-47-34-30-39. www. chateaux-hotels.com. 53 units. 1,100F–1,600F (167.20– 243.20, $159.50–$232) double; 2,350F (357.20, $340.75) suite. Half board 470F (71.45, $68.15) per person extra. AE, DC, MC, V. Closed Dec 3–Jan 13. From Tours, take N10 south for 7 miles to Montbazon, then take D17 a mile southeast. **Amenities:** Restaurant, bar; outdoor pool; fitness center; sauna; room service; baby-sitting; laundry/dry cleaning. *In room:* A/C, TV, minibar, hair dryer.

Tips **Château-Hopping Made Easy**

For folks who arrive in Tours to visit the châteaux of the Loire Valley, but who don't have a car, there's no longer a need to take the cumbersome local transport buses. Daily, year-round, the tourist office sponsors an armada of eight-passenger minibuses that depart from in front of the office between 9 and 9:30am and again between 1 and 1:30pm for tours of two to four châteaux, depending on the schedule. Based on which minibus you board, you might spend a half to a full day, costing from 100F to 185F (15.20 to 28.10, $14.50 to $26.85) per person.

The châteaux included in any given itinerary change frequently, but a full-day tour might feature brief visits to Chambord, Amboise, and Azay-le-Rideau. Since the trains from Paris take only 55 minutes each way, it makes a worthy side trip. Admission fees to the châteaux are not included in the price, but participation in the tour qualifies for reduced group rates.

Château de Beaulieu ✦✦   At this 17th-century country estate, you can experience the lifestyle of another era. Beyond the entrance, a double curving stairway leads to the reception hall. The bedrooms have mahogany and chestnut furniture, decorative fireplaces, and good plumbing. Nine are in the château (we recommend these); the others, a bit more sterile, are in a recently constructed pavilion nearby. All have elegant beds outfitted with comfortable mattresses.

67 rue de Beaulieu, 37300 Joué-les-Tours. ☎ **02-47-53-20-26.** Fax 02-47-53-84-20. 19 units. 520F–800F (79.05– 121.60, $75.40–$116) double. Half board 1,050F–1,350F (159.60– 205.20, $152.25–$195.75) for 2. AE, MC, V. Take D86 from Tours, then D207 for Beaulieu, 4¹⁄₂ miles southwest of Tours. **Amenities:** Restaurant, bar; pool and tennis courts across road; room service; laundry/dry cleaning. *In room:* A/C, TV, mini-bar, hair dryer.

TOURS AFTER DARK

Long a student town, Tours has a lively young population that demands a hip scene. Even during summer, when most students have left, the younger crowd still rules the hot spots. Place Plumereau (often shortened to "place Plume"), a square of medieval buildings, now houses a riot of restaurants and bars. In the warmer months, the square explodes with tables, which fill with people who like to see and be seen. This is the cruisy place to begin an evening out.

The most interesting clubs around place Plumereau include **Blues Rock Café,** 24 rue de la Monnaie (☎ 02-47-61-57-97), with its American memorabilia and young crowd. One popular place is the three-level bar at **37 rue Briçonnet** (☎ 02-47-05-77-17), whose tiers bear the names Le Louis XIV (the most formal and straight-laced), Le Duc (the most jazz-oriented), and Le Pharaon (the one in the cellar that plays the most disco). And perhaps the hottest place in town is **L'Excalibur,** 35 rue Briçonnet (☎ 02-47-64-76-78), with its disco beat and ultramodern video system. A clientele of all ages, many from the surrounding countryside, heads to **Le Pyms,** 170 av. de Grammont (☎ 02-47-66-22-22), an alternative disco open Tuesday through Sunday from 10:30pm to at least 4am.

If you're young, gay and you like to dance, check out **Stabily Club,** 71 rue Georges-Courteline (☎ 02-47-37-01-54). You'll want to drive here or walk in a group, as it's on a dark street in the middle of a run-down neighborhood. Inside, though, is a lively disco with a local male crowd that really packs the place on weekends. The dance floor has plenty of mirrors, flashing lights, and smoke.

12 Loches ✦✦

160 miles SW of Paris, 25 miles SE of Tours

Forever linked to legendary beauty Agnès Sorel, Loches is the *cité médiévale* of the valley, situated in the hills on the banks of the Indre. Known as the acropolis of the Loire, the château and its satellite buildings form a complex called the **Cité Royale** ✦. The House of Anjou, from which the Plantagenets descended, owned the castle from 886 to 1205. The kings of France occupied it from the mid-13th century until Charles IX became king in 1560.

Château de Loches ✦✦ at 5 place Charles-VII (☎ 02-47-59-01-32), is remembered for the *belle des belles* (beauty of beauties), Agnès Sorel. Inside is her tomb, where two angels guard her velvet cushion. In 1777, the tomb was opened, but all that remained of the 15th-century beauty were a set of dentures and some locks of hair. Maid of honor to Isabelle de Lorraine, she was singled out by Charles VII to be his mistress and had great influence on the king until her mysterious death. Afterward, Fouquet painted her as a practically topless Virgin Mary, with a disgruntled Charles VII looking on. (The original is in Antwerp, but the château has a copy.) The château also contains the oratory of Anne de Bretagne, decorated with ermine tails. One of its most outstanding treasures is *The Passion* triptych (1485) from the Fouquet school.

You can visit the château without a guide daily, July to mid-September from 9am to 7pm; mid-March to June and the last 2 weeks of September from 9:30am to 6pm; and October to mid-March from 9:30am to noon and 2 to 5pm. The dungeon opens 30 minutes after the castle and closes 1 hour after the castle. One ticket for both costs 32F (4.85, $4.65) for adults, 17F (2.630, $2.45) for children 7 to 18, 6 and under are free.

The château is the site of a *son-et-lumière* (sound-and-light) show depicting **Merlin the Magician,** "a fairy tale from the age of chivalry." The show is staged about 21 times during the months of July and August, beginning promptly at 10pm. It includes a cast of about a hundred local residents wearing medieval costumes, mingling history, lore, and legend into a highly entertaining program that's conducted entirely in French. Adults pay 70F (10.65, $10.15). Schedules vary and are announced only a few months prior to the event, so contact the tourist office of Loches (see below) if you're interested in attending.

You can visit the ancient keep (*donjon*), reached along the mail du Donjon, of the comtes d'Anjou during the same hours as the château. The Round Tower of Louis XI contains rooms used for torture; a favorite method involved suspending the victim in an iron cage. In the 15th century, the duke of Milan, Ludovico Sforza, was imprisoned in the Martelet, and he painted frescoes on the walls to pass the time; he died here in 1508.

Nearby, the Romanesque **Collegiale St-Ours** (Collegiate Church of St-Ours), 1 rue Thomas-Pactius (© **02-47-59-02-36**), spans the 10th to the 15th centuries. Its portal is decorated with sculpted figures, damaged but still attractive. Monumental stone pyramids (*dubes*) surmount the nave; the carving on the west door is exceptional. The church is open year-round daily from 9am to 7pm, except during class; free admission.

Finally, you may want to walk the ramparts and enjoy the view of the town, including a 15th-century gate and Renaissance inns.

Allow 3 hours to see Loches.

ESSENTIALS

GETTING THERE   Between 6 and 10 **buses** run here daily from Tours, costing 45F (6.85, $6.55) for the one-way, 50-minute trip. If you're **driving** from Tours, take N143 southeast to Loches.

VISITOR INFORMATION   The **Office de Tourisme** is near the bus station on place Wermelskirchen, which is referred to on some, but not all, maps as place de la Marne (© **02-47-91-82-82;** www.lochesentouraine.com).

ACCOMMODATIONS & DINING

For such a famous town, Loches is short on inns and notable restaurants. If you're here for lunch, we recommend the **Hôtel George-Sand,** 39 rue Quintefol (© **02-47-59-39-74;** fax 02-47-91-55-75), for its Touraine cuisine, including the filet of pike-perch from the Loire. It also rents 20 rooms for 270F to 450F (41.05 to 68.40, $39 to $65) for a double and 600F (91.20, $87) for a suite.

Grand Hotel de France 🖈   This is the town's leading inn. This charming and typically French hotel was a postal relay station until the mid-19th century. In

1932, three extra floors were added, and it was turned into an inn. Before the turn of the 20th century, its bedrooms were upgraded and redecorated with new beds and the small bathrooms restored. Each has a shower, but only half of them contain a tub. Many rooms overlook the courtyard, and these are the most tranquil. You can order meals in the petite dining room with wood paneling and crystal, or under the parasols in the courtyard.

6 rue Picois, 37600 Loches. ℂ **02-47-59-00-32.** Fax 02-47-59-28-66. 19 units. 300F–370F (47.50– 56.25, $43.50–$53.65) double. DC, V. Closed Jan 5–Feb 13. Parking 28F (4.25, $4.05). **Amenities:** Restaurant, bar. *In room:* TV.

13 Villandry

157 miles SW of Paris, 20 miles NE of Chinon, 11 miles W of Tours, 5 miles E of Azay-le-Rideau

The extravagant 16th-century–style gardens of the Renaissance **Château de Villandry** ★★★, 37510 Villandry (ℂ **02-47-50-02-09**), are celebrated throughout the Touraine. Forming a trio of superimposed cloisters with a water garden on the highest level, they were restored by the Spanish doctor and scientist Joachim Carvallo, grandfather of the present owner.

The grounds contain 10½ miles of boxwood sculpture, which the gardeners cut to style in only 2 weeks each September. Every square of the gardens is like a geometric mosaic. The borders represent the faces of love: tender, tragic (represented by daggers), and crazy (with a labyrinth that doesn't go anywhere). Pink tulips and dahlias suggest sweet love; red, tragic; and yellow, unfaithful. Crazy love is symbolized by all colors. The vine arbors, citrus hedges, and walks keep six men busy full time. One garden contains all the French vegetables except the potato, which wasn't known in France in the 16th century.

A feudal castle once stood at Villandry, but in 1536, Jean Lebreton, François I's chancellor, built the present château, whose buildings form a U and are surrounded by a two-sided moat. Near the gardens is a terrace from which you can see the small village and its 12th-century church.

Admission to the gardens with a tour of the château is 45F (6.85, $6.55) for adults, 38F (5.80, $5.50) for children. Visiting the gardens separately without a guide costs 33F (5, $4.80) for adults, 26F (3.95, $4.15) for children. The château is open mid-February to mid-November, and guided tours are conducted daily from 9am to 6:30pm. The gardens are open year-round from 9am to 5:30pm. Tours are given in French with leaflets in English.

There is no train service to Villandry. The nearest connection is the run from Tours to the town of Savonnières. From Savonnières, you can walk along the Loire for 2 miles to reach Villandry, rent a **bike** at the station, or take a **taxi.** You can also **drive,** following D7 from Tours. Allow 1½ hours to see Villandry.

ACCOMMODATIONS & DINING

Le Cheval Rouge MODERN FRENCH This is a well-known lunch stopover near the château, in spite of a sometimes unpleasant welcome and difficult staff. Set in a conservatively decorated dining room about 100 yards from the banks of the Cher, it won't be your most memorable meal in the Loire Valley. Specialties include lobster Thermidor, medallions of veal with morels, and turbot with hollandaise sauce. The inn also rents 20 rooms, all with private bathroom and telephone. A double is 270F (41.05, $43.20). Parking is free.

Villandry, 37510 Joué-les-Tours. ℂ 02-47-50-02-07. Fax 02-47-50-08-77. Reservations recommended. Main courses 95F–170F (14.45– 25.85, $15.20–$27.20); fixed-price menus 95F–180F (14.45– 27.35, $15.20–$28.80). MC, V. Tues–Sun noon–2pm and 7:30–9pm. Closed Feb to mid-March.

14 Langeais

161 miles SW of Paris, 16 miles W of Tours

Château de Langeais ★★ at 37130 Langeais (✆ **02-47-96-72-60**), is a true medieval fortress, a formidable gray pile that dominates the town. It's one of the few châteaux actually on the Loire. The facade is forbidding, but once you cross the drawbridge and go inside, you'll find the apartments so richly decorated that the severe effect is softened. The castle dates from the 9th century, when the dreaded Black Falcon erected the first dungeon in Europe, the ruins of which remain to this day. The present structure was built in 1465. The interior is well preserved and furnished thanks to Jacques Siegfried, who not only restored it over 20 years but also bequeathed it to the Institut de France in 1904.

On December 6, 1491, Anne de Bretagne "arrived at Langeais carried in a litter decked with gold cloth, dressed in a gown of black trimmed with sable. Her wedding gown of gold cloth was ornamented with 160 sables." Her marriage to Charles VIII was Langeais's golden hour. Their symbols—scallops, fleurs-de-lis, and ermine—set the motif for the Guard Room, while seven tapestries known as the Valiant Knights cover the walls of the Wedding Chamber.

In a bedchamber known as *The Crucifixion,* the 15th-century black-oak four-poster bed is reputed to be one of the earliest known. The room takes its name from a tapestry of the Virgin and St-John on flower-bedecked ground. A rare Flemish tapestry hangs in the Monsieur's Room. The Chapel Hall was built by joining two stories under a ceiling of Gothic arches. In the Luini Room is a large 1522 fresco by that artist, removed from a chapel on Lake Maggiore, Italy; it depicts St-Francis of Assisi and St-Elizabeth of Hungary with Mary and Joseph. The Byzantine Virgin in the Drawing Room is thought to be an early work of Cimabue, the Florentine artist. Finally, the Tapestry of the *Thousand Flowers* is a celebration of spring, a joyous riot of growth and symbol of life's renewal.

The château is open daily, July 15 to August from 9am to 9pm; April 1 to July 14 and September 1 to 30 from 9am to 6:30pm; October 1 to November 2 from 9am to 12:30pm and 2 to 6:30pm; and November 3 to March 31 from 9am to noon and 2 to 5pm (closed Christmas). Admission is 40F (6.10, $5.80) for adults, 35F (5.30, $5.10) for seniors, and 25F (3.80, $3.65) for children, 7 and under free. Allow 1½ hours to go through the château.

ESSENTIALS

GETTING THERE   Eighteen **trains** per day make a stop here en route from either Tours or Saumur. For schedules and information, call ✆ **08-36-35-35-39**. If you're **driving** from Tours, take N152 southwest to Langeais.

VISITOR INFORMATION   The **Bureau du Tourisme** is at place du 14 Julliet (✆ **02-47-96-58-22**).

ACCOMMODATIONS & DINING

Errard Hosten et Restaurant Langeais (Logis de France) ★ Value   This ivy-draped country inn offers an informal atmosphere and excellent food. The restaurant is expensive (and has received many honors), but the hotel charges reasonable rates for its well-furnished, comfortable rooms. Guests dine indoors or at tables set in the open courtyard under umbrellas and flowering trees. The *menu de prestige* includes a matelote of eel with Bourgueil red wine, or *homard* (lobster) *Cardinal.* The desserts may include soufflé au Grand-Marnier.

2 rue Gambetta, 37130 Langeais. © **02-47-96-82-12.** Fax 02-47-96-56-72. www.errard.com. 10 units. 300F–450F (46.60– 68.40, $43.50–$65.25) double; 550F (83.60, $79.75) suite. AE, MC, V. Closed Feb 15–March 30. Parking 30F (4.55, $4.35). **Amenities:** Restaurant; bar. *In room:* TV.

La Duchesse Anne   On the eastern outskirts of town, this hotel was conceived in the 18th century as a coaching inn, providing food and shelter for people and horses. The clean rooms are simply furnished but comfortable. They come in a variety of sizes and shapes, each with a good mattress and fine linen. Garden tables are set out for dining. The cuisine reflects the traditions of the Loire Valley and includes flavorful but not experimental dishes such as fresh salmon with beurre blanc sauce or guinea fowl with Bourgueil wine sauce. From April to October, the restaurant is open for lunch and dinner daily; the rest of the year, it's closed Friday night, Saturday at lunch, and Sunday night.

10 rue de Tours, 37130 Langeais. © **02-47-96-82-03.** Fax 02-47-96-68-60. 15 units, with private bathrooms. 310F–340F (47.10– 51.730, $44.95–$49.30) double. MC, V. **Amenities:** Restaurant; bar. *In room:* TV.

15 Azay-le-Rideau

162 miles SW of Paris, 13 miles SW of Tours

Its machicolated towers and blue-slate roof pierced with dormers shimmer in the moat, creating a reflection like a Monet painting. But the defensive medieval look is all for show: the Renaissance **Château d'Azay-le-Rideau** ★★, 37190 Azay-le-Rideau (© **02-47-45-42-04**), was created as a residence at an idyllic spot on the Indre River. Gilles Berthelot, François I's finance minister, commissioned the castle while his spendthrift wife, Philippa, supervised its construction. So elegant was the creation that the Chevalier King grew jealous. In time, Berthelot was accused of misappropriation of funds and forced to flee, and the château reverted to the king. He didn't live here, however, but granted it to "friends of the Crown." It became the property of the state in 1905.

Before entering, circle the château and note the perfect proportions of the crowning achievement of the Renaissance in the Touraine. Check out its most fancifully ornate feature, the bay enclosing a grand stairway with a straight flight of steps. The Renaissance interior is a virtual museum.

From the second-floor Royal Chamber, look out at the gardens. This bedroom, also known as the Green Room, is believed to have sheltered Louis XIII. The adjoining Red Chamber contains a portrait gallery that includes a *Lady in Red* and Diane de Poitiers (Henri II's favorite) in her bath.

The château is open daily: July to August from 9am to 7pm; April to June and October from 9:30am to 6pm; and November to March from 9:30am to 12:30pm and 2 to 5:30pm. Admission is 35F (5.30, $5.60) for adults and 23F (3.50, $3.70) for children. *Son-et-lumière* (sound-and-light) performances are staged from May to July at 10:30pm; in August at 10pm; and in September at 9:30pm. Tickets cost 60F (9.10, $9.60) for adults and 35F (5.30, $5.60) for children 12 and under. Allow 2 hours to see Azay-le-Rideau.

ESSENTIALS

GETTING THERE   To reach Azay-le-Rideau, take the **train** from either Tours or Chinon. Trip time is about 30 minutes; one-way fare is 27F ($4.30, $3.92). Both Tours and Chinon have express service to Paris. For SNCF bus and rail schedules to Azay-le-Rideau from virtually anywhere, call © **08-36-35-35-35.** If you're **driving** from Tours, take D759 southwest to Azay-le-Rideau.

Finds For Literary Fans: An Ode to Balzac

Three miles east of Azay-le-Rideau (take D17), you can visit **Saché,** the hometown of Honoré de Balzac, where he wrote *The Lily of the Valley* and declared his affection for the Touraine was like "the love of the artist for his art." Of interest to fans of the writer is the **Musée Balzac,** in the Château de Saché, 37190 Saché (② **02-47-26-86-50),** which contains the writer's bedrooms preserved as they were when he lived here.

A collection of Balzac's scribblings, first editions, etchings, letters, political cartoons, and even a copy of Rodin's sculpture of the writer are on display. The castle is open from July to August, daily from 10am to 6:30pm; March 15 to May 14 and in September, daily from 9:30am to noon and 2 to 6pm; May 15 to June 30, daily from 10am to 6pm; February to March 14 and in October and November, daily from 9:30am to noon and 2 to 5pm. Closed in January. Admission is 24F (3.65, $3.50) for adults, 17F (2.60, $2.45) for students and seniors, 13F (2.00, $1.90) for children 7 to 18, and free for children 6 and under.

VISITOR INFORMATION   The **Syndicat d'Initiative** (tourist office) is on place de l'Europe (② **02-47-45-44-40;** www.otsi.azay.le.rideau@wanadoo.fr).

ACCOMMODATIONS & Dining

We also recommend the restaurant at **Le Grand Monarque** (see below).

L'Aigle d'Or TRADITIONAL FRENCH   The service is professional, the welcome often charming, and the food the best in Azay. Within a dining room that's accented with ceiling beams, a fireplace, and pastel colors, you'll enjoy dishes that include a mousseline of scallops with crayfish coulis, and a *blanquette* (stew) of Loire valley whitefish prepared with one of the region's white wines. Desserts are made fresh daily and vary with the chef's moods. In summer, the party expands onto an outdoor terrace.

10 av. Adélaide-Riché. ② **02-47-45-24-58.** Reservations recommended. Main courses 95F–120F (14.45– 18.25, $13.80–$17.40); fixed price lunch 110F–160F (16.70–24.30, $15.95–$23.20); fixed price dinner 160F–265F (24.30– 40.30, $23.20–$38.45). V. Daily 12:30–2pm and 8:30–9pm. Closed Wed (year-round), Sun night (year-round); and Tues night Oct–May; also closed all of Feb and Nov 20–30.

Le Grand Monarque   The exterior of this hotel—located less than 500 feet from the château—is covered by a coat of ivy that seems to protect the interior from the modern world. As you enter the rustic manor house with its dark ceiling beams, you'll be transported to a different era. The large guest rooms are accented with deep-red tones and outfitted with antique furnishings. Half of the well-maintained bathrooms come with a combination tub and shower. In 1999, the hotel's government rating was increased from two-star to three-star status, thanks to renovations and improvements. You can enjoy a casual evening in the lounge area or in the warm dining room, whose fireplace you'd expect to see in the château across the way. During warmer months, you can dine out on the courtyard terrace. The restaurant is genuinely superb, thanks to the cuisine of talented chef Fréderic Arnault. Look for specialties that include a terrine of stingray with celery, steak of mullet prepared with the local wine of Azay, braised pig's foot served with veal drippings, and a kettle of crayfish prepared with a bouillon of exotic mushrooms.

3 place de la République, 37190 Azay-le-Rideau. ⓒ **02-47-45-40-08.** Fax 02-47-45-46-25. 25 units. 440F–650F (66.90– 98.80, $63.80–$94.25) double; 900F–950F (136.80– 144.40, $130.50–$137.75) suite. AE, MC, V. Closed Dec 15–Jan 31. Parking 40F (6.130, $5.80). **Amenities:** Restaurant, bar; room service; baby-sitting; laundry. *In room:* TV.

16 Chinon ★★

176 miles SW of Paris, 30 miles SW of Tours, 19 miles SW of Langeais

In the film *Joan of Arc,* Ingrid Bergman sought out the dauphin as he tried to conceal himself among his courtiers. The action took place in real life at the Château de Chinon, one of the oldest fortress-châteaux in France. Charles VII centered his government at Chinon from 1429 to 1450. In 1429, with the English besieging Orléans, the Maid of Orléans, that "messenger from God," prevailed upon the dauphin to give her an army. The rest is history. The seat of French power stayed at Chinon until the end of the Hundred Years War.

Today, Chinon remains a tranquil village known mainly for its delightful red wines. After you visit the attractions, we recommend taking a walk along the Vienne River; definitely stop to taste the wine at one of Chinon's terraced cafes.

Allow 3 hours to see Chinon.

ESSENTIALS

GETTING THERE   Three **trains** arrive daily from Tours (trip time: 1 hour), costing 52F (7.90, $7.55) one-way. For tickets and information, call ⓒ **08-36-35-35-35** in Tours. If you're **driving** from Tours, take D759 southwest through Azay-le-Rideau to Chinon.

VISITOR INFORMATION   The **Office de Tourisme** is at place Hoffheim (ⓒ **02-47-93-17-85**).

SPECIAL EVENTS   The best time to visit is the first weekend in August, for the celebrated **Marché Médiéval** (ⓒ **02-47-93-17-85**). This fair, marked by overtones of both the Middle Ages and the Renaissance, celebrates native son Rabelais with presentations of early music along with arts and crafts. The food is bountiful, and the wine flows freely as the whole town devotes itself to revelry.

EXPLORING THE TOWN & CHÂTEAU

Situated on the banks of the Vienne, the town of Chinon consists of winding streets and turreted houses, many built in the 15th and 16th centuries in the heyday of the court. For the best view, drive across the river and turn right onto quai Danton. From this vantage point, you'll be able to see the castle in relation to the village and the river. The gables and towers make Chinon look like a toy village. The most typical street is rue Voltaire, lined with 15th- and 16th-century town houses. At no. 44, Richard the Lion-Hearted died on April 6, 1199, from a mortal wound suffered during the siege of Chalus in Limousin. The Grand Carroi, in the heart of Chinon, served as the crossroads of the Middle Ages.

In between châteaux visits and vineyard tastings, you may want to pop into **Fleurisson Production,** 5 rue de l'Olive (ⓒ **02-47-93-21-79**). Expect a French twist to their grapes—they make not vino but *confiture de vin* (jam). Ask about purchasing products at the vineyard.

Château de Chinon ★★   The château consists of three separate buildings, two of which have been partially restored (they're still missing roofs). One of the restored buildings, Château du Milieu, dates from the 11th to the 15th centuries and contains the keep and clock tower, which houses a museum of Joan of Arc. The other, Château du Coudray, is separated from Château du Milieu by a moat, and contains the Tour du Coudray, where Joan of Arc once stayed. In the 14th century, the Knights Templar were imprisoned here (they're responsible for the graffiti) before meeting their violent deaths. Some of the grim walls from other dilapidated edifices remain, although many buildings—including the Great Hall where Joan of Arc sought out the dauphin—have been torn down; among the most destructive owners were the heirs of Cardinal Richelieu.

℧ 02-47-93-13-45. Admission 29F (4.40, $4.20) adults, 20F (3.05, $2.90) children 6–12, free 5 and under. July–Aug daily 9am–7pm; Mar 15–June and Sept daily 9am–6pm; Oct daily 9am–5pm; Nov 1–Mar 14 daily 9am–noon and 2–5pm.

Musée de la Devinière   The most famous son of Chinon, François Rabelais, the earthy and often bawdy Renaissance writer, walked the streets of Chinon and lived in a dwelling on rue de la Lamproie. (A plaque marks the spot where his father practiced law and maintained a home and office.) The above-mentioned site, in the suburb of La Devinière, 3½ miles west of Chinon, was an isolated cottage at the time of his birth. It was maintained, because of local superstition and custom, for the sole purpose of delivering the children of the Rabelais clan into the world.

The ground-floor rooms house literary works, prints, and documents of Rabelais and his contemporaries, thoroughly retracing the Rabelaisian era. Throughout the year, the museum hosts special events such as shows by local artists, displays of 16th-century clothing, and (in the courtyard at night) performances that bring to life some of Rabelais's own works.

La Devinière, on D117 near N751. ℧ 02-47-95-91-18, or 02-47-31-43-27 for information on theatrical performances. Admission 24F (3.65, $3.50) adults; 17F (2.60, $2.45) children, students 11–25, and seniors; free for children under 11. Tickets for theatrical performances 50F (7.60, $7.25). Jan 1–Mar 13 and Oct 1–Dec 31 daily 9:30am–12:30pm and 2–5pm; Mar 14–Apr 30 daily 9:30am–12:30pm and 2–6pm; May 1–Sept 14 daily 10am–7pm. From Chinon, follow the road signs pointing to Saumur and the D117.

ACCOMMODATIONS

Chris' Hôtel   This well-run hotel is housed in a 19th-century building near the town's historic district. Many of the rooms are small, but offer views of the castle and river. Most are furnished in a Louis XV style and all have modern amenities. Bathrooms are cramped, each with a shower only. Breakfast is the only meal served.

12 place Jeanne-d'Arc, 37500 Chinon. ℧ 02-47-93-36-92. Fax 02-47-98-48-92. Chrishotel@wanadoo.fr. 32 units. 260F–430F (39.50– 65.35, $37.70–$62.35) double. AE, DC, MC, V. Free parking. **Amenities:** Bar. In room: A/C, TV, hair dryer.

Hostellerie Gargantua   This 15th-century mansion has a terrace with a château view. Try to stop here for a meal, served in a stylish medieval hall; on weekends, the staff dons medieval attire. You can sample Loire sandre prepared with Chinon wine, or duckling with dried pears and smoked lard, followed by a medley of seasonal red fruits in puff pastry. Bedrooms have been renovated over the years, though they haven't replaced the mattresses frequently enough. Bathrooms are old-fashioned but in working order; half of them contain tubs.

73 rue Voltaire, 37500 Chinon. ℧ 02-47-93-04-71. fax 02-47-93-08-02. www.hostelleriegargantua.com. 8 units. 400F–600F (60.80– 91.20, $58–$87) double. MC, V. Free parking. **Amenities:** Restaurant, bar; room service; baby-sitting; laundry. In room: TV, hair dryer.

Hôtel Diderot   This sprawling aristocratic house from the 1700s offers a calm elegance. With its high black-slate roof and white-limestone walls, the hotel

---

Finds **In Pursuit of the Grape**

Chinon is famous for its wines, which crop up on prestigious lists around the world. These are sold in supermarkets and wine shops throughout the region, but the two most interesting stores are maintained by families who have been in the business longer than anyone can remember. At **Caves Plouzeau,** 94 rue Haute-St-Maurice (℃ **02-47-93-16-34**), the 12th-century cellars were dug to provide building blocks for the foundations of the nearby château. The present management dates from 1929; bottles of red or white are 30F to 45F (4.80 to 7.20, $4.35 to $6.53). You're welcome to climb down to the massive cellars, whose presence in the center of urban Chinon is a medieval oddity even by French standards. It's open for wine sales and visits from April to September, Tuesday through Saturday from 9:30am to noon and 2 to 6pm.

The cellars at **Couly-Dutheil,** 12 rue Diderot (℃ **02-47-97-20-20**), are suitably medieval, many carved into the rock undulating through the area's forests. This company produces largely Chinon wines (mostly reds), though it's justifiably proud of the Borgeuil and St-Nicolas de Borgeuil, whose popularity in North America has grown in recent years. Tours of the caves and a *dégustation des vins* (wine tasting) require an advance call and cost 30F (4.55, $4.35) per person. Visits are conducted Monday through Friday from 8am to noon and 2 to 5:45pm.

---

maintains a regal air. The friendly staff helps you settle into the large guest rooms, which feature hardwood floors, exposed beams, antique furniture, and cushy mattresses, plus tidily kept bathrooms, 17 of which come with both tub and shower. A sense of the past is preserved in the exposed beams and supports, the 18th-century staircase, and the 15th-century fireplace in the dining room, where breakfast is served. As a bonus, guests have use of a private garden and patio.

4 rue Buffon, 37500 Chinon. ℃ **02-47-93-18-87.** Fax 02-47-93-37-10. 27 units. 410F (62.30, $59.45) double. AE, DC, MC, V. Amenities: Restaurant, bar. *In room:* TV.

DINING

Au Plaisir Gourmand ✹✹ TRADITIONAL FRENCH   This is the premier restaurant in the area, owned by Jean-Claude Rigollet, who used to direct the chefs at the fabled Les Templiers in Les Bézards. The charming 18th-century building contains an intimate dining room with a limited number of tables. Menu items are likely to include roast rabbit in aspic with foie-gras sauce, oxtail in a Chinon red-wine sauce, and sautéed crayfish with a spicy salad. For dessert, try the prunes stuffed in puff pastry.

2 rue Parmentier. ℃ **02-47-93-20-48.** Reservations required. Main courses 80F–150F (12.15– 22.80, $11.60–$21.75); fixed-price menu 175F–340F (26.60– 51.70, $25.40–$49.30). AE, V. Tues–Sat noon–2pm and 7:30–9:30pm; Sun noon–2pm. Closed Feb.

NEARBY ACCOMMODATIONS & DINING

Château de Marçay ✹✹✹   Here you get the most elegant living in the area. This Relais & Châteaux began in the 1100s as a fortress and changed to its present form during the Renaissance. It remained untouched during the region's civil wars. The centerpiece of the wine-producing hamlet of Marçay, it's sumptuously decorated throughout. The main building houses the more opulent lodgings, while a handful of less expensive, less dramatic rooms are in a nondescript annex a short walk away. Menu specialties change with the season, and the chef works hard to maintain high standards. There's a panoramic view from the garden terrace and dining room, where the decor is elegantly rustic.

Marçay, 37500 Chinon. ☎ **02-47-93-03-47.** Fax 02-47-93-45-33. www.relaischateaux.fr/marcay. 34 units. 690F–1,450F (104.90– 220.40, $100.05–$210.25) double; 1,750F (266, $253.75) suite. Extra bed 160F (24.30, $23.20). AE, DC, MC, V. Closed 6 weeks mid-Jan to mid-March. Take D116 for 4¹/₂ miles southwest of Chinon. **Amenities:** Restaurant; bar; outdoor pool; tennis court; room service; laundry. *In room:* TV, hair dryer.

Manoir de la Giraudière   Built during the mid-1600s, this elegant manor house resembles a small château because of its use of *tuffeau* (the beige-colored stone used in residences of many of the French monarchs). Set in a 6-acre park surrounded by hundreds of acres of fields and forests, this two-star choice offers classic decor and modern comforts. Each good-size room comes with a fine bed and quality linen. About half of the bathrooms contain combination shower and tubs; the rest have showers only. Air-conditioning isn't necessary because the very thick walls act as natural insulation against the heat and cold. Note the 17th-century *pigeonnière* (dovecote) that doubles as a salon during warm weather.

Beaumont-en-Veron, 37420 Avoine. ☎ **02-47-58-40-36.** Fax 02-47-58-46-06. www.hotels-france.com/giraudiere. 25 units. 200F–590F (30.40– 89.70, $29–$85.55) double. AE, MC, V. Head 3 miles west of Chinon along D749 toward Bourgueil. **Amenities:** Restaurant; bar; room service; baby-sitting; laundry. *In room:* TV, hair dryer.

17 Ussé

183 miles SW of Paris, 9 miles NE of Chinon

At the edge of the hauntingly dark forest of Chinon, **Château d'Ussé** ★ (☎ **02-47-95-54-05**) was the inspiration for Perrault's legend of *The Sleeping Beauty* (*La Belle au bois dormant*). Conceived as a fortress, the complex of steeples, turrets, towers , and dormers was erected at the dawn of the Renaissance on a hill overlooking the Indre River. Two powerful families—the Bueil and the d'Espinay—lived here in the 15th and 16th centuries. The terraces, laden with orange trees, were laid out in the 18th century. When the need for a fortified château was gone, the north wing was demolished, to open up a greater view.

The château was later owned by the duc de Duras and then by Mme de la Rochejacquelin; its present owner, the marquis de Blacas, has opened many rooms to the public. The guided tour begins in the Renaissance chapel, with its sculptured portal and handsome stalls. You then proceed to the royal apartments, which are furnished with tapestries and antiques such as a four-poster bed draped in red damask. One gallery displays an extensive collection of swords and rifles. A spiral stairway leads to a tower with a panoramic view of the river and a waxwork Sleeping Beauty waiting for her prince to come.

The château is open February to October, daily from 9am to 6:30pm; it's closed November to January. Admission is 59F (8.95, $8.55) for adults, 19F (2.90, $2.75) for children 8 to 17, and free for children under 8. The château is best visited by **car** or on an organized **bus tour** from Tours. If you're **driving** from Tours or Villandry, follow D7 to Ussé. Allow 1¹/₂ hours for the tour.

18 Fontevraud-l'Abbaye ★★

189 miles SW of Paris, 10 miles SE of Saumur

You'll find the Plantagenet dynasty of England buried in the **Abbaye Royale de Fontevraud** (© **02-41-51-71-41**). Why here? These monarchs, whose male line ended in 1485, were also the comtes d'Anjou, and they left instructions that they be buried in their native soil.

In the 12th-century Romanesque church—with four Byzantine domes—are the remains of two English kings or princes, including Henry II of England, the first Plantagenet king, and his wife, Eleanor of Aquitaine, the most famous woman of the Middle Ages. Her crusading son, Richard the Lion-Hearted, was also entombed here. The Plantagenet line ended with the death of Richard III at the 1485 Battle of Bosworth. The tombs fared badly in the Revolution as mobs desecrating the sarcophagi and scattered their contents on the floor.

More interesting than the tombs, however, is the octagonal Tour d'Evraud, the last remaining Romanesque kitchen in France. A group of apsides, crowned by conically roofed turrets, surrounds the tower. A pyramid tops the conglomeration, capped by an open-air lantern tower pierced with lancets.

The abbey was founded in 1099 by Robert d'Arbrissel, who spent much of his life as a recluse. His abbey was like a public-welfare commune, liberal in its admission policies. One part, for example, was occupied by aristocratic ladies, many banished from court, including discarded mistresses of kings. The four youngest daughters of Louis XV were educated here as well.

The abbey is open daily, June to September from 9am to 7pm, and October to May from 9:30am to noon and 2 to 5:30pm. Admission is 30F (4.55, $4.35) for adults, 23F (3.50, $3.35) for ages 12 to 25, and free for children under 12. Allow 1½ hours for the abbey.

ESSENTIALS

GETTING THERE If you're **driving,** take N147 about 2½ miles from the village of Montsoreau. Four **buses** run daily from Saumur, costing 14F (2.15, $2.05) for the 30-minute, one-way trip.

VISITOR INFORMATION The **Office de Tourisme** is at the Chapelle Ste-Catherine (© **02-41-51-79-45**); it's open May 15 to September 30.

ACCOMMODATIONS

Hostellerie du Prieuré St-Lazare ★ *Finds* This is one of the most unusual hotels in Europe, set on 11th-century foundations within the perimeter of the legendary Abbaye Royale, in what once functioned as cells for penitent monks. It became a hotel in 1990. The guest rooms are well maintained and monastically simple, with white walls, modern furniture, and exposed sections of cream-colored tuffeau, the easy-to-carve rock used to build the abbey during the early Middle Ages. A third of the units come with combination shower and tubs.

49590 Fontevraud-l'Abbaye. © **02-41-51-73-16.** Fax 02-41-51-75-50. www.abbeyhotelfontevraud.com. 52 units. 380F–550F (57.75– 83.60, $55.10–$79.75) double; 630F (95.75, $91.35) triple. AE, MC, V. Closed Nov 15–Mar 15. **Amenities:** Restaurant, bar; baby-sitting; laundry. *In room:* TV, minibar.

DINING

Another choice is the restaurant at the **Hostellerie du Prieuré St-Lazare** (see above).

La Licorne ✦ MODERN FRENCH   For the perfect combination of medieval history and culinary sensuality, visit the abbey and then dine at this 30-seat restaurant set on a linden-lined walkway between the abbey and a nearby parish church. Its symmetrical proportions and neoclassical pilasters, built in the 1700s just before what the owners refer to as "La Révolution," evoke the *ancien régime* at its most graceful and opulent. In summer, guests are seated in the garden or in the elegantly rustic dining room. Chef Jean-Michel Bezille's menu almost always includes filet of beef flavored with smoked pork and shallots, roasted sandre with Szechuan peppers, crayfish-stuffed ravioli with morel sauce, filet of salmon with vanilla sauce, and luscious desserts like warm chocolate tart with pears and lemon-butter sauce.

Allée Ste-Catherine. ℂ **02-41-51-72-49.** Reservations required. Main courses 90F–180F (13.70– 27.35, $13.05–$26.10); fixed-price menu 140F–300F (21.30– 45.60E, $20.30–$43.50). AE, DC, MC, V. Tues–Sun noon–1:30pm; Tues–Sat 7–9pm. Closed 2 weeks in Jan.

19 Angers ✦✦✦

179 miles SW of Paris, 55 miles E of Nantes

Once the capital of Anjou, Angers straddles the Maine River at the western end of the Loire Valley. Though it suffered extensive damage in World War II, it has been restored, blending provincial charm with a suggestion of sophistication. The bustling regional center is often used as a base for exploring the château district to the west. With its skyscrapers and industrial complexes, it hardly suggests a sleepy Loire town; its preponderance of young people, including some 25,000 college students, keeps this vital city of 225,000 jumping until late at night.

Allow 3 hours to see the attractions at Angers.

ESSENTIALS

GETTING THERE   Twelve **trains** per day leave Paris's Gare de Montparnasse for the 90-minute trip; the cost is 243F (36.95, $35.25) one-way. From Saumur, 12 trains per day make the 30-minute trip; a one-way ticket costs 420F (6.40, $6.10). From Tours, seven trains per day make the 75-minute trip; a one-way ticket is 83F (12.60, $12.05). The Angers train station, at place de la Gare, is a convenient walk from the château. For train information and schedules, call ℂ **08-36-35-35-35.** If you're **driving** from Tours, take N152 southwest to Saumur, turning west on D952.

VISITOR INFORMATION   The **Office de Tourisme** is on place du Président-Kennedy (ℂ **02-41-23-51-11**).

EXPLORING THE TOWN

If you have some time for shopping, wander to the pedestrian zone in the center of town. The boutiques and small shops here sell everything from clothes and shoes to jewelry and books. For regional specialty items, head to **La Maison du Vin,** 5 place du Président-Kennedy (ℂ **02-41-88-81-13**), where you can learn about the area's many vineyards, taste their wares, and buy a bottle or two for gifts or an afternoon picnic. Another libation that's unique to Angers is Cointreau. **La Distillerie Cointreau,** rue Croix-Blanche in nearby St-Barthélémy d'Anjou (ℂ **02-41-30-50-50**), has a showroom where you can sample and stock up on this citrusy liqueur. To reach it from the center of Angers, follow the signs first to Paris, then to Cholet, then to St-Barthélémy. It's closed in January.

Château d'Angers ⭐⭐⭐ The moated Château d'Angers, dating from the 9th century, was once the home of the comtes d'Anjou. The notorious Black Falcon lived here, and in time, the Plantagenets also took up residence. From 1230 to 1238, the outer walls and 17 towers were built, creating a fortress prepared to withstand invaders. The château was favored by Good King René, during whose reign a brilliant court life flourished until he was forced to surrender Anjou to Louis XI. Louis XIV turned the château into a prison, dispatching his finance minister, Fouquet, here. During World War II, the Nazis used it as a munitions depot, and it was bombed by the Allies in 1944.

Visit the castle to see the **Apocalypse Tapestries** ⭐⭐⭐. This series of tapestries wasn't always so highly regarded—they once served as a canopy for orange trees, protecting the fruit from unfavorable weather; they were also used to cover the damaged walls of a church. Woven in Paris by Nicolas Bataille from cartoons by Jean de Bruges around 1375 for Louis I of Anjou, they were purchased for a nominal sum in the 19th century. The series of 77 pieces, illustrating the book of St-John, stretch a distance of 335 feet. One scene is called *La Grande prostituée;* another shows Babylon invaded by demons; yet another depicts a peace scene of two multiheaded monsters holding up a fleur-de-lis.

After seeing the tapestries, you can tour the fortress, including the courtyard, prison cells, ramparts, windmill tower, 15th-century chapel, and royal apartments.

📞 **02-41-87-43-47.** Fax 02-41-87-17-50. Admission 35F (5.30, $5.10) adults, 23F (3.50, $3.35) seniors and students 19–25, free for children 18 and under. June–Sept 15 daily 9:30am–7pm; Sept 16–May daily 10am–5pm.

Cathédrale St-Maurice ⭐⭐ The cathedral dates mostly from the 12th and 13th centuries; the main tower is from the 16th century. The statues on the portal represent everybody from the Queen of Sheba to David at the harp. Christ Enthroned is depicted on the tympanum; the symbols, such as the lion for St-Mark, represent the Evangelists. The stained-glass windows from the 12th through the 16th centuries have made the cathedral famous. The oldest one illustrates the martyrdom of St-Vincent (the most unusual is of St. Christopher with the head of a dog). All the Apocalypse Tapestries were once shown here; now only a few remain, with the majority on display in the nearby château. The 12th-century nave, a landmark in cathedral architecture, is a clear, coherent plan that's a work of harmonious beauty, the start of the Plantagenet architecture. If you're interested in a guided tour (offered in English in July and August), call the church's presbytery (see the number below). Tours are conducted erratically, often by an associate of the church, and usually with much charm and humor.

Place Freppel. 📞 **02-41-87-58-45.** Free admission, but donations appreciated. Daily 9am–7pm, sometimes later for special events.

Musée Lurcat ⭐⭐ The town's most intriguing museum is housed in the Ancien Hôpital St-Jean founded in 1174 to care for the sick. The museum is known for its famous tapestry called *The Song of the World* or *Le Chant do Monde,* designed by Jean Lurçat and executed in 10 panels between 1957 and 1966, depicting an abstract conglomeration of beneficent suns, popping champagne bottles, and life cycles of birth and death. You can visit a dispensary from the 17th century, with earthenware jars and trivets still on its wooden shelves, and see everything from a Romanesque cloister with a secret garden to a pewter vessel from 1720 that once contained an antidote for snake bites.

4 blvd. Arago. ℂ **02-41-24-18-45.** Tues–Sun 10am–noon and 2–6pm. Admission 25F (3.80, $3.65) adults, 15F (2.30, $2.20) students and children.

ACCOMMODATIONS

Hôtel d'Anjou   Situated next to a large park, this hotel is the best choice for overnighting in the area. Although comparable in price to the Quality Hôtel de France, it has more upscale appointments and amenities, along with a better restaurant. The guest rooms closer to the ground have higher ceilings and are more spacious. All accommodations and bathrooms were overhauled in 1998.

1 bd. Foch, 49100 Angers. ℂ **800/528-1234** in the U.S. or Canada, or 02-41-88-24-82. Fax 02-41-87-22-21. 53 units. 405F–905F (61.55– 137.55, $58.75–$131.25) double. AE, DC, MC, V. Parking 50F (7.60, $7.25). **Amenities:** Restaurant, bar; laundry/dry cleaning. *In room:* Minibar.

Quality Hôtel de France   This 19th-century hotel, one of the most respected in town, has been run by the Bouyers since 1893. It's the best choice near the railway station. Rooms are soundproofed, and many were renovated in the late 1990s. Bathrooms are very small with shower stalls only.

8 place de la Gare, 49100 Angers. ℂ **02-41-88-49-42.** Fax 02-41-86-76-70. hotel.de.france.anjou@ wanadoo.fr. 55 units. 450F–650F (68.40– 98.80, $65.25–$94.25) double. AE, DC, MC, V. Parking 40F (6.13E, $5.80). **Amenities:** 2 restaurants, bar; room service; laundry/dry cleaning. *In room:* A/C, TV, minibar, hair dryer, iron.

DINING

Hôtel d'Anjou (see above) boasts the town's best restaurant.

La Rose d'Or TRADITIONAL FRENCH   Conveniently located midway between the château and the railway station, La Rose d'Or serves a tried-and-true French menu. Examples include filet of zander cooked in Loire Valley wine; entrecôte of beef marinated in red Borgeuil wine; filet of skate (stingray) with Roquefort sauce; and a succulent roasted duckling that's stuffed with homemade foie gras. The pink-and-gray dining room is formal-looking, with Louis XVI furniture and glittering chandeliers.

21 rue Delaâge. ℂ **02-41-88-38-38.** Reservations recommended. Fixed-price menus 115F–185F (17.50– 28.10, $16.70–$26.85). MC, V. Tues–Sun noon–1:30pm, Tues–Sat 7–9pm.

Provence Caffè PROVENÇAL   This restaurant celebrates the herbs, spices, and seafood of Provence. The decor includes bundles of herbs, bright colors, and souvenirs of the Mediterranean; the ambience is casual and sunny. The chef here continues to delight with such dishes as a risotto served with asparagus and basil or with snails, grilled salmon with Provençal herbs, and a ballotine of chicken with ratatouille.

⌐ *Fun Fact*   A Toast with the Home Brew—Cointreau

Two brothers in Angers were confectioners who set out to create a drink of "crystal-clear purity." Today, some 13 million bottles of Cointreau are consumed annually. Packaged in a square bottle with rounded corners, Cointreau is made from twice-distilled alcohol from the peels of two types of oranges, bitter and sweet. The factory has turned out the drink since 1849. Often imitated, never duplicated, Cointreau flavors such drinks as the cosmopolitan, the kamikaze, the White Lady, and the sidecar.

---

9 place du Ralliement. ⓒ **02-41-87-44-15.** Reservations recommended. Main courses 85F (12.90, $12.35); fixed-price menu 98F–155F (14.90– 23.55, $14.20–$22.30). AE, MC, V. Tues–Sat noon–2pm and 7–10pm. Closed Aug.

ANGERS AFTER DARK

If you head to place du Ralliement and its fountain or rue St-Laud with its many bars and cafes, you'll find yourself in the center of Angers's nightlife. But for a great night of beer drinking with your friends, go to **Le Kent,** an Irish pub at 7 place Ste-Croix (ⓒ **02-41-87-88-55**), where you can choose from some 50 varieties of beer and 70 brands of whiskey. If you prefer quantity to quality when it comes to beer, stop by **Le Spirit Factory,** 14 rue Bressigny (ⓒ **02-41-88-50-10**). Just walk in and order *un mètre,* and for 98F (14.90, $14.20), you'll be served a meter-long wooden feeding trough full of beer (enough for 10 glasses), which many guests share with friends. If you've never had the pleasure of drinking a meter of beer before, here's a bit of etiquette: fill your drinking glass using the spout on the end of the trough and don't try to slurp your beer from the top, as that's *trop gauche,* even for this place.

If a night of dancing seems the perfect antidote to a day of château-gazing, consider **Disco Le Boléro,** rue Saint-Laud, adjacent to the Place de Ralliement (ⓒ **02-41-88-61-19**). It's open on Thursday, Friday, and Saturday nights from 10pm to dawn. There's no cover, but beer costs around 50F (7.60, $7.25). The club attracts a lot of singles, ranging in age from 25 to 45.

8

Normandy & Mont-St-Michel

Ten centuries have passed since the Vikings invaded of Normandy. The early Scandinavians might have come to ravish the land, but they stayed to cultivate it. The Normans produced great soldiers, none more famous than William the Conqueror, who defeated King Harold at the Battle of Hastings in 1066. The English and the French continued to do battle on and off for 700 years—a rivalry that came to a head at the 1815 Battle of Waterloo.

Much of Normandy was ravaged in the 1944 invasion that began June 6 when troops parachuted into Ste-Mère-Église and Bénouville-sur-Orne. The largest armada ever assembled was responsible for a momentous saga: the reconquest of continental Europe from the Nazis. Today many visitors come to Normandy to see the D-day beachheads.

Some of this province may remind you of a Millet landscape, with cattle grazing in verdant fields and wood-framed houses alongside modern buildings. Not far from the Seine you'll come upon the hamlet where Monet painted his waterlilies. Here and there you can find stained-glass windows and Gothic architecture that somehow survived the bombardments; however, many great buildings were leveled to the ground. And Normandy's wide beaches may attract families, but in August, the Deauville sands draw the chic-est of the chic from Europe and North America.

REGIONAL CUISINE Normandy is the land of the three Cs: cider, Calvados, and Camembert. Butter, cream, and other dairy products with such accompaniments as pear or apple cider and fiery apple brandy make up a large part of the diet. Norman cream is velvety in texture and ivory in color. The region's *sauce normande* might be called a plain white sauce anywhere else, but here it takes on added allure because of its richer taste.

Certain Norman towns and regions are associated with certain dishes—tripe à la Caen, sole from Dieppe, duck from Rouen, and soufflélike omelets from Mont-St-Michel. Auge Valley chicken, though not as highly praised as that of Bresse, also has a place in the diet. Locals adore *andouillet* (tripe sausage) from Vire, mussels from Isigny, oysters from Courseulles, cockles from Honfleur, and lobsters from La Hague. Highly prized lamb (*pré salé*) is raised on the salt meadows of Normandy.

The supple, fragrant cow's-milk Camembert, sold in a wooden box since 1880, is joined by other cheeses, including Pont-L'Evêque. Brillat-Savarin, with a high fat content of 75%, was invented in the 1930s by the cheese merchant Henri Androuët.

Normans consume cider at nearly every meal. *Bon bère* is the term for true cider, and sometimes it's so strong that it must be diluted. It takes 12 to 15 years to bring Calvados to taste-perfection (in America, Calvados may be called applejack). Many a Norman finishes a meal with black coffee and a glass of this strong drink, which is also used to flavor main courses.

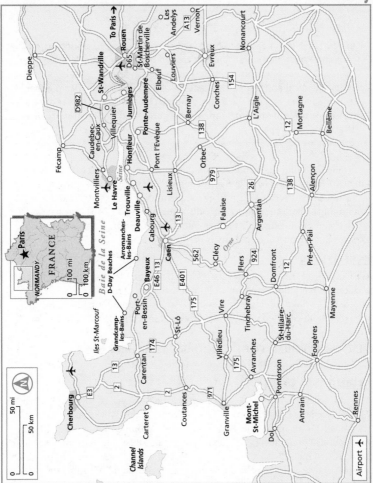

1 Rouen ★★★

84 miles NW of Paris, 55 miles E of Le Havre

The capital of Normandy, Rouen is the north's second most important center. It's a hub of commerce, the fifth-largest port in France. Rouen is a bustling, vibrant place, bursting with activity generated by the industrial businesses connected to the port and a lively scene generated by students at nearby universities and art schools. Today it's a city of half a million people holding memories of its former occupants, including the writers Pierre Corneille and Gustave Flaubert, along with Claude Monet, who endlessly painted the Cathédrale de Notre-Dame here, and even Joan of Arc ("Oh, Rouen, art thou then my final resting place?").

Victor Hugo called Rouen "the city of a hundred spires." Half of it was destroyed during World War II, mostly by Allied bombers, and many Rouennais

> **Tips** **Normandy in a Nutshell**
>
> On your first day, head for Rouen and spend the day exploring its old town and Rouen Cathedral. On your second day, go to Caen, William the Conqueror's seat of government. Stay in Caen or in Bayeux, where you can see its cathedral and the Bayeux tapestry. On your third day (from either Caen or Bayeux), explore the D-day beaches. On your fourth day, continue west toward Mont-St-Michel, an ancient abbey and one of the premier attractions of Europe.

were killed. During the reconstruction of the old quarters, some of the almost-forgotten crafts of the Middle Ages were revived. On the Seine, the city is rich in historic associations: William the Conqueror died here in 1087, and Joan of Arc was burned at the stake on place du Vieux-Marché in 1431.

The Seine, as in Paris, splits Rouen into a **Rive Gauche** (Left Bank) and **Rive Droite** (Right Bank). The old city is on the right bank.

ESSENTIALS

GETTING THERE From Paris's Gare St-Lazare, **trains** leave for Rouen about once every hour (trip time: 70 min.), costing from 105F (15.95, $15) one-way. The rail station is at rue Jeanne d'Arc. For train information and schedules, call © **08-36-35-35-35.** When **driving** from Paris, take A13 northwest to Rouen (trip time: 1½ hr.).

VISITOR INFORMATION The **Office de Tourisme** is at 25 place de la Cathédrale (© **02-32-08-32-40;** www.mairie-rouen.fr).

SEEING THE SIGHTS

Rue du Gros-Horloge ★★ The aptly named "Street of the Great Clock" runs between the cathedral and place du Vieux-Marché. Now a pedestrian mall, it's named for an ornate gilt Renaissance clock mounted on an arch, Rouen's most popular monument. The arch bridges the street and is connected to a Louis XV fountain with a bevy of cherubs and a bell tower. At night the bells still toll a curfew. In the past, the inside of the belfry could be visited for a view of the iron clockworks and the bells.

Place du Vieux-Marché ★ Joan of Arc was executed for heresy at the "Old Marketplace." Tied to a stake, she was burned on May 30, 1431. Her ashes were gathered and tossed into the Seine. A modern church with stained-glass windows from St-Vincent sits in the center of a monumental complex in the square; beside it a bronze cross marks the position of St. Joan's stake.

Cathédrale Notre-Dame de Rouen ★★★ Rouen's cathedral was immortalized by Monet in a series of Impressionist paintings of the three-portal facade with its galaxy of statues. The main door, Porte Central, is embellished with sculptures (some decapitated) depicting the Tree of Jesus. It's flanked by the 12th-century Porte St-Jean and Porte St-Etienne. Consecrated in 1063, the cathedral, a symphony of lacy stonework, was reconstructed after the bombings of World War II. Two soaring towers distinguish it: Tour de Beurre was financed by the faithful willing to pay in exchange for the privilege of eating butter during Lent and is a masterpiece of the Flamboyant Gothic style. Containing a carillon of 56 bells, the Tour Lanterne (Lantern Tower)—built in 1877 and utilizing 740 tons of iron and bronze—rises to almost 500 feet.

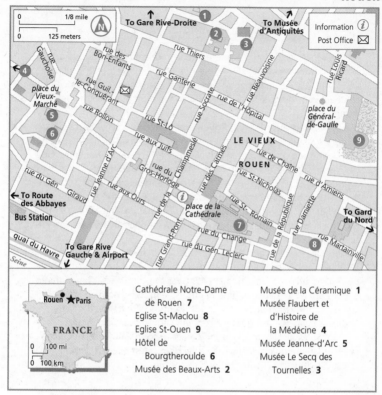

The cathedral's interior is fairly uniform. The nave has 11 bays; the choir is a masterpiece of harmony, with 14 soaring pillars. The Booksellers' Stairway, in the north wing of the transept, is adorned with a large rose window with stained glass that dates in part from the 1500s. The 13th-century chancel is beautiful, with relatively simple lines. Especially interesting is the **Chapelle de la Vierge,** adorned with the Renaissance tombs of the cardinals d'Amboise as well as Jean de Brézé. Also entombed inside is the heart of Richard the Lion-Hearted, a token of his affection for the people of Rouen.

Behind the cathedral is the **Palais de l'Archevêché** (Archbishop's Palace), which was bombed in the war. Now it stands naked against the sky. The broken arches and rosette windows witnessed the trial of Joan of Arc in 1431, and her rehabilitation was proclaimed here in 1456.

Place de la Cathédrale. Free admission. Mon–Sat 8am–7pm; Sun 8am–6pm. Closed during mass and on bank holidays.

Église St-Maclou ★★   St-Maclou was built in the Flamboyant Gothic style, with a step-gabled porch and handsome cloisters, and is known for the remarkable 16th-century panels on its doors. Our favorite (to the left) is the *Portail des Fontaines* (Portal of the Fonts). The church was constructed in 1200, rebuilt in 1432, and finally consecrated in 1521, though its lantern tower is from the 19th century. It sits on a square of old Norman crooked-timbered buildings. Inside, pictures dating from June 4, 1944, document St-Maclou's destruction.

A Drive Along the Route des Abbayes

Beginning at Rouen, the Seine winds through black forests and lush green countryside along the Route des Abbayes, eventually ending at Le Havre. As you make your way past the ruins of monasteries and châteaux, you'll agree that this is one of the most memorable routes in France.

Ten minutes after leaving Rouen (via D982), you arrive at the 11th-century **Abbaye St-George,** in St-Martin de Boscherville. Continue along D982 and then on D65 around the Seine for 12 miles to Jumièges. One of France's most beautiful ruins, **Abbaye de Jumièges** ★★★ was founded by St. Philbert in the 7th century and rebuilt in the 10th century. The abbey church was consecrated in 1067 by the archbishop of Rouen in the presence of William the Conqueror. The 30m (100-ft.)-high nave is complete, and the porch is surrounded by two towers 150 feet high.

Another 10 miles along the right bank of the Seine is St-Wandrille, 33 miles northwest of Rouen (reached via D982 from Jumièges). **Abbaye de St-Wandrille** was founded in 649. Over the centuries, it has suffered various attacks (by Vikings, among others), and today nothing remains of the 7th-century monastery. A huge 18th-century gate frames the entrance, and inside you can visit cloisters from the 14th to the 16th century.

From St-Wandrille, continue for 2 miles or so to **Caudebec-en-Caux** ★, set in an amphitheater along the Seine. Nearly destroyed in World War II, it has a Gothic church from the 15th century spared in the bombings.

Behind the cathedral, at 3 place Barthelemy. ✆ **02-35-71-71-72.** Free admission. Mon–Sat 10am–noon and 2–5pm; Sun 3–5pm. Closed Jan 1, May 1, July 14, Nov 11.

Église St-Ouen ★★   This church is the outgrowth of a 7th-century Benedictine abbey. Flanked by four turrets, its 115m (375-foot) octagonal lantern tower is called "the ducal crown of Normandy." One of the best-known Gothic buildings in France, the church represents the work of 5 centuries. Its nave is from the 15th century, its choir from the 14th (but with 18th-century railings), and its remarkable stained glass from the 14th to the 16th. On May 23, 1431, Joan of Arc was taken to the cemetery here, where officials sentenced her to be burned at the stake unless she recanted. She signed an abjuration, thus condemning herself to life imprisonment, but that sentence was later revoked.

Place du Général-de-Gaulle. Free admission. Mar–Oct Wed–Mon 10am–12:30pm and 2–6pm; Nov–Feb Wed and Sat–Sun 10am–12:30pm and 2–4pm.

Hôtel de Bourgtheroulde   This is one of the most frequently showcased Gothic buildings of Rouen, and headquarters of a local bank, Crédit Industrielle de Normandie (C.I.N.). Built in the 15th century by William the Red, and enlarged in the Renaissance, it's noteworthy for an interior courtyard, the only part you can visit regularly. In the courtyard, whose architecture warrants a stop, look back at the octagonal stair tower. The left gallery is entirely Renaissance.

15 place de la Pucelle (Square of the Maid). ✆ **02-35-08-64-00.** Free admission. Courtyard visits Mon–Fri 8:30am–6:30pm. Closed Sat and Sun except for special exhibitions. Call for details.

Henri IV considered it the handsomest chapel in his kingdom. On its west side is a trio of Flamboyant Gothic doorways, crowned by a rose window.

Drive west around the north bank of the Seine to **Villequier** ⭐, a tranquil village whose early-19th-century manor house functions as a reasonably priced 29-room hotel charging 350 to 400F (53.20 to 60.80, $51 to $58) for a double room. For information and reservations, contact the **Château-Hotel de Villequier,** 76490 Villequier (☎ **02-35-95-94-10**). Breakfast is the only meal served. It was in this town that Victor Hugo lost his daughter, along with her husband, in a seasonal tidal wave. You can visit the **Musée Victor-Hugo,** on quai Victor-Hugo (☎ **02-35-56-78-31**). It has the manuscript of his poem "Contemplations" and original excerpts from *The Hunchback of Notre Dame.* The museum is open from March to October, Wednesday to Monday, from 10am to 12:30pm and 2 to 6pm (it closes at 5pm from November to February). Throughout the year it's closed Sunday morning. Adults pay 20F (3.05, $2.90). It's free for students and for anyone under 18.

Some 33 miles to the west, along D81 and N182, is **Le Havre** ⭐⭐, France's major Atlantic port. The city was the target of more than 170 bombings during World War II, but its recovery was amazing. From here you can take boat tours to Trouville and Deauville, a pair of lovely resorts.

Musée des Beaux-Arts ⭐⭐⭐   This is one of France's most important provincial museums, with over 65 rooms of French art that ranges from medieval primitives to 20th-century contemporary paintings. You'll find portraits by David, works by Delacroix and Ingres (seek out his *La Belle Zélie*). A Gérard David retable, *La Vierge et les saints* (*The Virgin and the Saints*), is a masterpiece. One salon is devoted to Géricault, including a portrait of Delacroix. Other works are by Veronese, Velásquez, Caravaggio, Rubens, Poussin, Fragonard, and Corot; and several paintings are by Impressionists like Monet, including several versions of his Rouen Cathedral.

Place Verdel. ☎ **02-35-71-28-40.** Admission 20F (3.05, $2.90) adults, 13F (2.00, $1.90) for students, free for children 18 and under. Wed–Mon 10am–6pm.

Musée de la Céramique. ⭐⭐   One of the greatest treasures here is the 17th-century Rouen faïence, which has a distinctive dull Indian red color because of the unique color of the local clay. The exhibits provide a showcase for the talents of Masseot Abaquesne, the premier French artist in faïence and of the specific Rouen-style production (1650 to 1780). An exceptional showcase is devoted to chinoiserie from 1699 to 1745.

1 rue Faucon. ☎ **02-35-07-31-74.** Admission 15F (2.30, $2.20) for adults, 10F (1.50, $1.45) for students, free for children under 18. Wed–Mon 10am–1pm and 2–6pm.

Musée Le Secq des Tournelles (Wrought Ironworks Museum) ⭐
Housed in the 15th-century Église St-Laurent, this museum showcases a famous

traditional Norman art form. Its collection ranges from what the press once called "forthright masculine forging to lacy feminine filigree, from Roman keys to the needlepoint balustrade that graced Mme de Pompadour's country mansion." A Parisian aristocrat, Le Secq des Tournelles, began the collection in 1870. So passionately was he devoted to it that his wife divorced him. Donated to the city of Rouen, the collection now has some 14,000 pieces.

Rue Jacques-Villon. © 02-35-88-42-92. Admission 15F (2.30, $2.20) adults, 10F (1.50, $1.45) students, free for children under 18. Wed–Mon 10am–1pm and 2–6pm.

Musée Flaubert et d'Histoire de la Médécine Gustave Flaubert, author of *Madame Bovary*, was born in the director's quarters of Rouen's public hospital (his father was the director). He spent his first 25 years in the city; the room where he was born in 1821 is still intact. Family furniture and medical paraphernalia are also displayed. Only a glass door separated the Flauberts from the ward and its moaning patients.

In the Hôtel-Dieu, 51 rue de Lecat. © 02-35-15-59-95. Admission 12F (1.80, $1.75) adults, 8F (1.20, $1.15) for students and children under 16. Tues–Sat 10am–noon and 2–6pm. Closed holidays.

Musée Jeanne-d'Arc The life and the martyrdom of Joan of Arc, France's national heroine, are traced here. In a vaulted cellar are dioramas and waxworks and commentary in four languages, depicting her life—from Domrémy, where she was born, to her burning at the stake on the square in Rouen. The site also contains a research library on her life and the politics of her era.

33 place du Vieux-Marché. © 02-35-88-02-70. Admission 25F (3.80, $3.65) adults, 13F (2.00, $1.90) children and students. May–Sept 15 daily 9:30am–7pm; Sept 16–Apr daily 10am–noon and 2–6:30pm.

SHOPPING

Rouen was once one of France's major producers of the fine decorative ceramic ware known as *faïence de Rouen.* Examples of both antique and contemporary faïence still abound, and it's worth picking up one or two pieces for your home or even as gifts. For contemporary faïence, your best bet is **Faïencerie Augy,** 26 rue St-Romain (© **02-35-88-77-47**), where his artisans carry on the tradition of making faïence de Rouen.

Another Rouen specialty to watch for is *coffret de Rouen.* These little hand-painted wooden boxes were all the rage during the 18th and 19th centuries. The original versions continue to be popular, but watch out for modern forgeries.

Rouen has also become an antiques capital. The best hunting ground is in Vieux Rouen (the Old Town) along **rue Eau-de-Robec, place Barthélémy, rue Damiette,** and **rue St-Romain.** The first Saturday of every month you can find an **antiques fair** on rue Eau-de-Robec. The city also has two **flea markets,** one on Saturday and Sunday at place St-Mare and the other on Thursday at place des Emmurés. Medium- and large-scale antiques auctions take place throughout the year at the **Salles des Ventes,** 25 rue du Général-Giraud (© **02-35-71-13-50**) and 20 rue de la Croix-de-Fer (© **02-35-98-73-49**).

Other antiques shops worth visiting are **M. Bertran,** 108 rue Molière (© **02-35-98-24-06**), with a good selection of 18th- and 19th-century paintings; **E. Bertran,** 110 rue Molière (© **02-35-70-79-96**), with its collection of antique books dating back to the 1400s; **Antic St-Maclou,** 178 rue Martainville (© **02-35-89-52-61**), a shop specializing in estate jewelry and silver; **Patrick Chasset,** 12 rue de la Croix-de-Fer (© **02-35-70-59-97**), where you'll find toys and gaming cards from the 1700s and 1800s as well as bottles and glassware.

You'll find watercolors by local artists, as well as antique Norman and English engravings, at **Atelier St-Romain,** 28 rue St-Romain (© 02-35-88-76-17).

Lovers of chocolate will find a veritable paradise at **La Chocolatière,** 18 rue Guillaume-le-Conquérant (© **02-35-71-00-79**). If hats are your thing, head for **Monique,** 58 rue St-Romain (© **02-35-98-07-03**). Hats run the gamut here from funky to refined and elegant—and you won't be paying Parisian prices.

ACCOMMODATIONS

Hôtel Cardinal *(Value* You couldn't find a more ideally located hotel that is as affordable as this one. It's across from the cathedral (imagine waking up to the view of this majesty and the surrounding half-timbered buildings) and in the middle of a neighborhood known for antiques, art galleries, and fine dining. With this much to do, you won't mind the hotel's simplicity. Rooms are business-class plain with built-in furnishings and a small bathroom with tub or shower.

1 place de la Cathédrale, 76000 Rouen. © **02-35-70-24-42.** Fax 02-35-89-75-14. 18 units. 320F–420F (48.65– 63.85, $46.40–$60.90) double. MC, V. Parking 31F (4.70, $4.50) nearby. *In room:* TV, hair dryer.

Hôtel de Bordeaux Practically on the banks of the Seine, this hotel provides medium-size rooms with standard built-in furnishings. Most units were renovated in 2000. Each is acceptably comfortable, albeit just a bit sterile-looking. All have views of either the town's medieval rooftops or the cathedral. Accommodations on the upper floors get the bonus of a river view. About half the bedrooms come with a tub bath, the others with shower.

9 place de la République, 76000 Rouen. © **02-35-71-93-58.** Fax 02-35-71-92-15. interhotel. rouen@wanadoo.fr. 48 units. 320F–360F (48.65– 54.70, $46.40–$52.20) double. AE, DC, MC, V. **Amenities:** Bar; laundry. *In room:* TV.

Hôtel de Dieppe This Best Western across from the train station is run by the Gueret family, a tradition since 1880. Although modernized, it's still a traditional French inn. The only problem might be noise, but double-glazed windows help; after 10pm the last train from Paris arrives and the area quiets down. Rooms are compact, each with a firm mattress on a comfortable bed. Half the bedrooms have a full bath, the rest just a shower. In Le Quatre Saisons, the adjoining rôtisserie, you can enjoy dishes such as duckling *à la presse* and sole poached in red wine.

Place Bernard-Tissot, 76000 Rouen. © **800/528-1234** in the U.S. and Canada, or 02-35-71-96-00. Fax 02-35-89-65-21. www.bestwestern.fr. 41 units. 535F–635F (81.30– 96.50, $77.60–$92.10) double. AE, DC, MC, V. Parking 30F (4.55, $4.35). Bus: 1, 3, 5, 7, or 10. **Amenities:** Restaurant, bar; laundry; room service; baby-sitting. *In room:* TV, hair dryer.

Hôtel de la Cathédrale Built around a timbered and cobble-covered courtyard, this hotel is on a pedestrian street midway between the cathedral and the Église St-Maclou, opposite the Archbishop's Palace where Joan of Arc was tried. The recently remodeled rooms are well maintained and tastefully furnished, accessible by both stairs and an elevator. All the units contain a shower, but only a few come with tub baths as well. Breakfast is the only meal served.

12 rue St-Romain, 76000 Rouen. © **02-35-71-57-95.** Fax 02-35-70-15-54. 24 units. 310F–370F (47.10– 56.25, $44.95–$53.65) double. MC, V. Parking 31F (4.70, $4.50) nearby. Bus: 1, 3, 5, 7, or 10. **Amenities:** Laundry; baby-sitting. *In room:* TV.

Hôtel Le Viking The traffic noise can be bad, but the front rooms open onto charming views of the Seine. In July and August reserve well in advance because the hotel is packed. Rooms are small but comfortable. Each comes with a comfortable bed, plus a shower-only bathroom. Breakfast is the only meal served.

21 quai du Havre, 76000 Rouen. & 02-35-70-34-95. Fax 02-35-89-97-12. www.leviking.com. 37 units. 295F–325F (†44.85–†49.40, $42.80–$47.15) double. AE, DC, MC, V. Parking 45F (†6.85, $6.55). Bus: 1, 3, 5, 7, or 10. Amenities: Laundry; baby-sitting. In room: TV, hair dryer (in some rooms).

Mercure Centre ⚬★ In a town of lackluster hotels, the Mercure is a fine choice for an overnight stay. The functionally designed rooms, all almost exactly identical to those in hundreds of other Mercure hotels across Europe, are clean and well maintained, though perhaps a tad small. Each contains a comfortable bed with a good mattress. Breakfast is the only meal served.

Rue de la Croix-de-Fer, 76000 Rouen. ℂ **02-35-52-69-52.** Fax 02-35-89-41-46. 125 units. 480F–595F (72.95– 90.45, $69.60–$86.30) double; 890F–990F (135.30– 150.50, $129.05–$143.55) suite. AE, DC, MC, V. Parking 50F (7.60, $7.25). Métro: Palais de Justice. **Amenities:** Bar; room service (drinks only); baby-sitting. *In room:* A/C, TV, minibar, hair dryer.

DINING

Gill ⚬★⚬★⚬★ MODERN FRENCH The best place in town is located beside the traffic of the Seine's quays. The modern decor with high-tech accessories is an appropriate backdrop for the sophisticated cuisine of Gilles Tournadre. Who can resist the ravioli stuffed with foie gras and served in a bouillon sprinkled with fresh truffles? What about a terrine of artichoke flavored with fresh truffles, roasted white turbot with fresh asparagus flavored with Parmesan, or filet of sea bass with smoked salmon in red-wine sauce? The lobster fricassée with fresh mushrooms "from the woods" is another fine selection. Save room for the Calvados soufflé. It's a winner!

9 quai de la Bourse. ℂ **02-35-71-16-14.** Reservations recommended. Main courses 145F–195F (22.05– 29.65, $21.05–$28.30); fixed-price menus 220F–420F (3.45– 63.85, $31.90–$60.90). AE, DC, MC, V. May–Sept Tues–Sat noon–2pm and 7:30–9:45pm; Oct–Apr Wed–Sun noon–2pm, Tues–Sat 7:30–10pm. Métro: Théâtre-des-Arts. Closed 3 weeks in Aug.

Les Nymphéas ⚬★⚬★⚬★ MODERN FRENCH One of the most appealing restaurants in Rouen bears the name of a painting by Monet (*Waterlilies*). The setting is a 16th-century half-timbered house that fits gracefully into the centrally located neighborhood (Place du Vieux-Marché). It features a sophisticated and savory cuisine. The restaurant is celebrated for its warm foie gras; wild duckling Rouennais style, served with wild mushrooms and caramelized onions; and a *civet* (stew) of lobster with sauterne. Also look for veal chops with "*garniture bourgeois*," which includes long-simmered versions of pearl onions, bacon, and potatoes. An award-winning dessert that richly evokes the countryside of Normandy is a warm soufflé flavored with apples and Calvados.

9 rue de la Pie. ℂ 02-35-89-26-69. Reservations recommended. Main courses 150F–260F (22.80– 39.50, $21.75–$37.70); fixed-price menus 165F–380F (25.10–[e]57.75, $23.95–$55.10). AE, DC, MC, V. Tues–Sun noon–1:45pm; Tues–Sat 7:15–9:30pm.

Maison Dufour NORMAN One of Normandy's best-preserved 15th-century inns is flourishing under four generations of the Dufour family since 1906. The dining rooms are decorated with copper pots, wood carvings, curtains, and engravings. The food, reflecting Normandy's culinary traditions, is so outstanding it's hard to single out specialties. The home-smoked salmon, *canard* (duckling) *rouennais,* John Dory in cider sauce, and sole normande are exemplary.

The most appropriate dessert is a Calvados-flavored soufflé or a thin but wide slice of apple tart.

67 bis rue St-Nicholas. ✆ **02-35-71-90-62.** Reservations required. Main courses 80F–160F (12.15– 24.30, $11.60–$23.20); fixed-price menus 89F–230F (13.55– 34.95, $12.90–$33.35) at lunch, 120F– 230F (18.25– 34.95, $17.40–$33.35) at dinner. AE, MC, V. Tues–Sun noon–2pm; Tues–Sat 7–9:30pm. Métro: Palais de Justice.

Pascaline TRADITIONAL FRENCH   This informal bistro is often filled with regulars, though it's not as atmospheric or as charming as the Brasserie de la Grande Poste. The cheapest fixed-price menus are some of the best bargains in town, however. Menu items include seafood dishes like pavé of monkfish with roughly textured mustard sauce, a savory *pot-au-feu maison*, navarin of monkfish, tenderloin steaks, and cassoulet toulousain. Don't come for refined cuisine—instead, you can expect hearty and time-tested old favorites. Thursday night, when there's a live jazz and swing band, is especially appealing here.

5 rue de la Poterne. ✆ **02-35-89-67-44.** Reservations recommended. Main courses 59F–82F (8.95– 12.45, $8.55–$11.90); fixed-price menus (Mon–Fri only) 69F (10.50, $10) at lunch, 76.50F–99F (11.65– 15.05, $11.10–$14.35) at dinner. V. Daily noon–2:30pm and 7:30–11:30pm. Métro: Place du Palais de Justice.

ROUEN AFTER DARK

The citizens of Rouen usually start their nights on the town at a pub or cafe. The better ones frequented by 25- to 45-year-olds are the crowded **Café Leffe,** 36 place des Carmes (✆ **02-35-71-93-30**); and **La Taverne St-Amand,** 11 rue St-Amand (✆ **02-35-88-51-34**), with a friendly environment perfect for enjoying a mug of the best Irish, Belgian, and German beers. Across the street from the Taverne St-Amande, at 16 rue St-Amand, is an even smaller tavern, **La Bohème** (✆ **02-35-71-53-99**), a discotheque that offers a cozy, sometimes alcohol-sodden publike ambience that can be friendly and spontaneously charming. Many students call the **Underground Tavern,** 26 rue des Champs-Maillets (✆ **02-35- 98-44-84**), their home away from home. This place has both a street-level bar and an underground bar outfitted in wood and British bric-a-brac.

WINE BAR   If beer doesn't turn you on, try **Le Petit Zinc,** 20 place du Vieux-Marché (✆ **02-35-89-39-69**). This bistro-style wine bar, with its early 1900s decor, has one of the best wine selections in town. Of course, you can order Norman cider as well.

DISCO   At **Le Kiosk,** 43 bd. de Verdun (✆ **02-35-88-54-50**), 20-somethings rule the dance floor. Paying a cover of 90F (13.73, $13) will get you into the hard-edged techno music and psychedelic light action.

GAY & LESBIAN BARS   **Le Bloc House,** 138 rue Beauvoisine (✆ **02-35-07-71-97**), attracts a très cool crowd of mostly gay males from their 20s to their 40s who prefer the James Dean look. There's a full bar and lots of distractions, including house and techno music, pinball machines, video screens, billiards, and dartboards. **L'Opium,** 2 rue Malherbe (✆ **02-35-03-29-36**), open only on Friday, Saturday, and Sunday nights, is where the hip young gay and lesbian crowd comes to be seen and dance. Drag shows are popular every Sunday night. The cover is 50F (7.60, $7). The modern **Le Traxx,** 4 bis bd. Ferdinand-de-Lesseps (✆ **02-32-10-12-02**), attracts its share of young, well-connected gays and lesbians. It's known for light shows, techno, and a wild crowd until the wee hours. Here you'll pay 40 to 60F (6.10 to 9.10, $6 to $9) to get in, depending on the time and day. The price includes one drink.

Finds **Calvados, Madame Bovary & Flaubert**

For an evocation of old Normandy, motorists heading from Rouen to Deauville (the traditional route) will have a lasting memory if they stop in Pont-Audemer, 31 miles west of Rouen. Here on the banks of the River Risle, Pont-Audemer lies in the heart of Calvados country. William the Conqueror's father used to storm through this town of markets and tanners. In spite of war damage, Pont-Audemer retains much of its old look, especially if you wander its historic streets, rue de la Licorne (unicorn) and rue de la République, filled with half-timbered Norman buildings. Along rue de la République, look for the Église St-Ouen, dating from the 11th century.

For lunch, take Flaubert's advice and head for **Auberge du Vieux Puits,** 6 rue Notre-Dame-du-Pré (② 02-32-41-01-48), which the author used as one of the settings for his masterpiece, *Madame Bovary.* With is beamed ceilings and half-timbered walls, "The Inn of the Old Well" is still going strong. Order the duckling stew with sour cherries and finish with a slice of the three classic cheeses of Normandy: Camembert, Livarot, and pont-l'Evêque—washed down with Calvados, of course.

MUSIC   Rouen also has its cultural side. **Théâtre des Arts/Opéra Léonard de Vinci,** 7 rue du Dr.-Rambert (② 02-35-98-50-98), has a busy schedule of classical and contemporary operas. A variety of concerts are hosted at the **Église St-Maclou,** 3 rue Dutuit, and the **Église St-Ouen,** place du Général-de-Gaulle.

2 Honfleur ★★

125 miles NW of Paris, 39 miles NE of Caen

At the mouth of the Seine, opposite Le Havre, Honfleur is one of Normandy's most charming fishing ports. Having escaped major damage in World War II, the port looks like an antique, although it's a working one. Thanks to the pont de Normande bridge, which links it directly to Le Havre, visitors are now flocking here. Honfleur is 500 years older than Le Havre, dating from the 11th century. Early in the 17th century, colonists set out for Québec in Canada. The township has long been favored by artists, including Daubigny, Corot, and Monet.

ESSENTIALS

GETTING THERE   If you're **driving** in from Pont l'Evêque or other points south (including Paris), D579 leads to the major boulevard, rue de la République. Follow it to the town center. Driving time from Paris is 2½ hours.

There's no direct **train** service to Honfleur. From Paris, take one of five trains per day from Gare St-Lazare for the town of Lisieux. From there, buses continue the last 45 minutes onto Honfleur. From Rouen, take the train to Le Havre and transfer to a bus for the last 30-minute leg. Bus fare for either of the above routes is 42.50F (6.45, $6) each way. Three **Bus Verts** per day connect Caen and Honfleur (trip time: 2 hr.), costing 69 to 86F (10.50 to 13.05, $10 to $12) one-way. Call ② 02-31-89-28-41 for information and schedules.

VISITOR INFORMATION   The **Office de Tourisme** is on place Arthur-Boudin ((C) **02-31-89-23-30**).

SEEING THE TOWN

From place de la Porte-de-Rouen you can begin your tour of the town, which should take about an hour. Stroll along the **Vieux Bassin,** the old harbor, which has fishing boats and slate-roofed narrow houses. On the north side of the basin, the former governor's house, **Lieutenance,** which contains the administrative body of the nearby port, dates from the 16th century. Nearby is the **Église Ste-Catherine,** Place Ste-Catherine ((C) **02-31-89-11-93**), built of timber by shipbuilders in the 15th century. The church's belfry is on the other side of the street and is also of wood. The church is open daily 9am to noon and 2 to 6pm.

Musée Eugène-Boudin   This museum has a good collection of the painters who flocked to this port when Impressionism was born. The largest collection is of the pastels and paintings of Boudin, of course.

Place Erik-Satie. (C) **02-31-89-54-00.** Admission Jul–Sept 30F (4.50, $4.35), reduced admission 20F (3.00, $2.90) groups, seniors, students; Oct–Jun 25F (3.75, $3.63), 16F (2.40, $2.32) groups, seniors, students. Mar 15–Sep 30 10am–noon and 2–6pm daily except Tues; Oct 1–Mar 14 Mon and Wed–Fri 2:30–5pm and Sat–Sun 10am–noon and 2–5pm. Closed Jan to mid-Feb, Jul 14, Dec 25.

Musée du Vieux Honfleur   This place celebrates the unique cultural and aesthetic contribution of Normandy to the rest of Europe. Inside, you'll find old furniture, lace headdresses, embroideries, candle-making equipment, and farm implements, as well as several rooms outfitted with period art and antiques.

Quai St-Etienne. (C) **02-31-89-14-12.** Admission 25F (3.80, $3.65) adults, 15F (2.30, $2.20) students and ages 10–18, children under 10 free. Apr–Jun and Sept Tues–Sun 10am–noon and 2–6pm; Jul–Aug daily 10am–1pm and 2–6:30pm; Oct to mid-Nov and mid-Feb to Mar Tues–Fri 2–5:30pm and Sat–Sun 10am–noon and 2–5:30pm. Closed mid-Nov to mid-Feb.

Maisons Satie   Opened in 1998 in the house where he was born in 1866, this is a high-tech museum that honors Honfleur's native son Erik Satie. Satie was a "complete artist" who became most famous for his music, but who was also a painter, and as a muse and inspiration to Picasso, Braque, Cocteau, Débussy, Ravel, and Stravinsky. This is not a traditional museum. It incorporates a walk through exhibitions that include sound, light play, and recordings of Satie's compositions. These are transmitted via a high-tech helmet worn by each visitor, which allows a degree of play and experimentation with some of the exhibitions.

67 bd. Charles V. (C) **02-31-89-11-11.** Admission 30F (4.55, $4.35) adults, 20F (3.05, $2.90) ages 11–17, free for children under 10. Apr–Sept Wed–Mon 10am–7pm; Oct–Mar Wed–Mon 10:30am–6pm.

ACCOMMODATIONS

Restaurant/Hôtel L'Absinthe (see "Dining," below) also rents rooms.

Castel Abertine (★ (Finds)   Great care is taken to maintain the character of this home of Albert Sorel, a 19th-century historian/scholar. Today it is a handsome, welcoming hotel. All the individually decorated rooms have floor-to-ceiling windows that open up to views of gardens and century-old trees. Each was renovated in 1999 and has a comfortable mattress; many contain king-size beds. Bathrooms are small.

19 cours Albert-Manuel, 14600 Honfleur. (C) **02-31-98-85-56.** Fax 02-31-98-83-18. www.honfleurhotels. com. 26 units. 400F–700F (60.80– 106.40, $58–$101.50) double; 800F (121.60, $116) suite. AE, DC, MC, V. **Amenities:** Finnish sauna; laundry; room service; baby-sitting. *In room:* TV, hair dryer.

Hostellerie Lechat 🌟🌟 An undeniable sense of old-fashioned coziness abounds here. The comfortably furnished rooms, though modest, are excellent for an overnight stop and have comfortable mattresses. All the bathrooms contain a shower, but only about a third are equipped with tubs as well.

3 place Ste-Catherine, 14600 Honfleur. © **02-31-14-49-49.** Fax 02-31-89-28-61. www.honfleur.com. 23 units. 500F–550F (76– 83.60, $72.50–$79.75) double; 930F (141.35, $134.85) suite. AE, DC, MC, V. Closed Jan–Feb 15. Bus: 20 or 50. **Amenities:** Restaurant, bar; baby-sitting. *In room:* TV, hair dryer.

La Ferme St-Simeon 🌟🌟🌟 An old cider press is the focal point of this 17th-century half-timbered slate house, which has become one of Normandy's most elegant inns. The shimmering water of the English Channel drew artists in times past to this hilltop inn, said to be where Impressionism was born in the 19th century. Much of the hotel has terra-cotta floors, carved wood, and copper and faience touches. Rooms are decorated in an 18th-century style. Bathrooms are beautifully maintained, about half with a tub and shower combination.

Rte. Adolphe-Marais, 14600 Honfleur. © **02-31-81-78-00.** Fax 02-31-89-48-48. 34 units. 1,460F–3,510F (221.90– 533.50, $211.70–$508.95) double; 3,510F–5,400F (533.50– 820.80, $508.95–$783) suite. AE, V. **Amenities:** Restaurant, bar; indoor pool; sauna, laundry; room service; baby-sitting. *In room:* TV, mini-bar, hair dryer.

DINING

L'Assiette Gourmande 🌟🌟🌟 TRADITIONAL FRENCH This is the gourmet citadel of the area and the only one with a Michelin star. Located on the street level of the Cheval Blanc hotel, with which it's not associated, it's the domain of Gérard and Anne-Marie Bonnefoy, who serve dishes such as omelet au gratin studded with lobster chunks, escalope of warm foie gras with lentil-flavored cream sauce, roasted crayfish with a marinade of two vegetables, and roasted turbot with essence of chicken. Leave room for the *petit gâteau moelleux au chocolat* (very moist, deliberately overcooked chocolate-fudge cake).

2 quai des Passagers. © **02-31-89-24-88.** Reservations required. Main courses 150F–300F (22.80– 45.60, $21.75–$43.50); fixed-price menus 170F–450F (25.85– 68.40, $24.65–$65.25). AE, DC, MC, V. Tues–Sun noon–2:15pm and 7–9:45pm. Closed Jan.

Restaurant/Hôtel L'Absinthe 🌟🌟 TRADITIONAL FRENCH This tavern—named for the drink preferred by many 19th-century writers in Honfleur—is known by everyone in town for its beautiful decor, extravagant portions, and well-prepared savory cuisine. Owner Antoine Ceffrey will probably make an appearance in the dining rooms before the end of your meal. Menu choices may be veal kidneys with Calvados, baked turbot with pepper sauce, and attractive desserts like assorted fresh fruit with essence of raspberries.

If the food is so good that you can't bear to leave, you can rent one of the six simple but comfortable rooms (or the suite). All have satellite TV. A double is 550 to 750F (83.60 to 114, $80 to $109), and the suite is 1,350F (205.20, $196). Parking is available for 50F (7.60, $7).

10 quai de la Quarantaine, 14600 Honfleur. © **02-31-89-39-00.** Reservations required. Main courses 150F–250F (22.80– 38, $21.75–$36.25); fixed-price menus 179F–380F (27.20– 57.75, $25.95– $55.10). DC, MC, V. Daily 12:15–3pm and 7:15–10pm. Bus: 20 or 50.

3 Deauville 🌟🌟🌟

128 miles NW of Paris, 29 miles NE of Caen

Deauville has been associated with the rich and famous since it was founded as an upscale resort in 1859 by the duc de Morny, Napoléon III's half-brother. In

1913 it entered sartorial history when Coco Chanel launched her career here by opening a boutique selling tiny hats that challenged the then-current fashion of huge-brimmed hats loaded with flowers and fruit. (Coco's point of view: "How can the mind breathe under those things?")

ESSENTIALS

GETTING THERE   There are 6 to 10 daily **rail** connections from Paris's Gare St-Lazare (trip time: 2½ hr.), costing from 145F (22.05, $21) one-way. The rail depot is between Trouville and Deauville, south of the town. **Bus Verts du Calvados** (© 08-01-21-42-14) serves the lower Normandy coast from Caen to Le Havre. When **driving** from Paris (trip time: 2½ hr.), take A13 west to Pont L'Evêque. Then follow N177 traveling east to Deauville.

VISITOR INFORMATION   The **Office de Tourisme** is on place de la Mairie (© 02-31-14-40-00; www.deauville.org).

SPECIAL EVENTS   For a week in early September the **Deauville Film Festival** honors movies made in the United States. Actors, producers, directors, and writers flock here and briefly eclipse the high rollers at the casinos and the horse-race/polo crowd. For information, call the tourist office.

EXPLORING THE RESORT

Coco Chanel cultivated a tradition of elegance that survives here in Deauville, as well as in its smaller and less prestigious neighbor Trouville, on the opposite bank of the Toques (see below). Don't expect flashiness—in its way, the restrained and ever-so-polite Deauville is the most British seaside resort in France.

However, in its heart Deauville is less English than French, Parisian in particular. It has even been dubbed Paris's 21st arrondissement. Don't come here looking for medieval France. The aura is Edwardian. The crowds tend to be more urban and hip than the folk at resorts, say, near La Rochelle or in the remote stretches of Brittany. None of this comes cheaply—Deauville is stylish and not (by anyone's definition of the word) inexpensive.

With its golf courses, casinos, deluxe hotels, La Touques and Clairefontaine racetracks, regattas, yachting harbor, polo grounds, and tennis courts, Deauville is still a formidable contender for the business of the smart set. Looking for a charming place to stroll through the town? Head for the shop-lined **rue Eugène-Colas, place Morny** (named for the resort's founder), and **rue des Villas** (lined with holiday homes built by the well-heeled during France's gilded age).

BEACHES   Expect to spend time on Deauville's boardwalk, **Les Planches,** a wooden plank promenade running parallel to the beach; its edges are lined with formal beaux-arts or half-timbered Norman-inspired architecture. In summer, especially August, parasols dot the beach, and oiled bodies stretch out and seemingly cover every inch of sand.

The resort's only beach is **Plage de Deauville,** a long strip of sand that's part of Plage Fleurie. Flowers don't actually grow from the sand, but its name was part of a successful 19th-century marketing ploy developed by entrepreneurs to attract Parisians and, to a lesser extent, the English. Allegedly, its borders harbored some fragile flowers long before the mobs of sunbathers, high tides, and building sprees buried them forever, but today, if they bloom at all, they appear during April and May, when most people aren't likely to be here.

If you're looking for a gay and nudist beach, you'll have to go 24 miles from Deauville toward Caen, to **Merville-France-Ville,** but considering how permissive most Deauville fans are, many gays feel perfectly comfortable here.

Access to every beach in Normandy is free, although at least within Deauville itself, you'll pay about 8F (1.22, $1.35) per hour for parking in any of the many public parking lots beside the sea.

GOLF   On Mont Canisy, Deauville's **New-Golf Club** (℗ 02-31-14-24-24, see below) offers a tranquil country setting tinged by the sea's salty tang. The par-71, 18-hole course rolls through 6,490 yards of rapid greens and difficult roughs, with sweeping views of the Auge valley and the sea; and the par-36, 8-hole course runs 3,315 yards through a lush wooded setting. In addition, there's an indoor driving range, a putting green, a practice bunker, available instruction from three professionals, and a clubhouse with not only a bar and restaurant but also an exclusive line of golfing gear. A franchise of the Lucien Barrière chain of resorts, hotels, and casinos, the facility includes a palatial half-timbered hotel (see below). Greens fees for hotel residents are 250 to 400F (38– 60.80, $36–$58) Saturday and Sunday and 180 to 240F (27.35– 36.50, $26–$35) Monday to Friday. Nonguests pay a supplement of 20% above those rates.

HORSE RACES   Take a break from the sun and sand to watch the horse races, but only from late June to early September. At least one racing event is held every afternoon, either a race at 2pm or a polo match at 3pm. The venues are the **Hippodrome de Deauville La Touques,** boulevard Mauger (℗ **02-31-14-20-00**), in the heart of town, near the Mairie de Deauville (Town Hall); or the **Hippodrome de Deauville Clairefontaine,** route de Clairefontaine (℗ **02-31-14-69-00**), a bit farther afield but still within the city limits.

SHOPPING

This seaside town has a pedestrian shopping area between the polo field and the port; the main drags are rue Mirabeau, rue Albert-Fracasse, and the west end of avenue de la République. At **La Cave de Deauville,** 48 rue Mirabeau (℗ **02-31-87-35-36**), you'll be able to find a wide selection of apple ciders, cheeses, Calvados, and the aperitif known as pommeau.

For an overview of the agrarian bounty derived from the fertility of Norman soil, head for the **open-air market (Marché Publique)** that's conducted in the Place du Marché, immediately adjacent to the very central Place Morny. June to mid-September, it's open daily 8am till 1pm. The rest of the year, the market is held only on Tuesday, Friday, and Saturday mornings 8am to 1pm. In addition to fruits, vegetables, poultry, cider, wine, and cheeses, you'll find cookware, porcelain table settings, and cutlery for sale.

ACCOMMODATIONS
EXPENSIVE

Hôtel du Golf ✦✦✦   Golfers gravitate to this half-timbered hotel created by the Lucien Barrière chain in the late 1980s. Lavishly outfitted in an English country-house style, it's one of the few hotels in Normandy with its own golf course. If the links aren't your thing, you might consider the Normandy or Le Royal. Rooms come in a wide range of sizes; those in back open onto the links, those in front have better views of the Channel; some have balconies. The older ones aren't as good as the recently renovated ones. The best rooms are called

Prestige, featuring antique-style furnishings and French windows, along with spacious baths and balconies. Each comes with fine mattresses on quality beds.

At New-Golf Club, Mont Canísy, St-Arnoult 14800 Deauville. ✆ **02-31-14-24-00.** Fax 02-31-14-24-01. hoteldugolf@lucienbarriere.com. 178 units. 990F–2,500F (150.50– 380, $143.55–$362.50) double; 2,400F–4,000F (364.80– 608, $348–$580) suite. AE, DC, MC, V. Closed Nov–Dec 20. From Deauville, take D278 south for 1½ miles. **Amenities:** 2 restaurants, bar; laundry/dry cleaning; room service; outdoor heated pool; fitness center; sauna; 2 tennis courts; 27-hole golf course. *In room:* A/C, TV, minibar, safe.

Hôtel Normandy ✦✦✦   Resembling a Norman village, with turrets, gables, and windows piercing the sloping roofs, this year-round hotel is near the casino, in a park of well-manicured shrubs and flowers. It's Deauville's best and also its most legendary, though some discriminating people prefer Le Royal, which is almost as good. The interior is as warm and comfortable as a rambling country house, with chandeliers and Oriental carpeting. Rooms, in a constant state of refurbishment, are chicly styled and come in a range of shapes and sizes, with many luxuries such as deluxe mattresses, double glazing, and ample space. Sloping ceilings make the fourth-floor units feel cramped.

38 rue Jean-Mermoz, 14800 Deauville. ✆ **02-31-98-66-22.** Fax 02-31-98-66-23. www.lucienbarriere.com. 303 units. 1,190F–2,800F (180.93– 425.60, $172.55–$406) double; 2,700F–9,800F (410.40– 1,489.60, $391.50–$1,421) suite. AE, DC, MC, V. Free outside parking, 100F (15.20, $14.50) in garage. **Amenities:** Restaurant, bar; room service; laundry/dry cleaning; fitness room; steam room; 2 tennis courts; nursery. *In room:* TV, minibar, hair dryer, safe.

Le Royal ✦✦✦   Le Royal adjoins the casino and fronts a block-wide park near the Channel. An ideal place for a holiday, it rises like a regal palace, with columns and exposed timbers. Rooms range from sumptuous suites to cozy little nooks. Most were recently renovated, with thick rugs and comfortable mattresses. Those on the upper floors open onto the most panoramic views.

Bd. Eugène-Cornuché, 14800 Deauville. ✆ **02-31-98-66-33.** Fax 02-31-98-66-34. www.lucienbarriere.com/ deauville. 252 units. 1,380F–3,800F (209.75– 577.60, $200.10–$551) double; from 2,800F–16,000F (425.60– 2,432, $406–$2,320) suite. AE, DC, MC, V. Closed Nov to mid-Mar. **Amenities:** Restaurant, bar; heated outdoor pool; sauna; 2 recreation rooms; health club; room service; laundry/dry cleaning. *In room:* TV, minibar, hair dryer, safe.

INEXPENSIVE

Hôtel Ibis *Value*   Built in the 1980s as part of a nationwide chain, the Ibis is scenically located and offers some of the best values of any hotel in Deauville. The modern building overlooks the harbor. Rooms are comfortable but done in a dull chain style. Each was renovated during the late 1990s and has comfortable, but not particularly plush, beds. The restaurant offers a traditional French menu.

9 quai de la Marine, 14800 Deauville. ✆ **02-31-14-50-00.** Fax 02-31-14-50-05. ho795@accor-hotels.com. 95 units. 340F–475F (51.70– 72.20, $49.30–$68.90) double; 725F–790F (110.20– 120.130, $105.15–$114.55) duplex suite for 2 to 6. AE, DC, MC, V. Parking 42F (6.40, $6.10). **Amenities:** Restaurant; bar; baby-sitting. *In room:* TV.

Hôtel Le Trophée   This modern replica of a half-timbered medieval building is in the middle of Deauville, 500 feet from the beach. Rooms, with nondescript contemporary furniture, are on the small side, but have private balconies overlooking the shopping streets. Bathrooms are small. The roof has been converted into a sun terrace and provides a bird's-eye view of the town as well as a more private tanning area than the beach. If you plan on taking one or more of your meals here, eat at least one under the stars in the patio courtyard garden.

81 rue du Général-Leclerc, 14800 Deauville. ✆ **02-31-88-45-86.** Fax 02-31-88-07-94. 24 units. 400F–580F (60.80– 88.15, $58–$84.10) double; 750F–980F (114– 148.95, $108.75–$142.10) suite. AE, DC,

MC, V. Parking 50F (7.60, $7.25). **Amenities:** Restaurant, bar; room service; baby-sitting; pool. *In room:* TV, minibar, hair dryer.

L'Augeval ⟨★⟩ Across from the racetrack and mere blocks from the beach and casino, this rare gem provides you with a great mix of city flair and country charm. The former private villa was built in the early 1900s and sits in the middle of well-kept lawns and gardens. Rooms range from medium to spacious.

15 av. Hocquart-de-Turtot, 14800 Deauville. ⟨℃⟩ **02-31-81-13-18.** Fax 02-31-81-00-40. 32 units. 440F–870F (66.930– 132.25, $63.80–$126.15) double; 890F–1,400F (135.30– 212.80, $129.05–$203) suite. AE, DC, MC, V. Parking 50F (7.60, $7.25). **Amenities:** Restaurant, bar; room service; small heated pool; fitness room. *In room:* TV, minibar, hair dryer, Jacuzzi (some rooms).

DINING

Chez Miocque TRADITIONAL FRENCH Irreverent and hip, this cafe near the casino and the resort's boutiques does a bustling business at its sidewalk tables. The owner, known simply as Jack, speaks English and will welcome you for lunch or dinner or provide a convivial bar-type setting if you just want to stop in for a drink. The place serves hearty brasserie-style food, including succulent lamb stew with spring vegetables, filet of skate with cream-based caper sauce, mussels in white-wine sauce, and steaks. The portions are filling, and the atmosphere can be lively. The dish of the day is always from the sea.

81 rue Eugène-Colas. ⟨℃⟩ **02-31-88-09-52.** Reservations recommended. Main courses 100F–180F (15.20– 27.35, $14.50–$26.10). MC, V. May–Oct daily 9am–midnight; mid-Feb to Apr and Nov–Dec Fri–Mon noon–3pm and 7pm–midnight. Closed Jan 1 to mid-Feb.

Le Ciro's ⟨★★★⟩ FRENCH/SEAFOOD Hot on the resort's social scene, Le Ciro's serves Deauville's best seafood. It's expensive, but worth it. If you want a bit of everything, ask for the *plateau de fruits de mer,* with lobster and various oysters and clams. The most expensive item is grilled lobster. For an elaborate appetizer, we recommend a tartare of sea bass and salmon, or lobster salad with truffles. A marmite of scallops with sweet sauterne wine and saffron makes a superb main course. Classics like grilled beef filet with béarnaise and grilled lamb cutlets with thyme are also offered. The collection of Bordeaux wine is exceptional. The ambience here is airy, elegant, stylish, and evocative of the Belle Époque heyday of Deauville at its most appealing.

Promenade des Planches. ⟨℃⟩ **02-31-14-31-14.** Reservations required. Main courses 90F–350F (13.70– 53.20, $13.05–$50.75); fixed-price menu 205F (31.15, $29.75). AE, DC, MC, V. Daily noon–2:30pm and 7:30–10pm. Jan–Mar closed Tues night and all day Wed. Also closed 2 weeks in Jan.

Le Spinnaker ⟨★⟩ NORMAN Directed by the owner/chef, Pascal Angenard, this charming yellow-and-white restaurant features regional cuisine. The menu specialties are ultrafresh and richly satisfying, like terrine of foie gras with four spices, roast lobster with cider vinegar and cream-enriched potatoes, slow-cooked baby veal flank, and a succulent tart with hot apples. Pascal recommends the roast turbot flavored with shallots en confit. A fine array of wines can accompany your meal. There are nights when a dish here or there might not always be sublime, but usually most are excellent.

52 rue Mirabeau. ⟨℃⟩ **02-31-88-24-40.** Reservations required. Main courses 140F–310F (21.30– 47.10, $20.30–$44.95); fixed-price menus 180F–260F (27.35– 39.50, $26.10–$37.70). AE, DC, MC, V. Apr–Sept Tues–Sun 12:30–2:30pm and 7:30–10pm; Oct–Mar Wed–Sun 12:30–2:30pm and 7:30–10pm. Closed Jan.

DEAUVILLE AFTER DARK

Opened in 1912, the **Casino de Deauville,** rue Edmond-Blanc (⟨℃⟩ **02-31-14-31-14**), is one of France's premier casinos. Its original Belle Époque core has been expanded with a theater, a nightclub, two restaurants (Brunnel and le Cercle), and an extensive collection of slot machines (*machines à sous*). The casino makes an important distinction between the areas devoted to slot machines and more formal and elegant areas containing such games as roulette, baccarat, chemin de fer, 21, and poker. Areas containing slot machines are open daily 11am to 2am (to 3am Friday and Saturday), are accessible without cost or fee, and have no dress code. The more elegant and formal areas containing *"les jeux traditionnels"* are open daily at 4pm and close between 3 and 4am, depending on business and the day of the week. Entrance to the more formal (and more interesting) areas costs 70F (10.65, $10) per person. Men are requested to wear jackets (ties not required) in the formal areas of the casino. The most interesting nights here are Friday and Saturday, when the cabaret theater and all the restaurants are open. The theater presents glittering, moderately titillating shows at 10:30pm on Friday and Saturday. Entrance is 160F (24.30, $23) per person.

If it's a dance club you're looking for, head to the **Y Club,** 14 bis rue Désiré-le-Hoc (✆ 02-31-88-30-91), with its high-energy dance scene, or the **Snake Pit Club,** 13 rue Albert-Fracasse (✆ 02-31-88-17-64), where the energy level is less intense but by no means sleepy. If you want to say you've played miniature golf in France, stop by for a round at **Bar du Golf Miniature,** boulevard de la Mer (✆ 02-31-98-40-56), with its sophisticated little bar alongside that attracts a varied crowd. On Friday nights, a DJ spins the tunes. An alternative choice for salsa, merengue, and reggae is the **Brok Café,** 14 av. du Général-de-Gaulle (✆ 02-31-81-30-81). And if you want to re-create an almost Paleolithic sense of the restrained but decadent ambience of the 1970s, consider an hour or two within **Le Régine's,** inside Deauville's casino, rue Edmond-Blanc (✆ 02-31-88-07-21).

An alternative spot for dancing, 3 miles from Deauville, is **Dancing Les Planches,** Le Bois Lauret, Blonville (✆ 02-31-87-58-09). Here you'll find up-to-date music, an active dance floor, billiard tables, even an outdoor swimming pool flanking a warm-weather bar.

4 Trouville ★★

128 miles NW of Paris, 27 miles NE of Caen

Across the Touques River from its more fashionable (and expensive) rival Deauville, Trouville feels like a fisher's port, like the more charming Honfleur but with fewer boutiques and art galleries. Don't expect the grand beaux-arts atmosphere of Deauville—Trouville is more low-key. It's also less dependent on resort francs than its neighbor, for when the bathers leave its splendid sands, Trouville lives on—its resident population of fishers sees to that.

ESSENTIALS

GETTING THERE There are **rail** connections from Gare St-Lazare in Paris to Trouville (see the Deauville section earlier in this chapter). **Bus Verts du Calvados** services Trouville, Deauville, and the surrounding region, linking those towns with the rest of Normandy. For information about bus departures and fares in and out of Trouville, call the **Gare Routière** (✆ 08-01-21-42-14). If you're traveling by **car** from Deauville, simply travel west along D180 to Trouville.

VISITOR INFORMATION The **Office de Tourisme** is at 32 quai Fernand-Moureaux (✆ 02-31-14-60-70).

EXPLORING THE TOWN

In the heyday of Napoléon III, during the 1860s, boulevardiers used to bring their wives and families to Trouville and stash their mistresses in the then fledgling, and decidedly unstylish, Deauville, which was just beginning to emerge from what was at the time a marsh. Consequently, whereas Deauville is a planned city, with straight avenues and a sense of industrial-age orderliness, the narrow and labyrinthine alleyways of Trouville hint at its origins as a medieval fishing port.

Our recommendation? Stamp around Trouville, enjoying its low-key charm, and when you tire of it, join the caravan of traffic that heads across the river to the bright lights and glamour of Deauville (see above).

Les Planches is a rambling stretch of seafront boardwalk dotted with concessions on one side and a view of the sea on the other. In midsummer, expect lots of flesh sprawled on the sands before you in various states of undress—this is France. There's only one beach, **Plage de Trouville,** though when you've tired of it, you'll only have to cross the river to the Plage de Deauville. On Trouville's seafront promenade is the **Piscine de Trouville,** Promenade des Planches (© 02-31-14-48-10), a freshwater pool that gets very, very crowded in summer. An alternative option for pool swimming is at Deauville, just across the river. There, the **Piscine Olympique,** Bord de Mer (© 02-31-14-02-17), offers a larger alternative, albeit with seawater rather than fresh water. Entrance to either pool costs 32F (4.85, $4.65) adults, 23F (3.50, $3.35) children under 16, and both are open between late May and mid-September from 10am to 7pm.

SHOPPING

Trouville's main shopping streets are **quai Fernand-Moureaux, rue des Bains,** some sections of which are off-limits to conventional traffic, and to a lesser degree, the **rue du Général-de-Gaulle,** which has a greater concentration of everyday shops such as food outlets and hardware stores. And although the rue des Bains has its share of fashion boutiques and clothing stores, greater numbers of stylish shops lie within the neighboring resort of Deauville.

ACCOMMODATIONS

Hôtel Carmen *Value*   This highly recommended Logis de France, run by the Bude family, consists of two connected late-18th-century villas, one designed by a cousin of Georges Bizet. The management prefers that you take the half-board plan (breakfast and dinner). Rooms come in a variety of sizes; although most of them are rather small, they are fitted with a comfortable mattress on a good bed, plus a small shower-only bathroom. Some overlook a flower-filled courtyard.

24 rue Carnot, 14360 Trouville. © 02-31-88-35-43. Fax 02-31-88-08-03. 16 units, 15 with bathroom. 250F (38, $36.25) double without bathroom, 380F–460F (57.75– 69.90, $55.10–$66.70) double with bathroom. Half-board 240F (36.530, $34.80) extra per person. AE, DC, MC, V. **Amenities:** Restaurant; bar. *In room:* TV, minibar.

Le Beach Hotel   This hotel emerges out of a lackluster lot as a top accommodation, only 150 feet from the beach, facing Trouville harbor. Although a poor relation to the palace hotels of Deauville, it offers grand comfort at a more affordable price. Its average-size rooms have modern furniture and comfortable beds, plus ocean views. Most bathrooms have showers only.

1 quai Albert-1er, 14360 Trouville. © **02-31-98-12-00.** Fax 02-31-87-30-29. www.pierreetvacances.fr. 110 units. 585F–795F (88.90– 120.85, $84.85–$115.30) double; from 990F (150.50, $143.55) suite. AE, DC, MC, V. Closed Jan 4–28. Parking 50F (7.60, $7.25). **Amenities:** Excellent restaurant (Norman/International), bar; pool; room service; laundry. *In room:* TV, hair dryer.

DINING

La Petite Auberge NORMAN   If you want something inexpensive without sacrificing quality, head to this Norman bistro a block from the casino. Try the *soupe de poissons* (fish soup), one of the finest along the Flower Coast, or the seafood pot-au-feu, featuring filet of sole, scallops, monkfish, and salmon beautifully simmered together. You can also order grilled beef and stuffed rabbit braised in cider. Since the bistro seats only 30, reservations are vital in summer.

7 rue Carnot. ℭ **02-31-88-11-07**. Reservations required. Fixed-price menus 139F–220F (21.15– 33.45, $20.15–$31.90). AE, MC, V. Daily noon–2:30pm and 7–10pm. Sept–June closed Tues–Wed.

Les Vapeurs ★★ FRENCH/SEAFOOD   This Art Deco brasserie, one of the most popular on the Norman coast, is frequented by stylish Parisians on *le weekend*. Established in 1926, it has been called the Brasserie Lipp of Normandy. The windows face the port, and in warm weather you can dine at sidewalk tables. Seafood is the specialty: A wide range of shrimp, mussels laced with cream, crinkle-shelled oysters, and fish is served. Sauerkraut is also popular.

160 bd. Fernand-Moureaux. ℭ **02-31-88-15-24**. Reservations recommended. Main courses 100F–190F (15.20– 28.930, $14.50–$27.55). AE, MC, V. Daily noon–1am.

TROUVILLE AFTER DARK

If the casino in Deauville is too stuffy for your tastes, you'll feel more comfortable in its smaller, less grand, less architecturally distinctive sibling in Trouville, **Louisiane Follies,** place du Maréchal-Foch (ℭ **02-31-87-75-00**). Here you can try your hand in more of a New Orleans–style environment, with areas that add to the city-of-sin feel, like a blues/jazz bar and small-scale replica of Bourbon Street. Entrance to the area containing slot machines is free. It is open daily 10am to between 2 and 4am, depending on the day of the week and business. Entrance to the more formal area with roulette and blackjack tables costs 70F (10.65, $10) per person. The formal area is open daily 4pm till between 2 and 4am, depending on the day of the week and business. Men aren't required to wear jackets and ties here, bit tennis shoes are not allowed.

Trouville's leading nightclub and disco, **L'Embellie** (ℭ **02-31-87-75-02**), lies within the casino as well. Open nightly, it charges 100F (15.20, $15) for entrance, and the price includes one free drink.

5 Caen ★★★

148 miles NW of Paris, 74 miles SE of Cherbourg

Situated on the banks of the Orne, the port of Caen suffered great damage in the invasion of Normandy in 1944. Nearly three-quarters of its buildings, 10,000 in all, were destroyed, though the twin abbeys founded by William the Conqueror and his wife, Mathilda, were spared. The city today is essentially modern and has many broad avenues and new apartment buildings. Completely different from Deauville and Trouville, this capital of Lower Normandy is bustling, congested, and commercial (it's a major rail and ferry junction). The student population of 30,000 and the hordes of travelers have made Caen more cosmopolitan than ever.

ESSENTIALS

GETTING THERE   From Paris's Gare St-Lazare, 13 **trains** per day arrive in Caen (trip time: 2½ hr.), costing from 174F (26.45, $25) one-way. There are also six trains from Rouen (trip time: 1¾ hr.), costing from 11F (17.35, $17) one-way. When **driving** from Paris, travel west along A13 to Caen (driving time: 2½ hr.).

VISITOR INFORMATION   The **Office de Tourisme** is on place St-Pierre in the 16th-century Hôtel d'Escoville (© **02-31-27-14-14;** www.ville-caen.fr).

EXPLORING THE CITY

Abbaye aux Dames 🕉🕉   Founded by Mathilda, wife of William the Conqueror, this abbey embraces Église de la Trinité, which is flanked by Romanesque towers. Its spires were destroyed in the Hundred Years. In the 12th-century choir is the tomb of Queen Mathilda; note the ribbed vaulting.

Place de la Reine-Mathilde. © **02-31-06-98-98.** Free admission. Daily 2–5:30pm. Free guided 1-hr. tour of choir, transept, and crypt (in French) daily at 2:30 and 4pm.

Abbaye aux Hommes 🕉🕉   Founded by William and Mathilda, the abbey is adjacent to the Église St-Etienne, which you enter on place Monseigneur-des-Hameaux. During the height of the Allied invasion, denizens of Caen flocked to St-Etienne for protection. The church is dominated by twin 84m (276-ft.) Romanesque towers; its 15th-century spires helped earn Caen the appellation "city of spires." A marble slab inside the high altar commemorates the site of William's tomb. The Huguenots destroyed the tomb in an uprising in 1562, save for a hipbone that was recovered. However, during the French Revolution the last of William's dust was scattered to the wind. The hand-carved wooden doors and elaborately sculpted wrought-iron staircase are exceptional. From the cloisters you get a good view of the two towers of St-Etienne.

Esplanade Jean-Marie-Louvel. © **02-31-30-42-81.** Open for self-guided visits, without charge, daily 8:15am–7:30pm. Tours (in French) daily at 9:30 and 11am and 2:30 and 4pm for 10F (1.50, $1.45) for adults, 5F (.75, 75¢) for students, free for anyone under 18.

Caen Memorial (Le Mémorial de Caen)   The memorial stands 10 minutes away from the Pegasus Bridge and 15 minutes from the landing beaches. The museum presents a journey through history from 1918 to the present, recalling the unfolding and the meaning of World War II. It's also an ideal place to relax by walking through International Park or having brunch, tea, a cold buffet, or a drink in the restaurant, or browsing through the boutique for that special souvenir. Expect to spend at least 2½ hours at this site—anyone intrigued by 20th-century European history will be fascinated by the display here.

Esplanade Dwight-Eisenhower. © **02-31-06-06-44.** Admission 76F (11.55, $11) adults; 65F (9.930, $9.45) for students and ages 10–18; free to World War II veterans, war disabled, war widows, and children under 10. Daily 9am–6pm (open till 9pm from mid-July to mid-Aug). Closed Christmas, Jan 1–18.

The Château   Built on the ruins of a fortress erected by William the Conqueror in 1060, the grounds can be entered at Esplanade de la Paix. The gardens are ideal for strolling, and from the ramparts a panoramic view of Caen unfolds. Within the compound are two museums, including the **Musée de Normandie,** the former keep of the governor of the château. It is devoted to artifacts from Normandy, including archaeological finds, along with a collection of regional sculpture, paintings, and ceramics (© **02-31-30-47-50**). Admission is 10F (1.50, $1.45) and it is open Wednesday to Monday 9:30am to 12:30pm and 2 to 6pm. Also within the walls of the château is the **Musée des Beaux-Arts,** with a collection of old masters (not their finest works) including Titian, Rembrandt, Veronese, and Tintoretto (© **02-31-30-47-70**). Admission is 20F (3.05, $2.90), and it is open Wednesday to Monday 9:30am to 6pm.

SHOPPING

Caen has some good boutique-lined shopping streets, like **boulevard du Maréchal-Leclerc, rue St-Pierre,** and **rue de Strasbourg. Antiques** hunters should check out the shops along rue Ecuyère and rue Commerçantes, and the antiques show at the **Parc aux Expositions,** rue Joseph-Philippon (✆ **02-31-29-99-99**), in early December. The **markets** at place St-Sauveur on Friday mornings and place Courtonne on Sunday mornings also sell secondhand articles.

For reproduction antique furniture built to meet your specific needs, visit **La Reine Matilde,** 47 rue St-Jean (✆ **02-31-85-45-52**); it also sells decorative items, including a selection of bed linens and curtains. If you need some gift items, **Le Chocolatier Hotot,** 13 rue St-Pierre (✆ **02-31-86-31-90**), has a cornucopia of chocolate products as well as local jams and jellies; or you may want to stop by **Folklore,** 7 rue de Geole (✆ **02-31-86-34-13**), where you can find many regional items, like pottery, ciders, faïence, and decorative plates.

For objets d'art and paintings, check out **L'Atelier,** 33 rue Montoir-Poissonnerie (✆ **02-31-44-49-38**), which showcases local painter Gérard Boukhezer. If you're in the mood for browsing through worthy inventories of wine and *eaux-de-vie* from throughout France, head for **Nicolas,** rue Bellivet 10 (✆ **02-31- 85-24-19**).

ACCOMMODATIONS

Le Dauphin and **Le Manoir d'Hastings** (see "Dining," below) also rent rooms.

Holiday Inn ✪ This is the best hotel in town with a flavor that is both French and international. Across from the racecourse and opposite an angel-capped monument to a military hero, the hotel was built before World War II but was enlarged and modernized in 1991 when it adopted the Holiday Inn logo. Rooms are predictable, comfortable, and well maintained. The cozy bar is favored by Americans visiting the D-day beaches.

Place du Maréchal-Foch, 14000 Caen. ✆ **800/465-4329** in the U.S., or 02-31-27-57-57. Fax 02-31-27-57-58. www.holiday-inn.com. 88 units. 560F–695F (85.10– 104.25, $81.20–$100.80) double. AE, DC, MC, V. Bus: 1, 3, 4, 10, or 11. **Amenities:** Restaurant, bar; room service; baby-sitting. *In room:* A/C (in 44 units), TV, minibar (in 60%), hair dryer.

Hôtel Bristol Built after the devastating bombings of World War II and renovated in 1992, this hotel is on a block of modern apartments and shops, not far from the park. Consider the Bristol more of a bare-bones stopover than a charming inn. The prices are fair. Rooms are small but well kept, each with a comfortable bed and a shower-only bathroom. Breakfast is the only meal served.

31 rue du 11-November, 14000 Caen. ✆ **02-31-84-59-76**. Fax 02-31-52-29-28. 25 units. 230F–260F (34.95– 39.50, $33.35–$37.70) double. Rates include continental breakfast. DC, MC, V. Bus: 12. *In room:* No phone.

Hôtel de France The exterior of this six-story brick building is plain but reflects a bit of charm. Maybe it's the window boxes outside every room or the windows that swing open to let in breezes. Rooms are functional with simple furnishings. Mattresses are thin but still comfortable, especially at this price, and the small bathrooms come with showers. The public areas have a provincial charm. This hotel is a favorite with tour groups (often World War II veterans) and offers a restaurant that serves only these groups.

10 rue de la Gare, 14000 Caen. ✆ **02-31-52-16-99**. Fax 02-31-83-23-16. 47 units. 200F–300F (30.40– 5.60, $29–$43.50) double. MC, V. Free parking. **Amenities:** Restaurant (groups only). *In room:* TV.

Hôtel des Quatrans   This agreeable, unpretentious hotel was built after World War II, and thanks to continual renovations, remains one of Caen's best bargains. Don't expect luxury: The hotel has four floors and no elevator; rooms are old-fashioned and simple, and offer the most basic amenities, such as small shower-only bathrooms. Mattresses aren't particularly plush, but at these prices, who can complain? Breakfast is the only meal served, at 38F (5.80, $5.50).

17 rue Gémare, 14300 Caen. ✆ **02-31-86-25-57.** Fax 02-31-85-27-80. 36 units. 260F–290F (39.50–43.50, $37.70–$42.05) double. V. Free parking. Bus: 2 or 7. *In room:* No phone.

Hôtel Royal   This hotel is reliable and a bargain. The original Hôtel Royal was destroyed during a World War II bombing raid. The hotel was rebuilt several years later, and today it's surrounded by a busy commercial area of shops and restaurants as well as more tranquil pedestrian streets. The last renovation, completed in 1998, brought all the rooms up to an acceptable level of comfort, though space is a bit cramped. All the bedrooms contain a shower, and nearly three-fourths are also equipped with tub baths.

1 place de la République, 14000 Caen. ✆ **02-31-86-55-33.** Fax 02-31-79-89-44. 43 units. 300f–380F (45.60– 57.75, $43.50–$55.10) double. AE, MC, V. Parking 40F (6.10, $5.80). **Amenities:** Bar. *In room:* TV.

A NEARBY CHOICE

Relais Château d'Audrieu ★★   This château in a park offers the most luxurious accommodations near Caen. It was built of local stone (*pierre de Caen*) at the beginning of the 18th century. During the Allied invasion, some of the fiercest fighting took place right around this hotel. Notice the gashes and wounds in the trees in the surrounding park. The château functioned as a private home until 1976, when it was transformed into this hotel. Rooms are lovely and well appointed, with antiques, each with a carefully planned unique style. Beds are elegantly appointed with deluxe mattresses, tasteful linens, and beautiful fabrics.

14250 Audrieu. ✆ **02-31-80-21-52.** Fax 02-31-80-24-73. www.relaischateaux.fr/audrieu. 29 units. 790F–1,500F (120.10– 228, $114.55–$217.50) double; 2,250F–2,400F (342– 364.80, $326.25–$348) suite. AE, MC, V. Closed Nov 30–Feb 14. From Caen, take N13 for 11 miles west of Caen, then D158 for 2 miles to Audrieu. **Amenities:** Restaurant, bar; room service; baby-sitting; outdoor pool. *In room:* TV, Jacuzzi (some rooms), hair dryer.

DINING

La Bourride ★★★ NORMAN   Occupying a beautiful 17th-century house, this restaurant serves Caen's best food. The service includes tactful advice on wines to accompany any of the specialties, such as roasted pigeon with vanilla essence and salt. The namesake bourride is concocted from five kinds of fish, seasoned and simmered under the expert eye of Michel Bruneau. The signature dessert is *pommes, pommes, pommes,* which includes at least four variations of apples served on the same dessert plate. On it, look for tarte tatin, apple sorbet, aumônière of apples, and a surprise apple dish as well, all linked to Normandy's love of the apple and its derivatives.

15–17 rue du Vaugueux. ✆ **02-31-93-50-76.** Reservations required. Main courses 140F–230F (21.30– 34.95, $20.30–$33.35); fixed-price menus 340F–620F (51.70– 94.25, $49.30–$89.90). AE, DC, MC, V. Tues–Sat noon–2pm and 7:30–10pm. Closed 3 weeks in Jan, 2 weeks in late Aug. Bus: 1, 3, 4, 10, or 11.

Le Dauphin ★★ TRADITIONAL FRENCH   Although this establishment traces its history back to the Middle Ages, much of what you'll see today dates from a comprehensive restoration and reconstruction during the 1950s. All ingredients are market fresh; owners Stephane and Sylvie Pugnat prepare interesting items like ragoût of lobster with fresh pasta; sweetbreads forester style; gratin of oysters with a fondue of leeks; émincé of sole with fresh spinach; and chartreuse of partridge with crispy potatoes and slices of foie gras.

Le Dauphin also offers 22 well-furnished, richly accessorized guest rooms, each with comfortable beds, for 430F to 480F (65.35 to 72.95, $62 to $70) for a double, and 600F (91.20, $87) for a suite.

29 rue Gémare, 14300 Caen. ℂ 02-31-86-22-26. Fax 02-31-86-35-14. Reservations required. Main courses 75F–105F (11.40– 15.95, $10.90–$15.25); fixed-price menus 120F–380F (18.25– 57.75, $17.40–$55.10). AE, DC, MC, V. Sun–Fri noon–2:30pm; Mon–Sat 7:30–9:30pm. Hotel and restaurant closed 2 weeks in Feb; restaurant also closed July 17–Aug 6.

A NEARBY CHOICE

Le Manoir d'Hastings ★★ FRENCH/NORMAN This restaurant occupies a converted 17th-century monastery with an enclosed Norman garden. It's one of Normandy's most famous and charming inns (and a magnet for Parisians seeking a rustically elegant getaway). Many dishes are twists on Norman favorites, like cider-cooked lobster with Nantua sauce, delicately flavored sea bass, and filet of monkfish poached in port. Beef filets are stuffed with foie gras and scallops braised in an old-fashioned apple-based liqueur, Pommeau. Other choices include a mousseline of scallops with basil-flavored cream sauce, and filets of turbot and sea bass served on the same platter drenched in champagne sauce. For dessert, try the tarte normande flambéed with Calvados.

The manor also offers 15 handsome rooms in a stone-sided annex. Each has a garden view, bathroom, TV, minibar, and phone. A double goes for 500F to 800F (76 to 121.60, $73 to $116). Each of the rooms was overhauled and upgraded in the late 1990s, with improvements in the mattresses, furnishings, and fabrics. The hotel lies very close to Pegasus Bridge, one of the first strategic targets liberated by Allied soldiers after the invasion of Normandy in 1944.

Av. Côte-de-Nacre, 14970 Bénouville. ℂ 02-31-44-62-43. Fax 02-31-44-76-18. Reservations required. Main courses 80F–130F (12.15– 19.75, $11.60–$18.85); fixed-price menus 130F–360F (19.75– 54.70, $18.85–$52.20) at lunch, 175F–390F (26.60– 59.30, $25.40–$56.55) at dinner. AE, DC, MC, V. Sun 12:30–2pm; Tues–Sat 12:30–2pm and 7–9:30pm. Closed 2 weeks in Feb and Nov 12–Dec 4. From Caen, follow the signs north for Ouistreham, then turn off onto RD35. Stay on this road for 6½ miles, following the signs to Bayeux and Bénouville; the manor is next to the village church.

CAEN AFTER DARK

Take a walk down rue de Bras, rue St-Pierre, and the north end of rue Vaugueux to size up the action. If you want to connect with the hip 18-to-35 crowd, go to **Le Chic,** rue des Prairies St-Gilles (ℂ 02-31-94-48-72), where disco music begins at 10:30pm, and where you're likely to get a hint of the various scandals and infidelities that might be blossoming within this otherwise quiet Norman town. Another dance club is **Joy's/Le Paradis,** 10 rue de Strasbourg (ℂ 02-31-85-40-40), with a frenetic crowd and a techno beat.

A couple of the better pubs/bars are **Pub Concorde,** 7 rue Montoir-Poissonnerie (ℂ 02-31-93-61-29), with more than 150 beers to choose from, and **Le Dakota,** 54 rue de Bernières (ℂ 02-31-50-05-25). **Café des Beaux-Arts,** 88 rue de Geôle (ℂ 02-31-86-43-21), has become the hang-out-and-hang-about place where you can talk, play pinball, and listen to jazz, reggae, and salsa. There's no attitude here, just good music and fun people.

The town's most visible and popular gay bar is **Le Zinc,** 12 rue du Vaugueux (ℂ 02-31-93-20-30). It's open nightly from 11pm to as late as 5am.

Finds A Proustian Remembrance of "Balbec"

Torn from the pages of Marcel Proust's _Remembrance of Things Past_, the small resort of "Balbec" was really Cabourg, 15 miles northeast of Caen. Literary fans still come to this Second Empire resort, much of which looks as it did in the Belle Époque. It's still fashionable to stroll along boulevard des Angalis along the sandy beach. Cabourg is preferred by many visitors who otherwise shun the more commercialized Deauville and Trouville. Guests can check into the **Grand hotel,** promenade Marcel Proust (© **02-31-91-01-79;** fax 02-31-24-03-20), a holdover from the opulent days of the 19th century. Proust was a guest, and a bedroom called "Marcel Proust Memory" has been restored from a description in _Remembrance._

---

6 Bayeux ★★

166 miles NW of Paris, 16 miles NW of Caen

The ducs de Normandie sent their sons to this Viking settlement to learn the Norse language. Bayeux has changed a lot since then, but was spared from bombardment in 1944. This was the first French town liberated, and the citizens gave de Gaulle an enthusiastic welcome when he arrived on June 14. Today the town is filled with timbered houses, stone mansions, and cobblestone streets.

Visitors wanting to explore sites associated with "the Longest Day" flood the town, since many memorials (not to mention the beaches) are only 6 to 12 miles away. The cozy little streets are lined with shops, many selling World War II memorabilia, and more postcards and T-shirts than you'll ever need.

ESSENTIALS

GETTING THERE Between 6 and 14 **trains** depart daily from Paris's Gare St-Lazare (depending on the season and the day of the week), for the 2½-hour trip to Bayeux costing 192F (29.20, $28). Most of these trains stop in Caen en route. Travel time between Caen and Bayeux is about 20 minutes and costs 42F (6.40, $6). When **driving** to Bayeux from Paris (driving time: 3 hours), simply take E-46 west from Caen.

VISITOR INFORMATION The **Office de Tourisme** is at pont St-Jean (© **02-31-51-28-28**).

SPECIAL EVENTS The town goes wild with **Fêtes Médiévales** the first weekend in July, when Bayeux has 2 complete days of lunacy and revelry, filling the streets with wine and song outside the cathedral.

SEEING THE SIGHTS

Musée de la Tapisserie de Bayeux ★★★ Here you'll find the Bayeux tapestry—the most famous tapestry in the world. Actually, it's an embroidery on a band of linen, 231 feet long and 20 inches wide, depicting some 58 scenes in eight colors. Contrary to legend, it wasn't made by Queen Mathilda, the wife of William the Conqueror, but was probably commissioned in Kent and created by unknown embroiderers between 1066 and 1077. The first recorded mention of the embroidery was in 1476, when it was explained that it was used to decorate the nave of the Cathédrale Notre-Dame de Bayeux.

Housed in a Plexiglas case, the embroidery tells the story of the conquest of England by William the Conqueror, including such scenes as the coronation of Harold as the Saxon king of England, Harold returning from his journey to Normandy, the surrender of Dinan, Harold being told of the apparition of a comet (a portent of misfortune), William dressed for war, and the death of Harold. The decorative borders include scenes from *Aesop's Fables.*

Admission to this museum also gets you into two less significant museums, the **Musée Baron Gérard,** place de la Liberté (© **02-31-92-14-21**), and the **Musée de l'Art Sacré,** 6 rue Lambert le Forestier (© **02-31-92-73-80**), each within 200 yards of the main attraction. Both are open daily 10am to 12:30pm and 2 to 7pm (to 6pm in winter) and exhibit local examples of regional lace-work, religious statues, and religious and secular paintings.

Centre Guillaume-le-Conquérant, 13 rue de Nesmond. © **02-31-51-25-50**. Admission 41F (6.25, $5.95) adults, 16F (2.45, $2.30) students, free for children 9 and under. May–Aug daily 9am–7pm; mid-Mar to Apr and Sept 1 to mid-Oct daily 9am–6:30pm; mid-Oct to mid-Mar daily 9:30am–12:30pm and 2–6pm.

Musée Memorial de la Bataille de Normandie   Across from the cemetery, this museum deals with the military and human history of the Battle of Normandy (June 6 to August 22, 1944). In a low-slung building designed like a bunker are 440 feet of window and film displays, plus a diorama. Wax soldiers in their uniforms, along with the tanks and guns used to win the battle, are exhibited.

Bd. Fabian-Ware. © **02-31-92-93-41**. Admission 34F (5.15, $4.95) adults, 16F (2.45, $2.30) children, free for children under 10. May–Sept 15 daily 9:30am–6:30pm; Sept 16–Apr daily 10am–12:30pm and 2–6pm. Closed last 2 weeks in Jan.

Notre-Dame de Bayeux 🏛🏛   The cathedral was consecrated in 1077, but partially destroyed in 1105. Romanesque towers left over from that church rise on the western side. The central tower is from the 15th century, with an even later top. The nave is a fine example of Norman Romanesque style. Rich in sculpture, the 13th-century choir, a perfect example of Norman Gothic style, has handsome Renaissance stalls. The crypt was built in the 11th century and then sealed. Its existence remained unknown until 1412.

Rue du Bienvenu. © **02-31-92-01-85**. Free admission. Daily 9am–6pm (to 7pm July–Aug).

ACCOMMODATIONS

Family Home 🅺🆒   Ensconced in the town center, this 16th-century presby-tery, now a hotel, encompasses four connected buildings. Rooms are furnished with Norman antiques, and you can cook your own meals in the kitchen. Madame Lefèvre also serves large, varied meals of Normandy specialties at a communal table. The wine is a smooth Anjou red produced by Mme Lefèvre's family at their vineyards. Rooms are renovated at regular intervals. Rooms are a bit old fashioned, but each contains a soft, comfortable bed.

39 rue du Général-de-Dais, 14400 Bayeux. © **02-31-92-15-22**. Fax 02-31-92-55-72. family-home@ wanadoo.fr. 31 units. All the small bathrooms contain a shower (only 2 with a tub). 200F–230F (30.40– 34.95, $29–$33.35) double. Rates include breakfast. MC, V. **Amenities:** Restaurant; laundry. *In room:* TV.

Hôtel Churchill   Built in 1850, this hotel sits in the heart of the old town on a quiet pedestrian street near lots of boutiques, restaurants, and historic sites. Rooms are somewhat cramped but thoughtfully appointed with delicate

Louis XVI reproductions. Each was renovated in 1998. Large windows look out onto panoramic views of black slate rooftops and Bayeux's 11th-century cathedral. Seven of the 32 rooms contain tubs, the rest showers.

14 rue St-Jean, 14404 Bayeux. ⓒ **02-31-21-31-80.** Fax 02-31-21-41-66. 32 units. 380F–560F (57.75–85.10, $55.10–$81.20) double; 560F–730F (85.10– 110.95, $81.20–$105.85) suite. AE, DC, MC, V. Closed Nov 15–Mar 1. *In room:* TV.

Hôtel d'Argouges   Madame Auregan offers a pair of interconnected 18th-century town houses, with exposed beams, thick walls, and sloping ceilings. In good weather, you can enjoy the garden. Rooms are comfortable, intimate, and cozy with old-fashioned furniture and modern conveniences. Breakfast is the only meal served, but at least three restaurants are within a 2-minute walk.

21 rue St-Patrice, 14402 Bayeux. ⓒ **02-31-92-88-86.** Fax 02-31-92-69-16. dargouges@aol.com. 25 units. 400F–480F (60.80– 72.95, $58–$69.60) double. AE, DC, MC, V. Free parking. **Amenities:** Dining room; bar; laundry; room service; baby-sitting. *In room:* TV, hair dryer.

Hôtel de Luxembourg ⭐   After Le Lion d'Or (below), this Best Western is the area's finest hotel. The restored interior has terrazzo floors and a decor combining neoclassical and Art Deco. Rooms range in size from small to medium and have been overhauled with an eye to modern comfort, including firm mattresses and fine linen on the beds. All units come with small bathrooms with showers, and more than half also have tubs.

25 rue Bouchers, 14403 Bayeux. ⓒ **800/528-1234** in the U.S. and Canada, or 02-31-92-00-04. Fax 02-31-92-54-26. 22 units. 480F–630F (72.95– 95.75, $69.60–$91.35) double; from 850F–990F (129.20– 150.50, $123.25–$143.55) suite. AE, MC, V. **Amenities:** Restaurant, bar; room service; laundry. *In room:* TV, minibar, hair dryer.

Le Lion d'Or ⭐⭐⭐   This old-world hotel, the best in town, offers an open courtyard with lush flower boxes decorating the facade. As befits this old inn, rooms come in various shapes and sizes. The midsize bathrooms are well equipped, each with a shower and more than half with a tub. Guests are required to take at least one meal, but this shouldn't be a problem, as the traditional cuisine is inspired by the region's bounty. There are lots of reasonably priced wines.

71 rue St-Jean, 14400 Bayeux. ⓒ 02-31-92-06-90. Fax 02-31-22-15-64. lion-d-or.bayeux@ wanadoo.fr. 25 units. 450F–650F (68.40– 98.80, $65.25–$94.25) double; 630F–945F (95.75– 143.65, $91.35–$137.05) suite. AE, DC, MC, V. Closed Dec 20–Jan 20. **Amenities:** Restaurant, bar; laundry; baby-sitting. *In room:* TV, minibar.

7 The D-Day Beaches ⭐⭐

Arromanches-les-Bains: 169 miles NW of Paris, 6¹⁄₂ miles NW of Bayeux; Grandcamp-Maisy (near Omaha Beach): 186 miles NW of Paris, 35 miles NW of Caen

During a rainy week in June, 1944, the greatest armada ever known—soldiers and sailors, warships, landing craft, tugboats, jeeps—assembled along the southern coast of England. At 9:15pm on June 5, the BBC announced to the French Resistance that the invasion was imminent, signaling the underground to start dynamiting the railways. Before midnight, Allied planes began bombing the Norman coast. By 1:30am on June 6 (known forever after as "the Longest Day"), members of the 101st Airborne were parachuting to the ground on German-occupied French soil. At 6:30am the Americans began landing on the beaches, code-named Utah and Omaha. An hour later British and Canadian forces made beachheads at Juno, Gold, and Sword.

The Nazis had mocked Churchill's promise in 1943 to liberate France "before the fall of the autumn leaves." When the invasion did come, it was swift, sudden, and a surprise to the formidable "Atlantic wall." Today veterans walk with their children and grandchildren across the beaches where "Czech hedgehogs," "Belgian grills," pillboxes, and "Rommel asparagus" once stood.

ESSENTIALS

GETTING THERE   The best way to get to the D-day beaches is to **drive,** as public transportation is unreliable. The trip takes about 3 hours from Paris. Take A-13 west to Caen, continuing west on E46 to Bayeux. From Bayeux, travel north along D6 until you reach the coast at Port-en-Bessin. From here, D514 runs along the coastline; D-day sites are generally west of Port-en-Bessin. Parking is not a problem, as there are designated areas all along the roadway, most of them free. The best days to visit are during the week, because weekends (especially in summer) can be crowded with tourists and sunbathers alike.

Bus service from Bayeux is uneven and usually involves long delays. **Bus Verts** (© **02-31-92-02-92**) heads for Port-en-Bessin and points west, and bus 74 offers service to Arromanches and other points in the east. Bus 70 travels west from Bayeux to points west, towards Omaha Beach and the American cemetery.

VISITOR INFORMATION   The **Office de Tourisme** is at 4 rue du Maréchal-Joffre, Arromanches-les-Bains (© **02-31-22-36-45**), open April to September.

RELIVING THE LONGEST DAY

Start your exploration of the D-day beaches at the seaside resort of **Arromanches-les-Bains.** In June 1944, it was a fishing port, until it was taken by the 50th British Division. A mammoth prefabricated port known as Winston was towed across the English Channel and installed to supply the Allied forces. "Victory could not have been achieved without it," said Eisenhower. The wreckage of that artificial harbor—known as Mulberry—lies right off the beach, *la plage du débarquement.* The **Musée du Débarquement,** place du 6-Juin (© **02-31- 22-34-31**), features relief maps, working models, a cinema, and photographs, plus a diorama of the landing, with an English commentary. Admission is 35F (5.30, $5) for adults and 20F (3.05, $2.90) for students and children. May to September, it's open daily 9am to 6:30pm. October to April, it's open daily 10am to 12:30pm and 1:30 to 5pm.

Moving along the coast, you arrive at **Omaha Beach,** where you can still see the war wreckage. "Hanging on by their toenails," the men of the 1st and 29th American Divisions occupied the beach that June day. The code-name Omaha became famous, though up till then the beaches had been called St-Laurent, Vierville-sur-Mer, and Colleville. A monument commemorates the heroism of the invaders. Covering some 70 hectares (173 acres) at Omaha Beach, the **Normandy American Cemetery** (© **02-31-51-62-00**) is filled with crosses and Stars of David in Lasa marble. The remains of 9,386 American military dead were buried here on territory now owned by the United States, a gift from the French nation. The cemetery is open 9am to 5pm daily (to 6pm in summer).

Farther along the coast you'll see the jagged lime cliffs of the **Pointe du Hoc.** A cross honors a group of American Rangers, led by Lt.-Col. James Rudder, who scaled the cliffs using hooks to get at the pillboxes. The scars of war are more visible here than at any other point along the beach. Farther along the Cotentin Peninsula is **Utah Beach,** where the 4th U.S. Infantry Division landed at 6:30am. The landing force was nearly 2 miles south of its intended destination, but, fortunately, Nazi defenses were weak at this point. By midday the infantry had completely cleared the beach. A U.S. monument commemorates their heroism.

Nearby, you can visit the sleepy but historic hamlet of **Sainte-Mère-Église,** which was virtually unknown outside of France until the night of June 5 and June 6, when paratroopers dropped from the sky above the town. They were from the 82nd U.S. Airborne Division, under the command of General Matthew B. Ridgeway. Members of the 101st U.S. Airborne Division, commanded by General M.B. Taylor, were also involved. Also in Sainte-Mère-Église is Kilometer "0" on the Liberty Highway, marking the first of the milestones the American armies reached on their way to Metz and Bastogne.

There's a **tourist office** (ⓒ **02-33-21-00-33**), maintaining infrequent and irregular hours, even in the peak of midsummer.

ACCOMMODATIONS & DINING

Hôtel Duguesclin TRADITIONAL FRENCH   We recommend this Norman inn for lunch or even for an overnight. The fish soup, grilled scallops, Norman sole (if available), and grilled turbot with white butter are excellent. Everything tastes better with the dining room's country bread and Norman butter.

The hotel rents 25 simple, comfortable rooms, 7 with bathroom and all with TV. A double without bathroom is 175F to 190F (26.60 to   28.90, $25 to $28), and a double with bathroom goes for 200F to 300F (30.40 to   45.60, $29 to $44). About half are in a cozy and comfortable annex. Improvements are made virtually every year, including attention to the quality of the mattresses.

4 quai Crampon, 14450 Grandcamp-Maisy. ⓒ **02-31-22-64-22.** Fax 02-31-22-34-79. Reservations recommended. Main courses 55F–130F (8.35–   19.75, $8–$18.85); fixed-price menus 65F–200F (9.90–30.40, $9.45–$29). AE, MC, V. Free parking. Daily noon–2pm and 7–9pm. Closed Jan 15–Feb 15 and 1 week in Oct.

La Marée NORMAN   Set beside the port, this small, nautically decorated restaurant in a 1920s building is ideal for seafood devotees. Only fish that are caught within *La Manche* (the English Channel) or within a reasonable distance out in the Atlantic are served, guaranteeing an authentically local culinary experience. First, try the fresh oysters, then perhaps the grilled turbot served with oysters from the nearby coast. Sea bass with bacon and herbs is excellent, as is the sole à la Normande in a herb-flavored cream sauce. During clement weather, the dining room expands onto a terrace dotted with potted shrubs and flowers.

5 quai Henri Chéron. ⓒ **02-31-21-41-00.** Reservations required. Main courses 80F–160F (12.15–   24.30, $11.60–$23.20); fixed-price menus 98F–159F (14.90–   24.15, $14.20–$23.05). AE, DC, MC, V. Daily 12:30–2:30pm and 7–9:30pm. Closed Jan–Feb.

8 Mont-St-Michel 🅐🅐🅐

201 miles W of Paris, 80 miles SW of Caen, 47 miles E of Dinan, 30 miles E of St-Malo

One of Europe's great attractions, the island of **Mont-St-Michel** is surrounded by massive walls measuring more than half a mile in circumference. Connected to the shore by a causeway, it crowns a rocky islet at the border between Normandy and Brittany. The rock is 260 feet high.

ESSENTIALS

GETTING THERE   The most efficient way to reach isolated Mont-St-Michel is to **drive.** The best route involves going from Caen along N175 southwest to

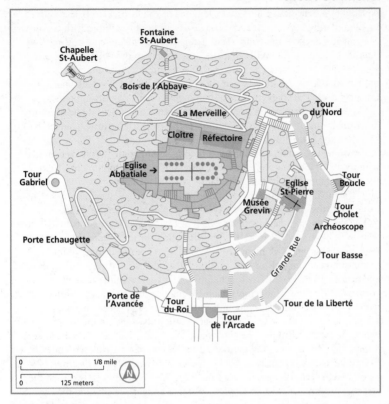

Fontaine St-Aubert
Chapelle St-Aubert
Bois de l'Abbaye
Tour du Nord
La Merveille
Cloître   Réfectoire
Eglise Abbatiale →
Tour Gabriel
Eglise St-Pierre
Tour Boucle
Musée Grevin
Tour Cholet
Archéoscope
Porte Echaugette
Tour Basse
Grande Rue
Porte de l'Avancée
Tour du Roi
Tour de la Liberté
Tour de l'Arcade

0   1/8 mile
0   125 meters
N

Pontorson, then taking E3 north to Mont-St-Michel. Total driving time from Paris is about 4½ hours.

There are no direct trains between Paris and Mont-St-Michel. We advise taking the high-speed **TGV train** from Paris's Gare Montparnasse to Rennes, where you can transfer to the **bus** run by **Les Couriers Bretons** (② 02-99-19-70-70 for reservations and information) for the 75-minute transfer to Mont-St-Michel. Depending on the season, there are between two and five bus departures from Rennes a day, most of which are configured to correspond to the arrival times in Rennes of the TGV. The same company also operates buses, between two and five a day, for a 75-minute ride to Mont-St-Michel from Saint Malo.

VISITOR INFORMATION   The **Office de Tourisme** is in the Corps de Garde des Bourgeois (the Old Guard Room of the Bourgeois), at the left of the town gates (② 02-33-60-14-30). The tourist office is closed two weekends (Saturday and Sunday) in January, and two weekends in February. Otherwise, it's open daily throughout the year.

EXPLORING MONT-ST-MICHEL

You'll have a steep climb up Grande Rue, lined with 15th- and 16th-century houses, to reach the **abbey** (② 02-33-89-80-00). Those who make it to the top can begin their exploration of the Marvel of the West. In the 8th century, St. Aubert, the bishop of Avranches, founded an oratory on the spot. It was replaced by a Benedictine monastery, founded in 966 by Richard I. That burned in 1203. Philip Augustus financed large parts of the abbey in the 13th century.

Ramparts encircle the church and a three-tiered ensemble of 13th-century buildings called **La Merveille** that rise dramatically to the pointed spire of the abbey church. This terraced complex is one of Europe's most important Gothic monuments, a citadel from which the concept of an independent France was nurtured during the darkest years of the English occupation of Aquitaine.

On the second terrace of La Merveille, midway up the rock, is one of Mont-St-Michel's largest and most beautiful rooms, a 13th-century banquet hall known as the **Salle des Chevaliers.**

Crowning the mountain's summit is the **Église Abbatiale** (not to be confused with the less important Église St-Pierre lower down on the mountain). Begun in the 11th century, the abbey church consists of a Romanesque nave and transept, plus a choir in the Flamboyant Gothic style. The rectangular refectory dates from 1212, the cloisters with their columns of pink granite from 1225.

The abbey is open daily (with mass daily at 12:15pm); May to September from 9am to 5:30pm, and October to April from 9:30am to 4:30pm. May to September, it also opens at night, every Monday to Saturday 9pm to 1am (last entrance is at midnight) for 60F (9.10, $9) adults, 40F (6.13, $6) students and persons 18 to 25, and free for children under 18. Nighttime visits allow newcomers to "meet the architecture on a more emotional level." Many visitors wander through the multilevel compound on their own, but if you're interested, there are guided tours—most in French, but occasionally some in English—on an extremely erratic schedule. The cost of any tour is 48F (7.30, $7) adults, 26F (3.95, $3.75) students and persons 12 to 25, and free for children under 12. Everything is closed January 1, May 1, November 1 and 11, and December 25.

The **Archeoscope,** chemin de la Ronde (*②* **02-33-48-09-37**), is a small theater that presents *L'Eau et La Lumière* (Water and Light), celebrating the legend and lore associated with the construction of Mont-St-Michel and its role as a preserver of French medieval nationalism during an era when most of France was swallowed up by foreign invaders. Shows are presented at intervals that begin every 30 to 60 minutes between 9:30am and 5:30pm, based on the season and demand, and last for 30 minutes each. An unusual diversion is the adjacent **Musée Maritime et Archéologique,** Grande Rue (*②* **02-33-60-14-09**), showcasing marine crafts throughout history and the world; information on the ecology of the local tidal flats; and illustrations of the French government's plans, beginning on a grand scale sometime during the lifetime of this edition, to reactivate the tidal cleansing of the nearby marshes. Finally, the **Musée Grevin** (Musée Historique de Mont-St-Michel), chemin de la Ronde (*②* **02-33-60-14-09**), traces the history of the abbey. Admission to each of these attractions is 45F (6.85, $7) adults and 20F (3.05, $2.90) for persons under 16; a combined ticket that's valid for all three attractions costs 75F (11.40, $11) adults and 45F (6.85, $7) children under 16. Each is open daily 9am to 5:30pm (last entrance). Note that locals regard these "attractions" as tourist traps, preferring to concentrate on the architectural and symbolic majesty of La Merveille instead.

ACCOMMODATIONS & DINING

Hôtel du Mouton-Blanc Occupying a pair of buildings, parts of which date from the 14th century, this inn stands halfway between the sea and the basilica and has been accepting guests since the 1700s. Rooms are small but cozy, a welcome haven against the Atlantic chill in winter and the hordes of visitors on the

Tips Sign of the Tides

Mont-St-Michel has been noted for its tides, the highest on the Continent, measuring at certain times a difference of 15m (50 ft.) between high and low tide. Unsuspecting visitors wandering across the sands have been trapped as the sea rushes toward the mont at a speed comparable to that of a galloping horse. However, the bay around the abbey has silted, not only because of the causeway (*la digue*) but because of barriers and dikes that have been erected. Today tides engulf the island less frequently. France will spend $110 million in the next few years replacing the mile-long "La Digue" with a bridge so that water can lap freely around the mont. Parking lots will be moved farther away, and ecology experts will work to encourage bird and marine life in the air and water.

narrow alleyways nearby in summer. All units are equipped with a small shower-only bathroom.

Tables are set in a rustic Norman-style dining room, accented with stone and roughly textured wood, on a terrace overlooking the sea. As in most restaurants here, popular dishes include omelets, along with fruits de mer, mussels in cream sauce, several preparations of lobster, and roast pork in cider sauce.

Grande Rue, 50116 Mont-St-Michel. ⓒ **02-33-60-14-08.** Fax 02-33-60-05-62. 15 units. 390F (59.30, $56.55) double. AE, MC, V. Closed Jan. **Amenities:** Restaurant.

La Mère Poulard NORMAN   This country inn is a shrine to those who revere the omelet that Annette Poulard created in 1888 when the hotel was founded. It's under the same ownership as the more rustic Terrasses Poulard (see below). Her secret has been passed on to the inn's operators: The beaten eggs are cooked over an oak fire in a long-handled copper skillet (you can buy one if you wish). The frothy mixture really creates more of an open-fire soufflé than an omelet. Other specialties are *agneau du pré salé* (lamb) raised on the saltwater marshes near the foundations of the abbey, and an array of fish, including lobster.

The guest house rents 27 rooms with TV, phone, minibar, and hair dryer; however, we suggest you opt for one of the other hotels recommended, and come here for the omelet. A double ranges from 500F to 950F (76 to 144.40, $73 to $138); a suite costs 1,600F (243.20, $232) with double occupancy.

Grande Rue, 50116 Mont-St-Michel. ⓒ **02-33-60-14-01.** www.mere-poulard.fr. Reservations recommended. Main courses 190F–350F (28.90– 53.20, $27.55–$50.75); fixed-price menus 250F–350F (38– 53.20, $36.25–$50.75). AE, DC, MC, V. Daily noon–10pm.

Les Terrasses Poulard   This inn was formed when two village houses—one medieval, the other built in the 1800s—were united. Today the hotel is one of the best in town, with an English-speaking staff and cozy rooms with comfortable beds, plus neatly maintained, shower-only bathrooms. The rates depend on the view: pedestrian traffic on the main street, the village, or the medieval ramparts. The largest and most expensive rooms have fireplaces. The restaurant, which is open every day throughout the year for lunch and dinner, offers a sweeping view over the bay to accompany its seafood and regional Norman specialties.

Grande Rue, 50116 Mont-St-Michel. ⓒ **02-33-60-14-09.** Fax 02-33-60-37-31. www.mere-poulard.fr. 29 units. 300F–900F (45.60– 136.80, $43.50–$130.50) double. AE, DC, MC, V. **Amenities:** Restaurant. *In room:* TV, minibar.

9

Brittany

In this ancient northwestern province, many Bretons stubbornly cling to their traditions. Deep in *l'Argoat* (the interior), many older folks live in stone farmhouses, as their grandparents did, and on special occasions the women still wear the trademark starched-lace headdresses. The Breton language is still spoken, but it's better understood by the Welsh and Cornish than by the French. Sadly, it may die out altogether, despite attempts to keep it alive.

Nearly every village and hamlet has its own *pardon,* a religious festival that can attract thousands of pilgrims in traditional dress. The best-known ones are on May 19 at Treguier (honoring St-Yves), on the second Sunday in July at Locronan (honoring St-Ronan), on July 26 at St-Anne-d'Auray (honoring the "mothers of Bretons"), and on September 8 at Le Folgoet (honoring *ar foll coat*—"idiot of the forest").

Traditionally, the province is divided into Haute-Bretagne and Basse-Bretagne. The rocky coastline, some 750 miles long, is studded with promontories, coves, and beaches. Like the prow of a ship, Brittany juts into the sea. The interior is a land of sleepy hamlets, stone farmhouses, and moors covered with yellow broom and purple heather. We suggest that first-time visitors stick to the coast, where you can see salt-meadow sheep grazing on pastureland whipped by sea breezes. If you're coming from Mont-St-Michel in Normandy, you can easily use St-Malo, Dinan, or Dinard as a base. Visitors coming from the château country of the Loire can explore the south Brittany coastline.

Brittany is a resort region. Many French families come here to go to the beach. British tourists frequent Dinard, although the water is often choppy and cold, with high waves sometimes suitable for surfing. If you're coming to Brittany to go to the beach, La Baule in the south is warmer, with a great beach, gourmet restaurants, and the finest hotels in the region.

REGIONAL CUISINE Breton cuisine derives its excellence from the flavors and freshness of its ingredients. Seafood is abundant: oysters, shellfish, barnacles, and crabs from the Breton coastline are famous throughout France. Many are served raw, especially Belon oysters, as appetizers (on a bed of seaweed with lemon/onion sauce and white wine).

Other regional specialties are *homard* (lobster) in cream sauce, grilled, or boiled; salmon *en brochette;* trout and *l'alose,* excellent with one of the Loire's fruity whites; and lamb and mutton, raised on the salt marshes. *Gigot à la bretonne* (leg of lamb), served with white beans, is one of France's great dishes. The ducklings of Nantes and chickens of Rennes are succulent, as are the strawberries of Plougastel.

Brittany is closely associated with crêpes, served plain, sweet, or salted, filled with jam, cheese, ham, salad, or eggs. Most villages have a crêperie, some of which sell crêpes right on the street.

The only famous wine produced in Brittany is muscadet, cultivated near Nantes, an excellent complement to seafood.

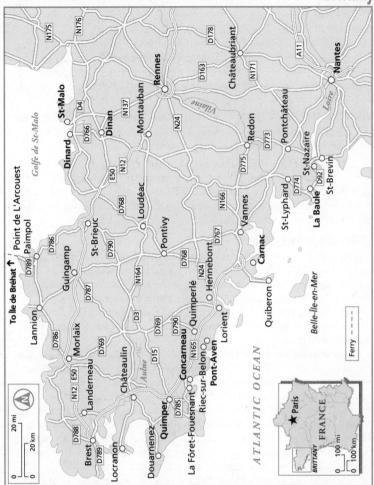

1 St-Malo ⓐⓐⓐ

257 miles W of Paris, 43 miles N of Rennes, 8 miles E of Dinard

Built on a granite rock in the Channel, St-Malo is joined to the mainland by a causeway. It's popular with the English, especially those from the Channel Islands, and, with its warm brown sands, makes a modest claim to be a beach resort. The peninsula curves around a natural harbor whose interior has been subdivided into several smaller basins. The walled city, one of the most impressive examples of civil architecture in Brittany, radiates outward from the town's château and its spiritual centerpiece, the Cathédrale St-Vincent, both of which lie near the peninsula's tip. The curse of St-Malo is the swarm of tour buses and their passengers engulfing the narrow. But there's charm in St-Malo, even though it's "merely the mock," having been virtually rebuilt after damage caused by World War II. The problem is trying to appreciate that charm while being trampled by millions of other travelers intent on the same pursuit.

ESSENTIALS

GETTING THERE   From Paris's Gare Montparnasse, about nine TGV **trains** per day make the journey via Rennes. Trip time is 3 hours; 306F (46.50, $44.35) one-way from Paris. For information and schedules, call © **08-36-35-35-35.** If you're **driving** from Paris, take A13 west to Caen, continuing southwest along N175 to the town of Miniac Morvan. From here, travel north on N137 directly to St-Malo. Driving time is 5 to 6 hours from Paris.

VISITOR INFORMATION   The **Office de Tourisme** is on esplanade St-Vincent (© **02-99-56-64-48**). A valid passport is necessary for the hydrofoil or car-ferry trips and tours to the Channel Islands.

SPECIAL EVENTS   One of the most important Breton *pardons* (festivals) is held at St-Malo in late January and early February: the **Pardon of the New-foundland Fishing Fleet** (*Pardon de St-Ouen*). The town's **Festival de la Musique Sacrée,** from mid-July to mid-August, offers evening concerts from time to time. Check with the Office de Tourisme for details.

EXPLORING THE CITY

For the best view of the bay and the islets at the mouth of the Rance, walk along the **ramparts** ★★★. These were built over several centuries, some of them from the 14th century. They were reconstructed in the 17th century, then restored in the 19th. You can begin at the 15th-century **Porte St-Vincent.**

At the harbor, you can book tours of the **Channel Islands.** Hydrofoils leave for the English island of Jersey (a passport is necessary, of course). Cost is 285F (43.30, $41.35).

At low tide, you can take a 25-minute stroll to the **Île du Grand-Bé** ★★, the site of the tomb of Chateaubriand, "deserted by others and completely surrounded by storms." The tomb, marked by a cross, is simple, unlike the man it honors, but the view of the Emerald Coast from here makes up for it.

Called the Bastille of the West, the forbidding-looking **Château de St-Malo** ★★, Porte St-Vincent (© **02-99-40-71-57**), and its towers shelter the **Musée de l'Histoire de St-Malo,** which is filled with insights into the role of St-Malo within Brittany and the rest of France, as well as souvenirs of the once-notorious pirates Duguay-Trouin and Surcouf, the most famous of the St-Malo privateers. Admission costs 28F (4.25, $4.05) for adults and 14F (2.15, $2.05) for students and children 18 and under. It's open daily from 10am to noon and from 2 to 6pm (closed Mondays from October to March). Free guided tours, conducted in English, are available on an as-needed basis, in July and August only.

After your visit to the château, try to carve out some time for wandering through the narrow streets and alleyways of St-Malo's historic core. Memories of the town's origins as a medieval fishing village confront you at nearly every turn.

St-Malo's **Cathédrale St-Vincent,** 12 rue St-Benoît (© **02-99-40-82-31**), is known for its 1160 nave vault. It's of the Angevin or Plantagenet style, elegantly marking the transition between Romanesque and Gothic. The cathedral also has a Renaissance west facade, with additions from the 18th century and a 15th-century tower. The 14th-century choir is surmounted by a triforium with tre-foiled arches and flanked by chapels. Admission is free, and it's open daily from 8am to 7pm.

BEACHES   As you drive along the coast, you'll find long stretches of sand interspersed with rocky outcroppings that suggest fortresses protecting Brittany from Atlantic storms. You can swim virtually wherever you like (beware of undertows in these storm-tossed waters!), but if you're staying in St-Malo, the two best beaches are **Plage de Bon Secours,** near the northern tip of the Vieille Ville, and **La Grande Plage du Sillon,** a longer stretch of tawny sand that begins at the eastern perimeter of the Vieille Ville.

SHOPPING   If you're in St-Malo on Tuesday or Friday between 8am and 12:30pm, and want to experience a great Breton **market,** head for the Place de la Poissonerie and the Halles au Blé, in the heart of the old city. You can't miss the activity, the bustle, and the hawking of country-fresh produce, cheeses, fish, and dozens of household items, including dishware, cooking utensils, and handcrafts.

For **boutique shopping,** head for rue St-Vincent, rue Porcon, rue Broussaus, rue Georges Clémenceau, rue Ville et Pépin, and rue de Dinan. Here you'll find everything from the trendy to the trashy. In particular, check out **Vêtements Marin-Marine,** 5 Grand' Rue (© **02-99-40-90-32**), for quality men's and women's fashions that include, of course, those great Breton wool sweaters, one of the town's best buys. For last-minute souvenirs, stop by **Aux Délices Mal-ouins,** 12 rue St-Vincent (© **02-99-40-55-22**).

For Breton handcrafts, try **Le Comptoir de Bretagne,** 3 rue Broussais (© **02-99-40-89-69**). In addition to hand-painted stoneware, books, and Gaelic CDs, you'll find Breton lace, Celtic souvenirs, and food items that include almond-flavored pastries and sugarcoated galettes. Other shops offering local crafts and Breton nostalgia include **Aux Arts Celtiques,** 4 rue de Dinan (© **02-99-40-05-41**), and **La Manne Bretonne,** 2 place Guy de Chambre (© **02-23-18-28-20**).

ACCOMMODATIONS

Hôtel Central   Located on a street near the harbor, this hotel is the best of a lackluster lot. It offers well-planned, standardized rooms, each renovated in the 1990s. The structure was rebuilt of granite blocks after the bombings of World War II, like much of the neighborhood surrounding it. Don't expect old-time touches; the furnishings are all contemporary. One of the most compelling reasons to stay here is the food: La Pêcharie restaurant serves wonderful seafood.

6 Grand' Rue, 35400 St-Malo. © **02-99-40-87-70.** Fax 02-99-40-47-57. www.hotel-central-st-malo.com. 46 units. 600F–800F (91.20– 121.60, $87–$116) double; 980F (148.95, $142.10) suite. Half board 170F (25.85, $24.65) per person extra. AE, DC, MC, V. Parking 60F (9.10, $8.70). **Amenities:** Restaurant, bar. *In room:* TV, minibar, hair dryer.

Hôtel de France et de Chateaubriand   This hotel, within the walls of old St-Malo, is a masterpiece of Napoléon III architecture. Guest rooms run from comfortably cozy to spacious and feature such details as cove moldings, plaster ceiling reliefs, and chandeliers. All contain period reproductions, and most have panoramic ocean views. The rooms were renovated in the 1990s and all have neatly tiled tub/shower combinations. In the chic bar, with gold-trimmed Corinthian columns, you can chat over drinks, play billiards, and listen to the pianist on the baby grand. A restaurant with four dining rooms serves breakfast, lunch, and dinner (closed January and February). Two less formal dining alternatives are the courtyard terrace and the sidewalk cafe in front of the hotel.

Place Chateaubriand, 35412 St-Malo. © **02-99-56-66-52.** Fax 02-99-40-10-04. hotel.france. chateaubriand@wanadoo.fr. 80 units. 434F–496F (65.95– 75.440, $62.95–$71.90) double. AE, DC, MC, V. Parking 50F (7.60, $7.25). **Amenities:** Restaurant, bar; room service; baby-sitting. *In room:* TV, hair dryer.

Hôtel de la Cité   You'd never guess that this inn is new. It was built in 18th-century style following the plan of the building that once stood here. The contemporary interior, however, is no match for the richly embellished facade. Like most modern chain hotels, it offers solid comforts but is short on style. The rooms range from cramped to spacious, and most come with a combination shower and tub. Those on the top floor break away from the norm with angled ceilings. As a saving grace, many units open onto views of the oft-turbulent sea.

Place Vauban, 35412 St-Malo. ℂ 02-99-40-55-40. Fax 02-99-40-10-04. 41 units. 535F–625F (81.30–95, $77.60–$90.65) double; 880F–1,196F (133.75– 181.840, $127.60–$173.40) suite. AE, DC, MC, V. Parking 60F (9.10, $8.70). *In room:* TV.

DINING

The **Hôtel Central** and **Hôtel de France et de Chateaubriand,** above, also have restaurants.

À la Duchesse Anne ✸✸✸ TRADITIONAL FRENCH   This leading restaurant, built into the ramparts, offers summer dining under a large canopy amid hydrangeas. Try the seafood specialties: the fish soup with chunks of fresh seafood, spiced and cooked in an iron pot, is excellent, as are the Cancale oysters. Main courses include grilled turbot with beurre blanc and pepper steak, and a superb version of grilled lobster. The equally tempting desserts may include the *fantaisie du chocolat,* several chocolate-based desserts artfully arranged on a platter. Year after year, this choice delivers the finest food in town.

5 place Guy-La-Chambre. ℂ 02-99-40-85-33. Reservations required. Main courses 100F–140F (15.20– 21.330, $14.50–$20.30). V. May–Nov Thurs–Tues 12:15–1:30pm and 7:15–9:15pm. Closed Dec–Jan.

Le Chalut ✸✸✸ TRADITIONAL FRENCH   The decor here is nautical, in green and blue. Chef Jean-Philippe Foucat's flavorful cuisine, based on fresh ingredients, includes a tart containing layers of salmon and scallops, bound together with lime juice; John Dory with wild mushrooms, essence of lobster, and fresh coriander; and a succulent version of line-caught sea bass with sherry sauce and braised endive. For dessert, try the gâteau of bitter chocolate with almond paste or the homemade ice cream flavored with malt whisky. The only complaint we've heard is that the place is touristy, but that's the curse of St-Malo in general.

8 rue de la Corne-de-Cerf. ℂ 02-99-56-71-58. Reservations required. Main courses 120F–150F (18.25– 22.80, $17.40–$21.75); fixed-price menu 115F–190F (17.50– 28.90, $16.70–$27.55) AE, V. Wed–Sun 12:15–1:30pm and 7:15–9:30pm.

ST-MALO AFTER DARK

For an evening of dinner and gambling, experience the **Casino,** 2 chaussée du Sillon (ℂ 02-99-40-64-00). Here you can take in a show and dinner sometimes accompanied by live music. The dress code is informally elegant, jacket for men.

   Bar La Belle Epoque, 11 rue de Dinan (ℂ 02-99-40-82-23), attracts a 20-and-over crowd with its inviting setting, complete with a fireplace that heats things up on cooler nights. Play a game of darts, study the exhibits of local artists' work, or, on weekends, enjoy live music while sipping a drink.

   For dancing, consider **l'Escalier,** La Buzardière (ℂ 02-99-81-65-56), open Thursday through Saturday from 9pm to 1am, with a blue-and-green decor and an occasional cover that doesn't exceed 50F (7.60, $7.25).

   Two popular bars include **L'Aviso,** 12 rue du Point du Jour (ℂ 02-99-40-99-08), which specializes in beers from everywhere; and **Cunningham's,**

2 rue des hauts Sablons (℗ **02-99-81-48-08**), outfitted like the interior of someone's upscale yacht. If you're on a pub-crawl, hunt for **Le O'Flaherty's,** 18 rue des Cordiers (℗ **02-99-56-87-54**), where you can experience a real Irish pub with a French twist. It serves six different draft beers and more than 40 whiskies.

2 Dinard ★★★

259 miles W of Paris, 14 miles N of Dinan

Dinard (not to be confused with its inland neighbor, Dinan) sits on a rocky promontory at the top of the Rance River, opposite St-Malo. Ferries ply the waters between the two resorts. Victorian-Gothic villas, many now hotels, overlook the sea, and gardens and parks abound. Dinard seems to have passed its prime, though a number of modern buildings dot the landscape. The old is still best here; for a look at what the Edwardians admired, go down the pointe de la Vicomte at the resort's southern tip or stroll along the promenade. You'll expect to see Maurice Chevalier with top hat and cane appear at any moment.

One of France's best-known resorts, Dinard offers well-sheltered bathing and bracingly healthful sea air in *La Manche* ("the Sleeve," the term given centuries ago to a body of water claimed by the British as the English Channel). During Queen Victoria's time, this town, once a tiny fishing port, became popular with the English, who wanted a continental holiday that was "not too foreign."

ESSENTIALS

GETTING THERE If you're **driving,** take D186 west from St-Malo to Dinard. SNCF **trains** go only as far as St-Malo; from there, you'll have to take one of the buses that depart from the St-Malo rail station daily for the 20-minute ride to Dinard. **Buses** arrive from many large cities in Brittany, including Rennes and St-Malo. For bus information, call **Compagnie T.I.V.** (℗ **02-99-40-83-33**). Between May and September, a **ferry** maintained by the **Emeraud-Lines** (℗ **02-99-46-10-45**) makes one daily trip from Dinan to Dinard. A **taxi** ride to Dinard from St-Malo is a particularly useful option, costing 100F (15.20, $14.50) during the day and around 150F (22.80, $21.75) on national holidays or evenings after 7pm. For taxi information, call (℗ **02-99-46-75-75**).

VISITOR INFORMATION The **Office de Tourisme** is at 2 bd. Féart (℗ **02-99-46-94-12**).

SPECIAL EVENTS From mid-June to mid-September, *musique-et-lumière* adds the drama of floodlights and recorded jazz, pop, or classical music to walks along the city's seafront Promenade du Clair-de-Lune.

ENJOYING THE RESORT

Dinard's main beach is **Plage de l'Écluse** or **La Grande Plage,** the strip of sand between the peninsulas that define the edges of the old town. Favored by families and vacationers, it's crowded on hot days. Smaller and more isolated, and accessible after a 20-minute hike east from Dinard that'll take you through the village of St-Enogat, is **Plage de St-Enogat.** There's also **Plage du Prieuré,** a 10-minute walk from the center; you may or may not like the many trees that shade the sand. Because there's such a difference between high and low tides here, the municipality has built swimming pool–style basins along the Plage de L'Écluse and the Plage de St-Enogat beaches to catch seawater during high tides. Most people, however, trek along the salt flats during low tides to bathe in the sea. For a trek that encircles most of the old town and encompasses views as far away as St-Malo, consider a walk to the Pointe du Moulinet, clearly signposted from the town's historic core.

Looking for a bona-fide pool that's covered, heated, filled with seawater, and open year-round? Head for the **Piscine Olympique,** boulevard du Président-Wilson (✆ **02-99-46-22-77**). Entrance is 25F (3.80, $3.65) for adults, 16F (2.45, $2.30) for children 5 to 16, free for children 4 and under. From July to mid-September, it's open Monday through Saturday from 10am to 12:30pm and 3 to 7:30pm, and Sunday to 6:30pm. The rest of the year, it runs on a schedule that varies according to the agendas of local school groups and swim teams.

GOLF   About 5 miles from Dinard is a par-68, 18-hole golf course, **Le Dinard Golf,** at St-Briac (✆ **02-99-88-32-07**), one of the finest in Brittany. It's set on sandy, terrain studded with tough grasses and durable trees and shrubs. You'll have to reserve your tee time in advance and present a membership card from a golf course in your hometown. Greens fees are 200F to 320F (30.40 to 48.65, $29 to $46.40), depending on the season. There are rental carts, and a limited number of clubs can be rented, but it's wiser to bring your own.

SHOPPING   For the usual selection of shops and boutiques, concentrate on rue du Maréchal-Leclerc, rue Levavasseur, and boulevard du Président-Wilson. Your best bet is the **Galerie Line Boutique,** 13 bd. du Président-Wilson (✆ **02-99-46-11-21**). The gallery scene offers you a chance to pick up some unique pieces at affordable prices. In the 15th-century medieval house containing **Atelier du Prince Noir,** 70 av. George-V (✆ **02-99-46-29-99**), you'll find a range of paintings and sculptures from some of the most talented artists in France. The gallery is closed from October to April. An equally worthwhile shopping destination is **Marinette,** 29 rue Jacques-Cartier (✆ **02-99-46-82-88**), whose premises originally functioned as a Protestant church. Within an old-fashioned and high-ceilinged set of antique-looking showrooms, you'll find upscale inventories of porcelain, stoneware, kitchen utensils, gift items, and fresh flowers.

ACCOMMODATIONS

Note that **Altaïr** and **Le Prieuré** (see "Dining," below) also rent rooms.

Grand Hôtel Barrière de Dinard ✦✦   Dinard's largest hotel, a member of the Lucien Barrière chain, dates from 1859. Its location, a 2-minute walk from the town center, commands an excellent view of the harbor. It rises in two wings, separated from each other by a heated outdoor pool. Most rooms have balconies and are equipped with traditional furnishings and combination tub and showers. The inviting bar is a popular spot before and after dinner. Fine meals, with generous portions, are offered in the dignified in-house restaurant, the George V.

46 av. George-V, 35801 Dinard. ✆ **02-99-88-26-26.** Fax 02-99-88-26-27. www.Lucienbarriere.com. 66 units. 900F–2,200F (136.80– 334.40, $130.50–$319) double; 1,750F–2,200F (266– 334.40, $253.75–$319) suite. AE, DC, MC, V. Closed late Jan–late Mar. **Amenities:** Restaurant; bar; indoor pool; fitness center; sauna; room service; baby-sitting; laundry. *In room:* TV, minibar, hair dryer.

Hôtel de la Reine-Hortense ✦   Though not as grand as the Grand, this is our second choice in Dinard. This hotel on the beach was built in 1860 as a retreat for one of the Russian-born courtiers of Queen Hortense de Beauharnais, daughter of Joséphine de Beauharnais (who went on to marry Napoléon) and mother of Napoléon III. It offers glamorously outfitted public salons and guest rooms decorated in either Louis XV or Napoléon III style. Most have private balconies; all have a deep-seated sense of nostalgia. All units contain combination tub and shower. One high-ceilinged room even has Hortense's silver-plated bathtub, dating from the early 19th century. Breakfast is the only meal served.

19 rue de la Malouine, 35800 Dinard. (℃ **02-99-46-54-31**. Fax 02-99-88-15-88. reine.hortense@ wanadoo.fr. 8 units. 980F–1,220F (148.95– 185.45, $142.10–$176.90) double; 1,800F–2,200F (273.60– 334.40, $261–$319) suite. AE, DC, MC, V. **Amenities:** Laundry. *In room:* TV, hair dryer.

Hôtel Printania This is a longtime favorite of nostalgia buffs, among them writers and artists. On August 15, 1944, this Breton hotel was damaged in a bombing raid, but the debris was removed in time for the Allied victory. The main villa boasts terraces and a glassed-in veranda with potted palms, while the sitting room has carved-oak furniture, old clocks, and provincial chairs. The guest rooms contain antiques and Breton decorations. Some contain *des lits Bretons* (Brittany-style beds), which surround the occupant with either curtains or paneled doors for coziness and protection from the howling winds outside. Each of the old-fashioned but well-kept bathrooms contains a tub and shower. Dinner here combines superb cookery with a view of the coast; the restaurant specializes in seafood and shellfish, and the waitresses wear traditional Breton costumes.

5 av. George-V, 35800 Dinard. (℃ **02-99-46-13-07**. Fax 02-99-46-26-32. printania@wanadoo.fr. 59 units. 350F–490F (53.20– 74.530, $50.75–$71.05) double. Half board 280F–400F (42.55– 60.80, $40.60–$58) per person. AE, MC, V. Closed mid-Nov to mid-Mar. **Amenities:** Restaurant, bar; room service; laundry. *In room:* TV.

DINING

Another choice is the restaurant at **Grand Hôtel Barrière de Dinard** (see "Accommodations," above).

Altaïr ✦ *Value* TRADITIONAL FRENCH Patrick Leménager, who operates the intimate Altaïr, serves excellent cuisine that includes sea scallops in puff pastry with coriander sauce; fresh salmon with herbs; ravioli with oysters, pulverized crayfish, and herbs; and duck breast with apple-and-honey sauce, followed by a soufflé of caramelized apples. The portions are generous, and most prices are a good value for the area. In warm weather, you may dine alfresco on the terrace. The Altaïr also rents 21 standard rooms with shower-only bathrooms and TVs. Each was renovated in the late 1990s. A double is 250F to 490F (38 to 74.50, $36.25 to $71.05) per person with half board.

18 bd. Féart, 35800 Dinard. (℃ **02-99-46-13-58**. Fax 02-99-88-20-49. Reservations recommended. Main courses 90F–180F (13.70– 27.35, $13.05–$26.10); fixed-price menu 95F–200F (14.45– 30.40, $13.80–$29). AE, DC, MC, V. Sun noon–2pm; Mon–Sat noon–2pm and 7–9:30pm. Closed Mon in winter. *In room:* TV.

Le Prieuré SEAFOOD Diners at this family-style, turn-of-the-20th-century seafood restaurant are greeted by a lively room full of seafaring bric-a-brac. The food is generously portioned and traditional, with no newfangled ideas from faraway Paris. Come with a hearty appetite and you'll be rewarded with dishes like sautéed sole in beurre blanc with baby potatoes, grilled salmon with a stir-fry of seasonal vegetables, and grilled eel with garlic mayonnaise. Desserts like ever-popular crème caramel round out the menu. One of the most appealing aspects of a meal here is the view out over the La Rance estuary. Le Prieuré also rents eight guest rooms, priced at 300F (45.60, $43.50) double. Each is simply outfitted with a comfortable bed, an armoire, a phone, a TV, and a shower-only bathroom.

Finds An Idyll on an Île

Île de Bréhat is home to some 500 hearty people who live most of the year isolated from others—until the summer crowds arrive to see their lovely island. The tiny island (actually two islands, Île Nord and Île Sud, linked by a bridge) is in the Golfe de St-Malo, north of Paimpol. A visit to Bréhat is an offbeat adventure, even to the French.

Walking is the primary activity here, and it's possible to stroll the marked footpaths around the island in a day. Cars aren't allowed, except those used by the police and fire departments. Some tractor-driven carts carry visitors on a 5-mile circuit of Bréhat, charging 38F (5.80, $5.50) for the 45-minute jaunt. A number of places rent bikes, but they aren't necessary.

The rich flora here astonishes many visitors, who get off the ferry expecting a windswept island—only to discover a more Mediterranean clime. Flower gardens are in full summer bloom, though both the gardens and houses appear tiny because of the scarcity of land. At the highest point, Chapelle St-Michel, you'll be rewarded with a panoramic view.

If you need information, there's a tourist office at Le Bourg, place du Bourg (© **02-96-20-04-15**). It's open from mid-June to mid-September.

Paimpol can be reached by **driving** on D768 west from Dinard to Lamballe; then E50 west to Plérin; then D786 north to Paimpol. To reach the island, take D789 3 miles north of Paimpol, where the peninsula ends at the pink-granite Pointe de l'Arcouest. From Paimpol, about 5 to 10 **CAT buses** make the 10-minute run to the point for a one-way fare of 14F (2.15, $2.05). Then catch one of the **ferries** operated by **Les Vedettes de Bréhat** (© **02-96-55-73-47**), which will take you to the Île de Bréhat. Ferries depart about every 30 minutes in summer, two or three times per day in off-season; the round-trip costs 40F (6.10, $5.80). Visitors in April, May, June, and September will find the island much less crowded.

---

1 place du Général-de-Gaulle, 35800 Dinard. © **02-99-46-13-74.** Fax 02-99-46-81-90. Reservations recommended. Main courses 75F–130F (11.40– 19.75, $10.90–$18.85); fixed-price menu 98F–250F (14.90– 38, $14.20–$36.25). MC, V. Tues–Sun 12:30–2pm; Tues–Sat 7:30–9pm. Closed Jan and 1 week in late Sept.

DINARD AFTER DARK

Like many of Brittany's seaside towns, Dinard has a **Municipal Casino,** boulevard du Président-Wilson (© **02-99-16-30-30**). It's liveliest from Easter to late October, when all its facilities, including a room for roulette and blackjack, are open. The rest of the year, only the slot machines are in operation. Regardless of season, the hours are Sunday through Thursday from 10am to 3am and Friday and Saturday from 10am to 4am. Admission is free; the management encourages men to wear ties, especially in the roulette and blackjack areas. Also on the premises is **La Brasserie de la Mer,** open year-round, daily from noon to 2:30pm and 7pm to midnight. An alternative is Dinard's newest contender, **Le Metro-Dôme,**

Le Haut-Chemin (no phone), which has earned the loyalty of many local residents thanks to a good selection of wine and an amiable ambience.

In the evenings from June to September, the **promenade du Clair-de-Lune** attracts a huge crowd of strollers for the *musique-et-lumière,* when the buildings and flowers along the promenade are illuminated and musical groups of just about every ilk—from rock to blues to jazz—perform.

3 Dinan ★★

246 miles W of Paris, 32 miles NW of Rennes

Once a stronghold of the ducs de Bretagne, Dinan is one of the best-preserved towns of Brittany, noted for houses built on stilts over the sidewalks. The 18th-century granite dwellings provide sharp contrast to the medieval timbered houses in this walled town with a once-fortified château. Dinan remains one of Brittany's prettiest towns, with a population of 14,000—it's not overrun like St-Malo.

ESSENTIALS

GETTING THERE   Although Dinan has a railway station, at this writing, the SNCF, because of budgetary constraints, has opted to avoid routing **trains** here. Consequently, railway passengers usually travel to Rennes, Dinard, or St-Malo, and from there, transfer to any of the SNCF **buses** (about five a day from each) that line up in front of the railway stations in those towns for ongoing transit to Dinan. Typical fare from St-Malo is 35F (5.30, $5.10) one way. For information about bus service into Dinan, call the town's Gare Routiêre (© **02-96-39-21-05**). If you're **driving** from Dinard, take highway D166 south to Dinan.

VISITOR INFORMATION   The **Office de Tourisme** is at 6 rue de l'Horloge (© **02-96-87-69-76**).

SPECIAL EVENTS   The most activity you'll see here occurs during the third weekend in July, during the 3-day **Fêtes des Remparts,** held in Dinan in even-numbered years. Duels from the Age of Chivalry are staged, and locals don medieval apparel for carousing in the streets of the city's historic core. In odd-numbered years, the venue is transferred to Dinan's sibling city, Québec, Canada.

EXPLORING THE TOWN

For a panoramic view of the valley, head for the **Jardin Anglais** (English Garden), a terraced garden that huddles up to the ramparts. A Gothic-style bridge spans the Rance River; it was damaged in World War II but has since been restored. Dinan's most typical and one of its most appealing streets is the sloping **rue du Jerzual,** flanked with some buildings dating from the 15th century. The street ends at the **Porte du Jerzual,** a 13th- and 14th-century gate. **Rue du Petit-Fort** and Place des Merciers contain a number of 15th-century *maisons.*

Dominating the city's medieval ramparts, **Château de Dinan Musée du Château,** rue du Château (© **02-96-39-45-20**), contains a 14th-century keep and a 15th-century tower, built to withstand sieges. Within the stones, you'll see the space for the portcullis and the drawbridge. Inside, you can view an exhibition of the architecture and art of the city, including locally carved sculpture from the 12th to the 15th centuries. Admission is 25F (3.80, $3.65) for adults and 10F (1.50, $1.45) for children 12 to 18, 11 and under are free. Between June and mid-October, the castle and its museum are open daily from 10am to

6:30pm. From mid-October to mid-November, hours are Wednesday through Monday from 10am to noon. In December, February, and March, hours are Wednesday through Monday from 1:30 to 5:30pm. In April and May, hours are Wednesday through Monday from 10am to noon and 2 to 6pm. Closed January.

The old city's **Tour de l'Horloge** (clock tower), on rue de l'Horloge (© 02-96-39-22-43), now classified a historic monument, boasts a clock made in 1498 and a great bell donated by Anne de Bretagne in 1507. You'll have a panoramic view of medieval Dinan from the 75-foot belfry. Admission is 18F (2.75, $2.60) for adults and 12F (1.80, $1.75) for children. The belfry is open June 15 to September 15, daily from 10am to 5:30pm.

The heart of Bertrand du Guesclin, who defended the town when the duke of Lancaster threatened it in 1359, was entombed in a place of honor in the **Basilique St-Sauveur,** place St-Sauveur (no phone); note the basilica's Romanesque portals and ornamented chapels. It's open daily from 9am to 7pm.

REGIONAL CRAFTS Dinan has attracted groups of craftspeople and artists for at least 20 years. The densest concentration of artists' studios is along either side of the **rue du Jerzual** and the **rue de la Port,** where art objects are crafted from glass, wood, silk, leather, and clay. You might be able to buy an item directly from the artisan, but more efficient is to visit galleries that sell art objects from a wide assortment of the town's artisans. Two of the best include **Galerie St-Sauveur,** 12 rue de la Port (© 02-96-85-26-62), and **Galerie Phonographe,** 2 rue de la Port (© 02-96-39-38-38), where wide cross-sections of paintings and crafts help provide perspective on the arts in Dinan.

ACCOMMODATIONS

Hôtel Arvor This is a comfortable, and relatively inexpensive hotel set within a former 14th-century Jacobin convent. The entrepreneur who oversaw its restoration in the early 1990s is Stephane Pierre, who manages the place today. During the renovation process, most of the building's interior was demolished and rebuilt. The result is a series of clean and comfortable, contemporary-looking bedrooms; they retain none of their original medieval characteristics, but provide a safe and cozy haven within one of Dinan's oldest neighborhoods. Breakfast is the only meal served, but many inviting restaurants lie within a short walk.

5 rue Pavie, 22100 Dinan. © **02-96-39-21-22.** Fax 02-96-39-83-09. 23 units. 290F–390F (44.10– 59.30, $42.05–$56.55) double. AE, MC, V. In room: TV, hair dryer.

Hôtel d'Avaugour ★★ This is the town's best inn, but it isn't expensive. It's hard to believe that what was once a gutted pair of stone-fronted buildings has been transformed into Dinan's most up-to-date hotel. Bedrooms are decorated with attention paid to detail, reflecting the historic charm of the area. The rooms contain new fabrics inspired by traditional 18th-century design, furniture reflecting the heritage of Dinan, canopied beds with plush mattresses, and mid-size bathrooms (most with tub and shower). Half of the units overlook the square; the others face the rear garden and were renovated in 1998.

1 place du Champs-Clos, 22100 Dinan. © **02-96-39-07-49.** Fax 02-96-85-43-04. avavgour.hotel@wanadoo.fr. 24 units. 420F–880F (63.85– 133.75, $60.90–$127.60) double; 900F–1,600F (136.80–243.20, $130.50–$232) suite. AE, DC, MC, V. In room: TV, hair dryer.

DINING

Chez La Mère Pourcel ★★ TRADITIONAL FRENCH This restaurant enjoys an outstanding reputation for regional food and an ambience that's old-fashioned and cozy. The menu is defined by the season, with concessions made to the chef's inspiration. Examples include grilled codfish with a garlic-flavored mayonnaise; grilled and oven-baked wild turbot, served with coconut and essence of shellfish; and a traditional whole roasted and deboned pigeon with apples, prunes, foie gras, and chopped cabbage. A unique experience is the *Menu Découverte* (Discovery Menu), five courses that will "surprise you" with whatever seasonal ingredients the chef found in local markets. Guests often opt to skip the desserts in favor of the well-chosen cheeses, many of which come from small local producers, and many of which are almost sinfully creamy.

3 place des Merciers. ℂ **02-96-39-03-80.** Reservations recommended. Main courses 92F–180F (14.00–27.35, $13.35–$26.10); fixed-price menu 97F–395F (14.75– 60.05, $14.05–$57.30). AE, DC, MC, V. Daily noon–2pm and 7:15–10pm. Closed Feb; from Mar–June and Sept–Jan closed for dinner Sun and all day Mon.

La Caravelle ⭐ *Value* TRADITIONAL FRENCH   We used to hail Jean-Claude Marmion as the most inventive chef in town. He still serves wonderful food, and his 140F (21.30, $20.30) menu is the town's best value, but some of the magic is gone now that he prepares only time-tested dishes. Specialties are scallops with flap mushrooms, John Dory with caramelized onions and a bro-chette of barnacles, and a caguerole (stew of oysters and lobsters). In season, he prepares game dishes like jugged hare and rabbit. When the spring turnips come in, he prepares them with a veal filet often served with onion compote.

14 place Duclos. ℂ **02-96-39-00-11.** Reservations required. Main courses 150F–350F (22.80– 53.20, $21.75–$50.75); fixed-price menu 140F–260F (21.30– 39.50, $20.30–$37.70). AE, MC, V. Mon–Tues and Thurs–Sat 7–9:30pm; closed Nov 12–Dec 3; from Dec–July closed Thurs–Tues noon–2pm.

DINAN AFTER DARK

The densest concentration of cafes and bars in Dinan lines either side of the **rue de la Cordonnerie,** which was nicknamed by long-ago sailors as *La rue de la Soif* ("the street where you go when you're thirsty"). One of the most appealing is **Le Bistrot d'en Bas,** 20 rue Haute-Voie (ℂ **02-96-85-44-00**), where many vintages of wine are sold by the glass along with an assortment of *tartines* (open-faced sandwiches) made with cheeses, meats, and patés. The town's most popu-lar disco is **Le Zéphire,** rue de Brest (ℂ **02-96-39-12-79**), which is busiest on weekends. It sometimes charges a cover of around 40F (6.10, $5.80).

4 Quimper ⭐⭐

342 miles W of Paris, 127 miles NW of Rennes

The town that pottery built, Quimper, at the meeting of the Odet and Steir rivers, is the historic capital of Brittany's most traditional region, La Cornouaille. Today, its faïence decorates tables from Europe to the United States. Skilled arti-sans have been turning out Quimper ware since the 17th century, using bold provincial designs. You can tour one of the ateliers during your stay; inquire at the tourist office (see below). Today's Quimper is rather smug and bourgeois, home to some 65,000 Quimperois, who walk narrow streets spared from World War II damage.

ESSENTIALS

GETTING THERE   Two or three regular **trains** from Paris arrive daily (trip time: 7½ hours). The speedier TGV has 12 trains per day from Paris (trip time: 4 to 5 hours). Fifteen trains also arrive from Rennes (trip time: 3 hours). For information and schedules, call ℂ **08-36-35-35-35.** If you're **driving** to Quim-per, the best route is from Rennes, taking E50/N12 west to just outside the town of Montauban and continuing west along N164 to the town of Châteaulin in western France. From Châteaulin, head south along N165 to Quimper.

VISITOR INFORMATION   The **Office de Tourisme** is on place de la Résistance (© **02-98-53-04-05**; www.bretagne-4villes.com).

SPECIAL EVENTS   During 6 days in late July, the **Festival de Cornouaille** adds a traditional flavor to the nightlife scene with Celtic and Breton concerts held throughout the city. For information, contact the Office de Tourisme.

EXPLORING THE TOWN

In some quarters, Quimper still maintains its old-world atmosphere, with footbridges spanning the rivers. At place St-Corentin is the **Cathédrale St-Corentin** ✪✪ (© **02-98-95-06-19**), characterized by two towers that climb 250 feet. The cathedral was built between the 13th and the 15th centuries; the spires were added in the 19th. Inside, note the 15th-century stained glass. It's open daily from 9am to 6:30pm.

Also on the square is the **Musée des Beaux-Arts** ✪✪, 40 place St-Corentin (© **02-98-95-45-20**), with a collection that includes Rubens, Boucher, Fragonard, and Corot, plus an exceptional exhibit from the Pont-Aven school (Bernard, Sérusier, Lacombe, Maufra, Denis). Admission is 25F (3.80, $3.65) for adults, 15F (2.30, $2.20) for ages 12 to 26, and free for children under 12. The gallery is open in July and August, daily from 10am to 7pm; September to June, it's open Wednesday through Monday from 10am to noon and 2 to 6pm.

Musée Departemental Breton, 1–3 rue Roi Gradlon (© **02-98-95-29-60**), is set within the medieval *Palais des Éveques de Cornouailles* (Palace of the Bishops of Cornwall), adjacent to the cathedral. The museum showcases the evolution of Breton national costumes, with examples of local handcrafts and furniture. It's an homage to the Breton aesthetic. It is open June through September, daily from 9am to 6pm; off-season, daily from 9am to noon and 2 to 5pm. Admission is 28F (4.25, $4.05) for adults, 15F (2.30, $2.20) for ages 11 to 26, and free for children under 11.

SHOPPING

When artisans from Rouen and other parts of France settled in Quimper, the city became forever associated with ceramics. The porcelain produced here is arguably the most recognized and the most popular French porcelain sold outside of France. Typical are chunky white pieces painted with blue and yellow Breton figures, fruits, and flowers. Although newer designs are sometimes proposed, the most popular patterns feature either a male *Breton* or a female *Bretonne,* both in profile and both in traditional Breton costume, each reeking of bucolic charm and simplicity. Today, that 19th-century design is copyrighted and fiercely protected.

The best shopping streets are **rue Kereron** and **rue du Parc,** where you'll find all kinds of Breton products, including pottery, dolls and puppets, clothing made from regional cloth and wool, jewelry, metal and wood crafts, lace, and even those beautiful Breton costumes.

One of the three sites where the stoneware is produced is open for tours. From 9am to 4:30pm Monday through Friday, between five and seven tours a day depart from the visitor information center of **H. B.–Henriot Faïenceries de Quimper,** rue Haute, Quartier Locmaria (© **02-98-90-09-36**). Tours last 40 to 45 minutes, are conducted in either English or French (or both), and cost 20F (3.05, $2.90) for adults and 10F (1.50, $1.45) for children 8 to 14, 7 and under free. On the premises is a store selling the most complete inventories of

Quimper porcelain in the world. You can invest in first-run (nearly perfect) pieces or slightly discounted "seconds," with flaws so small as to be nearly imperceptible. Anything you buy can be shipped.

For other Breton pottery and fine pieces of the faïence once heavily produced in this area, visit **François le Villec,** 4 rue du Roi-Gradlon (✆ **02-98-95-31-54**). Here you'll find quality tablecloths and other household linens.

With some 2 decades of experience and more than 1,200 square feet of showroom, **Le Grenier,** 60 rue du President Sadate (✆ **02-98-52-04-60**), is a treasure trove of antique furniture, bibelots, and paintings.

Another good choice for Breton art objects and artwork is **La Galerie le Cornet â Dés,** 1 rue Ste-Thérêse (✆ **02-98-53-37-51**), where hand-painted porcelain and antique and contemporary paintings will try to seduce you with their taste and appeal.

ACCOMMODATIONS

La Tour d'Auvergne _Value_ Although they're small and overlook a not particularly picturesque area about 200 yards from the cathedral, the rooms at this 19th-century inn are good value for Quimper. All doubles have private bathrooms (many with a combination tub and shower). The owner's grandparents bought the hotel in 1927, and one part or another has been renovated every year since.

One of the main draws is the kitchen's Breton cuisine. The best examples include a stewpot of scallops and chitterling sausages bound together with cider and rosemary, and breast of pigeon with a purée of garlic and foie gras, served with a _confit_ of the pigeon's thighs. Dessert might include an apricot and chocolate tart. Consider dining here even if you're not a guest.

13 rue des Réguaires, 29000 Quimper. ✆ **02-98-95-08-70.** Fax 02-98-95-17-31. www.la-tour-dauvergne.fr. 38 units. 575F–640F (87.40– 97.30, $83.40–$92.80) double. AE, DC, MC, V. Free parking. **Amenities:** Restaurant, bar; baby-sitting; laundry. _In room:_ TV.

Novotel _Kids_ In a garden a mile southwest of the town center, the Novotel, despite its blandness, is your best choice. Built in the 1980s with comfortable, standardized rooms, it boasts a Breton-style slate roof that would be the envy of any homeowner. It's ideal for motoring families (the pool is a magnet in summer) and is the best business-oriented hotel in the region. Each room has lots of space, plus a writing desk and midsize bathroom with a tub and shower combination.

17 rue Dupoher, pont de Poulguinan, 29000 Quimper. ✆ **02-98-90-46-26.** Fax 02-98-53-01-96. www.novotel. com. 92 units. 530F–600F (80.55– 91.20, $76.85–$87) double. Up to two children 16 and under stay free in parents' room and get free breakfast. AE, DC, MC, V. From the town center, follow the signs to route Pont-l'Abbé. **Amenities:** Restaurant, bar; heated outdoor pool; room service; baby-sitting; laundry. _In room:_ TV, minibar, hair dryer.

DINING

Another good choice is the restaurant at **La Tour d'Auvergne** (see above).

Le Capucin Gourmand ✦ TRADITIONAL FRENCH This popular restaurant offers some of the area's finest dining. The chef gives familiar dishes a twist by adding an unexpected ingredient or two. Delightful appetizers may include foie gras in a terrine, a dozen Breton oysters, or a plate of ravioli filled with basil-flavored lobster. As a main course, opt for a _blanquette_ of turbot with langoustines and artichokes or filet of sole with fresh basil. Breton lamb appears frequently, usually roasted and served in a made-from-scratch sauce, perhaps flavored with leeks.

Finds The Soul Food of the Breton—the Crêpe

Even more than oysters, nothing is more Breton than a crêpe. Locals consume two or three a day (at least). It's also a cheap way to fill up, as most crêpes cost from 8F (1.20, $1.15), although they could range up to 42F (6.40, $6.10) depending on the stuffing. For the greatest concentration of crêperies, walk across the river (onto the rue Ste-Catherine, where you'll find a string of crêperies dispensing their wares.

---

29 rue des Réguaires. ℂ 02-98-95-43-12. Reservations required in summer. Main courses 90F–120F (13.70– 18.25, $13.05–$17.40); fixed-price menu 93F–280F (14.15– 42.55, $13.50–$40.60). AE, DC, V. Tues–Sat noon–2pm; Tues–Sun 7–10pm.

NEARBY ACCOMMODATIONS & DINING

In an orchard district 8 miles from Quimper, the sleepy village of **La Forêt-Fouesnant** produces the best cider in the province and is home to one of Brittany's finest manor houses.

Manoir du Stang ★★★ To get to this 16th-century ivy-covered manor, you travel down a tree-lined avenue, through a stone gate into a courtyard. On your right is a formal garden; stone terraces lead to 25 acres of woodland. This is the domain of M. and Mme Guy Hubert, who provide gracious living in period rooms. Guests stay in the main building or in the even older but less desirable annex with a circular stone staircase. Your room is likely to be furnished with silk and fine antiques; each midsize bathroom comes with a combination tub and shower. One luxury is the maid who brings your breakfast on a tray each morning. The restaurant's specialties are grilled lobster with tarragon, côte of beef with green peppercorns, *fruits de mer* (seafood), and oysters house style.

29940 La Forêt-Fouesnant. ℂ and fax 02-98-56-97-37. 24 units. 600F–1,000F (91.20– 152, $87–$145) double. No credit cards. Free parking. Closed Oct–Apr. Drive a mile north of the village center and follow the signs from N783; access is by private road. **Amenities:** Restaurant, bar. *In room:* Hair dryer.

QUIMPER AFTER DARK

A trip down **rue Ste-Catherine** will lead to some of the best nightspots. The steadfastly Celtic bar **Céili Pub,** 4 rue Aristide-Briand (ℂ 02-98-95-17-61), was recently renovated and has lots of polished wood, regional music, and happy people—join in a game of darts with any of the regulars. **St. Andrew's Pub,** 11 place Styvel (ℂ 02-98-53-34-49), with its wood-and-leather interior and 44 varieties of beer and 37 whiskies, attracts a large number of Brits and Americans.

The young and stylish flock to **Les Naïades Discothèque,** boulevard Créac'h Gwen (ℂ 02-98-53-32-30), where you can dance to the latest tunes (there's sometimes a cover). **Le Coffee Shop,** 26 rue du Frout (ℂ 02-98-95-43-30), has a cool gay and lesbian crowd that unwinds to disco and techno.

5 Concarneau ★★

335 miles W of Paris, 58 miles SE of Brest

This port is a favorite of painters, who never tire of capturing on canvas the subtleties of the fishing fleet in the harbor. It's also our favorite of the coast communities—primarily because it doesn't depend on tourists for its livelihood.

In fact, its canneries produce nearly three quarters of all the tuna in France. Walk along the quays here, especially in the late evening, and watch the Breton fishers unload their catch; later, join them for a pint of potent cider in the taverns.

ESSENTIALS

GETTING THERE   There's no passenger rail service to Concarneau. If you're **driving,** the town is 13 miles southeast of Quimper along D783. A Caoudal **bus** (© 02-98-56-96-72) runs from Quimper to Concarneau (trip time: 40 minutes; 20F [3.05, $2.90]). A different bus runs 8 to 10 times per day from Resporden to Concarneau (trip time: 20 minutes).

VISITOR INFORMATION   The **Office de Tourisme** is on quai d'Aiguillon (© 02-98-97-01-44).

EXPLORING THE AREA

The town is built on three sides of a natural harbor whose innermost sheltered section is the Nouveau Port. In the center of the harbor, is the heavily fortified Ville-Close, an ancient hamlet surrounded by ramparts, some from the 14th century. From the quay, cross the bridge and descend into the town. Souvenir shops have taken over, but don't let that spoil it for you. You can easily spend an hour wandering the winding alleys, gazing up at the towers, peering at the stone houses, and stopping in secluded squares. For a splendid view of the port, walk the ramparts—it's free. Walks are possible mid-April to mid-June, daily from 10am to 6pm; and mid-June to mid-September, daily from 10am to 9:30pm. Access to the ramparts is closed between December and February, or whenever icy rain causes them to be slippery. The cost is 5F (.75, 75¢) per person.

Also in the old town is a fishing museum, **Musée de la Pêche,** rue Vauban (© 02-98-97-10-20). The 17th-century building contains ship models and exhibits tracing the development of the fishing industry all over the world; you can also view the preserved ship *Hemerica*. Admission is 36F (5.45, $5.20) for adults and 24F (3.65, $3.50) for children under 15. Year-round hours are daily from 10am to noon and 2 to 6pm. It's closed for 3 weeks in January.

BEACHES   Concarneau's largest and most beautiful beach, popular with families, is **Plage des Sables Blancs,** near the historic core. Within a 10-minute walk is **Plage de Cornouaille** and two small beaches, **Plage des Dames** and **Plage de Rodel,** where you'll find fewer families with children. The wide-open **Plage du Cabellou,** 3 miles west of town, is less congested than the others.

SEA EXCURSIONS   Boat rides are usually fine between June and September, but they're treacherous the rest of the year, when storms born in the central Atlantic unleash their forces onto the battered coastline. During midsummer, you can arrange deep-sea fishing with the captain of the *Santa Maria* (© 02-98-50-69-01). For excursions to anywhere along the coastline of southern Brittany, contact **Vedettes Glenn** (© 02-98-97-10-31), **Vedettes de l'Odet** (© 02-99-57-00-58), or **Vedettes Taxis** (© 02-99-50-72-12).

ACCOMMODATIONS

Hotel Les Halles   It's rated only two stars by the local tourist board, and there isn't a lot of historic charm associated with this three-story, cement-sided 1960s-era hotel. Yet it's affordable and warm, with bedrooms that are cozier than you might expect, and a location less than 150 yards west of the Vauban-designed fortifications encircling Concarneau's historic core. Rooms are upgraded frequently, each with a unique, discreetly contemporary decor and an eye for practicality.

Every unit is equipped with a small, shower-only bathroom. The city's covered food market, Les Halles (open daily from around 8am to around 1pm) lies within a short walk. Breakfast is the only meal served.

Place de l'Hotel de Ville, 29900 Concarneau. ✆ **02-98-97-11-41**. Fax 02-98-50-58-54. 23 units. 260F–350F (39.50– 53.20, $37.70–$50.75) double. AE, DC, MC, V. In room: TV.

DINING

La Coquille ✦ TRADITIONAL FRENCH This 30-year-old restaurant occupies one end of a stone-sided harborfront building; guests dine in a trio of rooms with exposed stone walls and ceiling beams. La Coquille serves primarily seafood, particularly lobster. Much of the food is prepared simply because the fish is so fresh and succulent, although a particularly excellent dish is scallop tart with shellfish and cream sauce. The service is bistro style (no great compliment), with a cheerful, old-fashioned kind of panache enhanced by the harbor view.

1 rue du Moros, at Nouveau Port. ✆ **02-98-97-08-52**. Reservations required Sat–Sun and in summer. Main courses 100F–150F (15.20– 22.80, $14.50–$21.75); fixed-price menu 160F–420F (24.30– 63.85, $23.20–$60.90). AE, DC, MC, V. Tues–Sun 12:30–1:30pm; Tues–Sat 7:30–9:30pm. Closed Jan.

NEARBY ACCOMMODATIONS & DINING

On the outskirts of the once-fortified town of **Hennebont,** 35 miles west of Concarneau, is the most delightful hotel in all of southern Brittany.

Château de Locguénolé ✦✦✦ This country estate, on 250 acres of parkland, is owned by the same family who ran it some five centuries ago. Now a Relais & Châteaux, with views over rugged coastline and an inlet, it's filled with antiques, tapestries, and paintings. The guest rooms vary widely in size and furnishings, but each has harmonious colors and, season permitting, sprays of flowers. The converted maids' rooms are smaller than the others yet still charming; some units are in a converted Breton cottage. Regardless of the size, each unit has a bathroom with a combination tub and shower.

Route de Port-Louis, 56700 Hennebont. ✆ **02-97-76-76-76**. Fax 02-97-76-82-35. www.chateau-de-locguenole.fr. 22 units. 680F–1,650F (103.35– 250.80, $98.60–$239.25) double; 1,950F–2,400F (296.40– 364.80, $282.75–$348) suite. AE, DC, MC, V. Closed Jan 2–Feb 11. From Hennebont, follow the signs to the château, 3 miles south. **Amenities:** Restaurant; room service; baby-sitting; laundry/dry cleaning. In room: TV, minibar, hair dryer, safe.

6 Pont-Aven ✦

324 miles W of Paris, 20 miles SE of Quimper, 10 miles S of Concarneau

Paul Gauguin loved this village with its white houses along the gently flowing Aven River. In the late 19th century, many painters followed him here, including Maurice Denis, Paul Sérusier, and Emile Bernard. The theories and techniques developed at the time have been known ever since as the School of Pont-Aven.

In the 16th-century **Chapelle de Trémalo,** less than a mile north of the town center, you can admire the crucifix that inspired two of Gauguin's paintings, *The Yellow Christ* (today in the Albright-Knox Art Gallery in Buffalo, New York) and *Self-Portrait with the Yellow Christ,* in the Musée d'Orsay. Every year, the local branch of the Société de Peinture organizes an exhibition of paintings, usually in the chapel, by other members of the School of Pont-Aven. The Chapel of Trémalo is privately owned; the only phone contact any casual visitor can have with it is through the Pont-Aven tourist office (see below). The owners unlock the chapel (its location is signposted) every morning at 9am, and close it between 7 and 8:30pm, depending on their whim and the season. In addition, there's a neighbor who appears magically to survey any possible danger. Entrance is free. The only address for the place is Chapelle de Trémalo, lieu-dit Trémalo.

ESSENTIALS

GETTING THERE   If you're **driving** from Quimperlé, head west along D783 toward Concarneau. SNCF **trains** stop at Quimperlé, where you can transfer to one of six daily **buses** for the 30-minute ride to Pont-Aven. Cost is 20F (3.05, $2.90) each way. For train information, call either the Pont-Aven tourist office (see below) or © **08-36-35-35-35.**

VISITOR INFORMATION   The **Office de Tourisme** is on place de l'Hôtel-de-Ville (© **02-98-06-04-70**).

ACCOMMODATIONS & DINING

Le Moulin de Rosmadec ★★★ *Finds* TRADITIONAL FRENCH   For a charming setting, nothing in Brittany compares to this 15th-century stone mill. Meals are served in a bilevel dining room with antique furnishings or, in good weather, on a flower-filled "island" terrace. The owners, M. and Mme Sebilleau, serve carefully prepared food, with specialties like trout with almonds, sole suprême with champagne, grilled lobster with tarragon, and duck breast with cassis. The fish dishes are sublime. Dessert includes a crêpe stuffed with strawberries and quince.

The Moulin rents four comfortable rooms for 480F (72.95, $69.60) double. Because of the hotel's location at the end of a quiet cul-de-sac in the heart of the village, its accommodations are quiet and calm.

29123 Pont-Aven. © **02-98-06-00-22.** Reservations recommended. Main courses 120F–160F (18.25– 24.30, $17.40–$23.20); fixed-price menu 168F–300F (25.55– 45.60, $24.35–$43.50); menu tradition (with oysters and lobster) 398F (60.50, $57.70). MC, V. Thurs–Tues 12:30–2pm and 7:30–9pm. Closed Feb, and Nov 15–Dec 1; from Sept–June, closed Sun night and Wed night. Free parking. *In room:* TV.

Moments **In the Footsteps of Gauguin**

In 1886, Paul Gauguin blazed the trail to the Breton village of Pont-Aven, and in time a pilgrimage of lesser artists trailed him. One of Gauguin's most memorable works, *The Yellow Christ,* exemplified the credo of the School of Pont-Aven. Breaking from mainstream Impressionism, Pont-Aven artists emphasized purer colors ("as true as nature itself"). They shunned perspective and simplified human figures.

Painters still flock here today. The tourist office sells a walking-tour guide (2F, .30, 30¢) that directs you on a trail once trotted by these great artists of the past.

Musée Municipal de Pont-Aven, place de l'Hotel de Ville (© **02-98-06-14-43**), provides one of the best overviews of the 19th-century painters inspired by the sea and landscapes of this wild region. Expect muted greens and blues and lots of Breton patriotism as interpreted through the most famous artistic movement to emerge from Brittany. Admission is 20F (3.05, $2.90) for adults and 15F (2.30, $2.20) for those 25 and under. Hours are July and August, daily from 10am to 7pm; September to June, daily from 10am to 12:30pm and 2 to 6pm.

7 Carnac ✶

302 miles W of Paris, 23 miles SE of Lorient, 62 miles SE of Quimper

In May and June, the fields here are resplendent with golden broom. Aside from being a seaside resort, Carnac is home to the hundreds of huge stones in the **Field of Megaliths** (six alignments), whose arrangement and placement remain a mystery. These stones date from Neolithic times. Many of them are set up in parallel rows. Scholars have debated the purpose of these stones for centuries, although most theories suggest they had astronomical or religious significance to the ancient people of the area. One theory is that some of the stones marked burial sites lost to antiquity. In all, the town contains 2,732 menhirs, some of them rising to heights of 60 feet. Their placement into 11 more or less straight lines is divided into at least three separate fields, whose exact divisions remain a mystery to modern anthropologists.

The park is open for unguided visits daily from October 1 to April 1; admission is free. In the busy summer months, the park is open for guided tours only, restricted to groups of 25 at a time with a limit of 180 for the entire day. The 90-minute tours are offered through the on-site visitor center and cost 32.50F (4.95, $4.70). Before heading here, call ☎ **02-97-52-89-99** to find out when group visits are scheduled and if the quota of visitors has been filled.

At Carnac Ville, **Musée de Préhistoire,** 10 place de la Chapelle (☎ **02-97-52-22-04**), displays collections from 450,000 B.C. to the 8th century. Admission is 30F (4.55, $4.35) for adults and 15F (2.30, $2.20) for children 10 to 18, 9 and under are free. The museum is open June 15 to September 15, daily from 10am to 6:30pm; September 16 to June 14, Wednesday through Monday from 10am to noon and 2 to 6pm; and October to May, Wednesday through Monday from 10am to noon and 2 to 5pm.

Even if Carnac didn't possess these prehistoric monuments, its pine-studded sand dunes would be worth the trip. Protected by the Quiberon Peninsula, **Carnac-Plage** is a family resort beside the ocean and alongside the waterfront boulevard de la Plage.

The center of Carnac is about half a mile from the sea. From the main square, rue du Tumulus leads north from the center of town to the **Tumulus St-Michel,** a Celtic burial chamber three-quarters of a mile from the center. Visitation has been halted until 2003 for an archaeological dig.

SHOPPING Carnac has two shopping areas: one along the beachfront called Carnac-Plage and the other about 1½ miles inland in Carnac proper. Along the beach, you'll run into your fair share of souvenir shops, but venture down avenue des Druids and avenue de l'Atlantique for more specialized galleries and antiques stores. Other good areas are rue St-Cornély and place de l'Église, with a host of clothing and shoe stores, antiques dealers, and jewelers.

For a treat, visit **L'Enfant d'Armor,** 2 place de l'Église (☎ **02-97-52-06-87**), which offers an array of Breton embroidery. It's open from April to September. **Kryso,** 10 rue St-Cornély (☎ **02-97-52-28-31**), sells unique creations of jewelry combining silver and semiprecious and precious stones, as well as mother-of-pearl. Go to **Clémentine,** avenue de l'Atlantique (☎ **02-97-52-96-34**), if you're in the market for quality household linens and dishware.

ESSENTIALS

GETTING THERE **Driving** is the most convenient way to get to Carnac. From Lorient, take N165 east to Auray, turning south on D768 to Carnac.

Public transport links are possible but inconvenient. Nine TIM **buses** (call
📞 **02-97-47-29-64** in Vannes, or 02-97-24-26-20 in Auray) run to Carnac
from Quiberon (trip time: 30 minutes). There are also at least nine TIM buses
from Auray to Carnac (trip time: 30 minutes). SNCF **trains** will take you as
far as Plouharnel, and from here you can catch one of seven buses per day (trip
time: 5 minutes). For train information and schedules, call 📞 **08-36-
35-35-35.**

VISITOR INFORMATION   The **Office de Tourisme,** on avenue des
Druides (📞 **02-97-52-13-52;** www.ot-carnac.fr), is open all year.

ACCOMMODATIONS & DINING

Hôtel Lann-Roz *Value*   Within walking distance of the water, this oasis for the
budget-minded is surrounded by a garden and lawns. Lann-Roz is managed by
the friendly Mme Le Calvez, who will invite you to have a drink on the veranda.
The midsize bedrooms are modestly yet comfortably furnished, each with a
small bathroom with combination tub and shower. In the typical Breton dining
room, the chef serves generous portions of regional food. Most of the menu
items are derived from local culinary traditions and are concocted with locally
produced ingredients. Examples include fresh Breton tuna with basil and fresh
noodles; a *rillette* (chunky terrine) of fish with shrimp and beurre blanc; house-
smoked salmon with a creamy chive sauce; and a platter containing both veal
chops and veal kidneys, prepared "in the style of Madame." Dessert might be an
apple and caramelized rhubarb tart. You don't have to be a guest to dine here.

36 av. de la Poste, 56340 Carnac. 📞 **02-97-52-10-48.** Fax 02-97-52-24-36. hotel-lann-roz@ infornie.fr. 12
units. 650F–750F (98.80– 114, $94.25–$108.75) double. Rates include half board. MC, V. Closed Jan;
Sept–May closed Mon nights. **Amenities:** Restaurant, bar. *In room:* TV.

Hôtel Le Diana 🖈   Located on the most popular beach, the Diana is the most
reliable and comfortable hotel in Carnac and better than its chief rival, the
Novotel. (See section 4, "Quimper," earlier this chapter.) The spacious, contemporary guest rooms contain balconies facing the sea, comfortable beds, sum-
mery furniture, and small bathrooms with tub and shower combinations. The
restaurant also faces the sea and serves standard seafood. You can sip drinks and
watch the crashing waves from the terrace.

21 bd. de la Plage, 56340 Carnac Plage. 📞 **02-97-52-05-38.** Fax 02-97-52-87-91. www.lediana.com.
32 units. 600F–1,350F (91.20– 205.20, $87–$195.75) double; 1,150F–1,750F (174.80– 266, $166.75–
$253.75) suite. AE, DC, MC, V. Closed Oct 4–Easter. **Amenities:** Restaurant, bar; open-air pool; sauna; room
service; baby-sitting; laundry/dry cleaning. *In room:* TV, minibar, hair dryer, safe.

CARNAC AFTER DARK

Carnac doesn't stay up very late, but a few places are worth checking out. The
Whiskey Club, 8 av. des Druides (📞 **02-97-52-10-52**), operates in an old
stone house with two floors devoted to entertainment. The first floor offers an
atmosphere conducive to conversation over drinks; the second floor is home to
dancing and loud music. **Les Chandelles,** avenue de l'Atlantique (📞 **02-97-
52-90-98**), pulls in a young, flashy crowd. The club plays mainly disco and
charges a 60F (9.10, $8.70) cover. As with most discos in France, no jeans or
sneakers are allowed. The professional crowd gathers at **Petit Bedon,** 108 av. des
Druides (📞 **02-97-52-11-62**). With its mixture of African and Mexican decor,
this is the place for dancing to rock of the 1960s. Though there's no cover, a beer
will set you back a hefty 50F (7.60, $7.25). There's also a restaurant.

The Wild, Wild Coast

If you take D768 south from Carnac and follow it onto the peninsula (formerly an island) connected to the mainland by a narrow strip of alluvial deposits, you'll come to the port of **Quiberon,** with its white-sand beach. You'll probably see the rugged Breton fishers hauling in their sardine catch.

This entire coast—the **Côte Sauvage,** or Wild Coast—is dramatic and rugged; the ocean breaks with fury against the reefs. Winds, especially in winter, lash across the dunes, shaving the short pines that grow here. On the landward side, the beach is calm and relatively protected.

Ten miles west of Brittany's shoreline is **Belle-Île-en-Mer,** an outpost of sand, rock, and twisted vegetation that the French love for summer holidays. For information, contact the local **Office de Tourism,** Quai Bonnelle le Palais (© **02-37-31-81-93**). Depending on the season, 4 to 12 ferries depart daily for this island from Port Maria in Quiberon (© **02-97-31-80-01**). The trip takes 45 minutes and costs 128F (19.45, $18.55) round-trip for adults, 69F (10.50, $10) for children. In summer, you must reserve space on board for your car. The ferry docks at **Le Palais,** a fortified 16th-century port that serves as the island's chief window to the rest of France. Storm-wracked and eerie, the local topography consists of rocky cliffs; a reef-fringed west coast; the **Grotte de l'Apothicairerie,** a cave (closed to visitors) whose name derives from stalactites shaped like apothecary jars; and a sense of isolation, despite a

8 La Baule ★★★

281 miles W of Paris, 49 miles NW of Nantes

Founded during the Victorian seaside craze, La Baule remains as inviting as the Gulf Stream that warms the waters of its 5-mile crescent of white-sand beach. Occupying the *Côte d'Amour* (Coast of Love), it competes with Biarritz today as the Atlantic coast's most fashionable resort. But La Baule is still essentially French, drawing only a small number of foreigners.

The gambler François André founded the casino and major resort hotels here. Pines grow on the dunes, and villas on the outskirts draw the wealthy chic from late June to mid-September; if you arrive at any other time, you might have La Baule all to yourself. While the movie stars and flashy rich go to Deauville or Cannes, La Baule draws a more middle-class crowd; however, the more reserved wealthy still come here—as the yachts in the harbor testify.

The town is north of a popular stretch of beachfront. The two main boulevards run parallel through the long, narrow town; the one closer to the ocean changes its name six times—at its most famous point, it's called boulevard de l'Océan.

Other than a rock outcropping much weathered by Atlantic storms, the beaches here are clean and sandy bottomed, providing safe swimming and lots of options for admiring flesh in all states of fitness.

scattering of hotels and seasonal restaurants. A drive around the island's periphery is about 35 miles, each rife with bracing Atlantic sights, breezes, and smells.

In the days before he was jailed for embezzlement, the Sun King's finance minister, Nicolas Fouquet, the inspirational force behind Vaux-le-Vicomte, erected a château on this island. Much later the "Divine" Sarah Bernhardt spent many pleasant summers here in a 17th-century fortress that was "always swarming with guests."

You'll find excellent accommodations in charming **Port de Goulphar,** on the southern shore on a narrow inlet framed by cliffs. The standout, and the only four-star hotel on the island, is the 43-unit Relais & Châteaux **Castel Clara,** Port de Goulphar, 56360 Bangor (℗ **02-97-31-84-21;** fax 02-97-31-51-69; www.relaischateaux.fr/castelclara). Few other places along the coast provide such a sense of isolated peace accompanied by ideal service and first-class cuisine. The rooms are comfortable and well furnished, with TVs, phones, and balconies facing the sea. The chef takes pride in his achievements, and the menu is a good showcase for his talents, particularly the seafood. The hotel also offers a large terrace with a solarium around a heated seawater pool. Depending on the season, rates for two (including half board) range from 1,290F to 2,160F (196.10 to 328.30, $187.05 to $313.20) double. The hotel is closed from November 15 to February 15.

Avenue du Général-de-Gaulle and avenue Louis-Lajarrige have the best shops and boutiques. Next to the casino on esplanade de François-André, you'll hit the shopping jackpot: a minimall with 40 or so French chain stores and boutiques.

ESSENTIALS

GETTING THERE   If you're **driving** from Nantes, take N165 northwest to Savenay, continuing west along D773 to La Baule. The **train** trip from Nantes is about an hour. Get off at the most central inner-city station, La Baule-Escoublac, or the more easterly and remote La Baule-Les Pins. For train information and schedules, call ℗ **08-36-35-35-35.**

VISITOR INFORMATION   The **Office de Tourisme** is at 8 place de la Victoire (℗ **02-40-24-34-44**).

ACCOMMODATIONS

Castel Marie-Louise ☆☆☆   This turn-of-the-20th-century Breton manor offers grand living in an oceanfront pine park. The public rooms are furnished in French provincial style, with tapestries of stylized animals. Guest rooms were renovated in the late 1990s. Most upper-floor units come with balconies; two are located in a tower. Furnishings reflect several styles: Louis XV, Directoire, and rustic. The excellent chef is reason enough to stay here, and even if you aren't a guest, you may want to stop in for a meal of regional-based fare that dares to be different. Specialties are lobster and home-smoked salmon and a dessert specialty of half-baked chocolate cake.

1 av. Andrieu, 44504 La Baule. ☎ **02-40-11-48-38**. Fax 02-40-11-48-35. www.relaischateaux.fr/marielouise. 31 units. 910F–3,200F (138.30– 486.40, $131.95–$464) double; 2,680F–3,200F (407.35– 486.40, $388.60–$464) suite. Half board 360F (54.70, $52.20) extra per person. AE, DC, MC, V. Closed Nov to mid-Dec. **Amenities:** Restaurant, bar; water sports; nearby golf; tennis court. *In room:* TV, minibar, hair dryer.

Hôtel Alexandra   Built in 1966 adjacent to the beach, the Alexandra boasts eight floors of modern rooms with balconies. There's an open-air terrace with umbrellas and sidewalk tables, plus planters of flowers and greenery. The ninth-floor solarium is a popular spot for drinks and coffee. The dining room has a view of the ocean. Note that the guest rooms here are basic, even by the admission of the staff, and completely unfrilly, the kind of boxy, functional atmosphere where you can track in sand and seashells and no one will mind.

3 bd. René-Dubois, 44500 La Baule. ☎ **02-40-60-30-06**. Fax 02-40-24-57-09. 36 units. 460F–850F (69.90– 129.20, $66.70–$123.25) double. AE, DC, MC, V. Closed Dec–Feb. Free parking. **Amenities:** Restaurant, bar; solarium. *In room:* TV, hair dryer.

Hôtel Bellevue-Plage   This hotel, which many prefer to the Alexandra, is more reliable than exciting, with a tranquil position in the center of the shoreline around the bay. Built around 1937, renovations have removed many of the original Art Deco features, leaving a modern, somewhat banal decor that's appropriate for a beach hotel. Rooms are comfortably furnished, each with a small bathroom with combination tub and shower. Guests gravitate to the rooftop solarium and the ground-floor restaurant with its sweeping view. Some consider the staff anonymous and rather detached. You'll find a beach, sailboats for rent, and access to spa facilities.

27 bd. de l'Océan, 44500 La Baule. ☎ **02-40-60-28-55**. Fax 02-40-60-10-18. www.hotel-bellevue-plage.fr. 35 units. 390F–900F (59.30– 136.80, $56.55–$130.50) double. AE, DC, MC, V. Closed mid-Nov to mid-Feb. **Amenities:** Restaurant, bar; sauna; room service; baby-sitting; laundry. *In room:* TV, minibar.

Hôtel La Palmeraie ★ *(Finds)*   In high-priced La Baule, this is a charmer. Built in the 1930s and renovated in the 1990s, it's named after eight large palms that thrive in the garden, thanks to the mild climate. Decorated in festive pink and white, La Palmeraie is near a beach and luxuriant with flowers in summer. The rooms are attractively decorated, often with English-style pieces. Each has high ceilings and dignified (sometimes antique) furniture. The only drawback: the soundproofed rooms aren't all that soundproof. Half board is obligatory in July and August; the food, however, is hardly in the league of that at the first-class hotels. The management and staff are helpful and even friendly.

7 allée des Cormorans, 44500 La Baule. ☎ **02-40-60-24-41**. Fax 02-40-42-73-71. 23 units. 350F–620F (53.20– 94.25, $50.75–$89.90) double; 700F (106.40, $101.50) suite. Half board (required July–Aug) 340F–450F (51.70– 68.40, $49.30–$65.25) per person extra. AE, DC, MC, V. Closed Oct–Apr 1. **Amenities:** Restaurant, bar. *In room:* TV.

DINING

Another choice is the restaurant at the **Castel Marie-Louise** (see "Accommodations," above).

Barbade *(Value)* CLASSIC FRENCH   Outfitted like an oversized greenhouse, and loaded with verdant plants and big windows, this restaurant offers competent, well-flavored cuisine that's fairly priced, particularly compared to many of the pricier establishments nearby. Menu items include sole meunière, grilled dorado, stuffed oysters, a hefty chunk of baked goat cheese with a crisp outer skin, and a dish of which the chef is particularly proud, freshwater crayfish in puff pastry.

bd. René Dubois (at the corner of the av. Ramblais). (*C* **02-40-17-57-57**. Reservations recommended. Main courses 90F–170F (13.70– 25.85, $13.05–$24.65); fixed-price menu 165F–185F (25.10– 28.10, $23.95–$26.85). MC, V. Daily noon–3pm and 8–11pm.

LA BAULE AFTER DARK

The most visible nighttime venue in town is the **Deauville Casino,** esplanade de François-André (*C* **02-40-11-48-28**), some areas of which are relatively stylish, but which can't compete with the glamour and high stakes at Deauville. No entrance fee is charged to the area containing the slot machines, which is accessible year-round daily from 10am to 4am. There is a fee—70F (10.65, $10.15)—for entrance to the area containing the *jeux traditionnels* of blackjack, roulette, and poker. That area is open between May and September, daily from 9pm to 5am. The casino is the site of a sometimes crowded disco, **L'Indiana** (*C* **02-40-11-48-28**), open from June to September, daily from 11:30pm to dawn; and the rest of the year, Wednesday through Sunday from 11:30pm to dawn. The cover is 70F (10.65, $10.15) and includes your first drink.

A stroll down avenue du Général-de-Gaulle or avenue Maréchale-de-Lattre-de-Tassigny will uncover any number of interesting bars and pubs. Newcomers feel welcome at **Le Bax,** 12 avenue de Pavie (*C* **02-40-60-90-00**), a cozy environment that survives despite the seasonal clientele. Other choices include **Klime Café,** 157 av. du Général-de-Gaulle (*C* **02-40-24-14-46**); **Le Sailor,** 305 av. Maréchale-de-Lattre-de-Tassigny (*C* **02-40-60-24-49**); and **Antidote,** 104 av. du Général-de-Gaulle (*C* **02-40-11-04-03**), the latter open only from June to September.

9 Nantes ★★★

239 miles W of Paris, 202 miles N of Bordeaux

Nantes is Brittany's largest town, although in spirit it seems to belong more to the Loire Valley's châteaux country. The mouth of the Loire is 30 miles away, and here it divides into several branches. A commercial and industrial city, Nantes is a busy port that suffered great damage in World War II. It's best known for the Edict of Nantes, issued by Henri IV in 1598, guaranteeing religious freedom to Protestants (it was later revoked). Many famous people, from Molière to Stendhal, have lived here. But Nantes hardly lives off its illustrious past. Now home to high-tech industries, it has some 30,000 college students and a population of half a million who welcome you as you make a stop between Brittany and points south or east in the Loire Valley.

Built on the largest of three islands in the Loire, the city expanded in the Middle Ages to the northern edge of the river, where its center lies today. The most prominent building is the **Château des Ducs de Bretagne,** which rises several hundred feet from a wide boulevard quai de la Fosse. At one end of this boulevard is the train station; at the other are the promenades beside the Loire.

ESSENTIALS

GETTING THERE If you're **driving,** take the A11 highway from Paris to Nantes. About 20 **trains** leave Paris, usually from Gare Montparnasse, for Nantes every day. The trip takes between 2 and 5½ hours, depending on the number of stops. The world's fastest train, the TGV Atlantique from Paris to Rennes and Nantes, is the best connection. Trains make the 3- to 4-hour trip from Bordeaux about 10 times a day. For information and schedules, call (*C* **08-36-35-35-35**.

VISITOR INFORMATION   The **Office de Tourisme** is at place du Commerce (℃ **02-40-20-60-00**; www.nantes-tourisme.com).

EXPLORING THE CITY

At the tourist office, you can buy a **Nantes City Card,** priced at 90F (13.70, $13.05) for 1 day, 160F (24.30, $23.20) for 2 days, or 200F (30.40, $29) for 3 days. It allows you to enter any of the museums and ride aboard any of the city's public conveyances.

Cathédrale St-Pierre ★★   Begun in 1434, this cathedral wasn't finished until the end of the 19th century. But despite all the time it took, it has remained architecturally harmonious—a rare feat. Two square towers dominate the facade, but more impressive is the 335-foot-long interior. Its pièce de résistance is Michel Colomb's Renaissance tomb of François II, duc de Bretagne, and his second wife, Marguerite de Foix. Another impressive work is the tomb of Gen. Juchault de Lamoricière, a native of Nantes and a great African campaigner; the sculptor Paul Dubois completed the tomb in 1879. After a 1972 fire destroyed the roof (rebuilt in 1975), the interior was restored. The white walls and pillars contrast with the rich colors of the stained-glass windows. The crypt, from the 11th century, shelters a museum of religions, although at press time it remains closed to the public due to terrorist threats.

Place St-Pierre. ℃ **02-40-47-84-64.** Free admission. Summer daily 9am–7pm; off-season daily 9am–6pm.

Château des Ducs de Bretagne ★★   Between the cathedral and the Loire is Nantes's second major sight, where the Edict of Nantes was signed. The castle was constructed in the 9th or 10th century, enlarged in the 13th century, destroyed, and then rebuilt into its present shape by François II in 1466. His daughter, Anne de Bretagne, continued the work. The castle is flanked by large towers and a bastion, and contains a symmetrical section (the Grand Gouvernement) built during the 17th and 18th centuries. The duchesse du Berry, royal courtesan, was imprisoned here, as was Gilles de Retz ("Bluebeard"), one of France's most notorious mass murderers. The castle's rich collections are being shaped into a museum of the history of Nantes from the 17th century to the present. Exhibitions are staged at the château pending completion of the museum.

4 place Marc-Elder. ℃ **02-40-41-56-56.** Admission 20F (3.05, $2.90) adults, 20F (3.05, $2.90) students, free for children 17 and under. July–Aug daily 10am–6pm; Sept–June Wed–Mon 10am–noon and 2–6pm.

Musée des Beaux-Arts de Nantes ★   In one of western France's most interesting provincial galleries, you'll find an unusually fine collection of sculptures and paintings from the 12th to the late 19th centuries. The street level is devoted to mostly French modern or contemporary art created since 1900, with special emphasis on painters from the 1950s and 1960s.

10 rue Georges-Clemenceau, east of place du Maréchal-Foch. ℃ **02-40-41-65-65.** Admission 20F (3.05, $2.90) adults, 10F (1.50, $1.45) students, children, and seniors. Free first Sun of the month and Fri 6–8pm. Mon and Wed–Thurs 10am–6pm; Fri 10am–8pm; Sat–Sun 10am–6pm.

Musée Jules Verne de Nantes   The novelist Jules Verne (*Journey to the Center of the Earth, Around the World in Eighty Days*) was born in Nantes in 1828, and literary fans seek out his house at 4 rue de Clisson in the Île-Feydeau. This museum is filled with memorabilia and objects inspired by his writings, from ink spots to a "magic" lantern with glass slides.

3 rue de l'Hermitage. ℃ **02-40-69-72-52.** Admission 8F (1.20, $1.15) adults, 4F (.60, 60¢) children and seniors. Mon and Wed–Sat 10am–noon and 2–5pm; Sun 2–5pm.

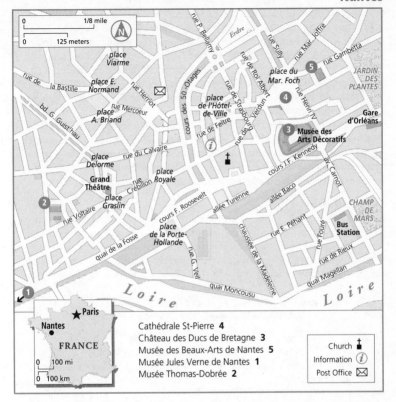

Cathédrale St-Pierre **4**
Château des Ducs de Bretagne **3**
Musée des Beaux-Arts de Nantes **5**
Musée Jules Verne de Nantes **1**
Musée Thomas-Dobrée **2**

Church ✝
Information ⓘ
Post Office ✉

Musée Thomas-Dobrée   This 19th-century neo-Romanesque mansion was
built by Thomas Dobrée, an important collector and traveler, whose parents left
him their whaling fortune in 1850. It stands in the town center, adjacent to the
15th-century manor of Jean V, where the bishops of Nantes occasionally lived.
Inside, you'll find Dobrée's varied and eclectic collection, gathered during the
height of France's gilded age, including prehistoric and medieval antiquities,
Flemish paintings from the 15th century, ecclesiastical relics, paintings by masters like Dürer, art objects from India, and the Dobrée family jewels. The collection, along with the building that contains it, was deeded to the city of
Nantes after the death of M. Dobrée in 1894.

18 rue Voltaire. ✆ **02-40-71-03-50.** Admission 20F (3.05, $2.90) adults; 10F (1.50, $1.45) children, students, and seniors. Tues–Sun 10am–noon and 1:30–5:30pm.

SHOPPING

Nantes overflows with shops and boutiques. The principal shopping streets are
rue du Calvaire, rue Crebillon, rue Boileau, rue d'Orléans, rue de la Marne, rue
de Verdun, and passage Pommeraye. Most of these encompass the shopping districts around place Graslin, place Royale, the château, and the cathedral. One of
the prime areas for antiques is around place Aristide-Briand and rue Mercoeur.

   The more interesting antiques dealers include **Antique Bijoux,** 21 rue Mercoeur (✆ **02-40-35-60-84**), specializing in antique and secondhand jewelry;
Jean-Yves Coue, 7 rue Mercoeur (✆ **02-40-08-29-95**), dealing in antique

primitive art from Africa, South and Central America, and the Pacific basin; and **L'Ecritoire Antiquités,** 12 rue Jean-Jaurès (℮ **02-40-47-78-18**), offering 18th- and 19th-century furniture and decorative pieces like historic mantels. **Robin Soustre,** 18 rue Mercoeur (℮ **02-40-48-51-79**), sells 19th-century furniture, usually mahogany, and antique porcelain. **Librairie Brocante du Palais,** 28 rue Jean-Jaurès (℮ **02-40-48-43-64**), offers engravings and antique books, while **Antiquité du Bouffay,** 17 rue de la Juiverie (℮ **02-40-12-11-87**), features small-scale art objects and antique furniture.

For other unique gifts, check out the stores of two talented master artisans: **Maison Devineau,** 2 place Ste-Croix (℮ **02-40-47-19-59**), which brings the art of wax-working to a new level, "growing" bushels of fruits and vegetables from liquid wax, and **Georges Gautier,** 9 rue de la Fosse (℮ **02-40-48-23-19**), where you'll find the town's best chocolates.

ACCOMMODATIONS

Hôtel Graslin *(Value)* Graslin is on a steep old street near the harbor, in the center of town. Tthere's a definite lassitude to the place, but the owners and managers, M. and Mme Roche, have given it many homelike touches, so it now offers more for the money than almost any other hotel in its price category. The comfortable rooms are bland and functional, with small, shower-only bathrooms.

1 rue Piron, 44000 Nantes. ℮ **02-40-69-72-91.** Fax 02-40-69-04-44. www.ifrance.com/graslin. 47 units. 350F–400F (53.20– 60.80, $50.75–$58) double. AE, DC, MC, V. *In room:* TV, hair dryer, safe.

L'Hôtel Within sight of the château and the cathedral, this hotel is, for the price, a perfect base in Nantes. Built in the early 1980s, the place is neat and modern but manages to maintain an inviting atmosphere. Guest rooms were renovated in the late 1990s and boast firm beds, rich colors, and contemporary furnishings. Some units have private balconies looking out over the château, while others open onto a garden and terrace. You'll find a paneled sitting area with couches and chairs next to the reception desk, as well as a softly lit breakfast room with terrace views.

6 rue Henri-IV, 44000 Nantes. ℮ **02-40-29-30-31.** Fax 02-40-29-00-95. www.ligneplus.com/lhotel. 31 units. 420F (63.85, $60.90) double. AE, DC, MC, V. Parking 35F (5.30, $5.10). **Amenities:** Room service; laundry/dry cleaning. *In room:* TV.

Mercure Beaulieu Situated on an island in the Loire, the Mercure offers well-furnished, soundproofed chambers. If you prefer contemporary comforts to historic charm, you'll be satisfied by the amenities and the alert, hardworking staff who know how to welcome international guests. The bedrooms were renovated in 2000 and offer mid-size bathrooms with a combination tub and shower. The restaurant and bar, Le Nautilus, offers a wide choice of seafood.

Île-Beaulieu, 44200 Nantes-Beaulieu. ℮ **02-40-95-95-95.** Fax 02-40-48-23-83. www.mercure.com. 100 units. 605F–645F (91.95– 98.05, $87.75–$93.55) double; 870F (132.25, $126.15) suite. AE, DC, MC, V. Free parking. Follow the blue NOVOTEL signs from any of the major traffic arteries in the city to a point 2 miles south of the town center. **Amenities:** Restaurant, bar; heated outdoor pool; tennis court. *In room:* A/C, TV, minibar, hair dryer.

DINING

L'Atlantide ★★★ MODERN FRENCH On the fourth floor of the complex that houses the city's chamber of commerce, this panoramic restaurant, with views sweeping out over the semi-industrial landscapes that surround it, serves the finest cuisine in the area. The world-renowned designer Jean-Pierre

Wilmotte created a nautical-looking enclave of pale hardwoods with lots of mirrors, but it's the innovative cooking of Jean-Yves Gueho that draws patrons. Menu items, steeped in the traditions of both the Loire Valley and the Breton coast, may include lobster salad with a crispy mixture of potatoes and olives; potato and herb tart capped with foie gras; Breton turbot with Cantonese spices; and braised sweetbreads with Anjou wine. An excellent dessert is bananas braised in local beer. The cellar is known for some of the finest vintages of Loire Valley wine anywhere, with special emphasis on Anjous and muscadets.

Centre des Salorges, 16 quai Ernest-Renaud. ℂ 02-40-73-23-23. Reservations required. Main courses 140F–160F (21.30– 24.30, $20.30–$23.20); fixed-price menus 155F–400F (23.55– 60.80, $22.50–$58) lunch, 200F–400F (30.40– 60.80, $29–$58) dinner. AE, V. Mon–Fri noon–2:30pm; Mon–Sat 7–10:30pm. Closed Aug 3–31.

La Cigale FRENCH/SEAFOOD   This is Nantes's most historic and charming brasserie, decorated in a sprawling Belle-Époque style that has changed little since the place opened in 1895 across from the landmark Théâtre Graslin. Menu items might include heaping platters of fresh shellfish, *confit des cuisses de canard* (duckling), an array of grilled steaks, and fresh scallops with green peppers and emulsified butter. It's usually quite loud, and the staff members tend to be overworked.

4 place Graslin. ℂ 02-51-84-94-94. Reservations recommended. Main courses 69F–92F (10.50– 14, $10–$13.35); fixed-price menu 75F–125F (11.40– 19, $10.90–$18.15). MC, V. Daily 11:45am–12:30am. Bus: 11 or 34.

Villa Mon Rêve MODERN FRENCH   This restaurant, housed in a stone-sided, late-19th-century villa built by a prosperous producer of fruits and vegetables, is set in a 1-acre garden awash with rose beds in summer. Chef Gérard Ryngel and his wife, Cécile, took over in 1979. Ryngel's repertoire includes regional specialties and his own creations: wild duck with Bourgeuil wine sauce, sandre from the Loire with beurre blanc, an unusual combination of veal sweetbreads with crayfish, and gazpacho studded with chunks of lobster. Especially unusual is roasted challons duckling served with caramelized muscadet wine. The wine list features more than 40 locally produced choices.

Route des Bords-de-Loire, Basse-Goulaine. ℂ 02-40-03-55-50. Reservations recommended. Fixed-price menus 168F–315F (25.55– 47.90, $24.35–$45.70). DC, MC, V. Daily noon–2pm and 7–9:30pm. Closed 2 weeks in early Nov and 2 weeks in Feb. Take D751 5 miles east of Nantes.

NANTES AFTER DARK

When the sun goes down, the town turns into one big party. On **place du Bouffay, place du Pilori,** and **rue Kervagen,** you'll find lots of cafes and pubs, many with live music and fun people. A younger crowd rules **rue Scribe.**

To beat that unshakable urge to check your e-mail before committing to an evening of fun, stop by **CyberHouse,** 8 quai de Versailles (ℂ 02-40-12-11-84); you'll pay 1F (.15, 15¢) per minute online and 13F (2.00, $1.90) for a beer. Afterward, catch some live blues, jazz, or rock at **Le Pub Univers,** 16 rue Jean-Jacques-Rousseau (ℂ 02-40-73-49-55); or techno and disco at **Quai West,** 17 quai François-Mitterrand (ℂ 02-40-47-68-45), which is open all night long. A great piano bar complete with dance floor and occasional jazz concerts is **Le Tie Break,** 1 rue des Petites-Ecuries (ℂ 02-40-47-77-00).

The pump-it-up dance scene has a huge following of everyone from students to seniors. **Balapapa,** 24 quai François-Mitterrand (ℂ 02-40-48-40-29), has a real cabaret feel in both its dance rooms. It plays an eclectic mix ranging from big band to funk and attracts a crowd just as diverse. The cover is 90F (13.70, $13.05). The over-30 crowd heads to the vintage 1970s disco **L'Evasion,** 3 rue de l'Emery (© **02-40-47-99-84**). Other discos that keep their dance floors packed are **New's,** place Émile-Zola (© **02-40-58-01-04**); **Le Royal Club Privé,** 7 rue des Salorges (© **02-40-69-11-10**); and **Wilton's Club,** 23 rue de Rieux (© **02-40-12-01-13**). Don't wear jeans to any of these places, and be prepared to pay 45F to 60F (6.85 to 9.10, $6.55 to $8.70) to get in.

The perennial favorite with gays and lesbians is **Le Plein Sud,** 2 rue Prémion (© **02-40-47-06-03**), where people meet and talk in a friendly atmosphere that welcomes everything from leather to lace. **Le Temps d'Aimer,** 14 rue Alexandre-Fourny (© **02-40-89-48-60**), is gay-friendly, though not exclusively gay. This disco with its small dance floor attracts a sophisticated crowd. The most you'll pay to get in is 60F to 80F (9.10 to 12.15, $8.70 to $11.60). The basement of **News** is another gay discotheque called **Le Privilége,** place Émile-Zola (© **02-40-58-01-04**). It's the favorite place for techno music lovers.

10

The Champagne Country

In about 3 days, you can take the Autoroute de l'Est (N3) from Paris and explore a region of beautiful cathedrals, historic battlefields, fantastic food, and world-famous vineyards, topping your tour with a glass or two of bubbly. On one of the Routes du Champagne, you can drive to the wine-producing center of Epernay, then on to Reims, some 90 miles northeast of Paris. After visiting Reims and its cathedral, you can leave on Route 31 east, heading toward Verdun, of World War I fame.

REGIONAL CUISINE Champagne's wine overshadows its cuisine, though several culinary specialties are unique to the district. Most are simple, hearty recipes developed over the centuries in country homes, using pork, beef, fish, and the area's fresh vegetables.

The tang and bite of the sparkling wines dissolve—in the most appetizing way—some of the flavorful grease and oils that are part of the local charcuteries and pâtés. Specialties include pork or sheep *andouillettes* (chitterlings) from Bar-sur-Aube and Bar-sur-Seine,

pig's feet from Ste-Menehould, and various pâtés made from offal, which many North Americans would never consider eating. A *matelote* is a stew, made with freshwater fish and red or white wine. Matelotes here usually employ champagne and carp, pike, and trout.

Most of the area's cheeses are made from cows' milk. The most famous are the *maroilles*, aged collectively (so their skins turn a terra-cotta red) in communal cellars. Some maroilles are sprinkled with tarragon, pepper, and paprika, and aged 2 months to produce the strong, aromatic Boulette d'Avesnes, which the French consume with beer. One cheese enjoying popularity in North America is Brie de Melun or Brie de Meaux—the best varieties are made in Champagne, preferably near Meaux.

The largest champagne producer here is Moët et Chandon, though there are excellent smaller vintners like Krug, Roederer, Böllinger, and Veuve Clicquot. Some of the still (non-sparkling) wines from the region, including blanc de blancs, are famous as well.

1 La Ferté-sous-Jouarre

41 miles E of Paris, 51 miles SW of Reims

In the village of Jouarre, 2 miles south of Ferté-sous-Jouarre, you can visit a 12th-century Benedictine abbey and explore one of the oldest crypts in France. At the **Tour de l'Abbaye de Jouarre,** 6 rue Montmorin (© **01-60-22-64-54**), those interested in medieval history will appreciate the documents referring to the Royal Abbey of Jouarre as well as the stones in the Merovingian crypt, which evoke the 7th century. There's also a collection of prehistoric artifacts, remnants of the Roman occupation, and sculptural fragments. The crypt and tower are open Wednesday through Monday 9am to noon and 2 to 5pm (until 6pm May through October). Admission to the crypt and tower is 30F (4.55, $4.35); to the crypt only, it's 20F (3.05, $2.90); and to the tower only, 15F (2.30, $2.20).

ESSENTIALS

GETTING THERE   If you're **driving,** take N3 along the Marne. About 10 **trains** per day make the 55-minute run from Paris's Gare de l'Est, stopping at Ferté-sous-Jouarre. From there, take a taxi 2 miles south to Jouarre and its abbey.

VISITOR INFORMATION   The most comprehensive and best equipped **Office de Tourisme** is adjacent to the tower and the abbey, at place de la Tour (𝒞 **01-60-22-64-54**), in Jouarre. There's a **Syndicat d'Initiative** (tourist office) at 26 place de l'Hôtel-de-Ville (𝒞 **01-60-22-63-43**), in Ferté-sous-Jouarre.

ACCOMMODATIONS

Château des Bondons ✹✹   Surrounded by a 60-acre park and forest, this château dates from the French Revolution. Not much of the furniture is original to the building, but overall, a sense of the English aesthetic, complete with chintz-patterned upholsteries and British antiques, fills many of the public areas. Bedrooms are most comfortable, and, as befits a château, come in a variety of shapes and sizes, filled with both old and new furnishings, plus combination tub and shower. Other than breakfast, no full-fledged meals are served, but room-service salads and cold platters are available most hours of the day and evening.

47–49 Rue des Bondons. 𝒞 **01-60-22-00-98.** Fax 01-60-22-97-01. chateau-des-bondons@ club-internet.fr 14 units. 550F–650F (83.60– 98.80, $79.75–$94.25) double; 900F–1,200F (136.80– 182.40, $130.50–$174) suite. AE, DC, MC, V. Follow the signs to Montménard; take D70 for 1½ miles east of the town center. **Amenities:** Restaurant, bar; limited room service. *In room:* TV, minibar, hair dryer.

DINING

Le Plat d'Étain TRADITIONAL FRENCH   This homey, conservative restaurant caters to the gastronomic needs of hundreds of art-history lovers who make the pilgrimage to see the world-famous Merovingian crypt, which is nearby. Expect exposed ceiling beams, lacy curtains, and tokens of old-fashioned France that might remind locals of the style of cuisine once prepared by their grandmothers. Examples include blanquette de veau, boeuf bourguignonne, and whatever is seasonal and appeals to the whims of the chef.

6 place Auguste-Tinchant. 𝒞 **01-60-22-06-07.** Reservations recommended. Main courses 75F–120F (11.40– 18.25, $10.90–$17.40; fixed-price menus 68F (10.35, $9.85) lunch, 95F–195F (14.45– 29.65, $13.80–$28.30) dinner). MC, V. Sat–Thurs noon–2:30pm; Sat and Mon–Thurs 6:30–10pm.

2 Château-Thierry

56 miles E of Paris, 6 miles SW of Reims

An industrial town on the Marne's right bank, Château-Thierry contains the ruins of a castle believed to have been constructed for the Frankish king Thierry IV. Château-Thierry gained fame for being the farthest point reached by the German offensive in the summer of 1918. Under heavy bombardment, French forces were aided by the Second and Third Divisions of the U.S. Expeditionary Force. The Battlefields of the Marne are a mile west of town; thousands of Allied soldiers who died fighting in World War I are buried here. Atop Hill 204 is a monument honoring American troops who lost their lives.

Château-Thierry is where the poet and fable writer Jean de la Fontaine (1621 to 1695) was born, in a stone-sided house built in 1452. Today, it contains one

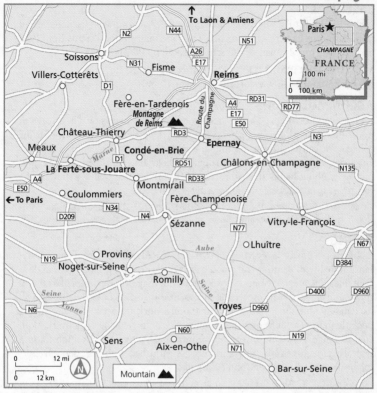

of France's most visited literary shrines, the **Musée Jean-de-la-Fontaine,** 12 rue
Jean de la Fontaine (② **03-23-69-05-60**). Located a few steps from place de
l'Hôtel-de-Ville, it contains a collection of his mementos, including editions of
his works from the Charles-Henri Genot collection, paintings and engravings
from the 17th to the 20th centuries. Copies of his fables (allegorical barnyard stories depicting the foibles of humans) and *contes* (short stories that are a lot racier
than his fables) are for sale in the bookshop. Hours are Wednesday through Monday from 10am to noon and 2 to 6pm. Admission is 20F (3.05, $2.90) for
adults and 10F (1.50, $1.45) for children; free to all on Wednesdays.

If you're interested in World War I relics, head 5 miles northwest of Château-
Thierry to the **Bois de Belleau** (Belleau Wood). The Battle of Belleau Wood
marked the second clash between American and German troops in World War
I and demonstrated the bravery of the U.S. soldiers in modern warfare. After a
bitter 2-week struggle, the woods were taken by the Second Division of the U.S.
Expeditionary Force under Maj. Gen. Omar Bundy. Though the Germans suffered many losses and some 1,650 prisoners were taken, U.S. casualties were
appalling: nearly 7,585 soldiers and 285 officers were wounded, killed, or missing in action. In 1923, the battleground was dedicated as a memorial to the men
who gave their lives here. The **American cemetery,** also known as Le Cimetière
de Belleau (② **03-23-70-70-90**), contains 2,288 graves. You'll also see a chapel
that was damaged in World War II.

ESSENTIALS

GETTING THERE   If you're **driving,** take A4 southwest from Reims or northeast from La Ferté-sous-Jouarre. There are frequent local **trains** from Paris and Reims. For information and schedules, call © **08-36-35-35-35.**

VISITOR INFORMATION   The **Office de Tourisme** is at 11 rue Vallée (© **03-23-83-10-14;** www.otsichateau-thierry.com).

ACCOMMODATIONS

Hôtel Île-de-France   This modern hotel is the leading choice in an area of not-so-hot options. Set in a park overlooking the green Marne Valley, near the ruins of the town's château, the four-story structure boasts balconies and dormers, a view of the town, and well-maintained bedrooms furnished in contemporary style. About half of the bathrooms come with a tub as well as a shower. The restaurant is not particularly noteworthy.

Rte. de Soissons, 02400 Château-Thierry. © **03-23-69-10-12.** Fax 03-23-83-49-70. 50 units. 380F (57.75, $55.10) double. AE, DC, MC, V. **Amenities:** Restaurant, bar; room service; baby-sitting; laundry. *In room:* TV.

DINING

Auberge Jean-de-la-Fontaine TRADITIONAL FRENCH   This restaurant is filled with paintings on wood panels dedicated to the fables of Jean de la Fontaine. The menu changes every 3 weeks, but may include dishes like salmon smoked in-house by the owners or an appetizer that showcases the duck "in all its states" (combining a portion of traditional duck breast, a taste of smoked duck thigh with a confit of gizzards, and a slice of homemade duck liver). Main courses range from a warm paté of freshwater sandre with Breton lobster to a typical regional dish of chitterling sausages garnished with pig's foot. Dessert might be crème brûlée with bitter almonds.

10 rue des Filoirs. © **03-23-83-63-89.** Reservations required. Main courses 60F–95F (9.10– 14.45, $8.70–$13.83); fixed-price menu (including aperitif, wine, and coffee) 220F (33.45, $31.90). AE, DC, MC, V. Tues–Sun 12:30–2pm; Tues–Sat 7:30–9:30pm. Closed Jan 5–18 and first 3 weeks of Aug.

3 Condé-en-Brie ⭐

55 miles E of Paris, 15 miles W of Epernay

West of Epernay, **Château de Condé** ⭐, rue du Château, 02330 Condé-en-Brie (© **03-23-82-42-25**), was inherited in 1814 by the comte de Sade, and remained in his family until 1983. The Sade name was besmirched by the marquis, an innovative writer (*Justine, Juliette, The 120 Days of Sodom*) whose sexual practices as described in his works gave us the word *sadism.*

   The castle was built in the late 12th century by Enguerran of Coucy. A part of the old keep still remains—two big rooms with great chimneys and thick walls. The castle was reconstructed in the Renaissance style at the beginning of the 16th century by Cardinal de Bourbon, a member of the royal family. His nephew, Louis de Bourbon, called himself the prince de Condé, most likely because he had many fond childhood memories of the place. After sustaining damage in the early 18th century, the château was rebuilt again—this time for the marquis de La Faye. The Italian architect Servandoni invited artists like Boucher and Watteau to do frescoes and paintings, which you can still see today. Servandoni decorated the largest room, making it a theater hall for music and entertainment. The present castle is an exceptional ensemble, with its paintings, woodwork, chimneys, and so-called Versailles floor.

In 1994, the new owners, the de Recheforts, discovered several Watteau paintings concealed behind mirrors installed during the 18th century. Now, at the push of a button, the mirrors open to reveal the previously hidden treasures.

Admission is 36F (5.45, $5.20) for adults and 18F (2.75, $2.60) for children 14 and under. The castle is open for tours from June to September, daily at 2:30, 3:30, 4:30, and 5:30pm. In May, it's open only on Sundays and bank holidays at the same hours.

If you're **driving** between Château-Thierry and Epernay on N3, head south at Dormans and follow the signs to Condé-en-Brie.

4 Reims ✫✫✫

89 miles E of Paris, 28 miles NW of Châlons-en-Champagne

Reims (pronounced *Rahns*), an ancient Roman city, was important at the time Caesar conquered Gaul. French kings came here to be crowned, and it's said that the French nation was born here in A.D. 498. Joan of Arc escorted Charles VII here in 1429, kissing the silly man's feet. But don't let this ancient background mislead you: As you approach Reims, you'll pass through prefabricated suburbs that look like apartment-house blocks in Eastern Europe. There are gems in Reims, including the cathedral, of course, but you must seek them out.

Most visitors come to Reims because it's the center of a wine-growing district whose bubbly is present at celebrations all over the world. The city today, with a population of 185,000, is filled with swank restaurants, ritzy champagne houses, large squares, and long, tree-lined avenues. The champagne bottled here is the lightest and subtlest in flavor of the world's wines. Make an effort to linger, exploring the vineyards and wine cellars, the Gothic monuments, and the battlefields. (The Germans occupied Reims in 1870, 1914, and 1940.)

ESSENTIALS

GETTING THERE   If you're **driving** from Paris to Reims, take A4 east. **Trains** depart from Paris's Gare de L'Est Station every 2 hours (trip time: 1½ hours). There are also five trains per day from Strasbourg (trip time: 4 hours). For train information and schedules, call ✆ **08-36-35-35-35.**

VISITOR INFORMATION   The **Office de Tourisme** is at 2 rue Guillaume-de-Machault (✆ **03-26-77-45-25**; www.tourism.fr/reims).

EXPLORING THE CITY

Cathédrale Notre-Dame de Reims ✫✫✫   This is one of the world's most famous cathedrals. It was restored after World War I, largely by U.S. contributions from John D. Rockefeller; mercifully, it escaped World War II relatively unharmed. Built on the site of a church that burned to the ground in 1211, it was intended as a sanctuary where French kings would be anointed. St-Rémi, the bishop of Reims, baptized Clovis, the pagan king of the Franks, here in A.D. 496. All of the kings of France from Louis the Pious (son of Charles the Great) in A.D. 815 to Charles X in 1825 were crowned here.

Laden with statuettes, its three western facade portals are spectacular. A rose window above the central portal is dedicated to the Virgin. The right portal portrays the Apocalypse and the Last Judgment; the left, martyrs and saints. At the western facade's northern door is a smiling angel. Lit by lancet windows, the immense nave has many bays.

Place du Cardinal-Luçon. ✆ **03-26-47-55-34**. Free admission. Daily 7:30am–7:30pm.

Palais du Tau ★★   Constructed in 1690 as the official residence of the bishops of Reims and set beside the cathedral, this stone mansion contains many statues that, until recently, decorated the cathedral facade. (Those there now are mostly copies.) Also on display are many holy relics associated with Reims, including a 12th-century chalice for the communion of French monarchs and a talisman supposedly containing a relic of the True Cross that Charlemagne is said to have worn.

Place du Cardinal-Luçon. ☎ **03-26-47-81-79.** Admission 36F (5.45, $5.20) adults, 23F (3.50, $3.35) students and those under 26. Daily 10am–noon and 2–5pm (until 6pm Sat–Sun).

Salle de Reddition   On May 7, 1945, the Germans surrendered to General Eisenhower in this structure, which was once a little schoolhouse near the railroad tracks. The walls of the room are lined with maps of the rail routes, exactly as they were on the day of surrender.

12 rue Franklin-D.-Roosevelt. ☎ **03-26-47-84-19.** Admission 10F (1.50, $1.45). Wed–Mon 10am–noon and 2–6pm. Closed May 1 and July 14.

Basilique St-Rémi ★★   This basilica is the oldest church in Reims, dating from 1007. Though an example of medieval French masonry at its most classic, it's often unfavorably compared to the more spectacular cathedral. Within the basilica complex is the former royal abbey of St-Rémi, who was once the guardian of the holy ampula used to anoint the kings of France. The abbey now functions as a museum with an extensive collection covering the history of Reims, regional archaeology, and military history. The architect Louis Duroché designed the majestic ornamental front of the main quadrangle as well as the Grand Staircase (1778), where you can admire one of the official portraits of the young Louis XV in his coronation robes. It also contains a Romanesque nave leading to a magnificent choir crowned with massive pointed arches. The nave, the transepts, one of the towers, and the aisles date from the 11th century; the portal of the south transept is in early-16th-century Flamboyant Gothic style. Some of the stained glass in the apse is from the 13th century. The tomb of St. Rémi is elaborately carved with Renaissance figures and columns.

53 rue St-Simon. ☎ **03-26-85-23-36.** Admission 10F (1.50, $1.45) adults, free for children and students. Mon–Fri 2–6:30pm; Sat–Sun 2–7pm.

Musée des Beaux-Arts   Housed in the 18th-century buildings belonging to the old Abbaye St-Denis, this fine provincial art gallery contains more than a dozen portraits of German princes of the Reformation by both "the Elder" and "the Younger" Cranach; the museum has owned this remarkable collection since it opened in 1795. You can see the *Toiles Peintes* (light painting on rough linen) that date from the 15th and 16th centuries and depict the *Passion du Christ* and *Vengeance du Christ.* Paintings and fine furniture from the 17th and 18th centuries are in the Salles Diancourt and Jamot-Neveux. There's an excellent series of 26 of Corot's tree-shaded walks.

8 rue Chanzy. ☎ **03-26-47-28-44.** Admission 10F (1.50, $1.45) adults, free for students and children under 12. Wed–Mon 10am–noon and 2–6pm. Closed Jan 1, May 1, July 14, Nov 1 and 11, and Dec 25.

EXPLORING THE CHAMPAGNE CELLARS ★★

Many of the vast champagne cellars of Reims extend for miles through chalky deposits. During the German siege of 1914 and throughout the war, people lived in them and even published a daily paper here. The cellars are open all year, but are most interesting during the fall grape harvest. After that, the wine is fermented in vats in the caves, then bottled with a small amount of sugar and natural yeast.

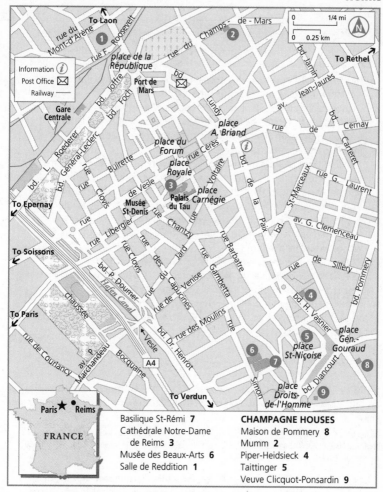

	CHAMPAGNE HOUSES
Basilique St-Rémi **7**	
Cathédrale Notre-Dame	Maison de Pommery **8**
de Reims **3**	Mumm **2**
Musée des Beaux-Arts **6**	Piper-Heidsieck **4**
Salle de Reddition **1**	Taittinger **5**
	Veuve Clicquot-Ponsardin **9**

The yeast feeds on the sugar and causes a second fermentation to take place—producing those fabulous bubbles. The wine growers wait until the sparkle has "taken" before they remove the bottles to racks or pulpits. For about 3 months, *remueurs* are paid to turn them a fraction every day, which brings the impurities (dead yeast cells and other matter) toward the cork. Eventually these sediments are removed and the wine is given its proper dosage (sugar dissolved in wine), depending on the desired sweetness. The process takes 4 or 5 years and is carried out in caves that are usually 100 feet deep and kept at a constant 50°F.

Maison de Pommery Among the most visited cellars are those under the Gothic-style buildings and spacious gardens of the Maison de Pommery. A magnificent 116-step stairway leads to a maze of galleries dug into the chalk that are more than 11 miles long and about 100 feet below ground. Various stages of champagne-making are shown, and it is available for sale in the gift shop.

Place du Général-Gouraud. ℂ **03-26-61-62-56.** Admission 50F (7.60, $7.25), free for children 11 and under. Apr–Oct daily 9am–7pm; Nov–Mar Mon–Fri 10am–6pm. Call in advance to book your visit.

Champagne: The Fizz & the Fun

The love of that effervescent mystery called champagne is nothing new. During the Renaissance, the only thing François I of France and Henry VIII of England could agree on was a preference for bubbly. Napoléon carted along cases of the stuff to his battlefronts. Casanova used it to liven up his legendary seductions, Mme de Pompadour employed it to tempt the Sun King, and Tallyrand imported cases of it to the Congress of Vienna for a different sort of seduction—procuring more favorable peace terms.

We all owe a toast or two to Dom Pérignon (1638 to 1715), that Benedictine monk who initiated the technique of adding cane sugar and natural yeast to the still wine to cause it, after years of fermentation, to foam. Without a complicated series of additives, double fermentations, cooling at precise temperatures, and turnings and twistings, champagne would be plain old table wine. Without the fizz, where would be the fun?

The best champagne grapes are grown in vineyards that meander like narrow ribbons along the bottomlands south of Reims. French vintners consider the best regions the Côte des Blancs, Montagne de Reims, and Vallée de la Marne; these are also the names for the three Routes du Champagne, signposted wine roads extending through the area.

Mumm   A visit here includes a video show and a cellar tour; a small museum exhibits casks and the ancient tools of a vintner. Champagne is available for purchase in the gift shop.

34 rue du Champ-de-Mars. ℂ **03-26-49-59-70.** Tours (in English) 30F (4.55, $4.35) adults, free for children 4 and under. Mar–Oct daily 9–11am and 2–5pm; Nov–Feb Mon–Fri 9–11am and 2–5pm, Sat–Sun and holidays 2–5pm.

Piper-Heidsieck   This firm—one of the oldest champagne houses in the world—was established in 1785. Here you explore the cellars in an electric-powered car (five occupants at a time) known as *une nacelle* and enjoy a tasting at the end of the tour. Champagne is available for purchase in the gift shop.

51 bd. Henri-Vasnier. ℂ **03-26-84-43-44.** Admission 40F (6.10, $5.80), children 11 and under free. Daily 9–11:45am and 2–5:15pm. Closed Tues–Wed from Dec–Feb.

Taittinger   Taittinger is a grand *marque* of French champagne, one of the few whose ownership is controlled by members of the family that founded it in 1930. It's one of the most visitor-friendly of the champagne houses. The Romanesque cellars were dug from the site of Gallo-Roman chalk mines in use between the 4th and the 13th century. Tours—including a film presentation, a guided cellar visit, and a surprisingly rich set of anecdotes about Reims, the champagne-making process, and Taittinger family lore—last about an hour.

9 place St-Niçaise. ℂ **03-26-85-45-35.** Admission 35F (5.30, $5.10). Mon–Fri 9:30am–noon and 2–4:30pm; Sat–Sun 9–11am and 2–5pm. Closed Sat–Sun from Dec–Feb.

The association of this bubbling wine with glamour, romance, and celebration is a triumph of marketing. Off the record, Burgundy's vintners will remind oenophiles that it takes a lot more work, with a greater chance of failure from uncontrollable variables, to produce a great bottle of still red than a jeroboam of sparkling Veuve Clicquot.

Nonetheless, the fascination with real champagne remains fervent, as shown by the increase in worldwide consumption of the stuff since Leslie Caron and Louis Jourdan sang about "The Night They Invented Champagne" in the 1958 movie *Gigi*.

And now a word about the word *champagne*. Since the days of the grand époque, when dandies drank bubbly out of ladies' slippers and beauties bathed in the stuff, the misuse of that word has aroused the wrath of even such venerable personages as the Veuve Clicquot herself. By law, only champagne made in France's Champagne region can be called champagne. Bubbly made in any other area of France must be categorized as sparkling wine produced via the *méthode champenoise*. In the U.S., each state has its own laws about this—in one state you can call your bubbly champagne while in another you cannot. But don't dare try that in France, as you'll face lengthy litigation. Just ask Yves St-Laurent, who once had the effrontery to name a new perfume he'd invented Champagne.

Veuve Clicquot-Ponsardin   You can visit part of the 16 miles of underground galleries on guided tours at Veuve Clicquot-Ponsardin. The highlight is the screening of a film about one of Champagne's grande dames, the Veuve Clicquot (Widow Clicquot).

1 place des Droits-de-l'Homme. (©) **03-26-89-54-41**. Free admission. Apr–Oct Mon–Sat; Nov–Mar Mon–Fri (advance appointments required).

SHOPPING

The main shopping district is conveniently located around the cathedral. Nearby streets to browse are the very long **rue de Vesle,** the **cours Langlet,** and the **place Drouet d'Erlon.**

You'll definitely want to include bottles of champagne on your shopping list. Many people opt to visit one of the major champagne houses in town; others get in their car and drive along the **Routes du Champagne,** three signposted wine roads that cover the region. This is where you'll find more of the smaller champagne makers. When you're making the rounds, be aware that most champagne houses prefer you to take the tour and not just stop in the shop. If you do take the tour, you'll at least get a glass of bubbly at the end. When purchasing here, be aware that the bottles are priced individually, but you can get discounts if you buy three or six bottles at a time. However, if you're looking for a good deal, you may want to buy at stores in town such as **Le Marché aux Vins, Pérandel,** 3 place Léon-Bourgeois ((©) **03-26-40-12-12**), where you can choose from a large selection of local champagnes and other wines. For complete information on the champagne houses in and around Reims, contact the Office de Tourisme.

Another specialty here is the light and delicious little pink cookie known as *biscuit de Reims.* Two of the best places to find them are **La Maison Fossier,** 25 cours Langlet (© **03-26-47-59-84**), and **Boutique Nominee,** place du Parvis (© **03-26-40-43-85**). For chocolate and candied specialties, try **La Petite Friande,** 15 cours Langlet (© **03-26-47-50-44**), where you can purchase liqueur-filled chocolate champagne bubbles and corks.

Parc des Expositions, route de Châlons-en-Champagne (2½ miles east of Reims), hosts a flea market the first Sunday of every month except August. On the first weekend of April, there's a huge "Euro" flea market, with more than 500 vendors, in the same location. The organization responsible for these events is **Artcom/Puces de Reims,** 82 rue Jacquart (© **03-26-02-04-06**).

ACCOMMODATIONS
EXPENSIVE
Boyer-les-Crayères ✦✦✦ There's no better place to stay or dine than at this hotel, which occupies one of the finest châteaux in eastern France. Set in a 14-acre park, it boasts 18-foot ceilings, burnished paneling, and luxurious furnishings. The bedrooms, with terraces and all the amenities, are individually decorated in a sophisticated country-manor style and usually available when a champagne mogul isn't in residence. The bathrooms are outfitted with deluxe toiletries and combination tub and shower. The restaurant is the greatest in the region (see "Dining," below).

64 bd. Henri-Vasnier, 51100 Reims. © **03-26-82-80-80.** Fax 03-26-82-65-52. www.gerardboyer.com. 19 units. 1,550F–2,050F (235.60– 311.60, $224.75–$297.25) double; 2,220F–2,650F (337.45– 402.80, $321.90–$384.25) suite. AE, DC, MC, V. Closed Dec 22–Jan 12. **Amenities:** Restaurant, bar; room service; baby-sitting; laundry/dry cleaning. *In room:* A/C, minibar, hair dryer.

Les Templiers ✦✦ This hotel, a short walk from the cathedral, may be small, but it's your best inner-city bet. A restored 1800s Mock-Gothic house, the place exhibits taste and sensitivity, with antiques, ornate ceilings, and hand-carved woodwork creating an inviting ambience. The guest rooms continue the 19th-century allure with color-coordinated fabrics and bold print wallcoverings. Each comes with a quality French mattress and a well-maintained private bathroom, most often with both tub and shower.

22 rue des Templiers, 51100 Reims. © **03-26-88-55-08.** Fax 03-26-47-80-60. http://wanadoo.fr/hotel. templiers 18 units. 990F–1,400F (150.50– 212.80, $143.55–$203) double; 1,800F (273.60, $261) suite. AE, DC, MC, V. Bus: G or H. **Amenities:** Bar; indoor heated pool; sauna; room service; laundry. *In room:* TV, minibar, safe.

MODERATE
L'Assiette Champenoise ✦ About 4 miles from Reims, this is the second-best hotel and restaurant in the area. Built in the 1970s among century-old trees, it occupies part of what was once a Norman estate. Rooms are attractively furnished and well maintained in a combination of French traditional and modern style, each with a combination tub and shower bathroom. Many come here just to enjoy the cooking of Jean-Pierre Lallement in the rustic dining room. The cuisine covers a medley of classics, some with an innovative twist. Try the John Dory with ragoût of vegetables, suckling veal with seven vegetables, or grilled duck liver with fondue of tomatoes. Homemade foie gras is always a reliable starter.

40 av. Paul-Vaillant-Couturier, 51430 Tinqueux. © **03-26-84-64-64.** Fax 03-26-04-15-69. www.chateau-muire.com. 62 units. 585F–970F (88.90– 147.45, $84.85–$140.65) double; 1,100F–1,500F (167.20– 228, $159.50–$217.50) suite. AE, DC, MC, V. Free parking. From Reims, take A4 west toward Paris and exit

at "Sortie 22-Tinqueux"; av. Paul-Vaillant-Couturier will lead you directly to Tinqueux. **Amenities:** Restaurant, bar; room service; laundry. *In room:* TV, minibar, hair dryer.

INEXPENSIVE

Best Western Hôtel de la Paix   Conveniently located between the train station and the cathedral, this is the only modern hotel in France that owns a medieval chapel (built for Benedictine nuns in the 1200s) overlooking its garden and pool. Constructed in 1946, it has been enlarged since then into the pleasant chain-hotel format you'll see today. The rooms are contemporary and well maintained, and many are air-conditioned. Furnishings are a bit sterile, but the beds are comfortable and most bathrooms have a combination tub and shower. The hotel's **Taverne du Maître Kanter** (© 03-26-47-00-45) serves excellent meals. The cuisine might include sauerkrauts, fish, grills, oysters, and casseroles.

9 rue Buirette, 51100 Reims. © **800/528-1234** in the U.S. and Canada, or 03-26-40-04-08. Fax 03-26-47-75-04. www.bestwestern.com. 106 units. 500F (76E, $72.50) double; 690F (104.90, $100.05) junior suite for 2 or 3 persons. AE, DC, MC, V. Parking 50F (7.60, $7.25). Bus: G or H. **Amenities:** Restaurant, bar; room service; laundry. *In room:* TV, minibar, hair dryer.

Grand Hôtel du Nord   This recently renovated old-fashioned hotel offers comfortably decorated rooms. They range in size from small to medium, each with a comfortable bed and shower-only bathroom. Two steps from the entrance, the liveliness of place Drouet-d'Erlon unfolds with its many boutiques, cafes, and cinemas. The hotel is also near the cathedral, the basilica, and various museums.

75 place Drouet-d'Erlon, 51100 Reims. © **03-26-47-39-03**. Fax 03-26-40-92-26. grandhoteldunord-reims@ wanadoo.fr. 50 units. 295F–330F (44.85– 50.15, $42.80–$47.85) double. AE, DC, MC, V. Parking 30F (4.55, $4.35). Take A4 (A26) motorway and exit at Reims-Centre. Bus: G or H. *In room:* TV, hair dryer.

Grand Hôtel L'Univers   In the heart of Reims, across from the train station, this five-story hotel offers small- to average-size bedrooms outfitted in a basic manner. All but three bathrooms have a combination tub and shower. This area can get noisy, but the rooms have double-pane windows. You can have breakfast in the American-style bar or dinner in the hotel's small but elegant restaurant, which specializes in traditional French cuisine and offers fixed-price menus.

41 bd. Foch, 51100 Reims. © **03-26-88-68-08**. Fax 03-26-40-95-61. www.ebc.fr/hotel-univers. 42 units. 425F–480F (64.60– 72.95, $61.65–$69.60) double. AE, DC, MC, V. **Amenities:** Restaurant, bar; babysitting; laundry. *In room:* TV, minibar, hair dryer.

Mercure Reims Cathédrale ⭐ *(Value)*   This hotel, part of a national chain, sits on the banks of the Marne Canal, a 5-minute walk from the town center. It's near the entrance to the autoroute, so it's easy to find. The good-size rooms have

---

(Finds **A Bucolic Retreat in Busy Reims**

Parc Leo-Lagrange is the largest park in central Reims, a tree-dotted haven favored by joggers and anyone looking for a respite from urban (and wine-related) life. Set within a 15-minute walk south of the cathedral, it's more English in its layout than French, and has none of the rigid symmetry and sculptures associated with formal French landscape design. There's also a section devoted to a children's playground.

all the modern conveniences including bathrooms with tub and shower; some units boast views of a scenic waterway. Furnishings are standard motel style.

31 bd. Paul-Doumer, 51100 Reims. (✆ **03-26-84-49-49.** Fax 03-26-84-49-84. h1248@accor-hotels. com. 126 units. 590F (89.730, $85.55) double; 790F–890F (120.10– 135.30, $114.55–$129.05) suite. AE, DC, MC, V. Parking 50F (7.60, $7.25). **Amenities:** Restaurant, bar; room service; baby-sitting; laundry. *In room:* TV, minibar, hair dryer.

DINING

L'Assiette Champenoise (see "Accommodations," above) also has an excellent restaurant.

Boyer-les-Crayères ✫✫✫ MODERN FRENCH   This grand restaurant has no equal in the champagne district. World-famous chef Gérard Boyer imbues each dish with his culinary imprint. One masterpiece is *salade du Père-Maurice*, with green beans, artichoke hearts, lemon, foie gras, truffles, and lobster. Other spectacular choices include turbot steak studded with truffles and served with foie gras, salsify braised in champagne and served with a truffle-flavored cream sauce, and a heavenly John Dury in a sherry and red port sauce flavored with Szechuan pepper and served with sautéed celery. Dessert might be an American-inspired brownie with almond-flavored chocolate truffles, accompanied by ice cream flavored with caramelized peanuts and a caramelized walnut sauce.

64 bd. Henri-Vasnier. (✆ **03-26-82-80-80.** Reservations required a few days in advance for weekday dinners, at least a month in advance for weekend dinners. Main courses 290F–360F (44.10– 54.70, $42.05–$52.20); fixed-price menu (including red Bordeaux and champagne) 1,200F (182.40, $174). AE, DC, MC, V. Wed–Sun noon–3pm; Tues–Sun 7:15–10pm.

Le Chardonnay ✫✫ TRADITIONAL FRENCH   This cozy enterprise serves superb cuisine in a much-restored building managed by members of the Lange family. You're likely to be greeted by Chantal and her daughters, the team that oversees the dining room that overlooks a flowering courtyard. The cuisine is remarkably consistent from week to week, with sauces often based on a gener-ous use of local wines. Examples include roasted rabbit with foie gras, veal stuffed with truffles and cooked in a clay pot, fricassee of lobster with tarragon vinegar, and nuggets of venison in a red wine–mushroom sauce.

184 av. d'Epernay. (✆ **03-26-06-08-60.** Reservations recommended. Main courses 90F–180F (13.70– 27.35; $13.05–$26.10); fixed-price menu 150F–420F (22.80[nd]63.85, $21.75–$60.90); "menu champagne" for 2 (including a bottle of a "champagne de marque") 880F (133.75, $127.60). AE, DC, MC, V. Sun–Fri noon–2:30pm; Mon–Sat 7:30–10pm. Drive a mile south of Reims's center, following the signs to Epernay.

Le Vigneron ✫ CHAMPENOISE   This sophisticated restaurant is firmly rooted in the traditions of Champagne: much of the cuisine is laced with one of the region's delectable wines. Wine experts grab the carte even before glancing at the menu. With 650 choices, it includes some museum-quality vintages, such as a Pol Roger 1892 (not for sale at any price) and a Veuve Clicquot 1923. Hervé Liegent and the charming staff offer such specialties as trout from the Marne prepared with crayfish sauce, poached eggs with a sauce made with *maroilles* (a mild locally fermented cheese), and lobster ragoût with champagne. A superb dessert is the *biscuits roses de Reims* served with a liqueur (*marc*) distilled from champagne. Try to step into the restaurant's small-scale museum, maintained in honor of the vintner's art, before you leave.

Place Paul-Jamot. (✆ **03-26-79-86-86.** Reservations recommended. Main courses 80F–140F (12.15– 21.30, $11.60–$20.30); fixed-price menu 150F–260F (22.80– 39.50, $21.75–$37.70). DC, MC, V. Mon–Fri 11:30am–2:30pm and 5:30–10pm. Closed Aug 1–15 and Dec 23–Jan 2.

NEARBY ACCOMMODATIONS & DINING

Château de Fère ★★ MODERN FRENCH   Set in a park, this fabulous restaurant occupies a 16th-century crenellated château with turrets. The only restaurant in Champagne with superior cuisine is Boyer-les-Crayères (above). Begin in the sunny garden, sipping an aperitif or a glass of champagne with juice from freshly crushed raspberries. Your imaginative meal might consist of specialties like foie gras of duckling with a confit of ginger and a sauce made from the sweet dessert wine Muscats de Venise; nuggets of suckling lamb cooked in a truffle-and-parsley-flavored crust; and deliberately undercooked Scottish salmon in a lemon-flavored sweet-and-sour sauce. The desserts are mouthwatering, but we prefer to order the *boulette d'Avesnes*, a cone of cheese flecked with herbs and crushed peppercorns and coated with paprika.

Also available are 25 luxurious guest rooms, each with minibar, TV, and phone. The doubles cost 850F to 1,300F (129.20 to 197.60, $123.25 to $188.50); the suites, 1,300F to 2,300F (197.60 to 349.60, $188.50 to $333.50).

To get here from Reims, take E46 northwest toward Soissons. At Fismes, take D367 toward Fère-en-Tardenois and follow the signs to the Château de Fère. About 1½ miles north of the restaurant, you'll see the ruins of a 12th-century fortified castle—also called the Château de Fère. The trip takes 35 minutes.

Rte. de Fismes (D967), 02130 Fère-en-Tardenois. (✆ **03-23-82-21-13.** Fax 03-23-82-37-81. Reservations required. Main courses 95F–230F (14.45– 34.95, $13.80–$33.35); fixed-price menus 200F (30.40, $29) lunch Mon–Fri, 290F–520F (44.10– 79.05, $42.05–$75.40) lunch Sat–Sun and dinner. AE, DC, MC, V. Daily noon–2:30pm and 7:30–9pm. Closed Jan.

REIMS AFTER DARK

Reims has the most vibrant nightlife in the Champagne region. The best place to start is **place Drouet-d'Erlon,** home to Reims's premier clubs. This is a university town, so for the most part students rule the night. Just follow them to the best venues.

For a beer, head to **The Glue Pot,** 49 place Drouet-d'Erlon (✆ **03-26-47-36-46),** with its heavy dose of noise and rowdy students; **Au Bureau,** 80 place Drouet-d'Erlon (✆ **03-26-40-33-06),** where a mixed-age crowd congregates in a typically Irish pub that has more than 120 types of beer; or the exotic **Au Lion de Belfort,** 37 place Drouet-d'Erlon (✆ **03-26-47-48-17),** where stuffed heads of hippos, elephants, and the like keep watch over the patrons. For a more sedate experience, try **L'Escalier,** 7 rue de Chativesle (✆ **03-26- 84-95-14),** where the atmosphere is more conducive to conversation with locals and other tourists.

The best dance floors in town are at **Le César Club,** 17 rue Lesage (✆ **03-26-88-33-83),** where techno is king and disco is dead; **Aquarium,** 93 bd. Général Leclerc (✆ **03-26-47-34-29),** attracting a mixed-age crowd of 25- to 40-year-olds; and **Le Tigre,** 2 bis av. Georges-Clemenceau (✆ **03-26-82-64-00),** with its decor of old French cars placed like artwork against the brick walls and mirrors. The fave of young gays and lesbians is **Bar Lilas,** 75 rue des Courcelles (✆ **03-26-47-02-81).** Everybody wears jeans; cover to any of these clubs is 50F (7.60, $7.25).

Another activity that draws a crowd is the free laser show on the exterior walls of the cathedral on Friday and Saturday nights in July and August. For details, call the **Centre National Arts et Technologies** (✆ **03-26-06-58-10).** If you want to enjoy a stage performance, **Comédie de Riems,** chaussée Bocquaine (✆ **03-26-48-49-10),** has a varied schedule, with tickets costing from 70F to 120F (10.65 to 18.25, $10.15 to $17.40), depending on the performance.

Moments The Route de Champagne

Whether for hiking or biking, the Montagne de Reims or "Route de Champagne" is the best place to experience the natural beauty of this vineyard-studded region. Montagne de Reims is a forested plateau south of Reims, where the slopes produce the grapes used to make bubbly.

Armed with a map from the tourist office in Reims or Epernay, you can explore this area along a series of trails called *sentiers de Grandes Randonnées,* along the top of the northern plateau of Montagne de Reims.

These trails are called GRs. Since you're not likely to have time to visit all of them, we recommend routes GR14 or GR141, forming a loop of some 50 kilometers (31 miles) around the plateau's eastern section, which takes in such towns as Verzy. There are several train stations along the way, including a convenient one at Verzy, which will take you back to Reims or Épernay should you tire before finishing the full loop.

5 Laon ★★ & Amiens ★★★: Side Trips from Reims

Laon is 28 miles NW of Reims, 74 miles SE of Amiens, 86 miles NE of Paris; Amiens is 68 miles NW of Reims, 75 miles N of Paris, 71 miles SW of Lille

North Americans tend to overlook France's northern region, but savvy travelers know that this pristine area offers restful alternatives to the densely populated tourist meccas of Paris and the Riviera. The landscape of this low-lying region, adjacent to Belgium's border, will be familiar to admirers of Matisse, who found much inspiration here. Amiens and Laon are the area's major draws.

From Reims, **Laon** would be a logical first stop, particularly for those traveling by rail who will have to transfer en route to Amiens. This site is the north's most intriguing for its history and setting. Over the years, it has witnessed much turbulence from its perch on a ridge above the plain and the Ardon River.

Amiens, on the Somme River, has subsisted as a textile center since medieval days. It was once the capital of Picardy, and its old town is a warren of jumbled streets and canals. Today, Amiens is renowned for its Gothic cathedral, one of the finest in France.

Beyond Amiens and Laon, the heavily forested **Ardennes** attracts lovers of nature and French poetry alike. Rimbaud lived and wrote here; other writers such as Victor Hugo, George Sand, and Alexandre Dumas also expounded upon its beauty in their writings. The sandy beaches of **Le Touquet-Paris-Plage** are the most fashionable and best equipped of the many resorts along the Channel. A mini–Monte Carlo, it was dubbed the "playground of kings" in the days before World War II. Many other stops merit a look if you have the time.

LAON

Arguably the single most intriguing town in the north of France, Laon is perched on a ridge that rises 328 feet above the plain and the Ardon River. The capital of the *département* of Aisne, Laon has had a long, turbulent history, due in large part to its remarkable location.

ESSENTIALS

GETTING THERE   If you're **driving** from Reims, go 28 miles on A26 north to Laon. **Trains** arrive from Paris's Gare du Nord at least 15 times a day (trip time: 1½ to 2 hours). Others arrive from Reims seven times a day (trip time: 45 minutes). For information and schedules, call ✆ **08-36-35-35-85.**

VISITOR INFORMATION   The **Office de Tourisme** is on place du Parvis (✆ **03-23-20-28-62;** www.ville-laon.fr).

EXPLORING THE TOWN

The Romans, recognizing Laon's strategic value, had it fortified. It was later besieged by Vandals, Burgundians, Franks, and many others. German troops entered in 1870 and again in the summer of 1914, holding it until the end of World War I. The town is still surrounded by medieval ramparts, regarded by many as the most rewarding attraction in the north. They appear to have survived intact from the Middle Ages and provide a ready-made itinerary for touring Laon. They aren't sound enough to be climbed on, so must be admired from below.

You don't have to huff and puff as you head from Laon's Basse Ville to its Haute Ville, thanks to a cable-operated tram, **Poma 2000** (✆ **03-23-79-07-59**), that shuttles passengers up and down the rocky hill at 3-minute intervals. It departs from the rail station on place de la Gare and ascends to the Hôtel-de-Ville on place du Général-Leclerc. The tram operates Monday through Saturday from 7am to 8pm. The cost is 6.40F (.95, 95¢) one-way and 6.50F (1.00, 95¢) round-trip. After visiting the cathedral, stroll down the pedestrian-only **rue Châtelaine,** Laon's major shopping street.

Cathédrale Notre-Dame de Laon ✦✦   Most visitors head to this famous cathedral with the huge carved oxen on its facade. Having escaped World War I unharmed, it stands on the spot where an ancient basilica stood until it was destroyed by fire in 1111. The structure has six towers, four of which are complete. Inside are stained glass, panels dating from the 13th century, and an 18th-century choir grille. Tours are conducted from Easter to October on Saturday and Sunday at 3pm, and can be arranged through the tourist office (see above); the cost is 35F (5.30, $5.10) for adults, children 5 to 16 are 20F (3.05, $2.90).

8 rue du Cloître, off place Aubry. ✆ **03-23-20-26-54.** Free admission. Daily 8:30am–6:30pm.

Musée Archéologique Municipal ✦   This museum was founded in 1861 and remained rather sleepy until 1937, when a collection of 1,700 artifacts (mainly from Greece, Rome, Egypt, Cyprus, and Asia Minor) was added, as well as a collection of French painting and sculpture.

32 rue George-Ermant. ✆ **03-23-20-19-87.** Admission 20F (3.05, $2.90) adults, 15F (2.30, $2.20) students and children, children 5 and under free. Wed–Mon 10am–noon and 2–6pm (to 5pm Oct–Apr).

ACCOMMODATIONS

Hostellerie St-Vincent   Situated at the edge of the city, near the point where the road from Reims (A26) enters the Basse Ville, this simple government-rated two-star hotel is the most modern and best in town, with basic but comfortable guest rooms, each with a shower-only bathroom. The restaurant is noted for its good food, served in a setting accented by lots of plants and a serpentine staircase that acts as the focal point of the dining room.

29 av. Charles-de-Gaulle, 02000 Laon. ✆ **03-23-23-42-43.** Fax 03-23-79-22-55. 47 units. 305F (46.35, $44.25) double. AE, MC, V. **Amenities:** Restaurant, bar. *In room:* TV.

Hôtel de la Bannière de France   This revered hotel, built in 1685, is located in the most historic part of Laon, Haute Ville. Despite its antique-looking facade, its interior has been completely modernized, though an attempt was made to maintain the ambience of a traditional French hotel. The rooms are small but cozy and comfortably furnished, each with a shower-only bathroom. The personality of the owner, Madame Lefevre, is most obvious in the traditional restaurant, open daily from noon to 2pm and 6:30 to 9:30pm. The flavorful menu items include trout poached in champagne; salad of scallops, crayfish, and foie gras; and delicious chocolate profiteroles.

11 rue Franklin-D.-Roosevelt, 02000 Laon. ✆ **03-23-23-21-44.** Fax 03-23-23-31-56. 18 units. 460F (69.90, $66.70) double. Rates include breakfast. AE, DC, MC, V. Closed May 1 and Dec 20–Jan 20. Parking 35F (5.30, $5.10). **Amenities:** Restaurant, bar. *In room:* TV.

DINING

Hostellerie St-Vincent and **Hôtel de la Bannière de France** (see "Accommodations," above) both contain very good restaurants.

Brasserie du Parvis PICARD/FRENCH   The allure here is the location opposite the main facade of the Cathedral of Laon. In warm weather, the outdoor tables facing the church are hard to snag. Inside, the owners redecorate frequently, focusing on whatever festival or calendar event happens to be in the minds of local residents, such as eclipses of the sun or moon and local medieval festivals. Menu items include a *ficelle Picard,* a kind of crêpe made with ham and mushrooms; a pungent tart of local maroilles cheese; and a very ethnic version of chitterling sausages, *les andouillettes de Troyes* with mustard sauce. More appetizing, at least to many North American palates, is a chicken cutlet with a mushroom cream sauce.

Place du Parvis. ✆ **03-23-20-27-27.** Reservations recommended. Main courses 39F–70F (5.95– 10.65, $5.65–$10.15); fixed-price menu 65F–145F (9.90– 22.05, $9.45–$21.05). MC, V. Daily 11:30am–3:30pm and 6–11pm.

AMIENS

A textile center since medieval days, Amiens was the ancient capital of Picardy, set on the south bank of the Somme, where it divides into a series of canals and irrigation networks. Its an old town, a jumble of narrow streets crisscrossed by canals that is run-down and seedy but still worth exploring. The city's focal point is its world-famous Gothic cathedral, one of France's finest. The edge of the modern town begins several blocks south of the cathedral, around the Tour Perret.

ESSENTIALS

GETTING THERE   If you're **driving** from Reims, take A26 north 28 miles to Laon, then travel west on N44 to N32, which becomes D934 en route to Amiens. The distance is 68 miles; however, the trek may take you more than 1½ hours because of the country roads you'll be traversing after you exit A26. Amiens is adjacent to the main autoroute (A1) connecting Paris with Lille. Driving time from Paris is about 90 minutes. Those coming from the northern suburbs of Paris prefer A16, which passes near Amiens on its way to Calais.

Reaching Amiens by **train** from Reims requires a transfer in Laon (which you can explore before continuing on) or Tergnier. Trains are relatively infrequent—only three a day—and take 80 minutes to 3 hours, depending on the schedule.

Many visitors come here straight from Paris, for Amiens sits astride the main rail lines connecting Paris's Gare du Nord with Lille. Depending on the season, four or five trains a day make the trip, taking 65 minutes each way. The rail station in Amiens is at place Alphonse-Fiquet, a 10-minute walk from the old town. For information and schedules, call © **08-36-35-35-35.**

VISITOR INFORMATION   The **Office de Tourisme** is at 6 bis rue Dusevel (© **03-22-71-60-50;** www.amiens.com/tourisme).

EXPLORING THE TOWN

Julius Caesar praised the fertility of the fields around Amiens. During the Middle Ages, **Les Hortillonnages** ⚘, an expanse of almost 600 acres at the eastern edge of the historic core, was set aside for the cultivation of pears, carrots, turnips, and all kinds of herbs and vegetables. Irrigated by a web of canals fed by the Somme, the district is still a commercial garden, producing ample amounts of foodstuffs. Not long ago, the harvest was floated on barges and in shallow-bottomed boats to the Quai Bélu, near the cathedral, for sale to consumers. Although today the produce is hauled from the fields into the town center by truck, the ritual retains its medieval name, the **Marché sur l'Eau,** though locals are increasingly referring to it as **Marché St-Leu.** The tradition continues every Thursday and Saturday from 8 to 11am, when the river's quays are transformed into a huge outdoor vegetable market.

A few paces north of the cathedral, straddling both banks of the Somme, is a cluster of carefully restored 13th- and 14th-century houses arranged within a labyrinth of narrow cobblestone streets. Known as the **Quartier St-Leu,** this is a neighborhood of gift shops, antiques shops, art galleries, boutiques, and cafes.

Jules Verne, author of *20,000 Leagues Under the Sea* and *Journey to the Center of the Earth,* is buried in Amiens, and you may want to visit him at the **Cimetière de la Madeleine,** rue St-Maurice, half a mile northwest of the town center. The beaux-arts tomb bears a representation of Verne as if physically rising from the dead. The cemetery is open daily from 9am to 7pm. Verne's home is located at 2 rue Charles-Dubois (© **03-22-45-37-84**). It's now a research center documenting his life and literary achievements; admission for members of the general public, however, is not encouraged.

Cathédrale Notre-Dame d'Amiens ⚘⚘⚘   At 469 feet long, this cathedral is the largest church in France. It was begun in 1220 to the plans of Robert de Luzarches and completed around 1270. Its original purpose was to house the head of St. John the Baptist, brought back from the Crusades in 1206. Two unequal towers were added later—the south one in 1366, the north one in 1402. The renowned architect Viollet-le-Duc restored the cathedral in the 1850s.

The Amiens cathedral is the crowning example of French Gothic architecture. In John Ruskin's rhapsodical *Bible of Amiens* (1884), which Proust translated into French, he extolled the door arches. The three portals of the west front are lavishly decorated, important examples of Gothic cathedral sculpture. The portals are surmounted by two galleries. The upper one contains 22 statues of kings; the large rose window is from the 16th century.

Inside are beautifully carved stalls and a Flamboyant Gothic choir screen. These stalls with some 3,500 figures were made by local artisans in the early 16th century. The interior is held up by 126 slender pillars, the zenith of the High Gothic in the north of France. The cathedral managed to escape destruction in World War II. In 1996, the *Portail de la Mère-Dieu* (Portal of the Mother of God), to the right of the cathedral's main entrance as you look over the facade, was restored at enormous expense.

Place Notre-Dame. ℂ **03-22-80-03-41.** Free admission. Guided tours 30F (4.55, $4.35), 12 and under free. Easter–Oct daily 8:30am–6:45pm; Nov–Mar daily 8:30am–noon and 2–5pm (to 6pm on Sat).

Musée de Picardie ★★   This museum occupies a building constructed from 1855 to 1867. The palace of the Napoleonic dynasty, inaugurated by Napoléon III, is divided into three sections, including one devoted to archaeology. Other sections include exhibits on the Roman occupation of Gaul, the Merovingian era, ancient Greece, and Egypt. One collection documents the Middle Ages with ivories, enamels, objets d'art, and sculpture. The sculpture and painting collection traces the European schools from the 16th to the 20th centuries, with works by El Greco, Maurice Quentin de La Tour, Guardi, and Tiepolo. Fragonard's *Les Lavandières* is his most beautiful work here.

48 rue de la République. ℂ **03-22-97-14-00.** Admission 20F (3.05, $2.90) adults, 12F (1.80, $1.75) students and children, free for children 15 and under. Temporary exhibitions may require a surcharge of 20F–35F (3.05– 5.30, $2.90–$5.13). Tues–Sun 10am–12:30pm and 2–6pm.

ACCOMMODATIONS

Hôtel Le Carlton ★   From a glance at this hotel's Napoléon III architecture, you'll immediately see that it's Amiens's stellar choice. Though it's geared toward business travelers, the guest rooms are luxurious, with rich furniture and murals. Appointments include quality mattresses, fine linens, and bathrooms with tub and shower combinations. The public areas range from an English bar to a deluxe brasserie-style restaurant. All feature elegant polished dark woods and deep hunter-green and burgundy walls.

42 rue de Noyon, 80000 Amiens. ℂ **03-22-97-72-22.** Fax 03-22-97-72-00. 25 units. 400F–640F (60.80– 97.30, $58–$92.80) double; 1,000F (152, $145) suite. AE, DC, MC, V. **Amenities:** Restaurant, bar; room service; laundry/dry cleaning. *In room:* A/C, TV, hair dryer.

Relais Mercure *Value*   This hotel lies directly opposite the main facade of the cathedral. It was purchased by France's biggest hotel conglomerate in 1997, and upgraded a year later. The renovation managed to preserve the stately facade and some of the antique beams in the bedrooms, while giving the interior a clean, unfussy, modern look. The pricier rooms contain cramped but cozy sitting areas; the less expensive units are smaller and more functional. Some have windows overlooking the cathedral. Rooms rarely rise above those of a good standard motel, but they do come with comfortable beds and bathrooms with combination tub and shower. Overall, the place provides good value, an unbeatable location, and the cost-consciousness of the Accor group.

Amiens Cathedrale, 17–19 place au Feurre, 8000 Amiens. ℂ **03-22-22-00-20.** Fax 03-22-91-86-57. 47 units. 490F–525F (74.50– 79.80, $71.05–$76.15) double. AE, DC, MC, V. Free parking. **Amenities:** Bar; babysitting; laundry. *In room:* A/C, TV.

DINING

Les Marissons PICARD/FRENCH   Two or three places around town match the quality of the food here, but none offer such a charming setting. The restaurant sits in a heavily timbered 15th-century building adjacent to one of the city's oldest bridges (pont de la Dodane). The cuisine is elegantly presented by chef Antoine Benoit, whose specialties include paté made from local ducklings, sea bass with apricots, roast lamb *pré-salé* from the salt marshes off the English Channel, scallops baked in their shells, and veal kidneys with rosemary sauce. In summer, you can dine on the terrace in the garden.

68 rue des Marissons. 📞 **03-22-92-96-66.** Reservations recommended. Main courses 125F–158F (19– 24, $18.15–$22.90); fixed-price menu 120F–295F (18.25– 44.85, $17.40–$42.80). AE, DC, MC, V. Mon–Fri noon–2pm; Mon–Sat 7:30–9:30pm. Closed Nov 1–11 and first week in Jan.

AMIENS AFTER DARK

You'll find the largest number of nightspots around quai Bélu. Try the **Riverside Café,** place du Don (📞 **03-22-92-50-30**), with its movie posters and photos of 1960s American icons filling the walls and an active young crowd filling the seats; or the **Bar Vents et Marées,** 48 rue du Don (📞 **03-22-92-37-78**), where you can absorb the fusion of rock and alcohol.

If you're big on musical events, head for a place next to the train station: **Le Grand Wazoo,** 5 rue Vulfran-Warmé (📞 **03-22-91-64-91**). Named in honor of Frank Zappa, this cool club with its exotic Arab decor draws a mixed crowd intent on listening to local musicians as well as groups famous throughout the continent. Concerts are generally scheduled on Fridays and Saturdays and range from techno and reggae to punk rock. The cover ranges from 10F to 40F (1.50 to 6.10, $1.45 to $5.80).

While you're checking out the scene along the canal area, stop in the old medieval house that's home to the traditional wine bar **La Queue de Vache** (the Cow's Tail), 51 quai Bélu (📞 **03-22-91-38-91**), where you'll be gregariously welcomed and immediately drawn into the heady atmosphere of half-timbered walls, fireplaces, live jazz, and (on occasion) accordion music. It's the ideal setting in which to drink good French wine and sample rich, chewy country breads along with aromatic cheeses.

For dancing, your best bet is **Le Nemo,** 9 rue des Francs-Mûriers (📞 **03-22-97-96-71**), with its spacious interior and frescoes of dolphins and marine life. The mainly young, hip crowd pays up to 35F (5.30, $5.10) to dive in here. The town's newest disco, **L'Amazone,** 14 rue des Archers (📞 **03-22-92-94-80**), welcomes a clientele mostly ages 28 to 45. A theme bar, **Le Texas Café,** 13 rue des Francs-Mûriers (📞 **03-22-72-19-79**), offers a roster of stiff drinks and a karaoke machine. And if you're gay and on the loose in Amiens, **Les Vaches Folles,** rue de la Dodane, in the Quartier St-Leu (no phone), will offer the chance to meet and talk with like-minded folks who might have dropped in for an after-dinner drink or to hear some music.

6 Epernay

87 miles E of Paris, 16 miles S of Reims

On the left bank of the Marne, Epernay rivals Reims as a center for champagne. Although it only has one sixth of Reims's population, Epernay today produces nearly as much champagne as its larger sibling. It boasts an estimated 200 miles or more of cellars and tunnels, a veritable warren for storing champagne. These caves are vast vaults cut into the chalk rock on which the town is built. Represented in Epernay are such champagne companies as Moët et Chandon (the largest), Pol Roger, Mercier, and de Castellane.

Epernay's main boulevards are the elegant residential avenue de Champagne, rue Mercier, and rue de Reims, all radiating from place de la République. Two important squares in the narrow streets of the commercial district are place Hughes-Plomb and place des Arcades.

Epernay has been either destroyed or burned nearly two dozen times, as it lay in the path of invading armies, particularly from Germany. Few of its old buildings have survived. However, check out avenue de Champagne for its neo-classical villas and Victorian town houses.

ESSENTIALS

GETTING THERE If you're **driving** to Epernay from Reims, head south on E51. Thirteen **trains** per day arrive from Paris (trip time: 1¼ hours); there are also 13 trains per day from Reims (trip time: 20 minutes). For train information and schedules, call ✆ **08-36-35-35-35.** The major **bus** link is STDM Trans-Champagne (✆ **03-26-65-17-07** in Epernay), operating four buses per day Monday through Saturday between Châlons-en-Champagne and Epernay (trip time: 45 minutes); a one-way fare is 34F (5.15, $4.95).

VISITOR INFORMATION The **Office de Tourisme** is at 7 av. de Champagne (✆ **03-26-53-33-00**).

EXPLORING THE TOWN

Boutiques and shops abound in the pedestrian district of **place des Arcades** and **rue du Général-Leclerc, rue St-Martin,** and **rue Porte Lucas.** Here you'll find stores selling gifts, clothes, antiques, books, and regional food items.

Of course, you may want to stock up on some vintages. You can go to the individual houses along avenue de Champagne—places like **Moët et Chandon,** 18 av. de Champagne (✆ **03-26-51-20-20**); and **Mercier,** 70 av. de Champagne (✆ **03-26-51-22-22**)—or try one of the champagne stores that represent a variety of houses. Two of the best include **La Cave Salvatori,** 11 rue Flodoard (✆ **03-26-55-32-32**); and **Le Domaine des Crus**, 2 rue Henri Durant (✆ **03-26-54-18-60**), known for a staggering array of champagnes. Also unusual is **La Boutique Achille Princier,** 9 rue Jean-Chandon-Moët (✆ **03-26-54-04-06**), which sells only the well-respected yet rather obscure champagne brand, Achille Princier.

For an antiques dealer with a wide inventory, head to **Antiquités Gallice,** 9 rue Gallice (✆ **03-26-54-23-84**), where absolute gems can be found scattered amid the bric-a-brac from many of the attics of old houses throughout the Champagne district. For regional antiques from the 18th and 19th centuries, try **Bonne Époque,** 106 av. Foch (✆ **03-26-54-11-39**).

For champagne gift items like flutes and corks as well as table decorations and linens, visit **La Boutique de Sophie,** 33 rue du Général-Leclerc (✆ **03-26-54-48-56**); **La Boutique Fromm,** 33 rue St-Thibault (✆ **03-26-55-25-64**); and **Camaieu,** 12 rue du Professeur-Langevin (✆ **03-26-51-83-83**).

Moët et Chandon Champagne Cellars An expert staff member gives guided tours in English, describing the champagne-making process and filling you in on champagne lore: Napoléon, a friend of Jean-Rémy Moët, used to stop by here for thousands of bottles on his way to the battlefront. The only time he didn't take a supply with him was at Waterloo—and look what happened. At the end of the tour, you're given a complimentary glass of bubbly. No appointment is necessary, except for large groups.

18 av. de Champagne. ✆ **03-26-51-20-20**. Admission 40F (6.10, $5.80). Daily 9:30–11:30am and 2–4:30pm. Closed holidays.

Mercier Since Mercier is near Moët et Chandon, you can visit them both on the same day. Mercier conducts tours in English of its 11 miles of tunnels from laser-guided trains. The caves contain one of the world's largest wooden barrels, with a capacity of more than 200,000 bottles. No appointment is necessary if there are fewer than 10 in your group.

70 av. de Champagne. Ⓒ **03-26-51-22-22**. Admission 35F (5.30, $5.10). Mon–Fri 9:30–11:30am and 2–4:30pm; Sat–Sun 9:30–11:30am and 2–5pm; Dec–Feb closed Tues–Wed.

ACCOMMODATIONS

Note that **Les Berceaux** (see "Dining," below) also rents rooms.

Best Western Hôtel de Champagne   Built in the 1970s about 200 yards from the Moët et Chandon showroom, near place de la République, this simple inn is one of the best of a modest lot in town. Some rooms are outfitted in modern style, while others look vaguely inspired by Louis XV; each comes with a small bathroom with shower. A buffet breakfast is served every morning.

30 rue Eugène-Mercier, 51200 Epernay. Ⓒ **800/528-1234** in the U.S. or Canada, or 03-26-53-10-60. Fax 03-26-51-94-63. www.bw-hotel-champagne.com. 33 units. 490F–560F (74.50– 85.10, $71.05–$81.20) double. AE, MC, DC, V. Free parking. **Amenities:** Restaurant, bar; room service; baby-sitting; laundry. *In room:* TV, minibar, hair dryer.

Royal Champagne ★★★   Constructed around what was originally built in the 1700s as a relay station for the French postal system, this hotel is a member of the prestigious Relais & Châteaux group. The establishment's historic core contains the reception, bar, and dining facilities; guest rooms are in town house–style accommodations overlooking the nearby vineyards. The units are rustic and very comfortable, exemplifying the coziness of wine-country living. Each comes with a sumptuous bed with luxury mattress and fine linen, plus a combination tub and shower.

The chef is known for classic dishes with an innovative twist. The food is exceptional, with specialties like lobster ragoût, John Dory with a purée of celery and a truffle-flavored cream sauce, and roast lamb with garlic.

51160 Champillon Belevue. Ⓒ **03-26-52-87-11**. Fax 03-26-52-89-69. www.relaischateaux.com. 25 units. 1,050F–1,400F (159.60– 212.80, $152.25–$203) double; 1,400F–1,800F (212.80– 273.60, $203–$261) suite. AE, DC, MC, V. Drive 4 miles from Epernay toward Reims on the Route du Vignoble (N2051); the hotel is in the hamlet of Champillon. **Amenities:** Restaurant, bar; room service; baby-sitting; laundry/dry cleaning. *In room:* TV, minibar, hair dryer.

DINING

The food at **Royal Champagne** (see "Accommodations," above) is excellent.

Les Berceaux ★★★ CHAMPENOIS   Chef/owner Patrick Michelon serves generous portions of flavorful, relatively conservative Champenois cuisine. The menu changes seasonally but always features fresh produce (from the region whenever possible) and superior cuts of fish, meat, and game. Particularly scrumptious are such dishes as roasted leg of lamb with an herb-flavored wine sauce; snails in champagne sauce; both warm and cold versions of foie gras; and a galette of guinea fowl in puff pastry, served with potatoes. At the wine bar, you can sample an assortment of vintages by the glass. Local wines, especially champagne, are showcased. If it errs at all, this place tends to be a bit pretentious, a flaw that you might be able to overcome with a touch of humor.

Available upstairs are 29 comfortably furnished bedrooms, each with TV and phone. A double with a tub and shower combination rents for 390F to 450F (59.30 to 68.40, $56.55 to $65.25).

13 rue Berceaux, 51200 Epernay. Ⓒ **03-26-55-28-84**. Fax 03-26-55-10-36. Reservations recommended. Main courses 150F–180F (22.80– 27.35, $21.75–$26.10); fixed-price menus 160F (24.30, $23.20) lunch Wed–Fri, 280F–360F (42.55– 54.70, $40.60–$52.20) dinner. AE, DC, MC, V. Wed–Sun noon–2:30pm and 7–9:30pm.

EPERNAY AFTER DARK

Start out with a stop at the chic cafe/bar **Le Progrès,** 5 place de la République (© **03-26-55-22-72**). This place lets you loosen up before the real festivities get under way. For a simple glass of wine or even Scotch (something you don't see enough of in this wine-crazed region), consider a visit to **Le Chriss Bar,** 38 rue de Sézanne (© **03-26-54-38-47**). A place that rocks and rolls a bit later into the night, sometimes with a live singer or musical act, is **Le Garden Club,** 5 av. Foch (© **03-26-54-20-30**), which has an atmosphere more in tune with Paris. **Le Tap-Too,** 5 rue des Près Dimanche (© **03-26-51-56-10**), attracts all ages and types to its four dance halls and six bars together in one big warehouse.

For live concerts and the occasional lighthearted theatrical performance, head over to the two-story American-style bar **La Marmite Swing,** 160 av. Foch (© **03-26-54-17-72**). Most acts take the stage on Friday and Saturday evenings, but the place continues to sizzle during the rest of the week as high-energy partyers work the crowd against a background of techno and rock. On performance nights, expect to pay a cover upward of 60F (9.10, $8.70).

11

Alsace-Lorraine

The provinces of Alsace and Lorraine, with ancient capitals at Strasbourg and Nancy, respectively, have been much disputed by Germany and France. Alsace has been called "the least French of French provinces," more reminiscent of the Black Forest across the Rhine. In fact, it became German from 1870 until after World War I and then was ruled by Hitler from 1940 to 1944. These days, both provinces are back under French control, though they remain somewhat independent.

In the Vosges Mountains you can follow **La Route des Crêtes** (Crest Road) or skirt along the foothills, visiting the wine towns of Alsace. In its cities and cathedrals, the castle-dotted landscape evokes memories of a past and (in battle monuments or scars) sometimes military glory or defeat. Lorraine is Joan of Arc country, and many of its towns still suggest their heritage from the Middle Ages.

There is no clear-cut dividing line that delineates Alsace from Lorraine. Alsace is more German, forming a fertile watershed between the mountains of the Vosges and the Black Forest of Germany. Lorraine, with its rolling landscape, is a poorer cousin and appears more French in character.

REGIONAL CUISINE The ample use of pork and goose fat in Alsatian dishes gives the cuisine a distinctive flavor. Alsace is a leader in the production of pâtés, with more than 40 varieties, so you really must visit a local *charcuterie* (delicatessen) for a sampling. Don't miss the richly flavorful pâté de foie gras (gooseliver pâté).

In Lorraine, the joyful excesses of cholesterol are even more exaggerated. In addition to butter and loads of cream, local chefs use large quantities of salted lard. Even local pot-au-feu (known as *une potes*) replaces beef with salted lard and local pork sausages.

Other regional specialties are *choucroute* (sauerkraut) with sausages, salted ham, pork chops, or (in deluxe versions) truffles; chicken with Riesling; trout in cream, with Riesling, or simply fried (*au bleu*); Alsatian *kouglof* (made with almonds, dried raisins, sugar, milk, flour, and eggs); and a simple tart made with flour, milk, and sugar called *un ramequin*.

The most famous Alsatian beer is Kronenbourg, which you'll find in of bars throughout France. There are more than 90 varieties of Alsatian wines, drunk from slender flutes whose glass is sometimes colored blue or green. The most celebrated Alsatian varietals are Riesling, gewürztraminer (traminer), and pinot blanc.

1 Strasbourg ✶✶✶

303 miles SE of Paris, 135 miles SW of Frankfurt

The capital of Alsace, Strasbourg is one of France's greatest cities and is also the birthplace of pâté de foie gras. And it was in Strasbourg that Rouget de Lisle first sang "La Marseillaise" (the French national anthem).

Strasbourg is one of France's major ports, only 2 miles west of the Rhine. In addition to being host to the Council of Europe, Strasbourg is the meeting place of the European Parliament, which convenes at the Palais de l'Europe.

In 1871, Strasbourg was absorbed by Germany and made the capital of the imperial territory of Alsace-Lorraine, but it reverted to France in 1918. One street is a perfect illustration of the city's identity crisis: more than a century ago it was avenue Napoléon. In 1871, it became Kaiser-Wilhelmstrasse, then turned into boulevard de la République in 1918. In 1940, it became Adolf-Hitler-Strasse, then ended up as avenue du Général-de-Gaulle in 1945.

One of the most happening cities of France, Strasbourg is the seat of the University of Strasbourg, once attended by the likes of Goethe, Napoléon, and Pasteur. Today, some 40,000 students follow in their footsteps.

ESSENTIALS

GETTING THERE The **Strasbourg-Entzheim Airport** (℡ **03-88-64-67-67**), 9 miles southwest of the city center, receives daily flights from many European cities, including Paris, London, Rome, and Frankfurt. You can get from the airport to the town center by using a well-defined combination of **shuttle buses** and **city trams.** They run at 30-minute intervals in the morning and every 15 minutes in the afternoon. The cost of 30F (4.55, $4.35) each way involves taking a shuttle bus to the south side of Strasbourg, to a junction point known as Baggersee. From there, you'll continue to the town center via a tram line. Combined travel time is between 35 and 40 minutes each way. For information, call **Autocars C.T.S.B** (℡ **03-88-77-70-70**).

At least nine **trains** a day arrive from Paris's Gare de l'Est (trip time: 4 hours). From Nancy, there are 13 trains a day (trip time: 90 minutes). For information and schedules, call ℡ **08-36-35-35-35.**

By **car,** the giant N83 highway crosses the plain of Alsace and becomes at times the A35 expressway. It links Strasbourg with Colmar and Mulhouse.

VISITOR INFORMATION The **Office de Tourisme** is on place de la Cathédrale (℡ **03-88-52-28-28;** www.strasbourg.com).

SPECIAL EVENTS **Wolf Music,** 24 rue de la Mésange (℡ **03-88-32-43-10**), puts on two summer festivals: the classical **Festival International de Musique,** in June, and the **Festival de Jazz** (℡ **03-88-15-29-19** for information), in the first week of July. Both feature performances by international artists and draw a large crowd despite the hefty ticket prices of 130F to 420F (19.75 to 63.85, $18.85 to $60.90); tickets go on sale in mid-April. The **Festival International des Musiques d'Aujourd'hui** is organized by the association Musica (℡ **03-88-23-47-23**). It takes place from the end of September to the first week of October and combines contemporary music concerts with movies and modern opera performances. Tickets are 80F to 110F (12.15 to 16.70, $11.60 to $15.95) and go on sale at the end of June.

EXPLORING STRASBOURG

Despite war damage, much remains of Old Strasbourg, including covered bridges and towers from its former fortifications, plus many 15th- and 17th-century dwellings with painted wooden fronts and carved beams.

The city's traffic hub is **place Kléber** ⚘, dating from the 15th century. Sit here with a tankard of Alsatian beer and get to know Strasbourg. The bronze statue in the center is of J. B. Kléber, born in Strasbourg in 1753; he became one of Napoléon's most noted generals and was buried under the monument.

Apparently his presence offended the Nazis, who removed the statue in 1940. This Alsatian bronze was restored to its proper place in 1945 at the Liberation.

Next, take rue des Grandes-Arcades southeast to **place Gutenberg,** one of the city's oldest squares and formerly a *marché aux herbes.* The central statue (1840) by David d'Angers is of Gutenberg, who perfected his printing press in Strasbourg in the winter of 1436 to 1437. The former town hall, now the **Hôtel du Commerce,** was built in 1582 and is one of the most significant Renaissance buildings in all Alsace. And anywhere within a few blocks of the city's **cathedral** will be loaded with medieval references and historic charm.

La Petite France ✪✪ is the most interesting quarter of Strasbourg. Its 16th-century houses are mirrored in the waters of the Ill River. In "Little France," old roofs with gray tiles have sheltered families for ages, and the cross-beamed facades with their roughly carved rafters are in typical Alsatian style. Rue du Bain-aux-Plantes is of particular interest. An island in the middle of the river is cut by four canals—for a good view, walk along rue des Moulins, branching off from rue du Bain-aux-Plantes.

Cathédrale Notre-Dame de Strasbourg ✪✪✪   The city's crowning glory stands as an outstanding example of Gothic architecture, representing a transition from the Romanesque. Construction began in 1176. The pyramidal tower in rose-colored stone was completed in 1439; at 469 feet, it's the tallest one dating from medieval times. This cathedral is still used for Roman Catholic worship

(*Finds* **Exploring Strasbourg by Boat**

One of the most romantic ways to spend your time in Strasbourg is to take an excursion on the **Ill River,** leaving from the Palais de Rohan. Daytime outings operate year-round, with night excursions from April to October. The 75-minute cruise is 41F (6.25, $5.95) for adults and 20.50F (3.10, $2.95) for children and includes a prerecorded commentary (in English and French) on the region's history. Between April and November, rides depart at 30-minute intervals daily between 9:30am and 9pm. Between December and March, there are departures only at 10:30am, 1pm, 2:30pm, and 4pm. Information is provided by the Strasbourg-Fluvial, 15 rue de Nantes (© **03-88-84-13-13**).

services. Religious ceremonies, particularly on feast days, meld perfectly with the majesty of this place. The tower can be visited by individual tourists only in the summer. The Office du Tourisme (see above) organizes tours for groups; call for the schedule.

Four large counterforts divide the **main facade** ✶✶✶ into three vertical parts and two horizontal galleries. Note the great **rose window,** which looks like real stone lace. The facade is rich in sculptural decoration: on the portal of the south transept, the Coronation and Death of the Virgin in one of the two tympana is the finest such medieval work. In the north transept, see also the facade of the **Chapelle St-Laurence,** a stunning achievement of the late Gothic German style.

A Romanesque **crypt** lies under the chancel, which is covered with square stonework. The stained-glass window is the work of Max Ingrand. The **nave** is majestic, with windows depicting emperors and kings on the north Strasbourg aisle. Five chapels are grouped around the transept, including one built in 1500 in the Flamboyant Gothic style. In the south transept stands the **Angel Pillar** ✶✶, illustrating the Last Judgment, with angels lowering their trumpets.

The **astronomical clock** ✶ was built between 1547 and 1574. It stopped working during the Revolution, and from 1838 to 1842 the mechanism was replaced. The clock is wound once a week. People flock to see its 12:30pm show of allegorical figures. On Sunday Apollo drives his sun horses, on Thursday you see Jupiter and his eagle, and so on. The main body of the clock has a planetarium based on the theories of Copernicus.

Place de la Cathédrale. © **03-88-21-43-34,** or 03-88-21-43-30 for the precise times of all the masses and offices. Tower 20F (3.05, $2.90) adults, 10F (1.50, $1.45) children, free for children 5 and under. Tower July–Aug daily 8:30am–7pm. (You may have to wait to climb the tower.) Close-up views of the clock available noon–12:30pm for 5F (.75, 75¢); tickets on sale daily in the south portal from 11:30am.

Église St-Thomas Built between 1230 and 1330, this Protestant church boasts five naves. It contains the **mausoleum** ✶✶ of Maréchal de Saxe, a masterpiece of French art by Pigalle (1777).

Rue Martin-Luther (along rue St-Thomas, near pont St-Thomas). © **03-88-32-14-46.** Free admission. Mar–Oct daily 10am–noon and 2–6pm; Nov–Dec daily 10am–noon and 2–5pm; Jan–Feb Sat–Sun 2–5pm.

Musée Alsacien ✶ This museum occupies three mansions from the 16th and 17th centuries and is like a living textbook of the folklore and customs of Alsace, containing arts, crafts, and tools of the old province.

Strasbourg

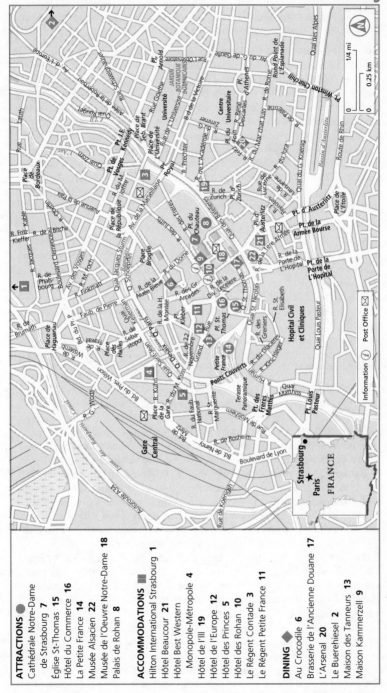

Information ⓘ   Post Office ⊠

23 quai St-Nicolas. ℭ **03-88-35-55-36.** Admission 20F (3.05, $2.90) adults, 10F (1.50, $1.45) students, free for children 11 and under. Mon and Wed–Sun 10am–noon and 1:30–6pm.

Musée de l'Oeuvre Notre-Dame ✦✦✦ This museum illustrates the art of the Middle Ages and Renaissance in Strasbourg and Alsace. Some of the pieces were once displayed in the cathedral, where copies have been substituted. The most celebrated prize is a stained-glass head of Christ (constructed around 1070) from a window said to have been at Wissembourg. There's also a stained-glass window depicting an emperor from around 1200. The medieval sculpture is of great interest, as are the works of Strasbourg goldsmiths from the 16th and 17th centuries. The winding staircase and interior are in the pure Renaissance style. The 13th-century hall contains the loveliest sculptures from the cathedral, including the wise and foolish virgins from 1280.

3 place du Château. ℭ **03-88-52-50-00.** Admission 20F (3.05, $2.90) adults, 10F (1.50, $1.45) children, free for children 5 and under. Tues–Sun 10am–6pm.

Palais de Rohan ✦✦ This palace, south of the cathedral, was built from 1732 to 1742. It's an example of supreme elegance and proportion. Noted for its facades and rococo interior, it's one of the crowning design achievements in eastern France. On the first floor is a fine-arts museum (Musée des Beaux Arts), with works by Rubens, Rembrandt, Van Dyck, El Greco, Goya, Watteau, Renoir, and Monet. A decorative-arts museum exhibits ceramics and the original machinery of the cathedral's first astronomical clock. Also on the premises are collections of artifacts excavated from nearby digs, focusing especially on art and utilitarian objects from the Roman and early medieval (Merovingian) eras.

2 place du Château. ℭ **03-88-52-50-00.** Admission 20F (3.05, $2.90) adults, 10F (1.50, $1.45) students, free for children under 16. Mon and Wed–Sat 10am–6pm; Sun 10am–5pm.

SHOPPING

Strasbourg overflows with antiques shops, artisans, craftspeople, and beer makers. Every well-accessorized home in Alsace stocks at least some of the napkins, aprons, tablecloths, and tea and bath towels of the Beauvillé textile mills. A premier outlet is **Nappes d'Alsace,** 6 rue Mercière, near the cathedral (ℭ **03-88-22-69-29**), which has one of the widest selections of textiles in town.

Bastian, 22–24 place de la Cathédrale (ℭ **03-88-32-45-93**), specializes in the 18th- and 19th-century ceramic tureens that Alsace produced with charm and abundance. Look for ragoût pots in the form of a cabbage, a trout, a boar's head, or a turkey, brightly painted in appetizing colors. There's also a selection of Louis XV and Louis XVI furniture, crafted in the region during the 18th and 19th centuries, that follows Parisian models from the same era.

Bastian's main competitor is **Antiquités de l'Ill,** 23 quai des Bateliers (ℭ **03-88-36-96-84**), in a Renaissance-style 17th-century building across from the Palais de Rohan. Standout items are polychromed Alsatian antiques (especially 18th- and 19th-century armoires and chests), Louis- and Directoire-style furnishings, and statues and antique paintings.

More affordable is **Arts et Collections d'Alsace,** 18 quai des Bateliers (ℭ **03-88-14-03-77**), which sells copies of articles found exclusively in Alsatian museums or prestigious private collections. Look for pieces in wood, glass, stone, and ceramic. A name you're likely to encounter is Soufflenheim, a provincial rococo pattern named after the Alsatian village where the style originated.

In that village 17 miles to the north, ceramics and pottery have been staples of the economy since the Bronze Age. Soufflenheim contains at least 15 outlets selling cake molds, tureens, saucers and cups, and dinnerware, usually in rustic patterns. One of the most prominent outlets is **Gérard Wehrling,** 64 rue de Haguenau (✆ **03-88-86-65-25**), known for pottery that can withstand the rigors of modern ovens, microwaves, and freezers. Expect to pay about 300F (45.60, $43.50) for a large casserole.

If you're driving, you may want to check out the villages of Obernai, Illhauesern, Ribeauvillé, and Schiltigheim. The last is beer-drinking territory; the others offer country wares, antiques, old-fashioned streets, and pure charm.

ACCOMMODATIONS
EXPENSIVE

Hilton International Strasbourg ★★★ The luxurious, seven-story steel-and-glass Hilton stands over a university complex and is opposite the Palais de la Musique et des Congrès. The decor incorporates five kinds of Iberian marble, much of it chosen to resemble the ruddy sandstone of the famous cathedral, visible from the hotel. The guest rooms contain tasteful artwork and spacious marble-trimmed bathrooms with combination tub and shower.

Av. Herrenschmidt, 67000 Strasbourg. ✆ **800/445-8667** in the U.S. and Canada, or 03-88-37-10-10. Fax 03-88-36-83-27. www.hilton-strasbourg.com. 246 units. 1,200F–1,700F (182.40– 258.40, $174–$246.50) double; from 2,700F (410.40, $391.50) suite. AE, DC, MC, V. Parking 65F–85F (9.90– 12.90, $9.45–$12.35). Take the Strasbourg-Centre exit from the auto route and follow signs to the Wacken, Palais des Congrès, and Palais de l'Europe. **Amenities:** Restaurant, two bars; room service; baby-sitting; laundry/dry cleaning. *In room:* A/C, TV, minibar, hair dryer.

Le Régent Petite France ★★ This is the first serious challenger to the Hilton in years. Many guests choose it for its more comfortable rooms and intriguing atmosphere. This site was once an ice factory, and many of the old steam machines were kept in place. The marble lobby sets the tone, with ice-cream colors and potted palms. Guest rooms come in various sizes, the best of which are quite spacious and open onto river views. The luxurious beds are among the city's finest, and the bathrooms are state of the art, with combination tub and shower. The staff is one of the most professional in Strasbourg.

5 rue des Moulins, 67000 Strasbourg. ✆ **800/223-5652** in the U.S. and Canada, or 03-88-76-43-43. Fax 03-88-76-43-76. www.regent-hotels.com. 72 units. 1,350F–1,680F (205.20– 255.35, $195.75–$243.60) double; 2,050F–2,600F (311.60– 395.20, $297.25–$377) suite. AE, DC, MC, V. **Amenities:** Restaurant, bar; fitness club; Jacuzzi; sauna; room service; laundry/dry cleaning. *In room:* A/C, TV, minibar, hair dryer.

MODERATE

Hôtel Beaucour ★★ This hotel is geared toward business travelers, but anyone will find it ideal—it's the city's most tranquil lodging. Situated at the end of a private street a few blocks east of the cathedral, it occupies a 17th-century building with timbered ceilings. Every guest room contains a whirlpool tub, a fax hookup, and computer connections, plus a bathroom with tub and shower. Furnishings are of standard international style, but comfortable. The hotel maintains an affiliation with three restaurants a short walk away. The concierge, who seems to know all the city's secrets, will make reservations for you.

5 rue Bouchers, 67000 Strasbourg. ✆ **03-88-76-72-00.** Fax 03-88-76-72-60. www.hotel-beaucour.com. 49 units. 780F (118.55, $113.10) double; from 950F (144.40, $137.75) suite. AE, DC, MC, V. Parking 45F (6.85, $6.55). Amenities: Laundry/dry cleaning. *In room:* TV, dataport, minibar, hair dryer.

Hôtel Best Western Monopole-Métropole This hotel is on a quiet street corner near the train station. Its modern lobby features a scattering of antiques, among them a 17th-century carved armoire and a bronze statue of a night watchman. An extension of the salon displays oil portraits of 18th-century Alsatian personalities and glass cases with pewter tankards and candlesticks. Breakfast (the only meal served) is presented in the high-ceilinged Alsatian-style dining room. The bedrooms are comfortable, especially in the selection of mattresses and crisp white linen. Each unit is unique; many contain Louis-Philippe antiques, and some bathrooms contain tubs. Léon and Monique Siegel are the proprietors; members of their family have owned this place since 1919.

16 rue Kuhn, 67000 Strasbourg. ✆ **800/528-1234** in the U.S. and Canada, or 03-88-14-39-14. Fax 03-88-32-82-55. www.bw-monopole.com. 90 units. 580F–810F (88.15– 123.10, $84.10–$117.45) double. AE, DC, MC, V. Parking 60F (9.10, $8.70). **Amenities:** Baby-sitting; laundry/dry cleaning. *In room:* TV, minibar, hair dryer, safe.

Hôtel de l'Europe

Behind a half-timbered facade a 3-minute walk west of the cathedral, this is one of the best-located, government-rated three-star hotels in town. Its roots go back to the 15th century, when it functioned as a coaching inn; it was enlarged with the annexation of an 18th-century house next door. Frequently renovated, it's comfortable and unpretentious, with an elevator and all the electronic gadgets you might want. About a third of the rooms are air-conditioned. They run the gamut from modern to a half-timbered fantasy directly under the roof (room 404), where angled beams evoke the original construction.

38–40 rue du Fosse-des-Tanneurs, 67000 Strasbourg. ✆ 03-88-32-17-88. Fax 03-88-75-65-45. www.hotel-europe.com. 60 units. 610F–980F (92.70– 148.95, $88.45–$142.10) double. AE, DC, MC, V. Parking 70F (10.65, $10.15). **Amenities:** 24-hour room service. *In room:* TV, minibar, hair dryer.

Hôtel des Rohan ⭐ *Value*

Located in the pedestrian zone 50 yards from the cathedral, this is one of the city's best values. The hotel is within walking distance of the Palais des Rohan. It offers a choice of elegantly furnished rooms, the cheapest of which are small and have a French bed called a *matrimonial*, a standard double bed. All units come with a shower-only bathroom.

17–19 rue du Maroquin, 67000 Strasbourg. ✆ 03-88-32-85-11. Fax 03-88-75-65-37. www.hotel-rohan. com. 36 units. 795F (120.85, $115.30) double. AE, DC, MC, V. Nearby underground parking 80F (12.15, $11.60). **Amenities:** Laundry/dry cleaning. *In room:* TV, minibar, hair dryer, safe.

Le Régent Contades ⭐⭐ *Finds*

Our favorite moderately priced choice in Strasbourg is this glorified B&B, housed in a three-story structure with dormers, close to the cathedral and the Rhine. Diplomats often guard it as a secret address, but the word is out. The hostelry is stylish and fashionable, and has an intelligent and helpful staff. The guest rooms are alluring, furnished with classic style. The most spacious units are in a new wing. Breakfast is the only meal served.

8 av. de la Liberté, 67000 Strasbourg. ✆ 03-88-15-05-05. Fax 03-88-15-05-15. www.regent-hoteles.com. 45 units. 695F–1,390F (105.65– 211.30, $100.80–$201.55) double; 1,690F–2,300F (256.90– 349.60, $245.05–$333.50) suite. Parking 95F (14.45, $13.80). AE, DC, MC, V. **Amenities:** Bar; fitness center; sauna; solarium; laundry. *In room:* A/C, TV, minibar, hair dryer.

INEXPENSIVE

Hôtel de l'Ill *Value*

A 5-minute walk from the cathedral, this government-rated two-star hotel is a good value. An inviting little place, it offers small, quiet, comfortably furnished rooms decorated in either modern or Alsatian traditional style. Those at the rear contain a private terrace or balcony, opening onto a view of neighboring gardens. Each room comes with a tidily kept, shower-only bathroom, but no amenities other than a phone. The breakfast room is decorated Laura Ashley style—well, except for the cuckoo clock, that is.

8 rue des Bateliers, 67000 Strasbourg. ✆ **03-88-36-20-01.** Fax 03-88-35-30-03. 27 units. 255F–395F (38.75– 60.05, $37.00–$57.30) double. MC, V. Parking 45F (6.85, $6.55). Bus: 10, direct from train station.

Hôtel des Princes _Value_   A 15-minute walk from the center of town, the Hôtel des Princes enjoys a three-star government rating and is one of the best values in the city. The management is helpful, and the rooms are furnished comfortably but simply, each with a shower-only bathroom. The hotel was renovated in 2000. A continental breakfast is the only meal served.

33 rue Geiler, Conseil de l'Europe, 67000 Strasbourg. ✆ **03-88-61-55-19.** Fax 03-88-41-10-92. www.hotel princes.com. 43 units. 460F–585F (69.90– 88.90, $66.70–$84.85) double. AE, MC, V. Bus: 2. **Amenities:** Baby-sitting; laundry/dry cleaning. _In room:_ TV, minibar.

DINING
VERY EXPENSIVE

Au Crocodile ★★★ ALSATIAN   A beautifully skylit restaurant, Au Crocodile serves the most inventive food in Strasbourg. There are only two restaurants in this entire region to equal it: Buerehiesel (see below) and the Auberge de l'Ill (see the "Colmar" section, later this chapter). Chef Emile Jung offers a wide array of dishes. Some of the best include a traditional, and unctuous, slab of gooseliver encased in a gewürztraminer aspic; sautéed scallops with a purée of celery and marsala-flavored butter sauce; a confit of quail with foie gras of duckling; and red snapper encased in a crust of confit of lemon and served with stewed artichokes. The menu continues to be charged with energy and inventiveness. Our major problem comes only when the bill (or _la note,_ as the French say) arrives, especially when you indulge in those high-priced wines.

10 rue de l'Outre. ✆ **03-88-32-13-02.** Reservations required. Main courses 195F–385F (29.65– 58.50, $28.30–$55.85); fixed-price menus 320F–460F (48.65– 69.90, $46.40–$66.70) lunch, 470F–740F (71.45– 112.50, $68.15–$107.30) dinner. AE, DC, MC, V. Tues–Sat noon–1:30pm and 7:30–9:30pm. Closed last 3 weeks of July and Dec 24–Jan 8.

Le Buerehiesel ★★★ MODERN FRENCH   Also known as Le Restaurant Westermann, Buerehiesel is famous for Antoine Westermann's _cuisine moderne,_ as well as for its prime location. It's in l'Orangerie, a beautiful park at the end of the allée de la Robertsau planned by the landscape artist Le Nôtre, who gave it to Joséphine during her marriage to Napoléon. In the kitchen, distantly remembered recipes are brought down from the attic and recycled in innovative and exciting ways. Of special merit are a pâté of roebuck in puff pastry, served with gooseliver; steamed turbot with shellfish, fennel, and confit of lemons; and a spectacular dessert, bitter chocolate in puff pastry, served with an essence of bitter oranges preserved in their own juices and Grand Marnier. We cannot praise the cuisine too highly. Even though the place elevates stuffiness to an art form, the movers and shakers of the European Union seem to lap it up.

4 parc de l'Orangerie. ✆ **03-88-45-56-65.** Reservations required. Main courses 230F–440F (34.95– 66.90, $33.35–$63.80); fixed-price menu 330F–840F (50.15– 127.70, $47.85nd]$121.80). AE, DC, MC, V. Thurs–Mon noon–2pm and 7:30–9:30pm. Closed 1 week in Dec, 1 week in Jan, 1 week in Feb, and first 2 weeks in Aug.

Finds **A Picnic in the Park**

One of the most popular green swaths in Strasbourg, usually loaded with picnickers, Frisbee players, and families, is **Park de l'Orangerie**, facing the Parlement Européen, a half mile north of the center of Strasbourg. (Bus 6, direction Bischhelim, goes here from the town center.)

MODERATE

L'Arsenal ALSATIAN   This restaurant is in a historic building and often counts European Parliament members among its patrons. The inventive regional menu changes often, but may feature young rabbit and gooseliver in jelly, veal escalope and calf's feet in red-wine sauce, duck roasted with pears and local wine, or salmon on a bed of sauerkraut. A specialty is *kugelhof* (pastry shell) with escargots—normally a sweet pastry, but the chef makes it salted with snails.

11 rue de l'Abreuvoir. © **03-88-35-03-69.** Reservations required. Main courses 80F–135F (12.15– 20.50, $11.60–$19.60); fixed-price menus 140F (21.30, $20.30) lunch, 165F (25.10, $23.95) dinner. AE, MC, V. Tues–Fri noon–2pm; Mon–Sat 7:15–9:30pm. Closed Aug 1–21.

Maison des Tanneurs ⊛ ALSATIAN   This place stands on a street in the Petite France quarter; inside, the overworked staff sometimes rushes from one task to another. Flowers and antiques create a warm atmosphere, and the terrace opens onto the canal. The restaurant has been called La Maison de la Chou-croute, as its sauerkraut-and-pork platter is the finest in the area. But the chef prepares many other dishes as well, including an extravagant parfait of foie gras with fresh truffles. We recommend main courses of crayfish tails in court bouil-lon, guinea fowl with green peppercorns served on a bed of sauerkraut, and *coq au Riesling* (chicken cooked in white wine and served with noodles).

42 rue du Bain-aux-Plantes. © **03-88-32-79-70.** Reservations required. Main courses 125F–170F (19–25.85, $18.15–$24.65); fixed-price menu 235F–285F (35.70– 43.30, $34.10–$41.35). AE, DC, MC, V. Tues–Sat noon–2:15pm and 7:15–10pm (also open for Sun lunch in Dec). Closed 3 weeks in midsummer.

Maison Kammerzell ⊛ *(Kids)* ALSATIAN   The gingerbread Maison Kam-merzell is a sightseeing attraction as well as a fantastic restaurant. The carved-wood framework was constructed during the Renaissance, and the overhanging stories in 1589. We suggest *la choucroute formidable* (for two), the Alsatian spe-cialty prepared with goose fat and Riesling wine, as well as Strasbourg sausages and smoked breast of pork. The owner, Guy-Pierre Baumann, also offers home-made foie gras, guinea hen with mushrooms, medallion of young wild boar, and other regional dishes.

A recent concession to modern cuisine is the chef's version of sauerkraut with fish. Families will want to take advantage of the free meals for children under 10 at lunch. The policy has made the place popular with big broods; if you want to eat your sauerkraut in peace and quiet, come for dinner.

16 place de la Cathédrale. © **03-88-32-42-14.** Reservations required. Main courses 89F–155F (13.55– 23.55, $12.90–$22.50); fixed-price menu 184F–295F (27.95– 44.85, $26.70–$42.80). AE, DC, MC, V. Daily noon–2:30pm and 7–11pm.

INEXPENSIVE

Brasserie de l'Ancienne Douane ⊛⊛ *(Value)* ALSATIAN   This is the largest and most colorful dining spot in Strasbourg. Established as part of a historic ren-ovation, it offers 600 seats indoors and 200 seats on a terrace. From the outside, along a street in the oldest part of town, you'll see the arcades of the lower floor and the small windows of the stone facade. The high-ceilinged rooms are some-what formal, with Teutonic chairs and heavily timbered ceilings. Among the Alsatian specialties are the well-known "sauerkraut of the Customs officers" and the foie gras of Strasbourg. Chicken in Riesling with Alsatian noodles, onion pie, and ham knuckle with potato salad and horseradish are also popular dishes.

6 rue de la Douane. © **03-88-15-78-78.** Reservations recommended. Main courses 45F–210F (6.85– 31.90, $6.55–$30.45); fixed-price menu 95F–135F (14.45– 20.50, $13.80–$19.60); children's menu 48F (7.30, $6.95). AE, DC, MC, V. Daily 11:30am–11pm.

NEARBY DINING

Many visitors drive north 7½ miles to the village of La Wantzenau, which has very good restaurants. From Strasbourg, take D468, which runs along the west bank of the Rhine.

À la Barrière ★★ TRADITIONAL/MODERN FRENCH   This restaurant is a 5-minute walk from the center of La Wantzenau. In a restrained Art Deco interior, the chef prepares a sophisticated cuisine. The menu might include fillet of sole with scallops and scampi in ginger sauce, roast rack of lamb with a potato casserole, and salmon steaks with sorrel. In autumn, the game dishes (especially pheasant and venison) are excellent.

3 rte. de Strasbourg, 67610 la Wantzenau. ℂ **03-88-96-20-23**. Reservations required. Main courses 90F–185F (13.70– 28.10, $13.05–$26.85); fixed-price menu 260F–400F (39.50– 60.80, $37.70–$58). AE, DC, MC, V. Thurs–Mon noon–2:30pm and 7–9:30pm. Closed Feb and Aug 7–30.

STRASBOURG AFTER DARK

For family fun in July and August, head to La Petite France and its ponts Converts around 9 or 10pm for *Les Nuits de Strass*—a water-show with fountains, lasers, music, and entertainers. Another bastion of outdoor entertainment is **place de la Cathédrale,** where you can find an assortment of street performers and artists. For a chance to see folk-dancing troupes from the world over, go to the **Palais des Rohan** around 8:30pm in summer. From mid-July to about August 8, additional open-air folk dances are presented within La Petite France on Monday night in the places des Tripiers, Tuesday in the place Benjamin Zix, and Wednesday in the place du Marché aux Chochons de Lait. Performance dates vary, so check with the Office de Tourisme (see "Essentials," above) for a precise schedule.

THE PERFORMING ARTS   For opera and ballet, try the **Opéra du Rhin,** 19 place Broglie (ℂ **03-88-75-48-01**); tickets range from 75F to 350F (11.40 to 53.20, $10.90 to $50.75). The **Orchestre Philharmonique de Strasbourg** gives concerts at the Palais de la Musique et des Congrès, place de Bordeaux (ℂ **03-88-15-09-00**). Tickets cost 100F to 250F (15.20 to 38, $14.50 to $36.25). The **Théâtre National de Strasbourg** plays a busy schedule at 1 av. de la Marseillaise (ℂ **03-88-24-88-24**). Tickets cost from 120F to 200F (18.25 to 30.40, $17.40 to $29).

CLUBS   For the club scene, head to the streets surrounding place de la Cathédrale: rue des Frères, rue des Soeurs, and rue de la Croix. For jazz and blues, your best bets are **Gayot,** 18 rue des Frères (ℂ **03-88-36-31-88**), with occasional guest performers; and the more refined though still sultry **Le Bistro Piano Bar,** 30 rue des Tonneliers (ℂ **03-88-23-02-71**), with a jazz piano player and free concerts Wednesday, Friday, and Saturday. **Café des Anges,** 5 rue Ste-Catherine (ℂ **03-88-37-12-67**), has an underground dance floor converted from a wine cellar as well as a ground-level bar area. The dance club never has a cover.

Le Seven, 25 rue des Tonneliers (ℂ **03-88-32-77-77**), has a below-street-level dance floor that features all types of music but disco. The place stays packed with a stylish crowd between ages 20 and 35. Cover ranges between 35F and 50F (5.30 and 7.60, $5.10 and $7.25).

One of the biggest and most visible discos in the region lies 4½ miles north of Strasbourg. (To get here, follow the signs to Wantzenau.) It's **Le Chalet,** 376 rte. de Wantzenau (ℂ **03-88-31-18-31**), where a 55F (8.35, $8) cover buys the first drink and the right to parade at will between two huge and distinctively

---

Moments Waking Up Sleepy Strasbourg

Strasbourg after dark can be a bit dull in summer, unless your idea of a good time is sitting in an open-air cafe enjoying the night breezes. In September and through late spring, the scene enlivens when the students return for the school year. The hottest place to go at night—and the best for live music—is the rowdy section between place de Zurich and place d'Austerlitz, across the canal from the old town (*vieille ville*). The sounds of everything from Cuban salsa to funk fill the night air.

---

different sections. One is designed for techno fans, another for less harsh dance music with a good mix of some disco classics.

GAY NIGHTLIFE Gays and lesbians should head for either **Le Sous-Sol,** 1 rue du Miroir (© **03-88-22-22-23**), most of whose clients are men; and **Le Monte Carl',** 1 quai Turkheim (© **03-88-22-35-02**), which attracts a mixed gay crowd with a somewhat higher percentage of lesbians.

2 La Route du Vin (Wine Road) ✶✶✶

The fastest route between Strasbourg and Colmar, 42 miles to the south, is the N83. But if you've got time, the famous *Route du Vin* (Wine Road) makes a rewarding experience. It rolls through 60 charming villages. Along the way are inns where you can sample the wine, take a leisurely meal, or spend the night.

The Wine Road runs along the Vosges foothills, with medieval towers and feudal ruins evoking faded pageantry. The slopes sometimes reaching a height of 1,450 feet, are covered with vines, as there's an estimated 50,000 acres of vineyards along this road. Some 30,000 families earn their living tending the grapes. The best time to go is for the harvest in September and October.

The traditional route starts at Marlenheim; signs are posted all along the way, so it's hard to get lost.

MARLENHEIM

This agreeable wine town, noted for its Vorlauf red wine, is 13 miles due west of Strasbourg on N4. You might want to visit even if you can't drive the full length of the Wine Road, as it offers an excellent inn.

Accommodations & Dining

Le Cerf ✶✶✶   In the heart of this medieval village, occupying a half-timbered building at least 300 years old, this hotel offers pleasantly furnished rooms adjoining an excellent restaurant. Robert Husser and his son, Michel, will feed you specialties like fresh foie gras, cassoulet of lobster, ballotine of quail (in fall only) with sweetbreads, ravioli stuffed with smoked foie gras, oysters cooked in court bouillon and flavored with herbs, and roast turbot with vegetables.

30 rue du Général-de-Gaulle, 67520 Marlenheim. © **03-88-87-73-73**. Fax 03-88-87-68-08. www. lecerf.com. 17 units. 550F–850F (83.60– 129.20, $79.75–$123.25) double; 1,250F (190, $181.25) suite. AE, DC, MC, V. Free parking. *In room:* TV, minibar, hair dryer.

WANGEN

One of the jewels along the route, Wangen (18.6 miles from Strasbourg) has a city gate crowned by a tower and twisting narrow streets. It's one of the most typical of the wine towns. The road from Wangen winds down to Molsheim.

MOLSHEIM ⚜

Molsheim (15½ miles from Strasbourg) retains its ramparts and a Gothic-Renaissance church built from 1614 to 1619. Its *Alte Metzig* (town hall) was erected by the Guild of Butchers and has a turret, gargoyles, loggia, and belfry, which houses a clock with allegorical figures striking the hour. The local **Office de Tourisme** is at 17 place de l'Hôtel de Ville (✆ **03-88-38-11-61**).

ROSHEIM ⚜

Nestled behind medieval fortifications, this wine-producing town (19½ miles from Strasbourg) is another of the 10 free Alsatian cities. It has a 12th-century Romanesque house and the Église St-Pierre et St-Paul, also Romanesque, from 2 centuries later; it's dominated by an octagonal tower. Medieval walls and gate towers evoke Rosheim's past. The **Office de Tourisme** is at place de la République (✆ **03-88-50-75-38**).

OBERNAI ⚜⚜

The patron saint of Alsace, Obernai, was born here, 20 miles from Strasbourg. With its old timbered houses and a colorful marketplace, **place du Marché**, this town is one of the most interesting stopovers on the Wine Road. There's a market on Thursdays from 8am to noon; go early. **Place de l'Étoile** is decked out in flowers, and the **Hôtel de Ville** has a delightful loggia (inside you can see the council chamber). An old watchtower, the **Tour de la Chapelle**, is from the 13th and 16th centuries. The town's six-pail **fountain** is one of the most spectacular in Alsace. The **Office de Tourisme** is at place du Beffroi (✆ **03-88-95-64-13**).

Accommodations & Dining

Le Parc ⚜⚜ This contemporary hotel, located in a park and most recently renovated in 1999, offers fine dining and many facilities you'd find in a health spa, with a traditional Alsatian motif and architectural style. City dwellers seeking some R&R appreciate the well-furnished, spacious guest rooms, each with a combination tub/shower bathroom. The good on-site restaurant serves dishes that vary depending on what's available in the local markets. These may include monkfish with mushrooms, duckling with apples and *cèpes* (flap mushrooms), salad of foie gras, salmon in red-wine sauce, and rich fruit desserts.

169 rte. d'Ottrott, 67210 Obernai. ✆ **03-88-95-50-08**. Fax 03-88-95-37-29. www.hotel-du-parc.com. 56 units. 720F–1,170F (109.45– 177.85, $104.40–$169.65) double; 1,570F–1,680F (238.65– 255.35,

---

⟮Finds⟯ Biking the Wine Road

A bike-rental outfitter is **La Vélocation de Strasbourg**, 10 rue des Bouchers (✆ **03-88-35-11-65**). Subsidized by the city, it's one of the cheapest places anywhere, with half-day rentals priced at 20F (3.05, $2.90), and full-day rentals at 30F (4.55, $4.35).

The tourist office provides free maps showing bike routes that fan from the city out into the countryside, with emphasis on cycle lanes (the French refer to them as *Les Pistes Cyclables*) that prohibit cars. One of these is a 17-mile southwesterly stretch from Strasbourg to the wine hamlet of Molsheim. You'll have a forest on one side, the banks of the Brûche River (a tributary of the Rhine) on the other, and little car traffic.

La Formidable Choucroute

There's no single recipe and no universal preparation, even in Alsace, but *choucroute garnie à l'alsacienne* is the dish most often associated with the province. Best consumed when the leaves start falling, it's a hearty dish intended to fortify against the coming winter. You'll know autumn is at hand when you see signs in restaurants announcing "Nouvelle Choucroute": the season's first batch of cabbage marinated for weeks in herbs and salt brine, with hints of crunchiness and acidity permeating the healthful fibers. Added zest comes from juniper berries, caraway seeds, fresh pepper, bouquet garni, bacon fat, and (in truly classic versions) a dollop or two of goose fat.

Choucroute and its perfect accompaniment, Riesling, are products of Alsace. Potatoes and cabbage are produced locally and can be stored in barrels in a cool cellar through a long winter. Since the Middle Ages, local farmers have produced vast amounts of pork products, some traditionally smoked over fir or cherrywood fires to impart the earthy taste that permeates the shredded cabbage. The version you'll likely encounter in restaurants will include only the choicest cuts of pork (a variety of chops, sausages, knuckles, and offal keeps even the most jaded diner from growing bored). Earthier, more traditional versions that many Alsatians are likely to remember from their childhoods include pork brains, entrails, feet, ears, tail, and pork-liver dumplings. Regardless of the ingredients, many diners find the result nothing less than *formidable*.

So how does a connoisseur identify the best choucroute? A worthy version is easy to digest, is free of excess grease and/or acidity, and doesn't float on a lake of juices. The dish should be cooked carefully so the potatoes don't turn to mush, and the meat and cabbage should gracefully blend so they coordinate with the flavors of an Alsatian Riesling. (Enjoying it with a hearty glass or two of beer is a dignified alternative, but if you opt for other types of liquid accompaniments, you're likely to be labeled an infidel.)

How can you tell whether the sauerkraut you're eating is authentically strasbourgeoise? The difference is in the sausage, which any charcuterie within 40 miles of either side of the Rhine could identify as *vraiment alsacien* (frankfurters best consumed with beer and mustard).

Riesling is the king of Alsatian wine, with its perfumed bouquet. Other regional wines are chasselas, knipperle, sylvaner, pinot blanc, muscat, pinot gris, pinot auxerrois, traminer, and gewürztraminer.

$227.65–$243.60) suite. AE, MC, V. Closed June 29–July 11 and Dec 8–Jan 6. **Amenities:** Restaurant, bar; indoor and outdoor pools; fitness center; Jacuzzi; sauna; steam room; room service; laundry. *In room:* A/C, TV, minibar, hair dryer.

BARR

The grapes for some of the finest Alsatian wines, sylvaner and gewürztraminer, are harvested here. The castles of Landsberg and Andlau stand high above the town. Barr (23 miles from Strasbourg) has many pleasant old timbered houses and a charming **place de l'Hôtel-de-Ville** with a town hall from 1640. Call ② **03-88-08-66-65** for tourist information.

MITTELBERGHEIM

This is a special village. Its **place de l'Hôtel-de-Ville** is bordered by houses in the Renaissance style.

ACCOMMODATIONS & DINING

Winstub Gilg ⭐   This is an excellent inn. Though parts of the building date from 1614, its showpiece is a two-story stone staircase, which is classified a historic monument It was carved by the medieval stonemasons who worked on the cathedral at Strasbourg. The bedrooms are attractively furnished, each with a combination tub and shower. Chef Georges Gilg and his son-in-law, Vincent Reuschlé, attract a loyal following with regional specialties like onion tart, sauerkraut, and foie gras in brioche. Main courses include stewed kidneys and sweetbreads, rack of lamb cooked pink and served with theme-flavored gravy, duck with oranges, and, in season, roast pheasant with grapes. The restaurant (but not the hotel) is closed Tuesdays and Wednesdays, the month of January, and from June 21 to July 8.

1 rte. du Vin, Mittelbergheim, 67140 Barr. ② **03-88-08-91-37**. Fax 03-88-08-45-17. 15 units. 285F–450F (43.30– 68.40, $41.35–$65.25) double. AE, DC, MC, V. **Amenities:** Restaurant, bar; room service; laundry. *In room:* TV, hair dryer.

ANDLAU

This gardenlike resort, 26 miles from Strasbourg, was once the site of an abbey dating from 887, founded by the disgraced wife of Emperor Charles the Fat. It has now faded into history, but a church remains that dates from the 12th century. In the tympanum are noteworthy Romanesque carvings. The **Office de Tourisme** (② **03-88-08-22-57**) is at 5 rue du Général-de-Gaulle.

DINING

Au Boeuf Rouge TRADITIONAL FRENCH   This bustling and unpretentious bistro has a busy bar area and a comfortably battered dining room. Its menu of classic and time-tested specialties includes homemade terrines, gamecock, fresh fish, and a tempting dessert cart. Noted chef Pierre Kieffer prepares a fabulous version of *quenelle* of brochette, a local whitefish, made according to the recipe of his grandmother. This isn't the most innovative cookery on the wine trail, but it is reliable and consistent. For dessert, have a thick slice of Bettelman, an Alsatian cake baked with apples and cherries. There's also a wine stube (tavern) on site. From March to October, you can sit out on the terrace in front of the restaurant in the traditional Parisian cafe style.

6 rue du Dr.-Stoltz. ② **03-88-08-96-26**. Reservations recommended. Main courses 88F–150F (13.40– 22.80, $12.75–$21.75); fixed-price menu 98F–178F (14.90– 27.05, $14.20–$25.80). AE, DC, MC, V. Fri–Wed 11am–2:30pm; Fri–Tues 6:30–9:30pm. Closed Jan 10–28 and 2 weeks between June and July.

DAMBACH

In the midst of its vineyards, Dambach (30 miles from Strasbourg) is one of the delights of the Wine Road. The town has ramparts and three fortified gates. Its timbered houses are gabled with galleries, and many contain oriels. Wrought-iron signs still tell you if a place is a bakery or a butcher shop. A short drive from the town leads to the **Chapelle St-Sebastian,** with a 15th-century ossuary. **The Office de Tourisme** (② **03-88-92-61-00**) is located in La Mairie (town hall).

AMMERSCHWIHR

Ammerschwihr, near the outskirts of Colmar (49 miles from Strasbourg), is a good stop to cap off your Wine Road tour. Once a free city of the empire, the town was almost destroyed in 1944 but has been reconstructed in the traditional style. More and more travelers visit to sample the wine, especially Käferkopf. Check out the town's gate towers, 16th-century parish church, and remains of early fortifications.

ACCOMMODATIONS & DINING

À l'Arbre Vert ✿ *Value*   If you want to call it an evening before you go on to Colmar, À l'Arbre Vert is a charming place to stay. Its public rooms are delightfully decorated, though the guest rooms are rather modest, each with a shower-only bathroom. The inn restaurant serves very good Alsatian specialties, including a savory scallop of gooseliver with pinot noir. You can dine here even if you aren't a guest at the hotel.

7 rue des Cigognes, 68770 Ammerschwihr. ✆ **03-89-47-12-23.** Fax 03-89-78-27-21. 17 units. 380F (57.75, $55.10) double. Half board 290F–370F (44.13– 56.25, $42.05–$53.65) per person extra. AE, DC, MC, V. Restaurant closed Mon dinner and all day Tues. **Amenities:** Restaurant. *In room:* TV.

Aux Armes de France ✿✿✿ FRENCH/ALSATIAN   This is the best restaurant along the Wine Road. Although you can rent a room here (doubles go for 380F to 480F (57.75 to 72.95, $55.10 to $69.60), the real reason to come is the cuisine. In a flower-filled setting, Philippe Gaertner and his staff receive many French and German gourmands. A specialty is fresh foie gras served in its own golden aspic. Main courses include classics with imaginative variations, such as roebuck (in season) in hot sauce and lobster fricassée with cream and truffles. The spicy duckling is particularly savory, as is the filet of sole with fresh noodles. The terrine of lobster and calf's head in aspic (called a *presskopf,* which we've never seen in any other restaurant in France) is particularly sought after by adventurous gastronomes. The pistachio parfait served with a brochette of exotic fruits is a dessert specialty.

1 Grand Rue, 68770 Ammerschwihr. ✆ **03-89-47-10-12.** Fax 03-89-47-38-12. Reservations required. Main courses 180F–290F (27.35– 44.10, $26.10–$42.05); fixed-price menu 390F–530F (59.30– 80.55, $56.55–$76.85); *menu dégustation* (tasting menu) 530F (80.55, $76.85). AE, DC, DISC, MC, V. Fri–Tues noon–2pm and 7–9pm.

SÉLESTAT

After passing through Chatenois, you'll reach Sélestat, 32 miles from Strasbourg. This was once a free city, a center of the Renaissance, and the seat of a great school. Towered battlements enclose the town. The **Bibliothèque Humaniste,** 1 rue de la Bibliothèque (✆ **03-88-58-07-20**), houses a rare collection of manuscripts, including Sainte-Foy's *Book of Miracles.* It's open Monday and Wednesday through Friday from 9am to noon and 2 to 6pm, and Saturday from 9am to noon. (In July and August, additional hours on Saturday and Sunday are from 2 to 5pm.). Admission is 20F (3.05, $2.90) for adults, 10F (1.50, $1.45) for students, and free for children under 13.

The Gothic **Église St-George** has some fine stained glass and a gilded and painted stone pulpit. Also try to visit the 12th-century **Église Ste-Foy,** built of red sandstone in the Romanesque style. One of the town's most noteworthy Renaissance buildings is the **Maison de Stephan Ziegler.**

The **Office de Tourisme** is in La Commanderie St-Jean, boulevard du Général-Leclerc (✆ **03-88-58-87-20**).

From Sélestat, you can take a detour about 2,500 feet up on an isolated peak to **Château Haut-Koenigsbourg** (© **03-88-82-50-60**), a 15th-century castle. It's the largest in Alsace and treats you to an eagle's-nest view. It once belonged to the Hohenstaufens; during the Thirty Years' War, the Swedes dismantled it, but it was rebuilt in 1901 after it was presented to Kaiser Wilhelm II. Admission is 42F (6.40, $6.10) for adults, 26F (3.95, $3.75) for students ages 18 to 25, and free for children under 18. It's open May through June and September, daily from 9am to 6pm; March through April and October, daily from 9am to noon and 1 to 5:30pm; February 6 to 28 and November through February, daily from 9:30am to noon and 1 to 4:30pm; and July through August, daily from 9am to 6:30pm.

DINING

La Couronne ★★★ ALSATIAN   This family-run place serves dishes reflecting the bounty of Alsace, prepared with finesse. A flower-filled vestibule leads to a trio of pleasant dining rooms. There is much charm here in the presentation of the food and the refined surroundings. The chefs know the classics well, but manage to give a personal twist to most dishes, turning out skillful concoctions that look as delectable as they taste. Alsatian dishes are given a light, modern interpretation without the heavy sauces and fats of yesterday. Only high-quality ingredients personally selected at market by the chefs are used, and there is a fine cellar plentiful in Alsatian wines. Menu choices may include noisettes of roebuck (from midsummer to Christmas), ragoût of fish, foie gras, *omble chevalier* (the elusive whitefish from Lake Geneva) with sauerkraut and cumin-laced potatoes, and frogs' legs served with a flan of freshwater shrimp.

45 rue de Sélestat-Baldenheim. © **03-88-85-32-22.** Reservations required. Main courses 90F–160F (13.70– 24.30, $13.05–$23.20); fixed-price menu 200F–420F (30.40– 63.85, $29–$60.90). AE, MC, V. Tues–Sun noon–2pm; Tues–Sat 7–9pm. Closed first week in Jan and last 2 weeks in July. From Sélestat, go 5½ miles east on D21; when the road forks, go to the right, taking D209 to the village of Baldenheim.

RIBEAUVILLÉ ★

At the foot of vine-clad hills, Ribeauvillé (53 miles from Strasbourg) is charming, with old shop signs, pierced balconies, turrets, and flower-decorated houses. See its Renaissance fountain and **Hôtel de Ville,** on place de la Mairie, which has a collection of silver-gilt medieval and Renaissance tankards known as *hanaps.* (These are showcased as part of free guided tours, offered May to September, Tuesday through Friday at 10am, 11am, 1:45pm, and 2:30pm.) Also of interest is the **Tour des Bouchers,** a "butchers' tower" of the 13th and 16th centuries, whose interior is closed to the public. The town is noted for its Riesling and traminer wines. In September, a "Day of the Strolling Fiddlers" fair is held. The **Office de Tourisme** is at 1 rue de Pierre de Coubertin (© **03-89-73-62-22**).

ACCOMMODATIONS & DINING

Clos St-Vincent ★★★   This is one of the most elegant choices along Route du Vin. Most of the individually decorated bedrooms have a balcony or terrace, but you get much more than a view of the Haut-Rhin vineyards and summer roses. The rooms, ranging from medium to large, are furnished with grand comfort; each has a deluxe mattress covered in fine linen and a bathroom with state-of-the-art plumbing and combination tub and shower. Arthur Chapotin's food is exceptional: hot duck liver with nuts, turbot with sorrel, roebuck (in season) in hot sauce, and veal kidneys in pinot noir. The wines are smooth, especially the Riesling and gewürztraminer, which seem to be the most popular.

Rte. de Bergheim, 68150 Ribeauvillé. (℗ **03-89-73-67-65.** Fax 03-89-73-32-20. closvincent@aol.com. 15 units. 835F–1,000F (126.90– 152, $121.10–$145) double; from 1,225F (186.20, $177.65) suite. Rates include breakfast. MC, V. **Amenities:** Restaurant, bar; indoor pool; baby-sitting, laundry/dry cleaning. *In room:* TV, minibar, hair dryer.

BERGHEIM

Renowned for its wines, this town (54 miles from Strasbourg) has kept part of its 15th-century fortifications. You can see timbered Alsatian houses and a Gothic church.

RIQUEWIHR ✸✸✸

This town (55 miles from Strasbourg), surrounded by some of the finest vineyards in Alsace, appears much as it did in the 16th century. With well-preserved walls and towers and great wine presses and old wells, it's one of the most rewarding destinations along the route. You can see Gothic and Renaissance houses, with wooden balconies, gables, and elaborately carved doors and windows. Its most interesting are **Maison Liebrich** (1535), **Maison Preiss-Zimmer** (1686), and **Maison Kiener** (1574). Try to peer into some of the galleried courtyards, where time seems frozen. **Tour de Dolder** (Dolder Belfry Tower) is from 1291. Nearby, the pentagonal **Tour des Voleurs** (Tower of Thieves, often called "the robbers' tower") contains a torture chamber. The château of the duke of Württemberg, from 1539, now the **Musée d'Histoire des P.T.T. d'Alsace,** or Alsace Postal History Museum (℗ **03-89-47-93-80**), offers exhibits devoted to postal and telecommunications history. The **Office de Tourisme** is shared with Ribeauvillé at 1 rue de Pierre de Coubertin (℗ **03-89-73-62-22**), in Ribeauvillé.

DINING

Auberge du Schoenenbourg ✸✸✸   We highly recommend the food here. You'll dine in a garden surrounded by vineyards at the edge of the village. The cuisine of François Kiener offers a delectable array of tantalizingly prepared fare. *Foie gras maison* is de rigueur, but salmon soufflé with sabayon truffles is an elegant surprise. Try the panache of fish with sorrel, ravioli of snails with poppy seeds, or tournedos in puff pastry with mushrooms and foie gras. Especially flavorful is a platter with portions of both smoked and fresh salmon, served with a creamy horseradish sauce and white, herb-flavored sauerkraut.

2 rue de la Piscine. (℗ 03-89-47-92-28. Reservations required. Main courses 150F–200F (22.80– 30.40, $21.75–$29); fixed-price menu 150F–440F (22.80– 66.90, $21.75–$63.80). AE, MC, V. Sun noon–2pm; daily 7–9:30pm. Closed Jan and on Wed in Nov–Dec and Feb.

KIENTZHEIM

Kientzheim is known for its wine, two castles, timber-framed houses, and walls from the Middle Ages. From here, it's just a short drive to Kaysersberg, also known for its vineyards. Tourist info can be found in Kaysersberg.

KAYSERSBERG ✸✸

Once a free city of the empire, Kaysersberg (58 miles from Strasbourg) lies at the mouth of the Weiss Valley, between two vine-covered slopes; it's crowned by a castle ruined in the Thirty Years' War. From one of the many ornately carved bridges, you can see the city's medieval fortifications along the top of one of the nearby hills. Many of the houses are Gothic and Renaissance, and most have half timbering, wrought-iron accents, leaded windows, and multiple designs carved into the reddish sandstone that seems to have been the principal building material.

In the cafes, you'll hear a combination of French and Alsatian. The language is usually determined by the age of the speaker—the older ones remain faithful to the dialect of their grandparents. Dr. Albert Schweitzer was born here in 1875; his house is near the bridge over the Weiss. You can visit the **Centre Culturel Albert-Schweitzer** from June to October, daily from 9am to noon and 2 to 6pm. The **Office de Tourisme** is at 31 rue du Geibourg (✆ **03-89-78-22-78**).

ACCOMMODATIONS & DINING

Au Lion d'Or FRENCH/ALSATIAN   This establishment boasts an exceptionally beautiful decor. A carved lion's head is set into the oak door leading into the restaurant, which has a beamed ceiling, stone detailing, brass chandeliers, and a massive fireplace. If you eat at an outdoor table, you'll have a view of one of Alsace's prettiest streets. A repertoire of classic Alsatian dishes appears on the menu including wild game, foie gras (which Alsatians claim to have invented), and any number of yummy pork dishes often shaped into hams and sausages. Sauerkraut, served either in its traditional meat-and-potato form or with fish, is an enduring specialty and a favorite with the loyal clientele.

66 rue du Général-de-Gaulle. ✆ **03-89-47-11-16**. Reservations required. Main courses 75F–150F (11.40– 22.80, $10.90–$21.75); fixed-price menu 85F–260F (12.90– 39.50, $12.35–$37.70). AE, MC, V. Thurs–Tues noon–2:30pm and 6:30–9:30pm. Closed Jan; Sept–June, closed Tues–Wed.

Chambard ⭐⭐⭐ FRENCH/ALSATIAN   The regional cuisine here is so good, it's well planning your wine tour to include a stopover. You'll recognize the restaurant—the finest in town—by the gilded wrought-iron sign above the cobblestones. Inside, you'll find a rustic ambience, with exposed stone and polished wood. Emotion and innovation combine to make a taste treat. Regional specialties with a few Mediterranean influences attest to the mastery of the kitchen. Oliver Nast, a chef of versatility and imagination, presents an impeccably flavored and very sophisticated cuisine. The chefs are known for sauerkraut served with a host of mostly smoked pork specialties, as well as foie gras and a pungent Munster cheese. Menu items include red snapper with herb sauce; an upscale version of a traditional Alsatian stew that's made partially with foie gras; and a traditional Alsatian cake (*kugelhof*) with cinnamon-flavored ice cream. All the best vintages from the "wine road of Alsace" emerge from the cellar.

The Chambard offers a 20-room hotel annex built in 1981 to match the other buildings on the street. It has a massive Renaissance fireplace that was transported from another building. A double goes for 650F to 750F (98.80 to 114, $94.25 to $108.75).

9–13 rue du Général-de-Gaulle, 68240 Kaysersberg. ✆ **03-89-47-10-17**. Fax 03-89-47-35-03. Reservations required. Main courses 140F–225F ([eu[21.30– 34.20, $20.30–$32.65); fixed-price menu 250F–410F (38– 62.30, $36.25–$59.45). AE, MC, V. Tues 7–9:30pm; Wed–Sun noon–2pm and 7–9:30pm. Restaurant closed Jan 1–7 and March 5–30.

ROUFFACH

Rouffach is south of Colmar. It's included here because of the excellent vineyard **Clos St-Landelin** (✆ **03-89-78-58-00**), on the Route du Vin, at the intersection of RN83 route de Soultzmatt. Rouffach is sheltered by one of the highest of the Vosges mountains, Grand-Ballon, which stops the winds that bring rain. That makes for a dry climate and a special grape. A clerical estate from the 6th century until the Revolution and celebrated over the centuries for the quality of wine it produces, Clos St-Landelin covers 37 acres at the southern end of the Vorbourg Grand Gru area. Its steep slopes call for terrace cultivation.

The soil that produces these famous wines is anything but fertile. Loaded with pebbles and high in alkalines, sand, and limestone, it produces low-yield, scraggly vines whose fruit (depending on where the vines are planted and their exposure to the sun) is used to make superb Rieslings, gewürztraminers, and pinot noirs. Since 1648, the Muré family has owned the vineyards, which now sprawl across 62 acres. In their cellar is the oldest wine press in Alsace, dating to the 13th century. The family welcomes visitors and speaks English.

3 Colmar (★(★(★

273 miles SE of Paris, 87 miles SE of Nancy, 44 miles SW of Strasbourg

One of the most attractive towns in Alsace, Colmar is filled with many medieval and early Renaissance buildings, with half-timbered structures, sculptured gables, and gracious loggias. Tiny gardens and wash houses surround many of the homes. Its old quarter looks more German than French, filled with streets of unexpected twists and turns. As a gateway to the Rhine country, Colmar is a major stopover south from Strasbourg. Situated near the vine-covered slopes of the southern Vosges, it's the third-largest town in Alsace.

Colmar today has been so well restored that it's now Alsace's most beautiful city, far more so than Strasbourg. While walking its streets, you'll find it hard to tell that Colmar was hard hit in two world wars.

ESSENTIALS

GETTING THERE   If you're **driving,** take N83 from Strasbourg; trip time is 1 hour. Because of Colmar's narrow streets, we suggest that you park in the Champ-de-Mars northeast of the rail station, and then walk a few blocks east to the old city. **Trains** link Colmar to Nancy, Strasbourg, and Mulhouse, as well as to Germany via Freiburg, across the Rhine. Nine trains per day arrive from Paris (trip time: 6 hours). For information and schedules, call ✆ **08-36-35-35-35.**

VISITOR INFORMATION   The **Office de Tourisme** is at 4 rue des Unter-linden (✆ **03-89-20-68-92;** www.ot-colmar.fr).

For information on winery visits, contact the **CIVA (Alsace Wine Commit-tee),** Maison du Vin d'Alsace, 12 av. de la Foire-aux-Vins (✆ **03-89-20-16-20**). It's usually open Monday through Friday from 9am to noon and 2 to 5pm. Make your arrangements far in advance.

SPECIAL EVENTS   Alsatian **folk dances** take place on place de l'Ancienne-Douane from mid-May to mid-September, Tuesdays at 8:30pm. If you want to listen to classical music, visit during the first 2 weeks in July for the **Festival International de Musique de Colmar,** when 24 concerts are held in various venues around the city such as churches and public monuments. **Les Mardis de la Collégiale,** at place de la Cathédrale (✆ **03-89-24-52-27**), offers organ and instrumental concerts every Tuesday at 8:45pm from the end of July to mid-September. And **L'Été Musical** (✆ **03-89-20-29-01**) presents classical instru-mental concerts once a week during August at the Église St-Pierre. Tickets for any of these range from 50F to 150F (7.60 to 22.80, $7.25 to $21.75). You can get complete information at the Office de Tourisme.

EXPLORING COLMAR

Colmar boasts lots of historic houses, many half-timbered and, at least in sum-mer, accented with geranium-draped window boxes. One of the most beautiful is the **Maison Pfister,** 11 rue des Marchands, at the corner of rue Mercière, a building with wooden balconies (1537). On the ground floor is a wine boutique owned by a major Alsace wine grower, **Mure,** proprietor of the vineyard Clos St-Landelin. (A cursory glance of its exterior may be all you'll get, as this isn't a public *maison.*)

If you take pont St-Pierre over the Lauch River, you'll have an excellent view of Old Colmar and can explore **Petite Venise** which is filled with canals.

SHOPPING If you're up for shopping, head for the old town of Colmar, particularly rue de Clefs, Grand Rue, rue des Têtes, and rue des Marchands.

Antiques abound, and you'll find a large grouping of stores in the old town, especially along rue des Marchands. Shops that deserve particular attention include **Gelsmar Dany,** 32 rue des Marchands (© 03-89-23-30-41), specializing in antique painted furniture; and **Antiquités Guy Caffard,** 56 rue des Marchands (© 03-89-41-31-78), with its mishmash of furniture, postcards, books, toys, bibelots, and the like. Also worth noting are **Lire & Chiner,** 36 rue des Marchands (© 03-89-24-16-78), and **Antiquité Arcana,** 13 place l'Ancienne Douane (© 03-89-41-59-81). For reproductions of objects found in Strasbourg's Alsacien Museum, such as glassware, jewelry, fabrics, and pottery, go to **Arts et Collections d'Alsace,** 1 rue des Tanneurs (© 03-89-24-09-78).

WINERIES Since Colmar is one of the gateways to the wine-producing Rhine country, local wine is one of the best purchases you can make. If you don't have time to head out to the vineyards along the Wine Road, stop in at **Cave du Musée,** 11 rue Kléber (© 03-89-23-85-29), for one of the largest selections of wines and liqueurs from the region as well as the rest of France.

If you have a car, you can drive to one of the most historic vineyards in Alsace-Lorraine. **Domaines Schlumberger,** at Guebwiller (where it's signposted), lies 16 miles southwest of Colmar. The cellars, established by the Schlumberger family beginning in 1810, are an unusual combination of early-19th-century brickwork and modern stainless steel. These grapes are turned into such famous wines of the region as Rieslings, gewürztraminers, muscats, sylvaners, and pinots (blancs, gris, noir). Views of the vineyards and the tasting rooms are available without an appointment, but tours of the cellars are conducted only whenever a staff member isn't too busy. Call © 03-89-74-85-75 before you go to find out when that might be.

Église des Dominicains This church contains one of the most famous artistic treasures of Colmar: Martin Schongauer's painting *Virgin of the Rosebush* (1473), all gold, red, and white, with fluttering birds. Look for it in the choir.

Place des Dominicains. © 03-89-24-46-57. Admission 8F (1.20, $1.15) adults, 6F (.90, 85¢) students, free for children 12 and under. Daily 10am–1pm and 3–6pm. Closed Jan–Mar.

Église St-Martin ✦ In the heart of Old Colmar is a collegiate church begun in 1230 on the site of a Romanesque church. It has a choir erected by William of Marburg in 1350 and is crowned by a steeple rising to 232 feet.

Place de la Cathédrale. © 03-89-41-27-20. Free admission. Daily 8am–6pm. Closed to casual visitors during mass.

Musée Bartholdi Statue of Liberty sculptor Frédéric-Auguste Bartholdi was born in Colmar in 1834. In this small, memento-filled museum, which is the house where he was born, there are Statue of Liberty rooms containing plans and scale models, as well as documents in connection with its construction and other works regarding U.S. history. Bartholdi's Paris apartment, with furniture and memorabilia, has been reconstructed here. The museum supplements its exhibits with paintings he collected of Egyptian scenes during his travels in 1856.

30 rue des Marchands. 🕐 **03-89-41-90-60.** Admission 20F (3.05, $2.90) adults, 15F (2.30, $2.20) children 12–18, free for children under 12. Wed–Mon 10am–noon and 2–6pm. Closed Jan–Feb.

Musée d'Unterlinden (Under the Linden Trees) ★★ This former Dominican convent (1232), the chief seat of Rhenish mysticism in the 14th and 15th centuries, was converted to a museum around 1850, and it's been a treasure house of the art and history of Alsace ever since.

The jewel of its collection is the **Issenheim Altarpiece (Le Retable d'Issenheim)** ★★★, painted by the Würzburg-born Matthias Grünewald, "the most furious of realists," around 1515. His colors glow and his fantasy will overwhelm you. One of the most exciting works in the history of German art, it's an immense altar screen with two-sided folding wing pieces—designed to show first the Crucifixion, then the Incarnation, framed by the Annunciation and the Resurrection. The carved altar screen depicts St. Anthony visiting the hermit St. Paul; it also reveals the Temptation of St. Anthony, the most beguiling part of a work that contains some ghastly misshapen birds, weird monsters, and loathsome animals. The demon of the plague, for example, is depicted with a swollen belly and purple skin; his body blotched with boils, and a diabolical grin on his horrible face.

Other attractions include the magnificent altarpiece (dating back to 1470) of Jean d'Orlier by Martin Schongauer, a large collection of religious wood carvings and stained glass from the 14th to the 18th centuries, and Gallo-Roman lapidary collections, including funeral slabs. Its armory collection includes ancient arms from the Romanesque to the Renaissance, featuring halberds and crossbows.

Place d'Unterlinden. 🕐 **03-89-41-89-23.** Admission 35F (5.30, $5.10) adults and seniors, 25F (3.80, $3.65) students and children 12–17, free for children under 12. Apr–Oct daily 9am–6pm; Nov–Mar Wed–Mon 10am–5pm. Closed on national holidays.

ACCOMMODATIONS

Rooms are also available in the **Hôtel des Têtes** (see "Dining," below).

Grand Hôtel Bristol This red sandstone hotel is the traditional first-class choice. Right at the train station, it provides well-maintained rooms with both modern and provincial decor. Accommodations are rather standardized and not quite as grand as the name of the hotel suggests. Each unit comes with a tidy, midsize bathroom, most with a combination tub and shower.

7 place de la Gare, 68000 Colmar. 🕐 **03-89-23-5959.** Fax 03-89-23-92-26. www.grand-hotel-bristol.fr. 70 units. 460F–770F (69.90– 117.05, $66.70–$111.65) double. AE, DC, MC, V. **Amenities:** Restaurant, bar; room service; laundry/dry cleaning. *In room:* TV, minibar, coffeemaker, hair dryer, iron, safe.

Hostellerie le Maréchal ★★ This hotel, the most tranquil in town, was formed when three 16th-century houses were joined. You climb a wide staircase to reach the guest rooms, most of which are air-conditioned. In the east wing is a small, partially timbered room with a sloping ceiling. Accommodations are generally small but neatly organized. There's a winter restaurant with a welcoming fireplace; in summer, the restaurant is moved to the terrace, where you can enjoy a water view. Feast on stuffed quail, good beef and veal dishes, and lamb Provençal—all accompanied by Tokay and Alsatian wines.

4–5 place des Six-Montagnes-Noires, 68000 Colmar. ℂ **03-89-41-60-32.** Fax 03-89-24-59-40. www.romantik hotels.com/colmar. 30 units. 600F–1,400F (91.20– 212.80, $87–$203) double; 1,600F (243.20, $232) suite. AE, MC, V. **Amenities:** Restaurant, bar; room service; laundry. *In room:* A/C, TV, minibar, hair dryer.

Le Colombier ⭐ This 14th-century, half-timbered ruin, successfully converted into an appealing hotel, is one of the finest in Colmar. The furnishings are streamlined, and the staff is engaging and helpful. But for the fact that it doesn't have a restaurant (breakfast is the only meal served), this government-rated three-star hotel would be worthy of four-star status. With the exception of the cozy unit beneath the steeply pitched pinnacle of the roofline, all of the guest rooms are high-ceilinged and come in a variety of sizes and shapes determined by the original layout. Each contains a comfortable mattress and fine linen, plus a small but tidy shower-only bathroom. Some rooms overlook the canals of the Petite Venise neighborhood; others open onto a half-timbered courtyard.

7 rue Turenne, 68000 Colmar. ℂ **03-89-23-96-00.** Fax 03-89-23-97-27. 24 units. 590F–1,180F (89.70– 179.35, $85.55–$171.10) double; 1,246F–1,508F (189.40– 229.20, $180.65–$218.65) suite. AE, DC, MC, V. **Amenities:** Laundry. *In room:* A/C, TV, minibar, hair dryer.

DINING

Fer Rouge ⭐⭐⭐ FRENCH/ALSATIAN This is one of the grandest restaurants in Colmar, serving up a flawless cuisine. In a half-timbered building on a cobblestone square in Colmar's historic core, Au Fer Rouge has stained-glass windows and window boxes that overflow with geraniums in summer. Inside, carved oak beams and brass and copper decorations provide a setting straight out of a Teutonic folktale. The owner has departed from the typical Alsatian fare in favor of more inventive styles. His specialties are scallops served with bacon and a pulverized essence of mussels, bound together with butter-sautéed endives; breast of pigeon smothered in "country-style cabbage" served with potatoes and port sauce; and breast of wild duckling grilled with its skin and served with a *parmentier* of its own thighs in a red-wine sauce and with wild mushrooms. A particularly succulent dessert is a slice of thin apple tart with cinnamon-flavored cream sauce and fresh-made vanilla ice cream.

52 Grand' Rue. ℂ **03-89-41-37-24.** Reservations required. Main courses 185F–250F (28.10– 38, $26.85–$36.25); fixed-price menu 295F–395F (44.85– 60.05, $42.80–$57.30); *menu dégustation* (tasting menu) 550F (83.60, $79.75). AE, DC, MC, V. Mon–Sat noon–2:15pm and 7:15–10pm. Closed Jan.

Maison des Têtes ⭐⭐⭐ TRADITIONAL FRENCH This Colmar monument, named for the sculptured heads on its stone facade, is the town's leading hotel and one of its top restaurants. It's reached via a covered cobblestone drive and open courtyard. The dining rooms are decorated with aged-wood beams and paneling, Art Nouveau lighting fixtures, and stained-glass and leaded windows. The food is excellent, including foie gras with truffles, *choucroute* (sauerkraut), seasonal roebuck with morels, roasted duck with two spices, and fresh trout or Rhine salmon braised in Riesling. The Alsatian wines are sublime.

The refined **Hôtel des Têtes** offers 18 nicely furnished rooms, each with minibar, TV, phone, and hair dryer, and some with Jacuzzi. The rates are 590F to 1,360F (89.70 to 206.70, $85.55 to $197.20) for a double and 1,360F to 1,500F (206.70 to 228, $197.20 to $217.50) for a suite.

In the Hôtel des Têtes, 19 rue des Têtes, 68000 Colmar. ℂ **03-89-24-43-43.** Reservations required. Main courses 92F–150F (14.00– 22.80, $13.35–$21.75); fixed-price menu 269F–355F (40.90– 53.95, $39–$51.50); *menu dégustation* (tasting menu) 350F (53.20, $50.75). AE, DC, MC, V. Sun noon–2pm, Tues–Sat noon–2pm and 7–9:30pm.

NEARBY ACCOMMODATIONS & DINING

Gourmets flock to Illhaeusern, 11 miles from Colmar, east of the N83 highway, for one reason—to dine at the Auberge de l'Ill, one of France's great restaurants. The signs for the restaurant, beside the main highway, are difficult to miss.

Auberge de l'Ill ★★★ MODERN FRENCH   This is the single greatest restaurant in eastern France. Run by the Haeberlin brothers in what used to be their family's 19th-century farmhouse, Auberge de l'Ill combines the finest-quality Alsatian specialties with *cuisine moderne* and classic offerings. You can enjoy your aperitif or coffee under the weeping willows in a beautiful garden, with a river view. Chef Paul Haeberlin takes dishes of Alsatian origin and makes them into *grande cuisine*—eel stewed in Riesling, *matelotes* (small glazed onions) in Riesling, and an inventive foie gras. His partridge, pheasant, and duckling are among the best in Europe. Two unsurpassed choices are his braised slices of pheasant and partridge served with a winey game sauce, chestnuts, wild mushrooms, and Breton cornmeal; and his salmon soufflé. Some dishes require 24-hour notice, so inquire when you make reservations.

You can spend the night at the **Hôtel de Berges** (② 03-89-71-87-87; fax 03-89-71-87-88) in a delightfully furnished, air-conditioned room, overlooking the Ill River. The 11 doubles cost 1,400F to 1,900F (212.80 to 288.80, $203 to $275.50).

Rte. de Collonges, 68970 Illhaeusern. ② 03-89-71-89-00. Fax 03-89-71-82-83. Reservations required, sometimes 6 weeks in advance on summer weekends. Main courses 160F–320F (24.30– 48.65, $23.20–$46.40); fixed-price menu 560F (85.10, $81.20). AE, DC, MC, V. Wed–Sun noon–2pm and 7–9:30pm. Closed Feb.

COLMAR AFTER DARK

Head for the smoky and seductive **Haricot Rouge,** 6 place de la Cathédrale (② 03-89-41-74-13), where rock concerts pull people in especially on Wednesday and Thursday nights, when live music is featured; or the local version of the Hard Rock Cafe known as **Rock Café,** 6 rue des Trois-Epis (② 03-89-24-05-36). Both places attract a cool crowd flaunting a little bit of a rough edge. For a softer atmosphere, try the piano bar **Louisiana Club,** 3A rue Berthe-Molly (② 03-89-24-94-18), where you can groove to authentic blues and jazz. If you can imagine a French version of a country/western bar, mosey on down to the **Country Bar,** 9 rte. d'Ingersheim (② 03-89-41-48-47), with its barnyard dance floor and ample supply of big belt buckles, cowboy boots, and 10-gallon hats.

4 La Route des Crêtes ★★★

From Basel to Mainz, a distance of some 150 miles, the Vosges mountain range stretches along the west side of the Rhine Valley, bearing a similarity to the Black Forest of Germany. Many German and French families spend their summer vacation exploring the Vosges. However, those with less time may want to settle for a quick look at these ancient mountains that once formed the boundary between France and Germany. The Vosges are filled with tall hardwood and fir trees and traversed by a network of twisting roads with hairpin curves. Deep in these mountain forests is the closest that France comes to having a wilderness.

EXPLORING THE AREA

You can explore the mountains by heading west from Strasbourg, but there's a more interesting route from Colmar. From that ancient Alsatian town, you can see some of the highest of the southern Vosges with their remarkable beauty. La Route des Crêtes (Crest Road) begins at **Col du Bonhomme,** to the west of Colmar. It was devised by the French High Command during World War I to carry supplies over the mountainous front. From Col du Bonhomme, you can strike out along this magnificent road, once the object of such bitter fighting but today a series of panoramic vistas, including one of the Black Forest.

By **Col de la Schlucht,** you'll have climbed 4,905 feet. Schlucht is a summer and winter resort, one of the most beautiful spots in the Vosges, with a panoramic view of the Valley of Münster and the slopes of Hohneck. As you skirt the edge of this glacier-carved valley, you'll be in the midst of a land of pine groves with a necklace of lakes. You may want to turn off the main road and go exploring in several directions, the scenery is that tempting. But if you're still on the Crest Road, you can circle **Hohneck,** one of the highest peaks at 5,300 feet, dominating the Wildenstein Dam of the Bresse winter-sports station.

At **Markstein,** you'll come to another pleasant resort. From here, take N430 and then D10 to **Münster,** where the savory cheese is made. You'll go via the Petit-Ballon, a landscape of forest and mountain meadows with lots of grazing cows. Finally, at **Grand-Ballon,** you'll have attained the highest point you can reach by car in the Vosges, 4,662 feet. Get out of your car and go for a walk— if it's a clear day, you'll be able to see the Jura, with the French Alps beyond, and can gaze on a lovely panorama of the Black Forest.

ACCOMMODATIONS & DINING IN MÜNSTER

Au Chêne Voltaire   This chalet-style inn, built in 1939 and renovated many times since, lies in an isolated section of the forest. The modern but no-frills rooms are in a separate building from the rustic core that contains the popular restaurant. The hotel isn't a destination itself; it's just good to keep in mind if you need to rest for the night before pressing on in the morning. Each unit comes with a small, shower-only bathroom. Otherwise, the bedrooms have no amenities except for a phone. You can dine here even if you're not a guest at the hotel.

Rte. du Chêne-Voltaire, at Luttenbach, 68140 Münster. ☎ **03-89-77-31-74.** Fax 03-89-77-45-71. 19 units, 15 with private bathroom. 270F (41.05, $39.15) double without bathroom, 300F (45.60, $43.50) double with bathroom. AE, DC, MC, V. Take D10 less than 1½ miles southwest from the center of Münster.

5 Nancy ★★★

230 miles SE of Paris, 92 miles W of Strasbourg

Nancy, in the northeast corner of France, was the capital of old Lorraine. The city was built around a fortified castle on a rock in the swampland near the Meurthe River. The important canal a few blocks east of the historic center connects the Marne to the Rhine. It once rivaled Paris as the center for Art Nouveau.

The city is serenely beautiful, with a historic tradition, cuisine, and architecture all its own. It has three faces: the medieval alleys and towers around the old Palais Ducal where Charles II received Joan of Arc, the rococo golden gates and fountains, and the dull modern sections with their university and industry.

With a population of 100,000, Nancy remains the hub of commerce and politics in Lorraine. The seat of the third-largest scientific university in France, it's a center of mining, engineering, metallurgy, and finance. Its 30,000 students, who have a passion for *le cool jazz,* keep Nancy jumping at night.

ESSENTIALS

GETTING THERE   **Trains** from Strasbourg arrive every 30 minutes (trip time: 1 hour); trains from Paris's Gare de l'Est pull in about every hour (trip time: 3 hours). For information and schedules, call ✆ **08-36-35-35-35.** If you're **driving** to Nancy from Paris, follow N4 east (trip time: 4 hours).

VISITOR INFORMATION   The **Office de Tourisme** is at place Stanislas (✆ **03-83-35-22-41;** www.ot-nancy.fr).

SPECIAL EVENTS   Serious jazz lovers come to town 2 weeks in October to attend the best-publicized music festival in Nancy, **Jazz Pulsations.** During this period, there is some kind of performance every night around sundown in a tent that's erected in the Parc de la Pépinière, a very short walk from the place Stanislas. Tickets range in price from 100F to 150F (15.20 to   22.80, $14.50 to $21.75). For information and ticket sales, call ✆ **03-83-35-40-86.**

EXPLORING NANCY

The most monumental square in eastern France and the heart of Nancy is **place Stanislas** ★★★, named for Stanislas Leczinski, the last of the ducs de Lorraine, ex-king of Poland, and father-in-law of Louis XV. His 18th-century building programs transformed Nancy into one of Europe's most palatial cities. The square stands between Nancy's two most notable neighborhoods: the **Ville Vieille,** in the medieval core in the northwest, centered around the cathedral, Grande-Rue, and the labyrinth of narrow meandering streets that funnel into it; and the **Ville Neuve,** in the southeast. Built in the 16th and 17th centuries, when streets were laid out in straight lines, Ville Neuve is centered on rue St-Jean.

Place Stanislas was laid out from 1752 to 1760 according to the designs of Emmanuel Héré. Its ironwork gates are magnificent. The square is fabled for the brilliant and fanciful railings, the work of Jean Lamour, a metal worker who achieved a kind of rococo fantasy. His gilded railings with their flowery decorations and crests evoke Versailles. The most imposing building on the square is the **Hôtel de Ville** (town hall); if you ask permission of the security guard at the entrance, you might be allowed into the building's majestic foyer to admire its grandiose inner staircase. It's edged with one of the wrought-iron masterpieces of eastern France, an 80-foot balustrade with a single-piece handrail, the masterpiece of Jean Lamour, who designed the square's screens and fountains. You can also visit the town hall, during July and August only, for a brief nocturnal display of the building's showcase salons. The civic authorities unlock the doors for public visits every evening between 10:30 and 11pm for a fee of 10F (1.50, $1.45). On the square's eastern side is the also-recommended **Musée des Beaux-Arts** (see below).

Arc de Triomphe, constructed by Stanislas from 1754 to 1756 to honor Louis XV, brings you to the place de la Carrière, a tree-lined promenade leading to the **Palais du Gouvernement,** built in 1760. This governmental palace adjoins the **Palais Ducal,** built in 1502 in the Gothic style with Flamboyant balconies.

Église des Cordeliers ★   This church, with a round chapel based on a design for Florence's Medici, contains the burial monuments of the ducs de Lorraine. The most notable are those of René II (1509), attributed to Mansuy Gauvain, and his second wife, Philippa of Gueldres, by Ligier Richier. The octagonal ducal chapel (1607) holds the baroque sarcophagi. The convent houses the

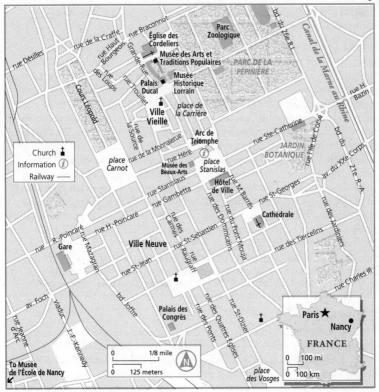

Musée des Arts et Traditions Populaires, which has antiques, porcelain, and reconstructed interiors of regional *maisons*.

66 Grande-Rue. ✆ **03-83-32-18-74.** Admission 20F (3.05, $2.90) adults, 15F (2.30, $2.20) students and children under 12. Combined ticket for the church and the Musée Historique Lorrain, 30F (4.55, $4.35) adults, 20F (3.05, $2.90) students and children. May–Sept Wed–Mon 10am–6pm; Oct–April Wed–Mon 10am–noon and 2–5pm.

Musée de l'École de Nancy ✿ Housed in a stunning turn-of-the-20th-century building is a museum displaying the works of Emile Gallé, the greatest artist of the Nancy style. See Gallé's celebrated "Dawn and Dusk" bed and our favorite, the well-known "mushroom lamp." Works by Eugène Vallin, another outstanding artist, are also on display.

38 rue Sergent-Blandan. ✆ **03-83-40-14-86.** Admission 30F (4.55, $4.35). Mon 2–6pm; Wed–Sun 10:30am–6pm. Guided tours available (in French) Fri, Sat, and Sun at 3pm for 40F (6.10, $5.80) extra.

Musée des Beaux-Arts ✿✿ Built in the 1700s, this is an outstanding regional museum, encompassing the Collection Galilée, works displayed in Paris between 1919 and 1930. It boasts a Manet portrait of the wife of Napoléon III's dentist—remarkable because of its brilliance and intensity, and because Manet portraits are rare. There are also works by Delacroix, Utrillo, Modigliani, Boucher, and Rubens. The Italians, like Perugino, Caravaggio, Ribera, and Tintoretto, are represented as well.

3 place Stanislas. ℂ **03-83-85-30-72.** Admission 35F (5.30, $5.10) adults, 20F (3.05, $2.90) students and children, free for children 12 and under. Wed–Mon 10am–6pm.

Musée Historique Lorrain ★★★ This is one of France's great museums, covering the art and history of the Lorraine region from ancient times. The first floor devotes an entire room to the work of Jacques Callot, the noted engraver who was born in Nancy in 1592. Galerie des Cerfs displays intricately woven tapestries. You'll see a vast collection of 17th-century Lorraine masterpieces by Jacques Beljlange, Jacques Callot, Georges de la Tour, and Claude Deruet, from when the duchy was known as a cultural center. The museum also has a room devoted to eastern France's Jewish history.

Until the Revolution this was a Franciscan convent. Franciscans were known as Cordeliers—hence, the name of the present Flamboyant Gothic church that adjoins the museum. The church is the burial site of the dukes of Lorraine. One of its greatest treasures is a reclining statue of the second wife of Rene II, Philippade Gueldra. In limestone, it is one of Nancy's most stunning examples of portraiture in the Renaissance era. Constructed in 1607, the octagonal Chapel of the dukes used the Medici Chapel in Florence as its role model.

In the Palais Ducal, 64 Grande-Rue. ℂ **03-83-32-18-74.** Admission 20F (3.05, $2.90) adults, 15F (2.30, $2.20) students and children, free for children 12 and under. Combined ticket for the museum and Église des Cordeliers 30F (4.55, $4.35) adults, 20F (3.05, $2.90) students and children. May–Sept Wed–Mon 10am–6pm; Oct–April Wed–Mon 10am–noon and 2–5pm.

SHOPPING

For glitz and glamour, your first stops should be along **rue Gambetta** and **rue des Dominicains,** where boutiques carry the best names in fashion and perfume. Along **rue St-Dizier,** you'll run across more down-to-earth shops selling clothes, shoes, jewelry, and leather goods at more affordable prices. The old town is home to small boutiques that carry antiques, arts and crafts, books, and bric-a-brac, as well as some clothing and jewelry.

For chic women's clothing and accessories, including the finest in handbags and shoes, try **Vanessa,** 14 place St-Epvre (ℂ **03-83-32-85-88**), or **Signatures,** 39 rue St-Jean (ℂ **03-83-32-93-30**). From the sophisticated to the trendy, men of class, or their partners who want them to dress the part, seek out **Alto Stratus,** 34 rue des Dominicains (ℂ **03-83-30-17-33**), and **Ecce Homo,** 2 bis rue d'Amerval (ℂ **03-83-32-12-82**).

Many of Nancy's antiques shops specialize in Art Nouveau. Visit **Jean Claude Jantzen,** 13 rue Stanislas (ℂ **03-83-35-20-79**), for the best pieces. If you'd like a more modern objet d'art, consider **Galerie Ovadia,** 14 Grande-Rue (ℂ **03-83-37-93-32**), with its offerings by contemporary masters of painting, sculpture, and intensely colorful mixed-media collages; and **Galerie Art International,** 17 rue d'Amerval (ℂ **03-83-35-06-83**), where you can choose from Lalique crystal, brightly colored vases and boxes known as Emaux de Longwy, and an assortment of lamps. **Daum Glassworks Showroom,** place Stanislas (ℂ **03-83-32-14-55**), offers exquisite crystal, especially items of the world-famous transparent-colored *pâté de verre*.

ACCOMMODATIONS

Albert-1er-Astoria Across from the railway station, this well-equipped hotel is run in a businesslike manner. Guests stay here for the price and central location. It offers comfortable if not plush rooms, with angular furniture and shower-only bathrooms. There is also a pleasant garden. Breakfast is the only meal served.

3 rue de l'Armée-Patton, 54000 Nancy. ✆ **03-83-40-31-24.** Fax 03-83-28-47-78. 85 units. 300F–400F (45.60– 60.80, $43.50–$58) double. AE, DC, MC, V. Parking 35F (5.30, $5.10). *In room:* TV.

Grand Hôtel de la Reine ✫✫✫   This is the grandest and most traditional hotel in Nancy. The 18th-century mansion was built simultaneously with the monumental square that contains it, and so prominently in the town's historic framework. The hotel is one of the showplaces of the upscale Concorde chain, operators of such bastions of luxury as Paris's Hôtel de Crillon. The Louis XV–style guest rooms boast draped testers over the comfortable beds, Venetian-style chandeliers, and gilt-framed mirrors. The Stanislas restaurant serves both classic and modern dishes.

2 place Stanislas, 54000 Nancy. ✆ **800/777-4182** in the U.S. and Canada, or 03-83-35-03-01. Fax 03-83-32-86-04. 48 units. 830F–1,600F (126.15– 243.20, $120.35–$232) double; from 2,200F (334.40, $319) suite. AE, DC, MC, V. Parking 80F (12.15, $11.60). **Amenities:** Restaurant, bar; room service; laundry. *In room:* A/C, TV, minibar, hair dryer.

Hôtel Mercure Nancy Centre Thiers ✫✫   Rising above every other building in Nancy, this seven-story hotel caters to both business and leisure travelers. Functional and efficient, with a hardworking staff, it's a top choice for Nancy but lacks the style of the Grand Hôtel de la Reine. The rooms are outfitted in a chain-format style that offers comfort, predictability, and warmth, with firm mattresses and serviceable bathrooms with a combination tub and shower.

11 rue Raymond-Poincaré, 54000 Nancy. ✆ **03-83-39-75-75.** Fax 03-83-32-78-17. 192 units. 595F–655F (90.45– 99.55, $86.30–$95) double; 1,000F (152, $145) suite. AE, DC, MC, V. **Amenities:** Restaurant, bar, room service, baby-sitting, laundry/dry cleaning. *In room:* A/C, TV, minibar, hair dryer.

DINING

The **Hôtel Mercure Nancy Centre Thiers** and **Grand Hôtel de la Reine** (see "Accommodations," above) also have decent restaurants.

Le Capucin Gourmand ✫✫ TRADITIONAL FRENCH   Chef Hervé Fourrière, a veteran of culinary apprenticeships at many of the grandest restaurants in France, is the owner of this gastronomic citadel that's outfitted with many examples of the hand-blown glass that's a trademark of the region. A massive glass chandelier overlooks the otherwise modern setting. Menu items include slices of pan-fried foie gras on a bed of lentils, cream of Canadian lobster soup served with truffle-stuffed ravioli, roasted pigeon in sherry sauce, a quartet of braised saltwater fish served with a confit of vegetables, and red snapper and scallops with finely chopped vegetables.

31 rue Gambetta. ✆ **03-83-35-26-98.** Reservations required. Main courses 95F–140F (14.45– 21.30, $13.80–$20.30); fixed-price menu 260F–340F (39.50– 51.70, $37.70–$49.30). AE, MC, V. Tues–Sun noon–2pm; Tues–Sat 7:30–10pm. Closed 2 weeks in Feb.

Les Pissenlits (The Dandelions) *Value* TRADITIONAL FRENCH   At this cost-conscious brasserie, the food is simple but flavorful and artfully prepared. Chef Jean-Luc Mengin's specialties are likely to include a matelot of freshwater zander with shallots; a dandelion salad with bacon and a creamy vinaigrette; aiguillettes of duckling with a spice-flavored honey sauce; and a traditional Alsatian stew. The chef's wife, Danièle, is one of the few fully accredited female wine stewards in France. The dining room is filled with Art Nouveau antiques, many of them crafted in Nancy.

27 rue des Ponts. (C) **03-83-37-43-97.** Reservations recommended. Main courses 52F–105F (7.90–15.95, $7.55–$15.25); fixed-price menu 102F–149F (15.50– 22.65, $14.80–$21.60). MC, V. Tues–Sat 11:45am–2pm and 7:15–11:30pm.

Restaurant Le Foy TRADITIONAL FRENCH This restaurant occupies the second floor of a building that's part of the 18th-century borders of place Stanislas. Outfitted with exposed timbers and Louis XIII furnishings, it sits above, but is independent of, a simple street-level brasserie (Café Foy) that serves less appealing food. The menu is a stylish roster of dishes such as roasted rabbit with violet-flavored mustard sauce, foie gras (a specialty of the house), crispy duck with braised cabbage, blanquette of lobster, and a local freshwater fish baked in a potato crust. Try a dessert that's unusual and heavenly: honey mousse cake prepared with brandy.

1 place Stanislas. (C) **03-83-32-21-44.** Reservations recommended. Main courses 85F–130F (12.90–19.75, $12.35–$18.85); fixed-price menu 120F–320F (18.25– 48.65, $17.40–$46.40). AE, MC, V. Thurs–Tues noon–2pm, Mon and Thurs–Sat 7–9:30pm. Closed Feb 15–Mar 10 and July 15–Aug 9.

NANCY AFTER DARK

As night approaches, most of the student population heads to the old town. **Le Blue Note,** 3 rue des Michottes ((C) **03-83-30-31-18**), has a room for weekly rock performances, a piano bar, a fireplace room with comfy armchairs, and an upbeat and rowdy beer hall. A cover of 60F (9.10, $8.70) is charged on concert nights. For a pub experience, go to the **Be Happy Bar,** 23 rue Gustave-Simon ((C) **03-83-35-56-41**), with 12 brands of beer on tap. It's got an English flavor and is full of characters playing games and guzzling beer into the night.

Nancy's most popular dance clubs are **Les Caves du Roi,** 9 place Stanislas ((C) **03-83-35-24-14**), with its techno crowd flailing around in the chrome-and-metallic space, and the wine-cellar-turned-rock-club called **Métro,** 1 rue du Général-Hoche ((C) **03-83-40-25-13**). Covers at these clubs range from 20F to 50F (3.05 to 7.60, $2.90 to $7.25), depending on the night and entertainment.

6 Domrémy-la-Pucelle

275 miles SE of Paris, 6½ miles NW of Neufchâteau

A pilgrimage center attracting tourists from all over the world, Domrémy is a plain village that would have slumbered in obscurity except for the fact that Joan of Arc was born here in 1412. Here she heard the voices and saw the visions that led her to play out her historic role as the heroine of France.

A residence traditionally considered her family's house, near the church, is known as **Maison Natale de Jeanne d'Arc,** 2 rue de la Basilique ((C) **03-29-06-95-86**). Here you can see the chamber where she was born. A museum beside the house shows a film depicting St. Joan's life. The house is open Wednesday through Monday: April to September from 9am to noon and 1:30 to 6pm; and October to March from 9:30am to noon and 2 to 5pm. Admission is 20F (3.05, $2.90) for adults, 10F (1.50, $1.45) for children 6 to 10, and free for children under 6.

Adjacent to the museum, on rue Principale, is **Église St-Rémi,** a much-reconstructed building whose 12th-century origins have mostly been masked by more recent repairs. All that remains from the age of Joan of Arc is a baptismal font and some stonework. Above the village, on a slope of the Bois-Chenu, is a monument steeped in French nationalism, the **Basilique du Bois-Chenu,** which was begun in 1881 and consecrated in 1926.

ESSENTIALS

GETTING THERE   If you're **driving** here, take N4 southeast of Paris to Toul, and from there, A31 south toward Neufchâteau/Charmes. Then take N74 southwest (signposted in the direction of Neufchâteau). At Neufchâteau, follow D164 northwest to Coussey. From here, take D53 into Domrémy.

There is no railway station in Domrémy—you must take one of four **trains** daily going to either Nancy or Toul, where bus and rail connections can be made to Neufchâteau. From here, there are three **buses** running daily to Domrémy. A one-way ticket costs 16F (2.45, $2.30). For bus information, call **Autocars Cariane** (✆ **03-29-94-15-54**). You can also take a **taxi** (✆ **03-29-06-12-13**) for about 100F (15.20, $14.50).

7 Verdun ⋆⋆

162 miles E of Paris, 41 miles W of Metz

Built on both banks of the Meuse and intersected by a series of canals, Verdun has an old section, the Ville Haute on the east bank, which includes the cathedral and episcopal palace. Today, stone houses on narrow cobblestone streets give Verdun a medieval appearance. However, most visitors come to see the famous World War I battlefields, 2 miles east of the town, off N3 toward Metz.

ESSENTIALS

GETTING THERE   Four or five **trains** (sometimes fewer) arrive daily from Paris's Gare de l'Est; you'll have to change at Châlons-en-Champagne. Several daily trains also arrive from Metz, after a change at Conflans. For train information and schedules, call ✆ **08-36-35-35-35. Driving** is easy, since Verdun is several miles north of the Paris-Strasbourg autoroute (A4).

VISITOR INFORMATION   The **Office de Tourisme** is on place de la Nation (✆ **03-29-86-14-18;** verduntourisme@wanadoo.fr). It's closed on bank holidays.

TOURING THE BATTLEFIELDS

At this garrison town in eastern France, Maréchal Pétain said, "They shall not pass!" And they didn't. Verdun is where the Allies held out against a massive assault by the German army in World War I. Near the end of the war, 600,000 to 800,000 French and German soldiers died battling over a few miles along the muddy Meuse between Paris and the Rhine. Two monuments commemorate these tragic events: Rodin's *Defense* and Boucher's *To Victory and the Dead.*

A tour of the battlefields is called the ***Circuit des Forts,*** covering the main fortifications. On the Meuse's right bank, this is a 20-mile run, taking in **Fort Vaux,** where Raynal staged a heroic defense after sending his last message by carrier pigeon. After passing a **French cemetery** of 16,000 graves, an endless field of crosses, you arrive at the **Ossuaire de Douaumont,** where the bones of those literally blown to bits were embedded. Nearby at the mostly underground **Fort de Douaumont,** the "hell of Verdun" was unleashed. From the roof you can look out at a vast field of corroded tops of "pillboxes." Then you proceed to the **Tranchée des Bäionettes** (Trench of Bayonets). Bayonets of French soldiers entombed by a shell burst from this unique memorial.

Within a few paces of the Tranchée des Bäionettes, you'll see the dignified premises of the **Mémorial de Verdun** (built around 1967), Fleury Devant Douaumont (✆ **03-29-84-35-34**), a museum that commemorates the weapons, uniforms, photographs, and geography of one of the most painful and bloody battles of World War I. From April to mid-September, it's open daily from 9am to 6pm. From February to March and again from mid-September to mid-December, it's open daily from 9am to noon and 2 to 6pm. It's closed the rest of the year. Entrance is 30F (4.55, $4.35) for adults and students; 15F (2.330, $2.20) children 11 to 16, and free for children under 11.

The other tour, *Circuit Rive Gauche,* is about a 60-mile run and takes in the **Butte de Montfaucon,** a hill on which Americans erected a memorial tower, and the **Cimetière Américain at Romagne,** with some 15,000 graves.

Because of inadequate public transportation, only visitors with cars should attempt to make these circuits.

ACCOMMODATIONS & DINING

Château des Monthairons ★★   This hotel, operated by the Thouvenin family, occupies an 1857 château crafted of blocks of pale stone. Bedrooms come in a variety of shapes and sizes. All of them, are fitted with luxury mattresses and quality linens. Bathrooms boast generous shelf space and a combination tub and shower. On the property are a pair of 15th-century chapels, a nesting ground for herons, and opportunities for canoeing and fishing.

Rte. D34, 55320 Dieue-sur-Meuse. ✆ 03-29-87-78-55. Fax 03-29-87-73-49. www.chateaudesmonthairons. fr. 20 units. 450F–1,090F (68.40– 165.70, $65.25–$158.05) double. AE, DC, MC, V. Drive 7½ miles south of Verdun on D334. **Amenities:** Restaurant, bar; room service; laundry. *In room:* TV, minibar, hair dryer.

Le Coq Hardi ★★   This is our favorite hotel in town, composed of four connected 18th-century houses near the Meuse. The interior contains church pews, antiques, and a Renaissance fireplace. Most of the well-maintained bedrooms have been decorated in regional style. Each has a comfortable mattress and an efficient but small shower-only bathroom.

The best food in town is served in the dining room, which has a painted ceiling, Louis XIII chairs, and two deactivated World War I bombshells at its entrance. Specialties are *salade Coq Hardi* with green mustard and pine nuts, Challons duck, cassolette of snails in champagne, and preparations of foie gras.

8 av. de la Victoire, 55100 Verdun. ✆ 03-29-86-36-36. Fax 03-29-86-09-21. www.coq-hardi.com. 35 units. 470F–790F (71.45– 120.10, $68.15–$114.55) double; from 1,200F (182.40, $174) suite. AE, MC, V. Parking 70F (10.65, $10.15). **Amenities:** Restaurant, bar; room service; laundry. *In room:* TV.

12

Burgundy

Vineyard castles and ancient churches mark the landscape of Burgundy, which is the land of the good life for those who savor fine cuisine and wines in historic surroundings. Burgundy was once a powerful independent province, its famed Valois dukes spreading their might across all of Europe from 1363 to 1477. In preserving its independence, Burgundy weathered many struggles, notably under Charles the Bold, who was always in conflict with Louis XI. When Charles died in 1477, Louis invaded and annexed the duchy. Nonetheless, the Habsburgs still maintained their claims to it. Even after its reunion with France, Burgundy suffered many more upheavals, including its ravaging during the Franco-Spanish wars beginning in 1636. Peace did not finally come to the region until 1678.

At the time of the Revolution, Burgundy disappeared as a political entity, and was subdivided into the *départements* of France, Yonne, Saône-et-Loire, and Côte-d'Or. The ducs de Bourgogne are but a memory, but they left a legacy of vintage red and white wines to please and excite the palate. The major wine-growing regions of Burgundy are Chablis, Côte de Nuits, Côte de Beaune, Côte de Chalon, Mâconnais, and Nivernais.

REGIONAL CUISINE For centuries the cuisine of Burgundy has been appreciated for the freshness and variety of its ingredients and the skill and finesse of its chefs. Many Roman historians, Charles VI, Escoffier, and Brillat-Savarin (who was born in the Burgundian town of Bugey) have praised the food and wine of Burgundy. There's something about the mild climate, rainfall, and nutrient-rich soil that produces some of the best beef (especially of the Charolais breed), mushrooms, grapes, fish, wild game, snails, fruit, and vegetables in Europe. The cuisine seems to have been invented for healthy appetites, and a typical Bourguignonne has been defined as someone who's both a gourmet and a gourmand.

Any sauce created with a dose of wine added to it (at least in Burgundy) is called *une meurette,* and you'll see lots listed as accompaniments to main courses on menus. These meurettes, whether bound with butter and flour or spiced with quantities of herbs and (occasionally) the blood of the slaughtered animal, are very flavorful and seem to make whatever wine you happen to be drinking taste even better. In the same vein, any cut of meat prepared *à la bourguignonne* is usually braised and served with a sauce made from wine (usually red), onions, mushrooms, and (except if it's served with fish) lardons.

One specialty is a succulent species of snail, cooked in the shell and flavored with garlic and butter. Other recipes handed down for generations are *coq au vin* (chicken with red wine, brandy, pulverized chicken livers, and blood) and chicken or ham cooked *en sauce* (made traditionally with white wine and cream) or *au sang* (with blood sauce, lard, and baby onions).

The region also produces fine cheese, sold in wine bars across Europe. Most visible is the goat cheese *crottin de chavignol,* made in Sancerre along with the superb white wine of the same name. The cheese and wine accompany each other splendidly. The blue-veined Gex has a flavor similar to Roquefort. All of the Epoisses cheeses are made in the Yonne valley.

Almost everyone appreciates the flavor of Dijon mustard, called the "king of French condiments." Any menu item followed by the adjective *dijonnaise* will have a sauce containing a liberal dose of that mustard. It's estimated that Dijon produces nearly three quarters of the mustard consumed in France.

And, of course, there are Burgundy's wines. Consisting of only 2% of all the wines produced in France (only one third the production of all the wines of Bordeaux), they include vintages sought the world over. The best are from the Côte d'Or, a narrow strip of gravel-studded soil usually divided into family-owned plots of fewer than 40 acres, which lies between Dijon and Santenay. In the Côte d'Or, the two major categories are the Côte de Nuits and the Côte de Beaune. Other burgundy categories are Gevrey-Chambertin, Chambolle-Musigny, Nuits-St-Georges, Beaune, Meursault, Chassagne-Montrachet, Santenay, and Pommard.

EXPLORING THE REGION BY CAR

Burgundy is perhaps the finest region in France to tour by car. Here's a suggested way to link together the best of the region.

Day 1 Begin at Burgundy's northwestern edge, in **Chablis.** Vineyards surround Chablis, the capital of Basse Bourgogne (Lower Burgundy). The town is more famous for its wine than for its monuments, but contains two interesting churches: the 12th-century Église St-Martin and the Église St-Pierre, which retains little of its Romanesque design. Chablis is not worth an overnight stop, though 9 miles to the east along D965, in the hamlet of **Tonnere,** is one of the best restaurants in the province: **Saint-Père,** 2 av. G. Pompidon (© **03-86-55-12-84**). It's open daily for lunch and dinner, but most visitors prefer it as a lunch stopover. Lunch costs 74F to 230F (11.25 to 34.95, $10.75 to $33.35) and dinner, 124F (18.85, $18.03). After a meal, backtrack about 15 miles east along D965 (passing through Chablis en route) to **Auxerre.**

Scene of many pivotal moments in French history, Auxerre is the site of one of France's most impressive churches, the Gothic **Cathédrale St-Etienne.** If you're looking for truly fine dining, drive north 17 miles to the hamlet of **Joigny** for **À la Côte St-Jacques** (see section 1, "Auxerre," later in this chapter). Return to Auxerre for the night or stay over in Joigny if you wish.

Day 2 Drive south from Auxerre along N151 and then east on D951 to the hamlet of **Vézelay**—if there's any Romanesque church in France that's a must-see, it's here. Marvel at the majesty of a pilgrimage site consecrated to Mary Magdalene. Ordinances encourage you to park at the bottom of the village and climb the cobblestone main street. A luxurious ending to your day is at the base of the hill on which the famous church sits: **L'Espérance** ★★★ St-Père-sous-Vézelay (© **03-86-33-39-10;** see "Dining," below), is

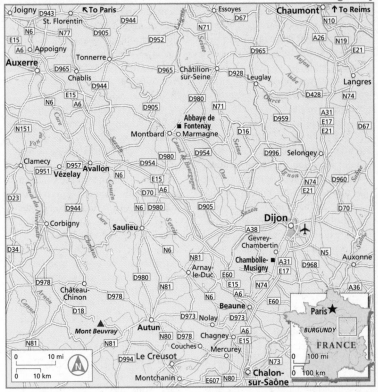

one of the best restaurants in the world. It's closed all day Tuesday and Wednesday at lunch, so you may want to plan your itinerary accordingly.

You can spend the night in Vézelay, driving 6 miles east on D957 to the town of **Avallon,** or continue south for 35 miles on well-signposted country roads to **Château-Chinon.** Wherever you spend the night, plan on an early departure the following day.

Day 3 From Château-Chinon, drive east 20 miles on D978 to visit one of the oldest towns in France, **Autun.** En route, you might wish to take the following detour: heading east on D978 toward Autun, turn right (south) at the town of Arleuf, going right onto D500. At a

fork, turn right to Glux and then follow the arrows to Mont Beuvray via D18. You reach the summit through D274. After 2 miles of climbing you'll be at **Oppidum of Bibracte,** home of the Eduens, a Gallic tribe. At this altitude of 2,800 feet, Vercingetorix organized the Gauls to fight Caesar's legions in A.D. 52. From here you'll have a splendid view of Autun and Mont St-Vincent. If the weather is clear, you can see the Jura and Mont Blanc. Leave Mont Beuvray via D274 and continue northeast to Autun.

At Autun, you'll find a historic town with ruins left by the ancient Romans, as well as a cathedral built in 1120 to hold the remains of St. Lazarus. Spend the night here.

Day 4 Start your day early, prepared for tours of various châteaux, fortresses, vineyards, and other historic sites. Your route will be loaded with appealing detours, so be as flexible as possible as you negotiate your way through a labyrinth of well-marked country roads leading toward Beaune.

Leave Autun on D973 east. After 6 miles, turn left onto D326 toward Sully. Here you'll find the **Château de Sully,** once known as the Fontainebleau of Burgundy; it's closed to the public, but a view from the outside might satisfy you. The gardens are open from Easter to September, daily from 8am to 6pm. Leave Sully, following signs to the small village of Nolay. Three miles past Nolay, you'll reach the **Château de La Rochepot** (☎ 03-80-21-71-37), a medieval-style fortress built during the Renaissance. It's open daily: April 1 to June 30 from 10 to 11:30am and 2 to 5:30pm; July to August from 10am to noon and 2 to 6pm; September from 10 to 11:30am and 2 to 5:30pm; and October from 10 to 11:30am and 2 to 4:30pm. Closed November to March. Admission is 34F (5.15, $4.95) for adults, 16F (2.45, $2.30) for children, free for children 12 and under.

Now head toward **Beaune** on D973, passing near some of the best-known **vineyards:** Chassagne-Montrachet, Puligny-Montrachet, Meursault, Auxey Duresses, Volnay, and Pommard. En route, stop at a restaurant whose setting is as interesting as its food. **Chagny,** 27 miles east of Autun and 11 miles southwest of Beaune, rarely attracts sightseers; gourmands from all over stop for a meal at **Lameloise,** 36 place d'Armes (☎ 03-85-87-65-65). It offers choices like lamb filet in a rice crêpe, Bresse pigeon, hot lemon

soufflé, and one of the broadest spectrums of burgundies in France. Reservations are required. Closed all day Wednesday and Thursday at lunch. Fixed-price menus cost 420F to 650F (63.85 to 98.80, $60.90 to $94.25).

Continue north to Beaune on D973, which will change to N74. You'll pass villages like Aloxe-Corton (where Charlemagne owned vineyards), and Comblanchien. In Vougeot, you can visit the **Château du Clos-de-Vougeot** (☎ 03-80-62-86-09), surrounded by France's most celebrated vineyards. The Renaissance château is associated with the Brotherhood of the Knights of Tastevin, revived in 1934 along medieval lines; it maintains a 12th-century cellar, open for visits April to September, daily from 9am to 7pm, and off-season, daily from 9 to 11:30am and 2 to 5pm. Admission is 20F (3.05, $2.90).

Resume north on N74, then branch off onto D122, which will take you through the hamlet of Chambolle Musigny, then to Morey St-Denis and the site of your overnight stay, **Gevrey-Chambertin.** It marks the beginning of the Côte de Nuits district, source of some of the world's most prestigious wines. Our favorite lodgings are **Arts et Terroirs** (☎ 03-80-3 4-30-76) and **Hôtel Les Grands Crus** (☎ 03-80-34-34-15), both of which rent simple rooms for about 620F(93, $90). For dinner, try **La Rôtisserie du Chambertin,** on Rue Chambertin (☎ 03-80- 34-33-20), for regional classics like *coq au vin,* or **Les Millésimes** ★★★, 25 rue de l'Église, at rue de Meixville (☎ 03-80-51-84-24), for a special night out, especially if you're a wine connoisseur.

Days 5 to 8 Continue north the short distance to **Dijon,** home to some of the region's spectacular architecture. Use Dijon as your base for several interesting side trips.

SIDE TRIPS FROM DIJON

Leave Dijon on A38 northwest toward Paris. You'll be traveling along a good road in the Vallée de l'Ouche, alongside the Burgundy Canal. At pont de Pany, on the outskirts of Sombernon, exit onto a local highway (D905) and continue northwest. On your left lies the artificial lake of Grosbois. The scenery is typical of agricultural France, with isolated farms, woods, and pastures.

Pass through Vitteaux; just before the next village, Posanges, stands a feudal château. You can't visit it, but it's worth a picture. Continue on D905 for a few miles until you come to a railroad crossing. On your left is another old castle, now part of a private farm. The next village you reach along D905 is Pouillenay. Follow the signs for a short detour to the hamlet of **Flavigny-sur-Ozerain.** Park your car outside the walls and walk through the old streets.

Leave Flavigny and follow the signs for a few miles on country roads to **Alise-Ste-Reine,** the site of the camp of Alesia, where Caesar wiped out a concentration of Gallic soldiers. Here, Millet sculpted a statue of Vercingetorix. You can explore the excavated ruins of a Roman-Gallic town and visit the **Musée Alesia,** rue de l'Hôpital (② **03-80- 96-10-95**); it's open June 30 to September 3, daily from 9am to 7pm; March 25 to June 30 and September 8 to November 5, daily from 10am to 6pm (closed November 5 to March 20). Admission is 28F (4.25, $4.05) for adults and 18F (2.75, $2.60) for students and children; children 6 and under are free. Alise-Ste-Reine honors a Christian girl decapitated for

refusing to marry a Roman governor, Olibrius. As late as the 17th century, a fountain at the site was said to have curative powers.

After Alise-Ste-Reine, you can head back to the village of Les Laumes, a railroad center. Before entering the village, make a U-turn to the right and take N454 to Baigneux-les-Juifs. After the village of Grésigny, on your left is a farm-fortress surrounded by water.

One mile farther, turn right toward the **Château de Bussy-Rabutin.** Roger de Rabutin, cousin of Mme de Sévigné, ridiculed Louis XIV's court, for which he spent 6 years in the Bastille. The château, with two round towers, has survived mostly intact, including the interior. The gardens and park are attributed to Le Nôtre. It's open Wednesday through Monday: April to September from 9am to noon and 2 to 6pm, and October to March from 10am to noon and 2 to 5pm. Admission is 10F (1.50, $1.45)

Going back to Grésigny, turn right before the farm-fortress, then go left. Outside the village, turn right toward Menetreux Le Pitois. You're off the main road and into the real countryside. Once back on D905, head on to **Montbard,** hometown of George-Louis Leclerc, comte de Buffon, one of the 18th century's great naturalists and author of *L'Histoire naturelle,* a 44-volume encyclopedia. The scientist's home is open, as well as a mini-museum of his life and work. The town is also the site of a hotel/restaurant, the **Hôtel de l'Ecu,** 7 rue Auguste-Carré (② **03-80-92-11-66**), where moderately priced meals are prepared in what was a postal relay station in the 1700s.

Continue east 6 miles to Marmagne, then turn left on D32 and head toward the **Abbaye de Fonte-nay** (© **03-80-92-15-00**). Isolated in a valley, Fontenay is one of Europe's most unspoiled 12th-century Cistercian abbeys. It was named as a World Heritage Site by UNESCO in 1981 and is open daily from 10am to noon and 2 to 6pm (to 5pm in winter). Admission is 47F (7.15, $6.80) for adults and 24F (3.65, $3.50) for children and students, children 6 and under free.

1 Auxerre 🟊 🟊

103 miles SE of Paris, 92 miles NW of Dijon

Auxerre was founded by the Gauls and enlarged by the Romans. Set on a hill overlooking the Yonne River, it's the capital of Lower Burgundy and the center of vineyards, some of which produce chablis. Joan of Arc spent several days here in 1429. Napoléon met Maréchal Ney on March 17, 1815, on the former emperor's return from Elba. Louis XVIII had sent Ney to stop Napoléon, but Ney embraced him and turned his army against the king. For that, Ney was later shot.

The city is a sleepy kind of place, as you'll see if you spend an afternoon with the Auxerrois reading a newspaper in a cafe. Its population of 42,000 will admit not a lot is happens around here these days—and that's how they like it.

ESSENTIALS

GETTING THERE   Visitors often **drive** here, since Auxerre is near A6/E1 (Autoroute du Soleil). Many of the **trains** going between Paris and Lyon stop at Auxerre. There are 12 trains per day from Paris and nine from Lyon; trip time is 2 hours from either. For train information and schedules, call © **08-36-35-35-35**.

VISITOR INFORMATION   The **Office de Tourisme** is at 1–2 quai de la République (© **03-86-52-06-19**; www.auxerre.com).

EXPLORING THE CATHEDRAL

The railway station lies at the eastern edge of town, about a mile from the historic center. Most of Auxerre is on the opposite (western) bank of the Yonne River. Its heart is between place du Maréchal-Leclerc (where you'll find the Hôtel de Ville) and the Cathédrale St-Etienne.

Cathédrale St-Etienne 🟊 🟊   Pay a visit to the Flamboyant Gothic Cathédrale St-Etienne, begun in the 13th century but not completed until the 16th. The front facade is remarkable, with sculptured portals. The stained glass, some of it original, is famous. In the crypt, which is all that remains of the Romanesque church that stood on this site, you can see 11th-century frescoes.

Every Sunday in July and August, you can attend an organ concert from 5 to 6pm; admission is free. And daily, June through August from 10 to 11:10pm and September from 9:30 to 10:40pm, there's a sound-and-light show depicting the history of the church. It's presented in English, French, and German for 35F (5.30, $5.10) for adults, free for children under 14.

© **03-86-52-23-29**. Free admission to church. Admission to crypt and museum 25F (3.80, $3.65). Daily 9am–6pm.

ACCOMMODATIONS

Hôtel Le Maxime   This family-run hotel contains attractive rooms, many with views of the river or the old city. Most retain their original wall and ceiling beams. Built as a private villa in 1850, and functioning as a hotel since 1900, this is a gracious, high-ceilinged, old-fashioned inn despite a thorough renovation that upgraded the rooms in 2000. All the bathrooms come with combination tub and shower. You can take breakfast in your room or in the quiet salon, amid Oriental rugs, polished paneling, and a sense of the gentility of an earlier era.

2 quai de la Marine, 89000 Auxerre. ✆ **03-86-52-14-19.** Fax 03-86-52-21-70. www.auxerre.com. 25 units. 470F–650F (71.45– 98.80, $68.15–$94.25) double. AE, DC, MC, V. Parking 20F (3.05, $2.90). **Amenities:** Two restaurants, bar; laundry/dry cleaning. *In room:* TV, minibar, hair dryer.

Inter Hôtel Normandie   This centrally located hotel (ca. 1960) offers traditional hospitality, combining antique furnishings with modern amenities. The tranquil and comfortably furnished rooms open onto garden views; each unit is different. Bathrooms come with showers only; some also have tubs.

41 bd. Vauban, 89000 Auxerre. ✆ **03-86-52-57-80.** Fax 03-86-51-54-33. www.acom.fr/normandie. 47 units. 330F–470F (50.15– 71.45, $47.85–$68.15) double. AE, DC, MC, V. Parking 30F (4.55, $4.35). **Amenities:** Small gym; room service. *In room:* TV, hair dryer.

Le Parc des Maréchaux ★★   A gem that outshines the competition, this was a private Napoléon III–style residence in the 19th century, set in its own 1-acre park. It's the most secluded choice in the area: on the western outskirts of town, surrounded by century-old trees. Decor of the public areas and the lounge is French Empire; the style of the bedrooms is less coherent, with a mixture of contemporary and Empire predominating. Each room comes with a combination tub and shower. The only meal offered is breakfast, though a limited roster of hot food can be served, on special request, in your bedroom or in one of the salons.

6 av. Foch, 89000 Auxerre. ✆ **03-86-51-43-77.** Fax 03-86-51-31-72. 25 units. 495F–575F (75.25– 87.40, $71.80–$83.40) double; 600F–650F (91.20– 98.80, $87–$94.25) triple or quad. AE, DC, MC, V. **Amenities:** Room service; laundry. *In room:* TV, minibar.

DINING

Le Jardin Gourmand ★★ FRENCH   The most sophisticated and charming restaurant in town specializes in *cuisine moderne du marché*, employing the freshest ingredients to create artfully presented menu items that change, often radically, eight times a year. The setting is an antique house located a 10-minute walk from the cathedral. In summer, an awning shades an outdoor terrace. Pierre Boussereau and Olivier Laplaine are devoted to cultivating fresh salad greens and herbs from their own garden, used to garnish such platters as a carpaccio of duck liver with *cornes de cerf* (stag's horn) and *pourpier d'Asie* (Asian purple-leaf). Other dishes might include a steak of calf's liver served with a thickened veal stock and fresh cardamon, rack of lamb with cinnamon and endive, roasted scallops served with the essence of pulverized pea pods, and red mullet with a sauce made from thickened fish stock and star anise.

56 bd. Vauban. ✆ **03-86-51-53-52.** Reservations required. Main courses 90F–170F (13.70– 25.85, $13.05–$24.65); fixed-price menus 180F (27.35, $26.10) lunch (except Sun), 250F–290F (38– 44.10, $36.25–$42.05) dinner. AE, MC, V. Thurs–Mon noon–2pm and 7:30–9:30pm. Closed 2 weeks in late Mar and 3 weeks in Nov.

NEARBY ACCOMMODATIONS & DINING

A la Côte St-Jacques ★★★ FRENCH   This top-echelon Relais & Châteaux property was massively upgraded in 2000. The 300-year-old foundation and 19th-century design contribute to the atmosphere in one of the region's most

Colette: An Unlikely Literary Heroine

"C'est Colette! C'est un miracle!"

That's what her fans had to say, and Colette's fans included the poet Stephen Koch (he claimed that she was the only writer who got it right when writing about sex), Proust, Updike, Woolf, Gide, and her beloved friend Cocteau. Auden compared her favorably to Tolstoy.

Born in 1873 to a one-legged, once-bankrupt tax collector from Provence and raised in the Burgundian village of St-Sauveur-en-Puisaye, Sidonie Gabrielle Colette was an unlikely literary heroine. As a school-girl, Colette fell for a would-be writer twice her age—known as Willy, pseudonym of Henri Gauthier-Villars—and married him at age 20. He exposed her to the world of Paris society and imposed a rigid writing discipline, locking her in a room until she finished a designated number of pages. Those pages were eventually compiled into four novellas known as the *Claudine* series. Published at yearly intervals between 1900 and 1903 under her husband's pseudonym, each was based on the experiences of a *libertine ingenue*, with an acute preoccupation for evoking the sounds, tastes, textures, colors, and interactions of that era's beautiful people. They began to explore a theme that Colette returned to again and again, with exquisite sensitivity: the pleasures and pains of love, permeated with a mix of naïveté and cunning.

In 1910, she divorced Willy and became a vaudeville entertainer in a Paris music hall. Later that year she was writing for *Le Matin,* whose editor was Henri de Jouvenel, whom she married in 1912. That partnership produced a daughter, Colette de Jouvenel (or *Bel Gazou,* "beautiful warbler," as her mother called her), and lasted until 1925. Then Colette met and married her third and final husband, Maurice Goudeket.

Two of Colette's most enduring works are *Chéri* (1920), the story of a youthful survivor of World War I who initiates a love affair with an older woman, and *Gigi* (1945), about a young girl reared to become a Parisian courtesan by two sophisticated and aging sisters. This work gained more popularity when Hollywood made it into a musical starring Leslie Caron and Louis Jourdan in 1958.

The former country girl's official awards eventually included membership in the Belgian Royal Academy (1935), France's Académie

luxurious hotels and restaurants. In addition to the main building, there's an annex across the road that's connected via an underground tunnel fashioned from rocks salvaged from old buildings. In one of the dining rooms that has welcomed such stars as Catherine Deneuve, you can enjoy specialties like a terrine of Brittany oysters, smoked sea bass served with Servruga caviar, Bresse chicken steamed in champagne, and turbot cooked in salt crust, served with a creamy medley of leeks and peas and an emulsion of liquefied bitter almonds.

The hotel rents 32 rooms, priced at 790F to 2,850F (120.10 to 433.20, $114.55 to $413.25) depending on size and views over the river. Each has a bathroom, TV, phone, minibar, and conservatively contemporary decor; half have air-conditioning. On the premises are a heated indoor pool and sauna.

Goncourt (elected a member in 1945, elected president in 1949), and the French Légion d'Honneur (elected a member in 1920, elected Grand Officer in 1953)—honors that until then had rarely been granted to women.

Literary fans around the world mourned the passing of Colette in 1954. In Paris, they shouted "Gigi!" or "Chéri!" as her body traveled from an elaborate ceremony in the courtyard of the Palais Royal to the Cimetière du Père-Lachaise, to be buried near Oscar Wilde and other literary icons.

Today, you can pay homage to Colette by journeying to the village of St-Sauveur-en-Puisaye, where you can visit the **Musée Colette** (© 03-86-45-61-95). It's open April to October, Wednesday through Monday from 10am to 6pm; November to March, Saturday and Sunday from 2 to 6pm. Admission is 28F (4.25, $4.05) for adults and 10F (1.50, $1.45) for students and children, children 6 and under free.

Colette fans from around the world—led by her daughter and only child—helped establish the museum. Her daughter died in 1981, before the shrine opened in 1995. Photographs in the museum serve as a guidebook to Colette's life. Pictured are Colette with her trio of husbands and even her lesbian lover, the marquise de Belboeuf. One depicts her going up in a balloon over Paris for *Le Matin*. She's seen with many of the leading legends of her day, including Sarah Bernhardt.

One room is a trompe-l'oeil copy of Colette's apartment in the Palais Royal (not open to the public) in Paris. You can also watch a 50-minute 1951 film of Colette in which she appears with Cocteau.

What comes as a surprise is that at a tearoom here you can order, among other items, *fra*, that salt cheese tart so beloved by Colette. Her other favorite Burgundian pastries are made fresh daily, including a pastry called *gâteau à six cornes* culled from a recipe of Colette's.

To reach the village, take the Autoroute du Soleil (A6) south from Paris toward Lyon, but exit at Joigny. Follow the signs for Toucy, where you go in the direction of Orléans-St-Fargeau. At the Toucy exit, St-Sauveur-en-Puisayne is signposted. If you're already in Auxerre, take D965 to Toucy.

14 Faubourg de Paris (N6), 89300 Joigny. © 03-86-62-09-70. Fax 03-86-91-49-70. Reservations required. Main courses 170F–480F (25.85– 72.95, $24.65–$69.60); fixed-price menus 390F–600F (59.33– 91.20, $56.55–$870) lunch, 820F–900F (124.65– 136.80, $118.90–$130.50) dinner. AE, DC, MC, V. Daily 12:15–2:45pm and 7:15–9:45pm. From Auxerre, head north on N6 (toward Sens) for 17 miles.

2 Vézelay ★★

135 miles SE of Paris, 32 miles S of Auxerre

Vézelay, a living museum of French antiquity, stands frozen in time. For many, the town is the high point of their trip through Burgundy. Because it contained what was believed to be the tomb of St. Mary Magdalene, that "beloved and pardoned sinner," it was one of the great pilgrimage sites of the Christian world.

Today, the medieval charm of Vézelay is widely known throughout France, and the town is virtually overrun with visitors in summer. The hordes are especially thick on July 22, the official day of homage to La Madeleine.

ESSENTIALS

GETTING THERE If you're **driving** from Paris, take A6 south to Auxerre, then continue south along N151 to Clamency, turning east along D951 to Vézelay. **Trains** travel from Auxerre to nearby Sermizelles, where a bus makes the run to Vézelay only on Saturday at noon. Then take a taxi for the 15-minute trip. For train information and schedules, call ℰ **08-36-35-35-35.**

VISITOR INFORMATION The **Office de Tourisme** is on rue St-Pierre (ℰ **03-86-33-23-69**), open daily April to September, and Friday through Wednesday from October to March.

EXPLORING THE TOWN

On a hill 360 feet above the countryside, Vézelay is known for its ramparts and houses with sculptured doorways, corbeled staircases, and mullioned windows. The site was an abbey founded by Girart de Roussillon, a comte de Bourgogne (troubadours sang of his exploits). Pope John VIII consecrated it in 878.

On March 31, 1146, St. Bernard preached the Second Crusade here; in 1190, the town was the rendezvous point for the Third Crusade, drawing such personages as Richard the Lion-Hearted and King Philippe-Auguste of France. Later, St. Louis of France came here several times on pilgrimages.

Park outside the town hall and walk through the medieval streets lined with 15th-, 16th-, and 18th-century houses, past flower-filled gardens.

If you're in the mood to shop, head for rue St-Etienne and rue St-Pierre. You'll find an assortment of stores selling religious books and statuary, including **Jerusalem,** 78 rue St-Pierre (ℰ **03-86-33-37-43**), and **Le Magasin du Pélerin,** place de la Basilique (ℰ **03-86-33-29-14**). For one-of-a-kind pieces by local artists, go to **Atelier Marie-Noëlle,** 69 rue St-Pierre (ℰ **03-86-33-26-02**), offering rich, colorful weavings and silk decorations; **Galerie Lieber,** 14 rue St-Etienne (ℰ **03-86-33-33-90**), which specializes in handmade jewelry using semiprecious and precious stones in both heavy and delicate settings of silver and gold; and **Jacques d'Aubres,** rue St-Etienne (ℰ **03-86-33-22-32**), with his unique textiles as well as stone and metal sculptures. You may also want to pick up a bottle or two of Vézelay wine at **La Cave Henry de Vézelay,** route de Nanchèvres in St-Père-sous-Vézelay (ℰ **03-86-33-29-62**).

Basilique Ste-Madeleine ★★ Built in the 12th century, France's largest and most famous Romanesque church is only 10 yards shorter than Notre-Dame de Paris. You enter the narthex, a vestibule of large dimensions, about 4,000 square feet. Raise your eyes to the doorway depicting Christ giving the apostles the Holy Spirit. From the Romanesque nave, with its white and gray stone of the traverse arches, you discover the light Gothic chancel. It's possible to visit the Carolingian crypt, where the tomb of Mary Magdalene formerly rested (today it contains some of her relics). There's a panoramic view from the back terrace.

ℰ **03-86-33-39-50.** Free admission. July–Aug daily 7am–7pm; Sept–June daily sunrise–sunset. Parking 10F (1.50, $1.45).

ACCOMMODATIONS

L'Espérance (see "Dining," below) also rents luxurious rooms.

Le Compostelle   This unpretentious, pleasant hotel occupies a late-19th-century building that was renovated in 1991. It's in the center of town, up the hill leading to the basilica, evoking in some ways an English country house . It's the best of the more affordable inns in town. Bedrooms are midsize but comfortably furnished, with a small, shower-only bathroom. Breakfast is the only meal served.

Place du Champ-de-Foire, 89450 Vézelay. ℭ **03-86-33-28-63**. Fax 03-86-33-34-34. 18 units. 275F–335F (41.80– 50.90, $39.90–$48.60) double. AE, MC, V. Closed Jan. *In room:* TV.

Poste et Lion d'Or ✸ *Value*   This is the local favorite, filled with character and tradition. Located on the main square, at the bottom of the hill that rises to the basilica, this hotel was built in the 17th century as a postal station. With a terrace and small garden, the Poste et Lion d'Or is a first-class place with surprisingly reasonable rates. Bedrooms are conservatively outfitted in a functional yet respectable way. Other than L'Espérance, which is in the countryside, it's the finest address in town, but only slightly better than Le Pontot.

The food is exceptional, especially the escargots de Bourgogne in chablis and stuffed trout with herbs. It's classic Burgundian—nothing experimental here.

Place du Champ-de-Foire, 89450 Vézelay. ℭ **03-86-33-21-23**. Fax 03-86-32-30-92. 39 units. 330F–650F (50.15– 98.80, $47.85–$94.25) double. AE, DC, MC, V. Closed mid-Nov to mid-Mar. Parking 40F (6.10, $5.80). **Amenities:** Restaurant, bar; room service; laundry. *In room:* TV.

Résidence-Hôtel Le Pontot ✸   Near the basilica, this tastefully renovated medieval structure is Vézelay's other leading in-town hotel. The guest rooms are decorated in a romantic French style—not to everyone's taste, but a lovely attempt at creating a cozy, homelike environment. Rooms range from small to spacious, with small, shower-only bathrooms. The hotel has bar service and a charming walled garden for breakfast, but no restaurant.

Place du Pontot, 89450 Vézelay. ℭ **03-86-33-24-40**. Fax 03-86-33-30-05. 11 units. 690F–920F (104.90– 139.85, $100.05–$133.40) double; 1,100F (167.20, $159.50) suite. DC, MC, V. Closed Nov–Easter. Parking 50F (7.60, $7.25). **Amenities:** Bar. *In room:* TV.

DINING

L'Espérance ✸✸✸ MODERN FRENCH   Few other restaurants in Burgundy are as richly or as frequently analyzed, assessed, and gossiped about as L'Espérance. Its acquisition and loss of Michelin accolades (its ratings bounce between two and three stars) are reported in the national press. Through it all, it never loses the support of its loyal fans. At press time, this legendary restaurant has just been demoted to the "mere mortal" (but much sought-after) status of a two-star monument by Michelin, but it still elicits our fervent loyalty.

The restaurant has the feel of an old-fashioned farm and bakery with a Napoléon III decor, emanating Burgundian wholesomeness as well as Parisian chic. It's in a fertile valley at the base of the most famous hill in Burgundy. Flagstone floors and big windows overlooking a garden create a backdrop for superb cuisine. Menu items change frequently but are likely to include an "ambrosia" of poultry with truffles and foie gras; oysters in a seawater-flavored aspic; a cream of truffle soup with an infusion of green olives; and a galette of new potatoes with caviar.

On the premises are 34 well-maintained and extremely comfortable rooms divided among three historic buildings. Each evokes French country living at its best. Doubles cost 800F to 1,400F (121.60 to 212.80, $116 to $203); suites 1,700F to 2,500F (258.40 to 380, $246.50 to $362.50). If there's any flaw, it involves a somewhat overworked staff, who struggle valiantly with the flow of traffic generated by the place's fame.

St-Père-sous-Vézelay, 89450 Vézelay. © **03-86-33-39-10.** Fax 03-86-33-26-15. www.relaischateaux.fr/ esperance. Reservations recommended. Main courses 300F–600F (45.60– 91.20, $43.50–$87); fixed-price menus 600F–990F (91.20– 150.50, $87–$143.55). Mid-June to mid-Oct Thurs–Mon noon–2pm, daily 7:30–9:30pm; mid-Oct to mid-June Thurs–Mon noon–2pm, Wed–Mon 7:30–9:30pm.

3 Avallon (★

133 miles SE of Paris, 32 miles SE of Auxerre

This old fortified town is shielded behind its ancient ramparts, upon which you can stroll. A medieval atmosphere still permeates Avallon, where you'll find many 15th- and 16th-century houses. At the town gate on Grande Rue Aristide-Briand is a clock tower from 1460. The Romanesque **Église St-Lazarus** dates from the 12th century and has two interesting doorways. The church is said to have received the head of St. Lazarus in 1000, thus turning Avallon into a pilgrimage site. Today, Avallon is visited mainly for its fabulous food.

ESSENTIALS

GETTING THERE   If you're **driving,** travel south from Paris along A6 to Auxerre; from Auxerre, take N6 south to Avallon. Ten **trains** arrive daily from Paris (trip time: 2 hours), and eight pull in from Dijon daily (trip time: 3 hours). For train information and schedules, call © **08-36-35-35-35. Buses** run from the railway junction of Montbard (a stop on the TGV lines from Paris) for Avallon, timed to coincide with the arrival of trains (about three a day). By train and bus, via Montbard, combined travel time from Paris is about 2 hours. For bus information, contact the railway station in Avallon at © **03-86-34-01-01.**

VISITOR INFORMATION   The **Office de Tourisme** is at 4–6 rue Bocquillot (© **03-86-34-14-19;** www.avallonnais-tourisme.com).

ACCOMMODATIONS & DINING

Château de Vault-de-Lugny ★★★   Between Avallon and Vézelay is this 16th-century moat-encircled château, with a fortress tower and peacocks on the grounds. There's an emphasis on service, with two staff members to every guest. The bedrooms and suites are sumptuous, with canopied beds, antique furnishings, and fireplaces. Each comes with a luxurious bathroom with a combination tub and shower. You can order cocktails in the salon, then proceed to dinner by candlelight. Fresh ingredients are the hallmark of the cuisine. A special bourguignon meal is offered nightly, consisting of typical regional dishes.

A Vault-de-Lugny, 89200 Avallon. © **03-86-34-07-86.** Fax 03-86-34-16-36. www.lugny.com. 12 units. 1,000F–1,500F (152– 228, $145–$217.50) double; 1,900F–2,900F (288.80– 440.80, $275.50–$420.50) suite. Rates include breakfast. AE, MC, V. Closed Mid-Nov to Mar 17. Take D957 from Avallon; turn right in Pontaubert (after the church) and follow signs to the château; Vault-de-Lugny is about 2 miles away. **Amenities:** Restaurant; bar; room service; baby-sitting. *In room:* TV, minibar, hair dryer, safe.

Moulin des Ruats ★ *Finds*   This country inn on the banks of the Cousin is enchanting. Once a flour mill, it has been a family hotel since 1924. Bedrooms are rustic and modern; try for one with a balcony overlooking the river. Many units have been recently renovated, some come with exposed beams and intimate alcoves. Each also contains a small bathroom with shower, some with a tub as well. The elegant dining room serves a menu of freshwater fish and boasts a fine wine list and a terrace. The meals are balanced, and everything has a certain zest and flavor. The restaurant is outstanding, more impressive than the hotel.

Vallée du Cousin, 89200 Avallon. ✆ **03-86-34-97-00.** Fax 03-86-31-65-47. www.moulin-des-ruats.com. 24 units. 400F–700F (60.80– 106.40, $58–$101.50) double. AE, DC, MC, V. Closed Nov 15–Feb 17; Mon–Tues closed at lunch. Take D427 2 miles outside town. **Amenities:** Restaurant, bar. *In room:* TV.

4 Autun ✦✦

182 miles SE of Paris, 53 miles SW of Dijon, 30 miles W of Beaune, 37 miles SE of Auxerre

Deep in burgundy country, Autun is one of the oldest towns in France. In the days of the Roman Empire, it was called "the other Rome." Some relics still stand, including the remains of the largest theater in Gaul, the Théâtre Romain, holding some 15,000 spectators. It was nearly 500 feet in diameter. Outside the town, you can see the tower of the Temple de Janus rising 80 feet over the plain.

Autun is a thriving provincial town of 20,000. Because it's off the beaten track, the hordes go elsewhere. Still, it has its memories, even of Napoléon, who studied here in 1779 at the military academy (today the Lycée Bonaparte).

ESSENTIALS

GETTING THERE   If you're **driving,** take D944 south from Avallon to the town of Château-Chinon. Then follow D978 east right into Autun. Autun has its own railway station; however, it isn't used very frequently. Many rail passengers find it more convenient to take one of the 10 **trains** a day from Paris (Gare de Lyon) or the eight trains a day from Lyon to the railway junction of Montchanin-le-Creusot, 25 miles to the south. From here, take a 45-minute bus connection to Autun, priced at around 50F (7.60, $8) each way. In Autun, **buses** arrive at a parking lot adjacent to the railway station on Avenue de la République. For bus information, call ✆ **03-85-86-92-55.** For railway information, call either the station in Autun at ✆ **03-85-52-28-01** or the national SNCF information line at ✆ **08-36-35-35-35.**

VISITOR INFORMATION   The **Office de Tourisme** is at 2 av. Charles-de-Gaulle (✆ **03-85-86-80-38;** www.ville-autun.fr).

SEEING THE SIGHTS

Once Autun was an important link on the road from Lyon to Boulogne, as reflected by the 55-foot high **Porte d'Arroux,** with its two large archways now used for cars and smaller ones for pedestrians. Also exceptional is the **Porte St-André** (St. Andrew's Gate), a quarter of a mile northwest of the Roman theater. Rising 65 feet, it has four doorways and is surmounted by a gallery of 10 arcades.

Cathédrale St-Lazare ✦✦   On the highest point in Autun, the cathedral was built in 1120 to house the relics of St. Lazarus. On the facade, the tympanum in the central portal depicts the Last Judgment—a triumph of Romanesque sculpture. Inside, a painting by Ingres depicts the martyrdom of St. Symphorien, who was killed in Autun. In the 1860s, Viollet-le-Duc, the architect who restored (sometimes with controversial results) some of the monuments of France, had to double the size of some of the columns supporting the cathedral's roof to avoid a collapse. New capitals matching the Romanesque style of the original building were crafted for placement atop the new columns. The original capitals, however, are now on display, more or less at eye level, in the Salle Capitulaire, one flight above street level. Especially noteworthy are *La*

Reveil des Mages (The Awakening of the Magi) and *La Fuite en Egypte* (The Flight into Egypt).

Place St-Louis. ☎ **03-85-52-12-37**. Free admission. Daily 8am–6pm (to 7pm July–Aug).

Musée Rolin ⭐ This 15th-century mansion was built for Nicolas Rolin (b. 1380), a famous lawyer in his day. An easy walk from the cathedral, the museum displays a collection of Burgundian Romanesque sculpture, as well as paintings and archaeological mementos. From the original Rolin collection are the *Nativity* by the Maître de Moulins, and a statue that's a masterpiece of 15th-century work, *Our Lady of Autun* (La Vierge d'Autun, also known as La Vierge Bulliot after the benefactor who donated the original statue back to the cathedral in 1948).

3 rue des Bancs. ☎ **03-85-52-09-76**. Admission 20F (3.05, $2.90) adults, 10F (1.50, $1.45) students and children. Apr–Sept, Wed–Mon 9:30am–noon and 1:30–6pm; Oct–Mar, Wed–Sat 10am–noon and 2–5pm, Sun 2–4pm.

NEARBY ATTRACTIONS

If you have a car, after visiting Autun you can tour one of Burgundy's finest wineries. **Domaine Protheau,** Château d'Etoyes (☎ **03-85-98-99-10**), lies at Mercurey, 25 miles southeast along D978. Among the selections are at least two appellations contrôlées, so you'll have a chance to immerse yourself in the subtle differences among reds (both pinot noirs and burgundies), whites, and rosés produced under the auspices of both Rully and Mercurey. The headquarters of the organization, founded in the 1740s, is a château built in the late 1700s and early 1800s. Free tours of the sprawling cellars and explanations of the various vintages it produces are offered, in French and halting English, daily from 9am to 6pm (call ahead to confirm). A *dégustation des vins* and the opportunity to haul a bottle or two away with you are included in every visit.

Two miles away, you can visit the **Château de Rully,** site of the **Domaine de la Bressande** (☎ **03-85-87-20-89**), a well-respected producer of white and, to a lesser extent, red burgundies. Originally built in the 12th century as a stronghold for the comte de Ternay, it offers tours to the public. The owner prefers you visit the château as part of a group; the cost is 35F (5.30, $5.10) per person. Individuals can visit between mid-July and mid-September daily at 4pm. This visit costs only 15F (2.30, $2.20), but it's more limited than the group tour.

ACCOMMODATIONS & DINING

Hostellerie du Vieux Moulin ⭐⭐ This fine hotel, a 10-minute walk north of the town center, contains Autun's best restaurant. At the edge of the Arroux River, within the stone walls of what was built in the 1870s as a grain mill, it boasts a warm ambience, a scattering of 19th-century regional antiques, and simple but comfortable bedrooms with small, shower-only bathrooms. Each is accented with reminders of the winemaking trade. Some units have TVs.

In summer, you can dine at a table overlooking the garden and the stream that abuts it. Menu items include filet of local sandre (whitefish) with basil-flavored cream sauce, Charolais beef simmered in red wine, and tournedos Tallyrand (named for a local bishop, not the politician, and the dish is flavored with shallots and red wine). Any of dozens of red burgundies can accompany your meal.

Porte d'Arroux, 71400 Autun. ☎ **03-85-52-10-90**. Fax 03-85-86-32-15. 16 units. 250F–350F (38– 53.20, $36.25–$50.75) double. MC, V. Closed Dec–Feb. **Amenities:** Restaurant, bar.

Hôtel des Ursulines The best hotel in Autun, the Ursulines offers attractively decorated rooms with views of the countryside and the distant Morvan mountains. This was built in the 1600s as an Ursuline convent, and about half the rooms lie within a comfortable annex that was added in 2000. Accommodations vary in shape and size; each comes with a fine mattress and quality linen, old or antique furniture, and a bathroom with combination tub and shower. Those set up under the mansard eaves of the old building are the cheapest, smallest, and also the coziest. The hotel is known for its cuisine.

14 rue Rivault, 71400 Autun. ℂ 03-85-86-58-58. Fax 03-85-86-23-07. 43 units. 410F–600F (62.30– 91.20, $59.45–$87) double; 830F (126.15, $120.35) suite. AE, MC, DC, V. **Amenities:** Restaurant, bar; baby-sitting; laundry. *In room:* TV, minibar, hair dryer.

5 Beaune ✶✶

196 miles SE of Paris, 24 miles SW of Dijon

This is the capital of the Burgundy wine country and one of the best-preserved medieval cities in the district, with a girdle of ramparts. Its history goes back more than 2,000 years. Beaune was a Gallic sanctuary, then a Roman town. Until the 14th century, it was the residence of the ducs de Bourgogne. When the last duke, Charles the Bold, died in 1477, Beaune was annexed by Louis XI. Visited today for its art, architecture, wines, and Burgundian cuisine, Beaune is a thriving town of some 20,000.

ESSENTIALS

GETTING THERE   If you're **driving,** note that Beaune is a few miles from the junction of four superhighways that fan out—A6, A31, A36, and N6. Beaune has good railway connections with Dijon, Lyon, and Paris. From Paris, there are four TGV **trains** per day (trip time: 2 hours); from Lyon, seven trains per day (trip time: 1½ hours); and from Dijon, 22 trains per day (trip time: 25 minutes). For train information and schedules, call ℂ **08-36-35-35-35.**

VISITOR INFORMATION   The **Office de Tourisme** is on rue de l'Hôtel-Dieu (ℂ **03-80-26-21-30;** www.ot-beaune.fr).

SPECIAL EVENTS   The town comes to life on the third Sunday in November, when wine buyers and oenophiles from the world over descend on the old town for a 3-day festival and wine auction called **Les Trois Glorieuses.** The town is packed with wineries offering free *dégustations*—and with tourists visiting the labyrinth of caves or wine cellars. With all the free spirits (both kinds), visitors crowding the streets can be more than a bit tipsy. It's a fun, funky, and always colorful event that really puts you in the mood to buy a lot of wine.

EXPLORING THE TOWN

North of the Hôtel-Dieu, the **Collégiale Notre-Dame,** on place du Général Leclerc (ℂ **03-80-26-22-70**), is an 1120 Burgundian Romanesque church. Some remarkable tapestries illustrating scenes from the life of the Virgin Mary are displayed in the sanctuary. You can view them from Easter to mid-November.

The best commercial shopping streets are rue de Lorraine, rue d'Alsace, rue Mauffoux, and place de la Madeleine. For smaller boutiques, stroll down the pedestrian rue Carnot and rue Monge. For antiques, concentrate your efforts around Rue Ziemand Place Ziem.

Beaune is one of the best towns in the region for sampling and buying famous Burgundy wines. You can tour, taste, and buy at **Marché aux Vins,** rue Nicolas-Rolin (ℂ **03-80-25-08-20**), housed in a 14th-century church. Its cellars are set in and among the ancient tombs, under the floor of the church. An interesting and unusual competitor, stocking most of the vintages of Burgundy, is **Cordelier**, 6 rue de l'Hôtel-Dieu (© **03-80-24-53-79**). Another cellar, **Caves Patriarche Père et Fils,** 7 rue du Collège (© **03-80-24-53-78**), is under the former Convent of the Visitandines with individual cellars from the 13th, 16th, and 17th centuries.

Musée de l'Hôtel-Dieu ★★   One of the town's most visible antique buildings is the Hôtel-Dieu. It thrived during the Middle Ages thanks to its ownership by an order of nuns associated with the famous vineyards of Aloxe-Corton and Meursault. It functioned as a hospital until 1970, and some sections are still devoted to a retirement home. It now contains the Musée de l'Hôtel-Dieu, displaying Flemish-Burgundian art such as Rogier van der Weyden's 1443 polyptych *The Last Judgment* ★★★. In the Chambre des Pauvres (Room of the Poor), you'll find painted, broken-barrel, timbered vaulting, with mostly authentic furnishings.

Rue de l'Hôtel-Dieu. © **03-80-24-45-00**. Admission 33F (5, $4.80) adults, 26F (3.95, $3.75) children. Apr–Nov 19 daily 9am–6:30pm; Nov 20–Mar daily 9–11:30am and 2–5:30pm.

Musée des Beaux-Arts et Musée Marey   This museum contains a rich Gallo-Roman archaeological section. The main gallery of paintings has works from the 16th to the 19th century, like Flemish primitives and many pieces by Felix Ziem, a precursor of the Impressionist school. Sculptures from the Middle Ages and the Renaissance are also displayed. A larger part of the museum honors the Beaune physiologist Etienne Jules Marey, who discovered the principles of the cinema long before 1895.

In the Hôtel de Ville (town hall), rue de l'Hôtel de Ville. © **03-80-24-56-92**. Free admission if you've paid for admission to the Musée du Vin (below). Daily 2–6pm. Closed Nov–Mar (except on the 3rd weekend in Nov).

Musée du Vin de Bourgogne ★   Housed in the former mansion of the ducs de Bourgogne, the Musée du Vin de Bourgogne traces the evolution of the region's winemaking. The collection of tools, objets d'art, and documents is contained in 15th- and 16th-century rooms. On display in the 14th-century press house is a collection of wine presses.

Rue d'Enfer. © **03-80-22-08-19**. Admission 25F (3.80, $3.65) adults, 15F (2.30, $2.20) students and children, free for children under 12. Daily 9:30am–6pm. Closed Tues Dec–Mar.

ACCOMMODATIONS

Hostellerie de Bretonnière *Value*   This is the best bargain in town: it's well run, with clean, quiet rooms. It's conveniently located a 5-minute walk from the center of town. The accommodations in the rear are the cheapest and most tranquil, though most visitors prefer those overlooking the garden. Rooms are small, but still adequate for an overnight stopover; each has a shower-only bathroom. There's no restaurant, but a continental breakfast is available.

43 rue de Faubourg Bretonnière, 21200 Beaune. © **03-80-22-15-77**. Fax 03-80-22-72-54. www. bretonniere.hotel.com. 24 units. 310F–460F (47.10– 69.90, $44.95–$66.70) double. AE, DC, MC, V. Free parking. *In room:* TV, hair dryer.

Hôtel de la Poste   Outside the town fortifications, this traditional hotel rivals but does not surpass the more elegant Cep (see below). The rooms overlook the ramparts or the vineyards; some have brass beds and midsize bathrooms with combination tub and shower. Menu specialties at the hotel restaurant, De La Poste, range from chicken fricassée with tarragon to sole in court bouillon with white butter. The bar and restaurant are in the belle-époque style.

1 bd. Georges-Clemenceau, 21200 Beaune. ℂ **03-80-22-08-11.** Fax 03-80-24-19-71. www.hoteldela postebeaune.com. 30 units. 700F–1,100F (106.40– 167.20, $101.50–$159.50) double; 1,250F–1,500F (190– 228, $181.25–$217.50) suite. AE, DC, MC, V. Parking 50F (7.60, $7.25). Amenities: Restaurant, bar; room service; laundry. *In room:* A/C, TV, minibar, hair dryer.

Hôtel Le Cep ★★★   The chic spot for oenophiles visiting Beaune is this mansion in the town center, fit enough for the ducs de Bourgogne. All the charm, grace, and style of Burgundy are reflected in this once-private residence. Each bedroom is individually decorated and named after a Grand Cru wine of the Côte-d'Or vineyards; our favorites are the Chambre Montrachet and the Chambre Meloisey. The luxurious bathrooms have combination tub and shower. On the grounds is Beaune's loveliest courtyard, with arcades and Renaissance stone medallions. A tower housing one of the city's most beautiful stone staircases rises from here. A former wine cellar is now the breakfast room (the only meal served). Beaune's finest restaurant, Bernard Morillon (see below), is next door.

27 rue Maufoux, 21206 Beaune. ℂ **03-80-22-35-48.** Fax 03-80-22-76-80. www.hotel-cep-beaune.com. 57 units. 800F–1,200F (121.60– 182.40, $116–$174) double; 1,500F–1,800F (228– 273.60, $217.50–$261) suite. AE, DC, MC, V. Parking 50F (7.60, $7.25). **Amenities:** Room service; laundry. *In room:* A/C, TV, minibar, hair dryer, safe.

DINING

Hôtel de la Poste (see "Accommodations," above) also has a good restaurant.

Bernard Morillon ★★ TRADITIONAL FRENCH   You'll dine here in a Directoire/Louis XV room on specialties like gratin of crayfish tails, an unusual version of *pigeonneau* made with fish served with a *fumet* of red wine, Bresse chicken with Gevrey-Chambertin wine, and deboned Bresse pigeon stuffed with foie gras and truffles. Bernard Morillon has a distinctive style, and his food always pleases. The desserts are sumptuous. To find a better restaurant, you'll have to journey outside town to the Hostellerie de Levernois (see below).

31 rue Maufoux. ℂ **03-80-24-12-06.** Reservations recommended. Main courses 120F–220F (18.25– 33.45, $17.40–$31.90); fixed-price menu 180F–480F (27.35– 72.95, $26.10–$69.60). AE, DC, DISC, MC, V. Tues 7:30–10pm, Wed–Sun noon–2pm and 7–10pm. Closed 3 weeks in Jan.

Relais de Saulx TRADITIONAL & MODERN FRENCH   In a 200-year-old stone-trimmed building named after one of the ancient and noble families of the Beaune region, Relais de Saulx is decorated with heavy timbers, oil paintings, and all the accoutrements you'd expect from one of the region's most respected restaurants. Chef Jean-Louis Monnoir prepares a sophisticated combination of traditional Bourguignon cuisine and up-to-date adaptations. Ongoing staples are Bresse chicken with a morel sauce, rack of lamb studded with rosemary and mountain herbs, lobster garnished with a sauce derived from the carapaces of shellfish, and roast pigeon whose sauces and garnishes vary according to the season (like baby asparagus tips in springtime and a wine-dark game sauce in winter). Monnoir's presentation is excellent, and his flavors sometime elicit gasps of delight. The skillfully compiled wine list includes many unusual local vintages.

6 rue Louis-Very. ℂ **03-80-22-01-35.** Reservations required for large groups. Main courses 140F–170F (21.30– 25.85, $20.30–$24.65); fixed-price menu 130F–330F (19.75– 50.15, $18.85–$47.85). MC, V. Tues–Fri noon–2pm; Mon–Sat 7–9:30pm. Closed 3 weeks in Dec.

NEARBY ACCOMMODATIONS & DINING

Hostellerie de Levernois ★★★ FRENCH   Jean Crotet and his sons, Christophe and Guillaume, offer grand cuisine in a stone-sided *maison bourgeoise* from the 1800s, set in an 8-acre park. Two of their trademark dishes are salmon smoked on the grounds and a delicious version of snails in puff pastry with a purée of watercress. Three kinds of fish arranged on the same platter, drenched with a garlic-tinged cream sauce, makes a worthy and memorable main course, as does a "canon" of roasted lamb with truffle sauce. There isn't a major emphasis on virtuoso techniques, just a powerful knowledge of first-class ingredients and what to do with them.

The inn also rents 16 carefully decorated rooms, each with TV, air-conditioning, and a bathroom with combination tub and shower, in a well-designed modern annex. Doubles cost 1,250F (190, $181.25); the suite goes for 1,700F (258.40, $246.50).

Rte. de Verdun-sur-le-Doubs, Levernois, 21200 Beaune. ℂ 03-80-24-73-58. Fax 03-80-22-78-00. levernois@ relaischateaux.fr. Reservations required. Main courses 150F–400F (22.80– 60.80, $21.75–$58); fixed-price menus 200F–680F (30.40– 103.35, $29–$98.60) lunch Mon–Fri, 330F–680F (50.15– 103.35, $47.85–$98.60) lunch Sat–Sun, 395F–535F (60.05– 81.30, $57.30–$77.60) dinner. AE, DC, MC, V. Summer Wed–Mon noon–2pm, Mon–Sat 7–9:30pm; off-season Thurs–Mon noon–2pm; Wed–Mon 7–9:30pm. Closed Mar 1–15. Take D970 south of Beaune for 2 miles, following the signs for Lons le Saunier.

BEAUNE AFTER DARK

Your best bets for a good time are the local nightclubs and discos. To hear solid jazz and rock and even flirt with some of the locals, step over to the **Cotton Bar,** 164 rte. de Dijon (ℂ **03-80-24-69-48**), which fills up early with a 30-plus crowd that seems to complete the retro ambience. If you've had enough wine tasting and are in the mood for an ale or two, try the English-style **Pickwick's Pub,** 2 rue Notre-Dame (ℂ **03-80-24-72-59**). For a little piano bar and karaoke, go to **Why Not,** 74 rue de Faubourg-Madeleine (ℂ **03-80-22-64-74**). For a more jolting, electric evening, head over to **Opéra-Night,** rue du Beaumarché (ℂ **03-80-24-10-11**), with its booming house music, immense dance floor, strobe lights, and mirrors revealing every angle imaginable. A more recently established competitor is **Disco Jazz Band,** 11 route de Seurre (ℂ **03-80-24-73-49**); both it and Opéra-Night charge a cover of up to 60F (9.10, $8.70).

6 Dijon ⟨★⟨★⟨★

194 miles SE of Paris, 199 miles NE of Lyon

Dijon is known overseas mainly for its mustard. Located in the center of the Côte d'Or, it's the ancient capital of Burgundy. Here, good food is accompanied by great wine. Between meals, you can enjoy the art and architecture.

The first impression, especially if you arrive at the rail station, is misleading. You'll think Dijon is a dreary modern city. Not so. Press on to the medieval core only a few blocks away. Many old streets and buildings have been restored. The once and future mayor, Robert Poujade (first elected in 1971), was the minister of environment in the Pompidou government (1969 to 74), and he thinks he's still back at his old job, wildly planting trees everywhere.

ESSENTIALS

GETTING THERE   The best way to reach Dijon is by **driving.** From Paris, follow A6 southeast to the town of Pouilly-en-Auxois, then east along A38 into Dijon. Dijon also has excellent rail and bus connections to the rest of Europe. A total of 25 **trains** arrive from Paris each day (trip time: 1¾ hours). Trains arrive from Lyon every hour (trip time: 2 hours). For train information and schedules, call ℂ **08-36-35-35-35.**

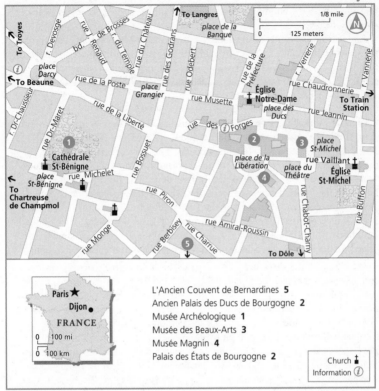

place de la Banque

To Langres

To Troyes

To Beaune

place Darcy

r. Devosge

bd. J. Renaud

rue de Brosses

r. du Temple

rue du Château

rue des Godrans

rue Odebert

rue de la Préfecture

r. Verrerie

rue Chaudronnerie

r. Vannerie

place Grangier

rue de la Poste

rue Musette

Église Notre-Dame

place des Ducs

To Train Station

rue Jeannin

r. Dr-Chaussier

r. Dr-Maret

rue de la Liberté

rue des Forges

rue Bossuet

place de la Libération

place St-Michel

rue Vaillant

Cathédrale St-Bénigne

rue Michelet

place du Théâtre

Église St-Michel

place St-Bénigne

To Chartreuse de Champmol

rue Piron

rue Monge

rue Berbisey

rue Charrue

rue Amiral-Roussin

rue Chabot-Charny

rue Buffon

To Dôle

To Dijon

0   1/8 mile
0   125 meters

Paris

Dijon

FRANCE

0   100 mi
0   100 km

L'Ancien Couvent de Bernardines **5**
Ancien Palais des Ducs de Bourgogne **2**
Musée Archéologique **1**
Musée des Beaux-Arts **3**
Musée Magnin **4**
Palais des États de Bourgogne **2**

Church
Information

VISITOR INFORMATION   The **Office de Tourisme** is on place Darcy (© **03-80-44-11-44;** www.ville-dijon.fr).

SPECIAL EVENTS   Between the end of June and the end of July, the streets of Dijon go through a lively renaissance when **Estivade** comes to town. This festival uses the city's streets as a stage for folk dances, music, and theatrical art that never fails to be a big hit. You can get a schedule of events from either the city tourist office (see above) or La Mairie (town hall; © **03-80-74-51-51**).

SEEING THE SIGHTS

One of the most historic buildings in this ancient province is the **Palais des Ducs et des États de Bourgogne,** which symbolizes the proudly independent (or semi-independent, depending on the era) status of this fertile region. Capped with an elaborate tile roof, it's a solid complex arranged around a trio of courtyards. The oldest section, only part of which you can visit, is the **Ancien Palais des Ducs de Bourgogne,** erected in the 12th century and rebuilt in the 14th. The newer section is the **Palais des États de Bourgogne,** constructed between the 17th and 18th centuries as a meeting place for the Burgundian parliament (it struggled to retain the duchy's semi-independent status against encroachments from the French monarchy). Today, as the palace is Dijon's *la mairie* (town hall), all of its newer section and a substantial part of its older section are reserved for the municipal government and can't be visited. However, there's a fine museum in the building that we highly recommend, the **Musée des Beaux-Arts** (see below).

A mile from the center of town on N5 stands the **Chartreuse de Champmol,** the Carthusian monastery built by Philip the Bold as a burial place; it's now a psychiatric hospital. Much of it was destroyed during the Revolution, but you can see the Moses Fountain in the gardens designed by Sluter at the end of the 14th century. The Gothic entrance is superb.

Musée Archéologique, 5 rue du Dr-Maret (© **03-80-30-88-54**), contains the findings unearthed from Dijon's many archaeological digs. A medieval nunnery, **L'Ancien Couvent des Bernardines,** 17 rue Ste-Anne (© **03-80-44-12-69**), is home to two separate museums. The convent's chapel is the site of the Musée d'Arts Sacrés, devoted to sacred art from regional churches. The convent's dignified cloister contains the **Musée de la Vie Bourguignonne** (also known as the Musée Perrin de Puycousin), which celebrates folkloric costumes, farm implements, and even some of the 19th- and early-20th-century storefronts from Dijon's commercial center. All three of the above charge 18F (2.75, $2.60) for adults, 9F (1.35, $1.30) for students and children, free for children 5 and under. All are open Wednesday through Monday 10am to noon and 2 to 6pm.

Musée des Beaux-Arts ★★   The part of the older palace that you can visit contains one of France's oldest and richest museums. It boasts exceptional sculpture, ducal kitchens from the mid-1400s (with great chimney pieces), a collection of European paintings from the 14th to the 19th century, and modern French paintings and sculptures. Take special note of the Salle des Gardes, the banquet hall of the old palace built by Philip the Good. The tomb of Philip the Bold was created between 1385 and 1411 and is one of the best in France: a reclining figure rests on a slab of black marble, surrounded by 41 mourners.

In the Palais des Ducs et des États de Bourgogne, cour de Bar. © **03-80-74-52-70.** Admission 22F (3.35, 3.20) adults, 10F (1.50, $1.45) seniors, free for students and children, free for everyone on Sun. Wed–Mon 10am–6pm.

Musée Magnin   Built in the 19th century as the home of an arts-conscious member of the grande bourgeoisie, it was willed, along with all its contents, to the city of Dijon as a museum following the death of the family's last descendant. It contains an eclectic display of 19th-century antiques and art objects, as well as a collection of paintings accumulated by, or painted by, the former owners.

4 rue des Bons-Enfants. © **03-80-67-11-10.** Admission 16F (2.45, $2.30) adults, free for students and children under 18. Tues–Sun 10am–noon and 2–6pm.

SHOPPING

Your shopping list might include robust regional wines, Dijon mustard, antiques, and the black-currant cordial called cassis (try a splash in champagne for a Kir Royale). The best streets to hone in on are rue de la Liberté, rue du Bourg, rue Bossuet, and rue Verrerie, the latter for antiques.

Dijon hosts a flea market, **Le Broc du Forum,** the last Sunday of every month at the Forum, rue du Général-Delaborde (© **03-80-74-31-23**), beginning at 9am and running through the afternoon. There's also a market at **Les Halles Centrales** in the rue Odebert, where fruits, vegetables, and foodstuffs are sold every Tuesday, Thursday, and Friday from 8am to noon, and every Saturday from 8am to around 5pm. A separate endeavor that specializes in used clothing, kitchen utensils, housewares, and flea-market castoffs, **Les Marchés autour des Halles,** operates along the market's periphery every Tuesday and Friday from 8am to noon, and every Saturday from 8am to around 5pm.

For the ideal picnic lunch, begin at the mustard shop of **La Boutique Maille,** 32 rue de la Liberté (℡ **03-80-30-41-02**), to purchase a supply of the world-famous condiment; head over to **Au Pain d'Autrefois,** 47 rue du Bourg (℡ **03-80-30-47-92**), for a baguette or round of your favorite chewy French bread; move on to **La Boucherie Nouvelle,** 27 rue Pasteur (℡ **03-80-66-37-10**), to choose one of its many selections of deli meats; follow that with a visit to the **Crémerie Porcheret,** 18 rue Bannelier (℡ **03-80-30-21-05**), to pick up several varieties of regional cheeses, including the citeaux, made by a group of brothers at a nearby monastery; and then finish at one of the three locations of **Mulot et Petitjean,** 1 place Notre-Dame, 16 rue de la Liberté, or 13 place Bossuet (℡ **03-80-30-07-10**), where you can pick up a bottle of wine and a gingerbread for dessert. Another source for wines is **Nicot,** rue J.-J.-Rousseau (℡ **03-80-73-29-88**).

For antiques, try **Monique Buisson,** 21 rue Verrerie (℡ **03-80-30-31-19**), where you'll find a good collection of regional furniture from the 1700s; **Dubard,** 25 bis rue Verrerie (℡ **03-80-30-50-81**), carries 18th-century decorative antiques as well as contemporary upholstery fabrics; and **Au Vieux Dijon,** 8 rue Verrerie (℡ **03-80-31-89-08**), has an assortment of 18th- and 19th-century vases, bibelots, and more refined examples of Burgundian furniture. Other recommended stops are **Galerie 6,** 6 rue Auguste-Comte (℡ **03-80-71-68-46**), offering a wide selection of antique paintings from the 1600s to the 1800s; and **Aux Occasions,** 29 rue Auguste-Comte (℡ **03-80-73-55-13**), where you can browse through a multitude of mainly English antiques from the 1800s as well as handmade Oriental rugs, both old and new. Also appealing is **Antiquaires Golmard,** 3 rue Auguste Comte (℡ **03-80-67-14-15**), which specializes in objects originating from the many private estates in the region.

ACCOMMODATIONS

La Toison d'Or (see "Dining," below) also rents rooms.

Hostellerie du Chapeau-Rouge ⭐ This Dijon landmark, with an acclaimed restaurant, is the town's best address. The hotel is filled with 19th-century antiques and has rooms with modern conveniences and comfortable furnishings. All of the bedrooms are air-conditioned, and all of the bathrooms have Jacuzzis. Since no other hotel restaurant in town serves comparable food, you may want to visit here even if you're not a guest. The supercharged chef offers Burgundian favorites, but has also broken new ground with mouthwatering fare, the specialties depending on what's good in any given season.

5 rue Michelet, 21000 Dijon. ℡ **800/528-1234** in the U.S. and Canada, or 03-80-50-88-88. Fax 03-80-50-88-89. www.bestwestern.com. 30 units. 930F (141.35, $134.85) double; 1,290F (196.10, $187.05) suite. AE, DC, MC, V. Parking 35F (5.30, $5.30). **Amenities:** Restaurant, bar; room service; laundry. *In room:* A/C, TV, minibar, hair dryer, safe.

Hôtel Ibis Central On a downtown square, this hotel is from 1930 and renovated by the Ibis chain into a streamlined design in the 1980s. It doesn't have the atmosphere and charm of some Dijon hotels, but we recommend it for its economy and its simple, businesslike and comfortable rooms, each with a small, shower-only bathroom. Bedrooms were renovated in 1998, with new mattresses added and improvements to the upholsteries, paint, and decor. The Central Grill Rôtisserie offers candlelit dinners and a view of Dijon (closed Sunday).

3 place Grangier, 21000 Dijon. ℡ **03-80-30-44-00.** Fax 03-80-30-77-12. 90 units. 355F–440F (53.95– 66.90, $51.50–$63.80) double. DC, MC, V. Parking 45F (6.85, $6.55). **Amenities:** Restaurant, bar; room service; laundry. *In room:* TV.

Hôtel Sofitel-La Cloche   This 15th-century historic monument, renovated in neoclassical style, is in the center of town. The interior features Oriental rugs and a pink-and-gray marble floor. The lobby bar is one of the most elegant places in town, with a view of the garden shared by an adjoining glassed-in tearoom. Although of chain format, the rooms are among the most comfortable in town. Most are medium; each has a quality mattress and a combination tub and shower.

14 place Darcy, 21000 Dijon. (℃) **03-80-30-12-32.** Fax 03-80-30-04-15. h1202@accov-hotels.com. 68 units. 900F–1,150 F(136.80– 174.80, $130.50–$166.75) double; 1,700F–2,000F (258.40– 304, $246.50–$290) suite. AE, DC, MC, V. Free parking. **Amenities:** Restaurant, bar; room service; laundry. *In room:* A/C, TV, minibar, hair dryer.

Hôtel Wilson ⭐ *Finds*   Our favorite nest in Dijon, opening onto a pleasant square, is this *ancien relais de poste* from the 17th century. The coaching inn has been tastefully restored. Although it has been modernized and decorated with traditional Burgundian wood furniture, many of the old time-darkened wood ceiling beams have been exposed, adding a hard-to-come-by charm. All units have small bathrooms, each with shower and some with a tub as well. A bonus is the neighboring restaurant, Thiebert, which serves a delectable French cuisine and is known for its wine cellar, which is especially rich in burgundies.

Place Wilson. (℃) **03-80-66-82-50.** Fax 03-80-36-41-54. 27 units. 410F–520F (62.30– 79.05, $59.45–$75.40) double. AE, MC, V. *In room:* TV.

DINING

The Hostellerie du Chapeau-Rouge (see above) boasts a marvelous restaurant.

La Toison d'Or ⭐ TRADITIONAL & MODERN FRENCH   This elegant and grand restaurant is accessible via an antique courtyard. On offer is traditional food that's hearty and satisfying, in a style somewhere between old-fashioned and conservatively modern. Amid stone walls, Oriental carpets, and Louis XII chairs, you'll enjoy specialties such as foie gras of duckling in puff pastry, served with a compôte of figs; marinated scallops and shrimp prepared tempura-style; and scallops and crayfish tails in a nage of spring vegetables and ginger.

On the premises, but with a decor and architectural style that's much more modern, is a simple 29-room hotel, Libertel Philippe-le-Bon, where each double room contains a bathroom, minibar, TV, and phone. Rates are 475F to 550F (72.20 to 83.60, $68.90 to $79.75).

18 rue Ste-Anne, 21000 Dijon. (℃) **03-80-30-73-52.** Fax 03-80-30-95-51. Hotel-libertel-philippe-le-bon@wanadoo.fr. Reservations required. Main courses 70F–150F (10.65– 22.80, $10.15–$21.75); fixed-price menu 175F–275F (26.60– 41.80, $25.40–$39.90) dinner. AE, DC, MC, V. Mon-Sat noon–1:30pm and 7–9:30pm.

Le Pré aux Clercs ⭐⭐⭐ BURGUNDIAN/FRENCH   In an 18th-century house across from the Palais des Ducs, this is one of Burgundy's finest restaurants, with a reputation that dates back to 1833. Its chef/owner, Jean-Pierre Billoux, assisted by his wife, Marie Françoise, prepares deceptively simple meals that have won acclaim. Menu items might include roast chicken steeped in liquefied almonds, terrine of pigeon, or thick-sliced filet of sole on a bed of tomato. The array of wines will be a joy to any connoisseur.

13 place de la Libération. (℃) **03-80-38-05-05.** Reservations required. Main courses 120F–200F (18.25– 30.40, $17.40–$29); fixed-price menus 200F–500F (30.40– 76, $29–$72.50) lunch, 260F–500F (39.50– 76, $37.70–$72.50) dinner. AE, DC, MC, V. Tues–Sun noon–2pm; Tues–Sat 7:30–9:30pm.

NEARBY DINING

Joël Perreaut's Restaurant des Gourmets ⭐⭐⭐ FRENCH   This restaurant is justification for journeying outside Dijon to a charming medieval village.

After Joël and Nicole Perreaut added an annex, modern kitchens, and a dining room, the place became well known as one of Burgundy's best restaurants. Within a modern-looking room whose large, sun-flooded windows overlook a garden, you can enjoy a seasonally changing menu that might include prof- iteroles of snails with fresh mint sauce; a Moroccan-inspired pastilla of mullet with spices; a cross-cut section of veal cooked for 7 hours with orange segments and served with parmesan cheese; and veal sweetbreads with a red-wine sauce and a purée of mushrooms. The cellar contains more than 600 wines, many of them burgundies from major as well as lesser-known, small-scale wineries whose value might not be immediately obvious.

8 rue Puits-de-Têt, 21160 Marsannay-la-Côte. (✆ **03-80-52-16-32**. Reservations required. Main courses 150F–270F (22.80– 41.05, $21.75–$39.15); fixed-price menu 170F–350F (25.85– 53.20, $24.65–$50.75); *menu dégustation* 460F (69.90, $66.70). AE, DC, MC, V. Wed–Sun noon–2pm; Tues–Sat 7–9:30pm. Closed first week of Jan, first 2 weeks of Feb, and Aug 1–15. Drive 6 miles south of Dijon on R.N. 17, following the signs for Beaune and then Marsannay-la-Côte.

DIJON AFTER DARK

Begin your evening at one of the many cafes or brasseries lining place Zola, rue des Godrans, place du Théâtre, or place Darcy, including the **Concorde,** 2 place Darcy (✆ **03-80-30-69-43**); **Brasserie du Théâtre,** 1 bis place du Théâtre (✆ **03-80-67-11-62**); and **La Comédie,** 3 place du Théâtre (✆ **03-80- 67-11-22**). All quickly fill up with young people who like to start the night with a drink and a look at others.

For a 30s-to-40s crowd who like to mingle in the low-key atmosphere of a piano bar, try **Hunky Dory,** 5 av. Foch (✆ **03-80-53-17-24**); **Le Messire,** 3 rue Jules-Mercier (✆ **03-80-30-16-40**); or **Le Cintra,** 13 av. Foch (✆ **03-80- 53-19-53**), with a piano bar upstairs and a cramped little disco down below. If the welcoming, boisterous (and often sloshed) atmosphere of an Irish pub is what you need, head over to **Le Kilkenny,** 1 rue Auguste-Perdrix (✆ **03-80-30-02-48**). Or for a more British spin, try **Le Brighton,** 33 rue Auguste-Comte (✆ **03-80- 73-59-32**), where you'll find a south-of-the-border dance club downstairs.

Two popular discos offering generic dance music and club atmosphere are **Le Rio,** 9 av. Maréchal Foch (✆ **03-80-43-50-23**), and **Le Klapton,** 5 rue Dauphine (✆ **03-80-50-06-54**). Appealing to a more sedate local crowd is **Le Privé,** 20 av. Garibaldi (✆ **03-80-73-39-57**), where there's a greater emphasis on slower, more romantic music. Other high-octane dance floors are at **L'An Fer,** 8 rue Pierre-Marceau (✆ **03-80-70-03-69**), with its 60F (9.15, $8.70) cover, gay-straight crowd, and Métro-station decor; and **Le Grizzli,** 131 av. Gustave-Eiffel (✆ **03-80-43-19-91**), where guys always pay the 40F (6.13E, $5.80) cover, but women get in free on Friday.

The opera season in Dijon stretches from the middle of October to May. The city's premier venue is the **Grand Théâtre de Dijon,** 2 rue Longepierre; call ✆ **03-80-68-46-40** for information on opera, operettes, dance recitals, and concerts. The city's second most visible cultural venue is the **Théâtre National Dijon-Bourgogne,** rue Monge (✆ **03-80-30-12-12**). Tickets for performances at either theater range from 100F to 250F (15.20 to 38, $14.50 to $36.25).

7 Saulieu ⊛

155 miles SE of Paris, 47 miles NW of Beaune

The town of Saulieu is interesting, but its food is what put it on the interna- tional map. Saulieu has enjoyed a reputation for cooking since the 17th century. Even Mme de Sévigné praised it in her letters. So did Rabelais.

The main sight is the **Basilique St-Andoche,** on place de la Fontaine (℡ **03-80-64-07-03**), which has some interesting decorated capitals. Next door in the art museum, the **Musée François-Pompon,** place de la Fontaine at rue Sallier (℡ **03-80-64-19-51**), you can see works by François Pompon, the sculptor of animals whose works are featured in Paris's Musée d'Orsay. Pompon's large statue of a bull stands on a plaza off the N6 at the entrance to Saulieu. Also featured in the museum are archaeological remnants from the Gallo-Roman era, sacred medieval art, and old tools showing some aspect of life in Burgundy several centuries ago. The museum is open from March to November, Wednesday through Monday from 10am to 12:30pm and 2 to 6pm. Admission is 20F (3.05, $2.90) for adults, 15 F (2.30, $2.20) for children 12 to 16.

ESSENTIALS

GETTING THERE   If you're **driving,** head along N80 from Montbard or N6 from Paris or Lyon. The **train** station is northeast of the town center. For train information and schedules, call ℡ **08-36-35-35-35.** Passengers coming from Paris sometimes opt to take the TGV from the Gare de Lyon, getting off in Montbard, 30 miles to the north. From Montbard, a series of **buses** carry passengers on to Saulieu about three times a day. For bus and rail information, call the **Gare SNCF** in Saulieu at ℡ **03-80-64-19-31.**

VISITOR INFORMATION   The **Office du Tourisme** is at 24 rue d'Argentine (℡ **03-80-64-00-21;** saulieu.tourism@wanadoo.fr.).

ACCOMMODATIONS & DINING

Bernard Loiseau-La Côte d'Or ★★★   This former stagecoach stop is an excellent choice, with one of the best-known restaurants in France. If you want to stay overnight, you'll find guest rooms with everything from Empire to Louis XV decor. Your bed will come complete with a comfortable mattress, but the bed itself is likely to be 200 years old.

Chef Alexandre Dumaine, the man who made this a world-famous restaurant, is gone, but the inventive Bernard Loiseau works to maintain his standards. (According to most, Loiseau has surpassed all previous standards, becoming one of Europe's culinary stars.) The cooking is less traditional, leaning away from heavy sauces to *cuisine légère.* The emphasis is on bringing out maximum taste with no excess fat or sugar. All the great burgundies are on the wine list.

21210 Saulieu. ℡ **03-80-90-53-53.** Fax 03-80-64-08-92. www.bernard-loiseau.com. 33 units. 1,250F–2,300F (190– 349.60, $181.25–$333.50) double; 2,500F–2,800F (380– 425.60, $362.50–$406) suite. AE, DC, MC, V. **Amenities:** Restaurant, bar; room serivce; laundry. *In room:* TV, minibar, hair dryer.

Hôtel de la Poste   Although leagues below the luxe Côte d'Or, this is the other leading inn, known for its Belle-Époque decor. Originally a 17th-century relay station, Hôtel de la Poste has been renovated by Guy Virlouvet. Each room has a bathroom with combination tub and shower. In the dining room, where antique timbers have been exposed, specialties include escalope of sea perch with baby vegetables, Charolais beef with marrow sauce, and kidneys in a sauce.

1 rue Grillot, 21210 Saulieu. ℡ **03-80-64-05-67.** Fax 03-80-64-10-82. 48 units. 355F–525F (53.95– 79.80, $51.50–$76.15) double; 685F–705F (104.10– 107.15, $99.35–$102.25) junior suite. AE, DC, MC, V. **Amenities:** Restaurant, bar; room service; laundry. *In room:* A/C, TV, minibar, hair dryer.

13

The Rhône Valley

The Rhône is as mighty as the Saône is peaceful, and these two great rivers form a part of the French countryside that travelers usually experience only briefly, glimpsing it as they rush south to the Riviera on the Mediterranean Express. But this land of mountains and rivers, linked by a good road network, invites more exploration than that: It's Beaujolais country, home to the city of Lyon, and a fabulous stop for gourmets; and it boasts Roman ruins, charming villages, castles, and even the Grand Canyon of France.

It was from the Rhône Valley that Greco-Roman architecture and art made their way to the Loire Valley, the château country, and to Paris. The district abounds in time-mellowed inns and gourmet restaurants, offering a cuisine that's among the finest in the world.

REGIONAL CUISINE Lyon and environs are the gastronomic capital of France. Excellent ingredients are available nearby—the best chicken and beef in France (from Bresse and Charolais, respectively), freshwater fish from the high lakes of the Savoy, and game from the dense forests.

Regional specialties are *quenelles de brochet* (pulverized brochet—a local whitefish—fashioned into cigar-shaped cylinders, served with white butter); Lyonnais sausages; many versions of chicken, especially garnished with truffles; an array of pâtés and terrines, often made from wild game. One excellent dish is *pommes de terres lyonnaises* (sautéed potatoes with onions).

As for wines, the vineyards along the Rhône are some of the oldest in France, established by the ancient Greeks. The better wines are sold under the names of the villages that produce them: Côtes-du-Rhône Ardèche, Côtes-du-Rhône Gigondas, Tavel, Châteauneuf-du-Pape, Muscat de Baumes-de-Venise, Condrieu, and Beaujolais. Beaujolais is the premier young wine of France. It's intended for early consumption—the annual release of a year's vintage is truly a national event.

1 Lyon ✦✦✦

268 miles SE of Paris, 193 miles N of Marseille

At the junction of the turbulent Rhône and the tranquil Saône, a crossroads of Western Europe, Lyon is the third-largest city in France. The city has a population of 400,000, with over a million more inhabitants spread across a large urban area. Lyon is the center of an industrial region, with textile manufacturing especially important. It's a leader in publishing and banking and is the world's silk capital. Some of the country's most highly rated restaurants, including Paul Bocuse, are found in and around Lyon. In fact, it's called the gastronomic capital of France. Such dishes as Lyon sausage, *quenelles* (fish balls), and tripe Lyonnais are world famous. The region's succulent Bresse poultry is the best in France.

Although you can dine better here than in any other French provincial city, there are disadvantages. There's urban sprawl and smog, along with some of the hottest and most humid summers in France. In spite of these drawbacks, Lyon is much more relaxed and friendlier than Paris. Parks in full bloom, skyscrapers and sidewalk cafes, a great transport system, concert halls, and a nightlife fueled by student energy await in Lyon, along with talented chefs, both young and old.

Lyon is the best base for exploring the Rhone region. It has the finest food in France and, although industrial and commercial on its fringes, has a historic core unequaled by anything else in the region.

ESSENTIALS

GETTING THERE If you're arriving from the north by **train,** don't get off at the first station, Gare La Part-Dieu; continue on to Gare de Perrache, where you can begin sightseeing. The high-speed TGV takes only 2 hours from Paris. Lyon makes a good stopover en route to the Alps or the Riviera. For train information and schedules, call ℂ **08-36-35-35-35.**

By **plane,** it's a 45-minute flight from Paris to Aéroport Lyon-Satolas (ℂ **04-72-22-72-21**), 15½ miles east of the city. Buses run from the airport into the center of Lyon every 20 minutes during the day. The 45-minute trip costs 52.50F (8, $7.60) each way. Call **Cie Satobus** (ℂ **04-72-68-72-17**) for information.

If you're **driving,** from Nice head west along E1/A7 toward Aix-en-Provence, continuing northwest toward Avignon. Bypass the city and continue north along the same route into Lyon. From Paris, head southeast along A8/E1 into Lyon. From Grenoble to the French Alps, head northeast along A48 until you hook up with the junction of A43, which will take you northeast into Lyon.

VISITOR INFORMATION The **Office de Tourisme** is on place Bellecour (ℂ **04-72-77-69-69;** www.Lyon-France.com).

SPECIAL EVENTS Festivals are so numerous in this city that they can become an everyday event, especially in summer. Music festivals reign supreme, with the most popular occurring on France's National Day of Music, around June 21. This **Fête de la Musique** is famous for turning the streets of Lyon into performance spaces for local bands. In December, the **Festival de Musique du Vieux-Lyon** takes place in various churches around the city. Tickets range from 75F to 225F (11.40 to 34.20, $10.90 to $32.65). For details, contact the festival's headquarters at 5 place du Petit-Collège (ℂ **04-78-38-09-09**).

ATTRACTIONS

The city sprawls over many square miles, divided, like Paris, into arrondissements. The heart straddles the Saône, around the east bank's place Bellecour and the west bank's Primatiale St-Jean. In 2000, four of Lyon's neighborhoods were added to UNESCO's list of sites that bear crucial interest for "la patrimoine universel." They include the slopes of the Croix Rousse, Fourvière, the "peninsula," and Vieux Lyon.

Begin your tour of Lyon at **place Bellecour,** one of France's largest and most charming squares. An equestrian statue of Louis XIV looks out on the encircling 18th-century buildings. Urban sociologists are proud of Lyon's efforts to decorate some of its drab facades with the kind of colorful, trompe l'oeil murals you might expect to see in a downtown neighborhood of Los Angeles. Among the most frequently cited works are the facade of the Musée Tony-Garnier, 4 rue des Serpollières, 8e, and the fresco "des Lyonnais célèbres," 2e.

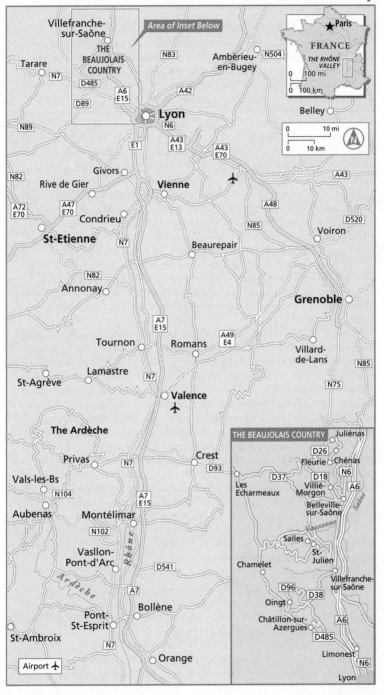

The Rhône Valley

Villefranche-sur-Saône

Area of Inset Below

★ Paris

FRANCE

THE RHÔNE VALLEY

0 ___ 100 mi
0 ___ 100 km

Tarare

THE BEAUJOLAIS COUNTRY

N83

Ambérieu-en-Bugey

N504

N7

D485

A6 E15

D89

Lyon

N6

Belley

0 ___ 10 mi
0 ___ 10 km

N89

E1

A43 E13

A43 E70

A43

N82

Givors

Rive de Gier

Vienne

A48

D520

A72 E70

A47 E70

Condrieu

N85

Voiron

St-Etienne

N7

Beaurepair

N82

Annonay

Grenoble

A7 E15

Tournon

Romans

A49 E4

Villard-de-Lans

N85

Lamastre

N7

St-Agrève

Valence

N75

The Ardèche

THE BEAUJOLAIS COUNTRY

Juliénas

D26

Fleurie

Chénas

Privas

N7

Crest

D93

Les Echarmeaux

D37

D18

Villié-Morgon

N6

A6

Vals-les-Bs

N104

Belleville-sur-Saône

Aubenas

Montélimar

Salles

St-Julien

N102

Rhône

Chamelet

Vasllon-Pont-d'Arc

D541

Oingt

D96

D38

Villefranche-sur-Saône

Ardèche

A7

Bollène

Châtillon-sur-Azergues

A6

Pont-St-Esprit

St-Ambroix

N7

D485

Limonest

N6

Airport ✈

Orange

Lyon

407

(*Moments*   **Entertainment Among the Ruins**

During July and August, when the heat can grow oppressive, consider attending one of the nocturnal events of **Les Nuits de Fourvière,** where dance recitals, concerts, and short plays are presented, under lights, amid the ruins of Lyon's ancient Roman theaters atop Fourvière Hill. For information and reservations, call (**04-72-61-77-77.**

IN VIEUX LYON ★★★

From place Bellecour, walk across pont Bonaparte to the right bank of the Saône River and **Vieux Lyon** (you can also take bus no. 1 or 31, or take the Métro from elsewhere in the city to get here). Covering about a square mile, Old Lyon contains an amazing collection of medieval and Renaissance buildings. Many houses were built five stories high by merchants to show off their new wealth. After years as a slum, the area is now fashionable, attracting antiques dealers, artisans, weavers, sculptors, and painters, who depict scenes along the characteristic **rue du Boeuf,** one of the most interesting streets for exploring.

Your first stop should be the **Primatiale St-Jean** (see below). South of the cathedral is the **Manécanterie,** 70 rue St-Jean ((**04-78-92-82-29**), noted for its 12th-century Romanesque facade and its role as a dormitory beginning in the 11th century. The boys who sang in the medieval choir lived here, making it the oldest residence in Lyon.

North of the cathedral is the most historically and architecturally evocative neighborhood of Old Lyon, with narrow streets, spiral stairs, hanging gardens, soaring towers, and unusual courtyards whose balconies seem to sit precariously atop medieval pilings or columns.

One architectural aspect of the city that's unique to Lyon is its *traboules,* a series of short covered passageways that interconnect longer avenues running parallel to one another. Scattered throughout Vieux Lyon, they're capped with vaulted masonry ceilings that open unexpectedly into flower-ringed courtyards.

While in Vieux Lyon, try to see the exceptional Gothic arcades of the 16th-century **Maison Thomassin,** place du Change, and the 16th-century **Hôtel du Chamarier,** 37 rue St-Jean, where Mme de Sévigné lived. You can admire but not enter these buildings. The neighborhood also contains the awesomely old **Église St-Paul,** 3 place Gerson ((**04-78-28-34-45**), consecrated in A.D. 549. A rebuilding began in 1084 after its destruction by the Saracens. Its octagonal lantern tower was completed in the 1100s, the rest of the premises in the 13th century. You can visit Monday through Saturday from noon to 6pm and Sunday from 2 to 6pm. Admission is free.

Musée Historique de Lyon ★   In the Hôtel de Gadagne, an early-16th-century residence, you'll find this museum's interesting Romanesque sculptures on the ground floor. Other exhibits are 18th-century Lyonnais furniture and pottery, antique ceramics from the town of Nevers, a pewter collection, and numerous paintings and engravings of Lyon.

In the same building is the **Musée de la Marionette** (same phone), which has three puppets by Laurent Mourguet, creator of Guignol, the best-known French marionette character. They have marionettes from other parts of France (Amiens, Lille, and Aix-en-Provence) and collections from around the world.

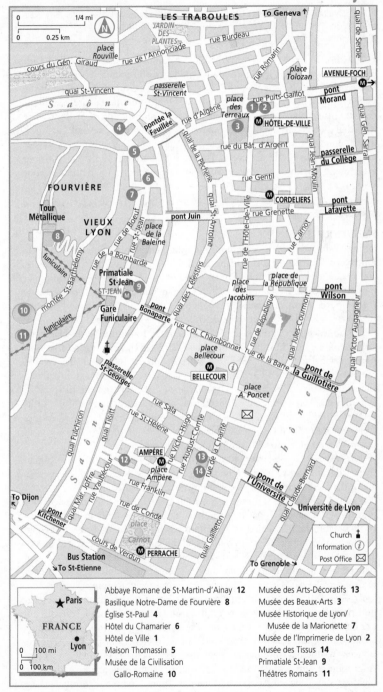

Lyon

LES TRABOULES

To Geneva ↑

quai de Serbie

JARDIN DES PLANTES

rue Burdeau

place Rouville

rue de l'Annonciade

cours du Gén. Giraud

passerelle St-Vincent

quai St-Vincent

S a ô n e

pont de la Feuillée

rue d'Algérie

rue Romarin

place Tolozan

AVENUE-FOCH Ⓜ →

pont Morand

place des Terreaux

rue Puits-Gaillot

① ②

③ Ⓜ HÔTEL-DE-VILLE

quai de la Pêcherie

rue du Bât. d'Argent

quai Gén. Sarrail

④

⑤

FOURVIÈRE

⑥

⑦

passerelle du Collège

quai Jean-Moulin

rue Gentil

Ⓜ CORDELIERS

rue de l'Hôtel-de-Ville

rue Grenette

pont Lafayette

Tour Métallique

VIEUX LYON

pont Juin

quai St-Antoine

rue de Boeuf

rue St-Jean

place de la Baleine

⑧

funiculaire

rue de la Bombarde

montée St-Barthélemy

quai des Célestins

rue Carnot

pont Wilson

quai Jules-Courmont

place de la République

place des Jacobins

Primatiale St-Jean

⑨

ST-JEAN Ⓜ

Gare Funiculaire

pont Bonaparte

rue Col. Chambonnet

rue de République

quai Augagneur

⑩

funiculaire

⑪

†

passerelle St-Georges

quai Fulchiron

place Bellecour

rue de la Barre

pont de la Guillotière

Ⓜ BELLECOUR ⓘ

place A. Poncet

✉

quai Victor Augagneur

R h ô n e

rue Sala

rue St-Hélène

quai Tilsitt

AMPÈRE

place Ampère Ⓜ

rue Victor-Hugo

rue August-Comte

rue de la Charité

⑫ ⑬

⑭

pont de l'Université

quai Claude-Bernard

To Dijon ↖

pont Kitchener

quai Mar. Joffre

rue Vaubecour

rue Franklin

rue de Condé

place Carnot

quai Gailleton

Université de Lyon

cours de Verdun

Ⓜ PERRACHE

To Grenoble →

Bus Station
↘ To St-Etienne

Church †
Information ⓘ
Post Office ✉

0 — 1/4 mi
0 — 0.25 km

N

1 place du Petit-Collège. (℃) **04-78-42-03-61.** Admission (including Musée de la Marionette) 25F (3.80, $3.65) adults, 13F (2, $1.90) students, free for children 18 and under. Both museums Wed–Mon 10:45am–6pm.

Primatiale St-Jean ⭐ This cathedral was built between the 12th and 15th centuries. Its apse is a masterpiece of Lyonnais Romanesque. The exceptional stained-glass windows are from the 12th to the 15th centuries. A highlight is the Flamboyant Gothic chapel of the Bourbons. On the front portals are medallions depicting the signs of the zodiac, the Creation, and the life of St. John. The cathedral's 16th-century Swiss astronomical clock is intricate and beautiful; it announces the hour daily at noon, 2pm, and 3pm in grand style: A rooster crows and angels herald the event. The treasury, on the right of the cathedral, was closed for renovation at press time, but might be open by the time of your visit.

Place St-Jean. (℃) **04-78-42-11-04.** Free admission. Mon–Fri 8am–noon and 2–7:30pm; Sat 2–5:30pm, Sun 8am–5pm.

IN FOURVIÈRE HILL ⭐

Rising to the west of Vieux Lyon on the west bank of the Saône is **Colline de Fourvière (Fourvière Hill)**. This wooded hill—on which numerous convents, colleges, and hospitals; two Roman theaters; and a superb Gallo-Roman museum have been established—affords a panoramic vista of Lyon, with its many bridges across two rivers, the rooftops of the medieval town, and (in clear weather) a view of the countryside extending to the snow-capped Alps.

Enthroned on its summit is the 19th-century **Basilique Notre-Dame de Fourvière,** 8 place de Fourvière (℃ **04-78-25-51-82**), rising fortresslike with four octagonal towers and crenellated walls. Its interior is covered with colored mosaics; adjoining it is an ancient chapel. The belfry is surmounted by a gilded statue of the Virgin. Admission is free; it's open daily from 6:30am to 7pm.

Jardin du Rosaire extends on the hillside between the basilica and the 13th-century Primatiale St-Jean. It's open daily between 7am and 7pm and provides a pleasant walk. You'll see a vast shelter for up to 200 pilgrims. An elevator takes you to the top of the towers, and two funiculars service the hill.

The excavated **Théâtres Romains,** Montée de Fourvière, a Roman theater/odeum is in a park south of the basilica at 6 rue de l'Antiquaille. The theater is the most ancient in France, built by order of Augustus from 17 B.C. to 15 B.C. and greatly expanded during the reign of Hadrian. The odeum, reserved for musical performances, apparently was once sumptuously decorated. Its orchestra floor, for example, contains mosaics of such materials as brightly colored marble and porphyry. The third building in the sanctuary was dedicated in A.D. 160 to the goddess Cybele, or Sibella, whose cult originated in Asia Minor. All that remains are the foundations, though they seem to dominate the theater (175 ft. by 284 ft.). They can be visited daily from 7am to 7pm.

An altar dedicated to a bull cult and a monumental marble statue of the goddess are shown in the **Musée de la Civilisation Gallo-Romaine,** 17 rue Cléberg (℃ **04-72-38-81-90**), a few steps from the archaeological site. The museum's collection of Gallo-Roman artifacts is the finest in France outside Paris. The site is open Wednesday through Sunday from 9:30am to noon and 2 to 6pm. Admission is 20F (3.05, $2.90) for adults, free for children 12 and under. Guides are available on Sundays and holidays from 2 to 6pm. Performances are given at both theaters in the summer.

ELSEWHERE AROUND THE CITY

In addition to the sites below, you might also check out the **Abbaye Romane de St-Martin-d'Ainay,** 11 rue Bourgelat (✆ 04-78-37-48-97), south of place Bellecour, near place Ampère. Lyon's oldest church dates from 1107. Admission is free; hours are daily from 8:30 to 11:30am and 3 to 6:30pm. The rue de l'Hôtel-de-Ville extends north from place Bellecour to **place des Terreaux,** dominated by the 1746 **Hôtel de Ville,** one of the most beautiful in Europe. The outside is dark and severe; the interior is brilliant but, alas, closed to the public.

Musée de l'Imprimerie de Lyon   Occupying a 15th-century mansion, this museum is devoted to Lyon's role in the world of printing. Exhibits include a page from a Gutenberg Bible, 17th- to 20th-century presses, 16th- to 19th-century woodcuts, and engravings. This is one of the most important printing museums in Europe, along with those at Mainz and Antwerp. It has a collection of books from "all epochs," including *incunabula,* books printed before Easter 1500.

13 rue de la Poulaillerie. ✆ **04-78-37-65-98**. Admission 25F (3.80, $3.65) adults, 13F (2, $1.90) students, free for children under 18. Wed–Sun 9:30am–noon and 2–6pm.

Musée des Arts-Décoratifs ★★   Housed in the 1739 Lacroix-Laval mansion by Soufflot (architect of the Panthéon in Paris), the Musée des Arts-Décoratifs contains furniture and objets d'art from the 17th and 18th centuries. The medieval and Renaissance periods are also represented. Look for a five-octave clavecin by Donzelague, the 18th-century creator of musical instruments.

34 rue de la Charité. ✆ **04-78-38-42-00**. Combined admission for this museum and Musée des Tissus 30F (4.55, $4.35) adults, 15F (2.30, $2.20) students, free for children 18 and under. Tues–Sun 10am–noon and 2–5:30pm.

Musée des Beaux-Arts ★★   On the south side of the square stands the Palais des Arts (also called the Musée de St-Pierre). This former Benedictine abbey was built between 1659 and 1685 in the Italian baroque style. Today, it's home to the Musée des Beaux-Arts. Renovated in 1998, it has an outstanding collection of paintings and sculpture. You enter via a courtyard graced with statuary and shade trees. The ground floor offers a display of 14th-century paintings. The collection includes Etruscan, Egyptian, Phoenician, Sumerian, and Persian art. See, in particular, Perugino's altarpiece. The top floor is one of France's richest 19th-century collections, with works by artists from Veronese, Tintoretto, and Rubens to Braque, Bonnard, and Picasso. Be sure to see Joseph Chinard's bust of Mme Récamier, the Lyon beauty who charmed Napoleonic Paris by merely reclining, and the Fantin-Latour masterpiece *Reading.*

20 place des Terreaux. ✆ **04-72-10-17-40**. Admission 25F (3.80, $3.65) adults, 13F (2, $1.90) students, free for children 17 and under. Wed–Mon 10:30am–6pm.

Musée des Tissus ★★★   Next door to the Musée des Arts-Décoratifs is an even more interesting collection, housed in the 1730 Palais de Villeroy. On view are priceless fabrics from all over the world, spanning 2,000 years. Some of the finest fabrics made in Lyon from the 18th century to the present are displayed. The 15th- and 16th-century textiles embroidered with religious motifs are noteworthy, as are the 17th-century Persian carpets. Look for the partridge-motif brocade for Marie Antoinette's bedchamber at Versailles, as well as a brocaded satin woven for Queen Victoria of 150 colors with birds of paradise and orchids.

34 rue de la Charité. ✆ **04-78-38-42-00**. Combined admission for this museum and Musée des Arts-Décoratifs 30F (4.55, $4.35) adults, 15F (2.30, $2.20) students, free for children 18 and under. Tues–Sun 10am–5:30pm.

OUTSIDE THE HEART OF THE CITY

One of Lyon's grandest archaeological sites, though minor in world terms, is **Amphithéâtre des Trois-Gauls,** rue du Jardin-des-Plantes, Croix-Rousse (no phone), in Lyon's 4th arrondissement, near the city's northern perimeter. Regrettably, you can view the site only from the outside. At the time of its construction, it was the centerpiece of Condate, a Gallic village near the junction of the Rhône and Saône that predated the arrival of the Romans by centuries. Various accounts have members of 60 Gallic tribes meeting here in the earliest example of a French parliamentary system. Based on those dimly remembered events, France's 2,000th anniversary was celebrated in Lyon in 1989.

On the opposite side of the Rhône, you can explore Lyon's largest public park and garden, the 260-acre **Parc de la Tête d'Or** (© 04-78-89-53-52). Its largest (but by no means only) entrance is on boulevard des Belges. It opened in 1857 with all the fountains, pedestrian walkways, and ornamental statues you'd expect. Surrounded by wealthy residential neighborhoods, the park has a lake, illuminated fountains, a zoo, a botanical garden with greenhouses, and a rose garden with some 100,000 plants. It's open throughout the year during daylight hours, and in May and June is particularly renowned for its profusion of roses.

At Rochetaillée-sur-Saône, 7 miles north of Lyon on D433, the **Musée Français de l'Automobile "Henri Malartre"** is housed in the Château de Rochetaillée, 645 chemin du Musée (© 04-78-22-18-80). Established by a wealthy benefactor (Henri Malartre) and taken over as a public museum by the city of Lyon in 1960, the collection includes 100 cars dating back to 1890, 65 motorcycles from 1903 and after, and 40 cycles dating back to 1848. The château is surrounded by a large park. Admission to the museum and château is 35F (5.30, $5.10) adults, free for children 18 and under. Both are open Tuesday through Sunday from 9am to 6pm.

SHOPPING

Since this is the third-largest city in France, you'll find a full array of shopping options. For small boutiques, art galleries, and local artists' studios and workshops, head to Vieux Lyon and the area around rue de la République, rue Victor Hugo, rue Mercière, and quai St-Antoine. For antiques, concentrate around rue Auguste-Comte as it approaches place Bellecour. And consider venturing to the **Cité des Antiquaires,** 117 bd. Stalingrad (© 04-72-44-91-98), with more than 100 antiques dealers.

Lyon remains a bastion for fashion: everything from the cutting edge to the classically elegant. The densest concentrations of retail shops in Lyon lie along the rue Émile Zola, rue de Presidént Edouard Herriot, and place Kléber.

For chic couture that rivals anything you'll find in Paris, try **George Rech,** 59 rue du Président-Herriot (© 04-78-37-82-90). And for a concentration of more than 200 shops and boutiques set side by side, wander down the walkways of the largest shopping center in Lyon, the **Centre Commercial de la Part-Dieu,** 17 rue du Dr. Bouchut (© 04-72-60-60-62). Although Lyon is not the major silk center of yesteryear, it still hangs on to several silk manufacturers; and a good selection of silk scarves, ties, sashes, and squares can be found at **La Maison des Canuts,** 10–12 rue d'Ivry (© 04-78-28-62-04), as well as at the famous Parisian supplier **Hermès,** 56 rue du Président-Herriot (© 04-78-42-25-14).

For a thoroughly Lyonnais gift, keep your eye out for **marionettes de Lyon.** These intricately crafted puppets are art forms in their own right, and at their best, each has a distinctive personality. The best selection and some of the finest craftsmanship are at **Maison de Guignol,** 60 rue du Lac (© **04-78-60-11-91**).

Bernachon, 42 cours Franklin-Roosevelt (© **04-78-24-37-98**), is home to Lyon's best chocolates and pastries. Here you'll find 30 varieties of bite-size pastries known as mini-gâteaux, 30 varieties of petits fours, and even dark, rich chocolates lightly dusted with 24-karat gold. Also at the Bernachon store is a small restaurant/tearoom called **Bernachon Passion.** Just down the way, you'll find the well-respected **Bocuse & Bernachon,** 46 cours Franklin-Roosevelt (© **04-72-74-46-19**), which sells both the chocolates of Bernachon and the upscale food products endorsed by gastronomic superstar Paul Bocuse.

ACCOMMODATIONS

Note that **Alain Chapel** (see "Dining," below) also rents rooms.

EXPENSIVE

Cour des Loges ✦✦✦   This luxury hotel in Old Lyon occupies several houses dating from the 14th to the 17th centuries. It offers beautifully furnished rooms and suites. Most units face gardens, the square, or a large sunlit lobby. The size and configuration of the rooms vary, but each comes with an immaculate tiled bathroom, most with both tub and shower. The staff is courteous, highly efficient, and the most savvy in Lyon.

6 rue du Boeuf, 69005 Vieux Lyon. © **04-72-77-44-44.** Fax 04-72-40-93-61. www.courdesloges.com. 62 units. 1,350F–2,000F (205.20– 304, $195.75–$290) double; 2,300F–3,000F (349.60– 456, $333.50–$435) suite. AE, DC, MC, V. Parking 130F (19.75, $18.85). Métro: St-Jean. **Amenities:** Restaurant, bar, wine cellar; indoor pool; Jacuzzi; sauna; 24-hr. room service; laundry/dry cleaning. *In room:* A/C, TV, minibar, hair dryer.

MODERATE

Libertel Hôtel des Beaux-Arts   Located in the center of Lyon, this is one of the best of the moderately priced choices. The lobby evokes the 1930s, whereas the guest rooms, though comfortable, are outfitted in businesslike modern style. Since this is a noisy part of the city, double-glazing on the windows helps shut out traffic sounds; the quieter rooms are in the rear. Each unit comes with a neat tiled bathroom, most with combination tub/shower. A large breakfast is the only meal served, though you may prefer having croissants and coffee at one of the cafes along place Bellecour.

75 rue du Président-Herriot, 69002 Lyon. © **04-78-38-09-50.** Fax 04-78-42-19-19. www.accorhotels.com. 75 units. 540F–720F (82.10– 109.45, $78.30–$104.40) double; 830F (126.15, $120.35) suite. AE, DC, MC, V. Métro: Cordelier. **Amenities:** Bar; room service; laundry. *In room:* A/C, TV, minibar, hair dryer.

Grand Hôtel Château Perrache ✦   This hotel near the Perrache train station offers Lyon's most traditional rooms. You will either love this monument to Art Nouveau or hate it, depending on your tastes. Admittedly, the old dame has seen better times. Romantics and nostalgia buffs love the creaky furnishings, the antiques, and the winter garden. Most of the old-fashioned bathrooms have dated bathtubs. Les Belles Saisons, the house restaurant, does more than just cater to the tired business traveler who doesn't want to leave the premises at night. Its finely honed cuisine is often innovative and features continental and regional dishes.

12 cours de Verdun, 69002 Lyon. © **800/MERCURE** or 04-72-77-15-00. Fax 04-78-37-06-56. www.accor hotels.com. 111 units. 880F–980F (133.75– 148.95, $127.60–$142.10) double. AE, DC, MC, V. Métro: Perrache. **Amenities:** Restaurant, bar; room service. *In room:* A/C, TV, minibar, hair dryer.

Hôtel Globe et Cécil *Value* Near place Bellecour, this hotel is a good value for Lyon, because of its location and attentive staff. The rooms are comfortable, attractively furnished, and individually decorated, each with a tidy shower-only bathroom. Breakfast is the only meal served, but many restaurants are nearby.

21 rue Gasparin, 69002 Lyon. ℭ **04-78-42-58-95.** Fax 04-72-41-99-06. 58 units. 720F–780F (109.45– 118.55, $104.40–$113.10) double. Rates include breakfast. AE, DC, MC, V. Parking 65F (9.90, $9.45). Métro: Bellecour. **Amenities:** Laundry. *In room:* A/C, TV.

INEXPENSIVE

Hôtel Bayard The foundations of this dignified town house date from the 16th century, and though the walls are more recent, each bedroom is outfitted in a style inspired by a period of French history. All units come with recently renewed and compact private bathrooms, most with shower only. The entire hotel was renovated in 1999. Enter via a narrow hallway, and climb one flight up to the reception area. Don't be put off by the staff, who may appear nonchalant.

23 place Bellecour, 69002 Lyon. ℭ **04-78-37-39-64.** Fax 04-72-40-95-51. www.hotelbayard.com. 15 units. 483F–563F (73.40– 85.60, $70.05–$81.65) double. AE, DC, MC, V. Parking 50F–65F (7.60– 9.90, $7.25–$9.45). Métro: Bellecour. **Amenities:** Room service; laundry. *In room:* TV, hair dryer, safe.

Hôtel Bellecordière A savvy gourmet traveler we know always stays at this nondescript hotel, preferring to spend her money on Lyon's .restaurants. The small accommodations are no-frills and, at their worst, a bit depressing. But each is neatly kept and equipped with a compact shower-only bathroom. Breakfast is the only meal served, but many worthwhile restaurants are within a short walk.

18 rue Bellecordière, 69002 Lyon. ℭ **04-78-42-27-78.** Fax 04-72-40-92-27. 45 units. 320F (48.65, $46.40) double. AE, MC, V. Métro: Bellecour.

La Résidence *Value* Long a favorite with budget travelers, this hotel is at the corner of a pedestrian zone in the center of Lyon. Beyond an ornate 19th-century facade, the bedrooms are comfortably, but not spectacularly, furnished. Half come with combination tub/showers. For the price, the place offers one of the best values in this rather overpriced city. Breakfast is the only meal served, but many restaurants are literally outside the door, as is some of the finest shopping.

18 rue Victor-Hugo, 69002 Lyon. ℭ **04-78-42-63-28.** Fax 04-78-42-85-76. www.hotel-la-residence.com. 67 units. 350F–380F (53.20– 57.75, $50.75–$55.10) double. AE, DC, MC, V. Métro: Bellecour. **Amenities:** Laundry. *In room:* TV.

DINING

The food in Lyon is among the finest in the world—with prices to match. However, we've found that a person of moderate means can often afford the most reasonable fixed-price menus even in the city's priciest establishments.

VERY EXPENSIVE

Alain Chapel ✸✸✸ MODERN FRENCH This Relais Gourmand occupies a 19th-century postal station that has evolved over years of architectural improvements into a comfortable, conservatively stylish place. Alain Chapel was one of the world's premier chefs, and after his death many claimed that the stellar reputation of his restaurant would tarnish; but under Philippe Jousse (who trained under Chapel), that hasn't been the case. Assisted by M. Chapel's widow, he continues to maintain the image of Lyon as a gastronomic capital, with perhaps a bit less emphasis on the media hype and glamour of his predecessor.

Menu items change with the seasons, but are likely to include lobster salad with pigeon necks and black truffles; Bresse chicken cooked in a pig's bladder, stuffed with foie gras and drizzled with foie-gras sauce; and puff pastry with apples and vanilla-flavored bourbon sauce and champagne-flavored sorbet. A particularly succulent and hearty main course is stuffed and braised oxtail with creamed leeks and a side dish containing the oxtail's herb-enriched consommé. End your meal with what the menu calls "some country cheeses," a particularly appealing assortment of unusual local cheeses whose presentation is charming.

Also available are 14 beautiful guest rooms, priced at 650F to 850F (98.80 to 129.20, $94.25 to $123.25) double.

N83 Mionnay, 01390 St-André-de-Corcy. © **04-78-91-82-02**. Fax 04-78-91-82-37. E-mail: chapel@relais chateaux.fr. Reservations required. Main courses 200F–300F (30.40– 45.60, $29–$43.50); fixed-price menus 380F (57.75, $55.10) lunch Wed–Fri, 610F–830F (92.70– 126.15, $88.45–$120.35) dinner. AE, DC, MC, V. Tues and Thurs 7:30–10:30pm, Wed and Fri–Mon 12:30–1:30pm and 7:30–10pm. Closed Jan. Take N83 12½ miles north of Lyon.

Léon de Lyon ★★★ MODERN FRENCH   Upstairs in what was once a private home, tables are placed in a series of small rooms that have welcomed many a famous guest, from Charles Aznavour to Bill Clinton. The atmosphere may be traditional and typical, but the food isn't. The owner, Jean-Paul Lacombe, has been called a challenger to the top chefs of Lyon, serving regional and modern cuisine with innovative flair. His brilliant use of Lyonnais offal might scare off some but will please the dedicated gastronome. Offerings might include pheasant soup with foie gras and red beans, pike *quenelles* (fish balls), or lobster with asparagus. More challenging fare ranges from local swine served with foie gras and an onion terrine to quenelles of brochet in local red wine served with lobster sauce and freshwater crayfish. The sorbets made with fresh fruits are a perfect ending.

1 rue Pleney. © **04-72-10-11-12**. Reservations required. Main courses 270F–520F (41.05– 79.05, $39.15–$75.40); fixed-price menus 290F (44.10, $42.05) lunch, 600F–850F (91.20– 129.20, $87–$123.25) dinner. AE, DC, MC, V. Tues–Sat noon–2pm and 7:30–10pm. Closed Aug 1–21. Métro: Hôtel-de-Ville.

Paul Bocuse ★★★ LYONNAISE   Paul Bocuse is one of the world's most famous contemporary chefs. He specializes in regional cuisine, though long ago he was the leading exponent of nouvelle cuisine (which he later called "a joke"). Since Bocuse (now in his 70s) is gone at least part of the time, other chefs must carry on with the mass production (for up to 180 diners) of the signature dishes the master created and on which there isn't a lot of variation.

You can't miss this place on the banks of the Saône. Tired of the conventional facades that shelter most French restaurants, Bocuse commissioned a local artist to paint the history of French cuisine, in cartoon form, on the outside of his place. The tale begins in the 1700s and proceeds through the years to its "defining moment"—a depiction of Bocuse himself. Inside, in one of three dining rooms, you can begin your meal with the famous black truffle soup, then try one of the most enduring dishes in the Bocuse repertoire: the perfumey Bresse chicken cooked in a pig's bladder. Other options include roast pigeon in puff pastry with baby cabbage leaves and foie gras, and red snapper served in a potato casing.

A boutique sells Bocuse's preferred wine, cognac, jams and jellies, coffees and teas, and cookbooks, all of which prominently display his image and logo.

Pont de Collonges, Collonges-au-Mont-d'Or. © **04-72-42-90-90**. Reservations required as far in advance as possible. Main courses 200F–300F (30.40– 45.60, $29–$43.50); fixed-price menus 630F–820F (95.75– 124.65, $91.35–$118.90). AE, DC, MC, V. Daily noon–1:30pm and 8–9:30pm. Take N433 5½ miles north of Lyon.

EXPENSIVE

La Mère Brazier ★★ TRADITIONAL FRENCH   This restaurant near pont Morand has grown from a 1921 lunch spot for silk workers to an internationally known gourmet restaurant that draws connoisseurs. It's managed by Carmen and Jacotte Brazier—the daughter-in-law and one of the granddaughters of its founder, Mme Brazier. The simple decor and wood paneling make an attractive setting for a leisurely lunch or an outstanding supper. Here you can order excellent regional dishes, accompanied by such local wines as Mâcon, Juliénas, Morgon, Chiroubles, and virtually every Côte du Rhone ever bottled. Appetizers include artichoke hearts stuffed with foie gras, as well as smoked Nordic salmon. Specialties are *volaille de Bresse demi-deuil* (boiled chicken with truffles under the skin, served with vegetables, rice, and bouillon) and superbly smooth *quenelles de brochet* (pike) au gratin. More-extravagant fare includes lobster Belle Aurore or *à la nage*. The service is solicitous.

12 rue Royale. ℂ 04-78-28-15-49. Reservations required. Main courses 120F–250F (18.25– 38, $17.40–$36.25); fixed-price menus 280F–330F (42.55– 50.15, $40.60–$47.85); business menu (Mon–Fri) 190F (28.90, $27.55). AE, DC, MC, V. Wed–Fri noon–1:45pm; Wed–Sat and Mon 7:30–10pm. Closed Apr 23–May 3 and July 22–Aug 22. Métro: Hôtel-de-Ville.

MODERATE

La Tassée *Value* FRENCH   The chef here isn't interested in fancy frills but does believe in serving good food at prices most people can afford. Huge portions are dished out, and you might be offered anything from strips of tripe to game or sole. Other favorites include quenelles of brochet with lobster sauce and sautéed chicken with drizzles of vinegar, tossed with freshly made pasta. On a recent visit, we arrived just when the Beaujolais nouveau had come in—a major event. The dining room boasts noteworthy 19th-century frescoes.

20 rue de la Charité. ℂ 04-72-77-79-00. Main courses 80F–190F (12.15– 28.90, $11.60–$27.55); fixed-price menus 165F–290F (25.10– 44.10, $23.95–$42.05). AE, DC, V. Mon–Sat noon–2:30pm and 7:15–10:15pm. July–Aug closed Sat–Sun. Métro: Bellecour.

Le Bistrot de Lyon TRADITIONAL FRENCH   This place stays hopping until the wee hours. It's on a street of bistros, with several wine bars mixed in. The setting is elegant and traditional, with marble-topped tables. You might want to stick to classic Lyonnais fare, like poached eggs in red-wine sauce; pot-au-feu, a stew with fresh vegetables; or braised chicken with herbs, white wine, and heaps of fresh pasta. The adventurous can immerse themselves in such earthy and savory Lyonnais classics as crispy pig's trotters with truffle-studded foie gras.

64 rue Mercière. ℂ 04-78-38-47-47. Main courses 65F–100F (9.90– 15.20, $9.45–$14.50); fixed-price menus 99F (15.05, $14.35) lunch, 140F–160F (21.30– 24.30, $20.30–$23.20) dinner. AE, MC, V. Daily noon–2:30pm and 7pm–1am. Métro: Cordelier.

INEXPENSIVE

Café des Fédérations TRADITIONAL FRENCH   This is one of the busiest, most animated, and sometimes most amusingly raucous bistros in Lyon. Open only on weekdays, catering to the office-worker crowd, it's operated with panache by a team of hardworking employees who would probably perform beautifully in the trenches of a war zone. All meals are set, fixed-price menus offering a selection of appetizers, main courses, and desserts. Each evokes old-time Lyonnais cuisine at its least pretentious, with such options as a green salad with bacon and croutons; eggs *en meurette* (poached in red wine); *andouillette*

Beaucoup Bocuse

A resurgence in interest in chef Paul Bocuse swept across Lyon in 1994 when he bought the **Brasserie Le Nord** ⚓, 18 rue Neuve ((ℂ **04-72-10-69-69**), a turn-of-the-20th-century brasserie that the master worked in as a teenager. Menu prices here—about 180F (27.35, $26.10) per person for a meal with wine and coffee—signaled that the last of the great chefs had finally decided to go for the mass market. And we're not complaining! It's the most popular restaurant in town, particularly with the bankers and merchants who pack the place at lunch. A short while later, Bocuse opened a twin of Le Nord, **Brasserie Le Sud,** place Antonin-Poncet (ℂ **04-72-77-80-00**), specializing in the cuisine of the French-speaking Mediterranean. Then in 1998, he opened **Brasserie de l'Est,** 11 place Jules-Ferry (ℂ **04-37-24-25-26**), offering a cuisine that incorporates the best of the Nord and the Sud, with a hint of Alsace and Lorraine thrown in for good measure. No prizes for guessing the name of his next brasserie if and when it opens.

At least some of the success of these brasseries stems from the Bocuse name, for he is the most prominent and enduring grand chef in France. His almost mythical restaurant in the Lyon suburb of Collanges-au-Mont-d'Or (see our review, above) has earned a trio of Michelin stars (the top rating) every year since 1965. Less secure chefs might tremble at the thought of the public scrutiny this involves, fearing that the laurels thrown by culinary critics will be ripped away later. But Bocuse, with his irrepressible ego, seems to thrill year after year to the notion that he's without parallel.

So, will the master be here when you drop in at his brasserie? Not necessarily. He may not even be found at Collanges-au-Mont-d'Or—or even in Lyon. Since creating some of the most award-winning dishes in Europe (black truffle soup, filet of sea bass *en croûte,* chicken cooked in a pig's bladder), Bocuse has launched his own line of vacuum-packed foods, endorsed a string of bakeries in Japan, purchased a Beaujolais vineyard, become interested in the French Pavilion at Walt Disney World's Epcot Center in Florida, and helped develop a collection of CDs (Matins et Câlins) designed to soothe the grumpy after-effects of too much wine and foie gras. He's in demand everywhere from Chicago to Tokyo, and virtually every agent in Hollywood salivates at the thought of getting him to endorse anything and everything—from T-shirts to slotted spoons.

His team quickly assures the press and diners that although "temporarily absent," Bocuse is present "in spirit." And in this case the spirit, as priests have affirmed for many years, is invariably stronger than the flesh.

(chitterling sausages) served with a *gratin dauphinois;* pork chops; and several kinds of sausage, usually with *pommes de terre dauphinoise.*

8 rue Major-Martin. ℂ **04-78-28-26-00.** Reservations recommended. Fixed-price menu 118F (17.95, $17.10) lunch, 148F (22.50, $21.45) dinner. V. Mon–Fri noon–2pm and 8–10pm. Closed Aug. Métro: Hôtel de Ville.

Le Borsalino FRENCH/LYONNAISE When a grander, more pretentious restaurant went out of business on this site in 1998, this less expensive new-comer moved in and still attracts a loyal clientele. The theme of the place involves images established by the movie *Borsalino,* a gangster film set in Marseille in the 1930s. Menu items change with the seasons, but might include ravioli stuffed with scallops; pave of rump steak with morels; frogs' legs with a watercress cream sauce; and house-style foie gras with shrimp. We admit that the place is a bit theme-ish, but it's all good-natured; the cuisine is actually rather good, and the prices are reasonable. The only drawback to this place is its limited hours.

42 rue Pierre-Corneille. ⓒ 04-72-75-90-66. Reservations recommended. Main courses 60F–85F (9.10– 12.90, $8.70–$12.35); fixed-price menus 97F–117F (14.75– 17.80, $14.05–$16.95). AE, DC, MC, V. Mon–Fri 11:30am–2:30pm, Thurs–Fri 7:30–10pm. Métro: Avenue-Foch.

LYON AFTER DARK

This cosmopolitan hub of entertainment and culture offers many options. At any newsstand, pick up a copy of the weekly guide *Lyon-Poche,* which lists all the cultural happenings around town, from bars and theaters to classical concerts.

For the theater or opera buff, Lyon's **Théâtre des Célestins,** 4 rue Charles-Dullin (ⓒ **04-72-77-40-00**), is the premier venue for comedy and drama; and the **Opéra,** place de la Comédie (ⓒ **04-72-00-45-45**), always has a lively and diverse season. A recent addition to Lyon's nightlife is **Halle Tony Garnier,** 20 place Antonin Perrin (ⓒ **04-72-76-85-85**). Named after one of the city's bene-factors, and originally built in the 19th century, its restored premises once func-tioned as a food market. Today, its immense space is known for its excellent acoustics and is the site of concerts, trade fairs, and temporary art exhibitions.

For the best pubs in town, go to the **Smoking Dog,** 16 rue Lainerie (ⓒ **04-78-28-38-27**), a happy neighborhood bar with a mixed-age crowd; or the **Barrel House,** 13 rue Ste-Catherine (ⓒ **04-78-29-20-40**), filled with a younger, English-speaking crowd bent on drinking themselves under the table.

Rock 'n' rollers head over to the old train station to one of the newest clubs, **Millennium,** 13 place J.-Ferry (ⓒ **04-72-74-04-41**), with its up-and-coming yuppies. Another club to check out is **Le Box-Office,** 30 bd. Eugène-Deruelle (ⓒ **04-78-95-37-02**), with its brash techno crew. The cover at these clubs ranges from 60F to 100F (9.10 to 15.20, $8.70 to $14.50). For jazz enthu-siasts, give a listen to what has become a Lyon tradition, **Le Hot Club,** 26 rue Lanterne (ⓒ **04-78-39-54-74**).

Surprisingly in a city this size, there are no exclusively gay and lesbian discos; the closest thing is a gay-friendly dance club called **Le Show-Biz,** 112 quai Pierre-Scize (ⓒ **04-72-00-22-55**), with its smoke machines, flashing lights, mirrors, and average cover of 60F (9.10, $8.70). It's a fun and safe place to let your hair down and burn off some calories. Bars include **Le Verre à Soi,** 25 rue des Capucins (ⓒ **04-78-28-92-44**), with a mixed gay and lesbian crowd; and the popular **Le Bar du Centre,** 3 rue Simon-Maupin (ⓒ **04-78-37-40-18**), where a guy can relax, have a drink, and strike up a conversation with what one of the bartenders called "the hottest men in Lyon."

2 The Beaujolais Country ⚹⚹

The vineyards of Beaujolais start about 25 miles north of Lyon. This wine-producing region is small—only 40 miles long and less than 10 miles wide—yet it's one of the most famous in the nation and known throughout the world because of the Beaujolais craze that began in Paris some 30 years ago. The United States is one of the big world markets for Beaujolais. In an average year, this region produces 30 million gallons of wine, more than 190 million bottles.

Most people don't come to the Beaujolais country to visit specific sites, but to drink the wine. There are around 180 châteaux scattered throughout this part of France, and at many of them you can sample and/or buy bottles of the Beaujolais.

This region is a colorful and prosperous rural part of France, with vineyards on sunlit hillsides, pleasant golden cottages where the vine growers live, and historic houses and castles. It has been called the Land of the Golden Stones. Don't expect many architectural monuments, though.

Unlike Alsace with its Route du Vin, the Beaujolais country doesn't have a defined route. You can branch off in many directions, stopping at whatever point or wine cellar intrigues you. Don't be worried about losing your way after meandering off the A6 superhighway. This is one of the easiest parts of eastern France to negotiate, with clear road signs. If you're in doubt, simply follow the signs to the region's capital and commercial center, Villefranche-sur-Saône.

If you're pressed for time, you can tie the highlights together in a one-way drive, beginning at the region's southern terminus, **Villefranche,** which you can access from A6 between Mâcon and Lyon. (If you're heading north to south, follow the drive in reverse order, beginning in Juliénas, accessible from A6.)

Start in Villefranche, marked with an exit off A6. After an excursion west on D38 to **Bagnol-en-Beaujolais,** return to Villefranche. From here, take the meandering D504 and D20, which make sharp bends toward the east en route to **St-Julien-sous-Montmelas.** From St-Julien, take D19 to **Salles-en-Beaujolais.** From Salles, take D62 and D19 to **Belleville-sur-Saône.** Then follow D37 and D68 to **Villié-Morgon.** From Villié-Morgon, take D68 and D266 to **Juliénas.**

VILLEFRANCHE-SUR-SAÔNE—CAPITAL OF BEAUJOLAIS

In Villefranche-sur-Saône, we advise you to go to the **Office du Tourisme,** 290 rue de Thizy, not far from the marketplace (© **04-74-07-27-40;** www.beaujo lais.com), for a booklet on the Beaujolais country. It offers a regional map and itineraries and lists some 30 villages and the wine-tasting cellars open to the public. The office is open Monday through Saturday from 9am to noon and 1:30 to 6:30pm (in July and August, also on Sunday from 9am to noon).

BAGNOLS-EN-BEAUJOLAIS

To reach Bagnols from Villefranche, head west on D38.

ACCOMMODATIONS & DINING

Château de Bagnols-en-Beaujolais ★★★   This is lordly living on a grand, superexpensive scale. France's premier château/hotel, this Renaissance ruin has been restored by 400 artisans and craftspeople for Helen Hamlyn and her husband, the publisher/philanthropist Paul Hamlyn, who spent between $6 and $12 million on the project. The mansion is filled with antiques, wall paintings, and art, much from the 17th century. The individually decorated guest rooms are sumptuous, with antique beds, period velvets, embroidered linen sheets, and down pillows; one unit is named for Mme de Sévigné, who spent a restless night here in 1673. The bathrooms contain tiled floors, brass fittings, and luxurious tubs. This place is not for the young and restless—you won't find a pool, gym, or tennis courts here. Elegant continental fare is served in the Guards Room.

69620 Bagnols. © **04-74-71-40-00.** Fax 04-74-71-40-49. www.bagnols.com. 20 units. 2,200F–3,800F (334.40– 577.60, $319–$551) double; 5,500F–6,500F (836– 988, $797.50–$942.50) suite. AE, DC, MC, V. Closed Jan 2–Mar 30. **Amenities:** Restaurant; bar; room service; laundry. *In room:* TV, minibar, hair dryer.

ST-JULIEN-SOUS-MONTMELAS

This charming village is 6½ miles northwest of Villefranche (take D504, then D20). It was the home of Claude Bernard, the father of physiology, born here in 1813. His small stone house—now the **Musée Claude-Bernard Hameau de Chatenay** (© **04-74-67-51-44**)—offers mementos of the scholar, and his instruments and books. The museum is open Wednesday through Sunday from 10am to noon and 2 to 6pm. Admission is 15F (2.30, $2.20) for adults and 10F (1.50, $1.45) for students and children. Closed in March.

SALLES-EN-BEAUJOLAIS

If you want to visit specific sites in the area, we suggest the **Église de Salles Arbuissonnas** (© **04-74-67-51-50**). Begun in A.D. 1090 and finally completed in the 1700s, this religious hideaway is mostly Romanesque, with an occasional Gothic overlay, especially in its doorways. Notice the Salle Capitulaire, where the ornate capitals of columns from throughout its long history are proudly displayed. The church is open daily, May to September from 9am to 7pm and October to April from 9am to 6pm. Admission is free. A guided tour, in French, costs 10F (1.50, $1.45). From St-Julien, take D19 a short distance to Salles.

BELLEVILLE-SUR-SAÔNE

For an excellent dining experience, drive north from Salles on D19 and D62 to Belleville-sur-Saône.

DINING

Le Rhône au Rhin ✪ MODERN FRENCH   Chef Michel Debize operates this out-of-the-way restaurant almost as a self-imposed refuge from the more congested regions of France. Consequently, you'll get the feeling that if he doesn't like you, he won't necessarily deal with you. All of that is forgotten once you try the well-flavored cuisine and align yourself with his escapist dream. Menu items change with the seasons but might include a terrine of foie gras with apples served in puff pastry, a tartare of raw salmon with lime juice, and a duo of salmon and crayfish in a potato galette. This restaurant doesn't attract the media attention it once did, but we think its cuisine remains as fine as ever.

10 av. du Port. © **04-74-66-16-23**. Reservations required. Main courses 75F–110F (11.40– 16.70, $10.90–$15.95); fixed-price menus 98F–265F (14.90– 40.30, $14.20–$38.45). MC, V. Tues–Sun noon–2pm; Tues–Sat 7–9:30pm.

VILLIÉ-MORGON

For another dining choice in the Beaujolais country, we suggest driving west from Belleville-sur-Saône on D37, north on D18 to Villié-Morgon. This village, and the region around it, contains around 250 wine producers. Their product, at its best, is usually judged one of the greatest Beaujolais wines in France.

In the basement of the Hôtel de Ville (town hall), place de l'Hôtel-de-Ville, is the **Caveau de Morgon** (© **04-74-04-20-99**), which assembles and "marries" a selection of the Villié-Morgon region's best wines into a well-respected brand name (Caveau de Morgon) whose marketing savvy benefits wine growers and consumers alike. (Whatever you do, don't use the word "blend" to describe this company's product, as it's usually received with something akin to horror.) The cellar is open for tours and sales daily from 9am to noon and 2 to 7pm (closed January 1 to 15). Admission is free. The town hall that contains it, incidentally, was built during the late 1600s, destroyed during the French Revolution, and reconstructed and modified several times since.

JULIÉNAS

Wines are also a reason to travel north on D266 and D68 to Juliénas. This village produces a full-bodied, robust wine. Go to the **Cellier dans l'Ancien Église** (© **04-74-04-41-43**), the old church cellar, to sip the wine. A statue of Bacchus with some scantily clad and tipsy girlfriends looks on from what used to be the altar. It's open daily from 10am to noon and 2:30 to 6:30pm (closed January to mid-May). Admission is 5F (.75, 75¢).

3 Roanne

242 miles SE of Paris, 54 miles NW of Lyon

This industrial town on the left bank of the Loire is often visited from Lyon or Vichy because it contains one of France's greatest three-star restaurants, the Hôtel-Restaurant Troisgros (see "Dining," below).

There's also a worthwhile museum. Housed in a neoclassic mansion built at the end of the 18th century, **Musée Joseph-Déchelette,** 22 rue Anatole-France (© **04-77-23-68-77**), offers an exceptional display of Italian and French earthenware from the 16th, 17th, 18th, and 20th centuries, as well as earthenware produced in Roanne from the 16th to the 19th centuries. Admission is 20F (3.05, $2.90); hours are Wednesday through Monday from 10am to noon and 2 to 6pm. On Sunday, the museum is open only in the afternoon, and on Friday there is no noontime break.

ESSENTIALS

GETTING THERE   There are **trains** and, to a lesser extent, **buses** from nearby cities, notably Lyon; the train is a lot more convenient. By train, Roanne lies 3 hours from Paris but only 1 hour from Lyon; for information and schedules, call © **08-36-35-35-35.** If you're **driving,** simply follow N7 northwest from Lyon to Roanne. From Paris, follow A6 south to the town of Nemours, continuing southwest along N7.

VISITOR INFORMATION   The **Office de Tourisme** is on 1 cours de la République (© **04-77-71-51-77**).

ACCOMMODATIONS & DINING

Hôtel-Restaurant Troisgros ★★★ FRENCH/LYONNAISE   This is one of the top 10 restaurants of France. It first acquired its reputation in the 1950s and has since factored into the itineraries of globe-trotting foodies, visiting heads of state, and very wealthy people touring the region. Come here with a respect for the French *grande bourgeoisie* and the enduring appeal of French culinary finesse. Don't expect anything wild and crazy. The place is too conservative and devoted to impeccably tailored service for anything radical or provocative.

Decorated in neutral colors and lined with contemporary artwork, the restaurant features superb cuisine at astronomical prices. Pierre (the father) and Michel (the son) Troisgros are the current bearers of the Troisgros flame, presenting a celebration of the bounty of the Lyonnais countryside. Dishes include warm oysters in butter sauce; fried foie gras served with marinated eggplant; salmon with sage sauce; and beef served with Fleurie wine and bone marrow. For dessert, ask to see one of the best assortments of esoteric cheeses in the region or perhaps enjoy a praline soufflé.

The hotel also rents 18 traditionally furnished bedrooms, priced from 800F to 2,200F (121.60 to 334.40, $116 to $319).

Place de la Gare, 42300 Roanne. ℂ **04-77-71-66-97.** Fax 04-77-70-39-77. Reservations required. Main courses 200F–550F (30.40– 83.60, $29–$79.75); fixed-price menus 760F–930F (115.50– 141.35, $110.20–$134.85). AE, DC, MC, V. Thurs–Mon noon–1:30pm and 7:30–9:30pm. Feb–Mar closed 3 weeks, Aug closed 2 weeks.

NEARBY ACCOMMODATIONS & DINING

In the satellite village of **Le Coteau,** you'll find several worthy restaurants. These two are our favorites. To get here, take N7 2 miles from the center of Roanne.

Auberge Costelloise ✦✦ FRENCH   Chef Christophe Suchon provides what this region needs: an attractive restaurant with fine cuisine and reasonable prices. Choose from one of the fixed-price menus, which change weekly; the cheapest one isn't available on Saturday night. Popular dishes are gâteau of chicken livers with essence of shrimp, sole filet with confit of leeks, and foie gras. You can order fine vintages of Burgundian wines by the pitcher. This is the place to head when you can't afford the dazzling but expensive food at Troisgros.

2 av. de la Libération, Le Coteau. ℂ **04-77-68-12-71.** Reservations required. Main courses 55F–140F (8.35– 21.30, $8–$20.30); fixed-price menus 140F–380F (21.30– 57.75, $20.30–$55.10). AE, MC, V. Tues–Sat noon–1:30pm and 7:45–9:15pm. Closed Dec 26–Jan 4 and Aug 7–Sept 5.

Hôtel Restaurant Artaud TRADITIONAL FRENCH   Nicole and Alain Artaud offer traditional French cuisine in an elegant dining room. Choices include monkfish salad with saffron, beef from local farms, and a variety of desserts. There's also a good selection of French wines.

The hotel has 25 well-appointed bedrooms with satellite TV; rates are 325F to 530F (49.40 to 80.55, $47.15 to $76.85).

133 av. de la Libération, 42120 Le Coteau. ℂ **04-77-68-46-44.** Fax 04-77-72-23-50. Reservations recommended. Main courses 55F–140F (8.35– 21.30, $8–$20.30); fixed-price menus 100F–260F (15.20– 39.50, $14.50–$37.70). AE, DC, V. Tues–Sat noon–2pm; Mon–Sat 7:30–9pm. Closed July 30–Aug 21.

4 Pérouges ✦✦

288 miles SE of Paris, 22 miles NE of Lyon

The Middle Ages live on. Saved from demolition by a courageous mayor in 1909 and preserved by the government, this village of craftspeople often attracts movie crews; *The Three Musketeers* (1973), starring Michael York, and *Monsieur Vincent* (1948) were filmed here. The town sits on what has been called an "isolated throne," atop a hill northeast of Lyon.

Follow rue du Prince, once the main business street, to place des Tilleuls, at the center of which is the ***Arbre de la Liberté*** (Tree of Liberty), planted in 1792 to commemorate the Revolution. Nearby, in what was originally built in the 14th century as a private home, is the **Musée du Vieux-Pérouges,** place de la Halle (ℂ **04-74-61-00-88**), displaying such artifacts as hand looms. It's open only from Easter to November 1, daily from 10am to noon and 2 to 6pm. Admission is 20F (3.05, $2.90). This price includes access to the museum and, through adjoining doors, to one of the finest houses in the village, the **Maison des Princes de Savoie,** with its watchtower (**La Tour de Guet**) and a replica of a 13th-century garden, the **Jardin de Hortulus.**

Wander through the town, soaking in the atmosphere of a stone-built village that's virtually unchanged since the birth of the modern age. During the 13th century, weaving was the principal industry here, and linen merchants sold their wares under the Gothic arcades and galleries on either side of the town's streets.

In the eastern sector of **rue des Rondes** are many houses of former hand weavers. The stone hooks on the facades were for newly woven pieces of linen.

ESSENTIALS

GETTING THERE   It's easiest to **drive** to Pérouges, though the signs for the town, especially at night, are confusing. From Lyon, take Route 84 northeast and exit near Meximieux.

VISITOR INFORMATION   The **Comité de Defense et de Conservation du Vieux-Pérouges** (a fancy name for the tourist office) is in the Hostellerie du Vieux-Pérouges, place des Tilleuls (© **04-74-61-00-88;** www.perouges.org).

ACCOMMODATIONS & DINING

Ostellerie du Vieux-Pérouges ★★   This is a treasure in a restored group of 13th-century timbered buildings. The Thibaut family runs a museum-caliber inn furnished with antiques, cupboards with pewter plates, iron lanterns hanging from medieval beams, refectory dining tables, and stone fireplaces.

The restaurant's food is exceptional, especially when accompanied by the local sparkling wine, Montagnieu, which has been compared to Asti Spumante. Specialties are *terrine truffée Brillat-Savarin* (stuffed filets of carp), *écrevisses* (crayfish) *pérougiennes,* and *galette pérougiennes à la crème* (a dessert crêpe). After dinner, ask for a glass of Ypocras, a unique liqueur made from a recipe dating to the Middle Ages.

Place des Tilleuls, 01800 Pérouges. © **04-74-61-00-88.** Fax 04-74-34-77-90. www.ostellerie.com. 28 units. 950F–1,300F (144.40– 197.60, $137.75–$188.50) double; 1,350F–1,450F (205.20– 220.40, $195.75–$210.25) suite. AE, MC, V. Free parking. **Amenities:** Restaurant, bar; room service; laundry. *In room:* TV, hair dryer.

5 Bourg-en-Bresse

264 miles SE of Paris, 38 miles NE of Lyon

The ancient capital of Bresse, this farming/business center lies on the border between Burgundy and the Jura and offers fabulous food.

ESSENTIALS

GETTING THERE   Bourg-en-Bresse is easily accessible by **train** from Paris, Lyon, and Dijon. Fifteen TGV trains arrive from Paris's Gare de Lyon each day (trip time: 2 hr.). From Lyon, 10 trains arrive per day (trip time: 40 to 80 min.). From Dijon, 5 trains arrive per day (trip time: 2 hr.). For information and schedules, call © **08-36-35-35-35.** If you're **driving** from Lyon, take A42 or N83 for the 40-minute trip; from Dijon, follow A31 to Mâcon and then switch to A40 for the 2-hour drive.

VISITOR INFORMATION   The **Office de Tourisme** is at 6 av. Alsace-Lorraine (© 04-74-22-49-40; www.bourg-en-bresse.org).

SEEING THE SIGHTS

If you have time, visit the **Église Notre-Dame,** off place Carriat. Begun in 1505, it contains some finely carved 16th-century stalls. It still acts as a functioning church complete with a resident priest. If you'd like to wander around town, check out the 15th-century houses on rue du Palais and rue Gambetta.

Église de Brou ★   Art lovers will want to stop at the Église de Brou to see its magnificent royal tombs. One of the great artistic treasures of France, this

Flamboyant Gothic monastery was built between 1506 and 1532 (the three cloisters between 1506 and 1512, the church between 1513 and 1532) for Margaret of Austria, the ill-fated daughter of Emperor Maximilian. Over the ornate Renaissance doorway, the tympanum depicts Margaret and her "handsome duke," Philibert, who died when he caught cold on a hunting expedition. The initials of Philibert (sometimes known as "the Fair") and Margaret are linked by love knots. The nave and its double aisles are admirable. Look for the ornate rood screen, decorated with basket-handle arching. Ask a guide for a tour of the choir, which is rich in decorative detail; the 74 choir stalls were made of oak in just 2 years by Flemish sculptors and local craftsmen. Vast sums of money were spent in 1998 and 1999 to repair the roof and some of the stonework.

The tombs form the church's treasure. The Carrara marble statues are of Philibert, who died in 1504, and Margaret, who remained faithful to his memory until her death in 1530. Another tomb is that of Marguerite de Bourbon, mother of Philibert and grandmother of François I, who died in 1483. See also the stained-glass windows inspired by a Dürer engraving and an alabaster retable depicting *The Seven Joys of the Madonna.*

Medieval and Renaissance art is not the only allure at this monument. Expositions of modern art are sometimes conducted inside.

63 bd. de Brou. ✆ **04-74-22-83-83.** Admission to church, cloisters, and museum 36F (5.45, $5.20) adults, 23F (3.50, $3.35) ages 18–25, free for children 17 and under. Apr to mid-June daily 9am–12:30pm and 2–6:30pm; mid-June to Sept daily 9am–6:30pm; Oct–Mar daily 9am–noon and 2–5pm. Closed Jan 1, May 1, Nov 1 and 11, Dec 25.

ACCOMMODATIONS

Hôtel du Prieuré ✿ Owned by Madame Alby, this is the town's most gracious hotel. Its angled exterior is surrounded by an acre of gardens and 400-year-old stone walls. The place is alluring in spring, when forsythia, lilacs, roses, and Japanese cherries fill the air with their perfume. Most of the bedrooms are large and tranquil, each outfitted in Louis XV, Louis XVI, or French country style. All come with a small bathroom, most with both tub and shower.

49–51 bd. de Brou, 01000 Bourg-en-Bresse. ✆ **04-74-22-44-60.** Fax 04-74-22-71-07. hotelduprieure@ wanadoo.fr. 14 units. 380F–580F (57.75– 88.15, $55.10–$84.10) double; 720F (109.45, $104.40) suite. AE, DC, V. Free parking. **Amenities:** Room service; laundry. *In room:* TV, hair dryer, iron.

Le Logis de Brou This is actually a much better hotel than its boxlike exterior suggests. The fully refurbished and soundproofed four-story property has landscaped grounds and is near the busy road running in front of the church. Each comfortably furnished guest room contains well-crafted reproductions of antique furniture, plus a small shower-only bathroom.

132 bd. de Brou, 01000 Bourg-en-Bresse. ✆ **04-74-22-11-55.** Fax 04-74-22-37-30. 30 units. 400F (60.80, $58) double. AE, MC, V. Parking 50F (7.60, $7.25). **Amenities:** Room service; laundry. *In room:* TV, iron/ ironing board, hair dryer.

DINING

Auberge Bressane ✿✿ TRADITIONAL FRENCH Bresse poultry is the best in France, and chef Jean-Pierre Vullin specializes in succulent *volaille de Bresse,* served five ways, including a delectable version in cream sauce with morels. He knows how to prepare other dishes equally well: You might enjoy a gâteau of chicken liver, crayfish gratin, or sea bass with fresh basil, accompanied by regional wines like Seyssel and Montagnieu. The staff, although not intentionally difficult, may appear slightly aloof.

166 bd. de Brou. ℂ **04-74-22-22-68**. Reservations recommended. Main courses 98F–300F (14.90– 45.60, $14.20–$43.50); fixed-price menus 110F–380F (16.70– 57.75, $15.95–$55.10). AE, DC, MC, V. Wed–Mon noon–1:30pm and 7:15–9:45pm.

Au Chalet de Brou ★★ TRADITIONAL FRENCH   You'll find flavorful but relatively inexpensive food in this unpretentious restaurant across from the village's most famous church. Specialties include a "cake" of chicken livers served with essence of tomato; quenelle of pike-perch with lobster sauce; frogs' legs in parsley sauce; and the all-time rave, any of at least a half-dozen kinds of Bresse chicken, served with your choice of a morel-flavored cream sauce, raspberry vinegar, or chardonnay sauce. Some purists (including us) opt for it simply grilled in order to appreciate the unadorned flavor of the bird in its own drippings. Dessert might be an apple tart presented, according to your choice, hot or semifrozen. This isn't the region's most glamorous or cutting-edge restaurant, but the prices are more than fair and the food is well prepared.

168 bd. de Brou. ℂ **04-74-22-26-28**. Reservations recommended. Main courses 80F–140F (12.15– 21.30, $11.60–$20.30); fixed-price menus 85F–200F (12.90– 30.40, $12.35–$29). MC, V. Sat–Thurs noon–2pm; Tues–Wed and Sat–Mon 7–9:30pm. Closed Dec 23–Jan 23.

6 Vienne ★★

304 miles SE of Paris, 19 miles S of Lyon

Serious gastronomes know Vienne because it boasts one of France's leading restaurants, La Pyramide. But even if you can't afford its haute cuisine, you may want to visit Vienne for its sights. Situated on the left bank of the Rhône, it's a wine center and the southernmost Burgundian town.

ESSENTIALS

GETTING THERE   **Trains** connect Vienne with the rest of France. Some trips require a transfer in nearby Lyon. For information and schedules, call ℂ **08-36-35-35-39**. **Buses** from Lyon arrive about eight times a day, taking about an hour for the transit; for information, contact Vienne's Gare Routière (ℂ **04-74-85-18-51**), adjacent to the railway station. If you're **driving** from Lyon, take either N7 (which is more direct) or A7, an expressway that meanders along the banks of the Rhône River.

VISITOR INFORMATION   The **Office de Tourisme** is at 3 cours Brillier (ℂ **04-74-53-80-30**).

SPECIAL EVENTS   In the first 2 weeks in July, Vienne comes to life with some of the biggest names in jazz during the annual **Festival du Jazz à Vienne**. Such notables as B. B. King, Sonny Rollins, the Count Basie Orchestra, Eric Clapton, and even Little Richard have played here. Tickets range from 100F to 550F (15.20 to 83.60, $14.50 to $79.75). You can get tickets and information from the **Théâtre Antique de Vienne**, 4 rue Chantelouve (ℂ **04-74-78-87-87**).

SEEING THE SIGHTS

Vienne contains many embellishments from its past, making it a *ville romaine et médiévale*. Near the center of town on place du Palais is the **Temple d'Auguste et de Livie**, inviting comparisons with the Maison Carrée at Nîmes. It was ordered built by Roman emperor Claudius and turned into a temple of reason during the French Revolution. Another outstanding monument is the small

Pyramide du Cirque Romain, part of the Roman circus. Rising 52 feet, it rests on a portico with four arches and is sometimes known as the tomb of Pilate.

Take rue Clémentine to the **Cathédrale St-Maurice** ✸✸, place St-Maurice (✆ **04-74-85-60-28**), which dates from the 12th century even though it wasn't completed until the 15th. It has three aisles but no transepts. Its west front is built in the Flamboyant Gothic style, and inside are many fine Romanesque sculptures.

In the southern part of town stands the **Église St-Pierre** ✸, at place St-Pierre (✆ **04-74-85-20-35**), a landmark with origins in the 5th century, making it one of the oldest medieval churches in France. Inside, the **Musée Lapidaire** (✆ **04-74-85-50-42**) displays architectural fragments and sculptures from excavations. The museum is open from April 1 to October 31, Tuesday through Sunday from 9:30am to 1pm and 2 to 6pm; the rest of the year, Tuesday through Saturday from 9:30am to 12:30pm and 2 to 5pm, Sunday from 2 to 6pm. Admission is 12F (1.80, $1.75) for adults, 8F (1.20, $1.15) for students and those under 26.

A large **Théâtre Romain** ✸, 7 rue du Cirque (✆ **04-74-85-39-23**), has been excavated east of town at the foot of Mont Pipet. Theatrical spectacles were once staged here for an audience of thousands. You can visit from April 1 to August 31, daily from 9:30am to 1pm and 2 to 6pm; the rest of the year, Tuesday through Saturday from 9:30am to 12:30pm and 2 to 5pm, Sunday from 1:30 to 5:30pm. Admission is 12F (1.80, $1.75) for adults, 8F (1.20, $1.15) for students and those under 26.

If you have time to make a side trip about an hour's drive south, in the village of Hauterives you'll find one of the world's strangest pieces of architecture, the **Palais du Facteur Cheval,** or Palace of the Mailman Cheval (✆ **04-75-68-81-19**). It represents the lifelong work of a French postman, Ferdinand Cheval; built of stone and concrete and elaborately decorated, often with clamshells, it's an unusual, eccentric palace of fantasy in a high-walled garden. During his lifetime, M. Cheval was ridiculed by his neighbors, but his palace has since been declared a national monument and a tribute to the aesthetic value, or mania, of the French individual. The work was finished in 1912, when Cheval was 76; he died 13 years later. The north end of the facade is in massive rococo style. The turreted tower is 35 feet tall, and the building is 85 feet long. The elaborate sculptural decorations include animals such as leopards and artifacts such as Roman vases. Admission is 30F (4.55, $4.35) for adults, 20F (3.05, $2.90) for children 6 to 16. The palace is open daily, mid-April to mid-September from 9am to 7pm, February to mid-April and mid-September to November from 9:30am to 5:30pm, and December and January from 10am to 4:30pm.

ACCOMMODATIONS

La Pyramide Fernand-Point (see "Dining," below) also offers rooms.

Hostellerie Beau-Rivage A Relais du Silence, this place originated around 1900 as a simple inn that offered food and wine to fishermen who traveled from Lyon to the well-stocked waters of this section of the Rhône. Since then, it has evolved into a stylish, nostalgic enclave of old-fashioned charm. The rooms are well furnished and, in some cases, discreetly grand and larger than you might expect. Each comes with a compact shower-only bathroom.

The Rhône passes by the dining terrace. The traditional cuisine is exceptional; try *quenelles* of pike; stuffed snails with new potatoes; and an intensely cultivated suprême of pigeon on a platter with a confit of pigeon, roasted foie gras, and turnips. The Côtes du Rhône wines complement the food well.

2 rue de Beau-Rivage, 69420 Condrieu. (C) **04-74-56-82-82**. Fax 04-74-59-59-36. 25 units. 550F–850F (3.60– 129.20, $79.75–$123.25) double. AE, V, DC. From Vienne, cross the Rhône on N86, head south 7½ miles; pass through Condrieu, on the southern outskirts, look for signs on the left. Amenities: Restaurant; room service; laundry. *In room:* TV, minibar.

DINING

La Pyramide Fernand-Point ★★★ MODERN FRENCH   This is the area's premier place to stay and/or dine, and for many it's the preferred stopover between Paris and the Riviera. The restaurant perpetuates the memory of a superb chef, Fernand Point. Through the continuing efforts of Patrick Henriroux, many of Point's secrets have been preserved, especially his sauces, touted as the best in the country. Menus change seasonally, but the cuisine is always imaginative and cerebral. Examples include a watercress and zander soup garnished with braised endive; peppered and roasted duckling with red cabbage, wild mushrooms, and liqueur-soaked grapes; suckling veal in puff pastry, served with truffles and braised salsify; and John Dory wrapped in Parma ham, soya-flavored endive, and a Tabasco-flavored sabayon. The cheese platter is absolutely wonderful, and desserts are as artfully caloric, and as stylish, as anything else in the Rhône Valley. The chef can appeal to the tastes of both traditionalists and adventurers.

The hotel offers 28 modern, air-conditioned guest rooms. Doubles are 960F to 1,200F (145.90 to 182.40, $139.20 to $174); suites go for 1,395F (212.05, $202.30).

14 bd. Fernand-Point, 38200 Vienne. (C) **04-74-53-01-96**. Fax 04-74-85-69-73. www.relaischateaux.fr/ pyramide. Reservations required. Main courses 210F–410F (31.90– 62.30, $30.45–$59.45); fixed-price menus 495F–720F (75.25– 109.45, $71.80–$104.40). AE, DC, MC, V. Thurs–Mon 12:30–1:30pm and 7:30–9:30pm. Closed Feb.

Le Bec Fin *Value* TRADITIONAL FRENCH   The best-prepared and most generously served fixed-price meals in town are available in this rustic setting. À la carte specialties are somewhat more sophisticated, including salads laced with all the region's delicacies (foie gras, smoked duckling, and the like), breast of duckling with a truffled sauce, filet of turbot, and monkfish with saffron.

7 place St-Maurice. (C) **04-74-85-76-72**. Reservations required. Main courses 80F–200F (12.15– 30.40, $11.60–$29); fixed-price menus 105F–320F (15.95– 48.65, $15.25–$46.40). AE, V. Tues–Sun noon–2pm; Tues and Thurs–Sat 7–9:30pm.

7 Valence ★

417 miles SE of Paris, 62 miles S of Lyon

Valence stands on the left bank of the Rhône between Lyon and Avignon. A former Roman colony, it later became the capital of the Duchy of Valentinois, set up by Louis XII in 1493 for Cesare Borgia.

Today, Valence is the market town and the major distribution point for the mammoth fruit and vegetable producers of the Rhône Valley. Perhaps it's altogether fitting that François Rabelais, who wrote of gargantuan appetites in his lusty prose, spent time here as a student.

Visitors can climb the ruined château atop the white stone **Mont Crussol.** The ruins date from the 12th century. A view of this castle is possible from the esplanade of the Champ de Mars. Valence is still the home of the Arsenal, one of France's oldest gunpowder factories.

The most interesting sight here is the **Cathédrale St-Apollinaire,** place de Ormeaux (✆ **04-75-43-13-32**), consecrated by Urban II in 1095, though it's been much restored since. Built in the Auvergnat-Romanesque style, the cathedral is on place des Clercs in the center of town. The choir contains the tomb of Pope Pius VI, who died here a prisoner at the end of the 18th century. It's open daily from 8am to 7pm.

Adjoining the cathedral is the **Musée Municipal,** 4 place des Ormeaux (✆ **04-75-79-20-80**), noted for its nearly 100 red-chalk drawings by Hubert Robert done in the 18th century. It also has a number of Greco-Roman artifacts. It's open daily from 2 to 6pm. Between June and September, it's also open on Wednesday, Saturday, and Sunday from 9am to noon. Admission is 15F (2.30, $2.20) for adults, free for children 15 and under.

On the north side of the square, on Grand-Rue, you'll pass **Maison des Têtes,** built in 1532 with sculpted heads of Homer, Hippocrates, Aristotle, and other Greeks.

ESSENTIALS

GETTING THERE   There are fast and easy **trains** from Lyon, Grenoble, and Marseille. For information and schedules, call ✆ **08-36-35-35-35.** If you're **driving** to Valence from Lyon, take A7 south. From Grenoble, follow E711 to outside the town of Voreppe, heading southwest along E713, merging to W532 into Valence. From Marseilles, follow A7 north.

VISITOR INFORMATION   The **Office de Tourisme** is at parvis de la Gare (✆ **04-75-44-90-40**).

ACCOMMODATIONS & DINING

Hotel-Restaurant Pic ★★★ FRENCH This is the least known of France's great restaurants, although it ranks among the top 10 in the country. The cooking and the wine list are exceptional, the latter featuring regional selections like Hermitage, St-Péray, and Côtes du Rhône. Alain Pic took over as chef when his renowned father, Jacques, died in 1992, and continues to perform admirably. The villa has a flower-garden courtyard and a dining room with big tables and ample chairs. Appetizers include ballotine of squab, pâté de foie gras, and breast of small game bird. For a main course, we recommend the sea bass in velvety velouté, crowned by caviar; chicken cooked in a pig's bladder; or lamb stew with basil, sweetbreads, and kidneys. In season, one of the chef's masterpieces is tender noisettes of venison in a wine-dark sauce as light as chiffon. The desserts are a rapturous experience, from the grapefruit sorbet to the cold orange soufflé. In addition to the restaurant, the establishment maintains a brasserie, l'Auberge du Pin, that serves well-flavored regional food without a lot of culinary fuss.

Pic also rents 13 well-furnished bedrooms, costing 750F to 2,000F (114 to 304, $108.75 to $290) per night.

285 av. Victor-Hugo. ✆ **04-75-44-15-32**. Fax 04-75-40-96-03. www.pic-valence.com. Reservations required. Main courses 240F–590F (36.50– 89.70, $34.80–$85.55); fixed-price menus 250F–720F (38– 109.45, $36.25–$104.40) lunch, 490F–720F (74.50– 109.45, $71.05–$104.40) dinner. AE, DC, MC, V. Tues–Sun noon–1:30pm; Tues–Sat 7:45–9:30pm. Closed 2 weeks in Jan.

8 The Ardèche ★★★

The Ardèche region began to draw foreign visitors only about a decade ago. Until then, it was almost unknown beyond the French borders, bypassed in favor of regions with more and better monuments and museums. Its wines aren't the finest in France, and its cuisine is fortifying country fare that nourishes the body but doesn't win awards. Although many districts of France contain buildings that have inspired architects around the world, the Ardèche is limited to stone-sided structures of rustic but not grandiloquent charm. But as urbanites and visitors began seeking the pleasures of escapes to the wilderness or adventures like kayaking down beautiful cliff-edged canyons, the Ardèche finally came of age.

The Ardèche occupies the eastern flank of the Massif Central (see chapter 21), a landscape of jagged, much-eroded granite and limestone highlands that ramble down to the western bank of the Rhône. It isn't the highest or most dramatic region—that honor goes to the Alps, whose peaks rise as much as three times higher. Although it defines itself as Le Midi (its southern border lies less than 25 and 31 miles from Avignon and Nîmes, respectively), its culture and landscape are more firmly rooted in the rugged uplands of France's central highlands.

Through its territory flow the streams and rivers that drain the snow and rain of the Massif Central. They include rivers with names like Ligne, Fontolière, Lignon, Tanargue, and, most important, Ardèche. They flow beside, around, and through rocky ravines, ancient lava flows, feudal ruins, and stone-sided villages perched in high-altitude sites originally chosen for their medieval ease of defense.

The most famous and oft-visited section of the Ardèche is its southern extremity, with granite-sided ravines 1,000 feet deep, gouged by millions of springtime floodings of the Ardèche River—no wonder it's called the Grand Canyon of France. This area draws thousands of tourists who, often with their children, take driving tours along the highways flanking the ravines.

We recommend that you stop in the southern Ardèche to admire the gorges only briefly. It's better to spend the night in the less touristy northern reaches than the honky-tonk commercialism that sometimes pervades the southern parts.

In the northern Ardèche, in the 28 miles of hills and valleys separating the hamlets of Vals-les-Bains and Lamastre, is a soft and civilized wilderness, with landscapes devoted to grape growing, sheep herding, and (more recently) hill trekking.

Vallon-Pont-d'Arc, the gateway to the gorges, was defined by one writer as a Gallic version of Gatlinburg, Tennessee. (For your overnight stop, we suggest you continue further north to the more picturesque towns of Vals-les-Bains or Lamastre.)

If you want to kayak in the gorges, go between early April and late November, when the waters are green and sluggish and safer than during the floods of winter and spring. In Vallon-Pont-d'Arc, you'll find at least three dozen rental agencies for everything from plastic kayaks to horses. One of the best outfitters is **Adventure Canoë,** place du Marché (B.P. 27), 07150 Vallon-Pont-d'Arc (© **04-75-37-18-14**), which arranges rentals of canoes and kayaks for rides through the gorges. A 3-hour *mini-descente* costs 200F (30.40, $29) for two participants riding a 4-mile route from Vallon-Pont-d'Arc to the downstream hamlet of Chames, or 100F (15.20, $14.50) for a kayak for one. A full-day *grande descente* for two riding a 19-mile downstream route from Vallon-Pont-d'Arc to St-Martin d'Ardèche costs 340F (51.70, $49.30) for two or 170F (25.85, $24.65) for one. A 2-day trip is 490F (74.50, $71.05) for two or 245F (37.25, $35.55) for one. Prices include transport by minivan back to Vallon-Pont-d'Arc at the end of the ride. Lunch is not included, so bring your own picnic. The makings for this are available at dozens of bakeries and delicatessens near each point of origin.

Despite the appeal of kayaking, most travelers stick with driving along the upper summits of the gorges.

The Grand Canyon of France

Measuring no more than 74 miles, the Ardèche isn't the longest, mightiest, or most influential river in France, but it flows faster, with more geological aftereffects, than any other. Originating on the eastern edge of the Massif Central at about 5,000 feet above sea level, the Ardèche descends faster, over a shorter distance, than any of its competitors. (In some sections, it falls as much as 3 ft. for every half-mile of its length, positively vertiginous compared with such placid rivers as the Seine and the Loire.) These changes in altitude, combined with cycles of heavy rainfall and drought, result in the most temperamental and changeable waterway in France.

The resulting ebbs and flows have created the Grand Canyon of France. Littered with alluvial deposits, strewn in ravines whose depth sometimes exceeds 950 feet, the river's lower extremity (its final 36 miles, before the waters dump into the Rhône) is one of the country's most unusual geological areas. A **panoramic road (D290)** runs along a rim of these canyons, providing views over an arid landscape of grasses, toughened trees, drought-resistant shrubs, and some of the most distinctively eroded deposits of granite, limestone, and basalt in Europe.

If you drive along this route, expect the type of cheap motels, family-fun emporiums, and fast-food joints you'd see near Yellowstone Park in the United States. There's no denying, however, the basic beauty of the site, which you can admire from a series of belvederes along the highway. The highway runs in a meandering line that's approximately parallel to the bluffs and corniches of the river's northwestern edge. Many of the belvederes have brown-and-white signs that encourage motorists to stop and walk for a few minutes along some of the well-marked footpaths.

The route, which you can traverse in a few hours even if you stop for sightseeing, stretches southeast to northwest between the towns of Vallon-Pont-d'Arc and Pont St-Esprit. Since the meandering corniche roads are a challenge, be especially careful. In particular, stay on the lookout for other vehicles weaving frighteningly as the drivers and passengers crane their necks to admire the scenery and furiously snap photos.

VALS-LES-BAINS

27 miles W of Montélimar, 86 miles SW of Lyon

In a depression of the valley of the Volane River, Vals-les-Bains is surrounded by about 150 springs whose existence was discovered relatively recently—around 1600. Scientists have never understood why each spring contains a different percentage of minerals: Most contain bicarbonate of soda, some are almost tasteless, and one—*La Source Dominique*—has such a high percentage of iron and arsenic that it's poisonous. Waters from Dominique are piped away from the town; others are funneled into a Station Thérmale adjacent to the town's casino.

In the park outside the Station Thérmale, a *source intermittante* erupts, Old Faithful style, to a height of around 25 feet every 6 hours or so. Small crowds gather for eruptions at 5:30am, 11:30am, 5:30pm, and 11:30pm.

A few steps away, the Belle-Époque casino, **Parc Thermal** (© **04-75-38-77-77**), is open daily from noon to 3am; admission is free. The only casino between Lyon and Aigues-Mortes, it's mobbed on weekends by local farmers and their families playing roulette or the slot machines, the only options offered. It's not at all glamorous; this isn't Monte Carlo. There's a bistro-style theme restaurant, Le Hollywood, on the premises, open nightly from 7pm to midnight. There's also a 600-seat theater for occasional plays or concerts, plus a movie theater.

Other than the surrounding scenery, the town's most unusual site is about 14 miles south, beside the highway to Privas. A ruined feudal château once stood here; it was richly embellished and enlarged in the 1700s and served as the home of the comtes du Valentinois. Ironically, it escaped the ravages of the Revolution only to fall into ruin in 1820, when its bankrupt owners sold its accessories and architectural ornaments to pay their debts. Today, only the 16th-century entrance gate remains relatively unharmed. The views over the confluence of two ravines and the valley below are worth the detour.

ACCOMMODATIONS

Grand Hôtel des Bains   This is the largest and best hotel in town, with a central wing built in 1860 in anticipation of a visit from Empress Eugénie. Alas, Eugénie, finding she was comfortable in the nearby resort of Vichy, canceled her visit. Despite the snub, the hotel added two additional wings in 1870 and has survived ever since, partly because of its cordial staff and its well-maintained, conservatively furnished rooms, most with both tubs and showers.

3 Montée de l'Hôtel-des-Bains, 07600 Vals-les-Bains. © **04-75-37-42-13**. Fax 04-75-37-67-02. grand.hotel.des.bains@wanadoo.fr. 63 units. 430F–495F (65.35– 75.25, $62.35–$71.80) double; 620F–750F (94.25– 114, $89.90–$108.75) suite. AE, DC, MC, V. Closed Nov–Mar. **Amenities:** Restaurant, bar; room service; laundry. *In room:* TV.

DINING

Restaurant Mireille TRADITIONAL FRENCH   Containing only 26 seats, this restaurant occupies the space below vaulted stone ceilings that for centuries sheltered a herd of goats. Known for its earthy warmth, Mireille serves an ambitious menu of carefully calibrated cuisine. Choices range from local mousse of flap mushrooms with scallops to filet of turbot with white butter.

3 rue Jean-Jaurès. © **04-75-37-49-06**. Reservations recommended. Fixed-price menus 85F–160F (12.90– 24.30, $12.35–$23.20). V. Daily noon–2pm; Thurs–Mon 7–9pm. Closed 2 weeks in Apr and 2 weeks in Sept.

LAMASTRE

26 miles N of Vals-les-Bains, 18 miles W of Valence

Near the Ardèche's northern frontier, the charming hamlet of Lamastre is known for its light industry (shoes, camping gear, furniture, and light machine tools). Many connoisseurs of Ardèche architecture view it as the most unaltered and evocative village in the district. Its most important site is its church, in Macheville, in the upper part of the village. Built of pink Romanesque stone, it boasts portions dating from the 12th century and is the frequent site of weddings, one of which you might get to view.

Don't expect lots of nightlife or razzle-dazzle here. Most visitors use the town as a base for striking out on nature walks and hikes through the surrounding hills and valleys. A network of brown-and-white signs clearly marks each trail.

ACCOMMODATIONS & DINING

Château d'Urbilhac ⭐ This is the only château in the Ardèche. Built in the 1500s, it was renovated in the 19th century and is sheathed in pink stucco. Rated three stars by the government, it boasts a large outdoor pool and tennis court. Bedrooms are midsize to spacious, coming in various shapes and sizes; most are equipped with a bathroom with both tub and shower. Other than a phone, there are few in-room amenities. The owner, Mme Marcelle Xampero, prepares evening meals and maintains the 115 acres around the building. The restaurant is usually closed at lunch except to hotel guests, and even at night, nonguests should phone in advance before their arrival.

Rte. de Vernoux, 07270 Lamastre. ℂ **04-75-06-42-11**. Fax 04-75-06-52-75. 12 units. 750F (114, $108.75) double. Rates include breakfast. AE, DC, V. Closed Sept 30–May 1. From the center of Lamastre, follow the signs to the château about 1 mile south. **Amenities:** Restaurant; outdoor pool; tennis court; room service; laundry.

Hôtel du Midi Built in 1925, with slightly faded rooms that retain a vague Art Deco allure, this place has been used as an overnight stop for both Charles de Gaulle and Elizabeth Bowes-Lyon, the Queen Mother of England. The inn is an old-fashioned choice with midsize to spacious bedrooms, each comfortably furnished and containing a bathroom with shower only or both shower and tub. Maintained by members of the Perrier family, this place is well known for its restaurant, which serves fixed-price menus. The food is among the area's best, including many updated takes on regional traditions.

Place Seignobos, 07270 Lamastre. ℂ **04-75-06-41-50**. Fax 04-75-06-49-75. 12 units. 465F–560F (70.70–85.10, $67.45–$81.20) double. AE, DC, DISC, MC, V. Closed late Dec–Feb. **Amenities:** Restaurant; room service; laundry.

14

The French Alps

No part of France has more dramatic scenery than the Alps, for the western ramparts of these mountains and their foothills are truly majestic. From the Mediterranean in the south to the Rhine in the north, they stretch along the southeastern flank of France. The skiing here has no equal in Europe. Some of the resorts are legendary, like **Chamonix-Mont Blanc,** the capital of Alpine skiing, with its 12-mile Vallée Blanche run. Mont Blanc, at 15,780 feet, is the highest mountain in western Europe.

Most of this chapter covers the area known as the Savoy (Savoie), taking in the French lake district, and the largest Alpine lake, which it shares with Switzerland The French call it Lac Léman but it's known as Lake Geneva in English.

From January to March, skiers flock to Chamonix-Mont Blanc, Megève, Val d'Isère, and Courchevel 1850; from July to September, spa fans head to Evian-les-Bains and Aix-les-Bains. Grenoble, the capital of the French Alps, is the gateway. It's 30 minutes by car from the Grenoble–St-Geoirs airport, 40 minutes from the Lyon-Satolas international airport, 90 minutes from Geneva's Cointrin airport. The city is connected to the Paris-Lyon-Marseille motorway on the west and to the Chambéry-Geneva motorway on the east.

REGIONAL CUISINE The cuisine of the Savoy is robust and straightforward, suited to the active lifestyle of the people. Most recipes depend on the region's superb raw ingredients: fresh produce, eggs, fish, meats, and—most important—cheese and milk.

Cheese making, a process developed over thousands of years, was fine-tuned in the Savoy (where cows and goats thrived on the grasses of the Alpine meadows). The region's most famous cheese is a form of Gruyère known as beaufort, which, is similar to Emmenthal "Swiss" cheese, but has hardly any holes. Aged for up to 2 years, it's best when made from milk produced between June and September, when the aroma of herbs and flowers is pungent. Another famous cheese is reblochon, a slightly bitter semihard variety that gourmets insist must be fermented at high altitude for full flavor. Another name for reblochon, in Savoyard dialect, is *tôme* (cheese) *de Savoie.*

Those who appreciate the pungent taste of goat cheese will search out the famous Savoyard chèvre: St-Marcellin, or (as its devoted aficionados call it) petit St-Marcellin. Once made solely from the milk of Alpine goats, it's now based on a combination of cows' and goats' milk; its exterior is firm and supple, but its interior runs with sweet creamy goodness. You'll find cheese fondue on almost every menu of the region.

The Savoy and its neighbor, the Dauphine, are famous for the ways cheese and milk are used to augment the flavors of other dishes. There's confusion in the non-French world about the meaning of *au gratin*. A concept developed in the rugged countryside here (the isolated Vercors southwest of Grenoble), it refers to the crusty top (not the ingredients) formed when certain ingredients are baked in a type of flat (usually oval) dish. "Au gratin" might be the most famous culinary concept to come out of the region and is seen on menus throughout the world. It usually implies the addition of cheese: A *gratin dauphinoise,* for example, is a baked casserole of sliced potatoes, usually with onions, cream, cheese, and sometimes eggs. A *gratin Savoyard* substitutes beef bouillon for the cream, omits the eggs, and sometimes adds cheese.

The lakes and streams of the Savoy have always yielded a healthy catch, such as trout, carp, grayling, pike, eel, perch, and a famous delicacy found only in the cold Alpine lakes of France and Switzerland, *omble chevalier.* In one recipe for the thousands of unnamed tiny fish, too small to fillet, they're seasoned, batter-fried, and served with a white Savoyard wine. As for vegetables, the traditional greens are those that endure a long growing season amid the Alpine snows. Most notable is the spikey-leafed cardoon.

The region's smoked hams, pâtés, and sausages (sometimes served with red lentils) are delicious, and the rich chocolate confections whipped up in elegant bakeries reflect the tastes of citizens who can permit themselves the treats—at this altitude, outdoor activities burn off the calories.

As for wines and spirits, the gentle foothills with southern exposure have produced good wines, although—with one exception—nothing like the vintages of Burgundy or Bordeaux. The famous red is the Montmélian, similar to a Beaujolais. The best-known white is a sparkling Seyssel, whose finest vintages have been compared to champagne. As in many mountain regions, the Alps produce potent eaux-de-vie (literally, waters of life), which are usually consumed to top off a full evening meal. Most celebrated is Gentian, flavored with a blue Alpine wildflower, and the famous Chartreuse, whose distinctive herbal green tint has become a common adjective. The local Marc de Savoie is a potent residue from the brandy-distillation process, guaranteed to give you a hangover.

1 Evian-les-Bains ✸✸✸

358 miles SW of Paris, 26 miles NE of Geneva

On the château-dotted southern shore of Lac Léman, Evian-les-Bains is one of the leading spa resorts in France. Its lakeside promenade, lined with trees and sweeping lawns, has been fashionable since the 19th century. Evian's waters became famous in the 18th century, and the first spa buildings were erected in 1839. Bottled Evian is considered beneficial for everything from baby's formula and salt-free diets to treatment of gout and arthritis.

Back in the days when Marcel Proust came here to enjoy the Belle-Époque grandeur, Evian was the haunt of the very rich. The hotel where Proust stayed, the Splendid, is no longer here, but he fashioned his "Balbec baths" after those of Evian. Today, the spa, with its lakefront promenade and elegant casino, attracts a broader range of clients—it's not just for the rich anymore.

In addition to its **spa buildings,** Evian offers an imposing **Ville des Congrès** (convention hall), earning the resort the title of "city of conventions." In summer, the **Nautical Center** on the lake is a popular attraction; it has a 328-foot pool with diving stage, a solarium, a restaurant, a bar, and a children's paddling pool.

The major excursion from Evian is a boat trip on Lake Geneva offered by the **Compagnie Générale de Navigation,** a Swiss outfit whose agent in Evian is the Office du Baigneur, place du Port (✆ **04-50-70-73-20**). Contact the company or head for the Office de Tourisme (see below) to pick up a schedule of prices and hours (in summer, night cruises are also offered). If you want to see it all, you can tour both the Haut-Lac and the Grand-Lac. The most popular of all trips is the crossing from Evian to Ouchy-Lausanne, Switzerland, on the north side.

Crescent-shaped **Lake Geneva** is the largest lake in central Europe; the name **Lac Léman** was revived in the 18th century. Covering about 225 square miles, the lake is formed by the Rhône and is noted for its exceptional blue color.

ESSENTIALS

GETTING THERE   Evian-les-Bains is easily reached from Geneva by **train.** In Geneva, the Gare des Eaux-Vives, on the eastern edge of the city on avenue de la Gare des Eaux-Vives, serves Evian-les Bains. For train information and schedules, call ✆ **08-36-35-35-35.**

Moments Driving the Route des Grandes Alpes

Evian can be a starting point for the 460-mile drive to Nice along the **Route des Grandes Alpes** ✮✮✮. This is one of Europe's great drives, linking Lake Geneva with the Riviera and crossing 35 passes along the way. Leaping from valley to valley, it's open from end to end only in summer, as many passes are closed in winter.

It's possible to make the drive in 2 days, but why hurry? The charm of this journey involves stopping at scenic highlights along the way, including Chamonix, Megève, and Val d'Isère. The most dramatic pass is the **Galibier Pass** (Col du Galibier), at 8,686 feet, marking the dividing line between the northern and southern parts of the French Alps.

En route to Nice, you'll pass through such towns as St-Veran, at 6,530 feet the highest community in Europe; Entrevaux, once a fortress town marking the dividing line between Upper Provence and the Alps; and Touet-sur-Var, a village filled with tall, narrow houses constructed directly against the towering rocky slope.

Evian can also be reached from Geneva by one of the popular **ferries** (CGN) that depart from quai du Mont-Blanc at the foot of the rue des Alpes or from Le Jardin Anglais. From May 28 to September 21, one ferry a day departs Geneva at 9am, arriving in Evian at 11:45am. The return from Evian is at 5:50pm daily, with an arrival in Geneva at 8:45pm. A first-class one-way ticket costs 180F (27.35, $26.10), a second-class ticket 130F (19.75, $18.85). For ferry information and schedules, call ℂ **022/312-52-23.**

If you're **driving** from Geneva, take N5 heading east along the southern rim of the lake. From Paris, take the A6 south. Before Macon, you'll see signs pointing to the turnoff for Thonon-Evian. At Thonon, N5 leads to Evian. Trip time is 5½ hours, although this can vary depending on traffic.

VISITOR INFORMATION The **Office de Tourisme** is on place d'Allinges (ℂ **04-50-75-04-26;** www.eviantourism.com).

TAKING THE WATERS AT EVIAN

The clear, cold waters at Evian, legendary for their health and beauty benefits, attract a distinguished clientele who possess both the time and the money to appreciate them.

For the most luxurious way to immerse yourself in the resort's hydro-rituals, check into either of these two hotels, both of which maintain private spa facilities open only to well-heeled residents: **Hotel Royal,** Rive Sud du Lac de Genève (ℂ **04-50-26-85-00**), or **Hotel Ermitage,** route Abondance (ℂ **04-50-26-85-00**). They offer the most expensive packages and are adept at pampering the bodies, souls, and egos of their world-class patrons.

More reasonably priced are the spa facilities at **Les Thermes de Evian,** place de la Libération (ℂ **04-50-75-02-30**). This public spa is adjacent to Débarcadère, just uphill from the edge of the lake. The treatments here are on a more democratic basis, and access is not restricted. The hotel spas are more likely to place an emphasis on beauty regimes and stress therapies, while the public facilities contain a broader range of services, including tanning, massage, and skin and beauty care (but no facilities for overnight guests).

For 360F (54.70, $52.20), you can indulge yourself with a *journée thermale*, which provides access to exercise rooms and classes, saunas, steam baths, floods of water from the Evian springs, and two massage sessions. You can also spend up to 1,000F (152, $145) extra per day on additional massage, health, and beauty regimes. The facilities are open Monday through Saturday from 9am to 8:30pm, with a 1-hour break between 1:30 and 2:30pm.

ACCOMMODATIONS

The **Hôtel-Restaurant Le Bourgogne** (see "Dining," below) also rents rooms.

Hôtel de la Verniaz et ses Chalets ★★★   This glamorous country house stands on a hillside with a view of woods, water, and the Alps. The well-furnished rooms are in either the main house or one of the separate chalets; the chalets have their own gardens and more privacy, but cost a small fortune. Throughout the hotel, you'll find comfortable, even plush, accommodations. Each unit comes with a luxurious bathroom with combination tub/shower.

Av. Verniaz, à Neuvecelle, 74500 Evian-les-Bains. © **800/735-2478** in the U.S. and Canada, or 04-50-75-04-90. Fax 04-50-70-78-92. www.relaischateaux.fr/verniaz. 38 units. 600F–1,350F (91.20– 205.20, $87–$195.75) double; 1,200F–1,600F (182.40– 243.20, $174–$232) suite; 1,300F–2,200F (197.60– 334.40, $188.50–$319) chalet. AE, DC, MC, V. Closed mid-Nov to mid-Feb. **Amenities:** Restaurant, bar; outdoor pool; tennis courts; room service; baby-sitting; laundry/dry cleaning. *In room:* TV, minibar, hair dryer, safe.

Hôtel Les Prés Fleuris ★★★   Beside a high-altitude Alpine lake 5 miles east of Evian, this Relais & Châteaux occupies a villa that evolved from an 1842 farmhouse. In summer, flower boxes are affixed to the windows and balconies, and the glass walls capitalize on the view. Each guest room is richly outfitted, often with antique or reproduction furnishings, plus a deluxe bathroom with combination tub/shower. In fair weather, tables are set under the trees for meals.

Rte. de Thollon, 74500 Evian-les-Bains. © **04-50-75-29-14.** Fax 04-50-74-68-75. 12 units. 1,000F–1,150F (152– 174.80, $145–$166.75) double; 1,300F–1,700F (197.60– 258.40, $188.50–$246.50) junior suite. AE, MC, V. Closed Oct to mid-May. **Amenities:** Restaurant, bar; room service; laundry/dry cleaning. *In room:* TV, minibar, hair dryer.

Hôtel Oasis *Value*   This is a large country house with a government two-star rating and modest prices. It lies about a 5-minute drive from the lake, in a 1-acre park with an outdoor swimming pool. Bedrooms are furnished with non-descript contemporary furniture and, in most cases, a combination tub/shower. An on-site restaurant serves solid, conservative food (including filets of lake perch, or *fera,* either meunière style or grilled) as part of fixed-price menus.

11 bd. du Bennevy, 74500 Evian-les-Bains. © **04-50-75-13-38.** Fax 04-50-74-90-30. www.oasis-hotel.com. 19 units. 300F–480F (45.60– 72.95, $43.50–$69.60) double. MC, V. Closed mid-Oct to mid-Mar. **Amenities:** Restaurant, bar; outdoor pool. *In room:* TV, minibar.

DINING

The restaurant at the **Hôtel Les Prés Fleuris** (see above) is an excellent dining choice.

Hôtel-Restaurant Le Bourgogne ★ TRADITIONAL FRENCH   Come here if you want a delectable meal, impeccable service, attractive setting, and excellent wine. Regional wines featured are Crépy and Rousette. Menu choices in the restaurant and in the brasserie are likely to include the house version of foie gras, beef served with either morels or a peppercorn poivrade sauce, and a poached version of the omble chevalier (local whitefish) with whiskey sauce.

Items in the brasserie are flavorful and unpretentious, such as robust portions of cassoulets, terrines of oxtail or salmon, magrêts of duckling, and steaks.

The inn also offers 31 comfortable rooms, each with TV and phone, costing 410F to 540F (62.30 to 82.10, $59.45 to $78.30) per night.

Place Charles-Cottet, 74500 Evian-les-Bains. 🕾 **04-50-75-01-05.** Fax 04-50-75-04-05. Reservations required. Main courses 69F–130F (10.50– 19.75, $10–$18.85); fixed-price menus 150F–280F (22.80– 42.55, $21.75–$40.60). AE, DC, MC, V. Daily noon–2pm and 7:30–10pm.

EVIAN-LES-BAINS AFTER DARK

In the town center is the **Casino Royal Evian,** domaine du Royal Club Evian, on the south bank of Lake Geneva (🕾 **04-50-26-87-87**), much visited by the Swiss from across the lake. It offers blackjack, baccarat, and roulette, among other games, and has its own disco (Le Flash) open Wednesday through Sunday from June to September, Friday and Saturday nights only from October to May. Hours are 10:30pm to 5am; the cover, which includes the first drink, is between 70F (10.65, $10.15) and 80F (12.15, $11.60), depending on the night. The casino offers more than 250 slot, roller, and video-poker machines and one of the largest machines in the world, the "Jumbo." The Jackpot Bar is open until the casino closes. Jackets for men are preferred at the casino, but not at the disco.

2 Annecy ★★★

334 miles SE of Paris, 35 miles SE of Geneva, 85 miles E of Lyon

Lac d'Annecy is the jewel of the Savoy Alps. The resort of Annecy, which is the region's capital, makes the best base for touring the Haute-Savoie. Once a Gallo-Roman town, the seat of the comtes de Genève, Annecy opens onto one of the best views of lakes and mountains in the French Alps. Since the 1980s, this has become a booming urban center that has managed to preserve its natural setting as well. In summer, its lakefront promenade is crowded and active.

ESSENTIALS

GETTING THERE   If you're **driving,** Annecy is near several highways: From Paris, take A6 southeast to Beaune, connect with A6/N6 south to Mâcon-Nord. Then follow A40 southeast to Seyssel, connecting with N508 going southeast to Annecy. Allow at least 5 hours for this trip. From Geneva, follow A40W to St. Julien, to the N201 south toward Annecy. Trip time is 30 minutes.

A car is useful but not essential in the Alps. Annecy has **train** and **bus** service from Geneva, Grenoble, and Lyon. Nine trains per day arrive from Grenoble (trip time: 2 hr.); about 10 trains from Paris (trip time: 3 hr., 40 min.). For train information and schedules, call 🕾 **08-36-35-35-35.**

There's also a nearby **airport** (🕾 **04-50-27-30-06**) in the hamlet of Meythet; it receives flights from Paris on **Air Liberté** (🕾 **04-50-27-30-06**).

VISITOR INFORMATION   The **Office de Tourisme** is at 1 rue Jean-Jaurès (🕾 **04-50-45-00-33;** www.lac-annecy.com).

SEEING THE SIGHTS

Built around the river Thiou, Annecy has been called the Venice of the Alps because of the canals that cut through the old part of town, **Vieil Annecy.** You can explore the arcaded streets where Jean-Jacques Rousseau arrived in 1728.

After seeing Annecy, consider a trek to the **Gorges du Fier** ★★, a dramatic river gorge 6 miles to the west. To reach it, take a train or a bus from in front of

---

Kids **The Lure of the Hills**

The Office de Tourisme (see above) distributes free pamphlets that discuss about a dozen easy, family-oriented hiking and biking excursions from Annecy. More-experienced hikers may wish to purchase a map with a detailed set of challenging walks (20F, 3.05, $2.90).

Walks in both of these categories last between 2 and 6 hours. Some begin in the center of Annecy; others require a trip by car or bus from one of several towns in the area, such as Saint-Jorioz and Sevrier, to the west, and Talloires, to the east. A travel agency in Annecy, **Agence Crolard,** place de la Gare (© **04-50-45-08-12**), sells bus tickets to the destinations around Annecy and Léman. It also arranges excursions by minibus to sites of panoramic interest in July and August.

Annecy's rail station, getting off at Poisy. From here, walk about a mile following the clearly marked signs. This striking gorge is one of the most interesting sights in the French Alps. A gangway takes you through a gully, varying from 10 to 30 feet wide, cut by the torrent through the rock; you'll hear the roar of the river at the bottom. Emerging from this labyrinth, you'll be greeted by a huge expanse of boulders. You can visit the gorge from June 15 to September 10, daily from 9am to 7pm; March 15 to June 14 and September 11 to October 15, daily from 9am to noon and 2 to 6pm. The site is closed to the public between October 15 and March 15. A hike through its well-signposted depths takes less than an hour and costs 27F (4.10, $3.90) for adults and 16F (2.45, $2.30) for children. Call © **04-50-46-23-07** for more information.

You can also take a cruise on the ice-blue lake for which the town is famous. Tours of **Lac d'Annecy,** offered from mid-March to late October, last an hour and come with a guide who points out, in English, the sights along the shore. Priced at 63F (9.60, $9.15) per person, the tours depart between one and six times a day, depending on the season. Inquire at the Office de Tourisme (see above), or call the **Compagnie des Bateaux du Lac d'Annecy** (© **04-50-51-08-40**) for more information.

Château de Montrottier   Within walking distance of the gorges is the 13th- and 14th-century Château de Montrottier. A once-feudal citadel partially protected by the rugged geology, its tower offers a panoramic view of Mont Blanc. Inside, a small museum showcases pottery, Asian costumes, armor, tapestries, and antiques, as well as some bronze bas-reliefs from the 16th century.

74330 Lovagny. © **04-50-46-23-02.** Admission 30F (4.55, $4.35) adults, 25F (3.80, $3.65) students, 20F (3.05, $2.90) children. Wed–Mon 10am–1pm and 2–5:30pm. Closed Oct 15–Mar 15.

Musée Château d'Annecy   This forbidding gray-stone monument, whose 12th-century pinnacle is known as the Queen's Tower, dominates the resort. It was in this castle that the comtes de Genève took refuge from their enemies in the 13th century. The château contains a museum of regional artifacts that include Alpine furniture, religious art, oil paintings, and modern works. One section is devoted to the geology and marine life of the region's deep, cold lakes.

Place du Château, 74000 Annecy. © **04-50-33-87-30.** Admission 30F (4.55, $4.35) adults, 10F (1.50, $1.45) ages 12–25, free for children 11 and under. June–Sept daily 10am–6pm; Oct–May Wed–Mon 10am–noon and 2–6pm.

ACCOMMODATIONS

Note that the **Auberge de l'Eridan** (see "Dining," below) also rents rooms.

Au Faisan Doré (Kids) Near the casino at the end of a tree-lined lakefront boulevard, this government-rated three-star hotel is 2 minutes on foot from the lake and Imperial Park. Owned by the Clavel family since 1919, it's a member of the Logis de France chain, which caters to families. The public and private rooms follow the decor of the Haute Savoy. Each guest room is cozy and comfortable, but not extravagant. Half of the units contain combination tub/showers. The chef serves three different fixed-price menus in the adjacent restaurant.

34 av. d'Albigny, 74000 Annecy. ℂ **04-50-23-02-46.** Fax 04-50-23-11-10. 40 units. 370F–500F (56.25– 76, $53.65–$72.50) double. AE, DC, MC, V. Closed Dec 20–Feb 1. Parking 50F (7.60, $7.25). **Amenities:** Restaurant, bar. *In room:* TV.

Demeure de Chavoire ★★ One of the most charming accommodations in the area is at Chavoires, about 2 miles west of Annecy. It's intimate and cozy, brightly decorated with well-chosen Savoy antiques. Large doors lead to the gardens overlooking the lake. The bedrooms have names rather than numbers, and each is uniquely decorated. Bathrooms are cramped but efficient, each with a shower only. But thoughtful extras, such as fruit in the rooms, make this a deserving selection—plus it's more tranquil than the hotels in the center of Annecy. The helpful staff will direct you to nearby restaurants.

71 rte. d'Annecy, 74290 Veyrier-du-Lac. ℂ **04-50-60-04-38.** Fax 04-50-60-05-36. www.demeure dechavoire.com. 13 units. 850F–1,200F (129.20– 182.40, $123.25–$174) double; 1,400F–1,700F (212.80– 258.40, $203–$246.50) suite. AE, DC, MC, V. From Annecy, follow signs to Chavoires and Talloires. **Amenities:** Bar; baby-sitting. *In room:* TV, minibar, coffeemaker, hair dryer, safe.

Hôtel du Nord (Value) A government-rated two-star hotel in the center of Annecy, the continually renovated du Nord is one of the better bargains—minutes from the train station and Lac d'Annecy. The staff speaks English and is extremely helpful. You'll appreciate the cleanliness and modernity of the soundproofed rooms; 20 come with shower only, and some units are air-conditioned. Breakfast is the only meal served, but the staff will direct you to reasonably priced restaurants nearby.

24 rue Sommeiller, 74000 Annecy. ℂ **04-50-45-08-78.** Fax 04-50-51-22-04. www.annecy-hotel-du-nord.com. 30 units. 278F–358F (42.25– 54.40, $40.30–$51.90) double. AE, MC, V. *In room:* TV.

DINING

Auberge de l'Eridan ★★★ MODERN FRENCH Famous throughout France because of the excellent and unusual cuisine of owner Marc Veyrat-Durebex, this world-class restaurant occupies a romanticized version of a Savoyard château at the edge of a lake in the village of Veyrier-du-Lac, about a mile from Annecy. Guests dine in a posh room with ceiling frescoes.

The chef has been dubbed *l'Enfant Terrible* of upscale Alpine cuisine. What you'll get here is a unique dining experience, marked by an almost ritualistic set of protocols regarding how to consume a meal. Fortunately, your waiter can advise you on the order in which a meal should be consumed. For example, a "declination of local cheeses" consists of three large ravioli, each stuffed with a different cheese—a mild cow cheese, a pungent goat cheese, and a very strong blue cheese, eaten in ascending order of strength. Ensuing platters contrast warm pâté of foie gras accompanied by mountain bayberries with a cold terrine of foie gras served with figs and bitter orange slices. Other menu choices include ravioli of vegetables, flavored with rare Alpine herbs gathered by

M. Veyrat-Durebex and his team in the mountains; pike-perch sausage; crayfish poached with bitter almonds; and poached sea bass with caviar. Especially interesting is rabbit served "in the style of yesterday and today," which showcases the evolution of cuisine from old-fashioned (a portion cooked in the rabbit's own blood) to modern (a portion of minced rabbit served in a contemporary presentation with a purée of celery) on a single platter. Desserts include a miniature chestnut cake served with essence of truffles. The wine list is excellent.

The Auberge rents some relatively expensive furnished rooms. Rates are 1,950F to 3,250F (296.40 to 494, $282.75 to $471.25) double; suites go for 3,250F to 3,650F (494 to 554.80, $471.25 to $529.25).

13 vieille rte. des Pensières, 74290 Veyrier-du-Lac. ℂ **04-50-60-24-00.** Fax 04-50-60-23-63. Reservations required. Main courses 295F–435F (44.85– 66.10, $42.80–$63.10); fixed-price menu 385F (58.50, $55.85) lunch Tues–Fri, 900F–1,004F (136.80– 152.60, $130.50–$145.60) dinner. AE, DC, MC, V. Daily noon–1:30pm; Tues–Sat 7:30–9:30pm. Closed Dec 6–Mar and Sept 2 to mid-June. From Annecy's lakefront blvd., follow signs to Veyrier-du-Lac, Chavoires, and Talloires.

Le Belvédère FRENCH/SEAFOOD   This is one of the most appealing reasonably priced restaurants in town. Located on a belvedere above Annecy, about a mile west of the town center, it provides views that extend up to 5 miles over mountains and lakes. Menu items include a salad of Breton lobster with freshwater crayfish and strips of foie gras; a platter containing scallops and red mullet with shellfish-flavored butter sauce; and an unusual "duet" of foie gras, one part of which is accompanied with a purée of figs, the other with a vanilla-flavored bourbon sauce. Dessert might be a "trilogy" of tropical-flavored sorbets.

Available for rent are 10 simple guest rooms, much less opulent than the restaurant. (They're often used by diners who discover they've had too much wine at dinner and prefer not to drive home.) The rooms with private bathroom go for 450F to 600F (68.40 to 91.20, $65.25 to $87).

7 chemin du Belvédère, 7400 Annecy. ℂ **04-50-45-04-90.** Fax 04-50-45-67-25. Reservations recommended. Main courses 80F–200F (12.15– 30.40, $11.60–$29); fixed-price menus 135F–350F (20.50– 53.20, $19.60–$50.75). AE, MC, V. Thurs–Tues 12:30–2:15pm; Mon and Thurs–Sat 8–9:30pm. From downtown Annecy, follow signs leading uphill to Le Semnoz.

Le Clos des Sens ★★ FRENCH/SAVOYARD   The charm of this restaurant derives from inspired cuisine based on local ingredients and a decor salvaged from several Savoyard chalets. The street-level introduction is a contemporary-looking, warmly outfitted bar; in the upstairs dining room, the food is elaborate, savory, and geared to the cold-weather climate. The best examples include a consommé of shrimp studded with chunks of firm crayfish meat; filets of fera (a fish living in Lac d'Annecy) that are partially smoked, partially marinated; a spit-roasted version of suckling pig served with polenta; and a dessert specialty of caramelized fennel served with tarragon-flavored ice cream.

13 rue Jean-Mermoz, Annecy-le-Vieux. ℂ **04-50-23-07-90.** Reservations recommended. Main courses 100F–180F (15.20– 27.35, $14.50–$26.10); fixed-price lunches 150F–400F (22.80– 60.80, $21.75–$58); fixed-price dinners 240F–400F (36.50– 60.80, $34.80–$58). AE, DC, MC, V. Wed–Sun noon–1:30pm; Tues–Sat 7:30–9:30pm.

ANNECY AFTER DARK

In the old town, you'll find bars, cafes, pubs, and (in warmer months) street dances, fairs, and even carnivals. A calmer alternative is an evening of theater or dance at the **Théâtre d'Annecy,** 1 rue Jean-Jaurès (ℂ **04-50-33-44-11**), where tickets cost 85F to 195F (12.90 to 29.65, $12.35 to $28.30).

If a long day has left you thirsty, try **Le Roi Arthur,** 14 rue Perrière (© **04-50-51-27-06**), where you can mingle with 20-somethings. A traditional Irish pub, **Le Captain Pub,** 11 rue Pont-Morenc (© **04-50-45-79-80**), has a selection of hearty ales on tap. **Le Vieux Necy,** 3 rue Filaterie (© **04-50-45-01-57**), attracts a younger, more boisterous crowd.

The best piano bar in town is **Le Duo,** 104 av. de Genève (© **04-50-57-01-46**), ideal for quiet conversation. If you're gay and looking for fun, Annecy's most visible and popular gay bars are the **Comedy Café and Night Bar,** 13 rue Royale, Galerie des Sorbiers (© **04-50-52-82-83**); and **Happy People Disco,** rue Carnot (no phone), where both locals and visitors can dance.

Of the dance clubs, the lively **Le Pop Plage,** 30 av. d'Albigny (© **04-50-23-12-86**), pulls in an older, more sophisticated crowd than **Le Garage,** rue Sommellier (© **04-50-45-69-40**), where the cover of around 75F (11.40, $10.90) buys the first drink. Both places are bastions of techno and rock and can charge a cover of as much as 100F (15.20, $14.50) on Fridays and Saturdays. Le Pop Plage is open in summer only.

For the most elegant evening on the town, head for the **Casino de l'Impérial,** 32 av. d'Albigny (© **04-50-09-30-00**), part of the Belle Époque–style Impérial Palace hotel on a peninsula jutting out into Lac d'Annecy. Entrance into the gaming rooms costs 70F (10.65, $10.15) and requires the presentation of a passport. It's open from 8:30pm to 2am (to 4am on Friday and Saturday). The area reserved for slot machines (where admission is free) is open daily 24 hours.

3 Talloires ★★

342 miles SE of Paris, 20 miles N of Albertville, 8 miles S of Annecy

The charming village of Talloires—it dates back to 866—is old enough to appear on lists of territories once controlled by Lothar II, great-grandson of Charlemagne. Chalk cliffs surround a pleasant bay, and at the lower end a wooden promontory encloses a small port. An 18-hole golf course and water sports like boating, swimming, water-skiing, and fishing make this a favorite spot with French vacationers. Talloires also boasts one of France's great restaurants, Auberge du Père-Bise, and a Benedictine abbey founded in the 11th century but now transformed into the deluxe Hôtel de l'Abbaye.

ESSENTIALS

GETTING THERE From Annecy, you can reach Talloires by **driving** south along N508 for 8 miles. There are about eight daily **buses** from Annecy to Talloires, which take 35 minutes and cost 15F (2.30, $2.20). In Talloires, buses stop in front of the post office. For information on bus routes in and out of Talloires, call the Gare Routière in Annecy at © **04-50-45-08-12.**

VISITOR INFORMATION The **Office de Tourisme** is on rue André-Theuriet (© **04-50-60-70-64;** talloirestourism@wanadoo.fr).

ACCOMMODATIONS

In addition to the following option, **Auberge du Père-Bise** and **Villa des Fleurs** (see "Dining," below) also rent luxurious rooms.

Hôtel de l'Abbaye ★★ What was a Benedictine monastery in the 16th century is now one of the grand inns of the Alps, a hotel since the French Revolution. With close-up views of the lake, it makes for a memorable stop even though it doesn't equal the cuisine or the luxury of the Auberge du Père-Bise (see below). Then again, it's a lot more affordable. The hotel is rich with beamed ceilings, antique portraits, leather chairs, French gardens, and carved balustrades. The great corridors lead to converted guest rooms, of which no two are alike. The furnishings include all the Louis periods as well as Directoire and Empire. In 1999, the hotel was thoroughly renovated. All units contain showers, and several have tubs as well. In summer, the restaurant expands onto a shaded lakefront terrace. Overall, the site is extremely pleasant for an escape from urban life.

Rte. du Port, 74290 Talloires. © **04-50-60-77-33.** Fax 04-50-60-78-81. www.abbaye-talloires.com. 32 units. 800F–1,990F (121.60– 302.50, $116–$288.55) double; 2,000F–2,650F (304– 402.80, $290–$384.25) suite. AE, DC, MC, V. Closed Jan to mid-Feb. **Amenities:** Restaurant, bar; sauna; room service; laundry/dry cleaning. *In room:* TV.

DINING

Auberge du Père-Bise ★★★ FRENCH   Since the 1950s, when millionaires and starlets were drawn here (and when being a millionaire meant something), Auberge du Père-Bise has radiated style and charm. A chalet built in 1901 and renovated many times since (most recently in 1996), it's one of France's most acclaimed—and expensive—restaurants. The elegant dining room has sparkling silverware and bowls of flowers, but in fair weather you can dine under a vine-covered pergola and enjoy the view of mountains and the lake. The kitchen excels at dishes like mousse of goose foie gras, layered potatoes with truffles and foie gras, delicate young lamb, and gratin of crayfish tails.

The inn also offers 34 guest rooms, each with minibar, TV, and phone; rates are 1,500F to 2,500F (228 to 380, $217.50 to $362.50) for a double and 2,500F to 3,000F (380   to 456, $362.50 to $435) for a suite. Because this place is so popular and intimate, it's wise to reserve at least 2 months in advance, especially in summer.

Rte. du Port, Bord du Lac, 74290 Talloires. © **04-50-60-72-01.** Fax 04-50-60-73-05. Reservations required. Main courses 220F–365F (33.45– 55.50, $31.90–$52.95); fixed-price menus 500F–920F (76– 139.85, $72.50–$133.40). AE, DC, MC, V. May–Oct daily noon–2pm and 7–9pm. Closed Nov to mid-Feb; closed Tues–Wed from Nov–Easter.

Villa des Fleurs *Value* TRADITIONAL FRENCH   This attractive *restaurant avec chambres* should be better known, because it's the best place in Talloires for the price. The proprietors, Marie-France and Charles Jaegler, along with their son, Sébastien, serve wonderfully prepared meals, which often include *salade landaise* with foie gras and filet of fera (a fish that lives in Lac d'Annecy) served with sage sauce. The dining room overlooks the water.

Eight simply furnished rooms are available for rent, each with minibar, phone, and Victorian-era decor. Doubles cost 490F to 610F (74.50 to   92.70, $71.05 to $88.45) and are at the top of a winding staircase—there's no elevator.

Rte. du Port, 74290 Talloires. © **04-50-60-71-14.** Fax 04-50-60-74-06. Reservations required. Main courses 115F–165F (17.50– 25.10, $16.73–$23.95); fixed-price menus 165F–290F (25.10– 44.10, $23.95–$42.05). AE, V. Wed–Sun noon–2pm; Tues–Sat 7–9pm. Closed Nov 15–Dec 15.

4 Aix-les-Bains ★★★

332 miles SE of Paris, 21 miles SW of Annecy, 10 miles N of Chambéry

On the eastern edge of Lac du Bourget, modern Aix-les-Bains is the most fashionable (and largest) spa in eastern France. The hot springs, which offered comfort to the Romans, are said to be useful for treating rheumatism.

ESSENTIALS

GETTING THERE   Some 20 **trains** per day arrive from Paris (trip time: 3½ hr.); 10 trains pull in from Annecy (trip time: 30 min.). For information and schedules, call ✆ **08-36-35-35-35. Buses** pull into Aix from Nice usually only once a day. For information on bus routes in and around the French Alps, call the Gare Routière in Chambéry at ✆ **04-79-69-11-88.** If you're **driving** to Aix-les-Bains from Annecy, follow RN 201 south.

VISITOR INFORMATION   The **Office de Tourisme et Syndicat d'Initiative** is on place Maurice-Mollard (✆ **04-79-35-05-92;** www.aixlesbains.com).

SEEING THE SIGHTS

The spa is well equipped for visitors: It contains flower gardens, a casino (the Palais de Savoie), a racecourse, a golf course, and Lac du Bourget, which has a beach. **Thermes Nationaux,** place Maurice Mollard (✆ **04-79-35-38-50**), lies in the center of town, near the casino, the Temple of Diana, and the Hôtel de Ville (town hall). Closer to the lake, a string of flowerbeds and ornamental shrubs border the town's waterside promenades, where you can take a lovely stroll.

Steamboats take visitors on a beautiful 4-hour **boat ride** on Lac du Bourget. A different 4-hour trip traveling up most of the length of the Canal de Savière (which links the lake with the Rhône) runs between March and November, either daily or four times a week, depending on the season, for 108F (16.40, $15.65) per adult, 67F (10.20, $9.70) per child under 12. For departure times (which change almost weekly throughout the season), contact the ferry operator, **Les Bateaux d'Aix** (✆ **04-79-63-45-00**). Boats depart from the piers of Grand Port, in the center of town. You can also take a bus ride from Aix to the town of Revard, at 5,080 feet, where you'll be rewarded with a panoramic view of Mont Blanc. For information, contact **Trans Savoie** (✆ **04-79-35-21-74**).

Abbaye d'Hautecombe 🌟🌟   This is the spiritual centerpiece of the French Alps and the mausoleum of many princes of the House of Savoy. It was built by a succession of monks from the Cîteaux, Cistercian, and Benedictine orders beginning in the 1100s and stands on a promontory over the western edge of Lac du Bourget, almost directly across the water from Aix-les-Bains. Before the 1500s, at least 40 members of the royal family of the Savoy were buried here.

After years of neglect, the church was reconstructed and embellished during the 19th century by Charles-Felix, king of Sardinia, in the Troubadour Gothic style. The fervently religious ecumenical community occupying the abbey organizes seminars, welcomes short- and medium-term devotees, and perpetuates the site's tradition of worship. Pilgrims are welcome to attend daily mass at noon.

73310 St-Pierre de Curtille. ✆ **04-79-54-26-12.** Tours are free, but donations are welcome. Self-guided half-hour tours with tape recording, in English and French, depart at 6-min. intervals Wed–Mon 10–11:30am and 2–5pm. You can reach the abbey by car or boat, with 2 to 5 steamers leaving daily Easter–Oct. To board, go to the landing stage at Aix-les-Bains; fare is 64F (9.75, $9.30) for adults, 42F (6.40, $6.10) for children under 12. The trip takes about 30 min. See Les Bateaux d'Aix, above, for steamer information.

Musée Faure   This is the town's most interesting museum, with a modern-art collection that includes sculptures by Rodin and works by Degas, Corot, and Cézanne. It's situated on a hill overlooking the lake and the town.

10 bd. des Côtes. ✆ **04-79-61-06-57.** Admission 20F (3.05, $2.90). Wed–Mon 10am–noon and 1:30–6pm.

Thermes Nationaux d'Aix-les-Bains   The Thermes Nationaux d'Aix-les-Bains was begun in 1857 by Victor Emmanuel II; the New Baths, launched in 1934, were expanded and renovated in 1972. To visit, go to the caretaker at the entrance opposite the Hôtel de Ville, the château of the marquises of Aix in the 16th century. Before you enter, you can visit the thermal caves. In the center of the spa are two Roman remains: a Temple of Diana and the 30-foot-tall triumphal Arch of Campanus. Of special interest are the mosaic-covered compartments that served as changing booths for members of the royal families of Europe. If historic origins don't appeal to you, just relax and bask in the warm waters.

Place Maurice-Mollard. ℭ **04-79-35-38-50.** Tours cost 26F (3.95, $3.75) and are given Apr–Oct Tues–Sat at 3pm.

ACCOMMODATIONS

Note that **Hôtel-Restaurant Davat** (see "Dining," below) also rents rooms.

Hostellerie Le Manoir ⭐   This architecturally interesting site—a stable until the present owners transformed it into a hotel in 1968—includes shutters, an overhanging roof, and paths weaving through turn-of-the-20th-century gardens with outdoor furniture placed under shade trees. You can order breakfast or dinner on a terrace bordering the garden. Most of the public rooms, as well as the guest rooms, open onto terraces. The decor is traditional, with antique and provincial furniture. Each unit's bathroom comes with a combination tub/shower.

37 rue Georges-1er, 73100 Aix-les-Bains. ℭ **04-79-61-44-00.** Fax 04-79-35-67-67. 73 units. 397F–795F (60.35– 120.85, $57.55–$115.30) double; 895F (136.05, $129.80) suite. AE, DC, MC, V. **Amenities:** Restaurant, bar; pool; Turkish bath; sauna; room service; laundry. *In room:* TV.

Hôtel Ariana ⭐⭐   The Ariana caters to a spa-oriented crowd that enjoys quiet walks in the surrounding park. The loggia-dotted glass exterior opens into an Art Deco interior highlighted by contrasting metal, wood, and fabrics, plus plenty of white marble and antique reproductions. Tunnel-like glass walkways connect it to the hotel's main core. The tastefully furnished guest rooms come in a range of sizes and styles, each comfortable and well appointed. Most have good-size bathrooms with combination tub/showers. Café Adelaïde functions as both a cafe and a restaurant, offering fine classic dishes.

Av. de Marlioz, à Marlioz, 73100 Aix-les-Bains. ℭ **04-79-61-79-79.** Fax 04-79-61-79-00. 60 units. 425F–720F (64.60– 109.45, $61.65–$104.40) double. AE, DC, V. **Amenities:** Restaurant, bar; 2 indoor pools; health club; sauna; room service; laundry. *In room:* A/C, TV, minibar, hair dryer.

DINING

Hôtel-Restaurant Davat ⭐ TRADITIONAL FRENCH   You'll enjoy the traditional cooking, gracious service, and selection of regional wines here. This is a leading restaurant and an excellent moderately priced lodging, where the chief attraction is the beautiful flower garden. The 20 rooms are simply furnished and cost from 230F to 280F (34.95 to 42.55, $33.35 to $40.60) for a double.

Au Grand Port, 73100 Aix-les-Bains. ℭ **04-79-63-40-40.** Reservations required. Main courses 85F–120F (12.90– 18.25, $12.35–$17.40); fixed-price menus 90F–250F (13.70– 38, $13.05–$36.25). AE, MC, V. Daily noon–1:30pm; Mon–Sat 7–9:30pm. Closed Jan–Feb.

Restaurant du Casino Grand Cercle FRENCH   No other setting in Aix-les-Bains provides as rich a beaux-arts environment as this restaurant, located within the town's casino. It occupies a corner of the area reserved for blackjack and roulette, giving diners a close-up view of the gamblers testing their luck. More impressive is the view that soars overhead. The most elaborate ceiling in the Alps is covered with the 1880s mosaics of Italian artist Salviati. Alas, the food is not as elaborate; anticipate conservative but flavorful dishes of veal, beef, and chicken, with a scattering of terrines, soups, and salads. But in terms of glamour and glitter in a beautiful place, it's one of the most enjoyable experiences in town.

Rue du Casino. (℃) **04-79-35-16-16.** Reservations recommended. Fixed-price menu with wine, including entrance to the casino and 50F (7.60, $7.25) worth of roulette tokens, 250F (38, $36.25). AE, DC, MC, V. Daily 8pm–midnight.

5 Grenoble ✶✶✶

352 miles SE of Paris, 34 miles S of Chambéry, 64 miles SE of Lyon

Because this city, the ancient capital of the Dauphine, is the commercial, intellectual, and tourist center of the Alps, it's a major stop for travelers (including those driving between the Riviera and Geneva).

A sports capital in both winter and summer, it also attracts many foreign students—its university has the largest summer-session program in Europe. Founded in 1339, the University of Grenoble has a student body of some 40,000 and is the heart of intellectual life in the region. With a population of 400,000, this town is also home to four other universities with a large influx of English and American students, giving it a cosmopolitan air.

ESSENTIALS

GETTING THERE An important rail and bus junction, Grenoble is easily accessible from Paris and all the cities in this chapter. About 11 **trains** per day arrive from Paris (trip time: 3 hr.); trains arrive almost every hour from Chambéry (trip time: 30 min.). For information and schedules, call (℃) **08-36-35-35-35.**

Grenoble's **Aéroport de St-Étienne de Saint-Geoirs** ((℃) **04-76-65-48-48**) is 24 miles northwest of the city center. Air France has a virtual monopoly on service, though there are charters from England, Turkey, Israel, and the Czech Republic. Five Air France flights per day leave from Orly Ouest (West); flight time is just under an hour and cost is about 2,000F (304, $290) round-trip. A shuttle bus meets every flight and takes passengers to and from Grenoble's center; the cost is 75F (11.40, $10.90) each way. For information on flights and bus transit to and from the airport, call the airport phone number listed above. A taxi to the town center costs around 350F (53.20, $50.75).

You can also fly into Lyon, which has many more flights per day. **Satobus** ((℃) **04-72-68-72-17**) meets most flights at the Lyon airport and takes passengers to Grenoble. Travel time is an hour; cost is 80F (12.15, $11.60) each way.

If you're **driving,** take A6 from Paris to Lyon and then continue along A48 into Grenoble. Depending on conditions, the drive should take 6 to 7 hours.

VISITOR INFORMATION Designed by the architect A. Wogenscky and constructed in 1968, the **Maison de la Culture,** 14 rue Paul Claudel ((℃) **04-76-51-33-71**), is a theater, dance recital space, and concert hall in the residential neighborhood of Malherbe. In the same building is the **Office de Tourisme,** 14 rue de la République ((℃) **04-76-42-41-41;** www.grenoble-isere-tourisme.com). The center is open Monday through Saturday from 9am to 6pm, Sunday from 9am to 1pm and 2 to 5pm.

SEEING THE SIGHTS

Grenoble lies near the junction of the Isère and Drac rivers. Most of the city is on the south bank of the Isère, though its most impressive monument, the **Fort de la Bastille,** stands on a rocky hilltop on the north bank (a cable car will carry you from the south bank across the river to the top of the fort). The center of Grenoble's historic section is the **Palais de Justice** and **place St-André.** The more modern part of town is southeast, centered on the contemporary **Hôtel de Ville** (town hall) and the nearby **Tour Perret.**

Begin at **place Grenette,** where you can enjoy a drink or an espresso at one of the cafes. This square enjoys many associations with Grenoble-born Stendhal, author of *The Red and the Black* and *The Charterhouse of Parma*. It was here that Antoine Berthet, supposedly the model for Stendhal's Julien Grel, was executed for attempted murder in 1827. The **Place aux herbes** and the **Place St-André** stand in the very heart of the *centre ville*. To miss these famous old squares would be like a visit to London without a stopover at Piccadilly Circus. Of the two, Place St-André, dating from the Middle Ages, is the most evocative of old Grenoble, graced on one side by the Palais de Justice and on the other by the Eglise St-André. The Palace of Justice was built in many stages, but the brick church went up in the 13th century. Two streets for strolling and browsing are rue de la Poste, within the medieval core, and rue J.-J.-Rousseau, a 5-minute walk southwest of the city. Much of this latter street is for pedestrians only.

Enjoy a ride on the **Téléférique de la Bastille** (© **04-76-44-33-65**), cable cars that haul you over the rocky banks of the Isère River and its valley. Between November and mid-March, the cable car operates daily from 10:30am to 6:30pm (from 11am on Mondays). The rest of the year, it operates daily from 9am to between midnight and 12:30am, depending on the season, except for Monday mornings, when operations begin at 11am. The cable car is completely closed for 2 weeks in January. A round-trip ticket costs 35F (5.30, $5.10) for adults, 28F (4.25, $4.05) for students, and 22F (3.35, $3.20) for children 5 to 18. From the belvedere where you land, you'll have a panoramic view of the city and the mountains that surround it. Come here for the view, not the remains of the fort. You can walk up in an hour or so if you're an Olympic athlete; the entrance is signposted to the west of Place St-André. However, we suggest you take the téléphérique to the top, then stroll down the mountain along the footpath, Montée de Chalmont, that winds its way through Alpine flower gardens and past old ruins before reaching a cobblestone walk that empties into the old town.

Musée Dauphinois 🔭   Housed in a 17th-century convent and enhanced by the cloister, gardens, and baroque chapel, the museum lies across the Isère in the Ste-Marie-d'en-Haut section of town. A collection of ethnographic and historic mementos of the Dauphine is displayed, along with folk arts and crafts. This place is a quick cram course on life in the Alps—no other museum gives such a detailed view of the people, often forced to struggle against ferocious weather to eke out a living. Furnishings, tools, artifacts, and miniature replicas of Alpine settings re-create the life here. Check out the special exhibition on skiing, tracing the earliest development of the sport to the 21st century's high-tech innovations.

30 rue Maurice-Gignoux. © **04-76-85-19-01**. Admission 20F (3.05, $2.90) adults, 10F (1.50, $1.45) children 12–16, free for children 12 and under. May–Oct Wed–Mon 10am–7pm; Nov–Apr Wed–Mon 10am–6pm. Closed Jan 1, May 1, Dec 25.

Musée de Grenoble 🟊🟊 Founded in 1796, this is one of the country's oldest art museums. It was the first French museum to focus on modern art, a fact appreciated by Picasso, who donated his *Femme Lisant* in 1921. Flemish and Italian Renaissance works are displayed, although it's the Impressionist paintings that generate the most interest. Note Matisse's *Intérieur aux aubergines* and Léger's *Le Remorqueur.* Ernst, Klee, Bonnard, Monet, Rouault—they're all here. There are a number of older paintings and sculptures, along with artifacts and relics dating from Roman times, including a well-preserved mosaic. The artistic highlight is a sculpted door panel from the 1400s of Jacob and his sons.

5 place de Lavalete. © **04-76-63-44-44.** Admission 25F (3.80, $3.65) adults; 15F (2.30, $2.20) children, students, and seniors. Wed 11am–10pm; Thurs–Mon 11am–7pm.

ACCOMMODATIONS

Hôtel d'Angleterre This hotel, located in the center of Grenoble, features tall windows and wrought-iron balconies; it opens onto a pleasant square with huge chestnut trees. Inside, the stylish salons boast wood-grained walls and ceilings and tropical plants. Some guest rooms look out on the Vercors Massif. Each small to midsize unit is comfortably furnished and comes with a shower-only bathroom. Breakfast is the only meal served.

5 place Victor-Hugo, 38000 Grenoble. © **04-76-87-37-21.** Fax 04-76-50-94-10. www.hotel-angleterre.fr. 62 units. 530F–830F (80.55– 126.15, $76.85–$120.35) double. AE, DC, MC, V. Parking 10F (1.50E, $1.45). **Amenities:** Room service; dry cleaning. *In room:* TV, minibar, coffeemaker, hair dryer, safe.

Hôtel Trianon Few other hotels in town have as effectively masked a banal 1950s design with such a dose of historic decorative styles. Trianon caters to business travelers during the week; it's a comfortable, well-managed hotel that survives on more than just tourism. The rates are reduced on weekends, when business is slower. The rooms are cramped but cozy, furnished in just about every Louis style; a handful are done in a "shepherd" decor that evokes a folkloric grange in the Alps. The midsize bathrooms are equipped with showers; some have tubs as well. You'll find this hotel a short walk south of the pedestrian-only district in the town center, near a well-known school, the Lycée Champollion.

3 rue Pierre-Arthaud, 38000 Grenoble. © **04-76-46-21-62.** Fax 04-76-46-37-56. 38 units. www.hotel-trianon.com. 299F–470F (45.45– 71.45, $43.35–$68.15) double. AE, DC, MC, V. Parking 37F (5.60, $5.35). **In-room amenities:** TV.

Park Hotel Concorde 🟊🟊 This is the most opulent and prestigious hotel in Grenoble, a government-rated four-star legend that welcomes most of the important politicians and entertainment-industry moguls who visit the region. It occupies the lower four floors of a mid-1960s tower mostly devoted to private condominiums, a short drive south of Grenoble's commercial center, close to City Hall. Each guest room is decorated differently, with a blend of dignified (sometimes antique) furniture, state-of-the-art lighting, and modern upholsteries. All of the bathrooms have both tub and shower; some have Jacuzzis as well.

10 place Paul-Mistral, 38027 Grenoble. © **04-76-85-81-23.** Fax 04-76-46-49-88. www.park-hotel-grenoble.fr. 50 units. 1,600F–1,910F (243.20– 290.30, $232–$276.95) double; 4,070F (618.65, $590.15) suite. Parking 80F (12.15, $11.60). AE, DC, MC, V. Tram: A (get off at Chavant). **Amenities:** Restaurant, bar; room service; baby-sitting; laundry. *In room:* A/C, TV, minibar, hair dryer, safe.

DINING

Le Berlioz TRADITIONAL FRENCH This appealing and tasteful restaurant occupies a century-old building in the heart of town. Inside, you'll find

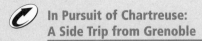

In Pursuit of Chartreuse: A Side Trip from Grenoble

Local monks are the custodians of the secret formula for the liqueur known as Chartreuse, which Maréchal d'Estrées gave them in 1605. It was an elixir involving the distillation of 130 herbs, believed to have been originated by an anonymous alchemist.

Eventually the formula found its way to **La Grande Chartreuse** (charterhouse), founded in 1084 about 20 miles north of Grenoble. The monastery is no longer open to the public, but you're allowed to visit the **Musée de la Correrie**, 38380 St-Pierre-de-Chartreuse (© **04-76-88-60-45**), housed in a 15th-century building at the head of the valley about 1½ miles from the monastery. Admission to the museum is 15F (2.30, $2.20) for adults and 10F (1.50, $1.45) for children. From April to June and September to October, it's open daily from 10am to noon and 2 to 6pm. In July and August, hours are daily from 9:30am to 6:30pm; it's closed the rest of the year. This unusual museum provides a glimpse into a monk's life; the sound you'll hear is chanting.

Even more interesting is a trip to **Voiron**, about 20 miles west of the monastery, where you can visit the **Caves de la Grande Chartreuse**, 10 bd. Edgar-Kofler (© **04-76-05-81-77**), the distillery where the famed liqueur is made. To reach the distillery from the monastery, follow the signs to Saint-Laurent du Pont, and then follow the signs to Voiron. Free tours are given in July and August, daily from 9am to 6:30pm; from Easter to June and from September to October, daily from 9 to 11:30am and 2 to 6:30pm; and from November to Easter, Monday through Friday 9 to 11:30am and 2 to 5:30pm. Dressed in chartreuse green, a guide will show you the copper stills and take you to the cellar, filled with gargantuan oak casks in which the liqueur matures for several years. At the end of the tour, you'll get a free taste of the yellow or fiery green Chartreuse or of a new product. You can also purchase bottles at a shop on the premises. It's said that only three monks and the father procurator have access to the formula.

Before you head out into the Massif de la Chartreuse, get a detailed map from the tourist office in Grenoble.

masses of fresh flowers, tables laid with silver and crystal, and cuisine by the talented young chef Hubert Festier. Menu items change with the seasons, but the stellar choices are likely to include scallops with a Chantilly cream sauce and truffles; a *cassolette* of scallops au gratin; and pressed breast of pigeon with a port wine sauce. Dessert might be a frozen mousse flavored with chartreuse liqueur.

4 rue Strasbourg. © **04-76-56-22-39.** Reservations required. Main courses 70F–170F (10.65– 25.85, $10.15–$24.65); fixed-price menus 120F–340F (18.25– 51.70, $17.40–$49.30). AE, DC, DISC, MC, V. Mon–Fri noon–2pm; Mon–Sat 7:30–10:30pm. Closed late July to mid-Aug.

Restaurant Pique-Pierre ⭐ TRADITIONAL FRENCH   One of the town's most appealing restaurants is this bastion of culinary finesse, about a mile north of the town center, set within a pleasant garden. Sheathed in burnished paneling, it offers a roster of oft-changing and delectable items that include such dishes as seafood salad with salmon and mussels, roasted pigeon in a foie-gras sauce, scallops au gratin, and roasted filet of duckling with a red-wine sauce. Of the 10 choices on the dessert list, our favorite is the bittersweet chocolate tarte.

Rte. Historique de Stendahl (N75), St-Martin-le-Vinoux. ☎ **04-76-46-12-88.** Reservations recommended. Main courses 60F–120F (9.10– 18.25, $8.70–$17.40); set-price menus 150F–300F (22.80– 45.60, $21.75–$43.50). AE, MC, V. Tues–Sun noon–2pm and 7–10pm. Closed last week in July and first 3 weeks of Aug. Bus 33.

GRENOBLE AFTER DARK

To get things started, walk to place St-André, place aux Herbes, or place de Gordes. On a good night, these squares overflow with young people, whose energy level builds in anticipation of an explosion of dancing and partying.

You may want to pace yourself, though, starting out on the sedate side at the **Cybernet Café,** 3 rue Bayard (☎ **04-76-51-73-18**). Here you'll find an unusual mix of soft candlelight and flea-market finds like car parts, signs, and bedposts, all interspersed among state-of-the-art computers. You'll pay 30F (4.55, $4.35) for 30 minutes of time online. Then you might check out **Le Jazz Club,** 7 rte. de Lyon (☎ **04-76-87-05-67**), for an evening of jazz.

Two popular sports pubs that host a wild crowd of students are **Le Couche Tard,** 1 rue Palais (☎ **04-76-44-18-79**), and **The London Pub,** 11 rue Brocherie (☎ **04-76-44-41-90**). **L'Entre-Pôt,** 8 rue Auguste-Gemin (☎ **04-76-48-21-48**), is a die-hard rock club famed for its live concerts.

For a great outdoor party, check out **Le Saxo,** 5 place d'Agier (☎ **04-76-51-06-01**). Its big patio, with speakers blasting techno and rock well into the early morning, has the feeling of a college party. If you're pumped up and need to cut loose on the dance floor, bop on over to **Le Mae Vas,** 1 rue Lamartine (☎ **04-76-87-23-48**), where the young rule the scene. The cover is 50F (7.60, $7.25).

Fans of virtually anything Irish—rugby, shamrocks, leprechauns, and blue-eyed Celts—gravitate to **Murphy's,** 5 place Vaucauson (☎ **04-76-85-30-30**). Guinness, Irish whisky, and all kinds of suds, both French and imported, flow freely. There's always recorded music and often the best Irish music in the Alps. Come to mingle and hear music, but know your soccer scores.

Less sports-oriented and more atuned to cutting-edge music from such centers as London or Los Angeles is **Le Styz,** 6 place Claveyson (☎ **04-76-44-09-99**). Expect a standard mix of hip-hop, R&B, soul, and techno, but be prepared for anything. The dance floor is too small, but used anyway. Young office workers head here after 5pm to sample one of 80 different cocktails featured, with beer and pastis being the drinks of choice.

(Moments   Arty Grenoble: A Sneak Preview

Most local artists label themselves as working in the style of *Ecole de Paris* or *Ecole de Provence*. The best way to enjoy a coffeehouse, an inexpensive brasserie-style meal, and a look at contemporary art in Grenoble today is to go to **Galerie Rome,** 1 rue Très Cloîtres (☎ **04-76-42-82-01**), where oversize, avant-garde paintings line the walls. Virtually everything displayed is for sale. Newer, smaller, and less time-tested is **Galerie Voltair,** 3 rue Voltaire (☎ **04-76-51-19-51**), whose repertoire changes frequently. Here you'll see a parade of some of the most creative Alpine statements in paintings, ceramics, and sculpture.

A restaurant frequented by gays is **La Crêperie,** l'Ange Bleu place de Metz (*Ⓒ* **04-76-87-55-89**). The town's most animated gay disco is **Le Georges V,** 124 cour Berriat (no phone), which does most of its business Thursday through Sunday beginning around 10:30pm.

6 Courchevel 1850 ✰✰

393 miles SE of Paris, 32 miles SE of Albertville, 60 miles SE of Chambéry

Courchevel has been called a resort of "high taste, high fashion, and high profile," a chic spot where multimillion-dollar chalets sit perched on pristine pine-covered slopes. Skiers and geographers know of it as part of Les Trois Vallées, sometimes called "the skiing supermarket of France." The resort, with 93 miles of ski runs in Courchevel and 375 miles of ski runs in the Trois Vallées region around it, employs as many workers in winter as in summer, many of whom do nothing more than manicure and maintain the top-notch ski conditions. Courchevel 1850 has excellent resorts and hotels—with price tags to match, so it largely draws the super-rich. Travelers on average budgets should avoid the place and head for more reasonably priced resorts, especially Chamonix (see below).

Courchevel maintains three ski schools with a staff of 450 instructors, a labyrinth of chairlifts, and over 200 ski runs, which are excellent in the intermediate and advanced categories. Also in Les Trois Vallées are the less well-known resorts of Méribel, Les Menuires, and Val Thorens, which you should avoid unless you direly need to save money. Courchevel consists of four planned ski towns, each marked by its elevation in meters. Thus there's less fashionable Courchevel 1300 (Le Prez), Courchevel 1550, and Courchevel 1650. Crowning them all is Courchevel 1850.

Courchevel 1850 is the most attractive ski mecca in the French Alps. It's also the focal point of a chair-hoist network crisscrossing the region. At the center of one of the largest ski areas in the world, Courchevel was built at the base of a soaring Alpine amphitheater whose deep snowfalls last longer than those at most other resorts because it faces the north winds. Expect reliable snow conditions, perfectly groomed runs, vertical cliffs, and enough wide runs to appease the intermediate skier as well. The glacier skiing draws experts from around the world. The whole complex of Les Trois Vallées is one vast ski circus.

SKI PASSES   A 1-day pass for Courchevel alone costs 197F (29.95, $28.55), but a 1-day pass to the facilities of Les Trois Vallées goes for 235F (35.70, $34.10). A 3-day pass costs 554F (84.20, $80.35) for Courchevel or 680F (103.35, $98.60) for Les Trois Vallées.

ESSENTIALS

GETTING THERE   If you're **driving** from Paris, take A6 to Lyon, then A42 to Chambéry, then A430 to Albertville. At Albertville, get on N90 to Moutiers; then follow the narrow roads 915 and 75 into Courchevel. Courchevel 1850 is the last stop on a steep Alpine road that dead-ends at the village center. Roads are kept open all year, but during winter snowstorms, driving can be treacherous. To go any higher, you'll have to take a cable car from the center of town. Most visitors drive here (you'll need snow tires and chains), but some buses link the city to railway junctions farther down the mountain.

The nearest **train** station is in Moutiers Salins. From Paris, five trains per day leave for Moutiers. The high-speed TGV covers the distance from Paris to

---

ⓘ Tips Le Snowboarding

Snowboarding ("Le Snowboarding" in French) is indulged and accepted at even the grandest Alpine resorts of France. For safety reasons, the *pistes* for snowboards are designated areas that are segregated from conventional ski runs. In the case of Courchevel, the site is identified as *Le Snowpark*. Peppered with all the moguls, hillocks, and obstacles a snowboarder would expect, it straddles the side of *La Piste des Chenus*, running parallel to conventional ski runs and accessible via la Telecabine des Chenus. Snowboarding is still a newcomer to the winter sports scene here, but as long as its participants don't do things too obviously unsafe or disruptive, the sport and its adherents are tolerated, albeit as something of a novelty. Most of the other ski resorts in the French Alps have added half-pipes and other trails exclusively for snowboarders.

Chambéry in about 3 hours. In Chambéry, transfer to another train going to Moutiers. From the station in Moutiers, you can catch the **bus** that takes you along the final lap of the journey into Courchevel. There are five buses per day Monday through Friday and 15 per day on Saturday and Sunday.

The nearest international **airport** is at Geneva. From here, you can catch a bus to Courchevel. There are three buses per day Monday through Friday and eight on Saturday and Sunday. The 4-hour ride costs 340F (51.70, $49.30) one-way. From the airport at Lyon, there are three to five buses a day to Courchevel; the 4-hour trip costs 270F (41.05, $39.15) one-way.

VISITOR INFORMATION   The **Office de Tourisme** is at La Croisette (© **04-79-08-00-29**).

ACCOMMODATIONS
EXPENSIVE

Hôtel Bellecôte ★★   This seven-story chalet, with direct access to the slopes, is known for its collection of unusual antiques. Bored with traditional Alpine motifs, proprietor Roger Toussaint scoured the bazaars of Afghanistan and the Himalayas for an array of objects that lend exotic warmth to the wood-sheathed walls and ceilings. Bedrooms are warmly outfitted with lots of varnished paneling, and each contains plush accessories as well as carved wooden objects from the Far or Middle East. The midsize bathrooms come equipped with combination tub/showers.

Lunch and dinner are offered daily. Full meals in the elegant dining room include cassolette of sweetbreads with flap mushrooms, frogs' legs Provençal, and chicken with morels. The impressive luncheon buffet has a dazzling array of seafood, like crayfish and urchins, followed by sauerkraut with pork. The best *fondant au chocolat* in the Alps is served here.

Rte. de Bellecôte, 73120 Courchevel 1850. © **04-79-08-10-19.** Fax 04-79-08-17-16. 53 units. 1,400F–1,950F (212.80– 296.40, $203–$282.75) per person double; 2,650F–3,080F (402.80– 468.15, $384.25–$446.60) per person suite. Rates include half-board. AE, DC, MC, V. Closed mid-Apr to Dec 20. **Amenities:** Restaurant; bar; indoor pool; fitness center; ski-rental shop; room service; laundry. *In room:* TV, minibar, hair dryer.

La Sivolière ★★   The secret of La Sivolière's success is the owner, Madeleine Cattelin, who has a rich knowledge of and appreciation for her native Savoy. The hotel was constructed in the 1970s by her husband, a building contractor, who used lots of pinewood boards and artfully rustic lichen-covered boulders. It's set near a small forest (*une sivolière*) in a sunny spot near the ski slopes. Each guest room contains tasteful furnishings and a sense of Alpine warmth. All units come with a bathroom with shower; some have a tub as well.

Quartier Les Chenus, 73120 Courchevel 1850. © 04-79-08-08-33. Fax 04-79-08-15-73. www.hotel-la-sivoliere.com. 32 units. 920F–2,520F (139.85– 383.05, $133.40–$365.40) double; 2,620F–3,250F (398.25– 494, $379.90–$471.25) suite. AE, MC, V. Closed mid-Apr to early Dec. Parking 90F (13.70, $13.05). **Amenities:** Restaurant, bar; sauna; room service; baby-sitting; laundry/dry cleaning. *In room:* TV.

Le Chabichou ★★   Within easy walking distance of many bars and clubs, this is one of the town's finest hotels, boasting a superb restaurant (see "Dining," below). Most of the guest rooms in this gingerbread-trimmed chalet are large and well furnished; their daring modern design might not appeal to everyone, however. Beds offer grand Alpine comfort, with quality mattresses and fine linens; the midsize bathrooms are luxurious with combination tub/showers.

Quartier Les Chenus, 73120 Courchevel 1850. © **04-79-08-00-55.** Fax 04-79-08-33-58. www.courchevel.com/chabichou. 44 units. 930F–1,770F (141.35– 269.05, $134.85–$256.65) per person double; 1,925F–2,150F (292.60– 326.80, $279.15–$311.75) per person suite. Rates include half-board. AE, DC, MC, V. Closed May–June and Sept to mid-Nov. **Amenities:** Restaurant, bar; sauna; Jacuzzi; exercise room; room service; baby-sitting; laundry/dry cleaning. *In room:* TV, minibar, hair dryer, safe.

Les Ducs de Savoie ★   This hotel, one of the largest at Courchevel, has elaborately scrolled pinewood and often rows of picturesque icicles hanging from the protruding eaves. There's an indoor pool with walls chiseled from mountain flagstones. Guests stay in spacious, pleasant bedrooms, each with a terrace. Evoking an Alpine theme, the recently modernized rooms are equipped with comfortable beds and bathrooms with combination tub/showers. The property is a few feet from the Téléski of the Jardin Alpin, and you can ski directly to the hotel's vestibule at the end of the day.

Au Jardin Alpin, 73120 Courchevel 1850. © 04-79-08-03-00. Fax 04-79-08-16-30. www.ducssavoie.com. 73 units. 990F–1,720F (150.50– 261.45, $143.55–$249.40) per person double. Rates include half-board. AE, MC, V. Closed Apr 16–Dec 20. Parking in covered garage 70F (10.65, $10.15). **Amenities:** Restaurant, bar; indoor pool; small fitness center; Jacuzzi; sauna; massage; baby-sitting; laundry/dry cleaning. *In room:* TV, hair dryer, safe.

MODERATE

Courcheneige (Kids)   A moderately priced choice, at least for Courchevel, this hotel is located at the heart of the slopes—you can virtually ski from your doorstep. Built like a chalet with sun-seeking balconies, its guest rooms for the most part open onto panoramas of the mountain ranges, including l'Aiguille du Fruit. Each comes with a midsize bathroom, most with a combination tub/shower; some rooms are large enough for a family of five. Regardless of how cold it is outside, it's always warm and cozy inside, especially in the art-filled and elegantly decorated public rooms. The cooking is excellent, with Alpine and international dishes, sometimes served outdoors on the terrace.

Rue Nogentil, 73120 Courchevel 1850. © 04-79-08-02-59. Fax 04-79-08-11-79. www.courcheige.com. 83 units. 650F–900F (98.80– 136.80, $94.25–$130.50) per person. Rates include half-board. AE, V. **Amenities:** Restaurant; fitness center; Jacuzzi; sauna; solarium; room service; laundry. *In room:* TV, hair dryer.

DINING

Chalet des Pierres FRENCH/SAVOYARD   This one is the best of the several lunch restaurants scattered across the slopes. Accented with weathered planking and warmed by open hearths, it sits in the middle of the Verdon slope, a few paces from the path of whizzing skiers. Lunch is served on a sun terrace, but most visitors gravitate to the rustic two-story interior, where blazing fire-places, hunting trophies, and a hip international crowd contribute to the charm of the place. Meals often include air-dried Alpine meat and sausages, the best *pommes frites* in Courchevel, pepper steak, fondue Savoyard, and *plats du jour* (plates of the day). Two particularly appealing dishes are a tart of Beauford cheese and a leg of lamb that's suspended, the traditional way, from a string within the chimney and left to slowly cook in the smoke from the smoldering fire.

Au Jardin Alpin. ✆ 04-79-08-18-61. Reservations required. Main courses 150F–225F (22.80– 34.20, $21.75–$32.65); fixed-price menus 320F–710F (48.65– 107.90, $46.40–$102.95) lunch, 400F–710F (60.80– 107.90, $58–$102.95) dinner. AE, MC, V. Daily 11:45am–5pm; Wed–Sat 7:30–10pm. Closed late Apr to early Dec.

La Bergerie TRADITIONAL FRENCH   Its uneven flagstone steps, stacks of carefully split firewood, and roughly weathered pine logs and planks testify to La Bergerie's 1830s origins as a shepherd's hut. A low-ceilinged dining room on the ground floor contains a dance floor and live entertainment. The ambience is warm, charming, and outdoorsy. Typical and well-prepared menu items are scallops in shallot butter, fondue bourguignonne, and raclette made with cheese imported from small-scale producers in Switzerland. An especially refined platter that usually meets with success is pâté of salmon that's smoked, poached, and grilled, then served with lemon-and-caviar *crème fraîche*.

Quartier Nogentile. ✆ 04-79-08-24-70. Reservations required. Main courses 70F–160F (10.65– 24.30, $10.15–$23.20); plat du jour (lunch) 140F (21.30, $20.30). AE, V. Restaurant daily noon–3pm, Tues–Sat 8–10pm; bar and cafe daily 10am–midnight. Closed late Apr to mid-Dec.

Le Bateau Ivre ✪✪✪ MODERN FRENCH   This restaurant, one of the greatest in the French Alps, is on the sixth floor of a hotel in the upper reaches of the resort and offers a panoramic view over the town and slopes. Its reputa-tion is the result of the efforts of the Jacob family, who prepare such dishes as polenta and escalopes of foie gras in vinaigrette and fricassée of lobster and truffles; we recommend the rack of lamb with olives and artichokes, suckling veal roasted in a sheathing of lard, and scallops scented with gentian, an Alpine flower.

In the Hôtel Pomme-de-Pin, quartier Les Chenus. ✆ 04-79-08-36-88. Reservations required. Main courses 240F–320F (36.50– 48.65, $34.80–$46.40); fixed-price menus 290F–790F (44.10– 120.10, $42.05–$114.55) lunch, 390F–790F (59.30– 120.10, $56.55–$114.55) dinner. AE, DC, V. Daily 12:30–2:15pm and 7:30–10pm. Closed Apr–Dec 20.

Le Chabichou ✪✪✪ MODERN FRENCH   This is the second-best restau-rant in town (only Le Bateau Ivre, above, is better). Le Chabichou is on the lobby level of the hotel of the same name; big windows showcase a view of the snow. The delectable cuisine includes a number of superlative dishes, like oyster soup with wild mushrooms, magrêt of duckling with honey sauce, Alpine curry, and a parmentier of confit of duckling with caramelized potatoes.

Quartier Les Chenus. ✆ 04-79-08-00-55. Reservations required. Main courses 130F–310F (19.75– 47.10, $18.85–$44.95); fixed-price menus 380F–750F (57.75– 114, $55.10–$108.75); skier's lunch 90F (13.70, $13.05) for hotel guests and 195F (29.65, $28.30) for nonguests. AE, DC, MC, V. Daily 12:30–2pm and 7:30–9:30pm. Closed May–June and Sept to mid-Nov.

COURCHEVEL AFTER DARK

A chic but seasonal resort, Courchevel offers nightlife that roars into the wee hours in midwinter but melts away with the snow. You'll never have to walk far from the center to sample the fun, since the area around **La Croisette** (departure point for most of the lifts) contains lots of restaurants, bars, and clubs that come and go. Some nightspots that have survived for a while:

Les Caves de Courchevel, Porte de Courchevel (℃ **04-79-08-12-74**), attracts an upscale crowd. A mock Tyrolean facade of weathered wood hides a club evoking a medieval cloister, with stone arches and columns. Full meals in the restaurant, open nightly from 11pm to 4am, begin at 250F (38, $36.25). Les Caves is open December to April, daily from 6pm to 6am. Also appealing is **Piggy's Pub,** La Croisette (℃ **04-79-08-00-71**), where stiff drinks and recorded music contribute to the sensation that you're far, far away from the French Alps.

La Grange, rue Park-City (℃ **04-79-08-37-99**), is an informal spot for music and dancing. If a spectacle is being staged on the night of your visit, the doors may open earlier. Drinks start at 100F (15.20, $14.50). It's open December to April 15 only, daily from 11pm to 4am.

The closest thing in town to a British pub is **Rhumerie Le Calico,** Au Forum (℃ **04-79-08-20-28**). A convivial bar with a blazing fireplace and a singer is **Le Grenier,** rue Park-City (℃ **04-79-08-36-47**). Both are open only from December to April.

7 Megève ★★★

372 miles SE of Paris, 45 miles SE of Geneva

Megève is famous as a summer resort amid pine forests, foothills, and mountain streams. But it's better known in winter as a cosmopolitan ski resort, with more than 180 miles of downhill runs plus nearly 50 miles of cross-country trails.

The village, with its turreted houses gathered around a 17th-century church, suggests what Megève looked like at the turn of the 20th century. After 1920, however, the new town came along and started attracting vacationers, especially skiers. Those who have made Megève their winter home include several members of the Rothschild family, one of whom, Mme Nadine de Rothschild, has an interest in the well-known Mont d'Arbois hotel. Hubert de Givenchy claims that the big draw of Megève is its *"parfum d'authenticité,"* from its scent of wood smoke to the sounds of heels and hooves clopping on cobblestones.

The interesting center contains **place de l'Église** and its famous hotel, the **Mont-Blanc,** south of the main arteries that cut through the valley. Rita Hayworth and Prince Aly Kahn were photographed nuzzling at this hotel in the 1950s. From 11am to 6am, the center of the old village is closed to traffic, except for pedestrians and sledges. You can shop at your leisure, stopping everywhere from the cobbler to the antiques dealer to the many boutiques.

Some of the resort's hotels and one of its most important cable-car depots are in the village of **Mont d'Arbois,** about a mile east of the center of Megève, at the end of a steep, narrow, and winding road. (In winter, it's unwise to drive up this road without chains on your snow tires.)

Tennis, horseback riding, and cable railways add to the attractions, with views of the Mont Blanc area from the top of each chairlift. The range of amusements includes a casino, clubs, and shows. Megève has more diversions than almost any of the French winter resorts and is a social center of international status.

ESSENTIALS

GETTING THERE Air France and Swissair both serve Geneva's **Cointrin Airport** (℃ **022/717-71-11**) with flights from all over Europe. Round-trip flights between Geneva and Paris cost from 1,900F to 2,450F (288.80 to 372.40, $275.50 to $355.25) each way. The airport is 43 miles to the southeast, from which there's bus service four times a day directly to Megève. The 90-minute transit costs 220F (33.45, $31.90). For information, contact Megève's tourist office (see below) or **Borini & Cie** (© **04-50-21-18-24**).

Many visitors come by **train.** Get off at the hamlet of Sallanches, 8 miles away. From Sallanches, about 10 buses a day make the trip to Megève at a cost of 40F (6.10, $5.80) one-way. Your journey from Paris to Megève will be faster on Saturday or Sunday, when the high-speed TGV travels directly to Sallanches, taking about 5½ hours. Monday through Friday, the TGV goes only as far as Annecy, after which travelers transfer onto slower trains to Sallanches. Total trip time is around 7½ hours. For train information, contact Megève's tourist office (see below) or the SNCF at © **08-36-35-35-35.**

Buses pull into town at the Autogare SNCF (also known as the Gare Routière de Megève), beside the highway running through the town center. For bus information, call © **04-50-21-23-42.**

If you're **driving** to Megève from Paris, take A6 southeast to Mâcon, connecting to the A40 east to St-Gervais, following N212 south straight into Megève. *Be alert:* Winter driving conditions can be perilous. Make sure your car has snow tires and chains.

VISITOR INFORMATION   The **Office de Tourisme** is on rue Monseigneur-Conseil (© **04-50-21-27-28**).

OUTDOOR PURSUITS ON THE SLOPES & BEYOND

You can take a chair hoist to **Mont d'Arbois,** at 6,000 feet, where a panorama unfolds for you, of not only Mont Blanc but also the Fis and Aravis massifs. Cable service operates from June 17 to September 5, every half-hour from 9am to 6pm. To reach the station, take route Edmond-de-Rothschild from the resort's center, past the golf course. The mountain was developed in the 1920s by the Rothschild family, whose search for solitude led them to this scenic outpost. Today, Mont d'Arbois is a pocket of poshness in an already posh resort.

The **French Ski School,** 176 rue de la Poste (© **04-50-21-00-97**), is one of Europe's foremost, with 250 instructors for adults and 32 for children. Classes include the complete French skiing method, modern ski techniques, monosurf-acrobatic skiing, cross-country skiing, and ski touring. The school is open from December 20 to the end of April, daily from 9am to 7pm.

Another option is the **École de Ski Internationale,** 3001 rte. Edmond-de-Rothschild (© **04-50-58-78-88**), which offers much the same facilities.

Much improvement has been made in sports facilities, including a Chamois gondola, which takes skiers to the mountain from the center of town; the Rocharbois cable car, linking the two ski areas of Mont d'Arbois and Rochebrune; and the addition of a gondola and chairlift at the Rochebrune Massif. Skiing here appeals to both intermediates and experts. A 3-day ski pass costs

---

Moments **Two Megève Highlights**

If you have the stamina, take the 9-mile footpath called the **Way of the Cross,** from the edge of town which links more than a dozen country chapels from the mid-19th century. Nothing is more memorable in Megève than the annual **Foire de la Croix,** on the last Sunday of September, marking the return of the herds from the high Alpine pastures. You can taste the farmers' bounty at dozens of stands at the fair, which has been a tradition here since 1282.

from 311F to 520F (47.25 to   79.05, $45.10 to $75.40). A 1-day pass costs 179F (27.20, $25.95).

Megève Palais des Sports et des Congrès (Sports Palace and Assembly Hall), route du Jaillet (© **04-50-21-15-71**), was built in 1968 as the town's showcase for ice sports, swimming, tennis, conventions, meetings, concerts, shows, and gala festivals. It contains two pools with a solarium, saunas, an indoor Olympic-size skating rink open throughout the summer, a curling track, a body-building room, a bar, a restaurant, a gymnasium, tennis courts, an auditorium, confer-ence rooms, and an exhibition gallery. Hours change with the seasons and any special competitions occurring inside, though in most cases it's open daily from 2:30 to 7:30pm. Annual closings occur during May and June.

ACCOMMODATIONS
EXPENSIVE

Chalet du Mont-d'Arbois ★★★   Built in 1928 by a Rothschild matriarch, in a design emulating Switzerland's chalets, this is the most opulent and stylish small resort on the mountain. Bedrooms are spacious, sunny, and sumptuous. Each unit has a good-size bathroom with combination tub/shower. The public rooms are the grandest in Megève, with fireplaces, beamed ceilings, antiques, and silver-plated replicas of alert deer. During part of the season, the hotel might be filled with friends of Mme Nadine de Rothschild, an author whose advice on how a woman should treat her husband became a bestseller in France.

Rte. du Mont-d'Arbois, 74120 Megève. © **04-50-21-25-03**. Fax 04-50-21-24-79. www.silicone.fr/arbois. 20 units. Winter 3,040F–5,480F (462.10– 832.95, $440.80–$794.60) double; off-season 2,760F–4,440F (419.45– 674.90, $400.20–$643.80) double. Rates include breakfast. Half-board 320F (48.65, $46.40) extra per person. AE, DC, MC, V. Closed Apr to mid-June and Oct to mid-Dec. **Amenities:** Restaurant, bar; 2 pools; sauna; Jacuzzi; room service; massage; baby-sitting; laundry/dry cleaning. *In room:* TV, minibar, hair dryer, safe.

Le Fer à Cheval ★★   This is the finest hotel in the center of the village. The guest rooms are beautifully maintained and have traditional styling, with qual-ity mattresses and linens. Most are spacious and sunny, each opening onto a view. All units come with a midsize bathroom with combination tub/shower.

36 rte. du Crêt-d'Arbois, 74120 Megève. © **04-50-21-30-39**. Fax 04-50-93-07-60. 47 units. Fer-a-cheval@ wanadoo.fr. 1,640F–2,120F (249.30– 322.25, $237.80–$307.40) double; 3,340F–4,265F (507.70– 648.30, $484.30–$618.45) suite. Rates include half-board. AE, MC, V. Closed Apr 8–June 7 and mid-Sept to early Dec. **Amenities:** 2 restaurants, bar; outdoor pool; fitness room; sauna; room service; baby-sitting; laundry/dry cleaning. *In room:* TV, minibar, hair dryer, safe.

Les Fermes de Marie ★★★   This is a unique inn. In 1989 the Sibuet fam-ily opened a hotel with a style that had not been seen before in Megève. The remnants of at least 20 antique barns and crumbling chalets were reassembled, then discreetly modernized in a desirable location at the eastern edge of the resort. The result is a compound of appealing, comfortable buildings loaded with atmosphere and eccentricities. The folkloric theme extends to the guest rooms, which look like attractive Alpine cabins. As you lie down for the night in your deluxe bed, you'll know you're experiencing the grandest comfort at the resort. Each well-kept bathroom comes with a combination tub/shower.

Chemin de Riante Colline, 74120 Megève. © **04-50-93-03-10**. Fax 04-50-93-09-84. www.fermesdemarie. com. 65 units. Winter 1,600F–2,900F (243.20– 440.80, $232–$420.50) double; 4,000F (608, $580) suite or chalet for 2. Off-season 1,400F–1,640F (212.80– 249.30, $203–$237.80) double; from 3,680F–4,000F (559.35–608, $533.60–$580) suite or chalet. Rates include half-board. AE, MC, V. Closed Apr 22–June 24 and mid-Sept to mid-Dec. **Amenities:** 3 restaurants, bar; 2 pools; health club; Jacuzzis; sauna; room service; baby-sitting. *In room:* TV, minibar, hair dryer, safe.

MODERATE

Au Coin du Feu Modern, spacious and comfortable, this is one of the best of the middle-bracket hotels of Megève, under the same management as the more glamorous Les Fermes de Marie (see above). It originated in the mid-1980s, when its owners maneuvered 23 bedrooms into the infrastructure of an older chalet. Rooms are cozy and medium-size, and each comes with a combination tub/shower. Public areas contain fireplaces (one of them monumental) and lots of exposed stone. You'll find the place within a 10-minute uphill walk from Megève's center, beside the path leading up to the Rochebrune cable car.

Rte. du Téléphérique de Rochebrune, 74120 Megève. ℂ **04-50-21-04-94.** Fax 04-50-21-20-15. www.coin dufeu.com. 23 units. Winter 686F–960F (104.25– 145.90, $99.45–$139.20) per person. Summer 720F–1,060F (109.45– 161.10, $104.40–$153.70) for 2 persons in a double. Rates include half-board. AE, MC, V. **Amenities:** Restaurant, bar with outdoor terrace; room service; laundry. *In room:* TV, minibar, hair dryer, safe.

Aus Vieux Moulin This building was conceived around 1910 as a water-powered grain mill that produced flour for the village. In 1994, new owners ripped out the then-obsolete mill machinery, added lots of wood paneling, and transformed the site into a cozy hotel. Bedrooms are decorated in a Loire Valley château–inspired style, with touches like black slate floors and coffered ceilings. Each bathroom comes with a combination tub/shower.

Av. Ambroise-Martin, 74120 Megève. ℂ **04-50-21-22-29.** Fax 04-50-93-07-91. www.vieuxmoulin.com. 37 units. 555F–865F (84.35– 131.50, $80.50–$125.45) per person. Rates include half-board. MC, V. Closed mid-Apr to mid-June and mid-Sept to mid-Dec. **Amenities:** Restaurant, bar; outdoor heated pool; exercise room; sauna; steam room; room service; laundry. *In room:* TV.

INEXPENSIVE

Hôtel Gai Soleil This choice boasts a charming setting at the base of hills at the eastern edge of town, between Megève's center and the Rochbrune slopes. Its design was inspired by a Swiss chalet, except for the broad staircase that sweeps down to the front. It has a heated outdoor pool; inside, it's warm and colorful, with lots of exposed wood and well-upholstered comfort. The cozy rooms are highlighted with varnished pine; however, they're not very large and aren't accessible via elevator. All but six have bathrooms with combination tub/shower.

Rue du Crêt-du-Midi, 74120 Megève. ℂ **04-50-21-00-70.** Fax 04-50-21-57-63. www.le-gai-soleil.fr. 21 units. 430F–650F (65.35– 98.80, $62.35–$94.25) double. Discounts of 20% to 50% for children, depending on age. AE, MC, V. Parking 25F (3.80, $3.65). **Amenities:** Restaurant; pool; exercise room; Jacuzzi; baby-sitting. *In room:* TV, minibar.

DINING

You can also try the restaurant at **Le Fer à Cheval** (see "Accommodations," above).

Chalet du Mont-d'Arbois ✦ MODERN FRENCH Often cited in French fashion magazines as one of the most elegant sites in Megève, this restaurant is known for the spit-roasted meats whose flavors and spices go well in this high-altitude, bracing climate. Accumulated mementos of the owners, the Roth-schilds, along with their association with some of the greatest vineyards in the world, are scattered throughout. Savory items include foie gras of duckling, omble chevalier (a local freshwater fish) meunière, spit-roasted turbot served with shellfish-studded risotto, and a dish that never fails to please: spit-roasted Bresse chicken in its own drippings. Out of respect for the small-scale spa that's located in this hotel, part of the menu is devoted to low-fat, low-sodium choices.

447 Chemin de la Rocaille. ✆ **04-50-21-25-03.** Reservations required. Main courses 170F–500F (25.85– 76, $24.65–$72.50); fixed-price menus 300F–350F (45.60– 53.20, $43.50–$50.75). AE, MC, V. Daily noon–2pm and 7:30–10pm. Closed Apr 6–June 11 and Oct to mid-Dec. In Jan, lunch is reserved for hotel guests only.

Le Prieuré TRADITIONAL FRENCH   This restaurant offers traditional French cooking, with specialties like foie gras de canard and salad made from crab, mussels, and lake fish. An excellent appetizer is melon with locally cured ham, which can be followed by grilled swordfish, grilled bass with fennel, or magrêt of duckling flavored with peaches. For dessert, try the half-baked chocolate cake. The restaurant is frequently cited as one of the best dining choices outside of the hotels.

Place de l'Église. ✆ **04-50-21-01-79.** Reservations required. Main courses 95F–280F (14.45– 42.55, $13.80–$40.60); fixed-price menus 129F–210F (19.60– 31.90, $18.70–$30.45). AE, DC, V. Daily noon–2:30pm and 7:30–10pm. Closed June–July 1, Nov, and Mon in off-season.

Les Enfants Terribles TRADITIONAL FRENCH   This acclaimed restaurant is still a hot spot on a cold night. In the adjoining bar, Jean Cocteau painted the wall frescoes that gave the place its name. Today, though far from being the most glamorous place in town, it's one of the more fun, ripe with the shenanigans of young vacationers and snow bunnies. Warmly outfitted with wood panels and rustic artifacts, it serves generous portions of dishes that include escalope of veal Savoyard; sole meunière; and beef served with either morels or a sauce of mustard, ground black pepper, and flambéed cognac. Stop in for nostalgia for the naughty old days of France in the 1950s, and judge for yourself.

In the Hôtel du Mont-Blanc, place de l'Église. ✆ **04-50-58-76-69.** Reservations required. Main courses 75F–180F (11.40– 27.35, $10.90–$26.10); fixed-price menu 125F–165F (19– 25.10, $18.15–$23.95). AE, DC. Wed–Mon noon–3pm and 7–11pm. Closed 3 weeks in Apr–May and Oct.

Restaurant Michel Gaudin ✪ TRADITIONAL FRENCH   This restaurant in the center of Megève benefits from the experience of its Brittany-born owner and namesake. M. Gaudin trained for many years at two of the most spectacularly prestigious restaurants of France, Taillevent (in Paris) and Troisgros (near Lyon). The conservative-looking, wood-paneled interior is less important than the well-flavored cuisine that's produced inside. Menu items focus on the savory and include such hearty culinary staples as terrine of foie gras; rack of lamb in the Breton style, in honor of the owners' home; smoked salmon; and a house specialty of roasted pigeon with honey and apricot sauce.

Carrefour d'Arly. ✆ **04-50-21-02-18.** Reservations recommended. Main courses 75F–195F (11.40– 29.65, $10.90–$28.30); fixed-price menus 120F–400F (18.25– 60.80, $17.40–$58). MC, V. Dec–Apr and July–Sept daily noon–2:30pm and 7–10:30pm; May, June, and Oct–Nov Thurs–Sun noon–2:30pm and 7–10:30pm.

MEGÈVE AFTER DARK

This town is a hotbed of intimate clubs and bars for après-ski fun. The ultimate is a jazz club by the name of **Club de Jazz des 5 Rues,** rue du Comte-de-Capré (✆ **04-50-21-24-36**), a rendezvous for such jazz notables as Claude Luter and Claude Bolling; it's open only during the peak winter season. However, if you're out and about looking to spot the rich and famous, head for the **Casino,** 115 av. Charles-Feige (✆ **04-50-93-01-83**), or its piano bar, **Palo Alto** (✆ **04-50-93-01-83**), where you might run into members of the French jet set. For a dance scene attracting the 18- to 25-year-old set, stop by the underground disco **Le Pallas,** route Edmond-de-Rothschild (✆ **04-50-91-82-70**), where a 90F (13.70, $13.05) cover gains you entrance to this techno/rock spot.

8 Chamonix–Mont Blanc ⟨⋆⟩⟨⋆⟩⟨⋆⟩

381 miles SE of Paris, 58 miles E of Annecy

At an altitude of 3,422 feet, Chamonix is the historic capital of Alpine skiing. This is the resort to choose if you're not a millionaire. Site of the first Winter Olympic Games in 1924, Chamonix is in a valley almost at the junction of France, Italy, and Switzerland. Skiers all over the world know of its 12-mile **Vallée Blanche run,** one of Europe's most rugged, and its longest. Because of its exceptional equipment—gondolas, cable cars, and chairlifts—Chamonix is among Europe's major sports resorts, attracting an international crowd. Thrill seekers also flock here for mountain climbing and hang gliding.

A charming old-fashioned mountain town, Chamonix has a breathtaking backdrop, **Mont Blanc** ⟨⋆⟩⟨⋆⟩⟨⋆⟩, western Europe's highest mountain at 15,780 feet. When two Englishmen, Windham and Pococke, visited Chamonix in 1740, they were thrilled with its location and later wrote a travel book that made the village famous. In 1786, Jacques Balmat became the first man to climb the mountain, though it was said no one could spend a night up there and survive. In the old quarter of town, a memorial to Balmat is in front of the village church.

Scheduled to reopen September 2001, the 7-mile **Mont Blanc Tunnel** (℃ **04-50-53-06-15**) made Chamonix a major stop along one of Europe's busiest highways. By going underground, the tunnel provides the easiest way to get past the mountains to Italy; motorists stop here even if they aren't interested in winter skiing or summer mountain climbing. Toll rates depend on the distance between the axles of your vehicle: 145F (22.05, $21.05) one-way for a small car and 195F (29.65, $28.30) for a big car or caravan trailer. Round-trip tickets are a significant discount, at 180F and 240F (27.35 and 36.50, $26.10 and $34.80), respectively—but you must return within 3 days of buying them.

Chamonix sprawls in a narrow strip along both banks of the Arve River. Its casino, rail and bus stations, and most restaurants and nightlife are in the town center. Cable cars reach into the mountains from the town's edge. Locals refer to Les Praz, Les Bossons, Les Moussoux, and Les Pélerins as satellite villages within Greater Chamonix, though technically Chamonix refers to only a carefully delineated section around place de l'Église.

ESSENTIALS

GETTING THERE   Most (but not all) **trains** coming from other parts of France or Switzerland require a transfer in such nearby villages as St-Gervais (in France) or Martigny (in Switzerland). Passengers from Aix-les-Bains, Annecy, Lyon, Chambéry, and, farther afield, Paris and Geneva are routed through these villages. There are two daily connections from Paris (trip time: 8 hr.); from Lyon, there are six rail links per day (trip time: 4 hr.). For more information and schedules for trains throughout France, call ℃ **08-36-35-35-35.**

Year-round, there's at least one daily **bus** from Annecy and Grenoble charging 96F and 161F (14.60 and 24.45, $13.90 and $23.35) each way, respectively, and from the Geneva airport, there are between two and six buses a day, depending on the season, charging 188F (28.60, $27.25) each way. Buses arrive and depart from a spot adjacent to the railway station in Chamonix. For reservations and information, call **Cie S.A.T.** (℃ **04-50-53-01-15**).

If you're **driving,** you probably won't have to worry about road conditions: Since Chamonix lies on a main road link between Italy and the Mont Blanc

Tunnel, conditions are excellent throughout the year. Even after a storm, roads are quickly cleared. From Paris you can follow A6 toward Lyon, taking the A40 toward Geneva. Before Geneva, turn south along A40 leading into Chamonix.

GETTING AROUND   Within Chamonix, a local network of small buses (*navettes,* usually painted yellow and blue) make frequent runs from points in town to many of the *téléphériques* (cable cars) and villages up and down the valley. Transit on any of them is usually included in the price of a lift ticket, but for nonskiers and summer visitors, the cost is 7.50F (1.15, $1.10) for each 3-mile sector you travel. For information, contact **Chambus** (© **04-50-53-38-03**).

VISITOR INFORMATION   Chamonix's **Office de Tourisme** is on place du Triangle-de-l'Amitié (© **04-50-53-00-24; www.chamonix.com**).

SPECIAL EVENTS   If you're here from mid-July to August, you may want to attend the classical and jazz concerts of the **Semaines Musicales du Mont-Blanc.** Concerts take place at the Grand Salle of "The Majestic," allée du Majestic, built during the Belle Époque as a particularly opulent hotel and later transformed into apartments. Tickets cost 75F to 150F (11.40 to 22.80, $10.90 to $21.75) and are available from the Office de Tourisme.

SKIING

With the highest mountain in western Europe as a backdrop, this is an area for the skilled skier. Regrettably, none of the five main ski areas spread along the valley floor are connected by lifts, and lines at the most popular areas are the longest in the Alpine world. Weather and snow conditions create crevasses and avalanches that may close whole sections for days, even threatening parts of the resort itself.

Skiing is not actually on Mont Blanc, but on the shoulders and slopes across the valley facing this giant. Vertical drops can be spectacular—with lift-serviced hills rising to as high as 10,500 feet. Glacier skiing begins at 12,465 feet. This is not for beginners or timid intermediate skiers, who should head for the resorts of Les Houches or Le Tour. World-class skiers come here to face the challenges of the high snows of Brévant, La Flégère, and especially Les Grands Monets, that fierce north-facing wall of snow that stretches about 3 city blocks wide.

A 1-day ski pass costs 160F (24.30, $23.20) and can be used only in the Brévant area. Better is the Chamski Pass, good for at least five major areas, for 240F (36.50, $34.80) for 1 day or 650F (98.80, $94.25) for 3 days.

SEEING THE AREA BY CABLE CAR

The belvederes you can reach from Chamonix by cable car or mountain railway are famous. For information on these rides, contact the **Société Touristique du Mont-Blanc,** 100 Parking de l'Aiguille du Midi (© **04-50-53-30-80**).

In town, you can board a cable car for the **Aiguille du Midi** ★★★ and on to Italy—a harrowing journey. The first stage, a 9-minute run to the Plan des Aiguilles at an altitude of 7,544 feet, isn't so alarming. But the second stage, to 12,602 feet, the Aiguille du Midi station, may make your heart leap, especially when the car rises 2,000 feet between towers. At the summit, you'll be 1,110 yards from Mont Blanc's peak. There's a commanding view of the Aiguilles of Chamonix and Vallée Blanche, the largest glacier in Europe (9.3 miles long and 3.7 miles wide). You also have a 125-mile view of the Jura and the French, Swiss, and Italian Alps.

You leave the tram station along a chasm-spanning narrow bridge leading to the third cable car and the glacial fields that lie beyond. Or you can end your journey at Aiguille du Midi and return to Chamonix. Generally, the cable cars operate year-round: in summer, daily from 6am to 5pm, leaving at least every 10 minutes; in winter, daily from 8am to 4pm, leaving every 10 minutes. The first stage, to Plan des Aiguilles, costs 88F (13.40, $12.75) round-trip, increasing to 220F (33.45, $31.90) for a round-trip from Chamonix to Aiguille du Midi.

You then cross over high mountains and pass jagged needles of rock and ice bathed in dazzling light. The final trip to **Pointe Helbronner,** in Italy—at 11,355 feet—requires a passport if you want to leave the station and descend on two more cable cars to the village of Courmayeur. From here, you can go to nearby Entrèves to dine at La Maison de Filippo, a "chalet of gluttony." The round-trip from Chamonix to Pointe Helbronner is 345F (52.45, $50.05); the cable car operates from mid-May to mid-October only.

Another cableway takes you up to **Brévent** ★★★, at 8,284 feet. From here, you'll have a first-rate view of Mont Blanc and the Aiguilles de Chamonix. The trip takes about 1½ hours round-trip. Cable cars operate year-round from 8am to 5pm. Summer departures are at least every half-hour. A round-trip costs 86F (13.05, $12.45).

Another aerial journey takes you to **Le Montenvers** ★★★ (© 04-50-53-12-54), at 6,276 feet. At the end of the cable-car run, you'll have a view of the 4-mile-long *mer de glace* (sea of ice, or glacier). Aiguille du Dru is a rock climb notorious for its difficulty. The trip takes 1½ hours, including a return by rail. Departures are from 8am to 6pm in summer, until 4:30pm in the off-season; service is usually year-round. The round-trip fare is 82F (12.45, $11.90).

You can also visit a cave, **La Grotte de Glace,** hollowed out of the *mer de glace;* a cable car connects it with the resort of Montenvers, and the trip takes 3 minutes. The train, cable car, and visit to the cave cost 120F (18.25, $17.40).

ACCOMMODATIONS
INEXPENSIVE

Au Bon Coin   This government-rated two-star hotel is very French Alpine. It has comfortable modern guest rooms, often with views of the mountainside. In autumn, the colors are spectacular. The rooms feature terraces where you can soak up the sun, even in winter. Each small to medium unit is equipped with a firm mattress; most have a shower-only bathroom. The chalet is tranquil, especially in the garden.

80 av. de l'Aiguille-du-Midi, 74400 Chamonix. © 04-50-53-15-67. Fax 04-50-53-51-51. 20 units, 16 with private bathroom. 352F (53.50, $51.05) double without bathroom, 462F (70.20, $67) double with bathroom. MC, V. Closed May–June and mid-Oct to mid-Dec. Free parking. *In room:* TV.

Chalet Hôtel Le Chantel   Within a 30-minute walk west from the city hall, this white-stucco hotel evokes a Swiss chalet with its dark-stained wood, balconies, and mountain panoramas. Originally built as a vacation home in 1952, it benefits from the care and attention of its owners, Peter and Françoise Schmid, who have added decorative touches akin to what you'd expect in a private home. The cozy knotty-pine–paneled rooms are small but offer fine Alpine comfort, each with a comfortable bed and a compact shower-only bathroom. Breakfast is the only meal served.

391 rte. des Pecles, 74400 Chamonix. © 04-50-53-02-54. Fax 04-50-53-54-52. 7 units. 370F–500F (56.25– 76, $53.65–$72.50) double. Rates include breakfast. MC, V. *In room:* TV.

Hôtel de l'Arve Originally a cafe around the turn of the 20th century, this place is now a comfortable hotel. Most of its stucco facade dates from the 1960s, and the interior is a simple setting with childproof, much-used furniture and accessories. Furnishings in the small to medium bedrooms are functional; the mattresses a bit worn but serviceable. The compact bathrooms contain shower stalls. This is a simple place that offers a friendly welcome, an appreciation for the great outdoors, and lovely views of the Arve River from many of the rooms. The setting is particularly convenient, just a 5-minute walk from the town hall.

60 impasse des Anémones, 74400 Chamonix. ℂ 04-50-53-02-31. Fax 04-50-53-56-92. www.hotelarve-chamonix.com. 39 units, 35 with private bathroom. 280F–384F (42.55– 58.35, $40.60–$55.70) double without bathroom. 318F–572F (48.35– 86.95, $46.10–$82.95) double with bathroom. Half-board 133F (20.20, $19.30) extra per person. AE, DC, MC, V. Closed Nov–Dec 20. **Amenities:** Restaurant. *In room:* TV.

DINING

Bartavel ITALIAN Decorated much like a tavern you might find in Italy, this restaurant offers a range of pastas and salads, plus a medley of rib-sticking platters designed to go well with cold air and high altitudes. Menu items include grilled steaks and chops, escalopes milanese or pizzaiola, several pizzas, and an array of simple desserts. Beer and wine flow liberally. Bartavel attracts a many outdoor enthusiasts, who appreciate its copious portions and reasonable prices.

26 cours du Bartavel (impasse du Vox). ℂ 04-50-53-97-19. Set-price menus 80F–100F (12.15– 15.20, $11.60–$14.50). AE, DC, MC, V. Thurs–Tues 11am–midnight.

La Casa Valerio ITALIAN This restaurant is the good-natured domain of long-time Chamonix resident Valerio Comazetto, whose clients have followed him from restaurant to restaurant for 2 decades. You might enjoy tapas at the cozy bar, filled with Chianti bottles and Alpine souvenirs, before proceeding upstairs to the dining room, where red-and-white checked tablecloths set the trattoria motif. You'll find the best pizzas in the region, many redolent of Mediterranean herbs; up to 40 kinds of fresh-made pastas, including succulent versions with salmon and thin-sliced *jambon de Parme.* More-substantial dishes include grilled calamari, mussels in white-wine sauce, and grilled steaks.

88 rue du Lyret. ℂ 04-50-55-93-40. Reservations not necessary. Pizzas, pastas, platters 60F–70F (9.10– 10.65, $8.70–$10.15). AE, DC, MC, V. Daily noon–2am.

Le Chaudron Value TRADITIONAL FRENCH There are a lot of fancier places in town, but for good value, honest cooking, and fine mountain ingredients, Le Chaudron emerges near the top of our list. Chef Pierre Osterberger cooks right in front of you, and you're sure to appreciate his specialties, which include house-style sweetbreads, rabbit stew with juniper berries, several robust beef dishes, and fondues, as well as many salads and desserts. The cellar is filled with well-chosen wines, including Château Mouton-Rothschild and Château Latour.

79 rue des Moulins. ℂ 04-50-53-40-34. Reservations recommended. Main courses 85F–180F (12.90– 27.35, $12.35–$26.10); fixed-price menus 145F–300F (22.05– 45.60, $21.05–$43.50). AE, MC, V. Daily 7pm–midnight. Closed June and Oct–Nov.

Restaurant Albert 1er MODERN FRENCH Although the hotel complex that contains this establishment features other, newer, eateries, this is the star. You'll dine in one of a trio of cozily decorated dining rooms, with bay windows opening onto views of Mont Blanc and walls accented with rustic artifacts and antique farm implements. Begin with chef Pierre Carrier's broth (*fumet*) of wild mushrooms garnished with ravioli stuffed with foie gras. Entrees include sweet onions cooked in rock salt, locally smoked salmon prepared with a caviar-flavored cream sauce, and foie gras of duck with truffled chicken rillettes. Try the classic honey ice cream with a raspberry coulis—there's nothing more succulent on the dessert menu. In summer, dine alfresco in the garden.

In the Hameau Albert 1er hotel, 119 impasse du Montenvers. © **04-50-53-05-09.** Reservations recommended. Main courses 185F–350F (28.10– 53.20, $26.85–$50.75); fixed-price menus 220F–650F (33.45– 98.80, $31.90–$94.25). AE, DC, MC, V. Fri–Mon and Wed 12:30–2pm; daily 7:30–9:30pm.

Restaurant Matafan 🌟 FRENCH/SAVOYARD This stellar restaurant offers a decor of soft pastels and hand-woven tapestries, arranged around a central pentagonal fireplace. Specialties change seasonally but may include omble chevalier (lake fish) meunière, medallions of veal in a white truffle sauce, rack of lamb roasted with herbs (for two), and sinful desserts like a mousse of apples and white chocolate. Many of the dishes are inspired by Savoy cooking, but with a refined touch. The excellent cellar contains more than 500 wines, many reasonably priced. In summer, you can lunch next to the pool in the garden.

In the Hôtel Mont-Blanc, 62 allée du Majéstic. © **04-50-53-05-64.** Reservations required. Main courses 140F–200F (21.30– 30.40, $20.30–$29); fixed-price menus 295F–350F (44.85– 53.20, $42.80–$50.75). AE, DC, MC, V. Daily noon–2pm and 7–10pm. Closed Oct 15–Dec 15.

CHAMONIX AFTER DARK

Nightlife in Chamonix runs the gamut from the classical and sublime to the campy and riotous. You'll find the highest concentration of bars and pubs along rue des Moulins and rue Paccard. The site most favored by hipsters between the ages of 18 and 50 is **l'Arbate Café,** 80 chemin du Spai (© **04-50-53-44-43**), a two-level, prosperous-looking chalet that projects cutting-edge music you might not have expected in an Alpine retreat. It serves the kind of drinks that can get a party rolling. Another choice is the sexy, high-energy, predominantly young **Dick's Tea Bar,** 80 rue des Moulins (© **04-50-53-19-10**), which occupies a converted water mill in the town center; and the British bastion, the **Mill Street Bar,** 123 rue des Moulins (© **04-50-55-80-92**), with tables spilling onto the sidewalk and English-language après-ski stories floating about.

The more sedate crowd enjoys the mellow atmosphere at **Le Blue Night Disco,** 22 rue Paccard (© **04-50-53-63-52**), where the dance floor occupies a very old vaulted cellar and the music is at such a level to allow conversation. The **Casino,** 12 place H.-B.-de-Saussure (© **04-50-53-07-65**), offers evenings of chance at the slot machines and the roulette and blackjack tables.

9 Val d'Isère 🌟🌟

413 miles SE of Paris, 73 miles E of Albertville, 81 miles E of Chambéry

Set in an open valley, and originally conceived as a hunting station for the ducs de Savoie, Val d'Isère (6,068 ft. above sea level) has grown into the centerpiece for some of Europe's most spectacular skiing. Less snobbish than Courchevel and less old-fashioned than Megève, it's a youthful, rather brash resort where virtually everyone comes to enjoy active, outdoor pursuits. Its fans compare it favorably to Chamonix, which—despite the allure of nearby Mont Blanc and some superb skiing—seems to be burdened with longer lift lines and a less accessible layout of ski lifts and slopes. In 1992 Val d'Isère hosted most of the men's downhill racing events for the Winter Olympics, which were headquartered at Albertville.

ESSENTIALS

GETTING THERE & GETTING AROUND **Driving** is the preferred way to get to and around Val d'Isère. Most motorists come from Albertville, accessible by superhighway from Paris. From Albertville, follow signs to Moutiers, then take RN202 to Bourg-St-Maurice (36 miles) and continue another 19 miles to Val d'Isère. The meandering RN202 is panoramic and breathtaking—for its views and its lack of guard rails along some sections. During snowfalls, chains on tires are required. When you get to the resort, we strongly advise you to park your car and not use it again until you're ready to leave. Parking problems here are legendary, and without chains, you'll risk getting stuck during snowfalls. You can walk to virtually anywhere in town faster than you can drive.

Two dozen red-and-white Train Rouge **shuttle buses,** each with a capacity of 100 people and their equipment, connect the hamlets at either end of the valley (Daille and Fornet) to the center. The central terminus is the Rond-Point des Pistes. Transit is free. In summer, service is available only in July and August.

Parking lots and garages are scattered around the valley and are clearly marked. Each charges around 80F (12.15, $11.60) per day, or 300F to 450F (45.60 to 68.40, $43.50 to $65.25) per week, depending on the season and the size of your car.

Nearby **airports** include Cointrin outside Geneva (© **022/717-71-11**), Lyon-Satolas (© **04-72-22-72-21**), Grenoble (© **04-76-65-48-48**), and Chambéry (© **04-79-54-49-54**). Bus and limo service are available from any airport via Cars Martin (© **04-79-06-00-42**).

The nearest **train** station is at Bourg-St-Maurice (© **04-79-07-10-10**), an Alpine village 19 miles west of Val d'Isère. For train information and schedules, call © **08-36-35-35-35.** From here, **buses** maintained by Cars Martin (© **04-79-07-04-49**) depart between 4 and 10 times a day, depending on the season, and cost 65F (9.90, $9.45) each way. Or you can take a **taxi** from Bourg-St-Maurice for a one-way fare of about 420F (63.85, $60.90) for up to four passengers. (Call **Altitude Taxis** at © **04-79-41-14-15,** or arrange pickup in advance with your hotel.)

VISITOR INFORMATION The resort's **Office de Tourisme,** rue Principale (© **04-79-06-06-60;** www.valdisere.com), is a font of information on outdoor activities. The widest spectrum of information on sports is available from the **Club des Sports (Sports Department),** B.P. 61, 73152 Val d'Isère (© **04-79-06-03-49**).

OUTDOOR PURSUITS ON & OFF THE SLOPES

As recently as 1930, Val d'Isère was little more than a mountain village near the Italian frontier, with a church and a handful of slate and stone houses accessible only via mule track. Today, the town is a mass of urban sprawl whose boundaries are defined by avalanche-prone walls that rise up to altitudes where snow is common even during spring and autumn. It's bisected by a gravel-bottomed stream, La Tarentaise. The developed (some say overdeveloped) sections of the resort sprawl along both sides of the highest road in Europe, RN202.

Don't expect a pristine-looking Alpine village. In Val d'Isère, traffic roars through the town center. Clusters of cheap restaurants, crêperies, and more than 125 stores and outlets line either side of the road. Since 1983, however, some of the worst of the town's architectural sins have been corrected, thanks to tighter building codes and greater emphasis on traditional chalet-style architecture.

Access to Val d'Isère, less than 6 miles from the Italian border, is inconvenient and time-consuming. Parking is a nightmare during busy seasons, and the medieval cluster of stone buildings that composed the original hamlet were long ago pushed into the background in the region's rush to modernize. But despite the commercialism, the town hums with the sense that its visitors are here to enjoy skiing. And few other European resorts can boast as logical a layout for a far-flung network of ski slopes.

Val d'Isère is the focal point for a network of satellite resorts scattered around the nearby valleys, including the architecturally uninspired Tignes (6,888 ft. above sea level), whose layout is divided into at least four resort-style villages. The most stylish and prosperous of these is Val Claret; less fortunate and successful are Tignes le Lac, Tignes les Boisses, and Tignes les Brévières.

Guarding one entrance to Val d'Isère is La Daille, a resort of mostly high-rise condominiums and time-shares. Standing sentry at the other is the medieval hamlet of Le Fornet, best known as the departure point for gondolas leading over a mountain ridge to the Pissaillas Glacier and another network of ski trails, the Système de Solaise. All these satellites lack the cachet and diversity of Val d'Isère's nightlife and dining. Public transport via the Train Rouge can pick you up and deposit you at the departure point to the terminus of virtually any ski lift or trail in the region.

Val d'Isère is legendary for its "death-defying" chutes and its off-piste walls. These slopes are for the experts, but the intermediate skier will also find open snowfields. The best place for intermediates is Tignes, with its wide variety of runs, including the Grande Motte at 11,150 feet. Skiers find enough variety here to stay 2 weeks and never repeat the slopes that stretch from the Pissaillas Glacier far above Val d'Isère to Tignes Les Brévières four valleys away.

There are only a few marked expert runs; it's the more accessible off-piste areas that lure experts from all over Europe and the United States. Most of these runs can be reached after short traverses from the Bellevarde, Solaiwse, and Fornet cable cars in Val d'Isère and the Grande Motte cable car in Val Claret.

At least a dozen **ski schools** flourish in winter. One of the largest and busiest is the **École de Ski Français,** or French National Ski School (℗ **04-79-06-02-34**), with 280 guides and teachers. Somewhat more personalized is **Snow Fun** (℗ **04-79-06-16-79**), with 60 guides. Purists usually gravitate to **Top Ski,** galerie des Cimes (℗ **04-79-06-14-80**), a small but choice outfit with 12 extremely well-trained guides catering exclusively to Alpine connoisseurs who want to ski off-piste (away from the officially recognized and maintained trails).

ACCOMMODATIONS

The staff at **Val Hôtel** (℗ **04-79-06-18-90;** fax 04-79-06-11-88), the resort's central reservations network, can book accommodations for you.

Hôtel Altitude This frequently renovated and oft-modernized chalet is from the 1970s, when it was built in true Savoyard style. It's frequently confused with the Hôtel Latitude nearby, because of the similarity of their names. The Altitude is comfortable and cozy, a short walk south of the town center, so you'll be able

---

(*Fun Fact* **Golden Boy**

Val d'Isère is the hometown of the legendary Jean-Claude Killy, who swept the gold in all three downhill skiing events (slalom, giant slalom, and downhill) at the 1968 Olympics held in nearby Grenoble.

Moments **Year-Round Skiing**

Although snow melts on the rock faces around town in summer exposing the gray bedrock, icy granules remain skiable year-round on the Pissaillas. The glacier is accessible via the Fornet cable car, on the northwestern edges of town. The tourist office considers the ski conditions safe and suitable only between June 28 and August 17. During that period, a lift ticket costs 108F (16.40, $15.65) for half a day, 136F (20.65, $19.70) for a full day, and 250F (38, $36.25) for 2 days. Note that these prices do not include medical and accident insurance, a limited policy that can be purchased for a supplement of 15F (2.30, $2.20) per day. Access to the glacier from Val Disole requires two cable-car transfers. For information, contact **Ski Lifts** (© **04-79-06-00-35**). Officially, the resort's sports activities slow down or stop altogether every year between early May and late June, and from early September to mid-November. In winter, when snow conditions are much, much better, half-day, full-day, and 2-day lift tickets sell for 159F (24.15, $23.05), 228F (34.65, $33.05), and 421F (64, $61.05), respectively.

to escape the crowds. Many guests return year after year, occupying elegantly appointed bedrooms with quality mattresses and fine linens. Each midsize bathroom comes with a combination tub/shower.

Rte. de la Balme, 73150 Val d'Isère. © **04-79-06-12-55**. Fax 04-79-41-11-09. www.skifrance.fr73304/altitude. 40 units. Winter 1,000F–1,480F (152– 224.95, $145–$214.60) double; summer 760F–900F (115.50– 136.80, $110.20–$130.50) double. Rates include half-board. V. Closed May 6–June 30 and Sept 9–Nov 1. **Amenities:** Restaurant; bar; outdoor pool; health club; sauna; room service; baby-sitting; laundry/dry cleaning. *In room:* TV, hair dryer.

Hôtel Christiania ★★   This is the best hotel in a town of worthy contenders. The stylishly designed 1949 lodging was almost completely rebuilt in 1991. Homage to its original design appears at unexpected moments, most obviously in the *Sputnik*-style furniture incorporated into a sunken lobby that's ringed with exposed stone, varnished pine, and blazing fireplaces. The guest rooms are deliberately cozy, with lots of pine trim and Alpine touches. The midsize bathrooms come equipped with tubs.

B.P. 48, 73152 Val d'Isère. © **04-79-06-08-25**. Fax 04-79-41-11-10. www.hotel-christiania.com. 69 units. 980F–1,700F (148.95– 258.40, $142.10–$246.50) per person double; 1,650F–2,300F (250.80– 349.60, $239.25–$333.50) per person suite. Rates include half-board. AE, MC, V. Closed May–Dec 5. **Amenities:** Restaurant; bar; indoor pool; exercise room; sauna; room service; massage; baby-sitting; laundry. *In room:* TV, hair dryer.

Hôtel Mercure Village   The success of this chain hotel is based on its relatively reasonable rates and its lack of the ostentation and glitter that permeate many of Val d'Isère's properties. Don't judge its charm by its rather uninspired four-story, chalet-style exterior: Inside are enough Alpine touches to evoke a bit of nostalgia. In the public areas are pinewood paneling and flowered curtains. The guest rooms are simpler and rather angular but still feature touches of varnished pine. Each midsize bathroom comes with a combination tub/shower. The hotel is in the town center, with easy access to the chairlifts and nightlife.

B.P. 45, 73152 Val d'Isère. © **04-79-06-12-93**. Fax 04-79-41-11-12. www.mercurevaldisere.com. 45 units. 640F–1,440F (97.30– 218.90, $92.80–$208.80) double; 920F–1,160F (139.85– 176.30, $133.40–$168.20) suite. Rates include breakfast. AE, DC, MC, V. Closed May 8–June 15. Parking 75F (11.40, $10.90). **Amenities:** 2 restaurants; bar; room service; laundry/dry cleaning. *In room:* TV, hair dryer, safe.

DINING

La Grande Ourse SAVOYARD   Although it's open for lunch, this restaurant doesn't take on its trademark coziness until after nightfall, when flickering candles and a blazing fireplace permeate the place with lots of Savoyard charm. It was built in 1937 by Jean Fautrier, an important painter who's almost unknown outside France. Its name derives from a mural that Fautrier painted of the zodiac, part of which features a large female bear. Menu items at lunch include grilled meats, pastas, salads, and simple but fortifying dishes of the day. Evening menus offer more sophisticated fare, like codfish steak braised with herbs, foie gras, and lemon juice; roast rack of lamb with herbs; lobster ravioli; and Savoyard fondue with three cheeses. Dessert may be a *tarte fine* with apples or a Gallic version of a North American brownie.

Sur le Front de Neige, adjacent to the church. © 04-79-06-00-19. Reservations recommended at dinner. Main courses 130F–180F (19.75– 27.35, $18.85–$26.10) dinner; fixed-price menus 130F (19.75, $18.85) lunch, 255F (38.75, $37) dinner. AE, DC, V. Daily noon–3pm and 7:30–9:30pm. Closed May 5–Nov 30.

La Vieille Maison (★) *Finds* SAVOYARD   Amid cozy but relatively new buildings in the satellite hamlet of La Daille, this former farmhouse is one of the valley's oldest chalets. Constructed 300 years ago, it has lots of exposed stone and a decor that's ripe with old-fashioned charm. Menu items are based on Savoyard themes, specializing in hearty cold-weather dishes like fondues and raclettes, many of which are prepared only for a minimum of two to four diners. Other choices range from filet mignon with lemon and sour cream to the specialty, Vieille Maison–style veal stuffed with ham and slathered with cheese. Hands-on chefs sometimes opt for La Viande à l'Auze—a superhot slab of rock is placed directly on your table so you can sizzle your beef strips yourself.

Vieux Village, La Daille. © 04-79-06-11-76. Reservations recommended. Main courses 95F–120F (14.45– 18.25, $13.80–$17.40), set menus (lunch only) 85F–120F (12.90– 18.25, $12.35–$17.40). AE, MC, V. Lunch daily noon–3pm; dinner daily 7–9:30pm. Closed May–June and Sept–Nov.

VAL D'ISÈRE AFTER DARK

The resort has its share of bars that come and go every season. Most are in the town's pedestrian zone or adjacent to rue Principale. One of the most reliable is **L'Aventure** (© 04-79-06-20-82). For an attractive-looking crowd, head to **Café Face**, rue Principale (© 04-79-06-04-93). If you want to dance, there are two discos, both mobbed in winter and dead during spring and autumn: **Dick's Tea Bar** (© 04-79-06-14-87), which also opens halfheartedly in July and August but only on evenings when business might justify the effort; and **Club 21** (© 04-79-06-04-93), open only in winter. Cover at both is around 75F (11.40, $10.90) and includes the first drink.

A SIDE TRIP TO ALBERTVILLE

The rail and highway junction of Albertville lies within **La Vallée de la Tarantaise,** a sinuous valley that climbs upward along a distance of 53 miles along Route 90. Route 90 extends from low-lying Albertville (at around 1,200 ft. above sea level) and branches into **La Vallée d'Isère,** whose focal point is the resort of Val d'Isère. Most visitors travel between the two points by car, although about five trains a day go uphill between Albertville and Bourg-St-Maurice. At Bourg-St-Maurice, a bus, whose departure is timed to coincide with the arrival of trains, continues for another 18 miles up to Val d'Isère. Train passengers should expect a total transit time of between 60 and 90 minutes, depending on the day of the week, and a one-way fare of around 95F (14.45, $13.80).

The 1992 Winter Olympics were held in Albertville, but you'd hardly know it these days. Even during the games, the town was little more than the administrative headquarters for an event that encompassed all of the Savoy region. The official name of those games (*Les Jeux d'Albertville et de La Savoie*) was chosen to downplay Albertville and to raise awareness of such Savoy resorts as Menuires, La Plagne, and Les Saisies. (It didn't do much good; they're still little-visited by foreigners.)

Today, few vestiges of the 1992 games remain in their original form within Albertville. The town is a dull railway and highway junction, and because of its location in a valley, not particularly panoramic. It's proud of the way it either demolished or transformed many of the Olympic structures into new uses, and 1992 is spoken of with nostalgia. Albertville's most visible monument to the 1992 games is the metal-sheathed **Halle Olympique**, avenue de Winnenden (© **04-79-32-84-11**), but frankly, we don't consider it a hot tourist ticket.

ACCOMMODATIONS & DINING

Hôtel Million ★★★ TRADITIONAL FRENCH   This is the area's finest choice, attracting gastronomes and sports enthusiasts. Set back from the main road, the Hôtel Million was established in 1770 by an ancestor of Philippe Million, the current owner and chef whose cuisine did much to put Albertville on the gourmet map. It's housed in a white building with strong horizontal lines and gables on a flagstone-covered square; the anterooms have authentic 19th-century decor, while the dining room itself has high ceilings and classic furnishings. Some of the traditional dishes derive from popular Savoy tastes of the 19th century, in particular the frogs' legs, freshwater fish from Lake Annecy, and freshwater crayfish. Other choices include fera (a whitefish found in Alpine lakes) served with wild celery and herb-flavored butter; sweetbreads with truffle sauce; and roasted rack of veal served with a fricassée of artichokes.

Available for overnight stays are 26 attractive bedrooms. Outfitted in rustic Alpine style, each contains a private bathroom, TV, phone, and more space than you'd expect. Weekends from December to April are the most expensive, when doubles rent for 550F to 750F (83.60 to 114, $79.75 to $108.75). The rest of the year, doubles cost 400F to 550F (60.80 to 83.60, $58 to $79.75).

8 place de la Liberté, 73200 Albertville. © **04-79-32-25-15**. Fax 04-79-32-25-36. Reservations recommended. Main courses 150F–260F (22.80– 39.50, $21.75–$37.70); fixed-price menus 150F–550F (22.80– 83.60, $21.75–$79.75). AE, DC, MC, V. Tues–Sun noon–2pm; Tues–Sat 7:45–9:30pm.

15

Provence: In the Footsteps of Cézanne & van Gogh

Provence has been called a bridge between the past and the present, where the past and present blend in a quiet, often melancholy way. Peter Mayle's *A Year in Provence* and its sequels have played a large role in the recent popularity of this sunny corner of southern France.

The Greeks and Romans first filled the landscape with cities boasting Hellenic theaters, Roman baths, amphitheaters, and triumphal arches. These were followed by Romanesque fortresses and Gothic cathedrals. In the 19th century, the light and landscapes here attracted painters like Cézanne and van Gogh.

Provence has its own language and its own customs. The region is bounded on the north by the Dauphine, on the west by the Rhône, on the east by the Alps, and on the south by the Mediterranean. In chapter 16, we'll focus on the part of Provence known as the Côte d'Azur, or French Riviera.

For more extensive coverage of this region, see *Frommer's Provence & the Riviera.*

REGIONAL CUISINE Part of the charm of Provence lies in its cuisine, which marries the traditions of the mountains and the seaside. The earliest contributors were the ancient Italians, for strong comparisons can be made between the Provençal and the Italian emphases on fresh fish and vegetables, olive oil, and garlic.

The best of Provençal produce includes melons from Cavaillon and tube-shaped onions known as *éschalotes-bananes.* The most famous vegetable dish is *ratatouille,* a stew of tomatoes, garlic, eggplant, zucchini, onions, and peppers, liberally sprinkled with olive oil and black pepper. A slightly different version is *soupe au pistou,* with the addition of basil, pounded garlic, vermicelli, string beans, and grilled tomatoes.

Each town along the Provence coast seems to have a fish-stew specialty. In Nice, stockfish is used in *stocaficada. Bourride* is made with whitefish, garlic, onions, tomatoes, herbs, egg yolks, saffron, and grated orange rind. Toulon has its *esquinado,* with saltwater crabs, vinegar, water, and pulverized mussels. The best, most authentic *bouillabaisse* is from Marseille.

Several Provençal meat dishes are welcome substitutes for the ubiquitous fish: *daube de boeuf* (beef stew); *fricassée de pintade* (guinea fowl), perhaps served with a mild purée of sweet garlic; and *fricassée* or *ragoût de cabri* (goat). Provence boasts scores of cheeses, among them Picadon, Pélardon, and St-Félicien; dozens of pastries and breads; and scented honeys.

The regional wines are almost as diverse as the cuisine. They include the vast family of the Côtes-du-Rhône, Gigondas, Châteauneuf-du-Pape, and Château de Fonsalette.

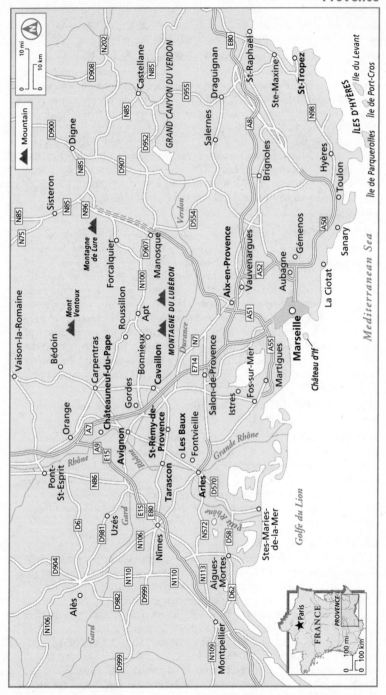

1 Orange ★★

409 miles S of Paris, 34 miles NE of Nîmes, 75 miles NW of Marseille, 16 miles S of Avignon

Orange gets its name from the days when it was a dependency of the Dutch House of Orange-Nassau. Actually, the last orange grove departed 2,000 years ago. The juice that flows in Orange today comes from its vineyards, which turn out a Côtes-du-Rhône vintage. Spread throughout the district are many caves, some of which offer *dégustations* to paying customers. (The tourist office can provide you with a list.)

Overlooking the Valley of the Rhône, today's Orange, with a sleepy population of about 30,000, boasts Europe's third-largest extant triumphal arch and best-preserved Roman theater. Louis XIV, who toyed with the idea of moving the theater to Versailles, said: "It is the finest wall in my kingdom." UNESCO has placed the arch on its World Cultural and Natural Heritage List.

ESSENTIALS

GETTING THERE   Orange sits on some of the major north-south rail and highway arteries, making arrivals by train, bus, or car convenient. Some 20 **trains** per day arrive from Avignon (trip time: 17 minutes), at a one-way fare of around 32F (4.85, $4.65). From Marseille, there are 14 trains per day (trip time: 1½ hours), for around 116F (17.65, $16.80) one-way. From Paris, there are 14 trains per day (trip time: 4½ hours) by TGV, which may require a transfer at Valence, Lyon, or Montélimar and ongoing transit by conventional train into Orange; a one-way fare is 362F (55, $52.50). For rail information and schedules, call ℂ **08-36-35-35-35.** For information on bus routes, contact the **Gare Routière** (ℂ **04-90-34-15-59**), on place Pourtoules, behind the Théâtre Antique. If you're **driving** from Paris, take A6 south to Lyon; then connect with A7 to Orange. The 425-mile drive takes 5½ to 6½ hours.

VISITOR INFORMATION   The **Office de Tourisme** is on cours Aristide-Briand (ℂ **04-90-34-70-88**).

SPECIAL EVENTS   From late June to mid-August, a drama, dance, and music festival called **Les Chorégies d'Orange** takes place at the Théâtre Antique, one of the most evocative ancient theaters in Europe. For information or tickets, visit the office on place Sylvain, adjacent to the theater; call ℂ **04-90-34-24-24;** or go to www.choregies.asso.fr. Recent productions have included *Tristan und Isolde* (presented in vocal and orchestral form, but without costumes), *Turandot,* and *Lucia di Lammermoor.*

EXPLORING THE TOWN

In the southern part of town, the **Théâtre Antique** ★★★, place des Frères-Mounet (ℂ **04-90-51-17-60**), dates from the days of Augustus. Built into the side of a hill, it once held 8,000 spectators in tiered seats. Carefully restored, the nearly 350-foot-long and 125-foot-high theater is noted for its fine acoustics. Today, it's used for outdoor entertainment. It's open daily: April to September from 9am to 6:30pm and October to March from 9am to noon and 1:30 to 5pm. Admission is 30F (4.55, $4.35) for adults, 25F (3.80, $3.65) for students, and 10F (1.50, $1.45) for children under 18.

To the west of the theater stood a huge temple, which, with a gymnasium and the theater, formed one of the greatest buildings in the empire. Across the street, the **Musée Municipal d'Orange,** place du Théâtre-Antique (ℂ **04-90-51-18-24**), displays fragments of the temple. Your ticket to the theater also admits you to the museum, which is open daily, April to September from 9:30am to 7:30pm and October to March from 9:30am to noon and 1:30 to 5:30pm.

Even older than the theater is the **Arc de Triomphe** ✦✦, on avenue de l'Arc-de-Triomphe. It has decayed, but its decorations and other elements are still fairly well preserved. Built to honor the conquering legions of Caesar, it rises 72 feet and is nearly 70 feet wide. Composed of a trio of arches held up by Corinthian columns, it was used as a dungeon for prisoners in the Middle Ages.

Before leaving Orange, head for the park, **Colline St-Eutrope,** adjacent to the Théâtre Antique, for a view of the valley with its mulberry plantations.

After exploring the town itself, you can drive south for 8 miles along A9 to **Châteauneuf-du-Pape,** where you can have lunch (any day but Monday) at the **Hostellerie du Château des Fines-Roches,** route d'Avignon (© **04-90-83-70-23**). Although the Hostellerie was built in the 19th century, it looks feudal, thanks to its many medieval features. If you're pressing on to Avignon, it's only another 8 miles south along any of at least three highways (each marked AVIGNON).

ACCOMMODATIONS

Hôtel Louvre et Terminus *Value*   Surrounded by a garden terrace, this conservatively decorated member of the Logis de France chain offers good value. Don't expect grandeur: Everything is simple, efficient, and rather brusque. Each unit comes with a compact shower-only bathroom. The hotel also has a modest but worthy restaurant, serving both lunch and dinner.

89 av. Frédéric-Mistral, 84100 Orange. © 04-90-34-10-08. Fax 04-90-34-68-71. 32 units. 380F–460F (57.75– 69.90, $55.10–$66.70) double; 680F (103.35, $98.60) suite. AE, DC, MC, V. Parking in garage 30F (4.55, $4.35). **Amenities:** Restaurant; dry cleaning. *In room:* A/C, TV, minibar.

Mercure Orange   This comfortable hotel is in a 20-year-old building whose wings curve around a landscaped courtyard. Its well-furnished rooms are arranged around a series of gardens, the largest of which contains a pool. They were all renovated in 1999, and each has a compact modern bathroom (most with tub/shower). Fixed-price menus are served in the poolside restaurant. This is your best bet for general overnight comfort far from the crowds.

80 rte. de Caderousse, 84100 Orange. © 04-90-34-24-10. Fax 04-90-34-85-48. 99 units. 520F–660F (79.05– 100.30, $75.40–$95.70) double. AE, DC, MC, V. Drive half a mile west of the city center, following directions to Caderousse. Free parking. **Amenities:** Restaurant; bar; pool; room service; laundry. *In room:* TV, minibar.

DINING

Le Parvis TRADITIONAL FRENCH *Kids*   Jean-Michel Berengier sets the best table in Orange, though the dining room is rather austere. He bases his cuisine on well-selected vegetables and the best ingredients from "mountain or sea." Try his escalope of braised sea bass with fennel or asparagus or his lamb with a garlic cream sauce. A can't-miss dish is the foie gras, which could be flavorfully followed by fresh seafood, whose preparation varies according to the season. (The staff prides itself on dozens of preparations.) The service is efficient and polite. A special children's menu is offered for 60F (9.10, $8.70).

3 cours Pourtoules. © 04-90-34-82-00. Reservations required. Main courses 70F–120F (10.65– 18.25, $10.15–$17.40); fixed-price menus 105F–265F ([eu]15.95– 40.30, $15.25–$38.45). AE, DC, MC, V. Tues–Sun noon–2:30pm; Tues–Sat 7:30–9:15pm. Closed Nov.

Shopping for *Brocante* in Provence

There's a big difference between antiques and fun, old junk in France. They even have different names. If you're into serious purchases, you may want to stick to well-established antiques stores, which are found in great abundance all over France, though concentrated mainly in Paris.

But if you prefer something more affordable, and your idea of fun is a flea market, then what you really want is *brocante.* You'll find brocante throughout France; your best bet is to head to the regular market in town on a specific day (the markets in Cannes are a good example; see chapter 16).

If you find yourself in Provence on a Sunday, head out bright and early (like 9am) for **Isle-sur-la-Sorgue,** a village that specializes in brocante. The town is 14 miles east of Avignon, 7 miles north of Cavaillon, and 26 miles south of Orange. There's a brocante market on both Saturdays and Sundays, but Sundays are much more fun because there's also a food market. *Warning:* Everything is over by 1pm.

If you're driving, try grabbing a parking space alongside the supermarket, Marché U. The town gets jammed, especially on Sundays. The Sorgue River isn't much bigger than a canal—the heart of town lies on the far side of the river, spanned by many footbridges. The brocante is on the near side of the river, a little farther downstream from the Marché U. If you drive by and shrug at the small number of dealers who are actually outside in the street and on the curb, be aware that every building on the side of the street facing the river hosts a warehouse filled with more dealers and more loot.

Although the prices aren't the lowest in France, this is a serious market. The market and stores offer top goods, frequently sold to dealers, and shipping can be arranged.

For lunch, there's (surprisingly for such a small place) a Michelin-starred restaurant: **La Prévôté,** 4 rue J.-J.-Rousseau (© **04-90-38-57-29**). You should make your reservation before arriving in town. In the rear of a flower-filled courtyard, chef Roland Mercier wows shoppers and locals with sublime cuisine. The cannelloni filled with fresh salmon and goat cheese is reason enough to cross the river. His tender duckling is flavored with honey from bees that flew over Provençal fields of lavender. The pièce de résistance is his hot chocolate tart. Fixed-price menus cost 150F to 330F (22.80 to 50.15, $21.75 to $47.85) at lunch, and 250F to 330F (38 to 50.15, $36.25 to $47.85) at dinner. Closed November, Sunday nights from October to June, and Mondays year-round.

NEARBY ACCOMMODATIONS & DINING

Château de Rochegude ★★ This Relais & Châteaux member stands on 25 acres of parkland. The castle is at the edge of a hill, surrounded by vineyards. The 12th-century turreted residence has been renovated by a series of distinguished owners, ranging from a pope to a dauphin. The current owners have made many additions, but ancient touches still survive. Each room is done in Provençal style, with fabrics and furniture influenced by the region's 18th- and 19th-century traditions. As befits a château, rooms come in many shapes and sizes, some quite spacious. All have bathrooms with tub/showers. Both the food and the service are exceptional. You can enjoy meals in the stately dining room, barbecue by the pool, and refreshments served on sunny terraces.

26790 Rochegude. ⓒ **04-75-97-21-10.** Fax 04-75-04-89-87. www.chateauderochegude.com. 29 units. 750F–2,100F (114– 319.20, $108.75–$304.50) double; 2,500F–3,200F (380– 486.40, $362.50–$464) suite. AE, DC, MC, V. Closed Nov–Apr 10. Free parking. The hotel is 8 miles north of Orange; take D976, following signs toward Gap and Rochegude. **Amenities:** Restaurant; bar; outdoor pool; room service; laundry. *In room:* A/C, TV, minibar, hair dryer.

2 Avignon ✷✷✷

425 miles S of Paris, 50 miles NW of Aix-en-Provence, 66 miles NW of Marseille

In the 14th century, Avignon was the capital of Christendom. The pope lived here during what the Romans called the Babylonian Captivity. The legacy left by that court makes Avignon one of the most beautiful of Europe's medieval cities.

Today, this walled city of some 100,000 residents is a major stopover on the route from Paris to the Mediterranean. It is increasingly known as a cultural center. Artists and painters have been moving here, especially to rue des Teinturiers. Experimental theaters, galleries, and cinemas have brought diversity to the inner city. The popes are long gone, but life goes on exceedingly well.

ESSENTIALS
GETTING THERE   There's frequent **train** service to Avignon. The TGV trains from Paris arrive at the Gare SNCF, on the boulevard Saint-Roch, 13 times a day (trip time: 3½ hr.); and 17 trains a day arrive from Marseille (trip time: 1½ hr.). For rail information and schedules, call ⓒ **08-36-35-35-35.** Avignon is also a junction for **buses** from throughout the region. For information, contact the Gare Routière, boulevard St-Roch (ⓒ **04-90-82-07-35**). If you're **driving** from Paris, take A6 south to Lyon; then take A7 south to Avignon.

VISITOR INFORMATION   The **Office de Tourisme** is at 41 cours Jean-Jaurès (ⓒ **04-32-74-32-74;** www.ot-avignon.fr).

SPECIAL EVENTS   The biggest celebration is the **Festival d'Avignon,** held during 3 weeks in July and the first week in August. The international festival focuses on avant-garde theater, dance, and music. Part of the fun is the bacchanalia that takes place nightly in the streets. The prices for rooms and meals skyrocket, so make reservations far in advance. Local authorities also crack down on festival-induced vagrancy. For information on dates, tickets, and venues, contact the **Bureaux du Festival,** 8 bis rue de Mons, 84000 Avignon (ⓒ **04-90-27-66-50**).

SEEING THE SIGHTS IN AVIGNON
Even more famous than the papal residency is the ditty *"Sur le pont d'Avignon, l'on y danse, l'on y danse."* Ironically, **pont St-Bénézet** ✷✷ was far too narrow for the *danse* of the rhyme. Spanning the Rhône and connecting Avignon with Villeneuve-lèz-Avignon, the bridge is now a ruin, with only four of its original 22 arches. According to legend, it was inspired by a vision that a shepherd named Bénézet had while tending his flock. The bridge was built between 1177 and 1185 and suffered various disasters from then on. (In 1669, half the bridge fell into the river.) On one of the piers is the two-story **Chapelle St-Nicolas**—one story in Romanesque style, the other in Gothic. The remains of the bridge are open daily from 9am to 6:30pm. Admission is 15F (2.30, $2.20) for adults and 7F (1.05, $1) for students and seniors.

Palais des Papes ✦✦✦   Dominating Avignon from a hilltop is one of the most famous, or notorious, palaces in the Christian world. Headquarters of a schismatic group of cardinals who came close to toppling the authority of the popes in Rome (see "A Tale of Two Papal Cities," below), this fortress-showplace is the monument most frequently associated with Avignon. You're shown through on a guided tour (usually lasting 50 minutes), which can be monotonous, as most of the rooms have been stripped of their once-legendary finery. The exception is the **Chapelle St-Jean,** known for its frescoes attributed to the school of Matteo Giovanetti and painted between 1345 and 1348. These frescoes present scenes from the life of John the Baptist and John the Evangelist. More Giovanetti frescoes can be found in the Chapelle St-Martial. The frescoes depict the miracles of St. Martial, the patron saint of Limousin.

The **Grand Tinel** (banquet hall) is about 135 feet long and 30 feet wide; the pope's table stood on the south side. The **pope's bedroom** is on the first floor of the Tour des Anges. Its walls are decorated in tempera foliage on which birds and squirrels perch. Birdcages are painted in the recesses of the windows. In a secular vein, the **Studium (Stag Room)**—the study of Clement VI—was frescoed in 1343 with hunting scenes. Added under the same Clement, who had a taste for grandeur, the **Grande Audience** (Great Audience Hall) contains frescoes of the prophets, also attributed to Giovanetti and painted in 1352.

Place du Palais. ✆ **04-90-27-50-00.** Admission (including tour with guide or cassette recording) 45F (6.85, $6.55) adults; 36F (5.45, $5.20) students, children, and seniors; 10F (1.50, $1.45) extra for special exhibitions. Daily Nov–Mar 9:30am–5:45pm; Apr–June and Aug–Oct daily 9am–7pm; July daily 9am–8pm.

Cathédrale Notre-Dame des Doms   Near the palace is the 12th-century Cathédrale Notre-Dame des Doms, containing the Flamboyant Gothic tomb of some of the apostate popes. Crowning the top is a statue of the Virgin from the 19th century. From the cathedral, enter the **promenade du Rocher-des-Doms** to stroll its garden and enjoy the view across the Rhône to Villeneuve-lèz-Avignon.

Place du Palais. ✆ **04-90-86-81-01.** Free admission. Hours vary according to religious ceremonies, but generally daily 9am–6pm.

La Fondation Angladon-Dubrujeaud ✦   It's been decades since the death of Jacques Doucet, the Belle-Époque dandy, dilettante, and designer of Parisian haute couture, but his magnificent art collection is on view to the general public. When not designing, Doucet collected the early works of a number of artists, among them Picasso, Braque, Max Jacob, and Marcel Duchamp. Today, you can wander through Doucet's former abode, viewing rare antiques; 16th-century Buddhas; Louis XVI chairs designed by Jacob; and canvases by Cézanne, Sisley, Degas, and Modigliani. Doucet died in 1929 at 76, his fortune so diminished that his nephew paid for his funeral, but his rich legacy lives on here.

5 rue Laboureur. ✆ **04-90-82-29-03.** Admission 30F (4.55, $4.35) adults, 20F (3.05, $2.90) students and youths 14–18, 10F (1.50, $1.45) children 7–13. Wed–Sun 1–6pm.

Musée Calvet ✦   Housed in an 18th-century mansion, the fine- and decorative-arts collections feature the works of Vernet, David, Corot, Manet, and Soutine, plus the most extensive collection of ancient silverware in provincial museums. Our favorite oil is by Brueghel the Younger, *Le Cortège nuptial* (The Bridal Procession). Look for a copy of Bosch's *Adoration of the Magi* as well.

65 rue Joseph-Vernet. ✆ **04-90-86-33-84.** Admission 30F (4.55, $4.35) adults, 15F (2.30, $2.20) students, free for children 17 and under. June–Sept Wed–Mon 10am–7pm; Oct–May Wed–Mon 10am–1pm and 2–6pm.

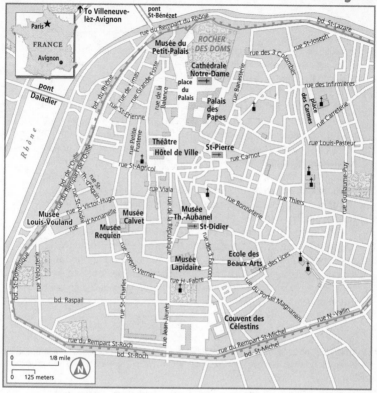

Musée Lapidaire   A 17th-century Jesuit church houses this collection of Gallo-Roman sculptures. This museum has been called a junkyard of antiquity: gargoyles, Gallic and Roman statues, and broken pillars confront you at every turn. Most of the pieces have known greater glory and placement (often in temples), so you can use your imagination to conjure up their lost splendor.

18 rue de la République. ℭ **04-90-85-75-38.** Admission 10F (1.50, $1.45) adults, 5F (.75, 75¢) students 12–18, free for children. Wed–Mon 10am–1pm and 2–6pm.

Musée Louis-Vouland   This collection, devoted to 17th- and 18th-century fine arts, is housed in a 19th-century mansion that opens onto a lovely garden. The treasure trove of lavish antiques and objets d'art includes Sèvres porcelain, the comtesse du Barry's tea set, tapestries from Aubusson and Gobelin, Persian rugs, antique clocks, chandeliers, and commodes to equal those at Versailles. Our favorites are the Louis XV inkpots with silver rats holding the lids.

17 rue Victor-Hugo. ℭ **04-90-86-03-79.** Admission 25F (3.80, $3.65) adults, 15F (2.30, $2.20) students. May–Oct Tues–Sat 10am–noon, Tues–Sun 2–6pm; Nov–Apr Tues–Sat 2–6pm.

Musée du Petit-Palais   The museum contains an important collection of paintings from the Italian schools of the 13th to 16th centuries, including works from Florence, Venice, Siena, and Lombardy. Salons display 15th-century paintings done in Avignon, and several galleries are devoted to Roman and Gothic sculptures.

A Tale of Two Papal Cities

In 1309, an ill Pope Clement V arrived in Avignon to live out the rest of his days as a guest of the Dominicans, the first of seven consecutive popes to live here rather than in Rome. Clement was succeeded in the spring of 1314 by John XXII, who, unlike the previous Roman popes, chose to live modestly in the Episcopal Palace. When Benedict XII took over, he enlarged and rebuilt the palace. Clement VI, who followed, built a more elaborate extension called the New Palace. During the 70 years that the papacy resided in Avignon, art and culture flourished— as did vice. Prostitutes went about peddling their wares in front of cardinals, merchants were robbed, and pilgrims from the hinterlands were tricked and swindled. The ramparts (still standing) were built at this time. They are characterized by their machicolated battlements, turrets, and old gates.

Pope Gregory XI, who succeeded Urban V in 1362, returned the papacy to Rome in 1378, setting off the Great Schism, during which one pope ruled in Rome and another (often referred to as an antipope) ruled in Avignon. The Schism continued for four popes and four antipopes until the 1417 election of Martin V produced an undisputed pope.

Place du Palais. ℭ **04-90-86-44-58.** Admission 30F (4.55, $4.35) adults, 15F (2.30, $2.20) students, free for children 18 and under. July–Aug Wed–Mon 10:30am–6pm; rest of year Wed–Mon 10am–noon and 2–6pm.

STEPPING BACK IN TIME IN VILLENEUVE-LÈZ-AVIGNON ✿

The modern world is impinging on Avignon, but across the Rhône at Villeneuve-lèz-Avignon, the Middle Ages slumber on. When the popes lived in exile at Avignon, wealthy cardinals built palaces (*livrées*) across the river. Many visitors prefer to stay or dine here rather than in Avignon.

In addition to the sights below, you might visit the **Église Notre-Dame,** place Meissonier, founded in 1333 by Cardinal Arnaud de Via. Its proudest possession is a 14th-century ivory Virgin. The church is open daily, April to September from 10am to 12:30pm and 3 to 7pm, October to March from 10am to noon and 2 to 5:30pm. From mid-September to mid-June, it's closed on Mondays. It's also closed in February. Admission is free, but to visit the cloisters, adults must pay 7F (1.05, $1), and students and children 12 to 17 must pay 5F (.75, 75¢).

Chartreuse du Val-de-Bénédiction Inside France's largest Carthusian monastery, built in 1352, you'll find a church, three cloisters, rows of cells that housed the medieval monks, and rooms depicting aspects of their daily lives. Part of the complex is devoted to a workshop (the Centre National d'Écritures et du Spectacle) for painters and writers, who live in the monastic cells rent-free for up to a year to pursue their craft. Exhibitions of photography and painting are presented throughout the year.

Pope Innocent VI (whose tomb you can view) founded this charterhouse, which became the country's most powerful. Inside one of the chapels, a remarkable *Coronation of the Virgin* by Enguerrand Charonton is enshrined; painted in

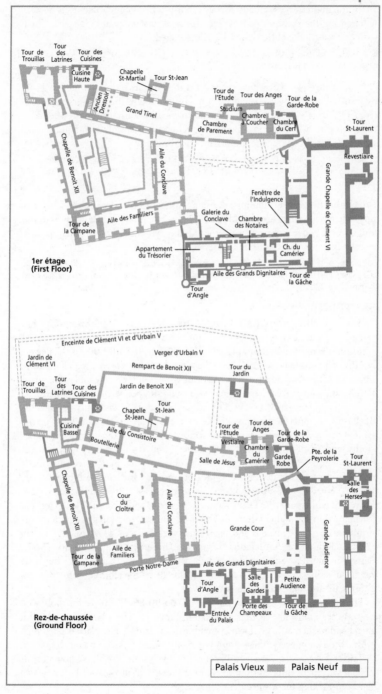

1er étage (First Floor)

Tour de Trouillas
Tour des Latrines
Tour des Cuisines
Cuisine Haute
Ancien Dressoir
Chapelle St-Martial
Tour St-Jean
Grand Tinel
Tour de l'Etude
Tour des Anges
Tour de la Garde-Robe
Studium
Chambre à Coucher
Chambre du Cerf
Tour St-Laurent
Chambre de Parement
Revestiaire
Chapelle de Benoît XII
Aile du Conclave
Fenêtre de l'Indulgence
Grande Chapelle de Clément VI
Tour de la Campane
Aile des Familiers
Galerie du Conclave
Chambre des Notaires
Appartement du Trésorier
Ch. du Camérier
Aile des Grands Dignitaires
Tour de la Gâche
Tour d'Angle

Rez-de-chaussée (Ground Floor)

Enceinte de Clément VI et d'Urbain V
Verger d'Urbain V
Jardin de Clément VI
Rempart de Benoit XII
Tour du Jardin
Jardin de Benoit XII
Tour de Trouillas
Tour des Latrines
Tour des Cuisines
Chapelle St-Jean
Tour St-Jean
Cuisine Basse
Aile du Consistoire
Tour de l'Etude
Tour des Anges
Tour de la Garde-Robe
Boutellerie
Vestiaire
Chambre du Camérier
Garde-Robe
Pte. de la Peyrolerie
Tour St-Laurent
Salle de Jésus
Salle des Herses
Chapelle de Benoît XII
Cour du Cloître
Aile du Conclave
Grande Cour
Grande Audience
Tour de la Campane
Aile de Familiers
Porte Notre-Dame
Aile des Grands Dignitaires
Tour d'Angle
Salle des Gardes
Petite Audience
Entrée du Palais
Porte des Champeaux
Tour de la Gâche

Palais Vieux   Palais Neuf

1453, the masterpiece contains a fringed bottom that's Bosch-like in its horror, representing the denizens of hell. The 12th-century graveyard cloister is lined with cells where the fathers prayed and meditated.

60 rue de la République. (℃ **04-90-15-24-24**. Admission 36F (5.45, $5.20) adults, 23F (3.50, $3.35) students, free for children 18 and under. Daily 9am–6:30pm.

Fort St-André ★ Crowning the town is the Fort St-André, founded in 1360 by Jean-le-Bon to serve as a symbol of might to the pontifical powers across the river. The Abbaye St-André, now privately owned, was installed in the 18th century. You can visit the formal garden encircling the mansion, a tranquil setting with a rose-trellis colonnade, fountains, and flowers.

Mont Andaon. (℃ **04-90-25-45-35**. Admission 25F (3.80, $3.65) adults, 15F (2.30, $2.20) students and ages 18–25, free for children under 17. Apr–Sept 9 daily 10am–1pm and 2–6pm; Oct–Mar daily 10am–1pm and 2–5pm.

Tour Philippe le Bel Philippe the Fair constructed the tower in the 13th century, when Villeneuve became a French possession; it served as a gateway to the kingdom. If you're game and have the stamina, you can climb to the top for a view of Avignon and the Rhône Valley.

Rue Montée-de-la-Tour. (℃ **04-32-70-08-57**. Admission 10F (1.50, $1.45) adults, 6F (.90, 85¢) students and children 12–17. Apr–Sept daily 10am–12:30pm and 2–7:30pm; Oct–Mar Tues–Sun 10am–12:30pm and 3–7pm. Closed Feb.

SHOPPING

Since the 1960s, **Antiquités Bourret,** 5 rue Limas (℃ **04-90-86-65-02**), has earned a reputation as a repository for 18th- and 19th-century Provençal antiques. **Véronique Pichon,** place Crillon (℃ **04-90-85-89-00**), is the newest branch of a porcelain manufacturer whose products have been a regional fixture since the 1700s. Manufactured in the nearby town of Uzès, the tableware, urns, statues, and lamps are priced well enough to be shipped virtually anywhere.

The Avignon branch of **Les Olivades,** 28 rue des Marchants (℃ **04-90-86-13-42**), is one of the most visible of a chain of outlets associated in the United States with Pierre Deux. Look for bedcovers, slipcovers, draperies, tablecloths, and fabrics by the yard. The fabrics, printed in a factory only 6 miles from Avignon, feature intricate designs in colors inspired by 19th-century models, as well as Créole designs. The idea behind **Les Indiens de Nîmes,** 4 rue Joseph-Vernet (℃ **04-90-86-32-05**), is to duplicate 18th- and 19th-century Provençal fabric patterns. They're sold by the meter and are available in clothing for men, women, and children. In addition, you can buy kitchenware and furniture inspired by Provence and the steamy wetlands west of Marseille.

The clothing at **Souleiado,** 5 rue Joseph-Vernet (℃ **04-90-86-47-67**), derives from a Provençal model, and even the Provençal name (meaning "first ray of sunshine after a storm"). Most, but not all, of the clothing is for women. Fabrics are also sold by the meter.

Hervé Baume, 19 rue Petite Fusterie (℃ **04-90-86-37-66**), is for those who yearn to set a table like that encountered in Provence. This place is stocked with merchandise such as handblown crystal hurricane lamps. The place is piled high with a little bit of everything—from Directoire dinner services to French folk art.

Jaffier-Parsi, 42 rue des Fourbisseurs (℃ **04-90-86-08-85**), is known for its copper saucepans shipped from the Norman town of Villedieu-les-Poêles, which has been making them since the Middle Ages.

If you seek a new point of view on all kinds of Provençal pottery, head for **Terre è Provence,** 26 rue République (© **04-90-85-56-45**). You can also pick up wonderful kitsch here—perhaps terra-cotta plates decorated with three-dimensional cicadas.

ACCOMMODATIONS

EXPENSIVE

Hôtel d'Europe ★★★   This deluxe hostelry, in operation since 1799, is almost the equal of the Mirande (below), though slightly cheaper. You enter the vine-covered hotel through a courtyard, where tables are set in the warmer months. The grand hall and salons boast antiques; the good-size guest rooms have a handsome decor and period furnishings. Three suites are perched on the roof, with views of the Palais des Papes. In some twin-bedded rooms, the beds are a bit narrow. Overall, rooms are comfortable, with touches of Gallic charm. The spacious bathrooms are handsomely equipped, each with a combination tub/shower. The restaurant, La Vieille Fontaine, is one of the best in Avignon.

12 place Grillon, 84000 Avignon. © **04-90-14-76-76.** Fax 04-90-85-43-66. www.hotel-d-europe.fr. 47 units. 690F–2,200F (04.90– 34.40, $100.05–$319) double; 3,000F–3,300F (456– 501.60, $435–$478.50) suite. AE, DC, MC, V. Parking 60F (9.10, $8.70). **Amenities:** Restaurant; bar; business service; room service; laundry/dry cleaning; pool; tennis arranged. *In room:* A/C, TV, hair dryer.

La Mirande ★★★   In the heart of Avignon (behind the Palais des Papes), this restored 700-year-old town house is one of France's grand little luxuries. The hotel treats you to 2 centuries of decorative art: from the 1700s Salon Chinois to the Salon Rouge, its striped walls in Rothschild red. In 1987, Achim and Hannelore Stein transformed it into a citadel of opulence. Room 20 is the most sought-after, its lavish decor opening onto the garden. But all the rooms are stunning, with exquisite decor, hand-printed fabrics on the walls, antiques, bedside controls, and huge bathtubs. The restaurant, among the finest in Avignon, deserves its one Michelin star. Chef Daniel Hébet has a light, sophisticated touch.

4 place Amirande, 84000 Avignon. © **04-90-85-93-93.** Fax 04-90-86-26-85. www.la-mirande.fr. 20 units. 1,700F–2,600F (258.40– 395.20, $246.50–$377) double; 3,700F (562.40, $536.50) suite. AE, DC, V. **Amenities:** Restaurant; bar; room service; baby-sitting; laundry/dry cleaning. *In room:* A/C, TV, minibar, hair dryer, safe.

MODERATE

Clarion Hotel Cloître St-Louis ★   This unusual hotel is housed in a former Jesuit school built in the 1580s. Much of the original premises remain, including the grand baroque facade, the wraparound arcades, and soaring ceiling vaults. Public areas have many of the original, intensely vertical lines. Bedrooms are more functional; they're the rather dull-looking result of several renovations. Rooms range from medium to spacious; some have sliding-glass doors overlooking the patio. Each unit has sleek modern lines without a lot of frilly extras; all but three have a combination tub/shower. Outbuildings and new construction include a wing designed by world-class architect Jean Nouvel.

20 rue Portail Boquier, 84000 Avignon. © **800/CLARION** in the U.S., or 04-90-27-55-55. Fax 04-90-82-24-01. www.cloitre-saint-louis.com. 80 units. 550F–1,400F (83.60– 212.80, $79.75–$203) double; 1,000F–1,800F (152– 273.60, $145–$261) suite. AE, MC, V. **Amenities:** Restaurant; bar; outdoor pool; room service; dry cleaning. *In room:* A/C, TV, minibar, hair dryer, safe.

INEXPENSIVE

Hôtel d'Angleterre   In the heart of Avignon, this Art Deco structure is the city's best budget hotel. The rooms are comfortably but basically furnished. Rooms are on the small side, and all except one come with a compact shower-only bathroom. Breakfast is the only meal served.

29 bd. Raspail, 84000 Avignon. ℂ **04-90-86-34-31.** Fax 04-90-86-86-74. www.hotelangleterre.fr. 40 units, 39 with private bathroom. 190F (28.90, $27.55) double without bathroom, 320F–450F (48.65– 68.40, $46.40–$65.25) double with bathroom. DC, MC, V. Closed Dec 20–Jan 20. Free parking. **Amenities:** Laundry/ dry cleaning. *In room:* TV, hair dryer.

Hôtel de l'Atelier   Villeneuve's budget offering is this 16th-century village house that has preserved much of its original style. Inside is a tiny duplex lounge with a stone fireplace. Outside, a rear garden, with potted orange and fig trees, provides fruit for breakfast. The immaculate rooms are comfortable and informal, but a bit dowdy. Each comes with a compact shower-only bathroom. A continental breakfast is the only meal served.

5 rue de la Foire, 30400 Villeneuve-lèz-Avignon. ℂ **04-90-25-01-84.** Fax 04-90-25-80-06. hotel.latelier@ libertisurf.fr. 23 units. 300F–600F (45.60– 91.20, $43.50–$87) double. AE, DC, MC, V. Free parking on street; 40F (6.130, $5.80) in nearby garage. *In room:* TV.

Hotel le Médièval   About 3 blocks south of the Palais des Papes, this three-story town house from the late 1600s is clean, and uncomplicated. Under beamed ceilings, the guest rooms are medium to spacious, each offering good comfort. Most peaceful are the units that overlook the inner courtyard, with its pots of flowers and shrubs. Those that overlook a congested medieval street corner might be noisier but have a rough-and-ready charm of their own. Most of the small bathrooms have a shower/tub.

15 rue Petite Saunerie, 84000 Avignon. ℂ **04-90-86-11-06.** Fax 04-90-82-08-64. hotel.medieval@ wanadoo.fr. 34 units. 250F–330F (38– 50.15, $36.25–$47.85) double. Extra bed 50F (7.60, $7.25). *In room:* TV.

DINING

Note that both **Hôtel d'Europe** and **La Mirande** (see "Accommodations," above) have excellent restaurants.

Brunel PROVENÇAL   This flower-filled air-conditioned restaurant is in the heart of Avignon. Managed by the Brunel family, it offers such specialties as warm pâté of duckling and breast of duckling with apples. The chef prepares a superb plate of wild mushroom–stuffed ravioli with roasted foie gras. The grilled John Dory is accompanied by artichoke hearts, and even the lowly pigs' feet emerge with a sublime taste. The excellent desserts are prepared fresh daily. Feel free to order house wines by the carafe.

46 rue de La Balance. ℂ **04-90-85-24-83.** Reservations required. Main courses 45F–85F (6.85– 12.90, $6.55–$12.35); fixed-price menus 55F–115F (8.35– 17.50, $8–$16.70) lunch, 170F (25.85, $24.65) dinner. MC, V. Mon–Sat noon–1:30pm; Tues–Sat 7:30–9:30pm.

Christian Etienne ★★★ PROVENÇAL   The stone house containing this restaurant is from 1180, built around the time as the Palais des Papes (next door). Owner Christian Etienne continues to reach new culinary heights. His dining room contains early-15th-century frescoes honoring the marriage of Anne de Bretagne to the French king in 1491. Several of the fixed-price menus present specific themes: Two feature seasonal tomatoes, mushrooms, or vegetables; one offers preparations of lobster; and the priciest relies on the chef's discretion (*menu confiance*) to come up with unique combinations. In summer, look for a vegetable menu where every course is based on ripe tomatoes; the main course is a mousse of lamb, eggplants, tomatoes, and herbs. A la carte specialties include filet of red snapper with black-olive coulis, rack of lamb with fresh thyme and garlic essence, and a dessert of fennel sorbet with saffron-flavored English cream sauce. Note for strict vegetarians: The vegetable menus aren't completely vegetarian; they're flavored with small amounts of meat or fish or, sometimes, meat drippings.

10 rue Mons. ✆ **04-90-86-16-50.** Reservations required. Main courses 170F–210F (25.85– 31.90, $24.65–$30.45); set-price lunch (Mon–Fri) 180F (27.35, $26.10); set-price dinners 320F–530F (48.65– 80.55 $46.40–$76.85). AE, DC, MC, V. July daily noon–1:30pm; Aug–June Tues–Sat noon–1:30pm and 7:30–9:30pm.

Hiély-Lucullus TRADITIONAL & MODERN FRENCH Before the arrival of Christian Etienne (see above), this Relais Gourmand reigned supreme in Avignon. The town's most fabled chef, Pierre Hiély, has retired, though he drops in occasionally to check on how his former sous chef, André Chaussy, is doing. He's doing just fine and continues to offer reasonable fixed-price menus (no a la carte). Try one of his appetizers, like *petite marmite du pêcheur,* a savory fish soup ringed with black mussels. A main-dish specialty is *pintadeau* (young guinea hen) with peaches. The pièce de résistance is *agneau des Alpilles grillé* (grilled alpine lamb). Dessert might be vanilla-bourbon cream in puff pastry. Carafe wines include Tavel Rosé and Châteauneuf-du-Pape.

5 rue de la République. ✆ **04-90-86-17-07.** Reservations required. Fixed-price menus 135F–225F (20.50– 34.20, $19.60–$32.65). MC, V. Thurs–Mon noon–1:30pm; Wed–Mon 7:30–9:30pm. Closed 2 weeks in June and 2 weeks in Jan.

La Fourchette *Value* TRADITIONAL & MODERN FRENCH This bistro offers creative cooking at a moderate price. There are two dining rooms, one like a summerhouse with walls of glass, the other like a tavern with oak beams. You might begin with fresh sardines flavored with citrus, ravioli filled with haddock, or a parfait of chicken livers with a spinach flan and a confiture of onions. For a main course, we recommend the blanquette of monkfish with endive or daube of beef with a gratin of macaroni.

7 rue Racine. ✆ 04-90-85-20-93. Set-price lunch 130F–160F (19.75– 24.30, $18.85–$23.20); set-price dinner 160F (24.30, $23.20). MC, V. Mon–Fri 12:30–2pm and 7:30–9:30pm. Closed Aug 5–29. Bus: 11.

AVIGNON AFTER DARK

Near the Palais des Papes is **Le Grand Café,** La Manutention (✆ **04-90-86-86-77**), a restaurant/bar/cafe that might become your favorite watering hole. The dance-club standby is **Les Ambassadeurs,** 27 rue Bancasse (✆ **04-90-86-31-55**), which is more animated than its competitor, **Piano Bar Le Blues,** 25 rue Carnot (✆ **04-90-85-79-71**); the cover at both is 10F (1.50, $1.45). Near Le Blues is a restaurant, **Red Zone,** 27 rue Carnot (✆ **04-90-27-02-44**), whose bar area is the site of live performances from whatever band happens to be in town.

Winning the award for having the most unpronounceable name is **Le Woolloomoolloo** (it means "Black Kangaroo" in an Aboriginal dialect of Australia), 16 bis rue des Teinturiers (✆ **04-90-85-28-44**). The bar and cafe complement a separate room devoted to the cuisine of France and a changing roster of cuisines from Asia, Africa, and South America. An alternative is **Bokao's Café,** 9 quai St-Lazare (✆ **04-90-82-47-95**), which offers both a restaurant and a disco as diversions during long sultry nights in Avignon. The most viable option for lesbians and gays is **L'Esclav,** 12 rue de Limas (✆ **04-90-85-14-91**), a bar and disco that are the focal point of the city's gay community.

3 St-Rémy-de-Provence ✫

438 miles S of Paris, 16 miles NE of Arles, 12 miles S of Avignon, 8 miles N of Les Baux

Nostradamus, the famous French physician/astrologer, was born here in 1503. Although he has many fans today, he does have detractors, like those who denounce him and his more than 600 obscure verses as psychotic.

St-Rémy is more closely associated with van Gogh. He committed himself to an asylum here in 1889 after cutting off his left ear. Between moods of despair, he painted such works as *Olive Trees* and *Cypresses*.

Come to sleepy St-Rémy not only for its memories and sights but also for a glimpse of small-town Provençal life. It's a market town of considerable charm that draws the occasional visiting celebrity trying to escape the spotlight.

ESSENTIALS

GETTING THERE   Local **buses** from Avignon (between four and nine per day) take 45 minutes and cost around 36F (5.45, $5.20) one-way. In St-Rémy, buses pull into the place de la République, in the town center. For bus information and schedules, call ✆ **04-90-14-59-00.** If you're **driving,** head south from Avignon along D571.

VISITOR INFORMATION   The **Office de Tourisme** is on place Jean-Jaurès (✆ **04-90-92-05-22**).

SEEING THE SIGHTS

Monastère St-Paul-de-Mausolée ✫✫   Visitors can see the 12th-century cloisters of the asylum that van Gogh made famous in his paintings. Now a psychiatric hospital, the former monastery is east of D5, a short drive north of Glanum (see below). You can't visit the cell where the artist was confined from 1889 to 1890, but it's worth coming here to explore the Romanesque chapel and cloisters with their circular arches and columns, which have beautifully carved capitals. On your way to the church, you'll see a bust of van Gogh.

Av. Edgar-le-Roy. ✆ 04-90-92-77-00. Admission 17F (2.60, $2.45) adults, 12F (1.80, $1.75) students and children 12–16. Apr–Oct daily 9:30am–7pm; off-season daily 11am–5pm.

Musée Archéologique   Located in the center of St-Rémy, the Musée Archéologique displays sculptures and bronzes from the Roman excavations at nearby Glanum. On the ground floor is an outstanding collection that includes altars, sarcophagi, obelisks, and fragments of columns and cornices from temples of pagan gods. In the courtyard are the ruins of baths from the 4th century A.D., along with ruins from a 5th century A.D. baptistery. Upstairs are a statue of a captured Gaul, fragments from a temple dedicated to the goddess Valetudo, and a low relief with the effigies of Fortuna and Hermes. There is also a prehistoric collection containing everything from bones to flints.

In the Hôtel de Sade, rue du Parage. ✆ 04-90-92-64-04. Admission 17F (2.60, $2.45) adults, 12F (1.80, $1.75) for children 18 and under. Open Jan by appointment only; Feb–Mar daily 10am–noon and 2–5pm; Apr–Sept daily 10am–noon and 2–7pm; Oct–Dec daily 10am–noon and 2–5pm.

Ruines de Glanum ✫   A Gallo-Roman settlement thrived here during the final days of the Roman Empire. Its historic monuments include a triumphal arch from the time of Julius Caesar, along with a cenotaph called the Mausolée des Jules. Garlanded with sculptured fruits and flowers, the arch dates from 20 B.C. and is the oldest in Provence. The mausoleum was raised to honor the grandsons of Augustus and is the only extant monument of its type. In the area are entire streets and foundations of private residences from the 1st-century town. Some remains are from a Gallo-Greek town of the 2nd century B.C.

Av. Vincent-van-Gogh (1 mile south of St-Rémy on D5). ℂ **04-90-92-23-79**. Admission 36F (5.45, $5.20) adults, 25F (3.80, $3.65) students and ages 12–25, free for children 11 and under. Apr–Sept daily 9am–7pm; Oct–Mar daily 9am–noon and 2–5pm. From the town center, follow the signs to Les Antiques.

ACCOMMODATIONS

Château de Roussan ★★ *(Finds* Although other château hotels are more stylish, this one is more evocative of another time and place. Its most famous resident, the Renaissance psychic Nostradamus, lived in an outbuilding a few steps from the front door. Today, you pass beneath an archway of 300-year-old trees leading to the neoclassical facade, constructed of softly colored local stone in 1701. Most rooms are spacious, the mattresses worn but still comfortable enough. Expect old-fashioned plumbing with combination tub/showers. As you wander the grounds, the history will envelop you, especially when you come upon the baroque sculptures lining the basin, fed by a stream. Be warned that the staff can be off-putting, but the rampant sense of mysticism and the historical importance of the place usually compensate for any Gallic crabbiness.

Rte. de Tarascon, 13210 St-Rémy-de-Provence. ℂ **04-90-92-11-63**. Fax 04-90-92-50-59. 21 units. 460F–790F (69.90– 120.10, $66.70–$114.55) double. AE, MC, V. **Amenities:** Restaurant, bar; laundry. *In room:* Hair dryer.

Hôtel Château des Alpilles ★★★ For luxury and refinement, this is the only château in the area the equal of Vallon de Valrugues (see below). When it was built in 1827 by the Pichot family, it housed Chateaubriand and other luminaries. When Françoise Bon converted this mansion in 1980, she wanted to create a "house for paying friends." The spacious rooms have combined the best of an antique framework with plush upholstery, rich carpeting, and vibrant colors. Each guest room boasts whimsical accessories, like a pair of porcelain panthers flanking one of the mantels, and travertine-trimmed baths with large windows. Units in the renovated 19th-century annex are just as comfortable as those in the main house. The midsize bathrooms have tub/showers.

Ancienne rte. du Grès, 13210 St-Rémy-de-Provence. ℂ **04-90-92-03-33**. Fax 04-90-92-45-17. 21 units. 1,000F–1,250F (152– 190, $145–$181.25) double; 1,520F–2,180F (231.05– 331.35, $220.40–$316.10) suite. AE, DC, MC, V. Closed Nov 15–Feb 15. **Amenities:** Restaurant; outdoor pool; two tennis courts; sauna; room service; laundry. *In room:* TV, minibar, hair dryer, safe.

Hôtel du Soleil Masses of ivy that cascade wonderfully down the facade of this hotel, a 4-minute walk south of the town center. It's set in a garden with venerable trees and a wrought-iron gazebo. Inside, the assortment of ceiling beams and Provençale accessories evoke the region around you. Bedrooms are simple but convenient, with tasteful settings and small, tiled bathrooms (some with both tub and shower). You'll want to spend part of your time beside the pool, ringed by chaise longues. Breakfast is the only meal served.

15 av. Pasteur, 13210 St-Rémy-de-Provence. ℂ **04-90-92-00-63**. Fax 04-90-92-61-07. hotelsoleil@ wanadoo.fr. 24 units. 315F–395F (47.90– 60.05, $45.70–$57.30) double. AE, DC, MC, V. Free parking. Closed Nov–Feb. **Amenities:** Pool. *In room:* TV, hair dryer, safe.

Les Antiques This moderately priced 19th-century villa lies in a 7-acre park with a pool. It contains an elegant lounge, which opens onto several salons, and Napoléon III furnishings. Some of the rooms are in a modern pavilion, with direct access to the garden. All are handsomely furnished, usually in pastels, some with flowered wallpapers. Units in the pavilion are more comfortable and spacious, though they don't have as much character as those in the main building. Each comes with a compact bathroom, most with tub/shower. Breakfast is the only meal available; in summer, it's served in what used to be the Orangerie.

15 av. Pasteur, 13210 St-Rémy-de-Provence. ℂ **04-90-92-03-02.** Fax 04-90-92-50-40. 27 units. 390F–900F (59.30– 136.80, $56.55–$130.50) double. AE, DC, MC, V. Closed mid-Oct to Apr 7. **Amenities:** Pool. *In room:* TV.

Vallon de Valrugues ★★★ Surrounded by a park, this Mediterranean hotel offers the best accommodations and restaurant in town. The owners, Françoise and Jean-Michel Gallon, offer beautifully furnished rooms and suites. They have recently been enlarged and renovated, with new marble bathrooms, all with tub and shower. The restaurant's terrace alone may compete with its cuisine, which is winning praise for innovative light dishes, such as John Dory with truffles and frozen nougat with a confit of fruits.

Chemin Canto-Cigalo, 13210 St-Rémy-de-Provence. ℂ **04-90-92-04-40.** Fax 04-90-92-44-01. www.valrugues-cassagne.com. 53 units. 880F–1,750F (133.75– 266, $127.60–$253.75) double; 2,680F–5,700F (407.35– 866.40, $388.60–$826.50) suite. AE, CB, DC, MC, V. Free parking. Closed 3 weeks in Feb. **Amenities:** Restaurant, bar; pool; putting green; two tennis courts; gym; sauna; horseback riding; room service; laundry. *In room:* Minibar, hair dryer, safe.

DINING

Another great choice is the restaurant at **Vallon de Valrugues** (see above).

Bar/Hôtel/Restaurant des Arts TRADITIONAL FRENCH This cafe/restaurant evokes the earthy pleasures of *gitanes* and *pastis,* and in many ways it hasn't changed a lot since the days of Albert Camus. The wait for dinner can be as long as 45 minutes, so you may want to spend time in the bar, with its wooden tables, paneling, copper pots, and slightly faded decor. Don't expect cutting-edge cuisine, as everything about this place, including the accents of the all-Provençal staff, is immersed in the Midi of long ago. The menu lists specialties like rabbit terrine, pepper steak with champagne, duckling in orange sauce, and three preparations of trout. *Warning:* Always call before heading here, and don't take the hours below too literally. The aging owner reserves the right to close whenever she is tired.

32 bd. Victor-Hugo, 13210 St-Rémy-de-Provence. ℂ **04-90-92-08-50.** Reservations recommended. Main courses 65F–160F (9.90– 24.30, $9.45–$23.20); fixed-price menus 120F–150F (18.25– 22.80, $17.40–$21.75). AE, DC, MC, V. Wed–Mon noon–2pm and 7:30–9:30pm. Closed Feb and Nov 1–12.

La Maison Jaune ★★ FRENCH/PROVENÇAL One of the most enduringly popular restaurants in St-Rémy is in the former residence of an 18th-century merchant. Today, in a pair of dining rooms occupying two floors, you'll appreciate cuisine prepared and served with flair by François and Catherine Perraud. In nice weather, additional seats are available on a terrace overlooking the Hôtel de Sade. Menu items include pigeon roasted in wine from Les Baux; grilled sardines served with candied lemon and raw fennel; artichoke hearts marinated in white wine and offered with tomatoes; and a succulent version of roasted rack of lamb served with a tapenade of black olives and anchovies.

15 rue Carnot. ℂ **04-90-92-56-14.** Reservations recommended. Main courses 120F–180F (18.25– 27.35, $17.40–$26.10); fixed-price menus 120F–320F (18.25– 48.65, $17.40–$46.40) lunch, 180F–320F (27.35– 48.65, $26.10–$46.40) dinner. MC, V. June–Sept Wed–Sun noon–2pm, Tues–Sun 7:30–9:30pm; Oct–May Tues–Sat noon–2pm, Mon–Sat 7:30–9:30pm.

4 Arles ★★★

450 miles S of Paris, 22 miles SW of Avignon, 55 miles NW of Marseille

Art lovers, archaeologists, and historians are attracted to this town on the Rhône, often called the soul of Provence. Many of its scenes, painted so luminously by van Gogh, remain to delight. The painter left Paris for Arles in 1888, the same year he cut off part of his left ear. He painted some of his most celebrated works here, including *Starry Night, The Bridge at Arles, Sunflowers,* and *L'Arlésienne.*

The Greeks are said to have founded Arles in the 6th century B.C. Julius Caesar established a Roman colony here in 46 B.C. Constantine the Great named it the second capital of his empire in 306, when it was known as "the little Rome of the Gauls." It wasn't until 1481 that Arles was incorporated into France.

Though Arles doesn't possess quite as much charm as Aix-en-Provence, it's still rewarding to visit, with first-rate museums, excellent restaurants, and summer festivals. The city today isn't quite as lovely as it was when Picasso came here, but it has enough of the antique charm of Provence to keep the appeal alive.

ESSENTIALS

GETTING THERE   Since Arles lies on the Paris-Marseille and the Bordeaux–St-Raphaël rail lines, connections from most cities of France pass through. Ten **trains** per day arrive from Avignon (trip time: 20 min.), 10 from Marseille (trip time: 1 hr.), and 10 from Aix-en-Provence (trip time: 1¾ hr.). For information and schedules, call ✆ **08-36-35-35-35.** There are about four **buses** per day from Aix-en-Provence (trip time: 1¾ hr.). For bus information, call ✆ **04-90-49-38-01.** If you're **driving,** head south along D570 from Avignon.

VISITOR INFORMATION   The **Office de Tourisme,** where you can buy a billet global (see below), is on the esplanade des Lices (✆ **04-90-18-41-20**).

EXPLORING THE TOWN

Go to the tourist office (see "Essentials," above), where you can purchase a **billet global,** the all-inclusive pass that admits you to the town's museums, Roman monuments, and major attractions, at a cost of 60F (9.10, $8.70) for adults and 40F (6.130, $5.80) for children.

Arles is full of Roman monuments. The vicinity of the old Roman forum is occupied by **place du Forum,** shaded by plane trees. The Café de Nuit,

---

Moments Le Olé

Bullfights, or *corridas,* in Arles are relatively infrequent, and don't generate as much excitement or passion as they do in Spain. They are conducted about five weekends a year, between Easter and late September. The bull is killed only on the Easter *corridas* (perhaps a reference to the death of Christ?); otherwise the bull is not killed, making the ritual less bloody than the Spanish version. Most bullfights begin around 5pm, though the Easter event begins at 11am. A seat on the worn stone benches of the Roman amphitheater costs 90F to 500F (13.70 to 76, $13.05 to $72.50). Tickets are usually available at the amphitheater a few hours before the beginning of every bullfight. For advance ticket sales via credit card, call ✆ **04-90-96-03-70.**

immortalized by van Gogh, once stood on this square. You can see two Corinthian columns and fragments from a temple at the corner of the Hôtel Nord-Pinus. South of here is **place de la République,** dominated by a 50-foot-tall blue porphyry obelisk. On the north is the **Hôtel de Ville** (town hall) from 1673, built to Mansart's plans and surmounted by a Renaissance belfry.

One of the city's great classical monuments is the Roman **Théâtre Antique** ✦✦, rue du Cloître (✆ **04-90-49-36-25**). Begun by Augustus in the 1st century, only two Corinthian columns remain. The theater was where the *Venus of Arles* was discovered in 1651. Take rue de la Calade from city hall. Admission is 17F (2.60, $2.45) for adults and 12F (1.80, $1.75) for children.

Nearby is the other monument, the **Amphitheater (Les Arènes)** ✦✦, rond-pont des Arènes (✆ **04-90-49-36-86**), also built in the 1st century. It seats almost 25,000 and still hosts bullfights in summer. You are warned to visit at your own risk, as the stone steps are uneven, and much of the masonry is worn to the point where it might be hazardous for older travelers or those with disabilities. For a good view, you can climb the three towers that remain from medieval times, when the amphitheater was turned into a fortress. The theater and Les Arènes are open daily: April 1 to September 31 from 10am to 12:30pm and 2 to 4:30pm; the rest of the year from 10 to 11:30am and 2 to 4pm. Admission is 15F (2.30, $2.20) for adults and 9F (1.35, $1.30) for children.

In an isolated spot 7½ miles north of Arles, **Les Olivades Factory Store,** chemin des Indienneurs, St-Etienne-du-Grès (✆ **04-90-49-19-19**), sits beside the road leading to Tarascon. Because of the wide array of art objects and fabrics inspired by the traditions of Provence, a trek out here is worth your while. Dresses, shirts for men and women, table linens, and fabric by the yard are all available at retail outlets of the Olivades chain throughout Provence, but the selection here is better and a bit cheaper.

Les Alyscamps ✦ Perhaps the most memorable sight in Arles, this was once a necropolis established by the Romans. After being converted into a Christian burial ground in the 4th century, it became a setting for legends and was even mentioned in Dante's *Inferno.* Today, it's lined with poplars and the remaining sarcophagi. Arlesiens escape here to enjoy a respite from the heat.

Rue Pierre-Renaudel. ✆ **04-90-49-36-87**. Admission 15F (2.30, $2.20) adults, 9F (1.35, $1.30) children. Mid-Sept to mid-June daily 9am–12:30pm and 2–7pm; mid-June to mid-Sept daily 9am–7pm.

Église St-Trophime ✦ This church is noted for its 12th-century portal, one of the finest achievements of the southern Romanesque style. Frederick Barbarossa was crowned king of Arles here in 1178. In the pediment, Christ is surrounded by the symbols of the Evangelists. The cloister, in both the Gothic and the Romanesque styles, is noted for its medieval carvings.

On the east side of place de la République. ✆ **04-90-96-07-38**. Free admission to church; cloister 15F (2.30, $2.20) adults, 9F (1.35, $1.30) students and children. Church daily 8:30am–6:30pm; cloister mid-June to mid-Sept daily 9am–12:30pm and 2–7pm.

Musée de l'Arles Antique ✦✦ Half a mile south of the town center, you'll find one of the world's most famous collections of Roman Christian sarcophagi, plus a rich ensemble of sculptures, mosaics, and inscriptions from the Augustinian period to the 6th century A.D. Eleven detailed models show ancient monuments of the region as they existed in the past.

Presqu'île du Cirque Romain. ✆ **04-90-18-88-88**. Admission 35F (5.30, $5.10) adults, 25F (3.80, $3.65) students, free for children under 12. Apr–Sept daily 9am–7pm; Oct–Mar daily 10am–5 pm.

In Search of van Gogh's "Different Light"

What strikes me here is the transparency of the air.
—Vincent van Gogh

Provence attracted artists long before the Impressionists. During the pope's residency at Avignon, a flood of Italian artists frescoed the palace in a style worthy of St. Peter's; and Provençal monarchs like King René imported painters from Flanders and Burgundy to adorn the public buildings. This continued through the 18th and 19th centuries, as painters drew inspiration from the dazzling light. Still, it wasn't until the age of the Impressionists that Provence really became known for its role in nurturing artists.

The Dutch-born Vincent van Gogh (1853 to 1890) moved to Arles in 1888 and spent 2 years in the historic towns of Les Baux, St-Rémy, and Stes-Maries, recording through the filter of his neuroses dozens of Impressionistic scenes now prized by museums. His search, he said, was for "a different light"; and when he found it, he created masterpieces like *Starry Night, Cypresses, Olive Trees,* and *Boats Along the Beach.*

Van Gogh wasn't alone in his pursuit of Provençal light. Gauguin joined him 8 months after his arrival and soon thereafter engaged him in a violent quarrel, which reduced the Dutchman to a morbid depression that sent him to a local sanitarium. Within 2 years, van Gogh returned to Paris, where he committed suicide in July 1890.

Things went somewhat better for Cézanne, who was familiar with the beauties of Provence from his childhood in Aix-en-Provence. He infuriated his father, a Provençal banker, by abandoning his studies to pursue painting. Later, his theories about line and color were publicized around the world. Although he migrated to Paris, he rarely set foot outside Provence from 1890 until his death, in 1904. Some critics have asserted that Cézanne's later years were devoted to one obsession: recording the line, color, and texture of Montagne-St-Victoire, a rocky knoll a few hours' horse ride east of Aix. He painted it more than 60 times. The bulk of the Provençal mountain, however, as well as the way shadows moved across its rocky planes, was decisive in affecting the Cubists, whose work Cézanne directly influenced.

Musée Réattu ✦   This collection of the local painter Jacques Réattu has been updated with more recent works, including etchings and drawings by Picasso. Other pieces are by Alechinsky, Dufy, and Zadkine. Note the Arras tapestries from the 16th century.

10 rue du Grand-Prieuré. ✆ **04-90-49-37-58.** Admission 20 F (3.05E, $2.90) adults, 15 F (2.30E, $2.20) children, free for children under 12. Mar daily 10am–12:30pm and 2–7pm; Apr–Sept daily 9am–12:30pm and 2–7pm; Oct daily 10am–12:30pm and 2–6:30pm; Nov–Feb 10am–12:30pm and 2–5:30pm.

Museon Arlaten ✦   This museum, whose name is written in Provençal style, was founded by poet Frédéric Mistral, leader of a movement to establish modern Provençal as a literary language, using the money from his Nobel Prize for literature in 1904. This is really a folklore museum, with regional costumes, portraits, furniture, dolls, a music salon, and one room devoted to mementos of Mistral. Among its curiosities is a letter (in French) from Theodore Roosevelt to Mistral, bearing the letterhead of the Maison Blanche in Washington, D.C.

29 rue de la République. ⓒ **04-90-96-08-23**. Admission 25F (3.80, $3.65) adults, 20F (3.05, $2.90) children, free for children under 12. Apr–Oct daily 9am–noon and 2–6:30pm; Nov–Mar Tues–Sun 9am–noon and 2–5pm.

ACCOMMODATIONS

Grand Hotel Nord Pinus *✸* Few other hotels in town evoke Provence's 19th-century charm as well as this one. Occupying a town house on a tree-lined square in the heart of Arles, it has public rooms filled with antiques, an ornate staircase with wrought-iron balustrades, and many of the trappings you'd expect in an upscale private home. Bedrooms are glamorous, even theatrical; they come in a range of shapes and sizes and are filled with rich upholsteries and draperies arranged artfully beside oversized French doors. Bathrooms contain combination tub/showers. You can't help but notice that many bullfighters and artists have stayed here—their photographs and framed artworks decorate the public areas.

Place du Forum, 13200 Arles. ⓒ **04-90-93-44-44**. Fax 04-90-93-34-00. www.nord-pinus.com. 24 units. 940F–1,090F (142.90– 165.70, $136.30–$158.05) double; 1,900F (288.80, $275.50) suite. AE, MC, V. Parking 50F–80F (7.60– 12.15, $7.25–$11.60) per night. **Amenities:** Restaurant, bar; room service; laundry/dry cleaning. *In room:* TV, minibar, hair dryer.

Hôtel Calendal *✸* *Value* Because of its reasonable rates, the Calendal is a bargain hunter's favorite. On a quiet square not far from the arena, it offers recently renovated rooms with bright colors, high ceilings, and a sense of spaciousness. Most have views of the hotel's garden, filled with palms and palmettos. Each unit comes with a compact shower-only bathroom. The restaurant has a limited menu featuring omelets, soups, and platters inspired by the cuisine of France and Provence.

5 rue Porte de Laure, 13200 Arles. ⓒ **04-90-96-11-89**. Fax 04-90-96-05-84. 38 units. 290F–480F (44.10– 72.95, $42.05–$69.60) double. AE, DC, MC, V. Bus: 4. **Amenities:** Restaurant; laundry.

Hôtel Jules César et Restaurant Lou Marquès *✸✸✸* This 17th-century Carmelite convent is now a stately country hotel with the best restaurant in town. Although it's in a noisy neighborhood, most rooms face the unspoiled cloister. You'll wake to the scent of roses and the sounds of birds singing. Throughout, you'll find a blend of antique neoclassic architecture and modern amenities. The decor is luxurious, with antique Provençal furnishings found at auctions throughout the countryside. The interior rooms are the most tranquil and also the darkest, though enlivened by bright fabrics. Most of the downstairs units are spacious, and although the upstairs rooms are small, they have a certain old-world charm. The rooms in the modern extensions are comfortable but lack character. Each bathroom comes with a combination tub/shower.

9 bd. des Lices, 13631 Arles CEDEX. ⓒ **04-90-52-52-52**. Fax 04-90-52-52-53. www.hotel-julescesar.fr. 58 units. 850F–1,250F (129.20– 190, $123.25–$181.25) double; from 1,500F (228, $217.50) suite. AE, DC, MC, V. Closed Nov 12–Dec 23. Parking 65F (9.90,$9.45). **Amenities:** Restaurant, bar; room service; laundry. *In room:* TV, minibar, hair dryer.

Hôtel Le Cloître *Value* This hotel, between the ancient theater and the cloister, is a great value. Originally part of a 12th-century cloister, it still has its original Romanesque vaultings. Throughout, you'll find a richly Provençal atmosphere, pleasant rooms with high ceilings and subtle references to the building's antique origins. Bedrooms are lean on amenities except for phones and small shower-only bathrooms. Some units have TVs available for a supplement of 20F (3.05, $2.90) per day. There's also a TV lounge and a breakfast salon.

16 rue du Cloître, 13200 Arles. © **04-90-96-29-50.** Fax 04-90-96-02-88. hotel_cloitre@hotmail.com. 30 units. 270F–390F (41.05– 59.30, $39.15–$56.55) double; 395F (60.05, $57.30) triple. AE, MC, V. Closed Nov–Mar 15. Parking 30F (4.55, $4.35). Bus: 4.

DINING

For a truly elegant meal, consider the **Restaurant Lou Marquês** at the Hôtel Jules César (see "Accommodations," above).

El Quinto Toro PROVENÇAL/SPANISH   Set a few steps from the Place du Forum, and outfitted with a decor inspired by the *corridas* (bullfights) held in and around Arles, this is a well-managed restaurant with no more than 30 seats and a following of local fans. Some of the best food is grilled over live coals that waft aromas from the kitchen into the dining rooms. You might begin with Spanish tapas, then follow with generous slabs of duck breast or fresh fish, both grilled and succulent. A specialty, not widely available, is wood-grilled bull steak from the Camargue. The owners pride themselves on the simplicity of their cuisine, and prefer to emphasize natural juices and flavors over fancy sauces. A wide selection of French and Spanish wines and beers accompanies your meal.

12 rue de la Liberté. © **04-90-49-62-29.** Reservations recommended in summer. Main courses 50F–80F (7.60– 12.15, $7.25–$11.60). AE, V. Thurs–Tues noon–2:30pm and 7–10:30pm.

L'Olivier 🍴 PROVENÇAL/FRENCH   On the western edge of the old town is one of the most charming restaurants in Arles, occupying a house whose foundations date from the 12th century. Inside, you'll find a warren of dining rooms with beamed ceilings, fireplaces, terra-cotta tiles, ladder-backed chairs, and the kind of antiques your French grandmother might have had in her home. Menu items vary with the season, but the best examples include fresh local asparagus garnished with sweetbreads on a bed of roasted tomatoes; fava-bean soup with garlic croutons and saffron-flavored rouille; codfish steak with a bouillon of garlic and fresh herbs; and baby pigeon roasted with foie gras–flavored butter.

1 bis rue Réattu. © **04-90-49-64-88.** Reservations recommended. Main courses 98F–170F (14.90– 25.85, $14.20–$24.65); set menus 178F–368F (27.05– 55.95, $25.80–$53.35). MC, V. Daily noon–1:15pm and 7:30–9:15pm.

ARLES AFTER DARK

Because of its relatively small population (around 50,000), Arles doesn't offer as many nightlife options as Aix-en-Provence, Avignon, Nice, or Marseille. The town's most appealing choice is the bar/cafe/music hall **Cargo de Nuit,** 7 av. Sadi-Carnot, route pour Barriol (© **04-90-49-55-99**). For a cover of 30F to 100F (4.55 to 15.20, $4.35 to $14.50), you'll get a dose of recorded blues, salsa, reggae, and Cubano music and access to a sprawling bar and restaurant that does everything it can to break what might have become too constant a diet of southern French cooking.

A good option farther from the city center, particularly for those in their 40s and 50s, is the very large **Le Krystal,** route de Pont-de-Crau (© **04-90-98-32-40**), about 6 miles south of Arles. The town's most animated cafe, where most of the singles go, is **Le Café van Gogh,** 11 place du Forum (© **04-90-96-44-56**). Overlooking an attractive plaza, it features live music and an ambience that the almost-young and the restless refer to as *super-chouette,* or "super cool."

5 Les Baux ⟨★⟨★⟨★

444 miles S of Paris, 12 miles NE of Arles, 50 miles N of Marseille

Cardinal Richelieu called Les Baux a nesting place for eagles. In its lonely position on a windswept plateau overlooking the southern Alpilles, Les Baux is a ghost of its former self. It was once the citadel of powerful seigneurs who ruled with an iron fist and sent their conquering armies as far as Albania. In medieval times, troubadours from all over the continent came to this "court of love," where they recited western Europe's earliest-known vernacular poetry. Eventually, the "Scourge of Provence" ruled Les Baux, sending his men throughout the land to kidnap people. If no one was willing to pay ransom for one of his victims, the poor wretch was forced to walk a gangplank over the cliff's edge.

Fed up with the rebellions against Louis XIII in 1632, Richelieu commanded his armies to destroy Les Baux. Today, the castle and ramparts are mere shells, though you can see remains of Renaissance mansions. Although foreboding, the dry countryside around Les Baux, which is nestled in a valley surrounded by shadowy rock formations, offers its own fascination. Vertical ravines lie on either side of the town. Vineyards—officially classified as Coteaux d'Aix-en-Provence—surround Les Baux, facing the Alpilles. If you follow the signposted route des vin, you can motor through the vineyards in an afternoon, perhaps stopping off at various growers' estates.

Now the bad news. Because of the beauty and drama of the area, Les Baux is virtually overrun with visitors; it's not unlike Mont-St-Michel in that respect.

ESSENTIALS

GETTING THERE   There's no rail station in Les Baux, so most **train** passengers get off at Arles. From Arles, there are four **buses** daily that stop at Les Baux (trip time: 25 min.) and an additional four or five that stop in nearby Maussane-les-Alpilles, 2 miles south. The bus makes fewer runs between November and March. For bus information, call ✆ **04-90-49-38-01** in Arles.

VISITOR INFORMATION   The **Office de Tourisme** is on Ilot Post Tenebras Lux (✆ **04-90-54-34-39**).

EXPLORING THE AREA

Les Baux is one of the most dramatic towns in Provence. You can wander through feudal ruins, called **La Ville Morte (Ghost Village)** ⟨★⟨★⟨★, at the northern end of town. The site of this castle or citadel covers an area at least five times that of Les Baux itself. As you stand at the ruins, you can look out over the Valley of Hell (*Val d'Enfer*) and even see the Mediterranean in the distance.

You can reach **La Citadelle** ⟨★⟨★, the castle ruins at the bottom of the town, by walking up rue du Château, which leads into the **Château des Baux** (✆ **04-90-54-55-56**). Allow at least an hour to explore. You enter the citadel by going through the **Hôtel de la Tour du Brau,** which houses the Musée du

---

⟨*Moments* **Les Baux with a View**

For the greatest drive in the area, take the panoramic route along D27 for about half a mile and bear right along a steep road. From this rocky promontory, you'll have the most spectacular view of Les Baux and even, in the far distance, of Arles and Camargue.

Château. The "Hôtel," which refers to a private mansion, was the residence of the powerful Tour de Brau family. The museum has exhibits related to the history of Les Baux, which will help you understand the other ruins within the compound. Models of the fortress in medieval times explain how the site has evolved architecturally.

After leaving the Hôtel de la Tour du Brau, you're free to wander through the citadel ruins, taking in such sites as the ruined chapel of St-Blaise (now housing a little museum devoted to the olive), replicas of medieval siege engines, grottoes used for storage or lodgings in the Middle Ages, the skeleton of a hospital built in the 16th century, a cemetery, and, finally, the **Tour Sarrisin** (Saracen Tower), which offers a view of the village and the citadel compound. Admission to the castle is 37F (5.60, $5.35) for adults, 28F (4.25, $4.05) for students, and 20F (3.05, $2.90) for children 7 to 17. The site is open daily from 9am to 8:30pm in July and August; daily from 9am to 7pm in March and in September through October; and daily from 10am to 5:30pm during other months.

In the village itself, you can visit the **Yves Brauyer Museum,** at the intersection of rue de la Calade and rue de l'Église (℡ **04-90-54-36-99**). The museum is devoted to a collection of the works of Yves Brayer (1907 to 1990), a figurative painter and Les Baux's famous native son (he's buried in the village cemetery). His works depict Italy, Morocco, and Spain, along with many bullfighting scenes. The museum is open April to October, Wednesday through Monday from 10am to 6:30pm; the rest of the year, Wednesday through Monday from 10am to noon and 2 to 5:30pm. Admission is 20F (3.05, $2.90) for adults, 10F (1.50, $1.45) for students and children.

Cathêdrale d'Images ☆ (℡ **04-90-54-38-65**) is one of the most remarkable cathedrals in Provence. It lies a quarter mile north of the village and can be reached along route du Val d'Enfer. Outside, you can marvel at the fact that the cathedral is carved out of the stone mountain. But it's as amazing inside, where the limestone surfaces of the large rooms and pillars become three-dimensional screens for a bizarre audio-visual show. Hundreds of projectors splash images from all directions. Photographer Albert Plecy created the site in 1977. It's open daily in summer from 10am to 7pm but closed from mid-January to March 4. Admission is 43F (6.55, $6.25) for adults, 27F (4.10, $3.90) for children under 18.

Musée des Santons is located in the town's **Ancien Hôtel de Ville,** place Louis Jou (no phone). Built in the 16th century as a chapel, "La Chapelle des Pénitents Blancs," the museum displays antique and idiosyncratic wood carvings, each representing a different saint or legend. It's open April to October, daily from 7am to 7pm, and November to March, daily from 10am to 6:30pm.

Head up to the much-praised **Place St-Vincent** for a sweeping view over the *Vallon de la Fontaine.* This is also the site of the much-respected **Église St-Vincent** (no phone), which is open April to October, daily from 9am to 6:30pm, and November to March, daily from 10am to 5:30pm. Its campanile is called *La Lanterne des Morts* (Lantern of the Dead). The windows were a gift from Rainier of Monaco, when he was the Marquis des Baux, during the 1980s. They are modern, based on designs of French artist Max Ingrand.

The Renaissance-era **Hôtel de Manville,** rue Frédéric Mistral, was built in the 16th century as a private mansion. Today, it functions as the **Mairie** (Town Hall) of Les Baux. You can visit its courtyard (its hours are the same as Musée des Santons, above). **Fondation Louis Jou** lies within the Renaissance-era

Hôtel Jean-de-Brion, rue Frédéric Mistral (✆ **04-90-69-88-03** or 04-90-54-34-17). It can be visited only by appointment, and does not maintain regular hours. Inside is an inventory of engravings and serigraphs by the recently departed artist Louis Jou, as well as a limited number of small-scale works by Rembrandt, Dürer, and Goya. Admission is 15F (2.30, $2.20).

ACCOMMODATIONS

La Riboto de Taven (see "Dining," below) has rooms for rent.

Auberge de la Benvengudo ✮ This auberge gives you the opportunity to spend the night in a converted 19th-century farmhouse surrounded by sculptured shrubbery, towering trees, and parasol pines. Extras include a pool, tennis court, and expansive terrace filled with the scent of lavender and thyme. The rooms are about equally divided between the original building, above the restaurant, and an attractive stone-sided annex. Regardless of their location, they're sunny, well-maintained, and recently renovated. Each has a private terrace or balcony and, in some cases, an antique four-poster bed. Five units come with shower only; the others have a combination tub/shower. The restaurant offers a delectable menu.

Vallon de l'Arcoule, rte. d'Arles, 13520 Les Baux. ✆ **04-90-54-32-54.** Fax 04-90-54-42-58. 24 units. 630F–800F (95.75– 121.60, $91.35–$116) double; 990F (150.50, $143.55) suite. AE, MC, V. Closed Nov–Mar 15. Take RD78 for a mile southwest of Les Baux, following signs to Arles. **Amenities:** Restaurant, bar; outdoor pool; tennis court; baby-sitting. *In room:* TV, hair dryer.

Hostellerie de la Reine-Jeanne ⟨Value⟩ This warm, well-scrubbed inn is the best bargain in Les Baux. You enter through a typical provincial French bistro. All the bedrooms are spartan but comfortable, and three even have their own terraces. Bathrooms are cramped, with a shower stall only; phones are the only in-room amenities. Fixed-price menus are sumptuously prepared by the chef.

Grand-Rue, 13520 Les Baux. ✆ **04-90-54-32-06.** Fax 04-90-54-32-33. 10 units. 280F–380F (42.55– 57.75, $40.60–$55.10) double. MC, V. Closed Nov 15–Feb 15 (open during the Christmas holidays). Free parking. **Amenities:** Restaurant.

La Cabro d'Or ✮✮✮ This is the less famous, less celebrated sibling of the also-recommended L'Oustau de Beaumanière, less than a half-mile away. You'll find some of the most comfortable accommodations in the region among these five low-slung stone buildings. The original building, a Provençal farmhouse, dates from the 18th century. The bedroom decor of unusual art and antiques evokes old-time Provence. Some rooms have sweeping views over the countryside, and each comes with a combination tub/shower. The dining room sits in a much-altered agrarian building from the 1800s. The massive ceiling beams are works of art in their own right. The restaurant is flanked by a vine-covered terrace with views of a pond, a garden, and a rocky and barren landscape that has been compared to the surface of the moon.

13520 Les Baux de Provence. ✆ **04-90-54-33-21.** Fax 04-90-54-45-98. www.lacabrodor.com. 31 units. 870F–1,270F (132.25– 193.05, $126.15–$184.15) double; from 1,920F (291.85, $278.40) suite. Off-season rates about 25% lower. Half-board 400F (60.80, $58) extra per person. AE, DC, MC, V. **Amenities:** Restaurant, bar; pool; two tennis courts; room service; laundry. *In room:* A/C, TV, minibar, hair dryer.

L'Oustau de Beaumanière ✮✮✮ This Relais & Châteaux member is one of southern France's most legendary hotels. Raymond Thuilier bought the farmhouse in 1945, and by the 1950s and 1960s, it was a rendezvous for the glitterati. Today, managed by its founder's grandson, it's not as glitzy, but the three stone houses, draped in flowering vines, still charm. The plush rooms evoke the

16th and 17th centuries. All units contain large sitting areas, and no two are alike. If there's no vacancy in the main building, the hotel will assign you to one of the annexes. If this is the case, request Le Manor, the most appealing. The spacious bathrooms contain tub/showers. In the stone-vaulted dining room, the chef serves specialties like ravioli of truffles with leeks, a *rossini* (stuffed with foie gras) of veal with fresh truffles, and roasted duckling with olives. The award-winning *gigot d'agneau* (lamb) *en croûte* has become this place's trademark.

Les Baux, 13520 Maussane-les-Alpilles. ℂ 04-90-54-33-07. Fax 04-90-54-40-46. www.oustaude beaumaniere.com. 27 units. 1,450F–1,550F (220.40– 235.60, $210.25–$224.75) double; 2,300F–2,500F (349.60– 380, $333.50–$362.50) suite. AE, DC, MC, V. Closed Jan 3–Mar 4. Restaurant closed Wed from Nov–Apr 1. **Amenities:** Restaurant, bar; outdoor pool; room service; laundry/dry cleaning. *In room:* A/C, TV, minibar, hair dryer.

DINING

L'Oustau de Beaumanière (see "Accommodations," above) boasts an excellent dining room.

La Riboto de Taven ★★★ Known for its flawless cuisine and market-fresh ingredients, this is one of the great restaurants of the area, a rival of Cabro d'Or. This 1835 farmhouse outside the medieval section of town has been owned by two generations of the Novi family. In summer, you can sit outdoors. Menu items may include sea bass in olive oil, fricassée of mussels flavored with basil, and lamb en croûte with olives—plus homemade desserts. The cuisine is a personal statement of Jean-Pierre Novi, whose cookery is filled with brawny flavors and the heady perfumes of Provençal herbs.

You can also stay in one of eight rooms large enough to be suites, for 900F to 1,100F (136.80 to 167.20, $130.50 to $159.50), breakfast included.

Le Val d'Enfer, 13520 Les Baux. ℂ 04-90-54-34-23. Fax 04-90-54-38-88. Reservations required. Main courses 150F–190F (22.80– 28.90, $21.75–$27.55); fixed-price menus 220F–450F (33.45– 68.40, $31.90–$65.25) lunch, 300F–450F (45.60– 68.40, $43.50–$65.25) dinner. AE, DC, MC, V. Tues noon–2pm; Thurs–Mon noon–2pm and 7:30–9pm. Closed Jan 3–Mar 15.

6 Aix-en-Provence ★★

469 miles S of Paris, 50 miles SE of Avignon, 20 miles N of Marseille, 109 miles W of Nice

Founded in 122 B.C. by a Roman general, Caius Sextius Calvinus, who named it Aquae Sextiae after himself, Aix (pronounced "ex") was a Roman military outpost and then a civilian colony, the administrative capital of a province of the late Roman Empire, the seat of an archbishop, and official residence of the medieval comtes de Provence. After the union of Provence with France, Aix remained a judicial and administrative headquarters until the Revolution.

The celebrated son of this old capital city of Provence, Paul Cézanne, immortalized the countryside. Just as he saw it, Montagne Ste-Victoire looms over the town today, though a string of high-rises has cropped up on the landscape. The most charming center in all Provence, this faded university town was once a seat of aristocracy, its streets walked by counts and kings.

Today, this city of some 150,000 is quiet in winter but active and bustling when the summer hordes pour in. Many of the local population are international students. (The Université d'Aix dates from 1413.) Émile Zola's absinthe has given way to pastis in the many cafes throughout the town. Summer is especially lively because of the frequent cultural events, ranging from opera to jazz, staged here from June to August. Increasingly, Aix is becoming a bedroom community for urbanites fleeing Marseille after 5pm.

ESSENTIALS

GETTING THERE   As a rail and highway junction, the city is easily accessible, with **trains** arriving hourly from Marseille (trip time: 40 min.). For rail information, call © **08-36-35-35-35**. Several **bus** companies serve Aix; call the **Gare Routière,** rue Lapierre (© **04-42-91-26-80**), for information. **SATAP** (© **04-42-26-23-78**) specializes in routes from Aix to Avignon, with up to four buses a day. If you're **driving** from Marseille, take A51 north to Aix-en-Provence; from Avignon, travel A7 south to Senas and then N7 southeast to Aix.

VISITOR INFORMATION   The **Office de Tourisme** is at 2 place du Général-de-Gaulle (© **04-42-16-11-61**).

SPECIAL EVENTS   Aix is more geared toward music than virtually any other city in the south of France. It offers at least four midsummer festivals that showcase music, opera, and dance. They include the **Saison d'Aix** (June to August), which focuses on symphonic and chamber music, and a **Jazz Festival** (June 28 to July 11) that attracts musicians from all over the world. For information, call the **Office des Fêtes et de la Culture,** Espace Forbin, Cours Gambetta (© **04-42-63-06-75**).

Also noteworthy is the **Festival International de Danse** (July 11 to 23), attracting classical and modern dance troupes from throughout Europe and the world. For information, call © **04-42-96-05-01**.

EXPLORING THE AREA

Aix's main street, **cours Mirabeau** ★★, is one of Europe's most beautiful. Plane trees stretch their branches across the top like an umbrella, shading it from the hot Provençal sun and filtering the light into shadows that play on the rococo fountains below. Shops and sidewalk cafes line one side of the street; sandstone *hôtels particuliers* (mansions) from the 17th and 18th centuries fill the other. The street begins at the 1860 fountain on place de la Libération, which honors Mirabeau, the revolutionary and statesman.

After touring Aix, you might consider a side trip to the **Château de Vauvenargues,** site of Pablo Picasso's last home. Reach it from Aix by driving 10 miles east on D10. You can't visit the château's interior, but Picasso and one of his wives, Jacqueline Roche, are buried nearby. Stop for a meal at **Au Moulin de Provence,** rue des Maquisards (© **04-42-66-02-22**).

Atelier de Cézanne   Cézanne was the major forerunner of Cubism. This house, surrounded by a wall and restored by American admirers, is where he worked. Repaired again in 1970, it remains much as Cézanne left it in 1906,

---

Moments Aix Through the Eyes of Cézanne

The best experience in Aix is a walk along the signposted route de Cézanne (D17), which winds eastward through the countryside toward Ste-Victoire. From the east end of cours Mirabeau, take rue du Maréchal-Joffre across boulevard Carnot to boulevard des Poilus, which becomes avenue des Écoles-Militaires and finally D17. The stretch between Aix and the hamlet of Le Tholonet is full of twists and turns where Cézanne often set up his easel to paint. The entire route makes a lovely 3½-mile stroll. Le Tholonet has a cafe or two where you can refresh yourself while waiting for one of the frequent buses back to Aix.

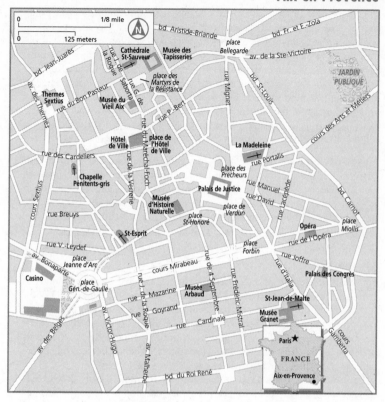

"his coat hanging on the wall, his easel with an unfinished picture waiting for a touch of the master's brush," as Thomas R. Parker wrote.

9 av. Paul-Cézanne (outside town). ℭ **04-42-21-06-53.** Admission 18F (2.75, $2.60) adults, 10F (1.50, $1.45) students and seniors, free for children 12 and under. Daily 10am–noon and 2–6pm (to 5pm Oct–Mar).

Cathédrale St-Sauveur ✦   The cathedral of Aix is dedicated to Christ under
the title St-Sauveur (Holy Savior or Redeemer). Its Baptistery dates from the 4th and 5th centuries, but the complex as a whole has seen many additions. It contains a 15th-century Nicolas Froment triptych, *The Burning Bush.* One side depicts the Virgin and Child; the other, Good King René and his second wife, Jeanne de Laval. Masses are conducted every Sunday at 9am, 10:30am, and 7pm.

Place des Martyrs de la Résistance. ℭ **04-42-23-45-65.** Free admission. Daily 7:30am–noon and 2–6pm.

Chapelle Penitents-gris (Chapelle des Bourras)   This 16th-century
chapel honoring St. Joseph was built on the ancient Roman Aurelian road linking Rome and Spain. Herbert Maza, founder and former president of the Institute for American Universities, restored the chapel. If you can't visit during the limited opening hours on Saturdays, you can call M. Borricand, rector of a group of local ecclesiastics, who'll arrange a rendezvous upon request.

15 rue Lieutaud. ℭ **04-42-26-26-72.** Free admission (donations welcome). July–Aug Sat 4:30–6pm; Sept–June Sat 2:30–4:30pm.

Musée Granet (Musée des Beaux-Arts)   This museum owns eight paintings by Cézanne, none of them major. The great painter had an antagonistic relationship with the people of Aix—so much so that a former director of the museum once claimed that the galleries "would never be sullied by a Cézanne." Housed in the former center of the Knights of Malta, the museum contains works by van Dyck, van Loo, and Rigaud; portraits by Pierre and François Puget; and (the most interesting) a *Jupiter and Thetis* by Ingres. Ingres also did an 1807 portrait of the museum's namesake, François Marius Granet.

Place St-Jean-de-Malte (up rue Cardinale). ℂ 04-42-38-14-70. Admission 18F (2.75, $2.60) adults, 10F (1.50, $1.45) students and children under 18. Wed–Mon 10am–noon and 2:30–6pm.

Musée des Tapisseries ✯   Three series of tapestries from the 17th and 18th centuries line the gilded walls of this former archbishop's palace. *The History of Don Quixote,* by Natoire, *The Russian Games,* by Leprince, and *The Grotesques,* by Monnoyer, were collected by archbishops to decorate the palace. The museum also exhibits rare furnishings from the 17th and 18th centuries.

28 place des Martyrs de la Résistance. ℂ 04-42-23-09-91. Admission 15F (2.30, $2.20) adults, free for ages 25 and under. Wed–Mon 10am–noon and 2–5:45pm.

SHOPPING

For the best selection of art objects and fabrics inspired by the traditions of Provence, head to **Les Olivades,** 15 rue Marius-Reinaud (℃ 04-42-38-33-66). It sells fabrics, shirts for women and men, fashionable dresses, and table linens.

Opened a century ago, **Bechard,** 12 cours Mirabeau (℃ 04-42-26-06-78), is the most famous bakery in town. It takes its work so seriously that it refers to its underground kitchens as a *laboratoire* (laboratory). The pastries are truly delectable, in most cases made fresh every day.

La Boutique du Pays d'Aix, in the Office de Tourisme, 2 place du Général-de-Gaulle (℃ 04-42-16-11-61), carries a wide selection of *santons* (carved figurines inspired by the Nativity of Jesus), locally woven textiles and carvings, and *calissons* (sugared confections made with almonds and a confit of melon).

Founded in 1934 on a busy boulevard about half a mile from the center of town, **Santons Fouque,** 65 cours Gambetta, route de Nice (℃ 04-42-26-33-38), stocks the largest assortment of *santons* in Aix. More than 1,800 figurines are cast in terra cotta, finished by hand, and decorated with oil-based paint according to 18th-century models. Each of the trades practiced in medieval Provence is represented, including shoemakers, barrel makers, coppersmiths, and ironsmiths, each poised to welcome the newborn Jesus. Figurines range in price from 22F to 5,600F (3.35 to 851.20, $3.20 to $812).

ACCOMMODATIONS
EXPENSIVE

Hôtel des Augustins ✯   Converted from the 12th-century Grands Augustins Convent in 1892, this hotel is beautifully restored, with ribbed-vault ceilings, stained-glass windows, stone walls, terra-cotta floors, and Louis XIII furnishings. The reception desk is in a chapel, and oil paintings and watercolors decorate the public rooms. This site won a place in history by sheltering an excommunicated Martin Luther on his return from Rome. The rooms are outfitted in a severe kind of monastic dignity, with dark wood furniture and high ceilings. Each unit comes with a good-size bathroom with combination tub/shower. Breakfast is the only meal served.

3 rue de la Masse, 13100 Aix-en-Provence. 𝄞 **04-42-27-28-59.** Fax 04-42-26-74-87. 29 units. 600 F–1,500 F (91.20E–228E, $87–$217.50) double. AE, DC, V. Nearby parking in private garage 50 F (7.60E, $7.25). **Amenities:** Laundry/dry cleaning. *In room:* TV, minibar, hair dryer.

Villa Gallici ⭐⭐⭐   This elegant, relentlessly chic inn is the most stylish hotel in town. The rooms, richly infused with the decorative traditions of Aix, speak of subtlety and charm. Some boast a private terrace or garden, and each comes with a combination tub/shower. The villa sits in a large enclosed garden in the heart of Aix, close to one of the best restaurants, Le Clos de la Violette (see "Dining," below). It's only a 5-minute walk to the town center.

Av. de la Violette (impasse des Grands Pins), 13100 Aix-en-Provence. 𝄞 **04-42-23-29-23.** Fax 04-42-96-30-45. www.villagallici.com. 22 units. 1,400F–3,300F (212.80– 501.60, $203–$478.50) double; 3,000F–3,300F (456– 501.60, $435–$478.50) suite. AE, DC, MC, V. **Amenities:** Restaurant, bar; spa; pool; baby-sitting; room service; laundry. *In room:* A/C, TV, minibar, hair dryer, safe.

MODERATE

Grand Hôtel Nègre Coste   This hotel, a former 18th-century town house, is so popular with the dozens of musicians who flock to Aix for the summer festivals that it's difficult to get a room at any price. Such popularity is understandable. Flowers cascade from jardinières, and windows are surrounded with 18th-century carvings. Inside, there's a wide staircase, marble portrait busts, and a Provençal armoire. The medium-size soundproof rooms contain interesting antiques. The higher floors overlook cours Mirabeau or the old city. Each unit comes with a compact bathroom with shower; some have tubs as well.

33 cours Mirabeau, 13100 Aix-en-Provence. 𝄞 **04-42-27-74-22.** Fax 04-42-26-80-93. 37 units. 420F–800F (63.85– 121.60, $60.90–$116) double. AE, DC, V. Parking 50F (7.60, $7.25). *In room:* A/C, TV.

INEXPENSIVE

Hôtel des Quatre Dauphins   This 18th-century town house is a short walk from place des Quatre Dauphins and the cours Mirabeau. Today, despite frequent modernizations, some of the original motifs remain. The medium-size bedrooms were refurbished in a simplified Provençal style, some with painted ceiling beams and casement windows that overlook the street. Five units come with a compact bathroom with tub/shower, the rest with shower only. You can have breakfast in your room or in a small salon.

54 rue Roux Alphéran, 13100 Aix-en-Provence. 𝄞 **04-42-38-16-39.** Fax 04-42-38-60-19. 13 units. 350F–450F (53.20– 68.40, $50.75–$65.25) double. MC, V. Nearby parking 55F (8.35, $8). *In room:* TV.

Hôtel La Caravelle *(Value)*   This conservatively furnished hotel, with a bas-relief of a three-masted caravelle on the stucco façade, is only a 3-minute walk from the center of town. It offers warm hospitality. One nice touch is the breakfast served in the stone-floored lobby. The majority of the rooms were restored between 1995 and 1998; they have double-glazed windows to help muffle the noise. Most bathrooms contain showers only.

29 bd. du Roi-René (at cours Mirabeau), 13100 Aix-en-Provence. 𝄞 **04-42-21-53-05.** Fax 04-42-96-55-46. 32 units. 330F–430F (50.15– 65.35, $47.85–$62.35) double. AE, DC, MC, V. *In room:* A/C, TV.

Novotel Aix Point de l'Arc *(Kids)*   You'll find this chain hotel at the end of a labyrinthine but well-marked route. The large rooms have been designed for European business travelers or traveling families, and each comes with a combination tub/shower. The hotel offers one of the most pleasant dining rooms in the suburbs, Côté Jardin, with big windows overlooking Rivière Arc de Méyran and an ivy-covered forest.

If this hotel is full, rooms are usually available at its twin, **Novotel Aix-Beaumanoir,** périphérique Sud (C **04-42-91-15-15;** fax 04-42-38-46-41), less than 500 yards away. It has a restaurant and an outdoor pool.

Périphérique Sud, arc de Méyran, 13100 Aix-en-Provence. C **800/221-4542** in the U.S., or 04-42-16-09-09. Fax 04-42-26-00-09. www.accor.com. 80 units. 550F (83.60, $79.75) double. AE, DC, MC, V. Take the ring road 2 miles south of the town center (exit at Aix-Est 3 Sautets). **Amenities:** Restaurant, bar; outdoor pool. *In room:* A/C, TV, minibar.

DINING
VERY EXPENSIVE

Le Clos de la Violette ★★★ MODERN FRENCH This innovative restaurant is a few steps from the also-recommended Villa Gallici (see "Accommodations," above) in an elegant neighborhood, which most visitors reach by taxi. The imposing Provençal villa has an octagonal reception area and several modern dining rooms. Menu items are stylish and seasonal, and include a medley of dishes richly attuned to the flavors of Provence. Examples include an upsidedown tart of snails with parsley juice; braised sea wolf with beignets of fennel; warm onion brioche with a fig-flavored vinaigrette and balsamic vinegar; and roasted Provençal lamb in puff pastry. An absolutely superb dessert is a "celebration" of Provençal figs, an artfully arranged platter containing a galette of figs, a tart of figs, a parfait of figs, and a sorbet of figs.

10 av. de la Violette. C **04-42-23-30-71.** Reservations required. Main courses 185F–250F (28.10– 38, $26.85–$36.25); fixed-price menus 300F–600F (45.60– 91.20, $43.50–$87) lunch, 600F (91.20, $87) dinner. AE, V. Mon 7:30–9:30pm; Tues–Sat noon–1:30pm and 7:30–9:30pm. Closed 2 weeks in Nov and 1 week in Feb.

MODERATE

Chez Maxime GRILLS/PROVENÇAL Located in the pedestrian zone, this likable restaurant reflects the skills and personality of its owner, Felix Maxime. You can eat on the sidewalk terrace or in the wood-trimmed stone dining room. To experience the true flavors of Provence, order the *tian* appetizer: layers of eggplant, peppers, and Mediterranean herbs in a terra-cotta pot, infused with garlic and olive oil, and baked until bubbly. Another superb beginning is *rillettes* (similar to a roughly textured pâté) of sea wolf with a garlicky *rouille* mayonnaise. Specialties include as many as 19 kinds of grilled meat or fish, cooked over an oak-burning fire, and several preparations of lamb. The wine list features more than 500 vintages, many of them esoteric bottles from the region.

12 place Ramus. C **04-42-26-28-51.** Reservations recommended. Main courses 85F–160F (12.90– 24.30, $12.35–$23.20); fixed-price menus 68F–98F (10.35– 14.90, $9.85–$14.20) lunch, 138F–270F (21– 41.05, $20–$39.15) dinner. MC, V. Mon 8–11pm; Tues–Sat noon–2pm and 8–11pm. Closed Jan 15–31.

Le Bistro Latin ★★ *Value* PROVENÇAL The best little bistro in Aix-en-Provence (for the price) is run by Gilles Holtz, who prides himself on the fixed-price menus. Guests dine in two intimate rooms: a street-level space and another in the cellar, decorated in Greco-Latin style. The staff is young and enthusiastic. Try the chartreuse of mussels, one of the meat dishes with spinach-and-saffron cream sauce, the scampi risotto, or crêpe of hare with basil sauce. We've enjoyed the classic cuisine on all our visits.

18 rue de la Couronne. C **04-42-38-22-88.** Reservations recommended. Fixed-price menus 75F–95F (11.40– 14.45, $10.90–$13.80) lunch, 129F–159F (19.60– 24.15, $18.70–$23.05) dinner. MC, V. Mon–Sat noon–2pm and 7–10:30pm.

Trattoria Chez Antoine Côte Cour PROVENÇAL/ITALIAN   This popular trattoria is in an 18th-century town house a few steps from place Rotonde. Regulars include Emanuel Ungaro and many film and fashion types who mingle with old-time "Aixers." Despite the grandeur, the ambience is unpretentious, even jovial. Crusty bread and small pots of aromatic purées (anchovy and basil) are placed at your table as you sit down. A simple wine, such as Côtes-du-Rhône, goes nicely with the hearty Mediterranean fare. Examples are a memorable pasta Romano flavored with calf's liver, flap mushrooms, and tomato sauce; ravioli with goat cheese; osso buco; a selection of *légumes farcies* (such as eggplant and zucchini stuffed with minced meat and herbs); and at least half a dozen kinds of fresh fish.

19 rue Mirabeau. (℃ 04-42-93-12-51. Reservations recommended. Main courses 65F–150F (9.90– 22.80, $9.45–$21.75). DC, MC, V. Tues–Sat noon–2:30pm; Mon–Sat 7:30pm–midnight.

AIX AFTER DARK

Aix is one of Provence's largest towns (after Marseille and Nice) and a university town to boot, making it a hotspot for animated nightlife. If you're a student or just want to act like one, head to **Babylon,** 4 bd. Carnot (℃ **04-42-21-47-44**), where live music enhances an everyday preoccupation with dating and mating.

Rockers go to **Le Mistral,** 3 rue Frédéric-Mistral (℃ **04-42-38-16-49**), where techno and house music blare long and loud. Its slightly more subdued competitor, **Le Richelm,** 24 rue de la Verrerie (℃ **04-42-23-49-29**), plays the same music but sometimes dips into 1970s and 1980s disco. Nearby is a woodsy-looking English pub that plays rock videos, **Bugsy,** 25 rue de la Verrerie (℃ **04-42-38-25-22**), where the good times are punctuated with bouts at billiard tables.

Less competitive and favored by those over 30 is the **Scat Club,** 11 rue de la Verrerie (℃ **04-42-23-00-23**), where a pianist and jazz trio provide music (jazz, soul, blues, and rock 'n' roll). Its rival is **Hot Brass,** chemin de la Pleine des Vergueiers (℃ **04-42-21-05-57**), attracting lots of off-duty photographers, artists, actors, and literary types who appreciate the drinks and live music.

7 Marseille ★★★

479 miles S of Paris, 116 miles SW of Nice, 19 miles S of Aix-en-Provence

Bustling Marseille, with more than a million inhabitants, is the second-largest city in France (its population surpassed Lyon in the early 1990s) and is the country's premier port. It's been called France's New Orleans. A crossroads of world traffic (Dumas called it "the meeting place of the entire world"), the city is ancient, founded by Greeks in the 6th century B.C. Marseille is a place of unique sounds, smells, and sights. It has seen wars and much destruction, but trade has always been its raison d'être.

Perhaps its most common association is with the national anthem of France, "La Marseillaise." During the Revolution, 500 volunteers marched to Paris, singing this rousing song along the way. The rest is history.

Although in many respects Marseille is big and sprawling, dirty and slumlike, there's much elegance and charm as well. The **Vieux Port,** the old harbor, is colorful, somehow compensating for the dreary industrial dockland nearby. Marseille is also the home of thousands of North and sub-Saharan Africans, creating a lively medley of races and creeds. A quarter of the population is of North African descent.

Marseille today actually occupies twice the amount of land space as Paris, and its age-old problems remain, including a drug industry, smuggling, corruption (often at the highest levels), the Mafia, and racial tension. Unemployment, as always, is on the rise. But despite all these difficulties, it's a bustling, always-fascinating city unlike any other in France. A city official proclaimed recently that "Marseille is the unbeloved child of France. It's attached to France, but has the collective consciousness of an Italian city-state, like Genoa or Venice."

ESSENTIALS

GETTING THERE   The **airport** (𝒞 **04-42-14-14-14**), 18 miles north of the center, receives international flights from all over Europe. From the airport, blue-and-white minivans (*navettes*) make the trip to Marseille's St-Charles rail station, near the Vieux-Port, for a one-way fee of 47F (7.15, $6.80). The minivans run daily at 20-minute intervals, from 6:20am to 10:50pm.

Marseille has **train** connections from hundreds of European cities, with especially good connections to and from Italy. The city is also the terminus for the TGV bullet train, which departs daily from Paris's Gare de Lyon (trip time: 4¾ hr.). Local trains leave Paris almost every hour, making a number of stops before reaching Marseille. For information and schedules, call 𝒞 **08-36-35-35-35.** **Buses** pull into Marseille at the Gare Routière, on the place Victor Hugo (𝒞 **04-91-08-16-40**), adjacent to the St-Charles railway station.

If you're **driving** from Paris, follow A6 south to Lyon; then continue south along A7 to Marseille. The drive takes about 7 hours.

GETTING AROUND   Parking and car safety are such potential hazards in Marseille that your best bet is to put your car in a garage and rely on public transportation. The city is sprawling, and public transportation will help you avoid the hassle of traffic.

Marseille is serviced by **Métro** lines 1 and 2, both of which stop at the main train station, Gare St-Charles, place Victor Hugo (𝒞 **08-36-35-35-35**). The Métro runs daily from 5am to 9pm. At the tourist office, pick up a free brochure outlining the public transportation routes of Marseille. If you're staying for 2 or 3 days, purchase a **Carte Liberté**—50F (7.60, $7.25) for 7 Métro transits, 100F (15.20, $14.50) for 14 Métro transits. These are available from **RTM,** 6–8 rue de Fabres (𝒞 **04-91-91-92-10**), open Monday to Friday from 8:30am to 6pm and Saturday from 9am to 5:30pm. You can also purchase tickets at Métro and bus stops, for 8F (1.20, $1.15) for a ride good for 70 minutes.

If you can't face the hassle of public transportation, call **Taxi Plus** (𝒞 **04-91-03-60-03**) or **Marseille Taxi** (𝒞 **04-91-02-20-20**).

VISITOR INFORMATION   The **Office de Tourisme** (Métro: Vieux-Port) is at 4 La Canebière (𝒞 **04-91-13-89-00;** www.marseille-tourisme.com).

SEEING THE SIGHTS

Many travelers never visit the museums, preferring to absorb the life of the city on its busy streets and at its cafes, particularly those along the main street, **La Canebière.** Known as "can of beer" to World War II GIs, it's the heart and soul of Marseille, even if it is the seediest main street in France. Lined with hotels, shops, and restaurants, the street is filled with sailors of every nation and people of every nationality, especially Algerians. (Some 100,000 North Africans live in the city and its tenement suburbs, often in communities that resemble *souks*.)

Canebière winds down to the **Vieux-Port** ✹✹, dominated by the massive neoclassical forts of St-Jean and St-Nicholas. The port is filled with fishing craft

Marseille

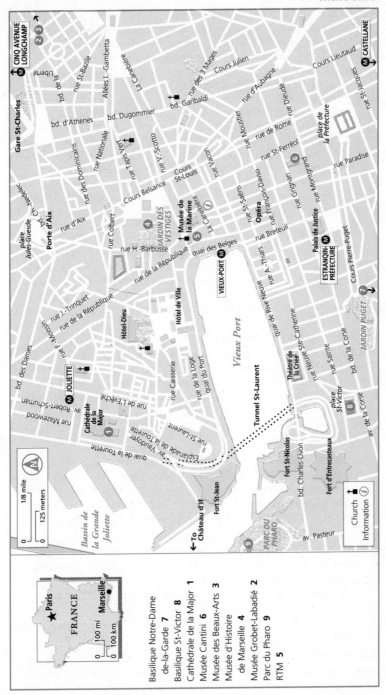

Basilique Notre-Dame
de-la-Garde **7**
Basilique St-Victor **8**
Cathédrale de la Major **1**
Musée Cantini **6**
Musée des Beaux-Arts **3**
Musée d'Histoire
de Marseille **4**
Musée Grobet-Labadié **2**
Parc du Pharo **9**
RTM **5**

and yachts and ringed with seafood restaurants. For a panoramic view, head for the **Parc du Pharo,** a promontory facing the entrance to the Vieux-Port. From a terrace overlooking the Château du Pharo, built by Napoléon III for his Eugénie, you can clearly see Fort St-Jean and the old and new cathedrals.

From quai des Belges at the Vieux-Port, you can take a 20-minute motorboat ride to **Château d'If,** for 50F (7.60, $7.25) round-trip. Boats leave every 60 to 90 minutes, depending on the season. For information, contact the **Groupement des Armateurs Côtiers,** quai des Belges (© **04-91-55-50-09;** Métro: Vieux-Port), open daily from 6:30am to 6:30pm. On the sparsely vegetated island of Château d'If (© **04-91-59-02-30** for information), François I built a fortress to defend Marseille. The site later housed a prison; carvings by Huguenot prisoners can still be seen. Alexandre Dumas used the château as a setting for *The Count of Monte Cristo,* though the adventure never really took place. Its most famous association—with the legendary Man in the Iron Mask— is also apocryphal. The château is open Tuesday through Sunday from 9am to 5:30pm (until 7pm from April to September). Admission to the island is 26F (3.95, $3.75) for adults and 15F (2.30, 2.20) for children.

If you're driving, continue from the old port to the **corniche Président-J.-F.-Kennedy,** a promenade running for about 3 miles along the sea. You'll pass villas and gardens and have a good view of the Mediterranean. To the north is the man-made **Port Moderne,** the "gateway to the East." Its construction began in 1844, and a century later the Germans destroyed it. Motorboat trips are conducted along the docks.

Basilique Notre-Dame-de-la-Garde   This landmark church crowns a limestone rock overlooking the southern side of the Vieux-Port. It was built in the Romanesque-Byzantine style popular in the 19th century and topped by a 30-foot gilded statue of the Virgin. Visitors come here not so much for the church as for the view—best seen at sunset—from its terrace. Spread out before you are the city, the islands, and the sea.

Rue Fort-du-Sanctuaire. © **04-91-13-40-80.** Free admission. Daily 7am–7pm (until 8pm mid-June to mid-Sept). Métro: Vieux-Port. Bus: 60.

Basilique St-Victor ✮   This semifortified basilica was built above a crypt from the 5th century, when St. Cassianus founded the church and abbey. You can visit the crypt, which also reflects work done in the 10th and 11th centuries.

Place St-Victor. © **04-96-11-22-60.** Admission to crypt 10F (1.50, $1.45). Crypt daily 10am–7pm. Head west along quai de Rive-Neuve (near the Gare du Vieux-Port). Métro: Vieux-Port.

Cathédrale de la Major   This was one of the largest cathedrals (some 450 feet long) built in Europe in the 19th century. Its interior is adorned with mosaic floors and red-and-white marble banners, and the exterior is in a bastardized Romanesque-Byzantine style. The domes and cupolas may remind you of Istanbul. This vast pile has almost swallowed its 12th-century Romanesque predecessor, built on the ruins of a Temple of Diana.

Place de la Major. © **04-91-90-53-57.** Free admission. Daily 9am–noon; Tues–Thurs 2–5:30pm; Fri–Sun 2:30–6pm. Métro: Joliette.

Musée Cantini   The temporary exhibitions of contemporary art staged here are often as good as the permanent collection. This museum is devoted to modern art, with masterpieces by Derain, Marquet, Ernst, Masson, Balthus, and others. It also owns a selection of works by important young international artists.

19 rue Grignan. ℭ **04-91-54-77-75.** Admission 12F (1.80, $1.75) adults, 6F (.90, 85¢) students, free for seniors and children 10 and under. June–Sept Tues–Sun 11am–6pm; Oct–May Tues–Sun 10am–5pm. Métro: Estrangin Préfecture.

Musée des Beaux-Arts ℛ   One of the most scenic sights is Palais Longchamp, with its fountain and colonnade, built during the Second Empire. This museum, housed in a northern wing of the palace, displays a vast array of paintings from the 16th to the 19th centuries, including works by Corot, Millet, Ingres, David, and Rubens. Particularly interesting is a gallery of Pierre Puget sculpture. One salon is devoted to Honoré Daumier, born in Marseille in 1808.

In Palais Longchamp, on place Bernex. ℭ **04-91-14-59-30.** Admission 12F (1.80, $1.75) adults, 6F (.90, 85¢) students and children 12–18. June 15–Sept 15 Tues–Sun 10am–7pm; Sept 16–June 14 Tues–Sun 10am–5pm. Métro: Cinq av. Longchamp or Réfomés.

Musée d'Histoire de Marseille   Visitors are allowed to wander through an archaeological garden where excavations are still going on, as scholars learn more about the ancient town of Massalia, founded by Greek sailors. Of course, many of the exhibits, such as old coins and fragments of pottery, only suggest their former glory. To help you more fully realize the era, you're aided by audiovisual exhibits and a free exhibition room. A medieval quarter of potters has been discovered, and the Louis XIV town is open to the public. You can also see what's left of a Roman wreck excavated from the site.

Centre Bourse, square Belsunce. ℭ **04-91-90-42-22.** Admission 12F (1.80, $1.75) adults, 6F (.90, 85¢) students and children 11–18. Mon–Sat noon–7pm. Métro: Vieux-Port.

Musée Grobet-Labadié ℛ   This private collection, bequeathed to the city in 1919, includes exquisite Louis XV and Louis XVI furniture, as well as an outstanding collection of medieval Burgundian and Provençal sculpture. Other exhibits showcase 17th-century Gobelin tapestries; 15th- to 19th-century German, Italian, French, and Flemish paintings; and 16th- and 17th-century Italian and French faïence.

140 bd. Longchamp. ℭ **04-91-62-21-82.** Admission 12F (1.80, $1.75) adults, 6F (.90, 85¢) students and children 11–18. Oct–May Tues–Sun 10am–5pm; June–Sept Tues–Sun 11am–6pm. Métro: Réformés.

SHOPPING

Only Paris and Lyon can compete with Marseille in breadth and diversity of merchandise. Your best bet is a trip to the **Vieux Port** and the streets surrounding it for a view of the folkloric things that literally pop out of the boutiques. Many of the shops are loaded with souvenirs like crèche-style *santons* (wooden figurines of saints). The best place for acquiring these is above the Vieux Port, behind the Théâtre National de la Criée. At **Ateliers Marcel Carbonel,** 47 rue Neuve-Ste-Catherine (ℭ **04-91-54-26-58**), more than 600 Nativity-related figures, available in half a dozen sizes, sell at prices starting at 60F (9.10, $8.70).

Bring an photo to the artists at **Amandine,** 69 bd. Eugène-Pierre (ℭ **04-91-47-00-83**), and they'll frost a cake with an amazing likeness. If you don't have a snapshot with you, choose from their roster of cakes, emblazoned with scenes of the Vieux Port or whatever. More traditional pastries and chocolates can be found at **Puyricard,** 25 rue Francis-Davso (ℭ **04-91-54-26-25**), with another location at 155 rue Jean-Mermoz (ℭ **04-91-77-94-11**). The treats include chocolates stuffed with almond paste (*pâté d'amande*) or *confits de fruits*.

Since medieval times, Marseille has thrived on the legend of Les Trois Maries—three saints named Mary, including everyone's favorite ex-sinner, Mary

Magdalene. Assisted by awakened-from-the-dead St. Lazarus, they reportedly came ashore near Marseille to Christianize ancient Provence. In commemoration of their voyage, small boat-shaped cookies *(les navettes)*, flavored with secret ingredients that include tons of orange zest, orange-flower water, and sugar, are forever associated with Marseille. They're sold throughout the city, most notably at **Le Four des Navettes,** 136 rue Sainte (© **04-91-33-32-12**). Opened in 1791, it sells the cookies for 45F ($7.20) per dozen and does very little else besides perpetuate the city's most cherished (and dubious) medieval myth.

Antiques from around Provence are sold along Cours Julien and in La Préfecture neighborhood. Two of the best include **Galerie Wulfram-Puget,** 39 rue de Lodi (© **04-91-76-42-85**), and **Antiquités François-Décamp,** 302 rue Paradis (© **04-91-81-18-00**). At **Felio,** 4 place Gabriel-Péri (© **04-91-90-32-67**), you'll find large-brimmed hats that would have thrilled ladies of the Belle Époque, as well as berets and other styles.

The souvenir shops along the **rue St-Féréol,** running perpendicular to La Canebière, as well as those near the Vieux Port, sell replicas of handcrafts from old Provence, including the cream-colored or pale-green bars of the city's local soap, savon de Marseille. Infused with a dollop of olive oil, the soap is known for its kindness to skin dried out by the sun and mistral. A large selection is available at **La Savonnerie du Sérail,** 50 bd. Anatle de la Forge (© **04-91-98-28-25**).

Looking for something that approximates, with a Provençal accent, the aura of a sun-flooded mall in California? Head for the most talked-about real-estate development in the city's recent history, **L'Escale Borély,** avenue Mendès-France. Only a 25-minute trip south of Marseille (take the Métro to rond-point du Prado; then transfer to bus no. 19), it incorporates shops, cafes, bars, and restaurants. For more on L'Escale Borély, see "Marseille after Dark," below.

You don't really think of Marseille as a place to shop for fashion, but the local fashion industry is booming. The fashion center is along **Cours Julien** and **rue de la Tour,** where you'll find many boutiques and ateliers. Much of the clothing reflects North African influences, though there is an array of French styles as well. Much of it is rich, brocaded, and ethnic—cut chic and close to the body.

ACCOMMODATIONS
VERY EXPENSIVE
L'Hôtel Le Petit Nice ★★★ This is the best hotel in Marseille. It opened in 1917, when the Passédat family joined two villas. The approach will take you past what looks like a row of private villas in a secluded area below the street paralleling the beach. The spacious Marina Wing across from the main building offers individually decorated rooms in the antique style, opening onto sea views. The rooms in the main house are more modern and avant-garde. Four units were inspired by the Cubist movement, with posh geometric appointments and bright colors. Each unit comes with a luxurious bathroom with tub/shower. The hotel restaurant is beautiful, with a view of the shore and the rocky islands off its coast. In summer, dinner is served in the garden facing the sea.

Corniche Président-J.-F.-Kennedy/Anse-de-Maldormé, 13007 Marseille. © **04-91-59-25-92.** Fax 04-91-59-28-08. www.petitnice-passedat.com. 16 units. 1,100F–2,900F (167.20– 440.80, $159.50–$420.50) double; 3,500F–4,500F (532– 684, $507.50–$652.50) suite. AE, DC, MC, V. Parking in garage 100F (15.20, $14.50); free in supervised outdoor parking lot. Closed 3 weeks in Nov. Métro: Vieux-Port. **Amenities:** Restaurant, bar; pool; solarium; room service; laundry. *In room:* A/C, TV, minibar, hair dryer, safe.

EXPENSIVE

Sofitel Marseille Vieux-Port ★★★   This hotel lacks the glamour and style of Petit Nice, but it is the highest rated in the center of the city, a seven-story palace standing above the embankments of the old port. Some of the guest rooms have panoramic views of the port of Old Marseille; others look out on the boulevard. All are fairly generous in size, up-to-date, comfortable, and furnished in Provençal style, with a combination tub/shower. In 1987, its owner, the Accor hotel giant, turned over 90 rooms to a new three-star Novotel (see below). Today, two entrances, staffs, and dining facilities coexist in the same building.

36 bd. Charles-Livon, 13007 Marseille. ℂ **04-91-15-59-00.** Fax 04-91-15-59-50. www.sofitel.com. 130 units. 1,050F–1,980F (159.60– 300.95, \$152.25–\$287.10) double; 3,000F–4,500F (456– 684, \$435–\$652.50) suite. AE, DC, MC, V. Parking 70F (10.65, \$10.15). Métro: Vieux-Port. **Amenities:** Restaurant, bar; room service; laundry/dry cleaning. *In room:* A/C, TV, minibar, hair dryer.

MODERATE

La Résidence du Vieux-Port   This old hotel has a touch of raffish charm and an unbeatable location: directly beside a harbor that was valued by the ancient Phoenicians. The guest rooms have loggia-style terraces opening onto the port; the rooms are simple but serviceable, each with a shower unit.

18 quai du Port, 13001 Marseille. ℂ **04-91-91-91-22.** Fax 04-91-56-60-88. 41 units. 610F–710F (92.70– 107.90, \$88.45–\$102.95) double; 860F–1,250F (130.70– 190, \$124.70–\$181.25) suite. AE, DC, MC, V. Parking 30F (4.55, \$4.35). Métro: Vieux-Port. **Amenities:** Cafe, bar; room service; laundry. *In room:* A/C, TV, minibar.

Novotel Vieux-Port *Value*   This Novotel was carved out of the more upscale Sofitel (see above) in 1987. Services are less extensive, amenities less plush, and spaces are a bit more cramped than at the Sofitel; but since this is one of the most reasonably priced hotels in town, no one seems to mind. The limited number of rooms overlooking the old port tends to fill up first. Each unit is outfitted in a chain-hotel format and comes with a small, well-equipped bathroom with tub/shower. The lattice-decorated restaurant, Côte Jardin, serves basic meals.

36 bd. Charles-Livon, 13007 Marseille. ℂ **04-96-11-41-11.** Fax 04-91-31-15-48. H0911@accor-hotels.com. 90 units. 640F–770F (97.30– 117.05, \$92.80–\$111.65) double. AE, DC, MC, V. Parking 45F (6.85, \$6.55). Métro: Vieux-Port. **Amenities:** Restaurant, bar; room service; laundry. *In room:* A/C, TV, minibar.

INEXPENSIVE

Hôtel Mascotte   Everything about this hotel evokes the grandeur of 19th-century port life in Marseille. It's located less than 2 blocks from the inner sanctums of the Vieux-Port, in the heart of town. The sun and mistrals of many seasons have battered the beaux-arts facade, decorated with ornate corbels and cornices. Inside, renovations have stripped the bedrooms of some of their old-fashioned charm but have left clean, efficient, soundproofed spaces. Each unit has a compact bathroom with shower. Breakfast is the only meal served, but considering the many dining options in the neighborhood, no one seems to care.

5 la Canebière, 13001 Marseille. ℂ **04-91-90-61-61.** Fax 04-91-90-95-61. 45 units. 485F–620F (73.70– 94.25, \$70.35–\$89.90) double. AE, DC, MC, V. Parking in nearby public lot 110F (16.70, \$15.95). *In room:* A/C, TV.

New Hôtel Bompard   This tranquil retreat is atop a cliff along the corniche, about 1½ miles east of Vieux Port. Partly because of its elegant garden, it might remind you of a well-appointed private home. The rooms contain traditional furniture, tasteful, subdued color schemes, and balconies or terraces overlooking the grounds. Each comes with a compact shower-only bathroom.

2 rue des Flots-Bleus, 13007 Marseille. ✆ 04-91-52-10-93. Fax 04-91-31-02-14. www.new-hotel.com. 46 units. 570F–650F (86.65– 98.80, $82.65–$94.25) double. Free parking. Bus: 61 or 83. *In room:* A/C, TV, minibar.

DINING
EXPENSIVE
Note that **L'Hôtel Le Petit Nice** (see "Accommodations," above) has a lovely restaurant.

Le Miramar ✦✦✦ SEAFOOD   Except at Petit Nice (see above), there is no grander dining in Marseille than at Le Miramar. Since the mid-1960s, bouillabaisse aficionados have been flocking here to savor what will surely be a culinary highlight of your trip. It's hard to imagine this was once a rough-and-tumble recipe favored by local fisherfolk, a way of using the least-desirable portion of their catch. Actually it's traditionally two dishes, beginning with a saffron-tinted soup followed by the fish poached in the soup. It's consumed with *une rouille,* a sauce of red chilies, garlic, olive oil, egg yolk, and cayenne. The version served here involves lots of labor and just as much costly seafood; its formula is so successful that the chefs spend part of their year teaching the technique to cooks in seminars as far away as Los Angeles. The setting is a big-windowed room with frescoes of underwater life. It's linked to an outdoor terrace that overlooks Marseille's most famous church, Notre-Dame-de-la-Garde.

12 Quai du Port. ✆ 04-91-91-10-40. Reservations recommended. Main courses 190F–300F (28.90– 45.60, $27.55–$43.50); bouillabaisse 300F (45.60, $43.50) per person (minimum 2 persons). AE, DC, MC, V. Tues–Sat noon–2pm and 7:15–10pm. Closed 2 weeks in Jan and 3 weeks in Aug. Métro: Vieux-Port/Hôtel de Ville.

MODERATE
Au Pescadou ✦ SEAFOOD   One of Marseille's finest seafood restaurants is maintained by three multilingual sons of the original owner, Barthélémy Mennella. Beside a busy traffic circle downtown, it overlooks a fountain, an obelisk, and a sidewalk display of fresh oysters. For an appetizer, try almond-stuffed mussels or "hors d'oeuvres of the fisherman." Main-dish specialties are bouillabaisse, *gigot de lotte* (monkfish stewed in cream sauce with fresh vegetables), and scallops cooked with morels.

19 place Castellane. ✆ 04-91-78-36-01. Reservations recommended. Main courses 78F–122F (11.85– 18.55, $11.30–$17.70); bouillabaisse 238F (36.20, $34.50) per person; fixed-price menus 188F (28.60, $27.25). AE, MC, V. Mon–Sat noon–2pm and 7–11pm; Sun noon–2pm. Closed July–Aug. Métro: Castellane.

Les Arcenaulx ✦ *Finds* PROVENÇAL   This is a dining oddity with a memorable cuisine. The stone premises, near the Vieux Port, were warehouses built by the navies of Louis XIV; they now contain this restaurant as well as two bookstores, all run by the charming sisters Simone and Jeanne Laffitte. Look for authentic Provençal cuisine with a Marseillais accent in such dishes as *baudroie* (kettle of seasonal fish) *à la Raimu*—named for a popular actor, it's equivalent to bouillabaisse. Equally tempting are artichokes *barigoule* (loaded with aromatic spices and olive oil), duckling with caramelized quince, and a worthy assortment of *petites légumes farcies* (Provençal vegetables stuffed with chopped meat and herbs).

25 cours d'Estienne d'orves. ✆ 04-91-59-80-30. Reservations recommended. Main courses 70F–110F (10.65– 16.70, $10.15–$15.95); fixed-price menus 155F–295F (23.55– 44.85, $22.50–$42.80). AE, DC, MC, V. Mon–Sat noon–2pm and 8–11:30pm. Métro: Vieux-Port.

Les Echevins PROVENÇAL/SOUTHWESTERN FRENCH   On the oppo-site side of the building from Les Arcenaulx (see above), this restaurant occupies what was built as a dorm for the prisoners forced to row the ornamental barges of Louis XIV during his inspections of Marseille's harbor facilities. Today, the setting contains crystal chandeliers, plush carpets, an enviable collection of antiques, and massive rocks and thick beams. You'll get a lot for your money, as the owners charge relatively reasonable prices and insist on using fresh ingredi-ents. Provençal dishes include a succulent version of baked sea wolf that's pre-pared as simply as possible—with herbs and olive oil. There's also roast codfish with aïoli and a delicious *baudroie* (a simpler bouillabaisse). Desserts usually include roasted figs served with sweet dessert wine.

44 rue Sainte. (? **04-96-11-03-11.** Reservations recommended. Main courses 115F–195F (17.50– 29.65, $16.70–$28.30); fixed-price menus 135F–280F (20.50– 42.55, $19.60–$40.60). AE, DC, MC, V. Mon–Fri noon–2:30pm and 7:30–11:30pm; Sat 7:30–11:30pm. Métro: Vieux-Port.

INEXPENSIVE

Ducs de Gascogne *Value* SOUTHWESTERN FRENCH   Popular and brisk, this restaurant thrives on the lunchtime business generated by the many chic boutiques in this commercial neighborhood near the Vieux Port. In an ochre dining room lined with red banquettes, guests enjoy a bistro-style cuisine that originates in the southwestern region of France. The menu is loaded with goose and duck specialties that many French diners associate with their grandmothers. Examples include confit of duckling, several preparations of foie gras, and fresh pasta with foie gras. Especially succulent is a heaping platter of duck and goose confits, rillettes, sausages, and liver, inspired by the Gers region of France.

39 rue Paradis, 1er. (? **04-91-33-87-28.** Reservations not necessary. Main courses 62F–115F (9.40– 17.50, $9–$16.70), set-price menu 80F (12.15, $11.60). AE, DC, V. Mon–Sat noon–2pm. Métro: Vieux Port or Estrangin.

Toinou SEAFOOD   Set in a massive building that overshadows every other structure nearby, this landmark restaurant serves more shellfish than any other restaurant in Marseille. Inside, a display of more than 40 different species of shellfish is laid out for the view of some of the canniest judges of seafood in France. Dining rooms are on three separate floors, served by a waitstaff who are very entrenched in their *marseillais* accents and demeanors. Don't come here unless you're really fond of shellfish, any species of which can be served raw or cooked. A dozen bivalved creatures, artfully arranged on a platter, will cost from 28F to 140F (4.25 to 21.30, $4.05 to $20.30). The wine list is extensive, with attractively priced whites from such regions as the Loire Valley.

3 cours St-Louis, 1er. (? **04-91-33-14-94.** Reservations recommended. Main courses 65F–85F (9.90– 12.90, $9.45–$12.35); set-price shellfish platter for 2 persons 240F (36.50, $34.80). DC, MC, V. Daily 11:30am–3pm and 6:30–11pm (to midnight Fri–Sat). Métro: Vieux Port.

MARSEILLE AFTER DARK

You can get an amusing (and relatively harmless) exposure to the town's saltiness during a walk around the **Vieux Port,** where a medley of cafes and restaurants angle their sightlines for the best view of the harbor. Select any that strikes your fancy (or just park yourself by the waterfront for a view of the passing parade).

Escale Borély, avenue Mendès-France, is a modern-day equivalent of the Vieux Port. It's a waterfront development south of the town center, only 20 min-utes away by Métro. About a dozen cafes as well as restaurants of every possible ilk present a wide choice of cuisines, plus views of in-line skaters on the prome-nade in front and the potential for dialogues with friendly strangers.

Unless the air-conditioning is powerful, Marseille's dance clubs produce a lot of sweat. The best of them is the **Café de la Plage,** in the Escale Borély (© **04-91-71-21-76**), where a 35-and-under crowd dances in an environment that's safer and healthier than many of the competitors'. Closer to the Vieux Port, you can dance and drink at the **Metal Café,** 20 rue Fortia (© **04-91-54-03-03**), where 20- to 50-year-olds listen to music that's been recently released in London and Los Angeles; or try the nearby **Trolley Bus,** 24 quai de Rive-Neuve (© **04-91-54-30-45**), best known for its techno, house, hip-hop, jazz, and salsa. Also very appealing, if only because people here seem to have more fun than at the usual run-of-the-mill pastis dive, is **Pêle-Mêle,** 8 place aux Huiles (© **04-91-54-85-26**), a many-faceted bar/disco/cafe and host of occasional live music.

If you miss free-form modern jazz and don't mind taking your chances in the less-than-completely-savory neighborhood adjacent to the city's rail station (La Gare St-Charles—a taxi here and back is recommended), consider dropping into **La Cave à Jazz,** rue Bernard-du-Bois (© **04-91-39-28-28**).

A cabaret that presents sexy performers, broad humor, and occasional political satire is **Le Chocolat Théâtre,** 59 cours Julien (© **04-91-42-19-29**), which also involves a restaurant. The venue and hours change weekly, so phone in advance.

The gay scene here isn't as interesting as it is in Nice, though there are a number of gay bars. **MP Bar,** 10 rue Beauveau (© **04-91-33-64-79**), is *le gay bar* in Marseille. It's open nightly from 6pm to sunrise. The youth-conscious **New Can Can,** 3–5 rue Sénac (© **04-91-48-59-76**), is an enormous venue that is everybody's favorite dance spot Thursday through Sunday from around 11pm to dawn. An alternative gay bar and disco, located in the sultry and central neighborhood near the Vieux Port, is **Le Crazy,** rue du Chantier (no phone). Customers here have known each other since forever, and a sailor or student from abroad will probably not buy his own drinks for very long. Its bar area and dance floor are especially busy every night from around 3am to sunrise.

8 Toulon

519 miles S of Paris, 79 miles SW of Cannes, 42 miles E of Marseille

This fortress and town is the principal naval base of France: the headquarters of the Mediterranean fleet, with hundreds of sailors wandering the streets. It's not as seedy, but also not as intriguing, as Marseilles. A beautiful harbor, it's surrounded by hills and crowned by forts, protected on the east by a breakwater and on the west by the great peninsula of Cap Sicié. The outer roads are known as the Grande Rade and the inner roads the Petite Rade. A winter resort colony lies on the outskirts. Like Marseilles, Toulon has a large Arab population. Note that there's racial tension here, worsened by the closing of the shipyards.

Park your car underground at place de la Liberté, then go along boulevard des Strasbourg, turning right onto rue Berthelot. This will take you into the pedestrian-only area in the core of the old city. It's filled with shops, hotels, restaurants, and cobblestone streets (but it can be dangerous at night). The best beach, **Plage du Mourillon,** is 1¼ miles east of the heart of town.

ESSENTIALS

GETTING THERE & GETTING AROUND **Trains** arrive from Marseille about every 30 minutes (trip time: 1 hr.). If you're on the Riviera, frequent trains arrive from Nice (trip time: 2 hr.) and Cannes (trip time: 80 min.). For rail information and schedules, call © **08-36-35-35-35.**

Three **buses** per day arrive from Aix-en-Provence (trip time: 75 min.). For information and schedules, call either **Cie Sodetrav** (© **04-94-12-55-12**) or **Littoral Cars** (© **04-94-74-01-35**).

If you're **driving** from Marseille, take A50 east to Toulon. When you arrive, park your car and get around on foot, as the *vieille ville* (old town) and most attractions are easy to reach. A municipal **bus** system serves the town as well. Tickets cost 8F (1.20, $1.15); a bus map is available at the tourist office.

VISITOR INFORMATION The **Office de Tourisme** is at place Raimu (© **04-94-18-53-00;** www.toulontourisme.com).

EXPLORING THE TOWN

In **Vieux Toulon,** between the harbor and boulevard des Strasbourg (the main axis of town), are many remains of the port's former days. Visit the **Poissonerie,** the covered market, bustling in the morning with fishmongers and buyers. Another colorful market, the **Marché,** spills over onto the streets around cours Lafayette. Also in old Toulon is the **Cathédrale Ste-Marie-Majeure,** built in the Romanesque style in the 11th and 12th centuries, then expanded in the 17th. Its badly lit nave is Gothic; the belfry and facade are from the 18th century. It's open daily from 8am to noon and 2 to 6pm.

In contrast to the cathedral, tall modern buildings line quai Stalingrad, opening onto **Vieille d'Arse.** On place Puget, look for the *atlantes* (caryatids), figures of men used as columns. These interesting figures support a balcony at the **Hôtel de Ville** (city hall) and are also included in the facade of the naval museum.

Musée de la Marine, place du Ingénieur-Général-Monsenergue (© **04-94-02-02-01**), contains figureheads and ship models. It's open in July and August, Wednesday through Monday from 10am to 6pm; September to June, Wednesday through Monday from 9:30am to noon and 2 to 6pm. Admission is 29F (4.40, $4.20) for adults and 19F (2.90, $2.75) for students and children.

Musée de Toulon, 113 bd. du Maréchal-Leclerc (© **04-94-36-81-00**), displays works from the 16th century to the present. There's a good collection of Provençal and Italian paintings, as well as religious works. The latest acquisitions include New Realism pieces and minimalist art. It's open daily from 1 to 6pm; admission is free.

Once you've covered the top attractions, we suggest taking a drive, an hour or two before sunset, along the **corniche du Mont-Faron.** It's a scenic boulevard along the lower slopes of Mont Faron, providing views of the busy port, the town, the cliffs, and, in the distance, the Mediterranean.

Earlier in the day, consider boarding a **téléphérique** (funicular) near the Altéa La Tour Blanche Hôtel (© **04-94-92-68-25**). It operates Tuesday through Sunday from 9:30 to 11:45am and 2:15 to 6:30pm; the round-trip cost is 38F (5.80, $5.50) for adults and 25F (3.80, $3.65) for children. It is not in service during windy conditions. At the top, enjoy the view and then visit the **Memorial du Débarquement en Provence,** Mont Faron (© **04-94-88-08-09**), which documents the Allied landings in Provence in 1944, among other exhibits. It's open in summer, daily from 9:30 to 11:45am and 2:30 to 5:45pm in winter, Tuesday through Sunday from 9:15 to 11:45am and 2 to 4:45pm. Admission is 25F (3.80, $3.65) for adults, 10F (1.50, $1.45) for children 5 to 12.

ACCOMMODATIONS

New Hôtel Tour Blanche   With excellent accommodations, attractive gardens with terraces, and a pool, this 1970s hotel is the best in Toulon. It lies in the hills about a mile north of the center of town, which gives it sweeping views of the port and sea from even the lower floors. Many rooms, especially those overlooking the bay, have balconies, and all are comfortably and simply outfitted in an international modern style. Showers are found in the compact bathrooms, but only a few have tub/showers. The restaurant, Les Terrasses, offers a panoramic view, fixed-price menus at 98F to 190F (14.90 to 28.90, $14.20 to $27.55), and food and wine whose selection is inspired by the culinary traditions of Provence and the Midi.

Bd. de l'Amiral-Vence, 83200 Toulon. ℂ **04-94-24-41-57.** Fax 04-94-22-42-25. www.new-hotel.com. 91 units. 460F–610F (69.90– 92.70, $66.70–$88.45) double. AE, DC, MC, V. Free parking. Bus: 40. From the town center, follow signs to the Mont Faron téléphérique and you'll pass the hotel en route. **Amenities:** Restaurant, bar; outdoor pool; room service; laundry. *In room:* A/C, TV, minibar, hair dryer.

DINING

La Chamade ✿✿✿ SOUTHERN FRENCH   The cuisine here is memorable, and the restaurant the finest for miles. It's located in the town center, in a nondescript building whose thick walls hint at its age. The chef, Francis Bonneau, is the disciple of some of the grandest restaurants of Paris and Brittany. He offers diners only one option: a fixed-price menu that includes an ever-changing choice of three appetizers, three main courses, and three desserts. Menu items change with the seasons but might include terrine of caramelized foie gras with dried fruit, an entire roasted pigeon prepared with lavender and Provençal honey, stuffed and deep-fried zucchini blossoms, sea bass with basil-flavored butter sauce, and risotto with local herbs. Desserts often include a craqueline of dates served with gentian, a herb that flourishes on Provence's hillsides, or frozen custard garnished with local strawberries marinated in red wine.

25 rue Denfert-Rochereau. ℂ **04-94-92-28-58.** Reservations recommended. Fixed-price menu 195F (29.65, $28.30). AE, MC, V. Mon–Fri noon–2:30pm and 7–9:30pm; Sat 7–9:30pm. Closed Aug 1–25. Bus: 1 or 21.

TOULON AFTER DARK

A town that's the temporary home of thousands sailors is bound to have a nightlife scene that's earthier, and a bit raunchier, than equivalent-sized towns elsewhere. A rough-and-ready bar that sports stiff drinks, live music, and a complete lack of pretension is **Le Bar 113,** 113 av. de Infanterie de la Marine (ℂ **04-94-03-42-41**). Adjacent to the port is the **Bar La Lampa,** Port de Toulon (ℂ **04-94-03-06-09**), where tapas and live music accompany copious amounts of beer and glasses of wine or whiskey. An even less formal hangout is **Bar à Thym,** 32 bd. Cuneo (ℂ **04-94-41-90-10**), where everybody seems to drink beer, gossip, and listen to live music.

Toulon is also home to one of the Azure Coast's best-known gay discos, **Boy's Paradise,** 1 bd. Pierre-Toesca (ℂ **04-94-09-35-90**), near the city's train station.

If you feel claustrophobic and want more resorty outlets, you might be happy at Hyère, about 16 miles east of Toulon, where there's an upscale disco, **Le Fou du Roy,** in the Casino des Palmiers (ℂ **04-94-12-80-80**). About 9 miles west of Toulon, in the port town of Sanary, **Mai-Tai,** route de Bandol (ℂ **04-94-74-23-92**), appeals to dancers under age 30.

16

The French Riviera

Each resort on the Riviera, known as the Côte d'Azur (Azure Coast), offers its own unique flavor and charms. This narrow strip of fabled real estate, less than 125 miles long located between the Mediterranean and a trio of mountain ranges, has always attracted the jet set with its clear skies, blue waters, and orange groves.

A trail of modern artists captivated by the brilliant light and setting of the Côte d'Azur has left a rich heritage: Matisse at Vence, Cocteau at Menton and Villefranche, Picasso at Antibes and seemingly everywhere else, Léger at Biot, Renoir at Cagnes, and Bonnard at Le Cannet. The best collection of all is at the Maeght Foundation in St-Paul-de-Vence.

The Riviera's high season used to be winter and spring only. In recent years, however, July and August have become the most crowded, and reservations are imperative. The average summer temperature is 75°F and average winter temperature 49°F.

The corniches of the Riviera, depicted in countless films, stretch from Nice to Menton. The Alps here drop into the Mediterranean, and roads were carved along the way. The lower road, 20 miles long, is the Corniche Inférieure. Along this road are the ports of Villefranche, Cap-Ferrat, Beaulieu, and Cap-Martin. The 19-mile Moyenne Corniche (Middle Road), built between World War I and World War II, runs from Nice to Menton, winding spectacularly in and out of tunnels and through mountains. The highlight is at mountaintop Eze. The Grande Corniche—the most panoramic—was built by Napoléon in 1806. La Turbie and Le Vistaero are the principal towns along the 20-mile stretch, which reaches more than 1,600 feet high at Col d'Eze.

Note: For more extensive coverage of this region, check out the book *Frommer's Provence & the Riviera.*

REGIONAL CUISINE In the 19th century a coastal strip of eastern Provence was deemed "the Riviera." Technically, the Riviera is part of Provence, and the culinary traditions of that region (see chapter 15) apply here, in slightly diluted forms.

On the Riviera you'll find high-toned bastions of French cuisine alongside budget joints catering to the latest culinary fads, juxtaposed in sometimes-uncomfortable proximity. The Riviera has more different types of restaurants and greater numbers of theme restaurants than anywhere else in France save Paris. So expect to find Provençal cuisine, with a generous dose of international sophistication.

1 St-Tropez ★★

543 miles S of Paris, 47 miles SW of Cannes

An air of hedonism runs rampant in this sun-kissed carnival town, but the true Tropezian resents the fact that the port has such a bad reputation. "We can be classy too," one native has insisted. Creative people in the lively arts along with ordinary folk create a varied mixture.

⎛ *Tips* **Surfing on the Riviera**

Before your tour of the Côte d'Azur, check out the website **www.crt-riviera.fr**. Activities are arranged by season, so you can get an idea of where you might like to go hiking, biking, or sunbathing. You can also get a **Carte Musée Côte d'Azur**, a pass good at 62 museums on the Riviera.

Brigitte Bardot's *And God Created Woman* put St-Tropez on the tourist map, but it has a history as well. Colette lived here for years. Even the diarist Anaïs Nin, confidante of Henry Miller, posed for a little cheesecake on the beach here in 1939 in a Dorothy Lamour–style bathing suit.

Artists, composers, novelists, and the film colony are attracted to St-Tropez in summer. Trailing them is a flamboyant parade of humanity unmatched anywhere on the Riviera. Some of the most fashionable yachts, bearing some of the most chic people, anchor here in summer, disappearing before the mistral of winter.

In 1995, Bardot pronounced St-Tropez dead—"squatted by a lot of no-goods, drugheads, and villains." She swore she'd never go back, at least in summer. But 1997 saw her return, as headlines in France announced that St-Tropez was "hot once again." Not only Bardot but other celebrities have been showing up, including Oprah, Quincy Jones, Barbra Streisand, Jack Nicholson, Robert De Niro, and even Elton and Sly (not together!).

ESSENTIALS

GETTING THERE   The nearest rail station is in St-Raphaël, a neighboring resort; at the Vieux Port, four or five **boats** per day leave the **Gare Maritime de St-Raphaël,** rue Pierre-Auble (*©* **04-94-95-17-46**), for St-Tropez (trip time: 50 minutes), costing 60F (9.10, $8.70) each way. Some 15 Sodetrav **buses** per day, leave from the Gare Routière in St-Raphaël (*©* **04-94-95-24-82**) and go to St-Tropez, taking 1½ to 2¼ hours, depending on the bus and the traffic, which during midsummer is usually horrendous. A one-way ticket costs 55F (8.35, $8). Buses run directly to St-Tropez from Toulon and Hyères. Buses also run directly to St-Tropez from its nearest airport, the airport at Toulon-Hyères, 35 miles away.

If you **drive,** note that parking in St-Tropez is very difficult, especially in summer. In 1998, of the situation was slightly relieved with the construction of a multistoried **Parc des Lices** (*©* **04-94-97-34-46**), beneath place des Lices, whose entrance is on avenue Paul-Roussel. Designed for 471 cars, this parking lot charges 8F to 13F (1.20 to 2.00, $1.15 to $1.90) per hour, depending on the season. Many visitors with expensive cars prefer this site, as it's more carefully guarded than any other lot. If you don't use it, you'll have to squeeze your car into tiny parking spaces wherever you can find them. **To get here from Cannes,** drive southwest along the coastal highway (RD98), turning eastward when you see the signs pointing to St-Tropez.

VISITOR INFORMATION   The **Office de Tourisme** is on quai Jean-Jaurès (*©* **04-94-97-45-21;** www.nova.fr/saint-tropez).

A DAY AT THE BEACH

The hottest Riviera beaches are at St-Tropez. The best for families are those closest to the center, including the **Plage de la Bouillabaisse** and **Plage des Graniers.** The more daring are the 6-mile sandy crescents at **Plage des Salins**

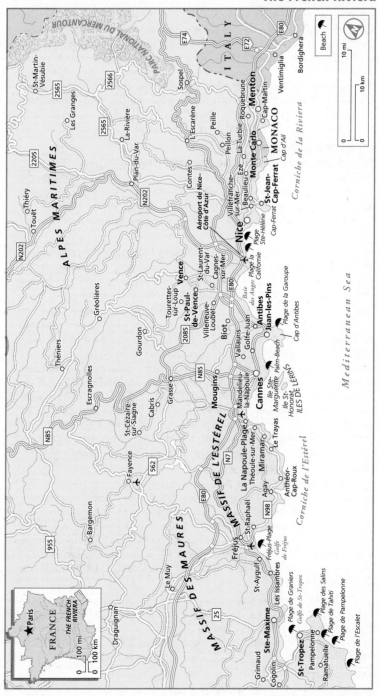

Beach

PARC NATIONAL DU MERCANTOUR

ITALY

Corniche de la Riviera

Mediterranean Sea

ALPES MARITIMES

MASSIF DE L'ESTÉREL

Corniche de l'Estérel

MASSIF DES MAURES

St-Martin-Vésubie

Sospel

E74

E72

E80

Menton
Ventimiglia
Bordighera

Roquebrune
La Turbie
Cap-Martin
MONACO
Monte-Carlo
Beaulieu-sur-Mer
Èze
St-Jean-Cap-Ferrat
Cap-Ferrat
Cap d'Ail

Les Granges

2566

2565

2565

La-Rivière
L'Escarène
Peille
Peillon
Peillon

Contes

Plan-du-Var

2205

N202

Thiéry
Touët

Aéroport de Nice-Côte d'Azur

Villefranche-sur-Mer

Nice

N202

St-Laurent-du-Var
Cagnes-sur-Mer

Plage Ste-Hélène
Plage la Californie

N202

Vence
Tourettes-sur-Loup
St-Paul-de-Vence

Baie des Anges

Plage la Garoupe

Gréolières

Villeneuve-Loubet
Biot

2085

Antibes
Juan-les-Pins
Cap d'Antibes

Théniers

Gourdon

Vallauris
Golfe-Juan

Palm-Beach
Plage
Ile Ste-Marguerite
Ile St-Honorat
ÎLES DE LÉRINS

Escragnolles

Grasse

N85

Mougins

Cannes

Mandelieu-la-Napoule

St-Cézaire-sur-Siagne
Cabris

N85

N85

Fayence

562

N7

La Napoule-Plage
Théoule-sur-Mer
Miramar
Le Trayas
Agay
Anthéor-Cap-Roux

E80

Bargemon

E80

N98

St-Raphaël
Fréjus

955

Le Muy

St-Aygulf

Fréjus-Plage
Golfe de Fréjus

Les Issambres

25

Draguignan

Ste-Maxime

Plage de Graniers
Golfe de St-Tropez
Plage des Salins
Plage de Tahiti

St-Tropez
Pampelonne
Plage de Pampelonne

Grimaud
Cogolin

Ramatuelle

Plage de l'Escalet

10 mi
10 km

and **Plage de Pampellone,** beginning some 2 miles from the town center and best reached by bike (see below) if you're not driving. Called "notoriously decadent," **Plage de Tahiti** occupies the north end of the 3½-mile-long Pampellone, lined with concessions, cafes, and restaurants. It's a strip of golden sand that has long been favored by exhibitionists wearing next to nothing (or nothing) and cruising shamelessly. If you ever wanted to go topless, this is the place to do it. Gay men tend to gravitate to **Coco Beach** in Ramatuelle, about 4 miles from the center of St-Tropez. Here a bar and restaurant, Le Coco Beach, rte. de l'Epi, Ramatuelle (© **04-94-79-83-25**), serve drinks and platters throughout the day.

OUTDOOR PURSUITS

BICYCLING & MOTOR-SCOOTERING   The largest outfitter for bikes and motor scooters is **Louis Mas,** 5 rue Josef-Quaranta (© **04-94-97-00-60**). You'll be required to leave a deposit of 1,000F (152, $145), payable with a major credit card, plus 48F (7.30, $6.95) per hour for a bike, 190F to 275F (28.90 to 41.80, $27.55 to $39.90) per hour for a motor scooter, depending on its size.

BOATING   The highly recommended **Suncap Company,** 15 quai de Suffren (© **04-94-97-11-23**), rents boats from 18 to 40 feet long. The smallest can be rented to qualified sailors without a captain, but the larger ones come with a captain at the helm. Prices begin at 3,000F (456, $435) per day.

GOLF   The nearest golf course, at the edge of Ste-Maxime, across the bay from St-Tropez, is the **Golf Club de Beauvallon,** boulevard des Collines (© **04-94-96-16-98**), a popular 18-hole course. Greens fees for 18 holes are 250F to 300F (38 to 45.60, $36.25 to $43.50) per person.

Sprawling over a rocky, vertiginous landscape that requires a golf cart and a lot of exertion is the Don Harradine–designed **Golf de Ste-Maxime-Plaza,** rte. du Débarquement, Ste-Maxime (© **04-94-55-02-02**). Built in 1991 with the four-star Plaza de Ste-Maxime, it welcomes nonguests; phone to reserve tee times. Greens fees for 18 holes are 250F to 300F (38 to 45.60, $36.25 to $43.50) per person; cart rental (capacity of two) is 125F (19, $18.15) per 18 holes.

SCUBA DIVING   A team of dive enthusiasts who are ready, willing, and able to show you the watery azure-colored depths off the coast of St-Tropez operate from the *Octopussy I* and *II.* Both are aluminum-sided, yellow-painted dive boats, built in the 1990s. They're based year-round in St-Tropez's Nouveau Port. Experienced divers pay 180F (27.35, $26.10) for a one-tank *"exploration"* dive, and novices are charged 280F (42.55, $40.60) for a *baptême,* that includes one-on-one supervision and a descent to a depth of around 15 feet; you have to have a license to dive here. For reservations and information, call or write Les *Octopussys,* Quartier de Berteau, Gassin, 83990 St-Tropez (© **04-94-56-53-10;** fax 04-94-56-46-59).

TENNIS   Anyone who phones in advance can use the eight courts (both artificial grass and "Quick," a form of concrete) at the **Tennis-Club de St-Tropez,** rte. des Plages, in St-Claude (© **04-94-97-15-52**), about half a mile from the resort's center. Open all the year, the courts rent for 100F (15.20, $14.50) per hour, 10am to 5pm, and 130F (19.75, $18.85) per hour after 5pm.

SHOPPING

Choses, quai Jean-Jaurès (© **04-94-97-03-44**), is a women's clothing store typical (but stocked better than some) of the many middle-bracket shops along the Riviera. Its specialty is clingy and often provocative T-shirt dresses. **Galeries**

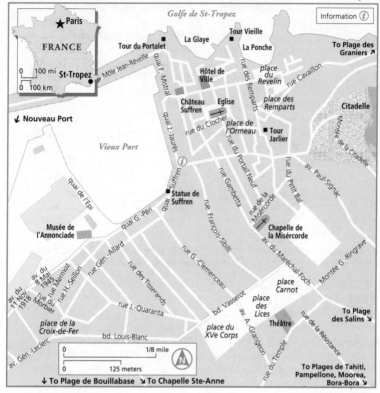

Golfe de St-Tropez

Paris

FRANCE

St-Tropez

0   100 mi
0   100 km

Information ⓘ

Tour Vieille
La Glaye
Tour du Portalet
La Ponche

To Plage des
Graniers ↗

Môle Jean-Réveille

quai F.-Mistral

Hôtel de
Ville

place
du
Revelin

rue Cavaillon

↙ Nouveau Port

Château
Suffren

Eglise

rue des Remparts

place des
Remparts

Citadelle

rue du Clocher

place de
l'Ormeau

Tour
Jarlier

Montée de la Citadelle

Vieux Port

quai J.-Jaurès

rue du Portail Neuf

ⓘ

av. Paul-Signac

quai de l'Epi

quai Suffren

Statue de
Suffren

rue Gambetta

rue de la
Misércorde

rue du Petit Bal

Musée de
l'Annonciade

quai G.-Péri

rue François-Sibilli

Chapelle de
la Misércorde

av. du Maréchal-Foch

Montée G.-Ringrave

rue Gén.-Allard

rue des Tisserands

rue G.-Clemenceau

place
Carnot

av. du
11 Nov.
1918

av. du
8 Mar
1945

rue du
Moralier

rue Mermoz

rue H.-Seillon

rue J.-Quaranta

bd. Vasserot

place
des
Lices

rue de la Résistance

To Plage
des Salins ↘

place de la
Croix-de-Fer

bd. Louis-Blanc

place du
XVe Corps

av. A.-Grangeon

Théâtre

av. Gén.-Leclerc

0   1/8 mile
0   125 meters

N

rue du Temple

To Plages de Tahiti,
Pampellone, Moorea,
Bora-Bora ↘

↓ To Plage de Bouillabase   ↘ To Chapelle Ste-Anne

Tropéziennes, 56 rue Gambetta (ⓒ **04-94-97-02-21**), crowds hundreds of unusual gift items—some worthwhile, some silly—into its showrooms near place des Lices. The inspiration is Mediterranean, breezy, and sophisticated.

In a resort that's increasingly loaded with purveyors of suntan lotion, touristy souvenirs, and T-shirts, **Jacqueline Thienot,** 12 rue Georges-Clemenceau (ⓒ **04-94-97-05-70**), maintains an inventory of Provençal antiques that's prized by dealers from as far away as Paris. The one-room shop is in a late-18th-century building that shows the 18th- and 19th-century antiques to their best advantage. Also sold are antique examples of Provençal wrought iron and rustic farm and homemaker's implements.

EXPLORING THE CITY

Château Suffren is east of the port at the top end of quai Jean-Jaurès. Home to occasional art exhibits, it was built in A.D. 980 by Comte Guillame I of Provence.

Near the junction of quai Suffren and quai Jean-Jaurès stands the bronze **Statue de Suffren,** paying tribute to Vice-Admiral Pierre André de Suffren. This St-Tropez native became one of the greatest sailors of 18th-century France, though he's largely forgotten today. In the Vieille Ville, one of the most interesting streets is **rue de la Misércorde.** It's lined with stone houses with artsy boutiques. This street evokes medieval St-Tropez better than any other in town.

At the corner of rue Gambetta is the **Chapelle de la Misércorde,** with a blue, green, and gold tile roof.

Two miles from St-Tropez, **Port Grimaud** ✮ makes an interesting outing. From St-Tropez, drive 3 miles west on A98 to Route 98, then 1 mile north to the Port Grimaud exit. If you approach the village at dusk, when it's bathed in Riviera pastels, it'll look like a hamlet from the 16th century. But this is a mirage. Port Grimaud is the dream fulfillment of its promoter, François Spoerry, who carved it out of marshland and dug canals. Flanking these canals, fingers of land extend from the main square to the sea. The homes are Provençal style, many with Italianate window arches. Boat owners can anchor at their doorsteps. One newspaper called the port "the most magnificent fake since Disneyland."

Musée de l'Annonciade (Musée St-Tropez) ✮✮   Near the harbor, this museum was installed in the former chapel of the Annonciade. It boasts one of the Riviera's finest modern art collections. Many of the artists, including Paul Signac, depicted the port of St-Tropez. The collection includes such works as Van Dongen's *Women of the Balustrade* and paintings and sculpture by Bonnard, Matisse, Braque, Dufy, Utrillo, Seurat, Derain, and Maillol.

Place Grammont. ☎ **04-94-97-04-01.** Admission 30F (4.55, $4.35) adults, 15F (2.30, $2.20) children. June–Sept Wed–Mon 10am–noon and 3–7pm; Oct and Dec–May Wed–Mon 10am–noon and 2–6pm.

ACCOMMODATIONS
VERY EXPENSIVE

Hôtel Byblos ✮✮✮   The builder said he created "an anti-hotel, a place like home." That's true if your home resembles a palace in Beirut with salons decorated with Phoenician gold statues from 3000 B.C. On a hill above the harbor, this complex boasts intimate patios and courtyards and retreats filled with antiques and rare objects like polychrome carved woodwork, marquetry floors, and a Persian-rug ceiling. Every room is unique. Unusual features, might be a fireplace on a raised hearth or a bed recessed on a dais. The rooms range from medium to spacious, often with high ceilings and antiques or reproductions and each with a luxury mattress on an elegant French bed. Some units have such special features as four-posters with furry spreads or sunken whirlpool baths. Le Hameau contains 10 duplex suites built around a small courtyard with an outdoor spa. Some rooms have balconies overlooking an inner courtyard; others open onto a terrace of flowers.

You can dine by the pool at Les Arcades, enjoying Provençal food, or try an Italian restaurant offering typical fare from France's neighbor. Later in the evening you can dance on a circular floor surrounded by bas-relief columns in the hotel's nightclub, Caves du Roy.

Av. Paul-Signac, 83990 St-Tropez. ☎ **800/223-6800** in the U.S. or Canada, or 04-94-56-68-00. Fax 04-94-56-68-01. www.byblos.com. 98 units, 10 duplex suites. 1,770F–4,590F (269.05– 697.70, $256.65–$665.55) double; from 3,800F (577.60, $551) junior suite; from 4,900F (744.80, $710.50) duplex suite. AE, DC, MC, V. Closed Oct 15–Easter. Parking 180F (27.35, $26.10) in garage. **Amenities:** 2 restaurants, 2 bars, nightclub; pool; spa; room service; massage; laundry/dry cleaning;. *In room:* A/C, TV, mini-bar, hair dryer, safe.

Hôtel Le Yaca ✮   Life here is called *la dolce vita.* Built in 1722 off a narrow street in the old part of town, this was the first hotel in St-Tropez. Colette lived here in 1927, and before that it was the home of pre-impressionists like Paul Signac. The high-ceilinged reception area boasts a view of an inner courtyard filled with flowers. Many rooms also have views of this courtyard; each was renovated in 2000. Some are on the upper floor, with terra-cotta floor tiles and massive ceiling timbers. Each has a comfortable bed, utilitarian furniture, and high ceilings, plus a roomy bath.

1 bd. d'Aumale, 83900 St-Tropez. © 04-94-55-81-00. Fax 04-94-97-58-50. www.hotel-le-yaca.fr. 27 units. 1,300F–2,900F (197.60– 440.80E, $188.50–$420.50) double; 3,600F–3,900F (547.20– 592.80, $522–$565.50) suite. AE, DC, MC, V. Closed mid-Oct to Easter. Parking 100F (15.20, $14.50). **Amenities:** Restaurant, bar; pool; room service; massage; baby-sitting; laundry/dry cleaning. *In room:* A/C, TV, minibar, hair dryer, safe.

EXPENSIVE

Hôtel La Ponche ★★ The same family has run this hotel overlooking the old fishing port for more than half a century. It's filled with the original airy paintings of Jacques Cordier, which adds to the elegant atmosphere. Each room has been newly redecorated and is well equipped, opening onto sea views. There are two or three rooms per floor. Sun-colored walls with subtle lighting evoke a homelike feeling. The beds are elegantly appointed with beautiful linen and quality mattresses, and the midsize to large bathrooms either come with a combination tub and shower or only a shower.

3 rue des Remparts, 83990 St-Tropez. © 04-94-97-02-53. Fax 04-94-97-78-61. www.laponche.com. 18 units. 820F–2,000F (124.65– 304E, $118.90–$290) double; 1,800F–2,800F (273.60– 425.60, $261–$406) suite. AE, MC, V. Closed Nov–Mar 15. **Amenities:** Restaurant, bar; pool; room service; laundry/dry cleaning. *In room:* A/C, TV, minibar, hair dryer, safe.

MODERATE

Hôtel Ermitage Attractively isolated amid the rocky heights of St-Tropez, this hotel was built in the 19th century as a private villa. Today its red-tile roof and green shutters shelter a plush hideaway. A walled garden is illuminated at night, and a corner bar near a wood-burning fireplace takes the chill out of blustery evenings. The small guest rooms are pleasantly but simply furnished, each with a compact shower-only bathroom. Breakfast is the only meal served.

Av. Paul-Signac, 83990 St-Tropez. © 04-94-97-52-33. Fax 04-94-97-10-43. 26 units. 490F–990F (74.50– 150.50, $71.05–$143.55) double. AE, DC, MC, V. **Amenities:** Bar; room service; baby-sitting; laundry/dry cleaning. *In room:* TV, hair dryer.

Hôtel La Tartane This small-scale hotel is between the center of St-Tropez and the Plage des Salins, about a 3-minute drive from each. There's a heated stone-rimmed pool in the garden, attractively furnished public rooms with terracotta floors, and an attentive management that works hard. The midsize guest rooms are bungalows surrounding the pool. Each comes with a small tiled bathroom with shower stall. Breakfasts are elaborate and attractive.

Rte. des Salins, 83990 St-Tropez. © 04-94-97-21-23. Fax 04-94-97-09-16. 16 units. 450F–1,000F (68.40– 152, $65.25–$145) double. AE, DC, V. Closed Oct–Mar. **Amenities:** Restaurant, bar; pool; baby-sitting; laundry/dry cleaning. *In room:* A/C, TV, minibar, safe.

Hôtel Sube If you want to be right on the port, this might be your first choice. It's directly over the Café de Paris in the center of a shopping arcade. The two-story lounge has a beamed ceiling and a glass front, allowing a great view of the harbor. The rooms aren't large but are comfortable and decorated in a provincial style. The more expensive units have nice views overlooking the port. Each comes with a private bathroom with a shower stall.

15 quai Suffren, 83900 St-Tropez. © 04-94-97-30-04. Fax 04-94-54-89-08. 30 units. 590F–1,500F (89.70– 228, $85.55–$217.50) double in high season; 390F–990F (59.30– 150.50, $56.55–$143.55) double in low season. AE, DC, MC, V. Parking nearby 200F (30.40, $29) in summer. Free in winter. **Amenities:** Restaurant/café, bar; room service. *In room:* A/C, TV.

DINING

Chez Maggi ★★ PROVENÇAL/ITALIAN This is St. Tropez's most flamboyant gay restaurant and bar but draws straight diners and drinkers as well. At least half its floor space is devoted to a busy bar, where patrons tend to range from 20 to 60. There are no tables in front. Consequently, cruising at Chez Maggi, in the words of loyal patrons, is *très crazée* and seems to extend for blocks in every direction, spilling over into the confines of Chez Joseph. Meals are served in an adjoining dining room. Menu items include chicken salad with ginger, goat-cheese salad, *petits farcis provençaux* (vegetables stuffed with minced meat and herbs), brochettes of sea bass with lemon sauce, and chicken curry with coconut milk, capers, and cucumbers.

7 rue Sibille. ✆ **04-94-97-16-12.** Reservations recommended. Main courses 70F–160F (10.65– 24.30, $10.15–$23.20); fixed-price menu 165F (25.10,$23.95). MC, V. Daily 7pm–midnight (restaurant); daily 7pm–3am (bar). Closed Oct to mid-Apr.

L'Echalotte ★ Value FRENCH This charming restaurant, with a tiny garden and simple dining room and tables that extend onto a veranda (weather permitting), serves good food at moderate prices. Because of demand, the tables may be difficult to get, especially in summer. The cuisine is solid, including grilled veal kidneys, crayfish with drawn-butter sauce, turbot filet with truffles, and some classic dishes of southwestern France, like three preparations of foie gras and magrêt of duckling. The menu includes several species of fish, like sea bass and daurade royale, which can be cooked in a salt crust.

35 rue Allard. ✆ **04-94-54-83-26.** Reservations recommended in summer. Main courses 80F–140F (12.15– 21.30, $11.60–$20.30); fixed-price menu 105F–160F (15.95– 24.30, $15.25–$23.20). AE, MC, V. Thurs 8–11:30pm, Fri–Wed 12:30–2pm and 8–11:30pm. Closed Nov 15–Dec 15.

Le Girelier PROVENÇAL The Rouets own this portside restaurant whose blue-and-white color scheme has become its own kind of trademark. They serve well-prepared grilled fish in many versions, as well as bouillabaisse, served only for two. Also available is a savory brochette of monkfish, a kettle of spicy mussels, and *pipérade* (a Basque omelet with pimientos, garlic, and tomatoes).

Quai Jean–Jaurès. ✆ **04-94-97-03-87.** Main courses 135F–500F (20.50– 76, $19.60–$72.50); fixed-price menu 200F (30.40, $29). AE, DC, MC, V. Daily noon–2pm and 7–11pm. Closed Jan–Mar and Nov 11–Dec 15.

Le Mouscardins ★★★ FRENCH/PROVENÇAL At the end of St-Tropez's harbor, this restaurant has won awards for culinary perfection. The dining room is in formal Provençal style with an adjoining sunroom under a canopy. We recommend the *moules* (mussels) *marinières* for an appetizer. A celebrated fish stew of the Côte d'Azur is offered, *bourride provençale,* and also an unusual main-course menu specialty, crushed chestnuts garnished with morels, crayfish, and truffles. The fish dishes are excellent, particularly the sauté of monkfish, wild mushrooms, and green beans. The dessert specialties are soufflés made with Grand Marnier or Cointreau.

1 rue Portalet. ✆ **04-94-97-29-00.** Reservations required. Main courses 160F–280F (24.30– 42.55, $23.20–$40.60); fixed-price menu 400F–500F (60.80– 76, $58–$72.50). AE, MC, V. Daily noon–2:30pm and 7:30–11:30pm. Closed Nov–Feb. Also closed at lunch July–Aug.

ST-TROPEZ AFTER DARK

On the lobby level of the Hôtel Byblos, **Les Caves du Roy,** avenue Paul-Signac (✆ **04-94-97-16-02**), is the most self-consciously chic nightclub in St-Tropez.

Entrance is free, but drink prices begin at a whopping 120F (18.25, $17.40).
Le Papagayo, in the Résidence du Nouveau-Port, rue Gambetta (© **04-94-
97-07-56**), is one of the largest nightclubs in town, with two floors, three bars,
and lots of attractive women and men from throughout the area. The decor was
inspired by the psychedelic 1960s. Entrance is 110F (16.70, $15.95) and
includes the first drink.

    Le Pigeonnier, 13 rue de la Ponche (© **04-94-97-84-26**), rocks, rolls, and
welcomes a crowd that's 80% to 85% gay, male, and between the ages of 20 and
50. Most of the socializing revolves around the long, narrow bar, where menfolk
from all over Europe seem to enjoy chitchatting. There's also a dance floor. For
another gay hotspot, check out the action at **Chez Maggi** (see "Dining," above).

    Below the Hôtel Sube, the **Café de Paris,** sur le Port (© **04-94-97-00-56**),
is one of the most consistently popular hangouts. An attempt has been made to
glorify a utilitarian room with early-1900s globe lights, an occasional 19th-
century bronze artifact, masses of artificial flowers, and a long zinc bar. The
crowd is irreverent and animated. Busy even in winter, after the yachting crowd
departs, it's open daily. The reporter Leslie Maitland aptly captured the kind of
crowd attracted to **Café Sénéquier,** sur le Port (© **04-94-97-00-90**). "What else
can one do but gawk at a tall, well-dressed young woman who appears *comme il
faut* at Sénéquier's with a large white rat perched upon her shoulder, with which
she occasionally exchanges little kisses, while casually chatting with her friends."

    If your idea of a night out is sitting in a cafe drinking wine, you can avoid
these expensive clubs and "hang out" at such joints as **Kelly's Irish Pub,** sur le
Port (© **04-94-54-89-11**), which draws mostly a foreign crowd to its site at the
end of Vieux Port. The tavern is casual, not chic. If you're nostalgic for a St-
Germain-des-Prés atmosphere, head for the old-fashioned **Café des Arts,** place
des Lices (© **04-94-97-02-25**), with its zinc bar attracting homesick Parisians.

2 La Napoule-Plage ⍟

560 miles S of Paris, 5 miles W of Cannes

This secluded resort is on the sandy beaches of the Golfe de la Napoule. In
1919, the fishing village was a paradise for the eccentric sculptor Henry Clews
and his wife, Marie, an architect. Fleeing America's "charlatans," whom he
believed had profited from World War I, this New York banker's son emphasized the fairy-tale qualities of his new home. His house is now the **Musée
Henry-Clews**—an inscription over the entrance reads ONCE UPON A TIME.

    The **Château de la Napoule** ⍟, boulevard Henry-Clews (© **04-93-
49-95-05**), was rebuilt from the ruins of a medieval château. Clews covered the
capitals and lintels with a grotesque menagerie—scorpions, pelicans, gnomes,
monkeys, lizards. Women, feminism, and old age are recurring themes in the
sculptor's work, as exemplified by the distorted suffragette depicted in his *Cat
Woman.* The artist admired chivalry and dignity as represented by *Don
Quixote*—to whom he likened himself. Clews died in Switzerland in 1937, and
his body was returned to La Napoule for burial. Marie Clews later opened the
château to the public as a testimonial to her husband. You can visit on a guided
French-English language tour, from March to October, Wednesday to Monday
at 3 and 4pm. In July and August, there's an extra tour at 5pm. It costs 25F
(3.80, $3.65) for adults and 20F (3.05, $2.90) for children. Free for children
under 5.

ESSENTIALS

GETTING THERE   La Mandelieu Napoule-Plage lies on the **bus** and **train** routes between Cannes and St-Raphaël. For information and schedules, call ☎ **08-36-35-35-35.** If you're **driving,** take A8 west from Cannes.

VISITOR INFORMATION   The **Office de Tourisme** is at 274 bd. Henry-Clews (☎ **04-93-49-95-31;** www.ot-mandelieu.fr).

ACCOMMODATIONS

Ermitage du Riou ✦✦   This old Provençal house, the most tranquil choice at the resort, was turned into a seaside hotel bordering the Riou River and the Cannes-Mandelieu golf club. The rooms are furnished in Provençal style with genuine furniture and ancient paintings. The rooms range from medium to spacious, each with an elegant bed with a quality mattress and fine linen. The most expensive ones have safes. All the rooms come with a good-size bathroom with combination tub and shower. Views are of either the sea or the golf course.

Bd. Henry-Clews, 06210 La Napoule. ☎ **04-93-49-95-56.** Fax 04-92-97-69-05. www.ermitage-du-riou.fr. 43 units. 735F–1,500F (111.70– 228, $106.60–$217.50) double; 2,020F–2,400F (307.05– 364.80, $292.90–$348) suite. AE, DC, MC, V. **Amenities:** Restaurant (seafood), bar; pool; solarium; garden; sauna. *In room:* A/C, TV, minibar, hair dryer.

La Calanque   The foundations of this hotel date from the Roman Empire, when it was an aristocrat's villa. The present hotel, run by the same family since 1942, looks like a hacienda, with salmon-colored stucco walls and shutters. Bedrooms range from small to medium, each with a comfortable mattress and a bathroom with tub or shower. The hotel's restaurant (see "Dining," below) spills onto a terrace and offers some of the cheapest fixed-price meals in La Napoule. Nonguests are welcome.

Av. Henry-Clews, 06210 La Napoule. ☎ **04-93-49-95-11.** Fax 04-93-49-67-44. 17 units. 500F–640F (76– 97.30, $72.50–$92.80) double. Rates include half board. MC, V. Closed Nov–Mar. **Amenities:** Restaurant, bar (guests only).

Royal Hôtel Casino ✦✦   A member of the Accor group, this Las Vegas–style hotel is on the beach near a man-made harbor, about 5 miles from Cannes. It was the first French hotel to include a casino and the last (before the building codes changed) to have a casino directly on the beach. It has one of the most contemporary designs on the Côte d'Azur. Most of the good-sized attractive rooms are angled toward a sea view; those facing the street are likely to be noisy, despite soundproofing. Each has a well-kept bathroom with a combination tub and shower. Le Féréol restaurant is recommended under "Dining," below.

605 av. du Général-de-Gaulle, 06212 Mandelieu La Napoule. ☎ **800/221-4542** in the U.S. or Canada, or 04-92-97-70-06. Fax 04-92-97-70-49. www.royal-hotel-casino.com. 213 units. 1,090F–2,190F (165.70– 332.90, $158.05–$317.55) double; 3,500F–12,000F (532– 1,824, $507.50–$1,740) suite. CB, DC, MC, V. Parking 65F (9.90, $9.45). **Amenities:** 2 restaurants, 3 bars; 2 tennis courts; exercise room; sauna; Turkish bath; room service; baby-sitting; laundry/dry cleaning. *In room:* A/C, TV, minibar, hair dryer.

DINING

La Calanque's restaurant (see "Accommodations," above) is open to nonguests.

Le Féréol ✦ TRADITIONAL/MODERN FRENCH   This well-designed restaurant services most of the culinary needs of the largest hotel (and only casino) in town. Outfitted in a nautical style, it offers one of the most impressive lunch buffets in the neighborhood. At night the place is candlelit and more elegant, and the view through bay windows over the pool is soothing. Menu items include foie gras, zucchini flowers with mousseline of lobster, mignon of veal with Parma ham and tarragon sauce, beef filet with a confit of shallots, sole braised with shrimp, and an émincée of duckling baked under puff pastry with cèpes. The dessert buffet offers an array of sophisticated pastries.

In the Royal Hôtel Casino, 605 av. du Général-de-Gaulle. ⓒ **04-92-97-70-00.** Reservations recommended. Main courses 115F–160F (17.50– 24.30, $16.70–$23.20); fixed-price lunch 170F–195F (25.85– 29.65, $24.65–$28.30). AE, DC, MC, V. Daily noon–2:30pm (to 3:30pm July–Aug) and 7–10:30pm (to 11pm July–Aug).

L'Oasis MODERN FRENCH   There's no more wonderful cuisine on the Western Riviera than the food here. At the entrance to the harbor of La Napoule, in an over-40-year-old house with a lovely garden and a re-creation of a mock-medieval cloister, this restaurant became world famous under the tutelage of the now-retired Louis Outhier. Today, his protégé, Stéphane Raimbault, prepares a sophisticated cuisine. Because Raimbault cooked in Japan for 9 years, many of his dishes are of the "East-Meets-West" variety. Menu choices might include roasted saddle of monkfish and squid risotto with ink sauce; medaillons of veal and duck in muscat wine-grape sauce; and snail-stuffed rack of local lamb with vegetables. The cellar houses one of the finest collections of Provençal wines anywhere. In summer, meals are served under the plane trees in the garden.

Rue Honoré-Carle. ⓒ **04-93-49-95-52.** Reservations required. Main courses 190F–340F (28.90– 51.70, $27.55–$49.30); fixed-price menus 250F (38, $36.25) lunch, 350F–750F (53.20– 114, $50.75–$108.75) dinner (without wine). AE, DC, MC, V. Daily noon–2pm and 7:30–10pm.

3 Cannes

562 miles S of Paris, 101 miles E of Marseille, 16 miles SW of Nice

When Coco Chanel went here and got a suntan, returning to Paris bronzed, she startled the milk-white society ladies. However, they quickly began copying her. Today the bronzed bodies—clad in nearly nonexistent swimsuits—that line the beaches of this chic resort continue the late fashion designer's example.

ESSENTIALS

GETTING THERE   Cannes is connected to each of the Mediterranean resorts, Paris, and the rest of France by rail and bus lines. **Trains** arrive frequently throughout the day. Cannes is only 15 minutes by train from Antibes and only 35 minutes from Nice. The TGV from Paris going via Marseille also services Cannes. (Transit from Paris to Cannes via TGV takes only about 3 breathless hours.) For rail information and schedules, call ⓒ **08-36-35-35-35.**

The Nice **international airport** is a 20-minute drive northeast. **Buses** pick up passengers at the airport every 40 minutes during the day, delivering them in Cannes at the Gare Routière, place de l'Hôtel de Ville (ⓒ **04-93-45-20-08**). Service to Cannes is also available from Antibes with one bus every half an hour.

By **car,** Cannes can be easily approached by two cities along the Riviera. From Marseille, take A51 north to Aix-en-Provence, continuing along A8 east to Cannes. From Nice, follow A8 southwest to Cannes.

VISITOR INFORMATION   The **Office de Tourisme** is in the Palais des Festivals, esplanade Georges-Pompidou (ⓒ **04-93-39-24-53;** www.cannes.com).

SPECIAL EVENTS   Cannes is at its most frenzied at the end of May, during the **International Film Festival** at the Palais des Festivals on promenade de la Croisette. It attracts not only film stars but seemingly every photographer in the world. On the seafront boulevards, flashbulbs pop as the stars and wannabes emerge and pose and pose and pose. You've got a better chance of being named prime minister of France than you do of attending one of the major screenings. (Hotel rooms and tables at restaurants are equally scarce during the festival.) But the people-watching is fabulous. If you find yourself here at the right time, you can join the thousands of others who line up in front of the Palais des Festivals, a.k.a. "the bunker," where the premieres are held. With paparazzi shouting, and gendarmes holding back the fans, the guests parade along the red carpet, stopping for a moment to strike a pose and chat with a journalist. *C'est Cannes!*

You may also be able to get tickets for some of the lesser films, which play 24 hours. For information, see "France Calendar of Events," in chapter 3 or access **www.festival-cannes.fr**.

From international regattas, to galas, *concours d'élégance,* and even a Mimosa Festival in February—something's always happening at Cannes, except in November, traditionally a dead month.

A DAY AT THE BEACH

Beachgoing in Cannes has more to do with exhibitionism and voyeurism than with actual swimming.

Plage de la Croisette extends between the Vieux Port and the Port Canto. Though the beaches along this billion-dollar stretch of sand aren't in the strictest sense private, they're *payante,* meaning you must pay between 90F and 100F (13.70 and 15.20, $13.05 and $14.50). You don't need to be a guest of the Noga Hilton, Martinez, Carlton, or Majestic to use the beaches associated with those hotels, though if you are you'll usually get a 50% discount. Each beach is separated from its neighbors by a wooden barricade that stops several feet from the sea, making it easy for you to stroll from one to another.

Why should you pay a fee at all? Well, it includes a full day's use of a mattress, a chaise lounge (the seafront isn't sandy or even soft, covered as it is with pebbles and dark-gray shingles), and a parasol, as well as easy access to freshwater showers and kiosks selling beverages. There are also outdoor restaurants where no one minds if you appear in your swimsuit.

For nostalgia's sake, our favorite beach is the one associated with the **Carlton** (see "Accommodations" below)—it was the first beach we went to, as teenagers, in Cannes. The merits of each of the 20 or so beaches along La Croisette vary daily depending on the crowd. And since every beach allows topless bathing (you must keep your bottom covered), you're likely to find the same forms of décolletage along the entire strip.

Looking for a free public beach where you'll have to survive without rentable chaises or parasols? Head for **Plage du Midi,** sometimes called Midi Plage, just west of the Vieux Port (© **04-93-39-92-74**), or **Plage Gazagnaire,** just east of the Port Canto (no phone). Here you'll find greater numbers of families with children and lots of caravan-type vehicles parked nearby.

OUTDOOR PURSUITS

BICYCLING & MOTOR-SCOOTERING Despite the roaring traffic, the flat landscapes between Cannes and such satellite resorts as La Napoule are well suited for riding a bike or motor scooter. The **Alliance Location de Cannes,** 9 rue des Frères Pradignac (© **04-93-38-62-62**), rents pedal bikes for 62F (9.40, $9) per day and requires a 1,000F (152, $145) deposit (payable with

Cannes

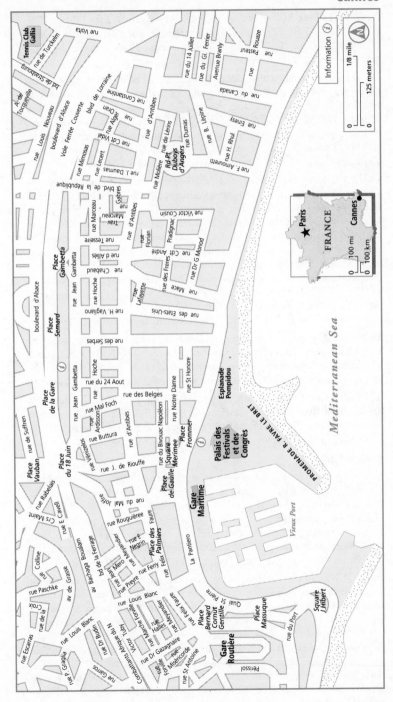

American Express, MasterCard, or Visa). Motor scooters rent for 175F to 200F (26.60 to 30.40, $25.40 to $29) per day and require a deposit of 4,000F to 10,000F (608 to 1,520, $580 to $1,450) per day. None of the motor scooters rented here requires a driver's license or special permit.

BOATING   Several companies can rent you a boat of any size, with or without a crew, for a day, a week, or a month. An outfit known for its short-term rentals of small craft, including motorboats, sailboats, and canoes, is **Elco Marine,** 110 bd. du Midi (✆ **04-93-47-12-62**). For access to larger boats, including motor-driven and sailing yachts and craft suitable for deep-sea fishing, try **MS Yachts,** 57 La Croisette (✆ **04-93-99-03-51**), or **Méditerranée Courtage** (Agence Y.P.), 22 quai Port Marseille (✆ **04-93-38-30-40**).

GOLF   One of the region's most challenging courses, **Country-Club de Cannes-Mougins,** 175 rte. d'Antibes, Mougins (✆ **04-93-75-79-13**), 4 miles north of Cannes, was a 1976 reconfiguration by Dye & Ellis of a plain course laid out in the 1920s. Noted for the olive trees and cypresses that adorn a relatively flat terrain, it has many water traps and a tricky layout loaded with technical challenges. It has a par of 72 and a much-envied role, since 1981, as host to the Cannes-Mougins Open, an important stop on the PGA European Tour. The course is open to anyone (with proof of handicap) willing to pay greens fees of 400F to 500F (60.80 to 76, $58 to $72.50), depending on the day of the week. An electric golf cart rents for 280F (42.55, $40.60), and golf clubs can be rented for 150F (22.80, $21.75). Reservations are recommended.

SWIMMING   Most of the larger hotels in Cannes have their own pools. The **Complexe Sportif Montfleury,** 23 av. Beauséjour (✆ **04-93-38-75-78**), boasts a large modern freshwater pool that's about 100 feet long. Anyone who pays the entrance fee of 25F (3.80, $3.65) can spend the entire day lounging beside it.

TENNIS   Its 10 tennis courts are one of the highlights of the **Complexe Sportif Montfleury,** 23 av. Beauséjour (✆ **04-93-38-75-78**). You'll find eight hard courts, at 80F (12.15, $11.60) per hour, and two clay courts, at 100F (15.20, $14.50) per hour.

SHOPPING

Cannes competes more successfully than many of its neighbors in a commercial blend of resort-style leisure, glamour, and media glitz. So you're likely to find branch outlets of virtually every stylish Paris retailer.

There's every big-name designer you can think of (Saint-Laurent, Rykiel, and Hermès) and designers you've never heard of (Claude Bonucci, Basile, and Durrani). There are also real-people shops; resale shops for star-studded castoffs; flea markets for fun junk; and a fruit, flower, and vegetable market.

ANTIQUES   In the Casino Croisette (also called the Palm Beach Casino) on La Croisette, Cannes hosts one of France's most prestigious **antiques salons,** conducted biannually in mid-July and late December or early January. Its organizers refuse to include low- or even middle-bracket merchandise. This is serious— not for the gilt-free crowd—with lots of 18th- and early-19th-century stuff. Admission is 70F (10.65, $10.15) per person. A bevy of services is available for crating, freighting and flying whatever you buy to wherever you want it. For dates and information, call or write the **Association des Antiquaires de Cannes,** 6 rue de Foresta, 06300 Nice (✆ **04-93-26-11-01**).

Looking for top-notch antiques dealers whose merchandise will wow you? Two of the city's most noteworthy dealers are **Hubert Herpin,** 20 rue Macé

(✆ **04-93-39-56-18**), and **Marc Franc,** 142 rue d'Antibes (✆ **04-93-43-86-43**). Within each of these stores, you'll find a wide selection of bronze and marble statues, marquetry, and 18th- and 19th-century furniture.

CHOCOLATE & JELLIED FRUITS   There are several famous chocolatiers in Cannes—try **Maiffret,** 31 rue d'Antibes (✆ **04-93-39-08-29**)—but the local specialty is *fruits confits* (jellied fruits, also called crystallized fruits), which became the rage in the 1880s. Maiffret sells these, especially in summer, when the chocolates tend to melt. Patés and confits of fruit, some of which decorate cakes and tarts, are also sold. Look for the Provençal national confection, *calissons,* crafted from almonds, a confit of melon, and sugar. A block away is **Chez Bruno,** 50 rue d'Antibes (✆ **04-93-39-26-63**). Opened in 1929 and maintained by a descendant of its founder, the shop is famous for fruits confits as well as its *marrons glacés* (glazed chestnuts), made fresh daily.

DEPARTMENT STORES   Near the train station in the heart of Cannes, **Galeries Lafayette** has a small branch at 6 rue du Maréchal-Foch (✆ **04-97-06-25-00**). It's noted for the upscale fashion in its carefully arranged interiors.

DESIGNER SHOPS   Most of the big names in designer fashion, for both men and women, line **promenade de la Croisette,** known as **La Croisette,** the main drag facing the sea. These stores are in a row, stretching from the Hôtel Carlton almost to the Palais des Festivals, with the best names closest to the **Gray-d'Albion,** 17 La Croisette (✆ **04-92-99-79-79**), which is both a mall and a hotel (how convenient). The stores in the Gray-d'Albion mall include **Hermès.** The mall is broken into two parts, so you go outdoors from the first part of the building, then enter again for the second part. It serves as the shopper's secret cutaway from the primary expensive shopping street, La Croisette, to the less expensive shopping street, **rue d'Antibes.**

FLEA MARKETS   Things are a lot less elevated at Cannes's two regular flea markets. Casual, dusty, and to an increasing degree filled with the castaways of estate sales, the **Marché Forville,** conducted in the neighborhood of the same name, near the Palais des Festivals, is a stucco structure with a roof and a few arches but no sides. Between Tuesday and Sunday, it's the fruit, vegetable, and flower market that supplies dozens of grand restaurants. But Monday is *brocante* day, when the market fills with offhanded, sometimes strident antiques dealers selling everything from grandmère's dishes to bone-handled carving knives.

Every Saturday, a somewhat disorganized and busy **flea market** is held outdoors, along the edges of the allée de la Liberté, across from the Palais des Festivals. Exact hours depend on the whims of whatever dealer happens to haul in a cache of merchandise, but they usually begin around 8am and run out of steam by around 4:30pm. *Note:* The vendors at the two flea markets may or may not be the same.

FOOD   Of the many streets that will attract with rustic and authentic Provençal allure, the most appealing, and the one lined with the greatest density of emporiums selling wine, olives, herbs, and oils, is the **rue Meynadier.**

A charmingly old-fashioned shop, **Cannolive,** 16–20 rue Vénizelos (✆ **04-93-39-08-19**), is owned by the Raynaud family, who founded the place in 1880. It sells Provençal olives and their by-products—*tapenades* (purées) that connoisseurs refer to as "Provençal caviar," black "olives de Nice," and green "olives de Provence," as well as three grades of olive oil from regional producers. Oils and food products are dispensed from no. 16, but gift items (fabrics, porcelain, and Provençal souvenirs) are sold next door.

MARKETS   At the edge of the Quartier Suquet, the **Marché Forville** is the town's primary fruit, flower, and vegetable market. On Monday it's a *brocante* market. See "Flea Markets," above.

PERFUME   The best shop is **Bouteille,** 59 rue d'Antibes (✆ **04-93-39-05-16**), also the most expensive. Its prices are high because it stocks more brands, has a wider selection, gives away more free samples, and presents you with a tote bag. A selection of other shops dots rue d'Antibes. Any may feature your favorite fragrance in a promotional deal. A final option for the reasonably priced perfumes is the boutiques associated with the Hôtel Gray-d'Albion.

SEEING THE SIGHTS

Cannes is sheltered by hills. For many visitors, it might as well consist of only one street, the **promenade de la Croisette** (or just La Croisette), curving along the coast and split by islands of palms and flowers.

A port of call for cruise liners, the seafront of Cannes is lined with hotels, apartment houses, and boutiques. Many of the bigger hotels, some dating from the 19th century, claim part of the beaches for the use of their guests. But there are also public areas. Above the harbor, the old town of Cannes sits on Suquet Hill, where you'll see the 14th-century **Tour de Suquet,** which the English dubbed the Lord's Tower.

Nearby is the **Musée de la Castre** ★, in the Château de la Castre, Le Suquet (✆ **04-93-38-55-26**), featuring paintings, sculpture, the decorative arts, and a section on ethnography, which includes objects from all over: from the Pacific islands to Southeast Asia, including Peruvian and Mayan pottery. There's also a gallery devoted to relics of ancient Mediterranean civilizations, from the Greeks to the Romans, from the Cypriots to the Egyptians. Five rooms are devoted to 19th-century paintings. The museum is open Wednesday to Monday: April to June from 10am to noon and 2 to 6pm, July to September from 10am to noon and 3 to 7pm, and October to March from 10am to noon and 2 to 5pm. Admission is 10F (1.50, $1.45), free for students and children 14 and under.

FERRYING TO THE ÎLES DE LÉRINS ★★

Across the bay from Cannes, the Lérins Islands are the most interesting excursion from the port. Ferryboats depart at 30-minute intervals throughout the day, beginning at 7:30am and lasting until 30 minutes before sundown. The largest of the ferryboat companies in Cannes is **Compagnies Estérel-Chanteclair** (✆ **04-93-39-11-82**), but other contenders include **Cie Horizon 4** (✆ **04-93-99-15-09**); **Compagnie Maritime Cannoise** (✆ **04-93-38-66-33**); and **Trans-Côte d'Azur** (✆ **04-92-98-71-30**). Departures are from the Gare Maritime des Îles, 06400 Cannes. Round-trip passage costs 55F (8.35, $8) per adult and 27F (4.10, $3.90) for children 5 to 10, free for children under 5.

ÎLE STE-MARGUERITE   This island was named after St. Honorat's sister, Ste. Marguerite, who lived here with a group of nuns in the 5th century. Today it is a youth center whose members (when they aren't sailing and diving) are dedicated to the restoration of the fort. From the dock, you can stroll along the island (signs point the way) to the Fort de l'Île, built by Spanish troops from 1635 to 1637. Below is the 1st-century B.C. Roman town where the unlucky man immortalized in *The Man in the Iron Mask* was imprisoned. You can visit his cell at Ste-Marguerite, in which seemingly every visitor has written his or her name. As you listen to the sound of the sea, you realize what a forlorn outpost this was.

Fun Fact Just Who Wore that Mask?

One of French history's most perplexing mysteries is the identity of the prisoner who arrived at Ste-Marguerite in 1698, wearing the *masque du fer*. Dumas fanned the legend that he was a brother of Louis XIV, and it has been suggested that the prisoner fathered a son who went to Corsica and "founded" the Bonaparte family. The most common theory is that the prisoner was a servant of the superintendent, Fouquet, named Eustache Dauger. At any rate, he died in the Bastille in Paris in 1703.

The **Musée de la Mer,** Fort Royal (© **04-93-38-55-26**), traces the history of the island, displaying artifacts of Ligurian, Roman, and Arab civilizations, plus the remains discovered by excavations, including paintings, mosaics, and ceramics. It's open July to September 10:30am to 12:15pm and 2:15 to 6:30pm; October to June it closes at sundown (4:30 to 5:30pm). Admission is 10F (1.50, $1.45) for adults and free for students and children 12 and under.

ÎLE ST-HONORAT   Only a mile long, but richer in history than its sibling islands, the Île St-Honorat is the site of a monastery whose origins go back to the 5th century. Today, the **Abbaye de St-Honorat** , Les Îles de Lérins, 06400 Cannes (© **04-92-99-54-00**), boasts a combination of medieval ruins and early-20th-century ecclesiastical buildings, and a community of about 30 Cistercian monks. Under controlled circumstances, if space is available, well-intentioned outsiders can visit and spend the night, but only for prayer and meditation. Most visitors opt to avoid the monastery, wandering through the pine forests on the island's western side, and sunbathing on its beaches.

ACCOMMODATIONS
VERY EXPENSIVE

Hôtel Carlton Intercontinental   Cynics say that one of the most amusing sights in Cannes is the view from under the grand gate of the Carlton. Here you'll see vehicles of every description dropping off huge amounts of baggage and numbers of fashionable (and sometimes not-so-fashionable) guests. It's the epitome of luxury and has become such a part of the city's heartbeat that to ignore it would be to miss the resort's spirit. The twin gray domes at either end of the facade are often the first things recognized by starlets planning their grand entrances, grand exits, and grand scenes in the hotel's public and private rooms.

Shortly after it was built in 1912, the Carlton attracted the most prominent members of Europe's *haut monde*. They were followed by battalions of the most important screen stars. Today the hotel is more democratic, hosting lots of conventions and motor-coach tour groups; however, in summer (especially during the film festival) the public rooms still are filled with all the voyeuristic and exhibitionistic fervor that seems so much a part of the Riviera. Bedrooms are plush and a bit airier than you might expect. The most spacious rooms are in the west wing, and many upper-floor rooms open onto waterfront balconies. The large bathrooms are in the grand *luxe* style, with a combination tub and shower.

58 bd. de la Croisette, 06400 Cannes. © **800/327-0200** in the U.S. or Canada, or 04-93-06-40-06. Fax 04-93-06-40-25. www.interconti.com. 338 units. 2,140F–4,775F (325.30– 725.80, $310.30–$692.40) double; from 6,815F (1035.90, $988.20) suite. AE, DC, MC, V. Parking 180F (27.35, $26.10). **Amenities:** 3 restaurants, bar; casino; indoor pool; health club; room service; laundry/dry cleaning. *In room:* A/C, TV, minibar, hair dryer, safe.

Hôtel Gray-d'Albion ★★ The smallest of the major hotels here isn't on La Croisette. But the rooms are outfitted with all the luxury a modern hotel can offer. Some critics consider the Gray-d'Albion among the most luxurious hotels in France. Groups form a large part of its clientele, but it also caters to the individual. All rooms are medium in size, blending contemporary and traditional furnishings; the generous-sized bathrooms have a combination tub and shower. Each unit has a balcony but the views aren't notable, except for rooms on the eighth and ninth floors, which have views of the Mediterranean.

38 rue des Serbes, 06400 Cannes. ℭ **04-93-99-79-79.** Fax 04-93-99-26-10. www.lucienbarrier.com. 189 units. 1,070F–2,170F (162.65– 329.85, $155.15–$314.65) double; from 3,170F (481.85, $459.65) suite. AE, DC, MC, V. Bus: 1. **Amenities:** restaurant, bar; sauna; salon; room service; baby-sitting; laundry/dry cleaning. In room: A/C, TV, minibar, hair dryer, safe.

Hôtel Martinez ★★ Lagging far behind the Carlton, this is often a convention hotel but is also a desirable property for the individual. When this Art Deco hotel was built in the 1930s, it rivaled any other hotel along the coast in sheer size alone. Over the years, however, it fell into disrepair and closed and reopened several times. But in 1982, the Concorde chain returned the hotel and its restaurants to their former luster, and today it competes with the Noga Hilton. The aim of the decor was a Roaring Twenties style, and all units boast full marble baths, wood furnishings, tasteful carpets, quality mattresses, and pastel fabrics. La Palme d'Or is among the finest restaurants in Cannes (see "Dining," below).

73 bd. de la Croisette, 06400 Cannes. ℭ **04-92-98-73-00.** Fax 04-93-39-67-82. www.hotel-martinez.com. 397 units. 1,500F–4,800F (228– 729.60, $217.50–$696) double; from 2,800F (425.60, $406) suite. AE, DC, MC, V. Parking 160F (24.30, $23.20). **Amenities:** 2 restaurants, bar; private beach; pool; 7 tennis courts; water-skiing school; room service; laundry/dry cleaning. *In room:* A/C, TV, minibar, hair dryer, safe.

Noga Hilton Cannes ★ Finished in 1992, this hotel is far superior to most Hiltons in the States. The owners procured one of Cannes's most sought-after sites, the lot occupied by the (since demolished) Palais des Festivals. This six-story place, with massive amounts of exposed glass, boasts a contemporary design recalling the best aspects of its older twin, the Noga Hilton in Geneva. You register in a soaring lobby sheathed with semitranslucent white marble. The soundproofed guest rooms are stylish, with balconies, bedside controls, luxury mattresses, combination shower and tub, and all the electronic accessories you'll need; the difference in rates is based on the sea view. Many of the appointments evoke a 1930s aura. The Prestige Rooms have large beds and elegant carpeting. Less desirable units are called Cityview and Gardenview rooms.

50 bd. de la Croisette, 06414 Cannes. ℭ **800-445-8667** in the U.S. or Canada, or 04-92-99-70-00. Fax 04-92-99-70-11. www.hiltoncannes.com. 234 units. 1,404F–4,497F (213.40– 683.55, $203.60–$652.05) double; 2,104F (319.80, $305.10) suite. AE, DC, MC, V. **Amenities:** 3 restaurants, 2 bars; casino; outdoor pool; health club; business center; shopping arcade; pier; baby-sitting; laundry/dry cleaning. *In room:* A/C, TV, minibar, hair dryer, safe.

MODERATE

Hôtel Brimer On a quiet street about 4 blocks from the seafront, this small hotel occupies the second floor of a four-story apartment building constructed in the 1970s. In 1998, it was renovated and upgraded by its owner, Brice Guëlle, who runs a tight ship. Bedrooms are well maintained, furnished unpretentiously but comfortable, and are relatively affordable in high-priced Cannes. Each of the midsize tiled bathrooms comes with a combination tub and shower. Breakfast is the only meal served, although there are many inexpensive bistros in the neighborhood.

6 rue Lecerf, 06400 Cannes. ☎ **04-93-38-69-54.** Fax 04-92-98-68-30. www.brimer.fr. 15 units. 450F–650F (68.40– 98.80, \$65.25–\$94.25) double; 700F–900F (106.40– 136.80, \$101.50–\$130.50) suite. AE, DC, MC, V. Parking 30F (4.55, \$4.35). **Amenities:** Laundry/dry cleaning. *In room:* TV, minibar, hair dryer.

Hotel Splendid ★ *(Value)*   Opened in 1871, this is a good conservative choice, a favorite of academicians, politicians, actors, and musicians. The Splendid's ornate white building with sinuous wrought-iron accents looks out onto the sea, the old port, and a park. The rooms boast antique furniture and paintings as well as videos; about half have kitchenettes. Each comes with a good mattress and a small but efficient bathroom with a combination tub and shower. The more expensive rooms have sea views.

Allée de la Liberté (4 and 6 rue Félix-faure), 06400 Cannes. ☎ **04-97-06-22-22.** Fax 04-93-99-52-02. 64 units. 730F–1,330F (110.95– 202.15, \$105.85–\$192.85) double; 1,200F–1,990F (182.40– 302.50, \$174–\$288.55) suite. Rates include continental breakfast. AE, DC, MC, V. Parking 40F (6.10, \$5.80). *In room:* A/C, TV.

Hôtel Victoria ★   The Victoria, a stylish modern hotel in the heart of Cannes, offers accommodations with period reproductions and refrigerators. Nearly half the rooms have balconies overlooking the small park and the hotel pool. Silk bedspreads and padded headboards with quality mattresses evoke a boudoir quality. The accommodations facing the park cost a little more but are worth it. Each unit is equipped with a modern tiled bathroom with either a shower or combination tub and shower. After a day on the beach, guests congregate in the paneled bar and sink comfortably into the couches and armchairs.

Rond-point Duboys-d'Angers, 06400 Cannes. ☎ **04-93-99-36-36.** Fax 04-93-38-03-91. hotelvictoria@ aol.com. 25 units. 790F–1,570F (120.10– 238.65, \$114.55–\$227.65) double. AE, DC, MC, V. Closed Nov–Dec. Parking 80F (12.15, \$11.60). **Amenities:** Pool. *In room:* A/C, TV, minibar.

INEXPENSIVE

Hôtel de Provence *(Value)*   Built in the 1930s and renovated in 1992, this hotel is small scale and unpretentious—a contrast to the intensely stylish, larger hotels with which it competes. Most of the rooms have private balconies, and many overlook the shrubs and palms of the hotel's walled garden. Bedrooms are showing their age but still offer fine comfort, and for Cannes this is a remarkable bargain. Most of the bathrooms are roomy, many with a combination tub and shower. In warm weather, breakfast is served under the flowers of an arbor.

9 rue Molière, 06400 Cannes. ☎ **04-93-38-44-35.** Fax 04-93-39-63-14. www.hotel-de-provence.com. 30 units. 490F–630F (74.50– 95.75, \$71.05–\$91.35) double. AE, MC, V. Parking 65F (9.90, \$9.45). **Amenities:** Bar. *In room:* A/C, TV, minibar, hair dryer, safe.

Hôtel Villa de l'Olivier *(Finds)*   Charming and personalized, this is a secret hideaway with a low-key management style. In the 1930s, it was a private villa and in the 1960s was transformed into a hotel, with a six-unit annex built in the garden. Today, you'll find buildings with lots of glass overlooking a kidney-shaped pool and a decor combining the French colonial tropics and Provence. The rooms are outfitted with upholstered walls, each in a different color and pattern, and lots of Provençal accessories. Bathrooms come in a variety of sizes, each with a combination tub and shower.

5 rue des Tambourinaires, 06400 Cannes. ☎ **04-93-39-53-28.** Fax 04-93-39-55-85. www.hotelolivier.com. 24 units. 490F–740F (74.50– 112.50, \$71.05–\$107.30); 1,600F2,000F (243.20– 304, \$232–\$290) suite. AE, DC, MC, V. Parking 60F (9.10, \$8.70). **Amenities:** Pool; room service; laundry. *In room:* A/C, TV.

DINING
VERY EXPENSIVE
La Palme d'Or ✸✸✸ MODERN FRENCH   Movie stars on the see-and-be-seen circuit head here during the film festival. It's a sophisticated rendezvous but also serves one of the Riviera's finest hotel cuisines. When the Taittinger family (of champagne fame) renovated this hotel, one of their primary concerns was to establish a restaurant that could rival the tough competition in Cannes. And they've succeeded. The result is this light wood-paneled Art Deco marvel with bay windows, a winter garden theme, and outdoor and enclosed terraces overlooking the pool, the sea, and La Croisette. Menu items change with the seasons but are likely to include warm foie gras with fondue of rhubarb; filets of fried red mullet with a beignet of potatoes, zucchini, and olive-cream sauce; or a medley of crayfish, clams, and squid marinated in peppered citrus sauce. A modernized version of a Niçoise staple includes three parts of a rabbit with rosemary sauce, fresh vegetables, and chickpea rosettes. The most appealing dessert is wild strawberries from nearby Carros, with a Grand Marnier–flavored nage and a "cream sauce of frozen milk." The service is worldly without being stiff.

In the Hôtel Martinez, 73 bd. de la Croisette. ℂ **04-92-98-74-14.** Reservations required. Main courses 250F–480F (38– 72.95, $36.25–$69.60); fixed-price menus 295F (44.85, $42.80) lunch Mon–Sat, 390F–820F (59.30– 124.65, $56.55–$118.90) at dinner. AE, DC, MC, V. Wed–Sun 12:30–2pm and 7:30–10:30pm (also Tues 7:30–10:30pm mid-June to mid-Sept). Closed Nov 15–Dec 20.

EXPENSIVE
Gaston-Gastounette ✸ TRADITIONAL FRENCH   This is the best restaurant for views of the marina. Located in the old port, it has a stucco exterior with oak moldings and big windows and a sidewalk terrace surrounded by flowers. Inside you'll be served any of three different bouillabaisses, ranging from full-flown authentic stewpots that are meals in their own right to less daunting versions designed as an appetizer. Other choices include baby turbot with hollandaise sauce; John Dory filets with wild mushrooms; an unusual Japanese-style broth flavored with monkfish, saltwater salmon, and chives; and a succulent platter of fried mixed fish with basil-flavored butter sauce. Profiteroles with hot chocolate sauce make a memorable dessert.

7 quai St-Pierre. ℂ **04-93-39-47-92.** Reservations required. Main courses 160F–300F (24.30– 45.60, $23.20–$43.50); fixed-price menu 125F–170F (19– 25.85, $18.15–$24.65) lunch, 200F (30.40, $29) dinner. AE, DC, MC, V. Daily noon–2pm and 7–11pm. Closed Nov 30–Dec 19.

La Mère Besson ✸ TRADITIONAL FRENCH   The culinary traditions of the late Mère Besson, who opened her restaurant in the 1930s, are carried on in one of Cannes's favorite places. The specialties are prepared with respect for Provençal traditions. Most delectable is *estouffade Provençal* (beef braised with red wine and rich stock flavored with garlic, onions, herbs, and mushrooms). You can sample a platter with codfish, fresh vegetables, and dollops of the famous garlic mayonnaise (*aïoli*) of Provence. Other specialties are fish soup, a *bourride Provençale* (a form of thick fish-and-vegetable stew), and shoulder of lamb with Provençal herbs and a purée of garlic.

13 rue des Frères-Pradignac. ℂ **04-93-39-59-24.** Reservations required. Main courses 75F–120F (11.40– 18.25, $10.90–$17.40); fixed-price menu 140F–170F (21.30– 25.85, $20.30–$24.65) at dinner. AE, DC, MC, V. Apr–Oct Tues–Fri 12:15–2pm and 7:30–10:30pm, Mon and Sat 7:30–10:30pm (open Sun in summer); Nov–Mar Mon–Sat 7:30–10:30pm. Bus: 1.

Le Festival ✸ TRADITIONAL FRENCH   Screen idols and sex symbols flood the front terrace of this place during the film festival. Almost every chair is emblazoned with the names of movie stars (who may or may not have graced it with their bottoms), and tables here are among the most sought-after entity in town. You can choose from the Restaurant or the less formal Grill Room. Meals in the Restaurant may include *bourride Provençale; soupe des poissons* (fish soup) with *rouille;* simply grilled fresh fish (perhaps with aïoli); bouillabaisse with lobster; pepper steak; and sea bass flambéed with fennel. Items in the Grill are more in the style of an elegant brasserie, served a bit more rapidly and without as much fuss but at more or less the same prices. An appropriate finish in either section might be a smoothly textured peach Melba.

55 bd. de la Croisette. ℭ **04-93-38-04-81**. Reservations required. Main courses 150F–300F (22.80– 45.60, $21.75–$43.50); fixed-price menu from 195F–225F (29.65– 34.20, $28.30–$32.65). AE, DC, MC, V. Daily 11:30am–3pm and 7:30–10pm. Closed Nov 20–Dec 26.

MODERATE

Le Marais TRADITIONAL/MODERN FRENCH   This is the most successful gay restaurant in Cannes, with a crowd of mostly gay men, sometimes with their entourages from the worlds of fashion and entertainment. The setting is a warm and appealing mix of Parisian and Provençal, with paneled walls and a bustling terrace that in its way is one of the most sought-after outdoor venues in town. Menu items include sea bream filet with olive-based tapenade sauce; a "triptych" of meats that includes magret of duck, beef filet, and shoulder of lamb with mint sauce. Know in advance that this is primarily a restaurant and doesn't cater to a crowd of folk coming in just to drink.

9 rue du Suquet. ℭ **04-93-38-39-19**. Reservations recommended. Main courses 80F–150F (12.15– 22.80, $11.60–$21.75); fixed-price menu 139F–190F (21.15– 28.90,$20.15–$27.55). MC, V. Tues–Sun 7:15–11pm.

Le Whatnut's TRADITIONAL FRENCH   Sophisticated, urbane, and permissive, this restaurant also features a bar and a dance floor where patrons can dance and drink till long after the usual dinner hour, and even arrive for a meal long after everything else is closed. The interior has trompe l'oeil and ornate plaster ceilings, and the outdoor terrace is accented with decorative columns and the smell of night-flowering vines. The menu isn't terribly long but is well chosen. Examples are a diet-conscious array of grilled fish, such as sea bass; a platter with shrimp and scallops; and filets of beef garnished with morels or foie gras. If you opt to come for just a drink, expect to pay from around 40F (6.10, $5.80) for a beer and from around 45F (6.85, $6.55) for a whisky and soda.

7 rue Marceau. ℭ **04-93-68-60-58**. Reservations recommended. Main courses 90F–135F (13.70– 20.50, $13.05–$19.60); fixed-price menu 130F–150F (19.75– 22.80, $18.85–$21.75). AE, DC, MC, V. May–Sept daily 6pm–midnight; Oct–Apr Wed–Sun 6pm–midnight. Bar open till 2:30am.

INEXPENSIVE

Au Bec Fin TRADITIONAL FRENCH   On a street halfway between the train station and the beach, this 1880s bistro isn't much on decor but offers especially good meals. Sometimes red carnations are brought in from the fields to brighten the tables. A typical meal might include salade Niçoise, the house specialty; then either a bourride (stew) of fish or a *caneton* (duckling) with *cèpes* (flap mushrooms); and finally a choice of cheese and dessert.

12 rue du 24-Août. ℭ **04-93-38-35-86**. Reservations required. Main courses 55F–70F (8.35– 10.65, $8–$10.15); fixed-price menu 115F–135F (17.50– 20.50, $16.70–$19.60). AE, DC, MC, V. Mon–Sat noon–2:30pm and 6–10:30pm. Closed Dec 15–Jan 15.

Le Monaco *Value* FRENCH/ITALIAN/PROVENÇAL Restaurant tabs on La Croisette often resemble the GNP of a small country. But believe it or not, pricey Cannes has working people who have to eat, and they go to Le Monaco, a blue-collar eatery with great food served bistro style. Menu choices include osso buco with sauerkraut, spaghetti bolognese, paella, couscous, roast rabbit with mustard sauce, mussels, trout with almonds, and minestrone with basil. Another specialty is grilled sardines, which many restaurants won't serve, considering them too messy and old-fashioned. Dessert might be a slice of orange tart.

15 rue du 24-Août. ℂ 04-93-38-37-76. Reservations required. Main courses 55F–90F (8.35– 13.70,$8–$13.05); fixed-price menu 95F–125F (14.45– 19, $13.80–$18.15). MC, V. Mon–Sat noon–2:30pm and 7–10:30pm. Closed Nov 10–Dec 10.

CANNES AFTER DARK

On the eighth floor (seventh in France) of the Hôtel Carlton Intercontinental, 58 bd. de la Croisette, is **Le Carlton Casino Club** (ℂ 04-92-99-51-00). It's smaller than its major competitor (the Casino Croisette), but the modern decor draws many devotees. Jackets are required for men, and a passport or government-issued ID card is required for admission. It's open daily from 7:30pm to 4am; however, access to the slot machines is from noon daily. Admission is 70F (10.65, $10.15).

The largest and most legendary casino in Cannes is the **Casino Croisette,** in the Palais des Festivals, 1 jetée Albert-Edouard, near promenade de la Croisette (ℂ 04-92-98-78-00). Within its glittering confines, you'll find all the roulette and blackjack you'd expect. Entrance into the gaming rooms costs 70F (10.65, $10.15). Men are required to wear a jacket and all guests must present their passport or ID card. The gaming room is open from 7:30pm till 4 or 5am. There are also slot machines available from 11am until closing; entrance is free and the dress code more relaxed. The casino also has one of the best nightclubs in town, **Jimmy's de Régine** (ℂ 04-93-68-00-07), open Thursday to Sunday from 11pm to dawn. Admission of 70F (10.65, $10.15) includes a drink.

Less formal, less rigidly stylish discos include **Jane's Club,** in the cellar of the Hôtel Gray-d'Albion, 38 rue des Serbes (ℂ 04-92-99-79-79), where male clients tend to wear jackets and ties and come in a wide range of ages. The hippest and most consistently in-demand club is **Le Cat-Corner,** 22 rue Macé (ℂ 04-93-39-31-31), where a multicultural blend of night owls, most under 35, come to dance, drink, talk, and flirt.

Gays and lesbians will feel especially comfortable in **Le Vogue,** 20 rue du Suquet (ℂ 04-93-39-99-18), a mixed bar open Tuesday to Sunday from around 9pm till 2:30am. Another gay option is **Disco Le Sept,** 7 rue Rouguière (ℂ 04-93-39-10-36), with two shows, each lasting 2 hours, that begin nightly at 11:30pm and at 2am. Entrance is free. Attracting an older, somewhat more conservative crowd of mostly gay men is the **Zanzi-Bar Pub,** La Pantièro, rue Félix-Faure (no phone), opposite Vieux Port.

4 Mougins

561 miles S of Paris, 7 miles S of Grasse, 5 miles N of Cannes

This once-fortified town on the crest of a hill provides an alternative for those who want to be near the excitement of Cannes but not in the midst of it. Picasso and other artists appreciated the sun-drenched hills covered with gnarled olive trees. The artist arrived in 1936 and in time was followed by Jean Cocteau, Paul Eluard, and Man Ray. Picasso decided to move here permanently, choosing as his refuge an ideal site overlooking the Bay of Cannes, near the Chapelle Notre-Dame de Vie, which Winston Churchill once painted. Here Picasso continued to work and spend the latter part of his life with his wife, Jacqueline. Fernand Léger, René Clair, Isadora Duncan, and even Christian Dior have lived at Mougins.

Mougins is a haven for those who feel that the Riviera is overrun, spoiled, and overbuilt. It preserves the quiet life even though it's a stone's throw from Cannes. The wealthy come from Cannes to golf here. Though Mougins looks serene and tranquil, it's actually part of the industrial park of Sophia Antipolis, a technological center where more than 1,000 companies have offices.

ESSENTIALS

GETTING THERE   The best way to get to Mougins is to **drive.** From Nice, follow E80/A8 west, then cut north on Route 85 into Mougins. From Cannes, head north of the city along N85. From La Napoule-Plage, head east toward Cannes on N7, then north at the signposted turnoff to Mougins up in the hills.

There's no rail station in Mougins, but there's daily **bus** service into Mougins from Cannes aboard the bus that travels from Cannes to Grasse. En route to Grasse, it stops in Mougins at Val de Mougins, about a 10-minute walk from the center. Fares from Cannes to Mougins are about 22F (3.35, $3.20) each way. For information about departure times and schedules, call **Rapides–Côte-d'Azur** at © **04-93-39-11-39.** Given the complexities of a bus transfer from Cannes, it'll invariably be a lot easier just to pay about 125F (19, $18.15) for a **taxi** to haul you and your possessions northward from Cannes.

VISITOR INFORMATION   The **Office de Tourisme** is at 15 av. Jean-Charles-Mallet (© **04-93-75-87-67**).

SEEING THE SIGHTS

For a look at the history of the area, head to the **Musée Municipal,** place du Village (© **04-92-92-50-42**), is in the St. Bernardin Chapel. It was built in 1618 and traces the history the area from 1553 to the 1950s. It's open December to October, Monday to Friday from 10am to noon and 2 to 6pm; free admission.

You can also visit the **Chapelle Notre-Dame de Vie,** Chemin de la Chapelle, a mile southeast of Mougins. The chapel, once painted by Churchill, is more famous for the priory next door where Picasso spent his last 12 years. It was built in the 12th century and then reconstructed in 1646; it was an old custom to bring stillborn babies to the chapel to have them baptized. The priory is still a private home occupied intermittently by the Picasso heirs. Alas, because of a series of break-ins, the chapel is only open during Sunday mass between 9 and 10am.

Musée de l'Automobiliste ★★ *Kids*   This is one of the top attractions on the Riviera. Founded in 1984 by Adrien Maeght, this ultramodern concrete-and-glass structure rises out of a green clearing. It houses temporary exhibitions but also owns one of Europe's most magnificent collections of prestigious automobiles. In all, there are more than 100 vehicles from 1908 until the present.

Aire des Bréguières. © **04-93-69-27-80.** Admission 40F (6.10, $5.80) adults, 25F (3.80, $3.65) children 11 and under. Oct and Dec–Mar daily 10am–6pm; Apr–Sept daily 10am–7pm.

ACCOMMODATIONS
EXPENSIVE

Le Moulin de Mougins (see "Dining," below) offers charming rooms and suites.

Mas Candille ★   An oasis of tranquility, this 200-year-old Provençal farmhouse was skillfully renovated in 2000. The public rooms contain many 19th-century furnishings, and some open onto the gardens. The renovated guest rooms are cozy, with traditional Provençal furnishings. Bathrooms are elegant and of good size, each with a combination tub and shower. The managers are always willing to provide whatever you need to make your room more comfortable. The dining room, with elegant stone detailing and a massive fireplace with a timbered mantel, serves exceptional food. Fresh salads and light meals are available throughout the day. In good weather, lunch is served on the terrace; dinner is served on the terrace in summer only.

Bd. Rebuffel, 06250 Mougins. ℭ **04-92-28-43-43.** Fax 04-92-92-85-56. 41 units. 1,875F–2,250F (281.25– 342, $135.40–$326.25) double; from 2,650F–4,900F (402.80– 744.80, $384.25–$710.50) suite. AE, DC, MC, V. **Amenities:** Restaurant; 2 outside pools; 1 tennis court; spa; room service; laundry. *In room:* A/C, TV, minibar, hair dryer, safe.

MODERATE

Manoir de l'Etang ★★   This 19th-century Provençal building in the midst of olive trees and cypresses is one of the choice places to stay on the Riviera. It boasts all the romantic extras associated with some Riviera properties, including a "love goddess" statuary in the garden and candlelit dinners around a pool, but it charges reasonable rates. The rooms are bright and modern—you'll feel almost as if you're staying in a private home. Some rooms are extremely spacious. Each boasts a quality mattress and fine linen, along with a midsize bathroom with a combination tub and shower. In winter, meals are served around a fireplace. The chef bases his menu on the freshest ingredients in any season.

Aux Bois de Font-Merle, allée du Manoir, 06250 Mougins. ℭ **04-92-28-36-00.** Fax 04-92-28-36-10. manoiretang@wanadoo.fr. 16 units. 600F–1,000F (91.20– 152, $87–$145) double; 1,350F–1,600F (205.20– 243.20, $195.75–$232) apt. AE, MC, V. Closed Nov–Feb. **Amenities:** Restaurant; bar; pool; room service; laundry. *In room:* A/C, TV, minibar.

DINING

L'Amandier de Mougins Café-Restaurant ★ *Value* NIÇOISE/PROVENÇAL The illustrious founder of this relatively inexpensive bistro is the world-famous Roger Vergé, whose much more expensive Moulin de Mougins is described below. A mass-market satellite to its exclusive neighbor, this restaurant serves relatively simple platters in an airy stone house. The specialties are usually based on traditional recipes and may include a terrine of the elusive Mediterranean hogfish with lemon; a tartare of fresh salmon and a céviche of tuna with hot spices; magrêt of grilled duckling with honey sauce and lemons, served with deliberately undercooked polenta; and rack of lamb served with a risotto of zucchini flowers.

Place du Commandant-Lamy. ℭ **04-93-90-00-91.** Reservations recommended. Main courses 70F–170F (10.65– 25.85, $10.15–$24.65); fixed-price menu 165F–200F (25.10– 30.40,$23.95–$29). AE, DC, MC, V. Daily noon–2:15pm and 8–10pm.

Le Moulin de Mougins ★★★ MODERN FRENCH   This place is among France's top 20 restaurants. A 10-foot-wide stone oil vat, with a wooden turn-screw and a grinding wheel, is near the entrance. This is the kingdom of Roger Vergé, the *maître cuisinier de France.* His specialties include *filets de rougets* (red mullet) with artichokes; *noisettes d'agneau* (lamb) de Sisteron with an eggplant cake in thyme-flavored sauce and *poupeton* (zucchini flowers) stuffed with a mix of truffles and pulverized mushrooms, served with truffle-flavored butter sauce; fricassée of lobster with sweet wine, cream sauce, and sweet peppers; and pepper steak "à la Mathurin," with grapes, pepper, and brandy. His forte is fish from the Mediterranean, bought fresh each morning. Dessert might be a lemon soufflé. Monsieur Vergé offers a lot of fantastic, even historic wines but also has a good selection of local vintages.

The mill offers four suites and three rooms, with air-conditioning, minibars, TVs, phones, and fax machines. The rooms are decorated with French antiques. These rent for 850F to 1,800F (129.20 to 273.60, $123.25 to $261).

Notre-Dame de Vie, 06250 Mougins. ☎ **04-93-75-78-24.** Fax 04-93-90-18-55. Reservations required. Main courses 195F–460F (29.65– 69.90, $28.30–$66.70); fixed-price menus 290F–750F (44.13– 114, $42.05–$108.75) lunch, 600F–750F (91.20– 114, $87–$108.75) dinner. AE, DC, MC, V. Tues–Sun noon–2:15pm and 8–10pm. Closed Dec 12–Jan 12.

5 Grasse ★★

563 miles S of Paris, 11 miles N of Cannes, 6 miles N of Mougins, 14 miles NW of Antibes

Grasse, a 20-minute drive from Cannes, is the most fragrant town on the Riviera, though it looks tacky and modern. Surrounded by jasmine and roses, it has been the capital of the perfume industry since the days of the Renaissance. It was once a famous resort, attracting such royalty as Queen Victoria and Princess Pauline Borghese, Napoléon's lascivious sister.

Today some three quarters of the world's essences are produced here from foliage that includes violets, daffodils, wild lavender, and jasmine. It takes 10,000 flowers to produce 2.2 pounds of jasmine petals. Almost a ton of petals is needed to distill 1½ quarts of essence. These figures are important to keep in mind when looking at that high price tag on a bottle of perfume.

ESSENTIALS

GETTING THERE   Buses pull into town at intervals of between 30 and 60 minutes every day from Cannes (trip time: 45 min). The one-way fare is 20F (3.05, $2.90). There are also about 30 buses every day arriving from Nice, a trip time of around 60 minutes. The one-way fare costs around 38F (5.80, $5.50). The buses disembark at the Gare Routière, avenue Thiers (☎ **04-93-36-37-37**), a 10-minute walk north of the town center. Visitors arriving by **car** take A8, which funnels in traffic from Monaco, Aix-en-Provence, and Marseille.

VISITOR INFORMATION   The **Office de Tourisme** is in the Palais des Congrès on place du Cours (☎ **04-93-36-66-66;** www.ville-grasse.fr).

SEEING THE SIGHTS

Musée d'Art et d'Histoire de Provence ★   This museum is in the Hôtel de Clapiers–Cabris, built in 1771 by Louise de Mirabeau, the marquise de Cabris and sister of Mirabeau. It includes paintings, four-poster beds, marquetry, ceramics, brasses, kitchenware, pottery, urns, and archaeological finds.

2 rue Mirabeau. ☎ **04-93-36-01-61.** Admission 20F (3.05, $2.90) adults, 10F (1.50, $1.45) children 8–16, free for children under 8. June–Sept daily 10am–7pm; Oct–May Wed–Mon 10am–12:30pm and 2–5:30pm.

Musée International de la Parfumerie   This museum will teach you everything about perfume. You learn that it takes a metric ton of flowers to make about a quart of fragrance; you'll also see interesting, often bizarre, exhibits relating to the perfume industry. One of the most fascinating displays a 3,000-year-old mummy's perfumed hand and foot. Apparently the flesh stayed preserved over the centuries because of some perfuming process. In the fourth-floor greenery, you can smell some of the base elements that go into the creation of celebrated perfumes.

8 place de Cours. ☎ **04-93-36-80-20.** Admission 20F (3.05, $2.90) adults, 10F (1.50, $1.45) children. Oct–May Wed–Mon 10am–12:30pm and 2–5:30pm; June–Sept Wed–Mon 10am–7pm.

Parfumerie Fragonard ⭐ One of the best-known perfume factories is named after an 18th-century French painter. This factory has the best villa, the best museum, and the best tour. An English-speaking guide will show you how "the soul of the flower" is extracted. After the tour, you can explore the museum of perfumery, which displays bottles and vases that trace the industry back to ancient times. Of course, if you're shopping for perfume and want to skip the tour, that's okay with the factories.

20 bd. Fragonard. ✆ 04-93-36-44-65. Daily 9am–6:30pm (Nov–Jan closed noon–2pm).

Parfumerie Molinard The firm is well known in the United States, and its products are sold at Saks, Neiman Marcus, and Bloomingdale's. In the factory you can witness the extraction of the essence of the flowers. You'll also learn all the details of the process of converting flowers into essential oils. You can admire a collection of antique perfume-bottle labels as well as see a rare collection of perfume *flaçons* (bottles) by Baccarat and Lalique.

60 bd. Victor-Hugo. ✆ 04-93-36-01-62. Free admission. May–Sept daily 9am–6:30pm; Oct–Apr daily 9am–12:30pm and 2–6pm.

Villa Fragonard The collection displayed here includes the paintings of Jean-Honoré Fragonard; his sister-in-law, Marguerite Gérard; his son, Alexandre; and his grandson, Théophile. Fragonard was born in Grasse in 1732. The grand staircase was decorated by Alexandre.

23 bd. Fragonard. ✆ 04-93-36-01-61. Admission 20F (3.05, $2.90) adults, 10F (1.50, $1.45) children. June–Sept Wed–Mon 10am–7am; Oct–May Wed–Mon 10am–12:30pm and 2–5:30pm.

ACCOMMODATIONS

La Bastide St-Antoine (Restaurant Chibois) (see "Dining," below) also rents rooms.

Hôtel La Bellaudière *Value* Part of the well-respected Logis de France chain, this completely unpretentious family-run hotel is 2 miles north of the town center in the hills above Grasse; the stone-sided farmhouse was built in stages beginning 400 years ago. Bedrooms are simple but severely dignified and outfitted with as many Provençal motifs as possible. Each unit has a small tiled bathroom with a shower. There's a view of the sea from many of the rooms, a garden terrace lined with flowering shrubs, and a sense of friendly cooperation from the hosts.

78 rte. de Nice, 06130 Grasse. ✆ 04-93-36-02-57. Fax 04-93-36-40-03. 17 units. 320F–440F (48.65–66.90, $46.40–$63.80) double. AE, DC, MC, V. Closed Nov 15–Feb 1. Free parking. **Amenities:** Restaurant. *In room:* TV.

DINING

La Bastide St-Antoine (Restaurant Chibois) ⭐⭐⭐ FRENCH/PROVENÇAL Dine here for one of the grandest culinary experiences along the Riviera. The fame that Jacques Chibois and his restaurant has attracted since 1996 is viewed with amazement and envy by every restaurateur in France. Occupying a 200-year-old Provençal farmhouse surrounded by 7 acres of stately trees and verdant shrubberies, the restaurant serves a sophisticated array of dishes. The best examples are the warm oysters with black olives, sage, and leeks and the roasted duckling served with a fondue of red cabbage, figs, and mushroom-studded mashed potatoes. Desserts might include strawberry soup with spice wine and an ice cream made with olives and a hint of olive oil. The chef also does wonders with wild duck.

In 1998, the owners added eight rooms and three suites, each with a whimsical Provençal style, air-conditioning, a minibar, a TV, a phone, upscale furnishings, and exceptionally comfortable beds. Doubles cost 950F to 1,700F (144.40 to 258.40, $137.75 to $246.50) and suites 1,800F to 2,500F (273.60 to 380, $261 to $362.50). Free parking is available.

48 av. Henri-Dunant. © 04-93-70-94-94. Reservations required. Main courses 170F–280F (25.85– 42.55, $24.65–$40.60); fixed-price menus 270F (41.05, $39.15) lunch Mon–Sat, 570F–750F (86.65– 114, $82.65–$108.75) dinner. AE, DC, MC, V. Daily noon–2pm and 8–10:30pm.

Restaurant Amphitryon TRADITIONAL FRENCH This is a more affordable option than the above, and the food is good. Many of the buildings lining this street, including the one that houses this restaurant, functioned as stables in the 19th century. Today, amid fabric-covered walls and soothing grays and off-whites, you can enjoy the flavorful cuisine of Michel André. The food is inspired by southwestern France, with plenty of foie gras and duckling, as well as lamb roasted with thyme and a ragoût of fish in red wine that has become one of the chef's most popular dishes. Also recommendable are the Mediterranean fish soup with Provençal rouille and braised sole with shallots and white wine.

16 bd. Victor-Hugo. © 04-93-36-58-73. Reservations recommended. Main courses 105F–175F (15.95– 26.60, $15.25–$25.430); fixed-price menu 127F–260F (19.30– 39.50, $18.40–$37.70). AE, DC, MC, V. Mon–Sat noon–1:30pm and 7:30–9:30pm. Closed Aug 1–Sept 1 and Dec 23–Jan 5.

6 Biot ⊛

570 miles S of Paris, 6 miles E of Cagnes-sur-Mer, 4 miles NW of Antibes

Biot has been famous for its pottery ever since merchants began to ship earthenware jars to Phoenicia and destinations throughout the Mediterranean. Biot was first settled by Gallo-Romans and has had a long, war-torn history. Somehow the potters still manage to work at their ancient craft. Biot is also the place Fernand Léger chose to paint until the day he died. A magnificent collection of his work is on display at a museum here.

ESSENTIALS
GETTING THERE Biot's **train station** is 2 miles east of the town center. There's frequent service from Nice and Antibes. For rail information and schedules, call © **08-36-35-35-35.** The **bus** from Antibes is even more convenient than the train. For bus information and schedules, call © **04-93-34-37-60** in Antibes. In Biot, buses pull into, and depart from, the Place Guynemer. To **drive** to Biot from Nice, take N7 west. From Antibes, follow N7 east.

VISITOR INFORMATION The **Office de Tourisme** is on rue St-Sebastien (© **04-93-65-78-00**).

EXPLORING THE TOWN
If you have time, you might explore the village. Begin at the muchphotographed **place des Arcades,** where you can see the 16th-century gates and the remains of the town's ramparts. Biot is known for its carnations and roses, which are sold on this lovely square. The **Église de Biot,** place des Arcades (© **04-93-65-00-85**), dates from the 15th century, when it was built by Italian immigrants who resettled the town after it was decimated by the Black Death. The church is known for two stunning 15th-century *retables:* the red-and-gold *Retable du Rosaire* by Ludovico Bréa and the recently restored *Christ aux Plaies* by Canavesio.

In the late 1940s, glassmakers created a bubble-flecked glass known as *verre rustique*. It comes in brilliant colors like cobalt and emerald and is displayed in many store windows on the main shopping street, **rue St-Sebastien.** The best place to watch the glassblowers and to buy glass, aside from the shops along rue St-Sebastien, is **Verrerie de Biot,** 5 chemin des Combes (© **04-93-65-03-00**), at the edge of town. Hours are Monday to Saturday 9:30am to 6:30pm. You can also visit the showroom on Sunday 10:30am to 1pm and 2:30 to 6:30pm. While you're here, you can call at **Galerie International du Verre,** where beautifully displayed glassworks are for sale, often at exorbitant prices. Even if you don't buy, you can admire these one-of-a-kind collector pieces.

There's also the **Galerie Jean-Claude Novaro** (also known as Galerie de la Patrimoine), place des Arcades (© **04-93-65-60-23**). Its namesake is known as the Picasso of glass artists. His works are pretty and colorful, though they sometimes lack the diversity and flair of works by some of the artists displayed at the Galerie International du Verre. Most of his glass art, except for some exhibition pieces, is for sale. You may also want to shop at **La Poterie Provençale,** 1689 rte. de la Mer (© **04-93-65-63-30**). Set adjacent to the Musée Fernand-Léger, about 2 miles southeast of town, it's one of the last potteries in Provence to specialize in the amphoralike containers known as *jarres*.

The **Musée d'Histoire Locale et de Céramique Biotoise,** 9 rue St-Sebastien (© **04-93-65-54-54**), has assembled the best work of local glassblowing artists, potters, ceramists, painters, and silver- and goldsmiths. It's open Wednesday to Sunday from 2 to 6pm, charging 10F (1.50, $1.45) for adults, 5F (.75, 75¢) for ages 6 to 16, and free for children under 6.

Musée National Fernand-Léger ★★ The artist's widow, Nadia Léger, assembled this collection and donated it to the French government after the artist's death. The stone-and-marble facade is enhanced by Léger's mosaic-and-ceramic mural. On the grounds is a polychrome ceramic sculpture, *Le Jardin d'enfant,* inside are two floors of geometrical forms in pure flat colors. The collection includes paintings, ceramics, tapestries, and sculptures showing the artist's development from 1905 until his death. His paintings abound with cranes, acrobats, scaffolding, railroad signals, buxom nudes, casings, and crankshafts. The most unusual work depicts a Léger Mona Lisa (*La Giaconde aux Clés*) contemplating a set of keys, a wide-mouthed fish dangling over her head.

Chemin du Val-de-Pome (on the eastern edge of town, beside the road leading to Biot's rail station). © **04-92-91-50-30**. Admission 30F–38F (4.55– 5.80, $4.35–$5.50) adults, 20F–28F (3.05– 4.25, $2.90–$4.05) ages 18–24 and seniors over 60, free for children 17 and under. (Prices vary depending on the exhibition.) Oct–June Wed–Mon 10am–12:30pm and 2–5:30pm; July–Sept Wed–Mon 10am–12:20pm and 2–6pm.

DINING

Les Terraillers ★★★ MEDITERRANEAN This stone-sided restaurant is about half a mile south of Biot, in what was built in the 1500s as a studio for the production of clay pots and ceramics. The cuisine of chef Claude Jacques and his young staff changes with the seasons and is more sophisticated and appetizing than of many competitors. Examples are a platter containing two preparations of pigeon (thigh and breast cooked in different ways) served with a corn galette and the pigeon's own drippings; roasted scallops with saffron and mussel-flavored cream sauce and a leek confit; a tart with artichoke hearts and tomatoes en confit with lobster salad; braised John Dory Provençal style, with olive oil and a fricassée of zucchini, artichokes, tomatoes, and olives; and ravioli filled with panfried foie gras served with essence of morels and mushroom duxelle.

11 rte. du Chemin-Neuf. © 04-93-65-01-59. Reservations required, as far in advance in possible. Main courses 180F–220F (27.35– 33.45, $26.10–$31.90); fixed-price menus 220F–390F (33.45– 59.30, $31.90–$56.55) lunch, 260F–390F (39.50– 59.30, $37.70–$56.55) dinner. AE, MC, V. Fri–Tues noon–2pm and 7–10pm. Thurs night July–Aug 7–10pm. Closed Nov. Take rte. du Chemin-Neuf, following the signs to Antibes.

7 Golfe-Juan & Vallauris ⭐

Golfe-Juan: 567 miles S of Paris, 4 miles E of Cannes; Vallauris: 565 miles S of Paris, 4 miles E of Cannes

Napoléon and 800 men landed at Golfe-Juan in 1815 to begin his Hundred Days. Protected by hills, this spot beside the coast was also the favored port for the American navy. Today it's primarily a family resort known for its beaches and a noteworthy restaurant (see "Dining," below for information on Chez Tétou).

The 1¼-mile-long RN135 leads inland from Golfe-Juan to Vallauris. Once merely a stopover along the Riviera, Vallauris (noted for its pottery) owes its reputation to Picasso, who "discovered" it. The master came to Vallauris after World War II and occupied a villa known as "The Woman from Wales."

ESSENTIALS

GETTING THERE You can **drive** to Golfe-Juan or Vallauris on any of the three east-west highways along the Riviera. Although route numbers are not always indicated, city names are clear once you're on the highway. From Cannes or Antibes, N7 east is the fastest route. From Nice or Biot, take A8/E80 west.

There's a sleepy-looking rail station in Golfe-Juan, on avenue de la Gare. To get here, you'll have to transfer from a **train** in Cannes. The train from Cannes costs around 10F (1.50, $1.45) each way. For railway information and schedules, call © 08-36-35-35-35. Alternatively, a flotilla of **buses**, operated by RCA (Rapides Côte-d'Azur; © 04-93-39-11-39), makes frequent transits from Cannes; the 20-minute trips cost 10F (1.50, $1.45) each way; and from Nice, the 60-minute trip costs 25F (3.80, $3.65) each way.

VISITOR INFORMATION There's an **Office de Tourisme** at 84 av. de la Liberté in Golfe-Juan (© 04-93-63-73-12) and another on square 8-Mai in Vallauris (© 04-93-63-82-58).

A DAY AT THE BEACH

Because of its position beside the sea, Golfe-Juan developed long ago into a warm-weather resort. The town's twin strips of beach are **Plages du Soleil** (east of the Vieux Port and the newer Port Camille-Rayon) and **Plages du Midi** (west of those two). Each stretches half a mile and charges no entry fee, with the exception of small areas administered by concessions that rent mattresses and chaises and offer access to kiosks dispensing snacks and cold drinks. Regardless of which concession you select (on Plage du Midi they sport names like Au Vieux Rocher, Palma Beach, and Corail Plage; on Plage du Soleil, Plage Nounou and Plage Tétou), you'll pay around 90F (13.70, $13.05) for a day's use of a mattress. Plage Tétou is associated with the upscale Chez Tétou (see "Dining," below). If you don't want to rent a mattress, you can cavort unhindered anywhere along the sands, moving freely from one area to another. Golfe-Juan indulges bathers who remove their bikini tops, but in theory it forbids nude sunbathing.

SEEING THE SIGHTS

Picasso's *Homme et Mouton* (Man and Sheep) is the outdoor statue at which Aly Kahn and Rita Hayworth were married. The council of Vallauris had intended to ensconce this statue in a museum, but Picasso insisted that it remain on the square "where the children could climb over it and the dogs water it unhindered."

Musée Magnelli, Musée de la Céramique & Musée National Picasso La Guerre et La Paix ✿ A chapel of rough stone shaped like a Quonset hut is the focal point of a three-in-one sightseeing highlight. The museum grew from the site of a chapel that Picasso decorated with two paintings: *La Paix* (Peace) and *La Guerre* (War). The paintings offer contrasting images of love and peace on the one hand and violence and conflict on the other. In 1970, a house painter gained illegal entrance to the museum and substituted one of his own designs, after whitewashing a portion of the original. When the aging master inspected the damage, he said, "Not bad at all." In July 1996, the site was enhanced with a permanent exposition devoted to the works of the Florentine-born Alberto Magnelli, a pioneer of abstract art whose first successes were acclaimed in 1915 and who died in 1971, 2 years before Picasso. A third section showcases ceramics, both traditional and innovative, from potters throughout the region.

Place de la Libération. ✆ 04-93-64-16-05. Admission 17F (2.60, $2.45) adults, 8.50F (1.30, $1.25) students, free for children under 16. Oct–Mar Wed–Mon 10am–noon and 2–6pm; Apr–Sept Wed–Mon 10am–6:30pm.

SHOPPING

A shop that rises far above its neighbors is the **Galerie Madoura,** avenue de Georges et Suzanne Ramié, in Vallauris (✆ **04-93-64-66-39**); it's the only shop licensed to sell Picasso reproductions. The master knew and admired the work of the Ramie family, who founded Madoura; it's open Monday to Friday from 10am to 12:30pm and 2:30 to 7pm (to 6pm October to March). Some of the reproductions are limited to 25 to 500 copies. Another gallery to seek out is the **Galerie Sassi-Milici,** 65 bis av. Georges-Clemenceau (✆ **04-93-64-65-71**), displaying works by contemporary artists.

Market day at Vallauris takes place every day except Monday from 7am to 12:30pm, at **place de l'Homme au Mouton,** with its flower stalls and local produce. For a souvenir, you may want to visit a farming cooperative, the **Cooperative Nérolium,** 12 av. Georges-Clemenceau (✆ **04-93-64-27-54**). It produces such foods as bitter-orange marmalade and quince jam, and scented products like orange flower water. Another unusual outlet for local products is the **Parfumerie Bouis,** 50 av. Georges-Clemenceau (✆ **04-93-64-38-27**).

La Boutique de l'Olivier, 46 av. Georges-Clemenceau (✆ **04-93-64-66-45**), is a specialist in objects made of olive wood. These include pepper mills, salad servers, cheese boards, free-form bowls, and bread-slicing boxes. **Terres à Terre,** 58 av. Georges-Clemenceau (✆ **04-93-63-16-80**), is known for its culinary pottery, made of local clay. This is an excellent outlet for picking up terra-cotta pottery. Gratin dishes and casseroles have long been big sellers here.

DINING

Chez Tétou ✿✿ SEAFOOD In its own amusing way, this is one of the Côte d'Azur's most famous restaurants, capitalizing on the beau monde who came here in the 1950s and 1960s. Retaining its Provençal earthiness despite its high prices, it has thrived in a white-sided beach cottage for more than 65 years. The list of appetizers is limited to platters of *charcuterie* (cold cuts) or several almost-perfect slices of fresh melon, as most diners order the house specialty, bouillabaisse. Also on the limited menu are grilled sea bass with tomatoes Provençal, *sole meunière,* and several preparations of lobster—the most famous of which is grilled and served with lemon-butter sauce, fresh parsley, and basmati rice. Your dessert might be a powdered croissant with grandmother's jams (winter) or a raspberry-and-strawberry tart (summer).

Av. des Frères-Roustand, sur la Plage, Golfe-Juan. © 04-93-63-71-16. Reservations required. Main courses 300F–350F (45.60– 53.20, $43.50–$50.75); bouillabaisse 410F–510F (62.30– 77.50, $59.45–$73.95). No credit cards. Thurs–Tues noon–11:30pm and 8–10:30pm. Closed Nov–Mar 6.

8 Juan-les-Pins ⭑⭑

567 miles S of Paris, 6 miles S of Cannes

This suburb of Antibes is a resort developed in the 1920s by Frank Jay Gould. At that time people flocked to "John of the Pines" to escape the "crassness" of Cannes. In the 1930s Juan-les-Pins drew a chic winter crowd. Today it attracts young Europeans from many economic backgrounds, in pursuit of sex, sun, and sea, in that order.

Juan-les-Pins is often called the "Coney Island of the Riviera," but anyone who calls it that hasn't seen Coney Island in a long time. One writer called it "a pop-art Monte Carlo, with burlesque shows and nude beaches," a description too provocative for such a middle-class resort. Another writer said that Juan-les-Pins is "for the young and noisy." Even F. Scott Fitzgerald decried it as a "constant carnival." If he could see it now, he'd know he was a prophet.

ESSENTIALS

GETTING THERE   Juan-les-Pins is connected by **rail** and bus to most other Mediterranean coastal resorts, especially Nice (trip time: 30 minutes). For rail information and schedules, call © **08-36-35-35-35.** There are also **buses** that arrive from Nice and its airport at 40-minute intervals throughout the day. A bus leaves for Juan-les-Pins from Antibes at place Guynemer (© **04-93-34-37-60**), daily every 20 minutes and costs 7.50F (1.15, $1.10) one way (trip time: 10 minutes). To **drive** to Juan-les-Pins from Nice, travel along N7 south; from Cannes, follow the signposted roads. Juan-les-Pins is just outside of Cannes.

VISITOR INFORMATION   The **Office de Tourisme** is at 51 bd. Charles-Guillaumont (© **04-92-90-53-05;** www.riviera.fr/tourisme.htm).

SPECIAL EVENTS   The town offers some of the best nightlife on the Riviera, and the action reaches its height during the annual jazz festival. The **Festival International de Jazz** descends at the end of July for 10 days, attracting jazz masters and their devoted fans. Concerts are presented within a temporary stadium, custom built for the event within Le Parc de la Pinède, which is then dismantled at the end of the festival. Tickets range 110F to 200F (16.70 to 30.40, $15.95 to $29) and can be purchased at the Office de Tourisme.

A DAY AT THE BEACH

Part of the reason people flock here is that the town's beaches actually have sand, unlike many of the other resorts along this coast, which have pebbly beaches. **Plage de Juan-les-Pins** is the town's most central beach. Its subdivisions, all public, include **Plage de la Salis** and **Plage de la Garoupe.** If you don't have your own beach chair, go to the concessions operated by each of the major beachfront hotels. Even if you're not a guest, you can rent a chaise and mattress for 80F to 120F (12.15 to 18.25, $11.60 to $17.40). The most chic of the lot is the area maintained by the Hôtel des Belles-Rives. Competitors more or less in the same category are La Jetée and La Voile Blanche, both opposite the tourist information office. Topless sunbathing is permitted, but total nudity isn't.

WATER SPORTS

If you're interested in scuba diving, check with your hotel concierge or one of these companies: **Club de la Mer,** Port Gallice (© **04-93-61-26-07**); or **EPAJ,** embarcadère Courbet (© **04-93-67-52-59**). **Water-skiing** is available at virtually every beach in Juan-les-Pins, including one outfit that's more or less permanently located on the beach of the Hôtel des Belles-Rives. Ask any beach attendant or bartender and he or she will guide you to the water-skiing representatives who station themselves on the sands. A 10-minute session costs about 150F (22.80, $21.75).

ACCOMMODATIONS
VERY EXPENSIVE

Hôtel des Belles-Rives ★★ This is one of the Riviera's fabled addresses, on a par with the equally famous Juana (below), though the Juana boasts a superior cuisine. Once it was a holiday villa occupied by Zelda and F. Scott Fitzgerald, and the scene of many a drunken brawl. In the following years, it hosted the illustrious, like the duke and duchess of Windsor, Josephine Baker, and Edith Piaf. A 1930s aura lingers through recent renovations. Double-glazing and air-conditioning help a lot. As befits a hotel of this age, rooms come in a variety of shapes and sizes, from small to spacious, but each is fitted with a luxurious bathroom with a combination tub and shower. The lower terraces are devoted to garden dining rooms and a waterside aquatic club with a snack bar and lounge, and a jetty extending into the water. Dinners are served in the romantic setting at La Terrasse (see "Dining," below) with a panoramic bay view.

33 bd. Baudoin, 06160 Juan-les-Pins. © 04-93-61-02-79. Fax 04-93-67-43-51. www.bellesrives.com. 45 units. 1,150F–2,900F (174.80– 440.80, $166.75–$420.50) double; from 3,200F (486.40, $464) suite. Half board 390F (59.30, $56.55) per person extra. AE, DC, DISC, MC, V. Closed mid-Oct to Mar. Free parking. **Amenities:** Restaurant, bar; private beach; landing dock; courtesy car; room service; baby-sitting; laundry/dry cleaning. *In room:* A/C, TV, minibar, hair dryer, safe.

Hôtel Juana ★★★ This balconied Art Deco hotel, owned by the Barache family since 1929, is separated from the sea by the park of pines that gave Juan-les-Pins its name and that was so beloved by F. Scott Fitzgerald. The hotel has a private swimming club where you can rent a "parasol and pad" on the sandy beach at reduced rates. Nearby is a park with umbrella-shaded tables and palms. The hotel is constantly being refurbished, as reflected in the attractive rooms with mahogany pieces, well-chosen fabrics, tasteful carpets, and large baths in marble or tile imported from Italy. The rooms often have such extras as balconies. We review La Terrasse restaurant below.

La Pinède, av. Gallice, 06160 Juan-les-Pins. © 04-93-61-08-70. Fax 04-93-61-76-60. www.hotel-juana.com. 50 units. 1,150F–2,850F (174.80– 433.20, $166.75–$413.25) double; from 2,800F (425.60, $406) suite. MC, V. Closed Nov–Mar. Parking 100F (15.20, $14.50). **Amenities:** Restaurant, 2 bars; private beach club and heated marble outdoor pool with solarium; bicycle rentals; concierge; secretarial services; room service; massage; baby-sitting; laundry/dry cleaning; . *In room:* A/C, TV, minibar, hair dryer, safe.

MODERATE

Hôtel des Mimosas This elegant 1870s-style villa sprawls in a tropical garden on a hilltop. The decor is a mix of high-tech and Italian-style comfort, with antique and modern furniture. Bedrooms come in a variety of shapes and sizes—some quite small—and each offers a compact shower-only bathroom. The rooms open onto balconies. A pool is set amid huge palm trees. The hotel is fully booked in summer, so reserve far in advance.

Rue Pauline, 06160 Juan-les-Pins. © 04-93-61-04-16. Fax 04-92-93-06-46. 34 units. 480F–690F (72.95– 103.50, $69.60–$100.05) double. AE, MC, V. Closed Sept 30–Apr 30. From the town center, drive a quarter mile west, following N7 toward Cannes. **Amenities:** Pool; dry cleaning. *In room:* TV, minibar, coffeemaker, safe.

INEXPENSIVE

Hôtel Cecil *Value*   Located 50 yards from the beach, this well-kept small hotel is one of the best bargains in Juan-les-Pins. The traditionally furnished rooms are well worn yet clean, ranging from small to midsize, each with a compact tiled bathroom with shower only. Owner/chef Michel Courtois provides a courteous welcome and good meals. In summer, you can enjoy his food on a patio.

Rue Jonnard, 06160 Juan-les-Pins. ℭ **04-93-61-05-12.** Fax 04-93-67-09-14. 21 units. Apr–Sept 600F (91.20, $87) double. AE, DC, MC, V. Closed Oct–Mar. Parking 50F (7.60, $7.25). **Amenities:** Restaurant, bar. *In room:* TV.

Hôtel Le Pré Catelan   In a residential area near the town park, this Provençal villa (built ca. 1900) features a garden with rock terraces, towering palms, lemon and orange trees, large pots of pink geraniums, and outdoor furniture. The atmosphere is casual, the setting uncomplicated and unstuffy. A full-scale renovation was completed in 2000. The more expensive rooms have terraces, but the furnishings are durable and rather basic. As is typical of such old villas, bedrooms come in a variety of shapes and sizes, each with a small shower-only bathroom. Despite the setting in the heart of town, the garden manages to provide a sense of isolation. Breakfast is the only meal served.

22 av. des Palmiers, 06160 Juan-les-Pins. ℭ **04-93-61-05-11.** Fax 04-93-67-83-11. trevoux@club-internet.fr. 24 units. 500F–650F (76– 98.80, $72.50–$94.25) double; 850F (129.20, $123.25) suite. AE, DC, MC, V. Closed Nov–Mar. **Amenities:** Pool. *In room:* TV, minibar.

DINING

La Romana FRENCH/INTERNATIONAL   Behind the casino, this unpretentious restaurant successfully caters its trade to the thousands of budget-conscious holidaymakers who flood the town every season. Don't expect grande cuisine, as the venue is too simple and too informal. What you'll get—amid a generic 1930s-style decor accented with touches of wrought iron—is pizzas, meal-size salads, mussels, fried fish and fried scampi, grilled steaks with French fries, and *plats du jour* whose composition changes every day.

21 av. Dautheville. ℭ **04-93-61-05-66.** Pizzas and pastas 57F–65F (8.65– 9.90,$8.25–$9.45); main courses 70F–140F (10.65– 21.30, $10.15–$20.30). DC, MC, V. Daily noon–2:30pm and 7pm–11pm.

La Terrasse ✦✦✦ FRENCH/MEDITERRANEAN   Bill Cosby loves this restaurant so much that he's been known to fly chef Christian Morisset to New York to prepare dinner for him. Morisset, who trained with Vergé and Lenôtre, cooks with a light, precise, and creative hand. His cuisine is the best in Juan-les-Pins and among the finest along the Riviera. The setting is lively and sophisticated, with a modern decor overlooking the garden and a glassed-in terrace whose roof opens for midsummer ventilation and a view of the stars. Menu items are steeped in the flavors of Provence. Examples include giant raviolis stuffed with fresh crayfish and olive-flavored essence of shellfish; and a rack of lamb from the salt marshes of Pauillac cooked in a clay pot, served with stuffed zucchini flowers and Provençal herbs. Dessert might include a Napoléon (*millefeuille*) of wild strawberries with mascarpone cream sauce.

In the Hôtel Juana, La Pinède, av. Gallice. ℭ **04-93-61-20-37.** Reservations required. Main courses 240F–390F (36.50– 59.33, $34.80–$56.55); fixed-price menus 290F (44.10, $42.05) lunch, 490F–660F (74.50– 100.30, $71.05–$95.70) dinner. AE, MC, V. July–Aug daily 12:30–2pm and 7:30–10:30pm; Apr–June and Sept–Oct Tues and Thurs–Sun 12:30–2pm, Thurs–Mon 7:30–10:30pm. Closed Nov–Mar.

Le Bijou FRENCH/PROVENÇAL This upscale brasserie flourishes beside the seafront promenade and has done so for about 80 years. The marine-style decor includes lots of varnished wood and bouquets of blue and white flowers in a mostly blue-and-white interior. Windows overlook a private beach whose sands are much less crowded than those of the public beaches nearby. Menu items are sophisticated and less expensive than you'd expect. Examples are an excellent version of bouillabaisse, grilled sardines, risotto with John Dory and truffled butter, steamed mussels with *sauce poulette* (frothy cream sauce with herbs and butter), grilled John Dory with a vinaigrette enriched by a tapenade of olives and fresh basil, and a super-size *plateau des coquillages et fruits de mer* (shellfish). Don't confuse this informally elegant place with its beachfront terrace, open only April to September daily from noon to 4pm. Here a lunch buffet—served to diners in swimsuits, which are strictly forbidden in the main restaurant several paces uphill—is 70F (10.65, $10.15) per person.

Bd. Charles-Guillaumont. (04-93-61-39-07. Reservations recommended. Main courses 175F–450F (26.60– 68.40, $25.40–$65.25); fixed-price menu 110F–280F (16.70– 42.55, $15.95–$40.60); shellfish platters 280F (42.55, $40.60); bouillabaisse 330F (50.15, $47.85). AE, DC, MC, V. Daily noon–2:30pm and 7:30–10:30pm (to 11:30pm June to mid-Sept).

JUAN-LES-PINS AFTER DARK

For starters, visit the **Eden Casino,** boulevard Baudoin in the heart of Juan-les-Pins ((**04-92-93-71-71**), and try your luck at the roulette wheel or at one of the slot machines. The area containing slot machines doesn't charge admission. It's open every day from 10am to 5pm. The area containing *les grands jeux* (blackjack, roulette, and chemin de fer) is open daily from 9:30pm to 5am and charges 70F (10.65, $10.15) per person.

For a more tropical experience, head to **Le Pam Pam,** route Wilson ((**04-93-61-11-05**), where you can sip rum drinks in an ambience created and celebrated by live reggae, Brazilian, and African performances of music and dance.

If you prefer some high-energy reveling, check out the town's many discos, the best of which are **Whisky à Gogo,** boulevard de la Pinède ((**04-93-61-26-40**), with its young trendsetters and pounding rock beat; the richly dramatic **Le J's,** avenue Georges-Gallice ((**04-93-67-22-74**), offering the latest music; and **Le Village,** 1 bd. de la Pinède ((**04-93-61-18-71**), which boasts an action-packed dance floor and hip DJs spinning the latest from the international music scene. The cover charge at these clubs is a stiff 100F (15.20, $14.50).

For a more relaxed evening, go to the British pub **Le Ten's Bar,** 25 av. du Dr.-Hochet ((**04-93-67-20-67**), where you'll find 56 brands of beer and a sociable crowd of young and old merrymakers. You could even choose the tranquil piano bar **Diamonds,** 25 rue du Dr.-Hochet ((**04-93-67-49-89**), with its older, more sophisticated crowd; or **Le Madison,** 1 av. Alexandre-III ((**04-93-67-83-80**), with the town's best jazz and blues.

9 Antibes & Cap d'Antibes ★★

567 miles S of Paris, 13 miles SW of Nice, 7 miles NE of Cannes

On the other side of the Baie des Anges (Bay of Angels), across from Nice, is the port of Antibes. This Mediterranean town has a quiet charm unique on the Côte d'Azur. Its little harbor is filled with fishing boats and pleasure yachts, and in recent years it has emerged as a new hot spot. The marketplaces are full of flowers, mostly roses and carnations. If you're in Antibes in the evening, you can watch fishers playing the popular Riviera game of boule.

Spiritually, Antibes is totally divorced from Cap d'Antibes, a peninsula studded with the villas and pools of the super-rich. In *Tender Is the Night*, F. Scott Fitzgerald described it as a place where "old villas rotted like water lilies among the massed pines." Photos of film and rock stars lounging at the Eden Roc have appeared in countless magazines.

ESSENTIALS

GETTING THERE **Trains** from Cannes arrive at the rail station, on place Pierre-Semard, every 20 minutes (trip time: 10 minutes), at a one-way fare of around 15F (2.30, $2.20). Trains from Nice arrive every 30 minutes (trip time: 18 minutes), charging a one-way fare of around 21F (3.20, $3.05). There's also a **bus** station, La Gare Routière, on place Guynemer (© **04-93-34-37-60**), that receives buses from throughout Provence.

If you're **driving**, take E1 east from Cannes, taking the turn-off to the south for Antibes, which will lead to the historic core of the old city. From Nice, take E1 west until you come to the turnoff for Antibes. From the center of Antibes, follow the coastal road, boulevard Leclerc, south until you come to Cap d'Antibes.

VISITOR INFORMATION The **Office de Tourisme** is at 11 place du Général-de-Gaulle (© **04-92-90-53-00;** www.riviera.fr/tourisme.htm).

SEEING THE SIGHTS

Musée Picasso ⭐⭐ On the ramparts above the port is the Château Grimaldi, once the home of the princes of Antibes of the Grimaldi family, who ruled the city from 1385 to 1608. Today it houses one of the world's great Picasso collections. Picasso came to town after his bitter war years in Paris and stayed in a small hotel at Golfe-Juan until the museum director at Antibes invited him to work and live at the museum. Picasso spent 1946 painting here. When he departed, he gave the museum all the work he'd done: 24 paintings, 80 pieces of ceramics, 44 drawings, 32 lithographs, 11 oils on paper, 2 sculptures, and 5 tapestries. In addition, there's a gallery of contemporary art exhibiting Léger, Miró, Ernst, and Calder, among others. Some of the works by these other artists might be in storage at the time of your visit, based on whatever temporary exhibition is being displayed.

Place du Château. © **04-92-90-54-26** for recorded message or 04-92-90-54-20 for an attendant. Admission 30F (4.55, $4.35) adults, 18F (2.75, $2.60) students and ages 15–24 and over 60, free for 18 and under. Tues–Sun 10–noon and 2–6pm (June–Sept, Tues–Sun 10am–6pm).

Musée Naval et Napoléonien *Kids* In this stone-sided fort and tower, built in stages between the 17th and the 18th century, you'll find a interesting collection of Napoleonic memorabilia, naval models, and paintings many of which were donated by at least two world-class collectors. A toy soldier collection depicts various uniforms, including one used by Napoléon in the Marengo campaign. A wall painting on wood shows Napoléon's entrance into Grenoble; another shows him disembarking at Golfe-Juan on March 1, 1815. In contrast to Canova's Greek-god image of Napoléon, a miniature pendant by Barrault reveals the general as he really looked, with pudgy cheeks and a receding hairline. In the rear rotunda is one of the many hats worn by the emperor. You can climb to the top of the tower for a view of the coast that's worth the admission price.

Batterie du Grillon, bd. J.-F.-Kennedy. © **04-93-61-45-32.** Admission 20F (3.05, $2.90) adults, 10F (1.50, $1.45) for students, persons under 25 and seniors. Mon–Fri 9:30am–noon and 2:15–6pm; Sat 9:30am–noon.

ACCOMMODATIONS
VERY EXPENSIVE

Hôtel du Cap–Eden Roc ★★★   Legendary for the glamour of both its setting and its clientele, this Second Empire hotel, opened in 1870, is surrounded by 22 splendid acres of gardens. It's like a great country estate, with spacious public rooms, marble fireplaces, scenic paneling, chandeliers, and upholstered armchairs. The guest rooms are among the most sumptuous on the Riviera, with deluxe mattresses. Even though the guests snoozing by the pool, which was blasted out of the cliffside at enormous expense, might appear artfully undraped during daylight hours, evenings here are intensely upscale, with lots of emphasis on clothing and style. The world-famous Pavillon Eden Roc, near a rock garden apart from the hotel, has a panoramic Mediterranean view. Venetian chandeliers, Louis XV chairs, and elegant draperies add to the drama. Lunch is served on an outer terrace, under umbrellas and an arbor.

Bd. J.-F.-Kennedy, 06600 Cap d'Antibes. ✆ **04-93-61-39-01.** Fax 04-93-67-76-04. www.edenroc-hotel.fr. 140 units. 2,500F–4,400F (380– 668.80, $362.50–$638) double; from 6,000F (912, $870) suite. No credit cards. Closed mid-Oct to Mar. Bus: A2. **Amenities:** Restaurant, 2 bars; pool; gym; sauna; secretarial service; room service; massage; baby-sitting; laundry/dry cleaning. *In room:* A/C, TV, hair dryer, safe.

Hôtel Imperial Garoupe ★★   Set within 50 yards of the beach, this hotel is the centerpiece of a 3½-acre park whose rows of pines block some of the sea views. It was built in 1993 by the heiress to the Moulinex housewares fortune. After an unprofitable first season, Gilbert Irondelle, son of the director of Antibes's hyper-expensive Hôtel du Cap, bought it and transformed it into a charming pocket of posh that's a bit less intimidating than the more monumental hotel run by his father. The luxurious rooms boast contemporary furnishings, luxury mattresses, and deluxe bathrooms with a combination tub and shower. The in-house restaurant serves a French and international cuisine.

770 Chemin de la Garoupe, 06600 Antibes. ✆ **800/525-4800** or 04-92-93-31-61. Fax 04-92-93-31-62. www.imperial-garoupe.com. 34 units. 3,000F–3,200F (450– 480, $435–$464) double; 3,950F–5,200F (592.59– 780, $572.75nd]$754) suite. AE, DC, MC, V. Free parking. Bus: A2. **Amenities:** Restaurant, bar; heated outdoor pool; room service; baby-sitting; laundry/dry cleaning. *In room:* A/C, TV, minibar, hair dryer.

MODERATE

Castel Garoupe *(Value)*   We highly recommend this Mediterranean villa, which was built in 1968 on a private lane in the center of the cape, because it offers tastefully furnished spacious rooms with fine mattresses and compact bathrooms with shower and tub. Many of the rooms have private balconies, and each has shuttered windows. There's a tranquil garden on the premises.

959 bd. de la Garoupe, 06160 Cap d'Antibes. ✆ **04-93-61-36-51.** Fax 04-93-67-74-88. www.castel garoupe.com. 27 units. 710F–890F (107.90– 135.30, $102.95–$129.05) double; 880F–1,040F (133.75– 156, $127.60–$150.80) studio apt with kitchenette. AE. Closed Nov to mid-Mar. Bus A2. **Amenities:** Outdoor pool; exercise room; room service; baby-sitting. *In room:* A/C, TV, kitchenette (in some), fridge, hair dryer, safe.

INEXPENSIVE

Auberge de la Gardiole ★   Monsieur and Mme Courtot run this country inn with a personal touch. The large villa, surrounded by gardens, is in an area of private estates. The charming rooms are on the upper floors of the inn and in the little buildings in the garden; they come in a variety of shapes and sizes, each furnished with a certain charm and an eye on comfort. Half the units come with showers and the others with a combination tub and shower. The cheerful dining room, serving French and Provençal cuisine, has a fireplace and hanging pots and pans; in good weather you can dine under a wisteria-covered trellis.

Chemin de la Garoupe, 06160 Cap d'Antibes. (℃ **04-93-61-35-03.** Fax 04-93-67-61-87. www.hotel-lagaroupe-gardiole.com. 17 units. 590F–790F (89.73– 120.10, $85.55–$114.55) double; 850F–1,300F (129.20– 197.60, $123.25–$188.50) suite. AE, MC, V. Closed Nov–Mar. Bus: A2. **Amenities:** Restaurant, bar; pool; room service; laundry. *In room:* A/C (in 15), TV, minibar, safe.

DINING

La Bonne Auberge ⊀ TRADITIONAL/MODERN FRENCH Though no longer the Riviera's most celebrated restaurant, this is still a desirable choice in its new incarnation. For many years following its 1975 opening, this was one of the most famous restaurants on the French Riviera. In 1992, in the wake of the death of its famous founder, Jo Rostang, his culinary heir, Philippe Rostang, wisely limited its scope and transformed it into a worthwhile but less ambitious restaurant. All that's available is a well-orchestrated fixed-price menu. Choices vary every 3 weeks but may include a Basque-inspired pipérade with poached eggs, sea wolf with soya sauce, savory swordfish tart, and chicken with vinegar and garlic. Dessert might be an enchanting peach soufflé.

Quartier de Brague, rte. N7. (℃ **04-93-33-36-65.** Reservations required. Fixed-price menu 220F (33.45, $31.90). MC, V. Wed–Sun noon–2pm; Tues–Sat 7–10pm. Closed mid-Nov to mid-Dec. Take coastal highway N7 east 2½ miles from Antibes.

La Taverne du Saffranier *Value* PROVENÇAL Earthy, irreverent, and occupying a century-old building in the Provençal motif, this brasserie serves a changing medley of local specialties. Portions are savory and generous. Examples are a platter of *petits farcis* (stuffed vegetables); *céviche,* the cold raw fish in hot sauce that's particularly refreshing on a hot day; a savory version of fish soup; and a medley of grilled fish (including sardines) that's served only with a dash of fresh lemon. The kitchen can also prepare its own version of bouillabaisse, but only if you give a day's notice. Lunch hours are very limited.

Place du Saffranier. (℃ **04-93-34-80-50.** Reservations recommended. Main courses 50F–130F (7.60– 19.75, $7.25–$18.85); fixed-price menu 64F (9.75, $9.30). No credit cards. Tues–Sun noon–12:30pm; Tues–Sat 7–10:30pm.

Restaurant de Bacon ⊀⊀⊀ SEAFOOD The Eden Roc restaurant at the Hôtel du Cap is more elegant, but Bacon serves the best seafood for miles around. Set among ultra-expensive residences, this restaurant on a rocky peninsula offers a panoramic coast view. Bouillabaisse aficionados claim that Bacon offers the best version in France. In its deluxe version, saltwater crayfish float atop the savory brew; we prefer the simple version—a waiter adds the finishing touches at your table. If bouillabaisse isn't to your liking, try fish soup with the traditional garlic-laden rouille sauce, fish terrine, sea bass, John Dory, or something from an exotic collection of fish unknown in North America. These include sar, pageot, and denti, prepared in several ways. Many visitors are confused by the way fish dishes are priced by the gram: A guideline is that light lunches cost around 250F to 400F (38 to 60.80, $36.25 to $58); dinners go for 550F to 800F (83.60 to 121.60, $79.75 to $116).

Bd. de Bacon. (℃ **04-93-61-50-02.** Reservations required. Fixed-price menu 280F–450F (42.55– 68.40, $40.60–$65.25); main courses 490F–650F (74.50– 98.80, $71.05–$94.25). AE, DC, MC, V. Tues–Sun 12:30–2pm and 8–10pm. Closed Nov–Jan.

10 Cagnes-sur-Mer (★

570 miles S of Paris, 13 miles NE of Cannes

Cagnes-sur-Mer, like the Roman god Janus, has two faces. Perched on a hill in the "hinterlands" of Nice, **Haut-de-Cagnes** is one of the most charming spots on the Riviera. At the foot of the hill is an old fishing port and rapidly developing beach resort called **Cros-de-Cagnes,** between Nice and Antibes.

For years Haut-de-Cagnes attracted the French literati, including Simone de Beauvoir, who wrote *Les Mandarins* here. A colony of painters also settled here; Renoir said the village was "the place where I want to paint until the last day of my life." Today the racecourse is one of the finest in France.

ESSENTIALS

GETTING THERE **Buses** from Nice and Cannes stop at Cagnes-Ville and at Béal/Les Collettes, within walking distance of Cros-de-Cagnes. For bus information, call (✆ **04-93-45-20-08** in Cannes or **04-93-85-61-81** in Nice. The climb from Cagnes-Ville to Haut-de-Cagnes is very strenuous, so between June and September, a minibus runs about every 30 minutes from place du Général-de-Gaulle in the center of Cagnes-Ville to Haut-de-Cagnes at a cost of 8F (1.20, $1.15) per person. By **car,** from any of the coastal cities of Provence, follow the A8 coastal highway, exiting at "Cagnes-sur-Mer/Cros-de-Cagnes."

VISITOR INFORMATION The **Office de Tourisme** is at 6 bd. Maréchal-Juin, Cagnes-Ville (✆ **04-93-20-61-64;** www.riviera.fr/tourisme.htm).

SPECIAL EVENTS The **Festival International de Peinture** (International Festival of Painting) is presented by Cagnes's Town Hall and the Musée d'Art Moderne Méditerranéen, during July and August in the Château Musée, 7 place Grimaldi. Painters from about 40 nations participate in the exposition and promotion of their works. For information, call (✆ **04-93-20-87-29.**

EXPLORING THE TOWN

Cros-de-Cagnes is known for 2¼ miles of seafront covered with light-gray pebbles that have been smooth by centuries of wave action. These beaches are identified as **Plages de Cros-de-Cagnes.** The expanse is punctuated by five concessions that rent beach mattresses and chaises for around 85F (12.90, $12.35). The best, or at least the most centrally located, are **Tiercé Plage** ((✆ **04-93-20-13-89), Le Cigalon** ((✆ **04-93-07-74-82),** and **La Gougouline** ((✆ **04-93-31-08-72).** As usual, toplessness is accepted but full nudity isn't.

The orange groves and fields of carnations of the upper village provide a beautiful setting for the narrow cobblestone streets and 17th- and 18th-century homes. Drive your car to the top, where you can enjoy the view from **place du Château** and have lunch or a drink at a sidewalk cafe.

Musée de l'Olivier & Musée d'Art Moderne Méditerranéen (★ The Château Musée was originally a fortress built in 1301 by Rainier Grimaldi I, a lord of Monaco and a French admiral (see his portrait inside the museum). Charts reveal how the defenses were organized. In the early 17th century, the dank castle was converted into a more gracious Louis XIII château, which now contains two museums. The Museum of the Olive Tree shows the steps in cultivating and processing the olive. The Museum of Mediterranean Modern Art displays works by Kisling, Carzou, Dufy, Cocteau, and Seyssaud, among others, with temporary exhibits. In one salon is an interesting trompe-l'oeil fresco, *La Chute de Phaeton.*

From the tower you get a panoramic view of the Côte d'Azur. The International Festival of Painting (see "Special Events," above) takes place here.

7 place Grimaldi. ✆ **04-93-20-87-29.** Admission to both museums 20F (3.05, $2.90) adults, 10F (1.50, $1.45) students, children under 12 free. May–Sept Wed–Mon 10am–noon and 2–6pm; Oct–Apr Wed–Mon 10am–noon and 2–5pm.

Musée Renoir & Les Collettes 🅰️   Les Collettes has been restored to what it looked like when Renoir lived here from 1908 until his death in 1919. He continued to sculpt here, even though he was crippled by arthritis. He also continued to paint, with a brush tied to his hand and with the help of assistants.

The house was built in 1907 in an olive-and-orange grove. There's a bust of Mme Renoir in the entrance room. You can explore the drawing room and dining room on your own before going up to the artist's bedroom. In his atelier are his wheelchair, easel, and brushes. From the terrace of Mme Renoir's bedroom is a stunning view of Cap d'Antibes and Haut-de-Cagnes. On a wall hangs a photograph of one of Renoir's sons, Pierre, as he appeared in the 1932 film *Madame Bovary.* Although Renoir is best remembered for his paintings, it was in Cagnes that he began experimenting with sculpture. The museum has 20 portrait busts and portrait medallions, most of which depict his wife and children. The curators say they represent the largest collection of Renoir sculpture in the world.

19 chemin des Collettes. ✆ **04-93-20-61-07.** Admission 20F (3.05, $2.90) adults, 10F (1.50, $1.45) children, under 12 free. May–Sept Wed–Mon 10am–noon and 2–6pm; Oct–Apr Wed–Mon 10am–noon and 2–5pm. Ticket sales end 30 min. before the lunch and evening closing hours.

SHOPPING

Terraïo, 12 place du Docteur-Maurel (✆ **04-93-20-86-83**), is a tiny gem. Art critics claim the stoneware sold in this shop perfectly captures the blue-green tones of the nearby Mediterranean. Part of that derives from artist/owner and native son, Claude Barnoin, who has spent nearly 25 years perfecting the mixture of copper-based glazes that produce these heavenly tones. The ashtrays, dinner services, and enormous showcase pieces produced in the artist's studio (which, alas, you cannot visit) are the pride of many private French and U.S. collections. Prices begin at around 100F (15.20, $14.50) for a simple ashtray, stretching to as much as 3,500F (532, $507.50) for something truly spectacular. The shop, which lies just across the square from the Château Musée of Haut-de-Cagnes, is open daily from 2 to around 6pm, except in midsummer, when it might close for an occasional day, based on the production schedule of the owner.

ACCOMMODATIONS
IN CAGNES-SUR-MER

Hôtel Le Chantilly *(Value)*   This is the best bargain for those who prefer to stay at a hotel near the beach. It won't win any architectural awards, but the owners have landscaped the property and made the interior as homey and inviting as possible, with Oriental rugs and potted plants. The rooms, for the most part, are small but cozily furnished and well kept, often opening onto balconies; each has a compact tiled bathroom with shower. In fair weather you can enjoy breakfast, the only meal served, on an outdoor terrace.

31 chemin de la Minoerie, 06800 Cagnes-sur-Mer. ✆ **04-93-20-25-50.** Fax 04-92-02-82-63. 20 units. 300F–390F (45.60– 59.30, $43.50–$56.55) double; 500F–640F (76– 97.30, $72.50–$92.80) suite. AE, DC, MC, V. Free parking. *In room:* TV, minibar.

IN HAUT-DE-CAGNES

Le Cagnard ★★ Several houses have been joined to form this handsome hostelry. The dining room is covered with frescoes, and there's vine-draped terrace. The rooms and salons are furnished with antiques, such as provincial chests, armoires, and Louis XV chairs. Each room has its own style: Some are duplexes; others have terraces and views of the countryside. The luxurious bathrooms are spacious, with a combination tub and shower. The cuisine of chef Jean-Yves Johany is reason enough to make the trip. Fresh ingredients are used in the delectable dishes placed on one of the finest tables set in Provence.

Rue du Pontis-Long, Le Haut-de-Cagnes, 06800 Cagnes-sur-Mer. ℂ 04-93-20-73-21. Fax 04-93-22-06-39. www.le-cagnard.com. 25 units. 1,100F–1,400F (167.20– 212.80, $159.50–$203) double; 1,600F–3,000F (243.20– 456, $232–$435) suite. AE, DC, MC, V. Parking 50F (7.60, $7.25). **Amenities:** Restaurant, bar; room service; laundry/dry cleaning. In room: A/C, TV, minibar, hair dryer, safe.

DINING

In Haut-de-Cagnes, the hotel **Le Cagnard** (see "Accommodations," above) has a remarkable restaurant.

IN HAUT-DE-CAGNES

À la Table d'Yves ★ Value FRENCH/PROVENÇAL Part of the charm of a meal here involves its setting in a 200-year-old village house. The menu items are reasonably priced and savory, reflecting the sophisticated training of chef/owner Yves Merville. Menu choices change virtually every day according to what's fresh in the markets, but they make ample use of fish, vegetables, cheeses, and herbs. Panfried foie gras is an ongoing favorite as well as the chef's idiosyncratic version of a dessert favorite, *pain perdu*. Other than that, take your pick from the day's assortment of bourrides, stews, blanquettes, fresh-grilled fish, soups, and roasts.

85 Montée de la Bourgade. ℂ 04-93-20-33-33. Reservations recommended. Main courses 80F–140F (12.15– 21.30, $11.60–$20.30); fixed-price menu 135F–240F (20.50– 36.50, $19.60–$34.80). MC, V. Fri–Mon noon–2pm and 7:30–10pm; Tues 7:30–10pm; Thurs 7:30–10pm.

Josy-Jo ★★ TRADITIONAL FRENCH The Cagnard (see "Accommodations," above) has a more elegant setting, but the food here is comparable to that of the famed citadel. Sheltered behind a 200-year-old facade covered with vines and flowers, this restaurant used to be the home and studio of Modigliani and Soutine, when they borrowed it from a friend during their hungriest years. The walls are covered with paintings, and everything is kept running smoothly by the good-natured Bandecchi family. Their cuisine is fresh and excellent, featuring grilled meats and a roster of fish. You can enjoy brochette of gigot of lamb with kidneys, four succulent varieties of steak, calves' liver, a homemade terrine of foie gras of duckling, stuffed provençal vegetables "in the style of Grandmother," and an array of salads.

8 place du Planastel. ℂ 04-93-20-68-76. Reservations required. Main courses 150F–180F (22.80– 27.35, $21.75–$26.10). AE, MC, V. Mon–Fri noon–2pm and 7:30–10pm; Sat 7:30–10pm.

IN CROS-DE-CAGNES

Loulou (La Réserve) ★★ FRENCH This restaurant, which enjoys a Michelin star along with Josy-Jo and Cagnard, makes the Cagnes area a gourmet enclave. It's across from the sea and named for a famous long-departed chef. Of particular note are brothers Eric and Joseph Campo, who prepare dishes that include spectacular versions of fish soup; shrimp that's steamed and then served with fresh ginger and cinnamon; and grilled versions of whatever catch the local suppliers might have brought in that day. These are served as simply as possible, usually with just a drizzling of olive oil and balsamic vinegar. Meat dishes include a flavor-filled version of veal kidneys with port sauce and delectable grilled steaks, chops, and cutlets. Dessert might include a tart of caramelized apples. In front is a glassed-in veranda that's a prime people-watching spot.

91 bd. de la Plage. ✆ **04-93-31-00-17.** Reservations recommended. Main courses 150F–365F (22.80– 55.50, $21.75–$52.95); fixed-price menu 235F (35.70, $34.10). AE, MC, V. Mon–Fri noon–1:30pm and 7–9:45pm; Sat 7–9:45pm. Closed for lunch July 14–Aug 31.

11 St-Paul-de-Vence ★★

575 miles S of Paris, 14 miles E of Grasse, 17 miles E of Cannes, 19 miles N of Nice

Of all the perched villages of the Riviera, St-Paul-de-Vence is the best known. It was popularized in the 1920s when many noted artists lived here, occupying the 16th-century houses flanking the narrow cobblestone streets. The feudal hamlet grew up on a bastion of rock, almost blending into it. Its ramparts (allow about 30 minutes to circle them) overlook a peaceful setting of flowers and olive and orange trees. They haven't changed much since they were constructed from 1537 to 1547 by order of François I. From the ramparts to the north you can look out on Baou de St-Jeannet, a sphinx-shaped rock that was painted into the landscape of Poussin's *Polyphème.*

ESSENTIALS

GETTING THERE   The nearest **rail** station is in Cagnes-sur-Mer. **Buses** depart from the station every 45 minutes for St-Paul-de-Vence. From Nice, about 20 daily buses head to the Gare Routière, near the railway station. For bus information, call **Cie SAP** at ✆ **04-93-58-37-60.** Buses stop in St-Paul near the post office, on the Route de Vence, about a quarter mile from the town center. If you're **driving** from Nice, take the coastal A8 highway east, turning inland at Cagnes-sur-Mer; then follow the signs northward to St-Paul-de-Vence.

VISITOR INFORMATION   The **Office de Tourisme** is at Maison Tour, 2 rue Grande (✆ **04-93-58-06-38;** www.riviera.fr/tourisme.htm).

EXPLORING THE TOWN

Note: Driving a car within the center of St-Paul's old town is prohibited, except to drop off luggage at your hotel. The pedestrian-only **rue Grande** is the most interesting street, running the length of St-Paul. Most of the stone houses along it are from the 16th and 17th centuries, many still bearing the coats-of-arms placed there by the original builders. Today most of the houses are antiques shops, art-and-craft galleries, and souvenir and gift shops; some are still artists' studios.

The village's chief sight is the **Collégiale de la Conversion de St-Paul** ★, constructed in the 12th and 13th centuries though much altered over the years. The Romanesque choir is the oldest part, containing some remarkable stalls carved in walnut in the 17th century. The bell tower was built in 1740. Look to the left as you enter: You'll see the painting *Ste-Cathérine d'Alexandrie,* which has been attributed to Tintoretto. The Trésor de l'Église is one of the most beautiful in the Alpes-Maritimes, with a spectacular ciborium. Look also for a low relief of the *Martyrdom of St-Clément* on the last altar on the right. In the baptismal chapter is a 15th-century alabaster Madonna. It's open daily 9am to 6pm (to 7pm during July and August). Admission is free.

Near the church is the **Musée d'Histoire de St-Paul,** place de Castre (℡ **04-93-32-53-09**), a minor museum in a 16th-century village house. It was restored and refurnished in a 1500s style, with many artifacts illustrating the history of the village. It's open daily from 10am to noon and 1:30 to 5:30pm. Admission is 20F (3.05, $2.90) adults, 12F (1.80, $1.75) students and children under 12, children under 5 free.

Foundation Maeght ⭐⭐⭐ This avant-garde building houses one of the most modern art museums in Europe. On a hill in pine-studded woods, the Foundation Maeght is like a Shangri-La. Nature and the creations of men and women blend harmoniously in this unique achievement of the architect José Luis Sert. Its white concrete arcs give the impression of a giant pagoda.

A stark Calder rises like some futuristic monster on the grassy lawns. In a courtyard, the bronze works of Giacometti form a surrealistic garden, creating a hallucinatory mood. Sculpture is displayed inside, but the museum is at its best in a natural setting of surrounding terraces and gardens. It's built on several levels, its many glass walls providing an indoor-outdoor vista. The foundation, a gift "to the people" from Aimé and Marguerite Maeght, also provides a showcase for new talent. Exhibitions are always changing. Everywhere you look, you see 20th-century art: mosaics by Chagall and Braque, Miró ceramics in the "labyrinth," and Ubac and Braque stained glass in the chapel. Bonnard, Kandinsky, Léger, Matisse, Barbara Hepworth, and many other artists are well represented. There is a library, a cinema, and a cafeteria here. In one showroom you can buy original lithographs by artists like Chagall and Giacometti and limited-edition prints.

Outside the town walls. ℡ **04-93-32-81-63**. Admission 50F (7.60, $7.25) adults, 40F (6.10, $5.80) students and ages 12–18, free for children under 12. July–Sept daily 10am–7pm; Oct–June daily 10am–12:30pm and 2:30–6pm.

ACCOMMODATIONS

La Colombe d'Or also rents deluxe rooms (see "Dining" below).

VERY EXPENSIVE

Le Mas d'Artigny ⭐⭐ This hotel, one of the Riviera's grandest, evokes a sprawling Provençal homestead set in an acre of pine forests. In the lobby is a constantly changing exhibit of art. Each of the comfortably large rooms has its own terrace or balcony, and suites have a private pool with hedges. Bathrooms are deluxe, with a combination tub and shower. For such an elegant hotel, the restaurant is a bit lackluster in decor, but it does have great views of the garden. Chef Francis Scordel regales you with his flavors of Provence, using only quality ingredients to shape his harmonious and rarely complicated cuisine. The wine cellar deserves a star for its vintage collection, but watch those prices!

Rte. de la Colle et des Hauts de St-Paul, 06570 St-Paul-de-Vence. ℡ **04-93-32-84-54**. Fax 04-93-32-95-36. www.mas-artigny.com. 83 units. 1,100F–2,600F (167.20– 395.20, $159.50–$377) double; 2,400F–3,700F (364.80– 562.40, $348–$536.50) suite. Rates about 30% lower in the off-season. AE, DC, MC, V. Parking 60F (9.10, $8.70) in a garage. From the town center, follow signs west about 1¼ miles. **Amenities:** Restaurant, bar; pool; tennis court; exercise room; sauna; mountain bikes; room service; laundry/dry cleaning. *In room:* A/C, TV, minibar, hair dryer, safe.

EXPENSIVE

Hôtel Le St-Paul ⭐⭐⭐ Converted from a 16th-century Renaissance residence and retaining many original features, this Relais & Châteaux member is in the heart of the medieval village. The rooms are decorated in a sophisticated

Provençal style, with sumptuous beds and midsize bathrooms with a combination tub and shower. One woman wrote us that while sitting on the balcony of room 30 she understood why Renoir, Léger, Matisse, and Picasso were inspired by Provence. Many rooms enjoy a view of the valley with the Mediterranean in the distance. The restaurant has a flower-bedecked terrace sheltered by the 16th-century ramparts as well as a superb dining room with vaulted ceilings.

86 rue Grande, 06570 St-Paul-de-Vence. ℂ 04-93-32-65-25. Fax 04-93-32-52-94. www.lesaintpaul.com. 19 units. 1,100F–1,800F (167.20– 273.60, $159.50–$261) double; 1,700F–3,700F (258.40– 562.40, $246.50–$536.50) suite. Half board 440F (66.90, $63.80) per person extra. AE, DC, MC, V. **Amenities:** Restaurant; 3 tennis courts; room service; baby-sitting; laundry/dry cleaning. In room: A/C, TV, minibar, hair dryer, safe.

MODERATE

Auberge Le Hameau ✪ (Value)   This romantic Mediterranean villa is on a hilltop on the outskirts of St-Paul-de-Vence, on the road to Colle at Hauts-de-St-Paul. Built as a farmhouse in the 1920s and enlarged and transformed into a hotel in 1967, it contains high-ceilinged rooms, each with a compact shower-only bathroom. You get a remarkable view of the surrounding hills and valleys. There's also a vineyard and a sunny terrace with fruit trees, flowers, and a pool.

528 rte. de la Colle (D107), 06570 St-Paul-de-Vence. ℂ 04-93-32-80-24. Fax 04-93-32-55-75. 17 units. 580F–790F (88.15– 120.10, $84.10–$114.55) double; from 900F (136.80, $130.50) suite. AE, MC, V. Closed Jan 6–Feb 15 and Nov 16–Dec 22. From the town, take D107 about a half mile, following the signs south of town toward Colle. **Amenities:** Pool. In room: A/C, minibar.

Les Bastides St-Paul   This hotel is in the hills outside town, a mile south of St-Paul and 2½ miles south of Vence. Divided into three buildings, it offers clean and comfortable carpeted rooms, each accented with regional artifacts and a terrace and garden. All the units come with a compact bathroom with a combination tub and shower. On the premises is a pool shaped like a clover leaf. The sensitive management staff is headed by the long-time hoteliers Marie José and Maurice Giraudet. Breakfast is served anytime you want it.

880 rte. des Blaquières (rte. Cagnes-Vence), 06570 St-Paul-de-Vence. ℂ 04-92-02-08-07. Fax 04-93-20-50-41. bastides@fr.fm.bastides.fr.fm. 19 units. 500F–750F (76– 114, $72.50–$108.75) double. AE, DC, MC, V. From the town center, follow the signs toward Cagnes-sur-Mer for 1 mile south. **Amenities:** Pool; room service. In room: A/C, TV, minibar, hair dryer (on request), safe.

Les Orangers (Finds)   Monsieur Franklin has created a beautiful "living oasis" in his villa. The scents of roses, oranges, and lemons waft through the air. The main lounge is impeccably decorated with original oils and furnished in a provincial style. Expect to be treated like a guest in a private home. The rooms, with antiques and Oriental carpets, have panoramic views, and each comes with a small bathroom with shower. Banana trees and climbing geraniums will accompany you while you relax on the sun terrace.

Chemin des Fumerates, rte. de la Colle (D107), 06570 St-Paul-de-Vence. ℂ 04-93-32-80-95. Fax 04-93-32-00-32. 5 units. 760F–1,200F (115.50– 182.40, $110.20–$174) double; 1,200F (182.40, $174) suite. Rates include breakfast. MC, V. Free parking. From the town center, follow the signs to Cagnes-sur-Mer for ½ mile south.

DINING

La Colombe d'Or ✪ TRADITIONAL FRENCH   This is one of the Riviera's most fabled inns. For a decade, "The Golden Dove" has been St-Paul's most celebrated restaurant, not for cutting-edge cuisine or wildly exotic experiments, but for its remarkable art collection. You can dine amid Mirós, Picassos, Klees,

Dufys, Utrillos, and Calders. In fair weather everyone tries for a seat on the terrace. You may begin with smoked salmon or foie gras from Landes if you've recently won at the casino. Otherwise, you can count on a soup made with fresh seasonal vegetables. The best fish dishes are poached sea bass with mousseline sauce and sea wolf baked with fennel. Tender beef comes with *gratin dauphinois* (potatoes), or you may prefer lamb from Sisteron. A classic finish to any meal is a *soufflé flambé au Grand-Marnier.*

The guest rooms (16 doubles, 10 suites) in this hotel contain French antiques and fabrics and accessories inspired by the traditions of Provence. They're scattered among three areas: the original 16th-century stone house, a more recent wing that stretches into the garden adjacent to the pool, and an even more modern annex, built in the 1950s and upgraded several times since. Some have exposed stone and heavy ceiling beams; all are comfortable and clean, with air-conditioning, minibars, TVs, and phones. Prices are 1,550F (235.60, $224.75) for a double and 1,800F (273.60, $261) for a suite.

1 place du Général-de-Gaulle, 06570 St-Paul-de-Vence. ⓒ **04-93-32-80-02**. Fax 04-93-32-77-78. Reservations required. Main courses 110F–250F (16.70– 38, $15.95–$36.25). AE, DC, MC, V. Daily noon–2pm and 7–10pm. Closed Jan 10–20 and Nov–Dec 20.

12 Vence (★)

1575 miles S of Paris, 19 miles N of Cannes, 15 miles NW of Nice

Travel into the hills northwest of Nice—across country studded with cypresses, olive trees, and pines, where flowers, especially carnations, roses, and oleanders, grow in profusion—and Vence comes into view. Outside the town, along boulevard Paul-André, two olive presses carry on with their age-old duties. But the charm lies in the **Vieille Ville** (Old Town). Visitors have themselves photographed on place du Peyra in front of the **Vieille Fontaine** (Old Fountain), a featured in several films. The 15th-century square tower is also a curiosity.

If you're wearing sturdy shoes, the narrow, steep streets of the Old Town are worth exploring. Dating from the 10th century, the cathedral on place Godeau is unremarkable except for some 15th-century Gothic choir stalls. But if it's the right day of the week, most visitors quickly pass through the narrow gates of this once-fortified walled town to where the sun shines more brightly—to see one of Matisse's most remarkable achievements, the Chapelle du Rosaire.

ESSENTIALS

GETTING THERE   Frequent **buses** (no. 400 or 410) originating in Nice take about an hour to reach Vence, and cost 22F (3.35, $3.20) each way. For bus information, contact the **Compagnie SAP** at ⓒ **04-93-58-37-60** for schedules. The nearest **rail station** is in Cagnes-sur-Mer, about 4½ miles from Vence. From here, about 20 buses per day make the trip to Vence. For train information, call ⓒ **08-36-35-35-35**. To **drive** to Vence from Nice, travel along N7 west to Cagnes-sur-Mer and then connect to D236 north to Vence.

VISITOR INFORMATION   The **Office de Tourisme** is on place Grand-Jardin (ⓒ **04-93-58-06-38**).

A MATISSE MASTERPIECE

Chapelle du Rosaire ★★   It was a beautiful golden autumn along the Côte d'Azur. The great Henri Matisse was 77, and after a turbulent introspective time he set out to design and decorate his masterpiece—"the culmination of a whole life dedicated to the search for truth," as he said. Just outside Vence, Matisse created the Chapelle du Rosaire for the Dominican nuns of Monteils. (Part of his action was a gesture of thanks for Sister Jacques-Marie, a member of the order who nursed him back to health after a debilitating illness.) From the front you might find it unremarkable and pass it by—until you spot a 40-foot crescent-adorned cross rising from a blue-tile roof.

Matisse wrote: "What I have done in the chapel is to create a religious space . . . in an enclosed area of very reduced proportions and to give it, solely by the play of colors and lines, the dimensions of infinity." The light picks up the subtle coloring in the simply rendered leaf forms and abstract patterns: sapphire blue, aquamarine, and lemon yellow. In black-and-white ceramics, St. Dominic is depicted in only a few lines. The most remarkable design is in the black-and-white tile Stations of the Cross, with Matisse's self-styled "tormented and passionate" figures. The bishop of Nice came to bless the chapel in the late spring of 1951 when the artist's work was completed. Matisse died 3 years later.

The price of admission includes entrance to **L'Espace Matisse,** a gallery devoted to the documentation of the way Matisse handled the design and construction of the chapel during its construction (1949 to 1951). It also contains lithographs and religious artifacts that concerned Matisse in one way or another.

Av. Henri-Matisse. ℂ **04-93-58-03-26.** Admission 13F (2.00, $1.90) adults, 5F (.75, 75¢) for persons 12 and under; contributions to maintain the chapel are welcomed. Unless special arrangements are made, the chapel is open Oct and Dec–June Tues and Thurs 10am–11:30am and 2:30–5:30pm; July–Sept Wed, Fri–Sat 2:30–5:30pm. Closed Nov.

ACCOMMODATIONS
VERY EXPENSIVE
Le Château du Domaine St-Martin ★★★   If you're heading into the hill-towns above Nice and you seek luxury and refinement, this is your address. This château, in a 35-acre park, was built in 1936 on the grounds where the Golden Goat treasure was reputedly buried. A complex of tile-roofed villas with suites was built in the terraced gardens. You can walk through the gardens on winding paths lined with tall cypresses, past the chapel ruins and olive trees. The spacious rooms are distinctively decorated, and the large rose-colored bathrooms have a combination tub and shower. The restaurant has a view of the coast and offers superb French cuisine. In summer, many guests prefer the poolside grill.

Av. des Templiers BP102, 06142 Vence. ℂ **04-93-58-02-02.** Fax 04-93-24-08-91. www.chateau-st-martin.com. 34 units, 6 cottages. 1,500F–5,000F (228– 760, $217.50–$725) double; 2,800F–15,000F (425.60– 2,280, $406–$2,175) cottage. AE, DC, MC, V. Closed mid-Oct to mid-Feb. From the town center, follow the signs toward Coursegoules and Col-de-Vence for 1 mile north. **Amenities:** Restaurant, bar; room service; laundry/dry cleaning. *In room:* A/C, TV, minibar, hair dryer, safe.

MODERATE
Hôtel Villa Roseraie ★ *Finds*   This charming hotel, a 5-minute walk from the center of Vence, is in a renovated 19th-century manor house. Marc Chagall lived for many years on a hill across from the hotel, which is within an easy walk of the Matisse chapel. The Martefon family has furnished their home with old-fashioned pieces, often antiques. The garden offers southern exposure and contains a moon-shaped pool. This *roseraie* (rose garden) is studded with magnolias, yucca, eucalyptus, banana trees, palms, and roses. Rooms 4, 5, and 8 have balconies, while rooms 12, 14, 15, and 16 have ground-floor patios. Mattresses are comfortable, and each unit comes with a neatly organized tiled bathroom with shower. There's no better way to start the day than with one of the fresh house-baked croissants.

Av. Henri-Giraud, rte. de Coursegoules, 06140 Vence. © **04-93-58-02-20.** Fax 04-93-58-99-31. 16 units. 510F–830F (77.50– 126.15, $73.95–$120.35) double. AE, MC, V. From the town center, drive for less than ¼ mile, following the signs toward Col-de-Vence. **Amenities:** Pool; room service; baby-sitting. *In room:* TV, minibar, hair dryer, safe (in some).

Relais Cantemerle ✦   One of the most appealing places in Vence is this artfully designed cluster that resembles an old-fashioned compound of Provençal buildings. Capped with rounded terra-cotta roof tiles, they surround a verdant lawn dotted with old trees, in the center of which is a pool. Public areas are stylishly outfitted with Art Deco furniture and accessories and include a richly paneled bar area and a flagstone terrace that's the site of sun-flooded meals. Rooms aren't overly large but contain unusual reproductions of overscaled Art Deco armchairs, louvered wooden closet doors, and balcony-style sleeping lofts with comfortable beds. All come with good-size bathrooms, most with a combination tub and shower. The restaurant serves worthwhile versions of regional and mainstream French cuisine.

258 chemin Cantemerle, 06140 Vence. © **04-93-58-08-18.** Fax 04-93-58-32-89. www.relais-cantemerle.com. 19 units. 750F (114, $108.75) double; 1,100F (167.20, $159.50) 1-bedroom duplex for 2; 1,350F (205.20, $195.75) 1-bedroom duplex for 3. 250F (38, $36.25) additional bed for 4th occupant. 290F (44.10, $42.05) supplement for half board. AE, MC, V. Closed mid-Oct to mid-Apr. **Amenities:** Restaurant, bar; room service; laundry. *In room:* A/C, TV, minibar, hair dryer.

INEXPENSIVE

Auberge des Seigneurs ✦   This 400-year-old stone hotel gives you a taste of Old Provence. Decorative objects and antiques are everywhere. The guest rooms are well maintained and comfortable, but the management dedicates its energy to the restaurant. Nevertheless, the rooms have lots of exposed paneling and beams, two have fireplaces, all have Provençal styling. Each unit comes with a small tiled bathroom with shower. Inside the dining room, there's a long wooden dining table, in view of an open fireplace with a row of hanging copper pots and pans. The cuisine of François I is served in an antique atmosphere with wooden casks of flowers and an open spit for roasting and grilling.

Place du Frêne, 06140 Vence. © **04-93-58-04-24.** Fax 04-93-24-08-01. 6 units. 384F–404F (58.35– 61.40, $55.730–$58.60) double. AE, DC, MC, V. Closed Nov–Mar 15. **Amenities:** Restaurant; room service. *In room:* Hair dryer.

DINING

Auberge des Seigneurs (see above) offers excellent dining at reasonable prices.

Jacques Maximin ✦✦✦ MODERN FRENCH   This deluxe dining room is justly hailed as one of the Riviera's grandest restaurants. The setting is an artfully rustic 19th-century manor house that was transformed in the mid-1980s into the private home of culinary superstar Jacques Maximin. Today, it's the target of pilgrimages by foodies and movie stars venturing north from the Cannes Film Festival, including Hugh Grant, Elizabeth Hurley, and Robert DeNiro. You can sample a menu firmly entrenched in the seasonal produce of the surrounding countryside. Stellar examples are salads made with asparagus and truffles, Canadian lobster, or fresh scallops; pigeon breast with cabbage with lentil cream sauce; peppered duck; and some of the best beef dishes in the region. Expect surprises from the capricious chef, whose menu changes virtually every day.

689 chemin de la Gaude. © **04-93-58-90-75.** Reservations required. Main courses 150F–380F (22.80– 57.75, $21.75–$55.10); fixed-price menus 240F–590F (36.50– 89.70, $34.80–$85.55) lunch, 350F–590F (53.20– 89.70, $50.75–$85.55) dinner. AE, DC, MC, V. Tues–Sun 12:30–2pm; Tues–Sat 7:30–10pm. From the historic core of Vence, drive SW for 2½ miles, following the signs to Cagnes-sur-Mer.

La Farigoule PROVENÇAL   Set within a century-old house that opens onto a rose garden, where tables are set out during summer, this restaurant specializes in Provençal cuisine. Menu items include a conservative but flavor-filled array of dishes that feature a *bourride Provençal* (a bouillabaisse with a dollop of cream and lots of garlic); shoulder of roasted lamb with a ragoût of fresh vegetables, served with fresh thyme; aïoli; and such fish dishes as dorado with a confit of lemons and fresh aromatic coriander.

15 rue Henri-Isnard. 🕐 **04-93-58-01-27.** Reservations recommended. Main courses 90F–150F (13.70– 22.80, $13.05–$21.75); fixed-price menu 160F–220F (24.30– 33.45, $23.20–$31.90). Thurs–Mon noon–2:30pm and 7:30–10:30pm.

13 Nice ⭐⭐⭐

577 miles S of Paris, 20 miles NE of Cannes

Nice is the capital of the Riviera, the largest city between Genoa and Marseille. It's also one of the most ancient, founded by the Greeks, who called it Nike (Victory). By the 19th century, the Victorian upper class and tsarist aristocrats were flocking here. But these days it's not as chichi and expensive, especially compared to Cannes. In fact, of all the major resorts of France, from Deauville to Biarritz to Cannes, Nice is the most affordable. It's also the best place to base yourself on the Riviera, especially if you're dependent on public transportation. You can go to San Remo, "the queen of the Italian Riviera," and return to Nice by nightfall. From the Nice airport, the second largest in France, you can travel by train or bus along the entire coast to resorts like Juan-les-Pins and Cannes.

Because of its brilliant sunshine and relaxed living, artists and writers have been attracted to Nice for years. Among them were Dumas, Nietzsche, Flaubert, Hugo, Sand, and Stendhal. Henri Matisse, who made his home in Nice, said, "Though the light is intense, it's also soft and tender." The city has, on average, 300 days of sunshine a year.

ESSENTIALS

GETTING THERE   Trains arrive at Gare Nice-Ville, avenue Thiers (🕐 **08-36-35-35-35**). From there you can take trains to Cannes, Monaco, and Antibes, with easy connections to anywhere else along the Mediterranean coast. There's a small-scale tourist center at the train station, open Monday to Saturday from 8am to 6:30pm and Sunday from 8am to noon and 2 to 5:30pm. If you face a long delay, you can eat at the cafeteria and even take showers at the station.

Visitors who arrive at **Aéroport Nice–Côte d'Azur** (🕐 **04-93-21-30-30**) can board a yellow-sided **bus,** known as the navette Nice-Aéroport, which travels several times a day between the railway station and the airport for 21F (3.20, $3.05) each way. They operate every day from 6am to 10:30pm or until the last incoming flight arrives, no matter how delayed. A **taxi** ride from the airport into the city center will cost at least 150F to 200F (22.80 to 30.40, $21.75 to $29) each way. Trip time is about 30 minutes.

⟨*Value* A Note on Nice Buses

If you plan on traveling a lot via the city's buses, consider buying a **Carte-Passe Niçoise,** available from the tourist office or on any bus. It allows unlimited transit on any city bus. The price is 25F (3.80, $3.65) for 1 day, 85F (12.90, $12.35) for 5 days, and 110F (16.70, $15.95) for a week.

VISITOR INFORMATION   Nice maintains three tourist offices, the largest and most central of which is at 5 promenade des Anglais (© **04-92-14-48-00;** fax 04-93-16-85-16) near place Massena. Additional offices are in the arrivals hall of the **Aèroport Nice–Côte d'Azur** (© **04-93-21-44-11**) and the railway station on avenue Thiers (© **04-93-87-07-07**). Any can make a hotel reservation (but only for the night of the day you happen to show up), charging a modest fee that varies according to the classification of the hotel you book.

GETTING AROUND   Most of the local buses in Nice create connections with one another at their central hub, the **Station Central,** 10 av. Félix-Faure (© **04-93-16-52-10**), which lies a very short walk from the place Masséna. Municipal buses each charge 8.50F (1.30, $1.25) for a ride within Greater Nice. To save money, consider the purchase of a five-ticket carnet for 34F (5.15, $4.95). Bus nos. 2 and 12 make frequent trips to the beach. Long-distance buses making the trek, say, between Nice and such long-haul destinations as Monaco, Cannes, St-Tropez, and other parts of France and Europe depart from the **Gare Routière,** 5 bd. Jean-Jaurès (© **04-93-85-61-81**).

You can rent bicycles and mopeds at **Nicea Rent,** 9 av. Thiers (© **04-93-82-42-71**), near the Station Centrale. From March through October, it's open daily from 9am to noon and 2 to 6pm (closed Sunday November to April). The cost begins at 100F (15.20, $14.50) per day, plus a 2,000F (304, $290) deposit. Credit cards are accepted.

SPECIAL EVENTS   The **Nice Carnaval** draws visitors from all over Europe and North America to this ancient spectacle. This "Mardi Gras of the Riviera" begins sometime in February, usually 12 days before Shrove Tuesday, celebrating the return of spring with three weeks of parades, *corsi* (floats), *veglioni* (masked balls), confetti, and battles in which young women toss flowers. Only the most wicked throw rotten eggs instead of carnations. Climaxing the event is a fireworks display on Shrove Tuesday, lighting up the Baie des Anges (Bay of Angels). King Carnival goes up in flames on his pyre but rises from the ashes the following spring. For information, contact the tourist office (see above).

Also important is the **Nice Festival du Jazz,** from July 10 to 17, when a roster of jazz artists perform in the ancient Arène de Cimiez. For information, contact the **Comité des Fêtes,** Mairie (town hall) de Nice, 5 rue de l'Hôtel-de-Ville, 06000 Nice (© **08-03-80-88-03**).

EXPLORING THE CITY

There's a higher density of museums in Nice than in many comparable French cities. If you decide to forgo the beach and devote your time to visiting some of the best-respected museums in the south of France, you can buy from the local tourist office a **Carte Passe-Musée** costing 70F (10.65E, $10.15) for 3 days or 140F (21.30E, $20.30) for 4 days. It allows you admission into seven of the city's largest museums. There are no reductions for students or children.

In 1822 the orange crop at Nice was bad and the workers faced a lean time. So the English residents put them to work building the **promenade des Anglais** ★★, a wide boulevard fronting the bay, split by "islands" of palms and flowers and stretching for about 4 miles. Fronting the beach are rows of grand cafes, the Musée Masséna, villas, and hotels—some good, others decaying.

Crossing this boulevard in the briefest of bikinis or thongs are some of the world's most attractive bronzed bodies. They're heading for the **beach**—"on the rocks," as it's called here. Tough on tender feet, the beach is made not of sand

Nice

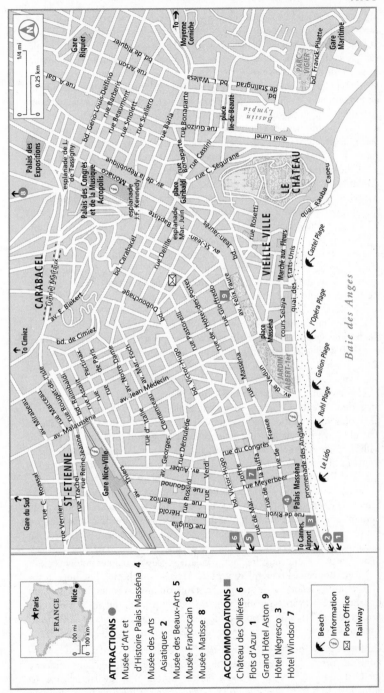

ATTRACTIONS ●
Musée d'Art et
d'Histoire Palais Masséna **4**
Musée des Arts
Asiatiques **2**
Musée des Beaux-Arts **5**
Musée Franciscain **8**
Musée Matisse **8**

ACCOMMODATIONS ■
Château des Olliéres **6**
Flots d'Azur **1**
Grand Hôtel Aston **9**
Hôtel Négresco **3**
Hôtel Windsor **7**

↙ Beach
ⓘ Information
⊠ Post Office
— Railway

FRANCE
★Paris
●Nice

0   100 mi
0   100 km

but of pebbles (and not too small ones). It's one of the least attractive aspects of the cosmopolitan resort city. Many bathhouses provide mattresses for a fee.

In the east, the promenade becomes **quai des États-Unis,** the original boulevard, lined with some of the best restaurants in Nice, all specializing in bouillabaisse. Rising sharply on a rock is the site known as **Le Château,** the spot where the ducs de Savoie built their castle, torn down in 1706. All that remains are two or three stones—even the foundations have disappeared in the wake of Louis XIV's destruction of what was viewed as a bulwark of Provençal resistance to his regime. The hill has been turned into a garden of pines and exotic flowers. To reach the site for the view, you can take an elevator; many prefer to take the elevator up, then walk down. The park is open daily from 8am to dusk.

At the north end of Le Château is the famous old **graveyard** of Nice, visited primarily for its lavishly sculpted monuments that form their own enduring art statement. It's the largest one in France and the fourth largest in Europe. To reach it, you can take a small canopied **Train Touristique de Nice** (© 04-93-92-45-59), which departs from the Jardin Albert-1er. It makes a 40-minute sightseeing transit past many of Nice's most heralded sites, including place Masséna, promenade des Anglais, and quai des États-Unis. With departures every 30 to 60 minutes, the train operates daily from 10am to 5pm (until 6pm in April, May, and September; until 7pm from June to August). There's no service between mid-November and mid-December and during most of January. Train rides last about 45 minutes. The price is 35F (5.30, $5.10) per person.

Continuing east from "the Rock" (the ruined site of Le Château), you reach the **harbor,** where the restaurants are even cheaper and the bouillabaisse is just as good. While sitting here lingering over a drink at a sidewalk cafe, you can watch the boats depart for Corsica. The port was excavated between 1750 and 1830. Since then an outer harbor, protected by two jetties, has been created.

The "authentic" Niçoise live in **Vieille Ville** ✿, the Old Town, beginning at the foot of "the Rock" and stretching out to place Masséna. Sheltered by sienna-tiled roofs, many of the Italianate facades suggest 17th-century Genoese palaces. The old town is a maze of narrow streets, teeming with local life and studded with the least expensive restaurants in Nice. Buy an onion pizza (*la pissaladière*) from one of the vendors. Many of the buildings are painted a faded Roman gold, and their banners are laundry flapping in the sea breezes.

While here, try to visit the **Marché aux Fleurs,** the flower market at cours Saleya. The vendors start setting up their stalls Tuesday to Sunday from 8am to 6pm in summer, and from 8am till between 2 and 4pm in winter, depending on the vendor's remaining inventory and energy level. A flamboyant array of carnations, violets, jonquils, roses, and birds of paradise is hauled in by vans or trucks, then displayed in the most fragrant, regularly scheduled market in town.

Nice's commercial centerpiece is **place Masséna,** with pink buildings in the 17th-century Genoese style and the **Fontaine du Soleil** (Fountain of the Sun) by Janoit, from 1956. Stretching from the main square to the promenade is the **Jardin Albert-1er,** with an open-air terrace and a Triton Fountain. With palms and exotic flowers, it's the most relaxing oasis in town.

Cathédrale Orthodoxe Russe St-Nicolas à Nice ✿ Ordered and built by none other than Tsar Nicholas II, this is the most beautiful religious edifice of the Orthodoxy outside Russia and is perfect expression of Russian religious art abroad. It dates from the Belle Époque, when some of the Romanovs and their entourage turned the Riviera into a stomping ground (everyone from grand dukes to ballerinas walked the promenade). The cathedral is richly ornamented and decorated with icons. You'll spot the building from afar because of its collection of ornate onion-shaped domes. Church services are held on Sunday morning.

Av. Nicolas-II (off bd. du Tzaréwitch). ✆ **04-93-96-88-02.** Admission 12F (1.80, $1.75). May–Sept daily 9am–noon and 2:30–6pm; Oct–Apr daily 9:30am–noon and 2:30–5pm. It's closed to purely touristic visits on Sun mornings. From the central rail station, head west along av. Thiers to bd. Gambetta; then go north to av. Nicolas-II.

Musée d'Art et d'Histoire Palais Masséna ⭐

The villa housing this collection was built in 1900 in the style of the First Empire as a residence for Victor Masséna, the prince of Essling and grandson of Napoléon's marshal. The city of Nice has converted the villa, next door to the Hôtel Negresco, into a museum of local history and decorative art. A remarkable First Empire drawing room furnished in the opulent taste of that era, with mahogany-veneer pieces and ormolu mounts, is on the ground floor. There's a representation of Napoléon as a Roman Caesar and a bust by Canova of Maréchal Masséna. The large first-floor gallery exhibits a collection of Niçoise primitives and also has a display of 14th- and 15th-century painters, as well as a collection of 16th- to 19th-century masterpieces of plates and jewelry decorated with enamel (Limoges). There are art galleries devoted to the history of Nice and the memories of Masséna and Garibaldi. Yet another gallery is reserved for a display of views of Nice during the 18th and 19th centuries. *Note:* At press time, the museum was closed for renovations, and is not scheduled to reopen until late 2003/early 2004.

65 rue de France. ✆ **04-93-88-11-34.** Admission 25F (3.80, $3.65) adults, 15F (2.30, $2.20) children. Free first Sun every month. May–Sept Tues–Sun 11am–noon and 3–6pm; Oct–Apr 2pm–5pm. Bus: 3, 7, 8, 9, 10, 12, 14, 22.

Musée des Beaux-Arts ⭐⭐

The collection is housed in the former residence of the Ukrainian Princess Kotchubey. There's an important gallery devoted to the masters of the Second Empire and belle époque, with an extensive collection of the 19th-century French experts. The gallery of sculptures includes works by J. B. Carpeaux, Rude, and Rodin. Note the important collection by a dynasty of painters, the Dutch Vanloo family. One of its best-known members, Carle Vanloo, born in Nice in 1705, was Louis XV's premier *peintre*. A fine collection of 19th- and 20th-century art is displayed, including works by Ziem, Raffaelli, Boudin, Renoir, Monet, Guillaumin, and Sisley.

33 av. des Baumettes. ✆ **04-92-15-28-28.** Admission 25F (3.80, $3.65) adults, 15F (2.30, $2.20) children under 16. Tues–Sun 10am–noon and 2–6pm. Bus: 3, 9, 12, 22, 23, 38.

Musée International d'Art Naïf Anatole–Jakovsky (Museum of Naïve Art) ⭐

This museum is housed in the beautifully restored Château Ste-Hélène in the Fabron district. The collection was once owned by the museum's namesake, for years one of the world's leading art critics. His 600 drawings and canvases were turned over to the institution and made accessible to the public. Artists from more than two dozen countries are represented here—from primitive painting to contemporary 20th-century works.

Av. Val-Marie. ✆ **04-93-71-78-33.** Admission 25F (3.80, $3.65) adults, 15F (2.30, $2.20) students and seniors, free for children 17 and under. Wed–Mon 10am–noon and 2–6pm. Bus: 9, 10, or 12; the walk from the bus stop takes 10 min.

Musée Naval (Naval Museum)

In the Tour Bellanda is the Naval Museum, sitting on "the Rock." The tower stands on a belvedere overlooking the beach, the bay, the old town, and even the terraces of nearby villas. Of the museum's old battle prints, one depicts the exploits of Caterina Segurana, the Joan of Arc of the Niçoise. During the 1543 siege by Barbarossa, she ran along the ramparts, raising her skirt to show her bottom to the Turks as a sign of contempt, though the soldiers were reported to have been more excited than insulted.

Parc du Château. ✆ **04-93-80-47-61.** Admission 15F (2.30, $2.20) adults, free for students and children under 16. June–Sept Wed–Sun 10am–noon and 2–7pm.

Palais Lascaris *Kids* The baroque Palais Lascaris in the city's historic core is linked to the Lascaris-Vintimille family, whose recorded history predates the year 1261. Built in the 17th century, it contains elaborately detailed ornaments. An intensive restoration undertaken by the city of Nice in 1946 brought back its original beauty, and the palace is now classified a historic monument. The most elaborate floor is the *étage noble,* retaining many of its 18th-century panels and plaster embellishments. A pharmacy, built around 1738, complete with many of the original Delftware accessories, is on the premises. Every Wednesday between 2 and 4pm, the museum appeals to children, inviting craftspeople to show the details of how they accomplish their art forms through live demonstrations.

15 rue Droite. ✆ **04-93-62-72-40.** Free admission. Tues–Sun 10am–noon and 2–6pm. Bus: 1, 2, 3, 5, 6, 14, 16, or 17.

NEARBY ATTRACTIONS IN CIMIEZ ★★

In the once-aristocratic hilltop quarter of Cimiez, Queen Victoria wintered at the Hôtel Excelsior and brought half the English court with her. Founded by the Romans, who called it Cemenelum, Cimiez was the capital of the Maritime Alps province. Recent excavations have uncovered the ruins of a Roman town, and you can wander among the diggings. The arena was big enough to hold at least 5,000 spectators, who watched contests between gladiators and wild beasts. To reach this suburb, take bus no. 15 or 17 from place Masséna.

Monastère de Cimiez (Cimiez Convent) ★ The convent embraces a church that owns three of the most important works from the primitive painting school of Nice by the Bréa brothers. See the carved and gilded wooden main altarpiece. In a restored part of the convent where some Franciscan friars still live, the Musée Franciscain is decorated with 17th-century frescoes. Some 350 documents and works of art from the 15th to the 18th century are displayed, and a monk's cell has been re-created in all its severe simplicity. See also the 17th-century chapel. In the gardens you can get a panoramic view of Nice and the Baie des Anges. Matisse and Dufy are buried in the cemetery.

Place du Monastère. ✆ **04-93-81-00-04.** Free admission. Museum, Mon–Sat 10am–noon and 3–6pm; church, daily 8:30am–7:30pm.

Musée Matisse ★ This museum honors the artist, who died in Nice in 1954. Seeing his nude sketches today, you'll wonder how early critics could have denounced them as "the female animal in all her shame and horror." The museum has several permanent collections, most painted in Nice and many donated by Matisse and his heirs. These include *Nude in an Armchair with a Green Plant* (1937), *Nymph in the Forest* (1935 to 1942), and a chronologically arranged series of paintings from 1890 to 1919. The most famous of these is *Portrait of Madame Matisse* (1905), usually displayed near a portrait of the artist's wife by Marquet, painted in 1900. There's also an ensemble of drawings and designs (*Flowers and Fruits*) he prepared as practice sketches for the Matisse Chapel at Vence. The most famous are *The Créole Dancer* (1951), *Blue Nude IV* (1952), and around 50 dance-related sketches he did between 1930 and 1931.

In the Villa des Arènes-de-Cimiez, 164 av. des Arènes-de-Cimiez. ℂ 04-93-53-40-53. Admission 25F (3.80, $3.65) adults, free for children 18 and under. Wed–Mon 10am–6pm (to 5pm off-season).

Musée National Message Biblique Marc-Chagall ★★ In the hills of Cimiez, this handsome museum, surrounded by shallow pools and a garden, is devoted to Marc Chagall's treatment of biblical themes. Born in Russia in 1887, Chagall became a French citizen in 1937. The artist and his wife donated the works—the most important Chagall collection ever assembled—to France in 1966 and 1972. Displayed are 450 of his oils, gouaches, drawings, pastels, lithographs, sculptures, and ceramics; a mosaic; three stained-glass windows; and a tapestry. Chagall decorated a splendid concert room with brilliantly hued stained-glass windows. Temporary exhibits are organized each summer featuring great periods and artists of all times.

Av. du Dr.-Ménard. ℂ 04-93-53-87-20. Admission 30F (4.55, $4.35) adults, 20F (3.05, $2.90) ages 18–24, free for children under 18. Fees may be higher for special exhibits. Wed–Mon 10am–5pm (until 6pm July–Sept).

OUTDOOR PURSUITS

BEACHES Nice's seafront offers at least seven public beaches. None of them has sand; they're covered with gravel (often the size of golf balls). The rocks are smooth but can be nettlesome to people with poor balance or tender feet. Tucked in between the public beaches are the private beaches of hotels such as the Beau Rivage. Most of the public beaches are divided into two sections: a free area and an area where you can avail yourself of the chaise longues, mattresses, parasols, changing cabanas, and freshwater showers. For the privilege, you'll pay 50F to 60F (7.60 to 9.10E, $7.25 to $8.70) for a half-day and 75F to 90F (11.40 to 13.70E, $10.90 to $13.05) for a full day. Nude sunbathing is prohibited, but toplessness is common. Take bus nos. 9, 10, 12, and 23 from the center of town to get to the beach.

GOLF The oldest golf course on the Riviera is about 10 miles from Nice: **Golf Bastide du Roi** (also known as the Golf de Biot), is at avenue Jules-Grec, Biot (ℂ 04-93-65-08-48). Open daily, this is a flat, not particularly challenging sea-fronting course. (Regrettably, it's necessary to cross over a highway midway through the course to complete the full 18 holes.) Tee times are 8am to 6pm; you can play until the sun sets. Reservations aren't necessary, though on weekends you should probably expect a delay. Greens fees are 240F (36.50, $34.80) for 18 holes; club rental is 80F (12.15, $11.60).

SCUBA DIVING The best outfit is the **Centre International de Plongée de Nice,** 2 ruelle des Moulins (ℂ 04-93-55-59-50), adjacent to the city's old port, midway between quai des Docks and boulevard Stalingrad. A *baptême* (initiatory dive for first-timers) costs 200F (30.40, $29) and a one-tank dive for experienced divers, with all equipment included, is 190F (28.90, $27.55); a license is required to dive.

TENNIS The oldest tennis club in Nice is the **Nice Lawn Tennis Club,** Parc Impérial, 5 av. Suzanne-Lenglen (ℂ 04-92-15-58-00), near the train station. It's open daily from 9am to 9pm (mid-October to mid-April) and charges 120F (18.25, $17.40) per person for 2 hours of court time, or a reduced rate of 300F (45.60, $43.50) per person for unlimited access to the courts for 1 week. The club contains a cooperative staff, a loyal clientele, 13 clay courts, and six hard-surfaced courts. Reserve a court the night before.

SHOPPING

You might want to begin with a stroll through the streets and alleys of Nice's historic core. The densest concentrations of boutiques are along **rue Masséna, place Magenta, avenue Jean-Médecin, rue de Verdun,** and **rue Paradis,** as well as on the streets funneling into and around them. Individual shops of note include **Gigi,** 7 rue de la Liberté (© 04-93-87-81-78), and **Carroll,** 9 rue de la Liberté (© 04-93-87-98-07), both of which sell sophisticated-looking clothing for women; and **Georges Rech Homme,** 10 rue de la Liberté (© 04-93-87-53-96), an emporium for menswear. Timeless and endlessly alluring are the products sold at **Yves Saint-Laurent Rive Gauche,** 4 av. de Suède (© 04-93-87-70-79), where the most upscale of the ready-to-wear St-Laurent line is sold, as well as the less expensive garments from the company's cost-conscious *Variations* line.

Opened in 1949 by Joseph Fuchs, the grandfather of the present English-speaking owners, the **Confiserie Florian du Vieux-Nice,** 14 quai Papacino (© 04-93-55-43-50), is near the Old Port. The specialty here is glazed fruits crystallized in sugar or artfully arranged into chocolates. Look for exotic jams (rose-petal preserves or mandarin marmalade) and the free recipe leaflet as well as candied violets, verbena leaves, and rosebuds. Prices for the sugary candied fruit are 115F to 215F (17.50 to   32.70, $16.70 to $31.20) per kilo.

Façonnable, 7–9 rue Paradis (© 04-93-87-88-80), is the original site that sparked the creation of several hundred branches around the world. This is one of the largest, with a wide range of men's suits, raincoats, overcoats, sportswear, and jeans. The look is youthful and conservatively stylish, for relatively slim (French) bodies.

If you're thinking of indulging in a Provençale *pique-nique,* **Nicola Alziari,** 14 rue St-François-de-Paule (© 04-93-85-76-92), will provide everything you'll need: from olives, anchovies, and pistous to aïolis and tapenades. It's one of Nice's oldest purveyors of olive oil, with a house brand that comes in two strengths: a light version that aficionados claim is vaguely perfumed with Provence, and a stronger version suited to the earthy flavors and robust ingredients of a Provençal winter. Also look for a range of objects crafted from olive wood.

Other shopping recommendations are **La Couquetou,** 8 rue St-François-de-Paule (© 04-93-80-90-30), selling *santons,* the traditional Provençal figurines. The best selection of Provençal fabrics is found at **Le Chandelier,** 7 rue de la Boucherie (© 04-93-85-85-19), where the designs of two of the region's best-known producers of cloth, Les Olivades and Valdrôme, are modeled on the burnt yellows and cerulean tones of Provence.

Nice is also known for its colorful street markets. In addition to the flower market, **Marché aux Fleurs** (see "Exploring the City," above) there's the main Nice flea market, **Marché à la Brocante,** also at cours Saleya, which takes place every Monday from 8am to 5pm. There's another flea market on the port, **Les Puces de Nice,** place Robilante, open Tuesday to Saturday from 9am to 6pm.

ACCOMMODATIONS
VERY EXPENSIVE

Hôtel Negresco ✦✦✦   The Negresco is one of the Riviera's many super-glamorous hotels, right in the heart of noisy Nice. Jeanne Augier has taken over the place and has triumphed. This Victorian wedding-cake hotel is named after its founder, Henry Negresco, a Romanian who died franc-less in Paris in 1920.

It was built on the seafront, in the French château style, with a mansard roof and domed tower; its interior design was inspired by the country's châteaux, and the decorators scoured Europe to gather antiques, tapestries, paintings, and art. Some of the guest rooms are outfitted in homage to the personalities who have stayed here: the Coco Chanel Room, for example. Others are fancifully modeled after literary or musical themes, such as La Traviata. In 1998, most of the bathrooms were upgraded. Suites and public areas are even grander, as is the case with the Louis XIV salon, reminiscent of the Sun King himself, and the Napoléon III suite, where swagged walls, a leopard-skin carpet, and a half-crowned canopy in pink create a sense of majesty. The most expensive rooms with balconies face the Mediterranean. The staff wears 18th-century costumes. The featured restaurant—one of the Riviera's greatest—is Chantecler (see "Dining," section below).

37 promenade des Anglais, 06007 Nice CEDEX. © **04-93-16-64-00.** Fax 04-93-88-35-68. www.hotel-negresco-nice.com. 158 units. 1,750F–2,450F (266– 372.40, $253.75–$355.25) double; from 3,000F (456, $435) suite. AE, DC, MC, V. Free parking in garage. **Amenities:** 2 restaurants; bar; fitness center; secretarial service; room service; massage; baby-sitting; laundry/dry cleaning. In room: A/C, TV, minibar, hair dryer.

Palais Maeterlinck ☆☆ On 9 landscaped acres east of Nice, this deluxe hotel occupies a fin-de-siècle villa that was inhabited between the World Wars by the Belgian-born writer Maurice Maeterlinck, winner of the Nobel Prize for Literature. While many visitors find the setting sumptuous, the service and experience of the staff pale in comparison to the Negresco. But on the plus side, since it's calmer and more tranquil than the hotels in more central locations, it enjoys the allure of verdant terraces and a large outdoor pool, set amid banana trees, olive trees, and soaring cypresses. A funicular will carry you down to the rock-strewn beach and marina. Each elegant guest room is outfitted in a different monochromatic color scheme and neoclassical Florentine styling, all with terraces opening onto views of Cap d'Antibes and Cap-Ferrat and with deluxe bathrooms. Le Mélisande is a gastronomic hideaway with a neo-Renaissance decor.

Basse Corniche, 06300 Nice. © **04-92-00-72-00.** Fax 04-92-04-18-10. www.palais-maeterlinck.com. 40 units. 1,450F–2,900F (220.40– 440.80, $210.25–$420.50) double; 2,500F–15,000F (380– 2,280, $362.50–$2,175) suite. AE, DC, MC, V. Drive 4 miles east of Nice along the Basse Corniche. **Amenities:** Restaurant; bar; room service; laundry/dry cleaning. In room: A/C, TV, minibar, hair dryer, safe.

EXPENSIVE

Grand Hôtel Aston ☆ This elegantly detailed 19th-century hotel is one of the most alluring in its price bracket. After radical renovations, the rooms are now outfitted with comfortable furnishings and restored bathrooms with a combination tub and shower. The prices of the rooms vary according to their views over the street, the splashing fountains of place Masséna, or the coastline panorama from the uppermost floor. On summer evenings, a garden-style bar, sometimes with dance music, provides diversions from a spot on the hotel's uppermost floor. The hotel is associated with Holland's Golden Tulip chain.

12 av. Félix-Faure, 06000 Nice. © **04-92-80-53-11.** Fax 04-93-80-40-02. www.hotel-aston.com. 160 units. 750F–1650F (114– 250.80, $108.75–$239.25) double. AE, DC, MC, V. Parking 100F (15.20, $14.50). Bus: 12. **Amenities:** Restaurant; bar; pool; room service; baby-sitting; laundry/dry cleaning. In room: A/C, TV, minibar, hair dryer, safe.

La Pérouse ☆ *Finds* Once a prison, La Pérouse has been reconstructed and is now a unique Riviera hotel. Set on a cliff, it's built right into the gardens of an ancient château-fort. There's no hotel in Nice with a better view over both the old city and the Baie des Anges. In fact, many people stay here just for the view alone. Inside, the hotel is like an old Provençal home, with low ceilings, white walls, and antiques. Most of the lovely rooms have loggias overlooking the bay. The spacious rooms are beautifully furnished, often with Provençal fabrics. The bathrooms are large, coming in Boticino marble, all with tubs and showers.

11 quai Rauba-Capéu, 06300 Nice. ℂ **04-93-62-34-63.** Fax 04-93-62-59-41. 63 units. 950F–2,350F (144.40– 357.20, $137.75–$340.75) double; 3,500F–4,500F (532– 684, $507.50–$652.50) suite. AE, DC, MC, V. Parking 80F (12.15, $11.60). **Amenities:** Restaurant; outdoor pool; exercise room; Jacuzzi; sauna; room service; laundry/dry cleaning; . *In room:* A/C, TV, minibar, hair dryer.

Westminster Concorde ⭐ This 1860 hotel stands prominently along the famous promenade. Its elaborate facade was restored in 1986 to its former grandeur, and many renovations were made. The contemporary rooms are comfortable and have soundproof windows; a few open onto balconies. Most rooms have high ceilings, antique mirrors, French windows, and brass beds, and each comes with a midsize tiled bathroom with tub and shower.

27 promenade des Anglais, 06000 Nice. ℂ **04-92-14-86-86.** Fax 04-93-82-45-35. www.westminster-nice.com. 100 units. 750F–1,360F (114– 206.70, $108.75–$197.20) double; from 2,000F (304, $290) junior suite. AE, DC, MC, V. Parking 130F (19.75, $18.85). Bus: 9, 10, or 11. **Amenities:** Restaurant; bar; room service; laundry/dry cleaning. *In room:* A/C, TV, minibar, hair dryer.

MODERATE

Château des Ollières ⭐ *Finds* This is a secret hideaway. The most appealing and unusual hotel to open in Nice in many years made its debut as a hotel in 1996, and as a restaurant a year later. It's conveniently located within a 5-minute walk of the Negresco and the promenade des Anglais. The setting is one of the largest tracts of privately owned land in Nice—a 20-acre park loaded with exotic trees and shrubs. The centerpiece is a Beaux-Arts villa built in the 1870s by a Russian prince who had fallen in love with the wife of the French ambassador to Turkey. Inside, you'll find a noteworthy collection of oil paintings and "neo-Napoléonienne" and Empire-inspired antiques. One of the highlights is a set that was custom-made for the dining room, when the villa was being constructed. The high-ceilinged guest rooms are outfitted in the same ornate style as the public areas. The hotel restaurant occupies both the villa's original dining room as well as a garden wing. Menus change weekly, according to the inspiration of the chef and the availability of fresh ingredients.

39 av. des Baumettes, 06000 Nice. ℂ **04-92-15-77-99.** Fax 04-92-15-77-98. www.chateaudesollieres.com. 8 units. 850F–2,200F (129.20– 334.40, $123.25–$319) double; 1,150F–3,000F (174.80– 456, $166.75–$435) suite. AE, MC, V. Bus: 38. **Amenities:** Restaurant; bar; room service; baby-sitting; laundry/ dry cleaning. *In room:* A/C, TV, minibar, hair dryer.

Hôtel Gounod ⭐ This winning choice lies in the city center, a 5-minute walk to the sea. It was built around 1910 in a neighborhood where the street names honor composers. The Gounod boasts ornate balconies, a domed roof, and an elaborate canopy of wrought iron and glass. The attractive lobby and adjoining lounge are festive and stylish, with old prints, copper pots with flowers, and antiques. The high-ceilinged guest rooms are quiet and usually overlook the gardens of private homes. The tiled bathrooms are small but efficiently organized, mainly with shower units. There aren't many amenities, but guests have free unlimited use of the pool, cafe-bar, and Jacuzzi at the Hôtel Splendid next door.

3 rue Gounod, 06000 Nice. ℂ **04-93-16-42-00.** Fax 04-93-88-23-84. www.gounod-nice.com. 46 units. 550F–750F (83.60– 114, $79.75–$108.75) double; 755F–1,100F (114.75– 167.20, $109.50–$159.50)

suite. AE, DC, MC, V. Closed Nov 20–Dec 20. Parking 75F (11.40, $10.90). Bus: 8. **Amenities:** Room service; massage; baby-sitting; dry cleaning. *In room:* A/C, TV, minibar, hair dryer.

Hotel Windsor *Value*   One of the most arts-conscious hotels in Provence is set within a *maison bourgeoise* (near the Negresco and the promenade des Anglais), built by disciples of Gustav Eiffel in 1895. Inside, you'll find an artful, artsy, somewhat claustrophobic environment. High points include a complicated fifth-floor superstructure, site of a health club, steam room, and sauna, and a one-of-a-kind series of frescoes that adorn each of the rooms. Attribute this to the heir and scion of the Redolfi family—the long-time owners of the place— who commissioned manifestations of his mystical and mythical visions after his years of traveling through Asia, Africa, and South America. Each midsize unit is individually furnished, mainly with a combination tub and shower. The garden contains scores of tropical and exotic plants, and the recorded sounds of birds singing in the jungles of the Amazon.

11 rue Dalpozzo, 06000 Nice. *C* **04-93-88-59-35.** Fax 04-93-88-94-57. www.webstore.fr/windsor. 29 units. 560F–760F (85.10– 115.50, $81.20–$110.20) double. AE, DC, MC, V. Parking 60F (9.10, $8.70). Bus: 9, 10, or 22. **Amenities:** Restaurant, bar; pool; gym; sauna; room service; baby-sitting; laundry/dry cleaning. *In room:* A/C, TV, minibar, safe.

Le Petit Palais   This whimsical hotel occupies a mansion built around 1890; in the 1970s it was the home of the actor and writer Sacha Guitry, a name that's instantly recognized in millions of French households. It lies about a 10-minute drive from the city center in the Carabacel residential district. Much of its architectural grace remains, as evoked by the Art Deco and Italianate furnishings, and Florentine moldings and friezes. The preferred rooms, and the most expensive, have balconies for sea views during the day and sunset watching at dusk. Bathrooms are small but efficient, each with a shower unit. Breakfast is served in a small but pretty salon.

10 av. Emile-Bieckert, 06000 Nice. *C* **04-93-62-19-11.** Fax 04-93-62-53-60. www.guide-gerard.com. 25 units. 435F–620F (66.10– 94.25, $63.10–$89.90) double. AE, DC, MC, V. Parking 50F (7.60, $7.25). **Amenities:** Room service; laundry. *In room:* TV.

INEXPENSIVE

Flots d'Azur   This three-story villa-hotel is next to the sea and a short walk from the more elaborate and costlier promenade hotels. While the rooms vary in size and decor, all have good views and sea breezes. Twelve of the rooms have TVs and minibars, and each comes with a tiled bathroom with shower. Double-glazed windows were recently added to cut down on the noise. There's a small sitting room and sun terrace in front, where a continental breakfast is served.

101 promenade des Anglais, 06000 Nice. *C* **04-93-86-51-25.** Fax 04-93-97-22-07. flotsazur@wanadoo.fr. 20 units. 300F–500F (45.60– 76, $43.50–$72.50) double. MC, V. Bus: 8. **Amenities:** Laundry/dry cleaning. *In room:* A/C, safe.

Hôtel de la Mer *Value*   You get a good deal here. In the center of Old Nice, this place was built around 1910, transformed into a hotel in 1947, and renovated in 1993. Despite that, it manages to keep its prices low. Ms. Feri Forouzan, the owner, welcomes you with personalized charm. Most guest rooms are of good size, each with a small bathroom with shower. From the hotel it's a 2-minute walk to the promenade des Anglais and the seafront. Breakfast is served in one of the public salons or your room.

4 place Masséna, 06000 Nice. *C* **04-93-92-09-10.** Fax 04-93-85-00-64. hotel-mer@wanadoo.fr. 12 units. 300F–450F (45.60– 68.40, $43.50–$65.25) double. AE, MC, V. Bus: 1, 2, 5, 15, or 17. **Amenities:** Room service; massage. *In room:* A/C, TV, minibar (in some).

Hôtel du Centre Near the train station, this simple, clean hotel is from 1947 but has been restored. The rooms are very close to the attractions and charms of downtown Nice with its bars. The small bathrooms are tiled and equipped with shower units. The staff is well versed in the many diversions of the city.

2 rue de Suisse, 06000 Nice. © **04-93-88-83-85.** Fax 04-93-82-29-80. www.webstore.fr/hotel-centre. 28 units. 257F–327F (39.05– 49.70, $37.25–$47.40) double. AE, MC, V. Parking 8F (1.20, $1.15). Bus: 23. *In room:* TV.

Hôtel Excelsior The Excelsior's ornate corbels and chiseled stone pediments rise grandly a few steps from the railway station. This much-renovated 19th-century hotel has a modern decor with durable rooms that have seen a lot of wear but are still comfortable. Furnishings, for the most part, are functional and conservative, each with a small shower-only bathroom. There's a reflecting pool in the lobby; the beach is a 20-minute walk through the residential and commercial heart of Nice.

190 av. Durante, 06000 Nice. © **04-93-88-18-05.** Fax 04-93-88-38-69. 45 units. 337F–577F (51.20– 87.70, $48.85–$83.65) double. AE, V. Parking 65F (9.90,$9.45). Bus: 1, 2, 5, 12, 18, 23, or 24. *In room:* TV.

Hôtel Magnan This well-run modern hotel was built around 1945 and has been renovated frequently since then. It's a 10-minute bus ride from the heart of town but only a minute or so from the promenade des Anglais and the bay. Many of the simply furnished rooms have balconies facing the sea, and some contain minibars. The look is a bit functional, but for Nice this is a good price, especially considering the comfortable beds. The bathrooms are small, each with a shower stall. Owner Daniel Thérouin occupies the apartment on the top floor, guaranteeing a closely supervised set up. Breakfast can be served in your room.

Square du Général-Ferrié, 06200 Nice. © **04-93-86-76-00.** Fax 04-93-44-48-31. hotelmagnan@wanadoo.fr. 25 units. 310F–400F (47.10– 60.80, $44.95–$58) double. AE, MC, V. Parking 35F (5.30, $5.10). Bus: 12, 23, or 24. *In room:* TV.

DINING
VERY EXPENSIVE

Chantecler ★★★ TRADITIONAL/MODERN FRENCH This is Nice's most prestigious and best restaurant. In 1989, a massive redecoration sheathed its walls with panels removed from a château in Puilly-Fussé; a Regency-style salon was installed for before- or after-dinner drinks; and a collection of 16th-century paintings, executed on leather backgrounds in the Belgian town of Malines, was imported. A much-respected chef, Alain Llorca, revised the menu to include the most sophisticated and creative dishes in Nice. They change almost weekly but may include turbot filet served with a purée of broad beans, sun-dried tomatoes, and asparagus; roasted suckling lamb served with beignets of fresh vegetables and ricotta-stuffed ravioli; and a melt-in-your-mouth fantasy of marbled hot chocolate drenched in almond-flavored cream sauce.

In the Hôtel Negresco, 37 promenade des Anglais. © **04-93-16-64-00.** Reservations required. Main courses 280F–570F (42.55– 86.65, $40.60–$82.65); fixed-price menus 300F (45.60, $43.50) lunch, 490F–700F (74.50– 86.65, $71.50–$82.65) dinner. AE, DC, MC, V. Daily 12:30–2:30pm and 7:30–10:30pm. Closed mid-Nov to mid-Dec. Bus: 8, 9, 10, or 11.

EXPENSIVE

Chez Michel (Le Grand Pavois) ★ SEAFOOD For treats from the sea, this is your best bet. This brasserie behind the Negresco was established by members of the family that own Chez Tétou, the stylish seafood restaurant in Golfe Juan that's beloved by movie stars, glitterati, and the merely rich. Jacques Marquise, one of the patriarchs of the Chez Tétou success story, is the creative force here; he's committed to maintaining prices 30% to 40% less than those charged by Chez Tétou. Bouillabaisse is the specialty, priced at 330F (50.15, $47.85) for a succulent version and at 450F (68.40, $65.25) for a royal version garnished with lobster and crayfish. Other delectable choices include sea bass in white wine, herbs, and lemon sauce; and fish (snapper, hogfish, sea bass, and John Dory) that's grilled and then flambéed with a combination of fennel and fennel-flavored brandy. The wine list has a number of reasonably priced bottles.

11 rue Meyerbeer. ℂ 04-93-88-77-42. Reservations required. Main courses 145F–400F (22.05– 60.80, $21.05–$58); fixed-price menus 130F (19.75, $18.85) lunch, 195F–300F (29.65– 45.60, $28.30–$43.50) dinner; bouillabaisse from 350F (53.20, $50.75). MC, V. Daily 7–11pm. Bus: 8.

La Merenda 🏵🏵 *Finds* NIÇOISE   Since there's no phone, you have to go by this place twice: once to make a reservation and once to dine. However, it's worth the effort, as this is the best bistro in Nice. Forsaking his chef's crown at the renowned Chantecler (above), Dominique Le Stanc opened this tiny bistro serving a sublime cuisine. Though he was born in Alsace, his heart and soul belong to the Mediterranean, the land of black truffles, wild morels, sea bass, and asparagus. His food is rightly called a lullaby of gastronomic unity, with texture, crunch, richness, and balance. Le Stanc never knows what he's going to serve until he goes to the market. Look for his specials on a chalkboard. Perhaps you'll find stuffed cabbage, fried zucchini flowers, or oxtail flavored with fresh oranges. Lamb from the Sisteron is cooked until it practically falls from the bone. Raw artichokes are paired with a salad of mâche. Service is discreet and personable. We wish we could dine here every day.

4 rue Terrasse. No phone. Reservations required. Main courses 160F–220F (24.30– 33.45, $23.20–$31.90). No credit cards. Mon–Fri noon–2pm and 7–9:30pm. Closed Aug 4–18, Dec 24–Jan 4, and Feb 16–22. Bus: 8.

MODERATE

Ane Rouge 🏵 PROVENÇAL   Facing the old port and occupying an antique building whose owners have carefully retained its ceiling beams and stone walls, this is one of the city's best-known seafood restaurants. In the two modern dining rooms noteworthy for their coziness, you can enjoy traditional specialties like bouillabaisse, bourride, filet of John Dory with roulades of stuffed lettuce leaves, mussels stuffed with breadcrumbs and herbs, and salmon in wine sauce with spinach. Service is correct and commendable.

7 quai des Deux-Emmanuels. ℂ 04-93-89-49-63. Reservations required. Main courses 125F–210F (19– 31.90, $18.15–$30.45); fixed-price menus 158F–345F (24– 52.45, $22.90–$50.05) lunch, 208F–345F (31.60– 52.45, $30.15–$50.05) dinner; bouillabaisse 280F (42.55, $40.60). AE, DC, MC, V. Thurs–Tues noon–2pm and 7:30–10:30pm. Closed 2 weeks in Feb. Bus: 30.

Brasserie Flo TRADITIONAL FRENCH   This is the town's most bustling brasserie. In 1991, the Jean-Paul Bucher group, a French chain noted for its skill at restoring historic brasseries, bought the premises of a faded early-1900s restaurant near place Masséna and injected it with new life. Its high ceilings are covered with their original frescoes. The place is brisk, stylish, reasonably priced, and fun. Menu items include an array of grilled fish, *choucroute* (sauerkraut) Alsatian style, steak with brandied pepper sauce, and fresh oysters and shellfish.

2–4 rue Sacha-Guitry. ℂ 04-93-13-38-38. Reservations recommended. Main courses 90F–140F (13.70– 21.30, $13.05–$20.30). Fixed-price menus 119F (18.10, $17.25) served only at lunch and after 10:30pm, 175F (26.60, $25.40) served anytime. AE, DC, MC, V. Daily noon–3pm and 7pm–midnight. Bus: 1, 2, or 5.

La Nissarda NIÇOISE/NORMAN   In the heart of town, about a 10-minute walk from place Masséna, this restaurant is maintained by a Normandy-born family who work hard to maintain the aura and the culinary traditions of Nice. In an intimate (40-seat) setting lined with old engravings and photographs of the city, the place serves a fixed-price menu of local versions of ravioli, spaghetti, carbonara, lasagna, and fresh-grilled salmon with herbs. A handful of Norman-based specialties also manage to creep into the menu, including escalopes of veal with cream sauce and apples.

17 rue Gubernatis. ℂ **04-93-85-26-29.** Reservations recommended. Fixed-price menu 100F–138F (15.20– 21.00, $14.50–$20). MC, V. Mon–Sat noon–2pm and 7–10pm. Closed Aug.

Le Safari ⭐ PROVENÇAL/NIÇOISE   The decor couldn't be simpler: a black ceiling, white walls, and an old-fashioned terra-cotta floor. The youthful staff is relaxed, sometimes in jeans, and always alert to the waves of fashion. Many diners prefer the outdoor terrace overlooking the Marché aux Fleurs but all appreciate the reasonably priced meals that appear in generous portions. Menu items include a pungent *bagna cauda*, in which vegetables are immersed in a sizzling brew of hot oil and anchovy paste; grilled peppers bathed in olive oil; *daube* (stew) of beef; fresh pasta with basil; and an omelet with *blettes* (tough but flavorful greens). The unfortunately named *merda de can* (dog shit) is gnocchi stuffed with spinach and is a lot more appetizing than it sounds.

1 cours Saleya. ℂ **04-93-80-18-44.** Reservations recommended. Main courses 80F–150F (12.15– 22.80, $11.60–$21.75); fixed-price menu 150F (22.80, $21.75). AE, DC, MC, V. Daily noon–2:30pm and 7–11:30pm. Closed Mon Nov–Mar. Bus: 1.

INEXPENSIVE

L'Olivier ⭐ PROVENÇAL/NIÇOISE   Opened in 1989, this charming restaurant lies beneath the arcades of place Garibaldi, just in back of the Museum of Modern Art. Named in honor of the premises' former occupant, a shop selling olives, olive oil, and anchovies, the restaurant serves an original cuisine based on modern versions of local culinary traditions. Well-prepared items include smoked slices of foie gras; deboned sea bass stuffed with shellfish and herbs and served with crabmeat sauce; roasted rabbit with sage-and-thyme sauce; and salmon-stuffed ravioli served with a sauce made from sea urchins. There's no menu—everything available that day is written on a chalkboard.

2 place Garibaldi. ℂ **04-93-26-89-09.** Reservations recommended. Main courses 55F–95F (8.35– 14.45, $8–$13.80). MC, V. Mon–Sat noon–2:30pm; Thurs–Sat and Mon–Tues 7:45–10pm. Closed Aug and 1 week in Jan.

Restaurant L'Estocaficada *(Finds* NIÇOISE   *Estocaficada* is the Provençal word for stockfish, Europe's ugliest fish. There might be a dried-out, balloon-shaped version on display in the cozy dining room. Brigitte Autier is the owner and chef, and her kitchens are visible from everywhere in the dining room. Descended from a matriarchal line (since 1958) of mother-daughter teams who've managed this place, she's devoted to the preservation of recipes prepared by her Niçoise grandmother. Examples are gnocchi, beignets, several types of *farcies* (tomatoes, peppers, or onions stuffed with herbed fillings), grilled sardines, or bouillabaisse served as a main course or in a mini-version. The place also serves pastas, one of which is garnished with three types of cheese.

2 rue de l'Hôtel-de-Ville. ℂ **04-93-80-21-64.** Reservations recommended. Main courses 55F–95F (8.35– 14.45, $8–$13.80); fixed-price menu 68F–125F (10.35– 19, $9.85–$18.15). AE, MC, V. Tues–Sat noon–2pm and 7–9:30pm. Bus: 1, 2, or 5.

NICE AFTER DARK

Nice has some of the most active nightlife along the Riviera, with evenings usually beginning at a cafe. At kiosks around town you can pick up a copy of *La Semaine des Spectacles,* which outlines the week's diversions.

The major cultural center on the Riviera is the **Opéra de Nice,** 4 rue St-François-de-Paule (☎ **04-92-17-40-40**), built in 1885 by Charles Garnier, fabled architect of the Paris Opéra. A full repertoire is presented, with emphasis on serious, often large-scale operas. In one season you might see *Tosca, Tristan und Isolde,* Verdi's *Macbeth,* Beethoven's *Fidelio,* and *Carmen,* as well as a *saison symphonique,* dominated by the Orchestre Philharmonique de Nice. The opera hall is also the major venue for concerts and recitals. Tickets are available (to concerts, recitals, and full-blown operas) up to about a day or two prior to any performance. You can show up at the box office (Tuesday to Friday 10am to 5:30 pm) or buy tickets in advance with a major credit card by phoning ☎ **04-92-17-40-40.** Tickets run 40F (6.10, $5.80) for nosebleed (and we mean it) seats to 800F (121.60, $116) for front-and-center seats on opening night.

Near the Hôtel Ambassador, **L'Ambassade,** 18 rue des Congrès (☎ **04-93-88-88-87**), was deliberately designed in a mock-Gothic style that includes the wrought-iron accents you'd expect to find in a château; it has two bars and a dance floor. At least 90% of its clients are straight and come in all physical types and age ranges. The cover is 100F (15.20, $14.50) and includes the first drink. Other contenders include **Blue Night Niels Club,** 67 rue des États-Unis (☎ **04-93-80-49-84**), where hip recorded music (including house, garage, techno, and whatever strikes the fancy of the DJ) attracts a high-energy, highly sociable crowd under 35 to boogie the night away.

The **Cabaret du Casino Ruhl,** in the Casino Ruhl, 1 promenade des Anglais (☎ **04-97-03-12-77**), is Nice's answer to the cabaret glitter that appears in more ostentatious forms in Monte Carlo and Las Vegas. It includes just enough flesh to titillate; lots of spangles, feathers, and sequins; a medley of cross-cultural jokes and nostalgia for the old days of French chanson; and an acrobat or juggler. The cover of 100F (15.20, $14.50) includes the first drink; dinner and the show, complete with a bottle of wine per person, costs 300F (45.60, $43.50). Shows are presented every Friday and Saturday at 10:30pm. No jeans or sneakers.

The casino contains an area exclusively for slot machines, open daily from 10am to 4 or 5am, entrance to which is free. A more formal gaming room (jacket required, but not a tie), with blackjack, baccarat, chemin de fer, and 21 tables, is open nightly, at a fee of 75F (11.40, $10.90) per person, every Monday to Friday from 8pm to 4am and every Saturday and Sunday from 5pm to 5am.

Le Relais, in the Hotel Negresco, 37 promenade des Anglais (☎ **04-93-16-64-00**), is the most beautiful bar in Nice, filled with white columns, an oxblood-red ceiling, Oriental carpets, English paneling, Italianate chairs, and tapestries. It was once a haunt of the actress Lillie Langtry. With its piano music and white-jacketed waiters, the bar still attracts a chic crowd.

GAY NIGHTLIFE

Increasingly, Nice remains the gay capital of southern France. You can make a night of it (or several nights of it) at the following establishments: **Latinos,** 6 rue Chauvain (☎ **04-93-85-01-10**), for "gay tapas"; **Café Chris,** 3 rue Smolett (☎ **04-93-26-75-85**), a gay cafe; and **Le C.D. Restaurant and Salad Bar,** 22 rue Benoit Bunico (☎ **04-93-92-47-65**), where you can cruise while you munch.

Near the Hôtel Negresco and promenade des Anglais, **Le Blue Boy,** 9 rue Spinetta (© **04-93-44-68-24**), is the oldest gay disco on the Riviera. With two bars and two floors, it's a vital nocturnal stop for passengers aboard the dozens of all-gay cruises that make regular calls at Nice. The cover varies from free to 50F (7.60, $7.25). A newer club, fun, but struggling for recognition is **Le Klub,** 10 rue Halevy (© **04-93-16-27-56**). No cover.

L'Ascenseur, 18 bis rue Emmanuel-Philibert (© **04-93-26-35-30**), is one of the most popular of the several new crops of gay bars in and around Nice. This is a bustling, friendly place with wood paneling, billiard tables, metallic accents, and some of the more appealing gay men in all of Europe. It's open Tuesday to Saturday from 9pm till at least 3am. There's no dance floor, but disco music plays as men (and to a lesser degree, lesbians) laugh, converse, and flirt.

14 Villefranche-sur-Mer ★

581 miles S of Paris, 4 miles E of Nice

According to legend, Hercules opened his arms and Villefranche was born. It sits on a big blue bay that looks like a gigantic bowl, large enough to attract U.S. Sixth Fleet cruisers and destroyers. Quietly slumbering otherwise, Villefranche takes on the appearance of an exciting Mediterranean port when the fleet's in. Four miles east of Nice, it's the first town you reach along the Lower Corniche.

ESSENTIALS

GETTING THERE **Trains** arrive from most towns on the Côte d'Azur, especially Nice (every 30 minutes), but most visitors **drive** via the Corniche Inférieure (Lower Corniche). For more rail information and schedules, call © **08-36-35-35-35.** There's no formalized **bus** station in Villefranche.

VISITOR INFORMATION The **Office de Tourisme** is on Jardin François-Binon (© **04-93-01-73-68;** www.villefranche-sur-mer.com).

EXPLORING THE TOWN

The vaulted **rue Obscure** is one of the strangest streets in France (to get to it, take rue de l'Église). In spirit it belongs more to a North African casbah. People live in tiny houses on this street, but occasionally there's an open space, allowing for a tiny courtyard.

Once popular with such writers as Katherine Mansfield and Aldous Huxley, the town is still a haven for artists, many of whom take over the little houses that climb the hillside. Two of the more recent arrivals who've bought homes in the area are Tina Turner and Bono (not together).

One artist who came to Villefranche left a memorial: Jean Cocteau, the painter, writer, filmmaker, and well-respected dilettante, spent a year (1956 to 1957) painting frescoes on the 14th-century walls of the **Romanesque Chapelle St-Pierre,** quai de la Douane/rue des Marinières (© **04-93-76-90-70**). He presented it to "the fishermen of Villefranche in homage to the Prince of Apostles, the patron of fishermen." One panel pays homage to the gypsies of the Stes-Maries-de-la-Mer. In the apse is a depiction of the miracle of St. Peter walking on the water, not knowing that he's supported by an angel. Villefranche's women in their regional costumes are honored on the left side of the narthex Cocteau. The chapel, which charges 12F (1.80, $1.75) admission, is open Tuesday to Sunday: July to September from 10am to noon and 4 to 8:30pm, October to March from 9:30am to noon and 2 to 5pm; April to June from 9:30am to noon and 2:30 to 7:30pm (closed mid-November to mid-December).

ACCOMMODATIONS

Hôtel Welcome   This is as good as it gets in Villefranche. The Welcome was a favorite of Jean Cocteau. In this six-floor villa hotel, with shutters and balconies, everything has been modernized and extensively renovated. Try for a fifth-floor room overlooking the water. All the midsize to spacious rooms are comfortably furnished, each with a small bathroom, mostly with a combination tub and shower. The sidewalk cafe is the focal point of town life. The lounge and the restaurant, St-Pierre, have open fireplaces and fruitwood furniture.

1 quai Courbet, 06230 Villefranche-sur-Mer. (℃) **04-93-76-27-62.** Fax 04-93-76-27-66. www.welcome hotel.com. 37 units. 540F–1,010F (82.13– 153.50, $78.30–$146.45) double. AE, DC, MC, V. Closed Nov 15–Dec 20. **Amenities:** Restaurant, bar; room service; baby-sitting; laundry. *In room:* A/C, minibar, safe.

DINING

La Mère Germaine FRENCH/SEAFOOD   This is the very best of a string of restaurants on the port. Plan to relax here over lunch while watching fishermen repair their nets. Mère Germaine opened the place in the 1930s, and her grandson, the likable Thierry Blouin, deftly handles the cuisine these days, producing a bouillabaisse that's celebrated across the Riviera. We recommend the grilled *loup* (sea bass) with fennel, salade Niçoise, sole Tante Marie (stuffed with mushroom purée), lobster ravioli with shellfish sauce, and beef filet with garlic and seasonal vegetables. The perfectly roasted *carré d'agneau* (lamb) is for two. Most dishes are at the lower end of the price scale.

Quai Courbet. (℃) **04-93-01-71-39.** Reservations recommended. Main courses 150F–570F (22.80– 86.65, $21.75–$82.65); fixed-price menu 233F (35.40, $33.80); bouillabaisse 337F (51.20, $48.85). AE, MC, V. Daily noon–2:30pm and 7–10pm. Closed Nov 12–Dec 24.

15 St-Jean-Cap-Ferrat ⟨★⟨★

583 miles S of Paris, 6 miles E of Nice

Of all the oases along the Côte d'Azur, no place has the snob appeal of Cap-Ferrat. It's a 9-mile promontory sprinkled with luxurious villas, outlined by sheltered bays, beaches, and coves. The vegetation is lush. In the port of St-Jean, the harbor accommodates yachts and fishing boats.

ESSENTIALS

GETTING THERE   Most visitors drive or take a **bus** or **taxi** from the rail station at nearby Beaulieu. Buses from the station at Beaulieu depart at hourly intervals for Cap-Ferrat. There's also bus service from Nice. For bus information and schedules, call (℃) **04-93-85-61-81.** By **car,** St-Jean-Cap-Ferrat is best reached from Nice by driving along N7 east.

VISITOR INFORMATION   The **Office de Tourisme** is on avenue Denis-Séméria ((℃) **04-93-76-08-90;** www.riviera.fr/tourisme.htm).

SEEING THE SIGHTS

One of the ways to enjoy the scenery here is to wander on some of the public paths. The most scenic goes from **Plage de Paloma** to **Pointe St-Hospice,** where a panoramic view of the Riviera landscape unfolds.

You can also wander around **St-Jean,** a colorful fishing village with bars, bistros, and inns. The beaches, although popular, are pebbly, not sandy. The best and most luxurious belongs to the Grand Hôtel du Cap-Ferrat (see below). It's open to nonguests who pay 100F (15.20, $14.50) to rent a mattress and an umbrella.

Everyone tries to visit the **Villa Mauresque,** avenue Somerset-Maugham, but it's closed to the public. Near the cape, it's where Maugham spent his final years. When tourists tried to visit him, he proclaimed that he wasn't one of the local sights. One man did manage to crash through the gate, and when he encountered the author, Maugham snarled, "What do you think I am, a monkey in a cage?"

Once the property of King Leopold II, of Belgium, the **Villa Les Cèdres** lies directly west of the port of St-Jean. Although the villa can't be visited, you can go to the **Parc Zoologique,** boulevard du Général-de-Gaulle, northwest of the peninsula, near Villa Les Cèdres (© **04-93-76-04-98**). It's open daily: April to October from 9:30am to 7pm (to 6pm in winter). Admission is 60F (9.10, $8.70) for adults, 42F (6.40, $6.10) for children under 18 and students. This private zoo is set in the basin of a now-drained lake and was Leopold's private domain. It houses a wide variety of reptiles, birds, and animals in outdoor cages. Six times a day there's a chimps' tea party, which explains Maugham's remark.

Musée Île-de-France ★★   Built by Baronne Ephrussi de Rothschild, this is one of the Côte d'Azur's most legendary villas. Born a Rothschild, the baronne married a Hungarian banker and friend of her father, about whom even the museum's curator knows little. She died in 1934, leaving the Italianate building and its magnificent gardens to the Institut de France on behalf of the Académie des Beaux-Arts. The wealth of her collection is preserved: 18th-century furniture; Tiepolo ceilings; Savonnerie carpets; screens and panels from the Far East; tapestries from Gobelin, Aubusson, and Beauvais; drawings by Fragonard; canvases by Boucher; rare Sèvres porcelain; and more. Covering 12 acres, the gardens contain fragments of statuary from churches, monasteries, and palaces. An entire section is planted with cacti.

Av. Denis-Séméria. © **04-93-01-33-09**. Admission 50F (7.60, $7.25) adults, 38F (5.80, $5.50) students and persons under 24, free for children under 9. Nov to mid-Feb Mon–Fri 2–6pm and Sat–Sun 10am–6pm; late Feb to Oct daily 10am–6pm.

HITTING THE BEACH

The town's most visible and popular beaches are **Plage Passable,** on the northeastern "neck" of the Cap-Ferrat peninsula, close to where it's connected to the French mainland; and **Plage Paloma,** near the peninsula's southernmost tip, and overlooked by the Chapelle St-Hospice. Neither has a sandy surface (they're composed of pebbles and gravel), but they do have snack bars, souvenir stands, and beachfront restaurants. Most hotel guests opt to remain around the pools of their hotels, and indeed, many hotels don't even have beaches of their own. A noteworthy exception is the Grand Hôtel du Cap-Ferrat (see below), which acquired a beach in the early 1900s.

ACCOMMODATIONS
EXPENSIVE

Grand Hôtel du Cap-Ferrat ★★★   One of the best features of this early-1900s palace is its location: at the tip of the peninsula in the midst of a 14-acre garden of semitropical trees and manicured lawns. It has been the retreat of the international elite since 1908 and occupies the same celestial status as the Réserve and Métropole in Beaulieu. Its cuisine even equals the Métropole's. Parts of the exterior have open loggias and big arched windows; you can also enjoy the views from the elaborately flowering terrace over the sea. Accommodations look as if the late Princess Grace might settle in comfortably at any minute. They're generally spacious and open to sea views, and each comes with a sumptuous bathroom. Rates include admission to the pool, Club Dauphin. The beach is accessible via funicular from the main building. The hotel is open year-round.

Bd. du Général-de-Gaulle, 06230 St-Jean-Cap-Ferrat. 🕿 800/225-4255 in the U.S. or Canada, or 04-93-76-50-50. Fax 04-93-76-04-52. www.grand-hotel-cap-ferrat.com. 53 units. 1,400F–7,200F (212.80– 1,094.40, $203–$1,044) double; 5,000F–18,800F (760– 2,857.60, $725–$2,726) suite. AE, DC, MC, V. Indoor parking 500F (76, $72.50); outdoor parking free. **Amenities:** 2 restaurants, 2 bars; Olympic-size heated pool; 2 tennis courts; sauna; hotel bicycles; room service; baby-sitting; laundry/dry cleaning. *In room:* A/C, TV, minibar, hair dryer, safe.

La Voile d'Or ★★ The "Golden Sail" is a tour de force, offering intimate luxury in a converted 19th-century villa set at the edge of the little fishing port and yacht harbor, with a panoramic coast view. It's equal in every way to the Grand Hôtel except for its cuisine, which is just a notch below. The guest rooms, lounges, and restaurant all open onto terraces. The rooms are individually decorated with hand-painted reproductions, carved gilt headboards, baroque paneled doors, parquet floors, antique clocks, and paintings, and each comes with a luxurious bathroom with a combination tub and shower. Guests gather on the canopied outer terrace for lunch, and in the evening dine in a stately room with Spanish armchairs and white wrought-iron chandeliers.

31 av. Jean-Mermoz, 06230 St-Jean-Cap-Ferrat. 🕿 **04-93-01-13-13.** Fax 04-93-76-11-17. www.lavoiledor.fr. 45 units. 1,210F–4,420F (183.90– 671.85, $175.45–$640.90) double; 2,860F–4,420F (434.70– 671.85, $414.70–$640.90) suite. Rates include continental breakfast. AE, MC, V. Closed Nov–Mar. Parking 100F (15.20, $14.50). **Amenities:** Restaurant, bar; 2 outdoor pools; exercise room; sauna; room service; baby-sitting; laundry/dry cleaning. *In room:* A/C, TV, minibar, hair dryer.

MODERATE

Hôtel Brise Marine This villa (built around 1878) with a front and rear terrace is on a hillside. A long rose arbor, beds of subtropical flowers, palms, and pines provide an attractive setting. The atmosphere is casual and informal, and the rooms are comfortably but simply furnished, each with a small tiled bathroom with shower and tub. You can have breakfast in the beamed lounge or under the rose trellis. The little corner bar is for afternoon drinks.

Av. Jean-Mermoz, St-Jean-Cap-Ferrat, 06230 Villefranche-sur-Mer. 🕿 **04-93-76-04-36.** Fax 04-93-76-11-49. www.hotel-brisemarine.com. 16 units. 750F–810F (114– 123.10, $108.75–$117.45) double. AE, DC, MC, V. Closed Nov–Jan. **Amenities:** Bar. *In room:* A/C, TV.

Hôtel Clair Logis *Value* This is a cozy retreat. Within an otherwise pricey resort strip of deluxe hotels and homes, this B&B was created by the grandmother of the present owners when she added two outbuildings to the grounds of her early-1900s villa, about a 10-minute walk from the beach. The hotel's most famous guest was de Gaulle, who lived in a room called Strelitzias (Bird of Paradise) during many of his retreats from Paris. The pleasant rooms, each named after a flower, are scattered over three buildings in the confines of the garden. The most romantic and spacious are in the main building; the seven rooms in the annex are the most modern but have the least character and tend to be smaller and cheaper. Each comes with a small bathroom with shower.

12 av. Centrale, 06230 St-Jean-Cap-Ferrat. 🕿 **04-93-76-04-57.** Fax 04-93-76-51-82. www.hotel-clair-logis.fr. 18 units. 690F–790F (104.90– 120.10, $100.05–$114.55) double. AE, DC, MC, V. Closed Jan 10 to mid-Mar and Nov–Dec 15. *In room:* TV, minibar, hair dryer.

DINING

Le Provençal ⭐ FRENCH/PROVENÇAL   With the possible exception of the Grand Hôtel's dining room, this is the grandest restaurant of this very grand resort. Near the top of Nice's highest peak, it has the most panoramic view, with sightlines that sweep, on good days, as far away as Menton and the Italian border. Many of the menu items are credited directly to the inspiration of "the Provençal" in the kitchens. Menu items include marinated artichoke hearts presented beside half a lobster, a *tarte fine* of potatoes with deliberately undercooked foie gras, rack of lamb with local herbs and tarragon sauce, and crayfish with asparagus and black-olive tapenade. The best way to appreciate the desserts is to order the house sampler, *les cinq desserts du Provençal*—five petite desserts that usually include macaroons with chocolate and crème brûlée. With the passage of years here, the cooking seems more inspired than ever.

2 av. Denis-Séméria. ⓒ 04-93-76-03-97. Reservations required. Main courses 250F–350F (38– 53.20, $36.25–$50.75); fixed-price menu 350F (53.20, $50.75). AE, MC, V. Apr–Sept daily noon–2:30pm and 7:30–11pm, Oct–Mar Tues–Sat noon–2:30pm and 7:30–11pm.

Le Sloop FRENCH/PROVENÇAL   This is the most popular and most reasonably priced bistro in this expensive area. Outfitted in blue and white inside and out, it sits at the edge of the port, overlooking the yachts in the harbor. A meal might begin with a salad of flap mushrooms steeped "en cappuccino" with liquefied foie gras or perhaps tartare of salmon with aïoli and lemon crêpes. This might be followed with a filet of deboned sea bass served with red-wine sauce or a mixed fish fry of three kinds of Mediterranean fish, bound together with olive oil and truffles. Dessert might include strawberry soup with sweet white wine and apricot ice cream or any of about seven other desserts, each based on "the red fruits of the region." The regional wines are reasonably priced.

Au Nouveau Port. ⓒ 04-93-01-48-63. Reservations recommended. Main courses 140F–160F (21.30– 24.30, $20.30–$23.20); fixed-price menu 160F (24.30, $23.20). AE, MC, V. June–Sept Wed 7–9:30pm, Thurs–Tues noon–2pm and 7–11pm; closed Tues lunch and Wed lunch July and Aug.

16 Beaulieu-sur-Mer ⭐⭐

583 miles S of Paris, 6 miles E of Nice, 7 miles W of Monte Carlo

Protected from the north winds blowing down from the Alps, Beaulieu-sur-Mer is often referred to as "La Petite Afrique" (Little Africa). Like Menton, it has the mildest climate along the Côte d'Azur and is popular with wintering wealthy. Originally, English visitors staked it out, after an English industrialist founded a hotel here between the rock-studded slopes and the sea. Beaulieu is graced with lush vegetation, including oranges, lemons, and bananas, as well as palms.

ESSENTIALS

GETTING THERE   Most visitors **drive** from Nice via the Moyenne Corniche or the coastal highway. **Train** service connects Beaulieu with Nice, Monaco, and the rest of the Côte d'Azur. For rail information and schedules, call ⓒ 08-36-35-35-35.

VISITOR INFORMATION   The **Office de Tourisme** is on place Georges-Clemenceau (ⓒ 04-93-01-02-21; www.riviera.fr/tourisme.htm).

FUN ON & OFF THE BEACH

Beaulieu does have a beach, but don't expect soft sands. The beaches aren't as rocky as those in Nice or other nearby resorts, but they're still closer to gravel than to sand. The longer of the town's two free public beaches is **Petite Afrique,** adjacent to the yacht basin; the shorter is **Baie des Fourmis,** beneath the casino. **Africa Plage** (℃ **04-93-01-11-00**) rents mattresses for 90F (13.70, $13.05) per day. They also sell snacks and drinks.

The town boasts an important church, the late-19th-century **Église de Sacré-Coeur,** a quasi-Byzantine, quasi-Gothic mishmash at 13 bd. du Maréchal-Leclerc (℃ **04-93-01-18-24**). With the same address and phone is the 12th-century Romanesque chapel of Santa Maria de Olivo, used mostly for temporary exhibits of painting, sculpture, and civic lore. Both sites are open daily from 8am to 7pm.

As you walk along the seafront promenade, you can see many stately Belle-Époque villas that evoke the days when Beaulieu was the very height of fashion. Although you can't go inside, you'll see signs indicating **Villa Namouna,** which once belonged to Gordon Bennett, the owner of the *New York Herald,* and **Villa Léonine,** former home of the marquess of Salisbury.

For a memorable 2-hour walk, start north of boulevard Edouard-VII, where a path leads up the Riviera escarpment to **Sentier du Plateau St-Michel.** A belvedere here offers panoramic views from Cap d'Ail to the Estérel. A 1-hour alternative is the stroll along **promenade Maurice-Rouvier.** The promenade runs parallel to the water, stretching from Beaulieu to St-Jean. On one side you'll see the most elegant of mansions set in well-landscaped gardens; on the other you'll get views of the Riviera landscape and the peninsular point of St-Hospice.

The **Casino de Beaulieu,** avenue Fernand-Dunan (℃ **04-93-76-48-00**), built in the Art Nouveau style in 1903, was revitalized with new management in 1997. The main part of the casino where the blackjack, roulette, and chemin de fer tables are housed is open every night from 8pm to dawn. The ambience is glamorous and men are required to wear jacket and tie. Entrance is 70F (10.65, $10.15). For more casual gambling, the casino has a separate area for slot machines only. Entrance is free and there's no dress code. This area is open every day from 11am to dawn. There is also a bar and a disco on the premises.

Villa Kérylos ⭐⭐ This is a replica of an ancient Greek residence, painstakingly designed and built by the archaeologist Theodore Reinach. Inside, the cabinets are filled with a collection of Greek figurines and ceramics. But most interesting is the reconstructed Greek furniture, much of which would be fashionable today. One curious mosaic depicts the slaying of the minotaur and provides its own labyrinth (if you try to trace the path, expect to stay for weeks).

Rue Gustave-Eiffel. ℃ **04-93-01-01-44.** Admission 40F (6.10, $5.80) adults, 20F (3.05, $2.90) children and seniors, under 5 free. Daily 10:30am–6pm.

ACCOMMODATIONS
VERY EXPENSIVE

La Réserve de Beaulieu ⭐⭐⭐ A Relais & Châteaux member, this pink-and-white fin-de-siècle palace is one of the Riviera's most famous hotels. Here you can sit, have an apéritif, and watch the sun set over the Riviera while a pianist treats you to Mozart. A number of the public lounges open onto a courtyard with bamboo chairs, grass borders, and urns of flowers. The social life revolves around the main drawing room. The guest rooms range widely in size and design; all are deluxe and individually decorated, with a beautiful view of the mountains or the sea. They come with deluxe mattresses and luxurious bathrooms with tubs and showers. Most of them overlook the Mediterranean, and some even have private balconies. The dining room has a frescoed ceiling, parquet floors, crystal chandeliers, and picture windows facing the Mediterranean.

5 bd. du Maréchal-Leclerc, 06310 Beaulieu-sur-Mer. ℂ 04-93-01-00-01. Fax 04-93-01-28-99. www.reserve
beaulieu.com. 38 units. High season 2,950F–4,150F (448.40– 630.80, $427.75–$601.75) double,
7,400F–12,000F (1,124.80– 1,824, $1,073–$1,740) suite; low season 980F–2,400F (148.95– 364.80,
$142.10–$348) double, 3,750F–6,150F (570– 934.80, $543.75–$891.75) suite. Rates even more astronomical during the Grand Prix of Monaco (June 1–4). AE, DC, MC, V. Closed Nov 20–Dec 20 and Jan–Mar.
Free parking. **Amenities:** Restaurant, bar; outdoor pool; room service; massage; baby-sitting; laundry/
dry cleaning. *In room:* A/C, TV, minibar, hair dryer, safe.

Le Métropole ★★   This Italianate villa is as good as it gets, except for La
Réserve de Beaulieu, offering some of the Riviera's most luxurious accommodations. It's classified as a Relais & Châteaux and is set on 2 acres of grounds discreetly shut off from the traffic of the resort. Here, you'll enter a world of
polished French elegance, with lots of balconies opening onto sea views. The
marble, Oriental carpets, and polite staff members set a pervasive tone. The
guest rooms are furnished in tasteful fabrics and flowery wallpapers, with deluxe
mattresses; the roomy bathrooms have tub/shower combinations. Though the
in-house restaurant lost a star from the Michelin judges in 2001, the food is
nonetheless superb. The restaurant has a seaside terrace/bar.

15 bd. du Maréchal-Leclerc, 06310 Beaulieu-sur-Mer. ℂ 04-93-01-00-08. Fax 04-93-01-18-51. www.le-
metropole.com/. 42 units. July–Sept 1,700F–3,400F (258.40– 516.80, $246.50–$493) double,
4,600F–5,900F (699.20– 896.80, $667–$855.50) suite; Sept–June 1,000F–2,900F (152– 440.80,
$145–$420.50) double, 2,700F–4,600F (410.40– 699.20, $391.50–$667) suite. Half board 450F (68.40,
$65.25) per person extra. AE, DC, MC, V. Closed Oct 20–Dec 20. **Amenities:** Restaurant, bar; outdoor pool;
concrete jetty for sunning; room service; laundry/dry cleaning. *In room:* A/C, TV, minibar, hair dryer, safe.

INEXPENSIVE

Hôtel Le Havre Bleu *Value*   This is a great little bargain if you don't need a lot
of services and amenities. Le Havre Bleu has one of the prettiest facades of any
inexpensive hotel in town. Housed in a former Victorian villa, the hotel has a
front garden dotted with flowering urns and arched ornate windows. The comfortable guest rooms are impeccable and functional. Each is a little bonebares of
in-room amenities, except for a phone, but all are equipped with a compact
bathroom with shower. Breakfast is the only meal served.

29 bd. du Maréchal-Joffre, 06310 Beaulieu-sur-Mer. ℂ 04-93-01-01-40. Fax 04-93-01-29-92. 22 units.
300F–350F (45.60– 53.20, $43.50–$50.75) double. AE, DC, MC, V. **Amenities:** None.

Hôtel Marcellin   The early-1900s Marcellin is a good budget selection in an
otherwise high-priced resort. The restored rooms come with homelike amenities
and a southern exposure. The rooms are small to midsize, but comfortably furnished. Corridor bathrooms are well kept and adequate; some units come with
a small tiled bathroom with shower. Except for a phone, in-room amenities are
skimpy. The location isn't bad either: amid the town's congestion, near its western periphery, only a 5-minute walk to the beach. Overall, this is a pleasant place
to stay. Breakfast is the only meal served, but many restaurants are nearby.

18 av. Albert-1er, 06310 Beaulieu-sur-Mer. ℂ 04-93-01-01-69. Fax 04-93-01-37-43. 21 units, 14 with bathroom. 180F (27.35, $26.10) double without bathroom, 250F–360F (38– 54.70, $36.25–$52.20) double
with bathroom; 500F–800F (76– 121.60, $72.50–$116) suite. MC, V. Closed Nov–Dec 15 and Feb.

Inter-Hôtel Frisia   Most of the Frisia's rooms, decorated in a modern style,
open onto views of the harbor. Expectedly, sea-view rooms are the most expensive. All the rooms contain a small bathroom, all but four equipped with a combination tub and shower, the others shower only. Public areas include a sunny

garden and inviting lounges. English is widely spoken here, and the management makes foreign guests feel especially welcome. Breakfast is the only meal served, but many reasonably priced dining places are nearby.

Bd. Eugène-Gauthier, 06310 Beaulieu-sur-Mer. ℂ 04-93-01-01-04. Fax 04-93-01-31-92. info@hotel-frisia.com. 34 units. 350F–730F (53.20– 110.95, $50.75–$105.85) double. AE, MC, V. Closed Nov 12–Dec 13. **Amenities:** Bar; baby-sitting; laundry/dry cleaning. *In room:* TV, minibar, hair dryer, safe.

DINING

La Pignatelle *Value* FRENCH/PROVENÇAL   Even in this super-expensive resort town, you can find an excellent and affordable Provençal bistro. After all, the locals have to eat somewhere and not every visitor can afford the higher-priced palaces. Despite its relatively low prices, La Pignatelle prides itself on the fact that all the products that go into its robust cuisine are fresh. Specialties include mushroom-stuffed ravioli with truffled cream sauce, a succulent *soupe de poissons* from which someone has labored to remove the bones, cassolette of mussels, monkfish steak garnished with olive oil and herbs, fricassee of sea bass with shrimp, and a *petite friture du pays* that incorporates very small fish with old Provençal traditions.

10 rue de Quincenet. ℂ 04-93-01-03-37. Reservations recommended. Main courses 75F–150F (11.40– 22.80, $10.93–$21.75); fixed-price menu 90F–145F (13.70– 22.05, $13.05–$21.05). AE, MC, V. Thurs–Tues noon–2pm and 7–9:30pm. Closed mid-Nov to mid-Dec.

Les Agaves ✶ MODERN FRENCH   One of the most stylish and artfully managed restaurants in Beaulieu is housed in an early-1900s villa across the street from the Beaulieu's railway station. U.S.-based publications such as *Bon Appétit* have praised the cuisine as delectable. Of particular note are curry-enhanced scallops with garlic-flavored tomatoes and parsley, terrine of pork with a confit of onions, lobster salad with mango, chopped shrimp with Provençal herbs, and several preparations of foie gras. Filet of sea bass with truffles and champagne sauce is particularly delectable.

4 av. Maréchal Foch. ℂ 04-93-01-13-12. Reservations recommended. Main courses 55F–190F (8.35– 28.90, $8–$27.55); fixed-price menu 185F (28.10, $26.85); bouillabaisse 250F (38, $36.25) per person. AE, MC, V. Tues–Sun noon–3pm; Tues–Sat 7:15–10:30pm. Closed Nov.

17 Eze & La Turbie ✶✶

585 miles S of Paris, 7 miles NE of Nice

The hamlets of Eze and La Turbie, though 4 miles apart, have so many similarities that most of France's tourist officials speak of them as if they're one. Both boast fortified feudal cores high in the hills overlooking the Provençal coast, and both were built during the early Middle Ages to stave off raids from corsairs who wanted to capture harem slaves and laborers. Clinging to the rocky hillsides around these hamlets are upscale villas, many of which have been built since the 1950s by retirees from colder climes. Closely linked, culturally and fiscally, to nearby Monaco, Eze and La Turbie have full-time populations of fewer than 3,000. The medieval cores of both contain art galleries, boutiques, and artisans' shops that have been restored.

Eze is accessible via the Moyenne (Middle) Corniche, La Turbie via the Grande (Upper) Corniche. Signs are positioned along the coastal road indicating the direction motorists should take to reach either of the hamlets.

The leading attraction in Eze is the **Jardin Exotique** ✶, boulevard du Jardin-Exotique (ℂ **04-93-41-10-30**), a lushly landscaped showcase of exotic plants set in Eze-Village, at the pinnacle of the town's highest hill. Admission is 15F (2.30, $2.20) for adult, 8F (1.20, $1.15) for students and persons 12 to 25, and free for children under 12. In July and August, it's open daily from 9am to 8pm; the rest of the year, it opens at 9am and closes between 5 and 7:30pm, depending on sunset.

La Turbie boasts a ruined monument erected by the ancient Roman emperor Augustus in 6 B.C., the **Trophée des Alps** (Trophy of the Alps). (Many locals call it La Trophée d'Auguste.) It rises near a rock formation known as La Tête de Chien, at the highest point along the Grand Corniche, 1,500 feet above sea level. The monument, restored with funds donated by Edward Tuck, was erected by the Roman Senate to celebrate the subjugation of the people of the French Alps by the Roman armies.

A short distance from the monument is the **Musée du Trophée des Alps,** rue Albert-1er, La Turbie (© **04-93-41-20-84**), a mini-museum containing finds from archaeological digs nearby and information about the monument's restoration. It's open daily from 9:30am to 5pm (until 6pm April to June, and until 7pm July to September). Admission is 26F (3.95, $3.75) for adults, 16F (2.45, $2.30) for students and ages 12 to 25, and free for children under 12. It's closed January 1, May 1, November, and December 25.

The **Office de Tourisme** is on place du Général-de-Gaulle, Eze-Village (© **04-93-41-26-00**).

ACCOMMODATIONS & DINING

Hostellerie du Château de la Chèvre d'Or ★★★ This is one of the grandest resort hotels along the Eastern Riviera. This miniature-village retreat was built in the 1920s in neo-Gothic style. It's a Relais & Châteaux in a complex of village houses, all with views of the coastline. But unlike most villages in the area, this mini-village doesn't have a beach. It's located on the side of a stone village off the Moyenne Corniche. The owner has had the interior of the "Golden Goat" flawlessly decorated to maintain its old character while adding modern comfort. The spacious bedrooms are sumptuous and filled with quality furnishings, and the large bathrooms have excellent fixtures including a combination tub and shower. Even if you don't stop in for a meal or a room, try to visit for a drink in the lounge, which has a panoramic view.

Rue du Barri, 06360 Eze-Village. © **04-92-10-66-66**. Fax 04-93-41-06-72. www.chevredor.com. 33 units. 1,800F–4,500F (273.60– 684, $261.50–$652.50) double; from 3,600F (547.20, $522) suite. AE, MC, DC, V. Closed mid-Nov to Mar. **Amenities:** 3 restaurants; bar; outdoor pool; room service; laundry/dry cleaning. *In room:* A/C, TV, minibar, hair dryer, safe.

18 Monaco ★★★

593 miles S of Paris, 11 miles E of Nice

Monaco, according to a famous quote from Somerset Maugham, is defined as "370 sunny acres peopled with shady characters." The outspoken Katharine Hepburn once called it "a pimple on the chin of the south of France." She wasn't referring to the principality's lack of beauty but rather to the preposterous idea of having a little country, a feudal anomaly, taking up some of the choicest coastline along the Riviera. Monaco became a property of the Grimaldi clan, a Genoese family, as early as 1297. It has maintained something resembling independence ever since. In a fit of impatience, the French annexed it in 1793, but the ruling family recovered it in 1814.

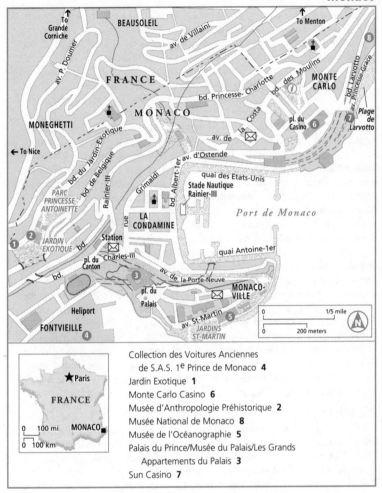

Collection des Voitures Anciennes
  de S.A.S. 1e Prince de Monaco **4**
Jardin Exotique **1**
Monte Carlo Casino **6**
Musée d'Anthropologie Préhistorique **2**
Musée National de Monaco **8**
Musée de l'Océanographie **5**
Palais du Prince/Musée du Palais/Les Grands
  Appartements du Palais **3**
Sun Casino **7**

Hemmed in by France on three sides and the Mediterranean on the fourth, tiny Monaco staunchly maintains its independence. Even Charles de Gaulle couldn't force Prince Rainier to do away with his tax-free policy. As almost everybody in an overburdened world knows by now, the Monégasques do not pay taxes. Nearly all their country's revenue comes from tourism and gambling.

Monaco, or more precisely its capital of Monte Carlo, has for a century been a symbol of glamour. Its legend was enhanced by the 1956 marriage of Prince Rainier III to American actress Grace Kelly. She had met the prince when she was in Cannes to promote *To Catch a Thief,* the Hitchcock movie she made with Cary Grant. A journalist arranged a *Paris Match* photo shoot with the prince, and the rest is history. A daughter, Caroline, was born in 1957; a son, Albert, in 1958; and a second daughter, Stephanie, in 1965. The Monégasques welcomed the birth of Caroline but went wild at the birth of Albert, a male heir. According to a 1918 treaty, Monaco would become an autonomous state under French protection should the ruling dynasty become extinct. However, the fact that Albert is still a bachelor has the entire principality concerned.

Though not always happy in her role, Princess Grace soon won the respect and admiration of her people. In 1982 she accidentally drove her sports car over a cliff. The Monégasques still mourn her death.

The second-smallest state in Europe (Vatican City is the tiniest), Monaco consists of four parts. The old town, **Monaco-Ville,** on a promontory, "the Rock," 200 feet high, is the seat of the royal palace and the government building, as well as the Oceanographic Museum. To the west of the bay, **La Condamine,** the home of the Monégasques, is at the foot of the old town, forming its harbor and port sector. Up from the port (walking is steep in Monaco) is **Monte Carlo,** once the playground of European royalty and still the center for wintering wealthy, the setting for the casino and its gardens and the deluxe hotels. The fourth part, **Fontvieille,** is a neat industrial suburb. Ironically, **Monte-Carlo Beach,** at the far frontier, is on French soil. It attracts a chic crowd, including movie stars in the skimpiest bikinis and thongs.

No one used to go to Monaco in summer, but now July and August tend to be so crowded it's hard to get a room. The Monégasques very frankly court an affluent crowd. But with the decline of royalty, Monaco has had to develop a broader base of tourism. You can now stay here moderately, though still not cheaply. As always, you can lose your shirt at the casinos. "Suicide Terrace" at the casino, though not used as frequently as in the old days, is still a real temptation to many who have gambled away family fortunes.

Even when family fortunes aren't slipping through the fingers of gamblers, the casino has been the subject of legends and the setting for many films (Richard Burton presented Elizabeth Taylor with the huge Koh-i-noor diamond here). Because Monaco is a tax haven, many celebrities have become residents, including Plácido Domingo, Claudia Schiffer, Boris Becker, and Ringo Starr.

ESSENTIALS

GETTING THERE   Monaco has rail, bus, and highway connections from other coastal cities, especially Nice. **Trains** arrive every 30 minutes from Cannes, Nice, Menton, and Antibes. For more rail information and schedules, call ℰ **08-36-35-35-35.** Monaco's railway station (Gare SNCF) is on avenue Prince Pierre. It's a long steep walk uphill from the train station to Monte Carlo. If you'd rather take a **taxi** but can't find one at the station, call ℰ **93-50-56-28** or 93-15-01-01. There are no border formalities for anyone entering Monaco from

---

⸨Tips⸩ Reach Out & Touch Someone in Monaco

To call Monaco from within France, dial 00 (the access code for all international long-distance calls placed from France), followed by Monaco's new country code, 377, and then the eight-digit local phone number. (Don't dial the 33 code; this is the country code for France, which no longer applies to Monaco.)

To call Monaco from North America, dial the international access code, 011, the country code, 377, then the eight-digit Monaco number.

To call any other country from within Monaco, dial 00 (the international access code), then the applicable country code, and the number. For example, to call Cannes, you would dial 00, 33 (France's country code), 4 (the city code, without the zero), and the eight-digit number.

mainland France. Monaco is a rather lengthy **drive** from Paris. Take A6 south to
Lyon. At Lyon, connect with A7 south to Aix-en-Provence; from here, take A6
south directly to Monaco. If you're already on the Riviera, drive from Nice along
N7 northeast. It's only 12 miles, but with traffic, the drive can take 30 minutes.

VISITOR INFORMATION   The **Direction du Tourisme** office is at 2A bd.
des Moulins (© **92-16-61-16;** www.monaco.net).

SPECIAL EVENTS   Some of the most-watched **car-racing events** in Europe
are held in January (Le Rallye) and May (the Grand Prix). Mid-April witnesses
one of the Riviera's most famous **tennis tournaments.** Every February, Monte
Carlo is home to a week-long convention that attracts media moguls from virtually everywhere: **Le Festival International de la Télévision,** wherein the
winning shows from all over the world are broadcast and judged on their individual merits. For information and further details, write or call Festival International de la Télévision, 4 bd. des Jardins Exotiques (© **93-10-40-60**).

FUN ON & OFF THE BEACH

BEACHES   Just outside the border, on French (not Monacan) soil, the
Monte-Carlo Beach Club adjoins the Monte-Carlo Beach Hotel, 22 av.
Princesse-Grace (© **04-93-28-66-66**). The beach club has thrived for years as
an integral part of Monaco's social life. Princess Grace used to come here in flowery swimsuits, greeting her friends and subjects with humor and style. The sand
is replenished at regular intervals, and you'll find two large pools (one for children), beach cabanas, a restaurant, a cafe, and a bar. As the temperature drops
in late August, expect the beach to close for the winter. The admission charge of
200F (30.40, $29) grants you access to the public changing rooms, toilets,
restaurants, and bar. A day's use of a private cubicle, where you can lock up your
street clothes, costs an extra 65F (9.90, $9.45). And a full day's rental of a mat-
tress for sunbathing costs 75F (11.40, $10.90). A fee of 1,000F (152, $145)
will get you a day's use of a striped private cabana. Most of the socializing occurs
around the edges of the Olympic-size pool. On the premises are bars and three
restaurants. As usual, topless is *de rigueur,* but bottomless isn't.

Monaco itself, the quintessential kingdom by the sea, also offers swimming
and sunbathing at the popular **Plage de Larvotto,** off avenue Princesse-Grace
(© **93-30-63-84**). There's no charge for entering this strip of beach, whose
sands are frequently replenished with sand hauled in by barge. The beach is open
to the public at all hours.

GOLF   The prestigious **Monte Carlo Golf Club,** Route N7, La Turbie
(© **93-41-09-11**), on French soil, is a par-72 golf course with scenic panoramas.
Certain perks (including use of electric golf buggies) are reserved for members.
Before they're allowed to play, nonmembers are asked to show proof of membership in another golf club and provide evidence of their handicap ratings.
Greens fees for 18 holes are 400F (60.80, $58) Monday through Friday and
500F (76, $72.50) Saturday and Sunday. Clubs can be rented for 80F
(12.15, $11.60). The course is open daily from 8am to sunset.

SPA TREATMENTS   In 1908, the Société des Bains de Mer launched a seawater (thalassotherapy) spa in Monte Carlo, inaugurated by Prince Albert I himself. However, it was bombed during World War II and didn't reopen until 1996.
Les Thermes Marins de Monte-Carlo, 2 av. de Monte-Carlo (© **92-16-
40-40**), is one of the largest spas in Europe. Spread over four floors are a pool, a
Turkish *haman,* a diet restaurant, a juice bar, two tanning booths, a fitness
center, a beauty center, and private treatment rooms. A day pass, giving access to

the sauna, steam rooms, fitness facilities, and pools costs 700F (106.40, $101.50). Hour-long massages cost an additional fee, from 300F to 600F (45.60 to 91.20, $43.50 to $87), depending on what type of massage you want.

SWIMMING Built to overlook the yacht-clogged harbor, the stupendous **Stade Nautique Rainier-III,** quai Albert-1er, at La Condamine (© **93-30-64-83**), a pool frequented by the Monégasques, was a gift from the prince to his loyal subjects. It's open May to October daily from 9am to 6pm (open till midnight in July and August); closed November to April. Admission is 25F (3.80, $3.65). In cooler weather, try the indoor **Piscine du Prince Héréditaire Albert,** in the Stade Louis II, at 7 av. de Castellane (© **92-05-42-13**). It's open Monday, Tuesday, Thursday, and Friday from 7:30am to 2:30pm; Saturday from 2 to 6pm; and Sunday from 9am to 1pm. Admission is 15F (2.30, $2.20).

TENNIS & SQUASH The **Monte Carlo Country Club,** in France on avenue Princesse-Grace, Roquebrune–St-Roman (© **04-93-41-30-15**), includes 21 clay and 2 concrete courts. The 220F (33.45, $31.90) entrance fee provides access to a restaurant, a health club with Jacuzzi and sauna, a putting green, a beach, squash courts, and the well-maintained tennis courts. Residents of the hotels administered by the Societé des Bains de Mer (the Hotel de Paris, the Hermitage, the Mirabeau, and the Monte Carlo Beach Club) pay half-price. Plan to spend at least half a day, ending a round of tennis with use of any of the other facilities. It's open daily from 8am to 8pm or 9pm, depending on the season.

SHOPPING

Cascio, Les Galeries du Metropole, 207 av. des Spélugues, (© **93-50-17-57**), sells only imitation gemstones. They're shamelessly copied from the real McCoys sold by Cartier and Van Cleef & Arpels. Made in Italy of gold-plated silver, the fake jewelry (the staff refers to it as Les Bijoux Fantaisies) costs between 200F and 2,000F (30.40 and 304, $29 and $290) per piece, thousands of francs less than what you might have paid for the authentic gems.

Boutique du Rocher, 1 av. de la Madone (© **93-30-91-17**), is the largest of two boutiques opened in 1966 by Princesse Grace as the official retail outlets of her charitable foundation. The organization merchandises Monégasque and Provençal handcrafts. A short walk from place du Casino, the shop sells carved frames for pictures or mirrors; housewares; gift items crafted from porcelain, textiles, and wood; toys; and dolls. On the premises are workshops where artisans produce the goods you'll find for sale. The organization maintains a second branch at 25 rue Émile de Loth, in Monaco-Ville (© **93-30-33-99**).

Brett Merrill, 17 bd. des Moulins (© **93-50-33-85**), is a menswear store aiming at a solid middle-bracket man who simply wants to dress appropriately and look good. You can pick up a swimsuit, shorts, slacks, a blazer, and a pair of socks to replace the ones you ruined by too many walking tours, at prices that won't require that you remortgage your house.

You don't have to be Princess Caroline to be able to afford to shop in Monaco, especially now that **FNAC** (© **93-10-81-81**), a member of the big French chain that sells records, CDs, tapes, and books, has opened in the heart of town at the **Galerie du Métropole,** 17 av. des Spélugues in the Jardins du Casino, alongside the Hôtel Métropole and across from the casino.

If you insist on ultra-fancy stores, you'll find them cheek by jowl with the Hôtel de Paris and the casino, lining the streets leading to the Hôtel Hermitage, or across from the gardens at the mini-mall Park Palace. Allée Serge-Diaghilev is just that, an alley, but a very tiny one filled with designer shops.

To get a better perspective on upper-middle-class shopping, visit the **Galarie du Metropole,** 17 av. des Spélugues. It has a few specialty shops worth visiting (especially if you aren't going into France). Check out **Geneviève Lethu** (© **93-50-09-41**) for colorful and country tabletop design; or **Manufacture de Monaco** (© **93-50-64-63**) for glorious bone china and elegant tabletop design. If the prices send you to bed, two doors away is a branch of the chic but often affordable French linen house **Yves Delorme** (© **93-50-08-70**). **Royal Food** (© **93-15-05-04**) is a tiny gourmet grocery store down a set of curving stairs hidden in the side entrance of the mall; here you can buy food items from France, Lebanon, and the United States, or stock up for *le pique-nique* or for your day trips. This market is open Monday to Saturday from 9:30am to 8pm.

For real-people shopping, stroll **rue Grimaldi,** the principality's most commercial street, near the fruit, flower, and food market (see below) and **boulevard des Moulins,** closer to the casino, where glamorous boutiques specialize in international chicness. There's also an all-pedestrian thoroughfare with shops less forbiddingly chic than those along boulevard des Moulins: **rue Princesse-Caroline** is loaded with bakeries, flower shops, and the closest thing you'll find to funkiness in Monaco. Also check out the **Formule 1** shop, 15 rue Grimaldi (© **93-15-92-44**), where everything from racing helmets to specialty keychains and T-shirts celebrates the roar of high-octane racing machines.

MARKETS   Should you be looking for the heart and soul of the real Monaco, get away from the glitz and head to place des Armes for the **fruit, flower, and food market** held daily from 7:30am to 1pm. It has an indoor and an outdoor market complete with a fountain, cafes, and hand-painted vegetable tiles set beneath your feet. While the outdoor market packs up promptly at noon, some dealers at the indoor market stay open to 2pm. If you prefer bric-a-brac, there's a small but very funky (especially for Monaco) flea market, **Les Puces de Fontvieille,** held Saturday from 10am to 5:30pm at the Espace Fontvieille, a panoramic open-air site near the heliport in Monaco's Fontvieille district.

SEEING THE SIGHTS

Les Grands Appartements du Palais ★   During summer, most day-trippers from Nice want to see the home of Monaco's royal family, the Palais du Prince, dominating the principality from "the Rock." A tour of the Grands Appartements allows you a glimpse of the Throne Room and some of the art (including works by Brueghel and Holbein) as well as Princess Grace's state portrait. The palace was built in the 13th century, and part dates from the Renaissance. You also see the chamber where England's George III died. The ideal time to arrive is 11:55am to watch the 10-minute **Relève de la Garde** (changing of the guard).

In a wing of the palace, the **Musée du Palais du Prince (Souvenirs Napoléoniens et Collection d'Archives),** place du Palais (© **93-25-18-31**), has a collection of mementos of Napoléon and Monaco itself. When the royal residence is closed, this museum is the only part of the palace the public can visit.

Place du Palais. © **93-25-18-31**. Combination ticket 50F (7.60, $7.25) adults, 25F (3.80, $3.65) children 8–14, free for children under 8. Palace, June–Sept daily 9:30am–6:30pm; Oct daily 10am–5pm. Closed Nov–May. Museum, June–Sept daily 9:30am–6:30pm; Oct–Nov 11 daily 10am–5pm; Dec 17–May Tues–Sun 10:30am–12:30pm and 2–5pm. Closed Nov 12–Dec 16.

Jardin Exotique ★★   Built on the side of a rock, the gardens are known for their cactus collection. They were begun by Prince Albert I, who was a naturalist and scientist. He spotted some succulents growing in the palace gardens and created this garden from them. You can also explore the grottoes here, as well as the **Musée d'Anthropologie Préhistorique** (© **93-15-80-06**). The view of the principality is splendid.

Bd. du Jardin-Exotique. © **93-15-29-80**. Admission to garden 41F (6.25, \$5.95) adults, 20F (3.05, \$2.90) children 6–18, free for children under 6. June–Sept daily 9am–7pm; Oct–May daily 9am–6pm.

Musée de l'Océanographie ★★ *Kids*   This museum was founded in 1910 by Albert I, great-grandfather of the present prince. In the main rotunda is a statue of Albert in his favorite costume: that of a sea captain. Displayed are specimens he collected during 30 years of expeditions. The aquarium, one of the finest in Europe, contains more than 90 tanks.

The collection is exhibited in the zoology room. Some of the exotic creatures here were unknown before he captured them. You'll see models of the ships aboard which he directed his scientific cruises from 1885 to 1914. The most important part of the laboratory has been preserved and reconstituted as closely as possible. Skeletons of specimens are on the main floor, including a giant whale that drifted ashore at Pietra Ligure in 1896. The skeleton is remarkable for its healed fractures sustained when a vessel struck the animal as it was drifting asleep on the surface. An exhibition devoted to the discovery of the ocean is in the physical-oceanography room on the first floor. Underwater movies are shown continuously in the lecture room.

Av. St-Martin. © **93-15-36-00**. Admission 60F (9.10, \$8.70) adults, 30F (4.55, \$4.35) children 6–18, free for children under 6. Apr–June and Sept daily 9am–7pm; July–Aug daily 9am–8pm; Mar and Oct daily 9:30am–7pm; Nov–Feb daily 10am–6pm.

Collection des Voitures Anciennes de S.A.S. le Prince de Monaco *Kids* Prince Rainier III has opened a showcase of his private collection of more than 100 vintage autos, including the 1956 Rolls-Royce Silver Cloud that carried the prince and princess on their wedding day. It was given to the royal couple by Monaco shopkeepers as a wedding present. A 1952 Austin Taxi on display was once used as the royal "family car." Other exhibits are a Woodie, a 1937 Ford station wagon used by Prince Louis II when on hunting trips, and a 1925 Bugatti 35B, winner of the Monaco Grand Prix in 1929. Other outstanding autos are a 1903 De Dion Bouton and a 1986 Lamborghini Countach.

Les Terrasses de Fontvieille. © **92-05-28-56**. Admission 30F (4.55, \$4.35) adults, 15F (2.30, \$2.20) students and children 8–14, free for children under 8. Daily 10am–6pm. Closed Nov.

Musée National de Monaco ★ *Kids*   In a villa designed by Charles Garnier (architect of Paris's Opéra Garnier), this museum houses one of the world's great collections of mechanical toys and dolls. See the 18th-century Neapolitan crib, which contains some 200 figures. This collection, assembled by Mme de Galea, was presented to the principality in 1972; it stemmed from the 18th- and 19th-century trend of displaying new fashions on doll models.

17 av. Princesse-Grace. © **93-30-91-26**. Admission 30F (4.55, \$4.35) adults, 20F (3.05, \$2.90) children 6–14, free for children under 6. Easter–Sept daily 10am–6:30pm; Oct–Easter daily 10am–12:15pm and 2:30–6:30pm.

ACCOMMODATIONS
VERY EXPENSIVE

Hôtel de Paris ★★★   On the resort's main plaza, opposite the casino, this is one of the world's most famous hotels. The ornate facade has marble pillars, and the lounge has an Art Nouveau rose window at the peak of the dome. The hotel is furnished with a dazzling decor that includes marble pillars, statues, crystal chandeliers, sumptuous carpets, Louis XVI chairs, and a wall-size mural. The guest rooms come in a variety of styles, with an elaborate period decor or a fashionably contemporary one. Some are enormous. Elegant tasteful fabrics, rich carpeting, and classic accessories make this a continuing favorite among the world's most discerning guests. Note that the rooms opening onto the sea aren't as spacious as those in the rear. The hotel's most famous dining options are Le Louis XV (see "Dining," below) and Le Grill. Both restaurants benefit from a collection of rare fine wines kept in a dungeon chiseled out of the rocks.

Place du Casino, 98000 Monaco. (C) **92-16-30-00.** Fax 93-16-38-50. www.montecarloresort.com. 197 units. 2,330F–3,900F (354.15– 592.80, $337.85–$565.50) double; from 4,362F (663, $632.50) suite. AE, DC, MC, V. Parking 130F (19.75, $18.85). **Amenities:** 3 restaurants, bar; Thermes Marins spa, connected to both the Hôtel de Paris and the Hôtel Hermitage, offering complete cures of thalassotherapy under medical supervision; large indoor pool; fitness center; 2 saunas; concierge; salon; room service; baby-sitting; laundry/dry cleaning; valet parking. *In room:* A/C, TV, safe, hair dryer.

Hôtel Hermitage ★★ Picture yourself sitting in a wicker armchair, being served drinks under an ornate stained-glass dome with an encircling wrought-iron balcony. You can do this at the clifftop Hermitage, with its wedding cake facade. The "palace" was the creation of Jean Marquet (who also created marquetry). Large brass beds anchor every room, wherein decoratively framed doors open onto balconies. Even the smallest rooms are medium size, the largest one fit for the biggest movie star with the most trunks. Large mirrors, elegant fabrics and upholstery, deluxe bathrooms, and sumptuous beds make living here idyllic. The newest rooms are in the Costa and Excelsior wings. They lack tradition but equal the accommodations in the main building, which many guests prefer because of its old-fashioned French decor and streetfront exposures. High-season rates are charged during Christmas, New Year's, Easter, and July and August.

Square Beaumarchais, 98005 Monaco CEDEX. (C) **92-16-40-00.** Fax 92-16-38-52. www.montecarloresort. com. 247 units. 2,230F–3,280F (338.95– 498.55, $323.35–$475.60) double; 5,150F–10,430F (782.80– 1,585.35, $746.75–$1,512.35) suite. AE, MC, V. Parking 120F (18.25, $17.40). **Amenities:** Restaurant, bar; indoor pool; health club; sauna; room service; baby-sitting; laundry/dry cleaning. *In room:* A/C, TV, minibar, hair dryer, safe.

Le Monte Carlo Grand Hôtel ★ Although a bit down the scale from the two previous choices, this is also a deluxe palace, built by the Loews Corporation but bought in 1998 by a consortium of local investors and renamed. It hugs the sea coast from below the terraces that support the famous casino, on one of the most valuable pieces of real estate along the Côte d'Azur. Architecturally daring when it was completed in 1975 (some of its foundations were sunk directly into the seabed, and some of the principality's busiest highways roar beneath it), the resort is now viewed as an integral enhancement of Monégasque life. It contains Monaco's highest concentration of restaurants, bars, and nightclubs—think of it as Las Vegas with a Gallic accent. The guest rooms are conservatively furnished in a style somewhere between Los Angeles and Miami. Each has a pastel-colored decor that's flooded with light from big windows and views over the town or the sea. All units contain large bathrooms with tubs and showers.

12 av. des Spélugues, 98007 Monaco CEDEX. (C) **93-50-65-00.** Fax 93-30-01-57. 619 units. 1,450F–2,750F (220.40– 418, $210.25–$398.75) double; 3,600F–9,800F (547.20– 1,489.60, $522–$1,421) suite. AE, DC, MC, V. Parking 120F (18.25, $17.40). **Amenities:** 3 restaurants, bar; outdoor pool; health club. *In room:* A/C, TV, minibar, hair dryer, safe.

Monte-Carlo Beach Hôtel ★ Despite its name, this hotel is in France, not Monaco. The most beautiful accommodation in the house is the spacious circular unit above the lobby. Eva Peron stayed here in 1947 during her infamous Rainbow Tour of Europe. Princess Grace came here almost every day in summer to paddle around the pool, a rendezvous for the rich and beautiful. All the spacious rooms are identically luxurious, right down to the sea view; the beautiful bathrooms include a combination tub and shower. The greatest choice of dining venues is available between June and September, when Le Restaurant serves gourmet meals at lunch and dinner. The reliable Le Rivage offers brasserie-style lunches and dinners near the pool, and is the only restaurant open year-round. Le Potinière features gastronomic lunches. La Vigie, a short walk from the hotel and accessible to several piers where yacht-owners can tie up their boats, presents a series of buffets inspired by the cuisine of Provence.

Av. Princesse-Grace, Monte-Carlo Beach, 06190 Roquebrune/Cap-Martin. ☏ **92-16-25-25.** Fax 92-16-26-26. www.montecarloresort.com. 45 units. 1,608F–2,887F (244.40– 438.80, $233.15–$418.60) double; 4,625F–6,495F (703– 987.25, $670.65–$941.80) suite. AE, DC, MC, V. Closed Dec–Feb. Free parking. The hotel is located on the France-Monaco border. **Amenities:** 4 restaurants, 2 bars; outdoor pool; room service; baby-sitting; laundry/dry cleaning. *In room:* A/C, TV, minibar, hair dryer, safe.

MODERATE

Hôtel Alexandra   This hotel is on a busy and often-noisy street corner in the center of the business district above the Casino Gardens. Its comfortably furnished guest rooms don't generate much excitement, but they're reliable and respectable, each with a compact bathroom with shower. The Alexandra knows it can't compete with the giants of Monaco and doesn't even try. But it attracts those who'd like to visit the principality without spending a fortune.

33 bd. Princesse-Charlotte, 98000 Monaco. ☏ **93-50-63-13.** Fax 92-16-06-48. 56 units. 650F–880F (98.80– 133.75, $94.25–$127.60) double. AE, DC, MC, V. Parking 45F (6.85, $6.55). *In room:* A/C, TV, hair dryer.

Hôtel du Louvre   Built like a traditional century-old mansion, this hotel is filled with antique furniture. The guest rooms are comfortable and come in a variety of shapes and sizes, each with a small bathroom with shower. Expect to pay higher prices for rooms facing the sea. Breakfast is the only meal served.

16 bd. des Moulins, 98000 Monaco. ☏ **93-50-65-25.** Fax 04-93-30-23-68. hotel-louvre@monte-carlo.mc. 33 units. 830F–1,030F (126.15– 156.55, $120.35–$149.35) double. AE, DC, MC, V. Parking 42F (6.40, $6.10). *In room:* A/C, TV, minibar.

INEXPENSIVE

Hôtel Cosmopolite   When it was built in the 1930s, this hotel was sited in the then-fashionable neighborhood a few steps downhill from the railway station. Today it's an appealingly dowdy Art Deco monument with three floors, no elevator, and comfortable but anonymous-looking rooms. Madame Gay Angèle, the English-speaking owner, is proud of her "Old Monaco" establishment. Her more expensive rooms have showers, but the cheapest way to stay here is to request a room without a shower—there are adequate facilities in the hallway.

4 rue de la Turbie, 98000 Monaco. ☏ **93-30-16-95.** Fax 93-30-23-05. 24 units, none with toilet, all with sink, some with shower. 228F–258F (34.65– 39.20, $33.05–$37.40) double without shower or toilet; 314F–338F (47.75– 51.40, $45.55–$49) with shower but without toilet. No credit cards. Free parking on street. *In room:* Hair dryer.

Hôtel de France   Not all Monégasques are rich, as a stroll along this street will convince you. Here you'll find some of the cheapest living and eating places in the high-priced principality. This 19th-century hotel, 3 minutes from the rail station, has modest furnishings but is clean and comfortable. The bedrooms and bathrooms are small, but there's comfort here, and each unit has a shower.

6 rue de la Turbie, 98000 Monaco. ☏ **93-30-24-64.** Fax 92-16-13-34. www.monte-carlo.MC/france. 26 units. 530F (80.55, $76.85) double; 650F (98.80, $94.25) suite. Rates include breakfast. MC, V. Parking 45F (6.85, $6.55). *In room:* TV.

DINING
VERY EXPENSIVE
Le Louis XV FRENCH/ITALIAN   In the Hôtel de Paris, the Louis XV offers what one critic called "down-home Riviera cooking within a Fabergé egg." When it lost one of its three Michelin stars in 2001, it made headlines. However, don't fear—the cuisine is as refined and elegant as it always was. Despite the place's regal trappings, the culinary star chef Alain Ducasse creates a refined but not overly adorned cuisine, served by the finest staff in Monaco. Everything is light, attuned to the seasons, with an intelligent and modern interpretation of both Provençal and northern Italian dishes. You'll find char-grilled breast of baby pigeon with sautéed duck liver and everything from truffles and caviar to the best stewed salt cod along the coast. Ducasse divides his time between this glittering enclave and his restaurants in Paris.

In the Hôtel de Paris, place du Casino. © **92-16-30-01.** Reservations recommended. Jacket and tie required for men. Main courses 310F–525F (47.10– 79.80, $44.95–$76.15); fixed-price menus 550F–1,050F (83.60– 159.60, $79.75–$152.25) lunch, 920F–1,050F (139.85– 159.60, $133.40–$152.25) dinner. AE, DC, MC. Thurs–Mon noon–3pm and 8–10pm. Between mid-June and Aug, Wed 8–10pm. Closed Feb 2–17 and Nov 28–Dec 28.

EXPENSIVE
Le Café de Paris ⭐ TRADITIONAL FRENCH   Its *plats du jour* are well prepared, and its location, the plaza adjacent to the casino and the Hôtel de Paris, provides you with a front-row view of the comings and goings of the nerve center of Monte Carlo. But to our tastes, this 1985 re-creation of old-time Monaco is a bit too theme-ish, a bit too enraptured with the devil-may-care glamour of early-1900s Monte Carlo. Despite that, the Café de Paris continues to draw patrons who appreciate the razzmatazz and all the glass and chrome. Menu items change frequently, and platters, especially at lunchtime, are appreciated by local office workers because they can be served and consumed relatively quickly, like fresh grilled sea bass and steak tartare with matchstick frites. Adjacent to the restaurant, you'll find (and hear) a jangling collection of slot machines and a cliché-riddled cluster of boutiques selling expensively casual resort wear and souvenirs.

Place du Casino. © **92-16-20-20.** Reservations recommended. Main courses 110F–220F (16.70– 33.45, $15.95–$31.90); fixed-price menu 200F–450F (30.40– 68.40, $29–$65.25). AE, DC, MC, V. Daily 8am–4am.

Rampoldi ⭐ FRENCH/ITALIAN   More than any other restaurant in Monte Carlo, Rampoldi is inextricably linked to the charming but somewhat dated interpretation of *La Dolce Vita.* Opened in the 1950s and staffed with a complementary mix of old and new, it has a spirit that's more Italian than French. It also serves some of the finest cuisine in Monte Carlo from an agreeable location at the edge of the Casino Gardens. Menu items include a succulent array of such pastas as tortelloni with cream and white truffle sauce; sea bass roasted in a salt crust; ravioli stuffed with crayfish; chateaubriand with béarnaise sauce; and veal kidneys in Madeira sauce. Crêpes Suzette makes a spectacular finish.

3 av. des Spélugues. © **93-30-70-65.** Reservations required. Main courses 120F–240F (18.25– 36.53, $17.40–$34.80); fixed-price menu 130F–250F (19.75– 38, $18.85–$36.25). AE, MC, V. Daily 12:15–2:30pm and 7:30–11:30pm.

MODERATE
Le Texan TEX-MEX/INDIAN   These Tex-Mex specialties have entertained even the most discriminating French taste buds. There's a handful of outdoor

tables, a long bar, a roughly plastered dining room draped with the flag of the Lone Star State, and a scattering of Mexican artifacts. You'll find Le Texan on a sloping residential street leading down to the old harbor—a world away from the glittering casinos and nightlife of the upper reaches. Menu items include T-bone steak, barbecued ribs, pizzas, nachos, tacos, a Dallasburger (*avec* guacamole), and the best margaritas in town. Ironically, thanks to several members of the kitchen staff who hail from India, this restaurant also manages to produce some great curry dishes (chicken, beef, and lamb), as well.

4 rue Suffren-Reymond. ✆ **93-30-34-54.** Reservations recommended. Main courses 78F–150F (11.85–22.80, $11.30–$21.75). AE, DC, MC, V. Daily noon–midnight.

INEXPENSIVE

Stars 'n' Bars (*Kids*) AMERICAN   This place revels in the cross-cultural differences that have contributed so much to Monaco's recent history. Modeled on the sports bars popular in the U.S., it features two dining and drinking areas devoted to American-style food, as well as a third-floor space, The Club, a sports bar with memorabilia donated by many athletes of note. There's even a disco every night after midnight between June and September, and Friday and Saturday nights the rest of the year. No one will mind if you drop in just for a drink, but if you're hungry, menu items read like an homage to the American experience. Try an Indy 500, a Triathlon salad or the Breakfast of Champions (eggs and bacon and all the fixings). If you've got kids under 12, order the Little Leaguer's Platter. Unless an artist of international note appears, there's never a cover charge.

6 quai Antoine-1er. ✆ **97-97-95-95.** Reservations recommended. Dinner salads and platters 60F–140F (9.10– 21.30, $8.70–$20.30); sandwiches 45F–80F (6.85– 12.15, $6.55–$11.60). AE, DC, MC, V. Tues–Sun 11am–midnight. (June–Sept, it's also open Mon 11am–midnight). Bar open till 3am.

MONACO AFTER DARK

CASINOS   Sun Casino, in the Monte Carlo Grand Hôtel, 12 av. des Spélugues (✆ **93-50-65-00**), is a huge room filled with one-armed bandits. It also features blackjack, craps, and American roulette. Additional slot machines are available on the roof starting at 11am—for those who want to gamble with a wider view of the sea. It's open daily from 5pm to 4am (to 5am for slot machines). Admission is free.

A speculator, François Blanc, developed the **Monte-Carlo Casino,** place du Casino (✆ **92-16-21-21**), into the most famous in the world, attracting the exiled aristocracy of Russia, Sarah Bernhardt, Mata Hari, King Farouk, and Aly Khan. The architect of Paris's Opéra Garnier, Charles Garnier, built the oldest part of the casino, and it remains an example of the 19th century's most opulent architecture. It's rather schizophrenically divided into an area devoted to the casino and others for different kinds of nighttime entertainment, including a theater (see below) presenting opera and ballet. Baccarat, roulette, and chemin-de-fer are the most popular games, though you can play *le craps* and blackjack as well. Admission 50F–100F (7.60– 15.20, $7.25–$14.50).

Salle Américaine, containing only slot machines, opens at noon, as do doors for roulette and *trente-quarante.* A section for roulette and chemin-de-fer opens at 3pm. Most of the facilities inside are operational by 4pm, when additional rooms open with more roulette, craps, and blackjack. The gambling continues until very late/early, the closing depending on the crowd. The casino classifies its "private rooms" as the more demure, nonelectronic areas devoid of slot machines. To enter the casino, you must carry a passport, be at least 21, and pay an admission of between 50F and 100F (7.60 and   15.20, $7.25 and $14.50), depending on where you want to go. In lieu of a passport, an identity card or driver's license will suffice. After 9pm, the staff will insist that gentlemen wear jackets and neckties for entrance into the private rooms.

The premises also contains a **Cabaret** in the Casino Gardens, where the show is preceded by the music of a well-rehearsed orchestra. A cabaret featuring lots of feathers, glitter, jazz dance, ballet, and Riviera-style seminudity is presented at 10pm Wednesday to Monday from mid-September to the end of June. If you want dinner with the show, service begins at 9pm and costs 450F (68.40, $65.25) per person (show included). If you just want to see the show, your drinks will cost from 150F (22.80, $21.75) each. For reservations, call ℂ **92-16-36-36.**

In the casino's **Salle Garnier,** where lots of gilt and Belle-Époque accents evoke the 19th-century opera house of Paris, concerts are held periodically; for information, contact the tourist office (see "Essentials," earlier in this section) or the Atrium du Casino (see below). The music is usually classical, featuring the Orchestre Philharmonique de Monte Carlo.

The casino also contains the **Opéra de Monte-Carlo,** whose patron is Prince Rainier. This world-famous house, opened in 1879 by Sarah Bernhardt, presents a winter and spring repertoire that traditionally includes Puccini, Mozart, and Verdi. The famed Ballets Russes de Monte-Carlo, starring Nijinsky and Karsavina, was created in 1918 by Sergei Diaghilev. The national orchestra and ballet company of Monaco appear here. Tickets may be hard to come by; your best bet is to ask your hotel concierge. You can make inquiries about tickets on your own at the **Atrium du Casino** (ℂ 92-16-22-99), open Tuesday to Saturday from 10am to 12:15pm and 2 to 5pm. Standard tickets are 150F to 800F (22.80 to 121.60, $21.75 to $116).

DANCING & DRINKING   Tiffany, avenue des Spélugues (ℂ **93-50-53-13**), is a favorite of the 25- to 30-year-old crowd who like a glamorous modern setting. Come on Sundays to catch some off-duty showgirls. **Le Symbole,** rue du Portier (ℂ **93-25-09-25**), is a hot spot for those under 30. The decor glitters in a high-tech gloss, and the music is disco. A slightly older group (ages 30 to 50) appreciates the **X-Club** (ℂ **93-30-70-55**) and **Le Living Room** (ℂ **93-50-80-31**), both at 7 av. des Spélugues, where crowds are international and dance-oriented. Neither enforces a cover charge, but drinks begin at around 70F (10.65, $10.15) each. Two piano bars, both nearly adjacent to one another at 11 av. Princesse-Grace, include **Le Sass-Café** (ℂ **93-25-52-00**) and the **Zebra Café** (ℂ **99-99-25-50**). Drinks cost from around 65F (9.93, $9.45) each. Toniest of all, and under the same management as the Hôtel de Paris and the Hermitage, is **Jimmy's,** in the Sporting d'Eté, av. Princesse-Grace (ℂ **92-16-22-77**), where drinks cost from around 100F (15.20, $14.50) each.

19 Roquebrune & Cap-Martin ★★ ★

Roquebrune: 592 miles S of Paris, 3 miles W of Menton, 36 miles NE of Cannes, 2 miles E of Monaco; Cap-Martin: 3 miles W of Menton, 1½ miles W of Roquebrune

Roquebrune, along the Grande Corniche, is a charming mountain village with vaulted streets. It has been restored, though some critics have found the restoration artificial. Today its rue Moncollet is lined with artists' workshops and boutiques with inflated merchandise.

Three miles west of Menton, Cap-Martin is a satellite of the larger resort that's been associated with the rich and famous since the empress Eugénie wintered there in the 19th century. In time, the resort was honored by the presence of Sir Winston Churchill, who came here often in his final years. Two famous men died here—William Butler Yeats in 1939 and Le Corbusier, who drowned while swimming off the cape in 1965. Don't expect to find a wide sandy beach—you'll encounter plenty of rocks, against a backdrop of pine and olive trees.

ESSENTIALS

GETTING THERE   To **drive** to Roquebrune and Cap-Martin, follow N7 east for 16 miles from Nice. Cap-Martin has **train** and bus connections from the other cities on the coast, including Nice and Menton. For more **railway** information and schedules, call ✆ **08-36-35-35-35.** To reach Roquebrune, you'll have to take a **taxi.** You can take a bus, but there's no formal bus station in Roquebrune; you get off on the side of the highway. For more information about **bus** routes, contact the Gare Routière in Menton (✆ **04-93-85-64-44**).

VISITOR INFORMATION   The **Office de Tourisme** is at 218 av. Aristide-Briand in Roquebrune (✆ **04-93-35-62-87**).

SEEING THE SIGHTS
IN ROQUEBRUNE

It'll take you about an hour to explore Roquebrune. You can stroll through its colorful covered streets, which retain their authentic look even though the buildings are now devoted to handcrafts, gift and souvenir shops, or art galleries. From the parking lot at place de la République, you can head for place des Deux-Frères, turning left into rue Grimaldi. Then head left to **rue Moncollet.** This long, narrow street is covered with stepped passageways and filled with houses that date from the Middle Ages, most often with barred windows. Rue Moncollet leads into **rue du Château,** where you may want to explore the château.

The only one of its kind, the **Château de Roquebrune** (✆ 04-93-35-07-22) was originally a 10th-century Carolingian castle; the present structure dates in part from the 13th century. Dominated by two square towers, it houses a museum. From the towers there's a panoramic view along the coast to Monaco. To wander the grounds, the castle gates are open daily from 10am to 12:30pm and 2 to 6pm. The interior is open daily: February through May 10am to 12:30pm and 2 to 6pm; June through September 10am to 12:30pm and 3 to 7:30pm; and October through January 10am to 12:30pm and 2 to 5pm. Admission is 20F (3.05, $2.90) for adults, 15F (2.30, $2.20) for seniors, and 10F (1.50, $1.45) for students and children 7 to 11, ages 6 and under are free.

Rue du Château leads to place William-Ingram. After crossing this square, you reach rue de la Fontaine. Take a left. This will lead you to the **Olivier millénaire** (millennary olive tree), one of the oldest in the world, having survived for at least 1,000 years.

Back on rue du Château you can reach the **Église Ste-Marguerite,** which hides behind a relatively common baroque facade. But this exterior masks the church from the 12th century. It's not entirely from that time, however, having seen many alterations over the years. The interior is of polychrome plaster. Look for two paintings by a local artist, Marc-Antoine Otto, who in the 17th century painted a Crucifixion (in the second altar) and a Pietà (above the entrance door). It's open Monday to Saturday from 2 to 5:30pm, Sunday from 8am to 3pm.

IN CAP-MARTIN

Cap-Martin is a rich town. At the center of the cape is a feudal tower that's today a telecommunications relay station. At its base you can see the ruins of the **Basilique St-Martin,** a priory constructed here by the monks of the Lérins Islands in the 11th century. After pirate raids in the centuries to come, notably around the 15th century, it was destroyed and abandoned. If you follow the road (by car) along the eastern shoreline of the cape, you'll be rewarded with a view of Menton against a backdrop of mountains. In the far distance looms the Italian Riviera, and you can see as far as the resort of Bordighera.

Although it takes about 3 hours, you can take one of the most interesting walks along the Riviera here. The coastal path, called **Sentier Touristique** ⚐, leads from Cap-Martin to Monte Carlo Beach. If you have a car, you can park it in the lot at avenue Winston-Churchill and begin your stroll. The path is marked by a sign labeled PROMENADE LE CORBUSIER. As you go along you'll be able to take in a view of Monaco set in a natural amphitheater. In the far distance, you'll view Cap-Ferrat and even Roquebrune with its château. The scenic path comes to an end at Monte Carlo Beach.

If you have a car, you can also take a **scenic 6-mile drive** ⚐, taking about an hour. Leave by D23, following the signs to Gorbio, a village perched on a hill and reached by this narrow, winding road. Along the way you'll pass homes of the wealthy and view a verdant setting with pines and silvery olives. The site is wild and rocky, the buildings having been constructed as a safe haven from pirate attacks. The most interesting street is rue Garibaldi, which leads past an old church to a panoramic belvedere.

ACCOMMODATIONS

Hôtel Victoria   This rectangular low-rise building is set behind a garden in front of the beach. Built in the 1970s, it was renovated in the mid-1990s in a neoclassical style that weds tradition and modernity. It's the "second choice" in town for those who can't afford the lofty prices of the more spectacular Vista Palace. Opening onto balconies fronting the sea, each of the midsize rooms is well furnished, with a neatly tiled bathroom with shower. The casual bar and lounge sets a stylishly relaxed tone. Breakfast is the only meal served.

7 promenade du Cap, 06190 Roquebrune/Cap-Martin. ☎ **04-93-35-65-90.** Fax 04-93-28-27-02. 32 units. 400F–580F (60.80– 88.15, $58–$84.10) double. AE, DC, MC, V. Closed Jan 5–Feb 5. Parking 50F (7.60, $7.25). **Amenities:** Bar. *In room:* A/C, TV, minibar, hair dryer.

Hôtel Vista Palace ⚐⚐⚐   This extraordinary hotel and restaurant stands on the outer ridge of the mountains running parallel to the coast, giving a spectacular "airplane view" of Monaco. And the design of the Vista Palace is just as fantastic: Three levels are cantilevered out into space so every room seems to float. Nearly all the rooms have balconies facing the Mediterranean. You live in *luxe* comfort here in grandly furnished bedrooms, with first-class bathrooms containing tubs and showers.

Grande Corniche, 06190 Roquebrune/Cap-Martin. ☎ **04-92-10-40-00.** Fax 04-92-10-40-40. www.web store.fr/vistapalace. 68 units. 1,250F–2,400F (190– 364.80, $181.25–$348) double; 2,400F– 7,200F (364.80– 1,094.40, $348–$1,044) suite. AE, DC, MC, V. Parking 130F (19.75, $18.85) in garage. **Amenities:** 3 restaurants; 3 bars; outdoor pool; health club; Jacuzzi; sauna; business center; room service; massage; baby-sitting; laundry/dry cleaning. *In room:* A/C, TV, minibar, hair dryer, safe.

DINING

You might also like to try **Le Vistaero** at the Hôtel Vista Palace (see above).

Au Grand Inquisiteur *(Finds)* TRADITIONAL FRENCH   This culinary find is a 28-seat restaurant in a two-room cellar near the top of the medieval mountaintop village of Roquebrune. On the steep, winding road to the château, this climate-controlled building is made of rough-cut stone, with large oak beams. The cuisine, though not the area's most distinguished, is quite good, especially the chef's duck special or scallops meunière. Most diners opt for one of the fresh fish choices. Other choices include stuffed zucchini flowers with morel sauce. The wine list is exceptional—some 150 selections, most at reasonable prices.

18 rue du Château. ℂ **04-93-35-05-37.** Reservations required. Main courses 80F–140F (12.15– 21.30, $11.60–$20.30); fixed-price menu 153F–225F (23.25– 34.20, $22.20–$32.65). MC, V. Wed–Sun noon–1:30pm and 7:30–10pm. July–Aug closed for lunch; also closed Mon for dinner. Closed: Nov–Dec 26.

20 Menton ★★

596 miles S of Paris, 39 miles NE of Cannes, 5 miles E of Monaco

Menton is more Italian than French. Right at the border of Italy, Menton marks the eastern frontier of the Côte d'Azur. Its climate, incidentally, is the warmest on the Mediterranean coast, attracting a large, rather elderly British colony throughout the winter. Because these senior citizens form a large part of the population of 130,000, Menton today is called "the Fort Lauderdale of France." Menton experiences a foggy day every 10 years—or so they say.

According to a local legend, Eve was the first to experience Menton's glorious climate. Expelled from the Garden of Eden along with Adam, she tucked a lemon in her bosom, planting it at Menton because it reminded her of her former stomping grounds. The lemons still grow in profusion here, and the fruit of that tree is given a position of honor at the Lemon Festival in February. Actually, the oldest Menton visitor may have arrived 30,000 years ago. He's still around—or at least his skull is—in the Municipal Museum.

Don't be misled by all those "palace-hotels" studding the hills. No longer open to the public, they've been divided up and sold as private apartments. Many of these early-1900s structures were erected to accommodate elderly Europeans, mainly English and German, who arrived carrying a book written by one Dr. Bennett in which he extolled the joys of living at Menton.

ESSENTIALS

GETTING THERE   Many visitors arrive by **car** on one of the corniche roads. Specifically, you can follow N7 east from Nice and arrive in 45 minutes.

There are good **bus and rail connections** that make stops at each resort along the Mediterranean coast, including Menton. Two trains per hour pull in from Nice (trip time: 35 minutes), and two trains per hour from Monte Carlo (trip time: 10 minutes). For rail information and schedules, call ℂ **08-36-35-35-35.** Two local bus companies, **Autocars Broch** (ℂ **04-93-31-10-52**) and **RCA** (ℂ **04-93-85-64-44**), run buses between Nice, Monte Carlo, and Menton, usually around two per hour, for a round-trip fee of 30F (4.55, $4.35) from Nice.

VISITOR INFORMATION   The **Office de Tourisme** is in the Palais de l'Europe, 8 av. Boyer (ℂ **04-92-41-76-76;** www.riviera.fr/tourisme.htm).

EXPLORING THE TOWN

On the Golfe de la Paix (Gulf of Peace), Menton, which used to belong to Monaco, is on a rocky promontory, dividing the bay in two. The fishing town, the older part with narrow streets, is in the east; the tourist zone and residential area are in the west.

Menton's beaches stretch for 2 miles between the Italian border and the city limits of Roquebrune and are interrupted only by the town's old and new ports. Collectively, they're known as **La Plage de la Promenade du Soleil** and with rare exceptions are public and free. Don't expect soft sand; the beaches are narrow, covered with gravel (or more charitably, big pebbles), and notoriously uncomfortable to lie on. Don't expect big waves or tides either.

So with no waves and no sand, who goes to the beach here? In the words of one nonswimming resident, mostly Parisians or residents of northern France, who are grateful for any escape from their urban milieux. Topless bathing is widespread, but complete nudity is forbidden.

Unlike in Cannes, where tens of thousands of chaises pepper the beaches, there aren't many options in Menton for renting mattresses and parasols; most people bring their own. Two exceptions are **Le Splendid Plage** (© 04-93-35-60-97) and **Les Sablettes** (© 04-93-35-44-77), both charging around 90F (13.70, $13.05) for use of a mattress. They're immediately to the east of the Vieux Port.

Musée Jean-Cocteau   The writer, artist, and filmmaker Jean Cocteau liked Menton, and this museum, in a 17th-century fort, contains two MacAvoy portraits of Cocteau: one while he was alive and another at his death. Some of the artist's memorabilia is here—stunning charcoals and watercolors, ceramics, signed letters, and 21 brightly colored pastels.

Bastion du Port, quai Napoléon-III. © **04-93-57-72-30.** Admission 20F (3.05, $2.90) adult, free for children under 18. Wed–Mon 10am–noon and 2–6pm.

La Salle des Mariages   Here Cocteau painted frescoes depicting the legend of Orpheus and Eurydice, among other things. A tape in English helps explain them. The room contains red-leather seats and leopard-skin rugs and is used for civil marriage ceremonies.

In the Hôtel de Ville (town hall), rue de la République. © **04-92-10-50-00.** Admission 10F (1.50, $1.45). Mon–Fri 8:30am–12:30pm and 1:30–5pm.

Musée de Préhistoire Régionale   This collection follows human evolution on the Côte d'Azur for the past million years. It emphasizes the prehistoric era, including the 25,000-year-old head of the Nouvel Homme de Menton (sometimes called "Grimaldi Man") found in 1884 in the Baousse-Rousse caves. Audiovisual aids (available in English), dioramas, and videos enhance the exhibition.

Rue Lorédan-Larchey. © **04-93-35-84-64.** Free admission. Wed–Mon 10am–noon and 2–6pm.

Musée des Beaux-Arts   Here you'll find 14th-, 16th-, and 17th-century paintings from Italy, Flanders, Holland, and the French schools. You'll also find modern paintings, including works by Dufy, Valadon, Derain, and Leprin.

In the Palais Carnoles, 3 av. de la Madone. © **04-93-35-49-71.** Free admission. Wed–Mon 10am–noon and 2–6pm.

ACCOMMODATIONS

Hôtel Aiglon *Kids*   A nugget along the coast, this hotel is a conversion from a Riviera villa. In a large park filled with Mediterranean vegetation, it offers a more intimate environment than any hotel in Menton in its league. The rooms come in various shapes and sizes, each well upholstered and containing quality mattresses on the elegant beds, plus good-sized bathrooms with tubs and showers. The magnet of the hotel is a heated pool surrounded by a veranda. The garden setting is beautifully maintained. An excellent Provençal-and-international cuisine is offered with view windows opening onto the pool and garden.

7 av. de la Madone, 06500 Menton. ② **04-93-57-55-55.** Fax 04-93-35-92-39. 30 units. 370F–790F (56.25– 120.10, $53.65–$114.55) double; 740F–1,100F (112.50– 167.20, $107.30–$159.50) suite. Half board 830F–1,250F (126.15– 190, $120.35–$181.25) double. AE, DC, MC, V. Closed Nov 6–Dec 18. Free parking. **Amenities:** Restaurant, bar; pool; garden; room service; baby-sitting; laundry. *In room:* TV, minibar, hair dryer.

Hôtel Princesse et Richmond   At the edge of the sea near the commercial district, this hotel boasts a facade of warm Mediterranean colors, with a sunny garden terrace. The owner rents comfortable, soundproof, and midsize rooms with modern and French traditional furnishings and balconies. The average sized bathrooms are equipped with tub and shower for the most part. Drinks are served on the roof terrace, where you can enjoy a view of the curving shoreline. A restaurant in the garden of the nearby Hôtel Aiglon, under the same ownership, offers lunch and dinner beside a heated pool you may use as well. The staff organizes sightseeing excursions.

617 promenade du Soleil, 06500 Menton. ② **04-93-35-80-20.** Fax 04-93-57-40-20. www.princess-richmond.com. 46 units. 362F–680F (55– 103.35, $52.50–$98.60) double; 800F–1,100F (121.60– 167.20, $116–$159.50) suite. AE, DC, V. Closed Nov 4–Dec 18. Parking 45F (6.85, $6.55). **Amenities:** Pool; Jacuzzi; exercise room; solarium. *In room:* A/C, TV, minibar, hair dryer.

DINING

La Calanque   FRENCH/SEAFOOD   Informal and earthy in a rustic Provençal way, this restaurant provides a waterside view and well-prepared food. In fair weather, tables are set under trees in full view of the harbor. We recommend the *soupe de poissons* (fish soup), and fresh sardines (grilled over charcoal and very savory). Other specialties include a savory bouillabaisse. You can count on an array of fresh fish and shellfish dishes prepared to perfection.

13 square Victoria. ② **04-93-35-83-15.** Main courses 60F–100F (9.10– 15.20, $8.70–$14.50); fixed-price menu 98F–165F (14.90– 25.10,$14.20–$23.95). MC, V. Tues–Sat noon–2pm and 7:15–9:30pm; Sun noon–2pm.

L'Albatros *Value*   FRENCH/PROVENÇAL   This charming little bistro along the port specializes in fish dishes from the Mediterranean. On the second floor and on the terrace you can enjoy a view over the old harbor and bay while sampling fresh fish. Menu items are conservative but savory, with lots of emphasis on Provençal interpretations of fish and seafood. An example is the succulent bouillabaisse, prepared only for a minimum of two diners and priced at 200F (30.40, $29) per person. There's also a *cassoulet des pêcheurs,* a stewpot brimming with herbs, saffron, and fish; and a thick and juicy charolais of beef with béarnaise sauce. Dessert might include baked apples with Armagnac.

31 quai Bonaparte. ② **04-93-35-94-64.** Reservations recommended. Main courses 50F–200F (7.60– 30.40, $7.25–$29); fixed-price menu 130F (19.75, $18.85). MC, V. Tues–Sun noon–3pm and 7pm–midnight.

Rocamadour PÉRIGORD   This pleasant restaurant overlooks the port. You dine at tables set under a canopy. Some specialties are from the Périgord region, including foie gras. *Magrêt de canard* (duckling) is another specialty. But basically the cookery is grounded in the rich tradition of the Côte d'Azur, with an emphasis on very fresh fish. A good example is filet of red snapper with a basil cream sauce. The restaurant was founded almost a century ago by a chef from Rocamadour, and the name of that town has stayed with the place.

1 square Victoria. ℂ **04-93-35-76-04.** Reservations recommended. Main courses 45F–145F (6.85– 22.05, $6.55–$21.05); fixed-price menu 95F–190F (14.45– 28.90, $13.80–$27.55). MC, V. Thurs–Tues noon–2:30pm and 7:30–10pm.

17

Languedoc-Roussillon

Languedoc, one of southern France's great old provinces, is a loosely defined area encompassing such cities as Nîmes, Toulouse, and Carcassonne. It's one of the leading wine-producing areas and is fabled for its art treasures.

The coast of Languedoc, from Montpellier to the Spanish frontier, might be called France's "second Mediterranean" (first place naturally goes to the Côte d'Azur). A land of ancient cities and a generous sea, it's less spoiled than the Côte d'Azur, with an almost-continuous strip of sand stretching west from the Rhône and curving toward the Pyrénées. In the days of Charles de Gaulle, the government began a project to develop the Languedoc-Roussillon coastline, and it has been a booming success. In July and August, the miles of sun-baking bodies along the coast attest to this success.

Ancient Roussillon is a small region of greater Languedoc, forming the Pyrénées Orientales *département.* This is the French Catalonia, inspired more by Barcelona in neighboring Spain than by Paris. Over its long, colorful history it has known many rulers. Part of the French kingdom until 1258, it was surrendered to James I of Aragón. Until 1344, it was part of the kingdom of Majorca, with Perpignan as the capital. By 1463, Roussillon was annexed to France again. Then Ferdinand of Aragón won it back, but by 1659, France had it again. Despite local sentiment for reunion with the Cataláns of Spain, France still firmly controls the land.

The Camargue is a marshy delta between two arms of the Rhône. South of Arles is cattle country. Wild black bulls are bred here for the arenas of Arles and Nîmes. The cattle is herded by *gardiens,* French cowboys, who ride small white horses, amazingly graceful, said to have been brought here by the Saracens. The gardiens can usually be seen in wide-brimmed black hats. The whitewashed houses, plaited-straw roofs, vast plains, endless stretches of sandbars, and the pink flamingos that inhabit the muddy marshes—all this qualifies as Exotic France.

REGIONAL CUISINE The cuisine of Languedoc-Roussillon is influenced by garlic, olive oil, and strong flavors. The region has plentiful game, trout, lamb, and seafood, usually prepared with local herbs, wine, and garlic.

One of the region's legendary dishes is usually prepared on a brazier in a boat on the open sea: the tripe (intestines) of tuna mixed with white wine and herbs, accompanied by a glass of seawater, whose salt alleviates some of the unpleasantness. A more palatable dish is *pouillade,* which requires the simultaneous preparation of two pots of soup (one made with cabbage, the other with white beans). Just before serving, the contents are mixed together in a serving bowl.

Other regional specialties are fish stews, foie gras, truffles, escargots, exotic mushrooms from the north-central areas, pâté of thrush from Rodez, cherries from Lodève, *aigo bouillido* (a soup made with garlic,

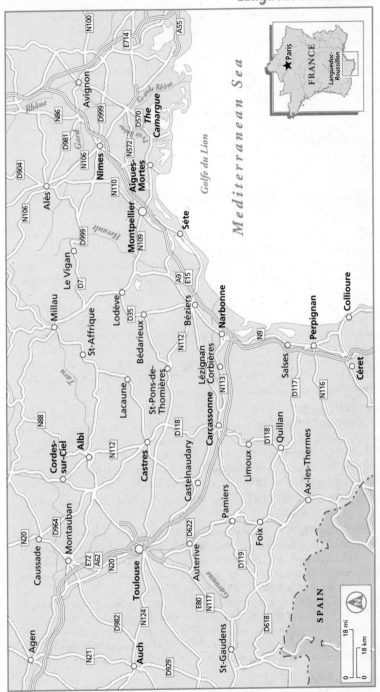

Mediterranean Sea

Golfe du Lion

Paris
FRANCE
Languedoc-Roussillon

SPAIN

N100
E714
A55
Avignon
Rhône
N86
D999
Grande Rhône
The Camargue
D570
D981
Gard
N106
Nîmes
P'tit Rhône
N572
Aigues-Mortes
D904
Alès
N106
N110
Montpellier
N109
Sète
D999
Hérault
Le Vigan
D7
A9
E15
Béziers
Millau
St-Affrique
Lodève
D35
Bédarieux
Narbonne
Tarn
N112
Lézignan Corbières
St-Pons-de-Thomières
N113
Perpignan
Collioure
Salses
Céret
D117
N116
Lacaune
Carcassonne
N88
Castres
D118
Quillan
D118
Limoux
Ax-les-Thermes
Cordes-sur-Ciel
Albi
N112
Castelnaudary
N20
D964
D622
Pamiers
Montauban
E72
A62
Auterive
Foix
Caussade
N20
Toulouse
D119
Garonne
N124
D982
E80
N117
St-Gaudens
D618
Agen
N21
Auch
D929

18 mi
18 km

601

eggs, herbs, and croûtons), *aligot* (a dish with garlic-laced cream, butter, potatoes, and cheese), and *cassoulet* of white beans and various meats. The region's most famous cheese is *pélardon*, made from goat's milk. The best-known pastry is the Alleluia. One of the region's most distinctive fish dishes is a *brandade de morue,* a stewed and baked form of codfish that was adopted long ago by the residents of Nîmes as uniquely theirs.

As for wine, Hérault, Aude, and Garde rank first, second, and third, respectively, in total wine production in France. Most of this is ordinary table wine. A few, however, have been granted an Appellation d'Origine Contrôlée. Some of the best are Fitou, produced in the Hautes-Corbières district near Narbonne, and Minervois, from west and northwest of Narbonne.

1 Nîmes ★★★

440 miles S of Paris, 27 miles W of Avignon

Nîmes, the ancient Nemausus, is one of the finest places in the world for wandering among Roman relics. The city grew to prominence during the reign of Caesar Augustus (27 B.C. to A.D. 14). Today, it possesses one of the best-preserved Roman amphitheaters in the world and a near-perfect Roman temple. The city of 135,000 is more like Provence than Languedoc, in which it lies. And there's a touch of Pamplona, Spain, in the festivals of the *corridas* (bullfights) at the arena. The Spanish image is even stronger at night, when the bodegas fill, usually with students, drinking sangria and listening to the sounds of flamenco.

By 1860, the togas of Nîmes's citizenry had long given way to denim, the cloth de Nîmes. An Austrian immigrant to Nîmes, Levi Strauss, exported this heavy fabric to California for use as work-pants material for gold diggers in those boomtown years. The rest, as they say, is history.

ESSENTIALS

GETTING THERE   Nîmes has bus and train service from the rest of France and is near several autoroutes. It lies on the main rail line between Marseille and Bordeaux. Six **trains** a day arrive from Paris (trip time: 4½ hr.). For train information and schedules, call © **08-36-35-35-35.** If you're **driving,** take A7 south from Lyon to the town of Orange, connecting here to A9 into Nîmes.

VISITOR INFORMATION   The **Office de Tourisme** is at 6 rue Auguste (© **04-66-58-38-00**).

SPECIAL EVENTS   Festivals, parties, and cultural events rule the summer nightlife scene. Once the warm weather hits, all sorts of activities take place at the arena, including concerts and theater under the stars. The Office de Tourisme has a complete list, or you can contact the **Bureau de Location des Arènes,** 4 rue de la Violette. (© **04-66-02-80-80**).

Every Thursday night during July and August, many of Nîmes's central squares burst forth with music, crowds of pedestrians, and one of the richest troves of paintings, crafts, used objects, and sculpture. Artists, musicians, and local residents gather in observance of the city's **Les Jeudis de Nîmes.** Of special interest are place de l'Horloge, place du Marché, and place aux Herbes.

EXPLORING THE CITY

If you really want to see all of the city's monuments and museums, consider buying a **billet global,** sold at the ticket counter of any of the local attractions. It

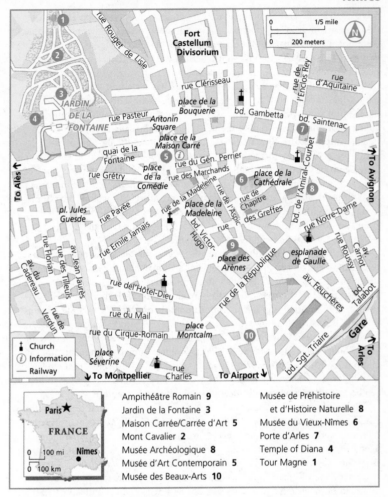

Fort Castellum Divisorium

Ampithéâtre Romain **9**
Jardin de la Fontaine **3**
Maison Carrée/Carré d'Art **5**
Mont Cavalier **2**
Musée Archéologique **8**
Musée d'Art Contemporain **5**
Musée des Beaux-Arts **10**

Musée de Préhistoire
  et d'Histoire Naturelle **8**
Musée du Vieux-Nîmes **6**
Porte d'Arles **7**
Temple of Diana **4**
Tour Magne **1**

FRANCE — Paris ★ — Nîmes ●

provides access for a 3-day period to all the cultural sites described below. The all-inclusive fee is 60F (9.10, $8.70) for adults and 30F (4.55, $4.35) for students and children 15 and under; entrance is free for children under 10.

The pride of Nîmes is the **Maison Carrée** ★★★, place de la Comédie (✆ **04-66-36-26-76**), built during the reign of Caesar Augustus. Consisting of a raised platform with tall Corinthian columns, it's one of Europe's most beautiful, and certainly one of the best preserved, Roman temples. It inspired the builders of La Madeleine in Paris as well as Thomas Jefferson. A changing roster of cultural and art exhibits is presented here, beneath an authentically preserved roof that the city of Nîmes repaired, at great expense, in 1996. The temple is open daily: October to May from 9am to 12:30pm and 2 to 6pm, June to September from 9am to noon and 2:30 to 7pm. Admission is free.

Across the square stands its modern-day twin, the **Carré d'Aer** (with one *e*), a sophisticated research center/exhibition space that contains a library, a newspaper kiosk, and an art museum. Its understated design was inspired by (but doesn't overpower) the ancient monument nearby. The most visible component is the **Musée d'Art Contemporain,** place de la Maison Carrée (with two *e*'s) (© **04-66-76-35-35**), whose permanent expositions are often supplemented by temporary exhibits of contemporary art. It's open Tuesday to Sunday from 10am to 6pm, charging 28F (4.25, $4.05) for adults and 20F (3.05, $2.90) for students and children 14 and under. *Note:* This modern building's terrace provides a panorama of most of the ancient monuments and medieval churches of Nîmes, above all of the neighborhood's roaring traffic.

The **Amphithéâtre Romain** ✮✮✮, place des Arènes (© **04-66-76-72-77**), a better-preserved twin to the one at Arles, is far more complete than Rome's Colosseum. It's two stories high—each floor has 60 arches—and was built of huge stones painstakingly fitted together without mortar. It once held more than 20,000 spectators who came to see gladiatorial combats and wolf or boar hunts. Today it's used for everything from ballet recitals to bullfights and is open daily from 9am to 6pm. Admission is 28F (4.25, $4.05) for adults and 20F (3.05, $2.90) for students and children 15 and under.

The **Jardin de la Fontaine** ✮✮, at the end of quai de la Fontaine, was laid out in the 18th century, using the ruins of a Roman shrine as a centerpiece. It was planted with rows of chestnuts and elms, adorned with statuary and urns, and intersected by grottoes and canals—making it one of the most beautiful gardens in France. Adjoining it is the ruined **Temple of Diana** ✮ and the remains of some Roman baths. Over the park, within a 10-minute walk north of the town center, rises **Mont Cavalier,** a low but rocky hill on top of which rises the sturdy bulk of the **Tour Magne** ✮, the city's oldest Roman monument. You can climb it for 15F (2.30, $2.20) for adults and 12F (1.80, $1.75) for students and children 14 and under; daily from 9am to 5pm (until 7pm May to September). It offers a panoramic view over Nîmes and its environs.

Nîmes is home to a great many museums. The largest and best respected, the **Musée des Beaux-Arts,** rue Cité-Foulc (© **04-66-67-38-21**), contains French paintings and sculptures from the 17th to the 20th century as well as Flemish, Dutch, and Italian works from the 15th to the 18th century. Seek out in particular one of G. B. Moroni's masterpieces, *La Calomnie d'Apelle,* and a well-preserved Gallo-Roman mosaic. The museum is open Tuesday to Sunday from 11am to 6pm. Admission is 28F (4.25, $4.05) for adults and 20F (3.05, $2.90) for students and children 14 and under.

If time allows, visit the **Musée du Vieux-Nîmes,** place de la Cathédrale (© **04-66-76-73-70**), housed in an episcopal palace from the 1700s. It's rich in antiques, including pieces from the 17th century. The museum is open Tuesday to Sunday from 11am to 6pm, charging 28 (4.25, $4.05) for adults and 20F (3.05, $2.90) for children.

One of the city's busiest thoroughfares, **boulevard de l'Amiral-Courbet,** leads to the **Porte d'Arles**—the remains of a gate built by the Romans during the reign of Augustus. Farther south, in the same stately building at 13 bis bd. l'Amiral-Courbet, are the **Musée de Préhistoire et d'Histoire Naturelle** (© **04-66-67-39-14**) and the **Musée Archéologique** ✮ (© **04-66-67-25-57**). Both are open Tuesday to Sunday from 11am to 6pm; a fee of 28F (4.25, $4.05) for adults and 20F (3.05, $2.90) for children admits you to both.

Outside the city, 14 miles northeast, the much-photographed **pont du Gard** spans the Gard River; its huge stones, fitted together without mortar, have evolved into one of the region's most vivid reminders of the ancient glory and technical competence of the Romans. Consisting of three tiers of arches arranged into gracefully symmetrical patterns, it dates from about 19 B.C. Frédéric Mistral, national poet of Provence and Languedoc, recorded a legend alleging that the devil constructed the bridge with the promise that he could claim the soul of the first person to cross it. To visit it, take highway N86 from Nîmes to a point 2 miles from the village of Remoulins, where signs are posted.

In April 2001, the touristic appeal of the pont du Gard was increased with the construction of a new museum, **La Grande Expo du Pont du Gard,** B.P. 7, 32110 Vers Pont du Gard (ⓒ **04-66-37-50-99**). Inside, four distinct expositions show details of its construction, its role throughout the Middle Ages in the development of the region, and insights into its symbolism as an enduring symbol of the architectural savvy of ancient Rome. Adjacent to the bridge itself, the museum is open daily from 10am to 7pm. Entrance costs 85F (12.90, $12.35) for adults, 40F (6.10, $5.80) for persons under 25 and students.

SHOPPING

If you'd rather concentrate on shopping, head to the center of town and **rue du Général-Perrier, rue des Marchands, rue du Chapître,** and the pedestrian **rue de l'Aspic** and **rue de la Madeleine.** A Sunday market runs from 8am to around 1pm in the lot of the **Stade des Castières,** site of most of the town's football (soccer) matches, adjacent to the boulevard Périphérique that encircles Nîmes.

To appease your sweet tooth, go to just about any pastry shop in town and ask for the regional almond-based cookies called *croquants villaret* and *caladons.* They're great for a burst of energy or for souvenirs. One of the best purchases you can make in Nîmes, especially if you're not continuing east into Provence, is a *santon.* These wood or clay figurines are sculpted into a cast of characters from Provençal country life and can be collected together to create a uniquely country-French nativity scene. For a selection of *santons* in various sizes, visit the **Boutique Provençale,** 10 place de la Maison Carré (ⓒ **04-66-67-81-71**), or **Au Papillon Bleu,** 15 rue du Général-Perrier (ⓒ **04-66-67-48-58**).

ACCOMMODATIONS

Hôtel l'Amphithéâtre The core of this hotel dates from the 18th century, when it was built as a private home. A stay here involves trekking to your room up steep flights of creaking stairs and navigating your way through a labyrinth of upper corridors. The small rooms are deliberately old-fashioned, usually containing antiques or antique reproductions and creaky albeit comfortable mattresses. The compact tiled bathrooms come with tub/shower combinations, except for four with shower only. The staff here grew jaded long ago to the fact that their hotel is less than perfect, but at these prices, who's complaining?

4 rue des Arènes, 30000 Nîmes. ⓒ **04-66-67-28-51.** Fax 04-66-67-07-79. http://multimania.com/hotel amphitheatre. 17 units. 265F–300F (40.30– 45.60, $38.45–$43.50) double; 325F–335F (49.40– 50.90, $47.15–$48.60) triple or quad. AE, MC, V. Closed Jan 2–20. Parking 50F (7.60, $7.25). *In room:* TV.

Hôtel Vatel Built around 1990, the hotel lies 2 miles north of the town center, within a cluster of other buildings that includes a technological university and a large hospital. It's efficiently staffed with students from the local hotel school, who work here as part of their on-the-job training. The rooms are streamlined, tasteful, and modern, with terraces. Each comes with a midsize bathroom with tub/shower combination. In all, the modern format of this hotel manages to provide a level of comfort that older hotels, in more historic but restricted settings, simply can't provide.

140 rue Vatel, B.P. 7128, 30913 Nîmes CEDEX. ✆ **04-66-62-57-57.** Fax 04-66-57-50. 46 units. 600F (91.20, $87) double; 1,200F (182.40, $174) suite. AE, DC, MC, V. From the A4 autoroute, exit at "Nîmes Ouest." **Amenities:** 2 restaurants, bar; pool; health club; solarium; sauna; tennis court. *In room:* A/C, TV, minibar, hair dryer.

Imperator Concorde A member of the Concorde chain, this is the largest and finest hotel in town, set behind the ancient Roman monuments—it's the one with the pale pink Italianate facade. With a recent major renovation, it's been much improved. The artful and cozy rooms have traditional or French furniture, either with fluted or cambriole-shaped legs, adhering to one or another of the Louis styles. You can order a meal in the hotel's verdant rear gardens or in a high-ceilinged dining room, L'Enclos de la Fontaine.

Quai de la Fontaine, 30900 Nîmes. ✆ **04-66-21-90-30.** Fax 04-66-67-70-25. www.concorde-hotels.com. 63 units. 590F–1,000F (89.70– 152, $85.55–$145) double; 1,200F (182.40, $174) suite. AE, DC, MC, V. Parking 70F (10.65, $10.15). **Amenities:** Restaurant, bar; room service; laundry/dry cleaning. *In room:* A/C, TV, minibar, hair dryer.

New Hôtel La Baume 🎨 *Finds* Our favorite nest in Nîmes sits in a 17th-century mansion. The designers were careful to preserve the original architectural heritage during its creation, and the result is a winning combination of modern and traditional. The rooms are fitted with exceptional charm, always in warm Provençal colors of ocher, burnt orange, and yellow. Each comes with a tiled bathroom, mostly with tub/shower combination. The hotel restaurant is also worth a visit, turning out such dishes as fresh salmon flavored with anise and chicken saltimbocca with ham.

21 rue Nationale, 30000 Nîmes. ✆ **04-66-76-28-42.** Fax 04-66-76-28-45. 34 units. 580F (88.15, $84.10) double. AE, DC, MC, V. Parking 40F (6.10, $5.80). **Amenities:** Restaurant, bar; breakfast-only room service; laundry/dry cleaning. *In room:* A/C, TV, minibar, hair dryer.

DINING

The dining room at the **New Hôtel La Baume** (see "Accommodations," above) is also a good choice.

Alexandre 🎨🎨🎨 TRADITIONAL FRENCH The most charming and amusing restaurant around is on the outskirts of Nîmes, 5 miles south of the center. Its setting is the elegantly rustic domain of Michel Kayser, who adheres to classic tradition, with subtle improvements. His charming wife, Monique, assists him in the dining room. Menu items are designed to amuse as well as delight the palate: *île flottante* with truffles and *velouté* of cèpe mushrooms, roasted pigeon stuffed with purée of vegetables and foie gras, braised turbot with lemon confit, and rack of lamb with sweetbreads. Especially appealing is the trolley loaded with goat cheeses from the region and worthy cheeses from other parts of France. The dessert trolley is incredibly hard to resist.

Rte. de l'Aéroport de Garons. ✆ **04-66-70-08-99.** Reservations required. Main courses 50F–200F (7.60– 30.40, $7.25–$29); fixed-price menus 215F–470F (32.70– 71.45, $31.20–$68.15) at lunch, 295F–470F (44.85– 71.45, $42.80–$68.15) at dinner. AE, MC, V. July–Aug Tues–Sun noon–1:45pm and 8–9:45pm; Sept–June Tues–Sun noon–1:45pm and Tues and Thurs–Sat 8–9:45pm. Closed 2 weeks in Feb. From the town center, take rue de la République southwest to av. Jean-Jaurès; then head south and follow the signs to the airport in the direction of Garons.

Restaurant au Chapon Fin ALSATIAN/LANGUEDOCIENNE This tavern/restaurant, on a little square behind St-Paul's, is run by M. and Mme Grangier. It has beamed ceilings, small lamps, and a black-and-white stone floor. Madame

Grangier is from Alsace, so you'll find both Alsatian and Languedocienne specialties. From the a la carte menu you can order foie gras with truffles, a casserole of roasted lamb and eggplant, *coq au vin* (chicken with wine), and entrecôte flambéed with morels. The proprietor makes his own *confit d'oie* (goose preserved in its own fat) from birds shipped in from Alsace.

3 rue du Château-Fadaise. ☎ **04-66-67-34-73**. Reservations required. Main courses 70F–149F (10.65– 22.65, $10.15–$21.60); fixed-price lunch 75F (11.40, $10.90). AE, DC, MC, V. Mon–Fri noon–2pm and 7:30–10pm; Sat 7:30–10pm. Closed Aug.

San Francisco Steak House STEAK/FRENCH   After traveling through the United States, the founders of this restaurant transported some ideas from California and created the most popular theme restaurant in Nîmes. You'll find the best steaks and seafood here, always in generous portions with plenty of flavor. In addition to the juicy steaks, you can order succulent veal or lamb chops. The trendiest dishes are grilled ostrich or bison steaks. Begin your meal with a shrimp-stuffed avocado or a salad of grapefruit and crayfish segments.

33 rue Roussy (near place de la Couronne). ☎ **04-66-21-00-80**. Reservations required. Main courses 70F–150F (10.65– 22.80, $10.15–$21.75). AE, DC, MC, V. Mon–Fri noon–2pm; Mon–Sat 7:30pm–midnight. Bus: 3 or 5.

Wine Bar Chez Michel *Value* TRADITIONAL FRENCH   This place is paneled with mahogany and has leather banquettes evocative of an early-1900s California saloon. Choices include an array of salads and platters. At lunch you can order a quick menu, including an appetizer, a garnished main course, and two glasses of wine. Typical dishes are magrêt of duckling and contrefilet of steak with Roquefort sauce. You can now enjoy lunch on the terrace in the courtyard. A restaurateur extraordinaire, Michel Hermet also makes his own wine within vineyards that have been associated with his family for many generations. There are more than 300 other varieties of wine to choose from, by the glass or the pitcher.

11 place de la Couronne. ☎ **04-66-76-19-59**. Main courses 60F–150F (9.10– 22.80, $8.70–$21.75); fixed-price menus 80F (12.15, $11.60) at lunch, 85F–130F (12.90– 19.75, $12.35–$18.85) at dinner. AE, DC, MC, V. Tues–Sat noon–2pm; Mon–Sat 7pm–midnight.

NÎMES AFTER DARK

Once the warm weather hits, all sorts of activities take place at the arena, including concerts and theater under the stars. The Office de Tourisme has a complete listing of events and schedules. Otherwise, for popular events like football (soccer), bullfights, and rock concerts, you can contact the **Bureau de Location des Arènes,** 4 rue de la Violette (☎ **04-66-02-80-80**). Tickets for more highbrow events, such as symphonic or chamber-music concerts, theater, and opera performances, are sold through **Hall du Théâtre,** 1 place de la Calade (☎ **04-66-36-65-00**).

If you like hanging out with a mix of French students and French soldiers, head to **Café Le Napoléon,** 46 bd. Victor-Hugo (☎ **04-66-67-20-23**). Popular with the intelligentsia is the **Haddock Cafe,** 13 rue de l'Agau (☎ **04-66-67-86-57**), with its weekly live rock concerts.

All the town's jazz aficionados know that **Le Diagonal,** 41 bis rue Emile-Jamais (☎ **04-66-21-70-01**), hosts the area's best jazz and blues concerts every Saturday. The flashy, sexy, and hip **La Comédie,** 28 rue Jean-Reboul (☎ **04-66-76-13-66**), is the hands-down best for dancing and attracts a pretty crowd of youthful danceaholics. A little less flashy, but a lot more fun, **Lulu**

Club, 10 impasse de la Curaterie (© **04-66-36-28-20**), is the gay and lesbian stronghold in Nîmes.

A newer contender for the nightlife attentions of the city's young and restless is **Le Cococlub,** 20 rue de l'Étoile (© **04-66-21-59-22**). Open every Wednesday to Saturday, beginning after 11pm, it rocks and rolls to music from Los Angeles and London. Clubs with dancing and/or entertainment generally impose a cover of 50F to 70F (7.60 to 10.65, $7.25 to $10.15).

Streets to explore for a healthy dose of nocturnal good times on virtually any night of the week include **place de la Maison Carrée** and **boulevard Victor-Hugo.**

2 Aigues-Mortes ★★

466 miles SW of Paris, 39 miles NE of Sète, 25 miles E of Nîmes, 30 miles SW of Arles

South of Nîmes, you can explore much of the Camargue by car. The most rewarding place to focus on is Aigues-Mortes, the city of the "dead waters." In the middle of dismal swamps and melancholy lagoons, Aigues-Mortes is France's most perfectly preserved walled town. Now 4 miles from the sea, it stands on four navigable canals. Louis IX and his crusaders once set forth from Aigues-Mortes, then a thriving port, the first in France on the Mediterranean. The **Ramparts** ★★, which still enclose the town, were constructed between 1272 and 1300. The **Tour de Constance** ★★ (© **04-66-53-61-55**) is a model castle of the Middle Ages, its stones looking out on the marshes. At the top, which you can reach by elevator, a panoramic view unfolds. Admission is 36F (5.45, $5.20) for adults, 23F (3.50, $3.35) for ages 18 to 25, and free for children 17 and under. The monument is open daily: May to August from 9:30am to 8pm, September 9:30am to 7pm, October to January 10am to 5pm, and February to April 10am to 6pm.

Frankly, the main allure in Aigues-Mortes involves the city itself and the way a sense of medievalism still permeates virtually every building, every rampart, and every cobble-covered street. The city's religious centerpiece is the **Église Notre-Dame des Sablons,** rue Jean-Jaurès (© **04-66-53-86-73**). Constructed of wood in 1183, it was rebuilt in stone in 1246 in the ogival style. Its stained-glass windows are modern, having been installed in 1980 as replacements for the badly damaged and weather-beaten originals. The church is open daily from 8:30am to 6pm.

ESSENTIALS

GETTING THERE   Five **trains** and four **buses** per day connect Aigues-Mortes and Nîmes. Trip time is about an hour. For information and schedules, call © **08-36-35-35-35.** If you're **driving** to Aigues-Mortes, take D979 south from Gallargues, or A9 from Montpellier or Nîmes.

VISITOR INFORMATION   The **Office de Tourisme** is at Porte de la Gardette (© **04-66-53-73-00**).

ACCOMMODATIONS

The **Restaurant Les Arcades** (see "Dining," below) also rents rooms.

Hostellerie des Remparts   Opened about 300 years ago, this weatherworn inn lies at the foot of the Tour de Constance, adjacent to the medieval fortifications. Popular and often fully booked (especially in summer), it evokes the defensive atmosphere of the Middle Ages, albeit with charm and a sense of

France's Cowboy Country: The Camargue

The Camargue, where the cowboys of France ride the range, is an alluvial plain inhabited by wild horses, fighting black bulls, roaming gypsies, pink flamingos, lagoons, salt marshes, wetlands, and gluttonous mosquitoes. Explore the rugged terrain by boat, bike, horse, jeep, or boat.

Possessing the most fragile ecosystem in France, the Camargue since 1970 has been a national park, known for its small white horses whose galloping ancestors were brought here by the Arabs in the Dark Ages. The horses roam wild in the national park, guarded by French cowboys known as *gardiens*, who wear large felt hats to protect themselves from the fierce sun and carry long three-pronged sticks to prod the cattle. These cowboys still live in thatched huts called *cabanes*. Ancestors of the gardiens may have been the first American cowboys, owing to the fact that they sailed on French ships to the port of New Orleans, where they rode the bayous of Louisiana and East Texas, rounding up cattle in French no less.

There's no more evocative sight on the landscape than watching these proud snow-white horses running at liberty through the marshlands, with hoofs so tough they don't need shoes. It is said that they evolved their long manes and long busy tails over the centuries to slap those pesky mosquitoes.

Exotic flora and fauna abound in this region where the delta of the mighty Rhône River empties into the Mediterranean. The birdlife is the most luxuriant in Europe and is especially known for its colonies of elegant pink flamingos (*flamants roses*). Evoking the Florida Everglades, the flamingos share living quarters with some 400 other bird species, including ibises, egrets, kingfishers, owls, wild ducks, swans, and ferocious birds of prey. The best place to see flamingo colonies is the area around Ginès, a hamlet along N570, lying 3 miles north of Camargue's capital, Stes-Maries-de-la-Mer.

Exploring the Camargue is best done on the back of one of those *camarguais* horses. These horses can take you into the interior, which you couldn't see otherwise, as they ford waters to places where the black bulls graze and wild birds nest. You'll find two to three dozen stables (depending on the time of year) along the highway from Arles to Stes-Maries. To stay competitive, virtually all of them charge the same daily rate of 350F (53.20, $50.75), with a picnic lunch included. These rides are aimed at the neophyte—not the champion equestrian. They're so easy that they're recommended even for those who have never been on a horse before.

nostalgia. The small rooms with simple furniture are accessible via narrow stone staircases; 13 contain TVs. The living here is rather plain and basic but is clean, decent, and well maintained, each unit having a small bathroom with shower. Breakfast is the only meal served.

6 place Anatole-France, 30220 Aigues-Mortes. ☎ **04-66-53-82-77.** Fax 04-66-53-73-77. 19 units. 280F–455F (42.55– 69.15, $40.60–$66) double. AE, DC, V.

Hôtel Les Templiers 🍸 The leading inn in town is a gem of peace and tranquility. Protected by the ramparts built by St. Louis, king of France, this 17th-century residence has been tastefully converted to receive guests. The small- to medium-size rooms are decorated in a Provençal style, with just enough decorative objects to lend a homelike aura. The midsize bathrooms come with a tub/shower combination (three have shower only). You can relax in the courtyard, where you can also enjoy breakfast. The restaurant is open only for dinner, serving regional cuisine.

23 rue de la République, 30220 Aigues-Mortes. © **04-66-53-66-56**. Fax 04-66-53-69-61. 10 units. 590F–800F (89.70– 121.60, $85.55–$116) double. AE, DC, V. Closed Nov–Jan. **Amenities:** Restaurant, bar; room service; laundry. *In room:* A/C, TV, hair dryer.

Hôtel St-Louis Even though not grand in any way, this is the town's second-place choice for lodging. Located near place St-Louis, the inn is not as fine as the Templiers (see above) but does offer comfortably furnished, but small, rooms, each with a compact bathroom with a shower. Many locals come here to enjoy the regional meals served in the dining room.

10 rue de l'Amiral-Courbet, 30220 Aigues-Mortes. © **04-66-53-72-68**. Fax 04-66-53-75-92. 22 units. 340F–510F (51.70– 77.50, $49.30–$73.95) double. AE, DC, MC, V. Closed Jan–Mar 10. Parking 70F (10.65, $10.15). **Amenities:** Restaurant, bar; room service. *In room:* TV, minibar.

DINING

Note that **Hôtel Les Templiers** (see "Accommodations," above) also has good restaurants.

Restaurant Les Arcades 🍸🍸 TRADITIONAL FRENCH There's no contest: This is the area's finest dining choice. This restaurant has several formal sections with ancient beamed ceilings or intricately fitted stone vaults. Almost as old as the nearby fortifications, the place is especially charming on sultry days, when the thick masonry keeps the interior cool. Good food is served at reasonable prices and is likely to include warm oysters, fish soup, pot-au-feu with three different meats, roasted monkfish in red-wine sauce, lobster fricassée, and grilled duckling.

The owner also rents 10 large, comfortable rooms, each with air-conditioning, TV, and phone. A double is 480F to 700F (72.95 to 106.40, $69.60 to $101.50), breakfast included.

23 bd. Gambetta, 30220 Aigues-Mortes. © **04-66-53-81-13**. Fax 04-66-53-75-46. Reservations recommended. Main courses 75F–165F (11.40– 25.10, $10.90–$23.95); fixed-price menus 130F–275F (19.75– 41.80, $18.85–$39.90). AE, DC, MC, V. Tues 7:30–9:30pm; Wed–Sun noon–2pm and 7:30–9:45pm (also open Mon night July–Aug). Closed 2 weeks in Mar and 2 weeks in Nov.

3 Montpellier ★ ★

471 miles SW of Paris, 100 miles NW of Marseille, 31 miles SW of Nîmes

The capital of Mediterranean (or Lower) Languedoc, the ancient university city of Montpellier is still renowned for its medical school, founded in the 13th century. Nostradamus qualified as a doctor here, and even Rabelais studied at the school. Petrarch came to Montpellier in 1317, staying for 7 years.

Today Montpellier is a bustling metropolis, one of southern France's fastest-growing cities, thanks to an influx of new immigrants. Except for some dreary suburbs, the city has a handsomely laid out core, with tree-flanked promenades, broad avenues, and historic monuments. Students make up a quarter of the population, giving the city a lively feel. In recent years, many high-tech corporations, including IBM, have settled in Montpellier.

ESSENTIALS

GETTING THERE   Some 20 **trains** per day arrive from Avignon (trip time: 1 hr.), 8 from Marseille (trip time: 45 min.), 1 every 2 hours from Toulouse (trip time: 2 hr.), and 10 per day from Perpignan (trip time: 1½ hr.). Eight trains per day arrive from Paris, calling for a change in Lyon (trip time: 4½ hr.). For rail information and schedules, call 🕿 **08-36-35-35-35.** Two **buses** a day arrive from Nîmes (trip time: 1¾ hr.).

If you're **driving,** Montpellier lies off A9, heading west.

VISITOR INFORMATION   The **Office de Tourisme** is at 30 av. Jean de Lattre de Tassigny (🕿 **04-67-60-60-60**).

SPECIAL EVENTS   From late June to early July, an array of classical and modern dance performances cascade into town for the **Festival International Montpellier Danse.** Tickets sell for 35F to 260F (5.30 to 39.50, $5.10 to $37.70) and can be purchased through the **Hôtel d'Assas,** 6 rue de la Vieille Aiguillerie (🕿 **04-67-60-83-60**). In late July, the **Festival de Radio France et de Montpellier** presents a variety of orchestral music, jazz, and opera. Tickets run 50F to 150F (7.60 to 22.80, $7.25 to $21.75); call 🕿 **04-67-02-02-01,** or contact the Corum Theater (🕿 **04-67-61-66-81**).

EXPLORING THE TOWN

Called the Oxford of France because of its burgeoning academic community, Montpellier is a city of young people, as you'll notice if you sit at a cafe opening onto the heartbeat **place de la Comédie,** admiring the theater, the 18th-century Fountain of the Three Graces, or whatever else amuses you. It's the living room of Montpellier, the ideal place to flirt, chat, people-watch, cruise, or just hang out.

Before leaving town, take a stroll along the 17th-century **promenade du Peyrou** ★★, a terraced park with views of the Cévennes and the Mediterranean. This is a broad esplanade constructed at the loftiest point of Montpellier. Opposite the entrance is an **Arc de Triomphe,** erected in 1691 to celebrate the victories of Louis XIV. In the center of the promenade is an equestrian statue of Louis XIV, and at the end is the **Château d'Eau,** a pavilion with Corinthian columns that serves as a monument to 18th-century classicism. Water travels here via a 9-mile-long conduit and an aqueduct.

Cathédrale St-Pierre   The town's spiritual centerpiece was founded in 1364. Once associated with a Benedictine monastery, the cathedral suffered badly in religious wars. (After 1795, the monastery was occupied by the medical school.) Today it has a somewhat bleak western front with two towers and a canopied porch.

Place St-Pierre. 🕿 **04-67-66-04-12.** Free admission. Daily 9am–noon and 2:30–7pm.

Jardin des Plantes   Paul Valéry met André Gide in the Jardin des Plantes, the oldest such garden in France. This botanical garden, filled with exotic plants and a handful of greenhouses, was opened in 1593.

163 rue Auguste-Broussonnet (reached from bd. Henri-IV). 🕿 **04-67-63-43-22.** Free admission. Tues–Sun 10am–5pm (to 7pm Apr–Sept).

Musée Fabre ★★   One of France's great provincial art galleries occupies the former Hôtel de Massilian, where Molière once played for a season. The collection originated with an exhibition of the Royal Academy that was sent to Montpellier by Napoléon in 1803. Its most important works, however, were given by

François Fabre, a Montpellier painter, in 1825. After Fabre's death, many other paintings from his collection were donated to the gallery. Several of these were of his own creation, but the more significant works were ones he had acquired—including Poussin's *Venus and Adonis* and Italian paintings like *The Mystical Marriage of Saint Catherine*. This generosity was followed by donations from other parties, notably Valedau, who in 1836 left his collection of Rubens, Gérard Dou, and Téniers.

39 bd. Bonne-Nouvelle. © **04-67-14-83-00.** Admission 20F (3.05, $2.90) adults, 10F (1.50, $1.45) students and persons 20 and under. Tues–Fri 9am–5:30pm; Sat–Sun 9:30am–5pm.

ACCOMMODATIONS

The **Jardin des Sens** (see "Dining," below) also rents rooms.

Hôtel du Palais *Finds* This hotel is one of the best bargains in the town. Built in the late 18th century, the Hôtel du Palais is set in the center, amid a labyrinth of narrow streets and monumental plazas and parks. Much of the decor dates from around 1983, when the hotel was richly restored to a motif that uses lots of fabrics, big curtains, and walls of public areas that are painted to resemble marble. The guest rooms are relatively large and appealing, thanks to thoughtful placements of antique reproductions and good maintenance. Breakfast is the only meal served.

3 rue du Palais, 34000 Montpellier. © **04-67-60-47-38.** Fax 04-67-60-40-23. 26 units. 350F–430F (53.20–65.35, $50.75–$62.35) double. AE, DC, MC, V. Parking 25F (3.80, $3.65). *In room:* A/C, TV, minibar.

La Maison Blanche Few other hotels in the south of France work so hard to emulate the gingerbread and French Créole ambience of this hotel. The rooms are stylishly furnished in rattan and wicker. Bathrooms are midsize to roomy, mostly with tub/shower combinations. Parts of the interior, especially the dining room, might remind you of Louis XIII's France more than Old Louisiana, but overall the setting is as charming and unusual as anything else in town.

1796 av. de la Prompignane, 34000 Montpellier. © **04-99-58-20-70.** Fax 04-67-79-53-39. 38 units. 490F–540F (74.50– 82.10, $71.05–$78.30) double; 780F (118.55, $113.10) suite. AE, DC, MC, V. Free parking. A 5-min. drive northeast of Montpellier's center: Take bd. d'Antigone east until you reach the intersection with av. de la Pompignane and head north until you see the hotel on your right. **Amenities:** Restaurant, bar; outdoor pool; room service; laundry. *In room:* A/C, TV, hair dryer.

Les Arceaux It's basic but still most acceptable, and the price is right. A hotel has stood at this prime location, right off the renowned promenade du Peyrou, since the early 1900s. The smallish rooms are pleasantly but simply furnished, and each comes with a compact bathroom with a shower unit. Breakfast is the only meal served. A shaded terrace adjoins the hotel.

33–35 bd. des Arceaux, 34000 Montpellier. © **04-67-92-03-03.** Fax 04-67-92-05-09. 18 units. 310F–340F (47.10– 51.70, $44.95–$49.30) double. MC, V. *In room:* TV.

Sofitel Antigone Situated in the heart of Montpellier, this modern hotel is a favorite with businesspeople. However, in summer, it does quite a trade with visitors. It's particularly distinguished for its pool, which, along with a bar and breakfast room, occupies most of the top floor. The rooms are chain format but first class. The best are on a floor known as Privilège, where you get such extras as all-marble baths. It's a winning choice, with the most efficient staff in the city. The bar, the Botanica, is one of the coziest hideaways in town.

1 rue Pertuisanes, 3400 Montpellier. 90 units. 950F–1,050F (144.40– 159.60, $137.75–$152.25) double; 1,700F (258.40, $246.50) suite. AE, DC, MC, V. Parking 70F (10.65, $10.15). **Amenities:** Bar; pool; room service; laundry. *In room:* A/C, TV, hair dryer.

Ulysse ☆ *Value* One of the city's better bargains, Ulysse delivers a lot of bang for your buck. There's a simplicity here, though the owners have worked hard—on a budget—to make the hotel as stylish as possible. The rooms, renovated in 1999, are unique in composition of colors and decorations. The furnishings are made with an original wrought-iron design, functional but with a certain flair. Much in-room comfort is found here, including fully equipped tub/shower baths.

338 av. de St-Maur, 34000 Montpellier. ℭ **04-67-02-02-30.** Fax 04-67-02-16-50. www.hotelulysse.com. 24 units. 320F–350F (48.65– 53.20, $46.40–$50.75) double. AE, DC, V. From bd. d'Antigone, head north along av. Jean-Mermoz to rue de la Pépinière; continue right for a short distance and take a sharp left at the first intersection, which leads to av. de St-Maur. **Amenities:** Room service. *In room:* TV, minibar.

DINING

La Réserve Rimbaud ☆ TRADITIONAL & MODERN FRENCH This memorable restaurant is located in a bulky manor house built in 1875 by a prosperous local family, the Rimbauds. It offers only about 30 seats in a setting that might've been plucked from the early 1900s. Menu items, prepared and presented by the English-speaking Tarrit family, change with the season but are likely to include truffle-studded chicken croquettes, monkfish with local herbs, curried crayfish, baked sea wolf with local herbs, stuffed calamari, warm foie gras with apples, fricassée of sole with baby vegetables, and chocolate cake with orange mousse and Grand Marnier sauce.

820 av. de St-Maur. ℭ **04-67-72-52-53.** Reservations recommended. Main courses 90F–160F (13.70– 24.30, $13.05–$23.20); fixed-price menus 180F–380F (27.35– 57.75, $26.10–$55.10). AE, DC, MC, V. Tues–Sat noon–2pm and 8–10pm; Sun noon–2pm. Closed Jan–Mar. Take N113 (av. de Nîmes) northeast toward Nîmes, follow it to the intersection with av. St-Lazare, and turn left; the restaurant is on right.

Le Chandelier ☆ FRENCH This is the most dramatic modern restaurant in Montpellier, with superb food prepared by Gilbert Furland, superb service choreographed by Jean-Marc Forest, and a sweeping view over an upscale residential neighborhood (l'Antigone). You'll find it on the 7th floor of a modern office building, with access to a large terrace. The staff searches for "temptations of the palate," which means you'll be presented with unusual flavor combinations. Examples are a sophisticated version of calamari fried with fresh thyme, an escalope of foie gras in orange sauce, an award-winning ragoût of lobster, and sautéed pigeon in a Provençal pistou (made of various vegetables and thick vermicelli). A particularly scrumptious dessert is a crispy tarte with caramelized mango.

Immeuble La Coupole Antigone, 267 rue Léon-Blum. ℭ **04-67-15-34-38.** Reservations recommended. Main courses 120F–220F (18.25– 33.45, $17.40–$31.90); fixed-price menus 220F (33.45, $31.90). Mon–Fri and Sat lunch, 290F–400F (44.10– 60.80, $42.05–$58) Sat night. AE, DC, MC, V. Tues–Sat noon–1:30pm; Mon–Sat 8–10pm.

Le Jardin des Sens ☆☆☆ FRENCH This is one of the great restaurants of southern France, awarded three Michelin stars. The chefs, twins Laurent and Jacques Pourcel, have taken Montpellier by storm, and their cuisine could be almost anything, depending on where their imaginations roam. The rich bounty of Languedoc is served, but only after going through a process designed to enhance its natural flavor. An appropriate starter might be ravioli stuffed with foie gras of duckling and flap mushrooms, floating in chicken bouillon fortified with truffles, broad beans, and crispy potatoes. Main courses of note are deshelled lobster, pressed flat and served with duck meat and vanilla oil; filet of dorado grilled with sesame and served with a marmalade of tomatoes, olives, and caramelized balsamic vinegar; a *tarte fine* with tomatoes, roasted monkfish, and essence of thyme; and a filet of pigeon stuffed with pistachios. A dessert specialty is a gratin of limes with slices of pineapple *en confit.*

Le Jardin des Sens also rents 14 deluxe guest rooms and 2 suites, each designed in cutting-edge modernism by Bruno Borrione, a colleague of Philippe Starck. They cost 980F to 1,380F (148.95 to 209.75, $142.10 to $200.10) for a double and 1,680F to 2,500F (255.35 to 380, $243.60 to $362.50) for a suite.

11 av. St-Lazare. (℃ **04-99-58-38-38.** Fax 04-67-72-13-05. jardinsens@relaischateaux.fr. Reservations required. Main courses 160F–280F (24.30– 42.55, $23.20–$40.60); fixed-price menus 260F (39.50, $37.70) at lunch (Mon–Fri); 490F–710F (74.50– 107.90, $71.05–$102.95) at dinner. AE, MC, V. Tues and Thurs–Sat noon–2pm; Mon–Sat 7:30–10pm.

L'Olivier ✦ *Finds* MODERN FRENCH   No restaurant, with the exception of Le Jardin des Sens, is improving more than this. Chef Michel Breton, assisted by his wife, Yvette, is becoming a name in the restaurant guides to the south of France. The establishment holds places for only 20 diners at a time, within a subdued and rather bland modern space accented only by a collection of contemporary paintings. But you don't come to L'Olivier to look at the walls. You come for Breton's salmon with oysters, warm monkfish terrine, stewed filet of lamb with crispy eggplant, frogs' legs with wild mushrooms, and haunch of rabbit stuffed with wild mushrooms. The welcome is warm and sincere.

12 rue Aristide-Olivier. (℃ **04-67-92-86-28.** Reservations required. Main courses 90F–160F (13.70– 24.30, $13.05–$23.20); fixed-price menus 218F (33.15, $31.60). AE, DC. Tues–Sat noon–1:30pm and 7:30–9:30pm. Closed Aug and holidays.

MONTPELLIER AFTER DARK

After the sun sets, head for **place Jean-Jaurès, rue de Verdun,** and **rue des Écoles Laïques,** or take a walk down **rue de la Loge** for its carnival atmosphere of talented jugglers, mimes, and musical artists.

Rockstore, 20 rue de Verdun (℃ **04-67-06-80-00**), with its 1950s rock memorabilia and live concerts, draws lots of students. Then walk up a flight of stairs to its disco, which pounds out techno and rock. The cover for the disco is 50F (7.60, $7.25). An exotic cocktail bar is **Viva Brazil,** 7 rue de Verdun (℃ **04-67-58-63-33**), where you chop your way through the lush rain-forest vegetation and friendly natives to reach the mirrored sanctuary of the dance floor. For the best jazz and blues in town, check out **JAM,** 100 rue Ferdinand-de-Lesseps (℃ **04-67-58-30-30**). In a noisy, smoky, and even gritty space, its regular concerts attract jazz enthusiasts from miles around. Concert tickets average 50F (7.60, $7.25).

A more recently inaugurated disco is **La Tipola,** route de Palavas (℃ **04-67-65-62-95**), a sparsely decorated modern bar/dance hall with a crowd that tends to be between 20 and 38 years old. Open every Wednesday to Sunday beginning around 10pm, it charges a 50F (7.60, $7.25) cover, a price that includes the first drink. Gays and lesbians gather at the town's most animated bar/disco, **La Villa Rouge,** route de Palavas (℃ **04-67-06-52-15**), a short distance from La Tipola (see above). Both of them lie about 3 miles south of the town center.

Le Corum (℃ **04-67-61-67-61**), the most up-to-date theater in town, is the site of many plays, dance recitals, operas, and symphonic presentations. It lies within the Palais des Congrès, esplanade Charles-de-Gaulle, in the heart of town. For complete ticket information and schedules, contact the Corum directly or an organization that's instrumental in its management, the **Opéra Comédie,** place de la Comédie (℃ **04-67-60-19-99**).

525 miles SW of Paris, 38 miles E of Carcassonne, 58 miles S of Montpellier

Medieval Narbonne was a port to rival Marseille in Roman times, its "galleys laden with riches." Since then, the Mediterranean has receded from Narbonne, and the town is now 5 miles inland.

Narbonne was the first town outside Italy to be colonized by the Romans. For that reason it's an intriguing place, steeped with antiquity. After Lyon, Narbonne was the largest town in Gaul, and even today you can still see evidence of the town's former wealth. Too far from the sea to be a beach town, it attracts history buffs and others aware of the memories of its glorious past.

Some 50,000 Narbonnais live here, in what's really a sleepy backwater. However, many locals are trying to make a go with their vineyards. Caves are open to visitors in the surrounding area (the tourist office will advise you). If you want to go to the beach, you'll have to head to the nearby sands at the village of **Gruis-son** and its adjoining beach, Gruisson-Plage, or the suburb of **St-Pierre la Mer** and its adjoining beach, Narbonne-Plage. Both lie 9 miles south from Narbonne. Buses from the town center are frequent, each marked with its destination.

ESSENTIALS

GETTING THERE   Narbonne has rail, bus, and highway connections with other cities on the Mediterranean coast and with Toulouse. Rail travel is the most popular way to get here, with 14 **trains** per day arriving from Perpignan (trip time: 50 min.), 13 per day from Toulouse (trip time: 1½ hr.), and 12 per day from Montpellier (trip time: 1 hr.). For rail information and schedules, call ✆ **08-36-35-35-35.** If you're **driving,** Narbonne is at the junction of A61 and A9, making it easily accessible from either Toulouse or the Riviera.

VISITOR INFORMATION   The **Office de Tourisme** is on place Roger-Salengro (✆ **04-68-65-15-60**).

EXPLORING THE TOWN

Few other cities in France contain such a massive medieval architectural block in their centers. Foremost among Narbonne's labyrinth of religious and civic buildings is the **Cathédrale St-Just** (★★, place de l'Hôtel-de-Ville, entrance on rue Gauthier (✆ **04-68-32-09-52**). Its construction began in 1272 but was never finished. Only the transept and a choir were completed; the choir is 130 feet high, built in the bold Gothic style of northern France. At each end of the transept are 194-foot towers from 1480. Inside is an impressive collection of Flemish tapestries. The cloisters are from the 14th and 15th centuries and connect the cathedral with the Archbishops' Palace (below). The cathedral is open daily: May to September from 10am to 7pm and October to March from 9am to noon and 2 to 6pm. Entrance is free.

The cathedral is attached to the **Palais des Archevêques** (Archbishops' Palace, sometimes referred to as the Vieux-Palais), place de l'Hôtel-de-Ville (✆ **04-68-90-30-30**). It was conceived as part fortress, part pleasure palace, with three military-style towers from the 13th and 14th centuries. The Old Palace on the right is from the 12th century and the so-called New Palace on the left is from the 14th. It's said that the old, arthritic, and sometimes very overweight archbishops were hauled up the interior's monumental Louis XIII–style stairs on mules. Part of the complex is devoted to the neo-Gothic **Hôtel de Ville** (town hall), which was reconstructed between 1845 and 1850 by

Viollet-le-Duc, a 19th-century architect involved with the refurbishment of such sites as the cathedral at Paris.

Today the once-private apartments of the former archbishops contain three museums. Admission is 10F (1.50, $1.45) to each museum (you can buy a global ticket that gets you into all three, plus the **Musée Lapidaire,** but it's no cheaper that way). Hours are the same at all three: April to September daily from 9:30am to 12:15pm and 2 to 6pm, October to March Tuesday to Sunday from 10am to noon and 2 to 5pm. For more information, call ℂ **04-68-90-30-54.**

The **Musée Archéologique** ✦ contains prehistoric artifacts, Bronze Age tools, 14th-century frescoes, and Greco-Roman amphorae. Several of the sarcophagi date from the 3rd century, and some of the mosaics are of pagan origin. The **Musée d'Art et d'Histoire de Narbonne** is three floors above street level in the archbishop's once-private apartments, the rooms in which Louis XII stayed during his siege of Perpignan. Their coffered ceilings are enhanced with panels depicting the nine Muses. A Roman mosaic floor and 17th-century portraits are on display. There's also a collection of antique porcelain, enamels, and a portrait bust of Louis XIV. In the **Horreum Romain,** you'll find a labyrinth of underground passages, similar to catacombs but with none of the burial functions, dug by the Gallo-Romans and their successors for storage of food and supplies during times of siege.

If you visit between mid-June and mid-September, you might want to participate in one of the occasional hikes up the steep steps of the **Donjon Gilles-Aycelin,** place de l'Hôtel-de-Ville. A watchtower and prison in the late 13th century, it has a lofty observation platform with a view of the cathedral, the surrounding plain, and the Pyrénées. Entrance costs 10F (1.50, $1.45) for adults and 5F (.75, 75¢) for students and children 11 to 18. The watchtower is open daily: April to September from 11am to 7pm and October to March from 10am to noon and 2 to 5pm.

You can see Roman artifacts at the **Musée Lapidaire,** place Lamourguier (ℂ **04-68-65-53-58**), in the 13th-century Notre-Dame de Lamourguier. The broken sculptures, Roman inscriptions, and relics of medieval buildings make up one of the largest (and most important) exhibits of this kind in France. At press time, this museum was closed for renovations, although it's expected to open during the life of this edition. Check with the tourist office for opening hours and prices at the time of your visit.

A final site worth visiting is the early Gothic **Basilique St-Paul-Serge,** rue de l'Hôtel-Dieu (ℂ **04-68-32-68-98**), built on the site of a 4th-century necropolis. It has an elegant choir with fine Renaissance woodcarvings and some ancient Christian sarcophagi. The chancel, from 1229, is admirable. The north door leads to the Paleo-Christian Cemetery, part of an early Christian burial ground. The basilica is open daily: April to September from 9am to 7pm and October to March from 9am to noon (plus Monday to Saturday 2 to 6pm).

ACCOMMODATIONS

Hôtel du Languedoc   This oft-modernized early-1900s hotel sits directly beside the canal de la Rhône. The public areas are airy and mostly outfitted in tones of Bordeaux. The rooms come in a wide variety of shapes and sizes, usually with some of the hotel's original wooden furniture and pastel color schemes. About half of the midsize bathrooms come with tub/shower combinations.

22 bd. Gambetta, 11100 Narbonne. ℂ **04-68-65-14-74.** Fax 04-68-65-81-48. www.hoteldulanguedoc.com. 40 units. 290F–380F (44.10– 57.75, $42.05–$55.10) double; 480F (72.95, $69.60) suite. AE, DC, MC, V. Parking 35F (5.30, $5.10). **Amenities:** Restaurant, bar/Breton style creperie; room service. *In room:* TV.

La Résidence ⭐ Our favorite hotel in Narbonne is near the Cathédrale St-Just. The 19th-century La Résidence, converted from a once-stately villa, is comfortable and decorated with antiques. The rooms are midsize to spacious, each comfortably and tastefully furnished, and the maintenance is the highest. All units come with a good-sized bathroom equipped for the most part with a tub/shower combination. The hotel doesn't have a restaurant but offers breakfast and a gracious welcome.

6 rue du 1er-Mai, 11100 Narbonne. © **04-68-32-19-41.** Fax 04-68-65-51-82. 25 units. 405F–470F (61.55– 71.45, $58.75–$68.15) double. AE, DC, MC, V. Parking 40F (6.10, $5.80). Closed Jan 16–Feb 14. *In room:* A/C, TV, minibar, hair dryer.

DINING

La Table St-Crescent ⭐⭐⭐ FRENCH/LANGUEDOCIENNE This is one of the region's best-respected restaurants. It's less than a mile east of town, beside the road leading to Perpignan, in a complex of wine-tasting boutiques established by a local syndicate of wine growers. The foundations of this place date, it's said, from the 8th century, when it functioned as an oratory (small chapel) and prayer site. Today, it's outfitted with nondescript modern furniture that's obviously little more than a foil for the cuisine of master chef Claude Giraud. He delivers a refined, brilliantly realized repertoire, with sublime sauces and sophisticated herbs and seasonings. Menu items change four times a year based on seasonality of ingredients and the inspiration of the owners. Main courses include sea bass marinated with olives, beef filet with foie gras and truffles, and a lasagne of grilled eggplant with a confit of tomatoes and oil of pistou. Especially succulent is roasted shoulder of lamb with crispy noodles and sweet garlic-and-sage sauce. Wine steward Sabrine Giraud (the chef's wife) will help you select the perfect accompaniment to your meal. The most unusual dessert is a platter piled high with four confections, each of which uses some variation on the olive.

In the Palais des Vins, rte. de Perpignan. © **04-68-41-37-37.** Reservations recommended. Main courses 50F–150F (7.60– 22.80, $7.25–$21.75); fixed-price menus 158F–258F (24– 39.20, $22.90–$37.40). Mon–Fri only. AE, DC, MC, V. Tues–Fri and Sun noon–2pm; Mon–Sat 7–9:30pm.

5 Collioure ⭐⭐

577 miles SW of Paris, 17 miles SE of Perpignan

You may recognize this port and its sailboats from the fauvist paintings of Lhote and Derain. It's said to resemble St-Tropez before being overrun, and in days past, Collioure attracted Matisse, Picasso, and Dali. It is the most authentically alluring port of Roussillon, a gem with a vivid Spanish and Catalan image and flavor. Some visitors believe it's the most charming village on the Côte Vermeille. The town's sloping narrow streets, charming semifortified church, antique lighthouse, and eerily introverted culture make it worth an afternoon's stopover. This is the ideal small-town antidote to the condominium-choked Riviera.

The two curving ports are separated from each other by the heavy masonry of the 13th-century **Château Royal,** place du 8-Mai-1945 (© **04-68-82-06-43**). The château, now a museum of painting and folkloric artifacts, is open daily: June to September from 10am to 6pm and October to May from 9am to 5pm (closed January 1, May 1, and December 25). Admission is 20F (3.05, $2.90) for adults and 10F (1.50, $1.45) for children; free for children under 7. Also try to visit the **Musée Jean-Peské,** route de Port-Vendres (© **04-68-82-10-19**), with its collection of works by artists who migrated here to paint. It's open in

July and August daily from 10am to noon and 3 to 7pm, September to June Wednesday to Monday from 10am to noon and 2 to 6pm. Admission is 12F (1.80, $1.75) for adults, 8F (1.20, $1.15) for children 12 to 16, and free for children under 12.

ESSENTIALS

GETTING THERE   Collioure is serviced by frequent **train** and bus connections, especially from Perpignan. For train information and schedules, call ✆ **08-36-35-35-35.** Many visitors **drive** along the coastal road (RN 114) leading to the Spanish border.

VISITOR INFORMATION   The **Office de Tourisme** is on place du 18-Juin (✆ **04-68-82-15-47**).

ACCOMMODATIONS

Casa Pairal ⚅   This family-operated hotel in a 150-year-old house is imbued with a certain charm. On sunny days, guests can take a dip in the outdoor pool, which sits in the shadow of century-old trees. The rooms are filled with charming old antiques blended with more-modern pieces. The best doubles have petit salons plus small balconies. All rooms except five have a complete tub/shower combination. Breakfast is the only meal served, but there are many restaurants nearby. The hotel lies 160 yards from the port and the beach.

Impasse des Palmiers, 66190 Collioure. ✆ 04-68-82-05-81. Fax 04-68-82-52-10. www.roussillhotel. 28 units. Summer 440F–790F (66.90– 120.10, $63.80–$114.55) double. AE, MC, V. Closed Nov–Mar. Parking 50F (7.60, $7.25). **Amenities:** Outdoor pool. *In room:* A/C, TV, minibar, hair dryer.

Les Caranques ⓥ𝖺𝗅𝗎𝖾   Constructed around the core of a private villa built after World War II and enlarged twice since then, this hotel is comfortably furnished, personalized, and one of the best bargains in town. The rooms are a bit small but neatly maintained, each with a shower-only bathroom. Set on the perimeter of Collioure, away from the crush (and the charm) of the center, the hotel features a terrace that opens onto a view of the old port. The terrace stretches from the hotel to the sea where guests can swim directly from the rocks.

Rte. de Port-Vendres, 66190 Collioure. ✆ 04-68-82-06-68. Fax 04-68-82-00-92. www.lescaranques.com. 22 units. 390F–440F (59.30– 66.90, $56.55–$63.80) double. AE, MC, V. Closed Oct 15–Mar.

Relais des Trois Mas et Restaurant La Balette ⚅⚅   This is not only the town's premier hotel but also the restaurant of choice. In the decor of its beautiful rooms, the hotel honors the famous artists who've lived at Collioure. The rooms, which lead to spacious baths with Jacuzzis, open onto views of the water. Even if you aren't a guest, you may want to take a meal in the dining room, with its vistas of the harbor. Christian Peyre is unchallenged as the best chef in town. His cooking is inventive—often simple but always refined.

Rte. de Port-Vendres, 66190 Collioure. ✆ 04-68-82-05-07. Fax 04-68-82-38-08. 23 units. 570F–1,640F (86.65– 249.30, $82.65–$237.80) double; 1,360F–2,680F (206.70– 407.35, $197.20–$388.60) suite. Half-board 395F (60.05, $57.30) extra per person (obligatory June–Sept). MC, V. Closed Nov 15–Dec 15. Parking 88F (13.40, $12.75). **Amenities:** Restaurant; bar; pool; room service. *In room:* A/C, TV, minibar, hair dryer.

DINING

The **Restaurant La Balette** at the Relais des Trois Mas (see "Accommodations," above) is the best dining room in town.

L'Andalou ⓥ𝖺𝗅𝗎𝖾 FRENCH/SPANISH   This cozy bistro/tavern, decorated with a hanging collection of flamenco dresses and depictions of the surrounding landscapes, is at the edge of Collioure's historic core. Your hosts are Manuel Fernandez, his wife, Caroline, and members of their family. Look for well-prepared Spanish-style dishes like parillade of seafood, garlic-laced *soupe de poissons,* or perhaps yellow Manchego cheese in a style you might have expected in Madrid. A particularly attractive bargain is the house paella, priced at 59F (8.95, $8.55) for one person or 175F (26.60, $25.40) for enough to feed the whole table. Snails are usually drenched in butter and roasted garlic, while a brochette andaluz brings grilled and herbed beef to new heights. Also look for thin-sliced Serrano ham and several preparations of mussels, including a grilled form (*à la plancha*) that's particularly delectable. A roster of French and Spanish wines (especially riojas) can accompany your meal.

10 rue de la République. ℂ **04-68-82-32-78.** Reservations recommended. Main courses 65F–75F (9.90– 11.40, $9.45–$10.90). Fixed-price menus 89F–109F (13.55– 16.55, $12.90–$15.80). AE, MC, V. Thurs–Tues noon–2:30pm and 7pm–midnight.

6 Perpignan ✶✶

562 miles SW of Paris, 229 miles NW of Marseille, 40 miles S of Narbonne

At Perpignan you may think you've crossed the border into Spain, for this was once Catalonia's second city, after Barcelona. Even earlier, it was the capital of the kingdom of Majorca. But when the Roussillon—the French part of Catalonia—was finally partitioned off, Perpignan became French forever, authenticated by the Treaty of the Pyrénées in 1659. However, Catalan is still spoken here, especially among country folk.

Today Perpignan is content to rest on its former glory. Its residents—some 110,000 in all—enjoy the closeness of the Côte Catalane and the mountains to their north. The pace is decidedly relaxed. You'll even have time to smell the flowers that grow here in great abundance.

This is one of the sunniest places in France, but summer afternoons in July and August are a cauldron. That's when many of the locals take the 6-mile ride to the beach to cool off. There's a young scene here that brings energy to Perpignan, especially along the quays of the Basse River, site of impromptu nighttime concerts, beer drinking, and the devouring of tapas, a tradition inherited from nearby Barcelona.

ESSENTIALS

GETTING THERE   Four **trains** per day arrive from Paris (trip time: 6 to 10 hr.); the high-speed TGV goes on to Montpellier. There are also at least 15 trains that pull into Perpignan from Nice (trip time: 6 hr.). For rail information and schedules, call ℂ **08-36-35-35-35.** If you're **driving** from the French Riviera, drive west along A9 to Perpignan.

VISITOR INFORMATION   The **Office Municipal du Tourisme** is within the Palais des Congrès, place Armand-Lanoux (ℂ **04-68-66-30-30;** www.little france.com).

SPECIAL EVENTS   During very hot July, **Les Estivales** causes the city to explode with a medley of music, expositions, and theater. For information, call ℂ **04-68-35-01-77.** Our favorite time to visit this area is during the **grape harvest** in September. If you visit at this time, you may want to drive through the Rivesaltes district bordering the city to the west and north. Temperatures have usually dropped by then.

Perpignan is host to one of the most widely discussed celebrations of photojournalism in the industry. Established in the late 1980s, it's the **Festival**

International de Photo-Journalisme, also referred to as **Le Visa pour l'Image.**
From September 1 to 16, at least 10 sites of historic, usually medieval, interest
are devoted to the exposition of photojournalistic expositions from around the
world. Entrance to all the expositions is free, and prizes are awarded by an international committee.

EXPLORING THE CITY

With its inviting pedestrian streets, Perpignan is a good town for shopping.
Catalan is the style indigenous to the area, and its influence is evident in the textiles, pottery, and furniture. For one of the best selections of Catalan pieces,
including pottery, furniture, carpets, and even antiques, visit the **Centre Sant-
Vicens,** rue Sant-Vicens (© **04-68-50-02-18**), site of about a dozen independent merchants. You'll find it 2½ miles south of the town center; follow the signs
pointing to Enne and Collioures. A competitor selling mostly Catalan-inspired
items for home decorating is **La Maison Quinta,** 3 rue des Grands-des-
Fabriques (© **04-68-34-41-62**), located in the town center.

A 3-hour guided **walking tour** is a good way to see the main attractions in
the town's historic core. Some tour leaders even lace their commentary with
English. These tours are conducted only between mid-June and mid-September,
at hours that change every day according to demand. They depart from the sidewalk in front of the tourist office and are priced at 25F (3.80, $3.65) per per-
son. For more details, contact the tourist office (see above).

Castillet ✦   This crenellated redbrick building is a combination gateway and
fortress from the 14th century. You can climb its bulky-looking tower for a good
view of the town. Also housed here is the **Musée des Arts et Traditions Populaires Catalans** (also known as La Casa Païral), which contains exhibitions of
Catalan regional artifacts and folkloric items, including typical dress.

Place de Verdun. © **04-68-35-42-05.** Admission 25F (3.80, $3.65) adults, 15F (2.30, $2.20) students and
children 17 and under. Mid-June to mid-Sept Wed–Mon 9:30am–7pm; mid-Sept to mid-June Wed–Mon
9am–6pm.

Cathédrale St-Jean ✦   The cathedral dates from the 14th and 15th centuries and has an admirable nave and interesting 17th-century retables. Leaving
via the south door, you'll find on the left a chapel with the *Devout Christ,* a magnificent wood carving depicting Jesus contorted with pain and suffering—his
head, crowned with thorns, drooping on his chest.

Place Gambetta/rue de l'Horloge. © **04-68-51-33-72.** Free admission. Daily 7:30am–noon and 3–7pm.

Palais des Rois de Majorque (Palace of the Kings of Majorca) ✦   Situated at the top of the town, the Spanish citadel encloses the Palace of the Kings
of Majorca. This structure from the 13th and 14th centuries, built around a
court encircled by arcades, has been restored by the government. You can see the
old throne room with its large fireplaces and a square tower with a double
gallery; from the tower there's a fine view of the Pyrénées. A free guided tour, in
French only, departs four times a day if demand warrants it.

Rue des Archers. © **04-68-34-48-29.** Admission 20F (3.05, $2.90) adults, 10F (1.50, $1.45) students,
free for children 7 and under. June–Sept daily 10am–6pm; Oct–May daily 9am–5pm.

Château de Salses   This fort has guarded the main road linking Spain and
France since the days of the Romans. Ferdinand of Aragón erected a fort here in
1497, hoping to protect the northern frontier of his kingdom. Even today, Salses
marks the language-barrier point between Catalonia in Spain and Languedoc in
France. This Spanish-style fort designed by Ferdinand is a curious example of an

Iberian structure in France, but in the 17th century it was modified by Vauban to look more like a château. After many changes of ownership, Salses fell to the forces of Louis XIII in September 1642; its Spanish garrison left forever. Some 2 decades later, Roussillon was incorporated into France.

In the town of Salses, 15½ miles north of the city center. (℃ **04-68-38-60-13**. Admission 32F (4.85, $4.65) adults, 21F (3.20, $3.05) under 25, free under 17. Apr–May and Oct daily 9:30am–12:30pm and 2–6pm; June and Sept daily 9:30am–6:30pm; July–Aug daily 9:30am–7pm; Nov–Mar daily 10am–noon and 2–5pm.

ACCOMMODATIONS

La Villa Duflot ★★★   This is the area's greatest hotel, yet its prices are reasonable for the luxury offered. Tranquillity, style, and refinement reign supreme. Located in a suburb, La Villa Duflot is a Mediterranean-style dwelling surrounded by a 3-acre park of pine, palm, and eucalyptus. You can sunbathe in the gardens surrounding the pool and order drinks at any hour at the outside bar. The good-size guest rooms are situated around a patio planted with century-old olive trees. All are spacious and soundproof, with solid marble tub/shower bathrooms and Art Deco interiors. The restaurant (see "Dining," below) is reason enough to stay here.

109 av. Victor-Dalbiez, 66000 Perpignan. (℃ **04-68-56-67-67**. Fax 04-68-56-54-05. www.little-france.com/villa.duflot. 24 units. 640–1,100F (97.30– 167.20, $92.80–$159.50) double. Half-board 560F–790F (85.10– 120.10, $81.20–$114.55) per person double occupancy. AE, DC, MC, V. To get here from the center of town, follow the signs to Perthus–Le Belou and the A9 autoroute, and travel 2 miles south of Perpignan's center. Just before you reach A9, you'll see the hotel. **Amenities:** Restaurant, 2 bars; outdoor pool; room service; laundry. *In room:* A/C, TV, minibar, hair dryer.

Park Hotel ★   This hotel, facing the Jardins de la Ville, offers well-furnished soundproofed rooms. Although the Park is solid and reliable, it's the town's second choice, having none of the glamour of the Duflot. The midsize to spacious rooms are comfortably furnished with taste but not much flair; each comes with an average-size bathroom, most often with tub/shower combination. The restaurant serves up first-class Mediterranean cuisine. Post-nouvelle choices include roast sea scallops flavored with succulent sea urchin velouté, various lobster dishes, and penne with truffles. As an accompaniment, try one of the local wines—perhaps a Collioure or Côtes du Roussillon. The hotel also houses Le Bistrot du Park, a less-expensive eatery specializing in seafood.

18 bd. Jean-Bourrat, 66000 Perpignan. (℃ **04-68-35-14-14**. Fax 04-68-35-48-18. 67 units. 350F–550F (53.20– 83.60, $50.75–$79.75) double. AE, DC, MC, V. Parking 50F (7.60, $7.25). **Amenities:** 2 restaurants, bar; room service; laundry. *In room:* A/C, TV, minibar, hair dryer.

DINING

There is also a wonderful restaurant in the **Park Hotel** (see above).

Côté Théâtre ★ MEDITERRANEAN   Here's your once-in-a-lifetime chance to dine in a 15th-century, dignified stone building that was the former home of a grand inquisitor for the Catholic church. The elaborately crafted wooden ceiling has been designated a historic monument in its own right. The restaurant attracts a quietly conservative crowd who dine under no pretenses. The cuisine is traditional, earthy, and completely unafraid of strong flavors. Menu items include calamari or octopus salad with herbs and vinaigrette; braised sea scallops with shallots; a variety of different fish hauled from local waters, sometimes prepared with flap mushrooms; and deboned and stuffed pig's foot.

7 rue du Théâtre. (℃ **04-68-34-60-00**. Reservations recommended. Main courses 95F–150F (14.45– 22.80, $13.80–$21.75); fixed-price menus 148F (22.50, $21.45) at lunch Mon–Fri, 230F–340F (34.95– 51.70, $33.35–$49.30) dinner and Sat lunch. AE, DC, MC, V. Tues–Sat noon–2pm; Mon–Sat 7:30–10:30pm. Closed 2 weeks in late July–early Aug.

La Villa Duflot ⭐ TRADITIONAL & MODERN FRENCH Slightly removed from the city center, this *restaurant avec chambres* (see also "Accommodations," above) is the most tranquil oasis in the area. Owner André Duflot employs top-notch chefs who turn out dish after dish with remarkable skill and professionalism. Try, for example, a salad of warm squid, a platter of fresh anchovies marinated in vinegar, an excellent foie gras of duckling, or lasagna of foie gras with asparagus points. A wonderful dessert is the chocolate cake with saffron-flavored cream sauce. On the premises is an American bar.

109 av. Victor Dalbiez, 66000 Perpignan. ✆ **04-68-56-67-67.** Fax 04-68-56-54-05. Reservations required. Main courses 95F–130F (14.45– 19.75, $13.80–$18.85); fixed-price menu 200F (30.40, $29) Sat–Sun only. Daily noon–2:30pm and 8–11pm. AE, MC, V. Take N9 from the town center leading to autoroute, exiting at Perpignan Sud (South) heading toward Argeles.

Le Bistrot Gourmand ⭐ *Finds* FRENCH/CATALONIAN In the heart of Perpignan's oldest neighborhood, this charming bistro serves excellent food. It's usually busier at lunch than at dinner. The best items on the menu include mussels in cream sauce, salmon steak with leek-flavored cream sauce, sea bass medallions with sweet white-wine sauce, and beef filet drenched in heady Banyuls wine. Those who crave strong Mediterranean flavors should try an *anchioade* (a paste of grilled anchovies), served with a medley of grilled Languedocien red peppers.

40 rue de la Fusterie. ✆ **04-68-51-21-14.** Reservations recommended. Main courses 60F–95F (9.10– 14.45, $8.70–$13.80); fixed-price menu 65F (9.90, $9.45) at lunch, 85F–115F (12.90– 17.50, $12.35–$16.70) at dinner. V. Mon–Sat noon–2pm and 7–10pm. Closed July–Aug.

PERPIGNAN AFTER DARK

Unlike the towns farther up north in France, Perpignan is permeated by Spanish and Catalan influences. This is especially evident at night, when a round of tapas and late-night promenades are among the evening's social activities. The streets radiating from **place de la Loge** contain a higher concentration of bars and nightclubs than any other part of town.

For a traditional Catalan-style bar with a hip staff, visit **Le Festival,** 40 place Rigaud (✆ **04-68-34-31-60**), a hot spot for tantalizing tapas and heady sangría. But the bars in the center of town, including the **Républic Café,** 2 place de la République (✆ **04-68-51-11-64**), can be stimulating alternatives with their vivacious student scene and live music. The most visible gay and lesbian hangout, featuring both a bar and a disco, is **Le Tapis Volé,** 3 rue Honoré-Daumier (✆ **04-68-63-90-79**), about a half-mile north of the town center. A wide range of savory tapas is served, mostly to a clientele of gay men and women, every day at **La Triquot,** 9 rue Lazare-Escarguel (✆ **04-68-35-19-18**), in the town center. The bar at this place is open Tuesday to Saturday from noon to 3pm, and 6pm to around midnight, depending on business, and tapas are served those same days from noon to 2pm and 7:30 to 10pm.

During summer, the nearby resort complex of **Canet-Plage,** 7½ miles east of Perpignan's historic core, contains a beachfront strip of seasonal bars and dance clubs that come and go with the tides and with midsummer tourism.

7 Carcassonne ⭐⭐⭐

495 miles SW of Paris, 57 miles SE of Toulouse, 65 miles S of Albi

Evoking bold knights, fair damsels, and troubadours, the greatest fortress city of Europe rises against a background of the snowcapped Pyrénées. Floodlit at night, it suggests fairy-tale magic, but back in its heyday in the Middle Ages, all wasn't so romantic. Shattering the peace and quiet were battering rams, grapnels, a mobile tower (inspired by the Trojan horse), catapults, flaming arrows, and the mangonel.

Today the city that served as a backdrop for the 1991 movie *Robin Hood, Prince of Thieves,* is overrun with hordes of visitors and tacky gift shops. But the elusive charm of Carcassonne still emerges in the evening, when thousands of day-trippers have departed and floodlights bathe the ancient monuments.

ESSENTIALS

GETTING THERE   Carcassonne is a major stop for **trains** between Toulouse and destinations south and east. There are 24 trains per day from Toulouse (trip time: 50 min.), 14 trains per day from Montpellier (trip time: 2 hr.), and 12 trains per day from Nîmes (trip time: 2½ hr.). For rail information and schedules, call ✆ **08-36-35-35-35.** If you're **driving,** Carcassonne lies on A61 south of Toulouse.

VISITOR INFORMATION   The **Office de Tourisme** is at 15 bd. Camille-Pelletan (✆ **04-68-10-24-30**) and in the medieval town at Porte Narbonnaise (✆ **04-68-10-24-36**). You can also try the website at www.francetourisme.fr.

SPECIAL EVENTS   The town's nightlife sparkles with real pizzazz during its major summer festivals. The whole month of July is devoted to the **Festival de Carcassonne,** when instrumental concerts, modern and classical dance, operas, and original theater shower the city. Tickets run 140F to 300F (21.30 to 45.60, $20.30 to $43.50) for adults or 60F (9.10, $8.70) for children under 15 and can be purchased by calling ✆ **04-68-11-59-15.** For more information, contact the **Théâtre Municipal** at ✆ **04-68-25-33-13.** On the night of July 14 on **Bastille Day,** one of the best fireworks spectacles in all of France lights up the skies at 10:30pm. In early August, the unadulterated merriment and good times of the Middle Ages overtake the city during the **Spectacles Musicaux.** For information, contact **Carcassonne Terre d'Histoire,** chemin de Serres (✆ **04-68-47-97-97**).

EXPLORING THE TOWN

Carcassonne consists of two towns: the **Bastipe St-Louis** (also known as the Ville Basse or Lower City) and the medieval **Cité.** The former has little of interest, but the latter is among the major attractions in France and the goal of many a pilgrim. The fortifications consist of the inner and outer walls, a double line of ramparts. The inner rampart was built by the Visigoths in the 5th century. Clovis, king of the Franks, attacked in 506 but failed. The Saracens overcame the city in 728, until Pepin the Short (father of Charlemagne) drove them out in 752. During a long siege by Charlemagne, the populace of the walled city was starving and near surrender until Dame Carcas came up with an idea. According to legend, she gathered up the last remaining bit of grain, fed it to a sow, then tossed the pig over the ramparts. The pig is said to have burst, scattering the grain. The Franks concluded that Carcassonne must have unlimited food supplies and ended their siege.

Carcassonne's walls were further fortified by the vicomtes de Trencavel in the 12th century and by Louis IX and Philip the Bold in the following century. However, by the mid-17th century the city's position as a strategic frontier fort was over, and the ramparts were left to decay. In the 19th century, the builders of the Lower Town began to remove the stone for use in new construction. But interest in the Middle Ages revived, and the government ordered Viollet-le-Duc (who restored Notre-Dame in Paris) to repair and, where necessary, rebuild the walls. Reconstruction continued until very recently. Within the walls resides a small populace.

In the highest elevation of the Cité, at the uppermost terminus of rue Principale (rue Cros Mayrevielle), you'll find the **Château Comtal,** place du Château (© **04-68-11-70-77**), a carefully restored 12th-century fortress that's open daily: October to May from 9:30am to 6pm and June to September from 9:30am to 7:30pm. Entrance includes an obligatory 50-minute guided tour, in French and broken English. The cost is 36F (5.45, $5.20) for adults and 23F (3.50, $3.35) for students and persons between 18 and 25. Entrance and participation in the tour are free for anyone under 18. The tour includes access to expositions that display the archaeological remnants that were discovered on-site, plus access to an explanation of the 19th-century restorations that brought the site to its present condition. It's also the only way you'll be able to climb onto the city's inner ramparts, walls that during medieval days provided additional barriers against enemies that might have already penetrated the city's outermost fortifications.

The second most-important monument in the fortifications is the **Basillique St-Nazaire** ⚐, La Cité (© **04-68-25-27-65**), dating from the 11th to the 14th century and containing some beautiful stained-glass windows and a pair of rose medallions. The nave is in the Romanesque style, but the choir and transept are Gothic. The organ, one of the oldest in southwestern France, is from the 16th century. The tomb of Bishop Radulph, from 1266, is well preserved. The cathedral is open daily: July and August from 9am to 7:30pm and off-season from 9:30am to noon and 2 to 5:30pm. Mass is celebrated on Sunday at 11am. Admission is free.

SHOPPING

Carcassonne, more than other French cities, is really two distinct shopping towns in one. In the modern lower city, the major streets for shopping, particularly if you're in the market for clothing, are **rue Clemenceau** and **rue de Verdun**. In the walled medieval city, the streets are chock-full of tiny stores and boutiques selling mostly gift items like antiques and local arts and crafts.

Stores worth visiting include **Cellier des Vigneronnes,** 13 rue du Grand Puits (© **04-68-25-31-00**), where you'll find a wide selection of regional wines ranging from simple table wines to those awarded the distinction of Appellation d'Origine Controlée. Some antiques stores of merit are **Mme Fage-Nunez,** 4 place du Château (© **04-68-25-65-71**), for antique furniture; **Antiquités Safi,** 54 rue de Verdun (© **04-68-25-65-71**), for paintings and art objects; and **Dominique Sarrante,** 13 Porte d'Aude (© **04-68-72-42-90**), for antique firearms.

ACCOMMODATIONS
IN THE CITÉ

Cité ⚐⚐⚐ Originally a palace for whatever bishop or prelate happened to be in control at the time, this is the most desirable hotel in town and has been since 1909. It's constructed into the actual walls of the city, adjoining the cathedral. The hotel has been acquired by the luxury Orient-Express Hotel group and fluffed up to the tune of $3 million. You enter into a long Gothic corridor/gallery leading to the lounge. Many rooms open onto the ramparts and a garden, and feature antiques or reproductions. A few rooms boast brass beds and four-posters, but unit 33 is the only one with a balcony, opening onto views of Carcassonne. Modern equipment has been discreetly installed throughout, including bathrooms of generous size with tub/shower combinations. The hotel is renowned for its restaurant, La Barbacane (see "Dining," below).

Place de l'Église, 11000 Carcassonne. © **04-68-71-98-71**. Fax 04-68-71-50-15. www.hoteldelacite.com. 61 units. 1,500F–2,400F (228– 364.80, $217.50–$348) double; 2,500F–3,500F (380– 532, $362.50–$507.50) suite. AE, DC, MC, V. Parking 90F (13.70, $13.05). **Amenities:** 2 restaurants, bar; outdoor pool; room service; laundry. *In room:* A/C, TV, minibar, hair dryer.

AT THE ENTRANCE TO THE CITÉ

Hôtel du Donjon ★★ *Value*   This little hotel is big on charm and the best value in the moderate range. Built in the style of the old Cité, it has a honey-colored stone exterior with iron bars on the windows. The interior is a jewel, reflecting the sophistication of owner Christine Pujol. Elaborate Louis XIII–style furniture graces the reception lounges. A newer wing contains additional rooms in a medieval architectural style, and the older rooms have been renewed. Their furnishings are in a severe style that's consistent with the artfully medieval look of the nearby ramparts. Each unit comes with a compact tiled bathroom, most with tub/shower. The hotel also runs the nearby Brasserie Le Donjon. In summer, the garden is the perfect breakfast spot.

2 rue du Comte-Roger, 11000 Carcassonne. © **800/528-1234** in the U.S. and Canada, or 04-68-11-23-80. Fax 04-68-25-06-60. www.hotel-donjon.fr. 63 units. 450F–570F (68.40– 86.65, $65.25–$82.65) double; 690F–1,300F (104.90– 197.60, $100.05–$188.50) suite. AE, DC, MC, V. Parking 26F (3.95, $3.75). **Amenities:** Restaurant, bar; room service; laundry. *In room:* A/C, TV, minibar, hair dryer.

IN VILLE-BASSE

Hôtel du Pont-Vieux   One of the best and most reasonably priced hotels in Carcassonne, this rustic boardinghouse lies at the foot of the medieval city. It has been completely restored without losing its provincial French charm. From the elegantly furnished lounge to the quiet reading room, it's cozy and inviting. The medium-size rooms have traditional furnishings and double-glazed windows to cut down on the noise. All except two rooms come with a tub/shower combination. An indoor garden provides a retreat from the crowds.

32 rue Trivalle, 11000 Carcassonne. © **04-68-25-24-99**. Fax 04-68-47-62-71. hoteldupontvieux@ minitel.net. 19 units. 260F–320F (39.50– 48.65, $37.70–$46.40) double; 420F–490F (63.85– 74.50, $60.90–$71.05) quad. Rates include breakfast. AE, DC, V. Parking 35F (5.30, $5.10). **Amenities:** Restaurant; room service; baby-sitting; laundry. *In room:* TV, minibar, hair dryer, safe.

Hôtel Montségur ★ *Value*   This circa 1887 stately town house with a mansard roof and dormers has a front garden that's screened from the street by trees and a high wrought-iron fence. Didier and Isabelle Faugeras have furnished the hotel with antiques, avoiding that institutional look. The rooms, furnished with antiques, are cheaper than you'd imagine from the looks of the place. Michelin ignores it, but this is a good and decent choice. A continental breakfast is available; Didier is the chef at the highly recommended Le Languedoc across the street (see "Dining," below).

27 Allée d'Iéna, 11000 Carcassonne. © **04-68-25-31-41**. Fax 04-68-47-13-22. www.hotelmontsegur.com. 21 units. 395F–495F (60.05– 75.25, $57.30–$71.80) double. AE, DC, MC, V. Free parking. **Amenities:** Restaurant, bar; room service; laundry. *In room:* A/C, TV.

DINING

Au Jardin de la Tour TRADITIONAL FRENCH   This restaurant with its verdant garden infuses greenery and charm into the city's tightly organized medieval core. It's housed in a building from the early 1800s. Within an environment bristling with rustic finds from local antique fairs, you can order from a large selection of salads, beef filet with morels, cassoulet, terrines of foie gras, and all kinds of grilled fish. The cookery is consistently good, relying on fresh ingredients deftly handled by a talented kitchen staff.

11 rue Porte-d'Aude. ℂ **04-68-25-71-24.** Reservations recommended in summer. Main courses 65F–140F (9.90– 21.30, $9.45–$20.30) at lunch, 80F–100F (12.15– 15.20, $11.60–$14.50) at dinner; set menus 90F–120F (13.70– 18.25, $13.05–$17.40). MC, V. Daily noon–2pm and 8–10pm. Closed Nov and Sun–Mon Dec–Easter.

La Barbacane ✪ TRADITIONAL & MODERN FRENCH   Named after the medieval neighborhood in which it sits, this restaurant enjoys equal billing with the celebrated hotel that contains it. Its soothing-looking dining room, whose walls are green with lots of paneling, features the cuisine of noted chef Franck Putelat. Menu items are based on seasonal ingredients, with just enough zest. Examples are green ravioli perfumed with *seiche* (a species of octopus) and its own ink, crisp-fried cod with black olives, saltwater crayfish with strips of Bayonne ham, Breton lobster with artichoke hearts and caviar, and organically fed free-range guinea fowl rubbed with vanilla and stuffed with truffles. A star dessert is a chestnut parfait with malt-flavored cream sauce and date-flavored ice cream.

In the Hôtel de la Cité, place de l'Église. ℂ **04-68-71-98-71.** Reservations recommended. Main courses 150F–360F (22.80– 54.70, $21.75–$52.20); fixed-price menus 390F–530F (59.30– 80.55, $56.55–$76.85). AE, DC, MC, V. Daily 7:30–10pm. Closed Dec–Mar.

Le Languedoc ✪✪ TRADITIONAL FRENCH   Acclaimed chef Didier Faugeras is the creative force behind the inspired cuisine here. The high-ceilinged century-old dining room is filled with antiques; a brick fireplace contributes to the warm Languedoc atmosphere. The specialty is *cassoulet au confit de canard* (the famous stew made with duck cooked in its own fat). It has been celebrated as a much-perfected staple here since the early 1960s. The *pièce de résistance* is tournedos Rossini, with foie-gras truffles and madeira sauce. A smooth dessert is flambéed crêpes Languedoc. In summer you can dine on a pleasant patio or in the air-conditioned restaurant. (Faugeras and his wife, Isabelle, are the owners of the worthy **Hotel Montségur,** just across the street.)

32 allée d'Iéna. ℂ **04-68-25-22-17.** Reservations recommended. Main courses 95F–140F (14.45– 21.30, $13.80–$20.30); fixed-price menus 135F–250F (20.50– 38, $19.60–$36.25). AE, DC, V. Sept–June Tues–Sun noon–2pm and Tues–Sat 7:30–9:30pm. July–Aug Tues–Sun noon–2pm and daily 7:30–9:30pm. Closed Dec 20–Jan 20 and the last week of June.

NEARBY ACCOMMODATIONS & DINING

Château St-Martin ✪ TRADITIONAL & MODERN FRENCH   One of Languedoc's most successful chefs operates out of this 16th-century château at Montredon, 2½ miles northeast of Carcassonne. Ringed by a wooded park, the restaurant serves the superb cuisine of co-owners Jean-Claude and Jacqueline Rodriguez. Dine inside or on the terrace. Recommended menu items are turbot with fondue of baby vegetables, sea bass with scallop mousseline, sole in tarragon, and *confit d'oie carcassonnaise* (goose meat delicately cooked in its own fat and kept in earthenware pots). Two other specialties are *cassoulet languedocienne* and *boullinade nouvelloise* (made with different sorts of fish that include scallops, sole, turbot, and most definitely not a rascasse or hogfish). On the premises are 15 simple, relatively new hotel rooms. Doubles rent for 500F (76, $72.50).

Montredon. ℂ **04-68-71-09-53.** Reservations required. Main courses 100F–170F (15.20– 25.85, $14.50–$24.65); fixed-price menus 170F–320F (25.85– 48.65, $24.65–$46.40). AE, DC, MC, V. Thurs–Tues noon–1:45pm and 7:30–9:45pm. Restaurant is 2½ miles northeast of La Cité. Follow the signs pointing to Stade Albert Domec.

Domaine d'Auriac ★★★ The premier place for food and lodging is this moss-covered 19th-century manor house, boasting gardens with reflecting pools and flowered terraces. The uniquely decorated rooms in this Relais & Châteaux member have a certain photo-magazine glamour; some are in an older building with high ceilings, whereas others have a more modern decor. Rooms range from midsize to spacious, each with an individualized decor and a good-sized bathroom with a tub/shower combination. Bernard Rigaudis sets a grand table in his lovely dining room. In summer, meals are served beside the pool on the terraces. Afterward you might work off lunch on the tennis courts or golf course. The menu changes about five or six times yearly but might include truffles and purple artichokes with essences of pears and olives.

Rte. St-Hilaire, 11000 Carcassonne. © 04-68-25-72-22. Fax 04-68-47-35-54. www.relaischateaux.fr. 26 units. 750F–2,500F (114– 2,500, $108.75–$362.50) double. AE, DC, MC, V. Closed Apr 30–May 8 and Jan. Free parking. Take D104 west 1½ miles from Carcassonne. **Amenities:** Restaurant, bar; laundry/dry cleaning; room service; baby-sitting; outdoor pool. *In room:* A/C, TV, minibar, hair dryer, safe.

CARCASSONE AFTER DARK

Carcassonne nightlife is centered along **rue Omer-Sarraut** (in La Bastide) and **place Marcou** (in La Cité). **La Bulle,** 115 rue Barbacane (© **04-68-72-47-70**), explodes with techno and rock dance tunes for an under-30 crowd that keeps the energy pumping and the place hopping till 4am. The cover charge begins at 50F (7.60, $7.25) per person. Another enduringly popular disco, 2½ miles southwest of town, is **Le Black Bottom,** route de Limoux (© **04-68-47-37-11**), which rocks to every conceivable kind of dance music every Thursday to Saturday beginning at 11pm. Entrance costs 60F (9.10, $8.70) per person.

8 Castres ★

452 miles SW of Paris, 26 miles S of Albi

Built on the bank of the Agout River, Castres is the gateway for trips to the Sidobre, the mountains of Lacaune, and the Black Mountains. Today the wool industry, whose origins go back to the 14th century, has made Castres one of France's two most important wool-producing areas. The town was formerly a Roman military installation. A Benedictine monastery was founded here in the 9th century, and the town fell under the comtes d'Albi in the 10th century. During the wars of religion, it was Protestant.

ESSENTIALS

GETTING THERE From Toulouse, there are eight **trains** per day (trip time: 1 hr.). For rail information and schedules, call © **08-36-35-35-35.** If you're **driving,** Castres is located on N126 east from Toulouse and along N112 south from Albi.

VISITOR INFORMATION The **Office de Tourisme** is at 3 rue Milhau Ducommun (© **05-63-62-63-62**).

EXPLORING THE TOWN

Église St-Benoît The town's most prominent church is an outstanding example of French baroque architecture. The architect Caillau began construction in 1677 on the site of a 9th-century Benedictine abbey, but the structure was never completed according to its original plans. The painting at the church's far end, above the altar, was executed by Gabriel Briard in the 18th century.

Place du 8-Mai-1945. © 05-63-59-05-19. Free admission. Mon–Sat 9am–noon and 1:30–6:30pm; Sun 8:30am–12:30pm. Oct–May, except for religious services, the church is closed to casual visitors every Sun.

Le Centre National et Musée Jean-Jaurès   Dedicated to the workers' movements of the late 19th and early 20th centuries, this collection includes printed material issued by various Socialist factions in France during this era. See, in particular, an issue of *L'Aurore* containing Zola's famous "J'accuse" article from the Dreyfus case. Paintings, sculptures, films, and slides round out the collection.

2 place Pélisson. ℂ **05-63-72-01-01.** Admission 10F (1.50, $1.45) adults, 5F (.75, 75¢) children under 14. Tues–Sun 9am–noon and 2–5pm (Apr–Sept opens at 10am Sun; July–Aug open Mon).

Musée Goya ⚑   The museum is located in the town hall, an archbishop's palace designed by Mansart in 1669. Some of the spacious public rooms have ceilings supported by a frieze of the archbishop's coats-of-arms. The collection includes 16th-century tapestries and the works of Spanish painters from the 15th to the 20th century. Most notable, of course, are the paintings of Francisco Goya y Lucientes, all donated to the town in 1894 by Pierre Briguiboul, son of the Castres-born artist Marcel Briguiboul. *Les Caprices* is a study of figures created in 1799 after the illness that left Goya deaf. Filling much of an entire room, the work is composed of symbolic images of demons and monsters, a satire of Spanish society.

In the Jardin de l'Evêché. ℂ **05-63-71-59-30.** Admission 20F (3.05, $2.90) adults, 10F (1.50, $1.45) children. Apr–Sept Tues–Sat 9am–noon and 2–5pm, Sun 10am–noon and 2–6pm; Oct–Mar Tues–Sun 9am–noon and 2–5pm (July–Aug, open Mon).

ACCOMMODATIONS

Hôtel Renaissance ⚑   The Renaissance is the best hotel in Castres. It was built in the 17th century as the courthouse, then functioned as a colorful but run-down hotel throughout most of the 20th century—until 1993, when it was discreetly restored. Today you'll see a severely dignified building composed of *colombages*-style half-timbering, with a mixture of chiseled stone blocks and bricks. Some rooms have exposed timbers; all are clean and comfortable, evoking the crafts of yesteryear. Each unit contains a midsize bathroom, and all but two are equipped with a tub/shower combination.

17 rue Victor-Hugo, 81100 Castres. ℂ **05-63-59-30-42.** Fax 05-63-72-11-57. 20 units. 410F–530F (62.30– 80.55, $59.45–$76.85) double; 600F–710F (91.20– 107.90, $87–$102.95) suite. AE, DC, MC, V. **Amenities:** Bar; room service; baby-sitting; laundry/dry cleaning. *In room:* TV, hair dryer, iron/ironing board.

DINING

Brasserie des Jacobins *Value* FRENCH/PROVENÇAL   This modern brasserie is a good bet for solid French and Provençal cuisine. So solid in fact, that the menu hasn't changed in years, and most of the patrons are local. Menu items include blanquettes of veal, cassoulets, and caramelized pork filets with Provençal herbs. The decor is rustic, the service is cordial, and many visitors find it especially suitable for a simple noontime meal.

1 place Jean-Jaurès. ℂ **05-63-59-01-44.** Reservations recommended. Main courses 40F–90F (6.10– 13.70, $5.80–$13.05). AE, MC, V. Daily noon–2:15pm and 7–10:30pm.

La Mandragore ⚑ LANGUEDOCIENNE   On an easily overlooked narrow street, this restaurant occupies a small section of one of the many wings of the medieval château-fort of Castres. The decor is consciously simple, perhaps as an appropriate foil for the stone walls and overhead beams. Sophie (in the dining room) and Jean-Claude (in the kitchen) Belaut prepare a regional cuisine that's among the best in town. Served with charm and tact, it might include artichokes with foie gras and truffle-flavored vinaigrette, roast pigeon stuffed with foie gras and served with gâteau of potatoes and flap mushrooms, tuna filet with sweet peppers and cured ham, and magrêt of duckling with truffle oil and braised leeks.

1 rue Malpas. ✆ 05-63-59-51-27. Reservations recommended. Main courses 75F–190F (11.40– 28.90, $10.90–$27.55); fixed-price menu 90F–265F (13.70– 40.30, $13.05–$38.45). AE, DC, V. Mon 7–10pm; Tues–Sat noon–2pm and 7–10pm.

9 Albi ⊛⊛⊛

433 miles SW of Paris, 47 miles NE of Toulouse

The "red city" (for the color of its bricks) of Albi straddles both banks of the Tarn River and is dominated by its brooding 13th-century cathedral. Toulouse-Lautrec was born in the Hôtel Bosc in Albi; it's still a private home and cannot be toured, but there's a plaque on the wall of the building, on rue Toulouse-Lautrec (no number) in the historic town center. The town's major attraction is a museum with a world-class collection of the artist's work.

ESSENTIALS
GETTING THERE   Fifteen **trains** per day link Toulouse with Albi (trip time: 1 hr.); there's also a direct Paris-Albi night train. For rail information and schedules, call ✆ **08-36-35-35-35.** If you're **driving** from Toulouse, take N88 northeast.

VISITOR INFORMATION   The **Office de Tourisme** is in the Palais de la Serbie, place Ste-Cécile (✆ **05-63-49-48-80**).

EXPLORING THE TOWN
Cathédrale Ste-Cécile ⊛⊛⊛   Fortified with ramparts and parapets and containing frescoes and paintings, this 13th-century cathedral was built by a local lord-bishop after a religious struggle with the comte de Toulouse (the crusade against the Cathars). Note the exceptional 16th-century rood screen with a unique suit of polychromatic statues from the Old and New Testaments.

Near place du Vigan, in the medieval center of town. ✆ 05-63-43-23-43. Cathédrale, 5F (.75, 75¢); treasury, 20F (3.05, $2.90). June–Oct daily 9am–7pm; Nov–May daily 9am–noon and 2:30–6:30pm.

Musée Toulouse-Lautrec ⊛⊛   The Palais de la Berbie (Archbishop's Palace) is a fortified structure dating from the late 13th century. Inside, the Musée Toulouse-Lautrec contains the world's most important collection of the artist's paintings, more than 600 in all. His family bequeathed the works remaining in his studio. The museum also owns paintings by Degas, Bonnard, Matisse, Utrillo, and Rouault.

Opposite the north side of the cathedral. ✆ 05-63-49-48-70. Admission 24F (3.65, $3.50) adults, 14F (2.15, $2.05) ages 12–18, free for children under 12. Apr–Sept daily 9am–noon and 2–6pm; Oct–Mar Wed–Mon 10am–noon and 2–5pm. Closed Dec 25, Jan 1.

ACCOMMODATIONS
Hostellerie St-Antoine ⊛⊛   The same family has owned this 250-year-old hotel for five generations; today it's managed by Jacques and Jean-François Rieux. Their mother focused on Toulouse-Lautrec when designing the hotel, since her grandfather was a friend of the painter and was given a few of his paintings, sketches, and prints. Several are in the lounge, which opens onto a rear garden. The rooms have been delightfully decorated, with a sophisticated use of color, good reproductions, and occasional antiques. They're generally spacious,

furnished with French provincial pieces. Most of the midsize bathrooms have tub/shower combinations. Even if you're not staying at the hotel, pay a visit to the dining room. The Rieux culinary tradition is revealed in their traditional yet creative cuisine, and everything tastes better washed down with Gaillac wines.

17 rue St-Antoine, 81000 Albi. © 05-63-54-04-04. Fax 05-63-47-10-47. www.saint-antoine-albi.com. 44 units. 780F–950F (118.55– 144.40, $113.10–$137.75) double; 950F–1,250F (144.40– 190, $137.75–$181.25) suite. AE, DC, MC, V. Parking 40F (6.10, $5.80). **Amenities:** Restaurant; room service; baby-sitting; dry cleaning. In room: A/C, TV, minibar, hair dryer.

Hôtel Chiffre _Value_ This hotel in the city center was built as lodgings for passengers on the mail coaches that hauled letters and people across southern France. Today, despite frequent renovations, it maintains the original porch that used to shelter carriages from the rain and sun. The rooms are outfitted with an artful kind of coziness, usually with upholstered walls in floral patterns, sometimes with views of the inner courtyard. The midsize bathrooms come with tub/shower combinations or just showers. The hotel restaurant, Bateau Ivre, is popular among locals because of its good-value fixed-price menus. The menu named for Toulouse-Lautrec consists of choices that were compiled after his death by his friends, who remembered the way he'd often prepare the dishes himself during his dinner parties, such as radishes stuffed with braised foie gras, supreme of sandre, and duckling roasted with garlic.

50 rue Séré-de-Riviéres, 81000 Albi. © **05-63-48-58-48.** Fax 05-63-47-20-61. www.hotelchiffre.com. 37 units. 380–470F (57.75– 71.45, $55.10–$68.15) double. AE, DC, MC, V. Parking 30F (4.55, $4.35). **Amenities:** Restaurant, bar; room service; laundry. In room: A/C (about 50%), TV, hair dryer.

La Réserve ★★★ This country-club villa set in a 4-acre park on the northern outskirts of Albi is managed by the Rieux family, who also run the Hostellerie St-Antoine. It was built in the Mediterranean style, with tennis courts, a pool, and a fine garden in which you can dine. The rooms, well furnished and color coordinated, contain imaginative decorations (but avoid those rooms over the kitchen); the upper-story rooms have sun terraces and French doors. The modern tiled bathrooms come with deluxe toiletries and showers.

Rte. de Cordes à Fonvialane, 81000 Albi. © **05-63-60-80-80.** Fax 05-63-47-63-60. www.relaischateaux.fr/reservealbi. 23 units. 850F–1,450F (129.20– 220.40, $123.25–$210.25) double; 1,950F (296.40, $282.75) suite. AE, DC, MC, V. Closed Nov–Apr. From the center of town, follow signs to Carmaux-Rodez until you cross the Tarn; then follow signs to Cordes. The hotel is adjacent to the main road leading to Cordes, 1¼ miles from Albi. **Amenities:** Restaurant, bar; outdoor pool; room service; baby-sitting; laundry/dry cleaning. In room: A/C, TV, minibar, hair dryer, safe.

DINING

La Réserve boasts a wonderful restaurant, as does **Hostellerie St-Antoine** (see "Accommodations," above).

Jardin des Quatre Saisons ★★ MODERN FRENCH The best food in Albi is served by Georges Bermond, who believes that menus, like life, should change with the seasons. That's how the restaurant got its name. The setting is a deceptively simple pair of modern dining rooms; the service is always competent and polite. Menu items have been fine-tuned to an artful science and include delicious fricassée of snails garnished with strips of the famous hams produced in the nearby hamlet of Lacaune and ravioli stuffed with pulverized shrimp and served with truffled cream sauce. Most delectable of all—an excuse for returning a second time—is a pot-au-feu of the sea with three or four species of fish garnished with crayfish-cream sauce. The wine list is the finest in Albi.

19 bd. de Strasbourg. ℭ **05-63-60-77-76.** Reservations recommended. Main courses 80F–125F (12.15– 19, $11.60–$18.15); fixed-price menus 95F–185F (14.45– 28.10, $13.80–$26.85). DC, MC, V. Tues–Sun noon–2:30pm; Tues–Sat 7–10pm.

Le Moulin de la Mothe ✸ MODERN FRENCH   One of the best aspects of this well-respected culinary staple is its location within a verdant park on the western bank of the Tarn, with sweeping views over the river and the cathedral. Michel and Marie-Claude Pellaprat celebrate local culinary traditions with verve. In dining rooms flooded with sunlight from big bay windows and surrounded by white brick walls and gleaming paneling, you can order dishes like fried foie gras garnished with local grapes, a "mosaic" of duck meat and fried duck liver, a salad of crisp-fried blood sausage with confit of onions and apples, and lobster salad garnished with red "Chinese" apples. Dessert might include an airy version of a pear soufflé.

Rue de Lamothe. ℭ **05-63-60-38-15.** Reservations recommended. Fixed-price menus 150F–185F (22.80– 28.10, $21.75–$26.85). Main courses 110F–145F (16.70– 22.05, $15.95–$21.05). AE, DC, MC, V. Thurs–Tues noon–2pm; Thurs–Sat and Mon–Tues 7:45–9:15pm. Closed 2 weeks in Feb and 1 week in Nov.

10 Cordes-sur-Ciel ✸✸

421 miles SW of Paris, 15½ miles NW of Albi

This remarkable site is like an eagle's nest on a hilltop, opening onto the Cérou valley. In days gone by, celebrities like Jean-Paul Sartre and Albert Camus considered this town a favorite hideaway.

Throughout the centuries, Cordes has been known for its textile, leather, and silk industries. Even today, it's an arts-and-crafts city, and many of the old houses on the narrow streets contain artisans—blacksmiths, enamelers, graphic artists, weavers, engravers, sculptors, and painters—plying their trades. Park outside; then go under an arch leading to the old town.

ESSENTIALS

GETTING THERE   If you're **driving,** take N88 northwest from Toulouse to Gaillac, turning north on D922 into Cordes-sur-Ciel. If you're coming by **train,** you'll have to get off in nearby Vindrac and walk, rent a bicycle, or take a taxi the remaining 2 miles to Cordes. For train information and schedules, call ℭ **08-36-35-35-35.**

VISITOR INFORMATION   The **Office de Tourisme** is in the Maison Fonpeyrouse, Grand-Rue Raymond VII (ℭ **05-63-56-00-52**).

EXPLORING THE TOWN

Often called "the city of a hundred Gothic arches," Cordes contains numerous *maisons gothiques* ✸✸ built of pink sandstone. Many of the doors and windows are fashioned of pointed (broken) arches that still retain their 13th- and 14th-century grace. Some of the best-preserved ones line **Grande-Rue,** also called **rue Droite.**

Musée d'Art et d'Histoire le Portail-Peint (Musée Charles-Portal) Small, quirky, and relatively unvisited even by residents of Cordes, this somewhat sleepy museum is named after a nearby gateway (the Painted Gate) that pierces the fortifications surrounding the city's medieval center. It's also named for Charles-Portal, an archivist of the Tarn region and a local historian. Set in a medieval house whose foundations date from the Gallo-Roman era, it contains artifacts of the textile industry, farming implements, samples of local embroideries, a reconstruction of an old peasant home, and a scattering of medieval pieces. If you happen to arrive when the museum is closed (which is frequently), ask someone at the tourist office to arrange a private visit at a convenient time.

Grande Rue Haute. ℂ 05-63-56-00-52. Admission 15F (2.30, $2.20) adults, 7F (1.05, $1) for children. Apr–June and Sept–Oct Sun and holidays 3–6pm; July–Aug daily 11am–12:30pm and 3:30–6:30pm. Closed Nov–Mar.

Musée Yves-Brayer   The Maison du Grand-Fauconnier (House of the Falcon Master), named for the falcons carved into the stonework of the wall, contains a grand staircase that leads to the Musée Yves-Brayer. Brayer came to Cordes in 1940 and became one of its most ardent civic boosters. After watching Cordes fall gradually into decay, he renewed interest in its restoration. The museum contains minor artifacts relating to the town's history; the most interesting exhibits are rather fanciful scale models of the town itself.

Grande-Rue. ℂ 05-63-56-00-40. Admission 15F (2.30, $2.20) adults, 7F (1.05, $1) children 11 and under. July–Aug daily 10:30am–12:30pm and 2–6pm; Sept–June Sat–Sun 10am–noon and 2–6pm.

Église St-Michel   The church dates from the 13th century, but many alterations have been made since. The view from the top of the tower encompasses much of the surrounding area. Most of the lateral design of the side chapels probably comes from the cathedral at Albi. Before being shipped here, the organ (dating from 1830) was in Notre-Dame de Paris.

Grande-Rue. The church can be visited only as part of guided visits arranged through the tourist office. With many exceptions, they're usually organized every day at 11am and 3pm, last for about an hour, and cost 25F (3.80, $3.65) for adults and 10F (1.50, $1.45) for students and children under 18.

ACCOMMODATIONS & DINING

Hostellerie du Parc *Value* TRADITIONAL FRENCH   This century-old stone house offers generous meals in a wooded garden or paneled dining room. The specialties include homemade foie gras, duckling, *poularde* (chicken) *occitaine,* rabbit with cabbage leaves, a ballotine of guinea fowl served with sweetbreads, duck braised with foie gras, and a confit of roasted rabbit with pink garlic from the nearby town of Lautrec. The hotel offers 17 simply furnished rooms; a double costs 320F to 470F (48.65 to 71.45, $46.40 to $68.15). The chef even offers French cooking lessons (in English).

Les Cabannes, 81170 Cordes. ℂ 05-63-56-02-59. Fax 05-63-56-18-03. Reservations recommended. Main courses 75F–135F (11.40– 20.50, $10.90–$19.60); fixed-price menus 107F–280F (16.25– 42.55, $15.50–$40.60). AE, DC, MC, V. Mon–Sat noon–2pm and 7–10pm; Sun noon–2pm. Nov–Mar, closed Mon and Sun at dinner. Take rte. de St-Antonin (D600) for about 1 mile west from the town center.

Maison du Grand Ecuyer ★★★ MODERN FRENCH   The medieval monument that contains this restaurant (the 15th-century hunting lodge of Raymond VII, comte de Toulouse) is classified as a national historic treasure. But despite its glamour and undeniable charm, the restaurant remains intimate and unstuffy. Chef Yves Thuriès prepares platters that have made his dining room an almost mandatory stop. Specialties include three confits of lobster, red mullet salad with fondue of vegetables, a confit of pigeon with olive oil and rosemary, and noisette of lamb in chicory sauce. The dessert selection is almost overwhelming.

The hotel contains 12 rooms and one suite, all with antiques and an undeniable sense of the Middle Ages blended discreetly with modern comforts. Doubles cost 750F to 850F (114 to 129.20, $108.75 to $123.25); the suite is

1,300F (197.60, $188.50). The most-desired room, honoring former guest Albert Camus, has a four-poster bed and a fireplace.

Rue Voltaire, 81170 Cordes. ℂ **05-63-53-79-50**. Fax 05-63-53-79-51. grand-ecuyer@thuries.fr. Reservations required. Main courses 150F–210F (22.80– 31.90, $21.75–$30.45); fixed-price menus 170F–470F (25.85– 71.45, $24.65–$68.15). AE, DC, MC, V. Easter–June Tues–Sun 7–9:30pm; July–Oct Wed–Sun noon–2pm and 7–9:30pm. Closed Oct 15–Easter.

11 Toulouse ★★★

438 miles SW of Paris, 152 miles SE of Bordeaux, 60 miles W of Carcassonne

The old capital of Languedoc and France's fourth-largest city, Toulouse (known as La Ville Rose) is cosmopolitan in flavor. The major city of the southwest, filled with gardens and squares, it's the gateway to the Pyrénées. Toulouse has a number of fine old mansions, most of them dating from the Renaissance, when this was one of the richest cities in Europe. Today Toulouse is an artistic and cultural center but also a high-tech center, home to two huge aircraft makers—Airbus and Aerospatiale. Also making the city tick is its extraordinarily high population of students: some 100,000 in all, out of a total population of 600,000.

Toulouse may be a city with a distinguished historical past, but it is also a city of the future and the center of the aerospace industry in France. The National Center for Space Research has been headquartered here for more than 3 decades. The first regularly scheduled airline flights from France took off from the local airport in the 1920s. Today long-range passenger planes of the Airbus consortium, the most important rival in the world to Boeing, are assembled in a gargantuan hangar in the suburb of Colombiers.

ESSENTIALS

GETTING THERE The Toulouse-Blagnac international **airport** lies in the city's northwestern suburbs, 7 miles from the center; for flight information, call ℂ **05-61-42-44-00. Air France** (ℂ **08-02-80-28-02**) has about 25 flights a day from Paris and 2 per day from London. **Air Liberté** (ℂ **08-03-80-58-05**) also flies from Paris about a dozen times each day.

Some 9 high-speed TGV **trains** per day arrive from Paris (trip time: 5 hr.), 8 from Bordeaux (trip time: 2¼ hr.), and 11 from Marseille (trip time: 4½ hours). For rail information and schedules, call ℂ **08-36-35-35-35.** The **drive** to Toulouse from Paris takes 6 to 7 hours. Take A10 south to Bordeaux, connecting to A62 to Toulouse. The Canal du Midi links many of the region's cities with Toulouse by waterway.

VISITOR INFORMATION The **Office de Tourisme** is in the Donjon du Capitole, rue Lafayette (ℂ **05-61-11-02-22;** www.ot-toulouse.fr).

EXPLORING THE CITY

In addition to the sights listed below, the architectural highlights include the Gothic brick **Église des Jacobins** ★★, parvis des Jacobins, in Old Toulouse, west of place du Capitole along rue Lakanal (ℂ **05-61-22-21-92**). The convent, daring in its architecture, has been restored and forms the largest extant monastery complex in France. It's open daily from 10am to 7pm. Admission to most of the complex is free, but a visit to the cloisters is 14F (2.15, $2.05) per person. Small, charming, and dating mostly from the 18th century, the

Basilique Notre-Dame La Daurade is at 7 quai de la Daurade (✆ **05-61-21-38-32**); its name derives from the gilding that covers its partially baroque exterior. It's open daily from 8am to 7pm. Admission is free.

In civic architecture, **Capitole** ⚘, place du Capitole (✆ **05-61-22-29-22**), is an outstanding achievement and one of the most potent symbols of Toulouse itself. Built in 1753, it houses the **Hôtel de Ville** (city hall), plus the **Théâtre du Capitole** (✆ **05-61-63-13-13**), devoted to concerts, ballets, and operas. Renovated in 1996, it's outfitted in an Italian-inspired 18th-century style with shades of scarlet and gold. Admission, which usually includes a view of the theater, is free. The Capitole complex is open Monday to Saturday from 9am to noon and 2 to 6pm (no afternoon hours on Saturday).

After all that sightseeing, head for **place Wilson,** a showcase 19th-century square (it's actually an oval) lined with fashionable cafes.

Basilique St-Sernin ⚘⚘⚘   Consecrated in 1096, this is the largest and finest Romanesque church extant in the Old World. One of its most outstanding features is the Porte Miègeville, opening onto the south aisle and decorated with 12th-century sculptures. The door opening into the south transept is the Porte des Comtes, its capitals depicting the story of Lazarus. Nearby are the tombs of the comtes de Toulouse. Entering by the main west door, you can see the double side aisles that give the church five naves, an unusual feature in Romanesque architecture. An upper cloister forms a passageway around the interior. Look for the Romanesque capitals surmounting the columns.

In the axis of the basilica, 11th-century bas-reliefs depict *Christ in His Majesty.* The ambulatory leads to the crypt (ask the custodian for permission to enter), containing the relics of 128 saints, plus a thorn said to be from the Crown of Thorns. The old baroque retables and shrine in the ambulatory have been reset; the relics here are those of the apostles and the first bishops of Toulouse.

13 place St-Sernin. ✆ **05-61-21-80-45**. Church, free admission; crypt 10F (1.50, $1.45). Church daily 10am–11:30am and 2:30–5pm, though please refrain from sightseeing during Sun morning masses. Crypt Mon–Sat 9am–noon and 2–6pm; Sun noon–6pm.

Cathédrale St-Etienne ⚘   Because of the eons required to build it (it was designed and constructed between the 11th and the 17th centuries), some critics scorn this cathedral for its mishmash of styles; nonetheless, it successfully conveys a solemn dignity. The rectangular bell tower is from the 16th century. A Gothic choir has been added to its unique ogival nave.

Place St-Etienne, at the eastern end of rue de Metz. ✆ **05-61-52-03-82**. Daily 8am–7pm.

Fondation Bemberg   Opened in 1995, this quickly became one of the city's most important museums. Housed in the magnificent Hôtel Assézat (built in 1555, with an unaltered 16th-century courtyard), the museum offers an overview of 5 centuries of European art. The nucleus of the collection represents the lifelong work of collector extraordinaire George Bemberg, who donated 331 works. The largest bequest was 28 paintings by Pierre Bonnard, including his *Moulin Rouge.* Bemberg also donated works by Pissarro, Matisse (*Vue d'Antibes*), and Monet, plus the Fauves. The foundation also owns Canaletto's much-reproduced *Vue de Mestre.* The mansion also houses the **Académie des Jeux-Floraux,** which since 1323 has presented flowers made of wrought metal to poets.

Place d'Assézat, rue de Metz. ✆ **05-61-12-06-89**. Admission 30F (4.55, $4.35). Tues–Wed and Fri–Sun 10am–6pm; Thurs 10am–9pm.

Toulouse

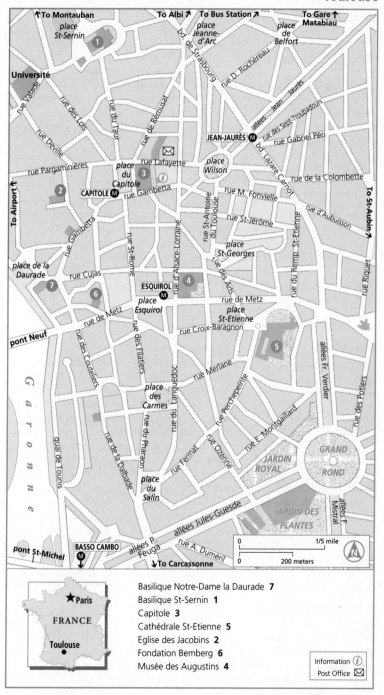

To Montauban ↑   ↗ To Albi   To Bus Station ↗   To Gare ↑ Matabiau

place St-Sernin

place Jeanne-d'Arc

place de Belfort

Université

bd. de Strasbourg

rue D. Rochereau

rue Valade

rue des Lois

rue du Taur

rue de Rémusat

rue Deville

allées Jean Jaurès

rue des Sept-Troubadours

JEAN-JAURÈS Ⓜ

rue Gabriel Péri

rue Pargaminières

place du Capitole

rue Lafayette

place Wilson

rue de la Colombette

CAPITOLE Ⓜ

rue Gambetta

rue M. Fonvielle

To Airport ↑

rue Gambetta

rue St-Rome

rue St-Antoine du Toulouse

rue St-Jérôme

rue d'Aubuisson

To St-Aubin ↑

place de la Daurade

rue Cujas

place St-Georges

rue d'Alsace-Lorraine

rue des Arts

rue du Remp.-St-Etienne

ESQUIROL Ⓜ

place Esquirol

rue de Metz

place St-Etienne

rue Riquet

pont Neuf

rue de Metz

rue des Filatiers

rue Croix-Baragnon

G a r o n n e

rue des Couteliers

rue Merlane

allées Fr. Verdier

place des Carmes

rue du Languedoc

rue Perchepinte

rue E. Montgaillard

allées des Potiers

quai de Tounis

rue du Pharaon

rue Fermat

rue Ozenne

JARDIN ROYAL

GRAND ROND

rue de la Dalbade

place du Salin

allées F. Mistral

JARDIN DES PLANTES

pont St-Michel

BASSO CAMBO Ⓜ

allées P. Feuga

allées Jules-Guesde

rue A. Duméril

↓ To Carcassonne

0		1/5 mile
0	200 meters	

Basilique Notre-Dame la Daurade **7**
Basilique St-Sernin **1**
Capitole **3**
Cathédrale St-Etienne **5**
Eglise des Jacobins **2**
Fondation Bemberg **6**
Musée des Augustins **4**

★ Paris

FRANCE

Toulouse ●

Information ⓘ
Post Office ✉

La Cité de l'Espace ⭐(*Kids*)   This is the place to go to learn what space exploration is all about and how it's done. Some half a million visitors a year come here to learn what it's like to program the launch of a satellite into orbit or how satellites are maneuvered in space. You learn, for example, how easy it is to lose a satellite in space by putting on a burst of speed at the wrong point during a launch. Life-size structural models abound, including a model of an astronaut riding an exercise bike in zero gravity. On the grounds you can walk through a replica of Russia's *Mir* space station. The place is both a teaching tool and a lot of fun to visit. The top floor focuses on exploration of the universe, with close-ups from fly-bys of the moons of Jupiter.

Av. Jean Gonord. ✆ **05-62-71-48-71.** Admission 69.40F (10.55, $10.05) adults, 59F (8.95, $8.55) senior citizens over 60, 48.20F (7.35, $7) children 6–17, free for children 6 and under; family tickets (2 adults, 2 children) 193F (29.35, $28). Tues–Fri 9:30am–6pm; Sat–Sun 9:30am–7pm. Exit 17 of the E. Peripheral Rte. Bus: 19 (only Sat–Sun).

Musée des Augustins ⭐⭐   Conceived as a convent, this museum's 14th-century cloisters contain the world's largest and most valuable collection of Romanesque capitals. The sculptures and carvings are magnificent, and there are some fine examples of early Christian sarcophagi. On the upper floors is a large painting collection, with works by Toulouse-Lautrec, Gérard, Delacroix, and Ingres. The museum also contains several portraits by Antoine Rivalz, a local artist of major talent.

21 rue de Metz. ✆ **05-61-22-21-82.** Admission 14F (2.15, $2.05), free for children 11 and under. Wed 10am–9pm; Thurs–Mon 10am–6pm. Closed May 1, Dec 25, Jan 1.

SHOPPING

When you're in the mood to shop, head for **rue d'Alsace-Lorraine,** which is especially rich in clothing and housewares. This town has a sprawling well-stocked shopping mall, the **Centre Commercial St-Georges,** rue du Rempart St-Etienne, where you can fill your suitcases with all kinds of glittery loot. But for upscale clothing boutiques, head for **rue Croix-Baragnon, rue des Arts,** and **rue St-Antoine du T.** The pearly gates of antiques heaven can be found on **rue Fermat.** More down-market antiques are spread out each Sunday from 8am to noon during the weekly **flea market** conducted adjacent to the Basilique St-Sernin. In addition to that, a once-a-month sale of knickknacks (*brocante*) takes place on the first weekend (Friday, Saturday, and Sunday) from 8am to 1pm.

   Olivier Desforges, 3 place St-Georges (✆ **05-61-12-07-00**), sells the most exotic and luxurious linens in town. Two additional shops that sell everything imaginable connected with violets include **Violettes & Pastels,** 10 rue St-Pantaléon (✆ **05-61-22-14-22**), and **Péniche Maison de la Violette,** Canal du Midi, just in front of the rail station (✆ **05-61-90-01-30**). Inventories include violet-scented perfume, and clothing—especially scarves—patterned with the dainty purple flower.

ACCOMMODATIONS
EXPENSIVE

Sofitel Toulouse Centre ⭐⭐ (*Kids*)   Business travelers deem this hotel the best in town (though we still prefer the Grand Hôtel de l'Opéra as the most tranquil retreat). Adjacent to place Wilson, this Sofitel employs a charming bilingual staff and offers rooms for travelers with disabilities, plus suites big enough to fit an entire family or serve as an office away from the office. The rooms are furnished in an international chain format, and each comes with a bathroom with tub/shower combination.

84 Allée Jean-Jaurès, 31000 Toulouse. ☎ **05-61-10-23-10.** Fax 05-61-10-23-20. www.sofitel.com. 119 units. 1,100F–1,200F (167.20– 182.40, $159.50–$174) double; 1,450F–1,850F (220.40– 281.20, $210.25–$268.25) suite. AE, DC, MC, V. Parking 80F (12.15, $11.60). Métro: Jean-Jaurès. **Amenities:** Restaurant, bar; children's programs; room service; baby-sitting; laundry/dry cleaning. In room: A/C, TV, minibar, hair dryer.

MODERATE

Grand Hôtel de l'Opéra ★★★   This is the most elegant oasis in Toulouse, and the owners have won several prestigious awards for transforming this 17th-century convent into a sophisticated hotel. The public rooms contain early-19th-century antiques and Napoleonic-inspired tenting over the bars. Some of the spacious and stylish guest rooms have urn-shaped balustrades overlooking formal squares, and all have high ceilings and modern amenities. The beds are elegantly attired in tasteful fabrics, fine mattresses, and soft pillows. Each comes with a well-maintained tiled bathroom, with a tub/shower combination. The hotel also runs a brasserie and the town's most prestigious restaurant (see "Dining," below).

1 place du Capitole, 31000 Toulouse. ☎ **05-61-21-82-66.** Fax 05-61-23-41-04. www.grand-hotel-opera.com. 54 units. 900F–1,600F (136.80– 243.20, $130.50–$232) double; 2,000F (304, $290) suite. AE, DC, MC, V. Parking 80F (12.15, $11.60). Métro: Capitole. **Amenities:** Restaurant, brasserie, bar; room service; laundry/dry cleaning. In room: A/C, TV, minibar, hair dryer, safe.

Hôtel des Beaux-Arts ★ 𝓥alue   This charming hotel occupies a richly dignified 250-year-old villa in the heart of town, on the banks of the Garonne. Despite the historic facade, the soundproof rooms are modern, refined, and comfortable. Each contains a quality mattress and some form of original modern art, plus a private bathroom, most with a shower. Breakfast is the only meal served; diners often head for the Brasserie des Beaux-Arts (see "Dining," below), in the same building but with an entrance around the corner.

1 place du pont-Neuf, 31000 Toulouse. ☎ **05-34-45-42-42.** Fax 05-34-45-42-43. contact@hoteldes beauxarts.com. 20 units. 630F–1,000F (95.75– 152, $91.35–$145) double; 1,100F (167.20, $159.50) junior suite. AE, DC, MC, V. Parking 45F (6.85, $6.55). **Amenities:** Nearby restaurant owned by hotel; room service; baby-sitting; dry cleaning. In room: A/C, TV, minibar, hair dryer, safe.

INEXPENSIVE

Hôtel Raymond-IV   Located on a quiet street close to the town center and the train station, this antique building contains pleasantly decorated rooms, each with bland but comfortable furniture and restful mattresses. All units come with a compact bathroom with shower. Although breakfast is the only meal served, the English-speaking staff will direct you to nearby restaurants.

16 rue Raymond-IV, 31000 Toulouse. ☎ **05-61-62-89-41.** Fax 05-61-62-38-01. 38 units. 550F–650F (83.60– 98.80, $79.75–$94.25) double. AE, DC, MC, V. Parking 40F (6.130, $5.80). Métro: Jean-Jaurès or Capitole. In room: TV, minibar.

DINING
EXPENSIVE

Chez Michel Sarran ★★★ MODERN FRENCH   At the most stylish restaurant in Toulouse, you can enjoy the cuisine of rising star Michel Sarran. The two beige-and-salmon dining rooms are in the heart of town, on two separate floors of a building near the Novotel Centre. The walls are upholstered with beige-toned linen from the Provençal upholsterer Soleiado. Sarran's wife, Françoise, oversees the dining rooms. The very fresh, very creative array of dishes have attracted diners as diverse as the prime minister of France and such show-biz types as Sophie Marceau and Gilbert Becaud. The food seems designed to bring out the flavors of southern and southwestern France. Examples are a platter of stuffed seasonal vegetables with anchovy-flavored mayonnaise and ratatouille; a *salade* of braised crayfish with crabmeat and a tapenade of olives; a creamy soup of Belon oysters and foie gras; grilled tuna with caramelized tomatoes and sweet Basque tomatoes stuffed with anchovies; and filet of lamb with prunes, almonds, apples, and thin-sliced ham. Dessert might include ravioli stuffed with creamed oranges and served with an aspic of sweet white Gaillac wine.

21 bd. Armand du Portal. ℭ **05-61-12-32-32.** Reservations recommended. Main courses 120F–300F (18.25– 45.60, $17.40–$43.50); fixed-price menus 250F–550F (38– 83.60, $36.25–$79.75). AE, MC, V. Mon–Fri noon–2pm and 7:30–10pm. Closed Aug and 1 week around Christmas. Métro: Capitole.

Le Pastel ⭐⭐ TRADITIONAL & MODERN FRENCH One of the most luxurious restaurants around Toulouse occupies a stone-sided manor house built around 1850. Today it's the domain of Paris-trained chef/entrepreneur Gérard Garrigues. The setting is as restful as the cuisine is superb: Terraces ringed with flowers and dining rooms accented with paintings by local artists contribute to the placidity. Menu items change about every 2 weeks. During our visit, the menu featured such game dishes as partridge and foie gras cooked in puffy pastry that seals in the juices; filet of sea bass prepared in a minestrone of shellfish; caramelized turnips served as a *"tarte tatin"* and topped with pan-seared foie gras; and pigeon stuffed with pine nuts and dried fruit, served on a bed of braised cabbage. Wine choices are as sophisticated as anything else you're likely to find in Toulouse.

237 rte. de St-Simon. ℭ **05-62-87-84-30.** Reservations required. Main courses 250F–300F (38– 45.60, $36.25–$43.50); fixed-price menus 180F–240F (27.35– 36.50, $26.10–$34.80) at lunch, 290F–450F (44.10– 68.40, $42.05–$65.25) at dinner. MC, V. Tues–Sat noon–2pm and 8–9:30pm. Métro: Basso-Cambo.

Les Jardins de l'Opéra ⭐⭐⭐ TRADITIONAL & MODERN FRENCH The entrance to the city's best restaurant is in the 18th-century Florentine courtyard of the Grand Hôtel. The dining area is a series of intimate salons, several of which face a winter garden and a reflecting pool. You'll be greeted by the gracious Maryse Toulousy, whose husband, Dominique, prepares what critics have called the perfect combination of modern and old-fashioned French cuisine. The outstanding menu listings are likely to include a salad of scallops and purple artichokes; ravioli with foie gras and truffles; red snapper filets with assorted shellfish and vegetables; tournedos of rabbit and fresh foie gras with pepper sauce; and leg of lamb stuffed with exotic mushrooms, braised in saffron. The *poivron rouge et calmar* (calamari stuffed with roasted red pepper and flavored with squid ink) is a tour de force. Desserts feature a sophisticated array of soufflés and tarts, some of which must be ordered at the beginning of the meal. If you forget, console yourself with the luscious roasted figs stuffed with vanilla ice cream and drenched with Banyuls wine.

In the Grand Hôtel de l'Opéra, 1 place du Capitole. ℭ **05-61-23-07-76.** Reservations required. Main courses 180F–390F (27.35– 59.30, $26.10–$56.55); fixed-price menus 230F (34.95, $33.35) at lunch, 300F–500F (45.60– 76, $43.50–$72.50) at dinner. AE, DC, MC, V. Tues–Sat noon–2pm and Mon–Sat 8–10pm. Closed Jan 1–4 and July 28–Aug 29. Métro: Capitole.

MODERATE

Brasserie des Beaux-Arts TRADITIONAL FRENCH This early-1900s brasserie offers an authentic Art Nouveau decor that's been enhanced because of its connection with the Jean Bucher chain. (They're the most successful directors of Art Nouveau French brasseries in the world, with at least a dozen similar places, some of which are classified as national historic monuments.) The carefully restored decor includes walnut paneling and many mirrors, and the cuisine emphasizes well-prepared seafood and all the predictable local dishes, including cassoulet, magrêt of duckling, lightly smoked salmon with lentils and mussels, and confit of duckling. Try the foie gras or country-style sauerkraut, accompanied by the house Riesling, served in an earthenware pitcher. During warm weather, eat on the terrace. The staff is likely to be hysterical during peak times, and when that happens, they tend to become less than suave.

1 quai de la Daurade. ℭ 05-61-21-12-12. Reservations recommended. Main courses 70F–160F (10.65– 24.30, $10.15–$23.20); fixed-price menus 123F and 176F (18.70 and 26.75, $17.85 and $25.50). AE, DC, MC, V. Daily noon–3:30pm and 7pm–1am. Métro: Esquirol.

Chez Émile/La Terrasse d'Émile 🌟 *Finds* TOULOUSIEN   In an old-fashioned house on one of Toulouse's most beautiful squares, this restaurant offers the specialties of chef Christophe Fasan. In winter, meals are served upstairs in a cozy enclave overlooking the square; in summer, the venue moves to the street-level dining room and flower-filled terrace. Menu choices include *cassoulet toulousain,* magrêt of duckling traditional style, a medley of Catalonian fish, and a very fresh parillade of grilled fish with a pungently aromatic cold sauce of sweet peppers and olive oil. The wine list is filled with intriguing surprises.

13 place St–Georges. ℭ **05-61-21-05-56.** Reservations recommended. Main courses 99F–150F (15.05– 22.80, $14.35–$21.75); fixed-price menus 110F–180F (16.70– 27.35, $15.95–$26.10) at lunch, 235F–255F (35.70– 38.75, $34.10–$37) at dinner. AE, DC, MC, V. Tues–Sat noon–2pm and 7–10:30pm (summer, also Mon 7–10:30pm). Métro: Capitole or Esquirol.

INEXPENSIVE

Eau de Folles TRADITIONAL FRENCH   Low prices and the variety of the menu keep patrons coming back to this place. In a room filled with mirrors, you can choose from 10 starters, 10 main courses, and 10 desserts on the fixed-price menu. Choices vary according to the inspiration of the chef and the availability of fresh ingredients. A typical meal might include a marinade of fish, followed by strips of duck meat with green pepper sauce and a homemade pastry such as a *tarte tatin.* Everything is very simple, served in a cramped but convivial setting.

14 Allée du President Roosevelt. ℭ **05-61-23-45-50.** Reservations recommended. Fixed-price menu 150F (22.80, $21.75). No credit cards. Mon–Sat 11:45am–2pm and 7:30pm–1am. Métro: Capitole.

NEARBY ACCOMMODATIONS & DINING

Hôtel de Diane 🌟 *Finds*   This hotel/restaurant surrounded by a 5-acre park is the most tranquil retreat near Toulouse. It occupies an early-1900s villa with comfortable but not particularly opulent rooms that appeal to people who want to be away from the traffic and congestion of the inner city. The bungalow-style units are built in a row facing the park. None has a kitchen, but each has a private terrace and parking. All come with midsize bathrooms, most often with tub/shower. The rustic atmosphere befits this getaway, which has a pool and groves of pines and venerable hardwoods.

3 rte. de St-Simon, 31100 St-Simon. ℭ **05-61-07-59-52.** Fax 05-61-86-38-94. 22 units, 13 bungalows. 450F (68.40, $65.25) double; 510F (77.50, $73.95) bungalow. AE, DC, MC, V. Free parking. Take D23 to exit 27, 5 miles east from Toulouse. **Amenities:** Restaurant; bar; pool; room service; laundry. *In room:* TV, minibar, hair dryer.

La Flanerie *Value*   Situated within a 6-acre garden that slopes down to the edge of the Garonne, this hotel is carved from an 1850 farm. The furnishings for the rooms have been carefully selected and include a high level of style and, in some cases, canopied beds and genuine antiques. A small shower-only bathroom comes with each unit.

Rte. de Lacroix-Falgarde, 31320 Vieille-Toulouse. ℂ **05-61-73-39-12.** Fax 05-61-73-18-56. 12 units. 400F–600F (60.80– 91.20, $58–$87) double. AE, DC, MC, V. Free parking. Bus: R. Take the D4 south of Toulouse for 5 miles. Closed Feb 1–15. **Amenities:** Pool. *In room:* A/C, TV, minibar.

TOULOUSE AFTER DARK

Toulouse has theater, dance, and opera that are often on a par with that found in Paris. The best way to stay on top of the city's arts scene is to pick up a copy of the free monthly magazine *Toulouse Culture* from the Office de Tourisme.

The city's most notable theaters are the **Théâtre du Capitole,** place du Capitole (ℂ **05-61-22-31-31**), which specializes in operas, operettas, and often works from the classical French repertoire; the **Théâtre de la Digue,** 3 rue de la Digue (ℂ **05-61-42-97-79**), site of ballets and works by local theater companies; and the **Halle aux Grains,** place Dupuy (ℂ **05-61-62-02-70**). Thanks to its role as the home of the well-regarded Orchestre du Capitole, under the direction of Michel Plasson, it's the venue for a variety of mostly classical concerts. Another contender is the **Théâtre Garonne,** 1 av. du Château d'Eau (ℂ **05-61-48-56-56**), site of everything from works by Molière to current existentialist dramas. Yet another important entertainment venue is the **Théâtre Zenith,** 11 av. Raymond-Badiou (ℂ **05-62-74-49-49**). Thanks to a large stage and a big seating capacity, it's usually the venue for rock concerts, variety acts, and musical comedies brought here from other European cities. A smaller competitor, with a roughly equivalent mix of music, theater, and entertainment, is the **Théâtre de la Cité,** 1 rue Pierre Baudis (ℂ **05-34-45-05-00**).

The liveliest squares to wander after dark are **place du Capitole, place St-Georges, place St-Pierre,** and **place Wilson.**

For bars and pubs, check out the Latin flair of **La Tantina de Bourgos,** 27 rue de la Garonette (ℂ **05-61-55-59-29**), which is always popular with the student scene; and the rowdier **Chez Tonton,** 16 place St-Pierre (ℂ **05-61-21-89-54**), with its *après-match* frolicking atmosphere complete with the winning teams' boozing it up. A particularly popular bar with both live and recorded music is **Monsieur Carnaval,** 34 rue Bayard (ℂ **05-61-99-14-56**), site of lots of jiving, rocking, and rolling *a la française.* To keep the party going, try out the rock club **Le Bikini,** route de Lacroix-Falgarde (ℂ **05-61-55-00-29**), with its occasional live concerts and endless supply of hot bods and a crowd that doesn't usually exceed age 25.

The disco/restaurant **L'Ubu,** 16 rue St-Rome (ℂ **05-61-23-26-75**), is where the stars come to eat, dance, and be seen. Mostly heterosexuals migrate to **Disco La Strada,** 4 rue Gabrielle-Peri (ℂ **05-34-41-15-65**), which begins to get animated every Wednesday to Saturday after 11pm; and a vaguely Iberian-looking establishment, **Bar La Bodega Bodega,** 1 rue Gabrielle-Peri (ℂ **05-61-63-03-63**). Site of recorded music and a scene that's more hip and fashionable than that at many of its competitors, it features recorded music and a venue where many friends seem to meet spontaneously over drinks.

As you first enter **Le New Shanghai,** 12 rue de la Pomme (ℂ **05-61-23-37-80**), you notice that this is a man's dance domain playing the latest in techno; then, venturing farther inside, you'll discover that it gives way to a darker, sexy cruise-bar environment with lots of hot men on the prowl. Plan on paying 40F (6.10, $5.80) to get in. Another gay disco, mostly favored by men, and among the most popular in the region is **On-Off,** 23 bd. Riquet (ℂ **05-61-62-35-91**). Lesbians appreciate **Le B. Machine,** 37 place des Carmes (ℂ **05-61-55-57-59**), the most popular women's bar in town, which plays recorded music but doesn't have a dance floor.

12 Auch ⓕ

451 miles SW of Paris, 126 miles SE of Bordeaux, 40 miles W of Toulouse

On the west bank of the Gers, in the heart of the ancient Duchy of Gascony, of which it was the capital, the lively market town of Auch is divided into upper and lower quarters, connected by several flights of steps. In the old part of town, the narrow streets (*pousterles*) center on **place Salinis,** from which there's a good view of the Pyrénées. Branching off from here, the **Escalier Monumental** leads down to the river, a descent of 232 steps.

North of the square is the **Cathédrale Ste-Marie** ⓕⓕ, place de la Cathédrale (ⓒ **05-62-05-72-71**). Built from the 15th to the 17th century, this is one of the handsomest Gothic churches in the south of France. It has 113 Renaissance **choir stalls** ⓕⓕⓕ made of carved oak and has impressive stained-glass windows, also from the Renaissance. Its 17th-century organ was one of the finest in the world at the time of Louis XIV. The cathedral is open daily from 8:30am to noon and 2 to 5pm (from 9:30am to noon and 2 to 5pm in winter).

Next to the cathedral stands an 18th-century **archbishop's palace** with a 14th-century bell tower, the **Tour d'Armagnac,** which was once a prison.

For shops and boutiques, walk down **rue Dessoles,** rue de Pouille, and **avenue de l'Alsace.** Here you'll find everything from confectionery shops to clothing stores. Also consider visiting the **Caves de l'Hôtel de France,** rue d'Etigny (ⓒ **05-62-61-71-71**), for a bottle or two of Armagnac. It has the best selection of this firewater, with more than 100 distilleries represented.

ESSENTIALS

GETTING THERE   Five to 10 SNCF **trains** or **buses** per day run between Toulouse and Auch (trip time: 1½ hr.); 6 to 13 SNCF buses arrive in Auch daily from Agen (trip time: 1½ hr.). For more information and schedules, call ⓒ **08-36-35-35-35.** If you're **driving** to Auch, take N124 west from Toulouse.

VISITOR INFORMATION   The **Office de Tourisme** is at place de la Cathédrale (ⓒ **05-62-05-22-89**).

ACCOMMODATIONS & DINING

Hôtel de France (Restaurant Gourmand du Terroir/Brasserie Le Neuvième) ⓕ   This is no longer a mandatory stop in southern France for serious foodies. The hotel is now a solid and reliable choice even if long stripped of its Michelin stars. A lot has changed here since the 1970s, when the Hôtel de France was celebrated. It was built around the much-modernized 16th-century core of an old inn. The rooms are comfortable, conservative, and furnished with French provincial pieces. Some, however, are a bit dowdy. The cuisine here somewhat slavishly follows many of the culinary trends established by the since-departed founder, André Daguin. Today, with kitchens directed by Roland Garreau, the cuisine is "innovative within traditional boundaries." The more glamorous of the two restaurants is Le Jardin des Saveurs. Menu choices include an assortment of preparations of foie gras from Gascony, brochette of oysters with foie gras, a duo of *magrêt de canard* (duck) cooked in a rock-salt shell and served with a medley of vegetables, and stuffed pigeon roasted with spiced honey. You might actually be happier within the hotel's less pretentious and much less expensive Brasserie Le Neuvième.

Place de la Libération, 32003 Auch CEDEX. ⓒ **05-62-61-71-84.** Fax 05-62-61-71-81. auchgarreau@intercom.fr. 29 units. 470F–770F (71.45– 117.05, $68.15–$111.65) double; 900F–1,900F (136.80– 288.80, $130.50–$275.50) suite. AE, DC, , V. Parking 40F (6.10, $5.80). **Amenities:** 2 restaurants, bar. *In room:* A/C, TV, minibar.

18

The Basque Country

The chief interest in the Basque country, a land rich in folklore and old customs, is focused on a small corner of southwestern France, near the Spanish border. Here you can visit the Basque capital, Bayonne, and explore the coastal resorts, Biarritz and St-Jean-de-Luz. In Bayonne's Roman arena, you can see a Spanish-style bullfight. The costume of the Basque men—beret and cummerbund—isn't as evident as it was, but you can still spot it here and there.

The vast Pyrénéan region is a land of glaciers, summits, thermal baths, subterranean grottoes and caverns, winter-sports centers, and trout-filled mountain streams. **Pau** is a good base for excursions to the western Pyrénées. **Lourdes** is the major religious pilgrimage center in France.

REGIONAL CUISINE Several distinct culinary traditions have flourished in and around the Pyrénées: those of the Basque, the Béarn, the Catalán, and the Landes region.

The food of the Pyrénées, also known as *bigorre,* is simple, hearty, and fresh, traditionally served on a table draped with the roughly woven, brightly striped cloths associated with the region. Basque cuisine transforms ordinary ingredients into aromatically tantalizing concoctions, usually with the liberal addition of pepper.

One delicacy is tuna grilled with local herbs over a wood fire and served with chopped garlic, parsley, vinaigrette sauce, and fresh pepper. Other regional specialties include *bigorneaux* (periwinkles), which diners skewer from their shells with toothpicks;

cèpes, meaty flap mushrooms braised with garlic and sprinkled with parsley; and lamb chops, pork chops, and Basque *bourrides* (fish stews), all with dollops of garlic. Basque bouillabaisse is called *ttoro,* and *chipirones* are cuttlefish, which the Basques stuff or stew after beating the flesh to break apart its toughness.

Basque country also produces *pipérade Basque,* scrambled eggs with tomatoes, onions, green peppers, and black pepper. Sausages popular here include *tripoxa,* made from calves' blood and hot peppers; *tripotcha,* from tripe of veal; and *loukinkas,* small garlic-laden sausages. A local sour cider is *pittara,* and the region's best wine is Irouléguy. Bayonne's chocolate is famous through France.

In the Béarn, centered around Pau, the wines are excellent and consumed with the contents of the family *toupi* (soup pot). Many kinds of onion, beet, sorrel, chicory, bacon/cabbage, and garlic/tomato soup are prepared in this pot. Thick, aromatic stews are called *garbure,* and they're not considered suitable unless the ladle can stand upright in the pot. With bread and wine, the garbure is a full meal. The wines of the Béarn are better than those of the Basque country and include its most famous vintage, Jurançon. Sadly for its regional pride, however, sauce béarnaise wasn't created here—it was invented by a Basque chef in Paris.

The Pyrénées are also inhabited by the Cataláns, who do much of their cooking in olive oil with lots of garlic. The Catalán national dish is *ouillade,*

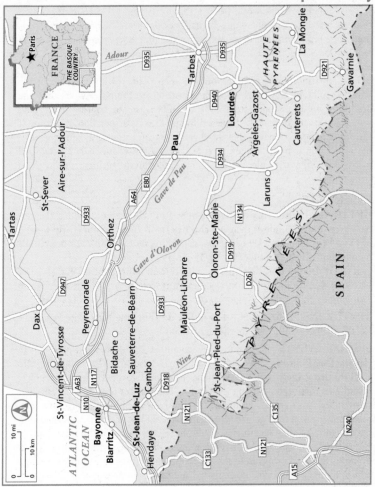

a constantly replenished pair of stew-pots that are never emptied, washed, or cleaned. Catalán bouillabaisse is called *bouillinade* and prepared with crayfish (among other fish) boiled in dry Banyuls wine.

Finally, in the northwestern Pyrénées, the traditional cooking medium is goose fat, which occasionally flavors the aromatic and delicious *cassoulet*. A cassoulet must always be cooked in a *cassoule* (earthenware pot), simmered in an oven for hours, and contain white beans and either goose meat, pork, lamb, partridge, or a combination of any of the above.

1 Lourdes ✦

497 miles SW of Paris, 25 miles SE of Pau

Muslims turn to Mecca, Hindus to the Ganges, but for Catholics, Lourdes is the world's most beloved shrine. Nestled in a valley in the southwestern part of the Hautes-Pyrénées, pilgrims journey here from all over the world. If you're coming in August, be sure to book your hotel as early as possible.

The Roman Catholic world believes that on February 11, 1858, the Virgin revealed herself to a shepherd girl, Bernadette Soubirous. Eighteen such apparitions were reported. Bernadette, subject of the film *Song of Bernadette* starring Jennifer Jones, died in a convent in 1879. She was beatified in 1925, and canonized in 1933.

Her apparitions put Lourdes on the map. The town has subsequently attracted millions of visitors, from the illustrious to the poverty-stricken. The devout are often disappointed by the commercialism of Lourdes today. And some vacationers are acutely disturbed by the human desperation of victims of various afflictions spending their hard-earned savings seeking a "miracle," then having to return home without a cure. However, the church has recognized many "cures" that took place after patients bathed in the springs, labeling them "true miracles."

ESSENTIALS

GETTING THERE   Six **trains** run from Pau (see section 2 in this chapter) daily (trip time: 30 min.); there are also five trains from Bayonne (trip time: 2 hr.) and Paris (trip time 5½ to 9½ hr., depending on the train). For train information and schedules, call © **08-36-35-35-35.**

If you're **driving** from Toulouse, take N117 west until you reach Tarbes. From here take N21 south to Lourdes. From Paris, follow A10 south to Vierzon, changing to N20 south to Limoges, continuing on N21 south to Lourdes.

VISITOR INFORMATION   The **Office de Tourisme** is on place Peyramale (© **05-62-42-77-40;** www.lourdes-france.com).

SPECIAL EVENTS   From July 1 to September 20, tourists and pilgrims can join the **Day Pilgrims** (*Pélerin d'un Jour*) (© **05-62-42-78-78**), a pilgrimage (in English) that gathers at 8:30am at the statue of the Crowned Virgin for a prayer meeting in the meadow facing the Grotto. The services include a 9:30am Stations of the Cross and an 11am mass. At 2:30pm, assembling at the same spot, pilgrims are taken on a guided visit to the Sanctuaries, or places associated with Bernadette. In the Sanctuaries you'll hear the story of Lourdes and of Bernadette, complete with a free 30-minute slide show (also in English). At 4:30pm there's a Procession of the Blessed Eucharist, starting from the Grotto. The 8:45pm Marian celebration, rosary, and torchlight procession all start from the Grotto as well.

EXPLORING THE TOWN & ITS ENVIRONS

At the **Grotto of Massabielle** the Virgin is said to have appeared 18 times to Bernadette between February 11 and July 16, 1858. This site is accessible to pilgrims both day and night, and mass is celebrated every day. The Statue of Our Lady depicts the Virgin in the posture she is said to have taken in the place she reputedly appeared, saying to Bernadette in Pyrénéan dialect, "I am the Immaculate Conception."

At the back of the Grotto, on the left of the altar, is the **Miraculous Spring** that reportedly spouted on February 25, 1858, during the ninth apparition, when Bernadette scraped the earth. The Virgin is said to have commanded her, "Go and drink at the spring and wash there." The water from this spring is collected in several reservoirs, from which you can drink.

The **Upper Basilica,** at place du Rosaire, was built in the 13th-century ogival style but wasn't consecrated until 1876. It contains one nave split into five equal bays. Votive tablets line its interior. On the west side of the square is the

Rosary Basilica, with two small towers. It was built in 1889 in the Roman-Byzantine style and holds up to 4,000 people. Inside, 15 chapels are dedicated to the "mysteries of the rosary."

The oval **Basilica of Pius X,** 1 av. Monseigneur Théas, was consecrated in 1958. An enormous underground chamber covered by a concrete roof, it's 660 feet long and 270 feet wide, holding as many as 20,000 people. It's one of the world's largest churches. It's open daily from 7am to 7pm. International masses are conducted in six languages, including English, every Wednesday and Sunday at 3:30am from Easter to October.

Nearby, the **Musée Ste-Bernadette** (© 05-62-42-78-78) contains scenes from the life of the saint; it's open daily from 10am to noon and 2:30 to 5pm (call ahead during winter). Bernadette devotees will also seek out the **Maison Natale de Bernadette,** rue Bernadette-Soubirous (© 05-62-42-16-36), where the saint was born on January 7, 1844, the daughter of a miller. Her former home is open November to March daily 3 to 5pm and April to October daily 9am to noon and 2 to 6:30pm. This was actually her mother's house. Bernadette's father, François Soubirous, had his home in another mill, **Moulin Lacadé,** at 2 rue Bernadette-Soubirous. You can visit daily from 9am to noon and 2 to 7pm in summer; in winter daily 2:15 to 5:45pm. Entrance to each of these sites costs 5F (.75, 75¢).

You can visit the privately owned and overly commercialized wax museum, **Musée Grévin,** 87 rue de la Grotte (© 05-62-94-33-74), where displays retrace not only Bernadette's life but also the life of Christ, with a bad reproduction of Leonardo da Vinci's *Last Supper*. In February, March, November, and December, it is open daily 2 to 6pm. April to October, hours are daily 9 to 11:30am and 1:30 to 6:30pm. Closed in January. Admission is 35F (5.30, $5) adults, 17.50F (2.65, $2.55) children ages 6 to 12, and children under 6 free.

If you want a panoramic view, take an elevator to the terrace of the **Château-Fort de Lourdes,** an example of medieval military architecture. The castle contains the **Musée Pyrénéen,** 25 rue du Fort (© 05-62-42-37-37), with regional handcrafts and costumes, including a collection of dolls in nuns' habits. In the courtyard are scale models of different styles of regional architecture. Both the château and the museum can be visited April to September, daily 9am to noon and 1:30 to 6:30pm; off-season it closes at 6pm and is closed Tuesday. Admission is 32F (4.85, $4.65) adults, 16F (2.45, $2.30) children 6 to 12, and children under 6 free.

A final site worth a brief visit is **Planète Aquarium,** 71 av. Alexandre Marqui (© 05-62-42-01-00), which features a collection of freshwater fish from the streams and lakes of the Pyrénées. Admission costs 55F (8.35, $8) adults, 39F (5.95, $6) students and persons under 25. The aquarium is open daily October to March, noon to 5pm; April to June and September 10am to 6pm; July and August 10am to 8pm.

OUTDOOR PURSUITS   Lourdes is a good base for exploring the Pyrénées. You can take tours into the snowcapped mountains across the border to Spain or go horseback riding near **Lac de Lourdes,** 2 miles northwest of town. Among the outstanding sites is **Bagnères-de-Bigorre**, a renowned thermal spa 14 miles east of Lourdes via D935. Visit **Pic du Jer** for a panoramic vista of the countryside—to get here board the funicular in Lourdes south of Esplanade des processions; one-way fare is 22F (3.35, $3.20) adults, 11F (1.65, $1.60) children under 18. The **Caves of Medous,** an underground river with stalactites, are located southeast of Lourdes via D26; they're open April to October and admission is 38F (5.80, $6) adults, 19F (2.90, $2.75) children under 18. For a full-day tour, go south of Lourdes along D921 to the **Heights of Gavarnie** (*Cirque de Gavarnie*), at 4,500 feet one of France's great natural wonders.

ACCOMMODATIONS

The two restaurants reviewed below also offer rooms.

Grand Hôtel de la Grotte ★   The Grand Hôtel is an old favorite, having catered to pilgrims (and to an increasing degree, tourists) since 1870. It's furnished in a comfortable upper-bourgeois French decor that's being updated. Some rooms on the upper floor open onto one of the most panoramic views in town, not only of the sanctuaries and the river but of the mountains. Rooms on the basilica side tend to be noisy. Each comes with a modernized midsize bathroom. The hotel has a garden beside the banks of the river Gave de Pau.

66–68 rue de la Grotte, 65000 Lourdes. ✆ **05-62-94-58-87.** Fax 05-62-94-20-50. www.hotel-grotte.com. 83 units. 430F–800F (65.35– 121.60, $62.35–$116) double; 1,300F (197.60, $188.50) junior suite. AE, DC, MC, V. Closed Oct 30–Mar. Bus: 2. **Amenities:** Restaurant (French/regional); room service; laundry. *In room:* A/C, TV, minibar.

Hôtel Adriatic   Built in the town center during the 1970s, this hotel offers clean, well-maintained, and uncluttered rooms, somewhat spartan, but comfortable. Bathrooms are small to midsize. The location is close to the shrines, the home of St. Bernadette, the parish church, and the town's fortified castle.

4 rue Baron-Duprat, 65100 Lourdes. ✆ **05-62-94-31-34.** Fax 05-62-94-14-70. 87 units. 315F–395F (47.90– 60.05, $45.70–$57.30) double. AE, MC, V. Closed mid-Dec to mid-Feb. Bus: 2. **Amenities:** Restaurant, bar; room service; laundry. *In room:* TV, minibar (23 rooms), hair dryer.

Hôtel Galilée et Windsor   This government-rated three-star hotel, often confused with the more comfortable, more expensive Gallia et Londres, remains a favorite ever since it was built after the war. Rooms are pleasant, if dull and anonymous-looking. Each is equipped with a small shower-only bathroom. Since this is one of the largest hotels in Lourdes, it's a magnet for religious groups.

10 av. Peyramale, 65100 Lourdes. ✆ **05-62-94-21-55.** Fax 05-62-94-53-66. 163 units. 450F–480F (68.40– 72.95, $65.25–$69.60) double. Rates include breakfast. AE, DC, MC, V. Closed Nov–Easter. **Amenities:** Restaurant (regional/continental), bar. *In room:* TV, minibar, hair dryer, safe.

Hôtel Gallia et Londres   This old-fashioned choice, dating from 1880, is still a viable candidate because of the major improvements and renovations it underwent in 1998. There was a complete overhaul of the bedrooms and an upgrade in the quality of the mattresses. All rooms contain a midsize bathroom. Most guests here are part of religious groups that tend to book en masse.

26 av. Bernadette-Soubirous, 65100 Lourdes. ✆ **05-62-94-35-44.** Fax 05-62-42-24-64. 90 units. 660F (100.30, $95.70) double. Rate includes breakfast. AE, MC, V. Closed Nov–Apr. **Amenities:** Restaurant, bar; free use of a pool next door; laundry. *In room:* TV, minibar.

Hôtel Notre-Dame de France   Located next to the Galilée et Windsor, this hotel is less than 100 yards from the main monument (the sanctuaries associated with the visions of Bernadette). Originally built around 1928, it underwent radical rebuilding in the late 1980s that eliminated virtually every vestige of its Art Deco detailing. It offers clean, simple, no-frills rooms with almost monastic furnishings, plus small bathrooms with shower units. Some pilgrims appreciate the emphasis here on religious activities. Overall, it's a worthy budget choice.

8 av. Peyramale, 65100 Lourdes. ✆ **05-62-94-91-45.** Fax 05-62-94-57-21. jean-michel.imbert@wanadoo.fr. 76 units. 340F–350F (51.70– 53.20, $49.30–$50.75) double. Half-board 290F (44.10, $42.05) extra per person. AE, MC, V. Closed Nov–Mar 15. Free parking. Bus: 2. **Amenities:** Restaurant, bar; laundry. *In room:* hair dryer.

DINING

Relais de Saux BIGORRE   This is the area's best restaurant, housed in an ivy-covered manor. It specializes in the mountain cuisine of the Pyrénées. The carved-wood fireplaces complement the beamed ceilings, silk-upholstered walls, and rustic artifacts. Innkeepers Madeleine and Bernard Heres supervise meals. Begin with a selection of hot or cold hors d'oeuvres, ranging from beet flan with cheese fondue to smoked swordfish. The boneless quail and the escalope of warm duck liver are especially delectable.

Upstairs are six guest rooms, some with large windows overlooking the garden. A double costs 500F to 580F (76 to 88.15, $73 to $84).

Rte. de Tarbes (N21), 65100 Lourdes. ✆ **05-62-94-29-61.** Fax 05-62-42-12-64. Reservations recommended. Fixed-price menus 140F–310F (21.30– 47.10, $20.30–$44.95) at lunch, 180F–310F (27.35– 47.10, $26.10–$44.95) at dinner. AE, DC, MC, V. Daily noon–2pm and 7:15–9:30pm. Take N117 2 miles northeast of Lourdes to the village of Saux. From there follow the signs to Tarbes.

Taverne de Bigorre et Hôtel d'Albret BIGORRE   This restaurant offers some of the best food in town; tournedos with flap mushrooms are a specialty. You can also order such country dishes as escalope of hot duck foie gras and duck steak kebab with green peppercorn sauce. The trout is especially good here, and an award-winning dessert is a frozen Grand Marnier soufflé with raspberry sauce and cream.

Hôtel d'Albret is one of the best budget hotels in Lourdes, with 27 comfortable rooms. A double costs 200F to 295F (30.40 to 44.85, $29 to $43), with half-board at 197F to 250F (29.95 to 38, $29 to $36) per person extra.

21 place du Champs-Commun, 65100 Lourdes. ✆ **05-62-94-75-00.** Fax 05-62-94-78-45. Reservations recommended. Main courses 60F–135F (9.10– 20.50, $8.70–$19.60); fixed-price menus 75F–150F (11.40– 22.80, $10.90–$21.75). AE, DC, MC, V. Daily noon–1:30pm and 7–9pm. Closed Nov 20–Mar 15.

2 Pau ★★★

477 miles SW of Paris, 122 miles SW of Toulouse

High above the banks of the Gave de Pau River, this year-round resort is a good place to pause in your trek through the Pyrénées. The British discovered Pau in the early 19th century, launching such practices as fox hunting, a custom that's lingered. Even if you're just passing through, go along boulevard des Pyrénées, an esplanade erected on Napoléon's orders, for a famous panoramic view.

Today Pau is the most cosmopolitan city in the western Pyrénées, the capital of the Pyrénées-Atlantiques *département*. It was once the capital of the Béarn region, the land of the kings of Navarre, the most famous and beloved of who was Henri IV. Its population of approximately 90,000 still observes some English traditions, such as afternoon tea. At one time the English formed 15% of the population, but with the arrival of two world wars, many of them left.

ESSENTIALS

GETTING THERE   Pau-Uzein airport is 7½ miles north of town; call ✆ **05-59-33-33-00** for flight information. There are good **train** connections from Biarritz (six per day taking 1½ hr.); for train information and schedules, call ✆ **08-36-35-35-35. Driving** to Pau is relatively easy because of its location along the N117 roadway, which is directly accessible from Toulouse. From Paris, take A10 south to Vierzon, changing to N20 south to Limoges, continuing on N21 south to Tarbes, and finally turning west along N117 to Pau.

VISITOR INFORMATION The **Office de Tourisme** is on place Royale (© **05-59-27-27-08**).

SPECIAL EVENTS For 2 days in May, there's the **Grand Prix de Pau,** where race cars from around France compete for speed records in what might remind you of a small-scale replica of the Grand Prix in Monaco. During June and early July, as part of the **Festival de Pau,** the municipality arranges for frequent theatrical, musical, and dance performances, either in public squares, in the streets, or in the courtyard of the château. Many of the events within the festival are presented in public venues for free; if there is a charge, it usually ranges from 80F to 200F (12.15 to 30.40, $12 to $29) for the various events. The local tourist office has complete details.

EXPLORING THE CITY

The heart of the commercial district is busy **place Clémenceau,** out of which radiate at least five boulevards. At the western end of town stands the **Château de Pau** ✪, 2 rue du Château (© **05-59-82-38-00**), dating from the 12th century and steeped in the Renaissance spirit of the bold Marguerite de Navarre, who wrote the bawdy *Heptaméron* at age 60. The castle has seen many builders and tenants. Louis XV ordered the bridge that connects the castle to the town, whereas the great staircase hall was commissioned by Marguerite herself. Around 1840, Louis-Philippe had the apartments redecorated. Inside are many souvenirs, including a crib made of a single tortoise shell for Henri de Navarre, who was born here. There's also a splendid array of Flemish and Gobelin tapestries. The great rectangular tower, **Tour de Gaston Phoebus,** is from the 14th century.

Another intriguing area within the château is **La Salle aux 100 Couverts,** site of some of the enormous receptions that were held here during the building's heyday. The château is open daily 9:30 to 11:45am and 2 to 5:15pm. Admission is 25F (3.80, $3.65) adults and 17F (2.60, $2.45) students 18 to 25, children under 18 free. **Musée des Beaux-Arts** ✪, rue Mathieu-Lalanne (© **05-59-27-33-02**), displays a collection of European paintings, including Spanish, Flemish, Dutch, English, and French masters, such as El Greco, Zurbarán, Degas, and Boudin. It's open Wednesday to Monday 10am to noon and 2 to 6pm. Admission is 10F (1.50, $1.45) adults and 5F (.75, 75¢) children.

SHOPPING

Pau affords ample opportunities for you to buy some authentic regional specialties, such as mouthwatering chocolates, sweet jams, and Basque antiques. The pedestrian **rue Serviez** and **rue des Cordelières** harbor an array of petit boutiques and shops that carry many of these items, as do **rue Louis-Barthou, rue Henry-IV,** and **rue du Maréchal-Foch.**

Pau is home to some of the best antiques shops in the region, such as **Champeau Paul,** 14 rue Castetnau (© **05-59-02-40-03**), with its mélange of 18th- to 20th-century treasures for the home. The area around the château is well known as the antiques center of town. On Saturday, Sunday, and Monday 10am to 6pm, you'll find a large **flea market** on place du Forail, selling everything from antiques to modern-day gadgets.

The best-known shop in Pau is the **Musée de la Confiture,** 48 rue du Maréchal Joffre (© **05-59-27-69-51**), which attracts gourmets from throughout France. It's owned by Mr. Miot, voted "Best Jammaker in France," and "best candy-maker in France" several years in a row. In addition to jams made from every Pyrénéan berry, the shop also stocks a selection of bonbons whose star and centerpiece, a *coucougnette*, is a jam-filled chocolate that he invented himself.

ACCOMMODATIONS

Hôtel Continental   The centrally located Continental is the largest, most prominent hotel in Pau. Renovated several times since its original construction around 1900, it's the best of a lackluster lot in town. Rooms are functionally decorated, modernized, and soundproofed. About 65 come with a midsize bathroom with tub and shower combination; the rest with shower units.

2 rue du Maréchal-Foch, 64000 Pau. ℂ 05-59-27-69-31 or 800/528-1234 in the U.S. Fax 05-59-27-99-84. www.bestwestern.com. 80 units. 400F–600F (60.80– 91.20, $58–$87) double. AE, DC, DISC, MC, V. Free parking in garage. **Amenities:** Restaurant; room service; baby-sitting; laundry. *In room:* TV, minibar, hair dryer.

Hôtel de Gramont   Within walking distance of the château and the rail station, this hotel is a truly impressive building. The châteaulike structure has street-level arcades and high-ceilinged soundproofed rooms. Although not as impressive as the exterior, the rooms are simply furnished with reasonably comfortable mattresses, plus small shower-only bathrooms.

3 place Gramont, 64000 Pau. ℂ **05-59-27-84-04.** Fax 05-59-27-62-23. www.hotel-gramont.fr. 36 units. 280F–400F (42.55– 60.80, $40.60–$58) double; 555F (84.35, $80.50) suite. AE, DC, DISC, MC, V. Closed Dec 23–Jan 2. *In room:* A/C (10 rooms), TV.

Hôtel Le Postillon   This is a cozy hotel, with French provincial decor and a flower-filled courtyard. Rooms are comfortably furnished, each individually decorated. Some have a balcony overlooking the garden. All come with small shower-only bathrooms. The reasonable price keeps the place consistently full. Breakfast is the only meal served, but there's a choice of restaurants nearby.

Place de Verdun, 10 cours Camou, 64000 Pau. ℂ **05-59-72-83-00.** Fax 05-59-72-83-13. 25 units. 265F–325F (40.30– 49.40, $38.45–$47.15) double. DC, V. Bus: 1. *In room:* TV.

Hôtel-Restaurant Corona   This is a solid choice if your expectations aren't too high. The French architect who designed this hotel had completed many commissions in Montréal. In honor of them, he added what were considered at the time many Canada-inspired touches, including the ample use of exposed pinewood. Situated about a mile east of the center of Pau, this hotel offers comfortable accommodations. Rooms range from midsize to spacious, and each comes with an adjoining bathroom.

71 av. du Général-Leclerc, 64000 Pau. ℂ **05-59-30-64-77.** Fax 05-59-02-62-64. 20 units. 250F–350F (38– 53.20, $36.25–$50.75) double. AE, DC, MC, V. **Amenities:** 2 restaurants, bar; laundry. *In room:* A/C, TV, hair dryer.

DINING

Au Fin Gourmet *(Value* BASQUE   This restaurant is maintained by Christian, Laurent, and Patrick, sons of the retired founder, Clément Ithurriague. It offers an outdoor terrace for warm-weather dining and a cuisine based almost exclusively on regional ingredients. Menu items include marinated codfish with herbs from the kitchen garden and bouillon-flavored potatoes, grilled duck liver with peppers, rack of lamb flavored with herbs from the Pyrénées in a parsley-enriched crust, sliced and sautéed foie gras, and braised stuffed trout. Dessert might include four different variations of caramel arranged on the same platter.

24 av. Gaston-Lacoste. ℂ **05-59-27-47-71.** Reservations recommended. Main courses 80F–130F (12.15– 19.75, $11.60–$18.85); fixed-price menus 100F–170F (15.20– 25.85, $14.50–$24.65). AE, DC, MC, V. Tues–Sun noon–2:15pm; Tues–Sat 7–10pm.

Chez Pierre ✿ BÉARNAISE/FRENCH   Year after year, we always have our finest meal in Pau at Chez Pierre, where regional products are spun into creative dishes. Chef Raymond Casau, who spent years apprenticing with some of the most successful chefs in France, is among the finest around, and his specialties are sole braised with wine, fresh salmon braised with Jurançon (a sweet, golden Pyrénéan wine), and a Béarnais version of cassoulet (it employs different sausages than the version found in Toulouse, and places a greater emphasis on confit of goose) One of the most attractive bars in town, outfitted like the club room of an English golf course, is adjacent to the dining rooms.

Rue Louis-Barthou. 📞 **05-59-27-76-86.** Reservations required. Main courses 115F–200F (17.50– 30.40,$16.70–$29); fixed-price menu 200F (30.40, $29). AE, DC, MC, V. Mon–Fri noon–2:30pm; Mon–Sat 7–10pm.

La Gousse d'Ail BASQUE   A few blocks from the château, this restaurant offers a stone, brick, and stucco interior with ceiling beams and a fireplace. The place is small-scale, medieval-looking, and permeated with a respect for the culinary techniques and ingredients of the Basque country. Fixed-price menus might include a version of scallops and shrimp cooked with Jurançon, fresh pasta with flap mushrooms and foie gras, or a confit of duck thighs with french fries that are cooked in the duck's own juices. Desserts and breads are homemade, and the menu changes with the season.

12 rue du Hédas. 📞 **05-59-27-31-55.** Fixed-price lunch 78F–207F (11.85– 31.45, $11.30–$30), fixed-price dinner 107F–207F (16.25– 31.45, $15.50–$30). MC, V. Sun–Fri noon–1:30pm; Mon–Sat 7–10:30pm.

ACCOMMODATIONS & DINING NEARBY

Some of the world's most discerning people head to the town of Eugénie-les-Bains, about 33 miles north of Pau, in search of the marvelous domain of Michel Guérard. The town has no rail station, so most people drive from Pau. To get there, take N134 north to the town of Garlin; then follow the unmarked road west to the town of Geaune and follow signs to Eugénie-les-Bains.

Les Prés d'Eugénie (Michel Guérard) ✿✿✿ BASQUE   This Relais & Châteaux is the creation of Michel Guérard, the innovative chef whose *cuisine minceur* started a culinary revolution in the early 1970s. It attracts a stream of diners who appreciate the calm surroundings, the much-publicized cooking, and the endless expansions of its owner. Offered here are both *cuisine minceur,* so that calorie counters can still enjoy well-seasoned flavors and fresh ingredients, and the heartier *cuisine gourmand,* whose traditions are influenced by Basque and classic French recipes. Dishes are constantly evolving here, usually tapping into a sense of regional sentimentality, as in the case of "bourgeois-style" veal chops fried "over low flame in a corner of the fireplace." Specialties include cream of crayfish soup, freshwater crayfish roasted with limes, whiting in white-wine sauce, mullet steamed with seaweed and oysters, lamb steamed with fennel, and a wide variety of simply steamed fish with fresh vegetables.

Those unwilling to pay the stratospheric prices in the main restaurant sometimes select a table in a satellite restaurant operated by M. Guérard called **La Ferme aux Grives.** The cuisine here focuses on more-rural specialties of the region, offering a single fixed-price menu at 220F (33.45, $32). Comfortable and rustically elegant, it's open for lunch and dinner every Wednesday to Sunday. A typical specialty includes brochettes of free-range chicken cooked on a skewer.

In addition to the restaurants, there are a variety of accommodations. The most comfortable, and expensive, are the eight high-ceilinged units within an outlying annex, **Le Couvent des Herbes.** They cost 1,800F to 2,300F (273.60 to 349.60, $261 to $334) for a double and from 2,500F to 3,000F (380 to 456, $363 to $435) for a suite. Slightly less glamorous are the 35 units within the main building, renting for 1,500F to 2,300F (228 to 349.60, $218 to $334) each, and from 2,500F to 3,000F (380 to 456, $363 to $435) for a suite. Rooms are decorated in the style of a manor house in the French countryside. Less expensive, and geared to the family-with-children trade, are the 32 units within **La Maison Rose,** where double occupancy costs from 490F to 1,300F (74.50 to 197.60, $71 to $189). Some units contain kitchenettes.

Eugénie-les-Bains, 40320 Beaune. ✆ **05-58-05-06-07.** Fax 05-58-51-10-10. Reservations recommended. Main courses 200F–380F (30.40– 57.75, $29–$55.10); fixed-price menus 650F–1,200F (98.80– 182.40, $94.25–$174). AE, DC, MC, V. Fri–Tues 12:30–2pm; Thurs–Tues 7:30–10pm (July–Aug, open daily). Closed Jan.

PAU AFTER DARK

The highest concentration of nightlife in Pau occurs within **Le Triangle,** an area in the town center flanked by the rue Emile-Garet, rue Lespy, and rue Castetnau. Within those confines, you'll find our favorite bars, **Le Garage,** 49 rue Emile-Garet (✆ **05-59-83-75-17**); the rough but congenial **Le Béarnais,** 3 rue Lespy (✆ **05-59-83-72-11**), with its fun staff and convivial atmosphere; and **Le Caveau,** 18 rue Castetnau (✆ **05-59-27-35-37**), more laid-back and not as loud. But if you need a more diverse and older crowd, check out the streets around the château. At **Le Paradis,** 11 place du Forail (✆ **05-59-84-06-73**), all ages mix, mingle, and bop the night away on the huge dance floor to the beat of Top-40 tunes. Covers range between 45F and 60F (6.85 and 9.10, $7 and $9).

3 Bayonne ★★

478 miles SW of Paris, 114 miles SW of Bordeaux

Bayonne is not only the leading port/pleasure-yacht basin of the Côte Basque, divided by the Nive and Adour rivers, it's also a cathedral city and capital of the Pays Basque. It's characterized by narrow streets, quays, and ramparts. Enlivening the scene are bullfights, *pelote* games (jai alai), and street dancing at annual fiestas. While here, you may want to buy some of Bayonne's chocolate at one of the arcaded shops along rue du Port-Neuf and then enjoy coffee at a cafe along place de la Liberté, the hub of town.

ESSENTIALS

GETTING THERE Bayonne is linked to Paris by 10 **trains** per day (trip time: 5½ to 8 hr.). Nine trains per day arrive from Bordeaux (trip time: 2½ hr.). For train information and schedules, call ✆ **08-36-35-35-35.**

There's **bus** service from Biarritz. (Bus no. 1 departs from Biarritz at 12-min. intervals throughout the daylight hours, depositing passengers on place de la Mairie in Bayonne.) There's also bus service between Bayonne and outlying towns and villages not serviced by train.

If you're **driving,** note that Bayonne is located near the end of the N117 roadway, easily accessible from Toulouse and other cities in the south of France. From Paris, take A10 south to Vierzon, changing to N20 south to Limoges, continuing on N21 south to Tarbes, finally turning west along N117 to Bayonne.

VISITOR INFORMATION The **Office de Tourisme** is on place des Basques (✆ **05-59-46-01-46;** www.bayonne-tourisme.com).

SPECIAL EVENTS The days around July 17 to 21 are the traditional start of the town's jazz festival called **Jazz aux Remparts.** Great musicians from as far away as the United States come here for a week of superb high-energy concerts. Tickets range between 120F and 200F (18.25 and 30.40, $17 and $29) and are available with complete details from the Théâtre Municipal (© **05-59-59-07-27**). During **Fête de Bayonne,** the first week in August, a frenzy of concerts and dancing fill the streets. The celebration is intense. For **free concerts** on fair-weather Thursday evenings in July and August, head to the gazebo on place de-Gaulle, where styles range from jazz to traditional Basque.

EXPLORING THE TOWN

The old town, **Grand Bayonne,** is inside the ramparts of Vauban's fortifications, on the left bank of the Nive. This part of town is dominated by the early 13th-century **Cathédrale Ste-Marie,** rue d'Espagne/rue des Gouverneurs (© **05-59-59-17-82**). The spiny 19th-century steeples of this cathedral are the most characteristic landmark in Bayonne. The cathedral is worth half an hour of your time and is a good retreat on a hot day. It was launched in 1258 when Bayonne was under British control, falling to the French in 1451. That explains the cathedral's ornamentation, mixing such elements as the English coat-of-arms (three leopards) with the fleur-de-lis of France. Some of the stained glass dates from the Renaissance, but the best statuary was smashed during the French Revolution. The gem of the complex—and reason enough to visit—is the wonderful 14th-century cloisters. They're like a secret garden from the Middle Ages. The cathedral is open daily 7:30am to noon and 3 to 7pm.

Musée Bonnat ★★ This museum owns one of the best collections of paintings in France. It's hardly the Louvre, but it encompasses hundreds of canvases, far too many to display in its limited space. Some of the greatest European masters are on parade here—not their masterpieces but a representative sampling of their work. If anybody's the star, it's Peter Paul Rubens (1577 to 1640), with an entire salon devoted to his paintings. The collection's strongest point is its 19th-century art. Otherwise, it's like an introduction to art history 101, with works by David, Degas, Goya, Ingres, da Vinci, El Greco, Tiepolo, and Rembrandt—a massive preview of European art from the 13th to the 20th century. Check out the often-overlooked collection of antiquities in the basement, a museum within a museum, with everything from Egyptian amulets to Greek vases—a whole show of the artifacts of long-vanished cultures.

5 rue Jacques-Lafitte. © **05-59-59-08-52**. Admission 20F (3.05, $2.90) adults, 10F (1.50, $1.45) students and children under 12. Wed–Mon 10am–noon and 2–6pm.

Musée Basque ★★ Bayonne's newest museum showcases the traditions, architecture, and decorative arts (including the textiles and furniture) of the Basques in a state-of-the-art format that's more advanced and sophisticated than any equivalent museum in the Basque-speaking world.

Quai des Corsaires. © **05-59-46-61-90**. Admission and hours not established at press time. Call tourist office for details.

SHOPPING

Most of Bayonne's specialty shops and boutiques lie inside the ramparts of the old town, Grand Bayonne. The pedestrian streets of **rue Port-Neuf** (aptly nicknamed the "street of chocolate shops"), **rue Victor-Hugo,** and **rue Salie** are the major venues. For antiques, walk along the rue des Faures and along the edges of **place Montaut,** behind the cathedral. Most of the modern shops and French chain stores are on **rue Thiers** and **quai de la Nive,** outside the old town. Visit **Maison de Blanc Berrogain,** place de 5 Cantons (© **05-59-59-16-18**), to get your Basque bath, kitchen, and bed linens. **Cazenave,** 19 rue Port-Neuf (© **05-59-59-03-16**), specializes in chocolats de Bayonne that include rich, dark, strong chocolate nougats; stop in the tearoom here for warm chocolate mousses.

You can also head for a 150-year-old shop in the shadow of Bayonne's cathedral, **La Maison Tajan,** 62–64 rue d'Espagne (© **05-59-59-00-39**), where you'll find the region's widest selection of glazed terra-cotta platters and pots, all safe for the oven and the microwave. Imported from Spain and decorated only with a translucent earth-toned glaze, they're among the best accessories for the slow-cooking processes necessary in preparing Basque cuisine.

The accessories of one Basque tradition have become something of a fine art. They are called *makilas,* which in olden days were used as either a walking stick, a cudgel, or—when equipped with a hidden blade—a knife. Today, carved makilas are sold in gentrified formats as collectors' items and souvenirs. For safety's sake, they almost never come with a blade. One of the best outlets in town for these objects is **Fabrication de Makilas,** 37 rue Vieille Boucherie (© **05-59-59-18-20**). Another famous product of the Basque country is its cured hams, which seem to taste best when shaved into paper-thin slices and consumed with one of the region's heady red wines. A site that both prepares and sells them is **Conserverie Artisanale de Jambon de Bayonne,** 41 rue des Cordeliers (© **05-59-25-65-30**), where the famous hams (sold in their entirety or sliced and sold by the pound) are available along with various pâtés, sausages, and terrines.

ACCOMMODATIONS

Best Western Grand Hôtel ⭐ This is the best hotel in town, built in 1835 amid the ruins of a medieval Carmelite convent. In 1991, after a renovation, it attained government-rated three-star status. Rooms are appointed with modern fittings, yet maintain a period feel. Each comes with a midsize bathroom.

21 rue Thiers, 64100 Bayonne. © **800/528-1234** in the U.S. and Canada, or 05-59-59-62-00. Fax 05-59-59-62-01. www.bestwestern.fr. 54 units. 420F–690F (63.85– 104.90, $60.90–$100.05) double. AE, DC, MC, V. Parking 55F (8.35, $8). **Amenities:** Restaurant; bar; room service; laundry. *In room:* TV, minibar, hair dryer, safe.

Mercure Agora Bayonne The second-best choice in Bayonne, the Mercure provides well-furnished rooms with views over the river Nive. Drinks are served on the terrace, which was carved out of a wooded setting beside the river. Rooms are typical chain-hotel style, each with a well-groomed private bathroom.

Av. Jean-Rostand, 64100 Bayonne. © **05-59-52-84-44.** Fax 05-59-52-84-20. h0953@accord-hotels.com. 109 units. 470F–495F (71.45– 75.25, $68.15–$71.80) double; 700F–820F (106.40– 124.65, $101.50–$118.90) suite. AE, DC, MC, V. **Amenities:** Restaurant; bar; laundry. *In room:* A/C, TV, minibar, hair dryer.

DINING

Cheval Blanc ⭐ BASQUE The finest restaurant in Bayonne occupies a half-timbered Basque-style house built in 1715 in the heart of the historic center. Menu items vary with the season but may include slices of foie gras with caramelized endive and pine nuts, ravioli stuffed with wild boar and flavored with local red wine and a confit of baby onions, and corn blinis with flap mushrooms. Dorado might be simmered in garlic and served with *crépinette de* *marmitako* (diced tuna with red and green peppers, bound in a pig's stomach). One of the best desserts is an *amandine bayonnais* with chocolate sauce.

68 rue Bourgneuf. ℂ **05-59-59-01-33.** Reservations recommended. Main courses 110F–195F (16.70– 29.65, $15.95–$28.30); fixed-price menus 135F–350F (20.50– 53.20,$19.60–$50.75). AE, DC, V. Tues–Sun noon–2pm; Mon–Sat 7:30–10pm. Closed Feb 2–Mar 2 and 1 week in June and Aug.

François Miura ★ *Finds* FRENCH Placed a few steps from the Église St-André, this restaurant occupies a late-19th-century cloister originally built for Visitandine nuns. The cuisine here is the most eclectic and personalized in town. Menu items are sophisticated, and composed with intelligence, including flavorful but complicated dishes such as escalope of sea bass with a confit of lemons, stuffed squid served with a confit of pig's foot flavored with squid ink and an essence of crayfish. Less daring examples include crayfish tails with leeks, mushrooms, and coriander sauce; warm calamari salad with two kinds of peppers; and braised rack of lamb with fresh vegetables and coriander sauce. Dessert may include a soufflé with pear liqueur.

24 rue Marengo. ℂ **05-59-59-49-89.** Reservations recommended. Main courses 100F–120F (15.20– 18.25, $14.50–$17.40); fixed-price menus 120F–190F (18.25–28.90, $17.40–$27.55). AE, DC, MC, V. Thurs–Tues noon–2pm; Mon–Tues and Thurs–Sat 8–10pm.

BAYONNE AFTER DARK

Rue des Tonneliers, rue Pannecau, and **rue des Cordeliers** are the liveliest areas after dark. The only pub in town is the **Killarney Pub,** rue des Cordeliers (ℂ **05-59-25-75-51**), where you'll find plenty of music and hearty laughter from a carefree group of rowdies. For a taste of local color, try **Le Cabaret La Luna Negra,** rue des Augustins (ℂ **05-59-25-78-05**), where the cover charge includes cabaret, jazz, or blues performances, and French popular songs. Danceaholics appreciate **Disco La Pompe,** 7 rue des Augustins (ℂ **05-59-25-48-12**), where the action starts around 11:30pm.

4 Biarritz ★★★

484 miles SW of Paris, 120 miles SW of Bordeaux

One of the most famous seaside resorts in the world, Biarritz was once a fishing village near the Spanish border. Favored by Empress Eugénie, the village soon attracted her husband, Napoléon III, who truly put it on the map. Later, Queen Victoria showed up often, and her son, Edward VII, visited more than once.

In the 1930s the prince of Wales (before he became, and then unbecame, Edward VIII) and the American divorcee he loved, Wallis Simpson, did much to make Biarritz more fashionable, as they headed south with these instructions: "Chill the champagne, pack the pearls, and tune up the Bugatti." Biarritz became the pre-jet set's favorite sun spot. Although those legendary days are long gone, the resort is still fashionable, but the unthinkable has happened: It now offers surf shops, snack bars, and even some reasonably priced hotels.

ESSENTIALS

GETTING THERE   Ten **trains** arrive daily from Bayonne (trip time: 10 min.), which has rail links with Paris and other major cities in the south of France. The rail station is 2 miles south of the town center, in La Négresse. For train information and schedules, call ℂ **08-36-35-35-35.** Bus no. 2 carries passengers at frequent intervals from the station to the center of Biarritz for a fee of 9F (1.37, $1.45) per person, or you can take a cab for not much more. If you're **driving,** Biarritz is located at the end of the N117 roadway, which is the

---

Moments Pyrénéan Golf

Biarritz devotes more of its landscapes and energies to golf than any other city in France, with 10 golf courses within a short drive of the town center. A setting that's conducive to practicing is the *Centre d'entraînement d'Ilbarritz-Bidart*, avenue du Château, 64210 Bidart (© **05-59-43-81-30**). Sprawling over 14 acres, it features a circular practice area that's set against a backdrop of the Pyrénées. The venue re-creates every possible golfing hazard and setback, from long shots to fussy putting-green dilemmas.

---

major thoroughfare for the Basque country. From Paris, take A10 south to Vierzon, changing to N20 south to Limoges, continuing on N21 south to Tarbes, and finally turning west along N117 to Biarritz.

VISITOR INFORMATION   The **Office de Tourisme** is on Square d'Ixelles (© **05-59-22-37-10**).

SPECIAL EVENTS   If you're in town in September, check out the concerts and ballet performances during the 3-week festival of **Le Temps d'Aimer.** Cultural events are presented in parks, churches, and auditoriums throughout town, with tickets to the various events ranging from 60F to 200F (9.10 to 30.40, $9 to $29) each. Other music is showcased at the **Les Fêtes Musicaux** festival for a 4-day period in late April, usually within the Casino Municipal and the Théâtre Gare du Midi, which was originally built as a railway station and later transformed into a concert space. For reservations and ticket sales to either of the above-mentioned festivals or for tickets to any of the cultural events within the Théâtre Gare du Midi, contact **Biarritz Tourisme** at © **05-59-22-37-10.**

  Biarritz is known as the surf capital of France. Each year in late July, cadres of surfboard enthusiasts descend on the town for a week for the annual **Biarritz Surf Festival.** You don't need to buy a ticket or show up at any particular time. The festival utilizes all the town's beachfronts, and a Hawaiian spirit permeates the Basque town as surfers re-create the California Dream and the search for the Endless Summer. If golf is your passion, consider visiting during a week in late July during the **Biarritz Cup,** a nationwide competition attended by mostly French golfers. This series of playoffs is held at the Golf du Phare, avenue Edith-Cavell (© **05-59-03-71-80**); it's usually televised. Established in 1888, the Golf du Phare is one of the oldest golf clubs in Europe. Information on all of the above-mentioned festivals is available from the tourist office.

A DAY AT THE BEACH

Along the seafront is the **Grande Plage.** During the Belle Époque, this was where Victorian ladies under parasols and wide-brimmed veiled hats would promenade. Today's women bathers don't dress up in such billowing skirts. Sometimes they don't even wear tops. The beach is also popular with surfers.

  Promenade du bord de mer, stretching 9 miles along the coast, is still a major attraction. The paths along this walk are often carved into cliffs, and sections have been planted as rock gardens with flowers, turning the area into a well-manicured public park. From here, you can head north to **Pointe St-Martin,** where you'll find more gardens and a staircase (look for the sign DESCENTE DE L'OCEAN) leading you to allée Winston-Churchill, a paved path going along **Plage Miramar.**

La Perspective de la Côte des Basques, a walk that goes up to another plateau, leads eventually to a beach that's one of the wildest and most exposed in France: **Plage de la Côte des Basques,** with breakers crashing at the base of the cliffs. This is where surfers head. For surfing rentals, contact **Ripcurl,** 2 av. de la Reine-Victoria (© **05-59-24-38-40**), or **Moraiz Surf Shop,** 4 place Bellevue (© **05-53-41-22-09**).

If you like your beaches calmer, head for the safest beach, the small horseshoe-shaped **Plage du Port-Vieux,** lining the path from plateau de l'Atalaye. Its tranquil waters, protected by rocks, make it a favorite with families.

EXPLORING THE TOWN

Église St-Martin, rue St-Martin (© **05-59-23-05-19**), is one of the few vestiges of the port's early boom days. In the 12th century, Biarritz grew prosperous as a whaling center until the animals left the Bay of Biscay, marking a decline in the port's fortune. The church dates from the 1100s and was restored in 1541 with a Flamboyant Gothic chancel. It's located away from the center of the resort and the town's beaches. Admission is free, and it's open daily 8am to 7:30pm.

Biarritz's turning point came with the arrival of the comtesse de Montijo, who spent lazy summers here with her two daughters. One of them, Eugénie, married Napoléon III in 1853 and prevailed on him to visit Biarritz the next year. The emperor fell under its spell and ordered the construction of the **Hôtel du Palais** (see below). The hotel remains the town's most enduring landmark, though it was originally dubbed "Eugénie's Basque folly." Edward VII stayed there in 1906 and again in 1910, only days before his death. Set in a commanding spot on Grande Plage, the hotel is worth a visit even if you're not a guest. You can view the palatial trappings of its public rooms.

Before the Russian Revolution of 1917, members of Russian nobility arrived, so many, in fact, that they erected the **Église Orthodoxe Russe,** 8 av. de l'Impératrice (© **05-59-24-16-74**). Across from the Hôtel du Palais, this Byzantine-Russian landmark was built in 1892 so that the wintering Russian aristocrats could worship when they weren't enjoying champagne, caviar, and Basque prostitutes. It's noted for its dome, the color of a blue sky on a sunny day.

After you pass the Hôtel du Palais, the walkway widens into **quai de la Grande Plage,** Biarritz's principal promenade. This walkway continues to the opposite end of the resort, where there's a final belvedere opening onto the southernmost stretch of beach. This whole walk would take about 3 hours.

At the southern edge of Grande Plage, steps will take you to **place Ste-Eugénie,** Biarritz's most gracious old square. Lined with terraced restaurants, it's the rendezvous point. Right below place Ste-Eugénie is the colorful **Port des Pêcheurs** (fishers' port). Crowded with fishing boats, it has old wooden houses and shacks backed up against a cliff. Here you'll find driftwood, rope, and plenty of lobster traps along with small harborfront restaurants and cafes.

The rocky **plateau de l'Atalaye** forms one side of the Port des Pêcheurs. Ordered to be carved by Napoléon III, a tunnel leads through the plateau to an esplanade. Here a metal footbridge stretches out into the sea to a rocky islet that takes its name **Rocher de la Vierge** (Rock of the Virgin) from the statue crowning it. Since 1865, this statue is said to have protected the sailors and fishers in the Bay of Biscay. Alexandre-Gustave Eiffel (he of the tower of the same name) directed the construction of the footbridge. This walk out into the terraced edge of the rock, with crashing surf on both sides, is the most dramatic in Biarritz. From this rock, you can see far to the south on a clear day, all the way to the mountains of the Spanish Basque country.

Once here, you can visit the **Musée de la Mer,** 14 plateau de l'Atalaye (© **05-59-24-02-59**), which houses 24 aquariums of fish native to the bay. The seals steal the show at their daily 10:30am and 5pm feedings. The museum also houses *requins* (sharks) that are fed on Tuesday and Friday at 11am and Wednesday and Sunday at 4:30pm. Admission is 47F (7.15, $7) adults, 30F (4.55, $4.35) students and children 5 to 16, children under 5 free. The museum is open May to June, Monday to Friday 9:30am to 12:30pm and 2 to 6pm, and Saturday and Sunday 9:30am to 7pm; July 1 to 13, daily 9:30am to 8pm; July 14 to August 30, daily 9:30am to midnight; and August 16 to September, Monday to Friday 9:30am to 6pm and Saturday and Sunday 9:30am to 7pm.

The only remaining building in town that was designed according to the specific tastes of the Empress Eugénie is **La Chapelle Impériale,** rue Pellot (no phone). Built in 1864 in an eclectic combination of Romanesque-Byzantine and Hispano-Moorish styles, it's open Tuesday, Wednesday, and Saturday 3 to 7pm. During July to September, it's open Monday to Saturday 3 to 7pm. Admission is free.

The town's newest museum, **Musée Asiatica,** 1 rue Guy Petit (© **05-59-22-78-78**), contains an unusual collection of Asian art, most of it from India, Nepal, Tibet, and China. The collection dates from prehistory to the current age. Admission is 45F (6.85, $7) adults, 25F (3.80, $3.65) persons 13 to 25, and 15F (2.30, $2.20) persons 8 to 12. It's open Tuesday to Friday 10am to 7pm, Saturday 10am to 8pm, Sunday 2 to 8pm.

SHOPPING

The major fashion boutiques, with all the big designer names from Paris, are centered on **place Clemenceau** in the heart of Biarritz. From this square, fan out to **rue Gambetta, rue Mazagran, avenue Victor-Hugo, avenue Edouard-VII, avenue du Maréchal-Foch,** and **avenue de Verdun.** Of particular interest are the exceptional Biarritz chocolates and confections and the select textiles that filter in from the Basque country.

The finest chocolatiers are **Pariès,** 27 place Clemenceau (© **05-59-22-07-52**), where you can choose from among seven varieties of *tourons,* ranging from raspberry to coffee; **Daranatz,** 12 av. du Maréchal-Foch (© **05-59-24-21-91**); and **Henriet,** place Clemenceau (© **05-59-24-24-15**), with its house specialty of *rochers de Biarritz:* morsels of candied orange peel and roasted almonds covered in creamy dark chocolate. The owners of this place also run the *Musée du Chocolat,* 14–15 av. Beaurivages (© **05-59-41-54-64**), where exhibits describe chocolate-making and its history. There's also a sales kiosk on-site for acquisition of the company's products. During July and August, it's open daily 10am to noon and 2:30 to 7pm. The rest of the year, it's open Monday to Saturday 10am to noon and 2:30 to 6pm. At the other end of the gastronomic spectrum, try **Mille et Un Fromages,** 8 rue Victor Hugo (© **05-59-24-67-88**), specializing in, as the name suggests, a myriad of tasty French cheeses as well as a host of hearty wines to accompany them.

Among antiques stores, your best bet is **Bakara,** 23 rue Mazagran (© **05-59-22-08-95**), with its special porcelain dolls. For the finest in Basque tablecloths, sheets, and other household linens, visit **St-Léon,** 18 av. Victor-Hugo (© **05-59-24-19-81**).

If a bottle of souvenir spirits appeals to you, join the stream of artists, actors, and gourmands who value **Arosteguy,** 5 av. Victor-Hugo (© **05-59-24-00-52**).

You can procure an affordable wine or bottle of deceptively potent spirits distilled from pears, plums, or raspberries.

Incidentally, **espadrilles,** the canvas-topped, rope-bottomed slippers, are sold at virtually every souvenir shop and department store in the region. A simple off-the-shelf model begins around 60F (9.10, $9), and made-to-order versions (special sizes, special colors) rarely rise above 400F (60.80, $58) per pair. Upscale espadrilles are made to order at **Maison Garcia,** pont de Baskutenea, in Bidart, a hamlet midway between Biarritz and St-Jean-de-Luz (© **05-59-26-51-27**). Opened in 1937, this is one of the last manufacturers to finish its product the old-fashioned way—by hand.

ACCOMMODATIONS

Café de Paris (see "Dining," below) also rents rooms.

Carlina Lodge *Value* This hotel manages to keep its prices low by providing almost no amenities other than daily maid service. But if you're looking for a bargain and you don't mind a no-frills setting, consider emulating the French, who often check into one of the rooms or apartments for a week or more. Built in 1972, it offers an exceptional view of the Pyrénées and the Atlantic. Don't expect much style in the rooms. There's a security code you'll punch into a keypad at night to regain admission to the lobby, since the staff goes home around nightfall. But many French clients consider this place roughly equivalent to their private apartments back in Paris, and the low prices justify the relative lack of comforts.

Bd. du Prince-de-Galles, 64200 Biarritz. © **05-59-24-42-14.** Fax 05-59-24-95-32. www.carlina.net. 18 units, 5 apts. with kitchenettes. 380F–600F (57.75– 91.20, $55.10–$87) double; 600F–1,300F (91.20– 197.60, $87–$188.50) apt. AE, DC, MC, V. Parking 30F (4.55, $4.35). *In room:* TV, minibar.

Château de Brindos ★★ This is one of the most architecturally and culturally unusual homes in the southwest of France, with a history firmly entrenched in the Jazz Age. Built by the American railway heiress Virginia Gould in 1920, it occupies 27 acres of park and garden set inland from the sea. With a facade inspired vaguely by the architecture of Spain, and an interior loaded with architectural remnants such as fireplaces and staircases from the Gothic age, this is the most romantic stopover on the Côte Basque. Rooms are spacious with antique furnishings and modern fittings, including large private bathrooms with combination tub and shower. Amenities include a private lake (where fishing can be arranged), tennis courts, and heated pool. The superb restaurant is set overlooking the lake.

Lac de Brindos, 64600 Anglet. © **05- 59-23-17-68.** Fax 05-59-23-48-47. www.chateau-de-brindos.com. 13 units. 700F–1,000F (106.40– 152, $101.50–$145) double; 1,000F–1,300F (152– 197.60, $145–$188.50) suite. AE, DC, MC, V. From town center, follow AEROPORT signs; after the second roundabout (*rond-point*), follow signs to château; it's about 1½ miles north of Biarritz. **Amenities:** Restaurant (Franco-Basque), bar; room service; laundry. *In room:* TV, hair dryer.

Hôtel Atalaye For economy with a bit of style, head here. In the heart of town on a tranquil spot overlooking the ocean, this circa 1900 hotel is open year-round, although it gets rather sleepy in winter. Rooms are well maintained and traditionally furnished; the small, tiled bathrooms come mainly with shower units. Breakfast is provided anytime you request it. The location is right off place Ste-Eugénie near the beaches, lighthouse, and casino.

Plateau de l'Atalaye, 64200 Biarritz. © **05-59-24-06-76.** Fax 05-59-22-33-51. 24 units. 250F–375F (38– 57, $36.25–$54.40) double; 350F–450F (53.20– 68.40, $50.75–$65.25) triple or quad. MC, V. *In room:* TV.

Hôtel du Palais ★★★ There is no finer hotel palace along the Basque coast. This has been the grand playground for the international elite for the past century. It was built in 1854 by Napoléon III as a private villa for Eugénie so she wouldn't get homesick for Spain. He picked the most ideal beachfront, in view of the rocks and rugged shoreline. Of course there are elaborately furnished suites here, but even the average rooms have period furniture and silk draperies, plus spacious private bathrooms. Try to get a room facing west to enjoy the sunsets over the Basque coast.

Av. de l'Impératrice, 64200 Biarritz. © **800/223-6800** in the U.S. and Canada, or 05-59-41-64-00. Fax 05-59-41-67-99. www.hotel-du-palais.com. 156 units. 1,650F–3,050F (250.80– 463.60, $239.25–$442.25) double; 2,750F–6,450F (418– 980.40, $398.75–$935.25) suite. AE, DC, MC, V. **Amenities:** 3 restaurants: the excellent Villa Eugénie (gourmet), La Rotonde (Basque/international), L'Hippocampe (lunch-only buffet), bar; room service; laundry/dry cleaning. In room: A/C, TV, minibar, hair dryer, safe.

Hôtel Plaza ★ Set near the casino and beach, this hotel is a gorgeous Art Deco monument. Built in 1928, it has remained virtually unchanged, except for discreet renovations, so it's classified as a historic monument and a civic treasure. Rooms retain their original Art Deco furnishings; they tend to be large and high ceilinged, and some have a private terrace. Those overlooking the back and side cost less than those with frontal sea views.

10 av. Edouard-VII, 64200 Biarritz. © **05-59-24-74-00.** Fax 05-59-22-22-01. hotel.plazabiarritz@ wanadoo.fr. 54 units. 380F–940F (57.75– 142.90, $55.10–$136.30) double. AE, DC, MC, V. Free parking. **Amenities:** Restaurant, bar; direct beach access; room service; laundry. In room: A/C, TV, minibar, safe, hair dryer.

DINING

The restaurant at **Château de Brindos** (see "Accommodations," above) also serves excellent Franco-Basque cuisine.

Auberge de la Négresse ★ Finds BASQUE Just 1½ miles south of Biarritz, this restaurant is named for a 19th-century slave who escaped from an American plantation by hiding in the bottom of a French ship. The inn she established on this site was used by Napoléon's army on its passage to Spain. The inn doubles as a delicatessen, but the two dining rooms also serve flavorful meals. Typical dishes include salmon cooked in parchment, an array of homemade terrines, fresh fish, roasted lamb, and steaks.

10 bd. Marcel Dassault. © **05-59-23-15-83.** Reservations required. Main courses 45F–80F (6.85– 12.15, $6.55–$11.60); fixed-price menus 70F–180F (10.65– 27.35, $10.15–$26.10). V. Tues–Sun noon–2:15pm and 7–10:15pm.

Café de Paris ★★★ BASQUE The supercharged chef here, Didier Oudill, is the hottest in town and has rescued the Café de Paris from its long decline. Although Oudill was the protégé of Michel Guérard, he has also come up with many interesting creations of his own. Along with colleague Edgar Duhr, he's not afraid to use Bayonne ham, Spanish merluza (hake), or even earthy fava beans. The setting is naturally elegant, from the mirrors that reflect how glamorous you look to the inevitable palm trees. Menu specialties include pink-cooked duck with vegetables in puff pastry. If you'd like to spend less, you can go to the bistro, where the menu changes often, though fish is always a feature.

The restaurant offers 18 comfortable guest rooms, each with a sea view. Decorated in a conservatively traditional style, each has a TV. They cost 770F to 1,300F (117.05 to 197.60, $112 to $189) for a double.

5 place Bellevue, 64200 Biarritz. © **05-59-24-19-53.** Fax 05-59-24-18-20. Reservations required. Restaurant, main courses 135F–260F (20.50– 39.50,$19.60–$37.70); fixed-price menus 240F–450F

(36.50– 68.40, \$34.80–\$65.25). Bistro, main courses 90F–130F (13.70– 19.75, \$13.05–\$18.85); fixed-price menu 135F–195F (20.50– 29.65,\$19.60–\$28.30). AE, DC, MC, V. Thurs–Tues noon–2:30pm and 7–10pm; also open Wed in July–Aug. Closed Nov to mid-Mar.

BIARRITZ AFTER DARK

Start the night by taking a stroll around **Port des Pêcheurs,** an ideal spot for people-watching, with its stable of sport fishers, restaurants, and fascinating crowds.

Fortunes have been made and lost at the town's own municipal **Casino,** boulevard du Général-de-Gaulle (© **05-59-22-77-77**), where you can easily catch gambling fever. While at the casino, check out its disco **Le Flamingo** (© **05-59-22-77-59**), with its stylish crowd of movers and shakers. Usually there's no cover.

The most hip and desirable nightclub in town is **Le Copacabana,** 24 av. Edouard-VII (© **05-59-24-65-39**), where Latin (especially Cuban) salsa is played along with virtually every other kind of danceable music. At **Le Cayo Coco,** rue Jaulerry (© **05-59-22-53-31**), Cubano music and tequila-based drinks set a steamy and danceable rhythmic tone. **Le Play Boy,** 15 place Clemenceau (© **05-59-24-38-46**), appeals to a diversified crowd ranging from 20 to 40. More appealing is **Disco Le Caveau,** 4 place Gambetta (© **05-59-24-16-17**), where a well-dressed and attractive combination of gay and straight people mingle together with ease. And for a site that's patronized almost exclusively by **gay men,** check out the pub-style **L'Opéra Café,** 31 av. de Verdun (© **05-59-24-27-85**).

5 St-Jean-de-Luz ⟨★⟨★

491 miles SW of Paris, 9 miles S of Biarritz

This Basque country tuna-fishing port and beach resort is ideal for a seaside vacation. St-Jean-de-Luz lies at the mouth of the Nivelle opening onto the Bay of Biscay, with the Pyrénées in the background. Tourists have been flocking here ever since the 19th century, when the town was "discovered" by H. G. Wells.

ESSENTIALS

GETTING THERE   Some 8 to 10 **trains** per day arrive from Biarritz (trip time: 15 min.), and there are also 10 trains per day from Paris (trip time: 5 to 10 hr.). For train information and schedules, call © **08-36-35-35-35. Buses** pulling into town from other parts of the Basque country arrive at the Gare Routière (© **05-59-26-06-99**), in front of the railway station. St-Jean-de-Luz is a short **drive** from Biarritz along N10 south on the west coast of the Basque country.

VISITOR INFORMATION   The **Office de Tourisme** is on place du Maréchal-Foch (© **05-59-26-03-16;** www.saint-jean-de-luz.com).

SPECIAL EVENTS   On Wednesday and Sunday nights during July and August, people pile into place Louis-XIV to take part in **Toro de Fuego,** a celebration of the bull, when revelers take to the streets, dance, and watch fireworks. The highlight of the festivities arrives when a snorting papier-mâché bull is carried through town. Between June 21 and 25, the city celebrates the *Festival of St-Jean (Festival Patronales de la Saint Jean)* with concerts in the streets and a series of food kiosks, usually selling Basque food, lined up along the harborfront. For

5 days in mid-October, there's a small-scale film festival showcasing the works of filmmakers from southwestern France. For a lineup of festivals, check with the Office de Tourisme (see above).

FUN ON & OFF THE BEACH

THE BEACH   The major draw here is the wide, gracefully curving stretch of the white-sand **Plage St-Jean-de-Luz;** it's one of the best beaches in all of France, and consequently very crowded in July and August. The beach lies in a half-moon–shaped bay between the ocean and the source of the Nivelle River.

THE PORT TOWN   Though tourism accounts for most of the revenue around here, fishing is still important. In fact, the town is the major fishing port along the Basque coast. Eating seafood recently plucked from the sea is one of the reasons to visit, especially when Basque chefs prepare the big catch into intriguing platters. This port's many narrow streets flanked by old houses are great for strolling.

EXPLORING THE TOWN

In the town's principal church, the 13th-century **Église St-Jean-Baptiste** ★★, at the corner of rue Gambetta and rue Garat (✆ 05-59-26-08-81), Louis XIV and the Spanish infanta, Marie-Thérèse, were married in 1660, as a celebration of the cessation of fighting between France and Spain over Hapsburg possessions in Holland and Flanders. The interior is among the most handsome of all Basque churches. Surmounting the altar is a statue-studded gilded retable. The interior can be visited daily 8am to noon and 2 to 6pm. At the harbor, the brick-and-stone **Maison de l'Infante,** in Louis XIII style, sheltered the Spanish princess. Admission is 25F (3.80, $3.65) adults, 13F (2, $1.90) students and children under 12.

The Sun King, meanwhile, dreamed of another woman at **La Maison de Louis XIV** (also known as the Château Lohobiague), on place Louis-XIV, the center of the old port (✆ **05-59-26-01-56**). Built in 1643 by a rich ship owner, Johannis of Lohobiague, the Maison de Louis XIV received its young namesake in 1660 for more than a month. The noble facade is distinguished by small towers built into each corner. The interior is in old Basque style, with beams and iron nails still visible. The second-floor stairwell leads to the apartments where Louis XIV stayed when he came to sign the Treaty of the Pyrénées and get married in the church of St-Jean-de-Luz to Maria-Thérèse. It's open June to October, daily 10:30am to noon and 2:30 to 6:30pm. Admission is 25F (3.80, $3.65) adults and 20F (3.05, $2.90) children.

SHOPPING

You'll find the best shopping along the pedestrian **rue Gambetta** as well as around the Église St-Jean-de-Luz. These are the spots where you can find just about anything, from clothes and leather handbags to books, chocolates, dishes, and linens.

You can also ramble around the port, sip pastis in a harborfront cafe, and debate the virtues of the beret. Then scout out **Maison Adam,** which has sold almond-based confections since 1660 from a boutique at 6 place Louis-XIV (✆ **05-59-26-03-54**). Specialties include sugared macaroons, *tournons* (an almond-paste confection flavored with everything from chocolate to confit of berries), and *canougat* (soft caramels). Closed January to March.

ACCOMMODATIONS

Hotel de Chantaco ★★ There's enough memorabilia from this mansion's heyday to remind you of the days when aristocrats from around Europe made it one of their preferred hotels. Surrounded by an 18-hole golf course and verdant parklands, within an hour from the beach, it resembles an eclectically designed country château that belonged to an erudite and somewhat eccentric industrialist. Rooms, improved in 2000, are luxurious, with lots of personalized touches and memorabilia from the gilded age. Breakfast is served beneath the wisteria-covered arches of an outdoor patio.

Gulf de Chantaco, Chantaco, 64500 St-Jean-de-Luz. © **05-59-26-14-76**. Fax 05-59-26-35-97. 23 units. 960F–1,600F (145.90– 243.20, $139.20–$232) double; 1,440F–1,900F (218.90– 288.80, $208.80–$275.50) suite. AE, DC, MC, V. Closed Nov–Easter. Free parking. Take D918 1 mile from the town center. **Amenities:** Restaurant, bar service in salon; outdoor pool; room service; baby-sitting; laundry. *In room:* A/C, TV, minibar, hair dryer, safe.

Hôtel Hélianthal ★ *Value* Efficient, well-designed, and comfortable, this hotel dates from the early 1990s. It was built on a site above a restaurant (l'Atlantique) that has been a city monument since the 1920s. Rising above the commercial heart of town, near the beach, it's rated three stars by the local tourist office, yet has on site at least some of the amenities you'd associate with a four-star, more expensive, property. Unfortunately, none of the Art Deco–style rooms overlooks the sea, but many have terraces, bay windows, or balconies. Each room comes with an immaculately kept bathroom. The big-windowed restaurant, L'Atlantique, offers a terrace overlooking the sea.

Place Maurice-Ravel, 64540 St-Jean-de-luz. © **05-59-51-51-51**. Fax 05-59-51-51-54. Helianthalinfouie@ infouie.fr. 100 units. 720F–1,195F (109.45– 181.65, $104.40–$173.30) double; 1,010F–1,560F (153.50– 237.10, $146.45–$226.20) 2-bedroom suite. AE, DC, MC, V. Parking 40f–65F (6.10– 9.90, $5.80–$9.45). **Amenities:** Restaurant, bar; pool; health club; sauna; room service; baby-sitting; laundry. *In room:* A/C, TV, minibar, hair dryer, safe.

Hôtel/Restaurant Lafayette This utterly unpretentious hotel and restaurant occupy a central location near place Louis-XIV and the town's beaches. Rooms evoke a dignified (albeit slightly battered) age, ranging from small to midsize; each comes with a compact bathroom with shower unit. The Basque cuisine prepared by the experienced matriarch Mayie Colombet is one of the most solidly reliable in town. Tried-and-true dishes include seafood casseroles, grilled duck, sea bass with thyme and lemon-butter sauce, and roast rack of lamb. The restaurant is closed on Monday from mid-November to mid-March, but during many school holidays, business is so good that Ms. Colombet usually decides to remain open anyway.

18–20 rue de la République, 64500 St-Jean-de-Luz. © **05-59-26-17-74**. Fax 05-59-51-11-78. 17 units. 250F–550F (38– 83.60, $36.25–$79.75) double with bathroom. AE, DC, MC, V. **Amenities:** Restaurant (Basque). *In room:* TV.

La Devinière *Value* Perhaps because of its small size, this is the best-furnished moderately priced hotel in St-Jean-de-Luz. It occupies the premises of what was originally a private town house and was brought to its present level of 18th-century elegance thanks to the unsold inventories of its antiques-dealer owner. Rooms are comfortable, well maintained, and filled, like the rest of the hotel, with attractive antiques. Each comes with a midsize bathroom.

5 rue Loquin, 64500 St-Jean-de-Luz. © **05-59-26-05-51**. Fax 05-59-51-26-38. 11 units. 650f–850F (98.80– 129.20, $94.25–$123.25) double. AE, DC, MC, V. Parking 40F (6.10, $5.80). **Amenities:** Tea salon.

DINING

The only really grand cuisine in town is served at the **Hôtel Grand,** but you might also like to check out the restaurant at the **Hôtel Hélianthal** or the reliable Basque food prepared at the **Hôtel/Restaurant Lafayette** (see "Accommodations," above).

Auberge Kaïku ⭐ BASQUE   On a narrow street off place Louis-XIV, Auberge Kaïku is the best restaurant in town outside the hotels. The structure, with hand-hewn beams and chiseled masonry, dates from 1540 and is said to be the oldest in town. The auberge is run by Emile and Jeanne Ourdanabia, who serve Basque cuisine that's been enhanced with modern touches. Examples are roast suckling Pyrénéan lamb, a parillade of shellfish, fried calamari with pasta and garlic, John Dory with fresh mint, grilled shrimp, filet of beef with essence of truffles, and duckling in honey. A particularly succulent starter is the salade Kaïku, garnished with panfried strips of foie gras and raspberry vinegar.

17 rue de la République. 🕐 **05-59-26-13-20**. Reservations recommended. Main courses 85F–145F (12.90– 22.05,$12.35–$21.05); fixed-price menus 150F–220F (22.80– 33.45, $21.75–$31.90). AE, MC, V. Mid-Sept to mid-June, Tues and Thurs–Sun 12:15–2:15pm and Thurs–Tues 7:15–10:30pm; mid-June to mid-Sept, Tues–Sun 12:15–2:15pm; daily 7:15–10:30pm. Closed mid-Nov to Dec 22.

Chez Maya (Petit Grill Basque) *Value* BASQUE   This small auberge is highly acclaimed for quality and value, with specialties that include a delectable fish soup and paella. Don't expect urban glitter. Things are too conservative and old-fashioned for that. The fixed-price menu is the best value in town. The chefs cook as their grandparents did, including all the old favorites, such as squid cooked in its own ink, and a local version of fish soup known as **Morro.**

4 rue St-Jacques. 🕐 **05-59-26-80-76**. Reservations recommended. Main courses 60F–100F (9.10–15.20, $8.70–$14.50); fixed-price menus 115F–160F (17.50– 24.30, $16.70–$23.20). AE, DC, MC, V. Thurs–Tues noon–2pm and 7–10pm. Closed Dec 20–Jan 20.

La Vieille Auberge BASQUE/LANDAISE   This Basque tavern specializes in seafood, and the owners claim that the fish soup is second to none. They offer good-value fixed-price menus, the most expensive of which is enormous. Generally, the recipes are part-Basque/part-Landaise, and each dish goes well with the *vin du pays,* especially mussels *à la crème.* A parillade of fish (mixed seafood grill) is particularly appealing.

22 rue Tourasse. 🕐 **05-59-26-19-61**. Reservations required. Main courses 60F–125F (9.10– 19, $8.70–$18.15); fixed-price menus 125F–135F (19– 20.50, $18.15–$19.60). MC, V. July–Aug, Wed–Mon noon–2pm, daily 7–10:30pm; Apr 2–June and Sept–Nov 11, daily noon–2pm, Thurs–Mon 7–10pm. Closed Oct–Mar.

ST-JEAN-DE-LUZ AFTER DARK

You can start by taking a walk along the promenade to watch the sunset. If you check out **place Louis-XIV,** you'll find a hotbed of activity at the surrounding cafes and bars.

A fun spot worth a visit is **Pub du Corsaire,** 16 rue de la République (🕐 **05-59-26-10-74**), one of the main places in town for simple, unpretentious merrymaking, good times, and revelry. It's all accompanied, of course, by copious amounts of drinking and old-fashioned rock 'n' roll. For dancing, virtually everyone heads north of town to the string of nightclubs and discos that stretch beside the R.N. 10. (Follow the signs from the town center for Biarritz.) The best of the lot include **Le Paseo,** R.N. 10 (🕐 **05-59-26-04-28**), about a half-mile north of town, which seems to be packed with nightlife maniacs under 25; and **Disco La Tupina,** R.N. 10 (🕐 **05-59-54-73-23**), about 2 miles north of town.

19

Bordeaux & the Atlantic Coast

From historic La Rochelle to the Bordeaux Wine District, the southwest of France is often a quick glimpse for visitors driving from Paris to Spain. However, this area is noted for its Atlantic beaches, medieval and Renaissance ruins, Romanesque and Gothic churches, vineyards, and charming old inns serving up splendid regional cuisine.

In our journey through this intriguing region, we detour inland for a snifter of cognac in Cognac and for trips to nearby art cities like Poitiers and Angoulême. If you can manage it, it's great to allow a week in this region—just enough time to sample the wine, savor the cuisine, and see at least some of the major sights.

REGIONAL CUISINE Major specialties from this region are *huîtres* (oysters) from Arcachon or Marennes, *jambon* (ham) from Poitou, *esturgeon* (sturgeon) or *saumon* (salmon) from the Gironde, *canard* (duck) from Challans, *chapon* (capon) or *poularde* (chicken) from Barbezieux, and *agneau* (lamb) from Pauillac.

Other specialties include *mouclade* (a mussel stew with cream or white wine and shallots), *lamproie* or *l'anguille à la bordelaise* (lamprey eels from local rivers, served with a blood-enriched red-wine sauce), *entrecôte à la bordelaise* (steak in a wine-laced brown sauce with shallots, tarragon, and bone marrow), *cèpes à la bordelaise* (flap mushrooms sautéed in oil, seasoned with chopped shallots and garlic), *escargots à la vigneronne* (snails simmered in a sauce of wine, garlic, and onions), and *chaudrée* (a local fish soup). The region's most famous cheese is chabichou, a goat cheese from Poitou; its best chocolate is les duchesses d'Angoulême.

Bordeaux wines include everything from the finest French vintages to ordinary table wines found on supermarket shelves. Among the best are the incomparable wines from the Médoc and Graves. Other reds include St-Emilion and Pomerol.

1 Poitiers ✦✦

207 miles SW of Paris, 110 miles SE of Nantes

This city, the ancient capital of Poitou, the northern part of Aquitaine, is filled with history. Everybody has passed through here—from England's Black Prince to Joan of Arc to Richard the Lion-Hearted.

Poitiers stands on a hill overlooking the Clain and Boivre rivers. It was this strategic location that tempted so many conquerors. Charles Martel chased out the Muslims in A.D. 732 and altered the course of European civilization. Poitiers was the chief city of Eleanor of Aquitaine, who had her marriage to pious Louis VII annulled so she could wed England's Henry II.

For those interested in antiquity, this is one of the most fascinating towns in France. That battle we learned about in history books was fought on September

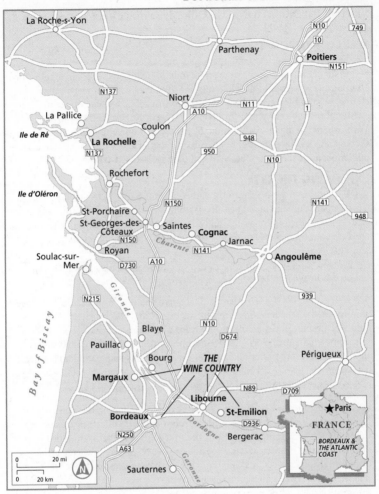

19, 1356, between the armies of Edward the Black Prince and King John of France. It was one of the three great English victories of the Hundred Years' War, distinguished by the use of the longbow in the skilled hands of English archers.

After decades of slumber, the town has really come alive, with the opening of **Futuroscope,** a futuristic cinema theme park. The thriving student population (a third of the 85,000 residents here are students) adds a slice of vitality as well.

ESSENTIALS

GETTING THERE   Rail service is available from Paris, Bordeaux, and La Rochelle. Around 18 of the fast TGV **trains** arrive daily from Paris (trip time: 1½ hours). Another 18 (regular speed) arrive daily from Bordeaux (1¾ hours), and 11 from La Rochelle (2 hours). For train information, call ✆ **08-36-35-35-35.** Bus services from Poitiers are so badly scheduled as to be virtually nonexistent. If you're **driving,** Poitiers is located on the A10 highway; from Paris, follow A10 south through the cities of Orléans and Tours, on to Poitiers.

VISITOR INFORMATION The **Office de Tourisme** is at 8 rue des Grandes-Écoles (✆ **05-49-41-21-24**).

SPECIAL EVENTS The most active time to visit is in July and August during the **Poitiers l'Été,** a festival of live jazz, opera, rock, and fireworks. Over that period the facade of Notre-Dame La Grande is highlighted in colored lights for 15 minutes every evening at 10:30pm; free concerts are held at various parks and churches around the city. Check with the tourist office for schedules.

Also of interest, every year for about 10 days in August, is the **Festival Colla Voce,** where the organs within some of the town's most important churches are showcased, usually with a series of recitals, most of them free. For more information, contact the tourist office or call ✆ **04-43-47-13-61.**

EXPLORING THE CITY

Baptistère St-Jean ✮ From the cathedral, you can walk to the most ancient Christian monument in France. It was built as a baptistery in the early 4th century on Roman foundations, and then extended in the 7th century. It contains frescoes from the 11th to the 14th centuries and a collection of funerary sculpture.

Rue Jean-Jaurès. Admission 4F (.60, 60¢). July–Aug daily 10am–12:30pm and 2:30–6pm; Apr–June and Sept–Oct daily 10:30am–12:30pm and 3–6pm; Nov–Mar Wed–Mon 2:30–4:30pm.

Cathédrale St-Pierre ✮ Here in the eastern sector of Poitiers, you'll find the twin-towered Cathédrale St-Pierre. It was begun in 1162 by Henry II of England and Eleanor of Aquitaine on the ruins of a Roman basilica. The cathedral was completed much later, but it has always been undistinguished architecturally. However, the interior, 295 feet long, contains some admirable stained glass from the 12th and 13th centuries.

Place de la Cathédrale. ✆ **05-49-41-23-76.** Free admission. Daily 8am–7pm (winter to 6pm).

Église Notre-Dame-la-Grande ✮✮ This church, built in the Romanesque-Byzantine style and richly decorated, is from the late 11th century. See in particular its western front, dating from the mid-12th century. Surrounded by an open-air market, the facade, carved like an ivory casket, is characterized by pinecone-shaped towers. It was thoroughly cleaned and restored in 1996. Carvings on the doorway represent biblical scenes.

Place Charles-de-Gaulle. ✆ **05-49-41-22-56.** Free admission. Daily 9am–7pm.

Église Ste-Radegonde A favorite place of pilgrimage in times gone by, this 11th-century structure in the eastern section of Poitiers commemorates the patroness of Poitiers, Radegonde. Her black marble sarcophagus is in the crypt. Radegonde, who died in A.D. 587, was the consort of Clotaire, king of the Franks.

Place St-Radegonde. ✆ **05-49-41-23-76.** Free admission. Apr–Sept daily 8:30am–7:30pm; Oct–Mar 8am–6pm.

Futuroscope ✮✮ *(Kids)* Drawing some three million visitors annually, this science amusement park is a wonderland of technology that lets you experience sounds, images, and sensations with the world's most advanced film-projection techniques and largest screens. Exhibitions include **Kinemax** (a rock crystal covered with mirrors with a 400-seat cinema); **Omnimax** (films projected onto a gigantic dome via a special fish-eye lens, putting you into the heart of the action); **Le Tapis Magique-Everest** (a film that shows you what it's like to fly above the Himalayas); and a 3-D cinema that takes you on a journey through the world's most impressive monuments and sites of natural beauty. Another subdivision of the park includes *Océan Oasis,* which leads you on an underwater exploration of a reef off the coast of Baja California.

About 5½ miles north of Poitiers in Jaunay-Clan. ⓒ **05-49-49-30-00.** Admission 145F–210F (22.05– 31.90, $21.05–$30.45) adults, 100F–145F (15.20– 22.05, $14.50–$21.05) children 5–12, free for children under 5. Daily 9am–6pm (between Apr and Nov, it's open daily from 8am until between 10pm and midnight, depending on the day of the week, the seasons, and the crowd). From Poitiers, bus 16 or 17 runs to the park; if you're driving, take N10.

Musée St-Croix   This museum, built on the site of the old abbey of St-Croix, has a fine-arts section devoted mainly to painting—especially 16th- and 17th-century Flemish art and 16th- to 18th-century Dutch paintings. Several works by Bonnard, Sisley, and Oudot are displayed, along with a bronze sculpture, *The Three Graces,* by Maillol. A separate archaeological section documents the history of Poitou, from prehistoric times to the Gallo-Roman era, the Renaissance, and up to the end of the 19th century.

Accessible from 3 bis, rue Jean Jaurès, 8600 Poitiers. ⓒ **05-49-41-07-53.** Admission 20F (3.05, $2.90) adult, free for children under 19. Oct–May Mon and Wed–Fri 1–5pm, Tues 10am–5pm, Sat–Sun 2–6pm; June–Sept Mon 1:15–6pm, Tues–Fri 10am–noon and 1:15–6pm, Sat–Sun 10am–noon and 2–6pm.

Palais de Justice   This structure incorporates the 14th-century keep and some other parts of a palace dating from the Gallo-Roman era. It was here that Joan of Arc was questioned by the doctors of the university who composed the French Court of Parliament, and also here that Richard the Lion-Hearted was proclaimed comte de Poitou and duc d'Anjou in 1170. Unfortunately, only one room within the stately municipal building can be visited, the **Salle des Pas Perdus.** Here, vaulted ceilings, majestic-looking columns, and an enormous fireplace mark the site where Eleanor d'Aquitaine conducted some of her receptions.

Place Lepetit. ⓒ **05-49-50-22-00.** Free admission. Mon–Fri 9am–6pm.

ACCOMMODATIONS

Grand Hôtel de l'Europe ✦   This is the town's leading inn. The isolation of this place enhances its sense of 1930s civility. Rooms are more modern and streamlined than the antique public areas would suggest. Each comes with a small bathroom with a combination tub and shower. Breakfast is the only meal served, in an old-fashioned dining room with tall windows and an elaborate fireplace.

39 rue Carnot, 86000 Poitiers. ⓒ **05-49-88-12-00.** Fax 05-49-88-97-30. 88 units. 330F–480F (50.15– 72.95, $47.85–$69.60) double. AE, DC, MC, V. Parking 40F (6.10, $5.80). **Amenities:** Breakfast-only room service; laundry. *In room:* TV, minibar (some rooms), hair dryer.

Hôtel du Plat d'Etain *Value*   One of the best bargains in Poitiers, this renovated hotel is on a narrow alley, close to place du Maréchal-Leclerc. Rooms are compact and simply but comfortably furnished, most with a small bathroom with a shower unit. Many restaurants and sights are nearby. Several readers have commented on the warmth of the staff. There's a guarded parking area.

7 rue du Plat-d'Etain, 86000 Poitiers. ⓒ **05-49-41-04-80.** Fax 05-49-52-25-84. 24 units, 21 with bathroom. 150F (22.80, $21.75) double without bathroom, 260F–300F (39.50– 45.60, $37.70–$43.50) double with bathroom. AE, DC, MC, V. Parking 20F (3.05, $2.90) Bus: 2A. *In room:* TV, minibar.

Le Chalet de Venise *Finds*   Those who don't want to stay in the town center will enjoy this reasonably priced inn. It's surrounded by trees and shrubbery, and its chalet opens onto the water. Rooms are simply furnished, clean, and comfortable, each with a small but neat shower-only bathroom. Drinks are served on a flagstone terrace overlooking one of the many tributaries of the region. The food is among the best in the Poitiers area, and portions are generous. Breakfast is served in a room overlooking a garden.

6 rue du Square (B.P. 4), 86280 St-Benoît-Bourg. © **05-49-88-45-07.** Fax 05-49-52-95-44. 12 units. 350F (53.20, $50.75) double. AE, DC, MC, V. Take D88 south 2½ miles from Poitiers to St-Benoît or A10 to exit 20, "Poitiers Sud." **Amenities:** Restaurant; laundry. *In room:* TV, minibar.

DINING

Le Chalet de Venise (see "Accommodations," above), serves some of the best food in the area.

Le Saint Hilaire ⭐ FRENCH/POITOU   This historic and unusual restaurant in Poitiers would be popular with foreigners if it were more centrally located. It's on a quiet street in the southern periphery of the medieval center. The fixed-price menus offer three types of cuisine: medieval, regional, and seasonal. The fare of André Point and his wife, Danielle, is superb, based on fresh seasonal ingredients. Examples include scallops marinated in lime juice; strips of pork braised with cabbage; and a beautiful slice of fresh, home-style foie gras prepared with cardamon. Especially succulent is a stew made from snails and local mushrooms, and rack of lamb with shallots and white beans. A light-textured dessert is a sorbet of fresh pears, flavored with pear-derived *eaux-de-vie*.

5 rue Théophraste-Renaudot. © **05-49-41-15-45.** Reservations recommended. Main courses 65F–145F (9.90– 22.05, $9.45–$21.05); fixed-price menu 95F–230F (14.45– 34.95, $13.80–$33.35) AE, DC, MC, V. Tues–Sat noon–2pm; Mon–Sat 7:30–9:45pm. Closed Jan 1–15; and Aug 6–20.

Maxime ⭐⭐ MODERN FRENCH   Maxime is the most sophisticated restaurant in town, and for some lucky reason it's ignored by the weekend crowds visiting Futuroscope. Christian Rougier, the hardworking chef, offers a menu that varies with the seasons but always includes ravioli with hot oysters and sometimes features baked back of rabbit stuffed with eggplant, mushrooms, and *fines herbes,* served with chardonnay sauce; roebuck with green garlic; stuffed snapper with roe sauce; fried foie gras served with asparagus; and an herb-laden roast rack of lamb from Montmorillon, a site famous for the quality of its lamb. Dessert might include au gratin of red berries with a champagne-based sabayon.

4 rue St-Nicolas. © **05-49-41-09-55.** Reservations recommended. Main courses 90F–165F (13.70– 25.10, $13.05–$23.95); fixed-price menu 115F–270F (17.50– 41.05, $16.70–$39.15) AE, DC, MC, V. Mon–Fri noon–2pm and 7:30–10pm. Closed 5 weeks over July–Aug.

POITIERS AFTER DARK

Some of the town's most popular techno- and electronic-music concerts occur at **Le Confort Moderne,** 185 rue du Faubourg du Pont-Neuf (© **05-49-46-08-08**), details for which are posted on virtually every billboard in town. A high-profile disco is **La Grand' Goule,** 46 rue du Pigeon-Blanc (© **05-49-50-41-36**), which doesn't get going until after 11pm. Two other nightclubs playing the latest music from Paris include **Le Loft,** 85 promenade des Courts (© **05-49-41-04-37**), and within a few steps, **L'Eclipse,** 55 promenade des Courts (© **05-49-88-34-21**). Both cater to a youthful, high-energy crowd who all seem to know each other. A final, somewhat more worldly looking alternative, is a two-in-one disco at 195 Avenue du 8 mai 1945 (© **05-49-57-08-21**). Inside, you'll find **Le Black House,** a bar and disco that attracts a higher-than-usual percentage of gay men and women, and its heterosexual alternative,

Le Privilège. The most frequented exclusively gay bar and disco in town is **Le George-Sand,** 25 rue St-Pierre-le-Puellier (© **05-49-55-91-58**). Another leading gay bar is **Le Victor–Victoria,** ave. de Nantes. (© **05-49-37-99-73**), where dance music filters in around a crowd otherwise devoted to drinking, talking, and flirting. Many gay students, often from countries other than France, hang out at cozy **Au Sixties,** 1 rue des Quatre Voûtes (© **05-49-52-19-44**).

2 La Rochelle ⋆⋆⋆

290 miles SW of Paris, 90 miles SE of Nantes, 100 miles S of Bordeaux, 88 miles NW of Angoulême

Once known as the French Geneva, La Rochelle is a historic port and ancient sailors' city, formerly the stronghold of the Huguenots. It was founded as a fishing village in the 10th century on a rocky platform in the center of a huge marshland. Eleanor of Aquitaine gave La Rochelle a charter in 1199, thereby freeing it from feudal dues. After becoming an independent city-state, the port capitalized on the wars between France and England. It was the departure point for the founders of Montréal and others who colonized Canada. From the 14th to the 16th centuries, La Rochelle was one of France's great maritime cities. It became the principal port between France and the colony of Canada, but France's loss of Canada ruined its Atlantic trade.

As a hotbed of Protestant factions, it armed privateers to prey on Catholic vessels but was eventually besieged by Catholic troops. Two men led the fight: Cardinal Richelieu (with, of course, his Musketeers) and Jean Guiton, formerly an admiral and then mayor of the city. When Richelieu blockaded the port, La Rochelle bravely resisted, but on October 30, 1628, Richelieu entered the city. Among the 30,000 citizens of the proud city, he found only 5,000 survivors.

Today La Rochelle, a city of 120,000, is the cultural and administrative center of the Charente-Maritime département. Its famous city lights have earned it the title "City of Light," like its grander sibling, Paris. While many of La Rochelle's sights are old, the city is riddled with high-rise condos and the largest pleasure-boat basin in Europe. In summer, the city is overrun with visitors.

ESSENTIALS
GETTING THERE   The La Rochelle-Laleu **airport** (© **05-46-42-30-26**) is on the coast, 3 miles north of the city. Rail connections from Bordeaux and Nantes are frequent. Six to eight **trains** from Bordeaux and Nantes arrive daily (trip time: 2 hours), and there are five to seven daily fast TGV trains from Paris Gare Montparnasse (3 hours). For train information and schedules, call © **08-36-35-35-35. Buses** pull into La Rochelle at the Gare Routière, on the Place de Verdun (© **05-46-34-02-22** for information). If you're **driving** to La Rochelle, it's best to stay near the A10 highway. Follow A10 south from Poitiers to exit Niort/St-Maixent, then take N11 east to the coast and La Rochelle.

VISITOR INFORMATION   The **Office de Tourisme** is on place de la Petite-Sirène, Le Gabut (© **05-46-41-14-68**).

SPECIAL EVENTS   The busiest month is July, when the **Festival International du Film de La Rochelle** rolls in at the beginning of the month. It attracts a huge following of fans, press, actors, directors, and, of course, paparazzi. Screenings are held around town; tickets cost from 40F to 55F (6.10 to 8.35, $5.80 to $8) each. For information, contact the festival's organizing office in the Maison de la Culture, rue St-Jean de Perot (© **05-46-51-54-00**). On the heels of this festival, during a 3-day period in mid-July, comes **Les**

Francofolies, a music festival with big names as well as not-so-famous groups, most of them pop musicians from the world over. The town is overrun with groupies and fans, and a festive party atmosphere prevails. Tickets range from 50F to 175F (7.60 to 26.60, $7.25 to $25.40) Call ✆ **05-46-28-28-28** for details. The Office de Tourisme can also provide details on both festivals.

La Rochelle is also the site of the biggest showcasing of boats and yachts in Europe, **Le Grand Pavois Salon Nautique.** It's a 5-day extravaganza that takes place yearly in early September. The action is based in and around La Rochelle's Port de Plaisance (Yacht Basin). Sellers and buyers of boats and marine hardware, as well as weekend sailors from everywhere, usually attend. For information about dates and venues, call ✆ **05-46-44-46-39.**

EXPLORING THE CITY

There are two sides to La Rochelle: the old and unspoiled town inside the Vauban defenses, and the tacky modern and industrial suburbs. Its **fortifications** have a circuit of 3½ miles with a total of seven gates.

The town, with its arch-covered streets, is great for strolling. The port is a bustling fishing harbor and one of the major sailing centers in western Europe. Try to schedule a visit in time to attend a fish auction. The best streets for strolling are **rue du Palais, rue Chaudrier,** and **rue des Merciers** with its ancient wooden houses. On the latter, seek out the houses at nos. 3, 5, 8, and 17.

Hôtel de Ville (City Hall) ★ The town's 14th-century showcase is constructed in Flamboyant Gothic style, with battlements. Inside you can admire the Henry II staircase with canopies and the marble desk of the heroic Jean Guiton. In 1996, major restoration work was needed after Corsican separatists bombed the building, causing heavy damage. Prime Minister Alain Juppé had left the building not long before the explosion occurred.

Place de la Mairie, in the city center. ✆ **05-46-41-14-68.** You must visit on a guided tour by reserving in advance. Tours 20F (3, $2.90) adults, 10F (1.5, $1.45) children ages 5–16, free for children under 4. In July–Aug, tours daily at 3pm and 4pm.

Musée d'Histoire Naturelle This ethnography and zoology museum is housed in an 18th-century building surrounded by a garden; the original paneling has been preserved. Clement de Lafaille, a former comptroller of war, assembled much of the collection, which has been enlarged since he donated it to the city. Displays include rare shellfish, a statue from Easter Island, an embalmed giraffe given to Charles X (the first of the species to be seen in France), and a parade boat encrusted with gems that was presented to Napoléon III by the king of Siam.

28 rue Albert-1er. ✆ **05-46-41-18-25.** Admission 22F (3.35, $3.20), free for children under 19. Tues–Fri 10am–12:30pm and 1:30–5:30pm; Sat–Sun 2–6pm.

Value **Buy a Combination Ticket**

You can buy a combination ticket good for entrance to the Musée des Beaux-Arts, Musée d'Obigny-Bernon, Musée du Nouveau-Monde, and Musée d'Histoire Naturelle at the tourist office or any of the four museums. The price of 42F (6.40, $6.10) allows an adult to visit all four museums over a period of eight days from the time of your purchase.

Musée d'Obigny-Bernon ✦ The most important artifacts pertaining to the history of ceramics and of La Rochelle are in this collection, which includes painted porcelain. Established in 1917, the museum also houses a superb collection of Far Eastern art.

2 rue St-Côme. ☎ **05-46-41-18-83**. Admission 23F (3.50, $3.35) adults, free for children under 19. Mon and Wed–Sat 10am–noon and 2–6pm; Sun 2–6pm.

Musée des Beaux-Arts ✦ The museum is housed in an Episcopal palace built in the mid-18th century. The art spans the 17th to the 19th centuries, with works by Eustache Le Sueur, Brossard de Beaulieu, Corot, and Fromentin. Some 20th-century pieces include works by Maillol and Léger.

28 rue Gargolleau. ☎ **05-46-41-64-65**. Admission 22F (3.35, $3.20) adults, 16F (2.45, $2.30) students, free for children under 19. Wed–Mon 2–5pm.

Musée du Nouveau-Monde The displays here trace the port's 300-year history with the New World. Exhibits start with the discovery of the Mississippi Delta in 1682 by LaSalle and end with the settling of the Louisiana territory. Other exhibits depict French settlements in the French West Indies, including Guadeloupe and Martinique.

In the Hôtel Fleuriau, 10 rue Fleuriau. ☎ **05-46-41-46-50**. Admission 23F (3.50, $3.35) adults, free for children under 19. Wed–Mon 10:30am–12:30pm and 1:30–6pm; Sun 3–6pm.

Tour de la Chaîne During the 1300s, this tower was built as an anchor piece for the large forged-iron chain that stretched across the harbor, as a means of closing it against hostile warships. Today, it's a sightseeing attraction in its own right, with unusual exhibits on the history of medieval naval warfare.

Quai du Gabut. ☎ **05-46-34-11-81**. Admission 25F (3.80, $3.65) adults, free for children under 18. Apr–Sept daily 10am–7pm; Oct–Mar 9:30am–12:30pm and 2–5:30pm.

Tour de la Lanterne ✦ Built between 1445 and 1476, this was once a lighthouse but was used mainly as a jail as late as the 19th century.

Opposite Tour St-Nicolas (see below). Admission 25F (3.80, $3.65) adults, 15F (2.30, $2.20) ages 18–25, free for children under 18. Apr–Sept daily 10am–7pm; Oct–Mar daily 10am–12:30pm and 2–5:30pm.

Tour St-Nicolas ✦ The oldest tower in La Rochelle, Tour St-Nicolas was built between 1371 and 1382. From its second floor you can enjoy a panoramic view of the town and harbor; from the top, however, you can see only the old town and Île d'Oléron.

Quai du Gabut. ☎ **05-46-41-74-13**. Admission 25F (3.80, $3.65) adults, 15F (2.30, $2.20) for ages 18–25, free for children under 18. Apr–Sept daily 10am–7pm; Oct–Mar daily 10am–12:30pm and 2–5:30pm.

SHOPPING

The main shopping streets are **rue du Palais, rue du Temple, rue de Merciers,** and **rue St-Yon,** where name-brand department stores as well as smaller shops sell everything from clothing to canned goods. If you want to explore antiques shops, art galleries, jewelry studios, and more high-end shops, enter the **old town.** On Saturday from 9am to around 6pm, an **antiques market** sets up along rue St-Nicholas with a multitude of dealers carrying mainly bric-a-brac and flea market items. For one of the largest selections of beachwear, parkas, windbreakers, and great wool pullover sweaters, stop in at the **Cooperative Maritime,** Port de Pêche, chef de Baie, place J. B. Moitessier (☎ **05-46-41-31-66**).

Finds **Sailing the Ports of La Rochelle**

La Rochelle has always made its living from the sea and ships that made its harbor their home. Four distinct harbors have grown up over the centuries, each a world unto itself, each rich with local nuance and lore. They include the historic Vieux-Port, the port de Plaisance (a modern yacht marina); the Port de Pêche (the fishing port); and the Port de Commerce, which is mostly used by large-scale container ships.

The best way to appreciate them is to visit the tourist office (see "Essentials" above), which acts as a clearing house for the outfitters that maintain tours of these four harbors. You can address your queries to any of them (Ste. Inter-Iles, Croslères Océanes, Navi-Promer, Cap l'ouest, and Re Croisières), but because their phones are hysterically busy in summer (or never answered), it's best to contact the tourist office, which is fairly objective about the merits of the offerings of each of the four. Every day midsummer, there are about a half-dozen tours of the city's four ports. In winter, they're offered about three times a day, Saturday and Sunday only. Prices range from 60F to 90F (9.10 to 13.70, $8.70 to $13.05) per person, and last between 70 and 95 minutes each, depending on the tour and the company. Rides are very touristy with a guy with a microphone speaking in French.

Another option involves taking tours from the Vieux-Port of La Rochelle to Ile de Ré. Ile de Ré has 43 miles of white sandy beaches and lies 16 miles across the sea from La Rochelle. It is an island of nature preserves with bike and hiking paths. Easter to November, there are five to seven departures a day. The rest of the year there are two or three departures every Saturday and Sunday, and about one a day Monday to Friday. Tours allow brief promenades on some of the islands, and cost, round-trip, between 90F to 160F (13.70 to 24.30, $13.05 to $23.20) per person, depending on the itinerary.

ACCOMMODATIONS

Hotel de France et d'Angleterre et de Champlain ★★ Close to the major parks and the old port, this is the most gracious choice in La Rochelle. It's furnished with a winning combination of antiques and art objects. This is complemented with a genial staff. Rooms are tasteful and dignified, many with a nautical theme. Each comes with a midsize bathroom with a combination tub and shower. One of the best aspects of the hotel is its romantic garden brimming with flowers, shrubbery, and shade trees. Breakfast is the only meal served.

20 rue Rambaud, 17000 La Rochelle. ✆ **800/528-1234** in the U.S. or Canada, or 05-46-41-23-99. Fax 05-46-41-15-19. 36 units. 400F–600F (60.80– 91.20, $58–$87) double; 780F (118.55, $113.10) suite. AE, DC, MC, V. Parking 48F (7.30, $6.95) . **Amenities:** Breakfast-only room service; laundry. *In room:* A/C, TV, minibar, hair dryer.

Hôtel Les Brises ★ *Value* This tranquil, seaside hotel opposite the new Port des Minimes offers a view of the soaring 19th-century column dedicated to the Virgin. You can enjoy the view from the front balconies as well as the parasol-shaded patio. The immaculate rooms have cherrywood furniture, plus comfortable beds and neatly organized and compact bathrooms with shower units. Breakfast is the only meal served.

Chemin de la Digue de Richelieu, 17000 La Rochelle. ℭ 05-46-43-89-37. Fax 05-46-43-27-97. 48 units. 450F–645F (68.40– 98.05, $65.25–$93.55) double; 985F (149.70, $142.85) suite. AE, DC, MC, V. **Amenities**: Breakfast-only room service; laundry. *In room:* TV.

Novotel La Rochelle Centre ⚹   This hotel, one of the best in town, occupies a desirable verdant location in the Parc Charruyer, a greenbelt about a 5-minute walk from the town center. Rooms are standardized and well maintained, with big windows overlooking the park. Each comes with a midsize bathroom with a combination tub and shower.

1 av. de la Porte-Neuve, 17000 La Rochelle. ℭ 05-46-34-24-24. Fax 05-46-34-58-32. 94 units. 560F–680F (85.10– 103.35, $81.20–$98.60) double. Children 15 and under stay free in parents' room. AE, DC, MC, V. **Amenities**: Restaurant, bar; outdoor pool; room service; laundry. *In room:* TV, minibar.

DINING

Bar/Bistro André *Value*   Regrettably, seafood is an expensive item anywhere in France, and it's a bit of a splurge, but worth it. One plate of food at the lower end of the price scale is a big meal unto itself. Menu items are based on the seafaring traditions of La Rochelle, and include savory versions of fish soup; all kinds of shellfish; an unusual version of *cabillaud fume* (home-smoked codfish) served with a garlic-flavored cream sauce; a local version of curried mussels (*mouclade*); and a local saltwater fish not very common in other parts of France, filet of *maigre* served with a chive-flavored cream sauce. The restaurant is set between the square overlooking the port and one of the oldest streets in town.

5 rue St-Jean/Place de la Chaine. ℭ 05-46-41-28-24. Reservations recommended. Main courses 72F–128F (10.95– 19.45, $10.45–$18.55); fixed-price menu 122F (18.55, $17.70). AE, MC, V. Daily noon–2:30pm and 7–10:30pm.

Le Bistrot Rochelais *Value* TRADITIONAL FRENCH   The affordable meals here are attuned to modern tastes, even though based on traditional recipes. Since 1998, the well-prepared food and hardworking staff have gained the respect of other restaurants nearby. Menu items are savory and surprisingly sophisticated: Examples include a mixed platter of fish with curry sauce, braised filet of pork, a salad of mâche, grilled scallops, and vinaigrette; fresh codfish with a purée of garlic; and a filet of sea bass with asparagus.

14 rue St-Jean-du-Perot. ℭ 05-46-41-17-03. Reservations required in summer. Main courses 60F–110F (9.10– 16.70, $8.70–$15.95) fixed-price menu 89F–120F (13.55– 18.25, $12.90–$17.40) AE, DC, MC, V. Daily noon–midnight.

Les Quatre Sergents TRADITIONAL FRENCH   This restaurant is housed in a fanciful Art Nouveau greenhouse some visitors compare to the framework of the Eiffel Tower. Specialties include seafood ragoût, duxelles of turbot, brochettes of crayfish, mussels in curry sauce, and several regional favorites that have been going strong for the better part of 100 years.

49 rue St-Jean-du-Pérot. ℭ 05-46-41-35-80. Reservations required. Main courses 65F–100F (9.90– 15.20, $9.45–$14.50); fixed-price menu 80F–190F (12.15– 28.90, $11.60–$27.55) AE, DC, MC, V. Tues–Sun noon–2pm; Tues–Sat 7:30–10pm.

Relais Gourmand–Richard Coutanceau ⭑⭑⭑ MODERN FRENCH This is not only the most glamorous restaurant in La Rochelle but also one of the finest along the coast Delectable cuisine is served in this circular concrete pavilion in a pine-filled park. Clearly an artist, Richard Coutanceau, the owner and genius chef, offers his "modernized" cuisine that often includes fresh local shellfish; lobster-filled ravioli with zucchini flowers; freshwater crayfish in aspic with oysters; and roasted turbot with tomato-enriched béarnaise.

Plage de la Concurrence. (05-46-41-48-19. Reservations required. Main courses 135F–195F (20.50– 29.65, $19.60–$28.30); fixed-price menu 250F–480F (38– 72.95, $36.25–$69.60) AE, DC, MC, V. Mon–Sat noon–2pm and 7:30–9:30pm.

LA ROCHELLE AFTER DARK

To find the heart of La Rochelle's nightlife from July to September, head for **quai Duperré** and **cours des Dames.** Once the sun starts to set, cars are cleared away and the area becomes one big pedestrian zone peppered with street performers. It's a fun, almost magical area that sets the tone for the rest of the night.

Later you might find yourself at **MacEwan's,** 7 rue de la Chaîne ((**05-46-41-18-94**). At cour du Temple, you'll find two little hotbeds of fun. The proudly French-style **Le Piano Pub,** 12 cour du Temple ((**05-46-41-03-42**), hosts regular rock concerts that keep the 18- to 35-year-old crowd coming back for more. With its staunchly English decor of wood and leather, **Le Mayflower,** 14 bis cour du Temple ((**05-46-50-51-39**), is just as popular with the same age group. Both places are loud, boisterous, and very friendly. A recent newcomer to the scene is **Music-Hall Cohiba,** place du Maréchal Foch. (**05-46-41-27-77,** a disco and bar that's steeped with the music and aesthetics of Cuba.

Gays are often attracted to the mixed crowds at **Le Tuxedo Café,** 21 Place du Maréchal Foch ((**05-46-50-01-22**).

3 Cognac

297 miles SW of Paris, 23 miles NW of Angoulême, 70 miles SE of La Rochelle

The world enjoys 100 million bottles a year of the nectar known as cognac, which Victor Hugo called "the drink of the gods." Sir Winston Churchill required a bottle a day. It's worth a detour to visit one of the château warehouses of the great cognac bottlers. Martell, Hennessy, and Otard welcome visits from the public and even give you a free drink at the end of the tour.

ESSENTIALS

GETTING THERE Cognac's rail station is south of the town center. Seven **trains** per day arrive from Angoulême (trip time: 1 hour), and seven trains pull in from Saintes (20 minutes). For train information and schedules, call (**08-36-35-35-35. Bus** travel is scarce in this part of France. For information contact La Gare Routière ((**05-45-82-01-99**), which is located next to the railway station.

If you're **driving** to Cognac, the best route is from Saintes (which lies along the major route A10); follow N141 west.

VISITOR INFORMATION The **Office de Tourisme** is at 16 rue du 14-Juillet ((**05-45-82-10-71;** www.tourism-cognac.com).

SPECIAL EVENTS Cognac grapes are among the last to be picked in France. Harvest time usually begins in mid-October.

For the ultimate in the newest whodunit movies, come to town in late March and early April for the **Festival du Film Policier.** Screenings of crime films by each year's new wave of directors are held in theaters around town. Contact the **Bureau National de Cognac** ((**05-45-35-60-89**) for complete information.

EXPLORING THE TOWN

Many visitors don't realize that this unassuming town of some 22,000 people is actually a town, and not just a drink. Cognac may be beautiful to drink, but it's not beautiful to make. A black fungus that lives on the vapors released by the cognac factories has turned the town's buildings an ugly gray. But while the fumes may blacken the houses, they also fill the air here with a kind of sweetness.

If you'd like to visit a distillery, go to its main office during regular business hours and request a tour. The staffs are generally receptive, and you'll see some brandies that have aged for as long as 50 or even 100 years. You can ask about guided tours at the tourist office. The best distillery tour is offered by **Hennessy** ✿, 1 rue de la Richonne (© 05-45-35-72-68). It's open daily 10am to 6pm (closed January 1, May 1, and December 25). Guided tours cost 30F to 50F (4.55 to 7.60, $4.35 to $7.25), depending on how many glasses of cognac you consume at the end of your tour. Tours last 75 minutes.

To buy bottles of cognac, you can visit one of the distilleries, take the tour, have a free taste, and then purchase a bottle or two. In addition to Hennessy, you can try **Camus,** 29 rue Marguerite-de-Navarre (© 05-45-32-28-28); **Martell,** place Edouard-Martell (© 05-45-36-33-33); and **Rémy-Martin,** domaine de Merpins, route de Pons (© 05-45-35-76-66). If you're short on time, opt for **La Cognathèque,** 10 place Jean-Monnet (© 05-45-82-43-31), which prides itself on having the widest selection of cognac from all the distilleries, though you'll pay extra for the convenience of having everything under one roof. Another cognac producer with a well-recognized product is **Otard,** 127 Bd. Denfert-Rochereau (© 05-45-36-88-86).

At the **Musée de Cognac,** 48 bd. Denfert-Rochereau (© 05-45-32-07-25), you can see a collection including exhibits on popular arts and traditions (local artifacts in the cognac industry) as well as archaeological exhibits, plus a fine arts collection (painting, sculpture, decorative arts, and furniture). It's open Wednesday to Monday, June to September 10am to noon and 2 to 6pm, and October to May 2 to 5:30pm. Admission is 13F (2, $1.90), 6.50F (1, 95¢) for students, and children under 18 are free.

Cognac has two beautiful parks: the **Parc François-1er** and the **Parc de l'Hôtel-de-Ville.** The Romanesque-Gothic **Église St-Léger,** rue d'Angoulême (© 05-45-82-05-71), is from the 12th century, and its bell tower is from the 15th. The town is imbued with memories of François I, who was born in the **Château de Cognac** (© 05-45-36-88-86), which today belongs to the Otard cognac firm.

ACCOMMODATIONS

Domaine du Breuil ✿✿ This 18th-century manor house, studded with magnificent windows, is set in an 18-acre landscaped park 2 minutes from the center of Cognac. Cognac aficionados and those in town to do business with the factories head here for the hospitality; the, well-appointed rooms; and excellent cuisine from the southwest of France. Rooms have a pristine simplicity but are well furnished and well maintained, each with a compact bathroom with a combination tub and shower. The food is reason enough to visit, and, naturally, you'll finish off with a cognac in the bar to aid digestion.

104 rue Robert-Daugas, 16100 Cognac. © 05-45-35-32-06. Fax 05-45-35-48-06. 24 units. 300F–400F (45.60– 60.80, $43.50–$58) double. AE, MC, V. **Amenities:** Restaurant, bar; room service; laundry. *In room:* TV, hair dryer.

Hostellerie Les Pigeons Blancs ⭐ This stylish hotel is named after the white pigeons that nest in its moss-covered stone walls. The angular farmhouse with sloping tile roofs was built in the 17th century as a coaching inn. For many years, it was the home of the Tachet family, until they transformed it into a hotel and restaurant in 1973. It's a mile northwest of the town center and offers elegant guest rooms. The midsize to spacious, well-furnished rooms are comfortably furnished, each equipped with an average sized bathroom with a combination tub and shower. The restaurant is recommended (see "Dining," below).

110 rue Jules-Brisson, 16100 Cognac. ℂ **05-45-82-16-36.** Fax 05-45-82-29-29. 6 units. 400F–600F (60.80– 91.20, $58–$87) double. AE, DC, V. Closed Jan 1–15. **Amenities:** Restaurant; room service; laundry. *In room:* TV, hair dryer.

Hôtel Ibis Clean and unpretentious, this hotel is identified by townspeople as either the Ibis or the Urbis, though management suggests the name Ibis. The pleasant rooms are outfitted in a standardized modern style with comfortable bedding, each with a compact bathroom with shower. Some overlook a garden. Breakfast is the only meal served, but sometimes the management will prepare you a simple platter if you prefer to dine in.

24 rue Elisée-Mousnier, 16100 Cognac. ℂ **05-45-82-19-53.** Fax 05-45-82-86-71. 40 units. 350F–360F (53.20– 54.70, $50.75–$52.20) double. AE, DC, MC, V. Parking 25F (3.80, $3.65). **Amenities:** Garden; room service; laundry/dry cleaning. *In room:* TV, minibar.

DINING

The restaurant at **Domaine du Breuil** (see "Accommodations," above) also offers worthwhile meals.

Hostellerie Les Pigeons Blancs ⭐⭐ MODERN FRENCH This restaurant, run by the Tachet family, has two elegant dining rooms with exposed ceiling beams and limestone fireplaces. Menu offerings depend on the availability of ingredients but might include warm oysters with mushrooms and a champagne-flavored cream sauce; lobster with champagne sauce and bay leaves; roasted sea bass served with spice-flavored butter sauce; slices of warm goose liver with pears and white wine; and a particularly succulent version of duck steak with warm mandarin oranges and caramelized vinegar. The flavor combinations always seem successful here.

110 rue Jules-Brisson. ℂ **05-45-82-16-36.** Reservations recommended. Main courses 90F–160F (13.70– 24.30, $13.05–$23.20); fixed-price menus 120F–320F (18.25– 48.65, $17.40–$46.40) lunch, 178F–320F (27.05– 48.65, $25.80–$46.40) dinner. AE, DC. Daily noon–2pm; Mon–Sat 7–10pm. Closed Jan 1–15.

NEARBY ACCOMMODATIONS & DINING

Moulin de Cierzac ⭐ *Finds* The site of this restaurant and hotel has been around for 150 years. This former mill house is set beside a flowing stream at the southern periphery of a village (St-Fort-sur-le-Né), 8 miles south of Cognac. Loaded with character, and under the dedicated management of the well-respected team of Georges Renault and his wife Evelyne, it's best known as the site of a superb restaurant, more so than a hotel. Many diners, however, do opt to spend the night here in one of the quaint, charmingly decorated rooms.

Cuisine is crafted by M. Geslin, a gifted chef whose reputation is of the highest caliber. He makes abundant use of local products, especially the foie gras, vegetables, nuts, and berries of the region. Fixed-price menus cost 138F to 258F (21 to 39.20, $20 to $37.40); main courses 85F to 135F (12.90 to

20.50, $12.35 to $19.60) and are served at lunch and dinner daily except Monday. Advance reservations are highly recommended. Come for the crust-covered version of warm foie gras of duckling, served with sesame, pineapple, and essence of morels; strips of veal braised in local wine, served with mashed potatoes; and desserts such as a grapefruit-flavored "cappuccino" served with Szechuan pepper.

Rte. de Barbezieux, 16130 St-Fort-sur-le-Né. (℃ **05-45-83-01-32.** Fax 05-45-83-03-59. www.moulin decierzac.com. 10 units. 295F–480F (44.85– 72.95, $42.80–$69.60) double. AE, DC, MC, V. Closed mid-Jan to mid-Feb. From Cognac, drive 8 miles south of town, following the signs for Bordeaux and Barbezieux. **Amenities:** Restaurant; room service; laundry. *In room:* TV, hair dryer.

4 Angoulême (★(★

275 miles SW of Paris, 72 miles NE of Bordeaux

The old town of Angoulême, population 46,000, hugs a hilltop between the Charente and Aguienne rivers. You can visit it on the same day you visit Cognac. The town was the center of the French paper industry in the 17th century, a tradition carried on today: Angoulême remains the center of French comic-strip production. Rolling off the presses are the latest adventures of Tintin, Astérix, and Lucky Luke. During the last week of January, Angoulême is the site of the **Festival de la Bande Dessinée (Festival of Cartoons),** the centerpiece of which is the **Centre National de la Bande Dessinéet de l'Image (NOBI),** see "Exploring the Town," below. During its run, cartoon artists from around the world gather to present, on-screen, examples of their work and lecture onlookers about their art form. For more information, contact NOBI (℃ **05-45-38-65-65**) directly, or the local tourist office.

ESSENTIALS

GETTING THERE   There are 12 regular **trains** and 8 to 10 TGV trains every day from Bordeaux (trip time: 1½ hours by regular train, 55 minutes by TGV). There are also four to five trains daily from Saintes and another five from Poitiers (1 hour from either city). From Paris, there are seven trains daily (3 hours). For train information and schedules, call ℃ **08-36-35-35-35.** If you're **driving,** take N10 northeast to Angoulême.

VISITOR INFORMATION   The **Office de Tourisme** is at 7 bis rue du Chat (℃ **05-45-95-16-84**).

EXPLORING THE TOWN

The hub of the town is **place de l'Hôtel-de-Ville.** The town hall was erected from 1858 to 1866 on the site of the palace of the ducs d'Angoulême, where Marguerite de Navarre, sister of François I, was born. All that remains of the palace are the 15th-century Tour de Valois and 13th-century Tour de Lusignan.

The **Cathédrale St-Pierre** (★, place St-Pierre (℃ **05-45-95-20-38**), was begun in 1128 and restored in the 19th century. Flanked by towers, its facade boasts 75 statues, each in a separate niche, representing the Last Judgment. This is one of France's most startling examples of Romanesque-Byzantine style. Some of its restoration was questionable, however. The architect, Abadie (designer of Sacré-Coeur in Paris), tore down the north tower, then rebuilt it with the original materials in the same style. In the interior you can wander under a four-domed ceiling. It's open Monday to Saturday 8am to 7pm and Sunday 9am to 6:30pm.

Adjoining is the former bishops' palace, which has become the **Musée des Beaux-Arts,** 1 rue Friedland (✆ 05-45-95-07-69), and features a collection of European paintings, mainly from the 17th to the 19th century. The most interesting exhibits are the African art, ethnological, and archaeological collections. It's open Monday to Friday noon to 6pm and Saturday and Sunday 2 to 6pm. Admission is 15F (2.30, $2.20) adults, 5F (.75, 75¢) students and children under 18.

Angoulême is the European capital of the cartoon industry, with strong historic and creative links to many of the pop-art and cartoon themes that are today part of the overall cultural fabric of French life. The art form's focal point is the **Centre National de la Bande Dessinée at de l'Image,** 121 rue de Bordeaux (✆ 05-45-38-6565). Inside you'll find a museum devoted to famous (and usually original) cartoons and their creation, a library, a bookshop, and creative people who come here for insights into the entertainment industry. It's open Tuesday to Friday 10am to 6pm, Saturday and Sunday 2 to 6pm. July and August, it's open on the above-mentioned days to 7pm. Entrance costs 30F (4.55, $4.35) adults, 20F (3.05, $2.90) persons aged 7 to 18 and students, and free for children under 7.

Finally, you can take the **promenade des Remparts** ★★, a boulevard laid on the site of the demolished walls that once surrounded the city. From certain points, you'll have superb views of the valley almost 250 feet below.

ACCOMMODATIONS

Mercure Hôtel de France ★★ This grand hotel stands in the center of the old town on extensive grounds. Rooms are generally spacious, with high ceilings and French provincial furnishings; each comes with a fair-sized bathroom with a combination tub and shower. Beds are comfortable with firm mattresses. A formal restaurant offers excellent food and polite service. Specialties include foie gras, sole meunière, and trout with almonds. Lunch is served Monday to Friday; dinner is offered nightly.

1 place des Halles, 16000 Angoulême. ✆ **05-45-95-47-95.** Fax 05-45-92-02-70. 89 units. 540F (82.10, $78.30) double; 640F (97.30, $92.80) suite. AE, DC, MC, V. Parking 42F (6.40, $6.10). **Amenities:** Restaurant, bar; room service; laundry; baby-sitting. In room: A/C, TV, minibar, hair dryer.

Relais Mercure Angoulême Nord *Kids* This dependable hotel is the area's family-friendly choice. The grounds are filled with evergreens and well-maintained lawns. Rooms are simple and chain-hotel uniform, each featuring a double bed with a comfortable mattress, a couch that transforms into a twin, and a midsize bathroom with a combination tub and shower. The sunny, modern restaurant serves a variety of local and international specialties, but the cuisine is no reason to stay here.

Rte. de Poitiers, 16430 Champniers. ✆ **05-45-68-53-22.** Fax 05-45-68-33-83. 103 units. 395F (60.05, $57.30) double. AE, DC, MC, V. Take N10 from Angoulême about 4 miles toward Poitiers. **Amenities:** Restaurant; room service; laundry. In room: A/C, TV, hair dryer.

DINING

La Ruelle ★★ FRENCH This first-class restaurant, in the center of the oldest part of town, is the town's best. Christophe Combeau, and his wife, Virginie, are the only shining lights in Angoulême's dim culinary scene. Count on classic French recipes with a modern twist. The best specialties include ravioli stuffed with a confit of duckling, served with a vegetable bouillon with herbs; filet of fried red snapper with polenta, with starfruit sauce; shoulder of lamb cooked with herbs and baby vegetables; and a semisoft warm chocolate cake served with coffee liqueur and essence of oranges.

6 rue Trois-Notre-Dame. ℂ 05-45-92-94-64. Reservations recommended. Main courses 90F–160F (13.70– 24.30, $13.05–$23.20); fixed-price menus 130F (19.75, $18.85) lunch, 170F–240F (25.85– 36.50, $24.65–$34.80) dinner. AE, DC, MC, V. Tues–Fri noon–2pm; Mon–Sat 7:30–10pm. Closed two weeks in August.

NEARBY ACCOMMODATIONS & DINING

Le Moulin du Maine-Brun ★★   Today it's the premier place to stay and dine in this area. But this Relais du Silence (part of a chain of hotels noted for their tranquility) was originally a flour mill. It's surrounded by 80 acres of lowlands, about half of which are now devoted to the production of cognac. The maître d'hôtel's preferred brand is the one made in the hotel's distillery: Moulin du Domaine de Maine-Brun. These are the most luxurious accommodations around. Rooms are individually decorated with 18th- and 19th-century French period furniture but with new mattresses. The restaurant serves splendid fare; specialties include terrine of foie gras with cognac, a tartare of raw salmon with lime-flavored chive sauce, and a ragoût of four kinds of fish and shellfish cooked with leeks and local white wine.

R.N. 141, Lieu-Dit la Vigerie, 16290 Asnières-sur-Nouère. ℂ 05-45-90-83-00. Fax 05-45-96-91-14. hostellerie-du-maine-brun@wanadoo.fr .20 units. 630F–760F (95.75– 115.50, $91.35–$110.20) double; 950F–1300F (144.40– 197.60, $137.75–$188.50) suite. AE, DC, MC, V. Hotel and restaurant closed Nov–Jan. Take R.N. 141 4½ miles west of Angoulême and turn right at Vigerie. **Amenities:** Restaurant; bar; room service; laundry. *In room:* TV, minibar, hair dryer.

5 Bordeaux ★★★

359 miles SW of Paris, 341 miles W of Lyon

On the Garonne River, the great port of Bordeaux, the capital of Aquitaine, is the center of the world's most important wine-producing area. It attracts many visitors to the offices of wine exporters here, most of whom welcome guests. (For a trip through the surrounding Bordeaux Wine Country, refer to section 6, "The Wine Country," later in this chapter.)

Bordeaux is a city of warehouses, factories, mansions, and exploding suburbs, as well as wide quays 5 miles long. Now the fifth-largest French city, Bordeaux belonged to the British for 300 years, and even today is considered the most "un-French" of French cities.

It may not exude the joie de vivre of Paris, but Bordeaux is a major cultural center and a transportation hub between southern France and Spain. With a population of some 650,000, much of Bordeaux is looking seedy, but the worn-out docklands to the south of the center are slated for urban renewal.

ESSENTIALS

GETTING THERE   The local **airport,** Bordeaux-Mérignac (ℂ **05-56-34-50-50** for flight information), is served by flights from as far away as London and New York. It's 6½ miles west of Bordeaux in Mérignac. A **shuttle bus** connects the airport with the train station, departing every 30 minutes from 6am to 10:30pm (trip time: 40 minutes), and costing 37F (5.60, $5.35) one-way for adults and 29F (4.40, $4.20) for students, children under 6 free.

The railway station, Gare St-Jean, is on the west bank of the river, within a 30-minute walk (or 5-minute taxi ride) of the center of the old town. Some 12 to 15 **trains** from Paris arrive per day (trip time: 3 hours by TGV). For train information and schedules, call ℂ **08-36-35-35-35.**

Bordeaux is easily reached **by car.** From Paris, follow A10 south through the cities of Orléans, Tours, and Poitiers into Bordeaux (trip time: about 5 hours). Be aware that navigating the city streets of Bordeaux is fraught with hazards: narrow 18th-century alleys, massive traffic jams on the quays beside the Garonne, and simply too many cars and people. Consequently, expect a lack of easily available parking within the city's historic core, and head, whenever possible, for any of the blue-and-white "P" signs that indicate public garages.

VISITOR INFORMATION The **Office de Tourisme** is at 12 cours du 30-Juillet (© 05-56-00-66-00; www.bordeaux-tourisme.com).

EXPLORING BORDEAUX

Wine exporters welcome guests who come to sample wines and learn about the industry. In section 6, "The Wine Country," later in this chapter, we take a tour of the Bordeaux Wine Country. Plan your trip with maps and guides that are available free from the **Maison du Vin (House of Wine),** 3 cours du 30-Juillet (© **05-56-00-22-88**), opposite the tourist office. To make the rounds of the vineyards, consider alternative forms of transport: bus, bicycle, or even walking.

STROLLS THROUGH TOWN You can traipse around the **old town** on your own, since it's fairly compact, or take advantage of the 2-hour **walking tour** the tourist office (see above) arranges daily at 10am (year-round) and at 3pm (mid-July to mid-August only). Conducted in both French and English, tours begin at the tourist office, cost 40F (6.10, $5.80) per adult and 35F (5.30, $5.10) for students and children 17 and under, and take in all the most important sites. We strongly recommend these, as they correspond to the opening hours of each of the monuments listed below. Reserve in advance, call to confirm that the tour is on for the day of your arrival. Additionally, April 15 to November 15, every Wednesday and Saturday, there's a bus tour, with French and English commentary, that departs daily at 10am from in front of the tourist office.

If you go it alone, your tour of Old Bordeaux can begin at **place de la Comédie,** at the very heart of this old city, a busy traffic hub that was once the site of a Roman temple. On this square, one of the great theaters of France, the **Grand Théâtre** ★★, was built between 1773 and 1780 as testimony to the burgeoning prosperity of Bordeaux's emerging bourgeoisie. A colonnade of 12 columns graces its facade. Surmounted on these are statues of goddesses and the Muses. If you'd like to visit the richly decorated interior, ask the porter; you can also phone the tourist office about the schedule for one of the weekly guided tours of the site. They cost 30F (4.58, $4.80) per adult, 20F (3.05, $2.90) per child, and are scheduled to coincide with French school holidays.

From here you can walk north to **esplanade des Quinconces,** the largest square of its kind in Europe. It was laid out between 1818 and 1828, and covers nearly 30 acres. A smaller but lovelier square is **place de la Bourse** ★, bounded by quays opening onto the Garonne. It was laid out between 1728 and 1755; the fountain of the Three Graces is at its center. Flanking the square are the Custom House and the Stock Exchange.

CHURCHES The largest and most ostentatious church in Bordeaux, and the city's religious centerpiece, is the **Cathédrale St-André** ★★, place Pey-Berland (© **05-56-81-64-36**), near the southern perimeter of the old town. The sculptures on the 13th-century Porte Royale (Royal Door) are admirable; see also the 14th-century sculptures on the North Door. Separate from the rest of the

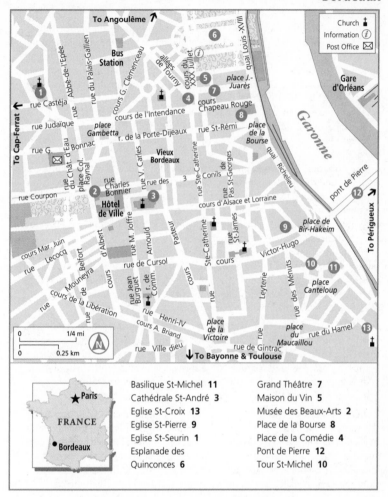

church is the 155-foot **Tour Pey-Berland,** a belfry begun in the 15th century. Foundations date from 900 years ago. The church is open July to September, daily 7:30 to 11:30am and 2 to 6:30pm. Off-season, it's closed Sunday afternoons. The tower is open daily 10am to 5pm (to 6pm in April, May, June, and September, and to 7pm in July and August). Tower admission is 25F (3.80, $3.65) for adults and 15F (2.30, $2.20) for those 25 and under. Organ recitals are held Tuesdays in summer from 6:30 to 7:30pm. Admission is free.

Bordeaux, always a magnet for power, money, and ecclesiastical zeal, has four other important churches, each with an unusual charm. Foremost among these is the **Basilique St-Michel** ⋆, place St-Michel (place Canteloup). The church itself is incredibly charming, but more impressive is the **Fleche St-Michel** across the street. This tower, erected in 1472, is the tallest stone tower in France, rising 374 feet. The tower (and the 228 steps you'll have to climb to reach its summit) is open for visits June to September, daily 3 to 7pm, for 15F (2.30, $2.20).

From the top, you are confronted with sweeping views out over the port. The rest of the year, unless you receive special permission from the tourist office, you'll have to appreciate the architecture of the tower from the ground. During July and August, every Friday 5 to 7pm, the bells in the tower are activated as part of a (free) carillon concert that can be heard throughout the neighborhood.

Another interesting church is **Basilique St-Seurin,** place des Martyrs de la Résistance (℗ **05-56-48-22-08**), whose most ancient sections, such as its crypt, date from the 5th century. See the porch leftover from an earlier church; it has some capitals from the Romanesque era. It's open daily 8am to noon and 2 to 7:30pm. During July and August, it's the site of free organ recitals every Thursday at 6pm.

The **Abbatiale Ste-Croix,** place Pierre-Renaudel, gained attention in musical circles around the world when its organ, a musical marvel built by a monk, Dom Bedos, was restored to its original working order in 1996. You can hear it during the free organ recitals conducted here every Wednesday at 6pm during July and August. The church itself, a severe Romanesque structure from the 11th and 12th centuries, is revered for its stately dignity.

For information about any of the four "secondary" churches above, you can call the **Presbytère de l'Église St-Michel** (℗ **05-56-94-30-50**), but the kindly prelates who answer are likely to speak only French. Opening hours of each vary slightly, according to the day's schedule for masses and celebrations, but are usually Monday to Saturday 8am to 6pm and Sunday 9am to noon.

A MUSEUM   **Musée des Beaux-Arts** ✹✹, 20 cours d'Albret (Jardin du Palais-Rohan) (℗ **05-56-10-20-30**), has an outstanding collection ranging from the 15th to the 20th centuries. Works by Perugina, Titian, Rubens, Veronese, Delacroix, and Marquet are displayed. The museum is open Monday and Wednesday to Friday 11am to 6pm and Saturday and Sunday 2-6pm. Admission is 25F (3.80, $3.65) adults; children and students free.

BOAT RIDES   The **pont de Pierre,** with 17 arches, stretches 1,594 feet across the Garonne and is one of the most beautiful bridges in France. Ordered built by Napoléon I in 1813, the bridge can be crossed on foot for a view of the quays and the port. But for an even better view we suggest a **tour of the port,** which lasts about 1½ hours and goes up the river and all around the harbor. It departs from the Embarcadères des Quinconces, on quai Louis-XVIII in the center of town. It's open year-round. The cost is 55F (8.35, $8) for adults and 35F (5.30, $5.10) for children under 10. For exact times and a wide selection of other cruises, call the tourism office (see "Essentials," above) or **the boat captains' office** near the quai (℗ **05-56-52-88-88**). Ask about the occasional floating concerts at night. Note that tours may be canceled without warning.

You may enjoy a **cruise** on one of France's mightiest (and least-visited) rivers, the Garonne. In July and August, **Alienor Loisirs,** Hangar 7, quai Louis-XVIII (℗ **05-56-51-27-90**), offers a Sunday-afternoon ride downriver from Bordeaux to the château town of Blaye. Boarding at the company's dock begins at around 11am for an 11:30am departure. Lunch is served on board, and between 2 and 4pm you enjoy a shore excursion in Blaye. The return to Bordeaux is usually scheduled for around 6:30pm the same day. The cost, lunch included, is 270F (41.05, $39.15), 115F (17.50, $16.70) children under 12. The rest of the year, roughly equivalent excursions are offered, depending on the number of prepaid advance reservations. Closed each February. For more information, call the Bordeaux tourist office or Alienor Loisirs.

SHOPPING

If you want antiques, concentrate your search around **rue Bouffard, rue des Remparts,** and **rue Notre-Dame,** where you'll find a market area known as **Village Notre-Dame,** housing all sorts and sizes of antiques shops. Another haven is the neighborhood around **Église St-Michel,** particularly the passage St-Michel, a narrow alleyway a few stops from the church.

If you need to fill up some empty suitcases with new clothes, go to the couture quarter around **place des Grands Hommes** with its many upscale, trendy, and classic clothing emporiums. If you're out for a younger, more casual style, try the shops (and also the many restaurants) around **place du Parlement.** And for the highest concentration of shops in town, head for the **Rue Ste-Catherine,** the longest pedestrian street in France, and site of at least 100 boutiques that range from the most luxurious to the cheapest.

The better-known choices include the haute couture boutique of the Bordeaux designer **Jacqueline Dourthe,** 18 rue Lafaurie-de-Monbadon (✆ **05-56-52-35-78**), where you can find everything from cocktail and evening dresses to the most luxurious wedding gowns; and **La Soierie,** 54 cours George Clemenceaux (✆ **05-56-51-23-75**), which carries a complete line of chic women's silk garments.

Galerie Condillac, 24 rue Condillac (✆ **05-56-79-04-31**), is one of the classier art houses that specializes in mostly local artists who paint with strong, vibrant colors. A relatively cramped but choice emporium for French crystal and antique engravings is **Maurice Mazuque,** 6 rue du Parlement Ste-Catherine. For a sugar rush, head over to **Cadiot Badie,** 26 allées de Tourny (✆ **05-56-44-24-22**), where you'll find everything from sinfully good pralines to creamy and decadent Bordeaux truffles.

ACCOMMODATIONS

Hôtel Continental ⭐ *(Value)*   To get a certain class, charm, and elegance in Bordeaux at this price is a rarity. In the center of the golden triangle, on a semipedestrian mall dotted with boutiques, this 18th-century town house wins new fans every year. You'll get a warm welcome and a fine dose of Bordelaise hospitality. Rooms, although a bit small (especially the singles), are warmly decorated and furnished, each with a compact bathroom with a combination tub and shower. A few have balconies, but space is at an absolute minimum.

10 rue Montesquieu, 33000 Bordeaux. ✆ **05-56-52-66-00.** Fax 05-56-52-77-97. www.hotel-le-continental. com. 50 units. 370F–580F (56.25– 88.15, $53.65–$84.10) double;1,200F (182.40, $174) suite. AE, DC, MC, V. **Amenities:** Breakfast-only room service. *In room:* A/C, TV, minibar.

Hôtel de Sèze *(Value)*   This hotel occupies an 18th-century building that's an antique in its own right, roughly equivalent to many others in its historic neighborhood. The hotel is such a well-known value that you should make reservations as early as possible. Rooms, which are scattered over four floors, are comfortable and well furnished; the cheapest has only a bed and bathroom (with shower only).

23 allées de Tourny, 33000 Bordeaux. ✆ **05-56-52-65-54.** Fax 05-56-48-98-00. 24 units. 300F–450F (45.60– 68.40, $43.50–$65.25) double. AE, DC, MC, V. Parking 40F (6.10, $5.80). *In room:* TV, minibar.

Hôtel Majestic   Set back from quai Louis-XVIII, which opens onto the Garonne, this choice is sheltered in a sturdy 18th-century town house, which has been carefully restored to offer modern comforts. In the historic and commercial heart of Bordeaux, it lies on a tranquil street near the Grand Theater.

Finds Buying Wine in Bordeaux

Many visitors come to Bordeaux to buy wine. There are inexpensive wines, but it doesn't make sense to blow your one-bottle-per-adult liquor allowance on a 15F (2.30, $2.20) bottle. Try to pick one that carries personal significance because you've visited the vineyard, or chat up the experts at some of the wine shops. We recommend **La Vinothèque,** 8 cours du 30-Juillet (✆ **05-56-52-32-05**); and **Badie,** 62 allées de Tourny ((✆ **05-56-52-23-72**). The best spots for red Bordeaux wines from small houses are **Château Lespare,** Beychac-et-Caillau, 24 miles north of Bordeaux (✆ **05-57-24-51-23**); **Château Bel Air,** Naujan-et-Postiac, 9 miles east of Bordeaux (✆ **05-57-84-55-08**); and **Château Les Bouzigues,** Saintes Gemmes, 47 miles south of Bordeaux (✆ **05-56-61-65-92**).

Rooms are decorated in a traditional French provincial style and contains soundproofing plus a midsize bathroom with a combination tub and shower. A carefully prepared continental breakfast is the only meal served, but room service is always available. The street outside is one of the most bustling in Bordeaux, with boutiques, museums, cafes, and restaurants.

2 rue de Condé, 33000 Bordeaux. ✆ **05-56-52-60-44.** Fax 05-56-79-26-70. www.hotel-majestic.com. 50 units. 390F–620F (59.30– 94.25, $56.55–$89.90) double. AE, DC, V. Parking 60F (9.10, $8.70). **Amenities:** Room service; laundry. *In room:* A/C, TV, minibar.

Mercure Bordeaux Mériadeck ✪ This hotel, in a sleek building facing a shopping mall in the Mériadeck business district, and only a 5-minute walk from the town center, offers modern comforts that are popular with business travelers and groups. The well-furnished rooms with modern amenities and comfortable mattresses attract vine growers and wine merchants from abroad. The best rooms are on the sixth floor (some are showing signs of wear and tear). Each is well furnished and comfortable, coming with an average sized bathroom with a combination tub and shower. La Brasserie du Festival, the main restaurant, is one of the finest hotel grills.

5 rue Robert-Lateulade, 33000 Bordeaux. ✆ **05-56-56-43-43.** Fax 05-56-96-50-59. www.mercure.com. 194 units. 590F–690F (89.70– 104.90, $85.55–$100.05) double; 1,000F (152, $145) suite. AE, DC, MC, V. Bus: 7 or 8. **Amenities:** Restaurant, bar; room service; laundry. *In room:* A/C, TV, minibar, hair dryer.

Mercure Château Chartrons ✪✪ This is one of Bordeaux's leading hotels. Near the landmark place Tourny, it opened in 1991. Rooms are decorated with memorabilia of the wine trade. Each comes with a midsize modern bathroom with a combination tub and shower. The bar has an impressive array of local vintages sold by the glass. The restaurant, Le Chai St-Louis, serves bistro-style specialties.

81 cours St-Louis, 33300 Bordeaux. ✆ **05-56-43-15-00.** Fax 05-56-69-15-21. www.mercure.com. 144 units. 580F–650F (88.15– 98.80, $84.10–$94.25) double; 790F (120.10, $114.55) suite. AE, DC, MC, V. Parking 45F (6.85, $6.55). **Amenities:** Restaurant, bar; room service; laundry. *In room:* A/C, TV, minibar, hair dryer.

Novotel Bordeaux Centre ✪ Built in 1989, this first-class hotel is in the heart of the city near the railway station, a short walk from the rue Sainte Catherine, quai des Chartrons, and the cathedral. Rooms are comfortable, with good-quality mattresses. All have standard motel-like bathrooms with a combination tub and shower. Some are suitable for individuals with disabilities.

45 cours du Maréchal-Juin, 33000 Bordeaux. © **05-56-51-46-46**. Fax 05-56-98-25-56. www.novotel.com. 140 units. 570F (86.65, $82.65) double; 850F (129.20, $123.25) suite. Children 15 and under stay free in parents' room. AE, DC, MC, V. Free parking. **Amenities:** Restaurant, bar; room service; laundry. *In room:* A/C, TV, minibar, hair dryer.

Tulip Inn Le Bayonne Etche-Ona ★★ In 1997, two antique, stone-fronted town houses, Le Bayonne Hotel and its equally but less elegant neighbor, Hôtel Etche-Ona, were radically upgraded and joined to form this entity. The aura of the 1930s has been retained, and many features have been added, most notably soundproofing and comfortable furnishings, along with midsize bathrooms, all with a combination tub and shower. Many attractions, including several good restaurants, the cathedral, place de la Bourse, the quays, and the Grand Théâtre, are nearby. Breakfast is the only meal served.

15 cours de l'Intendance (with entrances at 4 rue Martignac and 11 rue Mautrec), 33000 Bordeaux. © **05-56-48-00-88**. Fax 05-56-48-41-60. www.bordeaux-hotel.com. 63 units. 560F–650F (85.10– 98.80, $81.20–$94.25) double; 1,200F (182.40– $174) suite. AE, DC, MC, V. 70F (10.65, $10.15). **Amenities:** 2 bars; room service; baby-sitting; dry cleaning. *In room:* A/C, TV, minibar, hair dryer, safe.

DINING

You can also try the restaurant at **Mercure Château Chartrons** (see "Accommodations," above).

La Chamade *(Finds* TRADITIONAL FRENCH You'll have a delightful time at La Chamade, in a vaulted 18th-century cellar of honey-colored stone. Specialties include roasted foie gras with confit of leeks and scallops with truffles. The fish is steamed to perfection and served simply, often with a warm vinaigrette of tomatoes and basil. The owner, M. Lasserre, has an impressive collection of Bordeaux wines.

20 rue des Piliers-de-Tutelle. © **05-56-48-13-74**. Reservations required. Main courses 100F–250F (15.20– 38, $14.50–$36.25); fixed-price menu 100F–350F (15.20– 53.20, $14.50–$50.75) AE, DC, MC, V. Sun–Tues and Thurs–Fri noon–2:30pm. Closed last week July and first week Aug.

La Forge ★ *(Value* FRENCH Jean-Michel Pouts, a former chef on the ocean liner *France*, owns this bistro. The well-prepared specialties include brochette of pork with Gruyère, savory grilled meats, and an excellent cassoulet. The fixed-price menus are among the best value in town. The restaurant's devotion to a regional repertoire and attempts to keep prices down are most admirable. The savory *cassoulet maison* (a stewed combination of white beans, duck, pork, onions, and carrots) is excellent.

8 rue du Chai-des-Farines. © **05-56-81-40-96**. Reservations recommended. Main courses 60F–100F (9.10– 15.20, $8.70–$14.50); fixed-price menu 92F–160F (14– 24.30, $13.35–$23.20). AE, DC, MC, V. Tues–Sat noon–1:30pm and 7:30–10pm. Closed mid-Aug to mid-Sept.

La Tupina ★ TRADITIONAL FRENCH One of Bordeaux's most talented chefs runs this cozy restaurant with a summer terrace near quai de la Monnaie. It's been called "a tribute to country kitchens and the grandmothers who cooked in them." Jean-Pierre Xiradakis's specialty is duck, so your meal might begin with croutons spread with duck rillettes, and his salads often use duck giblets, skin, and livers. Regional specialties include roasted shoulder of lamb with white beans, *cassoulet maison,* and steaks grilled and barbecued at the table. Desserts usually include pears marinated in red Bordeaux wine.

6 rue de la Porte de la Monnaie. © **05-56-91-56-37**. Reservations recommended. Main courses 85F–295F (12.90– 44.85, $12.35–$42.80); fixed-price menus 100F (15.20, $14.50) lunch, 200F–300F (30.40– 45.60, $29–$43.50) dinner. AE, DC, MC, V. Daily noon–2pm and 7–11pm.

Le Chapon-Fin ★★★ MODERN FRENCH Under the guidance of Francis Garcia from Barcelona, this is the leading restaurant in Bordeaux, serving an even more refined cuisine than that found at the also-highly rated La Chamade (see above). The dining room boasts several banquettes in artificial stone grottoes; a pivoting skylight lets in summer breezes. A meal might include truffle flan with essence of morels, gratin of oysters with foie gras, crayfish-stuffed ravioli with lime sauce, sliced Atlantic lobster tail served with artichokes, white beans, serrano ham, and a superb array of cheeses and desserts. The wines are usually selected from the most respected and expensive French vintages.

5 rue Montesquieu. ✆ **05-56-79-10-10**. Reservations required. Main courses 180F–250F (27.35– 38, $26.10–$36.25); fixed-price menus 160F–425F (24.30– 64.60, $23.20–$61.65) lunch, 275F–425F (41.80– 64.60, $39.90–$61.65) dinner. AE, DC, MC, V. Tues–Sat noon–2pm and 7:30–10pm.

Le Vieux Bordeaux ★ MODERN FRENCH Nearly a neighborhood institution, this restaurant ranks among the top five in highly competitive Bordeaux. The decor is an almost-incongruous mix of exposed wood and modern accents, with a summer terrace. Specialties include pavé of fresh salmon with warm oysters; salad of crabmeat and sea urchins with vinaigrette; and "oriental" (sweet-and-sour) pigeon with lime sauce. Dessert might be a slice of "half-baked, half raw" chocolate cake served with mocha sauce.

27 rue Buhan. ✆ **05-56-52-94-36**. Reservations recommended. Main courses 80F 165F (12.15– 25.10, $11.60–$23.95); fixed-price menu 165F–300F (25.10– 45.60, $23.95–$43.50). AE, DC, MC, V. Mon–Fri noon–2pm and 8–10:30pm; Sat 8–10:30pm. Closed 2 weeks in Feb and 3 weeks in Aug.

NEARBY ACCOMMODATIONS & DINING

Restaurant St-James/Hôtel Hautrive ★★★ MODERN FRENCH This is the domain of Jean-Marie Amat, whose specialties are based on local seasonal ingredients. These may revolve around *cèpes* (the district's meaty flap mushrooms), game (venison and pheasant), *girolles* (another kind of mushroom), or fruit. In a modern dining room whose windows offer a view of some of the most famous vineyards in Europe, you can enjoy such dishes as terrine of mixed wild game and foie gras with a chanterelle salad and stewed rhubarb; a salad of raw scallops with balsamic vinegar; pigeon grilled with spices and presented Moroccan-style, as a pastilla; and roasted lobster served with potatoes and garlic cloves. Dessert might include a confit of figs, cooked with a crusty-crispy top and served with mandarin sorbet. You can dine less expensively in the brasserie, Le Bistroy, where meals average 160F (24.30, $23.20) without beverage.

Adjacent is the Hôtel Hautrive, whose 15 elegant rooms and three suites are scattered among four modern pavilions. Doubles go for 800F to 1,200F (121.60 to 182.40, $116 to $174); suites cost 1,400F to 1,700F (212.80 to 258.40, $203 to $246.50)

3 place Camille-Hostein, 33270 Bouliac. ✆ **05-57-97-06-00**. Fax 05-56-20-92-58. Reservations required. Main courses 140F–300F (21.30– 45.60, $20.30–$43.50); fixed-price menu 460F (69.90, $66.70). AE, DC, MC, V. Apr–Nov Wed–Sun noon–2pm and 8–10pm; Dec–Mar daily 8–10pm. Closed Jan. From Bordeaux, follow the signs south to Toulouse/Bayonne. At the périphérique encircling Bordeaux, follow the signs toward Paris; take exit 23 and follow the signs to Bouliac.

BORDEAUX AFTER DARK

Pick up a copy of *Clubs et Concerts* at the Office de Tourisme or *Bordeaux Plus* at one of the newsstands; both detail the goings-on in and around town.

Taking in a play or an opera could make for a good start to your evening. **Grand Théâtre,** place de la Comédie (✆ **05-56-00-85-20**), has a very busy and diverse performance schedule.

There's gambling, drinking, dining, and lots of opportunities for people-watching at **Casino de Bordeaux**, in the Hotel Sofitel Bordeaux Lac, Bd. Jean Gabriel Domergue (✆ **05-57-19-32-51**). Open daily 8pm to 3am, and charging 65F (9.90, $9.45) for entrance to its gaming rooms, it offers live piano-bar music every Wednesday to Saturday nights, and a well-choreographed restaurant where fixed-menus prices are 200F (30.40, $29) each.

For street life that's out-in-the-open and sometimes animated, head for the inner core of Bordeaux by night, to streets that include place de la Victoire, place St-Pierre, place du Parlement, place Camille Jullian, and—for a site particularly swarming with students—place Gambetta.

For some of the best pubbing around, hit the **Connemara Irish Pub,** 18 cours d'Albret (✆ **05-56-52-82-57**), where the Guinness flows freely and a noisy crowd gathers to hear traditional Irish music; or **Dick Turpin's Bar,** 72 rue du Loup (✆ **05-56-48-07-52**), which specializes in just about every brand of whiskey imaginable. With its white piano and live jazz, the piano and jazz club **Black Jack,** 35 place Gambetta (✆ **05-56-81-71-38**), creates a soft, stylish ambience that pulls in a sophisticated middle-aged crowd.

More raucous partiers head for the immense **L'Ane Qui Tousse,** 57 rue de Bègles (✆ **05-56-92-52-98**), with its two dance floors and tropical motifs. Frat types congregate at **Le Plana,** 22 place de la Victoire (✆ **05-56-91-73-23**), where the space around the bar turns into a makeshift dance floor once the party gets going. An even better choice for dancing is **Sénéchal,** 57 bis quai de Paludate (✆ **05-56-85-54-80**), with its 1970s decor and a just as classic 25- to 45-year-old crowd. A popular, and very hip, disco favorite that's spiced up with the occasional live cabaret or musical act is **Le Caesar's,** quai Louis XVIII (✆ **05-56-51-99-41**). At **Bar Le Moyen-Age,** 8 rue des Remparts (✆ **05-56-44-12-87**), a mostly **gay male** crowd congregates in a medieval-looking cellar.

6 The Wine Country

The major Bordeaux wine districts are Graves, Médoc, Sauternes, Entre-deux-Mers, Libourne, Blaye, and Bourg. North of the city of Bordeaux, the Garonne River joins the Dordogne. This forms the Gironde, a broad estuary at the heart of the wine country. More than 100,000 vineyards produce some 70 million gallons of wine a year, some of which are among the greatest reds in the world. (The white wines are lesser known.)

Some of the famous vineyards are pleased to welcome visitors, providing you don't arrive at the busy harvest time. However, most vineyards aren't likely to have a permanent staff to welcome you. Don't just show up. Call first or check with local tourist offices about appropriate times to visit.

VISITOR INFORMATION The best-respected source of information about the wines of Bordeaux (and French wines in general) is the **Centre d'Information, de Documentation, et de Dégustation (CIDD),** 30 rue de la Sablière, 75014 Paris (✆ **01-45-45-44-20;** fax 01-45-42-78-20). This self-funded school presents about a dozen courses throughout the year addressing all aspects of wine tasting, producing, buying, and merchandising. They will also send information to anyone anticipating a tour of the vineyards of France, either in the region around Bordeaux, or elsewhere.

Before heading out on this wine road, make sure you get a detailed map from the Bordeaux tourist office (see "Essentials" in section 5, "Bordeaux," earlier in this chapter), since the "trail" isn't well marked. From Bordeaux, head north toward Pauillac on D2, the wine road, called the Route des Grands-Crus.

LIBOURNE

This is a sizable market town with a railway connection. At the junction of the Dordogne and Isle rivers, Libourne is roughly the center of the St-Emilion, Pomerol, and Fronsac wine districts. In the town, a large colonnaded square still contains some houses from the 16th century, including the **Hôtel-de-Ville** (town hall). You can also explore the remains of 13th-century ramparts. In the town center is the **Office de Tourisme,** 40 place Abel-Surchamp (© **05-57-51-15-04**), where you can get details on visiting the Bordeaux vineyards.

NEARBY ACCOMMODATIONS & DINING

La Bonne Auberge This family hotel is located near an intersection of two busy highways. Although basic, the rooms are comfortable and welcoming, each coming with a small shower-only bathroom. This still feels more like a *restaurant avec chambres* than a full-fledged hotel. The food served here is good and plentiful. Serious diners go to the restaurant at the top of the exterior stairs; there's also a brasserie on the ground level. A fixed-price menu in the brasserie is 59F to 70F (8.95 to   10.65, $8.55 to $10.15), whereas the fixed-price menu in the restaurant goes for 74F to 207F (11.25 to   31.45, $10.75 to $30) Specialties are grilled salmon with shallot-flavored butter, omelets, lamb with parsley, snails in red-wine sauce, sweetbreads with mushrooms, and entrecôte in bordelaise-wine sauce. The restaurant is open daily for lunch and dinner; November to March, it's closed Saturday for lunch and Monday for dinner. Reservations for the restaurant are necessary.

Rue du 8-Mai-1945 et av. John-Talbot, 33350 Castillon-la-Bataille. © **05-57-40-11-56.** Fax 05-57-40-21-66. 10 units. 150F–330F (22.80–   50.15, $21.75–$47.85) double. AE, MC, V. Closed last 2 weeks in Nov. From Libourne, follow the signs to Bergerac; take the highway for 18 miles to Castillon-la-Bataille, then continue to the far end of the village. **Amenities:** restaurant. *In room:* TV.

MÉDOC ⭐

The Médoc, an undulating plain covered with vineyards, is one of the most visited regions in southwestern France. Its borders are marked by Bordeaux and the Pointe de Grave. Throughout the region are many châteaux producing grapes; only a handful of these, however, are worthy of your attention. The most visited château is that of Mouton-Rothschild, said to be second only to Lourdes among attractions in southwestern France, in spite of the red tape involved in visiting.

In Haut-Médoc, the soil isn't especially fertile but absorbs much heat during the day. To benefit from this, the vines are clipped close to the ground. The French zealously regulate the cultivation of the vineyards and the making of the wine. Less than 10% of the wines from the region are called Bordeaux. These are invariably red, including famous labels like Château Margaux, Château Latour, Château Mouton, and Château Lafite. Most of these are from grapes grown some 3,000 feet from the Gironde River.

EXPLORING THE AREA

Château Lafite This site is second only to the nearby Château Mouton-Rothschild. Count on spending at least an hour here. The vinothèque contains many vintage bottles, several dating from 1797. The Rothschilds purchased the château in 1868.

On D2. © **05-56-73-18-18**, or 01-53-89-78-00 for appointments. Free admission. Tours by appointment only. Mon–Fri 9–11am and 2–5pm. Closed Aug–Oct.

Château Margaux Known as the Versailles of the Médoc, this Empire-style château was built in the 19th century near the village of Margaux. The estate covers more than 650 acres, of which 193 acres produce Château Margaux and Pavillon Rouge du Château Margaux; almost 30 acres are devoted to producing Pavillon Blanc du Château Margaux. There are no tours of the chateau; you can only admire it from the outside. To see the vat rooms and wine cellars, make an appointment by letter or phone.

On D2, 33460 Margaux. ℰ **05-57-88-83-83.** chateau-margot@chateaux-margaux.com. Vat rooms and wine cellars open by appointment only. Mon–Fri 10am–noon and 2–4pm. Closed Aug–Oct.

Château Mouton-Rothschild ⭐ Thousands of tourists visit this château, one of the many former homes of the baron Philippe de Rothschild and his American-born wife, Pauline. Today their daughter, Philippine de Rothschild, carries on their work. The welcoming room is furnished with a collection of sculptures and paintings that portray wine as art, plus a 16th-century tapestry depicting the grape harvest. An adjoining museum, in former wine cellars, has art from many eras, much of it related to the cultivation of the vineyards. Note the collection of modern art, including a statue by the American sculptor Lippold.

Le Pouyalet, 33250 Pauillac. ℰ **05-56-73-21-29.** Tours 30F (4.55, $4.35) per person without a tasting, 80F–150F (12.15– 22.80, $11.60–$21.75) per person with a tasting. Tours by appointment only. Apr–Oct Sat–Thurs 9am–4pm, Fri 9am–3:30pm; Nov–Mar Mon–Fri 9am–4pm. Call to make an appointment well in advance to see the cellars.

Société Duboscq Your free visit to the cellars here will be followed by a complimentary *dégustation des vins* of whichever product you request. A relative newcomer whose prestige has grown rapidly, Duboscq offers excellent opportunities for studying the ancient fermentation process in its modern forms and the maturation process in new oak casks.

Château Haut-Marbuzet, 33180 St-Estephe ℰ **05-56-59-30-54.** Free admission. Mon–Sat 8am–noon and 2–5pm. Tours in English on Tues.

DINING

Auberge André *Finds* TRADITIONAL FRENCH This charming hideaway is located at the edge of Cambes, a village with no more than 100 residents, in a century-old farmhouse whose terrace offers a sweeping view of the Garonne. Menu items might include filet of eel with parsley-butter sauce, lamprey eels in bordelaise-wine sauce, *confit de canard,* filet of sea bass infused with essence of laurel, salmon cooked with port and, over autumn and winter, an impressive collection of game.

Le Grand Port, 33880 Cambes. ℰ **05-56-21-34-69.** Reservations recommended. Main courses 75F–118F (11.40– 17.95, $10.90–$17.10); fixed-price menu 135F–245F (20.50– 37.25, $19.60–$35.55). AE, MC, V. June–Sept Tues–Sun noon–2pm, Mon–Sat 8–10:30pm; Oct–May Wed–Sun noon–2pm, Wed–Sat 8:30–10:30pm.

ST-EMILION ⭐⭐

Surrounded by vineyards, St-Emilion is on a limestone plateau overlooking the Valley of the Dordogne; a maze of wine cellars has been dug from the limestone beneath the town. The wine made in this world-famous district has been called "Wine of Honor," and British sovereigns nicknamed it "King of Wines." The town, constructed mostly of golden stone and dating from the Middle Ages, is also known for its macaroons.

St-Emilion maintains the ancient tradition of La Jurade, a society dedicated to maintaining the highest standard for the local wine and promoting and honoring it around the world. Members of this society wear silk hats and scarlet robes edged with ermine, and the Syndicat Viticole, which watches over the quality of wine, have all been around the world to promote the wines with this appellation.

ESSENTIALS

GETTING THERE St-Emilion lies 22 miles northeast of Bordeaux between Libourne, 5 miles away, and Castillon-la-Bataille, (7 miles away. **Trains** from Bordeaux make the 45-minute trip to St-Emilion three times per day. Trains from other parts of France usually require transfers in either Bordeaux or Libourne, a 10-minute train ride from St-Emilion.

VISITOR INFORMATION The **Office de Tourisme** is on place des Créneaux (© **05-57-55-28-28**).

EXPLORING THE TOWN

At the heart of St-Emilion is **place du Marché,** between two hills. An old acacia tree marks the center. St-Emilion is loaded with unusual monuments, some of which were dug, for defensive reasons, into the limestone bedrock that adds such verve to the vineyards. Foremost of these is the **Église Monolithe** ✿, place du Marché (© **05-57-55-28-28**), the largest underground church in Europe, carved by Benedictine monks during the 9th to 12th centuries. Its facade is marked by three 14th-century bay windows. A 14th-century sculpted portal depicts the Last Judgment and resurrection of the dead. The church is 37 feet high, 67 feet wide, and 125 feet long. It can be visited only as part of organized tours, in English and French. Tours depart from the tourist office at 10, 10:45, and 11:30am and 2, 2:45, 3:30, 4:15, and 5pm. April to October, an additional tour is offered at 5:45pm; during July and August, another tour is at 6:30pm. They include a visit to the Église Monolithe, as well as the Benedictine catacombs and the 13th-century **Chapelle de la Trinité** and its underground grotto (the Hermitage, the site where St-Emilion sequestered himself for the latter part of his life). The entire complex was kept alive during the heyday of its use by underground springs, which were surrounded in the 1500s by ornate balustrades. The tour, which lasts 45 minutes, costs 33F (5, $4.80) for adults, 20F (3.05, $2.90), for students, and 16F (2.45, $2.30) for children 13 to 18; children under 13 free.

The city contains two additional monuments that can be visited without an organized tour. The first is the **Bell Tower** (*clocher*) of the above-mentioned Église Monolithe. It rises from a position on place des Créneaux, near place du Marché. Built between the 1100s and the 1400s, it's the second-highest tower in La Gironde and for years after its construction was the only above-ground landmark that indicated the position of the underground church. You can climb the bell tower 9am to 5pm every day except Christmas and New Year's Day for a fee of 6F (.90, 85¢). Naturally, views from the top are panoramic.

Finally, you may want to visit the **Château du Roi** (© **05-57-24-61-07**), founded by Henry III of the Plantagenet line during the 13th century. Don't expect a full-fledged castle. The tower was the first section built, and the limited construction that followed was either demolished later or never completed. Until 1608, it functioned as the local Town Hall. From its summit, on a clear day, you can see as far away as the Dordogne. You can climb the tower during daylight hours every day except Christmas and New Year's Day, 9:30am to noon and 1:45 to 6pm (to 6:30pm April to September) for 6F (.90, 85¢).

ACCOMMODATIONS & DINING

Hostellerie de Plaisance ✿✿ This 200-year-old stone building, set on 14th-century foundations, is the best choice in this medieval town. The well-styled rooms, some with views of stone monuments and towers, welcome sophisticated wine tasters and buyers from all over the world. Some rooms are quite small, but the best doubles have terraces where you can enjoy breakfast. Each comes with a midsize bathroom with a combination tub and shower. The cuisine of Christophe Canati is the best known and most praised in the area. He's at his best when working with the region's bountiful seasonal ingredients, especially game dishes, usually available October to February. Otherwise, menu items include a salad of grilled quail with avocados; a civet of sturgeon cooked with local red wine; a *timbale* of filets of sole with crayfish tails; a ballotine of foie gras with shallots and grilled toast; and filet mignon of veal with wild mushrooms. Top it all off with a warm soufflé flavored with pear liqueur and served with nougat ice cream and chocolate sauce.

Place du Clocher, 33330 St-Emilion. ⓒ **05-57-55-07-55.** Fax 05-57-74-41-11. 16 units. 650F–1,500F (98.80– 228, $94.25–$217.50) double; 1,400F–1,900F (212.80– 288.80, $203–$275.50) suite. AE, DC, MC, V. Closed Jan. **Amenities:** Restaurant, bar; room service; laundry. *In room:* A/C, minibar, hair dryer, safe.

20

The Dordogne & Périgord: Land of Prehistoric Caves, Truffles & Fine Wine

Lovers of foie gras and truffles, not to mention nature lovers, have always sought out the Dordogne and Périgord regions of France. Our first stop, Périgueux, was the capital of the old province of Périgord. After following the trail of the Cro-Magnon people to prehistoric caves, we'll visit Cahors, the ancient capital of Quercy, then Montauban, where the great painter Ingres was born. But the towns themselves aren't the stars—it's the unspoiled fertile countryside that holds the fascination. In some villages the Middle Ages seem to live on. It's said that there are no discoveries to be made in France, but you can make many discoveries if you give yourself adequate time to visit a region too often neglected by North Americans.

REGIONAL CUISINE   Ask gastronomes about the cuisine of the Dordogne and Périgord, and the first thing to come to mind will be truffles, one of the most sought-after delicacies in France. The region produces more than 30 types. They all grow underground, without a root or stem, at the base of one type of oak tree in light soil of a certain degree of acidity. They give off a distinctive odor, said by one 19th-century gastronome "to epitomize the perfumed soul of the Périgord." Because truffles grow underground, truffle hunters have traditionally used carefully trained dogs to smell out their location. Trained pigs have also been used to find them, but

unlike dogs, pigs tend to eat truffles they find before the hunter can retrieve them.

Equally famous are the region's pâtés, which, when studded with "black diamonds" (truffles), have conquered many a resistant appetite. These are made from the enlarged livers of geese that have been force-fed a diet of rich corn. Some pâtés are still made of unadulterated goose liver, but the more frequently seen version is a ballotine of foie gras. This contains goose liver mixed with white turkey meat and then covered with meat gelatin.

One characteristic of the region's cuisine is the stuffing used for many roasts and joints. It usually includes breadcrumbs, truffles, and segments of goose liver. The most famous sauce here is sauce Périgueux, made from sweet madeira wine and truffles. Anything prepared *à la périgourdine* includes a garnish of truffles to which foie gras has been added. Another staple of the cuisine is *cèpes* (flap mushrooms). Other regional specialties are *bréjaude* (cabbage and bacon soup served with rye bread) and *lièvre en chabessal* (freshly killed rabbit stuffed with highly seasoned pork, ham, and veal).

Rich in nutrients, the soil here produces huge quantities of walnuts, vegetables, and fruits. In this region, you'll also find succulent beef and veal. The Limousin breed of cows has been exported to Australia and South America, where it has thrived.

The most famous wines here are the red and white Bergerac, the red Pécharmant, and the deep-red Cahors. Cahors is aged for a dozen years before reaching a suitable sophistication. The Montbazillac is a sweet, tawny dessert wine whose grapes have been deliberately permeated with a whitish-green mold known as *pourriture noble* (noble rot). When it's fermented, this improves the flavor of the wine, partly by reducing its acidity and partly because of a mystery that only Dionysius could fully understand.

1 Périgueux ✶

301 miles SW of Paris, 53 miles SE of Angoulême, 70 miles NE of Bordeaux, 63 miles SW of Limoges

This is the city of foie gras and truffles. Capital of the old province of Périgord, Périgueux stands on the Isle River. In addition to its food products, the region is known for its Roman ruins and medieval churches. The city is divided into three sections: the Cité (old Roman town), Le Puy St-Front (the medieval town) on the slope of the hill, and to the west, the modern town.

Périgueux today is a sleepy provincial backwater, with a population of 35,000. Its attractions probably won't hold your interest more than a day, but it's a gateway to the Dordogne Valley and the cave paintings at Les Eyzies.

ESSENTIALS

GETTING THERE   **Trains** run frequently from Paris, Lyon, and Toulouse, plus many regional towns. Six trains per day arrive from Paris (trip time: 6 to 7 hours), four trains from Lyon (7 hours), 10 trains from Bordeaux (2½ hours), and seven trains from Toulouse (4 hours). For train information and schedules, call ✆ **08-36-35-35-35.** The local bus station, Gare Routière, place Francheville (✆ **05-53-08-43-13**), adjacent to the tourist office, only provides infrequent services to villages in the surrounding district. When **driving** from Bordeaux, take N89 east. From Paris, take A10 south to Orléans, connect to A71 south to Vierzon, continue along A20 south to Limoges, and then connect to N21 south to Périgueux.

VISITOR INFORMATION   The **Office du Tourisme** is at 26 place Francheville (✆ **05-53-53-10-63**).

EXPLORING THE TOWN

You may want to rent a bike and explore the surrounding countryside; a map is available from the tourist office. Rent from **MBK,** 15 cours Fénelon (✆ **05-53-53-44-62**), or **Cycle Evasion Peugeot,** 46 rond-point de Chanzy (✆ **05-53-05-21-80**). They both charge 60F (9.10, $8.70) per day or 120F (18.25, $17.40) for 3 days.

Périgueux is a treasure trove of Gallo-Roman antiquities. The most visible of these is the **Tour de Vésone,** a partially ruined site that stands 85 feet tall beyond the railway station, half a mile southwest of town. There, you'll find the remains of a Roman temple dedicated to the goddess Vesuna.

The **Jardin des Arènes,** a vast amphitheater that once held as many as 22,000 spectators, is another reminder of Roman days. Now in ruins, the amphitheater, with a diameter of 1,312 feet, dates from the 2nd or 3rd century. The site is open daily: May to August 7:30am to 9pm and September to April 8am to 6pm. Admission is free. Near the arena are the remains of the **Château Barrière,** rue Turenne, built in the 11th or 12th century on Roman foundations. June to August, Périgueux's tourist office offers organized walking tours of the city that incorporate both its ancient Roman and medieval attractions. During that period, tours depart Monday to Saturday at 10:30am (focusing on ancient Roman and early medieval architecture) and 2:30pm (focusing on late medieval and Renaissance architecture). Each tour lasts 2 hours and costs 30F (4.55, $4.35) for adults and 23F (3.50, $3.35) for students and children under 18.

Gastronomy reigns supreme in Périgueux, especially when it comes to smooth, melt-in-your-mouth foie gras. Stores that sell this regional delicacy abound. The best foie gras emporiums include **La Maison Léon,** 9 place de la Clautre (✆ **05-53-53-29-96**), and **À la Cathédrale,** 9 rue des Chaînes (✆ **05-53-53-47-04**). But if you want an adventure, then head for a real goose farm by the name of **À la Ferme de Puy Gauthier,** about 15 minutes south of town in the village of Marsaneix (✆ **05-53-08-87-07**), where they make their own home-style foie gras. To get there, follow the signs to Brive. Those who enjoy outdoor marketplaces should head for the open-air food market at **place St-Louis,** open every Wednesday and Saturday from 8am to around 5pm. Fresh foie gras, sold either in its natural state or factored into terrines and pâtés, is available from

Finds **Biking Through the Dordogne**

The Dordogne's rivers meander through countryside that's among the most verdant and historic in France. This area is relatively underpopulated, but it's dotted with monuments, feudal châteaux, 12th-century villages, and charming churches.

As you bike around, the rural character of the area unfolds before you. Unlike in more pretentious regions of France, no château, hotel, or inn treats you disdainfully if you show up on two rather than four wheels. (*Au contraire,* the staff will probably offer advice on suitable bike routes for your departure.) If you're ever in doubt about where your handlebars should lead you, know that you'll rarely go wrong if your route parallels the riverbanks of the Lot, the Vézère, the Dordogne, or any of their tributaries. Architects and builders since the 11th century have added greatly to the visual allure of their watersides.

The SNCF makes it easy to transport a bike on the nation's railways. However, if you don't want to bring your own wheels on the train, there are plenty of rental shops throughout the region. (We recommend rentals in this chapter's sections on Périgueux, Les Eyzies-de-Tayac, and Montauban.)

Locally there are many organizations through the Dordogne that can help you with organizing bike trips. An authority on bike tours through the region is **Animation Vézère,** Base des Eyzies, Les Eyzies (© **05-53-06-92-92**). Two worthy competitors that also arrange canoe and kayak expeditions are **Canoé Loisin,** in the hamlet of Sailat (© **05-53-28-23-43**), and **Canoé Dordogne,** in the hamlet of La Roque Gageac (© **05-53-29-58-50**). The ultimate authority on the many bike, canoeing, and hiking expeditions throughout the region is **Le Comité Départemental du Tourism,** 25 rue du Président Wilson, 24000 Périgueux (© **05-53-35-50-24**), which provides information about the attractions and allure of all the towns within the département.

---

many different vendors November to March. A different series of food markets are held every Wednesday morning, 8am to around 1pm, in the **place Francheville,** the **place Bugeaud,** and the above-mentioned place St-Louis.

Cathédrale St-Front ☆   In Le Puy St-Front (the medieval quarter) rises this cathedral, the last of the Aquitanian-domed churches and one of the largest churches in southwestern France. Built 1125 to 1150, it was dedicated to St. Front, a local bishop. The cathedral's bell tower rises nearly 200 feet, overlooking the marketplace. With its five white domes and colonnaded turrets, St-Front evokes memories of Constantinople. The interior is built on the plan of a Greek cross, unusual for a French cathedral. On the tour, you can walk between the domes and turrets, looking out over Vieux Périgueux with its old houses running down to the Isle. In rare cases, qualified students of art history or architecture are admitted to the crypt and cloisters, which date from the 9th century, although those are otherwise closed to the public. Mass is celebrated every Monday to Thursday and Saturday at 9am, Friday at 6:30pm, and Sunday at 11am.

Place de la Clautre. © **05-53-53-23-62.** Free admission. Daily 8am–noon and 2:30–7pm (winter, closes at dusk).

Église St-Etienne-de-la-Cité ⋆   Périgueux's other remarkable church—this one in the Cité area on rue de la Cité—was a cathedral until 1669, when it lost its position to St-Front. The church was built in the 12th century but has been much damaged since. It contains a 12th-century bishop's tomb and a carved 17th-century wooden reredos depicting the Assumption of the Madonna.

10 av. Cavaignac. ℂ **05-53-53-21-35.** Free admission. Daily 8am–7pm.

Musée de Périgord ⋆   Built on the site of an Augustinian monastery, this museum has an exceptional collection of prehistoric relics, sculptures, and Gallo-Roman mosaics. Many of the artifacts were recovered from digs in the Périgord region, which is rich in prehistoric remains.

22 cours Tourny. ℂ **05-53-06-40-70.** Admission 20F (3.05, $2.90) adults, 10F (1.50, $1.45) students and children under 12. Nov–Mar Wed–Mon 10am–5pm; Apr–Oct Wed–Mon 9am–6pm.

ACCOMMODATIONS & DINING

Hôtel Bristol   This modern hotel is centrally located behind a small parking lot and offers comfortable rooms, often with sleek styling. It's your best bet among a limited, lackluster selection. Bathrooms are a bit small but come with a combination tub and shower. Breakfast is the only meal served, but it's only a 5-minute walk to the town's best restaurants and major points of interest. The owners have spent much of their lives in North America and offer both a French and English welcome to all international travelers.

39 rue Antoine-Gadaud, 24000 Périgueux. ℂ **05-53-08-75-90.** Fax 05-53-07-00-49. bristol.hotel@ wanadoo.fr. 29 units. 345F–415F (52.45– 63.10, $50.05–$60.20) double. AE, MC, V. Closed Dec 23–Jan 4. **Amenities:** Breakfast room service; laundry. *In room:* A/C, TV, minibar.

L'Oison ⋆⋆⋆ MODERN FRENCH   To live and dine in a style you'd expect from the region of truffles and foie gras, visit L'Oison. In 1995, the most acclaimed restaurant in Périgueux moved to the finest hotel, the 19th-century Château des Reynats. This slate-roofed manor offers an Empire dining room in which you can enjoy the *cuisine du marché* of the talented chef Régis Chiorozas. Menu items elevate the cuisine of the region to sublime levels, as is the case with his unusual version of lasagne with foie gras and liquefied truffles; pigeon with spices; and *sandre* with Sevruga caviar.

The château also rents 37 beautiful rooms, costing 640F to 690F (97.30 to 104.90, $92.80 to $100.05) for a double, or 800F to 1,050F (121.60 to 159.60, $116 to $152.25) for a suite.

In the Château des Reynats, at Chancelade, 24650 Périgueux. ℂ **05-53-03-53-59.** Fax 05-53-03-44-84. Reservations recommended. Main courses 95F–200F (14.45– 30.40, $13.80–$29); fixed-price menus 140F (21.30–$20.30) lunch, 190F–350F (28.90– 53.20, $27.55–$50.75) dinner. AE, DC, MC, V. Mid-Mar to June and Sept–Dec Tues–Sun noon–2pm and 7:30–10pm; July–Aug open daily noon–2pm and 7:30–10pm. Closed Jan to mid-Mar.

PÉRIGUEUX AFTER DARK

If the weather is good, start your evening with a walk over to **place St-Silain, place St-Louis,** and **place du Marché,** where you'll most likely stumble onto a great little bar or even a bit of live impromptu music.

If you're in the mood for a beer and a *Cheers*-type of atmosphere, go to the **Gordon Pub,** 12 rue Condé (ℂ **05-53-35-03-74**). A regular stop for the dance-crazed youth of town is **La Régence,** 16 rue des Chancelier-de-l'Hôpital (ℂ **05-53-53-10-55**), with its booming techno-rock beat and more than ample supply of pheromones. If you prefer to while the night away, over-drinks and good conversation, stop by **Café Le St-Louis,** place St-Louis (© **05-53-53-53-90**), or **Café La Rotonde,** 9 cours Montaigne (© **05-53-08-30-31**), or **Café de Paris,** 19 cours Montaigne (© **05-53-08-29-15**). You can always find a full house at **L'An des Rois,** 51 rue Aubarède (© **05-53-53-01-58**), the only gay and lesbian disco and bar in town. There are separate areas for men and women. The cover is 60F (9.10, $8.70).

2 Lascaux (Montignac) 🖈

308 miles SW of Paris, 29 miles SE of Périgueux

The **Caves at Lascaux,** near the Vézère River town of Montignac in the Dordogne region, contain the most beautiful and most famous cave paintings in the world. Unfortunately, you can't view the actual paintings, because the caves have been closed to the general public to prevent deterioration, but a replica gives you a clear picture of the remarkable works.

They were discovered in 1940 by four boys looking for a dog and were opened to the public in 1948, quickly becoming one of France's major attractions, drawing 125,000 visitors annually. However, it became evident that the hordes of tourists had caused atmospheric changes in the caves, endangering the paintings. Scientists went to work to halt the deterioration, known as "the green sickness."

ESSENTIALS

GETTING THERE   Because of infrequent use, Montignac no longer maintains its own railway station. Rail passengers must get off at the neighboring hamlet of Condat-Le-Lardin, 6 miles to the northeast. From here, taxis (© **05-53-51-27-62**), which usually wait at the railway station, take visitors the remaining distance to Montignac for 150F (22.80, $21.75). If there are no taxis waiting, a railway station employee will call one for you. For **train information** about rail travel to Condat or anywhere else in France, call © **08-36-35-35-35.**

There are no **bus connections** from Condat to Montignac. There are bus connections from Sarlat, but because they're relatively infrequent, the easiest way to reach Montignac is **driving** northeast from Eyzies on N704 for 12 miles.

VISITOR INFORMATION   The **Office de Tourisme** is on place Bertrand-de-Born (© **05-53-51-82-60**) in Montignac.

EXPLORING THE CAVES & OTHER ATTRACTIONS

Public visits to Lascaux I ceased in 1964. Permission to visit for research purposes is given only to qualified archaeologists: Apply for permission to **Direction Régionale des Affaires Culturelles (D.R.A.C.),** Service Régional de l'Archéologie, 54 cours Magendie, 33074 Bordeaux CEDEX (© **05-57-95-02-02**). If you want to contact the staff at the famous cave, call © **05-53-51-90-29.** *Warning:* It's not easy to get around the rigid protocol regarding visits to the interior.

Lascaux II   A short walk downhill from the real caves leads to Lascaux II, an impressive reproduction of the originals, duplicated in concrete, molded above ground. The 131-foot-long reproduction displays some 200 paintings so that you'll at least have some idea of what the "Sistine Chapel of Prehistory" looks like. Here you can see majestic bulls, wild boars, stags, "Chinese horses," and lifelike deer, the originals of which were painted by Stone Age hunters 15,000 to 20,000 years ago. Try to show up as close to opening time as possible—the number of visitors per day is limited to 2,000, and tickets are usually sold out by 2pm. During the winter, you can buy tickets directly at Lascaux II, but from April to October you must purchase them from a kiosk adjacent to the tourist office, place Bertran de Born, in Montignac. For information, call the number below.

ⓒ **05-53-51-95-03.** Admission 50F (7.60, $7.25) adults, 25F (3.80, $3.65) children 6–12, free for children under 6. Feb–Mar and Nov Tues–Sun 10am–noon and 2–5pm; Apr–June and Sept daily 9:30am–6:30pm; July–Aug 9am–7pm; Oct 10am–noon and 2–6pm. Closed Jan.

Le Thot *(Kids)* On the premises are a zoo with live animals, two projection rooms showing short films on the discovery of cave art at Lascaux, and exhibitions relating to prehistoric communities in the Dordogne. After your visit to Le Thot, walk out on the terrace for a view of the Vézère Valley and the Lascaux hills.

4½ miles southwest of Montignac along D706 (follow the signs pointing to the hamlet of Les Eyzies). ⓒ **05-53-50-70-44.** Admission 30F (4.55, $4.35) adults, 15F (2.30, $2.20) children 6–12, free for ages 5 and under. You'll save some money by buying a combination ticket that grants access to both Lascaux II and Le Thot for 57F (8.65, $8.25) adults and 30F (4.55, $4.35) children 6–12. Feb–Mar and Nov Tues–Sun 10am–noon and 2–5pm; Apr–June and Sept daily 9:30am–6:30pm; July–Aug 9am–7pm; Oct 10am–noon and 2–6pm. Closed Jan.

Site Préhistorique de Regourdou *(Kids)* About 500 yards uphill from the barricaded grotto of Lascaux, a narrow road branches off through a forest until it reaches this site, discovered in 1954, and believed to be a center for a prehistoric bear cult. Discovered at the site were the sepulcher and skeleton of a Neanderthal man, surrounded by the sepulcher and skeletons of several bears. Also on the site is an archeological museum, and about 20 semitame, semiwild bears that roam freely around a naturalized habitat that's carefully barricaded against transgressions from most humans. The only way to experience this site is by means of guided tours that are conducted in both French and English. They depart at frequent intervals during the site's opening hours, as listed below.

ⓒ **05-53-51-81-23.** Admission 30F (4.55, $4.35) adults, 20F (3.05, $2.90) children 6–12, free for children under 6. July–Aug daily 10am–7pm; Sept–June daily 10am–6pm.

ACCOMMODATIONS & DINING

Château de Puy Robert ★★★ This mansion, set on 16 acres, about a 15-minute walk from the grottoes, was built in 1860 as a country home. Rooms are handsomely furnished. Those in the annex are more modern and contemporary looking, whereas the 15 rooms in the original manor house have a more pronounced sense of nostalgia. Many offer views over the Vézère Valley. Each ranges from midsize to spacious and comes with a good-sized bathroom with a combination tub and shower. The owners and most of the staff migrate to Courchevel to operate a ski hotel in the Alps during the winter, so they're not always on their toes at the beginning and end of this hotel's season. The chef, Alain Bideau, plays a active role in configuring the cuisine at the in-house restaurant, treading a delicate line between traditional and postnouvelle cuisine.

Rte. 65, 24290 Montignac Lascaux. ⓒ **05-53-51-92-13.** Fax 05-53-51-80-11. 38 units. 710F–1,500F (107.90– 228, $102.95–$217.50) double; 1,860F (282.70, $269.70) suite. AE, DC, MC, V. Closed Oct 25–May. **Amenities:** Restaurant, bar; outdoor pool; baby-sitting; laundry,. *In room:* A/C, TV, minibar, hair dryer, safe.

Hôtel Le Relais du Soleil d'Or ★ In the heart of Montignac, this place functioned during the 1800s as a postal relay station, providing food and lodging to travelers. Today, it offers traditionally furnished rooms and a landscaped garden. Rooms range from small to medium, each fitted with a compact shower-only bathroom. The main restaurant serves traditional Dordogne fare such as stewed snails with garlic; and a magret of duckling prepared with three different flavorings: cèpes (flap) mushrooms, morels, and truffles. Dessert might be a slice of walnut cake served with vanilla-walnut sauce. The less formal Le Bistrot offers salads, snacks, and simple platters.

16 rue du 4-Septembre, 24290 Montignac Lascaux. ℂ 05-53-51-80-22. Fax 05-53-50-27-54. www. soleil-dor.com. 32 units. 450F–550F (68.40– 83.60, $65.25–$79.75) double; 550F–825F (83.60– 125.40, $79.75–$119.65) suite. AE, DC, MC, V. Closed mid-Jan to mid-Feb. **Amenities:** 2 restaurants, bar; outdoor pool; room service; laundry. In room: TV, minibar, hair dryer.

3 Les Eyzies-de-Tayac ★ ★

331 miles SW of Paris, 28 miles SE of Périgueux

When prehistoric skeletons were unearthed here in 1868, the market town of Les Eyzies suddenly became an archaeologist's dream. This area in the Dordogne Valley was found to be one of the richest in the world in ancient sites and deposits. Some of the caves discovered contain primitive drawings made 30,000 years ago. The most beautiful and most famous, of course, are at Lascaux. (See section 2 above.) Many caves around Les Eyzies are open to the public.

ESSENTIALS

GETTING THERE   Local **trains** run from nearby Le Buisson, 12 miles away, which has direct connections from larger cities like Bordeaux. The several daily trains from Périgueux are more direct. For train information and schedules, call ℂ 08-36-35-35-35. A **drive** to Les Eyzies-de-Tayac will be a rural route from Périgueux, starting along D710 southeast to the town of Le Bugue, then following the rural road east for a short drive. Look out for the road sign leading into Les Eyzies-de-Tayac.

VISITOR INFORMATION   The **Office de Tourisme,** place de la Mairie (ℂ 05-53-06-97-05), is open year-round.

EXPLORING THE AREA

If you want to pedal around the countryside, you can rent bicycles at the tourist office, beginning at 40F (6.10, $5.80) per half day or 60F (9.10, $8.70) per full day. A 200F (30.40, $29) deposit is required; MasterCard and Visa are accepted.

Whether you're biking or driving, some of the loveliest villages include Beynac-et-Cazenac, 9 miles southeast of Les Eyzies, and Sarlat-la-Canéda, 4½ miles northeast of Beynac. Other smaller villages lie beside the road that meanders through Dordogne Valley, including Castelnaud, La Roque-Gageac, Domme, and Montfort. Throughout the region, routes are country roads marked only with signs leading to the above-mentioned destinations.

Make a special effort to relax within the shadow of the severely foreboding **Château de Beynac,** 24220 Beynac (ℂ 05-53-29-50-40), a 13th-century curiosity that opened its doors to visitors in 1961. The Grosso family has been renovating the monument for almost 40 years. (By their own calculations, at their present pace, they estimate that renovations on their monument won't be complete until 2060.) Once it was the gathering place for the aristocracy of Périgord; today, its view over the valley, coupled with its evocative sense of history, make a visit here worthwhile. March to September, it's open daily 10am to 6pm and October to February, it's open daily 11am to sundown. Guided tours (in French and broken English) are conducted at 30-minute intervals year-round 10am to noon and 2 to 6pm. (There are no guided tours December to February.) Admission, with or without the tour, costs 40F (6.10, $5.80) per adult, children 22F (3.35, $3.20). There's a worthy restaurant nearby, within the **Hôtel Bonnet** (© **05-53-29-50-01**), which occupies the site of a converted forge and blacksmith's shop in the center of town.

Sarlat-la-Canéda, 6 miles northeast, is home of the unusual **Cathédrale St-Sacerdos** as well as the **Maison de la Boétie,** located at place André-Malraux, which belonged to one of France's most famous Renaissance writers, Etienne de la Boétie. One of the town's most endearing restaurants is the **Hostellerie Marcel,** 50 av. de Selves (© **05-53-59-21-98**).

Grotte de Font-de-Gaume ★

This is one of the few authentic caves still open to visitors, though access is very limited in summer. Alas, some of the markings you see aren't from the Magdalenian ages, but from British students on a holiday back in the 18th century. Here depictions of bison, reindeer, and horses, along with other animals, reveal the skill of the prehistoric artists. *Note:* Only 200 visitors per day are permitted in the caves. In midsummer, demand far exceeds the supply of tickets, so call and reserve far in advance if you're coming between April and September.

Less than 1 mile outside Les Eyzies on D47. © **05-53-06-86-00.** Admission 36F (5.45, $5.20) adults, 23F (3.50, $3.35) ages 18–25, free for children under 18. Apr–Sept Thurs–Tues 9am–noon and 2–6pm; Oct–Mar Thurs–Tues 9:30am–noon and 2–5:30pm. Closed holidays.

Grotte des Combarelles

Discovered at the turn of the 20th century, the Grotte des Combarelles has many drawings of animals, including musk oxen, horses, bison, and aurochs. Think of it as a gallery of Magdalenian art. Tickets are limited to 70 per day, but you can make reservations up to a year in advance by calling the number below.

On D47, 10½ miles north of Bergerac. © **05-53-06-86-00.** Admission 36F (5.45, $5.20) adults, 23F (3.50, $3.35) ages 18–25, free for children under 18. Apr–Sept Thurs–Tues 9am–noon and 2–6pm; Oct–Mar Thurs–Tues 10am–noon and 2–6pm. Closed holidays.

Grotte du Grand-Roc (Cave of the Big Rock) ★★

This is one of most interesting caves. Upon entering you'll come on a tunnel of stalagmites and stalactites. The cave is about a mile northwest of Les Eyzies on the left bank of the Vézère (signs point the way on D47).

On D47. © **05-53-06-92-70.** Admission 40F (6.10, $5.80) adults, 21F (3.20, $3.05) children 6–12, free for ages 5 and under. June–Sept daily 9:30am–6pm; Oct–May Sun–Fri 10am–5pm. Closed Jan.

Musée National de la Préhistoire ★

Prehistoric artifacts from local excavations are displayed in this late-16th-century fortress-castle overlooking Les Eyzies. On the terrace is a statue of a Neanderthal man. One building displays a reconstructed Magdalenian tomb containing a woman's skeleton.

© **05-53-06-45-45.** Admission 22F (3.35, $3.20) adults, 15F (2.30, $2.20) ages 18–25, free for children under 18. Dec–Mar Wed–Mon 9:30am–noon and 2–5pm; Apr–June and Sept–Nov Wed–Mon 9:30am–noon and 2–6pm; July–Aug daily 9:30am–7pm.

Tips The Scoop on Cave Tickets

To prevent deterioration of the art, only a limited number of visitors are allowed into the caves of Les Eyzies-de-Tayac each day. But tickets are available up to a year in advance. If you plan on visiting these caves, call and reserve tickets as far in advance as possible.

ACCOMMODATIONS & DINING

Hostellerie du Passeur *Value* This is the best bet for the frugal traveler. This well-maintained hotel contains simple but cozy rooms. On-site there is also a family-run restaurant with well-crafted cuisine. The fixed-price menus represent some of the best values in town. They contain such dishes as roasted rabbit with liquefied truffles and flap mushrooms; and scallops also served with flap mushrooms. Dessert might include a frozen walnut soufflé. During good weather, you can enjoy your meal on a shaded terrace.

Place de la Mairie, 24620 Les Eyzies-de-Tayac. *©* **05-53-06-97-13.** Fax 05-53-06-91-63. 20 units. 280F–450F (42.55– 68.40, $40.60–$65.25) double. MC, V. Closed Nov–Jan. **Amenities:** Restaurant, bar; room service; laundry. *In room:* TV.

Hôtel Le Centenaire ✰✰✰ Nothing in this whole area equals the charms of this oasis, which is even better known for its cuisine than for its hotel rooms. Part of the Relais & Châteaux chain, it has undergone extensive renovations. The very comfortable rooms are conservatively modern, each of good size, coming with a deluxe bathroom with a combination tub and shower. The chef, Roland Mazère, creates a light, modern French cuisine, the finest of any restaurant mentioned in this chapter. His menu might include terrine of fresh foie gras, brochette of salmon; *noisettes d'agneau* (lamb); a terrine of flap mushrooms; and Rossini-style goose steak (sliced and layered with foie gras). Dessert might be a semisoft chocolate cake studded with walnuts.

Rocher de la Penne, 24620 Les Eyzies-Tayac-Sireuil. *©* **05-53-06-68-68.** Fax 05-53-06-92-41. www.hotel ducentenaire.fr. 20 units. 700F–1,200F (106.40– 182.40, $101.50–$174) double; 1,500F–2,000F (228– 304, $217.50–$290) suite. AE, DC, MC, V. Closed Nov–Apr 1. **Amenities:** restaurant, bar; heated pool; health club; shopping gallery; room service;, laundry. *In room:* TV, minibar, hair dryer.

Hôtel Les Glycines ✰ *Finds* We'd stay here just for the beautiful flower garden. Since 1862, this establishment has offered substantial regional cuisine, comfortable accommodations, and dozens of charming touches, such as drinks served on a veranda with a grape arbor. Rooms are quaint with a regional charm. Each is midsize to spacious with a compact bathroom, most with a combination shower and tub. Restaurant specialties include macaroni laced with foie gras, flap mushrooms, and truffles; *confit de canard* with truffle juice; and escalope of duck liver with lime juice.

Rte. de Périgueux (D47), 24620 Les Eyzies-Tayac-Sireuil. *©* **05-53-06-97-07.** Fax 05-53-06-92-19. www.les-glycines-dordogne.com. 23 units. 398F–650F (60.50– 98.80, $57.70–$94.25). DC, MC, V. Closed Nov to mid-Mar. **Amenities:** Restaurant, bar; outdoor pool; room service; laundry. *In room:* TV, hair dryer.

4 Rocamadour ✰✰✰

336 miles SW of Paris, 41 miles SE of Sarlat-la-Canéda, 34 miles S of Brive, 39 miles NE of Cahors

The Middle Ages seem to live on here. After all, Rocamadour reached the zenith of its fame and prosperity in the 13th century. Make an effort to see it even if it's out of your way. The setting is striking, one of the most unusual in Europe: Towers, old buildings, and oratories rise in stages up the side of a cliff on the right slope of the usually dry gorge of Alzou. The population has held steady at around 5,000 for many years.

The faithful continue to arrive today as they did more than 8 centuries ago. As a pilgrimage site, Rocamadour is billed as "the second site of France," with Mont-St-Michel ranking first, of course. Summer visitors descend in droves, and vehicles are prohibited. Park in one of the big lots and make your way on foot.

ESSENTIALS

GETTING THERE The best way to reach Rocamadour is **by car.** From Bordeaux, travel east along N89 to Brive-la-Gaillarde, connecting to N205 east into Cressensac, continuing along N140 south into Rocamadour.

Rocamadour and neighboring Padirac share a **train** station that isn't really convenient to either—it's 3 miles east of Rocamadour on N140, serviced by infrequent trains from Brive in the north and Capdenac in the south. Most visitors avoid the inconvenience and drive. For train information and schedules, call ✆ **08-36-35-35-35.** The bus service in and out of town is so infrequent as to be almost nonexistent.

VISITOR INFORMATION The **Office de Tourisme** is in the Hôtel de Ville, rue Roland-le-Preux (✆ **05-65-33-62-59**).

Exploring THE TOWN

The **site** ★★★ of this gravity-defying village rises abruptly across the landscape. Its single street, lined with souvenir shops, runs along the side of a steep hill. It's best seen when approached from the road coming in from the tiny village of L'Hospitalet. Once in Rocamadour, you can take a flight of steps (or an elevator) from the lower town (Basse Ville) to the town's **Cité Religieuse,** a cluster of chapels and churches halfway up the cliff.

There's a fee of 27F (4.10, $3.90) one-way or 48F (7.30, $6.95) round-trip to ride both of the town's two elevators. One goes from the Basse Ville to the Cité Religieuse; the other goes from the Cité Religieuse to the panoramic medieval ramparts (*le château*) high above the town.

The **Château de Rocamadour** (le château) is perched on a rock spur above the town center. You can reach it via the curvy "chemin de la Croix." It was built in the 14th century and restored by the local bishops in the 19th century. Its interior is strictly off-limits except for guests of the church officials who live and work here. You can, however, walk along its panoramic **ramparts** ★★, which are open daily 8am to 8pm. Admission to the ramparts costs 17F (2.60, $2.45) adults, and 13F (2, $1.90) children 5 to 12, ages 4 and under free.

The most photogenic entrance to the Basse Ville is through the **Porte de Figuier** (Fig Tree Gate), through which many of the most illustrious Europeans of the 13th century passed.

One of the oldest places of pilgrimage in France, Rocamadour became famous as a cult center of the black Madonna. It was supposedly founded by Zacchaeus, who entertained Christ at Jericho. He's claimed to have come here with a black wooden statue of the Virgin, although some authorities have suggested that this statue was carved in the 9th century.

Basilique St-Sauveur Against the cliff, this basilica was built in the Romanesque-Gothic style from the 11th to the 13th centuries. It's decorated with paintings and inscriptions, recalling visits of celebrated persons, including Philippe the Handsome. In the Chapelle Miraculeuse, the "holy of holies," the mysterious St. Amadour is said to have carved out an oratory in the rock. Hanging from the roof of this chapel is one of the oldest clocks known, dating back to the 8th century. Above the altar is the venerated statue of the black Madonna, which Zacchaeus reportedly brought here. The Romanesque Chapelle St-Michel is sheltered by an overhanging rock; inside are two frescoes rich in coloring, dating from the 12th century. Above the door leading to the Chapelle Notre-Dame is a large iron sword that, according to legend, belonged to Roland.

Place St-Amadour. ✆ 05-65-33-23-23. Free admission. Daily 9am–7pm.

Cité Religieuse   This is the town's religious centerpiece, a site oft visited both by casual tourists and devoted pilgrims. Site of many conversions, with mystical connotations that date back to the Middle Ages, it's accessible from the town below via the **Grand Escalier,** a stairway of 216 steps. Even today, devout pilgrims make this difficult journey on their knees in penance: A recent devotee was the French composer Francis Poulenc, who remained in Rocamadour after a religious conversion he experienced here, and in honor of which he composed his *Litanies à la Vierge Noire.* Climbing its weathered steps will lead to the **Parvis des Églises,** place St-Amadour, with seven chapels.

Place de la Carreta. Free admission, but donation to churches and guides appreciated. Guided tours of the chapels June–Sept 15, daily at 9am, 10am, 2pm, and 3:30pm. Suggested donation for tour: 22F (3.35, $3.20) adults, 15F (2.30, $2.20) children 8–18, free for children under 8.

Musée d'Art Sacré & Trésor Francis Poulenc   This artistic highlight of the religious complex, which was radically enlarged and renovated in 1996, contains a gold chalice presented by the 19th-century pope, Pius II, among other treasures. There is a panoramic elevator between the different floors.

Parvis du Sanctuaire. ⓒ 05-65-33-23-30. Admission 30F (4.55, $4.35) adults, 17F (2.60, $2.45) children 10–18, free for children under 10. Jan–June and Sept–Dec Mon–Fri 10am–noon and 2–pm; July–Aug daily 9am–7pm.

ACCOMMODATIONS & DINING

Hôtel Beau-Site et Le Jehan de Valon ★★   With its entrance evoking a medieval hall, this is the area's finest inn, a place with original character. The stone walls were built in the 15th century by an Order of Malta commander. Today the rear terrace provides a sweeping view of the Val d'Alzou. The reception area has heavy beams and a cavernous fireplace. Rooms (in the main building and a less desirable annex) are comfortable; each contain a midsize bathroom, most with a combination tub and shower. The restaurant serves a regional cuisine prepared by the Menot family, who've owned the place for generations. Specialties include foie gras of duck with dark truffles; rack of locally raised lamb; raw marinated salmon with green peppercorns; and braised and then roasted duck served with truffled mashed potatoes. Dessert might be a slice of country-style fruit pie, served with caramel and whortleberry sauce, or a cake of caramelized walnuts.

Cité Médiévale, 46500 Rocamadour. ⓒ 800/528-1234 in the U.S. or Canada, or 05-65-33-63-08. Fax 05-65-33-65-23. www.bw-beausite.com. 43 units. 385F–520F (58.50– 79.05, $55.85–$75.40) double; 584F–730F (88.75– 110.95, $84.70–$105.85) suite. AE, DC, MC, V. Closed Nov to mid-Feb. **Amenities:** Restaurant, bar; room service, laundry. *In room:* A/C (23 rooms), TV, hair dryer.

Hôtel Domaine de La Rhue ★ *(Finds)*   The charming owners, Christine and Eric Jooris, gutted a 19th-century stable and turned it into a series of spacious rooms, each individually decorated in superb taste. Some have terraces, and all are equipped with compact bathrooms, mainly with shower units. On the lower level is an inviting reception and breakfast room with a welcoming fireplace. The Joorises, who speak English, are most helpful in directing you to the best places for dinner in the center of Rocamadour, which is only a few minutes' drive away. Christine enjoys mapping out perfect tours of the nearby villages and plotting the best direction from which to approach each town and/or castle so as to have a commanding view from the distance and to take advantage of afternoon sun for photographs. Eric is a pilot and takes guests for a 45-minute hot-air balloon ride over the canyon of Rocamadour for 800F (121.60, $116).

46500 Rocamadour. ℂ **05-65-33-71-50.** Fax 05-65-33-72-48. www.domainedelarhue.com 14 units. 390F–590F (59.30– 89.70, $56.55–$85.55) double. DC, MC, V. Closed Nov–Easter. Follow route D673, then N140 signposted Rhue for a total of 3¼ miles from town. **Amenities:** Indoor pool. *In room:* TV, minibar (some rooms), hair dryer.

NEARBY ACCOMMODATIONS & DINING

Château de Roumégouse ⭐ If you prefer to be away from the tourist bustle, try this Relais & Châteaux in Roumégouse. The 15th-century château overlooking the Causse is surrounded by 12 acres of parkland. Each room is unique in both decor and architecture and is fitted with antique furniture and paintings. Each spacious room comes with a well-maintained but compact bathroom with a combination tub and shower.

N140, Rignac, 46500 Gramat. ℂ **05-65-33-63-81.** Fax 05-65-33-71-18. www.integra.fr/relaischateaux.fr/ roumegouse. 15 units. 710F–1,210F (107.90– 183.90, $102.95–$175.45) double; 1,400F–1,700F (212.80– 258.40, $203–$246.50) suite. AE, DC, MC, V. Closed Nov–Mar. Take N140 to Roumégouse, 4 miles southeast of Rocamadour. **Amenities:** Restaurant, bar; room service; laundry. *In room:* A/C, TV, minibar, hair dryer.

5 Cahors ⭐⭐

336 miles SW of Paris, 135 miles SE of Bordeaux, 55 miles N of Toulouse

The ancient capital of Quercy, Cahors was a thriving university city in the Middle Ages, and many antiquities from its illustrious past life remain. However, Cahors is best known today for the almost-legendary red wine that's made principally from the Malbec grapes grown in vineyards around this old city in central France. Firm but not harsh, Cahors is one of the most deeply colored fine French wines.

ESSENTIALS

GETTING THERE To **drive** to Cahors from Toulouse, follow A62 north to its junction with N20, continuing along N20 north into Cahors.

Cahors is serviced by **train** from Toulouse, Brive, and Montauban. You may have to transfer in neighboring towns. For train information and schedules, call ℂ **08-36-35-35-35.** There's infrequent bus service from some of the outlying villages, several of which are of historic interest, but it's vastly easier to drive.

VISITOR INFORMATION The **Office de Tourisme** is on place François-Mitterrand (ℂ **05-65-53-20-65;** www.quercy.net).

SPECIAL EVENTS The **Festival de Blues** turns this town upside down for 3 days in mid-July when famous blues groups, including some from the United States, descend on different venues around Cahors. Tickets are 80F to 200F (12.15 to 30.40, $11.60 to $29), and exact dates and performing artists can be obtained from the Office de Tourisme (see above). For tickets, contact **Mme Nicola Tertre,** 349 rue Wilson, 46000 Cahors (ℂ **05-65-35-22-29**).

EXPLORING THE AREA

The town is on a rocky **peninsula** ⭐ almost entirely surrounded by a loop of the Lot River. It grew up near a sacred spring that still supplies the city with water. At the source of the spring, the **Fontaine des Chartreux** stands by the side of the **pont Valentré** (also called the pont du Diable), a bridge with a trio of towers. It's a magnificent example of medieval defensive design erected between 1308 and 1380. It was restored in the 19th century. The pont, the first medieval fortified bridge in France, is the most colorful site in Cahors, with crenellated parapets, battlements, and seven pointed arches.

Cahors's heritage includes rich tradition of wine making. The wines of Cahors are characterized by a heady robustness that mellows over time. Three local wineries of exceptional merit, each within a short drive from Cahors, include Domaine de Lagrezette, in the hamlet of Caillac (© 05-65-20-07-420); Domaine de Haute Serre, in Cieurac (© 05-65-30-70-10); and the Domaine de St-Didier Parnac, in Parnac (© 05-65-30-70-10). Their dark wines are of consistently high quality and easily hold their own with any of the region's rich, hearty dishes. The Office de Tourisme (see above) provides detailed information and maps to these wineries.

Dominating the old town, the **Cathédrale St-Etienne** ✿, 30 rue de la Chanterie (© **05-65-35-27-80**), was begun in 1119 and reconstructed between 1285 and 1500. It was the first cathedral in the country to have cupolas, giving it a Romanesque-Byzantine look. One remarkable feature is its finely sculptured Romanesque north portal, carved around 1135 in the Languedoc style. It's open daily 8am (scheduled hour for daily mass) to 6 or 7pm, depending on the season. Adjoining the cathedral are the remains of a Gothic cloister from the late 15th century. The cloister is open only May to October, daily 8am to 7pm. Admission is 15F (2.30, $2.20) adults, 10F (1.50, $1.45) persons 8 to 18 and students, children under 8 free.

SIDE TRIPS   Cahors is a starting point for an excursion to the **Célé and Lot valleys,** a long journey that many French are fond of taking in summer, a round-trip of about 125 miles. If you have time for sightseeing, the trip should last 2 days. The Office de Tourisme (see above) provides maps that offer itineraries.

Grotte du Pech-Merle (© **05-65-31-27-05**), a prehistoric cave near Cabrerets, 21 miles east of Cahors (take D653), was once used for ancient religious rites. The wall paintings, footprints, and carvings are approximately 20,000 years old. The cave may be explored only April to October, daily from 9:30am to noon and 1:30 to 5pm. Admission is 45F (6.85, $6.55) adults and 30F (4.55, $4.35) children, 5 and under are free. There are 2 miles of chambers and galleries open to the public, especially interesting for those familiar with geology. The Aurignacian- and Magdalenian-age art includes drawings of mammoths, bison, aurochs, horses, deer, mountain goats, and women.

ACCOMMODATIONS

Hôtel de France   This hotel, between pont Valentré and the train station, provides the best rooms in the town center. They're well furnished and modern in design. Each unit comes with an average-size bathroom, most often with a shower unit. The room service is efficient, but breakfast is the only meal served.

252 av. Jean-Jaurès, 46000 Cahors. © **05-65-35-16-76.** Fax 05-65-22-01-08. 79 units. 370F (56.25, $53.65) double. AE, DC, MC, V. Closed Dec 20–Jan 5. Parking 40F (6.10, $5.80). *In room:* A/C (40 rooms), TV, minibar.

Hôtel Terminus ✿   On the avenue leading from the railway station into the heart of town, this hotel still oozes with the turn-of-the-last-century character of its original stone construction. Rooms are conservative, yet tastefully decorated with lots of floral prints, fresh flowers, and firm comfortable mattresses. Bathrooms are average size, most with a combination tub and shower. On the premises is Le Balandre, which was awarded a Michelin star in 2001. Even if you don't opt for a meal in its Art Deco dining room or on its outdoor terrace, you might want to step into its 1920s-style bar for a drink.

5 av. Charles-de-Freycinet, 46000 Cahors. ℭ **05-65-53-32-00.** Fax 05-65-53-32-26. Terminus-balandre@ wanadoo.fr. 22 units. 550F–1,100F (83.60– 167.20E, $79.75–$159.50) double. AE, DC, MC, V. Free parking in open courtyard, 45F (6.85, $6.55) in covered garage. Closed last 2 weeks in Nov. **Amenities:** Restaurant, bar; room service; laundry. *In room:* TV, minibar, hair dryer.

DINING

The **Hôtel Terminus** restaurant, Le Balandre (see "Accommodations," above), has won a Michelin star. Popular with a young crowd is **Les Terrasses Valentré** (ℭ **05-65-35-95-88**), a block to the left of pont Valentré. Here you can order a beer, meet some locals, and take in one of the best river views in town.

La Taverne ⟨★⟩ TRADITIONAL FRENCH   This restaurant serves outstanding local cuisine in a rustic atmosphere. The finely crafted cuisine of Quercy is featured here, along with other regional specialties. Typical dishes are truffles in puff pastry, tournedos with foie gras and truffles, duck filet with morels, breast of chicken with morels, and fresh fish.

Place Escorbiac. ℭ **05-65-35-28-66.** Reservations recommended. Main courses 45F–95F (6.85– 14.45, $6.55–$13.80); fixed-price menu 75F–149F (11.40– 22.65, $10.90–$21.60). MC, V. Mon–Fri noon–2pm and 7–9:30pm (July–Aug also open daily for lunch and dinner). Closed Feb and Sat–Sun during winter.

6 Montauban ⟨★⟩

404 miles SW of Paris, 45 miles NW of Albi, 31 miles N of Toulouse

This pink-brick capital of the Tarn-et-Garonne is the city of the painter Ingres and the sculptor Bourdelle. Montauban, on the right bank of the Tarn, is one of the most ancient of southwest France's towns, still dominated by the fortified Église St-Jacques. The most scenic view of Montauban is at the 14th-century brick bridge, pont Vieux, which connects the town to its satellite of Villebourbon.

Jean-Auguste-Dominique Ingres, an admirer of Raphael and a student of David, was born in 1780 in Montauban. His father, an ornamental sculptor and painter, recognized his son's artistic abilities early and encouraged him. He was noted for his nudes and historical paintings, now fine examples of neoclassicism. One of his first exhibitions of portraits in 1806 met with ridicule, but later generations have been more appreciative. His work is displayed in town at the **Cathédrale Notre-Dame** and the **Musée Ingres** (see below).

ESSENTIALS

GETTING THERE   If you're **driving,** R.N. 20 (Paris-Toulouse-Andorra, Spain), R.N. 113 (Bordeaux-Marseille), and the A61 motorway run through the Tarn-et-Garonne. Seven **trains** arrive here daily from Paris (trip time: 4½ to 6 hours); trains arrive every hour from Toulouse (25 minutes). For train information and schedules, call ℭ **08-36-35-35-35.** For **bus** information contact the Gare Routière (ℭ **05-63-93-34-34**).

VISITOR INFORMATION   The **Office de Tourisme** is on 4 rue du Collège (ℭ **05-63-63-60-60**).

SPECIAL EVENTS   The major festival that takes place in Montauban occurs in May and early June. The **Festival Alors Chante** in June showcases French music and song and offers performances by some of the biggest French stars. From July 17 to 26 the Festival de Jazz fills the outdoor venues with blues and jazz concerts, including the wildly popular Baltimore Baptist Church Choir. The

Office de Tourisme has information on both events, or contact **Synergie Club** (© **05-63-20-46-72**) for specifics on the Festival de Jazz.

EXPLORING THE AREA

You can rent bicycles at **Denayrolles,** 878 av. Jean-Moulin (© **05-63-03-62-02**), open Monday 2 to 7pm and Tuesday to Saturday 8:15am to noon and 2 to 7pm. A credit card or cash deposit of 1,500F (228, $217.50) is required.

Shoppers may want to pick up some foie gras and other goose products at the **Conserverie Artisanale Larroque,** 1300 av. de Falguières (© **05-63-63-45-40**). Or visit **Pecou,** 10 rue de la République (© **05-63-63-06-38**) for a supply of Montauriol (a chocolate-covered cherry with a shot of Armagnac) and Boulet de Montauban (a chocolate-covered roasted hazelnut). For a collectible specialty of the town, go to the **Librairie Deloche,** 21 rue de la Résistance (© **05-63-63-22-66**), where you can buy a *pigeonnier miniature*—miniature models of pigeon coops that were built on local farms to attract pigeons for their "fertilizer." Deloche carries 30 models of various architectural styles and a selection of books on pigeonniers.

In addition to taking in the Ingres masterpieces in the museum listed below, head for the **Cathédrale Notre-Dame,** place Roosevelt, a classical building framed by two square towers. In the north transept is the painting the church commissioned from Ingres, *Vow of Louis XIII.* It's open daily 9am to noon and 2 to 6pm.

Musée Ingres ★★ Upon his 1867 death the artist bequeathed to Montauban more than two dozen paintings and some 4,000 drawings (more than any other museum except the Louvre in Paris). They're displayed at this 17th-century bishops' palace. One painting in the collection is *Christ and the Doctors,* a work Ingres completed at 82. The *Dream of Ossian* was intended for Napoléon's bedroom in Rome. On the ground floor are works by Antoine Bourdelle, who was heavily influenced by Rodin. The two busts Bourdelle sculpted of Ingres and of Rodin are particularly outstanding.

19 rue de l'Hôtel-de-Ville. © **05-63-22-12-91.** Admission 25F (3.80, $3.65) adults, free children under 18. July–Aug daily 9:30am–noon and 1:30–6pm; Sept–June Tues–Sun 10am–noon and 2–6pm.

ACCOMMODATIONS

The **Hôtel Orsay** (see below) also rents rooms.

Hostellerie Les Coulandrières *(Finds* This inn, 2 miles northwest of Montauban's center in the village of Montbeton, occupies the site of an old farm. The original buildings house the reception area, bar, and restaurant. Set in a 10-acre park, it offers pleasant, traditionally furnished rooms in a nearby annex built around 1975. Rooms are midsize to spacious, most with a combination tub and shower. The inn also makes an excellent dining choice, as the chefs deftly handle first-class ingredients. In summer, grills are a specialty.

Rte. de Castelsarrasin, 82290 Montbeton, near Montauban. © **05-63-67-47-47.** Fax 05-63-67-46-45. 22 units. 470F–500F (71.45– 76, $68.15–$72.50) double. Half board 380F–410F (57.75– 62.30, $55.10–$59.45) per person, double occupancy. AE, DC, MC, V. Free parking. **Amenities:** Restaurant, bar; pool; miniature golf course; room service; laundry. *In room:* TV, hair dryer.

Hôtel Mercure Montauban ★ In a town not known for its inns, this is a shining light. One of the most dramatic hotel renovations in the district occurred in 1999. Today, it's the most appealing modern hotel in town, with relatively large rooms, each with comfortable mattresses. All units come with midsize bathrooms, most with a combination tub and shower. The restaurant, La Brasserie Bourdelle, named after a local sculptor, serves fixed-price menus.

12 rue Notre-Dame, 82000 Montauban. ℂ **05-63-63-17-23.** Fax 05-63-66-43-66. 44 units. 540F (82.10, $78.30) double. AE, DC, MC, V. Parking 25F (3.80, $3.65). **Amenities:** Restaurant, bar; room service; laundry. *In room:* A/C, TV, hair dryer.

DINING

The two accommodations recommended above also have decent restaurants.

Hôtel Orsay et Restaurant La Cuisine d'Alain ✦ MODERN FRENCH This is the best restaurant in town, as chef Alain Blanc is talented and inventive. Try his terrine of lentils flavored with the neck of a fattened goose en confit, filet of beef with liver and apple flan, or escalope of foie gras with apples. The amazing dessert trolley offers plenty of choices. Built a century ago, and renovated in frequent stages by the hardworking staff ever since, the Hôtel Orsay has 20 well-decorated but unpretentious rooms, with doubles running 250F to 350F (38 to 53.20, $36.25 to $50.75).

Face Gare (across from the train station). ℂ **05-63-66-06-66.** Fax 05-63-66-19-39. Reservations recommended. Main courses 95F–140F (14.45– 21.30, $13.80–$20.30); fixed-price menu 130F–295F (19.75– 44.85, $18.85–$42.80). AE, DC, MC, V. Tues–Sat 12:30–2pm; Mon–Sat 7:30–9:30pm. Closed Dec 23–Jan 6, a week in May, and the 2nd and 3rd weeks in Aug.

MONTAUBAN AFTER DARK

Our favorite nightspot here is **Le Santa Maria,** quai Montmurat (ℂ **05-63-91-99-09**), close to the Musée d'Ingres. Theme nights include salsa, merengue, rock, and retro disco. The place gets lively after 9:30pm. Less stylish is **Bar Le Flamand,** 8 rue de la République, near the cathedral (ℂ **05-63-66-12-20**), with an easygoing crowd and a broad roster of Belgian beers.

21

The Massif Central

In your race south to Biarritz or through the Rhône Valley to the Riviera, you'll pass through the Massif Central, the agricultural heartland of France. Here you'll find ancient cities, lovely valleys, and a wonderful provincial cuisine. With its rolling farmlands, isolated countryside, and châteaux and manor houses (many of which you can stay in and dine in), this is one of the most unspoiled parts of France—your chance to see a life too rapidly fading.

From the spa at Vichy to the volcanic *puys* of the Auvergne, there's much of interest here and much to learn about the art of good living. We begin in George Sand country in the province of Berry and then proceed to the Auvergne Limousin.

REGIONAL CUISINE Fans of this region's cuisine often praise it for its simple honesty and adherence to tradition, though its critics claim that it lacks finesse and creativity. Everyone, however, agrees that this is a family-inspired rural cuisine, based on generous quantities of fresh ingredients and few pretensions.

Characteristic dishes are soup (*une potée*) made with cabbage and about a dozen other ingredients, usually including fresh and salted pork; and stuffed sheep's foot cooked in a sheep's stomach. Among the region's cheeses are enormous wheels known as Cantal, bleu d'Auvergne, St-Nectair, and a goat cheese called *le cabecou,* which appears on cheese trays in restaurants throughout France. The Massif Central is famous for its desserts, in particular cherry tarts (sometimes with the cherry pits still in place) and many exceptional pastries.

The climate and soil aren't conducive to grape growing, so most regional wines are straightforward table wines. The best local spirits are several types of distilled alcohol served after meals. These are usually distilled from the fermented essence of flowers and herbs, including strawberries, raspberries, blossoms from the linden tree, myrtle, and a mountain flower called *gentiane.*

1 Bourges ★★★

148 miles S of Paris, 43 miles NW of Nevers, 95 miles NW of Vichy, 175 miles NW of Lyon

Once the capital of Aquitaine, Bourges lies in the heart of France; you can easily tie in a visit here from Orléans at the eastern end of the Loire Valley. The commercial/industrial center of Berry, this regional capital is still off the beaten path for most tourists, even though it boasts a rich medieval past still in evidence today. Its history goes back far beyond the Middle Ages: In 52 B.C. Caesar called it the finest city in Gaul. Today Bourges remains a rather sleepy provincial town, awakened only by the life surrounding the Institut Universitaire de Technologie.

ESSENTIALS

GETTING THERE   There are good road and rail connections from Tours and other regional cities. Four **trains** arrive daily from Paris (trip time: 2½ hr.); sometimes a transfer is required at nearby Vierzon. Eight trains a day arrive from Tours, taking 1½ hours. For information and schedules, call ℂ **08-36-35-35-39**. If you're **driving** from Paris, take A10 south to Orléans and then Route 20 to Vierzon, where you pick up Route 76 east into Bourges. From Tours, head east along Route 76.

VISITOR INFORMATION   The **Office de Tourisme** is at 21 rue Victor-Hugo (ℂ **02-48-23-02-60**; www.ville-bourges.fr).

SPECIAL EVENTS   The energy level really picks up between April and August, thanks to several colorful music festivals. The **Festival Printemps de Bourges,** offers dozens of concerts ranging from traditional French to international rock. Most events cost between 30F and 170F (4.55 and 25.85, $4.35 and $24.65), though any number of seemingly spontaneous performances always pop up along the sidewalks for everyone to enjoy at no charge. For tickets and more information, contact the **Association Printemps de Bourges,** 22 rue Henri-Sellier (ℂ **02-48-70-61-11**). At the beginning of June, a younger, more free-form and high-impact music scene explodes during the **Festival International des Groupes de Musique Experimentale de Bourges,** during which groups such as U2 have appeared. For information, call ℂ **02-48-20-41-87**. **Un Été à Bourges** kicks off yearly in late June and runs until mid-September. During this time, the streets are once again filled with musical performers and actors. More-structured performances also take place, with tickets at 30F to 200F (4.55 to 30.40, $4.35 to $29). For more information, call ℂ **02-48-57-81-10** or contact the tourist office.

SEEING THE SIGHTS

Cathédrale St-Etienne ✿✿✿   Situated on the summit of a hill dominating the town, this is one of the most beautiful Gothic cathedrals in France. Its construction began at the end of the 12th century and wasn't completed until a century and a half later; additions have been made. Flanked by asymmetrical towers, it has five magnificent doorways, including one depicting episodes in the life of St. Stephen. The cathedral has a vaulted roof and five aisles and is remarkably long (407 feet deep); it's distinguished for its stained-glass windows, best viewed with binoculars. Many were made between 1215 and 1225. One impressive scene, *A Meal in the House of Simon,* shows Jesus lecturing Simon on forgiveness as Mary Magdalene repents at his feet. To climb the north tower for a view of the cathedral and Bourges, buy a ticket from the custodian. The same ticket allows you to explore the church's 12th-century crypt, the largest in France. In the crypt rests the tomb (built between 1422 and 1438) of Jean de Berry, who ruled this duchy in the 14th century. Fanatically dedicated to art, he directed a "small army" of artisans, painters, and sculptors. The recumbent figure is the only part of the original tomb that has survived.

After your visit, you may want to wander through the **Jardins de l'Archevêché,** the archbishop's gardens, credited to Le Nôtre. From these gardens you'll have a good view of the eastern side of the cathedral.

Place Etienne-Dolet. ℂ **02-48-65-72-89**. Cathedral, free admission; tower and crypt, 36F (5.45, $5.20) adults, 29F (4.40, $4.20) ages 18–25, free for children under 17. Combination ticket to both cathedral and Palais Jacques-Coeur 50F (7.60, $7.25) for everyone. Cathedral, Apr–Sept daily 9am–6pm; Oct–Mar daily 9am–4pm. Crypt cannot be visited Sun 8am–1pm during mass.

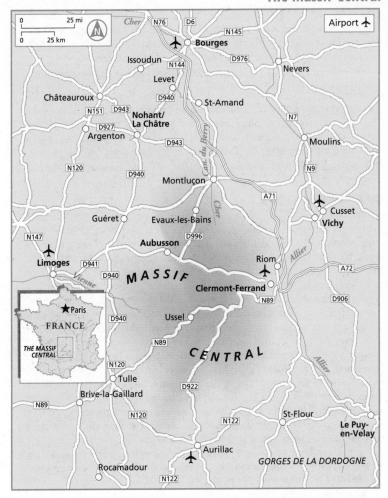

Palais Jacques-Coeur ★★ This is one of the country's greatest secular Gothic structures. Take a guided tour through the four buildings around a central court, constructed around 1450 by the finance minister/banker Jacques Coeur, who had amassed a fortune. Monsieur Coeur never got to enjoy the palace, however. After a trial by a jury of his creditors, he was tossed into prison by Charles VII and died there in 1456. His original furnishings no longer remain, but the decor and wealth of detail inside the palace form a remarkable view of 15th-century opulence. In the dining hall is a monumental chimneypiece, and in the great hall are sculptures from the 15th and 16th centuries.

Rue Jacques-Coeur. ✆ **02-48-24-06-87.** Admission 36F (5.45, $5.20) adults, 23F (3.50, $3.35) ages 18–25 and over 60, free for children 17 and under. Combination ticket to cathedral and Palais Jacques-Coeur 50F (7.60, $7.25) for everyone. The palace can be seen only on a 60-min. guided tour in French (English speakers receive a printed English-language text of the commentary). Tours daily at 9, 10, and 11am and at 2, 3, and 4pm; Apr–Oct, additional tour 5pm; July–Aug, additional tour 6pm.

Hôtel Lallemant The Renaissance Hôtel Lallemant, north of the cathedral, has been transformed into a museum of decorative art. The mansion was built for a textile merchant; today its galleries display a colorful history of Bourges. Exhibits include china, objets d'art, ceramics, and antique furniture.

6 rue Bourbonnoux. ℂ **02-48-57-81-17.** Free admission. Tues–Sat 10am–noon and 2–6pm; Sun 2–6pm.

Musée du Berry The museum is inside the Hôtel Cujas, built about 1515. On display is a collection of Celtic and Gallo-Roman artifacts; impressive are the 280 funerary sculptures. Some rooms are devoted to finds from Egyptian archaeological digs, along with medieval masterpieces of sculpture from around 1400, and some rooms on the second floor have ethnological exhibitions.

4 rue des Arènes. ℂ **02-48-70-41-92.** Free admission. Mon and Wed–Sat 10am–noon and 2–6pm; Sun 2–6pm.

ACCOMMODATIONS

Hôtel de Bourbon/Grand Hôtel Mercure et Restaurant St-Ambroix ★★
This is the finest hotel in Bourges, and its cuisine is the best in the entire area. In the early 1990s, the Mercure chain converted a ruined 17th-century abbey into this first-class hotel. The cheerful rooms are comfortable (except for the half-timbered sloping rooms beneath the mansard roof on the third floor, which are short on style). Each unit comes with a small but modern bathroom, mainly with a tub/shower combination. Despite this, the stonework of the exterior and the public areas are quite beautiful. The setting is convenient for train travelers, as it lies almost adjacent to the rail station. The refined cuisine of Pascal Auger is a draw, even for locals. Under the vaulted ceiling of a former Renaissance chapel, you can select delectable main courses—perhaps baked saddle of lamb (pink and juicy) or *escalope de foie gras de canard* (duckling). The *noix de ris de veau braisée* (sweetbreads) is among the finest you're likely to sample. The menu changes four times a year but invariably offers cannelloni stuffed with green asparagus, small shellfish, shallots, exotic mushrooms, and thin-sliced cured ham as well as chicken sautéed with walnuts and served with fresh pasta with squid ink and slices of leeks stewed with essence of orange.

Bd. de la République, 18000 Bourges. ℂ **02-48-70-70-00.** Fax 02-48-70-21-22. 59 units. 580–760F (88.15– 115.50, $84.10–$110.20) double; 990F (150.50, $143.55) suite. AE, DC, V. Free parking. **Amenities:** Restaurant, bar; room service; laundry. *In room:* A/C, TV, hair dryer.

Le Christina This is a simple but comfortable inn, built in the 1930s and renovated many times since. It rises three and five stories (depending on which part of the hotel you're in). All the units contain a small bathroom with a shower. The location, a few steps from the cathedral and the Palais Jacques-Coeur, is especially convenient. Breakfast is the only meal served, but there are several simple brasseries within walking distance.

5 rue de la Halle, 18000 Bourges. ℂ **02-48-70-56-50.** Fax 02-48-70-58-13. 71 units. 259F–399F (39.35– 60.65, $37.55–$57.85) double. AE, DC, MC, V. Parking 30F (4.55, $4.35). *In room:* TV.

DINING

Jacques-Coeur ★ TRADITIONAL FRENCH François Bernard serves tasty traditional bourgeois cuisine amid a medieval Gothic decor, though the food at Hotel de Bourbon et Restaurant St-Ambroix (see "Accommodations," above) is better. Specialties here include veal kidneys *berrichonne,* frogs' legs sautéed with herbs, *scallops à la façon* (with a *concasse* of tomatoes, snail-flavored butter, and *beignets* of onion), fresh filets of mackerel marinated in local white wine, and chicken *en barbouille* (with a sauce made of wine and blood). The desserts are all homemade and tempting, and service is politely efficient. The featured wines from a balanced list include Quincy and Menetou-Salon, two excellent but not very well-known vintages from the region. Of the two dining rooms, the one on the upper floor is more interesting, with exposed beams and plaster impressions of scallop shells on its ceiling (ca. 1947).

3 place Jacques-Coeur. ℃ 02-48-70-12-72. Reservations required. Main courses 65F–135F (9.90– 20.50, $9.45–$19.60); fixed-price menus 160F–190F (24.30– 28.90, $23.20–$27.55). AE, DC, MC, V. Sun–Fri noon–2:15pm; Mon–Fri 7:15–9:15pm. Closed July 23–Aug 23 and Dec 24–Jan 2.

BOURGES AFTER DARK

Most of the best clubs are in Bourges's old town. Try **Le Pub Birdland,** 4 av. Jean-Jaurès (℃ 02-48-70-66-77), a good old-fashioned drinking establishment with wood interior, young crowd of heavy-duty beer drinkers, and jazz and rock. **Beau Bar,** rue des Beaux-Arts (℃ 02-48-24-40-49), pulls in a very bohemian crowd—artists, poets, songwriters, and the like—whereas the most popular bar in town, **La Comédie,** 10 place Mirepied (℃ 02-48-65-95-85), packs its below-street-level vaulted dance floor with young hot bodies. A 50F (7.60, $7.25) cover charge is sometimes imposed.

For something a little different, head over to **La Soupe aux Choux,** part of the restaurant Le Guillotin, place Gordaine (℃ 02-48-65-43-66), where you can take in an evening of *cafe-théâtre.* Shows can be anything from musical performances to stand-up comics; tickets run around 70F (10.65, $10.15).

2 Nohant/La Châtre

180 miles S of Paris, 19 miles S of Châteauroux

George Sand was the pen name of Amandine Lucile Aurore Dupin, baronne Dudevant, the French novelist born in 1804. Her memory is forever connected to this little Berry hamlet near the Indre Valley.

In her early life she wrote bucolic tales of peasants, but she also penned romantic novels in which she maintained that women were entitled to as much freedom as men. Among her 80 novels, some of the best known were *François le Champi* and *La Mare au Diable.* She was also known for her love affairs, of which her two most notorious were with the poet Alfred de Musset, and with the composer Frédéric Chopin. By the time of her death in Nohant in 1876, George Sand had become a legend.

ESSENTIALS

GETTING THERE   If you're **driving,** it's a 1-hour trip from Bourges to La Châtre via D940 south. The closest **train** station is in Châteauroux, with a connecting bus to Nohant/La Châtre. From Bourges, you can buy a combination train/bus ticket to La Châtre via Châteauroux. Five daily trains make the run to Châteauroux, where you'll then transfer to a bus to complete the 2½-hour trip. For complete train information, call ℃ 08-36-35-35-35.

VISITOR INFORMATION   The nearest **Office de Tourisme** is on square George-Sand (℃ 02-54-48-22-64) in La Châtre.

IN THE FOOTSTEPS OF GEORGE SAND

La Maison de George Sand ✪   It was at the Château de Nohant, known today as La Maison de George Sand, that the famous novelist learned the ways and thoughts of the peasants. During her time here, she entertained some of the

---

Finds **A Secret Hideaway in George Sand Country**

On the grounds of the château (see above) is a *pigeonnier*—an aviary for raising pigeons that's now a guesthouse/cottage with a kitchenette, a salon, and a private garden. The rate is 1,000F (152, $145) per day, double occupancy.

---

intellectual and artistic elite of Europe—Flaubert, Balzac, Delacroix, Liszt, and Gautier. The building, which its guides define as a *maison bourgeoise*, set in its own 7-acre park, was constructed of stone in 1763 and purchased in 1793 by the family of George Sand. Today, it houses the mementos of Sand and her admirers and friends, with ample testimonials to the literary conceits and eccentricities of one of France's most enduringly famous female writers. You can see the boudoir where she wrote *Indiana*, the popular novel published when she was 28. You can also visit her private bedchamber/study. At Nohant, George Sand staged theatricals, dramatizing several of her novels—not very successfully, according to reports. Today, *fêtes romantiques de Nohant* are sometimes staged, with an impressive list of musical performers.

36400 Nohant-Vic. ☎ **02-54-31-06-04.** Visits only with a 45-min. guided tour in French (non-French speakers can follow the lecture with a printed text) for 32F (4.85, $4.65) adults, 23F (3.50, $3.35) for students and persons 17–25, free for children 17 and under. Daily 10:30–11:15am and 2:30–5:30pm. (July–Aug daily 9:30am–5:30pm). Tours depart at regular intervals according to the number of people waiting and/or the day's schedule.

ACCOMMODATIONS & DINING

Auberge de la Petite Fadette *(Value)* This compound of 19th-century, ivy-covered buildings abuts a château and is the focal point for one of the smallest villages in the region. Since 1890 the compound has been owned by four generations of the Chapleau family; it was renovated in 1995. A scattering of antiques decorates the interior. The rooms are cozy and comfortable, although a bit small, and each comes with a compact bathroom with shower.

Nohant-Vic, 36400 La Châtre. ☎ **02-54-31-01-48.** Fax 02-54-31-10-19. www.aubergepetitefadette.com. 10 units. 350F–700F (53.20– 106.40, $50.75–$101.50) double. AE, MC, V. **Amenities:** Restaurant; room service; laundry. *In room:* TV.

Château de la Vallée Bleue ⋆⋆ This is the area's prestige address. This charming small château was built in 1840 by Dr. Pestel so he could be close to his patient, George Sand. It's now a hotel/restaurant owned by Gérard Gasquet. The rooms have been named after the doctor's former guests, including Musset, Delacroix, Flaubert, Chopin, and Liszt. All rooms have dignified, sometimes antique furniture, and six have a complete bathroom with tub/shower combination. There's also a 10-acre wooded park. The excellent regional specialties are characterized as cuisine *actuelle,* with an accent on presentation; they include goat cheese and carp with lentils and chicken à la George Sand (with crayfish sauce). For dessert, try a delectable pear baked in pastry.

Rte. de Verneuil, St-Chartier, 36400 La Châtre. ☎ **02-54-31-01-91.** Fax 02-54-31-04-48. www.chateau valleebleue.com. 15 units. 395F–725F (60.05– 110.20, $57.30–$105.15) double; 875F (133,$126.90) suite. MC, V. Hotel closed Sun night. Hotel and restaurant closed mid-Nov to mid-Mar. **Amenities:** Restaurant; pool; room service; laundry. *In room:* TV, minibar, hair dryer.

3 Vichy (★(★(★

216 miles S of Paris, 33 miles NE of Clermont-Ferrand, 108 miles NW of Lyon

This world-renowned spa on the northern edge of the Auvergne, in the heart of Bourbon country, is noted for its sparkling waters (said to alleviate liver and stomach ailments). It looks much as it did a century ago, when princes and industrial barons filled its rococo casino. (The casino you'll visit today isn't the one that thrived during the spa's 19th-century heyday. That edifice, at 5 rue du Casino, now functions as a convention hall. Within its premises, Diaghilev produced his first ballet and Strauss directed *Salomé*.)

Since 1861, when Napoléon III was a frequent visitor, much has been done to add to the spa's fame. During the 1980s, the hotels and baths of Vichy underwent a modernization program to keep up with the times and other baths of France, much to the pleasure of their clients and their ever-changing tastes.

The city's current reputation for health and relaxation has been aided greatly by the Perrier craze that has swept most of the world. The Perrier Company has a contract to bottle Vichy water for sale elsewhere and also runs the city's major attractions. Vichy is a sports-and-recreation center, boasting a casino, theaters, regattas, horse racing, and golf. The **Parc des Sources,** a promenade with covered walks, is the center of Vichy's fashionable life, which is at its peak from May to the end of September.

ESSENTIALS

GETTING THERE   Vichy lies on the heavily traveled Paris–Clermont-Ferrand rail line. Some 20 **trains** per day arrive from Clermont-Ferrand (trip time: 30 min.); 10 trains per day arrive from Paris (trip time: 3 hr.). For train information and schedules, call © **08-36-35-35-35. Bus** service into town is possible, though it's usually not as convenient or well orchestrated as the train. The Gare Routière (© **04-70-98-41-33**) lies adjacent to the rail station. If you're **driving** to Vichy from Paris, take A10 south to Orléans, then connect to A71 south. At the Gannat/Vichy exit, follow N209 east to Vichy.

VISITOR INFORMATION   The Office de Tourisme is at 19 rue du Parc (© 04-70-98-71-94).

ACCOMMODATIONS

Aletti Palace Hôtel (★★   This early-1900s hotel, the largest and, in some ways, most stately in town, contains all the grand vistas and elegant accessories of the Belle Époque. The rooms are high ceilinged and comfortably furnished. Many have balconies overlooking the wooded park and casino, and all come with spacious bathrooms with tub/shower combinations. If you ask, the staff will tell you about the role of this monument (under a different name, the Thermal Palace) during the tenure of the collaborationist Vichy government: It

---

Moments Creating a New You

For a rejuvenating sojourn at a spa and health farm, contact the **Centre Thermal des Dômes,** c/o Novotel Thermalia (© **04-70-31-04-39**), or the **Centre des Célestins,** c/o Hôtel les Célestins (© **04-70-30-82-00**). For questions about Vichy's spas and hydrotherapy facilities, call © **04-70-97-39-59.**

housed the headquarters of Vichy France's Ministry of War. These days, the hotel has a good restaurant and offers a bar and a terrace with a view of Vichy.

3 place Joseph-Aletti, 03200 Vichy. ℂ **800/528-1234** in the U.S., or 04-70-31-78-77. Fax 04-70-98-13-82. 133 units. 650F–940F (98.80– 142.90, $94.25–$136.30) double; 1,030F–1,190F (156.55– 180.90, $149.35–$172.55) suite. AE, DC, MC, V. **Amenities:** Restaurant, bar; room service; baby-sitting; laundry. *In room:* TV, hair dryer.

Hôtel Chambord *Value* This is one of the best bets for a spa holiday on a budget. This pleasant hotel, built near the rail station in the 1930s, has high ceilings and a bit more space than you might find in newer buildings. Its rooms were renovated in 1998, with rejuvenated bathrooms. The Escargot Qui Tette restaurant offers well-prepared meals in a sunny setting with reasonable prices.

82–84 rue de Paris, 03200 Vichy. ℂ **04-70-30-16-30**. Fax 04-70-31-54-92. 28 units. 200F–300F (30.40– 45.60, $29–$43.50) double. AE, DC, MC, V. **Amenities:** Restaurant, bar; room service; laundry. *In room:* TV.

DINING

Brasserie du Casino TRADITIONAL FRENCH Since the 1920s, this is the leading brasserie in Vichy, a preferred stop for actors and musicians visiting from Paris to perform at the casino. The de Chassat family is charming and especially solicitous to foreigners. Their restaurant, known for its sheathing of copper and Art Deco mahogany, is busy at lunch, but the real charm comes out at night, when a pianist entertains. Specialties are duck breast with a confit of figs, *paupiette* of rabbit with shallots, fish that derives "from all the seas and oceans that border France," and veal liver with fondue of onions.

4 rue du Casino. ℂ 04-70-98-23-06. Reservations recommended at lunch. Main courses 85F–120F (12.90– 18.25, $12.35–$17.40). Fixed-price menus 89F–149F (13.55– 22.65, $12.90–$21.60) at lunch (Mon–Tues and Thurs–Sat); 149F ([eu]22.65, $21.60) at dinner. MC, V. Thurs–Tues noon–1:30pm and Mon–Tues and Thurs–Sat 7–9:30pm. Closed Nov.

L'Alambic ⭐ MODERN FRENCH There are only 18 seats at this small restaurant. And because this spot has the best food in Vichy, they fill up quickly. Since 1989, Jean-Jacques Barbot has run a busy place, appealing to what one food critic called "the jaded palates of Vichy." If you're in the mood for vichyssoise—the soup that bears this town's name but was invented elsewhere—the version made here is particularly delicious, studded with mussels and crayfish tails. Other choices are ravioli stuffed with a mousse of red snapper and crayfish tails, homemade foie gras and smoked salmon, a casserole with crayfish, pork leg with truffles and lentils, and ravioli stuffed with confit of duckling and snails.

8 rue Nicolas-Larbaud. ℂ **04-70-59-12-71**. Reservations required for certain seatings. Main courses 75F–140F (11.40– 21.30, $10.90–$20.30); fixed-price menus 160F–280F (24.30– 42.55, $23.20–$40.60). MC, V. Wed–Sun noon–1:30pm and 7:30–9:30pm. Closed Feb 15–Mar 10 and Aug 20–Sept 15.

VICHY AFTER DARK

Head straight for the **Casino Elysée Palace,** passage Clémenceau (ℂ **04-70-98-50-41**). Built around 1900 as the Hôtel Elysée Palace, it was converted into the more glamorous of the town's two casinos in the early 1990s. But don't expect the imperial grandeur that Napoléon III would have met. Today, it's a lot more modern and informal. An area devoted to slot machines, where entrance is free, is open Sunday to Thursday from 11am to 3am, to 4am on Friday and Saturday. A separate area featuring roulette and blackjack is open Monday, Tuesday, and Friday from 8pm to 4am and Saturday and Sunday from 4pm to 4am. Entrance is 70F (10.65, $10.15) per person. Men must wear jackets in this area.

A less impressive place to gamble, with only whirring slot machines and roulette (no blackjack), is an annex of the old-casino-turned-convention-center, **Le Grand Café,** 5 rue du Casino (℗ **04-70-97-16-45**). It shares its space with, as you guessed, a cafe and restaurant. Entrance is free.

4 Clermont-Ferrand ✶✶

248 miles S of Paris, 110 miles W of Lyon

This old city in south-central France was the ancient capital of the Auvergne. Ever since then, Clermont-Ferrand has seen a long parade of history. It was created in 1731 by a merger of two towns, Clermont and Montferrand. The city is surrounded by hills, and in the distance stands one of the great attractions of Auvergne, the volcanic mountain Puy-de-Dôme.

Today Clermont-Ferrand is hardly celebrated for its ancient appearance and medieval streets. Much of the town looks as if it were created in the stark 1960s and 1970s, with unimpressive buildings, car dealerships, and plenty of shopping malls. It's not a town in which we'd choose to linger, but it's an important rail hub in this region, and has a number of attractions that do bring in visitors.

ESSENTIALS

GETTING THERE   Rail lines converge on Clermont-Ferrand from all parts of France, including Marseille, Toulouse, and Paris's Gare de Lyon. Trains from small towns in the Auvergne usually require a connection. For train information and schedules, call ℗ **08-36-35-35-35.** Clermont-Ferrand is best approached by **car** from two cities. A lengthy drive from Paris begins along A10 south to Orléans, continuing south along A71 to Clermont-Ferrand. From Lyon, take A47 west to St-Etienne, traveling northwest on A89 to Clermont-Ferrand.

Clermont-Ferrand is the biggest hub of **Regional Airlines** (℗ **04-73-62-71-76**). Consequently, the **Aéroport de Clermont-Aulnat** (℗ **04-73-62-71-00**), about 3 miles southwest of the town center, receives about 130 flights a day from all over France as well as parts of Italy and Germany. **Air France** (℗ **08-02-80-28-02**) flies here from Paris for around 2,000F (304, $290) round-trip. Buses meet every flight and take passengers either to town, to the bus station, or to the rail station. Cost is 25F (3.80, $3.65) per person each way. Service to Paris is provided by Air France Service, flying to about a dozen other points within France, as well as to some of the airports of Germany and Italy.

Passengers arriving by bus pull into the **Gare Routière,** boulevard François-Mitterrand (℗ **04-73-93-13-61** for information), on the southern periphery of town. Overall, train travel into Clermont-Ferrand is, in virtually every case, more convenient and efficient than bus service.

VISITOR INFORMATION   The Office de Tourisme et des Congrès is on place de la Victoire (℗ **04-73-98-65-00**). This tourist office is unique in France because it also houses an interesting museum called the **Espace Art Roman.** Here an interactive presentation combines a slide show with captioned photographs and archaeological remnants depicting Auvergne as a rich repository of Romanesque architecture and artifacts. The slide show takes 30 minutes, and it's worth spending another hour digesting all the additional information. Admission is free. Between May and September, the tourist office is open daily 9am to 7pm; from October to April, hours are Monday to Saturday from 9am to 6pm and Sunday 2 to 6pm.

SPECIAL EVENTS If you're in town at the end of January, check out one of the 40 screenings during the weeklong **Festival du Court Métrage.** The works, by up-and-coming directors, are shown in seven theaters, mainly concentrated on boulevard François-Mitterrand. Tickets are 20F (3.05, $2.90) per showing, with discounts for packages of 20 showings, and can be purchased through Sauve Qui Peut le Court Métrage, La Jetée, 4 place Michel de l'Hôpital (© **04-73-91-65-73**).

EXPLORING THE ENVIRONS: A SPECTACULAR VOLCANIC LANDSCAPE

The region surrounding Clermont-Ferrand is one of France's most geologically distinctive. In 1977, the government designated 946,000 acres as the **Parc Naturel Régional des Volcans d'Auvergne.** The park contains 186 villages as well as farms with herds of cows and goats that produce the Auvergne's cheeses and charcuteries. Scattered among them are at least 90 extinct volcanic cones (*puys*), which rise dramatically and eerily above the pine forests.

The highest and oldest of these is **Puy-de-Dôme** ✿✿✿, 4,800 feet above sea level, a site used for worship since prehistoric times by the Gauls and the Romans. In 1648, Pascal used this mountaintop for his experiments that proved Torricelli's hypothesis about how altitudes affect atmospheric pressure. And in 1911, one of the most dramatic events in French aviation occurred at Puy-de-Dôme when Eugène Renaux, with a passenger, flew nonstop from Paris in just over 5 hours, to land precariously on its summit and collect a 100,000F ($14,500) prize. From the summit you'll have a panoramic view—on a clear day you can see as far east as Mont Blanc. Shuttle buses run daily from the base to the summit in July and August and Sundays in September from 11am to 6pm, costing 21F (3.20, $3.05) round-trip. You can drive your car to the summit daily, before 11am only, for 22F (3.35, $3.20).

The different areas of the park contain radically dissimilar features. **Les Puys** (also known as Monts Dômes) are a minichain of 112 extinct volcanoes (some capped with craters, some with rounded peaks) packed densely into an area 3 miles wide by 19 miles long. Each dome is unique: Some were built up by slow extrusions of rock; others were the source of vast lava flows. Those with craters at their summits were the sites of violent explosions whose power stands in direct contrast to the region's peace and quiet today. The geological fury that created these hills ended between 5,000 and 6,000 years ago, but the rectangle of extinct volcanoes is aligned along one of the most potentially unstable fault lines in France, the San Andreas fault of the French mainland.

This region is relatively underpopulated, so you may not be aware of the park's boundaries during your explorations. Details about trekking and camping are available from the Parc Naturel Régional des Volcans d'Auvergne, Montlosier, 63970 Aydat (© **04-73-65-64-00**), 12½ miles southwest of Clermont-Ferrand. A branch office is at the Château St-Etienne, 15000 Aurillac (© **04-71-48-68-68**). You can buy at least half a dozen guidebooks covering specific hikes and walks (from 2 to 6 hours in duration) at either branch.

SEEING THE SIGHTS IN TOWN

Begin your tour in the center of Clermont, the bustling **place de Jaude,** where you can sample a glass of regional wine at a cafe. Later, walk north on rue du 11-Novembre, which branches off from the main plaza. This street leads to **rue des Gras,** the most interesting artery of Clermont.

Most of the interesting old buildings are in **Vieux-Clermont,** whose focal point is **place de la Victoire,** site of the black-lava **Cathédrale Notre-Dame de l'Assomption** ★★ (© **04-73-92-46-61**). One of the great churches of central France, it dates to the 13th and 14th centuries. Structural additions were made in the 19th century. Its most outstanding feature is the series of stained-glass windows from the 13th and 14th centuries. Admission is free; it's open Monday to Saturday from 9:30am to noon and 2 to 6:30pm and Sunday from 9am to noon and 2 to 5pm.

After leaving the cathedral, explore the buildings in this historic neighborhood. In particular, look for the **Maison de Savaron,** 3 rue des Chaussetiers, constructed in 1513. It's noted for the exceptional beauty of its courtyard and its Renaissance vaulting. The site is occupied today by a crêperie, **Le Quinze-Treize** (© **04-73-84-87-33**), where you can enjoy either a meal-sized (salted) or dessert-style (sugared) crêpe beneath the artfully crafted vaulting. It's open daily for lunch and dinner.

Several blocks northeast of the cathedral is the finest example of Auvergnat Romanesque architecture, made of lava from volcanic deposits in the region: the **Église Notre-Dame-du-Port** ★★, rue du Port (© **04-73-91-32-94**). Dating from the 11th and 12th centuries, the church has four radiating chapels and a transept surmounted by an octagonal tower. The crypt holds a 17th-century "black Madonna." UNESCO lists the entire complex as a World Heritage Site. Admission is free; it's open daily from 8am to 7pm (to 8pm from June to mid-October).

Between the two churches stands the Renaissance **Fontaine d'Amboise,** on place de la Poterne, its pyramid supporting a statue of Hercules. Nearby is **square Pascal,** commemorating the birth of mathematician Blaise Pascal in 1623 in a house on rue des Gras. Regrettably, the house was demolished in 1958, but a statue was erected in honor of the native son.

Musée Bargoin   The collection here consists of objects excavated from Auvergnat sites founded by the Gallo-Romans and their predecessors: pottery shards, bronzes, wood carvings, and an array of works noteworthy for anyone interested in France's prehistoric and pre-Roman origins. There's also an unusual collection of antique Oriental carpets. In the same building, maintaining the same hours and prices, is the **Musée des Tapis d'Art** (© **04-73-90-57-48**), with a collection of around 80 rare and very rare Middle Eastern and east Asian carpets. Each is artfully lit and suspended from walls and ceilings, and together they represent the evolution of the carpet as a prayer aid and a decorative work of art. Don't expect anything French within the confines of this place, since the carpets produced in nearby Aubusson are, ironically, completely omitted.

45 rue de Ballainvilliers. © **04-73-91-37-31.** Admission 25F (3.80, $3.65) adults, 13F (2, $1.90) children 12–17 and students, free for children 11 and under. Tues–Sun 10am–6pm.

Musée d'Art Roger Quilliot   This museum is 2 miles north of Clermont's center, in an award-winning building erected in 1992. This is the cultural showcase of the Auvergne. When it was created, multiple works of art were culled from other museums throughout the Auvergne, then reassembled into a format that displays European art and culture in chronological order. Visitors navigate their way in a circular pattern through rooms devoted to French, Italian, and Flemish works, progressing from the 7th to the 20th century.

Place Louis-Deteix. © **06-73-16-11-30.** Admission 24F (3.65, $3.50) adults, 13F (2, $1.90) children 13–16 and students, free for children 12 and under. Tues–Sun 10am–6pm.

ACCOMMODATIONS

Hôtel Gallieni *(Value)*   This is not the best hotel in town, but it's still a good value. The Gallieni has a completely unassuming 1960s style, with rooms that, for the most part, have been recently renovated and are comfortably furnished, though somewhat uninspired. The small bathrooms are tidily organized, each with a shower. Much emphasis is placed on its role as an overnight stop for farmers and sales representatives of companies selling farm equipment, so as a casual visitor you might feel somewhat in the minority. A simple bistro, Le Clos Maréchal, offers affordable meals.

51 rue Bonnabaud, 63000 Clermont-Ferrand. © **04-73-93-59-69.** Fax 04-73-34-89-29. 80 units. 320F–360F (48.65– 54.70, $46.40–$52.20) double. AE, MC, V. Parking 25F (3.80, $3.65). **Amenities:** Restaurant; room service. *In room:* TV, minibar.

Mercure Gergovie *(★)*   A favorite of the business traveler, this early 1970s hotel is the best of a fairly lackluster lot. It was radically renovated and upgraded in 1997. Its location near the lovely Jardin Lecoq is great for jogging and taking strolls. The rooms are well furnished and very clean; most are spacious. Each unit comes with a midsize bathroom with a tub/shower combination. Everything about the hotel is functional and businesslike, but not necessarily exciting. The restaurant, La Retirade, is a worthwhile choice.

82 bd. François-Mitterrand, 63000 Clermont-Ferrand. © **04-73-34-46-46.** Fax 04-73-34-46-36. 123 units. 630F (95.75, $91.35) double. AE, DC, MC, V. Parking 42F (6.40, $6.10). **Amenities:** Restaurant, bar; room service, baby-sitting; laundry. *In room:* A/C, TV, minibar, hair dryer.

DINING

Brasserie Daniele Bath *(★)* *(Value)* MODERN FRENCH   For years Jean-Yves Bath reigned supreme as the leading chef of the city and became a local culinary legend. Gourmets in the area lamented when he sold the restaurant to his sous chef and departed for Paris. Their concern was groundless. The new owner/chef retained all the recipes from his previous employer and has added many imaginative dishes of his own. Lots of superb flavors go into the locally inspired yet grandly creative cuisine. Begin with such delights as a tarte of scallops with black truffles; a rabbit, shrimp, and tomato strudel; or perhaps a small lasagne of salmon with black olives. The fish is truly excellent and changes seasonally, and you can also count on any number of savory meat dishes, including roast lamb with glazed turnips. Pigeon is another specialty, served with roasted foie gras.

Place du Marché-St-Pierre. © **04-73-31-23-22.** Reservations required. Main courses 85F–180F (12.90– 27.35, $12.35–$26.10); fixed-price menus 130F (19.75, $18.85). V. Tues–Sat noon–1:30pm and 7:30–10:30pm. Closed 3 weeks in Feb and 2 weeks in Sept.

Emmanuel Hodencq *(★★)* TRADITIONAL & MODERN FRENCH   The namesake of this restaurant is the culinary king of the roost, having topped even the long-time favorite, Le Clavé (below). The dynamic young chef is equally at home among traditional or *moderne* cookery, and his dishes almost waltz out of the kitchen and onto your table for a delectable offering. Local "wheeler-dealers" (a reference to Michelin tires) and politicos hang out here, enjoying the food. Expect a menu composed of the best of local produce—perhaps foie gras in a caramel vinegar or roasted pigeon with chanterelles. Grilled red mullet is a perfect dish, as is the medallion of veal in a grainy mustard sauce.

Place Marché St-Pierre. © **04-73-31-23-23.** Reservations required. Main courses 200F–550F (30.40– 83.60, $29–$79.75). AE, DC, MC, V. Tues–Fri noon–2pm and 7:30–10pm; Sat 7:30–10pm; Sun noon–2pm.

Le Clavé ✦ MODERN & TRADITIONAL FRENCH   This well-known restaurant inside a 19th-century stone house serves some of the most creative and intelligent food in the region. Menu items are both classic and contemporary. Main-course choices include foie gras with garnishes tailored to the seasons (fresh fruit in summer, asparagus tips in spring); warm chiffonnade of shellfish; roasted lobster served with a truffle-studded risotto; John Dory in mushroom-flavored cream sauce, roasted rabbit with galette of sweet polenta and tarragon sauce; and filet of Salers beef with sauce Périgueux (foie gras and truffles), accompanied by roasted potatoes drizzled with a local cheese. Dessert might include roasted slices of pineapple and grapefruit, each served with its own sherbet.

10–12 rue St-Adjutor. ℂ **04-73-36-46-30.** Reservations required. Main courses 120F–190F (18.25– 28.90, $17.40–$27.55); fixed-price menus 190F–250F (28.90– 38, $27.55–$36.25). MC, V. Mon–Sat noon–2pm and 7:30–10:30pm.

CLERMONT-FERRAND AFTER DARK

A very hip crowd gathers all year at **Le Blue Sport Café,** 68 place de l'Étoile (ℂ **04-73-36-08-92**), where jazz and rock blend with a lively pub atmosphere to create one of the most popular meeting places around. For the best cafe/bar in town, complete with regular jazz and rock concerts, go to **Le 15e Avenue,** rue des Petits Gras (no phone). Always in danger of closing down for lack of funds, it's informal, with a schedule of events that's usually planned at the last minute. Two discos that are a lot more certain to survive deep into the millennium include **Le Frog,** 12 rue des Petits Gras (ℂ **04-73-37-99-73**), and **Le Symbol,** 11 rue de Serbie (ℂ **04-73-31-01-01**). Both attract a crowd over 25, including lots of single, divorced, or nominally married people looking for a dance and perhaps a fling. If you're gay and looking for a night on the town, consider the most visible gay disco in Clermont, **Le Zyzy Folies,** 31 rue Anatole-France (ℂ **04-73-90-21-21**). You might also consider dropping into the previously recommended Le Frog. It's not altogether gay, but its trendiness and hipness make it an agreeable place for lots of outwardly gay clients (along with everyone else).

5 Aubusson

236 miles S of Paris, 55 miles E of Limoges, 59 miles NW of Clermont-Ferrand

In the Creuse Valley, the little market town of Aubusson enjoys world renown for its carpets and tapestries. Aubusson is characterized by clock towers, bridges, peaked roofs, and turrets—all of which inspired the painter Gromaire's widely reproduced cartoon *View of Aubusson.* Against the gray granite, rainbow-hued skeins of wool hang from windows. The workshops of the craftspeople are spread throughout the town; many are open to the public (just ask). The origin of the industry is unknown. Some credit the Arabs who settled here in 732. Others think the craft came from Flanders in the Middle Ages. For years, the favorite subject was *The Lady and the Unicorn,* the original of which was discovered in the nearby Château de Boussac. Many tapestry reproductions of the works of 18th-century painters like Boucher and Watteau have been made. Since World War II, designs by painters like Picasso, Matisse, and Braque have been stressed.

The **Musée Départemental de la Tapisserie,** avenue des Lissiers (ℂ **05-55-66-33-06**), has exhibits related to the 600-year-old tradition of the Aubusson carpet- and tapestry-weaving industry. The displays also highlight the 20th-century rebirth of the Aubusson carpet and the art of tapestry weaving. The museum is open Wednesday to Monday from 9:30am to noon and 2 to 6pm (in summer from 9am to 6pm). Admission is 20F (3.05, $2.90) for adults, 75F (11.40, $10.90) for children 12 to 16, and free for children 11 and under. The **Maison du Tapissier,** rue Vieille (© 05-55-66-32-12), exhibits old carpets and displays a reconstruction of an old carpet-weaving studio. It's open daily from 9:30am to 12:30pm and 2:30 to 6pm, from mid-June to September, and Tuesday to Saturday off-season (same hours). Admission is 17F (2.60, $2.45) for adults, free for persons under 12.

ESSENTIALS

GETTING THERE Aubusson does have **rail** service, much of it indirect, from Clermont-Ferrand and Paris, among other cities. Ten trains leave from Paris's Gare d'Austerlitz for Aubusson with a change in Limoges. From Clermont-Ferrand to Aubusson, four trains depart daily for a nearly 4-hour trip (with a minimum of two stops). For complete train information, call © 08-36-35-35-35. Passengers interested in bus transit usually find that the routes leading into town only service the towns and communities in the neighborhood, with inconvenient connections from other parts of France. For information, call La Gare Routière (© 05-55-10-31-00). If you're **driving** from Clermont-Ferrand, take D941 west to Aubusson. The trip takes between 1 and 1½ hours.

VISITOR INFORMATION The Office de Tourisme is on rue Vieille (© 05-55-66-32-12).

ACCOMMODATIONS & DINING

Le Lion d'Or *Value* Hardly a fancy choice, this is a solid and reliable inn, occupying a building erected around 1800 on the town's main square. It's unpretentious but still one of the town's best choices, with polite but no-nonsense management by Jean-Pierre Clerc. The rooms are simple yet comfortable, each with a small shower-only bathroom. The street level contains a restaurant that serves the town's best food. In summer, lunch and dinner are offered daily, but between October 15 and April 15 no meals are served on Sunday nights. Meals feature such dishes as stingray with butter-flavored cabbage, and a local specialty, a *fondue Creusoise,* a choice you might have more readily expected in the French Alps. It consists of a pot of melted local cheese (Le Creusois) served with strips of locally cured ham, French fries, and salad.

Place du Général-Espagne, 23200 Aubusson. © **05-55-66-13-88.** Fax 05-55-66-84-73. 11 units. 270F–300F (41.05– 45.60, $39.15–$43.50) double. AE, MC, V. **Amenities:** Restaurant; room service; laundry. *In room:* TV.

6 Limoges ✦

246 miles S of Paris, 193 miles N of Toulouse, 58 miles NE of Périgueux

Limoges, the ancient capital of Limousin in west-central France, is world famous for its exquisite porcelain and enamel works, the latter a medieval industry revived in the 19th century and still going strong today. In fact, Limoges is the economic capital of western France. Occupying the Vienne's right bank, the town has historically consisted of two parts: the Cité, with its narrow streets and old maisons on the lower slope; and the town proper at the summit.

ESSENTIALS

GETTING THERE Limoges has good **train** service from most regional cities, with direct trains from Toulouse, Poitiers, and Paris. Ten trains depart daily from Paris's Gare d'Austerlitz for Limoges (trip time: 3 hr.). For complete train information, call ✆ **08-36-35-35-35. Bus** transit in and out of the small towns and villages nearby can be arranged through the Gare Routière, place des Charentes (✆ **05-55-10-31-00**). If you're **driving** from Aubusson, take D941 west for the 1-hour trip.

VISITOR INFORMATION   The **Office de Tourisme** is on boulevard de Fleurus (✆ **05-55-34-46-87;** www.en-france.com).

EXPLORING THE TOWN

If you'd like to see an enameler at work or a porcelain factory producing its wares, ask at the tourist office (see above) for a list of workshops, or go directly to the famous Pavillon de la Porcelaine (below).

To stock up on local porcelain, try these three **Prestige de Limoges** shops owned by the same company: At 2 bd. Louis-Blanc (✆ **05-55-34-44-15**), you'll find Limoges's own "unblemished crystal" as well as crystal from Lalique, St. Louis, and Baccarat, and silverware from Christofle and Puiforcat. At 13 and 27 bd. Louis-Blanc (✆ **05-55-34-58-61**), you can buy porcelain from Haviland, Bernardaud, Raynaud, and Lafarge, as well as slightly imperfect seconds.

For a sales-oriented overview of the abundance of locally made porcelain that's available, visit any of three branches of the **Société Lachaniette,** which lie, respectively, at nos. 2, 13, and 27 bd. Louis-Blanc. They share a communal switchboard at ✆ **05-55-34-58-61.** At nos. 13 and 27, you'll find examples of porcelain from each of the manufacturers in Limoges, including Haviland, Bernardaud, Raynaud, and Laure Japy (formerly known as Laforge). At no. 2, you'll find mostly crystal from Lalique, St. Louis, and Baccarat, and silverware from Christofle and Puiforcat. Specific inventories are shifted among the three branches as new collections are released, but overall, by wandering among all three, you'll get a fast overview of what's available.

Thanks to the rich deposits of kaolin (known locally as "white gold") that were found near Limoges in the 18th century, more than 30 manufacturers of delicate porcelain have set up operations through the years in and around the town. Many of them maintain factory outlets, sometimes offering good-quality seconds at reduced prices. Some of the best outlets, with the widest inventories, are as follows: For a thoroughly antique style of porcelain, visit the **Ancienne Manufacture Royale,** 7 place Horteils, in Limoges' suburb of Aixe-sur-Vienne (✆ **05-55-70-44-82**), 3½ miles west of Limoges. Within the center of town, you'll find **Raynaud,** 14 ancienne route d'Aixe (✆ **05-55-01-77-65**), and **Chastagner,** 20 av. des Casseaux (✆ **05-55-33-45-74**). Largest of all, with the most evolved sense of public relations and marketing, is **Bernardaud,** 27 rue Albert-Thomas (✆ **05-55-10-55-91**), where a small-scale museum (focusing on past porcelain-related triumphs) and a tearoom adjoin the showroom.

Pavillon de la Porcelaine   Haviland has been exporting its porcelain to the United States and other countries since 1842, when a group of American entrepreneurs immigrated to France from Boston to found the first American-owned company ever established in Europe. Over the years, it has used the designs of artists like Gauguin and Dali. In the museum, you can see the masterpieces as well as original pieces created for the U.S. White House. Later, visit an air-conditioned room where you can learn the history of this unusual company as well as follow the manufacturing process with the help of a video shown on a giant screen. A large shop also sells the porcelain at factory prices.

Av. John-Kennedy. ✆ **05-55-30-21-86.** Free admission. Apr–Oct daily 8:30am–7:30pm; Nov–Mar daily 9:30am–7pm.

Musée National de la Porcelaine Adrien-Dubouché ★★ This museum, housed in a 19th-century building, boasts the largest public collection of Limoges porcelain. Its 12,000 pieces illustrate the history of glassmaking and ceramics (porcelain, glazed earthenware, stoneware, and terra cotta) throughout the ages. In France, its porcelain collection is second only to that of Sèvres. The main gallery contains whole dinner sets of noted figures and some contemporary Limoges ware.

Place Winston-Churchill, 87000 Limoges. ✆ **05-55-33-08-50**. Admission 22F (3.35, $3.20) adults, 15F (2.30, $2.20) ages 18–25, free for children 17 and under. July–Aug Wed–Mon 10am–5:45pm; Sept–June Wed–Mon 10am–12:30pm and 2–5:45pm.

Cathédrale St-Etienne The cathedral was begun in 1273 but took many years to complete. The choir, for example, was finished in 1327, but work continued in the nave until almost 1890. The cathedral is the only one in the old province of Limousin to be built entirely in the Gothic style. The main entrance is through Porte St-Jean, which has beautifully carved wooden doors from the 16th century (constructed at the peak of the Flamboyant Gothic style). Inside, the nave appears so harmonious it's hard to imagine that its construction took 6 centuries. The rood screen is of particular interest, built in 1533 in the ornate style of the Italian Renaissance. The cathedral also contains some admirable bishops' tombs from the 14th to the 16th centuries.

Place de la Cathédrale. ✆ **05-55-34-53-81**. Free admission. Summer daily 10am–6pm; winter daily 10am–5pm.

Musée Municipal de l'Évêché-de-l'Émail Adjoining the cathedral in the Jardins de l'Evêché—which offer a view of the Vienne and the pont St-Etienne from the 13th century—the old archbishops' palace has been turned into the Musée Municipal. The elegant 18th-century building has an outstanding collection of Limoges enamels from the 12th century, as well as some enamel paintings by Leonard Limousin, who was born in 1505 in Limoges and went on to win world acclaim and the favor of four monarchs. Limoges was also the birthplace of Renoir, and the museum displays several works by this world-class artist.

Place de la Cathédrale. ✆ **05-55-34-44-09**. Free admission. June–Sept daily 10–11:45am and 2–6pm; Oct–May Wed–Mon 10am–11:45 and 2–5pm.

Église St-Michel-des-Lions Construction of this church was launched in the 14th century, and work continued into the 15th and 16th centuries. Although the church is not as interesting as older Romanesque churches scattered in other parts of the Auvergne, it's the headquarters of the cult of St-Martial, a Limoges hometown bishop (and saint) who died in the 3rd century. The church is the home of what's reputed to be his skull, which is stored in an elaborately enamelled reliquary. "Les Ostensions" is a religious procession, established in 994, that occurs every 7 years, when the skull—which some adherents credit with mystical powers—is removed from storage and exhibited as part of religious ceremonies that attract as many as 100,000 devout adherents. The next such procession is scheduled for 2002.

Place St-Michel. ✆ **05-55-34-18-13**. Free admission. Mon–Sat 8am–noon and 2–6pm; Sun 8am–11:45 and 4–6pm.

ACCOMMODATIONS

Hôtel Royal Limousin ★ This is the town's leading inn, built in the 1960s adjacent to a municipal parking lot in the center of Limoges. The rooms are outfitted in a modern chain-hotel style but are generally large and have midsize bathrooms, mostly with tub/shower combinations. Accommodations on the noisier avenue Carnot side rent for less than those on the quieter place de la République side. The only drawback is that the hotel is often booked by summer group tours and porcelain collectors. There's no restaurant, but the staff refers hotel guests to the restaurant next door, under separate management.

Place de la République, 87000 Limoges. ⓒ **05-55-34-65-30.** Fax 05-55-34-55-21. 77 units. 510F–615F (77.50– 93.50, $73.95–$89.20) double; 680F–1,200F (103.35– 182.40, $98.60–$174) suite. AE, DC, MC, V. **Amenities:** Breakfast room service; laundry. *In room:* TV, minibar, hair dryer.

Hotel St-Martial Located just north of the city center, this modern hotel is the most recent manifestation of a building erected around 1900, but frequent renovations have kept it looking fresh. The quiet rooms are simply but comfortably furnished in a modern style, each with a small bathroom with shower. Breakfast is the only meal served, but the management can direct you to the half dozen or so restaurants on rue Garibaldi, a short walk away.

21 rue Armand-Barbès, 87000 Limoges. ⓒ **05-55-77-75-29.** Fax 05-55-79-27-60. 30 units. 370F (56.25, $53.65) double. AE, V. Parking 40F (6.10, $5.80). *In room:* TV.

DINING

Philippe Redon ✦ TRADITIONAL FRENCH In a 19th-century house a few steps from the produce market, owner/chef, Philippe Redon, the finest cook in Limoges, presides over a youthful team of waiters. The restaurant contains a 1930s Art Deco–style interior accented with exposed stone and flowers. Menu items vary with the availability of local ingredients. Examples include lobster casserole with delectable fresh seasonings, slices of foie gras and duckling, and sea bass grilled or roasted to perfection.

3 rue Aguesseau. ⓒ **05-55-34-66-22.** Reservations recommended. Fixed-price menus 160F–290F (24.30– 44.10, $23.20–$42.05). AE, DC, V. Mon–Fri noon–2:30pm; Tues–Sat 7–10pm. Closed Aug 1–15 and Jan 1–15.

NEARBY ACCOMMODATIONS & DINING
IN ST-MARTIN-DU-FAULT

La Chapelle St-Martin ★★★ This is the best place in the environs if you enjoy early-1900s living and superb food in the tradition of the Relais & Châteaux group. The hotel is graciously situated in a private park with two ponds. Your host, Gilles Dudognon, requests that you reserve well in advance. The rooms are individually decorated and tasteful, and some are suitable for travelers with disabilities. Each has a 19th-century theme (usually Directoire or Empire). The hotel contains deluxe bathrooms with tub/shower combinations. The restaurant offers excellent food, using raw materials selected and handled with care and deftness by the chefs.

87510 Nieul. ⓒ **05-55-75-80-17.** Fax 05-55-75-89-50. www.chapellesaintmartin.com. 13 units. 690F–980F (104.90– 148.95, $100.05–$142.10) double; 1,300F–1,500F (197.60– 228, $188.50–$217.50) suite. AE, MC, V, DC. Restaurant closed Mon. Free parking. Take N147 and D35 7 miles northeast from Limoges. **Amenities:** Restaurant; room service; laundry. *In room:* TV, hair dryer.

IN NIEUIL

To get to Nieuil from Limoges, take N141 west of the town center (signposted Angoulême). The town of Nieuil is signposted at the town of Suaux. Follow the signs for about a mile east of the village toward Fontafie. Nieuil lies 7½ miles northwest of Limoges. *Note:* Don't confuse Nieuil with La Chapelle St-Martin at Nieul (with a slightly different spelling).

Château de Nieuil ★★   This fabled old inn comes with quite a pedigree. The château, built in the 16th century as a hunting lodge for François I, was transformed in 1937 into the first château-hotel in France. Restored by the comte de Dampierre early in the 1800s after its destruction in the Revolution, it has remained in the antique-collecting family of Jean-Michel Bodinaud since around 1900. Today 400 acres of park and forest lead up to a series of beautifully maintained gardens, the pride of the owners. The cuisine, crafted and supervised by Mme Luce Bodinaud, is superb, focusing on classic traditions and regional recipes. A typical dish is stuffed cabbage (*farci Charentais*), though you may prefer the filet of beef du Limousine or a selection of fish that includes filet of sole in the style *pêcheurs d'Oléron*, prepared with a compôte of leeks and crayfish. Nonguests can dine here if they call ahead.

16270 Nieuil. (℃ **05-45-71-36-38.** Fax 05-45-71-46-45. www.relaischateaux.fr/nieuil. 14 units. 900F–1,600F (136.80– 243.20, $130.50–$232) double; 1,800F–2,400F (273.60– 364.80, $261–$348) suite. AE, DC, MC, V. Closed Nov–Apr. **Amenities:** Restaurant; pool; 2 tennis courts; room service; laundry. *In room:* A/C, TV, minibar, hair dryer.

7 Le Puy-en-Velay ★★★

325 miles S of Paris, 80 miles SE of Clermont-Ferrand

Le Puy-en-Velay (usually shortened to Le Puy) is one of the most extraordinary sights in France. Steep volcanic spires, left over from geological activity that ended millennia ago, are capped with Romanesque churches, a cathedral, and medieval houses that rise sinuously from the plain below. The history of Le Puy is centered around the cult of the Virgin Mary, an attachment that prompted the construction of many of the city's churches.

Le Puy today is a provincial French city of steep cobblestone streets with lots of rather shabby buildings (many of which are now being restored). Much of the population of approximately 22,000 lives off the tourist trade, and today's visitors follow in the footsteps of Charlemagne, "the first tourist" here. Le Puy remains a major pilgrimage destination of France, although it is not as famous as Lourdes.

Le Puy is defined as the capital, within France, of lentils. Lentils produced within a predefined distance of Le Puy are categorized, in a way that emulates the country's most prestigious wines, as A.O.C. (Appellation d'Origine Controlée). The town is also the point of departure for many pilgrims who follow the road to Santiago de Compostela in northwest Spain. As such, there's a special blessing given in honor of pilgrims every morning at 7am in the cathedral (see below). Because of the vast numbers of pilgrims who have traditionally stopped at Le Puy and its cathedral, the town, as well as the entire length of the chemin de St-Jacques de Compostelle, is listed by UNESCO as a site of importance to the Universal Patrimony.

ESSENTIALS

GETTING THERE   Passengers arriving in Le Puy from anywhere in Europe must change **trains** at the railway junction of St-Georges d'Aurac. From here, small trains, timed for convenient connections, travel along the 17-mile spur route that connects Le Puy's small railway station to the rest of the lines of the SNCF. For train information and schedules, call (℃ **08-36-35-35-35. Bus service** in and out of Puy-en-Velay is relatively inefficient and of use only to passengers coming in and out of the small-scale villages within the Auvergne. Even buses from Clermont-Ferrand take at least 3 hours for the relatively short distance. For **bus** information, contact La Gare Routière at ℭ **04-71-09-25-60.** If you're **driving,** the best way to reach Le Puy is from St-Etienne, traveling southwest along N88. From Clermont-Ferrand, drive south along N88 to Lempdes, continuing southeast along N102 to Le Puy.

VISITOR INFORMATION   The **Office de Tourisme** is on place du Breuil (ℭ **04-71-09-38-41**).

SEEING THE SIGHTS

Puy is the historic center of the French lace industry; you'll find lace shops on every block. But to be assured of handmade authenticity, look for the words *dentelle du puy.* As decreed by a 1931 local government ordinance, the display of this mark on lace is a privilege reserved for the real thing. The best selections of local lace can be found at **Spécialités du Velay,** 1 bd. St-Louis (ℭ **04-71-09-09-34**); **Lucia Dentelles,** 28 place du plot (ℭ **04-71-09-60-69**); and **Aux Souvenirs du Puy,** 60 rue Raphaël (ℭ **04-71-05-76-71**).

Cathédrale Notre-Dame ★★★   This Romanesque cathedral was conceived as a site for shelter and prayer for medieval pilgrims heading to the religious shrines of Santiago de Compostela in northwestern Spain. Marked by vivid Oriental and Byzantine influences, it's worth a visit. The cloisters contain carved capitals dating from the Carolingian era. The Chapelle des Reliques et Trésor d'Art Religieux contains fabrics and gold and silver objects from the church treasury, as well as an unusual enameled chalice from the 12th century.

Place du For. ℭ **04-71-05-45-52.** Admission to cathedral free; to cloisters and Chapel of Relics 26F (3.95, $3.75) adults, 16F (2.45, $2.30) ages 12–24, free for children 11 and under. Cathedral, daily 8:30am–7:30pm (Oct–Feb until 6:30pm). Cloisters and Chapel of Relics, Oct–Mar daily 9:30am–noon and 2–4pm; Apr–June daily 9:30am–12:30pm and 2–6pm; July–Sept daily 9:30am–6:30pm.

Chapelle St-Michel-d'Aiguilhe ★★   This 10th-century chapel, perched precariously atop a volcanic spur that rises abruptly from hilly terrain, is one of the city's most dramatic sights. It sits on the northwestern perimeter of Le Puy. Reaching its summit requires a very long climb up rocky stairs. When you get here, you'll be struck by the Oriental influences in the floor plan, the arabesques, and the mosaics crafted from black stone. On view are some 12th-century murals and an 11th-century wooden depiction of Christ.

Atop the Rocher St-Michel. ℭ **04-71-09-50-03.** Admission 15F (2.30, $2.20) adults, 8F (1.20, $1.15) children 13 and under. Mid-June to mid-Sept daily 9am–7pm; mid-Sept to early June daily 9 or 10am–noon and 2–5 or 6pm, depending on the hours of sunrise and sunset; Dec 20–31 2–4pm only.

Musée Crozatier   If you appreciate handcrafts, you'll enjoy the displays of lace, some from the 16th century, at this museum, which also has a collection of carved architectural embellishments from the Romanesque era and paintings from the 14th to the 20th century.

In the Jardin Henri-Vinay. ℭ **04-71-09-38-90.** Fax 04-71-02-18-09. m-crozat@mail.es-conseil.fr. Admission 20F (3.05, $2.90) adults, 10F (1.50, $1.45) children, free for children 5 and under. May–Sept Wed–Mon 10am–noon and 2–6pm; Oct–Apr Mon and Wed–Sat 10am–noon and 2–4pm; Sun 2–4pm.

ACCOMMODATIONS

Hôtel Brivas *Value*   Set about a 2-minute drive southwest of the town center, adjacent to Le Dolaizon river, this hotel is the newest and most modern in town. The rooms are clean, streamlined, and simple with basic furnishings, each with a small bathroom with shower. The hotel and its restaurant cater to tour bus groups. The restaurant offers a fixed-price menu.

Av. Charles-Massot, 43750 Vals-Près-Le-Puy. ℂ **04-71-05-68-66.** Fax 04-71-05-65-88. brivas@aol.com.fr. 47 units. 330F–430F (50.15– 65.35, $47.85–$62.35) double. AE, MC, V. Closed Dec 26–Jan 15. **Amenities:** Restaurant; room service; laundry. *In room:* TV.

Hôtel Régina ⋆ In no way is this hotel grand, but it's the finest in town. In 1998, a radical renovation brought it up to the best standards in town. Built late in the 19th century and operated by extended members of a local family (the Venosinos), it offers simple but thoughtfully decorated rooms. All units contain midsize bathrooms, mostly with tub/shower combinations. It's conveniently located close to the heart of town.

The in-house brasserie offers affordable platters of food that begin at 78F (11.85, $11.30) and fixed-price menus at 85F to 230F (12.90 to 34.95, $12.35 to $33.35). In the afternoon, it turns into a tea salon that attracts many local retirees and shopkeepers.

34 bd. du Maréchal-Fayolle, 43000 Le Puy-en-Velay. ℂ **04-71-09-14-71.** Fax 04-71-09-18-57. 27 units. 350F–395F (53.20– 60.05, $50.75–$57.30) double; 600F–650F (91.20– 98.80, $87–$94.25) suite. AE, MC, V. Parking 28F (4.25, $4.05). **Amenities:** Brasserie; room service; laundry. *In room:* TV, minibar, hair dryer.

DINING

Le Bateau Ivre FRENCH/AUVERGNAT Set in the heart of town and devoted to the traditions of the region, this restaurant occupies a pair of rustically old-fashioned dining rooms in a house whose interior is much older than its 19th-century facade. Monsieur Datessen, your host, prepares a variety of dishes utilizing the robust wines of the region, as well as lentils, which crop up in appealing and flavorful ways. Specialties include roasted versions of the Auvergne's black lambs, prepared with thyme and mashed potatoes studded with morels; beef of the Salers breed with local red wine and marrow sauce; roasted pigeon with foie gras and a confit of grapes; and local whitefish (*omble chevalier*) served at least four different ways. Dedicated pilgrims to Le Puy always have this restaurant marked as the "serious" dining choice. Notice the lace that covers the windows and wooden tables: It was all handmade in Le Puy, mainly by elderly women working in their living rooms.

5 rue Portail-d'Avignon. ℂ **04-71-09-67-20.** Reservations recommended. Main courses 60F–110F (9.10– 16.70, $8.70–$15.95); fixed-price menus 115F–190F (17.50– 28.90, $16.70–$27.55). AE, MC, V. Tues–Sat noon–2:30pm and Mon–Sat 7:30–10pm. Closed 1 week in June and Nov 1–15.

Appendix A: France in Depth

France remains one of the world's most talked about, and most written about destinations. It's packed with diversions and distractions of every sort: cultural, culinary, sensual, you name it. And perhaps that's why France has been called *le deuxième pays de tout le monde:* everyone's second country.

The French claim credit for developing Gothic style architecture and the cathedrals that stand as legacies of soaring stone. And ever since the Middle Ages, creators of everything from palaces to subway stations have drawn at least some inspiration from designs born in France. The thrilling monuments tell the stories of an land that has shaped, and been shaped, by the rise and fall of rulers and empires since ancient times; a country that has been the scene of and the subject of thousands of bloody battles. France has entered the millennium as part of an ever more unified Europe, but remains, and probably always will, indescribably, unalterably, *French.*

History 101

EARLY GAUL

When the Romans considered France part of their empire, their boundaries extended deep into the forests of the Paris basin and up to the edges of the Rhine. Part of Julius Caesar's early reputation came from his defeat of King Vercingetorix at Alésia in 52 B.C., a victory he was quick to publicize in one of the ancient world's literary masterpieces, *The Gallic Wars.* In that year the Roman colony of Lutetia (Paris) was established on an island in the Seine (Île de la Cité).

As the Roman Empire declined, its armies retreated to the colonies that had been established along a strip of the Mediterranean coast—among others, these included Orange, Montpellier, Nîmes, Narbonne, and Marseille, which retain some of the best Roman monuments in Europe.

As one of their legacies, the Roman armies left behind the practice of Christianity. The Roman Church, for all its abuses, was the only real guardian of civilization during the anarchy following the Roman decline.

Dateline

- 121 B.C. The Romans establish the province of Gallia Narbonensis to guard overland routes between Spain and Italy; its borders correspond roughly to today's Provence.
- 58–51 B.C. Julius Caesar conquers Gaul (north-central France).
- 52 B.C. The Roman city of Lutetia, later Paris, is built on a defensible island in the Seine.
- 2nd century A.D. Christianity arrives in Gaul.
- 485–511 Under Clovis I, the Franks defeat the Roman armies and establish the Merovingian dynasty.
- 768 Charlemagne (768–814) becomes the Frankish king and establishes the Carolingian dynasty; from Aix-la-Chapelle (Aachen), he rules lands from northern Italy to Bavaria to Paris.
- 800 Charlemagne is crowned Holy Roman Emperor in Rome.
- 814 Charlemagne dies, his empire breaks up.
- 1066 William of Normandy (the Conqueror) invades England; his conquest is completed by 1087.

continues

A form of low Latin was the common language, and it evolved into the archaic French that both delights and confuses today's medieval scholars.

The Christianity adopted by many of the chieftains was viewed as heretical by Rome. Consequently, when Clovis (king of Gaul's Franks and founder of the Merovingian dynasty) astutely converted to Catholicism, he won the approval of the pope, the support of the powerful archbishop of Reims, and the loyalty of the many Gallic tribes who'd grown disenchanted with anarchy. (Clovis's baptism is viewed as the beginning of a collusion between the Catholic church and the French monarchy that flourished until the 1789 Revolution.) At the Battle of Soissons in 486, Clovis defeated the last vestiges of Roman power in Gaul. Other conquests included expansions westward to the Seine, then to the Loire. After a battle in Dijon in 500, he became the nominal overlord of the king of Burgundy. Seven years later, his armies drove the Visigoths into Spain, giving most of Aquitaine, in western France, to his newly founded Merovingian dynasty. Trying to make the best of an earlier humiliation, Anastasius, the Byzantium-based emperor of the Eastern Roman Empire, finally gave the kingdom of the Franks his legal sanction.

After Clovis's death in 511, his kingdom was split among his squabbling heirs. The Merovingian dynasty survived in fragmented form for another 250 years. During this period, the power of the bishops and the lords grew, entrenching the complex hierarchies of what we today know as feudalism. Although apologists for the Merovingians are quick to point out their achievements, the quasi-anarchy of their reign has been (not altogether unfairly) identified by many as the Dark Ages.

- 1140 St-Denis Cathedral, the first example of Gothic architecture, is completed.
- 1270 Louis IX (St. Louis), along with most of his army, dies in Tunis on the Eighth Crusade.
- 1309 The papal schism—Philip the Fair establishes the Avignon papacy, which lasts nearly 70 years; two popes struggle for domination.
- 1347–51 The bubonic plague (Black Death) kills 33% of the population.
- 1431 The English burn Joan of Arc at the stake in Rouen for resisting their occupation of France.
- 1453 The French drive the English out of all of France except Calais; the Hundred Years' War ends.
- 1515–47 France captures Calais after centuries of English rule.
- 1562–98 The Wars of Religion: Catholics fight Protestants; Henri IV converts to Catholicism and issues the Edict of Nantes, granting limited rights to Protestants.
- **1643–1715** The reign of Louis XIV, the Sun King; France develops Europe's most powerful army, but wars in Flanders and court extravagance sow seeds of decline.
- 1763 The Treaty of Paris effectively ends French power in North America.
- 1789–94 The French Revolution: The Bastille is stormed on July 14, 1789; the Reign of Terror follows.
- 1793 Louis XVI and Marie Antoinette are guillotined.
- 1794 Robespierre and the leaders of the Reign of Terror are guillotined.
- 1799 Napoléon enters Paris and unites diverse factions; his victories in Italy solidify his power in Paris.
- 1804 Napoléon crowns himself emperor in Notre-Dame de Paris.
- 1805–11 Napoléon and his armies successfully invade most of Europe.
- 1814–15 Napoléon abdicates after the failure of his Russian campaign; exiled to Elba, he returns. On June 18, 1815, defeated at Waterloo, he's exiled to St. Helena, and dies in 1821.
- 1830–48 The reign of Louis-Philippe.

continues

THE CAROLINGIANS

From the wreckage of the intrigue-ridden Merovingian court emerged a new dynasty: the Carolingians. One of their leaders, Charles Martel, halted a Muslim invasion of northern Europe at Tours in 743 and left a much-expanded kingdom to his son, Pepin. The Carolingian empire eventually stretched from the Pyrénées to deep in the German forests, encompassing much of modern France, Germany, and northern Italy. The heir to this vast land was Charlemagne. Crowned emperor in Rome on Christmas Day in 800, he returned to his capital at Aix-la-Chapelle (Aachen) and created the Holy Roman Empire. Charlemagne's rule saw a revived interest in scholarship, art, and classical texts called the Carolingian Renaissance.

Despite Charlemagne's magnetism, cultural rifts formed in his sprawling empire, most of which was eventually divided between two of his three squabbling heirs. Charles of Aquitaine annexed the western region; Louis of Bavaria took the east. Historians credit this division with the development of modern France and Germany as separate nations. Shortly after Charlemagne's death, his fragmented empire was invaded by Vikings from the north, Muslim Saracens from the south, and Hungarians from the east.

THE MIDDLE AGES

When the Carolingian dynasty died out in 987, Hugh Capet, comte de Paris and duc de France, officially began the Middle Ages with the establishment of the Capetian dynasty. In 1154 the annulment of Eleanor of Aquitaine's marriage to Louis VII of France and subsequent marriage to Henry II of England placed the western half of France under English control, and vestiges of their power remained for centuries. Meanwhile,

- 1848 A revolution topples Louis-Philippe; Napoléon III (nephew of Napoléon I) is elected president.
- 1851–71 President Napoléon names himself Emperor Napoléon III.
- 1863 An exhibition of paintings marks the birth of Impressionism.
- 1870–71 The Franco-Prussian War: Paris falls; France cedes Alsace-Lorraine but aggressively colonizes North Africa and Southeast Asia.
- 1873 France loses Suez to the British; financial scandal wrecks an attempt to dredge the canal.
- 1889 The Eiffel Tower is built for Paris's Universal Exhibition and the Revolution's centennial; architectural critics howl with contempt.
- 1914–18 World War I; French casualties exceed five million.
- 1923 France occupies the Ruhr, Germany's industrial zone, collecting enormous war reparations.
- 1929 France retreats from the Ruhr and the Rhineland and constructs the Maginot Line, dubbed "impregnable."
- 1934 The Great Depression; a political crisis is spurred by clashes of left and right.
- 1936 Germans march into the demilitarized Rhineland; France takes no action.
- 1939 France and Britain guarantee to Poland, Romania, and Greece protection from aggressors; Germany invades Poland; France declares war.
- 1940 Paris falls to Germany on June 14; Marshal Pétain's Vichy government collaborates with the Nazis; General de Gaulle forms a government-in-exile in London to direct French resistance fighters.
- 1944 On June 6, the Allies invade the Normandy beaches; other Allied troops invade from the south; Paris is liberated in August.
- 1946–54 War in Indochina; French withdraw from Southeast Asia; North and South Vietnam are created.
- 1954–58 The Algerian revolution and subsequent independence from

continues

vast forests and swamps were cleared (often by the Middle Ages' hardest-working ascetics, Cistercian monks), the population grew, great Gothic cathedrals were begun, and monastic life contributed to every level of a rapidly developing social order. Politically driven marriages among the ruling families more than doubled the size of the territory controlled from Paris, a city increasingly recognized as the country's capital. Philippe II (reigned 1179 to 1223) infiltrated more prominent families with his genes than anyone else in France, successfully marrying members of his family into the Valois, Artois, and Vermandois. He also managed to win Normandy and Anjou back from the English.

Louis IX (St. Louis) emerged as the 13th century's most memorable king, though he ceded most of the hard-earned military conquests of his predecessors to the English. Somewhat of a religious fanatic, he died of illness (with most of his army) in 1270 in a boat off Tunis. The vainglorious and not-very-wise pretext for his trip was the Eighth Crusade. At the time of his death, Notre-Dame and the Sainte-Chapelle in Paris had been completed, and the arts of tapestry making and stonecutting were flourishing.

During the 1300s, the struggle of French sovereignty against the claims of a rapacious Roman pope tempted Philip the Fair to support a pope based in Avignon. (The Roman pope, Boni-

France; refugees flood France; the Fourth Republic collapses.

- **1958** De Gaulle initiates the Fifth Republic, calling for a France independent from the United States and Europe.
- **1960** France tests an atomic bomb.
- **1968** Students riot in Paris; de Gaulle resigns.
- **1981** François Mitterrand becomes the first Socialist president since World War II.
- **1989** The bicentennial of the French Revolution and the centennial of the Eiffel Tower.
- **1993** Conservatives topple the Socialists, as Edouard Balladur becomes premier.
- **1994** The Channel Tunnel opens to link France with England.
- **1995** Jacques Chirac wins the French presidency and declares a war on unemployment; his popularity wanes and much unrest follows; terrorists bomb Paris several times.
- **1997** Strict immigration laws are enforced, causing strife for many African and Arab immigrants and dividing the country. French voters elect Socialist Lionel Jospin as the new prime minister.
- **1998** France hosts, wins the World Cup.
- **2000** The euro is officially introduced. France gives legal status to unmarried couples.
- **2001** France buries its national currency, the French franc, and switches to the euro, the equivalent of a European dollar.

face VIII, whom Philip insulted and then assaulted in his home, is said to have died of the shock.) During one of medieval history's most bizarre episodes, two popes ruled simultaneously, one from Rome and one from Avignon. They competed for control of Christendom until years of political intrigue turned the tables in favor of Rome, and Avignon relinquished its claim in 1378.

The 14th century saw an increase in the wealth and power of the French kings, an increase in prosperity, and a decrease in the power of the feudal lords. The death of Louis X without an heir in 1316 prompted more than a decade of scheming and plotting before the eventual emergence of the Valois dynasty.

The Black Death began in 1348, killing an estimated 33% of Europe's population, decimating the population of Paris, and setting the stage for the exodus of the French monarchs to safer climes in such places as the Loire Valley. A financial crisis, coupled with ruinous harvests, almost bankrupted the nation.

During the Hundred Years' War, the English made sweeping inroads into France in an attempt to grab the throne. At their most powerful, they controlled almost all the north (Picardy and Normandy), Champagne, parts of the Loire Valley, and the huge region called Guyenne. The peasant-born charismatic visionary Joan of Arc rallied the French troops as well as the timid dauphin (crown prince), whom she managed to have crowned as Charles VII in the cathedral at Reims. As threatening to the Catholic church as she was to the English, she was declared a heretic and burned at the stake in 1431. Led by the newly crowned king, a barely cohesive France initiated reforms that strengthened its finances and vigor. After compromises among various factions, the French drove the discontented English out, leaving them only the Norman port of Calais.

In the late 1400s, Charles VIII married Brittany's last duchess, Anne, for a unification of France with its Celtic-speaking western outpost. In the early 1500s, the fascinating François I, through war and diplomacy, strengthened the monarchy, rid it of its dependence on Italian bankers, coped with the intricate policies of the Renaissance, and husbanded the arts into a form of patronage that French monarchs continued to endorse for centuries.

Meanwhile, the growth of Protestantism and the unwillingness of the Catholic church to tolerate it led to civil strife. In 1572, Catherine de Médici ordered the St. Bartholomew's Day Massacre of hundreds of Protestants. Henri IV, tired of the bloodshed and fearful that a Catholic Spain would meddle in the religious conflicts, converted to Catholicism in 1593. Just before being stabbed by a half-crazed monk, he issued the Edict of Nantes in 1598, granting freedom of religion to Protestants in France.

THE PASSING OF FEUDALISM

By now France was rid of all but a few of the vestiges of feudalism. In 1624, Louis XIII appointed a Catholic cardinal, the duc de Richelieu, his chief minister. Amassing enormous power, Richelieu virtually ruled the country until his death in 1642. His sole objective was investing the monarchy with total power—he committed a series of truly horrible acts trying to attain this goal and paved the way for the eventual absolutism of Louis XIV.

Although he ascended the throne when he was only 9, with the help of his Sicilian-born chief minister, Cardinal Mazarin, Louis XIV was the most powerful monarch Europe had seen since the Roman emperors. Through a brilliant military campaign against Spain and a judicious marriage to one of its royal daughters, he expanded France to include the southern provinces of Artois and Roussillon. A series of diplomatic and military victories along the Flemish border expanded the country north and east. The estimated population of France at this time was 20 million, as opposed to 8 million in England and 6 million in Spain. French colonies in Canada, the West Indies, and America (Louisiana) were stronger than ever. The mercantilism that Louis's finance minister, Colbert, implemented was one of the era's most important fiscal policies, increasing France's power and wealth. The arts flourished, as did a sense of aristocratic style that's remembered with a bittersweet nostalgia today. Louis's palace of Versailles is the perfect monument to the most flamboyant and excessive era in French history.

Louis's ambitions so threatened the rest of Europe that, led by William of Orange, its kingdoms united to hold him in check. France conducted a series of expensive wars that, coupled with high taxes and bad harvests, stirred up much discontent. England was a threat to France within Europe and in the global rush for colonies. The Atlantic ports, especially Bordeaux, grew and prospered with France's success in the West Indian slave and sugar trades. Despite the country's power, the number of French colonies diminished, due to the naval power of the English. The rise of Prussia as a militaristic neighbor was also problematic.

THE REVOLUTION & THE RISE OF NAPOLÉON

Meanwhile, the Enlightenment was training a new generation of thinkers for the struggle against absolutism, religious fanaticism, and superstition. Europe was never the same after the Revolution of 1789, though the ideas that engendered it had been brewing for more than 50 years. On August 10, 1792, troops from Marseille, aided by a Parisian mob, threw the dim-witted Louis XVI and his Austrian-born queen, Marie Antoinette, into prison. After months of bloodshed and bickering among competing factions, the two monarchs were executed.

France's problems got worse before they got better. In the ensuing bloodbaths, moderates and radicals were guillotined in view of a bloodthirsty crowd that included voyeurs like Dickens's Mme Defarge, who brought her knitting every day to place de la Révolution (later renamed place de la Concorde) to watch the beheadings. The drama surrounding the collapse of the *ancien régime* and the executions of Robespierre's Reign of Terror provides the most heroic and horrible anecdotes in French history. From this era emerged the Declaration of the Rights of Man, an enlightened document published in 1789; its influence has been cited as a model of democratic ideals since. The implications of the collapse of the French aristocracy shook the foundations of every monarchy in Europe.

Only the militaristic fervor of Napoléon Bonaparte could reunite France and bring an end to the chaos. A political and military genius who appeared on the landscape when the French were sickened by the anarchy following their Revolution, he restored a national pride that had been tarnished. He also established a bureaucracy and a code of law that has been emulated around the world. In 1799, at the age of 30, he entered Paris and was crowned First Consul and Master of France. Soon after, a victory in his Italian campaign solidified his power at home. A brilliant politician, he made peace through a compromise with the Vatican, quelling the atheistic spirit of the earliest days of the Revolution.

Napoléon's victories made him the envy of Europe. Beethoven dedicated his Eroica symphony to Napoléon—but retracted the dedication when Napoléon committed what Beethoven considered atrocities. On the verge of conquering all Europe, Napoléon's infamous retreat from Moscow during the winter of 1812 reduced his army to tatters, as 400,000 Frenchmen died in the Russian snows. Napoléon was then defeated at Waterloo by the combined armies of the English, Dutch, and Prussians. Exiled to the British-held island of St. Helena in the South Atlantic, he died in 1821, probably the victim of an unknown poisoner.

THE BOURBONS & THE SECOND EMPIRE

In 1814, following the destruction of Napoléon and his dream, the Congress of Vienna redefined the map of Europe. The new geography was an approximation of the boundaries that had existed in 1792. The Bourbon monarchy was reestablished, with reduced powers for Louis XVIII, an archconservative, and a changing array of leaders who included the prince de Polignac and, later, Charles X. A renewal of the ancient régime's oppressions, however, didn't sit well in a France that had already spilled so much blood in favor of egalitarian causes.

In 1830, after censoring the press and dissolving Parliament, Louis XVIII was removed from power after more uprisings. Louis-Philippe, duc d'Orléans, was elected king under a liberalized constitution. His reign lasted for 18 years of prosperity during which England and France more or less collaborated on matters of foreign policy. The establishment of an independent Belgium and the French conquest of Algeria (1840 to 1847) were to have resounding effects on French politics a century later. It was a time of wealth, grace, and expansion of the arts for most French people, though the industrialization of the north and east produced some of the 19th century's most horrific poverty.

A revolution in 1848, fueled by a financial crash and disgruntled workers in Paris, forced Louis-Philippe out of office. That year, Napoléon I's nephew, Napoléon III, was elected president. Appealing to the property-protecting instinct of a nation that hadn't forgotten the upheavals of less than a century before, he initiated a repressive government in which he was awarded the status of emperor in 1851. Rebounding from the punishment they'd received during the Revolution and the minor role they'd played during the First Empire, the Second Empire's clergy enjoyed great power. Steel production was begun, and a railway system and Indochinese colonies established. New technologies fostered new kinds of industry, and the bourgeoisie flourished. And Baron Georges-Eugène Haussmann radically altered Paris by laying out the grand boulevards the world knows today.

By 1866, an industrialized France began to see the Second Empire as more of a hindrance than an encouragement to expansion. The dismal failure of colonizing Mexico and the increasing power of Austria and Prussia were setbacks to the empire's prestige. In 1870, the Prussians defeated Napoléon III at Sedan and held him prisoner with 100,000 of his soldiers. Paris was besieged by an enemy who only just failed to march its vastly superior armies through the capital.

After the Prussians withdrew, a violent revolt ushered in the Third Republic and its elected president, Marshal MacMahon, in 1873. Peace and prosperity slowly returned, France regained its glamour, a mania of building occurred, the Impressionists made their visual statements, and writers like Flaubert redefined the French novel into what today is regarded as the most evocative in the world. The Eiffel Tower was built as part of the 1889 Universal Exposition.

By 1890, a new corps of satirists (including Zola) had exposed the country's wretched living conditions, the cruelty of the country's vested interests, and the underlying hypocrisy of late-19th-century French society. The 1894 Dreyfus Affair exposed the corruption of French army officers who had destroyed the career and reputation of a Jewish colleague (Albert Dreyfus), falsely and deliberately punished—as a scapegoat—for treason. The ethnic tensions identified by Zola led to further divisiveness in the rest of the 20th century.

THE WORLD WARS

International rivalries, thwarted colonial ambitions, and conflicting alliances led to World War I, which, after decisive German victories for 2 years, degenerated into the mud-slogged horror of trench warfare. Mourning between four and five million casualties, Europe was inflicted with psychological scars that never healed. In 1917, the United States broke the deadlock by entering the war.

After the Allied victory, economic problems, plus demoralization stemming from years of fighting, encouraged the growth of socialism and communism. The French government, led by a vindictive Georges Clemenceau, demanded every centime of reparations it could from a crushed Germany. The humiliation associated with this has been cited as the origin of the German nation's almost obsessive determination to rise from the ashes of 1918 to a place in the sun.

The worldwide depression had devastating repercussions in France. Poverty weakened the Third Republic to the point where coalition governments rose and fell with alarming regularity. The crises reached a crescendo on June 14, 1940, when Hitler's armies marched down the Champs-Elysées, and newsreel cameras recorded French people openly weeping. The north of France was occupied by the Nazis, and a puppet French government was established at Vichy under the authority of Marshal Pétain. The immediate collapse of the French army is viewed as one of the most significant humiliations in modern French history.

Pétain and his regime cooperated with the Nazis in shameful ways. Not the least of their crimes included the deportation of more than 75,000 French Jews to German work camps. Pockets of resistance fighters (le maquis) waged small-scale guerrilla attacks against the Nazis throughout the course of the war, and free-French forces continued to fight along with the Allies on battlegrounds like North Africa. Charles de Gaulle, the irascible giant whose personality is forever associated with the politics of his era, established himself as the head of the French government-in-exile, operating first from London and then from Algiers.

The scenario ended on June 6, 1944, when the largest armada in history landed on the beaches of Normandy. Paris rose in rebellion before the Allied armies arrived, and on August 26, 1944, Charles de Gaulle entered the capital as head of the government. The Fourth Republic was declared even as Nazi snipers continued to shoot from scattered rooftops throughout the city.

THE POSTWAR YEARS

Plagued by the bitter residue of colonial policies that France had established during the 18th and 19th centuries, the Fourth Republic witnessed the rise and fall of 22 governments and 17 premiers. Many French soldiers died on foreign soil as once-profitable colonies in North Africa and Indochina rebelled. It took 80,000 French lives to put down a revolt in Madagascar. After a bitter defeat in 1954, France ended the war in Indochina and freed its former colony. It also granted internal self-rule to Tunisia and (under slightly different circumstances) Morocco.

Algeria was to remain a greater problem. The advent of the 1958 Algerian revolution signaled the end of the Fourth Republic. De Gaulle was called back from retirement to initiate a new constitution, the Fifth Republic, with a stronger set of executive controls. To nearly everyone's dissatisfaction, de Gaulle ended the Algerian war in 1962 by granting the country independence. Screams of protest resounded, but the sun had set on most of France's far-flung empire. Internal disruption followed as numbers of *pieds-noirs* (French-born residents of Algeria recently stripped of their lands) flooded back into metropolitan France, often into makeshift refugee camps in Provence and Languedoc.

In 1968, social unrest and a violent coalition hastily formed between the nation's students and blue-collar workers led to the collapse of the government. De Gaulle resigned when his attempts to placate some of the marchers were defeated. The reins of power passed to his second-in-command, Georges Pompidou, and his successor, Valérie Giscard d'Estaing, both of whom continued de Gaulle's policies emphasizing economic development and protection of France as a cultural resource to the world.

THE 1980s THROUGH THE TURN OF THE MILLENNIUM   In 1981

François Mitterrand was elected the first Socialist president of France since World War II (with a close vote of 51%). In response, many wealthy French decided to transfer their assets out of the country, much to the delight of banks in Geneva, Monaco, the Cayman Islands, and Vienna. Though reviled by the rich and ridiculed for personal mannerisms that often seemed inspired by Louis XIV, Mitterrand was reelected in 1988. During his two terms he spent billions of francs on his *grands projets* (like the Louvre pyramid, Opéra Bastille, Cité de la Musique, and Grande Arche de la Défense).

In 1992, France played a leading role in the development of the European Union (EU), 15 countries that will ultimately abolish all trade barriers among themselves and share a single currency, the euro. More recent developments include France's interest in developing a central European bank for the regulation of a shared intra-European currency, a ruling that some politicians have interpreted as another building block in the foundation of a united Europe.

In April 1993, voters dumped the Socialists and installed a conservative government. Polls cited corruption, unemployment, and urban insecurity as reasons for this. The Conservative premier Edouard Balladur had to "cohabit" the government with Mitterrand, whom he blamed for the country's economic problems. Diagnosed with terminal cancer near the end of his second term, Mitterrand continued to represent France with dignity, despite his illness. The battle over who would succeed him was waged against Balladur with epic rancor by Jacques Chirac, survivor of many terms as mayor of Paris. Their public discord was among the most venomous since the days of Pétain.

On his third try, on May 7, 1995, Chirac won the presidency with 52% of the vote and declared war on unemployment. Mitterrand turned over the reins of government on May 17 and died shortly thereafter. But Chirac's popularity faded in the wake of unrest caused by an 11.5% unemployment rate, a barrage of terrorist attacks by Algerian Muslims, and an economy struggling to meet European Union entry requirements.

A wave of terrorist attacks from July to September 1995 brought an unfamiliar wariness to Paris. Six bombs were planted, killing seven people and injuring 115. Algerian Islamic militants, the suspected culprits, may have brought military guards to the Eiffel Tower, but they failed to throw France into panic.

Throughout 1995 and early 1996, France infuriated everyone from the members of Greenpeace to the governments of Australia and New Zealand by resuming its long-dormant policy of exploding nuclear bombs on isolated Pacific atolls. This policy continued until public outcry, both in France and outside its borders, exerted massive pressure to end the tests.

In May 1996, thousands of Parisian workers took to the streets, disrupting passenger train service to demand a workweek shorter than the usual 39 hours. They felt that this move would help France's staggering unemployment figures. Employers resisted this idea, claiming that even if the workweek were cut to 35 hours, businesses wouldn't be able to take on many new employees.

The drama of 1996 climaxed with the heat of the summer, when the police took axes to the doors of the Paris church of St-Bernard de la Chapelle. Nearly 300 African immigrants were removed by force and deported. Strikes and protests continued to plague the country, and Chirac's political horizon became dimmer—with a 12% unemployment rate and crime on an alarming increase. Terrorist scares continued to flood the borders of France throughout 1997, forcing a highly visible police force, as part of a nationwide program known as Vigipirate, to take to the streets. One of the offshoots of the Vigipirate program involved the closing of the crypts of many of France's medieval churches to visitors, partly in fear of a terrorist bomb attack on national historic treasures.

In the spring of 1998, Conservatives were ousted in a majority of France's regional provinces, amounting to a powerful endorsement for Prime Minister Lionel Jospin's Socialist-led government.

In 1999, France joined with other European countries in adopting the euro as its standard of currency. The new currency will accelerate the creation of a single economy comprising nearly 300 million Europeans, with a combined gross national product approaching $9 trillion, larger than that of the United States.

France moved into the millennium by testing the practicality of new and progressive social legislation. On October 13, 1999, the French Parliament passed a new law giving legal status to unmarried couples, including homosexual unions. The law allows couples of same sex or not to enter into a union and be entitled to the same rights as married couples in such areas as housing, inheritance, income tax, and social welfare. In 2000 France, it is estimated that some five million couples live together without benefit of marriage. The law faced extreme opposition, especially from conservative lawmakers who plan to appeal to the Constitutional Council to see if the law is indeed constitutional. The Catholic church also denounced the new law, calling it "an assault on the family."

One of the most enduring symbols of France, its French franc, was assigned to the dustbin of history in 2001, as the country joined 11 other EU nations in a switch to the euro, which stands now as a virtual European dollar.

Appendix B:
Glossary of Useful Terms

A well-known character is the American or lapsed Canadian who returns from a trip to France and denounces the ever-so-rude French. But it is often amazing how a word or two of halting French will change your hosts' disposition. At the very least, try to learn a few numbers, basic greetings, and—above all—the life-raft phrase, *Parlez-vous anglais?* (Do you speak English?). As it turns out, many people do speak a passable English and will use it liberally, if you demonstrate the basic courtesy of greeting them in their language. Go out, try our glossary, and don't be bashful. *Bonne chance!*

BASICS

English	French	Pronunciation
Yes/No	**Oui/Non**	wee/nohn
Okay	**D'accord**	dah-core
Please	**S'il vous plaît**	seel voo play
Thank you	**Merci**	mair-see
You're welcome	**De rien**	duh ree-ehn
Hello (during daylight hours)	**Bonjour**	bohn-jhoor
Good evening	**Bonsoir**	bohn-swahr
Good-bye	**Au revoir**	o ruh-vwahr
What's your name?	**Comment vous appellez-vous?**	ko-mahn-voo-za-pell-ay-voo?
My name is	**Je m'appelle**	jhuh ma-pell
Happy to meet you	**Enchanté(e)**	ohn-shahn-tay
How are you?	**Comment allez-vous?**	kuh-mahn-tahl-ay-voo?
Fine, thank you, and you?	**Trés bien, merci, et vous?**	Tray bee-ehn, mare-ci, ay voo?
So-so	**Comme ci, comme ça**	kum-see, kum-sah
I'm sorry/excuse me	**Pardon**	pahr-dohn
I'm so very sorry	**Désolé(e)**	day-zoh-lay
That's all right	**Il n'y a pas de quoi**	eel nee ah pah duh kwah

GETTING AROUND/STREET SMARTS

English	French	Pronunciation
Do you speak English?	**Parlez-vous anglais?**	par-lay-voo-ahn-*glay?*
I don't speak French	**Je ne parle pas français**	jhuh ne parl pah frahn-*say*
I don't understand	**Je ne comprends pas**	jhuh ne kohm-*prahn* pas
Could you speak more loudly/ more slowly?	**Pouvez-vous parler plus fort/ plus lentement?**	Poo-*vay* voo par-lay ploo for/ploo lan-te-*ment?*
Could you repeat that?	**Répetez, s'il vous plaît**	ray-pay-*tay,* seel voo *play*
What is it?	**Qu'est-ce que c'est?**	kess-kuh-*say?*

English	French	Pronunciation
What time is it?	**Qu'elle heure est-il?**	kel uhr eh-*teel*?
What?	**Quoi?**	kwah?
How? or What did you say?	**Comment?**	ko-*mahn*?
When?	**Quand?**	kahn?
Where is?	**Où est?**	ooh-eh?
Who?	**Qui?**	kee?
Why?	**Pourquoi?**	poor-*kwah*?
here/there	**ici/là**	ee-*see*/lah
left/right	**à gauche/à droite**	a goash/a drwaht
straight ahead	**tout droit**	too-drwah
I'm American	**Je suis américain(e)**	jhe sweez a-may-ree- *kehn*
Canadian	**canadien(e)**	can-ah-dee-*en*
British	**anglais(e)**	ahn-*glay* (*glaise*)
Fill the tank (of a car), please	**Le plein, s'il vous plaît**	luh plan, seel-voo-*play*
I'm going to	**Je vais à**	jhe vay ah
I want to get off at	**Je voudrais descendre à**	jhe voo-*dray* day-son drah-ah
airport	**l'aéroport**	lair-o-*por*
bank	**la banque**	lah bahnk
bridge	**pont**	pohn
bus station	**la gare routière**	lah gar roo-tee-*air*
bus stop	**l'arrêt de bus**	lah-*ray* duh boohss
by means of a bicycle	**en vélo/par bicyclette**	uh *vay*-low, par bee-see-*clet*
by means of a car	**en voiture**	ahn vwa-*toor*
cashier	**la caisse**	lah *kess*
cathedral	**cathedral**	ka-tay-*dral*
church	**église**	ay-*gleez*
dead end	**une impasse**	ewn am-*pass*
driver's license	**permis de conduire**	per-*mee* duh con-*dweer*
elevator	**l'ascenseur**	lah sahn *seuhr*
entrance (to a building or a city)	**une porte**	ewn port
exit (from a building or a freeway)	**une sortie**	ewn sor-*tee*
gasoline	**du pétrol/de l'essence**	duh pay-*trol*/de lay-*sahns*
ground floor	**rez-de-chausée**	ray-de-show-*say*
highway to	**la route pour**	la root por
hospital	**l'hôpital**	low-pee-*tahl*
insurance	**les assurances**	lez ah-sur-*ahns*
luggage storage	**consigne**	kohn-*seen*-yuh
museum	**le musée**	luh mew-*zay*
no entry	**sens interdit**	sehns ahn-ter-*dee*
no smoking	**défense de fumer**	day-*fahns* de fu-may
on foot	**à pied**	ah pee-*ay*
one-day pass	**ticket journalier**	tee-kay jhoor-nall-ee-*ay*
one-way ticket	**aller simple**	ah-*lay* sam-pluh
police	**la police**	lah po-*lees*
rented car	**voiture de location**	vwa-*toor* de low-ka-see *on*

English	French	Pronunciation
round-trip ticket	**aller-retour**	ah-*lay* re-*toor*
second floor	**premier étage**	prem-ee-*ehr* ay-*taj*
slow down	**ralentir**	rah-lahn-*teer*
store	**le magazin**	luh ma-ga-*zehn*
street	**rue**	roo
suburb	**banlieu/environs**	bahn-*liew*/en-veer-*ohn*
subway	**le métro**	le may-tro
telephone	**le téléphone**	luh tay-lay-*phone*
ticket	**un billet**	uh *bee*-yay
ticket office	**vente de billets**	vahnt duh bee-*yay*
toilets	**les toilettes/les WC**	lay twa-*lets*/les vay-*say*
tower	**tour**	toor

NECESSITIES

English	French	Pronunciation
I'd like	**Je voudrais**	jhe voo-*dray*
a room	**une chambre**	ewn *shahm*-bruh
the key	**la clé (la clef)**	la clay
How much does it cost?	**C'est combien?/ ça coûte combien?**	say comb-bee-*ehn?*/ sah coot comb-bee-*ehn?*
That's expensive	**C'est cher/chère**	say share
Do you take credit cards?	**Est-ce que vous acceptez les cartes de credit?**	es-kuh voo zaksep-*tay* lay kart duh creh-*dee?*
I'd like to buy	**Je voudrais acheter**	jhe voo-dray ahsh-*tay*
aspirin	**des aspirines/ des aspros**	deyz ahs-peer-*een*/ deyz ahs-*proh*
cigarettes	**des cigarettes**	day see-ga-*ret*
condoms	**des préservatifs**	day pray-ser-va-*teef*
dictionary	**un dictionnaire**	uh deek-see-oh-*nare*
dress	**une robe**	ewn robe
envelopes	**des envelopes**	days ahn-veh-*lope*
gift	**un cadeau**	uh kah-*doe*
handbag	**un sac**	uh sahk
hat	**un chapeau**	uh shah-*poh*
magazine	**une revue**	ewn reh-*vu*
map of the city	**un plan de ville**	unh plahn de *veel*
matches	**des allumettes**	dayz a-loo-*met*
necktie	**une cravate**	uh cra-*vaht*
newspaper	**un journal**	uh zhoor-*nahl*
phonecard	**une carte téléphonique**	uh cart tay-lay-fone-*eek*
postcard	**une carte postale**	ewn carte pos-*tahl*
road map	**une carte routière**	ewn cart roo-tee-*air*
shirt	**une chemise**	ewn che-*meez*
shoes	**des chaussures**	day show-*suhr*
skirt	**une jupe**	ewn jhoop
soap	**du savon**	dew sah-*vohn*
socks	**des chaussettes**	day show-*set*
stamp	**un timbre**	uh *tam*-bruh
trousers	**un pantalon**	uh pan-tah-*lohn*
writing paper	**du papier è lettres**	dew pap-pee-*ay* a *let*-ruh

IN YOUR HOTEL

English	French	Pronunciation
Are taxes included?	**Est-ce que les taxes sont comprises?**	ess-keh lay taks son com-*preez?*
balcony	**un balcon**	uh bahl-cohn
bathtub	**une baignoire**	ewn bayn-*nwar*
for two occupants	**pour deux personnes**	poor duh pair-*sunn*
hot and cold water	**l'eau chaude et froide**	low showed ay fwad
Is breakfast included?	**Petit déjeuner inclus?**	peh-*tee* day-jheun-*ay* ehn-*klu?*
room	**une chambre**	ewn *shawm*-bruh
shower	**une douche**	ewn dooch
sink	**un lavabo**	uh la-va-*bow*
suite	**une suite**	ewn sweet
We're staying for . . . days	**On reste pour . . . jours**	ohn rest poor . . . jhoor
with air-conditioning	**avec climatization**	ah-*vek* clee-mah-tee-zah-ion
without	**sans**	sahn
youth hostel	**une auberge de jeunesse**	oon oh-bayrge-duh-jhe-*ness*

IN THE RESTAURANT

English	French	Pronunciation
I would like	**Je voudrais**	jhe voo-*dray*
to eat	**manger**	mahn-*jhay*
to order	**commander**	ko-mahn-*day*
Please give me	**Donnez-moi, s'il vous plaît**	doe-nay-*mwah*, seel voo play
an ashtray	**un cendrier**	uh sahn-dree-*ay*
a bottle of	**une bouteille de**	ewn boo-*tay* duh
a cup of	**une tasse de**	ewn tass duh
a glass of	**un verre de**	uh vair duh
a plate of breakfast	**une assiette de le petit-déjeuner**	ewn ass-ee-*et* duh luh puh-*tee* day-zhuh-*nay*
cocktail	**un apéritif**	uh ah-pay-ree-*teef*
check/bill	**l'addition/la note**	la-dee-see-*ohn*/la noat
dinner	**le dîner**	luh dee-*nay*
knife	**un couteau**	uh koo-*toe*
napkin	**une serviette**	ewn sair-vee-*et*
platter of the day	**un plat du jour**	uh plah dew jhoor
spoon	**une cuillère**	ewn kwee-*air*
Cheers!	**A votre santé!**	ah vo-truh sahn-*tay!*
Can I buy you a drink?	**Puis-je vous acheter un verre?**	*pwee*-jhe voo *zahsh*-tay uh *vaihr?*
fixed-price menu	**un menu**	uh may-*new*
fork	**une fourchette**	ewn four-*shet*
Is the tip/service included?	**Est-ce que le service est compris?**	ess-ke luh ser-*vees* eh com-*pree?*
Waiter!/Waitress!	**Monsieur!/ Mademoiselle!**	mun-*syuh*/ mad-mwa-*zel*
wine list	**une carte des vins**	ewn cart day *van*

English	French	Pronunciation
appetizer	une entrée	ewn en-*tray*
main course	un plat principal	uh plah pran-see-*pahl*
tip included	service compris	sehr-*vees* cohm-*pree*
wide-ranging sampling of the chef's best efforts	menu dégustation	may-*new* day-gus-ta-see-*on*
drinks not included	boissons non comprises	bwa-*sons* no com-*pree*

NUMBERS & ORDINALS

English	French	Pronunciation
zero	zéro	*zare*-oh
one	un	oon
two	deux	duh
three	trois	twah
four	quatre	*kaht*-ruh
five	cinq	sank
six	six	seess
seven	sept	set
eight	huit	wheat
nine	neuf	noof
ten	dix	deess
eleven	onze	ohnz
twelve	douze	dooz
thirteen	treize	trehz
fourteen	quatorze	kah-*torz*
fifteen	quinze	kanz
sixteen	seize	sez
seventeen	dix-sept	deez-*set*
eighteen	dix-huit	deez-*wheat*
nineteen	dix-neuf	deez-*noof*
twenty	vingt	vehn
twenty-one	vingt-et-un	vehnt-ay-*oon*
twenty-two	vingt-deux	vehnt-*duh*
thirty	trente	trahnt
forty	quarante	ka-*rahnt*
fifty	cinquante	sang-*kahnt*
sixty	soixante	swa-*sahnt*
sixty-one	soixante-et-un	swa-*sahnt*-et-*uh*
seventy	soixante-dix	swa-sahnt-*deess*
seventy-one	soixante-et-onze	swa-sahnt-et-*ohnze*
eighty	quatre-vingts	kaht-ruh-*vehn*
eighty-one	quatre-vingt-un	kaht-ruh-vehn-*oon*
ninety	quatre-vingt-dix	kaht-ruh-venh-*deess*
ninety-one	quatre-vingt-onze	kaht-ruh-venh-*ohnze*
one hundred	cent	sahn
one thousand	mille	meel
one hundred thousand	cent mille	sahn meel

English	French	Pronunciation
first	**premier**	*preh*-mee-ay
second	**deuxième**	*duhz*-zee-em
third	**troisième**	*twa*-zee-em
fourth	**quatrième**	*kaht*-ree-em
fifth	**cinquième**	*sank*-ee-em
sixth	**sixième**	*sees*-ee-em
seventh	**septième**	*set*-ee-em
eighth	**huitième**	*wheat*-ee-em
ninth	**neuvième**	*neuv*-ee-em
tenth	**dixième**	*dees*-ee-em

THE CALENDAR

English	French	Pronunciation
Sunday	**dimanche**	dee-*mahnsh*
Monday	**lundi**	luhn-*dee*
Tuesday	**mardi**	mahr-*dee*
Wednesday	**mercredi**	mair-kruh-*dee*
Thursday	**jeudi**	jheu-*dee*
Friday	**vendredi**	vawn-druh-*dee*
Saturday	**samedi**	sahm-*dee*
yesterday	**hier**	ee-*air*
today	**aujourd'hui**	o-jhord-*dwee*
this morning/ this afternoon	**ce matin/ cet après-midi**	suh ma-*tan*/ set ah-preh mee-*dee*
tonight	**ce soir**	suh *swahr*
tomorrow	**demain**	de-*man*

Appendix C:
Glossary of Basic Menu Terms

You're hungry, you don't want brains, but you don't understand a thing on the menu. What to do? Use the following list of menu terms (organized by food type) to help determine what exactly you're ordering.

Note: To order any of these items from a waiter, simply preface the French-language name with the phrase, "Je voudrais" (jhe voo-*dray*), which means, "I would like . . ." *Bon appétit!*

MEATS

French	English	Pronunciation
De l'agneau	Lamb	Duh l'ahn-*nyo*
Des ailes de poulet	Chicken wings	Dayz ehl duh poo-lay
De l'aloyau	Sirloin	Duh l'ahl-why-*yo*
Du bifteck	Steak	Dew beef-*tek*
De la blanquette	Stewed meat with white sauce, enriched with cream and eggs	Duh lah blon-*kette*
Du boeuf à la mode	Marinated beef braised with red wine and served with vegetables	Dew bewf ah lah *mhowd*
De la cervelle	Brains	Duh lah ser-*vel*
Du Chateaubriand	Double tenderloin, a long muscle from which filet steaks are cut	Dew sha-tow- bree-*ahn*
Du coq au vin	Chicken, stewed with mushrooms and wine	Dew cock o vhaihn
Des cuisses de grenouilles	Frogs' legs	*Day cweess duh gre* noo *yuh*
Du gigot	Haunch or leg of an animal, especially that of a lamb or sheep	*Dew jhi*-goh
Du jambon	Ham	*Dew jham*-bohn
Du lapin	Rabbit	*Dew lah*-pan
Du pot au feu	Beef stew	*Dew poht o* fhe
Du poulet	Chicken	*Dew poo*-lay
Des quenelles	Rolls of pounded and baked chicken, veal, or fish, often pike, usually served warm	*Day ke*-nelle
Des ris de veau	Sweetbreads	*Day ree duh* voh

French	English	Pronunciation
Des rognons	Kidneys	*Day row*-nyon
Un steak au poivre	Filet steak, embedded with fresh green or black peppercorns, flambéed and served with a cognac sauce	*Uh stake o pwah*-vruh
Du veau	Veal	*Dew voh*

FISH & SEAFOOD

French	English	Pronunciation
De l'anguille	Eel	Duh l'ahn-*ghwee*-uh
De la bouillabaisse	Mediterranean fish soup or stew made with tomatoes, garlic, saffron, and olive oil	Duh lah booh-ya-*besse*
Du brochet	Pike	Dew broh-*chay*
Des crevettes	Shrimp	Day kreh-*vette*
Du hareng	Herring	*Dew ahr*-rahn
Du homard	Lobster	*Dew oh*-mahr
Des huîtres	Oysters	*Dayz hoo-ee-truhs*
Du loup de mer	Wolf fish, a Mediterranean sea bass	Dew loo-*duh*-mehr
Des moules	Mussels	*Day moohl*
Des moules marinières	Mussels in herb-flavored white wine with shallots	*Day moohl mar-ee-nee*-air
Du poisson de rivière, or poisson d'eau douce/ du poisson de mer	Fish (freshwater) and fish (saltwater)	*Dew pwah-sson duh ree-vee*-aire, *dew pwah-sson d'o* dooss/*dew pwah-sson duh* mehr
Du saumon fumé	Smoked salmon	*Dew sow-mohn fu*-may
Du thon	Tuna	*Dew tohn*
De la truite	Trout	*Duh lah tru*-eet

SIDES/APPETIZERS

French	English	Pronunciation
Du beurre	Butter	Dew bhuhr
De la choucroute	Sauerkraut	Duh lah chew-*kroot*
Des escargots	Snails	Dayz ess-car-*goh*
Du foie	Liver	Dew fwoh
Du foie gras	Goose liver	Dew fwoh grah
Du pain	Bread	Dew pan
Des rillettes	Potted and minced pork and pork byproducts, prepared as a roughly chopped pâté	*Day ree*-yett
Du riz	Rice	*Dew ree*

FRUITS/VEGETABLES

French	English	Pronunciation
De l'ananas	Pineapple	Duh l'ah-na-*nas*
De l'aubergine	Eggplant	Duh l'oh-ber-*jheen*
Du choux	Cabbage	Dew *shoe*
Du citron/ du citron vert	Lemon/lime	Dew cee-*tron*/dew cee-*tron* vaire
Des épinards	Spinach	Dayz ay-pin-*ar*
Des fraises	Strawberries	Day frez
Des haricots verts	Green beans	*Day ahr-ee-coh* vaire
Une orange	Orange	*Ewn or-an-*jhe
Un pamplemousse	Grapefruit	*Uh pahm-pluh-*moose
Des petits pois	Green peas	*Day puh-tee* pwah
Des pommes frites	French-fried potatoes	*Day puhm* freet
Des pommes de terre	Potatoes	*Day puhm duh* tehr
Du raisin	Grapes	*Dew ray-*zhan

BEVERAGES

French	English	Pronunciation
De la bière	Beer	Duh lah bee-*aire*
Boissons non compris	Drinks not included	*Bwa-son nohn com-*pree
Un café	Coffee	Uh-ka-*fay*
Un café au lait	Coffee (with milk)	Uh ka-fay o *lay*
Un café crème	Coffee (with cream)	Uh ka-fay krem
Un café decaffeiné (un déca; slang)	Coffee (decaf)	Un ka-fay day-kah-fay-*e-nay* (uh day-kah)
Un café noir	Coffee (black)	Uh ka-fay-nwahr
Un espresso (un express)	Coffee (espresso)	Un ka-fay ek-*sprehss-o* (uh ek-*sprehss*)
Du jus d'orange	Orange juice	*Dew joo d'or-an-*jhe
De l'eau	Water	Duh lo
Du lait	Milk	*Dew* lay
Du thé	Tea	*Dew* tay
Une tisane	Herbal tea	*Ewn tee-*zahn
Du vin blanc	White wine	*Dew vhin* blahn
Du vin rouge	Red wine	*Dew vhin* rooj

DESSERTS

French	English	Pronunciation
De la crème brûlée	Thick custard dessert with a caramelized topping	Duh lah krem bruh-*lay*
Du fromage	Cheese	*Dew fro* mahjz
Du gâteau	Cake	*Dew gha-*tow
De la glace à la vanille	Vanilla ice cream	*Duh lah glass a lah vah-*ne-yuh
Une tarte	Tart	*Ewn tart*
Une tarte tatin	Caramelized upside-down apple pie	*Ewn tart tah-*tihn

SPICES/CONDIMENTS

French	English	Pronunciation
De la crème fraîche	Sour heavy cream	Duh lah krem *fresh*
De la moutarde	Mustard	*Duh lah moo*-tard-*uh*
Du poivre	Pepper	*Dew pwah*-vruh
Du sel	Salt	*Dew* sel
Du sucre	Sugar	*Dew suh*-kruh

COOKING METHODS

French	English	Pronunciation
À la Bourguignon	In the style of Burgundy, usually with red wine, mushrooms, bacon, and onions	Ah lah Boor-geehn-*nyon*
Un confit	Method of cooking whereby anything (including fish, meat, fruits, or vegetables) is simmered in a reduction of its own fat or juices	Uh khon-feeh
Cuit au feu de bois	Cooked over a wood fire	Kwee o fhe duh *bwoi*
À la Lyonnais	A method of food preparation native to Lyon and its region that usually includes wine sauce accented with shredded and sautéed onions	*Ah lah lee-ohn*-nehz
En papillotte	Cooked in parchment paper	*Ehn pah-pee*-yott
Une terrine	Minced and potted meat, seasoned and molded into a crock	*Ewn tair*-ee
Vol-au-vent	Puff pastry shell	*Vhol-o*-vhen

Index

FROMMER'S® COMPLETE TRAVEL GUIDES

Alaska
Amsterdam
Argentina & Chile
Arizona
Atlanta
Australia
Austria
Bahamas
Barcelona, Madrid & Seville
Beijing
Belgium, Holland &
  Luxembourg
Bermuda
Boston
British Columbia & the
  Canadian Rockies
Budapest & the Best of Hungary
California
Canada
Cancún, Cozumel & the
  Yucatán
Cape Cod, Nantucket &
  Martha's Vineyard
Caribbean
Caribbean Cruises & Ports
  of Call
Caribbean Ports of Call
Carolinas & Georgia
Chicago
China
Colorado
Costa Rica
Denmark
Denver, Boulder & Colorado
  Springs
England
Europe

European Cruises & Ports of Call
Florida
France
Germany
Greece
Greek Islands
Hawaii
Hong Kong
Honolulu, Waikiki & Oahu
Ireland
Israel
Italy
Jamaica
Japan
Las Vegas
London
Los Angeles
Maryland & Delaware
Maui
Mexico
Montana & Wyoming
Montréal & Québec City
Munich & the Bavarian Alps
Nashville & Memphis
Nepal
New England
New Mexico
New Orleans
New York City
New Zealand
Nova Scotia, New Brunswick &
  Prince Edward Island
Oregon
Paris
Philadelphia & the Amish
  Country
Portugal

Prague & the Best of the Czech
  Republic
Provence & the Riviera
Puerto Rico
Rome
San Antonio & Austin
San Diego
San Francisco
Santa Fe, Taos & Albuquerque
Scandinavia
Scotland
Seattle & Portland
Shanghai
Singapore & Malaysia
South Africa
Southeast Asia
South Florida
South Pacific
Spain
Sweden
Switzerland
Texas
Thailand
Tokyo
Toronto
Tuscany & Umbria
USA
Utah
Vancouver & Victoria
Vermont, New Hampshire
  & Maine
Vienna & the Danube Valley
Virgin Islands
Virginia
Walt Disney World & Orlando
Washington, D.C.
Washington State

FROMMER'S® DOLLAR-A-DAY GUIDES

Australia from $50 a Day
California from $70 a Day
Caribbean from $70 a Day
England from $70 a Day
Europe from $70 a Day

Florida from $70 a Day
Hawaii from $70 a Day
Ireland from $60 a Day
Italy from $70 a Day
London from $85 a Day

New York from $80 a Day
Paris from $80 a Day
San Francisco from $60 a Day
Washington, D.C.,
  from $70 a Day

FROMMER'S® PORTABLE GUIDES

Acapulco, Ixtapa &
  Zihuatanejo
Alaska Cruises & Ports
  of Call
Amsterdam
Australia's Great Barrier Reef
Bahamas
Baja & Los Cabos
Berlin
Boston
California Wine Country
Charleston & Savannah
Chicago

Dublin
Hawaii: The Big Island
Hong Kong
Houston
Las Vegas
London
Los Angeles
Maine Coast
Maui
Miami
New Orleans
New York City
Paris

Phoenix & Scottsdale
Portland
Puerto Rico
Puerto Vallarta, Manzanillo &
  Guadalajara
San Diego
San Francisco
Seattle
Sydney
Tampa & St. Petersburg
Vancouver
Venice
Washington, D.C.

FROMMER'S® NATIONAL PARK GUIDES

Family Vacations in the
  National Parks
Grand Canyon

National Parks of the American
  West
Rocky Mountain
Yellowstone & Grand Teton

Yosemite & Sequoia/
  Kings Canyon
Zion & Bryce Canyon

FROMMER'S® MEMORABLE WALKS

Chicago	New York	San Francisco
London	Paris	Washington, D.C.

FROMMER'S® GREAT OUTDOOR GUIDES

Arizona & New Mexico	Northern California	Southern New England
New England	Southern California & Baja	Vermont & New Hampshire

FROMMER'S® BORN TO SHOP GUIDES

Born to Shop: France	Born to Shop: Italy	Born to Shop: New York
Born to Shop: Hong Kong, Shanghai & Beijing	Born to Shop: London	Born to Shop: Paris

FROMMER'S® IRREVERENT GUIDES

Amsterdam	Los Angeles	Seattle & Portland
Boston	Manhattan	Vancouver
Chicago	New Orleans	Walt Disney World
Las Vegas	Paris	Washington, D.C.
London	San Francisco	

FROMMER'S® BEST-LOVED DRIVING TOURS

America	France	New England
Britain	Germany	Scotland
California	Ireland	Spain
Florida	Italy	Western Europe

THE UNOFFICIAL GUIDES®

Bed & Breakfasts in California	Golf Vacations in the Eastern U.S.	New Orleans
Bed & Breakfasts in New England	The Great Smokey & Blue Ridge Mountains	New York City
Bed & Breakfasts in the Northwest	Inside Disney	Paris
Bed & Breakfasts in Southeast	Hawaii	San Francisco
Beyond Disney	Las Vegas	Skiing in the West
Branson, Missouri	London	Southeast with Kids
California with Kids	Mid-Atlantic with Kids	Walt Disney World
Chicago	Mini Las Vegas	Walt Disney World for Grown-ups
Cruises	Mini-Mickey	Walt Disney World for Kids
Disneyland	New England with Kids	Washington, D.C.
Florida with Kids		World's Best Diving Vacations

SPECIAL-INTEREST TITLES

Frommer's Britain's Best Bed & Breakfasts and Country Inns
Frommer's France's Best Bed & Breakfasts and Country Inns
Frommer's Italy's Best Bed & Breakfasts and Country Inns
Frommer's Caribbean Hideaways
Frommer's Adventure Guide to Australia & New Zealand
Frommer's Adventure Guide to Central America
Frommer's Adventure Guide to India & Pakistan
Frommer's Adventure Guide to South America
Frommer's Adventure Guide to Southeast Asia
Frommer's Adventure Guide to Southern Africa
Frommer's Gay & Lesbian Europe
Frommer's Exploring America by RV
Hanging Out in England

Hanging Out in Europe
Hanging Out in France
Hanging Out in Ireland
Hanging Out in Italy
Hanging Out in Spain
Israel Past & Present
Frommer's The Moon
Frommer's New York City with Kids
The New York Times' Guide to Unforgettable Weekends
Places Rated Almanac
Retirement Places Rated
Frommer's Road Atlas Britain
Frommer's Road Atlas Europe
Frommer's Washington, D.C., with Kids
Frommer's What the Airlines Never Tell You

Let Us Hear From You!

Dear Frommer's Reader,

You are our greatest resource in keeping our guides relevant, timely, and lively. We'd love to hear from you about your travel experiences—good or bad. Want to recommend a great restaurant or a hotel off the beaten path—or register a complaint? Any thoughts on how to improve the guide itself?

Please use this page to share your thoughts with me and mail it to the address below. Or if you like, send a FAX or e-mail me at frommersfeedback@hungryminds.com. And so that we can thank you—and keep you up on the latest developments in travel—we invite you to sign up for a free daily Frommer's e-mail travel update. Just write your e-mail address on the back of this page. Also, if you'd like to take a moment to answer a few questions about yourself to help us improve our guides, please complete the following quick survey. (We'll keep that information confidential.)

Thanks for your insights.

Yours sincerely,

Michael Spring

Michael Spring, *Publisher*

Name (Optional) ———————————————————————————————

Address————————————————————————————————————

——

City————————————————————————————— **State**——— **ZIP**———

Name of Frommer's Travel Guide ———————————————————————

Comments————————————————————————————————————

——

——

——

——

——

——

——

——

Please tell us a little about yourself so that we can serve you and the Frommer's community better. We will keep this information confidential.

Age: ( )18-24; ( )25-39; ( )40-49; ( )50-55; ( )Over 55

Income: ( )Under $25,000; ( )$25,000-$50,000; ( )$50,000-$100,000; ( )Over $100,000

I am: ( )Single, never married; ( )Married, with children; ( )Married, without children; ( )Divorced; ( )Widowed

Number of people in my household: ( )1; ( )2; ( )3; ( )4; ( )5 or more

Number of people in my household under 18: ( )1; ( )2; ( )3; ( )4; ( )5 or more

I am ( )a student; ( )employed full-time; ( )employed part-time; ( )not employed at this time; ( )retired; ( )other

I took ( )0; ( )1; ( )2; ( )3; ( )4 or more leisure trips in the past 12 months

My last vacation was ( )a weekend; ( )1 week; ( )2 weeks; ( )3 or more weeks

My last vacation was to ( )the U.S.; ( )Canada; ( )Mexico; ( )Europe; ( )Asia; ( )South America; ( )Central America; ( )The Caribbean; ( )Africa; ( )Middle East; ( )Australia/New Zealand

( )I would; ( )would not buy a Frommer's Travel Guide for business travel

I access the Internet ( )at home; ( )at work; ( )both; ( )I do not use the Internet

I used the Internet to do research for my last trip. ( )Yes; ( )No

I used the Internet to book accommodations or air travel on my last trip. ( )Yes; ( )No

My favorite travel site is ( )frommers.com; ( )travelocity.com; ( )expedia.com; other_____

I use Frommer's Travel Guides ( )always; ( )sometimes; ( )seldom

I usually buy ( )1; ( )2; ( )more than 2 guides when I travel

Other guides I use include _____

What's the most important thing we could do to improve Frommer's Travel Guides?

_____

_____

_____

_____

Yes, please send me a daily e-mail travel update. My e-mail address is

_____

Mail to: Michael Spring, Publisher and Vice President, Frommer's Travel Guides
909 Third Ave., New York, NY 10022   FAX: 212.884.5432